Saint Thomas Aquinas

Commentary on the Gospel of Matthew, Chapters 13-28

Translated by Jeremy Holmes
Edited by The Aquinas Institute

Biblical Commentaries

Volume 34
Latin/English Edition of the Works of St. Thomas Aquinas

The Aquinas Institute for the Study of Sacred Doctrine
Lander, Wyoming
2013

This printing was funded in part by donations made in memory of:
Marcus Berquist, Rose Johanna Trumbull, John and Mary Deignan,
Thomas and Eleanor Sullivan, and Fr. John T. Feeney and his sister Mary.

The printing was also made possible by a donation from Patricia Lynch,
and by a donation made in honor of Fr. Brian McMaster.

Published with the ecclesiastical approval of
The Most Reverend Paul D. Etienne, DD, STL
Bishop of Cheyenne
Given on July 16, 2013

Copyright © 2013
The Aquinas Institute for the Study of Sacred Doctrine
165 Dupont Drive
Lander, WY 82520
www.TheAquinasInstitute.org

Printed in the United States of America

PUBLISHER'S CATALOGING-IN-PUBLICATION DATA

Thomas Aquinas, Saint, 1225?-1274
 Commentary on the Gospel of Matthew, chapters 13-28 / Saint Thomas Aquinas; edited by The Aquinas Institute; translated by Jeremy Holmes
 p. 488 cm.
 ISBN 978-1-62340-016-3

1. Bible. N.T. Matthew--Commentaries--Early works to 1800. I. Title. II. Series

BS2575.T4612 2013
226'.2'07--dc23   2013942432

Notes on the Text

Sacred Scripture

The text of Sacred Scripture presented at the beginning of each lecture is given in Latin, English, and Greek. Since St. Thomas appears to be familiar with more than one translation, quotes from memory, and often enough paraphrases, it has proven difficult to reconstruct the version of Scripture St. Thomas was working with. However, the closest available version of Scripture to St. Thomas's text was found to be the Clementine Vulgate of 1598, and this version of the Vulgate is the one found at the beginning of each lecture. The choice of an English version of Scripture to parallel to the Vulgate was therefore the Douay-Rheims. Both of these versions have been slightly modified to fit the text of St. Thomas. The Greek text is from the Nestle-Aland, Novum Testamentum Graece, 27th Revised Edition, edited by Barbara Aland, Kurt Aland, Johannes Karavidopoulos, Carlo M. Martini, and Bruce M. Metzger in cooperation with the Institute for New Testament Textual Research, Münster/Westphalia, © 1993 Deutsche Bibelgesellschaft, Stuttgart. Used with permission. The numbering of Scripture in the lecture headings and the English translation of the commentary is taken from the Nestle-Aland 27th Revised Edition and the RSV, while the numbering St. Thomas uses in the Latin text has been kept intact.

Latin Text of St. Thomas

The Latin text used in this volume is based on the 1951 Marietti edition. It has been scanned and edited by The Aquinas Institute.

English Translation of St. Thomas

The English translation used in this volume was prepared by Jeremy Holmes. It has been edited and revised by The Aquinas Institute.

The Aquinas Institute requests your assistance in the continued perfection of these texts.
If you discover any errors, please send a note to us by e-mail: editor@theaquinasinstitute.org.

Dedicated with love to
Our Lady of Mt. Carmel

Contents

CHAPTER 13
- Lecture 1 - Matthew 13:1–23 1
- Lecture 2 - Matthew 13:24–30 18
- Lecture 3 - Matthew 13:31–43 26
- Lecture 4 - Matthew 13:44–58 35

CHAPTER 14
- Lecture 1 - Matthew 14:1–14 45
- Lecture 2 - Matthew 14:15–36 52

CHAPTER 15
- Lecture 1 - Matthew 15:1–20 65
- Lecture 2 - Matthew 15:21–28 77
- Lecture 3 - Matthew 15:29–38 82

CHAPTER 16
- Lecture 1 - Matthew 16:1–12 89
- Lecture 2 - Matthew 16:13–19 95
- Lecture 3 - Matthew 16:20–28 104

CHAPTER 17
- Lecture 1 - Matthew 17:1–13 113
- Lecture 2 - Matthew 17:14–27 124

CHAPTER 18
- Lecture 1 - Matthew 18:1–11 135
- Lecture 2 - Matthew 18:12–22 144
- Lecture 3 - Matthew 18:23–35 151

CHAPTER 19
- Lecture 1 - Matthew 19:1–30 157

CHAPTER 20
- Lecture 1 - Matthew 20:1–16 183
- Lecture 2 - Matthew 20:17–34 193

CHAPTER 21
- Lecture 1 - Matthew 21:1–22 205
- Lecture 2 - Matthew 21:23–46 219

CHAPTER 22
- Lecture 1 - Matthew 22:1–14 231
- Lecture 2 - Matthew 22:15–22 239
- Lecture 3 - Matthew 22:23–33 244
- Lecture 4 - Matthew 22:34–46 249

CHAPTER 23
- Lecture 1 - Matthew 23:1–12 257
- Lecture 2 - Matthew 23:13–33 265
- Lecture 3 - Matthew 23:34–39 279

CHAPTER 24
- Lecture 1 - Matthew 24:1–14 ... 285
- Lecture 2 - Matthew 24:15–22 ... 293
- Lecture 3 - Matthew 24:23–41 ... 298
- Lecture 4 - Matthew 24:42–51 ... 315

CHAPTER 25
- Lecture 1 - Matthew 25:1–13 ... 321
- Lecture 2 - Matthew 25:14–30 ... 329
- Lecture 3 - Matthew 25:31–46 ... 345

CHAPTER 26
- Lecture 1 - Matthew 26:1–16 ... 357
- Lecture 2 - Matthew 26:17–25 ... 367
- Lecture 3 - Matthew 26:26 ... 373
- Lecture 4 - Matthew 26:27–29 ... 381
- Lecture 5 - Matthew 26:30–46 ... 387
- Lecture 6 - Matthew 26:47–56 ... 401
- Lecture 7 - Matthew 26:57–75 ... 408

CHAPTER 27
- Lecture 1 - Matthew 27:1–26 ... 419
- Lecture 2 - Matthew 27:27–66 ... 432

CHAPTER 28
- Lecture 1 - Matthew 28:1–20 ... 455

Commentary on the Gospel of Matthew, Chapters 13-28

Chapter 13

Lecture 1

13:1 In illo die exiens Iesus de domo, sedebat secus mare. [n. 1078]

13:2 Et congregatae sunt ad eum turbae multae, ita ut in naviculam ascendens sederet, et omnis turba stabat in littore, [n. 1080]

13:3 et locutus est eis multa in parabolis, dicens: ecce exiit qui seminat seminare, [n. 1082]

13:4 et dum seminat, quaedam ceciderunt secus viam, et venerunt volucres, et comederunt ea. [1088]

13:5 Alia autem ceciderunt in petrosa, ubi non habebant terram multam, et continuo exorta sunt, quia non habebant altitudinem terrae; [n. 1089]

13:6 sole autem orto aestuaverunt; et quia non habebant radicem, aruerunt. [n. 1090]

13:7 Alia autem ceciderunt in spinas, et creverunt spinae, et suffocaverunt ea. [n. 1090]

13:8 Alia autem ceciderunt in terram bonam, et dabant fructum, aliud centesimum, aliud sexagesimum, aliud trigesimum. [n. 1091]

13:9 Qui habet aures audiendi, audiat. [n. 1093]

13:10 Et accedentes discipuli dixerunt ei: quare in parabolis loqueris eis? [n. 1098]

13:11 Qui respondens ait illis: quia vobis datum est nosse mysterium regni caelorum, illis autem non est datum. [n. 1101]

13:1 Ἐν τῇ ἡμέρᾳ ἐκείνῃ ἐξελθὼν ὁ Ἰησοῦς τῆς οἰκίας ἐκάθητο παρὰ τὴν θάλασσαν·

13:2 καὶ συνήχθησαν πρὸς αὐτὸν ὄχλοι πολλοί, ὥστε αὐτὸν εἰς πλοῖον ἐμβάντα καθῆσθαι, καὶ πᾶς ὁ ὄχλος ἐπὶ τὸν αἰγιαλὸν εἱστήκει.

13:3 Καὶ ἐλάλησεν αὐτοῖς πολλὰ ἐν παραβολαῖς λέγων· ἰδοὺ ἐξῆλθεν ὁ σπείρων τοῦ σπείρειν.

13:4 καὶ ἐν τῷ σπείρειν αὐτὸν ἃ μὲν ἔπεσεν παρὰ τὴν ὁδόν, καὶ ἐλθόντα τὰ πετεινὰ κατέφαγεν αὐτά.

13:5 ἄλλα δὲ ἔπεσεν ἐπὶ τὰ πετρώδη ὅπου οὐκ εἶχεν γῆν πολλήν, καὶ εὐθέως ἐξανέτειλεν διὰ τὸ μὴ ἔχειν βάθος γῆς·

13:6 ἡλίου δὲ ἀνατείλαντος ἐκαυματίσθη καὶ διὰ τὸ μὴ ἔχειν ῥίζαν ἐξηράνθη.

13:7 ἄλλα δὲ ἔπεσεν ἐπὶ τὰς ἀκάνθας, καὶ ἀνέβησαν αἱ ἄκανθαι καὶ ἔπνιξαν αὐτά.

13:8 ἄλλα δὲ ἔπεσεν ἐπὶ τὴν γῆν τὴν καλὴν καὶ ἐδίδου καρπόν, ὃ μὲν ἑκατόν, ὃ δὲ ἑξήκοντα, ὃ δὲ τριάκοντα.

13:9 ὁ ἔχων ὦτα ἀκουέτω.

13:10 Καὶ προσελθόντες οἱ μαθηταὶ εἶπαν αὐτῷ· διὰ τί ἐν παραβολαῖς λαλεῖς αὐτοῖς;

13:11 ὁ δὲ ἀποκριθεὶς εἶπεν αὐτοῖς· ὅτι ὑμῖν δέδοται γνῶναι τὰ μυστήρια τῆς βασιλείας τῶν οὐρανῶν, ἐκείνοις δὲ οὐ δέδοται.

13:1 That same day, Jesus, going out of the house, sat by the sea. [n.1078]

13:2 And great multitudes gathered together about him, so that he went up into a boat and sat there, and all the multitude stood on the shore. [n. 1080]

13:3 And he told them many things in parables, saying: behold, the sower went out to sow. [1082]

13:4 And while he was sowing, some fell by the way side and the birds of the air came and ate them up. [n. 1088]

13:5 And some others fell upon stony ground, where they did not have much earth, and they sprang up immediately, because they had no deep soil. [n. 1089]

13:6 But when the sun came up they were scorched, and because they had no root, they withered away. [n. 1090]

13:7 And others fell among thorns, and the thorns grew up and choked them. [n. 1090]

13:8 And others fell upon good ground, and they produced fruit, some a hundredfold, some sixtyfold, and some thirtyfold. [n. 1091]

13:9 He who has ears to hear, let him hear. [n. 1093]

13:10 And his disciples came and said to him: why do you speak to them in parables? [n. 1098]

13:11 He answered and said to them: because it is given to you to know the mysteries of the kingdom of heaven, but it is not given to them. [n. 1101]

13:12 Qui enim habet, dabitur ei, et abundabit; qui autem non habet, et quod habet, auferetur ab eo. [n. 1102]

13:13 Ideo in parabolis loquor eis, quia videntes non vident, et audientes non audiunt, neque intelligunt, [n. 1107]

13:14 et adimpletur in eis prophetia Isaiae dicentis: *auditu audietis, et non intelligetis, et videntes videbitis, et non videbitis.* [n. 1109]

13:15 *Incrassatum est enim cor populi huius, et auribus graviter audierunt, et oculos suos clauserunt, ne quando videant oculis, et auribus audiant, et corde intelligant, et convertantur, et sanem eos.* [n. 1111]

13:16 Vestri autem beati oculi, quia vident, et aures vestrae, quia audiunt. [n. 1115]

13:17 Amen quippe dico vobis, quia multi prophetae et iusti cupierunt videre quae videtis, et non viderunt, et audire quae auditis, et non audierunt. [n. 1117]

13:18 Vos ergo audite parabolam seminantis. [n. 1120]

13:19 Omnis qui audit verbum regni, et non intelligit, venit malus, et rapit quod seminatum est in corde eius; hic est qui secus viam seminatus est. [n. 1122]

13:20 Qui autem super petrosa seminatus est, hic est qui verbum audit, et continuo cum gaudio accipit illud: [n. 1125]

13:21 non habet autem in se radicem, sed est temporalis. Facta autem tribulatione et persecutione propter verbum, continuo scandalizatur. [n. 1127]

13:12 ὅστις γὰρ ἔχει, δοθήσεται αὐτῷ καὶ περισσευθήσεται· ὅστις δὲ οὐκ ἔχει, καὶ ὃ ἔχει ἀρθήσεται ἀπ' αὐτοῦ.

13:13 διὰ τοῦτο ἐν παραβολαῖς αὐτοῖς λαλῶ, ὅτι βλέποντες οὐ βλέπουσιν καὶ ἀκούοντες οὐκ ἀκούουσιν οὐδὲ συνίουσιν,

13:14 καὶ ἀναπληροῦται αὐτοῖς ἡ προφητεία Ἠσαΐου ἡ λέγουσα· ἀκοῇ ἀκούσετε καὶ οὐ μὴ συνῆτε, καὶ βλέποντες βλέψετε καὶ οὐ μὴ ἴδητε.

13:15 ἐπαχύνθη γὰρ ἡ καρδία τοῦ λαοῦ τούτου, καὶ τοῖς ὠσὶν βαρέως ἤκουσαν καὶ τοὺς ὀφθαλμοὺς αὐτῶν ἐκάμμυσαν, μήποτε ἴδωσιν τοῖς ὀφθαλμοῖς καὶ τοῖς ὠσὶν ἀκούσωσιν καὶ τῇ καρδίᾳ συνῶσιν καὶ ἐπιστρέψωσιν καὶ ἰάσομαι αὐτούς.

13:16 ὑμῶν δὲ μακάριοι οἱ ὀφθαλμοὶ ὅτι βλέπουσιν καὶ τὰ ὦτα ὑμῶν ὅτι ἀκούουσιν.

13:17 ἀμὴν γὰρ λέγω ὑμῖν ὅτι πολλοὶ προφῆται καὶ δίκαιοι ἐπεθύμησαν ἰδεῖν ἃ βλέπετε καὶ οὐκ εἶδαν, καὶ ἀκοῦσαι ἃ ἀκούετε καὶ οὐκ ἤκουσαν.

13:18 Ὑμεῖς οὖν ἀκούσατε τὴν παραβολὴν τοῦ σπείραντος.

13:19 παντὸς ἀκούοντος τὸν λόγον τῆς βασιλείας καὶ μὴ συνιέντος ἔρχεται ὁ πονηρὸς καὶ ἁρπάζει τὸ ἐσπαρμένον ἐν τῇ καρδίᾳ αὐτοῦ, οὗτός ἐστιν ὁ παρὰ τὴν ὁδὸν σπαρείς.

13:20 ὁ δὲ ἐπὶ τὰ πετρώδη σπαρείς, οὗτός ἐστιν ὁ τὸν λόγον ἀκούων καὶ εὐθὺς μετὰ χαρᾶς λαμβάνων αὐτόν,

13:21 οὐκ ἔχει δὲ ῥίζαν ἐν ἑαυτῷ ἀλλὰ πρόσκαιρός ἐστιν, γενομένης δὲ θλίψεως ἢ διωγμοῦ διὰ τὸν λόγον εὐθὺς σκανδαλίζεται.

13:12 For he who has, to him it will be given, and he will abound; but he who has not, from him will be taken away even that which he has. [n. 1102]

13:13 Therefore, I speak to them in parables, because seeing they see not, and hearing they hear not, neither do they understand. [n. 1107]

13:14 And the prophecy of Isaiah is fulfilled in them, which said: *by hearing you will hear, and will not understand: and seeing you will see, and will not perceive.* [n. 1109]

13:15 *For the heart of this people has grown gross, and with their ears they have been dull of hearing, and their eyes they have shut: lest at any time they should see with their eyes, and hear with their ears, and understand with their heart, and be converted, and I should heal them.* [n. 1111]

13:16 But blessed are your eyes, because they see, and your ears, because they hear. [n. 1115]

13:17 For, amen, I say to you, many prophets and just men have desired to see the things that you see, and have not seen them, and to hear the things that you hear and have not heard them. [n. 1117]

13:18 Hear therefore the parable of the sower. [n. 1120]

13:19 When anyone hears the word of the kingdom, and does not understand it, there comes the wicked one, and snatches away that which was sown in his heart; this is he who received the seed by the way side. [n. 1122]

13:20 And he who received the seed upon stony ground is he who hears the word and immediately receives it with joy. [n. 1125]

13:21 However, he has no root in himself, but endures only for a time, and when there comes tribulation and persecution because of the word, he quickly falls away. [n. 1127]

13:22 Qui autem seminatus est in spinis, hic est qui verbum Dei audit, et sollicitudo saeculi istius, et fallacia divitiarum suffocat verbum, et sine fructu efficitur. [n. 1129]	**13:22** ὁ δὲ εἰς τὰς ἀκάνθας σπαρείς, οὗτός ἐστιν ὁ τὸν λόγον ἀκούων, καὶ ἡ μέριμνα τοῦ αἰῶνος καὶ ἡ ἀπάτη τοῦ πλούτου συμπνίγει τὸν λόγον καὶ ἄκαρπος γίνεται.	**13:22** And he who received the seed among thorns is he who hears the word, and the care of this world and the deceitfulness of riches chokes up the word, and he becomes fruitless. [n. 1129]
13:23 Qui vero in terram bonam seminatus est, hic est qui audit verbum, et intelligit, et fructum affert, et facit aliud quidem centesimum, aliud autem sexagesimum, aliud vero trigesimum. [n. 1131]	**13:23** ὁ δὲ ἐπὶ τὴν καλὴν γῆν σπαρείς, οὗτός ἐστιν ὁ τὸν λόγον ἀκούων καὶ συνιείς, ὃς δὴ καρποφορεῖ καὶ ποιεῖ ὃ μὲν ἑκατόν, ὃ δὲ ἑξήκοντα, ὃ δὲ τριάκοντα.	**13:23** But he who received the seed upon good ground, is he who hears the word, and understands, and bears fruit; and one yields a hundredfold, and another sixty, and another thirty. [n. 1131]

1077. Supra proposita est doctrina evangelica, et confutati sunt adversarii, hic ostendit virtutem evangelicae doctrinae; et

primum verbis;

secundo factis in capite XIV.

Et circa primum

primo ponuntur circumstantiae doctrinae;

secundo Christi doctrina;

tertio effectus.

Secunda ibi *ecce exiit qui seminat seminare*; tertia ibi *intellexistis haec omnia?*

Et primo ponit quatuor circumstantias, scilicet locum, tempus, dispositionem audientium et dispositionem loquentis.

1078. Tempus tangit, cum dicit *in die illo*. Ex quo datur intelligi quod tangit ordinem rei gestae. Aliter enim non posset intelligi, nisi ly *die* sumatur pro tempore.

1079. Deinde tangitur circumstantia loci, *sedebat secus mare* et cetera. Et hoc potest exponi secundum expositionem litteralem et mysticam.

Litteralem tangit Chrysostomus. Quia enim supra dixerat, quod loquente eo ad turbas dixit quidam, *ecce mater tua* etc., ibi exposuerat Chrysostomus quod aliquid humanum senserant, ideo Dominus voluit exire, ut eorum, scilicet fratrum, nequitiam reprimeret. Et exivit etiam, ut matri honorem deferret. Unde Ex. XX, 12: *honora patrem et matrem tuam*.

Mystice per domum Iudaea intelligitur, de qua exiens propter infidelitatem, venit ad mare, scilicet ad gentes, quae turbatae erant per infidelitatem; infra XXIII, 38: *ecce relinquetur vobis domus vestra deserta*; sicut Ier. XII, v. 7: *reliqui domum meam, dimisi haereditatem meam, dedi dilectam animam meam in manibus inimicorum eius*. Mare dicitur mundus; Ps. CIII, 25: *hoc mare magnum et spatiosum manibus, illic reptilia, quorum non est numerus* et cetera. Vel aliter per domum intelligitur interior mens; Sap. VIII, 16:

1077. Above the evangelical teaching was set forth, and the adversaries were refuted; here he shows the power of the evangelical teaching. And

first, by words;

second, by the deeds (Matt 14).

And concerning the first,

first, the circumstances of the teaching are set down;

second, Christ's teaching;

third, the effect.

The second is at *behold the sower went out to sow*; the third, at *have you understood all these things?* (Matt 13:51).

And first, he sets down four circumstances, namely the place, the time, the arrangement of the hearers, and the position of the one speaking.

1078. He touches on the time when he says, *the same day*. From which one is given to understand that he touches upon the order of history, for it cannot be understood in another way than that the *day* is taken for time.

1079. Then the circumstance of place is touched upon: He *sat by the sea*. And this can be explained according to a literal explanation and a mystical one.

Chrysostom touches upon the literal. For since it was said above that while he was speaking to the crowds, someone said, *behold your mother and your brethren* (Matt 12:47), Chrysostom had explained there that they felt something human, so the Lord wished to go out, that he might reproach their, namely the brothers', wickedness. And he also went out that he might show honor to his mother. Hence, *honor your father and your mother* (Ex 20:12).

Mystically, by the house is understood Judea, from whom he went out due to infidelity and came to the sea, namely to the gentiles, who were disturbed by infidelity; below, *behold, your house will be left to you, desolate* (Matt 23:38); as in, *I have forsaken my house, I have left my inheritance: I have given my dear soul into the land of her enemies* (Jer 12:7). The world is called the sea; *so is this great sea, which stretches wide its arms: there are creeping things without number, creatures, little and great* (Ps 103:25). Or in another way, by the house is understood the interior mind; *when I go into my house, I will repose myself with her*

intrans in domum meam, conquiescam cum illa. Unde aliquando exit de secreto contemplationis ad publicum doctrinae.

1080. *Et congregatae sunt ad eum turbae*. Hic ponit auditores: cum enim mens exit ad publicum doctrinae, tunc multi possunt audire et proficere; Eccli. ult., 31: *appropinquate ad me, indocti, et congregate vos in domum disciplinae*.

1081. Deinde ponitur dispositio docentis et audientium; unde dicitur *ita ut in naviculam ascendens sederet*. Et quare in naviculam? Potest esse ratio litteralis, quia multi auditores erant, ideo voluit eos habere ante faciem, ut melius intelligerent. Omnia enim ante ipsum; Iob XIII, 1: *ecce omnia vidit oculus meus*.

Alia ratio mystica est, quia per navem Ecclesia ex gentibus collecta significatur, ubi sedet per fidem, et docet eos qui stant in littore, scilicet catechumenos, qui parati sunt ad fidem. Vel aliter, quod Iesus in mari, auditores autem in littore stant, in hoc dat exemplum praedicatoribus, quod scilicet non exponant subditos suos periculis. Et hoc significatur Ex. XIII, 17, quod cum Moyses educeret populum suum, non eduxit eos per viam terrae Philisthiim, reputans ne forte poeniterent, et reverterentur in Aegyptum. Ideo Iesus in turbine sedit, alios autem extra dimisit; ideo dicitur *et omnis turba stabat in littore*.

1082. Sequitur modus doctrinae *et locutus est eis multa in parabolis*. Ratio duplex est. Una est, quia per huiusmodi parabolas absconduntur sacra ab infidelibus, ne blasphement: supra enim dictum est: *nolite sanctum dare canibus*: ideo quia multi blasphemabant, ideo voluit loqui in parabolis. Unde Lc. VIII, 10: *vobis datum est nosse mysterium regni Dei, ceteris autem in parabolis*.

Secunda ratio est, quia per huiusmodi parabolas homines rudes melius docentur. Unde homines, scilicet rudes, quando divina sub similitudinibus explicantur, melius capiunt, et retinent. Ideo Dominus loqui voluit in parabolis, ut melius memoriae commendarent. Quia enim noverat quod digni doctrinam suam reciperent, voluit eam sic tradere, ut magis memoriter tenerent; in Ps. LXXVII, 2: *aperiam in parabolis os meum*.

1083. Et quare multas proposuit parabolas? Ratio una est, quia in multitudine hominum diversi diversimode sunt affecti; ideo diversificare debuit, ut congrueret diversis affectibus. Alia ratio est, quia spiritualia semper sunt occulta; ideo per temporalia non plene manifestari possunt, ideo per diversa habent manifestari; Iob XI, 5:

(Wis 8:16). Hence sometimes he goes out from the hidden place of contemplation to the public place of teaching.

1080. *And great multitudes gathered together about him*. Here he sets down the hearers; for when the mind goes out to the public place of teaching, then many can hear and profit; *draw near to me, you unlearned, and gather yourselves together into the house of discipline* (Sir 51:31).

1081. Then are set down the arrangement of the one teaching and of those listening; hence it says, *so that he went up into a boat and sat there*. And why in a boat? There can be a literal reason, that there were many hearers, so he wanted to have them before his face, that they might understand better. For all things are before him; *behold my eye has seen all these things* (Job 13:1).

Another reason is a mystical one, that the boat signifies the Church gathered from the gentiles, where he sits through faith, and teaches those who stand on the shore, namely the catechumens, who are prepared for faith. Or in another way, that Jesus stands on the sea, and the listeners on the shore, and in this he gives an example for preachers, namely that they should not expose themselves to dangers. And this is signified, because when Moses led his people out, he did not lead them through the way of the Philistine's land, considering lest they should repent, and turn back into Egypt (Exod 13:17). This is why Jesus sits in the crowd, but sends the others outside; so it says, *and all the multitude stood on the shore*.

1082. There follows the manner of teaching: *and he told them many things in parables*. There are two reasons. One is that by such parables sacred things are hidden from the unbelieving, lest they blaspheme. For it was said above, *do not give what is holy to dogs* (Matt 7:6), because of the fact that many blaspheme, and for this reason he willed to speak in parables. Hence *to you it is given to know the mystery of the kingdom of God; but to the rest in parables* (Luke 8:10).

The second reason is that by such parables unrefined men are better taught. Hence men, namely the unrefined ones, grasp and retain things better when divine things are explained under likenesses. For this reason the Lord willed to speak in parables, that they might better commit the teachings to memory. For since he had known that those worthy would receive his teaching, he willed to hand it over to them in such a way that they would hold it more by memory; *I will open my mouth in parables* (Ps 77:2).

1083. And why did he set forth many parables? One reason is that in a multitude of men, different men are affected in different ways; so he ought to have diversified his teaching that it might fit with the different affections. Another reason is because spiritual things are always hidden, so they cannot be made entirely clear by temporal things,

utinam loqueretur Deus tecum, et aperiret labia sua tibi, ut ostenderet tibi secreta sapientiae.

1084. ***Exiit qui seminat seminare*** et cetera. Hic ponitur parabolica doctrina.

Et intendit tria.

Primo ponit impedimentum evangelicae doctrinae;

secundo profectum;

tertio dignitatem.

Secunda ibi ***simile est regnum caelorum fermento*** etc.; tertia ibi ***simile est regnum caelorum homini quaerenti bonas margaritas*** et cetera.

Circa primum

primo ponit impedimenta ab intra;

secundo quae ab extra, in sequenti parabola.

Prima in tres: quia

primo ponitur parabola;

secundo assignatur;

tertio exponitur.

Secunda ibi ***et accedentes discipuli*** etc.; tertia ibi ***vos ergo audite parabolam seminantis***.

In prima tria facit.

Primo describitur studium seminantis;

secundo impedimentum seminis;

tertio fructus.

Secunda ibi ***et cum seminat, quaedam ceciderunt secus viam*** etc.; tertia ibi ***alia vero ceciderunt in terram bonam*** et cetera.

1085. Dicit ergo ***exiit qui seminat seminare***. Qui exit est Christus. Exit enim tripliciter. Ab occulto patris, non mutans locum. Item exiit a Iudaea ad gentes. Item a profundo sapientiae ad publicum doctrinae. ***Exiit*** ergo ***qui seminat***, scilicet semen doctrinae. Unde Christus seminat sicut baptizat, ut habetur Io. IV. Semen enim est principium fructus. Unde omnis bona operatio est a Deo; Phil. I, 6: *qui incepit in nobis opus bonum, perficiet* et cetera.

Et in hoc removetur error dicentium quod initium boni operis est a nobis; quod falsum est. Unde Gregorius: *in vanum laborat praedicator, nisi intus insit gratia Salvatoris.* Unde dicit ***exiit qui seminat seminare*** et cetera. Videtur ista involvere verba; sed non involvit, quia seminator exiit aliquando ad seminandum, et aliquando ad metendum; sic Christus in principio exit ad seminandum; Prov. c. XI, 18: *seminanti iustitiae merces fidelis.* ***Exiit*** ergo ***qui seminat seminare***.

1086. Et quid? Semen suum. Quidam enim exeunt seminare iniquitatem; Iob IV, 8: *vidi eos qui operantur iniquitatem, et seminant dolores, et metunt eos.* Sed iste

and so they have to be manifested through diverse things; *I wish that God would speak with you, and would open his lips to you, that he might show you the secrets of wisdom* (Job 11:5–6).

1084. Behold the sower went out to sow. Here the teaching in parables is set down.

And he intends three things:

first, he sets out an impediment to the evangelical teaching;

second, the profit;

third, the dignity.

The second is at **the kingdom of heaven is like leaven** (Matt 13:33); the third is at **again the kingdom of heaven is like a merchant seeking good pearls** (Matt 13:45).

Concerning the first,

first, he sets out impediments from within;

second, those which are from outside, in the following parable.

The first, in three parts, for

first, the parable is set out;

second, it is applied;

third, it is explained.

The second is at **and his disciples came and said**; the third, at **hear therefore the parable of the sower**.

In the first, he does three things:

first, the zeal of the one sowing is described;

second, the impediment to the seed;

third, the fruit.

The second is at **and while he was sowing some fell by the way side**, the third, at **and others fell upon good ground**,

1085. He says then, **behold the sower went out to sow**. He who goes out is Christ, for he goes out in three ways: from the secrecy of the Father, not changing place; likewise, he went out from the Jews to the gentiles; likewise, from the depth of wisdom to the public place of teaching. **The sower went out to sow**, namely the seed of teaching. Hence Christ sows just as he baptizes (John 4). For seed is the principle of fruit. Hence every good working is from God; *he, who has begun a good work in you, will perfect it* (Phil 1:6).

And this removes the error of those who say that the beginning of good works is from us, which is false. Hence Gregory: *in vain does the preacher labor, unless the grace of the Savior is present within.* Hence he says, **the sower went out to sow**. He seems to convolute these words; but he does not convolute them, because he sometimes went out for sowing, and sometimes for reaping. Thus Christ in the beginning goes out for sowing; *to him who sows justice, there is a faithful reward* (Prov 11:18). **The sower** therefore **went out to sow**.

1086. And to sow what? His seed. For certain ones went out to sow iniquity; *I have seen those who work iniquity, and sow sorrows, and reap them* (Job 4:8). But this one went

exiit seminare semen suum. Istud semen est verbum Dei, quod procedit essentialiter. Unde est verbum Patris; Eccli. I, 5: *fons sapientiae verbum Dei*.

Sed quid facit? Similes ei a quo procedit, quia facit filios Dei; Ps. LXXXI, 6: *ego dixi: dii estis, et filii Excelsi omnes*. Io. X, 35: *illos dixit deos ad quos sermo Dei factus est*. Et ibid. c. I, 12: *dedit eis potestatem filios Dei fieri*. **Exiit** ergo et cetera.

1087. Sed videamus de impedimento seminis. Tripliciter enim impeditur, quia tria requiruntur. Requiritur enim quod memoria conservetur. Unde Prov. VI, 21: *liga eas in corde tuo iugiter*. Secundum est, quod radicetur per amorem; Ps. CXVIII, 140: *ignitum eloquium tuum vehementer, et servus tuus dilexit illud*. Tertio requiritur sollicitudo; I ad Tim. VI, 11: *sectare iustitiam, pietatem, fidem, caritatem, patientiam, mansuetudinem* et cetera.

Haec tria per tria tolluntur. Memoria per vanitatem; amor, sive caritas, per duritiam; sollicitudo per germinationem vitiorum.

1088. Unde dicit **et dum seminat, quaedam ceciderunt secus viam**. Via patens est omni viatori, sic cor quod cuilibet exponitur cogitationi; Ez. XVI, 25: *ad omne caput viae aedificasti signum prostitutionis tuae, et abominabilem fecisti decorem tuum*.

Unde quando in corde vano et instabili cadit verbum Dei, cadit secus viam, et subiacet duplici periculo. Sed Matthaeus non ponit nisi unum, scilicet **volucres caeli comederunt illud**. Lucas vero ponit duo, videlicet quia conculcatur, item rapitur a volucribus. Sic quoniam vani recipiunt verbum Dei, conculcatur per vanam cogitationem, vel pravam societatem. Quare multum gaudet Diabolus, quando potest auferre et conculcare semen istud. Habacuc I, 13: *quare respicis contemptores, et taces impio conculcante iustiorem se*?

1089. Secundum est cordis duritia; Iob penult., 15: *cor eius indurabitur quasi lapis, et stringetur quasi malleatoris incus*. Et hoc opponitur caritati, quia amoris est liquefacere; Cantic. V, 6: *anima mea liquefacta est, ut dilectus locutus est* et cetera. Durum enim est quod est in se constrictum, et propriis metis arctatum. Amor facit transferre amantem in amatum: unde diffunditur.

Dicit ergo **alia ceciderunt in petrosa loca** et cetera. Ez. XXXVI, 26: *auferam a vobis cor lapideum et dabo vobis cor carneum*. Aliqui enim sunt qui ita habent cor privatum omni amore, quod omni carne carent. Aliqui vero habent bonum affectum, sed parum habent: unde non habent profundum. Habere profundum est, quum finis et affectus est profundus. Ille ergo habet profundum amorem, qui omnia diligit propter Deum, et nihil

out to sow his seed. That seed is the word of God, which proceeds essentially. Hence it is the word of the Father; *the word of God on high is the fountain of wisdom* (Sir 1:5).

But what does he produce? Things similar to him from whom he proceeds, because he produces sons of God; *I have said: you are gods and all of you the sons of the Most High* (Ps 81:6). *He called them gods, to whom the word of God was spoken* (John 10:35). And *he gave them power to be made the sons of God* (John 1:12). **He went out to sow**, therefore.

1087. But let us see the impediment to the seed. For it is impeded in three ways, because three things are required. For it is required that the memory of the word be preserved. Hence, *bind them in your heart continually* (Prov 6:21). The second is that it be rooted through love; *your word is exceedingly refined: and your servant has loved it* (Ps 118:140). Third, concern is required; *pursue justice, godliness, faith, charity, patience, mildness* (1 Tim 6:11).

These three things are taken away by three things. Memory, by vanity; love or charity, by hardness; concern, by the sprouting up of vices.

1088. Hence he says, **and while he was sowing some fell by the way side**. The way is open to every traveler; so is the heart which is exposed to any thought whatever. *At every head of the way you have set up a sign of your prostitution: and have made your beauty to be abominable* (Ezra 16:25).

Hence when the word of God falls into a vain and unstable heart, it falls **by the way side**, and is subject to two dangers. But Matthew only sets down one, namely **the birds of the air came and ate them up**. But Luke sets down two, namely that it is trampled underfoot, and likewise it is snatched by the birds (Luke 8:5). For this is how the vain receive God's word: it is trampled by vain thoughts, or corrupt society. For which reason the devil rejoices greatly when he can steal away and trample down this seed. *Why do you look upon those who do unjust things, and hold your peace when the wicked devours the man who is more just than himself?* (Hab 1:13).

1089. The second is hardness of heart; *his heart shall be as hard as a stone, and as firm as a smith's anvil* (Job 41:15). And this is opposed to charity, because it belongs to love to melt the heart; *my soul melted when he spoke* (Song 5:6). For that is hard which is constrained within itself, and bound to its own measurement. Love works to transfer the one loving into the one loved; hence the one loving is spread out.

He says therefore, **and some others fell upon stony ground**. *I will take away the stony heart out of your flesh, and will give you a heart of flesh* (Ezra 36:26). For there are some men who have a heart deprived of all love, because they lack all flesh. But some have a good affection, but have too little; hence they have no depth. To have depth is when the end and affection are profound. So that man has a profound love who loves all things for God's sake, and sets

nothing before the love of God. Hence some are well delighted in God, but more in other things; and these are not melted, and such do not have much soil. And soil signifies softness. Hence it is taken for a hardened mind.

There follows **and they sprang up immediately**, because those who think profoundly think for a long time; but those who do not think profoundly rush forth at once into work. Hence they go out quickly; *for before the harvest it was all flourishing, and it shall bud without perfect ripeness* (Isa 18:5). Hence they hear readily, but are not rooted in it, because they do not have the profundity of the soil of love and charity. *That Christ may dwell by faith in your hearts; being rooted and founded in charity* (Eph 3:17).

1090. The third danger is the destruction of the fruit, because if a man loves riches more, when a time of tribulation comes he takes what he loves more. Hence, **when the sun came up they were scorched**, namely through weakness. *He who would kill by the sword, must be killed by the sword. Here is the patience and the faith of the saints* (Rev 13:10). **And because they had no root, they withered away**, because God was not the root. *My strength is dried up like a potsherd* (Ps 21:16). Sometimes in Scripture, 'rock' is taken for those who are good, sometimes for those who are bad. Similarly with 'soil' and 'sun.' Hence there are some who are well moved, but afterwards carry themselves heedlessly. But not so Paul, who said *but I chastise my body, and bring it into subjection, lest perhaps, when I have preached to others, I myself should become a castaway* (1 Cor 9:27).

And others fell among thorns. Now, the thorns are anxieties, resentments, brawls, and suchlike. *Do not sow upon thorns* (Jer 4:3); *I passed by the field of the slothful man, and there follows, and by the vineyard of the foolish man* (Prov 24:30). **And the thorns grew up and choked them**.

But someone could say: it was the stupidity of the one sowing. It can be said that if this speech had been made about sensible land, it would be true; but mention was made of the spiritual, so it does not work, since the parable is referred back to various matters.

1091. The impediments having been set forth, he treats of the fruit of the seed: **and others fell upon good ground, and they produced fruit**. The soil which is not beside the way, which is not rocky, which is not thorny, is good soil, namely a good heart; and if the seed is sown there, it bears fruit; *for the Lord will give goodness: and our earth will yield her fruit* (Ps 84:13).

1092. But what does it bear? **Some a hundredfold, some sixtyfold, and some thirtyfold**. Some refer this to a reward which is in heaven, because some have a hundredfold, *for the fruit of good labors is glorious* (Wis 3:15).

1093. Others refer the thirtyfold fruit to the faith of the Trinity, the sixtyfold to the fruit of good works, the hundredfold to heavenly contemplation. But this cannot be,

potest esse, quia auditor est qui facit fructum. Item praemium recipitur. Unde oportet retorqueri ad perfectionem iustitiae.

Fructus igitur est proprie ultimum quod expectatur in arbore: sic fructus iustitiae qui habetur ex praedicatione. Et haec est *centesima* etc., quia triplex est perfectio, minor, maior et media, ita quod centesima martyrum, sexagesima virginum, trigesima est coniugatorum. Et quare? *Quia* et cetera. Sed perfectio virginum sexagesima, quia tunc debent vacare a malitia; ideo haec perfectio est virginum et quiescentium, qui separati sunt a mundo. Per trigesimum perfectio militantium in hac vita, quia tales apti sunt ad bellum.

1094. Alii assignant per computationem in manu etc. ut in Glossa habetur.

1095. Aliter potestis secundum numerum numerorum. Semen enim fructificat in perfectione. Videatis ergo quod semen est mandatum Dei: trigesimus numerus ex trinario et denario componitur, sexagesimus ex sex et decem, centesimus ex ductu denarii in seipsum. Ternarius est numerus completus, et habet communem perfectionem; senarius similiter est numerus perfectus, quia nihil deest ei, habet enim perfectionem integritatis; denarius est numerus perfectus, quia est primus limes numerorum, unde habet perfectionem finis.

Sic triplex est perfectio. Communis iustitia, et sic est perfectio trinarii, quae habetur per tricenarium numerum; sed cum plus habet ultra communem, tunc dicitur facere sexagesimum fructum; sed quando perfectus est, et iam praegustat suavitatem, tunc pervenit ad centesimum fructum.

1096. Vel aliter secundum Augustinum, secundum quod tripliciter homines se habent ad tentationes. Quidam enim graviter tentantur, sed resistunt fortiter; et hi habent fructum trigesimum. Alii parum tentantur, sed surgunt; et hi habent sexagesimum. Centesimum vero habent qui iam in quieta pace manent.

1097. Et quia hoc parabolice dictum est, ideo subdit *qui habet aures audiendi*, scilicet cordis interius *audiat* per intellectum.

1098. *Et accedentes discipuli* et cetera. Supra posita est parabola, hic assignatur ratio: et

circa hoc ponuntur duo hic.
Primo ponitur interrogatio discipulorum;
secundo responsio, ibi *qui respondens* et cetera.
1099. Dicit ergo *accedentes discipuli dixerunt ei*.

because the hearer is the one who bears the fruit. Likewise, a reward is received. Hence it must be referred to the perfection of justice.

Fruit, therefore, is properly the last thing which is expected in a tree; just so the fruit of justice, which is had from preaching. And this is *some a hundredfold, some sixtyfold, some thirtyfold*, because perfection is threefold: the lesser, the greater, and the middle, such that the hundredfold is of martyrs, the sixtyfold of virgins, the thirtyfold of those who are married. And why? *He who has ears to hear, let him hear*. But the perfection of virgins is sixtyfold, because they should be empty of malice; therefore this is the perfection of virgins and of those who keep quiet, who are separated from the world. The thirtyfold signifies the perfection of those who fight in this life, because such men are suited to war.

1094. Others give a reason by the calculation in the hand, as is had in the Gloss.

1095. In another way, you can explain it according to the number of the numbers. For seed bears fruit in perfection. Consider then that the seed is God's commandment: the number thirty is put together out of three and ten; sixty out of six and ten; one hundred from leading ten into itself. Three is the complete number, and has the common perfection; similarly, six is a perfect number, because nothing is lacking to it, for it has the perfection of integrity; ten is a perfect number, because it is the first boundary of numbers, so it has the perfection of an end.

Thus perfection is threefold: common justice, and such is the perfection of the number three, which is had through the number thirty; but when one has more, beyond the common, then he is said to bear fruit sixtyfold; but when he is perfect, and already tastes the sweetness, then he arrives at the hundredfold fruit.

1096. Or in another way, according to Augustine, according as men carry themselves in three ways with regard to temptations. For some are heavily tempted, but resist bravely, and these have the thirtyfold fruit. Others are tempted only a little, but rise up; and these have the sixtyfold. But those who already abide in restful peace have the hundredfold.

1097. And because this was spoken as a parable, he adds, *he who has ears to hear*, namely with the heart, interiorly, *let him hear* with the understanding.

1098. *And his disciples came and said to him: why do you speak to them in parables?* Above, the parable was set forth; here the explanation is given. And

concerning this two things are set down:
first, the disciples' questioning is set down;
second, the response, at *he answered and said to them*.
1099. It says then, *and his disciples came and said to him*.

Incidit quaestio litteralis: quoniam ipse erat in navicula, quomodo ergo accesserunt ad eum?

Sciendum quod ipsi erant in navicula cum Christo; accesserunt autem per sollicitudinem mentis, vel etiam corporaliter, quia cum parum distarent ab eo, venerunt magis prope: vel cum essent extra, venerunt ad eum. Sic nos, si velimus accedere ad eum, illuminabimur; Ps. XXXIII, 6: *accedite ad eum, et illuminamini*.

Et duo attenduntur. Primo datur exemplum non importune interrogandi; unde dum doceret turbas, non interrogaverunt eum; Eccle. c. III, 7: *tempus tacendi, et tempus loquendi*. **Quare in parabolis loqueris eis?**

Item hic considerandum est, quod debet semper fieri quod de salute hominum est.

1100. Unde sequitur responsio *qui respondens ait illis*. Et

primo ponitur Dei ordinatio;

secundo quaedam ratio assignatur.

1101. Dicit, ideo dico quod in parabolis loquor, **quia vobis datum est nosse mysterium regni caelorum, illis autem non est datum**: in quibus verbis tria ponuntur. Primo quod quidam sunt intelligentes, quidam non. Et non est attribuendum alicui, sed Deo ordinanti; ideo datum est vobis, aliis non. Et ideo est divina ordinatio. Item magnae utilitatis est, quia est quaedam notificatio beatitudinis: unde magna est utilitas, inquantum dat vobis cognitionem de mysteriis divinis; Ier. IX, 12: *quis est vir sapiens qui intelligat hoc, et ad quem verbum oris Domini fiat, ut annuntiet illud?* Item est signum divini amoris; Io. XV, 15: *vos autem dixi amicos, quia omnia quaecumque audivi a Patre meo, nota feci vobis*. Item hoc fit ex dono, non ex merito; Phil. I, 29: *quia vobis datum est pro Christo non solum ut in eum credatis, sed ut etiam pro illo patiamini*. Et hoc est **mysterium regni caelorum** Dei, et hoc a Deo; I ad Cor. IV, 7: *quid autem habes, quod non accepisti?*

1102. Qui enim habet, dabitur ei et abundabit. Aliquid enim est quod habet homo cui datur. Et quid est illud?

Dicendum quod quatuor sunt praeparatoria ad hoc quod detur aliquid. Primum est desiderium. Unde si vis habere scientiam, praeoccupat desiderium, ut habetur Sap. VI, v. 21: *concupiscentia sapientiae deducit ad regnum perpetuum*. Et supra VII, 7: **petite, et accipietis**. Unde **qui habet**, desiderium, **dabitur ei, et abundabit**, quia *ipse est qui dat abundanter omnibus, et non improperat*, Iac. c. I, 5. **Qui autem non habet**, et si aliquam videatur habere aptitudinem ad sapientiam, vel iustitiam, et sit tepidus id quod videtur habere, et non habet,

A literal question comes up: since he was in the boat, how did they approach him?

One should know that they were in the boat with Christ; now, they approached him through anxiety of mind, or even bodily, because when they stood a little ways off from him, they came nearer. Or when they were outside, they came to him. In the same way we, if we wish to approach him, will be enlightened; *come to him and be enlightened* (Ps 33:6).

And two things are considered. First, an example is given of not asking rudely; hence they did not ask him while he was teaching the crowds. *A time to keep silence, and a time to speak* (Eccl 3:7). **Why do you speak to them in parables?**

Likewise, one should consider here that what concerns the salvation of men should always come about.

1100. Hence the response follows: **he answered and said to them**. And

first, God's ordination is set down;

second, a certain reason is given.

1101. He says, I say that I speak in parables for this reason, **because to you it is given to know the mysteries of the kingdom of heaven; but it is not given to them**. Three things are set down in these words. First, that there are some who understand, and some who do not. And this should not be attributed to anyone but God who ordains it; it was given to you for this reason, and not to the others. And therefore it is the divine ordination. Likewise, it is of great use, because it is a certain expression of beatitude; hence its usefulness is great, insofar as it gives you a knowledge of the divine mysteries. *Who is the wise man, that may understand this, and to whom the word of the mouth of the Lord may come that he may declare this?* (Jer 9:12). Likewise, it is a sign of divine love; *but I have called you friends: because all things whatsoever I have heard of my Father, I have made known to you* (John 15:15). Likewise, this comes about by a gift, not by merit; *for unto you it is given for Christ, not only to believe in him, but also to suffer for him* (Phil 1:29). And this is **the mysteries of the kingdom of heaven** of God, and this is from God; *or what have you that you have not received?* (1 Cor 4:7).

1102. For he who has, to him will be given, and he will abound. For there is something which the man to whom it is given has. And what is it?

One should say that there are four things preparatory to something being given. The first is desire. Hence if you wish to have knowledge, first take hold of desire, as is written, *therefore the desire of wisdom brings to the everlasting kingdom* (Wis 6:21). And above, **ask, and it will be given to you** (Matt 7:7). Hence, **he who has** desire, **to him it will be given, and he will abound**, because it is *God, who gives to all men abundantly, and does not upbraid* (Jas 1:5). **But he who has not** and if he seems to have some aptitude for wisdom, or justice, and what he seems to have is lukewarm,

auferetur ab eo. Unde Chrysostomus: *si vides tepidum, debes admonere quod desistat: et si non vult, dimitte eum*. Apoc. III, 16: *utinam calidus esses, aut frigidus; sed quia tepidus es, et nec frigidus, nec calidus, incipiam te evomere ex ore meo*.

1103. Secundum quod requiritur est studium; et haec est expositio Remigii. Unde qui habet bonum ingenium, et non studet, non proficiet. Unde qui habet studium, illi dabitur sapientia, et **abundabit**; Prov. II, v. 4: *si quaesieris eam quasi pecuniam, et sicut thesauros effoderis illam, tunc intelliges timorem Domini, et scientiam Dei invenies*. **Qui autem non habet**, studium, quod videtur habere, scilicet ingenium naturale, non proficiet, sed **auferetur ab eo**.

1104. Tertium quod requiritur est caritas: quia caritas omnium virtutum radix est et omnium bonorum operum. Apostolus ad Eph. III, 17: *in caritate radicati et fundati*. Unde si habes, scilicet caritatem, prorumpes in omne opus bonum; Apostolus I Cor. XIII, 4: *caritas patiens est, benigna est*. Unde si non habes, totum siccatur. Unde quodcumque bonum habet homo sine caritate, nihil est, quia *qui non diligit, manet in morte*, I Io. III, 14.

1105. Quartum quod requiritur, est fides, quia qui fidem non habent, alia bona parum valent; Sap. I, 2: *apparet autem eis qui fidem habent in illum*. Et Rom. X, 10: *corde creditur ad iustitiam, ore autem confessio fit ad salutem*. Et **qui non habet** iustitiam fidei, id quod videtur habere, sive naturale, sive morale, **auferetur ab eo**. Apostolus ad Rom. XIV, 23: *omne quod non est ex fide, peccatum est*. Dico ergo quod **datum est vobis**, quia vos habetis fidem, **illis autem non est datum**.

1106. Sed hic cavendum est de quodam errore, quia videtur quod ex studio et bonis naturalibus possemus acquirere gloriam aeternam. Sed Paulus dicit: *quid habes quod non accepisti?* Unde et desiderium, et studium, et caritas, et fides, omnia haec sunt a Deo.

1107. Ideo in parabolis loquor eis et cetera. Hic adaptat ad propositum; et duo facit.

Primo applicat quantum ad Iudaeos;

secundo quoad apostolos, ibi **vestri autem beati oculi** et cetera.

Et primo duo facit.

Primo adaptat ne ex odio videretur dicere;

secundo inducit auctoritatem, ibi **et adimpletur in eis prophetia Isaiae**.

1108. Notate quod monens ad salutem, manifestat doctrinam suis actibus. Unde Act. I, 1: *coepit Iesus facere et docere*. Et Io. XV, 24: *si opera non fecissem quae nullus alius fecit, peccatum non haberent*. Item: *si locutus non fuissem eis, peccatum non haberent*. Unde ante

and he does not have, **from him will be taken away even that which he has**. Hence Chrysostom: *if you see someone lukewarm, you should warn him to stop; and if he will not, leave him. But because you are lukewarm, and neither cold, nor hot, I will begin to vomit you out of my mouth* (Rev 3:16).

1103. The second thing which is required is zeal; and this is the explanation of Remigius. Hence he who has good natural disposition and is not zealous about it will not profit. Hence he who has zeal, to him will be given wisdom, and **he will abound**; *if you seek her as money, and dig for her as for a treasure: then will you understand the fear of the Lord, and will find the knowledge of God* (Prov 2:4–5). **But he who has not** the zeal which he seems to have, namely a natural disposition, will not profit, but it **will be taken away from him**.

1104. The third thing which is required is charity, because charity is the root of all virtues and of all good works. The Apostle: *being rooted and founded in charity* (Eph 3:17). Hence if you have, namely charity, you rush out into every good work; the Apostle: *charity is patient, is kind* (1 Cor 13:4). Hence if you do not have it, the whole is dried up. Hence whatever good a man has without charity is nothing, because *he who does not love, abides in death* (1 John 3:14).

1105. The fourth thing which is required is faith, because he who does not have faith will gain but little of the other goods; *he shows himself to those who have faith in him* (Wis 1:2). And *with the heart, we believe unto justice; but, with the mouth, confession is made unto salvation* (Rom 10:10). And **he who has not** the justice of faith, that which he seems to have, whether natural or moral, **will be taken away from him**. The Apostle: *for all that is not of faith is sin* (Rom 14:23). I say therefore that **to you it is given** that you have faith, **but it is not given to them**.

1106. But here one should beware a certain error, because it seems that we can acquire eternal glory out of zeal and natural goods. But Paul says, *what have you that you have not received?* (1 Cor 4:7). Hence even desire, and zeal, and charity, and faith; all these things are from God.

1107. Therefore, I speak to them in parables. Here he applies it to the matter at hand; and he does two things:

first, he applies it with regard to the Jews;

second, as regards the apostles, at **but blessed are your eyes, because they see**.

And first he does two things:

first, he adapts it lest he seem to speak from hatred;

second, he brings in an authority, at **and the prophecy of Isaiah is fulfilled in them**.

1108. Note that while he admonishes to salvation, he manifests his teaching in actions. Hence, *Jesus began to do and to teach* (Acts 1:1). And, *if I had not done among them the works that no other man has done, they would not have sin* (John 15:24). Likewise, *if I had not come, and spoken to*

sine parabolis locutus est eis, sed modo post operationem miraculorum *in parabolis loquor eis, quia videntes non vident*. Vident miracula, non vident effectum. Vel sic *videntes*, scilicet exterius, *non vident* interius. Is. XLIII, v. 8: *educ foras populum caecum, et oculos habentem, surdum, et aures ei sunt* et cetera. *Et audientes non audiunt, nec intelligunt*. *Audiunt* verba quibus excitari deberent ad bonum, tamen *non audiunt*, idest non habent effectum; Ez. II, 7: *si forte audiant et quiescant*. Et ibid. XXXIII, 31: *in canticum oris sui vertunt illos*. Et quid est quod non vident? Quia non intelligunt; Ps. LXXXI, 5: *nescierunt, neque intellexerunt, in tenebris ambulant*.

1109. Consequenter inducitur auctoritas Isaiae prophetae. *Et adimpletur in eis prophetia Isaiae dicentis: 'auditu audietis, et non intelligetis'* etc., quod scribitur Is. VI, v. 9; sed ibi dicitur imperative, hic praenunciative. Ibi: *audite audientes, et nolite intelligere, et videte visionem, et nolite cognoscere*.

Et tanguntur tria.
Primo Iudaeorum duritia;
secundo causa;
tertio illius causae effectus.
Secunda ibi *'incrassatum est enim cor populi huius'*; tertia ibi *'ne quando videant'* et cetera.

1110. Et quia duo dixerat, scilicet de auditu et de visu; ideo duo dicit *'audietis'*, auditu scilicet exteriori, audietis doctrinam Christi *'et non intelligetis'*, mysteria; Ps. XXXV, v. 4: *noluit intelligere ut bene ageret*; Osee c. IV, 6: *quia tu scientiam repulisti, repellam te, ne sacerdotio fungaris mihi*. *'Et videntes videbitis, et non videbitis.'* Videbitis carnem Christi visu exteriori, et non considerabitis virtutem eius. *Palpavimus sicut caeci parietem, et quasi absque oculis attrectavimus*, etc., Is. LIX, 10.

1111. Sequitur ratio *'incrassatum est enim cor populi huius'* et cetera. Quia enim de auditu fecerat mentionem, et intelligere proprie est mentis; ideo *'cor populi huius'*, idest mens, *'incrassatum est'*, idest excaecatum. Quare? Quia sicut ad visionem corporalem puritas requiritur, sic ad spiritualem. Unde intellectus dicitur vis superior, quoniam maxime spiritualis. Incrassatur intellectus, quando applicatur grossis et terrenis, sed quando abstrahitur, subtiliatur, sicut in apostolis; II ad Cor. IV, 18: *non contemplantibus nobis quae videntur, sed quae non videntur*. Unde isti non considerabant nisi terrena. *Animalis homo non percipit quae sunt Spiritus Dei*, Apostolus I ad Cor. II, 14; Deut. XXXII, 15: *incrassatus,*

them, they would not have sin (John 15:22). Hence before, he spoke to them without parables, but now, after the working of miracles, *I speak to them in parables, because seeing they see not*. They see miracles; they do not see the effect. Or thus: *seeing*, namely exteriorly, *they see not* interiorly. *Bring forth the people that are blind, and have eyes: that are deaf, and have ears* (Isa 43:8). *And hearing they hear not, neither do they understand*. *They hear* words, by which they should be urged on to good, yet *they hear not*, i.e., they do not have the effect. *If perhaps they will hear, and forbear* (Ezek 2:7). And, *my people sit before you: and hear your words, and do them not: for they turn them into a song of their mouth* (Ezek 33:31). And why is it that they do not see? Because they do not understand; *they have not known nor understood: they walk on in darkness* (Ps 81:5).

1109. Next, the authority of Isaiah the prophet is brought in. *And the prophecy of Isaiah is fulfilled in them, who said: 'by hearing you will hear, and will not understand'*, which is written in Isaiah, but there it is said imperatively (Isa 6:9), here pronunciatively. There: *hearing, hear, and understand not: and see the vision, and know it not* (Isa 6:9).

And three things are touched upon:
first, the hardness of the Jews;
second, the cause;
third, the effect of this cause.
The second is at *'for the heart of this people has grown gross'*; the third, at *'lest at any time they should see with their eyes.'*

1110. And because he had said two things, namely about hearing and about vision, he says two things: *'you will hear'*, i.e., with exterior hearing you shall hear Christ's teaching *'and will not understand'* the mysteries; *he would not understand that he might do well* (Ps 35:4); *because you have rejected knowledge, I will reject you, that you will not do the office of priesthood to me* (Hos 4:6). *'And seeing you will see, and will not perceive.'* You will see Christ's body with exterior sight, and you will not consider his power. *We have groped for the wall, and like the blind we have groped as if we had no eyes* (Isa 59:10).

1111. There follows the reason: *'for the heart of this people has grown gross.'* For since he had mentioned the hearing, and to understand is proper to the mind, he says, *'the heart of this people'*, i.e., the mind, *'has grown gross'*, i.e., blinded. Why? Because just as purity is required for bodily vision, so it is required for spiritual vision. The intellect is made gross when it is applied to things which are gross and earthly, but when it is drawn away, it is made fine, as in the apostles: *while we do not look at the things which are seen, but at the things which are not seen* (2 Cor 4:18). Hence these men will only consider earthly things. *But the sensual man does not perceive these things that are of the Spirit of God*, says the Apostle (1 Cor 2:14); *the beloved grew fat, and*

impinguatus, dilatatus, dereliquit Deum factorem suum, et recessit a Deo salutari suo.

Item sciendum quod quando homo audit quae non placent, non potest de facili intelligere: ergo isti male intelligebant, quia eis non placebant verba sua. Ideo dicitur: **'et auribus graviter audierunt'**; Io. VI, 61: *durus est hic sermo, et quis potest hunc audire?*

'Et oculos suos clauserunt' et cetera. Contingit quod aliquis habet oculos, et non videt, quia claudit oculos: unde ipse sibi facit impedimentum. Aliqua vero sunt ita occulta, ut nisi multum infigat intuitum, non potest videre; sed si res sit in medio, sicut paries, non potest homo non videre nisi claudat oculos. Ideo si Dominus non fecisset miracula aperta, non esset mirum si non crederent; sed apertissima fecit, ideo ipsi cognoscerent, nisi clauderent oculos; Dan. XIII, 9: *declinaverunt oculos suos, ut non viderent caelum* et cetera.

Unde notandum quod in ista obduratione causa per se est homo, Deus vero non indurat nisi in non impartiendo gratiam. Deus ergo indurat, quia non dat gratiam; sed homo quia imponit sibi impedimentum lumini. Ideo istis imputatur quod oculos clauserunt.

1112. 'Ne quando videant oculis.' Hic ponitur damnum quod consequuntur. Unde potest intelligi dupliciter. Ita quod ly **'ne quando'** referatur ad totum sequens, ut sit sensus: ita clauserunt oculos, **'ne quando'** etc., et hoc modo intelligitur quod sit ex eorum malitia, quidam enim peccant ex infirmitate, quidam ex industria, sive ex certa malitia. Unde isti hoc attendentes clauserunt oculos ne intelligant; unde tacita est eorum malitia. **'Ne convertantur, et sanem eos'**, scilicet si convertantur; Ier. III, 14: *convertimini, filii revertentes* et cetera. Et haec expositio est Chrysostomi. Et ponuntur tria: ne videant, ne audiant, ne corde intelligant, et respondent tribus supradictis.

Augustinus aliter exponit dicens **'ne quando videant'**, cum modo non videant oculis, **'et auribus audiant, et corde intelligant, et convertantur, et sanem eos.'** Unde dicit Augustinus quod possent haec verba habere duplicem sensum, quia aliquando ponitur **'ne quando'** pro eo quod est ut possit accidere, ut habetur II ad Tim. II, 25: *ne quando det illis Deus poenitentiam ad cognoscendam veritatem.* Aliquando vero ponitur pro eo quod est ne possit contingere, idest hoc contingeret nisi argueremus et cetera.

kicked: he grew fat, and thick and gross, he forsook God who made him, and departed from God his savior (Deut 32:15).

Likewise, one should know that when a man hears something which does not please him, he cannot easily understand it. Therefore these men understood badly, because his words did not please them. For this reason it says, **'and with their ears they have been dull of hearing'**; *this saying is hard, and who can hear it?* (John 6:61).

'And their eyes they have shut.' It happens that someone has eyes, and does not see because he closes his eyes. Hence he himself sets up an impediment for himself. Indeed, there are some things hidden in such a way that a man cannot see them unless he gives it a long stare; but if a thing is in the middle, like a wall, a man cannot not see it unless he shuts his eyes. So if the Lord had not done manifest miracles, it would not be a marvel if they did not believe; but he worked the most manifest miracles, so they would have known if they had not closed their eyes. *And they perverted their own mind and turned away their eyes that they might not look unto heaven, nor remember just judgments* (Dan 13:9).

Hence one should notice that in this stubbornness the cause *per se* is man; indeed, God does not harden the heart except in not imparting grace. Therefore God hardens, because he does not give grace; but a man hardens because he sets up for himself an impediment to the light. Therefore it is imputed to them that they closed their eyes.

1112. 'Lest at any time they should see with their eyes.' Here the curse which they obtain is set down. Hence it can be understood in two ways. In one way, such that the **'lest at any time'** is referred to the whole of what follows, so that the sense is: they have closed their eyes, in this way, **'lest'** sometime they should see, and in this way it is understood that it is out of their malice, for some men sin out of weakness, and some on purpose, or out of certain malice. Hence these men, considering this, closed their eyes lest they should see; hence their malice is unmentioned. Lest they should **'be converted, and I should heal them'**, namely if they converted; *return, O revolting children, says the Lord, for I am your husband* (Jer 3:14). And this is Chrysostom's explanation. And three things are set down: lest they should see, lest they should hear, lest they should understand with the heart; and these correspond to the three things said above.

Augustine explains it in another way, saying, **'lest at any time they should see with their eyes'**, since they do not see with their eyes at the moment, **'and hear with their ears, and understand with their heart, and be converted, and I should heal them.'** Hence Augustine says that these words can have a double sense, because sometimes **'lest at any time'** is set down for that which is in order that it may happen, as is written, *with modesty admonishing them that resist the truth: if perhaps God may give them repentance to know the truth* (2 Tim 2:25). But sometimes it is set down for that which is lest it should happen, i.e., this would happen unless we were to argue.

1113. Et quid est ergo quod dicit *'incrassatum est'*? Solvit Augustinus quod aliquando contingit quod homo superbus est, et videtur ei, quod sit valde bonus; et permittit Dominus cadere in alia peccata ut sanet eum a superbia sua. Tales sunt praesumptuosi, de quibus Rom. X, 3: *ignorantes Dei iustitiam, et suam quaerentes statuere, iustitiae Dei non sunt subiecti*. Quia igitur isti superbi erant, ideo permisi ut excaecarentur, ut videant et audiant, et sanem eos.

Et haec expositio habetur ex littera Marci c. IV, 12. Sed littera Ioannis XII, 40 contradicit quia ibi dicit, *propterea non poterant credere, quia Isaias dixit: 'excaecavit oculos eorum; et induravit cor eorum, ut non videant oculis, et non intelligant corde, et convertantur, et sanem eos.'* Non ergo sunt excaecati, ut crederent, sed ut non crederent.

1114. Sed, secundum Augustinum, hic est quaestio gravis, quia si excaecati sunt, ut non credant; ergo non debet eis imputari.

Solvit Augustinus: possumus dicere, quod hoc quod excaecati sunt, ex praecedentibus peccatis meruerunt. Rom. I, 21: *obscuratum est insipiens cor eorum; dicentes enim se esse sapientes, stulti facti sunt*, et sequitur post, *propter quod Deus tradidit eos* et cetera. Ideo propter peccata induravit, et aures aggravavit, non indurando, sed non impartiendo gratiam propter peccata eorum.

Et possumus aliter dicere, secundum Augustinum: *'incrassatum est cor populi huius'*; ut non videant, et convertantur, scilicet statim, sed permanentes crucifigant Christum, et post videntes miracula convertantur. Et dicit Augustinus quod videtur haec sententia extorta, si non videmus ita accidisse de facto. Aliqui enim non reducuntur ad humilitatem nisi in grave peccatum cadant: sic Dominus istis fecit.

1115. Vestri autem beati oculi qui vident, et aures vestrae quae audiunt et cetera. Supra ostendit Dominus miseriam Iudaeorum qui videntes non videbant, hic ostendit beatitudinem apostolorum qui videbant et audiebant. Et

primo ostendit beatitudinem;

secundo signum ostendit, ibi **amen quippe dico vobis** et cetera.

1116. Dicit ergo, quod videntes non vident, **sed vestri oculi sunt beati**. Sed si istud referatur ad oculos exteriores et aures, ita beatificantur oculi Iudaeorum sicut apostolorum. Ideo dicit Hieronymus quod oportet intelligere duplices oculos, scilicet exteriores, quibus communiter omnes viderunt: et de his non loquitur; vel interiores, quibus apostoli soli viderunt. Ad Eph. I, 17:

1113. So why does he say, *'has grown gross'*? Augustine solves it, saying that sometimes it happens that a man is proud, and it seems to him that he is very good; and the Lord permits him to fall into other sins that he might heal him of his pride. Such are the presumptuous, of whom it says, *for they, not knowing the justice of God, and seeking to establish their own, have not submitted themselves to the justice of God* (Rom 10:3). Therefore, since they were proud, I have permitted them to be blinded, that they might see and hear, and I might heal them.

And this explanation comes from another text (Mark 4:12). But the text of John contradicts what he says there, *therefore they could not believe, because Isaiah said again: 'he has blinded their eyes, and hardened their heart, that they should not see with their eyes, nor understand with their heart, and be converted, and I should heal them'* (John 12:39–40). Therefore, they were not blinded in order that they should believe, but in order that they should not believe.

1114. But, according to Augustine, there is a grave question here, because if they were blinded so that they would not believe, then it should not be imputed to them.

Augustine solves it: we can say that they had merited the fact that they were blinded by preceding sins. *Their foolish heart was darkened. For professing themselves to be wise, they became fools* (Rom 1:21–22), and afterwards there follows: *wherefore God gave them up, to the desires of their heart* (Rom. 1:24). Therefore he hardened them on account of sins, and made heavy their ears, not by hardening, but by not imparting grace on account of their sins.

And we can say otherwise, according to Augustine: *'for the heart of this people has grown gross'*, that they might not see, and be converted, namely at once, but that persisting, they might crucify Christ, and afterward be converted when they see miracles. And Augustine says that this opinion seems wrenched out of the text, if we do not see it to have happened this way in fact. For some are not brought down to humility unless they fall heavily into sin: thus the Lord did to these.

1115. But blessed are your eyes, because they see, and your ears, because they hear. Above, the Lord showed the misery of the Jews, who seeing did not see; here he shows the blessedness of the apostles, who saw and heard. And

first, he shows their blessedness;

second, he shows a sign, at **for, amen, I say to you**.

1116. He says then that seeing they do not see, **but blessed are your eyes**. But if this is referred to exterior eyes and ears, in this way the eyes of the Jews would be blessed just as the apostles'. Therefore Jerome says that one must understand double eyes, namely the exterior ones, with which all see in common, and he does not speak of these; or the interior eyes, with which only the apostles saw.

That the God of our Lord Jesus Christ, the Father of glory, may give unto you the spirit of wisdom and of revelation, in the knowledge of him: the eyes of your heart enlightened (Eph 1:17–18). Hence similarly also, there are certain exterior ears, and certain interior ones, about which it was said above: **he who has ears to hear, let him hear**. *The Lord God has opened my ear, and I do not resist: I have not gone back* (Isa 50:5).

He attributes blessedness in seeing to them, because the blessedness on the way consists only in a participation of eternal blessedness, which consists in vision, for the glory of man is in the vision of God; *let not the wise man glory in his wisdom*, and there follows: *but let him who glories glory in this, that he understands and knows me* (Jer 9:23–24).

1117. Then he sets forth a sign: *for, amen, I say to you*. Augustine says, *blessed is he who has all that he wants*. Hence blessed are they to whom are given all the things the ancients wanted, namely the prophets and the just. For any just man is a king; hence it says *the king, who sits on the throne of judgment, scatters away all evil with his look* (Prov 20:8). And this is because **they have desired to see the things that you see**. If therefore they desired and did not have, and you have, then already you perceive a certain participation of beatitude.

1118. But why does he say, **and have not seen them**? Does it not say *Abraham your father rejoiced that he might see my day: he saw it, and was glad*? (John 8:56). Likewise, *I saw the Lord sitting upon a throne high and elevated* (Isa 6:1). And the same thing about the passion; hence, *we have seen him, and there was no sightliness* (Isa 53:2).

One solution is that some saw and some did not. But, as Jerome says, this is dangerous to say. Or otherwise, that they saw, but not so manifestly. *Which in other generations was not known to the sons of men, as it is now revealed to his holy apostles and prophets in the Spirit* (Eph 3:5). Or in another way, that the whole is referred to the vision and hearing of bodily presence, because to see Christ in the body was desirable to just men. An example is had in Simeon (Luke 2:10). Hence, **blessed are your eyes, because they see**.

1119. And did not the Jews see? I say that it says about these that they did not see, because they only saw exteriorly.

But the contrary is had in John, where it says, *blessed are they that have not seen, and have believed* (John 20:29).

One should say that there is the blessedness of the thing which is had by participation, and the blessedness of hope which is had in meriting. Hence blessed are they who did not see with the blessedness of hope or merit, and blessed are they who saw with the blessedness of the thing or participation; hence it says about Abraham: *your father rejoiced that he might see my day: he saw it, and was glad* (John 8:56).

1120. *Hear therefore the parable of the sower*. Here the explanation is set down. And

first, he concludes that they were worthy;

secundo exponit.

1121. Dicit ergo *vos ergo audite* etc., quia scilicet estis digni vos audire, et non solum audire, sed per me audire; Prov. I, 5: *audiens sapiens sapientior erit*.

1122. *Omnis qui audit verbum regni* et cetera. Hic exponit; et quia fecerat mentionem de duplici terra, ideo primo exponit quod dixerat de terra mala, secundo de terra bona, ibi *qui vero in terram bonam seminatus est* et cetera.

Item, in terra mala posuerat tres differentias, quia quaedam secus viam quaedam in petrosa, quaedam in spinosa. Et hoc exponit.

Et ad huius intellectum debetis scire, quod audire verbum Dei debet habere effectum unum, ut infigatur in corde unde: *beatus qui in lege domini meditatur die ac nocte*, Ps. I, 2. Alibi *in corde meo abscondi eloquia tua, ut non peccem tibi*. Item alius effectus est ut perducatur in opus. In quibusdam enim impeditur primus, in quibusdam secundus.

1123. De primo ponitur. Et sciendum quod littera habet interpositionem, et debet sic intelligi. *Omnis qui audit verbum regni, et non intelligit, venit malus, et rapit quod seminatum est in corde eius*. Et hic est qui est secus viam. Et quare non intelligit? Quia *venit malus* homo etc., unde *omnis qui audit verbum regni*, idest Christi praedicantis regnum caelorum, quia Christus solum regnum Dei praedicavit: Moyses enim terrenum regnum praedicavit. Unde Petrus, Io. VI, 69: *Domine, ad quem ibimus? Verba vitae aeternae habes*. Aliqui, sicut infideles, non audiunt; Is. LXV, 12: *locutus sum, et non audivistis* et cetera. Aliqui sunt qui audiunt; *beati qui audiunt verba Dei*, Lc. XI, 28. *Sed non intelligit*. Glossa: *quia audit non ex affectu unde non recondit in corde*. Ps. XXXV, 4: *noluit intelligere ut bene ageret*.

1124. Et quid erit de isto? Capitur a furibus, quia detinetur mens a cogitationibus, et ita rapitur; et hoc est quod dicit *venit malus*, scilicet Diabolus, quia malus non natura, sed perversitate: *et rapit*, scilicet occulte, seducendo, et inducendo vanam cogitationem, *quod seminatum est in corde eius*, scilicet semen: *hic est qui seminatus est secus viam*.

Seminatus aliquando nominat quod seminatur, aliquando agrum qui seminatur: unde cum dicit *quod seminatum est*, intelligitur semen; cum vero dicitur *qui seminatus est*, intelligitur ager. Homo enim dicitur ager, de quo agro habetur Prov. XXIV, 27: *diligenter exerce*

second, he explains.

1121. He says then, *hear therefore the parable*, namely because you are worthy to hear, and not only to hear, but to hear through me; *a wise man shall hear and shall be wiser* (Prov 1:5).

1122. *When anyone hears the word of the kingdom*. Here he explains the parable; and because he had mentioned the twofold soil, first he explains what he had said about the bad soil, second about the good soil, at *but he who received the seed upon good ground*.

Likewise, he had set out three differences in the bad soil, for some seed fell beside the way, some in a rocky place, some on thorny soil. And he explains this.

And to understand this, you should know that the hearing of God's word should have one effect, that it be implanted in the heart. Hence: *on his law he shall meditate day and night* (Ps 1:2). In another place, *your words have I hidden in my heart, that I may not sin against you* (Ps 118:11). Likewise another effect is that it should be brought forth into work. For in some the first effect is impeded, in other things the second.

1123. The explanation of the first is set down. And one should know that the text has an interposition, and should be understood in this way. *When any one hears the word of the kingdom, and does not understand it, there comes the wicked one, and snatches away that which was sown in his heart*. And this is the one who is beside the way. And why does not he understand? Because *there comes the wicked one*, i.e., a wicked man, hence, *any one hears the word of the kingdom*, i.e., of Christ preaching the kingdom of heaven, because only Christ preached the kingdom of God: for Moses preached an earthly kingdom. Hence Peter says: *Lord, to whom will we go? You have the words of eternal life* (John 6:69). Some men, such as the infidels, do not hear; *I spoke, and you did not hear* (Isa 65:12). There are some men who hear; *blessed are they who hear the word of God* (Luke 11:28). But he *does not understand it*. The Gloss: *because he does not hear out of affection, he does not hide it away in his heart. He would not understand that he might do well* (Ps 35:4).

1124. And what will happen to this one? He is seized by robbers, because the mind is detained by thoughts, and so he is snatched away. And this is what he says, *there comes the wicked one*, namely the devil, because evil is not by nature, but by perversity, *and snatches away*, that is, secretly, by seducing and by introducing vain thoughts, *that which was sown in his heart*, namely the seed: *this is he who received the seed by the way side*.

The *sown* sometimes names what is sown, and sometimes the field which is sown. Hence when he says, *that which was sown*, the seed is understood; but when it says, *who was sown*, the field is understood. For a man is called a field, about which field it says, *prepare your work without*

agrum tuum et cetera. Et quomodo *secus viam*? Quoniam non custoditur, contra illud Prov. IV, 23: *omni custodia serva cor tuum, quoniam ex ipso vita procedit*. Sic homo dicitur seminatus secus viam, qui verbum recipit, sed non custodit.

1125. Secundus effectus est producere in opus; unde Iac. I, 22: *estote factores verbi, et non auditores tantum*. Effectus autem iste impeditur per prospera et adversa. De eo qui impeditur per adversa dicit *qui autem super petrosa seminatus est* et cetera.

Primo ergo ponit principium boni;

secundo occasionem mali, ibi **non habent autem in se radicem**;

tertio malum, ibi **facta autem tribulatione** et cetera.

1126. Petra est malum cor, in quod non potest penetrare verbum, sicut in terra petrosa, et ubi est parum de terra; sic aliqui non exponunt cor suum penetrabile. Tunc enim dicitur penetrabile, quando nihil praeponit verbo, ita quod verbum habeat ut radicem principalem. Unde Ez. XI, 19: *auferam a vobis cor lapideum* et cetera. **Hic verbum audit, et continuo cum gaudio suscipit illud**, ideo delectatur de iustitia, et pronus fit ad bonum. Ad Gal. III, 5: *qui tribuit vobis Spiritum Sanctum, operatur in vobis virtutes*.

1127. Et sic delectatur; sed non potest figi, quia **radicem non habet**, quia in lapide seminatur. Radix autem caritas est. Ad Eph. c. III, 17: *in caritate radicati et fundati* et cetera. **Sed temporalis est**, et ad tempus gaudet; Eccli. VI, 10: *est amicus socius mensae, et non permanebit in die necessitatis*. Haec est ergo occasio, quia non habet radicem.

1128. Et quomodo est? Quia male figitur. Unde dicit *facta tribulatione et persecutione propter verbum* etc., ut quando occurrunt adversantes contra fidem, et tribulationes per interiores vel exteriores adversitates propter doctrinam verbi, vel propter fidem **continuo scandalizantur**, quia a fide resiliunt; Ps. CXVIII, 165: *pax multa diligentibus legem tuam, et non est illis scandalum*. Ille qui perseverat, est amicus.

Et dicit **continuo**: quia etsi caritatem habeant, ex multa tribulatione possent scandalizari. Sed quando continuo ex parva tribulatione quis scandalizatur, non est radicatus in caritate; unde I ad Cor. X, 13: *fidelis Deus, qui non permittit hominem tentari ultra quam possit, sed faciet etiam cum tentatione proventum*. Et ad Hebr. XII, 4: *nondum enim restitistis usque ad sanguinem*. Et secundum Hieronymum **continuo**, quia distanter inter istum et illum.

1129. *Qui autem seminatus est in spinis* et cetera. Hic ponitur impedimentum bene fructificandi, quod

and diligently till your ground (Prov 24:27). And how is it *by the way side*? Because it is not taken care of, contrary to *with all watchfulness keep your heart, because life issues out from it* (Prov 4:23). Thus a man is said to be sown by the way side, because he receives the word, but does not take care of it.

1125. The second effect is to lead one forth into work; hence, *but be doers of the word, and not hearers only* (Jas 1:22). Now, this effect is impeded by prosperity and by adversity. Of him who is impeded by adversity he says, **he who received the seed upon stony ground**.

First, then, he sets down the principle of good;

second, the occasion of evil, at **however, he has no root in himself**;

third, the evil, at **and when there comes tribulation, and persecution**.

1126. The rock is an evil heart, into which the word cannot penetrate, just as into rocky ground, and where there is too little soil. In this way, some men do not put forth their heart as penetrable. For it is called penetrable when nothing is set before the word, such that he has the word as a principal root. Hence, *I will take away the stony heart* (Ezek 11:19). This one **hears the word and immediately receives it with joy**, because he is delighted with justice, and becomes inclined to good. *He therefore who gives to you the Spirit, and works miracles among you* (Gal 3:5).

1127. And he is delighted so; but it cannot be thrust in, because **he has no root in himself**, because it is sown on a rock. Now, the root is charity. *Being rooted and founded in charity* (Eph 3:17). **But endures only for a time**, and rejoices for a time, *and there is a friend, a companion at the table, and he will not abide in the day of distress* (Sir 6:10). This then is the occasion, that he does not have a root.

1128. And how is this? Because he is badly established. Hence he says, **when there comes tribulation and persecution because of the word**, as when adversaries rise up against the faith, and afflictions through interior or exterior hardships on account of the teaching of the word, or on account of the faith, **he quickly falls away**, because he shrinks back from the faith. *Much peace have they who love your law, and to them there is no stumbling block* (Ps 118:165). He who perseveres is a friend.

And he says, **quickly**, because even if they have charity, they could fall away because of many afflictions. But when someone falls away immediately because of a small affliction, he is not rooted in charity; hence, *God is faithful, who will not suffer you to be tempted above that which you are able: but will make also with temptation issue, that you may be able to bear it* (1 Cor 10:13). And, *for you have not yet resisted unto blood, striving against sin* (Heb 12:4). And according to Jerome, he says, **quickly**, because standing between this and that.

1129. *And he who received the seed among thorns*. Here is set down the impediment to bearing fruit well,

aliquando fit ex prosperitatibus, et aliquando ex adversitatibus; unde dicit *qui autem in spinis seminatus est, hic est qui audit verbum Dei*. Istae spinae sunt sollicitudines huius saeculi; sicut enim spinae pungunt, et non sinunt hominem quiescere, sic nec istae sollicitudines. Ideo nolite seri super spinas. *Sollicitudo huius saeculi et fallacia divitiarum suffocat verbum.*

Sollicitudo quoad futura, *fallacia divitiarum*, quoad praesentia: unde cum abundant divitiae, fallaces sunt; I ad Tim. VI, 17: *divitibus huius saeculi praecipe non sublime sapere neque sperare in incerto divitiarum.* Item cum desiderantur, fallunt quantum ad satietatem, quia non satiant. Item sollicitant; ideo Dominus apostolis suis prohibet, *nolite solliciti esse quid manducetis, aut bibatis*, supra VI, 31.

1130. *Suffocat verbum.* Superius dixit *aruit*, hic *suffocat*.

Scitis enim quod candela potest extingui vel propter defectum humoris, et tunc arescit: aliquando propter superfluitatem, et tunc suffocatur; sic et vita naturalis, quae fundatur in calido et humido, potest deficere propter abundantiam humoris, vel propter defectum. Similiter tribulationes aliquando subtrahunt humores consolationis praesentis, et tunc redditur instabile, et arescit: aliquando accrescunt, et tunc suffocatur; ideo semen est sine fructu; unde dicit *et sine fructu efficitur*. Ad Rom. VI, 21: *quem ergo fructum habuistis in illis in quibus nunc erubescitis?* Et sequitur, *servi autem facti Deo, habetis fructum vestrum in sanctificationem*; ad Eph. V, 9: *fructus enim lucis in omni bonitate, et iustitia, et veritate.*

1131. *Qui vero in terram bonam seminatus est* et cetera. Exposita triplici differentia ad malum, subiungit ad bona, quam distinguit per tres effectus, quia primo *audit*, item plus *et intelligit*, item *fructum affert, et facit aliud quidem centesimum, aliud autem sexagesimum, aliud vero trigesimum.* Exponatur sicut supra.

Sciendum tamen quod Augustinus Lib. II, cap. 23 *de Civ. Dei*, ponit expositionem quorumdam qui volebant sic interpretari, quia in die, cum Dominus veniet ad iudicium, multi sancti orabunt pro multis; et secundum quod erunt meliores, plures eis dabuntur. Unde quibusdam dabuntur triginta, quibusdam sexaginta, quibusdam centum. Sed hoc est contra fidem: quia peccata mortalia non dimittentur, quia sine caritate non possunt dimitti; unde mortalia contraria sunt caritati, venialia non: ideo et cetera.

which sometimes comes from prosperities, and sometimes from adversities; hence he says, *and he who received the seed among thorns is he who hears the word*. These thorns are the anxieties of this age; for just as thorns prick, and do not let a man be at rest, so neither do these anxieties. Therefore do not be sown upon thorns. *The care of this world and the deceitfulness of riches chokes up the word.*

Care as regards the future, *deceitfulness of riches* as regards the present. Hence when riches abound, there are deceptions; *charge the rich of this world not to be highminded, nor to trust in the uncertainty of riches* (1 Tim 6:17). Likewise, when they are desired, they deceive as regards satisfaction, because they do not satisfy. Similarly, they disturb; therefore the Lord forbade his disciples, *do not be solicitous therefore, saying, what will we eat: or what will we drink?* (Matt 6:31).

1130. *Chokes up the word*. Above he said, **withered away**, here **chokes**.

For you know that a candle can be put out because of a lack of moisture, and then withers away; sometimes a candle is put out because of an excess of moisture, and then it is suffocated. So it is also with natural life, which is founded on heat and moisture: it can fail because of an abundance of moisture, or because of a lack. Similarly, afflictions sometimes take away the moisture of present consolation, and then a man is rendered unstable and withers away; sometimes they swell up and then he is suffocated. For this reason the seed is without fruit; hence he says, *and he becomes fruitless*. *What fruit therefore had you then in those things, of which you are now ashamed?* (Rom 6:21). And there follows: *become servants to God, you have your fruit unto sanctification* (Rom 6:22). *For the fruit of the light is in all goodness, and justice, and truth* (Eph 5:9).

1131. *But he who received the seed upon good ground*. Having explained the three differentiations with regard to evil, he adds next something with regard to good, which he distinguishes by three effects, because first he **hears**, likewise further **and understands**, likewise **bears fruit; and one yields a hundredfold, and another sixty, and another thirty**. This is explained as above.

Yet one should know that Augustine, in *The City of God* (Bk. II, Ch. 23), sets out the explanation of certain men who wanted to interpret it in this way, that on the day when the Lord shall come for judgment, many saints will pray for many men; and according as they are better, more will be given to them. Hence to certain men will be given thirtyfold, to certain ones sixtyfold, to certain ones a hundredfold. But this is against the faith, because mortal sins will not be forgiven, since without charity they cannot be forgiven; hence mortal sins are against charity, while venial sins not.

Lecture 2

¹³:²⁴ Aliam parabolam proposuit illis, dicens: simile factum est regnum caelorum homini qui seminavit bonum semen in agro suo. [n. 1133]

¹³:²⁵ Cum autem dormirent homines, venit inimicus eius, et superseminavit zizania in medio tritici, et abiit. [n. 1135]

¹³:²⁶ Cum autem crevisset herba, et fructum fecisset, tunc apparuerunt et zizania. [n. 1141]

¹³:²⁷ Accedentes autem servi patrisfamilias dixerunt ei: domine, nonne bonum semen seminasti in agro tuo? Unde ergo habet zizania? [n. 1143]

¹³:²⁸ Et ait illis: inimicus homo hoc fecit. Servi autem dixerunt ei: vis, imus, et colligimus ea? [n. 1144]

¹³:²⁹ Et ait: non ne forte colligentes zizania, eradicetis simul et triticum. [n. 1147]

¹³:³⁰ Sinite utraque crescere usque ad messem, et in tempore messis dicam messoribus: colligite primum zizania, et alligate ea fasciculos ad conburendum, triticum autem congregate in horreum meum. [n. 1150]

¹³:²⁴ Ἄλλην παραβολὴν παρέθηκεν αὐτοῖς λέγων· ὡμοιώθη ἡ βασιλεία τῶν οὐρανῶν ἀνθρώπῳ σπείραντι καλὸν σπέρμα ἐν τῷ ἀγρῷ αὐτοῦ.

¹³:²⁵ ἐν δὲ τῷ καθεύδειν τοὺς ἀνθρώπους ἦλθεν αὐτοῦ ὁ ἐχθρὸς καὶ ἐπέσπειρεν ζιζάνια ἀνὰ μέσον τοῦ σίτου καὶ ἀπῆλθεν.

¹³:²⁶ ὅτε δὲ ἐβλάστησεν ὁ χόρτος καὶ καρπὸν ἐποίησεν, τότε ἐφάνη καὶ τὰ ζιζάνια.

¹³:²⁷ προσελθόντες δὲ οἱ δοῦλοι τοῦ οἰκοδεσπότου εἶπον αὐτῷ· κύριε, οὐχὶ καλὸν σπέρμα ἔσπειρας ἐν τῷ σῷ ἀγρῷ; πόθεν οὖν ἔχει ζιζάνια;

¹³:²⁸ ὁ δὲ ἔφη αὐτοῖς· ἐχθρὸς ἄνθρωπος τοῦτο ἐποίησεν. οἱ δὲ δοῦλοι λέγουσιν αὐτῷ· θέλεις οὖν ἀπελθόντες συλλέξωμεν αὐτά;

¹³:²⁹ ὁ δέ φησιν· οὔ, μήποτε συλλέγοντες τὰ ζιζάνια ἐκριζώσητε ἅμα αὐτοῖς τὸν σῖτον.

¹³:³⁰ ἄφετε συναυξάνεσθαι ἀμφότερα ἕως τοῦ θερισμοῦ, καὶ ἐν καιρῷ τοῦ θερισμοῦ ἐρῶ τοῖς θερισταῖς· συλλέξατε πρῶτον τὰ ζιζάνια καὶ δήσατε αὐτὰ εἰς δέσμας πρὸς τὸ κατακαῦσαι αὐτά, τὸν δὲ σῖτον συναγάγετε εἰς τὴν ἀποθήκην μου.

¹³:²⁴ He proposed another parable to them, saying: the kingdom of heaven is like a man who sowed good seed in his field. [n. 1133]

¹³:²⁵ But while men were asleep, his enemy came and oversowed weeds among the wheat and went away. [n. 1135]

¹³:²⁶ And when the seed had grown, and had produced fruit, then the weeds appeared as well. [n. 1141]

¹³:²⁷ And the servants of the master of the house came and said to him: lord, did you not sow good seed in your field? Why then does it have weeds? [n. 1143]

¹³:²⁸ And he said to them: an enemy has done this. And the servants said to him: do you wish us to go and gather it up? [n. 1144]

¹³:²⁹ And he said: no, lest perhaps in gathering up the weeds, you root up the wheat also together with it. [n. 1147]

¹³:³⁰ Allow both to grow until the harvest, and in the time of the harvest I will say to the reapers: gather up the weeds first, and bind it into bundles to burn, but gather the wheat into my barn. [n. 1150]

1132. Supra posuit parabolam, in qua ostendebatur impedimentum evangelicae doctrinae ab extrinseco, hic ponitur alia parabola, in qua ponitur impedimentum de audienda doctrina, quod est ab intrinseco, quia in hac ad nos trahuntur ea, de quibus ingenia solent sollicitari.

Primo ergo docet de origine boni et mali;

secundo de processu;
tertio de fine.
Secundum ibi *cum autem crevisset* et cetera. Tertium ibi *et in tempore messis dicam messoribus* et cetera.

Circa primum notantur duo.
Primo de origine boni;
secundo mali, ibi *cum autem dormirent homines* et cetera.

1132. Above, he set out a parable, in which was shown an impediment from the outside to the evangelical teaching; here is set down another parable, in which is set down an impediment from the inside to hearing the teaching, for in this one those things about which natural dispositions are usually anxious are brought out.

First, then, he teaches about the origin of good men and evil men;

second, about their progress;
third, about the end.
The second is at *and when the seed had grown*. The third is at *and in the time of the harvest I will say to the reapers*.

Concerning the first, two things are recorded:
first, concerning the origin of good men;
second, of evil men, at *but while men were asleep, his enemy came*.

1133. Dicit ergo *aliam parabolam proposuit illis*. Et quibus? Eis. Dico non apostolis tantum, sed etiam turbis. Unde cum primam in navi exposuisset apostolis, convertit se ad turbas. *Aliam*, non *alteram*; quia non solum proposuit duas parabolas, sed plures; 'alterum' vero unum de duobus dicitur. Plures autem posuit, ut pluribus dispositionibus subveniret. Quidam enim afficiuntur in uno, quidam in alio.

1134. *Simile factum est regnum caelorum homini qui seminavit bonum semen in agro suo*. In regno continetur rex, et hi qui reguntur: et isti sunt homines caelestes, qui facti sunt aequales Angelis; Ps. XC, 11: *angelis suis mandavit de te, ut custodiant te in omnibus viis tuis* et cetera.

Homini qui seminavit bonum semen. Tres parabolae ponuntur consequenter de semine. Prima de semine seminato; secunda de semine inspirato; tertia de semine multiplicato. Secundum intentionem litterae, aliter quam supra accipitur semen. Seminatur enim semen quod seminatur in homine, et hoc est verbum Dei, sicut habetur Lc. XXII. Hic autem accipitur ipse homo, in quo seminatur. Et hoc patet, quia infra dicit quod semen istud sunt filii regni; unde non est alia facienda expositio ab ea quam Dominus fecit.

Et dicitur *semen*, quia sicut semen est principium propagationis, sic homines boni fundamentum totius fidei; unde ex apostolis tota Ecclesia pullulavit. Unde Is. I, 9: *nisi Dominus reliquisset nobis semen, quasi Sodoma fuissemus*. Et istud fuit bonum semen, de quo Is. VI, 13: *semen sanctum erit id quod steterit in ea*.

Istud seminavit Christus, et ubi? *In agro suo*, idest in mundo. Mundus enim dicitur ager, in quo sunt boni ac mali, quem Dominus per creationem edidit; unde Io. I, 10: *mundus per ipsum factus est*. Et in Ps. XLIX, 11: *pulchritudo agri mecum est*.

1135. *Cum autem dormirent homines* et cetera. Habito de origine boni, hic agit de origine mali. Et

> primo ponitur occasio malitiae illatae;
> secundo ordo.
> Et primo ponitur occasio duplex:
> una est ex parte custodum,
> secunda ex parte seminantis.

1136. Ex parte custodum dicit *cum autem dormirent homines* etc., idest praepositi humani generis, qui positi sunt ad custodiendum *dormirent*, scilicet per dormitionem mortis. Sancti scilicet apostoli qui noverunt quod haeretici in Ecclesia miscuerunt se tritico; unde Paulus: *scio quod post decessum meum intrabunt lupi rapaces in vos, non parcentes gregi*.

1133. It says then, *he proposed another parable to them*. And to whom? To those. Not to the apostles alone, I say, but also to the crowds. Hence when he had first explained the first parable to the apostles in the boat, he turned himself toward the crowds. *Another*, not *the other*, because he set out not only two parables, but many, while 'the other' means one of two. But he set out many, so that he might aid many dispositions. For some are affected in one way, some in another.

1134. *The kingdom of heaven is like a man who sowed good seed in his field*. In the kingdom there are the king and those who are ruled, and these are heavenly men, who are made equal to the angels; *for he has given his angels charge over you; to keep you in all your ways* (Ps 90:11).

A man who sowed good seed in his field. In what follows, three parables are set down about seed. First, about the seed sown; second, about the seed breathed in; third, about the seed increased. According to the intention of the letter, seed is taken differently than it was above. There, seed is sown which is sown in a man, and this is the word of God (Luke 8:11). But here the man himself is taken up, in whom it is sown. And this is clear, because he says below that this seed is the children of the kingdom; hence one should not give another explanation than the one which the Lord gave.

And it says, *seed*, because just as seed is the principle of propagation, so good men are the foundation of the whole faith; hence the whole Church sprouted forth from the apostles. Hence, *except the Lord of hosts had left us seed, we had been as Sodom* (Isa 1:9). And this was the good seed, of which: *that which will stand in it, will be a holy seed* (Isa 6:13).

Christ sowed this, and where? *In his field*, i.e., in the world. For the world is called a field, in which there are good men and evil, whom the Lord put out by creation; hence, *and the world was made by him* (John 1:10). And, *with me is the beauty of the field* (Ps 49:11).

1135. *But while men were asleep, his enemy came*. Having treated of the origin of good men, here he treats of the origin of evil men. And

> first, the occasion of the malice brought in is set out;
> second, the order.
> And first, two occasions are set out:
> one is on the part of the guard,
> the second on the part of the one sowing.

1136. On the part of the guard, he says, *but while men were asleep*, i.e., the human race set in charge, which was set up to guard, *were asleep*, namely through the sleep of death. The saints were the apostles, who knew that heretics in the Church had mingled themselves with the wheat; hence Paul: *I know that, after my departure, ravening wolves will enter in among you, not sparing the flock* (Acts 20:29).

1137. Deinde ponitur alia occasio; unde dicit ***venit inimicus*** etc., idest diabolus; Ps. LXXIII, 23: *superbia eorum qui te oderunt, ascendit semper*: eorum qui te oderunt, idest daemonum. Haec autem inimicitia est secundum perversitatem voluntatis.

Sed est quaestio. Estne hoc verum quod aliqua res odiat Deum?

Dicendum, quod amor non est nisi rei cognitae. Dupliciter autem potest cognosci Deus: in se, vel in suis effectibus. In se impossibile est quin ametur: quicquid enim amatur, amatur sub specie boni. Cum ergo sit prima bonitas, odiri non potest. Sed in effectibus suis non est impossibile. Daemones enim inquantum sunt, eum amant a quo sunt; sed aliqui effectus displicent eis, quod scilicet contra voluntatem suam puniantur, quod non ad voluntatem suam puniant homines, et similia.

1138. Sequitur de ordine ***et superseminavit zizania***. Singula verba habent magnam significationem. Videamus ergo quid est quod seminatur, et qualis est ordo.

Quod seminatur est zizania, quae similis est tritico, et lolium vocatur. Quid significatur per zizaniam? Filii nequam, et omnes qui iniquitatem diligunt, specialiter haeretici. Tria sunt genera malorum: pravi Catholici, schismatici et haeretici. Mali Catholici per paleas significantur, de quibus supra cap. III, 12: *paleas comburet igni*. Schismatici per aristas. Haeretici per zizaniam. Seminantur ergo in agro, idest in hoc mundo. Item zizania habet similitudinem cum tritico, sic isti praetendunt speciem boni, ut habetur I Tim. I, 7: *volentes esse legis doctores, et non intelligentes neque quae loquuntur, neque de quibus affirmant*.

1139. Et nota quod dicitur supra ***seminavit***, et hic non; quia prius fuerunt Catholici, quam haeretici. Diabolus enim videns Ecclesiam dilatari, invidit, et seminavit corruptivum, et movit corda haereticorum, ut magis noceret; unde *ex nobis erant*, secundum quod habetur in I canonica Ioannis II, 19, *sed ex nobis non erant, quia si ex nobis fuissent, permansissent utique nobiscum*.

1140. Item dicit ***in medio tritici***. Non curat diabolus quod aliqui sint haeretici inter gentiles, quia omnes possidet, sed in medio tritici et fidelis populi. Et hoc est quod dicitur Iob IV, 18: *et in angelis suis reperit pravitatem*. Et Augustinus dicit, quod nulla societas est ita bona quin aliquis sit pravus: unde in societate apostolorum unus fuit malus, scilicet Iudas.

Item dicit ***et abiit***: ubi signatur malitia daemonis. ***Abiit***, idest occultum se reddidit. Quando enim instigat, non semper cooperatur: si enim ad votum omnia succederent, de facili posset discerni; ideo aliquando malitiae

1137. Then the other occasion is set down; hence he says, ***his enemy came***, i.e., the devil; *the pride of those who hate you ascends continually* (Ps 73:23), of those who hate you, i.e., the demons. Moreover, this enmity is according to a perversity of the will.

But there is a question. Is this true, that something hates God?

One should say that there is no love except of something known. Now, God can be known in two ways: in himself, or in his effects. In himself it is impossible that he not be loved: for whatever is loved, is loved under the appearance of the good. Since then he is the first goodness, he cannot be hated. But in his effects it is not impossible. For the demons, insofar as they exist, love him from whom they exist; but some effects displease them, namely that they are punished against their will, that they do not punish men according to their own will, and similar things.

1138. There follows concerning the order, ***and oversowed weeds***. The individual words have a great significance. So let us see what is sown, and in what sort of order.

What is sown is a weed, which is similar to wheat, and is called *lolium*. What is signified by the weed? The wicked children, and all who delight in iniquity, especially heretics. There are three kinds of evil men: corrupted Catholics, schismatics, and heretics. Bad Catholics are signified by chaff, of whom it says above, *the chaff he will burn with unquenchable fire* (Matt 3:12). The schismatics, by ears of corn. Heretics, by weeds. So they are sown in the field, i.e., in this world. Likewise, the weed has a likeness to the wheat; even so, these men put on the appearance of good men, as it says: *desiring to be teachers of the law, understanding neither the things they say, nor of what they affirm* (1 Tim 1:7).

1139. And note that above it is said that he ***sowed***, and not here; because they were Catholics before they were heretics. For the devil, seeing the Church grow, is envious, and sows the corruptive, and moves the hearts of heretics, that he may harm the more; hence *they went out from us*, according as is said in the first canonical epistle of John, *but they were not of us. For if they had been of us, they would no doubt have remained with us* (1 John 2:19).

1140. Likewise he says, ***among the wheat***. The devil does not care that there are some heretics among the gentiles, because he is the master of them all; but he wants heretics among the wheat and the faithful people. And this is what is said, *in his angels he found wickedness* (Job 4:18). And Augustine says that there is no society so good but that someone is corrupted; hence in the society of the apostles there was one evil man, namely Judas.

Likewise he says, ***and went***; here the demon's malice is signified. ***And went away***, i.e., he hid himself. For when he incites, he does not always cooperate: for if everything followed his wish he could easily be detected. Therefore

1141. Next, he treats of the progress of the good men and evil men: *and when the seed had grown*. And that you may understand, three things are considered:

first, the manifestation of the good and the bad is set down;

second, the zeal of the good men against the evil;

third, tolerance.

1142. He says then, *and when the seed had grown, and had produced fruit, then the weeds appeared as well*. For it was not apparent from the beginning, when it was sown, but when the seed had grown. And this can be referred both to the wheat and to the weeds. Augustine explains it as about the wheat, because when a man is small, he cannot discern; but when he grows, and bears fruit, and becomes spiritual, then he knows; *but the spiritual man judges all things* (1 Cor 2:15).

Chrysostom explains it as about the weed, because at first it does not appear, since heretics at first hide their knowledge, for at first they say some good things and preach to the laity, and afterward they plant some evils among the clerics, which are freely heard; and thus they turn the people away from love of the clerics, and so by consequence from love of the Church. But afterward, when they undertake teaching, they manifest their malice. For at first they only said light things, but afterward they manifest themselves and their teaching, which is understood by wine; about which wine it is said: *it goes in pleasantly, but in the end, it will bite like a snake* (Prov 23:31–32).

1143. *And the servants of the master of the house came and said to him*. Here something is set out about the zeal of the good men against the evil. And

first, they inquire about the origin of the evil men;

second, they are moved with zeal to wipe out the evil men, at *and the servants said to him: do you wish us to go?*

1144. He says, *and the servants of the master of the house came*. First, one should see who these servants are. Below, he speaks about the reapers; but these are not servants, but angels. These are good men; and this is not unfitting, since the Lord is called both the gate and the gatekeeper. *And the servants of the master of the house came* by faith; *come to him and be enlightened* (Ps 33:6). *And said to him: lord, did you not sow good seed in your field?* Did not the apostles sow good teaching? Yes, certainly. *And God saw all the things that he had made, and they were very good* (Gen. 1:31). *Why then does it have weeds?* There is a similar question: *yet I planted you a chosen vineyard, all true seed: how then are you turned unto me into that which is good for nothing, O strange vineyard?* (Jer 2:21).

The Lord responds: *And he said to them: an enemy has done this*. And notice that this is not from the first origin, but about that in man which is from the devil; *but by the*

diaboli intravit mors in orbem terrarum. Homo dicitur diabolus per defectum a deitate; Ps. IX, 20: *exurge, Domine, non confortetur homo*. Hic homo dicitur **inimicus** propter consummatam malitiam; Gen. III, 15: *inimicitias ponam inter te et ipsum*.

1145. Servi autem dixerunt. Hic dicitur quod servi moventur zelo ad extirpationem malorum. ***Vis, imus, et colligimus ea?***

Dicuntur hic de ipsis duo laudabilia, quia moventur ad destruendum malum; I ad Cor. c. V, 13: *auferte malum ex vobis ipsis*. Item aliud laudabile, quia hoc facere nolunt proprio motu, sed iussu Domini; unde Tob. IV, v. 20: *omni tempore benedic Deum, et omnia consilia tua in ipso permaneant*.

1146. Et ait illis. Nota, hoc est tertium, scilicet de sustinentia malorum; de hoc Eccle. VIII, 11: *etenim quia cito non profertur contra malos sententia, filii hominum absque timore perpetrant mala*. Et

primo ostendit propositum;

secundo rationem assignat;

tertio ponit terminum sustinentiae, quia semper non sustinebit.

1147. Dicit ergo **non**, idest non volo quod colligatis adhuc; II Petr. ult., 9: *non tardat Dominus promissionem suam, sed patienter expectat*.

1148. Ne forte, hic ponit rationem. Et prima fronte notare debetis, quod bonum est magnum, et victoriosum supra malum, quia bonum potest esse sine malo, malum autem non sine bono; ideo sustinet Dominus multa mala, ut veniant vel etiam ne pereant multa bona. Ideo dicit **ne forte colligentes zizania**, idest malos, vel haereticos etc., **eradicetis simul et triticum**.

1149. Quatuor de causis contingit quare mali non debeant eradicari propter bonos. Una causa est, quia per malos exercitantur boni; I Cor. XI, 19: *oportet haereses esse, ut qui probati sunt, manifesti fiant in vobis*; Prov. XI, 29: *qui stultus est, serviet sapienti*. Si non fuissent haeretici, non claruisset scientia sanctorum, Augustini, et aliorum. Unde qui vellet malos eradicare, eradicaret et multa bona.

Item contingit quod qui modo malus est, postea bonus fit, ut Paulus. Unde si occisus fuisset Paulus, careremus doctrina tanti magistri, quod absit. Ideo si vis eradicare, eradicabis simul et triticum, scilicet eum, qui erit triticum; Ps. LXVII, 23: *dixit Dominus, ex Basan convertam, convertam in profundum maris*.

Tertia ratio, quia aliqui videntur mali, et non sunt; ideo si velles evellere malos, statim multos bonos extirpares. Et hoc apparet, quia noluit Deus quod colligerentur,

envy of the devil, death came into the world (Wis 2:24). A man is called the devil by a falling away from the deity; *arise, O Lord, let not man be strengthened* (Ps 9:20). This man is called an **enemy** on account of complete malice; *I will put enmities between you and the woman* (Gen 3:15).

1145. And the servants said to him. Here it says that the servants are moved with zeal to wipe out the evil men. ***Do you wish us to go and gather it up?***

Two praiseworthy things are said about these men here, because they are moved to the destruction of evil; *put away the evil one from among yourselves* (1 Cor 5:13). Likewise another praiseworthy thing, because they do not want to do this by their own proper motion, but by the Lord's command; hence *bless God at all times: and desire of him to direct your ways* (Tob 4:20).

1146. And he said. Notice, this is the third, namely about putting up with the evil men; about this, *for because sentence is not speedily pronounced against the evil, the children of men commit evils without any fear* (Eccl 8:11). And

first, he makes clear the thing at hand;

second, he gives the reason;

third, he sets down a limit to the toleration, because he will not always put up with them.

1147. He says then, **no**, i.e., I do not wish that you should collect them yet; *the Lord . . . deals patiently for your sake, not willing that any should perish* (2 Pet 3:9).

1148. Lest perhaps; here he sets forth the reason. And in the first part you should note that the good is great and victorious over evil, because good can be without evil, but not evil without good. Therefore, the Lord puts up with many evils that many goods might come, or also lest they perish. Therefore he says, **no, lest perhaps gathering up the weeds**, i.e., the evil men, or heretics, **you root up the wheat also together with it**.

1149. There are four reasons why evil men should not be wiped out for the sake of good men. One reason is because good men are exercised by the evil; *for there must be also heresies: that they also, who are approved, may be made manifest among you* (1 Cor 11:19); *The fool shall serve the wise* (Prov 11:29). If there had not been heretics, the knowledge of the saints, of Augustine and of others, would not have shone forth. Hence he who would wipe out evil men would wipe out many good things as well.

Likewise, it happens that one who for a while is evil afterwards becomes good, like Paul. Hence if Paul had been killed, we would lack the teaching of so great a master, which God forbid. Therefore, if you wish to wipe them out, you will wipe out at the same time the wheat also, namely him who will be wheat; *the Lord said: I will turn them from Basan, I will turn them into the depth of the sea* (Ps 67:23).

The third reason is because some men seem evil and are not; therefore if you wish to root up evil men, right away you will wipe out many good men. And this is clear,

donec ad perfectam maturitatem pervenirent; unde I ad Cor. IV, 5: *nolite ante tempus iudicare*.

Quarta ratio est, quia aliquis quandoque est magnae potestatis; ideo si excludatur, trahit multos secum, et sic cum illo malo multi pereunt. Ideo congregatio non excommunicatur, nec princeps populi, ne cum uno multi cadant. De tali intelligitur quod dicitur in Apocalypsi XII, 4, quod draco traxit tertiam partem stellarum secum et cetera. Et Gen. c. XVIII, 25: *absit a te ut hanc rem facias, et occidas iustum cum impio*.

1150. Sed numquid semper parcetur eis? Non, sed usque ad tempus; unde dicit **sinite utraque crescere usque ad messem** et cetera. Similis sententia habetur Apoc. ult., 11: *qui nocet, noceat adhuc, et qui in sordibus est, sordescat adhuc*.

1151. Sinite utraque crescere usque ad messem. Contra istam sententiam obiicitur, quia dicitur Is. I, 16: *auferte malum cogitationum vestrarum* et cetera. Item I Cor. V, v. 7: *expurgate vetus fermentum, ut sitis nova conspersio sicut estis azymi* et cetera. Quid ergo dicit **sinite** et cetera?

Chrysostomus dicit quod loquitur de occisione. Unde haeretici non sunt occidendi, quia inde multa mala sequerentur. Augustinus in epistola quadam dicit, quod fuit sibi visum aliquando quod non deberent occidi; sed post experimento didicit quod multi convertuntur per violentiam: Dominus enim quosdam violenter trahit, sicut traxit Paulum. Unde iste coacte conversus plus profecit quam omnes alii qui voluntarie crediderunt. Et hanc opinionem, vel quaestionem, tractavit Augustinus. Unde secundum sententiam Chrysostomi, si non possit sine periculo, non debet fieri, sed ubi maius periculum timetur.

Et hoc patet inducendo in omnibus, quia etsi mali sunt, prosunt ad exercitationem. Quia tamen magis timendum est ne evangelica doctrina per eos in aliis pereat, ideo et cetera. Item aliqui qui modo sunt mali, fiunt post boni. Verum est quod statim non debent occidi, sed, sicut habetur ad Titum III, 10, *haereticum post primam et secundam monitionem devita*.

Ad aliud quod tertio opponitur, quia scilicet multi videntur mali qui sunt boni, verum est, si fieret indiscrete, sicut habetur I ad Tim. IV.

Item quod dictum est, quod princeps populi excommunicari non debet, si videas quod maius sit scandalum si excommunicetur quam in eo quod delinquit, non debet excommunicari; sed si aliquid egisset quod esset ad periculum fidei, sine dubio excommunicari debet, quodcumque inde accidat damnum.

because God did not will that they should be gathered until they came to perfect maturity; hence, *therefore judge not before the time* (1 Cor 4:5).

The fourth reason is that sometimes someone has great power; so if he were cut off, he would drag many with him, and thus with the evil man many would perish. Therefore the congregation is not excommunicated, nor the prince of a people, lest with one man many should fall. About such men is understood what is said, that the dragon dragged a third part of the stars with him (Rev 12:4). And *far be it from you to do this thing, and to slay the just with the wicked* (Gen 18:25).

1150. But will he always spare them? No, but only for a time; hence he says, **allow both to grow until the harvest**. A similar thought is found: *he who hurts, let him hurt still: and he who is filthy, let him be filthy still* (Rev 22:11).

1151. Allow both to grow until the harvest. Against this sentence it is objected: *take away the evil of your devices from my eyes, cease to do perversely* (Isa 1:16). Likewise, *purge out the old leaven, that you may be a new paste, as you are unleavened* (1 Cor 5:7). Why then does he say, **allow both to grow until the harvest**?

Chrysostom says that he speaks about killing. Hence heretics should not be killed, because many evils would follow from that. Augustine says in a certain epistle that for a while it seemed to him that they should not be killed; but afterward he learned by experience that many are converted by violence; for the Lord draws certain men violently, as he drew Paul. Whence this man, forcibly converted, was more profitable than many others who believed voluntarily. And Augustine investigated this opinion or question. Hence according to Chrysostom's thought, if it cannot be done without danger, it should not be done, but only where a greater danger is feared.

And this is clear by induction from all the particulars, because even if they are evil, they are useful for exercise. Nevertheless, because one should fear even more lest the evangelical teaching perish in others through them, the conclusion follows. Likewise, some men who are evil for a while become good afterward. It is true that they should not be killed right away, but, as is said, *a man that is a heretic, after the first and second admonition, avoid* (Titus 3:10).

As regards something which is opposed to the third thing, namely that many seem evil who are good, this is true, if they become indiscreet (1 Tim 4).

Likewise, what was said, that the prince of a people should not be excommunicated, if you should see that there will be a greater scandal if he is excommunicated than in the fact that he does wrong, he should not be excommunicated; but if he had done something which was dangerous to the faith, without doubt he should be excommunicated, whatever damage might come from it.

1152. *Et in tempore messis dicam messoribus* et cetera. Supra Dominus exposuit parabolice originem boni et mali, et processum utriusque, hic agitur de similitudine utriusque. Et

primo ponitur tempus finis;

secundo ponuntur ministri;

tertio modus et ordo, quorum unumquodque ordinatur ad finem.

1153. Tempus tangitur, cum dicitur *in tempore messis* et cetera. Tempus messis est tempus collectionis fructus, qui expectatur ex seminibus.

Duplex est autem collectio: una in Ecclesia praesenti, alia in caelesti. Et ideo duplex est messis: quaedam congregationis fructuum in praesenti; de hac Io. IV, 35: *levate oculos vestros, et videte regiones, quoniam albae sunt iam ad messem*. Item tempus messis in triumphanti Ecclesia; unde infra, eodem dicitur, quod **messis est consummatio saeculi**; ergo usque ad illud tempus differtur.

1154. Qui sunt ministri? Messores. Unde **dicam messoribus**. Messores primae messis fuerunt apostoli: ipsi enim collegerunt et converterunt totum mundum, de quibus Io. IV, 38: *misi vos metere quod non seminastis*. In secunda messe messores erunt angeli; Apoc. XIV, 15 dictum est cuidam angelo: *mitte falcem tuam, et mete: quia venit hora ut metatur, quoniam aruit messis terrae* et cetera. Quae enim mediante Deo fiunt, credendum quod fiant ministerio angelorum; unde dicitur de angelis Ps. CII, 21: *ministri eius, qui facitis voluntatem eius*.

1155. Sed videamus ordinem, et quo modo assequantur finem, et quem finem. Et

primo de malis;

secundo de bonis.

1156. De malis sciendum, quod primo colliguntur; secundo alligantur; tertio comburuntur.

In primo est separatio malorum a bonis. Quamdiu durat tempus istud, mali cum bonis sunt, zizania cum tritico, lilium inter spinas, ut habetur Cant. II, 2; infra XXV, 31: **cum venerit filius hominis, separabit bonos a malis, haedos ab agnis**. Unde dicit **colligite primum zizania** et cetera. Modo quasi indiscrete accidunt bona et mala bonis et malis: et hoc est quod dicitur Eccle. IX, 3, *quod hoc pessimum est inter omnia, quae sub caelo fiunt, quia eadem cunctis eveniunt*; sed tunc bona

1152. *And in the time of the harvest I will say to the reapers*. Above, the Lord explained in a parable the origin of good men and of evil, and the progress of each; here he treats of a similitude of both. And

first, the time of the end is set down;

second, the ministers are set down;

third, the manner and order, each of which is ordered to the end.

1153. The time is touched upon when it says, *in the time of the harvest*. The time of the harvest is the time of collecting the fruit which is expected from the seeds.

Now, there are two collections: one in the present Church, another in the heavenly. And therefore, there are two harvests: one of the gathering of fruit in the present; concerning this: *behold, I say to you, lift up your eyes, and see the countries; for they are white already to harvest* (John 4:35). Likewise, the time of the harvest in the Church triumphant; hence below, it is said by this same evangelist that **the harvest is the end of the world** (Matt 13:39). Therefore it is put off until that time.

1154. Who are the ministers? The reapers. Hence, **I will say to the reapers**. The reapers of the first harvest were the apostles, for they themselves gathered and converted the whole world, of whom John says, *I have sent you to reap that in which you did not labor* (John 4:38). In the second harvest, the reapers will be angels; it is said to a certain angel: *thrust in your sickle, and reap, because the hour is come to reap: for the harvest of the earth is ripe* (Rev 14:15). For those things which come about by one mediating to God, one should believe that they come about by the ministry of the angels; hence it says of the angels, *you ministers of his that do his will* (Ps 102:21).

1155. But let us see the order, and in what manner the end is attained, and what end. And

first, concerning the evil men;

second, concerning the good.

1156. Concerning the evil, one should know that first, they are gathered; second, they are bound; third, they are burned.

In the first, there is the separation of the evil from the good. However long that time lasts, the evil are with the good, the weed with the wheat, the lily among the thorns, as it is said (Song 2:2); below, **and when the Son of man will come . . . he will separate them one from another, as the shepherd separates the sheep from the goats** (Matt 25:31–32). Hence he says, **gather up the weeds first**. Good things and bad things happen to good men and bad men in an indiscriminate manner, so to speak; and this is

reddentur bonis, et mala malis. Ne ergo involvantur, oportet quod separentur et alligentur.

Unde *et alligate ea*. In alligatione perpetuitas poenae signatur; Ps. CXLIX, 8: *ad alligandos reges eorum in compedibus* etc.; infra XXII, 13: **ligatis manibus et pedibus, proiicite eum in tenebras exteriores**, quod signat impoenitentiam et irrevocationem aeternae damnationis. *In fasciculos*. Omnes erunt separati a visione Dei: poena damni erit aequalis omnibus, ideo ponentur *in fasciculos*, sicut habetur Lev. XIII, ubi docetur discernere inter sanguinem et sanguinem, inter lepram et lepram; et Is. XXVII, 8: *in mensura contra mensuram*.

Et ad quid? *Ad comburendum*, idest igni aeterno tradentur. De isto dicitur Lc. XVI, v. 24: *quia crucior in hac flamma*.

1157. Deinde cum dicitur **triticum autem congregate in horreum meum**, ponitur finis bonorum, et, e contrario, tria ponuntur, scilicet puritas, et unitas, et tranquillitas.

Puritas, cum dicitur *triticum*. Sed notate quod zizania fuit colligata, ideo non fuit excussa, triticum vero fuit excussum. Et hoc significat quod mali cum suis inquinamentis in infernum mittentur; sed boni penitus erunt purgati; Is. XXXV, 8: *via sancta vocabitur, non transibit per eam pollutus*.

Item est inter eos unitas; unde **congregate**. Inter malos semper sunt iurgia, ideo non habent unitatem; sed boni congregantur; Ps. XLIX, 5: *congregate illi sanctos eius, qui ordinant testamentum eius super sacrificia* etc.; et infra XXIV, 28: **ubi corpus, ibi congregabuntur et aquilae**.

Item erit inter eos tranquillitas; unde dicit **in horreum meum**. Horreum fit ad conservationem messis; sic illa patria erit horreum sanctorum, ubi erunt cum laude et laetitia sempiterna, ut habetur Is. XXXV, 10.

what is said, that *this is a very great evil among all things that are done under the sun, that the same things happen to all men* (Eccl 9:3); but at that time good things will be rendered to good men, and evil things to evil men. So lest they get entangled, it is necessary that they be separated and bound.

Hence, **and bind it**. In the binding is indicated the everlastingness of the punishment; *to bind their kings with fetters* (Ps 149:8). Below, **bind his hands and feet, and cast him into the exterior darkness** (Matt 22:13), which indicates the impenitence and irrevocation of eternal damnation. **Into bundles**. They all will be separated from the vision of God: the punishment of the damned will be equal for all. For this reason they will be put **into bundles**, as is said in Leviticus, where it teaches how to discern between blood and blood, between leper and leper (Lev 13); and *in measure against measure* (Isa 27:8).

And for what? **To burn**, i.e., they will be handed over to eternal fire. About this fire it says, *for I am tormented in this flame* (Luke 16:24).

1157. Then when it says, **but gather the wheat into my barn**, the end of the good men is set down, and, by way of contrast, three things are set down, namely purity and unity and tranquility.

Purity, when it says, **wheat**. But notice that the weeds were bound, and so were not shaken out, but the wheat was shaken out. And this signifies that the evil men with their defilements will be cast into hell; but the good men will be thoroughly purged. *It will be called the holy way: the unclean will not pass over it* (Isa 35:8).

Likewise, there is unity among them; hence **gather**. Among evil men there are always quarrels, so they do not have unity; but the good are gathered together. *Gather together his saints to him: who set his covenant before sacrifices* (Ps 49:5), and below, **wherever the body will be, there will the eagles also be gathered together** (Matt 24:28).

Likewise there will be among them tranquility; hence he says, **into my barn**. A barn is made for the preservation of the harvest; even so this homeland will be a barn for the saints, where they will be with eternal praise and joy, as is said (Isa 35:10).

Lecture 3

¹³:³¹ Aliam parabolam proposuit eis, dicens: simile est regnum caelorum grano synapis, quod accipiens homo seminavit in agro suo: [n. 1159]

¹³:³² quod minimum quidem est omnibus seminibus; cum autem creverit, maius est omnibus oleribus, et fit arbor, ita ut volucres caeli veniant, et habitent in ramis eius. [n. 1160]

¹³:³³ Aliam parabolam locutus est eis: simile est regnum caelorum fermento, quod acceptum mulier abscondit in farinae satis tribus, donec fermentatum est totum. [n. 1165]

¹³:³⁴ Haec omnia locutus est Iesus in parabolis ad turbas, et sine parabolis non loquebatur eis, [n. 1170]

¹³:³⁵ ut impleretur quod dictum erat per Prophetam dicentem: *aperiam in parabolis os meum, eructabo abscondita a constitutione mundi.* [n. 1173]

¹³:³⁶ Tunc dimissis turbis, venit in domum, et accesserunt ad eum discipuli eius dicentes: edissere nobis parabolam zizaniorum agri. [n. 1175]

¹³:³⁷ Qui respondens ait illis: qui seminat bonum semen est Filius hominis: [n. 1178]

¹³:³⁸ ager autem est mundus; bonum vero semen, hi sunt filii regni; zizania autem filii sunt nequam; [n. 1179]

¹³:³⁹ inimicus autem qui seminavit ea, est diabolus; messis vero consummatio saeculi est; messores autem angeli sunt. [n. 1180]

¹³:⁴⁰ Sicut ergo colliguntur zizania, et igni comburuntur, sic erit in consummatione saeculi. [n. 1182]

¹³:³¹ Ἄλλην παραβολὴν παρέθηκεν αὐτοῖς λέγων· ὁμοία ἐστὶν ἡ βασιλεία τῶν οὐρανῶν κόκκῳ σινάπεως, ὃν λαβὼν ἄνθρωπος ἔσπειρεν ἐν τῷ ἀγρῷ αὐτοῦ·

¹³:³² ὃ μικρότερον μέν ἐστιν πάντων τῶν σπερμάτων, ὅταν δὲ αὐξηθῇ μεῖζον τῶν λαχάνων ἐστὶν καὶ γίνεται δένδρον, ὥστε ἐλθεῖν τὰ πετεινὰ τοῦ οὐρανοῦ καὶ κατασκηνοῦν ἐν τοῖς κλάδοις αὐτοῦ.

¹³:³³ Ἄλλην παραβολὴν ἐλάλησεν αὐτοῖς· ὁμοία ἐστὶν ἡ βασιλεία τῶν οὐρανῶν ζύμῃ, ἣν λαβοῦσα γυνὴ ἐνέκρυψεν εἰς ἀλεύρου σάτα τρία ἕως οὗ ἐζυμώθη ὅλον.

¹³:³⁴ ταῦτα πάντα ἐλάλησεν ὁ Ἰησοῦς ἐν παραβολαῖς τοῖς ὄχλοις καὶ χωρὶς παραβολῆς οὐδὲν ἐλάλει αὐτοῖς,

¹³:³⁵ ὅπως πληρωθῇ τὸ ῥηθὲν διὰ τοῦ προφήτου λέγοντος· ἀνοίξω ἐν παραβολαῖς τὸ στόμα μου, ἐρεύξομαι κεκρυμμένα ἀπὸ καταβολῆς [κόσμου].

¹³:³⁶ Τότε ἀφεὶς τοὺς ὄχλους ἦλθεν εἰς τὴν οἰκίαν. καὶ προσῆλθον αὐτῷ οἱ μαθηταὶ αὐτοῦ λέγοντες· διασάφησον ἡμῖν τὴν παραβολὴν τῶν ζιζανίων τοῦ ἀγροῦ.

¹³:³⁷ ὁ δὲ ἀποκριθεὶς εἶπεν· ὁ σπείρων τὸ καλὸν σπέρμα ἐστὶν ὁ υἱὸς τοῦ ἀνθρώπου,

¹³:³⁸ ὁ δὲ ἀγρός ἐστιν ὁ κόσμος, τὸ δὲ καλὸν σπέρμα οὗτοί εἰσιν οἱ υἱοὶ τῆς βασιλείας· τὰ δὲ ζιζάνιά εἰσιν οἱ υἱοὶ τοῦ πονηροῦ,

¹³:³⁹ ὁ δὲ ἐχθρὸς ὁ σπείρας αὐτά ἐστιν ὁ διάβολος, ὁ δὲ θερισμὸς συντέλεια αἰῶνός ἐστιν, οἱ δὲ θερισταὶ ἄγγελοί εἰσιν.

¹³:⁴⁰ ὥσπερ οὖν συλλέγεται τὰ ζιζάνια καὶ πυρὶ [κατα]καίεται, οὕτως ἔσται ἐν τῇ συντελείᾳ τοῦ αἰῶνος·

¹³:³¹ He proposed another parable to them, saying: the kingdom of heaven is like a grain of mustard seed, which a man took and sowed in his field. [n. 1159]

¹³:³² Which is indeed the least of all seeds; but when it is grown, it is greater than all herbs, and becomes a tree, so that the birds of the air come, and dwell in its branches. [n. 1160]

¹³:³³ Another parable he spoke to them: the kingdom of heaven is like leaven, which a woman took and hid in three measures of meal, until the whole was leavened. [n. 1165]

¹³:³⁴ All these things Jesus spoke in parables to the multitudes and without parables he did not speak to them. [n. 1170]

¹³:³⁵ So that what was spoken by the Prophet might be fulfilled, saying: *I will open my mouth in parables, I will utter things hidden from the foundation of the world.* [n. 1173]

¹³:³⁶ Then having sent away the multitudes, he came into the house, and his disciples came to him, saying: expound the parable of the weeds of the field to us. [n. 1175]

¹³:³⁷ He answered and said to them: he who sowed the good seed is the Son of man. [n. 1178]

¹³:³⁸ And the field is the world. And the good seed are the children of the kingdom. And the weeds are the children of the wicked one. [n. 1179]

¹³:³⁹ And the enemy who sowed them is the devil. But the harvest is the end of the world. And the reapers are the angels. [n. 1180]

¹³:⁴⁰ Therefore, even as weeds are gathered up, and burnt with fire, so will it be at the end of the world. [n. 1182]

13:41 Mittet Filius hominis angelos suos, et colligent de regno eius omnia scandala, et eos qui faciunt iniquitatem, [n. 1182]	13:41 ἀποστελεῖ ὁ υἱὸς τοῦ ἀνθρώπου τοὺς ἀγγέλους αὐτοῦ, καὶ συλλέξουσιν ἐκ τῆς βασιλείας αὐτοῦ πάντα τὰ σκάνδαλα καὶ τοὺς ποιοῦντας τὴν ἀνομίαν	13:41 The Son of man will send his angels, and they will gather out of his kingdom all scandals, and those who work iniquity. [n. 1182]
13:42 et mittent eos in caminum ignis: ibi erit fletus et stridor dentium. [n. 1183]	13:42 καὶ βαλοῦσιν αὐτοὺς εἰς τὴν κάμινον τοῦ πυρός· ἐκεῖ ἔσται ὁ κλαυθμὸς καὶ ὁ βρυγμὸς τῶν ὀδόντων.	13:42 And they will cast them into the furnace of fire, where there will be weeping and gnashing of teeth. [n. 1183]
13:43 Tunc iusti fulgebunt sicut sol in regno Patris eorum. Qui habet aures audiendi, audiat. [n. 1185]	13:43 τότε οἱ δίκαιοι ἐκλάμψουσιν ὡς ὁ ἥλιος ἐν τῇ βασιλείᾳ τοῦ πατρὸς αὐτῶν. ὁ ἔχων ὦτα ἀκουέτω.	13:43 Then the just will shine as the sun, in the kingdom of their Father. He who has ears to hear, let him hear. [n.1185]

1158. Per duas ostendit impedimentum evangelicae doctrinae. Sed quia posset aliquis dicere: *si ita est, quod ita impeditur, quod quaedam secus viam, quaedam super petram etc., videtur quod non possit proficere*; ideo subdit de profectu parabolice, quod scilicet profecerit propter duo. Primo propter parvitatem apparentem; secundo propter occultationem. Ideo duas parabolas ponit.

Secunda ibi **aliam parabolam locutus est eis**.

Tertio confirmat modum per auctoritatem prophetae, ibi **haec omnia locutus est Iesus in parabolis**.

Circa primum
primo agit de seminatione;
secundo de parvitate seminis;
tertio de magnitudine fructus.

Secundum ibi **quod minimum quidem est omnibus seminibus**; tertium ibi **quod cum creverit maius est omnibus oleribus**.

1159. Dicit ergo **simile est regnum caelorum grano synapis** et cetera. In regno est rex, princeps, subditi, et etiam incarcerati. Item divitiae et cetera. Ideo ad haec omnia possumus assimilare regnum.

Quod ergo dicit quod **simile est regnum caelorum grano synapis**, potest exponi, sicut dicit Hieronymus, quod per granum synapis doctrina evangelica intelligitur. Et quare? Quia granum istud fervidum est; item venena repellit. Et hoc significatur, quia doctrina evangelica per fidem facit fervescere; infra XVII, v. 19: *si habueritis fidem sicut granum synapis, dicetis monti huic, transi hinc, et transibit; et nihil impossibile erit vobis*. Item excludit errores; unde utilis est ad arguendum, ut habetur II ad Timoth. III, 16.

Quod accipiens homo seminavit. Homo iste est Christus, qui seminavit istud semen; vel quilibet homo

1158. He has shown the impediment to the evangelical teaching by two things. But since someone could say: *if it is true that it is impeded in this way, because some are beside the way, some on a rock, etc., then it seems that it cannot make progress*; for this reason he adds next a parable about the progress, namely that it will progress on account of two things: first, on account of its apparent smallness; second, on account of its being hidden. Therefore he sets forth two parables.

The second is at **another parable he spoke**.

Third, he confirms the manner by the authority of a prophet, at **all these things Jesus spoke in parables to the multitudes**.

Concerning the first parable,
he first treats of the sowing;
second, of the smallness of the seed;
third, of the largeness of what is produced.

The second is at **which is indeed the least of all seeds**; the third at **but when it is grown, it is greater than all herbs**.

1159. He says then, **the kingdom of heaven is like a grain of mustard seed**. In a kingdom there are the king, the prince, the subjects, and also the imprisoned. Likewise, riches, etc. Therefore we can liken the kingdom to all these things.

So what he says, that **the kingdom of heaven is like a grain of mustard seed**, can be explained, as Jerome says, according as by the grain of mustard is understood the evangelical teaching. And why? Because this grain is hot; likewise, it drives away poison. And this is signified because the evangelical teaching makes one grow hot through faith; below, *if you have faith as a grain of mustard seed, you would say to this mountain: remove from here, and it would be removed; and nothing will be impossible to you* (Matt 17:20). Likewise, it excludes errors; hence it is useful for reproving, as is said (2 Tim 3:16).

Which a man took and sowed. This man is Christ, who sowed this seed; or any man at all who sows the evangelical

qui doctrinam evangelicam seminat. **In agro suo**, idest in corde suo, quando ei praebet assensum. Christus seminavit, quia fidem dedit in qua salvi sumus; Eph. II, 8: *gratia enim salvati estis per fidem, et non ex vobis, Dei enim donum est*. Item quilibet, qui obedit, seminat in agro, idest in corde; Prov. XXIV, 27: *diligenter exerce agrum tuum*.

In isto agro sunt diversa semina, quae sunt diversa dogmata. Dogmata Hieronymi et Augustini magna videntur, et confirmantur magnis argumentis: similiter doctrina legis.

1160. Sed doctrina legis evangelicae modica apparuit, quia praedicabat Deum passum, crucifixum et huiusmodi. Et quis posset hoc credere? I ad Cor. I, 18: *verbum crucis pereuntibus quidem stultitia est, his autem qui salvi fiunt, idest nobis, virtus Dei est*. Et ideo dicit **quod minimum quidem est omnibus seminibus**; unde primo minima apparuit.

1161. Sequitur magnitudo. Et primo ponitur magnitudo; secundo confirmatur, ibi **cum autem creverit**, idest pullulaverit, **maius est omnibus oleribus**, quia doctrina evangelica magis fructificavit quam doctrina legis, quia doctrina legis non fructificavit nisi inter Iudaeos; unde dicebatur Ps. CXLVII, 20: *non fecit taliter omni nationi, et iudicia sua non manifestavit eis*. Non enim fuit aliquis philosophus qui aliquam patriam potuerit totam convertere ad suam doctrinam: si enim aliquis philosophus, sicut Plato, dixisset quod talis et talis veniet, non crederetur ei. Ps. CXVIII, 85: *narraverunt mihi iniqui fabulationes, sed non ut lex tua*.

1162. Maior est ergo in soliditate, in generalitate et in utilitate.

In soliditate **et fit arbor**, quia aliae doctrinae sunt olera mollia, nihil firmum habentia, quia rationi humanae subiecta, Sap. IX, 14: *cogitationes enim mortalium timidae, et incertae providentiae nostrae*, sed haec est arbor firma; Ps. CXVIII, 89: *in aeternum, Domine, permanet verbum tuum*; Lc. XXI, 33: *caelum et terra transibunt, verba autem mea non transibunt*. Ideo sicut haec arbor se habet ad alias arbores, ita haec doctrina ad alias. **Ita ut volucres caeli veniant, et habitent in ramis eius**.

Item praeest in generalitate doctrinae: quia haec scientia multos ramos habet, et exhibet homini quae sunt necessaria ad vitam. Unde si sunt coniugati, habent per istam qualiter se regere debent; si clerici quomodo vivant, et sic de aliis: ideo diversa dogmata sunt diversi rami.

Item praeest utilitate, quia volucres habitant in ramis eius, idest omnes qui habent animum in caelis; ad Phil. III, 20: *nostra conversatio est in caelis*. Isti veniunt et meditantur, et quiescunt: qui enim habitant in terra, non sunt volucres; II ad Cor. IV, 18: *non contemplantibus*

teaching. **In his field**, i.e., in his heart, when he submits his assent to it. Christ sowed, because he gave the faith in which we are saved; *for by grace you are saved through faith, and that not of yourselves, for it is the gift of God* (Eph 2:8). Likewise, any man who obeys sows in the field, i.e., in the heart; *diligently till your ground* (Prov 24:27).

There are different seeds in this field, which are the different doctrines. The doctrines of Jerome and of Augustine seem tremendous, and are confirmed by tremendous arguments; similarly the teaching of the law.

1160. But the teaching of the evangelical law appeared small, because it preached God suffering, crucified, and so on. And who can believe this? *For the word of the cross, to those indeed who perish, is foolishness; but to those who are saved, that is, to us, it is the power of God* (1 Cor 1:18). And for this reason he says that it **is indeed the least of all seeds**; hence it appeared least, at first.

1161. There follows the largeness. And first, the largeness is set out; second, it is confirmed, at **but when it is grown**, i.e., sprouted up, **it is greater than all herbs**, because the evangelical teaching bears more fruit than the teaching of the law, since the teaching of the law bore fruit only among the Jews; hence it was said, *he has not done in like manner to every nation: and his judgments he has not made manifest to them* (Ps 147:9). For there was no philosopher who was able to convert some entire homeland to his teaching; for if some philosopher, like Plato, had said that such and such shall come, they would not have believed him. *The wicked have told me fables: but not as your law* (Ps 118:85).

1162. Therefore, it is greater in solidity, in generality, and in utility.

In solidity: **and becomes a tree**, because the other teachings are soft herbs, having nothing firm, because they are subjected to human reason. *For the thoughts of mortal men are fearful, and our counsels uncertain* (Wis 9:14), but this is a firm tree; *for ever, O Lord, your word stands firm in heaven* (Ps 118:89); *heaven and earth will pass away, but my words will not pass away* (Luke 21:33). Therefore, just as this tree relates to the other trees, so this teaching to the others. **So that the birds of the air come, and dwell in its branches**.

Likewise, it is foremost in generality of teaching, because this knowledge has many branches, and shows a man what things are necessary for life. Hence if there are married people, they can know by this how they should conduct themselves; if clerics, how they may live, and so with the others. For this reason the different doctrines are the different branches.

Likewise it is foremost in usefulness, because the birds dwell in its branches, i.e., all who those who have their spirit in the heavens; *but our conversation is in heaven* (Phil 3:20). These come and meditate and rest: for those who dwell on earth are not birds. *While we look not at the things which*

nobis quae videntur, sed quae non videntur: quae enim videntur, temporalia sunt; quae autem non videntur, aeterna sunt.

1163. Chrysostomus exponit de apostolis, quos comparavit grano synapis quia erant spiritu ferventes; et istud **seminavit homo**, idest Christus, **in agro**, idest in Ecclesia, ex quo tota fructificatio accidit Ecclesiae: et fuerunt modici et abiecti; nulla enim scientia divulgata est per tam deiectos homines; unde apostolus, I Cor. I, 27: *non multi sapientes, sive potentes, non multi nobiles; sed quae stulta sunt mundi elegit Deus ut confundat sapientes* et cetera. **Sed cum creverit, maius est**, effectum, **omnibus**, quia apostoli maiorem fecerunt fructum. Alexander convertit unam partem mundi ad se, Roma similiter, sed numquam tantum sicut isti, qui tantum fecerunt. **Ut volucres caeli**, idest boni, **requiescant in ramis**, idest in doctrinis eorum; Zach. VIII, 23: *apprehendent fimbriam viri Iudaei dicentes: ibimus vobiscum; audivimus enim, quoniam Deus vobiscum est.*

1164. Hilarius exponit de Christo qui fuit granum synapis propter fervorem, quia plenus Spiritu Sancto, quod **seminavit**, postea in morte, **in agro**, idest in populo, quod minimum fuit propter contemptum infidelium; Is. LIII, 2: *vidimus eum, et non erat ei aspectus, et desideravimus eum, despectum et novissimum virorum, virum dolorum, et scientem infirmitatem.* **Et maius est omnibus oleribus**, idest omnibus perfectis. *Non adaequabitur ei aurum.* Et comparantur perfecti oleribus, quia olus datur infirmis: *qui infirmus est, olera manducet.* Sed doctrina Christi perfectis datur, et sic fit arbor. Et hoc significatur per arborem, de qua habetur Dan. IV, 7.

1165. Aliam parabolam locutus est eis. Hic ponitur parabola de profectu, et ostenditur mirabilis, quia de semine occulto; unde dicit **simile est regnum caelorum fermento, quod acceptum mulier abscondit in farinae satis tribus, donec fermentatum est totum.**

Notate quod non est inconveniens idem aliquando in bonum, aliquando in malum interpretari, sicut petra aliquando interpretatur Christus, aliquando contrarium, ut duritia; Ez. XXXVI, 26: *auferam a vobis cor lapideum de carne vestra.* Ita fermentum aliquando interpretatur in malum, inquantum habet corruptionem; I ad Cor. V, 7: *expurgate vetus fermentum* et cetera. Item ibid.: *non in fermento veteri neque in fermento malitiae et nequitiae, sed in azymis sinceritatis et veritatis.* Sed secundum quod habet fervorem et virtutem dilatandi, sic sonat in bonum.

1166. Quid ergo significatur per illud? Significantur quatuor. Chrysostomus dicit, quod istud fermentum

1163. Chrysostom explains this as about the apostles, whom he compares to a grain of mustard because they were hot in spirit; and **a man**, i.e., Christ, **sowed** it **in his field**, i.e., in the Church, from which all the Church's fruit-bearing arises. And they were ordinary and downcast, for now knowledge has been spread through such downcast men; hence the apostle, *not many wise according to the flesh, not many mighty, not many noble: but the foolish things of the world has God chosen, that he may confound the wise* (1 Cor 1:26–27). **But when it is grown, it is greater** in its effect **than all**, because the apostles bore greater fruit. Alexander converted one part of the world to himself, and Rome likewise, but never so much as these, who have done so much. **So that the birds of the air**, i.e., good men, **dwell in the branches**, i.e., in their teachings; *ten men of all languages of the gentiles will take hold, and will hold fast the skirt of one that is a Jew, saying: we will go with you: for we have heard that God is with you* (Zech 8:23).

1164. Hilary explains it as about Christ, who was a grain of mustard on account of fervor, because he was filled with the Holy Spirit, whom he **sowed** afterward in death **in a field**, i.e., in the people, which was smallest of all on account of unbelievers' contempt. *We have seen him, and there was no sightliness, that we should be desirous of him: despised, and the most abject of men, a man of sorrows, and acquainted with infirmity* (Isa 53:2–3). And **it is greater than all herbs**, i.e., than all the perfect. *Gold or crystal cannot equal it* (Job 28:17). And the perfect are compared to herbs, because an herb is given to the sick: *he who is weak, let him eat herbs* (Rom 14:2). But Christ's teaching is given to the perfect, and so it becomes a tree. And this is signified by the tree, which is spoken of in Daniel (Dan 4:7).

1165. Another parable he spoke to them. Here is set down a parable about the progress, and it is shown to be marvelous, because it comes from a hidden seed; hence he says, **the kingdom of heaven is like leaven, which a woman took and hid in three measures of meal, until the whole was leavened**.

Note that it is not unfitting that the same thing is sometimes interpreted as good, sometimes as evil, as a rock is sometimes interpreted as Christ, sometimes the contrary, as hardness; *I will take away the stony heart out of your flesh* (Ezek 36:26). So leaven is sometimes interpreted as evil, insofar as it has corruption; *purge out the old leaven* (1 Cor 5:7). Similarly, in the same place, *not with the old leaven, nor with the leaven of malice and wickedness; but with the unleavened bread of sincerity and truth* (1 Cor 5:7–8). But according as it has fervor and the power of enlarging, it connotes good.

1166. So what is signified by it? Four things are signified. Chrysostom says that this leaven is the apostles. **A woman**,

sunt apostoli. ***Mulier***, divina sapientia, ***abscondit***, eos, ***in farinae satis tribus***, idest in tribulationibus oppressit. Sed primo ***accepit***; unde Io. XV, 19: *ego vos elegi de mundo ut eatis*. Quos misit inter fideles, posuit ***in farinae satis tribus***. Satus est mensura, et valet modium et dimidium; idest in tribus mensuris farinae.

Et quare in tribus? Ponitur finitum pro infinito, quia inter multas gentes. Vel propter tres partes mundi, quia ad omnes missi; vel propter gentes, quae a tribus filiis Noe ortae sunt. ***Donec fermentatum est totum***, idest donec omnes converterentur ad Deum; Ps. XVIII, 5: *in omnem terram exivit sonus eorum, et in fines orbis terrae verba eorum*.

1167. Vel aliter, secundum Augustinum, per fermentum fervor caritatis significatur, quia sicut fermentum dilatat, sic caritas; Ps. CXVIII, 32: *viam mandatorum tuorum cucurri, cum dilatasti cor meum*. ***Mulier***, ratio vel anima, ***abscondit in tribus***, idest in toto corde, in tota anima, in totis viribus. Vel per tria sata tres status, scilicet praelatorum, contemplativorum et activorum, qui per Noe, Iob et Daniel intelliguntur. Vel possunt referri ad fructum centesimum, sexagesimum et trigesimum.

1168. Hieronymus exponit de doctrina evangelica, quam ***mulier***, idest sapientia, ***abscondit in tribus satis***, quae sunt spiritus et anima, vel irascibilis, et concupiscibilis, et rationalis. Vel aliter, per mulierem intelligitur fides; per tria sata, tres personae in divinis.

1169. Hilarius exponit de Christo, qui est fermentum, quod per providentiam patris in mundo absconsum est in lege triplici, lege naturae, lege Mosaica, et lege evangelica.

1170. ***Haec omnia locutus est Iesus in parabolis*** et cetera. Positis diversis parabolis ad turbas, hic confirmat, vel approbat per auctoritatem prophetae.

Et dividitur in tres; quia
primo ponitur consuetudo Christi circa parabolicam lectionem;

secundo adhibetur auctoritas;

tertio ponitur praecedentium expositio.

Secunda ibi ***ut adimpleretur quod dictum est per Prophetam***; tertia ibi ***tunc dimissis turbis, venit in domum***.

1171. Dicit ergo ***haec omnia locutus est Iesus in parabolis ad turbas***. Quare ergo turbis loqueretur in parabolis, ratio est duplex: quia in turba permixti erant aliqui fideles, et aliqui infideles, item aliqui benigni, et aliqui maligni: propter malignos et infideles loquebatur sic, ut non intelligerent, ut supra dictum est, ***ut videntes non videant***, propter fideles, ut melius capiant, melius

divine wisdom, **hid** them **in three measures of meal**, i.e., pressed them down with afflictions. But first she **took** them; hence, *I have chosen you; and have appointed you, that you should go* (John 15:16). Those who are sent from among the faithful are placed **in three measures of meal**. A measure makes a peck and a half; i.e., in three measures of flour.

And why in three? The finite is set down in place of the infinite, because they were placed among many nations. Or because of the three parts of the world, since they were sent to all men; or because of the nations, which arose from the three sons of Noah. **Until the whole was leavened**, i.e., until all were converted to God; *their sound has gone out into all the earth: and their words unto the ends of the world* (Ps 18:5).

1167. Or in another way, according to Augustine, the leaven signifies fervor of charity, because just as leaven enlarges, so does charity; *I have run the way of your commandments, when you enlarged my heart* (Ps 118:32). **A woman**, reason or the soul, **hid it in three**, i.e., in the whole heart, in the whole soul, in all the powers. Or by the three measures are understood three states, namely that of prelates, that of contemplatives, and that of the active, who are understood through Noah, Job, and Daniel. Or they can be referred to the hundredfold, sixtyfold, and thirtyfold fruit.

1168. Jerome explains it as about the evangelical teaching, which **a woman**, i.e., wisdom, **hid in three measures**, which are the spirit and the soul, or the irascible, concupiscible, and rational powers. Or in another way, by the woman is understood faith; by the three measures, the three persons in the divinity.

1169. Hilary explains it as about Christ, who is the leaven which, by the Father's providence, was hidden in the world in three laws: the law of nature, the Mosaic law, and the evangelical law.

1170. ***All these things Jesus spoke in parables to the multitudes***. The various parables spoken to the crowds being set down, here he confirms, or commends the parables through the authority of a prophet.

And it is divided in three parts, for
first, Christ's custom of selecting parables is set down;

second, an authority is brought in;

third, an explanation of what came before is set down.

The second is at ***so that what was spoken by the Prophet might be fulfilled***; the third, at ***then having sent away the multitudes***.

1171. It says then, ***all these things Jesus spoke in parables to the multitudes***. So there are two reasons why he spoke to the crowds in parables: because in the crowds there were mixed together some who believed and some who did not believe, likewise some well disposed and some ill disposed: he spoke this way because of the ill disposed and those who did not believe, that they might not understand,

retineant. Et hoc habetur Marci IV, 33 s. Paulus I ad Cor. c. III, 1: *non potui vobis loqui quasi spiritualibus, sed quasi carnalibus*.

1172. *Et sine parabolis non loquebatur eis*. Hoc videtur falsum, quia in sermone Domini in monte, et in multis aliis non loquebatur in parabolis.

Chrysostomus sic solvit, quod verum est de ista tota locutione, quia istam totam praedicationem ad turbas parabolice locutus est. Augustinus sic, quod ideo non sine parabolis, quia aliquam locutionem non est locutus ad turbas, quin permiscuerit aliquam parabolam. Unde in sermone Domini in monte permiscuit, ubi dixit *nesciat sinistra tua quid faciat dextera tua*. Et dicit, quod si aliquando inveniatur sine parabola, dicendum quod evangelistae non secundum ordinem narraverunt: unde etsi non sit scripta, parabola intelligi debet, propter hoc quod ibi dicit, quod sine parabolis non loquebatur eis, et nisi commisceret parabolas.

1173. *Ut adimpleretur quod dictum est per Prophetam dicentem: 'aperiam in parabolis os meum.'*

Dupliciter locutus est Dominus humano generi. Primo in prophetis; secundo in seipso; Is. LII, 6: *ecce ego qui loquebar, ecce adsum*. Utrobique parabolice locutus est, in prophetis multipliciter, et per seipsum similiter: quod enim factum est in prophetis, signum fuit eius quod faciendum erat per Christum; unde dicit, ego Dominus, qui aperui os prophetarum in parabolis, aperiam in meipso.

1174. *'Eructabo abscondita a constitutione mundi.'* In apertione oris est manifestatio secretorum, ut supra; eructatio ex intimis est. Tunc eructat quando de profundo sapientiae emittit; Ps. XLIV, 2: *eructavit cor meum verbum bonum*. Sapientia Domini abscondita est; Iob XXVIII, 21: *abscondita est ab oculis omnium viventium*; Io. I, 18: *Deum nemo vidit umquam; unigenitus Filius, qui est in sinu Patris, ipse enarravit* et cetera. Eructavit abscondita, et quae fuerunt occulta a mundi constitutione; ad Eph. III, 5: *quod aliis generationibus non est agnitum filiis hominum, sicuti nunc revelatum est sanctis apostolis eius, et prophetis in Spiritu*.

Vel aliter. *'Eructabo ea'*, quae sunt *'a constitutione mundi'*, quae *'sunt abscondita.'* Et quare? Quia ipse est *'a constitutione mundi'* et ipse nobis revelavit seipsum per ea quae fecit; Rom. I, 20: *invisibilia Dei per ea quae facta sunt intellecta conspiciuntur*.

1175. *Tunc dimissis turbis, venit in domum*. Hic exponitur una de praemissis parabolis. Et

as was said above, *seeing, they see not*; and because of those who believed, that they might better grasp and better retain it. Mark also says this (Mark 4:33). Paul: *I, brethren, could not speak to you as unto spiritual, but as unto carnal* (1 Cor 3:1).

1172. *And without parables he did not speak to them*. This seems false, because in the sermon on the mount and in many others he did not speak in parables.

Chrysostom solves it in this way, that it is true of this whole speech, because this whole preaching was spoken to the crowd in parables. Augustine solves it in this way, that it was not without parables because no speech was spoken to the crowds but that he mingled with it some parable. Hence in the Lord's sermon on the mount, where he says, *do not let your left hand know what your right hand is doing* (Matt 6:3). And he says that, if there is sometimes found a speech without a parable, one should say that the evangelists did not recount everything in order; hence even if it is not written, a parable should be understood, because of what he says here, that he did not speak to them without parables, and unless he mixed in parables.

1173. *So that what was spoken by the Prophet might be fulfilled, saying: 'I will open my mouth in parables'* (Ps 77:2).

The Lord has spoken to the human race in two ways. First, in prophets; second, in himself; *I myself that spoke, behold I am here* (Isa 52:6). Either way, he spoke in parables, in the prophets in many ways, and through himself similarly: for what was done in the prophets was a sign of what was to be done through Christ. Hence he says, I the Lord, who opened the mouths of the prophets in parables, I will open in my own self.

1174. *'I will utter things hidden from the foundation of the world.'* In the mouth's opening is the manifestation of secrets, as above; utterance is from the innermost parts. Somone utters when he sends forth from the depth of wisdom; *my heart has uttered a good word* (Ps 44:2). The Lord's wisdom is hidden; *it is hid from the eyes of all living* (Job 28:21); *no man has seen God at any time: the only begotten Son who is in the bosom of the Father, he has declared him* (John 1:18). He uttered hidden things, and things which were hidden from the foundation of the world; *which in other generations was not known to the sons of men, as it is now revealed to his holy apostles and prophets in the Spirit* (Eph 3:5).

Or in another way: *'I will utter things'* which are *'from the foundation of the world'*, which are *'hidden.'* And why? Because he himself is *'from the foundation of the world'*, and he himself revealed himself to us by the things which he did; *for the invisible things of him . . . are clearly seen, being understood by the things that are made* (Rom 1:20).

1175. *Then having sent away the multitudes, he came into the house*. Here one of the preceding parables is explained. And

primo describitur locus;
secundo discipulorum interrogatio;
tertio expositio.

1176. Dicit ergo **tunc dimissis turbis, venit in domum**. In quo datur nobis exemplum, quod si velimus secreta investigare, debemus in secretum intrare; Sap. VIII, 16: *intrans in domum meam, conquiescam cum illa*; Eccli. XXXII, 15: *praecurre in domum tuam, et illic avocare, et illic lude, et age conceptiones tuas, et non in delictis et verbo superbo* et cetera.

1177. Et accesserunt ad eum discipuli eius dicentes: edissere nobis parabolam zizaniorum agri etc., quia de ista magis dubitabant. Aliquando prae reverentia accedere non audebant, ut habetur Io. IV, 27, quod nemo dixit ei, quare cum muliere loqueretur et cetera. Sed hic specialem audaciam acceperunt, quia audierant **vobis datum est nosse mysteria regni caelestis**. Sic si aliquid mysticum velimus acquirere, debemus ad eum accedere; Ps. XXXIII, 6: *accedite ad eum, et illuminamini*.

1178. Qui respondens ait. Hic ponitur expositio parabolae zizaniae.

Et primo quoad primam seminationem;
secundo quoad superseminationem;
tertio quoad utrumque.

1179. Et primo exponit quid sit seminator, quid ager, quid semen. **Qui seminat bonum semen est Filius hominis**. Nominat se Filium hominis, tum propter humilitatem, tum ut repellat haereticos futuros: quidam enim Deum esse negaverunt, quidam vero hominem. Unde dicit se Filium hominis, quod ad hominem pertinet; et seminare spirituale, ad Deum pertinet. Ps. IV, 7: *signatum est super nos lumen vultus tui, Domine* et cetera.

Ager est mundus, quem ipse creavit; unde supra dixit, **in agro suo**; Io. I, 11: *in propria venit* et cetera. Item ibidem: *mundus per ipsum factus est*. **Bonum vero semen hi sunt filii regni**, ex quo alii propagati sunt, qui fuerunt boni filii; *quod si filii, et haeredes*, ad Rom. VIII, 17.

1180. Deinde exponit quod ad superseminationem pertinet, et dicit quid sit semen. **Zizania autem filii sunt nequam**; Is. I, 4: *vae populo gravi iniquitate, semini nequam, filiis sceleratis*.

Deinde quis seminator, dicens **inimicus autem, qui seminavit ea, est diabolus**, qui induxit peccatum; Sap. II, 24: *invidia diaboli intravit mors in orbem terrarum*.

1181. Consequenter agitur de distinctione, et tria facit: primo ponitur tempus; secundo ministri; tertio distinctio.

first, the place is described;
second, the disciples' question;
third, the explanation.

1176. Then having sent away the multitudes, he came into the house; in which an example is given to us, that if we wish to search after secret things, we should enter into a hidden place; *when I go into my house, I will repose myself with her* (Wis 8:16); *and at the time of rising be not slack: but be first to run home to your house, and there withdraw yourself, and there take your pastime. And do what you have a mind, but not in sin or proud speech* (Sir 32:15–16).

1177. And his disciples came to him, saying: expound the parable of the weeds of the field to us, because they were more uncertain about this one. Sometimes they dared not approach, out of reverence, as when no one asked him why he was speaking with the woman (John 4:27). But here they received a special audacity, because they had heard **to you it is given to know the mysteries of the kingdom of heaven**. Thus if we wish to search after some mystical thing, we should approach him; *come to him and be enlightened* (Ps 33:6).

1178. He answered and said to them. Here the explanation of the parable of the weed is set down. And

first, as regards the first sowing;
second, as regards the sowing over;
third, as regards both.

1179. And first, he explains what the sower is, what the field is, and what the seed is. **He who sowed the good seed is the Son of man**. He names himself the Son of man both on account of humility, and to drive back future heretics; for some have denied that he is God, while some have denied that he is man. Hence he calls himself the Son of man, which pertains to man; and to sow spiritually pertains to God. *The light of your countenance O Lord, is signed upon us* (Ps 4:7).

And the field is the world, which he himself created; hence he said above, **in his field**. *He came unto his own* (John 1:11). Similarly in the same place, *the world was made by him* (John 1:10). **And the good seed are the children of the kingdom**, out of which others have been propagated who have been good children; *and if sons, heirs also*, (Rom. 8:17).

1180. Then he explains what pertains to the sowing over, and says what the seed is. **And the weeds are the children of the wicked one**. *Woe to the sinful nation, a people laden with iniquity, a wicked seed, ungracious children* (Isa 1:4).

Then who the sower is, saying, **and the enemy who sowed them is the devil**, who introduced sin; *but by the envy of the devil, death came into the world* (Wis 2:24).

1181. Next he treats of the separation, and he does three things: first, the time is set down; second, the ministers; third, the separation.

Tempus ponit *messis vero consummatio saeculi est*. Sicut est dictum, collectio prima facta est per apostolos, de qua Io. IV, 35: *levate oculos vestros et videte regiones, quia albae sunt iam ad messem*. Alia vero, in qua erit fructus collectio, de qua ad Galat. ult., 8: *quae seminaverit homo, haec et metet*. *Messores vero angeli sunt*. Sicut enim in praesenti Ecclesia ministri boni sunt homines, sic tunc erunt angeli.

1182. Consequenter ponit finem utriusque, ibi, *sicut ergo colliguntur zizania*, et cetera. Et primo quoad malos; secundo quoad bonos; tertio excitat ad spiritualem sensum.

Dicit ergo *sicut zizania colliguntur, et igni comburuntur, sic erit in consummatione saeculi. Mittet Filius hominis angelos suos*, haec verba ostendunt eum esse hominem et Deum, *et colligent de regno eius omnia scandala*. Retorquet ad peccata, quae fiunt in proximum. Quod autem sequitur *et eos qui faciunt iniquitatem*, refert ad alia peccata. Quod autem dicitur *regnum*, intelligitur praesens Ecclesia, quia in triumphanti non sunt scandala, et homo sciet per tribulationem praecedentem finale iudicium. Augustinus dicit, quod non legimus quod mali sunt ad remunerandum bonos, sed boni inveniuntur aliquando punire malos. Quod ergo dicit *omnia*, intelligendum est in praesenti Ecclesia, immittendo tribulationes, per quas etiam boni et mali puniuntur. Chrysostomus exponit per regnum caelestem patriam. Et quod dicitur *omnia scandala*, non intelligitur quod ibi sint, sed quod non sint.

1183. Unde colligent, et separabunt malos a bonis, ne sint cum eis *et mittent eos in caminum ignis*. Poena damni est carentia divinae visionis. Sed tangitur poena sensus, cum dicitur *et mittent eos in caminum ignis*; Apoc. penult., 27: *non intrabit in eam aliquod coinquinatum*. *Et mittet eos*, idest Filius hominis potestate iudicatoria, *in caminum ignis*; unde dicetur: *ite, maledicti, in ignem aeternum*.

1184. *Ibi erit fletus et stridor dentium*. Hoc expositum est; tamen potest ex hoc haberi quod damnati et in anima et in corpore punientur; unde supra X, 28: *eum timete qui potest animam et corpus mittere in gehennam*. Fletus enim pertinet ad oculos, stridor ad dentes; oculi autem et dentes sunt membra corporalia, in quo significatur veritas resurrectionis. Item per fletum, qui ex fumo cito generatur, significatur poena ignis; per stridorem dentium frigus. Iob XXIV, 19: *ad nimium calorem transeat ab aquis nivium*.

Vel aliter, quod fletus ex tristitia, stridor ex ira, unde Act. VII, 54 dicitur, quod *stridebant dentibus in eum*. Is.

He sets down the time: *but the harvest is the end of the world*. As was said, the first gathering was done by the apostles, about which John says, *behold, I say to you, lift up your eyes, and see the countries; for they are already white to harvest* (John 4:35). But there is another, which will be the gathering of the fruit: *what things a man will sow, those also will he reap* (Gal 6:8). *And the reapers are the angels*. For just as in the present Church the ministers are men, so then they will be angels.

1182. Next, he sets out the end of both, at *even as the weeds therefore are gathered up*. And first, as regards the evil; second, as regards the good; third, he urges them on to the spiritual sense.

He says then, *therefore, even as the weeds are gathered up, and burnt with fire, so will it be at the end of the world. The Son of man will send his angels*, and these words show that he is man and God, *and they will gather out of his kingdom all scandals*. This refers to sins which are committed against one's neighbor. But what follows, *and those who work iniquity*, refers to other sins. And what is said, *kingdom*, is understood as the present Church, because there are no scandals in the Church triumphant, and a man will know the final judgment by its preceding afflictions. Augustine says that we do not read that the evil are for rewarding the good, but the good are sometimes found to punish the evil. So what he says, *all*, should be understood in the present Church, by admitting afflictions through which both the good and the evil are punished. Chrysostom explains the kingdom as the heavenly homeland. And the fact that it says, *all scandals*, does not mean that they are there, but that they are not.

1183. Hence they will gather, and will separate the evil from the good, lest the good should be with them, *and they will cast them into the furnace of fire*. The punishment of the damned is the lack of divine vision. But the punishment of the sense is touched upon when it says, *and they will cast them into the furnace of fire*; *there shall not enter into it any thing defiled* (Rev 21:27). And the Son of man with judicial power *will cast them into the furnace of fire*; hence it shall be said, *depart from me, you cursed, into everlasting fire* (Matt 25:41).

1184. *There will be weeping and gnashing of teeth*. This was explained; yet one can gather from this that the damned will be punished both in soul and in body; hence above, *fear him who can destroy both soul and body in gehenna* (Matt 10:28). For weeping pertains to the eyes, gnashing to the teeth; but eyes and teeth are bodily members, in which the truth of the resurrection is indicated. Likewise by weeping, which is produced quickly by smoke, is indicated the punishment of fire; by gnashing of teeth, cold. *Let him pass from the snow waters to excessive heat, and his sin even to hell* (Job 24:19).

Or in another way, that the weeping is out of sorrow, the gnashing out of anger; hence Acts says that *they gnashed*

penult., 14: *servi mei gaudebunt prae exultatione cordis, et vos clamabitis prae dolore cordis, et prae contritione cordis ululabitis*. Lc. VI, 25: *vae vobis qui ridetis, quia plorabitis*. Item in stridore signatur impatientia et rixa; Apoc. XVI, v. 10: *qui manducaverunt linguas suas propter impatientiam sustinendi*.

1185. Tunc iusti fulgebunt sicut sol in regno Patris eorum. Hic exponit quoad bonos; et in eis erit duplex fulgor, scilicet in anima, per quem Deum videbunt; Ps. XXXV, v. 10: *in lumine tuo videbimus lumen*, scilicet increatum; Is. LVIII, 11: *et implebit splendoribus animam tuam*. Et derivabitur ad corpus; ad Phil. III, 21: *reformabit corpus humilitatis nostrae configuratum corpori claritatis suae*. Sap. III, 7: *fulgebunt iusti, et tamquam scintillae in arundineto discurrent* et cetera.

Quod dicit **sicut sol**, non est intelligendum absolute per omnimodam aequalitatem: maiorem enim habebunt splendorem; sed quia in istis sensibilibus quod magis splendet est sol. Convenit autem cum sole, quia sicut sol non mutatur, sic nec iustus; Eccli. XXVII, 12: *homo sanctus in sapientia manet sicut sol; stultus autem ut luna mutatur*.

1186. Deinde excitat ad spiritualem sensum: **qui habet aures audiendi**, scilicet interiores, **audiat**, intelligendo Is. l, 5: *Dominus aperuit mihi aurem*.

with their teeth at him (Acts 7:54). *My servants will praise for joyfulness of heart, and you will cry for sorrow of heart, and will howl for grief of spirit* (Isa 65:14). *Woe to you that now laugh: for you shall mourn and weep* (Luke 6:25). Likewise, in gnashing is indicated impatience and quarrels; *they gnawed their tongues for pain* (Rev 16:10).

1185. Then the just will shine as the sun, in the kingdom of their Father. Here he explains it with respect to the good; and in them there will be a twofold brightness, namely in the soul, through which they will see God; *in your light we shall see light* (Ps 35:10), namely uncreated light. *And the Lord will give you rest continually, and will fill your soul with brightness* (Isa 58:11). And it will be channeled to the body; *who will reform the body of our lowness, made like to the body of his glory* (Phil 3:21). *The just will shine, and will run to and fro like sparks among the reeds* (Wis 3:7).

What he says, **as the sun**, should not be understood absolutely, equal in every way: for they shall have a greater splendor. But he says this because among sensible things what shines most brightly is the sun. Moreover, they are like the sun because, just as the sun is not changed, so neither the just man; *a holy man continues in wisdom as the sun: but a fool is changed as the moon* (Sir 27:12).

1186. Then he urges them on to the spiritual sense: **he who has ears to hear**, namely interior ears, **let him hear**, by understanding. *The Lord God has opened my ear* (Isa 50:5).

Lecture 4

¹³:⁴⁴ Simile est regnum caelorum thesauro abscondito in agro, quem qui invenit homo, abscondit, et prae gaudio illius vadit, et vendit universa quae habet, et emit agrum illum. [n. 1188]

¹³:⁴⁵ Iterum simile est regnum caelorum homini negotiatori quaerenti bonas margaritas. [n. 1193]

¹³:⁴⁶ Inventa autem una pretiosa margarita, abiit, et vendidit omnia quae habuit, et emit eam. [n. 1193]

¹³:⁴⁷ Iterum simile est regnum caelorum sagenae missae in mare, et ex omni genere piscium congreganti. [n. 1196]

¹³:⁴⁸ Quam, cum impleta esset, educentes, et secus litus sedentes, elegerunt bonos in vasa sua, malos autem foras miserunt. [n. 1198]

¹³:⁴⁹ Sic erit in consummatione saeculi. Exibunt angeli, et separabunt malos de medio iustorum, [n. 1199]

¹³:⁵⁰ et mittent eos in caminum ignis: ibi erit fletus et stridor dentium. [n. 1200]

¹³:⁵¹ Intellexistis haec omnia? Dicunt ei: etiam. [n. 1201]

¹³:⁵² Ait illis: ideo omnis scriba doctus in regno caelorum similis est homini patrifamilias, qui profert de thesauro suo nova et vetera. [n. 1204]

¹³:⁵³ Et factum est, cum consummasset Iesus parabolas istas, transiit inde. [n. 1208]

¹³:⁵⁴ Et veniens in patriam suam docebat eos in synagogis eorum, ita ut mirarentur, et dicerent: unde huic sapientia haec, et virtutes? [n. 1209]

¹³:⁴⁴ Ὁμοία ἐστὶν ἡ βασιλεία τῶν οὐρανῶν θησαυρῷ κεκρυμμένῳ ἐν τῷ ἀγρῷ, ὃν εὑρὼν ἄνθρωπος ἔκρυψεν, καὶ ἀπὸ τῆς χαρᾶς αὐτοῦ ὑπάγει καὶ πωλεῖ πάντα ὅσα ἔχει καὶ ἀγοράζει τὸν ἀγρὸν ἐκεῖνον.

¹³:⁴⁵ Πάλιν ὁμοία ἐστὶν ἡ βασιλεία τῶν οὐρανῶν ἀνθρώπῳ ἐμπόρῳ ζητοῦντι καλοὺς μαργαρίτας·

¹³:⁴⁶ εὑρὼν δὲ ἕνα πολύτιμον μαργαρίτην ἀπελθὼν πέπρακεν πάντα ὅσα εἶχεν καὶ ἠγόρασεν αὐτόν.

¹³:⁴⁷ Πάλιν ὁμοία ἐστὶν ἡ βασιλεία τῶν οὐρανῶν σαγήνῃ βληθείσῃ εἰς τὴν θάλασσαν καὶ ἐκ παντὸς γένους συναγαγούσῃ·

¹³:⁴⁸ ἣν ὅτε ἐπληρώθη ἀναβιβάσαντες ἐπὶ τὸν αἰγιαλὸν καὶ καθίσαντες συνέλεξαν τὰ καλὰ εἰς ἄγγη, τὰ δὲ σαπρὰ ἔξω ἔβαλον.

¹³:⁴⁹ οὕτως ἔσται ἐν τῇ συντελείᾳ τοῦ αἰῶνος· ἐξελεύσονται οἱ ἄγγελοι καὶ ἀφοριοῦσιν τοὺς πονηροὺς ἐκ μέσου τῶν δικαίων

¹³:⁵⁰ καὶ βαλοῦσιν αὐτοὺς εἰς τὴν κάμινον τοῦ πυρός· ἐκεῖ ἔσται ὁ κλαυθμὸς καὶ ὁ βρυγμὸς τῶν ὀδόντων.

¹³:⁵¹ Συνήκατε ταῦτα πάντα; λέγουσιν αὐτῷ· ναί.

¹³:⁵² ὁ δὲ εἶπεν αὐτοῖς· διὰ τοῦτο πᾶς γραμματεὺς μαθητευθεὶς τῇ βασιλείᾳ τῶν οὐρανῶν ὅμοιός ἐστιν ἀνθρώπῳ οἰκοδεσπότῃ, ὅστις ἐκβάλλει ἐκ τοῦ θησαυροῦ αὐτοῦ καινὰ καὶ παλαιά.

¹³:⁵³ Καὶ ἐγένετο ὅτε ἐτέλεσεν ὁ Ἰησοῦς τὰς παραβολὰς ταύτας, μετῆρεν ἐκεῖθεν.

¹³:⁵⁴ καὶ ἐλθὼν εἰς τὴν πατρίδα αὐτοῦ ἐδίδασκεν αὐτοὺς ἐν τῇ συναγωγῇ αὐτῶν, ὥστε ἐκπλήσσεσθαι αὐτοὺς καὶ λέγειν· πόθεν τούτῳ ἡ σοφία αὕτη καὶ αἱ δυνάμεις;

¹³:⁴⁴ The kingdom of heaven is like a treasure hidden in a field. Which a man, having found it, hides, and out of joy goes, and sells all that he has, and buys that field. [n. 1188]

¹³:⁴⁵ Again the kingdom of heaven is like a merchant seeking good pearls. [n. 1193]

¹³:⁴⁶ Who upon finding one pearl of great price, went his way, and sold all that he had, and bought it. [n. 1193]

¹³:⁴⁷ Again the kingdom of heaven is like a net cast into the sea, which gathered together all kinds of fish. [n. 1196]

¹³:⁴⁸ Which, when it was filled, they drew out, and sitting by the shore, they put the good into vessels, but the bad they threw out. [n. 1198]

¹³:⁴⁹ So will it be at the end of the world. The angels will go out, and will separate the wicked from among the just, [n. 1199]

¹³:⁵⁰ and will cast them into the furnace of fire, where there will be weeping and gnashing of teeth. [n. 1200]

¹³:⁵¹ Have you understood all these things? They say to him: yes. [n. 1201]

¹³:⁵² He said to them: therefore every scribe, instructed in the kingdom of heaven, is like a man who is a householder, who brings up out of his treasure new things and old. [n. 1204]

¹³:⁵³ And it came to pass, when Jesus had finished these parables, that he went from there. [n. 1208]

¹³:⁵⁴ And coming into his own country, he taught them in their synagogues, so that they wondered and said: how does this man come by this wisdom and these miracles? [n. 1209]

13:55 Nonne hic est fabri filius? Nonne mater eius dicitur Maria, et fratres eius Iacobus, et Ioseph, et Simon, et Iudas? [n. 1210]	**13:55** οὐχ οὗτός ἐστιν ὁ τοῦ τέκτονος υἱός; οὐχ ἡ μήτηρ αὐτοῦ λέγεται Μαριὰμ καὶ οἱ ἀδελφοὶ αὐτοῦ Ἰάκωβος καὶ Ἰωσὴφ καὶ Σίμων καὶ Ἰούδας;	**13:55** Is not this the carpenter's son? Is not his mother called Mary, and his brothers James, and Joseph, and Simon, and Jude? [n. 1210]
13:56 Sorores eius nonne omnes apud nos sunt? Unde ergo huic omnia ista? [n. 1210]	**13:56** καὶ αἱ ἀδελφαὶ αὐτοῦ οὐχὶ πᾶσαι πρὸς ἡμᾶς εἰσιν; πόθεν οὖν τούτῳ ταῦτα πάντα;	**13:56** And his sisters, are they not all with us? From where therefore, does he have all these things? [n. 1210]
13:57 Et scandalizabantur in eo. Iesus autem dixit eis: non est propheta sine honore, nisi in patria sua et in domo sua. [n. 1211]	**13:57** καὶ ἐσκανδαλίζοντο ἐν αὐτῷ. ὁ δὲ Ἰησοῦς εἶπεν αὐτοῖς· οὐκ ἔστιν προφήτης ἄτιμος εἰ μὴ ἐν τῇ πατρίδι καὶ ἐν τῇ οἰκίᾳ αὐτοῦ.	**13:57** And they were scandalized in his regard. But Jesus said to them: a prophet is not without honor, except in his own country, and in his own house. [n. 1211]
13:58 Et non fecit ibi virtutes multas propter incredulitatem illorum. [n. 1214]	**13:58** καὶ οὐκ ἐποίησεν ἐκεῖ δυνάμεις πολλὰς διὰ τὴν ἀπιστίαν αὐτῶν.	**13:58** And he did not perform many miracles there, because of their unbelief. [n. 1214]

1187. Supra Dominus parabolice ostendit doctrinae evangelicae et impedimentum, et profectum; nunc autem ostendit eius dignitatem per quasdam parabolas, quas discipulis exposuit.

Dignitas ostenditur quantum ad tria: quantum ad copiositatem, quantum ad pulchritudinem, quantum ad eius communitatem.

Secunda ibi *iterum simile est regnum caelorum homini negotiatori* etc.; tertia ibi *iterum simile est regnum caelorum sagenae missae in mare* et cetera.

1188. Dico ergo, quod copia doctrinae evangelicae est in similitudine thesauri, quia sicut thesaurus est copia divitiarum, sic doctrina evangelica; Is. XXXIII, 6: *divitiae salutis sapientia et scientia; timor Domini ipse est thesaurus eius*.

Circa istud sic procedit.

Primo ponitur thesaurus absconditus;

secundo inventio;

tertio acquisitio et cetera.

Secunda ibi *quem qui invenit* etc.; tertia ibi *et prae gaudio illius vadit* et cetera.

1189. Iste thesaurus multipliciter potest exponi. Secundum Chrysostomum est evangelica doctrina, de qua II ad Cor. IV, v. 7: *habemus hunc thesaurum in vasis fictilibus*, qui absconditus est in agro huius mundi, scilicet ab oculis immundorum; Sup. c. XI, 25: *abscondisti haec a sapientibus et prudentibus*.

Secundum Gregorium dicitur caeleste desiderium; Is. XXXIII, 6: *timor Domini ipse est thesaurus eius*. Iste est absconditus in agro disciplinae spiritualis; quia exterius videtur contemptibilis, interius vero dulcedinem habet; Prov. XXIV, 27: *diligenter exerce agrum tuum*.

Secundum Hieronymum est Verbum Dei, de quo ad Col. II, 3: *in quo sunt omnes thesauri sapientiae, et scientiae absconditi*, quem abscondit in agro sui corporis, quia latebat in carne. Is. II, 7: *et non est finis thesaurorum eius*.

1187. Above the Lord made clear in a parable both the impediment to and the progress of the evangelical teaching; and now he shows its dignity through certain parables, which he set forth to the disciples.

The dignity is shown with respect to three things: with respect to abundance, with respect to beauty, and with respect to its commonness.

The second is at **again the kingdom of heaven is like a merchant**, the third, at **again the kingdom of heaven is like a net cast into the sea**.

1188. I say, therefore, that the abundance of the evangelical teaching is like a treasure, because just as a treasure is an abundance of riches, so the evangelical teaching; *riches of salvation, wisdom and knowledge: the fear of the Lord is his treasure* (Isa 33:6).

Concerning this, he proceeds in this way:

first, the hidden treasure is set down;

second, the finding;

third, the acquisition.

The second is at **which a man having found it, hides**; the third, at **and out of joy goes**.

1189. This treasure can be explained in many ways. According to Chrysostom it is the evangelical teaching: *but we have this treasure in earthen vessels* (2 Cor 4:7), which is hidden in the field of this world, namely hidden from the eyes of the unclean. Above, *you have hidden these things from the wise and prudent* (Matt 11:25).

According to Gregory it names heavenly desire; *the fear of the Lord is his treasure* (Isa 33:6). This is hidden in the field of spiritual discipline, because exteriorly it seems contemptible, but interiorly it has sweetness. *Diligently till your ground* (Prov 24:27).

According to Jerome it is the Word of God, *in whom are hid all the treasures of wisdom and knowledge* (Col 2:3), which he hid in the field of his body, because he was hidden in the flesh. *There is no end of his treasures* (Isa 2:7). For this

Ideo aliter intelligitur sacra doctrina, quae absconditur in agro Ecclesiae; Sap. VII, 14: *infinitus enim thesaurus est hominibus*.

1190. ***Quem qui invenit homo abscondit***. Invenitur in omnibus per fidem. Non enim potest in aliquibus esse, nisi per fidem; Sap. I, 2: *invenitur ab his qui non tentant illum; apparet autem eis, qui fidem habent in illum*. Sed oportet quod abscondatur, secundum quod dicitur Ps. CXVIII, 11: *in corde meo abscondi eloquia tua*. Quod autem absconditur, non debet esse ex invidia, sed ex cautela.

Quare autem abscondi debeat, multiplex est ratio. Una quia magis fructificat et proficit, quia magis exardescit; sicut enim ignis conclusus magis calefacit, sic verbum quando est absconditum; Ier. XX, 9: *factum est verbum Domini quasi ignis aestuans, claususque in ossibus meis, et defeci, ferre non sustinens*. Et in Ps. XXXVIII, 4: *concaluit cor meum, et in meditatione mea exardescet ignis intra me*. Item est quod absconditur ob inanem gloriam: si enim fumigat exterius, subiacet periculo. Ideo Dominus supra VI, 6: *ora Patrem tuum in abscondito*. Item quia sic tutius custoditur; quando enim est in publico, tunc invenit qui rapit. Is. XXXIX, 4: *qui ostendit thesauros nuntiis regis Babylonis*, et subditur: *ecce venient dies, et auferentur omnia quae in domo tua sunt*.

1191. Sed quid est quod dictum est supra c. V, 15: *luceant opera vestra bona*?

Solvitur ob distinctionem temporum: quia quando primo invenitur, bonum est quod abscondatur; sed quando homo confirmatus est, tunc bonum est quod manifestetur; Eccli. XLI, v. 17: *thesaurus invisus, et sapientia abscondita, quae utilitas in utrisque?* Gregorius dicit, quod debet esse apertus in effectu, absconditus in corde. Unde dicit sic: *opus sit in publico, quamquam intentio maneat in occulto*.

1192. ***Prae gaudio illius vadit, et vendit universa quae habet***. Hoc est tertium de acquisitione, quia gaudet. Iob c. III, 21: *quasi effodientes thesaurum, gaudentque vehementer cum invenerint sepulcrum*. Quando per fidem invenerit **prae gaudio vadit**, et incipit proficere **et vendit omnia**, idest contemnit, ut spiritualia habeat, **et emit agrum illum**; hoc est vel bonam societatem sibi exquirit, vel emit sibi otium quod non habet, scilicet pacem spiritualem. Ad Phil. III, 8: *omnia arbitratus sum ut stercora, ut Christum lucrifacerem*; Cant. VIII, 7: *si dederit homo omnem substantiam domus suae pro dilectione, quasi nihil despiciet eam* et cetera.

1193. ***Iterum simile est regnum caelorum homini negotiatori*** et cetera. Hic ostenditur pulchritudo, vel caritas. **Simile est regnum**.

reason, in another way, it is understood as sacred teaching, which is hidden in the field of the Church; *for she is an infinite treasure to men* (Wis 7:14).

1190. ***Which a man, having found it, hides***. It is found in all through faith. For it cannot be in anyone except through faith; *for he is found by those who do not tempt him: and he shows himself to those who have faith in him* (Wis 1:2). But it is necessary that it be hidden, according to what is said in the Psalm, *your words have I hidden in my heart* (Ps 118:11). But that it is hidden should not be out of envy, but out of caution.

And there are many reasons why it should be hidden. One, because it bears fruit more and profits more, since it blazes up more; for just as fire closed in heats more, so a word which is hidden bears more fruit. The word of the Lord was made *in my heart as a burning fire shut up in my bones, and I was wearied, not being able to bear it* (Jer 20:9). And in the Psalm, *my heart grew hot within me: and in my meditation a fire shall flame out* (Ps 38:4). Similarly, it is what is hidden from vainglory, for if it smoked exteriorly, it would be subject to danger. For this reason the Lord said above, *pray to your Father in secret* (Matt 6:6). Similarly, because in this way it is more safely guarded; for when it is in public, then he who steals it away finds it. *He showed them the storehouses of his aromatical spices, and of the silver, and of the gold*, and it adds below, *behold the days will come, that all that is in your house . . . will be carried away into Babylon* (Isa 39:2–6).

1191. But why was it said above, ***so let your light shine before men***? (Matt 5:16).

This is resolved by distinguishing between times, because when it is first found it is good that it be hidden; but when a man has become strong, then it is good that it be made manifest; *wisdom that is hid, and a treasure that is not seen, what profit is there in them both?* (Sir 41:17). Gregory says that it should be open in effect, hidden in the heart. Hence he speaks thus: *let the work be in public, however much the intention remains hidden*.

1192. ***And out of joy goes, and sells all that he has***. This is the third part, about the acquisition, because he rejoices. *They who dig for a treasure: and they rejoice exceedingly when they have found the grave* (Job 3:21). When by faith he finds it, ***out of joy goes*** and begins to progress, ***and sells all that he has***, i.e., despises all that he has, that he may have what is spiritual, ***and buys that field***; that is, either he seeks out good company, or he buys the leisure which he does not have, namely spiritual peace. *And count them but as dung, that I may gain Christ* (Phil 3:8); *if a man should give all the substance of his house for love, he will despise it as nothing* (Song 8:7).

1193. ***Again the kingdom of heaven is like a merchant***. Here the beauty, or charity, is shown. ***The kingdom of heaven is like***.

Ista parabola exponitur multipliciter. Chrysostomus et Hieronymus exponunt de evangelica doctrina. Multae sunt doctrinae falsae. Istae non sunt margaritae. Homo ergo qui quaerit diversas doctrinas, invenit unam, scilicet evangelicam doctrinam, quae una est propter veritatem. Virtutes enim multae sunt, sed veritas una. Unde Dionysius dicit quod virtus dividit, sed veritas unitatem dat. Unde ad designandam veritatem vocat **unam**. Item dicitur **una** propter diversam doctrinam prophetarum. ***Abiit, et vendidit***, idest omnes doctrinas et prophetarum, et philosophorum pro ista dimisit. Prov. XXV, 12: *inauris aurea, et margarita fulgens, qui arguit sapientem, et aurem obedientem* et cetera.

1194. Gregorius istam dicit esse caelestem gloriam, quia bonum est naturaliter desiderabile, et homo semper vult commutare minus bonum pro maiori bono. Summum bonum hominis est gloria caelestis; hanc cum invenerit, debet omnia dimittere pro ista; Ps. XXVI, 4: *unam petii a Domino, hanc requiram, ut inhabitem in domo Domini omnibus diebus vitae meae.*

1195. Augustinus tripliciter exponit. ***Simile est regnum caelorum*** etc., idest quaerenti bonos homines a quibus informetur, quia unus pollet in una virtute, alius in alia. Et cum invenerit eam, scilicet Christum, in quo omnes virtutes sunt in summo, ***abiit*** et cetera.

Item aliter per bonas margaritas signantur diversa praecepta, et omnia ad vitam necessaria. Et dum invenerit unam, idest unum mandatum, scilicet caritatis, ***abiit*** et cetera. Io. XIII, v. 34: *mandatum novum do vobis, ut diligatis invicem, sicut dilexi vos, ut et vos diligatis invicem* et cetera. Et Apostolus Rom. XIII, v. 10: *plenitudo legis est dilectio.*

Item aliter per margaritas intelliguntur diversae scientiae, quas quaerendo invenimus principium omnium scientiarum, scilicet Verbum Dei, de quo Eccli. I, 5: *fons sapientiae Verbum Dei.* Unde debes omnia vendere pro isto, et terrena, et animam, et corpus, quia cum vendis ista, teipsum habes, et es dominus tui. Ad Phil. III, 8: *omnia arbitratus sum ut stercora, ut Christum lucrifaciam.* Unde omnia debes dare pro isto lucro, sicut dabat Paulus, II Cor. V, 14: *unus pro omnibus mortuus est, ut et qui vivunt, iam non sibi vivant, sed ei, qui pro ipsis mortuus est, et resurrexit.*

1196. *Iterum simile est regnum caelorum sagenae missae in mare* et cetera. Hic ponitur alia parabola. Secundo ponitur expositio non quantum ad totum, sed quoad partem, ibi ***sic erit in consummatione saeculi***.

Et in ista duo fiunt.

Primo ponitur communitas huius doctrinae;

This parable is explained in many ways. Chrysostom and Jerome explain it as about the evangelical teaching. There are many false teachings. These teachings are not pearls. So the man who seeks different teachings finds one, namely the evangelical teaching, which is one on account of truth. For there are many powers, but one truth. Hence Dionysius says that power divides, but truth gives unity. Hence to designate the truth, he calls it ***one***. Similarly, it is called ***one*** on account of the diverse teaching of the prophets. He ***went his way, and sold***, i.e., abandoned all teachings both of the prophets and of the philosophers for this one. *As an earring of gold and a bright pearl, so is he who reproves the wise, and the obedient ear* (Prov 25:12).

1194. Gregory says that this is heavenly glory, because the good is naturally desirable, and man always wants to exchange a lesser good for a greater good. Man's highest good is heavenly glory; when he has found this, he should abandon all things for it. *One thing I have asked of the Lord, this will I seek after; that I may dwell in the house of the Lord all the days of my life* (Ps 26:4).

1195. Augustine explains it in three ways. ***The kingdom of heaven is like a merchant***, i.e., like one seeking good men by whom he may be formed, because one man is strong in one virtue, another man in another. And when he had found one pearl, namely Christ, in whom all the virtues are in the highest degree, ***he went his way***.

Similarly, in another way, the good pearls signify the different commandments, and all things necessary for life. And when he found one, i.e., the one commandment, namely of charity, ***he went his way***. *A new commandment I give unto you: that you love one another, as I have loved you, that you also love one another* (John 13:34). And the Apostle: *love therefore is the fulfilling of the law* (Rom 13:10).

Similarly, in another way, by pearls are understood the different sciences, which we find by seeking the principle of all sciences, namely the Word of God, about whom Sirach says, *the Word of God on high is the fountain of wisdom* (Sir 1:5). Hence you should sell all things for it, both earthly things, and the soul, and the body, because when you sell these things, you have yourself, and you are master of yourself. *I count all things to be but loss for the excellent knowledge of Jesus Christ* (Phil 3:8). Hence you should give away all for this profit, as Paul gave; *one died for all, then all were dead. And Christ died for all; that they also who live, may not now live to themselves, but unto him who died for them, and rose again* (2 Cor 5:14).

1196. *Again the kingdom of heaven is like a net cast into the sea*. Here another parable is set down. Second, an explanation is set down, not with regard to the whole, but as regards a part, at ***so will it be at the end of the world***.

And in this two things are done:

first, the commonness of this teaching is set down;

secundo distinctio, ibi *cum impleta esset* et cetera.

1197. Dicit ergo *simile est regnum caelorum sagenae*. Ista sagena est quoddam instrumentum, quod circumdat magnam partem maris; unde potest per eam significari vel doctrina, vel Ecclesia: quia primi doctores fuerunt piscatores; supra IV, 18: *erant enim piscatores*. Haec ponitur in mari, idest in mundo; Ps. CIII, 25: *hoc mare magnum et spatiosum* et cetera. *Et ex omni genere piscium congreganti*. Ecce communitas. Lex enim non erat data nisi uni genti; Ps. CXLVII, 20: *non fecit taliter omni nationi, et iudicia sua non manifestavit eis*. Lex evangelica congregat omnes; ad Rom. I, 14: *Graecis et barbaris, sapientibus et insipientibus debitor sum*. Et Mc. ult., 15: *ite, praedicate Evangelium omni creaturae*.

1198. Sed numquid idem erit finis omnium? Modo omnes simul sunt in sagena, sed in fine omnes separabuntur; unde dicit *quam, cum impleta esset*, idest quando tot electi intraverint ut sit completus numerus electorum *educentes, et secus littus sedentes* et cetera.

Per littus finis mundi significatur, quia non erit apud sanctos turbulentia, sed erunt in quiete bona. Et dicit *sedentes*, quod pertinet ad iudiciariam potestatem. Infra XIX, v. 28: *vos qui secuti estis me, in regeneratione, cum sederit Filius hominis in sede maiestatis suae, sedebitis et vos super sedes duodecim, iudicantes duodecim tribus Israel*. *Elegerunt bonos in vasa*, idest in caelestia habitacula; Io. XIV, 2: *in domo Patris mei mansiones multae sunt*. Et dicit *vasa* pluraliter propter diversitatem retributionum; Lc. c. XVI, 9: *recipiant vos in aeterna tabernacula*. *Malos autem foras miserunt*, quia omnes immundi eiicientur.

1199. *Sic erit in consummatione saeculi*. Hic exponit parabolam. Et notandum quod exponit solum quoad malos.

Sed tunc est quaestio, quare magis exponit de malis, quam de bonis.

Dicendum, quod fecerat mentionem de sagena, qua, quando pisces capiuntur, mali eiiciuntur, et vivunt; boni autem occiduntur, et comeduntur. Ideo posset aliquis dicere, quod ita esset ex parte ista; ideo ut excludat illud, exponit dicens *exibunt angeli*, non quod discedant ab intimis contemplationis, quia ubicumque sunt, contemplantur Deum; sed quia progrediuntur ad exterius ministerium. Daniel c. IX, 22 dicitur de quodam angelo: *egressus sum, ut docerem te*.

Et separabunt malos de medio iustorum. Modo mali sunt inter bonos, zizania in medio tritici, lilium inter spinas, sed separabuntur ex communione bonorum; et ex hoc est mala excommunicatio; ista tamen signum illius, sed tamen alia, quia Ecclesia saepe decipitur, sed

second, the separation, at *which, when it was filled, they drew out*.

1197. He says then, *the kingdom of heaven is like a net*. This net is a certain instrument which encloses a large part of the sea; hence it can signify either teaching, or the Church, since the first teachers were fishermen. Above, *for they were fishermen* (Matt 4:18). This is placed in the sea, i.e., in the world; *so is this great sea, which stretcheth wide its arms* (Ps 103:25). *Which gathered together all kinds of fish*. Behold, the commonness. For the law was only given to one race; *he has not done in like manner to every nation: and his judgments he has not made manifest to them* (Ps 147:9). The evangelical law gathers all together; *to the Greeks and to the barbarians, to the wise and to the unwise, I am a debtor* (Rom 1:14). And, *go into the whole world, and preach the Gospel to every creature* (Mark 16:15).

1198. But there will not be the same end for all, will there? For a while all will be in the net together, but in the end all will be separated; hence he says, *which, when it was filled*, i.e., when all the elect have entered so that the number of the elect is complete, *they drew out, and sitting by the shore*.

The shore signifies the end of the world, because there will be no disturbance among the saints, but they will be in good peace. And he says, *sitting*, which pertains to the judiciary power. Below, *you, who have followed me, in the regeneration, when the Son of man will sit on the seat of his majesty, you also will sit on twelve seats judging the twelve tribes of Israel* (Matt 19:28). *They put the good into vessels*, i.e., into heavenly dwelling places; *in my Father's house there are many mansions* (John 14:2). And he says, *vessels*, in the plural because of the diversity of rewards; *that when you will fail, they may receive you into everlasting dwellings* (Luke 16:9). *But the bad they threw out*, because all the unclean shall be cast out.

1199. *So will it be at the end of the world*. Here he explains the parable. And one should notice that he explains it only as regards the evil.

But then there is a question, why he explains more about the evil than about the good.

One should say that he had mentioned a net, from which, when fish are captured, the bad are thrown out, and live, while the good are killed and eaten. So someone could say that it will be this way on the part of these men; to exclude this, he explains, saying, *the angels will go out*, not that they withdraw from the inmost contemplation, because they contemplate God wherever they are, but because they go forth to exterior service. Daniel says about a certain angel, *I am now come forth to teach you* (Dan 9:22).

And will separate the wicked from among the just. For now, the evil are among the good, the weed in the midst of the wheat, the lily among the thorns, but they will be separated out from the communion of the good; and from this is evil excommunication. Yet this one is a sign of that, and

tunc non erit deceptio. Haec est de qua dicit Apostolus I Cor. XVI, 22: *si quis non amat Dominum nostrum Iesum Christum, sit anathema*. Unde dicitur: *tollatur impius ne videat gloriam Dei*.

1200. Sequitur de poena sensus *et mittent eos in caminum ignis*. Hoc exponitur ut supra.

Sed est quaestio, quare iteravit hoc Dominus, quia videtur idem esse quod parabola de zizania.

Dicendum, quod idem est quantum ad aliquid, quia hic per sagenam intelliguntur et boni et mali; unde significat eos qui non sunt praecisi ab Ecclesia. Sed per zizaniam significantur illi qui sunt praecisi per diversitatem dogmatum, et hi non sunt de Ecclesia.

1201. *Intellexistis haec omnia? Dicunt ei, etiam*. Postquam Dominus complevit parabolicam doctrinam, et quoad discipulos, hic determinat de effectu; et

primo in discipulis;
secundo in turbis, ibi *et factum est* et cetera.

Effectus in discipulis fuit intellectus: unde tria ponuntur.
Primo examinatio;
secundo professio;
tertio designatio eorum ad futurum officium.

1202. Notandum autem, quod cum multa locutus esset ad turbas et discipulos, quia futuri erant magistri, ideo oportebat quod intelligerent.

Et nota quod de tribus examinabantur. Primo de intellectu *intellexistis haec omnia?* Item de amore, Io. ult., 15: *Simon, amas me plus his?* Item de possibilitate ad passionem; infra XX, 22: *potestis bibere calicem, quem ego bibiturus sum?* Ps. XCI, 15: *bene patientes erunt ut annuntient*.

1203. Licet autem humilitatis sit quod homo non se extollat; ingratus tamen est si beneficium non recognoscat. Is. LXIII, 7: *miserationum Domini recordabor*. Ideo respondent et *dicunt ei etiam*. Ibi ponitur professio eorum attribuentium sermoni Christi. Ps. CXVIII, 130: *declaratio sermonum tuorum illuminat, et intellectum dat parvulis*.

1204. *Ideo omnis scriba doctus* et cetera. Hic ostendit officium quod imminebat eis, quasi iam examinatis. Et haec conclusio dupliciter potest sequi ex praemissis. Primo retorquendo hoc quod dictum est de thesauro. Potest ergo esse sensus, ut Dominus velit istud exponere: vos dicitis, quod intelligitis. Si intelligitis, potestis scire

yet different, because the Church is often deceived, but at that time there will be no deception. This is what the Apostle speaks about when he says, *if any man does not love our Lord Jesus Christ, let him be anathema* (1 Cor 16:22). Hence it is said, *let the impious man be taken away, lest he see the glory of God*.

1200. There follows, concerning the punishment of the senses, *and will cast them into the furnace of fire*. This is explained above.

But there is a question as to why the Lord repeated this, because it seems to be the same as the parable of the weed.

One should say that it is the same only in a certain respect, because here the net indicates both the good and the bad; hence it signifies those who are not cut off from the Church. But the weed signifies those who are cut off by a difference of doctrine, and these are not of the Church.

1201. *Have you understood all these things? They say to him: yes*. After the Lord completed the teaching in parables, and with respect to the disciples, here he describes the effect; and

first, in the disciples;
second, in the crowds, at *and it came to pass, when Jesus had finished these parables*.

The effect in the disciples was understanding; hence three things are set down:
first, the inquiry;
second, the declaration;
third, their appointment to a future office.

1202. But one should note that while he had spoken many things to the crowds and the disciples, since they were going to be teachers, it was necessary for this reason that they understand.

And notice that they are questioned about three things. First, about understanding: *have you understood all these things?* Similarly, about love, *Simon son of John, do you love me more than these?* (John 21:15). Similarly, about the ability for suffering; below, *can you drink the chalice that I will drink?* (Matt 20:22). *They will still increase in a fruitful old age: and will suffer well, that they may show, that the Lord our God is righteous* (Ps 91:15).

1203. Now, although it belongs to humility that a man not extol himself, yet he is ungrateful if he fails to recognize a benefit. *I will remember the tender mercies of the Lord* (Isa 63:7). For this reason they answer, and *say to him, yes*. Here their declaration is set down, giving tribute to Christ's word. *The declaration of your words gives light: and gives understanding to little ones* (Ps 118:130).

1204. *Therefore every scribe instructed in the kingdom of heaven*. Here he shows the office which was in store for them, as for those already examined. And this conclusion can follow from the premises in two ways. First, by referring this to what was said about the treasure. So the sense can be that the Lord willed to explain this: you say that you

quod thesaurus est sacra doctrina. De isto thesauro poteritis proferre nova et vetera.

Et notandum quod isti dicuntur scribae, quia possunt conferre in regno caelorum, et in doctrina sacra, ubi nova et vetera continentur. Et dicuntur scribae per idoneitatem, quia scribae, idest docti; Dan. XII, 10: *porro docti intelligent*; infra XXIII, 34: ***ecce ego mitto ad vos sapientes et scribas***. Item dicuntur scribae ex officio, quia sunt notarii Christi, quia scripserunt mandata Christi in tabulis cordis sui; Prov. VI, 21: *liga ea in corde tuo iugiter*. Item in cordibus aliorum. Unde Apostolus II ad Cor. III, 2: *epistola vestra scripta est in cordibus nostris*.

Similis est patrifamilias, scilicet Christo. Ipse enim est Dominus, ut habetur supra XIII, v. 52. ***Qui profert de thesauro nova et vetera***, officia novae legis. Nova enim lex novos sensus addit super veterem, et Christus hos exposuit; et ideo debet nobis sufficere ut sit similis Christo, sicut supra X, 25 habetur: ***sufficit discipulo si sit sicut magister eius***.

1205. Vel potest dici: simile est cuicumque alii patri, qui profert de scientia divinitus sibi data nova et vetera. Non sic Manichaei, quia non proferebant vetera. Cant. VII, 13: *omnia nova et vetera servavi tibi*. Ergo potest referri de expositione parabolae.

1206. Secundum Augustinum sic exponitur ***ideo omnis scriba doctus*** et cetera. Vos intellexistis qualiter locutus sum turbis parabolice, et exercitati estis, ut quod parabolice dictum est, secundum sensum spiritualem intelligatis. Unde debetis intelligere, ut ea, quae in veteri lege leguntur, sciatis exponere per novam. Unde quae in Veteri dicuntur, sunt figurae Novi Testamenti. Unde Apostolus I ad Cor. X, 11: *omnia in figura contingebant eis*. Et haec revelata sunt in passione. Unde infra XXVII dicitur quod, patiente Domino, velum templi scissum est. Unde Christus ante passionem in parabolis locutus est, ut auditis his intelligant ea, quae in Veteri Testamento dicuntur, esse dicta in figura aliarum rerum, licet essent res gestae. ***Omnis ergo Scriba doctus in regno caelorum similis est homini patrifamilias, qui profert de thesauro suo nova et vetera***.

1207. Vel, secundum Gregorium, quod vetera referantur ad omnia ea quae ad peccatum referuntur, nova quae ad gratiam Christi: unde nova dicuntur praemia vitae aeternae, vetera poena inferni. Ille ergo profert nova

understand. If you understand, you are able to know that the treasure is sacred teaching. From this treasure you will be able to bring forth things new and old.

And one should notice that these men are called scribes, because they can discuss the kingdom of God and sacred teaching, wherein things new and old are contained. They are also called scribes by fitness, because they are scribes, i.e., instructed; *the learned shall understand* (Dan 12:10); below, ***behold I send to you prophets, and wise men, and scribes*** (Matt 23:34). Similarly, they are called scribes from their office, because they are Christ's secretaries, since they wrote down Christ's commandments on the tablets of their hearts; *bind them in your heart continually* (Prov 6:21). Likewise in the hearts of others. Hence the Apostle: *you are our epistle, written in our hearts* (2 Cor 3:2).

Is like a man who is a householder, namely Christ. For he himself is the Lord, as is said above (Matt 13:52). ***Who brings up out of his treasure new things and old***, the duties of the new law. For the new law adds new senses over the old, and Christ explains this; and for this reason it should be enough for us to be like Christ, as is said above, ***it is enough for the disciple that he be like his master*** (Matt 10:25).

1205. Or one can say: he is like any other head of a household, who brings forth the knowledge divinely given to him, new and old. Not so the Manichees, because they did not bring forth the old. *The new and the old, my beloved, I have kept for you* (Song 7:13). So it can be referred to the explanation of the parable.

1206. According to Augustine, it is explained in this way. ***Therefore every scribe, instructed in the kingdom of heaven, is like a man who is a householder***. You have understood how I spoke to the crowds in parables, and you have been examined, that you may understand what was said in parables according to the spiritual sense. Hence you should understand, so that you may know to explain those things which are written in the Old Law through the New. Hence those things said in the Old are figures of the New Testament. Hence the Apostle: *now all these things happened to them in figure* (1 Cor 10:11). And these things were revealed in the passion. Hence below, it says that, while the Lord was suffering, the veil in the temple was rent (Matt 27). Hence Christ spoke in parables before the passion, that having heard these things, they might understand those things which are written in the Old Testament to be said as figures of other things, even though they were historical. ***Therefore every scribe, instructed in the kingdom of heaven, is like a man who is a householder, who brings up out of his treasure new things and old***.

1207. Or, according to Gregory, the old things refer to all those things which are attributed to sin, and the new to those things which are attributed to the grace of Christ. Hence the new things refer to the reward of eternal life,

et vetera, qui non solum praemia, sed poenam etiam inferni considerat.

1208. *Et factum est, cum consummasset Iesus parabolas istas* et cetera. Hic ponitur effectus in turbis: duplex, scilicet et admirationis, et scandalizationis. Et

primo locus describitur;
secundo admiratio;
tertio improbatio.

1209. Dicit ergo *factum est cum consummasset Iesus parabolas istas, transiit inde.*

Notandum, quod non videtur, quod statim transierit. Unde non servat ordinem historiae; sed **transivit**, quia ad intelligendum non erant idonei; ideo ad alia se transtulit, secundum illud Eccli. XXXII, 6: *ubi auditus non est, non effundas sermonem.* Et cap. XXII, v. 9: *cum dormiente loquitur, qui narrat stulto sapientiam.* **Et veniens in patriam suam**. Patria sua aliquando dicitur Nazareth, ubi nutritus est, et ibi fecit pauca miracula: aliquando Bethlehem, in qua natus est; aliquando Capharnaum, quia miracula fecit ibi.

1210. *Et docebat in synagogis eorum* et cetera. Sequitur admiratio. Et primo ponitur admiratio; secundo causatur effectus.

Dicit *ita ut mirarentur*. Non erat mirum si mirabantur; Ps. CXVIII, 129: *mirabilia testimonia tua.* Admirabantur unde illae virtutes essent: admiratio enim ex hoc causatur, quod videtur effectus, et nescitur causa. Isti effectum manifestum videbant, sed causam nesciebant; unde dicebant: *unde huic sapientia et virtutes?* Sed haec stulta admiratio, quia I ad Cor. I, 24 habetur, *quod ipse est Dei virtus et sapientia.* Sed non cognoscebant, ideo admirabantur.

Et ponunt admirationem suam, et cognitionem suam: unde dicebant *nonne hic est fabri filius?* Ipse enim putabatur filius Ioseph, qui non erat faber ferrarius, sed lignarius: quamvis etiam posset dici Filius Fabri, *qui fabricatus est auroram et solem.* Ps. LXXIII, 16. **Nonne mater eius dicitur Maria?** Omnia noscebant quae erant humanitatis. De Maria habetur supra I, 18: *cum esset desponsata mater Iesu Maria Ioseph* et cetera. *Et fratres eius Iacobus et Ioseph, Simon et Iudas.* Elvidius intellexit istos esse filios Mariae. Sed hoc falsum est, sed fuerunt consobrini eius. Vel dicuntur fratres, quia de cognatione Ioseph, qui putabatur esse pater Iesu. Gen. XIII, 8: *non sit contentio inter me et te: fratres enim sumus,* dixit Abraham ad Lot: cum tamen Lot esset filius fratris. Et eodem modo intelligendum est quod sequitur: *et sorores eius nonne omnes apud nos sunt?* Ideo ex his

while the old things refer to the punishment of hell. Therefore, that man brings forth things new and old who considers not only the reward, but also the punishment of hell.

1208. *And it came to pass, when Jesus had finished these parables, that he went from there.* Here the effect on the crowds is set down: there are two, both wonderment and scandal. And

first, the place is described;
second, the wonderment;
third, the reproval.

1209. *And it came to pass, when Jesus had finished these parables, that he went from there.*

One should note that it does not seem that he passed on immediately. Hence Matthew does not preserve the order of history. But **he went**, since they were not fit for understanding; for this reason he carried himself on to others, according to, *where there is no hearing, do not pour out words* (Sir 32:6). And, *he speaks with one who is asleep, who utters wisdom to a fool* (Sir 22:9). **And coming into his own country**. His own country is sometimes called Nazareth, where he grew up, and there he worked few miracles; sometimes Bethlehem, in which he was born; sometimes Capharnaum, because he worked miracles there.

1210. And *he taught them in their synagogues*. There follows the wonderment. And first, the wonderment is set down; second, the effect is caused.

It says, *so that they wondered*. It was no wonder that they wondered; *your testimonies are wonderful* (Ps 118:129). They wondered at where these powers were from, for wonderment is caused by the fact that the effect is seen and the cause is unknown. These people saw the manifest effect, but they did not know the cause; hence they said, *how does this man come by this wisdom and miracles?* But this was foolish wonderment, because it says in Corinthians that he himself is *the power of God, and the wisdom of God* (1 Cor 1:24). But they did not know this, so they wondered.

And they set out their wonderment and their knowledge; hence they said, *is not this the carpenter's son?* For he was considered the son of Joseph, who was not a craftsman with iron, but with wood; although he could also be called the Son of the Craftsman *who crafted the morning light and the sun* (Ps 73:16). *Is not his mother called Mary?* They knew everything that belonged to his humanity. Concerning Mary, it is written above, *when his mother, Mary, was espoused to Joseph* (Matt 1:18). *And his brethren James, and Joseph, and Simon, and Jude*. Helvidius understood these to be sons of Mary. But this is false; they were his first cousins on his mother's side. Or they are called brothers because of blood relation to Joseph, who was thought to be Jesus's father. *Let there be no quarrel, I beseech you, between me and you . . . for we are brethren* (Gen 13:8), said Abraham to Lot, while nevertheless Lot was the son of his brother. And in the same way one should understand what follows: *and his sisters, are they not all with us?* So from

quae secundum carnem erant, in admirationem prodibant dicentes: *unde ergo huic omnia ista?*

1211. Sed notandum quod admiratio quandoque habet debitum effectum, scilicet Dei glorificationem, ut supra III, 5, aliquando vero scandalizationem: unde dicit *et sic scandalizabantur in eo*.

Sed quae est ratio, quod admiratio aliquando pariat gloriam, aliquando scandalum? Ratio est, quia quidam ea quae audiunt, interpretantur in peius, ideo tales necessario scandalizantur. In canonica Iudae, 10: *quaecumque quidem ignorant, blasphemant*.

1212. Sed aliqui qui sunt bene dispositi, semper in melius interpretantur. De primis erant isti; ideo eos reprehendit; et primo verbo; secundo facto, cum dicit *Iesus autem dixit eis: non est propheta sine honore nisi in patria sua*. Dominus seipsum prophetam nominat: nec mirum, quia Moyses etiam ipsum prophetam nominaverat, Deut. XVIII, v. 15: *prophetam suscitabit tibi de gente tua, et de fratribus tuis* et cetera. Et potest dici, quod propheta dicitur esse, qui aliquid dicit quod est supra humanum intellectum per revelationem; et sic Iesus dicitur propheta, quia mens eius illuminata est ab angelis et Deo. Vel potest dici aliquis propheta a *procul*, et *phanos*, quod est illuminatio: et sic Iesus non potest dici propheta: *si quis fuerit inter vos propheta Domini, in visione apparebo ei* et cetera. Sic habet textus. Sed si fuerit aliquis propheta, loquatur in aenigmatibus: sic non fuit Christus propheta, quia dixit quae vere scivit; Eccli. XXXIV, 9: *qui multa didicit, narrabit intellectum*. In prophetis Veteris Testamenti non invenimus aliquem honoratum a suis, sed magis ab alienis, ut legitur in Ieremia, qui fuit captus a suis, sed civitate capta, ab extraneis liberatus: sic etiam fuit de Christo, qui ab extraneis honorabatur, a suis despiciebatur.

1213. Et quae est ratio, quare nullus in patria sua honoratur? Una ratio est, quia quando est in patria sua, multi qui cognoscunt infirma sua, semper reducunt in memoriam infirma: hoc enim est a malitia hominum, ut magis infirma cogitent quam perfecta. Alia potest assignari, quia dicit Philosophus quod populus multum paralogizatur, quia credunt quod in aliquo pares, in omnibus pares sint. Unde quando aliquis est in patria sua, cum vident eum parem sibi in aliquo vel in genere, vel aliis, credunt quod non possit esse maior; ideo bene dicit *non est propheta sine honore nisi in patria sua et domo sua*.

1214. Unde sequitur *et non fecit ibi multas virtutes*; non quia non potuerit, quia omnipotens erat, sed non

these things which were according to the flesh, they passed on to wonderment; hence *from where therefore does he have all these things?*

1211. But one should note that wonderment sometimes has its due effect, namely the glorification of God, as above (Matt 3:5); but sometimes the effect is scandal: hence it says, *and they were scandalized in his regard*.

But why is it that wonderment sometimes gives birth to glory, sometimes to scandal? The reason is that some men interpret what they hear for the worse, so such men are necessarily scandalized. In the canonical letter of Jude, *but these men blaspheme whatever things they do not know* (Jude 1:10).

1212. But there are some who are well disposed; they always interpret what they hear for the better. These men were of the first sort, so he reproached them. And first, by word; second, by deed, when it says, *but Jesus said to them: a prophet is not without honor, except in his own country*. The Lord calls himself a prophet; nor is this a marvel, since Moses also called him a prophet: *the Lord your God will raise up to you a prophet of your nation and of your brethren like unto me* (Deut 18:15). And it can be said that a prophet is said to be one who says something which is beyond human understanding, by revelation; and in this way Jesus is called a prophet, because his mind was illumined by angels and by God. Or someone can be called a prophet from *procul* (at a distance) and *phanos*, which is illumination; and in this way Jesus cannot be called a prophet: *if there is among you a prophet of the Lord, I will appear to him in a vision, or I will speak to him in a dream* (Num 12:6). So the text has it. But if someone is a prophet, he speaks in enigmas; in this way Christ was not a prophet, because he spoke what he truly knew. *He who has learned many things, will show forth understanding* (Sir 34:9). In the prophets of the Old Testament we find no one honored by his own, but more by foreigners, as is written in Jeremiah, who was captured by his own, but when the city was taken, he was freed by outsiders. It was also this way with Christ, who was honored by outsiders, but looked down on by his own.

1213. But why is it that no one is honored in his own homeland? One reason is that when he is in his homeland, many who know his weaknesses always recall the weaknesses to mind; for this is due to men's malice, that they consider more the weaknesses than the perfect things. Another reason can be given, for the Philosopher says that many people are deceived by a fallacious argument, because they think that things equal in one respect are equal in all respects. Hence when someone is in his homeland, since they see him equal to themselves in one respect, either in race or other things, they believe that he cannot be greater in other respects. So he says well, *a prophet is not without honor, except in his own country, and in his own house*.

1214. Hence there follows *and he did not perform many miracles there*; not because he could not, for he was

fecit, quia ad hoc faciebat ut sibi crederetur. Sed ipsi eum despectui habebant, quia in malum interpretabantur, ideo non erant dispositi ad fidem: aliquas tamen fecit, ut inexcusabiles redderentur; et ideo dicit *non multas*, quia aliquas. Et hoc ***propter incredulitatem eorum***.

omnipotent, but he did not work miracles because his miracle working was so that people might believe in him. But these people held him in contempt, since they interpreted his words and deeds for evil, and so they were not disposed to faith. Yet he worked some, that they might be rendered inexcusable; and for this reason it says, ***not many***, because he did work some. And this was ***because of their unbelief***.

Chapter 14

Lecture 1

¹⁴:¹ In illo tempore audivit Herodes tetrarcha famam Iesu, [n. 1216]

¹⁴:² et ait pueris suis: hic est Ioannes Baptista, ipse surrexit a mortuis, et ideo virtutes operantur in eo. [n. 1219]

¹⁴:³ Herodes enim tenuit Ioannem, et alligavit eum, et posuit in carcerem propter Herodiadem uxorem fratris sui. [n. 1221]

¹⁴:⁴ Dicebat enim illi Ioannes: non licet tibi habere eam. [n. 1223]

¹⁴:⁵ Et volens illum occidere, timuit populum, quia sicut prophetam eum habebant. [n. 1224]

¹⁴:⁶ Die autem natalis Herodis saltavit filia Herodiadis in medio, et placuit Herodi, [n. 1225]

¹⁴:⁷ unde cum iuramento pollicitus est ei dare quodcumque postulasset ab eo. [n. 1227]

¹⁴:⁸ At illa praemonita a matre sua, da mihi, inquit, hic in disco caput Ioannis Baptistae. [n. 1228]

¹⁴:⁹ Et contristatus est rex; propter iuramentum autem et eos qui pariter recumbebant, iussit dari, [n. 1229]

¹⁴:¹⁰ misitque, et decollavit Ioannem in carcere. [n. 1231]

¹⁴:¹¹ Et allatum est caput eius in disco, et datum est puellae, et illa attulit matri suae. [n. 1233]

¹⁴:¹ Ἐν ἐκείνῳ τῷ καιρῷ ἤκουσεν Ἡρῴδης ὁ τετραάρχης τὴν ἀκοὴν Ἰησοῦ,

¹⁴:² καὶ εἶπεν τοῖς παισὶν αὐτοῦ· οὗτός ἐστιν Ἰωάννης ὁ βαπτιστής· αὐτὸς ἠγέρθη ἀπὸ τῶν νεκρῶν καὶ διὰ τοῦτο αἱ δυνάμεις ἐνεργοῦσιν ἐν αὐτῷ.

¹⁴:³ Ὁ γὰρ Ἡρῴδης κρατήσας τὸν Ἰωάννην ἔδησεν [αὐτὸν] καὶ ἐν φυλακῇ ἀπέθετο διὰ Ἡρῳδιάδα τὴν γυναῖκα Φιλίππου τοῦ ἀδελφοῦ αὐτοῦ·

¹⁴:⁴ ἔλεγεν γὰρ ὁ Ἰωάννης αὐτῷ· οὐκ ἔξεστίν σοι ἔχειν αὐτήν.

¹⁴:⁵ καὶ θέλων αὐτὸν ἀποκτεῖναι ἐφοβήθη τὸν ὄχλον, ὅτι ὡς προφήτην αὐτὸν εἶχον.

¹⁴:⁶ Γενεσίοις δὲ γενομένοις τοῦ Ἡρῴδου ὠρχήσατο ἡ θυγάτηρ τῆς Ἡρῳδιάδος ἐν τῷ μέσῳ καὶ ἤρεσεν τῷ Ἡρῴδῃ,

¹⁴:⁷ ὅθεν μεθ᾽ ὅρκου ὡμολόγησεν αὐτῇ δοῦναι ὃ ἐὰν αἰτήσηται.

¹⁴:⁸ ἡ δὲ προβιβασθεῖσα ὑπὸ τῆς μητρὸς αὐτῆς· δός μοι, φησίν, ὧδε ἐπὶ πίνακι τὴν κεφαλὴν Ἰωάννου τοῦ βαπτιστοῦ.

¹⁴:⁹ καὶ λυπηθεὶς ὁ βασιλεὺς διὰ τοὺς ὅρκους καὶ τοὺς συνανακειμένους ἐκέλευσεν δοθῆναι,

¹⁴:¹⁰ καὶ πέμψας ἀπεκεφάλισεν [τὸν] Ἰωάννην ἐν τῇ φυλακῇ.

¹⁴:¹¹ καὶ ἠνέχθη ἡ κεφαλὴ αὐτοῦ ἐπὶ πίνακι καὶ ἐδόθη τῷ κορασίῳ, καὶ ἤνεγκεν τῇ μητρὶ αὐτῆς.

¹⁴:¹ At that time, Herod the tetrarch heard of the fame of Jesus. [n. 1216]

¹⁴:² And he said to his servants: this is John the Baptist; he is risen from the dead, and therefore mighty works are performed in him. [n. 1219]

¹⁴:³ For Herod had apprehended John, and bound him, and put him into prison, because of Herodias, his brother's wife. [n. 1221]

¹⁴:⁴ For John said to him: it is not lawful for you to have her. [n. 1223]

¹⁴:⁵ And he wanted to put him to death, but he feared the people: because they esteemed him as a prophet. [n. 1224]

¹⁴:⁶ But on Herod's birthday, the daughter of Herodias danced before them, and pleased Herod. [n. 1225]

¹⁴:⁷ Upon which, he promised with an oath to give her whatever she would ask of him. [n. 1227]

¹⁴:⁸ But she, being instructed before by her mother, said: give me here, in a dish, the head of John the Baptist. [n. 1228]

¹⁴:⁹ And the king was struck sad, but because of his oath, and because of those who sat with him at table, he commanded it to be given. [n. 1229]

¹⁴:¹⁰ And he sent, and beheaded John in the prison. [n. 1231]

¹⁴:¹¹ And his head was brought in a dish, and it was given to the girl, and she brought it to her mother. [n. 1233]

14:12 Et accedentes discipuli eius tulerunt corpus eius, et sepelierunt illud, et venientes nuntiaverunt Iesu. [n. 1234]	14:12 καὶ προσελθόντες οἱ μαθηταὶ αὐτοῦ ἦραν τὸ πτῶμα καὶ ἔθαψαν αὐτὸ[ν] καὶ ἐλθόντες ἀπήγγειλαν τῷ Ἰησοῦ.	14:12 And his disciples came and took the body, and buried it, and came and told Jesus. [n. 1234]
14:13 Quod cum audisset Iesus, secessit inde in navicula in locum desertum seorsum. Et cum audissent turbae, secutae sunt eum pedestres de civitatibus. [n. 1235]	14:13 Ἀκούσας δὲ ὁ Ἰησοῦς ἀνεχώρησεν ἐκεῖθεν ἐν πλοίῳ εἰς ἔρημον τόπον κατ᾽ ἰδίαν· καὶ ἀκούσαντες οἱ ὄχλοι ἠκολούθησαν αὐτῷ πεζῇ ἀπὸ τῶν πόλεων.	14:13 When Jesus had heard, he retired from there by boat, into a desert place which was set apart. And the multitudes, having heard of it, followed him on foot out of the cities. [n. 1235]
14:14 Et exiens vidit turbam multam, et misertus est eis, et curavit languidos eorum. [n. 1238]	14:14 Καὶ ἐξελθὼν εἶδεν πολὺν ὄχλον καὶ ἐσπλαγχνίσθη ἐπ᾽ αὐτοῖς καὶ ἐθεράπευσεν τοὺς ἀρρώστους αὐτῶν.	14:14 And, coming out, he saw a great multitude, and had compassion on them, and healed their sick. [n. 1238]

1215. Supra, ostendit Dominus virtutem evangelicae doctrinae sub quibusdam parabolis, hic ostendit factis; et tria facit.

Primo ostendit ad quos effectus se extendat per similitudinem factorum;

secundo ostendit sufficientiam evangelicae doctrinae;

tertio quomodo in puritate conservanda sit.

Secundum in cap. XV tertium in cap. XVI.

Circa primum

primo ponitur falsa opinio;

secundo occasio;

tertio improbatur opinio.

Secunda ibi *Herodes tenuit Ioannem* etc.; tertia ibi *quod cum audisset Iesus, secessit inde*.

1216. Dicit ergo *in illo tempore audivit Herodes tetrarcha famam eius*. Et non est retorquenda ad illum diem, sed ad tempus in generali; quia Marcus VI, 1 et Lucas c. IV, 16 non eodem ordine narrant, quia istud narrant post missionem discipulorum, ut habetur Marci VI. Unde incertum est qui servent ordinem historiae. Tamen quod dicitur *in illo tempore*, dicitur, ut denotetur negligentia Herodis, quia post miracula tunc primo audivit famam de Iesu: haec enim desidia solet esse in divitibus, quod non curant de parvis rebus. I Tim. ult., 17: *divitibus huius saeculi praecipe non sublime sapere, neque sperare in incerto divitiarum* et cetera.

1217. *Audivit Herodes tetrarcha*, ad differentiam Herodis regis, sub quo natus est Christus, ut habetur supra cap. II. Unde, illo defuncto, reversus est Christus de Aegypto. Iste Herodes fuit filius eius, et fuit tetrarcha. Pater eius constitutus est rex a Romanis, et habuit sex filios, quorum duos interfecit in vita sua, alium primogenitum interfecit in morte, cum iam faceret se proferri in regem, patre adhuc vivente. Ipso mortuo, Archelaus accepit sibi regnum, et sequens malitiam paternam, non potuit tolerari a Iudaeis. Tunc accesserunt ad Romanos,

1215. Above, the Lord showed the power of the evangelical teaching under certain parables; here he shows it by deeds. And he does three things:

first, he shows to what effects it extends itself, through the likeness of deeds;

second, he shows the sufficiency of the evangelical teaching;

third, how it should be preserved in purity.

The second is in chapter fifteen; the third, in chapter sixteen.

Concerning the first,

first, a false opinion is set down;

second, the occasion;

third, the opinion is disproven.

The second is at *for Herod had apprehended John*; the third, at *when Jesus had heard, he retired from there*.

1216. It says then, *at that time, Herod the tetrarch heard the fame of Jesus*. And it should not be referred to that very day, but to that general time, because Mark and Luke do not tell it in the same order, since these both tell it after the sending out of the disciples (Mark 6:14; Luke 9:7). Hence it is uncertain who preserves the order of history. Nonetheless, it says, *at that time*, to point out Herod's negligence, because it was after the miracles that he first heard the fame of Jesus; for this laziness is common among the rich, that they have no care of little things. *Charge the rich of this world not to be highminded, nor to trust in the uncertainty of riches* (1 Tim 6:17).

1217. *Herod the tetrarch*, to distinguish him from Herod the king, under whom Christ was born, as is said above (Matt 2). Hence, when that man died, Christ returned from Egypt. This Herod was his son, and was a tetrarch. His father was made a king by the Romans, and had six sons, two of whom he killed during his life; another, the firstborn, he killed at his own death, since he would have made himself be exalted to the kingship while his father was still living. With this one dead, Archelaus took the kingship for himself, and following his father's malice, he could not be

et divisum est regnum in quatuor partes: duae partes traditae sunt Archelao, alia Herodi, et alia pars Philippo. Unde iste erat tetrarcha et princeps super quartam partem regni.

1218. *Audivit famam Iesu.* Ex hoc reprehensibilis erat, quod tanto tempore iam vixerat, et miracula fecerat, et tamen tunc primo audivit; unde impletur illud Iob XXVIII, v. 22: *perditio et mors dixerunt: auribus nostris audivimus famam eius.*

1219. *Et ait pueris suis: hic est Ioannes Baptista* et cetera. Aliqui dixerunt quod ipse tenuit dogma de transfusione animarum: Plato enim et Pythagoras posuerunt, quod anima exiens ab uno corpore subintrat aliud corpus. Hanc opinionem Herodes tenens, ut dicunt, credebat quod anima Ioannis transisset in animam Christi. Sed hoc non potest esse, quia parum ante interfecerat eum; Iesus autem erat triginta annorum; unde hoc non credidit. Item iam miracula fecerat ante decollationem, et ante incarcerationem, ut habetur Io. III. Herodes tamen laudandus est, quia resurrectionem credidit, de qua Iob XIV, v. 14: *putasne homo mortuus rursum vivat?* Item aliam bonam conditionem habuit, quod credidit quod fiat resurrectio in meliori statu; ideo credidit quod tunc operaretur miracula, quae ante resurrectionem non fecerat; ideo dicit *et ideo virtutes operantur in eo*, quia ad altiorem statum advenit; unde resurgent homines in meliori statu. Unde Apostolus I Cor. XV, 43: *seminatur in infirmitate, resurget in virtute.*

1220. Sed hic est quaestio, quia dicit Lucas, quod audivit et dubitavit; unde dixit, *Ioannem ego decollavi*; hic autem dicit sine dubitatione, dum dicit, *hic est Ioannes*.

Solvit Augustinus, quod non a se, sed audivit ab aliis. Unde cum primo audivit, dubitavit, sed crescente fama consensit. Unde Lucas primum recitavit, sed secundum Matthaeus. Vel aliter potest dici quod etiam Matthaeus dubitationem Herodis tangit, ita quod legatur interrogative *hic est Ioannes?*

1221. *Herodes enim tenuit Ioannem.* Haec facta sunt ante; unde non sequitur ordinem, sed ex incidenti determinat de morte Ioannis.

Sed est quaestio, quare Evangelistae ex incidenti determinant de Ioanne, et hoc quaerit Chrysostomus. Solvit autem, quia principaliter facta Christi intenderunt, alia vero solum secundum quod referebantur ad Christum.

Ideo hic ex consequenti determinat mortem Ioannis. Et

primo determinat incarcerationem;

1218. *Herod the tetrarch heard the fame of Jesus.* And for this he was worthy of blame, because Jesus had lived such a long time, and had done miracles, and yet now he first heard; hence Job is fulfilled, *destruction and death have said: with our ears we have heard the fame of it* (Job 28:22).

1219. *And he said to his servants: this is John the Baptist.* Some have said that this man held the doctrine of the transfusion of souls, for Plato and Pythagoras claimed that the soul, leaving one body, entered into another body. Herod, holding this opinion, as they say, believed that John's soul had passed over into Christ's soul. But this cannot be, because he had killed him only a little before, while Jesus was thirty years old; hence he did not believe this. Likewise, he had already worked miracles before the beheading and before the imprisonment (John 3). Yet Herod should be praised, because he believed in the resurrection, about which Job says, *will man that is dead, do you think, live again?* (Job 14:14). Likewise, he had another good condition, namely that he believed that there would be a resurrection to a better state; for this reason, he believed that miracles were worked then which John had not done before his resurrection; so he says, *and therefore mighty works are performed in him* because he has come to a higher state. Hence men will rise in a better state. Hence the Apostle: *it is sown in dishonour, it will rise in glory* (1 Cor 15:43).

1220. But there is a question here, because Luke says that he heard and doubted (Luke 9:7); hence he says, *John I have beheaded; but who is this of whom I hear such things?* (Luke 9:9). But here he speaks without doubt when he says, *this is John*.

Augustine solves it, saying that he did not know of Christ on his own, but heard from others. Hence when he first heard, he doubted; but as Christ's fame grew, he agreed. Hence Luke recounts the first, but Matthew the second. Or in another way, it can be said that Matthew also touches upon Herod's doubt, so that it would be read interrogatively: *is this John?*

1221. *For Herod had apprehended John.* These things were done before; hence the order is not followed, but from the incident of Herod's hearing about Christ he describes John's death.

But there is a question as to why the Evangelists tell about John from an incident. Chrysostom asks this, and solves it, saying that the Evangelists aimed primarily at the deeds of Christ, and at others only according as they were referred to Christ.

So consequently he describes John's death here. And

first, he describes the imprisonment;

second, the death, at *but on Herod's birthday*.

Concerning the first, he does three things:

first, he sets out the imprisonment;

second, the cause;

third, the beheading.

1222. ***For Herod had apprehended John, and bound him, and put him into prison***. He touches upon the order, since first he arrested him, bound him, and imprisoned him; moreover, so it happened with Christ.

1223. He touches upon the cause when he says, ***because of Herodias, his brother's wife***. Herod and Philip were brothers. Philip had the daughter of Areta, the king of the Arabs. He had enmity with this king of the Arabs, and with his brother Herod also, so that the king of the Arabs, in hatred of Philip, took his daughter and granted her to Herod.

About this John, you should understand that he was a man of great virtue; hence it is said of him, *and he will go before him in the spirit and power of Elijah* (Luke 1:17). Likewise, you should notice that he is also called a martyr, because he died for the defense of the faith; for he died for the truth, and Christ is Truth.

For he was saying to Herod, ***it is not lawful for you to have her***. One should know that Antipater, the father of Herod the king, was a foreigner, but a proselyte; hence his children were Jews. But it had been commanded in the law that, while the brother was living, another may not have his brother's wife. For this reason John, as one jealous for the law, was saying, ***it is not lawful for you to have her***.

1224. ***And he wanted to put him to death, but he feared the people***. Sometimes it happens that when someone does not want to avoid a sin, he falls into a greater sin. *Cursing, and lying, and killing, and theft, and adultery have overflowed, and blood has touched blood* (Hos 4:2). Hence when he did not want to avoid adultery, he fell into murder. And when he wanted to murder him, ***he feared the people***. The agitation of the people is greatly to be feared; *of three things my heart has been afraid . . . the accusation of a city, and the gathering together of the people, and a false calumny* (Sir 26:5–7). Likewise, the fear of the Lord takes away an evil desire; but the fear of man does not, although it makes one put it off. So since he could not do it, due to fear of the people, he put it off.

1225. ***But on Herod's birthday***. Here he does three things concerning the killing, since he could not do it due to fear of the people:

first, the things that came before are set down;

second, the killing;

third, what followed.

Concerning the first, three things which came before are set down: the dance; the promise; the request.

1226. He says then, ***but on Herod's birthday***. It was the custom among the ancients that they would celebrate their birthdays, contrary to, *a good name is better than precious*

dies nativitatis. Non legitur quod aliqui celebraverint diem natalis nisi iste, et Pharao rex Aegypti.

Unde ***die natalis filia Herodiadis***, sic vocabatur, ***saltavit in medio***, idest in triclinio, et in hoc culpabilis redditur, quia in lascivia oblitus est aulam regiam, in qua non debebant haec fieri, et placuit Herodi, contra illud Eccli. IX, 4: *cum saltatrice non sis assiduus*.

1227. Et sequitur ***unde cum iuramento pollicitus*** et cetera. Ecce incauta promissio, et temerarium iuramentum. Eccli. XXIII, 9: *iurationi non assuescat os tuum, multi enim casus in illa*.

1228. ***Et praemonita a matre sua, da mihi,*** inquit, ***hic in disco caput Ioannis Baptistae***. Hic ponitur petitio mulieris. Mulieres aliquando sunt piae, et mobilem affectum habent; unde quando sunt piae, maxime sunt piae, sed quando sunt crudeles, maxime sunt crudeles; Eccli. XXV, 22: *non est caput nequius super caput colubri; non est ira super iram mulieris*. Et ibidem dicitur: *brevis omnis malitia super malitiam mulieris*. Vix enim cogitaret homo quae cogitat perversa mulier. Mater ergo petit ut saturaret iram suam. Item timebat ne aliquando Herodes propter verba Ioannis converteretur, et dimitteret eam.

1229. *Et contristatus est rex propter iusiurandum*. Hic determinatur quomodo occiditur. Chrysostomus: *hic datur exemplum quod honestas etiam ab impiis honoratur, ut habetur Sap. V, 1*.

Hieronymus dicit, quod modo est contristatus, qui ante voluit interficere, sed timuit populum. Quare ergo dicit quod est contristatus? Solvit. Consuetudo est hominum ut recitent quod videtur hominibus: sicut dicebant Christum filium Ioseph, quia ita putabant, ut habetur Lc. III. Unde dicit ***contristatus***, quia ita videbatur hominibus.

1230. Sequitur executio. Et primo ponitur praeceptum; secundo executio.

Propter iusiurandum, et propter simul discumbentes. In hoc stultus fuit, quia de re inhonesta non est timendum iuramentum, quia eo quod iuro, sum periurus; Ier. IV, 2: *iurabitis in iudicio*, scilicet cum discretione, *in iustitia et veritate*. Item si iurasset, quod in semet faceret, intelligi debebat 'in honestis.' Unde quod in se facere non debuit, alii nec praecipere debuit; Zac. VIII, 17: *iuramentum mendax ne diligatis*. ***Et propter simul discumbentes***, ut omnes faceret homicidii participes, omnes enim rogabant pro puella. ***Iussit dari***.

1231. ***Misitque et decollavit Ioannem***. Hic ponitur executio. Hic adimpletur quod dixerat: *illum oportet*

ointments: *and the day of death than the day of one's birth* (Eccl 7:2). It is not written that anyone celebrated a birthday except this man and Pharaoh the king of Egypt.

Hence, ***but on Herod's birthday, the daughter of Herodias***, for so she was called, ***danced before them***, i.e., in the dining room, and in this she is rendered culpable, because in wantonness she forgot the royal hall, in which these things should not take place, and pleased Herod, contrary to Sirach, *do not use much the company of her who is a dancer* (Sir 9:4).

1227. And there follows, ***upon which, he promised with an oath***. Behold, an incautious promise, and a reckless oath. *Do not let your mouth be accustomed to swearing: for in it there are many falls* (Sir 23:9).

1228. ***But she, being instructed before by her mother, said: give me here, in a dish, the head of John the Baptist***. Here the woman's request is set down. Women are sometimes pious, and they have easily moved affections; hence when they are pious, they are the most pious of all, but when they are cruel, they are the most cruel of all. *There is no head worse than the head of a serpent: and there is no anger above the anger of a woman* (Sir 25:22–23). And it says in the same place, *all malice is short to the malice of a woman* (Sir 25:26). For a man would scarcely think of what a corrupted woman thinks. So the mother asked to satisfy her own anger. Likewise, she feared, lest sometime Herod should be converted by John's words, and send her away.

1229. ***And the king was struck sad, but because of his oath***. Here is described how he is killed. Chrysostom: *here an example is given that honesty is honored even by the impious, as is said in Wisdom* (Wis 5:1).

Jerome notes that he is saddened now, who before wished to kill him, but feared the people. So why does it say that he was saddened? He solves it. It is customary for men to recount what appears true to men; just as they said that Christ was the son of Joseph, because so they thought (Luke 3). Hence he says he was ***struck sad***, because so it seemed to men.

1230. There follows the execution. And first, the command is set out; second, the execution.

Because of his oath, and because of those who sat with him at table. In this he was foolish, because one should not fear an oath in a dishonest matter, because by the fact that I swear, I am false; *and you will swear*, namely with discretion, *in truth, and in judgment* (Jer 4:2). Likewise, if he had sworn that he would do something himself, he should have been understood to mean 'among honorable things.' Hence what he should not do himself, neither should he have commanded others to do; *do not love a false oath* (Zech 8:17). ***And because of those who sat with him at table***, that he might make them all partakers of murder, for they all were asking on the girl's behalf. ***He commanded it to be given***.

1231. ***And he sent, and beheaded John***. Here the execution is set down. Here is fulfilled what he had said, *he must*

crescere, me autem minorari, quia Christus in cruce extensus, iste decollatus. Item decollatio Ioannis signum fuit, quod auctoritate legis debebant amittere Christum et legem.

1232. Consequenter ponuntur subsequentia decollationis. Et primo ponitur redditio promissi; secundo sepultura.

1233. Dicit ergo *et allatum est caput eius in disco*. Et in hoc reprehensibilis fuit Herodes, quia crudelitatem exercuit inter voluptates: unde dicitur quod quidam balivus amabat quamdam meretriculam, et cum esset in gremio, dixit illa quod numquam vidit hominem interfici. Et cum esset in prandio, fecit adduci quemdam morte dignum, et fecit coram illa decollari: quod sciverunt Romani, et exul factus est a Roma. Sic iste etiam missus fuit in exilium.

1234. *Et accedentes discipuli eius tulerunt corpus eius, et sepelierunt illud*. Hic agitur de sepultura Ioannis, et computatur inter opera misericordiae; et tamen videtur quod misericordia ad mortuum non pertineat, quia si ad eum pertineat, videtur quod non sit verum quod dicit Dominus: *nolite timere eos qui occidunt corpus*.

Quare ergo computatur inter opera misericordiae? Dicendum, quod etsi non serviatur ei secundum effectum, quem modo habet, servitur tamen ei secundum affectum, quem modo habet cum mortuo.

Unde *tulerunt corpus eius, et sepelierunt*; dicitur quod apud Sebastem, cum sit ibi prope. Post videns Iulianus apostata multos venientes ad eius reliquias, fecit eum comburi, excepto capite.

Et venientes nuntiaverunt Iesu. Unde discipuli Ioannis, qui primo calumniabantur Iesum, Ioanne mortuo, redierunt ad Iesum, et fuerunt ei familiares: sic aliqui in tempore tribulationis convertuntur ad Christum; Osee VI, 1: *in tribulatione sua mane consurgent ad me*.

1235. *Et cum audisset Iesus secessit in navicula in locum desertum seorsum*. Supra posita est opinio Herodis de Christo, et occasione huius introducta est narratio de Ioanne; nunc autem ostenditur opinio Herodis esse falsa. Duo dixerat: quia Christus erat Ioannes quem occiderat, item quod resurgens virtutes operabatur.

Dicit ergo *quod cum audisset Iesus, secessit inde in navicula* et cetera.

1236. Quare secessit? Assignat quatuor rationes Hieronymus. Prima, ut parceret inimicis suis, ne ex homicidio in homicidium ruerent; Osee IV, 2: *sanguis sanguinem tetigit*. Item, ut passionem differret; unde ipse dicit Io. VII, 6: *tempus meum nondum advenit*. Item, ut nobis exemplum daret ne nos ingeramus passionibus: non enim est virtus se passionibus ingerere, sed praesumptio.

increase, but I must decrease (John 3:30), because Christ was stretched out on the cross, this man beheaded. Likewise, John's beheading was a sign that by the authority of the law they should lose both Christ and the law.

1232. Next, those things which followed the beheading are set down. And first, the fulfillment of the promise; second, the burial.

1233. It says then, *and his head was brought in a dish*. And in this, Herod was reprehensible, because he practiced cruelty among pleasures. Hence it is said that a certain chief magistrate loved a certain harlot, and when she was in his lap she said that she had never seen a man be killed. And since he was at lunch, he had a certain man worthy of death led out, and had him beheaded in front of her. The Romans came to know of it, and he was exiled from Rome. So also this man was sent into exile.

1234. *And his disciples came and took the body, and buried it*. Here it treats of John's burial. This is reckoned among the works of mercy; yet it seems that mercy does not pertain to a dead man, because if it pertained to him, it seems that what the Lord said would not be true, *and do not fear those who kill the body* (Matt 10:28).

Why then is it reckoned among the works of mercy? One should say that even if it is no use to him according to an effect which he has now, nevertheless it is a service to him according to affection, which he now has with the dead.

Hence they *took the body, and buried it*; it is said that they buried it in Sebaste, since he was near there. Afterward, when Julian the apostate saw many people coming to his relics, he had him burned, except for the head.

And came and told Jesus. Hence John's disciples, who at first were slandering Jesus, returned to Jesus when John was dead, and were intimate with him. In this way, some are converted to Christ in times of affliction; *in their affliction they will rise early to me* (Hos 6:1).

1235. *When Jesus had heard, he retired from there by boat, into a desert place which was set apart*. Above, Herod's opinion about Christ was set down, and with this as the occasion, the story about John was introduced. But now Herod's opinion about John is shown to be false. He had said two things: that Christ was John whom he killed, and that he worked miracles after rising from the dead.

Therefore it says, *when Jesus had heard, he retired from there by boat*.

1236. Why did he withdraw? Jerome gives four reasons. First, to spare his enemies, lest they rush on from murder into murder; *blood has touched blood* (Hos 4:2). Similarly, to delay the passion; hence he himself says, *my time is not yet come* (John 7:6). Likewise, to give us an example, lest we throw ourselves into sufferings: for it is no virtue to throw oneself into sufferings, but presumption. Hence above,

Unde supra X, 33: *si persecuti fuerint vos in una civitate, fugite in aliam*. Item, ut ostenderet quanta devotione audiebant turbae verbum Dei, quia etiam in periculo sequebantur eum; Deut. XIII, 3: *tentat vos Dominus Deus vester, ut palam sciat utrum diligatis eum*.

1237. Item notandum, quod quatuor ponit quae turbam debeant retrahere a sequela Christi. Primum est, quod secessit **in navicula**, item quod **in locum desertum**, item quod non erant ibi aliqua nemora, quia erat desertum, item non iuxta viam, ad quam homines libenter se divertunt; sed iste secessit **seorsum**. Hoc autem fecit ut magis devotio turbae sit approbanda. Item Chrysostomus dicit quod secessit ut hominem approbaret; ideo noluit secedere nisi nuntiata morte Ioannis.

1238. Sequitur *et cum audissent turbae* et cetera. Hic agitur de mirabilibus. Et primo tangitur devotio turbarum; secundo tanguntur mirabilia.

Dicit ergo *et cum audissent turbae, secutae sunt eum pedestres de civitatibus*; ubi tangitur devotio turbarum et pauperum hominum, qui devotionis causa Dominum sequuntur. Osee VI, 1: *in tribulatione sua mane consurgent ad me*.

Et exiens vidit turbam multam et cetera. Hic tangit mirabilia quae operatus est Dominus exiens de deserto: et recte, quia dum in caelis erat, non quaerebant eum turbae; Io. c. XVI, 28: *exivi a Patre, et veni in mundum*. *Vidit turbam*. Unde excitatur ad misericordiam; unde sequitur *et misertus est eis*; unde statim fecit eis misericordiam: Ps. LXXXV, 15: *miserator et misericors Dominus, patiens, et multae misericordiae, et verax*.

Sequitur effectus huius misericordiae *et curavit languidos eorum*, scilicet gratis, et non rogatus. Ps. CVI, 20: *misit verbum suum, et sanavit eos*.

and when they persecute you in this city, flee into another (Matt 10:23). Similarly, to show with how great a devotion the crowds heard the word of God, because even in danger they followed him; *the Lord your God tries you, that it may appear whether you love him* (Deut 13:3).

1237. Likewise, one should notice that he sets down four things which should hold the crowd back from following Christ. The first is that he withdrew **in a boat**; also that it was **in a desert place**; and that there were no forests there, since it was a desert; likewise, it was not some place close to the road, to which men gladly turn themselves, but rather he withdrew **apart**. And he did this so that the crowd's devotion might be the more commended. Similarly, Chrysostom says that he withdrew that he might commend a man; so he did not want to withdraw except when John's death was reported.

1238. There follows **and the multitudes, having heard of it**. Here it treats of miracles. And first, the devotion of the crowds is touched upon; second, the miracles are touched upon.

It says then, **and the multitudes, having heard of it, followed him on foot out of the cities**; here the devotion of the crowds is touched upon, and of poor men, who follow the Lord out of devotion. *In their affliction they will rise early to me* (Hos 6:1).

And, coming out, he saw a great multitude. Here it touches upon the miracles which the Lord worked when he came out from the desert: and rightly, because when he was in heaven, the crowds did not seek him; *I came forth from the Father, and have come into the world* (John 16:28). **He saw a great multitude**. Hence he is roused to mercy; hence there follows, **and had compassion on them**. Hence at once he works mercy for them; *and you, O Lord, are a God of compassion, and merciful, patient, and of much mercy, and true* (Ps 85:15).

There follows the effect of this mercy: **and healed their sick**, that is, freely and unasked. *He sent his word, and healed them* (Ps 106:20).

Lecture 2

14:15 Vespere autem facto accesserunt ad eum discipuli eius dicentes: desertus est locus et hora iam praeteriit; dimitte turbas ut euntes in castella emant sibi escas. [n. 1240]

14:16 Iesus autem dixit eis: non habent necesse ire, date illis vos manducare. [n. 1241]

14:17 Responderunt ei: non habemus hic nisi quinque panes et duos pisces. [n. 1243]

14:18 Qui ait eis: afferte mihi illos huc. [n. 1244]

14:19 Et cum iussisset turbam discumbere super foenum, acceptis quinque panibus et duobus piscibus, aspiciens in caelum, benedixit et fregit et dedit discipulis panes, discipuli autem turbis; [n. 1246]

14:20 et manducaverunt omnes, et saturati sunt, et tulerunt reliquias duodecim cophinos fragmentorum plenos. [n. 1250]

14:21 Manducantium autem fuit numerus quinque millia virorum, exceptis mulieribus et parvulis. [n. 1252]

14:22 Et statim compulit discipulos ascendere in naviculam, et praecedere eum trans fretum, donec dimitteret turbas. [n. 1253]

14:23 Et dimissa turba, ascendit in montem solus orare. Vespere autem facto solus erat ibi. [n. 1256]

14:24 Navicula autem in medio mari iactabatur fluctibus, erat enim contrarius ventus. [n. 1260]

14:25 Quarta autem vigilia noctis venit ad eos ambulans supra mare. [n. 1262]

14:15 Ὀψίας δὲ γενομένης προσῆλθον αὐτῷ οἱ μαθηταὶ λέγοντες· ἔρημός ἐστιν ὁ τόπος καὶ ἡ ὥρα ἤδη παρῆλθεν· ἀπόλυσον τοὺς ὄχλους, ἵνα ἀπελθόντες εἰς τὰς κώμας ἀγοράσωσιν ἑαυτοῖς βρώματα.

14:16 ὁ δὲ [Ἰησοῦς] εἶπεν αὐτοῖς· οὐ χρείαν ἔχουσιν ἀπελθεῖν, δότε αὐτοῖς ὑμεῖς φαγεῖν.

14:17 οἱ δὲ λέγουσιν αὐτῷ· οὐκ ἔχομεν ὧδε εἰ μὴ πέντε ἄρτους καὶ δύο ἰχθύας.

14:18 ὁ δὲ εἶπεν· φέρετέ μοι ὧδε αὐτούς.

14:19 καὶ κελεύσας τοὺς ὄχλους ἀνακλιθῆναι ἐπὶ τοῦ χόρτου, λαβὼν τοὺς πέντε ἄρτους καὶ τοὺς δύο ἰχθύας, ἀναβλέψας εἰς τὸν οὐρανὸν εὐλόγησεν καὶ κλάσας ἔδωκεν τοῖς μαθηταῖς τοὺς ἄρτους, οἱ δὲ μαθηταὶ τοῖς ὄχλοις.

14:20 καὶ ἔφαγον πάντες καὶ ἐχορτάσθησαν, καὶ ἦραν τὸ περισσεῦον τῶν κλασμάτων δώδεκα κοφίνους πλήρεις.

14:21 οἱ δὲ ἐσθίοντες ἦσαν ἄνδρες ὡσεὶ πεντακισχίλιοι χωρὶς γυναικῶν καὶ παιδίων.

14:22 Καὶ εὐθέως ἠνάγκασεν τοὺς μαθητὰς ἐμβῆναι εἰς τὸ πλοῖον καὶ προάγειν αὐτὸν εἰς τὸ πέραν, ἕως οὗ ἀπολύσῃ τοὺς ὄχλους.

14:23 καὶ ἀπολύσας τοὺς ὄχλους ἀνέβη εἰς τὸ ὄρος κατ' ἰδίαν προσεύξασθαι. ὀψίας δὲ γενομένης μόνος ἦν ἐκεῖ.

14:24 τὸ δὲ πλοῖον ἤδη σταδίους πολλοὺς ἀπὸ τῆς γῆς ἀπεῖχεν βασανιζόμενον ὑπὸ τῶν κυμάτων, ἦν γὰρ ἐναντίος ὁ ἄνεμος.

14:25 τετάρτῃ δὲ φυλακῇ τῆς νυκτὸς ἦλθεν πρὸς αὐτοὺς περιπατῶν ἐπὶ τὴν θάλασσαν.

14:15 And when it was evening, his disciples came to him, saying: this is a desert place, and the hour is now past; send away the multitudes, so that, going into the towns, they may buy themselves food. [n. 1240]

14:16 But Jesus said to them: they have no need to go; you give them something to eat. [n. 1241]

14:17 They answered him: we have nothing here except five loaves and two fish. [n. 1243]

14:18 He said to them: bring them here to me. [n. 1244]

14:19 And when he had commanded the multitudes to sit down on the grass, he took the five loaves and the two fish, and looking up to heaven, he blessed, and broke, and gave the loaves to his disciples, and the disciples gave them to the multitudes. [n. 1246]

14:20 And they all ate and were filled. And they took up what remained, which was twelve full baskets of fragments. [n. 1250]

14:21 And the number of those who ate was five thousand men, besides women and children. [n. 1252]

14:22 And at once, Jesus obliged his disciples to go up into the boat and go before him over the water, until he dismissed the people. [n. 1253]

14:23 And having dismissed the multitude, he went up into a mountain to pray alone. And when it was evening, he was there alone. [n. 1256]

14:24 But the boat, out on the sea, was tossed by the waves, because the wind was contrary. [n. 1260]

14:25 In the fourth watch of the night he came to them, walking on the sea. [n. 1262]

14:26 Et videntes eum supra mare ambulantem, turbati sunt, dicentes, quia phantasma est. Et prae timore clamaverunt. [n. 1267]

14:27 Statimque Iesus locutus est eis dicens: habete fiduciam, ego sum, nolite timere. [n. 1268]

14:28 Respondens autem Petrus dixit: Domine, si tu es, iube me ad te venire super aquas. [n. 1270]

14:29 At ipse ait: veni. Et descendens Petrus de navicula ambulabat super aquam, ut veniret ad Iesum. [n. 1271]

14:30 Videns vero ventum validum timuit. Et cum coepisset mergi, clamavit dicens: Domine, salvum me fac. [n. 1272]

14:31 Et continuo Iesus extendens manum apprehendit eum, et ait illi: modicae fidei, quare dubitasti? [n. 1275]

14:32 Et cum ascendisset in naviculam, cessavit ventus. [n. 1276]

14:33 Qui autem in navicula erant, venerunt, et adoraverunt eum dicentes: vere Filius Dei es. [n. 1277]

14:34 Et cum transfretassent, venerunt in terram Genesareth. [n. 1278]

14:35 Et cum cognovissent eum viri loci illius, miserunt in universam regionem illam, et obtulerunt ei omnes male habentes, [n. 1280]

14:36 et rogabant eum ut vel fimbriam vestimenti eius tangerent. Et quicumque tetigerunt, salvi facti sunt. [n. 1281]

14:26 οἱ δὲ μαθηταὶ ἰδόντες αὐτὸν ἐπὶ τῆς θαλάσσης περιπατοῦντα ἐταράχθησαν λέγοντες ὅτι φάντασμά ἐστιν, καὶ ἀπὸ τοῦ φόβου ἔκραξαν.

14:27 εὐθὺς δὲ ἐλάλησεν [ὁ Ἰησοῦς] αὐτοῖς λέγων· θαρσεῖτε, ἐγώ εἰμι· μὴ φοβεῖσθε.

14:28 ἀποκριθεὶς δὲ αὐτῷ ὁ Πέτρος εἶπεν· κύριε, εἰ σὺ εἶ, κέλευσόν με ἐλθεῖν πρός σε ἐπὶ τὰ ὕδατα.

14:29 ὁ δὲ εἶπεν· ἐλθέ. καὶ καταβὰς ἀπὸ τοῦ πλοίου [ὁ] Πέτρος περιεπάτησεν ἐπὶ τὰ ὕδατα καὶ ἦλθεν πρὸς τὸν Ἰησοῦν.

14:30 βλέπων δὲ τὸν ἄνεμον [ἰσχυρὸν] ἐφοβήθη, καὶ ἀρξάμενος καταποντίζεσθαι ἔκραξεν λέγων· κύριε, σῶσόν με.

14:31 εὐθέως δὲ ὁ Ἰησοῦς ἐκτείνας τὴν χεῖρα ἐπελάβετο αὐτοῦ καὶ λέγει αὐτῷ· ὀλιγόπιστε, εἰς τί ἐδίστασας;

14:32 καὶ ἀναβάντων αὐτῶν εἰς τὸ πλοῖον ἐκόπασεν ὁ ἄνεμος.

14:33 οἱ δὲ ἐν τῷ πλοίῳ προσεκύνησαν αὐτῷ λέγοντες· ἀληθῶς θεοῦ υἱὸς εἶ.

14:34 Καὶ διαπεράσαντες ἦλθον ἐπὶ τὴν γῆν εἰς Γεννησαρέτ.

14:35 καὶ ἐπιγνόντες αὐτὸν οἱ ἄνδρες τοῦ τόπου ἐκείνου ἀπέστειλαν εἰς ὅλην τὴν περίχωρον ἐκείνην καὶ προσήνεγκαν αὐτῷ πάντας τοὺς κακῶς ἔχοντας

14:36 καὶ παρεκάλουν αὐτὸν ἵνα μόνον ἅψωνται τοῦ κρασπέδου τοῦ ἱματίου αὐτοῦ· καὶ ὅσοι ἥψαντο διεσώθησαν.

14:26 And seeing him walking on the sea, they were troubled, saying: it is an apparition. And they cried out for fear. [n. 1267]

14:27 And immediately Jesus spoke to them, saying: be of good heart, it is I, fear not. [n. 1268]

14:28 And Peter answering, said: Lord, if it is you, bid me come to you upon the waters. [n. 1270]

14:29 And he said: come. And Peter descended from the boat and walked upon the water to come to Jesus. [n. 1271]

14:30 But seeing the strong wind, he was afraid, and when he began to sink, he cried out, saying: Lord, save me. [n. 1272]

14:31 And immediately Jesus, stretching out his hand, took hold of him, and said to him: O you of little faith, why did you doubt? [n. 1275]

14:32 And when they had come up into the boat, the wind ceased. [n. 1276]

14:33 And those who were in the boat came and adored him, saying: indeed, you are the Son of God. [n. 1277]

14:34 And having passed over the water, they came into the country of Gennesaret. [n. 1278]

14:35 And when the men of that place knew about him, they sent into all of that country, and brought to him all who were diseased. [n. 1280]

14:36 And they asked him that they might touch but the hem of his garment. And as many as touched it were made well. [n. 1281]

1239. Postquam exclusit Herodis opinionem, hic tangit doctrinae Christi virtutem. Triplex enim est virtus eius: reficit, liberat et infirmos sanat.

Prima igitur virtus ostenditur, quia pascit turbas;

secunda, quia discipulos a periculis maris liberat;

tertia, quia multos sanat.

1239. After excluding Herod's opinion, here he touches upon Christ's power. For his power is threefold: he refreshes, sets free, and heals the sick.

First, therefore, his power is shown, by his feeding the crowds;

second, by his freeing the disciples from the dangers of the sea;

third, by his healing many people.

Secunda ibi *et statim impulit discipulos ascendere in naviculam*; tertia ibi *et cum transfretassent* et cetera.

Circa primum tria. Quia
primo ponitur voluntas reficiendi;
secundo distributio cibi;
tertio plenitudo refectionis.

Secunda ibi *Iesus autem dixit eis* etc., tertia ibi *et manducaverunt omnes* et cetera.

1240. Dicit ergo *vespere autem facto*, scilicet solis occubitu, per quod significatur mors Christi, quia tunc tradidit corpus suum in cibum; unde I Cor. XI, 24: *hoc facite in meam commemorationem*. Et: *mortem Domini annuntiabitis donec veniat*.

Deinde inducit necessitatem ex loco: *desertus est locus*. Hic videtur illa eadem fieri quaestio quae habetur in Ps. LXXVII, 19. Nam quomodo poterat Dominus mensam parare in deserto? Item si iuxta villam esset locus, potuisset credi quod inde habuisset cibos, sed locus erat desertus.

Item ponitur necessitas ex hora, quia dicit *et hora iam praeteriit*, qua possint sibi acquirere cibos. *Dimitte turbas*. Ex hoc videtur, quod discipuli ita fuerunt intenti suavitati sermonis Christi, quod magis delectabantur in audiendo Christum, quam in procurando sibi victum: unde parum curabant de corporis refectione. Habetur enim Lc. XXI, v. 37: *erat autem diebus docens in templo, noctibus autem morabatur in monte*.

Item alia occasio, quia iam vespere erat. De ista fame habetur Amos VIII, 11: *mittam famem in terra, non famem panis, neque sitis, sed audiendi verbum Domini*. Et in hoc significatur devotio turbarum, item dilectio et reverentia ad Christum, quia non recesserunt ab eo, quamvis vespere esset.

Sed hic est quaestio litteralis, quia in Ioanne habetur, quod Iesus interrogavit Philippum; hic autem habetur, quod discipuli interrogaverunt Christum.

Solvit Augustinus. Non est hoc inconveniens, quod id quod unus dimisit, alter dicat. Unde primo dixerunt illi Christo; secundo elevans oculos Iesus interrogavit discipulos.

1241. *Iesus autem dixit eis*. Hic ponit distributionem cibi: et
circa hoc tria facit.
Primo ponitur imperium Christi;
secundo quantitas ciborum;
tertio modus et ordo distribuendi.

The second is at *and at once Jesus obliged his disciples to go up into the boat*; the third, at *and having passed over the water*.

Concerning the first, three things:
first, the will to refresh is set down;
second, the distribution of food;
third, the fullness of the refreshing.

The second is at *but Jesus said to them*; the third at *and they all ate*.

1240. It says then, *and when it was evening*, namely when the sun had set, which signifies the death of Christ, because that was when he gave over his own body for food; hence *this do for the commemoration of me* (1 Cor 11:24). And: *you will show the death of the Lord, until he come*, (1 Cor 11:26).

Then he introduces the crowd's need, based on the place: *this is a desert place*. Here that same question seems to come up which is written in the Psalm: *and they spoke ill of God: they said: can God furnish a table in the wilderness?* (Ps 77:19). For how could the Lord prepare a table in the desert? Similarly, if the place were next to a village, one could have thought he would get food from there, but it was a desert place.

Likewise, their need is set out based on the time, since it says, *and the hour is now past*, in which they could acquire food for themselves. *Send away the multitudes*. From this it appears that the disciples were so eager for the sweetness of Christ's words that they were more delighted with hearing Christ than with obtaining food for themselves; hence they cared little for the refreshment of the body. For this is written: *and in the daytime, he was teaching in the temple; but at night, going out, he abode in the mount* (Luke 21:37).

Likewise another occasion for the miracle, for it was already evening. Concerning this hunger it says, *I will send forth a famine into the land: not a famine of bread, nor a thirst of water, but of hearing the word of the Lord* (Amos 8:11). And this indicates the devotion of the crowds, and their love and reverence for Christ, because they did not leave him, even though it was evening.

But there is a literal question here, because in John it says that Jesus questioned Philip (John 6:5); but here it says that the disciples questioned Christ.

Augustine solves it. It is not unfitting that what one leaves out, the other says. Hence first they spoke to Christ; second, lifting up his eyes, Jesus questioned the disciples.

1241. *But Jesus said to them*. Here the distribution of food is set down. And
concerning this he does three things:
first, Christ's command is set down;
second, the quantity of the food;
third, the manner and order of distribution.

Secunda ibi *responderunt ei* etc.; tertia ibi *afferte mihi illos* et cetera.

1242. Duo dixerant. Primo ut dimitteret turbas; item quod quaererent escas sibi: et ad haec duo respondet Christus. Vos dicitis: **dimitte turbas**, sed **non habent necesse ire**, quia hic est *qui dat escam omni carni*, Ps. CXXXV, 25. Item vos dicitis quod quaerant escas, sed non est necesse, quia vos potestis dare escas caelestes; unde dicit **date illis vos manducare**. Unde datur exemplum quod spirituales escae praeponendae sunt carnalibus.

1243. Sequitur quantitas ciborum **responderunt ei: non habemus nisi quinque panes et duos pisces**. Ex hoc possumus notare, quod apostoli ita erant dediti sermoni Dei, quod non curabant etiam de cibis quaerendis. Ad Rom. XIII, 14: *et carnis curam ne feceritis*.

Mystice per quinque panes doctrina legis; Eccli. XV, 3: *pavit eos pane vitae et intellectus*. Per duos pisces doctrina Psalmorum et prophetarum importatur; vel secundum Hilarium, per duos pisces doctrina prophetarum et Ioannis Baptistae, ut duae personae excellentes in lege, scilicet regalis et sacerdotalis.

1244. Qui ait: afferte mihi illos. Hic ponitur modus distributionis; et

primo ponitur praesentatio;

secundo dispositio turbarum;

tertio oratio;

quarto distributio.

1245. Unde dicit **qui ait**. Ipse, qui omnipotens erat, creare poterat panes novos; sed voluit ex factis panibus reficere.

Sed quae est causa? Ratio litteralis secundum Chrysostomum est, ut confutaret haeresim Manichaeorum, qui has creaturas a diabolo dixerunt factas, contra illud quod scribitur I ad Tim. IV, 4: *omnis creatura Dei bona est*. Unde si a diabolo essent, in eis tanta miracula non fecisset. Item, ut ostenderet se Dominum in terra et in mari. Ille qui in Gen. I, 11 dixit, *germinet terra herbam virentem*, et qui dixit: *producant aquae reptile animae viventis* etc., ille idem panes multiplicat. Item ad designandum quod legem veterem non reprobavit, sed in novam convertit: ideo dicit **afferte mihi**, quia quae in veteri lege scripta sunt, ad novam debent referri. Unde ipse dixit, Io. V, v. 46: *si crederetis Moysi, crederetis forsitan et mihi*.

1246. Et cum iussisset turbam discumbere super foenum et cetera. Hic ponitur dispositio hominum, quia fecit sedere super foenum; Is. XL, 6: *omnis caro foenum*. Sedere ergo super foenum non est nisi carnem mortificare.

The second is at **they answered him**; the third, at **bring them here to me**.

1242. They had said two things: first, that he should send away the crowds; likewise, that they should seek food for themselves; and Christ responds to these two things. You say, **send away the multitudes**, but **they have no need to go**, because here is the one *who gives food to all flesh* (Ps 135:25). Likewise, you say that they should seek food, but that is not necessary, because you can give them heavenly food; hence he says, **you give them something to eat**. Hence an example is given that spiritual food should be preferred to bodily food.

1243. There follows the quantity of the food. **They answered him: we have nothing here, except five loaves and two fish**. From this we can note that the apostles were so devoted to God's word that they did not take care even to seek out food. *And do not make provision for the flesh* (Rom 13:14).

Mystically, the five loaves signify the teachings of the law; *with the bread of life and understanding, she will feed him* (Sir 15:3). The two fishes bring in the teaching of the Psalms and the prophets; or according to Hilary, the fishes signify the teachings of the prophets and of John the Baptist, as two persons excelling in the law, namely the royal and the priestly.

1244. He said to them: bring them here to me. Here the manner of distribution is set down; and

first, the presentation is set down;

second, the arrangement of the crowd;

third, the speech;

fourth, the distribution.

1245. Hence it says, **he said**. He who was omnipotent was able to create new loaves; but he willed to refresh the crowds out of bread already made.

But why? The literal reason, according to Chrysostom, is to refute the heresy of the Manichees, who said that these creatures were made by the devil, contrary to what is written, *for every creature of God is good* (1 Tim 4:4). Hence if they were from the devil, he would not have worked such a great miracle in them. Likewise, to show that he is Lord on land and sea. He who said, *let the earth bring forth the green herb* (Gen 1:11), and who said, *let the waters bring forth the creeping creature* (Gen 1:20), this same one multiplies the loaves. Likewise, to indicate that he did not reject the old law, but transformed it into the new; for this reason he says, **bring them here to me**, because those things which are written in the old law should be referred to the new. Hence he himself said, *for if you did believe Moses, you would perhaps believe me also* (John 5:46).

1246. And when he had commanded the multitudes to sit down on the grass. Here the arrangement of the men is set down, because he made them sit on the grass; *all flesh is grass* (Isa 40:6). So to sit down on the grass is nothing other

Ad Col. III, 5: *mortificate membra vestra quae sunt super terram*. Item per foenum significatur lex. Quia isti erant Iudaei, sublevabantur per legem; ideo noluit eos sedere in terra.

1247. *Acceptis quinque panibus et duobus piscibus* et cetera. Notandum quod Dominus faciens miracula aliquando orat, aliquando non orat. Aliquando orat, ut hic, ut verum hominem se ostendat: aliquando etiam maiora facit, et non orat, ut Deum se ostendat. ***Aspiciens in caelum benedixit***.

In caelum, scilicet ad Patrem. Ps. CXX, 1: *levavi oculos meos in montes, unde veniet auxilium mihi*. ***Benedixit***, quia per sermonem Dei omnia benedicuntur.

Nota quod nostrum benedicere non est factivum, sed significativum; Dei autem benedicere est factivum; unde benedictio ad multiplicationem pertinet, unde Gen. I, 22: *benedixit, et dixit: crescite, et multiplicamini, et replete terram*.

1248. Consequenter agitur de distributione ***fregit et dedit discipulis suis***; in quo significatur quod prima distributio facta est discipulis a capite Christo; I ad Cor. XI, 3: *omnis viri caput Christus est*. Sed ***fregit***, ut notaret suam distributionem. Is. LVIII, 7: *frange esurienti panem tuum*. ***Et dedit discipulis***, quasi mediatoribus. Infra XXVI, 26: *accipite et comedite*; I ad Cor. XI, 28: *et sic probet se homo, ut de pane illo edat, et de calice bibat* et cetera. ***Discipuli autem dederunt turbis***, ut distributores.

1249. Sed quomodo multiplicati sunt? Dicendum, quod fragmenta multiplicata sunt.

Et dicunt quidam hoc posse fieri naturaliter: sicut enim materia se habet ad quamlibet formam, ita se habet ad quamlibet quantitatem. Sed hoc est stultum, quod materia se habeat ad quamlibet quantitatem materialem: hoc enim non potest fieri nisi per rarefactionem; haec autem rarefactio determinata est in naturalibus.

Quidam dicunt quod multiplicat, sicut ex paucis granis multa grana; sed ibi per naturam, hic per operationem Christi. Unde manus Christi fuerunt quasi terra, fragmenta quasi semina: unde sicut semina multiplicantur, sic fragmenta. Sed non solum ista, sed per conversionem alterius materiae in ipsam, hoc miraculum factum est.

1250. Sequitur de plenitudine refectionis, et hoc quantum ad duo: quantum ad saturitatem, et quantum ad residuum. Unde dicitur ***manducaverunt omnes, et saturati sunt***, secundum illud Ps. XXI, 27: *edent pauperes, et saturabuntur* et cetera. ***Et tulerunt reliquias duodecim cophinos fragmentorum plenos***. Hic tangitur plenitudo refectionis sub multitudine reliquiarum.

than to mortify the flesh. *Mortify therefore your members which are upon the earth* (Col 3:5). Likewise, grass signifies the law. Since these men were Jews, they were supported by the law; so he did not want them to sit on the ground.

1247. ***He took the five loaves and the two fish***. One should note that the Lord sometimes prays when he works a miracle, and sometimes he does not pray. Sometimes he prays, as here, to show that he is a true man; and sometimes he works greater things and does not pray, to show that he is God. ***And looking up to heaven, he blessed***.

Up to heaven, namely to the Father. *I have lifted up my eyes to the mountains, from where help will come to me* (Ps 120:1). He ***blessed***, because all things are blessed by God's word.

Notice that our blessing is not operative, but significative; but God's blessing is operative, hence the blessing pertains to the multiplication. Hence *and he blessed them, saying: increase and multiply* (Gen 1:22).

1248. Next, it treats of the distribution: ***and broke, and gave the loaves to his disciples***, which signifies that the first distribution was made to the disciples by Christ the head; *the head of every man is Christ* (1 Cor 11:3). But he ***broke*** to mark his own distribution. *Deal your bread to the hungry* (Isa 58:7). ***And gave the loaves to his disciples***, as to mediators. Below, *take, and eat* (Matt 26:26); *but let a man prove himself: and so let him eat of that bread, and drink of the chalice* (1 Cor 11:28). ***And the disciples gave them to the multitudes*** as distributors.

1249. But how were they multiplied? One should say that the fragments were multiplied.

And some men say that this can happen naturally: for just as matter can take on any form, so it can take on any quantity. But this is foolish, that matter can take on any material quantity: for this can only happen through rarefaction, and this rarefaction is limited in natural things.

Some say that he multiplies just as many grains are produced from a few grains; only there it happens through nature, here through Christ's operation. Hence Christ's hand was like the earth, the fragments like the seeds; hence just as seeds are multiplied, so were the fragments. But not only that, but this miracle was worked by the conversion of another matter into it.

1250. This next part deals with the fullness of the refreshing, and this in two respects: as regards satisfaction, and as regards what was left over. Hence it says, ***and they all ate, and were filled***, in accord with *the poor will eat and will be filled* (Ps 21:27). ***And they took up what remained, which was twelve full baskets of fragments***. Here the fullness of the refreshing is touched upon as regards the multitude of remains.

1251. Sed quare voluit dominus colligi reliquias? Litteralis causa est quam ponit Chrysostomus. Voluit primo quod colligerent discipuli, ne videretur phantasma, item ne ab eis daretur oblivioni. Et quod tulerunt duodecim cophinos, hoc fuit secundum numerum duodecim apostolorum, ut quilibet tolleret suum, ita quod essent in memoria omnium.

Mystice per fragmenta intelligitur sensus spiritualis, qui a turbis non capitur, sed in cophinis, idest in sapientibus; I ad Cor. I, 26: *videte vocationem vestram, fratres, quia non multi sapientes secundum carnem, non multi potentes, non multi nobiles; sed quae stulta sunt mundi elegit Deus, ut confundat sapientes* et cetera.

1252. Deinde ponitur numerus manducantium *fuit autem numerus manducantium quinque millia virorum*: ut de uno pane mille secundum Hilarium. Hoc etiam post ascensionem factum est, quando ad vocem apostolorum uno die quinque millia conversi sunt. *Exceptis mulieribus et parvulis*, qui sunt ignorantes, et computari non sunt digni. Simile habetur in Lib. Machabaeorum quod parvuli et mulieres non computantur ad bellum.

Item notate, quod istud miraculum statim factum est post occisionem Ioannis, et erat prope Pascha, et Christus iam praedicaverat per annum, et revoluto anno passus est Christus.

1253. *Et statim impulit Iesus discipulos*. Hic figuratur virtus doctrinae Christi, quia liberativa est a periculis, quia discipulos a periculis liberavit.

Unde tria facit.
Primo ponitur occasio subeundi periculum;
secundo periculum;
tertio liberatio.

Secunda ibi *et dimissa turba, ascendit in montem* etc.; tertia ibi *quarta autem vigilia noctis venit ad eos, ambulans supra mare*.

1254. Occasio periculi fuit praeceptum Christi: frequenter enim volentes obtemperare voluntati Dei, periculis exponuntur, ut ait Apostolus, II ad Cor. XI, 26: *periculis fluminum, periculis latronum, periculis ex genere, periculis ex gentibus, periculis in civitatibus, periculis in solitudine, periculis in mari, periculis in falsis fratribus.* Unde *statim impulit eos intrare naviculam*. Unde statim facto miraculo voluit separari a turbis.

1255. Et hoc fecit triplici ratione. Primo ut ostenderet miraculi veritatem, ne propter eius praesentiam illud accidisse dicerent: ipse enim Veritas est, ut habetur Io. XIV, 6. Secundo, ut doceret nos inanem gloriam vitare; ideo post facta miracula recedit; Io. c. VIII, 50: *ego gloriam meam non quaero* et cetera. Item ut discretionis virtutem ostenderet: discretionis est separare se, et

1251. But why did the Lord will that the remains be gathered? The literal cause is what Chrysostom sets down. First, he willed that the disciples should gather the bread lest it seem to be a phantasm; similarly, lest they forget it. And that they took up twelve baskets was according to the number of the twelve apostles, as each one took up his own basket, such that it would be in each one's memory.

Mystically, the fragments indicate the spiritual sense, which is not grasped by the crowds, but in baskets, i.e., in wisdom; *for see your vocation, brethren, that there are not many wise according to the flesh, not many mighty, not many noble: but the foolish things of the world has God chosen, that he may confound the wise* (1 Cor 1:26–27).

1252. Then the number of those who ate is set down: *and the number of those who ate, was five thousand men*, so that from one loaf a thousand ate, according to Hilary. This was also done after the ascension, when at the apostles' call five thousand were converted in one day. *Besides women and children*, who are ignorant, and unworthy to be counted. A similar thing is written in the Book of Machabees, that the children and women are not counted for war.

Notice also that this miracle was worked immediately after the killing of John, and was near the time of the Passover, and Christ had already preached for a year; and one year later Christ suffered.

1253. *And at once Jesus obliged his disciples*. Here the power of Christ's teaching is represented, for he freed the disciples from danger.

Hence he does three things:
first, the occasion for going into danger is set down;
second, the danger;
third, the liberation.

The second is at *and having dismissed the multitude, he went up into a mountain to pray alone*; the third, at *and in the fourth watch of the night, he came to them, walking on the sea*.

1254. The occasion of the danger was Christ's command: for often those who wish to obey God's will are exposed to dangers, as the Apostle says, *in journeying often, in perils of waters, in perils of robbers, in perils from my own nation, in perils from the gentiles, in perils in the city, in perils in the wilderness, in perils in the sea, in perils from false brethren* (2 Cor 11:26). Hence, *at once, Jesus obliged his disciples to go up into the boat*. Hence at once, when the miracle was done, he wished to be separated from the crowds.

1255. And he did this for three reasons. First, to show the truth of the miracle, lest they should say that it happened because of his presence; for he himself is Truth (John 14:6). Second, to teach us to avoid vainglory; so he withdraws after working a miracle; *I do not seek my own glory* (John 8:50). Likewise, to show the virtue of discretion: for it pertains to discretion to separate oneself and to

quiescere; Sap. VIII, 16: *intrans in domum meam conquiescam cum illa.*

Sed notandum quod utitur impulsione, quia durum erat eis separari a Christo, ut dicit Petrus, Io. VI, 69: *Domine, ad quem ibimus? Verba vitae aeternae habes.* Item ostendit affectum turbarum, scilicet cum quo ardore sequebantur eum; Cant. I, 2: *oleum effusum nomen tuum, ideo adolescentulae dilexerunt te.*

1256. ***Et dimissa turba, ascendit in montem solus orare***. Sequitur de periculo, et ostenditur periculum ex tempore; ex loco; ex vento.

1257. Et primo ponitur absentia Christi, quia cum esset cum discipulis **ascendit in montem solus orare**. Ipse venerat plantare fidem nostram, ideo operabatur aliquando humanum, aliquando divinum; quod enim panes multiplicavit hoc Dei fuit; quod oravit, humanum fuit, non quod indigeret, sed ut exemplum daret: omnis enim Christi actio nostra est instructio. Io. XIII, 15: *exemplum dedi vobis, ut sicut facio, ita et vos faciatis.*

1258. Et dat nobis exemplum quomodo ad orandum: et ad orationem requiritur quies mentis, elevatio, solitudo.

Quies ostenditur, quia **dimissa turba**, quae designat cogitationes perturbantes cum quibus non potest homo orare, ideo ostium cordis claudere docet; supra VI, 6: **cum autem oraveris, intra cubiculum** et cetera. Item elevatio; Thren. III, 28: *sedebit solitarius et levabit se supra se.* Item solitudo. Osee II, 14: *ducam eam in solitudinem, et loquar ad cor eius.* Per montem intelligitur caelum: caelo enim nihil excelsius. **Et dimissis turbis**, idest dimissis mortalibus ivit in caelum, et ipse solus ascendit, et propria virtute. Michaeae II, v. 13: *ascendit ante eos pandens iter.* Item ascendit orare; ad Hebraeos VII, 25: *per semetipsum accedens.*

1259. Sed hic videtur esse quaestio, quia Ioannes videtur dicere quod pavit turbas in monte, ut habetur Io. VI, 3, hic autem dicitur quod post refectionem turbarum ascendit in montem.

Sed respondetur, quod in monte pavit, sed post in altiorem locum montis ascendit.

Item est alia quaestio, quia habetur Io. VI, v. 15 quod ipse fugit, quia voluerunt eum facere regem; hic autem dicitur quod ascendit orare.

Augustinus dicit, quod eadem potest esse causa et fugiendi, et orandi.

rest; *when I go into my house, I will repose myself with her* (Wis 8:16).

But one should notice that he compels the disciples to go, because it was hard for them to be separated from Christ, as Peter says, *Lord, to whom will we go? You have the words of eternal life* (John 6:69). Similarly, it shows the crowds' affection, that is, with what ardor they followed him; *your name is as oil poured out: therefore young maidens have loved you* (Song 1:2).

1256. And having dismissed the multitude, he went up into a mountain to pray alone. What follows concerns the danger, and the danger is made plain from the time, the place, and the wind.

1257. And first, Christ's absence is set down, because while he was with the disciples, **he went up into a mountain to pray alone**. He had come to plant our faith, so sometimes he worked a human thing, sometimes a divine thing: for instance, that he multiplied the loaves was divine; that he prayed was human. It was not that he needed it, but that he might give an example: for Christ's every action is our instruction. *For I have given you an example, that as I have done to you, so you do also* (John 13:15).

1258. And he gives us an example of how to pray; and for prayer is required quiet of mind, elevation, and solitude.

The quiet is shown because he **dismissed the people**, which designates disturbing thoughts, with which a man cannot pray. So he teaches us to close the door of the heart; above, **but when you will pray, enter into your chamber, and having shut the door** (Matt 6:6). Also, elevation; *he will sit solitary and will lift up above himself* (Lam 3:28). Likewise, solitude: *therefore, behold I will allure her, and will lead her into the wilderness: and I will speak to her heart* (Hos 2:14). By the mountain is understood heaven, for nothing is higher than heaven. **And having dismissed the multitude**, i.e., having sent away mortal things, he went into heaven, and he alone ascended, and by his own power. *He will go up who will open the way before them* (Mic 2:13). Likewise, he ascended to pray; *whereby he is able also to save forever those who come to God by him; always living to make intercession for us* (Heb 7:25).

1259. But there seems to be a question here, because John seems to say that he fed the crowds on the mountain (John 6:3–5), but here it says that after refreshing the crowds, he went up onto the mountain.

But it is responded that he fed them on the mountain, and afterward went up onto a higher place on the mountain.

There is also another question, because it says in John that he fled, because they wanted to make him king (John 6:15); here, however, it says that he went up to pray.

Augustine says that the same thing can be the cause both of the fleeing and of the praying.

1260. Post describitur periculum ex tempore, quia nox erat, et in nocte maius est periculum maris; ideo dicit: **vespere autem facto**. Et significatur eius passio, quia in passione solus ascendit; Act. I, 9: *videntibus illis elevatus est, et nubes suscepit eum ab oculis eorum*.

Navicula autem in medio maris iactabatur fluctibus. Per naviculam significatur Ecclesia, per mare mundus: Ps. CIII, 25: *hoc mare magnum et spatiosum manibus*. Et haec Ecclesia, Christo ascendente, remansit in mari, et in periculis maris mundi. Quando enim aliquis magnus impugnat Ecclesiam, tunc agitatur fluctibus. Ps. LXXXVII, 8: *et omnes fluctus tuos induxisti super me*. Sed quia Christus orat, non potest submergi, quamvis fluctuet et elevetur. Gen. VII, 17: *et elevaverunt arcam in sublime a terra*.

1261. Item agitatur a vento: iste ventus est impetus diabolicae incitationis. Iob I, v. 19: *quia venit ventus a regione deserti et concussit quatuor angulos domus*; Is. XXV, v. 4: *spiritus robustorum quasi turbo impellens parietem*.

1262. Quarta autem vigilia noctis venit ad eos, ambulans supra mare. Posito periculo, ponitur liberatio a periculo:

et circa hoc duo facit.

Primo ponitur auxilium;

secundo effectus. Secunda ibi **qui autem in navicula erant, venerunt et adoraverunt eum**.

Tria pericula posuerat: primo obscuritatem noctis, periculum maris, periculum venti. Et

contra primum ponit visitationem suam;

contra secundum certitudinem sui, ibi **statimque Iesus locutus** etc.;

contra tertium porrigit manum **et continuo Iesus extendens manum, apprehendit eum**.

Item tranquillitatem maris **et cum ascendisset in naviculam, cessavit ventus**.

Circa primum ponitur sua visitatio;

secundo effectus suae visitationis, ibi **videntes autem eum supra mare ambulantem, turbati sunt**.

1263. Dicit ergo **quarta vigilia noctis venit ad eos**. Hic tangitur et adventus eius, et tempus, quia **quarta vigilia**. Hieronymus dicit, quod antiqui dividebant noctem in quatuor partes. In prima quidam vigilabant, in secunda alii, in tertia alii, et in quarta alii; et illi qui vigilaverant quiescebant. Unde dicit quod **in quarta vigilia** etc., quia tota nocte fuerant in mari.

1264. Venit ad eos ambulans supra mare. Et quare? Assignat Chrysostomus rationem litteralem, dicens quod tantum tardavit ut magis desideraretur.

1260. Afterward, the danger is described from the time, because it was night, and the danger of the sea is greater at night. For this reason it says, **and when it was evening**. And his passion is signified, because in the passion he alone ascended; *while they looked on, he was raised up: and a cloud received him out of their sight* (Acts 1:9).

But the boat, out on the sea, was tossed by the waves. The boat signifies the Church, and the sea signifies the world; *so is this great sea, which stretches wide its arms* (Ps 103:25). And this Church, when Christ ascended, remained in the sea, and in the dangers of the sea of the world. For when someone great fights against the Church, then it is shaken about by the waves. *All your waves you have brought in upon me* (Ps 87:8). But because Christ prays, it cannot be submerged, however much it is tossed on the waves and lifted up. *And the waters increased, and lifted up the ark on high from the earth* (Gen 7:17).

1261. It is also driven about by the wind: this wind is the assault of diabolical instigation. *A violent wind came on a sudden from the side of the desert, and shook the four corners of the house* (Job 1:19); *for the blast of the mighty is like a whirlwind beating against a wall* (Isa 25:4).

1262. In the fourth watch of the night, he came to them, walking on the sea. With the danger set down, here the liberation from danger is set down.

And concerning this, he does two things:

first, the help is set down;

second, the effect. The second is at **and those who were in the boat came and adored him**.

Three dangers had been set down: first, the obscurity of night time; second, the danger of the sea; third, the danger of the wind. And

against the first, he sets his visitation;

against the second, the certitude of himself, at **and immediately Jesus spoke to them**;

against the third, he stretches out a hand: **and immediately Jesus, stretching out his hand, took hold of him**.

Also, the tranquillity of the sea: **and when they had come up into the boat, the wind ceased**.

Concerning the first, his visitation is set down;

second, the effect of his visitation, at **and seeing him walking on the sea, they were troubled**.

1263. It says then, **in the fourth watch of the night, he came to them**. Here it touches upon his coming, and upon the time, that it was **in the fourth watch**. Jerome says that the ancients divided the night into four parts. In the first, certain men watched, others in the second, others in the third, and others in the fourth; and those who had watched rested. Hence it says that it was **in the fourth watch**, because they had been on the sea the whole night.

1264. He came to them, walking on the sea. And why? Chrysostom gives a literal reason, saying that he delayed so long so that he would be the more desired. *My soul has*

Is. XXVI, 9: *anima mea desideravit te in nocte*. Item, ut discerent quod si statim non haberent auxilium, quod non desisterent, quoniam oportet semper orare.

Mystice per quatuor horas significantur quatuor status. Primo status legis: secundo status prophetarum; tertio tempus gratiae; quarto ascensus in caelum, in quo statu cessavit tempestas. Unde in quarta vigilia venit sicut in fine noctis; unde Iac. ult., 8: *patientes estote et vos, et confirmate corda vestra, quoniam adventus Domini appropinquabit*.

1265. Sed qualiter venit? **Ambulans supra mare**. Et quare sic voluit venire? Ut se ostenderet Dominum maris; Ps. LXXXVIII, 10: *tu dominaris potestati maris, motum autem fluctuum eius tu mitigas*. Item, ut ostenderet illusores potestatis huius saeculi: diabolus enim semper illudit potestati huius saeculi; Ps. CIII, 26: *draco iste quem formasti ad illudendum ei*. Sed istam potestatem Dominus fregit; Ps. LXXIII, 14: *tu confregisti capita draconis*; et significat quod Ecclesia non potest tribulationes sustinere, nisi secundum quod voluit ipse.

1266. Opinio fuit hic, quod in hac vita Dominus accepit quatuor dotes, subtilitatis in nativitate, impassibilitatis quando ieiunavit quadraginta diebus, vel transubstantiando sacramentum Eucharistiae, agilitatis hic, claritatis in transfiguratione. Sed hoc non credo: credo enim quod miraculose fecit.

1267. *Et videntes eum*. Hic ponitur effectus praesentiae Christi, scilicet turbatio discipulorum; unde ponitur turbatio, ponitur causa, ponitur signum.

Et dicit *et videntes eum turbati sunt* et cetera. Debetis scire, quod quando auxilium divinum est magis propinquum, permittit Dominus magis affligi, ut tunc magis cum devotione et gratiarum actione recipiatur auxilium eius. Item magis timor crevit, quia frequenter ex timore homines convertuntur.

Et quare? Quia crediderunt phantasma esse; unde *dicentes, quia phantasma est*, non credentes esse verum corpus de Virgine. Mystice enim significatur quod antequam Christus veniat, multi multa phantastica dicent, ut habetur infra XXIV, 23 s.

Et prae timore clamaverunt: clamor enim est signum timoris, sicut etiam in omni tribulatione ad Dominum debemus clamare; Ps. CXIX, 1: *ad Dominum cum tribularer clamavi, et exaudivit me*.

1268. *Statimque locutus est eis* et cetera. Hic ponitur auxilium. Quia in obscuritate erant, ideo certitudinem dat:

et tria facit.
Primo certificat verbis;
secundo petit signum Petrus factis;
tertio conceditur ei.

desired you in the night (Isa 26:9). Also, so that they would learn that if they do not have help right away, they should not give up, because one must always pray.

Mystically, the four hours signify four states. First, the state of the law; second, the state of the prophets; third, the time of grace; fourth, the ascent into heaven, in which state time ceases. Hence in the fourth watch he came as at the end of the night; hence *be therefore also patient, and strengthen your hearts: for the coming of the Lord is at hand* (Jas 5:8).

1265. But how did he come? **Walking on the sea**. And why did he will to come this way? To show that he is the Lord of the sea; *you rule the power of the sea: and appease the motion of the waves thereof* (Ps 88:10). Also, to point to those who mock the power of this age, for the devil always mocks the power of this age; *this sea dragon which you have formed to play in it* (Ps 103:26). But the Lord breaks this power; *you have broken the heads of the dragon* (Ps 73:14); and it signifies that the Church cannot withstand afflictions, except according as he himself wills it.

1266. There was an opinion here that the Lord received the four endowments in this life: subtility in birth, the inability to suffer when he fasted forty days or when transubstantiating the sacrament of the Eucharist, agility here, and brilliance in the transfiguration. But I do not believe this: I believe that he did it miraculously.

1267. *And seeing him walking on the sea*. Here the effect of Christ's presence is set down, namely the troubling of the disciples; hence the troubling is set down, the cause is set down, and a sign is set down.

And it says, *and seeing him walking on the sea, they were troubled*. You should know that when divine aid is nearer, the Lord permits one to be afflicted all the more, so that then he may receive his help with more devotion and thanksgiving. Similarly, fear increases more, because often men are converted out of fear.

And why were they troubled? Because they thought he was a ghost; hence, *saying: it is an apparition*, not believing it to be a true body from the Virgin. For mystically, it is signified that before Christ comes, many men will say many fantastical things, as is said below (Matt 24:23).

And they cried out for fear, for a cry is a sign of fear, as also in every affliction we should cry out to the Lord; *in my trouble I cried to the Lord: and he heard me* (Ps 119:1).

1268. *And immediately Jesus spoke to them*. Here the help is set down. For they were in darkness, so he gives certitude.

And he does three things:
first, he confirms by words;
second, Peter asks for a sign in deeds;
third, it is granted to him.

1269. Tria posuerat: turbationem timoris, falsitatem opinionis, item desperationem: et contra ista tria facit, quia *statim locutus est eis*. Unde quando quis clamat ad Dominum, si opus est, statim venit; Is. c. XXX, 19: *ad vocem clamoris tui, statim cum audierit, respondebit tibi*. Item, quia erant desperantes, dicit eis *nolite timere*. Idem habetur Ioannis XVI, 33: *in mundo pressuram habebitis, sed confidite, quia ego vici mundum*: in me autem quietem. Item, quia phantasma credebant, ideo dicit eis *ego sum*. Et quare dicit sic? Quia ex modo loquendi suo poterant certificari; Io. X, 3: *oves meae vocem meam audiunt*. Item ut se verum Deum ostenderet. Simile habetur Ex. III, 13: *qui est, misit me*, dixit Moyses. Item contra hoc quod turbati erant, dixit *nolite timere*. Is. LI, v. 12: *quis es tu ut timeas ab homine mortali, et a filio hominis, qui quasi foenum ita arescit?* Et Prov. XXVIII, 1: *iustus autem quasi leo confidens absque terrore erit*.

1270. *Respondens Petrus dixit: Domine, si tu es, iube me ad te venire super aquas*. Quia auxilium contulerat verbis, ideo Petrus petit signum factis. Petrus autem in persona totius fiducialiter petiit, et dixit *si tu es, iube me ad te venire*. Hic est magna fiducia Petri. Non dixit, *ora pro me*, sed dixit *iube me ad te venire*, quia ipse confessus est *tu es Christus Filius Dei vivi*. Unde ex fide quam iam conceperat, audacter confidit in eius potestate. Esther XIII, 9: *Domine, in potestate tua cuncta sunt posita, et non est qui resistere possit voluntati tuae*. Et hoc dixit ex solo desiderio, non ut tentaret, nec ex infidelitate. I ad Thess. I, 3: *memores fidei vestrae, et operis, et laboris* et cetera.

1271. Deinde ponitur signum; unde dixit *veni*. *Et descendens Petrus de navicula, ambulabat super aquam, ut veniret ad Iesum*. Et hoc contra Manichaeos qui dixerunt, quod Christus non habebat verum corpus: quia si Christus non habebat, quia ambulabat super aquas, sic nec Petrus.

Per hoc quod post quartam vigiliam adhuc imminebat periculum, significatur quod in quarto adventu, quod erit purgandum purgabitur in electis. Ps. XCVI, 3: *ignis ante ipsum praecedet, et inflammabit in circuitu inimicos eius*.

1272. *Videns autem ventum validum* et cetera. Hic ponitur tertium auxilium, quia liberavit Petrum a submersione. Et

primo ponitur causa;
secundo petitio Petri;
tertio auxilium Christi.

1273. *Videns autem ventum validum timuit*. In mari ventus non habet continuum impetum, similiter nec in terra; unde interpellabatur quando Petrus intravit mare;

1269. Matthew had set down three things: the disturbance of fear, the falsity of opinion, and the desperation; and against these he does three things, for *immediately Jesus spoke to them*. Hence when someone cries out to the Lord, if it is beneficial, he comes at once; *at the voice of your cry, as soon as he will hear, he will answer you* (Isa 30:19). Also, since they were despairing, he says to them, *fear not*. The same thing is said in John, *in the world you will have distress: but have confidence, I have overcome the world* (John 16:33), and in me there is rest. Also, since they thought he was a ghost, he says to them, *it is I*. And why does he speak this way? Because they could be certain from his way of speaking; *my sheep hear my voice* (John 10:27). Also, to show that he is the true God. A similar thing is written in Exodus: *HE WHO IS, has sent me to you*, Moses said (Exod 3:14). Likewise, against the fact that they were troubled, he said, *fear not*. *Who are you, that you should be afraid of a mortal man, and of the son of man, who will wither away like grass?* (Isa 51:12). And *the just, bold as a lion, will be without dread* (Prov 28:1).

1270. *And Peter answering, said: Lord, if it is you, bid me come to you upon the waters*. Since he had bestowed help in words, Peter asked for a sign in deeds. Now, Peter asked confidently, in the person of the whole of those present, and said, *if it is you, bid me come to you*. Here is Peter's great faith! He did not say, *pray for me*, but said, *bid me come to you*, because he himself had confessed, *you are the Christ, the Son of the living God* (Matt 16:16). Hence out of the faith which he had already conceived, he confided boldly in his power. *O Lord, Lord, almighty king, for all things are in your power, and there is none who can resist your will* (Esth 13:9). And he said this out of desire alone, not to tempt, nor out of disbelief. *Being mindful of the work of your faith, and labor, and charity* (1 Thess 1:3).

1271. Then the sign is set down; hence he said, *come*. *And Peter descended from the boat and walked upon the water to come to Jesus*. And this is against the Manichees, who said that Christ did not have a true body: for if Christ did not have a true body, since he walked on water, then neither did Peter.

The fact that danger still threatened after the fourth watch signifies that in the fourth coming, whatever should be purged in the elect will be purged. *A fire will go before him, and will burn his enemies round about* (Ps 96:3).

1272. *But seeing the strong wind*. Here the third help is set down, namely that he saved Peter from sinking beneath the water. And

first, the cause is set down;
second, Peter's petition;
third, Christ's help.

1273. *But seeing the strong wind, he was afraid*. The wind does not have a constant force at sea, nor on the land. Hence it had stopped momentarily when Peter entered the

sed cum fuit super mare, flavit fortiter, et tunc timuit. Ex hoc est considerandum quod dicit, quod periculosius erat supra mare quam in navi, ideo Dominus aliquando fortes in periculo maris submergi permittit. Unde Apostolus I ad Cor. X, 12: *qui existimat se stare, videat ne cadat*.

Sed quare permisit in periculo? Primo praecepit ire, ut virtus eius ostendatur, quia uterque ambulabat, et hoc viderunt discipuli. Sed quod permiserit mergi Petrum, hoc fecit, ut experiretur quid posset de se. Unde quod ivit supra mare, hoc fuit virtute Christi; quod autem coepit mergi, hoc fuit infirmitatis Petri, sicut Paulus, II ad Cor. XII, 7: *ne magnitudo revelationum extollat me, datus est mihi stimulus carnis meae, angelus satanae, qui me colaphizet*. Permisit etiam Dominus Petrum mergi, quia futurus erat pastor. Voluit ergo et virtutem ostendere, et infirmitatem. Item hoc fecit ad compescendam aemulationem discipulorum: quia enim viderunt eius periculum, cessavit aemulatio eorum.

1274. ***Et cum coepisset mergi, clamavit: Domine, salvum me fac***. Simile habetur in Ps. LXVIII, 2: *salvum me fac, Domine, quoniam intraverunt aquae usque ad animam meam*.

1275. ***Et continuo Iesus extendens manum apprehendit eum***. Christus duo facit, quia et auxilium impendit, et infidelitatem arguit. Auxilium impendit, quia manum porrigit; Ps. CXLIII, 7: *emitte manum tuam de alto, libera me, et eripe me de aquis multis*. Et Iob XIV, 15: *operi manuum tuarum porriges dexteram*. Deinde de infidelitate eum arguit, et ait illi: ***modicae fidei, quare dubitasti?*** In quo significatur quod si fidem certam habuisset, submergi non potuisset, ideo stabiles esse debemus in fide. Idem habetur supra VIII, 26: ***quid timidi estis, modicae fidei?***

1276. ***Et cum ascendisset in naviculam, cessavit ventus***. Hic ponitur quartum auxilium contra ventum. Ps. CVI, 25: *dixit, et stetit spiritus procellae*. Unde signum est, quod cum Christus est cum suis, nil perversi habent; unde Apoc. VII, 16: *non esurient, neque sitient ultra*.

1277. Sequitur liberationis effectus *qui autem in navicula erant, venerunt, et adoraverunt eum*, scilicet discipuli, vel nautae. Supra VIII, 27: ***qualis est hic, quia venti et mare obediunt ei? Vere Filius Dei es***. Per hoc autem significatur, quod quando Dominus cum fidelibus est, tunc veraciter credunt; I Io. II, 28: *filioli, manete in eo, ut, cum apparuerit, habeamus fiduciam, et non confundamur ab eo in adventu eius*.

1278. ***Et cum transfretassent, venerunt in terram Genesareth***. Hic ponitur virtus Christi. Et

sea; but while he was on the sea, it blew harder, and then he became afraid. From this one should consider what it says, that it was more dangerous on the sea than in the boat; so the Lord sometimes permits the strong to be submerged in the danger of the sea. Hence the Apostle: *wherefore he who thinks himself to stand, let him take heed lest he fall* (1 Cor 10:12).

But why did he let him be in danger? First, he commanded him to walk to show his strength, because both walked, and the disciples saw this. But that he permitted Peter to sink was so he would find out what he could do on his own. Hence that he went over the sea, this was by Christ's power; but that he began to sink, this was from Peter's weakness, as Paul says, *and lest the greatness of the revelations should exalt me, there was given me a sting of my flesh, an angel of satan, to buffet me* (2 Cor 12:7). The Lord also permitted Peter to sink because he was a future shepherd. So he wanted to show both strength and weakness. Likewise, he did this to restrain the disciples' jealousy, for since they saw his danger, their jealousy ceased.

1274. ***And when he began to sink, he cried out, saying: Lord, save me***. A similar thing is said in the Psalms, *save me, O God: for the waters are come in even unto my soul* (Ps 68:2).

1275. ***And immediately Jesus, stretching out his hand, took hold of him***. Christ does two things, for he both extends help and reproaches unbelief. He extends help, because he stretches out his hand; *put forth your hand from on high, take me out, and deliver me from many waters* (Ps 143:7). And, *to the work of your hands you will reach out your right hand* (Job 14:15). Then he reproves him for unbelief, and says to him: ***O you of little faith, why did you doubt?*** Which signifies that if he had had certain faith, he could not have been submerged; therefore, we should be steadfast in faith. The same thing is said above, ***why are you fearful, O you of little faith?*** (Matt 8:26).

1276. ***And when they had come up into the boat, the wind ceased***. Here the fourth help is set down, against the wind. *And he turned the storm into a breeze: and its waves were still* (Ps 106:29). Hence it is a sign that when Christ is with his own, nothing ruinous can happen; hence, *they will no more hunger nor thirst* (Rev 7:16).

1277. There follows the effect of the liberation: *and those who were in the boat came and adored him*, namely the disciples, or the sailors. Above, ***what manner of man is this, for the winds and the sea obey him?*** (Matt 8:27). ***Indeed you are the Son of God***. Now, this signifies that when the Lord is with the faithful, then they truly believe; *and now, little children, abide in him, that when he appears, we may have confidence, and not be confounded by him at his coming* (1 John 2:28).

1278. ***And having passed over the water, they came into the country of Gennesaret***. Here Christ's power is set down. And

primo describitur locus;
deinde devotio hominum;
et post virtus operativa.

1279. Dicit ergo *et cum transfretassent, venerunt in terram Genesareth*, qui locus est ex alia parte maris, et interpretatur 'ortus': unde post periculum venerunt ad refrigerium.

1280. Deinde sequitur devotio turbarum: *et cum cognovissent eum viri loci illius, miserunt in universam regionem illam, et obtulerunt ei omnes male habentes* etc., quia non solum suos infirmos obtulerunt, sed miserunt pro extraneis. Unde cum cognovissent per famam et per doctrinam, miserunt pro infirmis, et obtulerunt ei; unde omnes credebant in eum, tantae erat virtutis sermo eius; et hoc significatur Is. ult., 19: *mittam ex eis, qui salvati fuerint, ad gentem in mare* et cetera.

1281. Item devotio etiam demonstratur, quia non solum petebant, quod imponeret manus, sed eum tantum *rogabant, ut vel fimbriam vestimenti eius tangerent*. Per fimbriam significantur minima praecepta, vel caro Christi, vel sacramentum baptismi. *Et quicumque tetigerunt*, scilicet per fidem, *salvi facti sunt*. Unde Mc. ult., 16: *qui crediderit et baptizatus fuerit salvus erit*.

first, the place is described;
then, men's devotion;
and afterwards, the power at work.

1279. It says then, *and having passed over the water, they came into the country of Gennesaret*, which is a place on the other side of the sea, and is interpreted 'sunrise': hence after the danger, they came to refreshment.

1280. Then there follows the crowd's devotion: *and when the men of that place knew about him, they sent into all that country, and brought to him all who were diseased*, because they not only brought their own sick, but also sent for outsiders. Hence, when they had known him through fame and through teaching, they sent for the sick and brought them to him. Hence they all believed in him, so great was the power of his word; and this is signified in Isaiah, *I will send of those who will be saved, to the gentiles into the sea* (Isa 66:19).

1281. Their devotion is also proven because they did not just ask that he lay hands on them, but *they asked him that they might touch but the hem of his garment*. The hem signifies the least commandments, or Christ's flesh, or the sacrament of baptism. *And as many as touched*, namely through faith, *were made whole*. Hence, *he who believes and is baptized, will be saved* (Mark 16:16).

Chapter 15

Lecture 1

¹⁵:¹ Tunc accesserunt ad eum ab Ierosolymis scribae et Pharisaei, dicentes: [n. 1283]

¹⁵:² quare discipuli tui transgrediuntur traditiones seniorum? Non enim lavant manus suas, cum panem manducant. [n. 1284]

¹⁵:³ Ipse autem respondens ait illis: quare et vos transgredimini mandatum Dei propter traditionem vestram? [n. 1286]

¹⁵:⁴ Nam Deus dixit: *honora patrem et matrem*, et: *qui maledixerit patri vel matri, morte moriatur*. [n. 1288]

¹⁵:⁵ Vos autem dicitis: quicumque dixerit patri vel matri: munus quodcumque est ex me, tibi proderit, [n. 1291]

¹⁵:⁶ et non honorificabit patrem suum, aut matrem suam; et irritum fecistis mandatum Dei propter traditionem vestram. [n. 1293]

¹⁵:⁷ Hypocritae, bene prophetavit de vobis Isaias dicens: [n. 1294]

¹⁵:⁸ *populus hic labiis me honorat, cor autem eorum longe est a me*. [n. 1295]

¹⁵:⁹ *Sine causa autem colunt me docentes doctrinas mandata hominum*. [n. 1296]

¹⁵:¹⁰ Et convocatis ad se turbis, dixit eis: audite et intelligite. [n. 1297]

¹⁵:¹¹ Non quod intrat in os, coinquinat hominem, sed quod procedit ex ore, hoc coinquinat hominem. [n. 1300]

¹⁵:¹² Tunc accedentes discipuli eius dixerunt ei: scis quia Pharisaei audito verbo scandalizati sunt? [n. 1303]

¹⁵:¹ Τότε προσέρχονται τῷ Ἰησοῦ ἀπὸ Ἱεροσολύμων Φαρισαῖοι καὶ γραμματεῖς λέγοντες·

¹⁵:² διὰ τί οἱ μαθηταί σου παραβαίνουσιν τὴν παράδοσιν τῶν πρεσβυτέρων; οὐ γὰρ νίπτονται τὰς χεῖρας [αὐτῶν] ὅταν ἄρτον ἐσθίωσιν.

¹⁵:³ ὁ δὲ ἀποκριθεὶς εἶπεν αὐτοῖς· διὰ τί καὶ ὑμεῖς παραβαίνετε τὴν ἐντολὴν τοῦ θεοῦ διὰ τὴν παράδοσιν ὑμῶν;

¹⁵:⁴ ὁ γὰρ θεὸς εἶπεν· τίμα τὸν πατέρα καὶ τὴν μητέρα, καί· ὁ κακολογῶν πατέρα ἢ μητέρα θανάτῳ τελευτάτω.

¹⁵:⁵ ὑμεῖς δὲ λέγετε· ὃς ἂν εἴπῃ τῷ πατρὶ ἢ τῇ μητρί· δῶρον ὃ ἐὰν ἐξ ἐμοῦ ὠφεληθῇς,

¹⁵:⁶ οὐ μὴ τιμήσει τὸν πατέρα αὐτοῦ· καὶ ἠκυρώσατε τὸν λόγον τοῦ θεοῦ διὰ τὴν παράδοσιν ὑμῶν.

¹⁵:⁷ ὑποκριταί, καλῶς ἐπροφήτευσεν περὶ ὑμῶν Ἡσαΐας λέγων·

¹⁵:⁸ ὁ λαὸς οὗτος τοῖς χείλεσίν με τιμᾷ, ἡ δὲ καρδία αὐτῶν πόρρω ἀπέχει ἀπ' ἐμοῦ·

¹⁵:⁹ μάτην δὲ σέβονταί με διδάσκοντες διδασκαλίας ἐντάλματα ἀνθρώπων.

¹⁵:¹⁰ καὶ προσκαλεσάμενος τὸν ὄχλον εἶπεν αὐτοῖς· ἀκούετε καὶ συνίετε·

¹⁵:¹¹ οὐ τὸ εἰσερχόμενον εἰς τὸ στόμα κοινοῖ τὸν ἄνθρωπον, ἀλλὰ τὸ ἐκπορευόμενον ἐκ τοῦ στόματος τοῦτο κοινοῖ τὸν ἄνθρωπον.

¹⁵:¹² Τότε προσελθόντες οἱ μαθηταὶ λέγουσιν αὐτῷ· οἶδας ὅτι οἱ Φαρισαῖοι ἀκούσαντες τὸν λόγον ἐσκανδαλίσθησαν;

¹⁵:¹ Then scribes and Pharisees came to him from Jerusalem, saying: [n. 1283]

¹⁵:² why do your disciples transgress the tradition of the elders? For they do not wash their hands when they eat bread. [n. 1284]

¹⁵:³ But he answered and said to them: why do you also transgress the commandment of God for the sake of your tradition? [n. 1286]

¹⁵:⁴ For God said: *honor your father and mother*: And: *he who will curse father or mother, let him die the death*. [n. 1288]

¹⁵:⁵ But you say: whoever will say to father or mother: whatever gift proceeds from me, will profit you, [n. 1291]

¹⁵:⁶ and he will not honor his father or his mother, then you have made void the commandment of God for the sake of your tradition. [n. 1293]

¹⁵:⁷ Hypocrites, well has Isaiah prophesied of you, saying: [n. 1294]

¹⁵:⁸ *this people honors me with their lips: but their heart is far from me*. [n. 1295]

¹⁵:⁹ *And in vain do they worship me, teaching doctrines and commandments of men*. [n. 1296]

¹⁵:¹⁰ And having called the multitudes to himself, he said to them: hear and understand. [n. 1297]

¹⁵:¹¹ It is not what goes into the mouth that defiles a man; but what comes out of the mouth, this defiles a man. [n. 1300]

¹⁵:¹² Then his disciples came, and said to him: do you know that the Pharisees, when they heard this saying, were scandalized? [n. 1303]

15:13 At ille respondens ait: omnis plantatio quam non plantavit Pater meus caelestis, eradicabitur. [n. 1306]	**15:13** ὁ δὲ ἀποκριθεὶς εἶπεν· πᾶσα φυτεία ἣν οὐκ ἐφύτευσεν ὁ πατήρ μου ὁ οὐράνιος ἐκριζωθήσεται.	**15:13** But he answered and said: every plant which my heavenly Father has not planted, will be rooted up. [n. 1306]
15:14 Sinite illos, caeci sunt, et duces caecorum. Caecus autem si caeco ducatum praestet, ambo in foveam cadunt. [n. 1308]	**15:14** ἄφετε αὐτούς· τυφλοί εἰσιν ὁδηγοὶ [τυφλῶν]· τυφλὸς δὲ τυφλὸν ἐὰν ὁδηγῇ, ἀμφότεροι εἰς βόθυνον πεσοῦνται.	**15:14** Leave them alone; they are blind and leaders of the blind. And if the blind lead the blind, both will fall into the pit. [n. 1308]
15:15 Respondens autem Petrus, dixit ei: edissere nobis parabolam istam. [n. 1310]	**15:15** Ἀποκριθεὶς δὲ ὁ Πέτρος εἶπεν αὐτῷ· φράσον ἡμῖν τὴν παραβολὴν [ταύτην].	**15:15** And Peter answering, said to him: explain this parable to us. [n. 1310]
15:16 At ille dixit: adhuc et vos sine intellectu estis? [n. 1312]	**15:16** ὁ δὲ εἶπεν· ἀκμὴν καὶ ὑμεῖς ἀσύνετοί ἐστε;	**15:16** But he said: are you also still without understanding? [n. 1312]
15:17 Non intelligitis, quia omne quod in os intrat, in ventrem vadit, et in secessum emittitur? [n. 1314]	**15:17** οὐ νοεῖτε ὅτι πᾶν τὸ εἰσπορευόμενον εἰς τὸ στόμα εἰς τὴν κοιλίαν χωρεῖ καὶ εἰς ἀφεδρῶνα ἐκβάλλεται;	**15:17** Do you not understand, that whatever enters the mouth, goes into the belly, and is cast out in private? [n. 1314]
15:18 Quae autem procedunt de ore, de corde exeunt, et ea coinquinant hominem. [n. 1317]	**15:18** τὰ δὲ ἐκπορευόμενα ἐκ τοῦ στόματος ἐκ τῆς καρδίας ἐξέρχεται, κἀκεῖνα κοινοῖ τὸν ἄνθρωπον.	**15:18** But the things which proceed forth from the mouth, come forth from the heart, and those things defile a man. [n. 1317]
15:19 De corde enim exeunt cogitationes malae, homicidia, adulteria, fornicationes, furta, falsa testimonia, blasphemiae. [n. 1317]	**15:19** ἐκ γὰρ τῆς καρδίας ἐξέρχονται διαλογισμοὶ πονηροί, φόνοι, μοιχεῖαι, πορνεῖαι, κλοπαί, ψευδομαρτυρίαι, βλασφημίαι.	**15:19** For from the heart come forth evil thoughts, murders, adulteries, fornications, thefts, false testimonies, blasphemies. [n. 1317]
15:20 Haec sunt quae coinquinant hominem; non lotis autem manibus manducare, non coinquinat hominem. [n. 1317]	**15:20** ταῦτά ἐστιν τὰ κοινοῦντα τὸν ἄνθρωπον, τὸ δὲ ἀνίπτοις χερσὶν φαγεῖν οὐ κοινοῖ τὸν ἄνθρωπον.	**15:20** These are the things that defile a man. But to eat with unwashed hands does not defile a man. [n. 1317]

1282. Supra Dominus sub figuris virtutem suae doctrinae ostendit, nunc ostendit sufficientiam eius.

Ostenditur autem dupliciter.

Primo, quod non requirit observantias legis;

secundo quod non solum uni genti Iudaeorum data sit, sed et gentilibus, ibi *egressus inde Iesus secessit in partes Tyri et Sidonis*.

Circa primum tria facit.

Primo tanguntur circumstantiae accusationis;

secundo accusatio;

tertio expositio.

Secunda ibi *quare discipuli transgrediuntur traditiones seniorum?* Tertia ibi: *non enim lavant manus suas cum panem manducant*.

1283. Aggravatur autem malitia eorum ex tribus. Primo ex tempore, quia tunc quando haec signa faciebat et miracula, ipsi faciebant signa iniquitatis, unde

1282. Above, the Lord showed the power of his teaching under figures; now he shows its sufficiency.

And he shows it in two ways:

first, because it does not require the observance of the laws;

second, because it is given not only to the one nation of the Jews, but also to the gentiles, at *and Jesus went from there and retired to the coasts of Tyre and Sidon* (Matt 15:21).

Concerning the first, he does three things:

first, the circumstances of the accusation are touched upon;

second, the accusation;

third, the explanation.

The second is at *why do your disciples transgress the tradition of the elders?* The third is at *for they do not wash their hands when they eat bread*.

1283. Now, their malice is made worse by three things. First, by the time, because while he was working signs and miracles, these men were working signs of iniquity; hence

malignabantur. Supra XI, 25: *abscondisti haec a sapientibus et prudentibus* et cetera. Item redditur aggravatio ex loco, quia cum Iudaei essent diffusi per Iudaeam, illi tamen qui erant in Ierusalem, erant sapientes, et tamen erant deteriores. Is. XXVI, 10: *in terra sanctorum iniqua gessit, non videbit gloriam Domini*. Item aggravatur ex conditione personarum, quia de magnis venerunt scribae, qui erant magis litterati, et Pharisaei, qui reputabantur magis sancti. Ier. V, 5: *ibo ad optimates, et loquar eis; ipsi enim cognoverunt viam Domini*.

1284. Deinde ponitur id in quo accusabant eos: *quare discipuli tui transgrediuntur traditiones seniorum?* Praeceptum erat, ut habetur Deut. IV, 2: *non addetis ad verbum, quod vobis loquor, nec auferetis ex eo*. Unde addentes traditiones, contra legem faciebant; non quod non liceret constituere aliquid, sed quod ita praecipiebant observari sicut legem Domini.

1285. *Non enim lavant manus suas* et cetera. Hic exponitur, quae sunt eorum traditiones. Hoc tamen exponitur magis Mc. VII, v. 2: ibi enim dicitur, quod *cum vidissent quosdam de discipulis eius communibus manibus*, idest non lotis, *manducare panes, vituperaverunt*.

Et potest hoc esse ad litteram, quia non lavabant manus. Quare? Quia ita solliciti erant verbo Dei, quod etiam tempus non habebant: unde ex sollicitudine circa spiritualia non se lavabant eo modo sicut Iudaei, sicut habetur Marci VII, 4 quod omnes Iudaei nisi crebro lavent manus, non manducant: ideo discipuli non lavabant secundum ritum eorum. Unde carnaliter intelligebant quod dicitur Is. I, 16: *lavamini, mundi estote*. Unde ipsi ad litteram intelligebant, lavantes quod erat exterius, et non quod interius.

1286. *Ipse autem respondens ait illis*. Dominus duo facit: quia non respondet excusando discipulos, sed ostendit quod ipsi non sunt digni, qui reprehenderent eos. Supra VII, 5: *hypocrita, eiice primum trabem de oculo tuo*. Constat, quod transgredi mandatum Dei est gravius quam traditiones hominum: et ideo qui transgrediebantur mandata Dei, in maioribus delinquebant.

Ideo
primo ostendit eos transgressores legis;
secundo quod mandatum transgrediuntur.

1287. Dicit ergo *quare vos transgredimini mandatum Dei*, et non observatis, *propter traditionem vestram?* Rom. X, 3: *ignorantes Dei iustitiam, et suam quaerentes statuere, iustitiae Dei non sunt subiecti*. Is. III, v. 8: *lingua eorum et adinventiones eorum contra Dominum, ut provocarent oculos maiestatis eius*.

they were slandering him. Above, *you have hidden these things from the wise and prudent* (Matt 11:25). It is also made worse by the place, because while the Jews were scattered throughout Israel, yet those who were in Jerusalem were wise, and yet were worse. *In the land of the saints he has done wicked things, and he shall not see the glory of the Lord* (Isa 26:10). It is also made worse by the condition of the persons, because the scribes, who were more learned, and the Pharisees, who were reputed to be holier, came from among the great. *I will go therefore to the great men, and I will speak to them: for they have known the way of the Lord* (Jer 5:5).

1284. Then the thing about which they were accusing them is set down: *why do your disciples transgress the tradition of the elders?* It had been commanded, *you shall not add to the word that I speak to you, neither shall you take away from it* (Deut 4:2). Hence when they added traditions, they acted against the law; not because it was unlawful to establish something, but because they commanded that it be observed just as the law of the Lord.

1285. *For they do not wash their hands*. Here is explained what their traditions are. Yet this is explained more in Mark, for it says there that *when they had seen certain of his disciples with common hands*, i.e., unwashed, *eating bread, they reproached them* (Mark 7:2).

And this can be literal, that they did not wash their hands. Why? Because they were so anxious for the word of God that they did not even have time to wash their hands. Hence out of concern for spiritual things, they did not wash themselves in the same way as the Jews, as it is written in Mark, that all the Jews would not eat unless they washed their hands frequently (Mark 7:4). So the disciples did not wash according to their ritual. Hence they understood carnally what is said: *wash yourselves, and be clean* (Isa 1:16). Hence they understood it literally, washing what was exterior, and not what was interior.

1286. *But he answered and said to them*. The Lord does two things, for he does not respond by excusing the disciples but by showing that those who would reproach them are unworthy. Above, *you hypocrite, first cast the beam out of your own eye* (Matt 7:5). It is agreed that to transgress God's commandment is more grave than to transgress the traditions of men; and therefore, those who transgressed God's commandments committed a greater offense.

Therefore,
first, he points out that they are transgressors of the law;
second, which commandment they transgress.

1287. He says then, *why do you also transgress the commandment of God* and do not observe it, *for the sake of your tradition?* For they, not knowing the justice of God, and seeking to establish their own, have not submitted themselves to the justice of God (Rom 10:3). *Their tongue, and their devices are against the Lord, to provoke the eyes of his majesty* (Isa 3:8).

1288. Deinde cum dicit *nam Deus dixit* etc., ponit quod est istud mandatum, quod est scilicet de honoratione parentum. Et

primo ponit mandatum;
secundo poenam.

1289. Unde dicit *nam Deus dixit: 'honora patrem et matrem tuam.'* Et notandum, quod honor non est nisi reverentia exhibita in testimonium virtutis. Ille enim exhibet reverentia, qui quae necessaria sunt administrat: unde non solum tenetur homo assurgere, sed etiam necessaria ministrare. Eccli. II, 21: *qui timent Dominum, custodient mandata illius*. Et quod debeatur talis honor, patet, quia Tobias mutuavit Gabelo, quod agere praeceperat Dominus. Ex. XX, 12 statim addit poenam: *ut sis longaevus super terram*. Item Lev. XX, 9.

1290. Addit poenam transgressoribus: *'qui maledixerit patri suo et matri suae, morte moriatur.'* Et sic in benedictione non solum intelligitur, quod ore benedicas, sed etiam quod benedictionem impendas; Prov. c. XX, 20: *qui maledixit patri suo et matri, extinguetur lumen eius in mediis tenebris*.

Sed quia posuit incitativum ex parte poenae, quare non posuit praemium ex obedientia? Quia homines magis terrentur a poena, quam desiderent praemium; nam et brutum a poena terretur. Ex hoc enim habetur, quod si qui detrahunt patri et matri, sunt digni morte; ergo qui movent alios eis detrahere, sunt digni morte; quare non sunt digni accusatione. Ergo vos non estis digni accusare eos.

1291. *Vos autem dicitis* et cetera. Hic tangit quomodo transgrediuntur. Et

primo hoc ostendit;
secundo auctoritatem ponit.
Et circa
primum ostendit ritum suum;
secundo quid sequebatur.

1292. Dicit *vos dicitis, quicumque dixerit patri vel matri* et cetera. Multis modis hoc legitur. Uno modo, ut sit constructio perfecta, et tunc sic *quicumque*, idest quivis, *dixerit*, idest dicere poterit. Alio modo, ut sit imperfecta, sic *quicumque dixerit* etc. supple, *servat mandatum, et est immunis a poena*.

Quid est hoc dictum? Tripliciter exponitur. Rabanus dicebat, quod spirituale bonum praeferendum est temporali; ideo dicebant his qui habebant patres pauperes, ut dicerent eis: pater, non displiceat tibi si non do tibi necessaria, quia munus quod offero, proficit tibi spiritualiter. Sed hoc non erat verum, secundum illud: *dona iniquorum non probat Altissimus*. Et Prov. c. XXVIII, 24: *qui subtrahit aliquid a patre suo et a matre et non dicit*

1288. Then when he says, *for God said*, he sets down what this commandment is, which is of course about honoring parents. And

first, he sets down the commandment;
second, the punishment,.

1289. Hence he says, *for God said: 'honor your father and mother'* (Exod 20:12). And one should note that honor is nothing but reverence shown in testimony to virtue. For he shows reverence who supplies whatever things are necessary: hence a man is not only bound to stand up, but also to supply what is needed. *Those who fear the Lord, keep his commandments* (Sir 2:21). And that such honor is due is clear, because Tobias lent money to Gabelus, which the Lord had commanded. Exodus immediately adds the punishment: *that you may be longlived upon the land which the Lord your God will give you* (Exod 20:12). Likewise Leviticus (Lev 20:9).

1290. He adds the punishment for transgressors: *'he who will curse father or mother, let him die the death.'* And thus by blessing is understood not only that you bless with your mouth, but also that you yourself bestow the blessing; *he who curses his father, and mother, his lamp will be put out in the midst of darkness* (Prov 20:20).

But since he sets out the incentive on the side of punishment, why did not he set out the reward of obedience? Because men are more terrified by punishment than they would desire a reward; for even a brute is terrified by punishment. For it is known from this that if anyone slanders his father and mother, he is worthy of death; therefore, those who move others to slander them are worthy of death, which is why they are not fit to make accusations. Therefore you are not worthy to accuse them.

1291. *But you say*; here he touches on how they transgress. And

first, he points this out;
second, he sets out an authority.
And concerning
the first, he points out their own rite;
second, what followed.

1292. *But you say: whoever will say to father or mother*. This is read in many ways. In one way, as a construction of the perfect, and then it is this way: *whoever*, i.e., anyone you please, *will say*, i.e., will be able to say. In another way, as it is imperfect, in this way: *whoever will say*, supply, *keeps the commandment, and is free from punishment*.

What is this saying? It is explained in three ways. Rabanus said that a spiritual good should be preferred to a temporal one; for this reason, they said to those who had poor parents that they should say to them: father, let it not displease you if I do not give you the necessary things, because the service which I offer profits you spiritually. But this was not true, according to *the Most High approves not the gifts of the wicked* (Sir 34:23). And, *he who steals any thing from*

hoc esse peccatum, particeps homicidae est. Ideo si aliquis habet patrem, vel matrem, et non possent vivere sine eo, qui diceret ei, *vade ultra mare, vel intra religionem*, in hanc sententiam incidit.

Alia est expositio. Hieronymus autem legit interrogative, idest **numquid proderit tibi?** Habetur Lev. XXII, 2, quod alienigena non poterat sumere quae consecrata erant Domino, ideo filios qui habebant patres pauperes, monebant quod offerrent Deo. Et si patres vellent sustentari ex eis, dicerent eis: si aliquid accipias ex illo quod Deo debeo offerre, numquid proderit tibi? Non, immo magis erit tibi in damnationem.

Augustinus sic exponit. Dicebant Iudaei, quod pueri dum erant sub tutela patris, eis tenebantur. Unde quando parvi sunt filii, patres offerunt pro filiis, et valet eis; sed quando liberi arbitrii sunt, tunc non valet devotio aliena. Unde dicebant quod omnis qui ad hunc statum potest pervenire et patri suo dicere **munus quod ex me est, tibi proderit**; non tenebatur patri.

1293. Sed ex ista doctrina sequuntur duo inconvenientia. Unum contra proximum, aliud contra Dominum. Contra proximum, quia qui sic diceret, et qui sic instructus est, non honorificat patrem suum. Unde Rom. I, v. 30: *inventores malorum, parentibus non obedientes*. Et sequitur: *qui talia agunt digni sunt morte*. Item contra Deum; unde dicit **et irritum fecistis mandatum Dei**, quasi dicat: non solum fecistis contra proximum, immo etiam irritum fecistis mandatum Dei propter traditionem vestram.

1294. Hypocritae. Proprie dicebantur hypocritae, qui intrabant theatrum, et habebant unam personam, et simulabant aliam cum larvis. Isti ergo hypocritae sunt, qui exterius aliud praetendunt quam habeant interius; unde interius intendebant lucra, exterius movebant homines ad offerendum Deo. Iob c. XXXVI, 13: *simulatores et callidi provocant iram Dei, neque clamabunt cum vincti fuerint*.

Bene prophetavit de vobis Isaias. Hoc habetur Is. XXIX, 13.

Primo ponit duplicitatem eorum;

secundo inutilitatem servitii, ibi *'sine causa autem colunt me.'*

1295. Dicit ergo *'populus hic labiis me honorat, cor autem eorum longe est a me.'* Et hoc ad litteram, quia honorabant labiis, sed corde longe erant a Deo; quia Christum in nomine Dei venientem non recipiebant. Vel sic. *'Populus hic labiis me honorat'* etc., quod enim dicunt, quod homo debet offerre Deo, videtur quod honorent Deum, *'cor autem eorum longe est'*, quia non tendebant ad honorem Dei, sed ad cupiditatem: unde

his father, or from his mother: and says, this is no sin, is the partner of a murderer (Prov 28:24). Therefore, if someone has a father, or a mother, and they cannot live without him, he who says to him, *go across the sea and enter religion*, falls under this judgment.

There is another explanation. Jerome reads it interrogatively, i.e., **will it profit you?** It says in Leviticus that a foreigner could not take for himself what had been consecrated to the Lord; therefore, they advised children who had poor fathers that they should offer to God (Lev 22:2). And if the fathers wished to be supported by them, they would say to them: if you take something from what I should offer to God, will it profit you? No, but rather it will be unto your condemnation.

Augustine explains it in this way. The Jews said that children, while they were under the father's guardianship, were bound to him. Hence when children were small, fathers offered on behalf of the children, and that was profitable for them. But when they are of free judgment, then another's devotion is no use. Hence they said that anyone who can arrive at this state and say to their father, **whatever gift proceeds from me, will profit you**, was not bound to the father.

1293. But two unfitting things follow from this teaching: one against one's neighbor, another against the Lord. Against one's neighbor, because he who speaks in this way and who instructs others in this way does not honor his father. Hence, *inventors of evil things, disobedient to parents* (Rom 1:30). And there follows, *they who do such things are worthy of death* (Rom 1:32). Likewise, against God; hence he says, **you have made void the commandment of God**, as though to say, not only have you acted against your neighbor, but you have even made God's commandment useless for the sake of your tradition.

1294. Hypocrites. Those were called hypocrites in the proper sense who went into the theater and, having one person, imitated another with a mask. Therefore, these men are hypocrites who pretend exteriorly something other than what they have interiorly; hence interiorly they aimed at gain, but exteriorly they moved men to offer to God. *Dissemblers and crafty men prove the wrath of God, neither will they cry when they are bound* (Job 36:13).

Well has Isaiah prophesied of you. It is in Isaiah that this is written (Isa 39:13).

First, he sets down their duplicity;

second, the uselessness of their service, at *'and in vain do they worship me.'*

1295. He says then, *'this people honors me with their lips: but their heart is far from me.'* And this is literal, because they honored with lips, but were far away from God in heart, because they did not receive Christ, who came in the name of God. Or in this way: *'this people honors me with their lips'*, for what they say, that a man should offer to God, seems to honor God, *'but their heart is far from me'*, because they were not aiming at the honor of God, but at

1296. But is this fiction of any use to them? No, because it does not please the Lord; hence there follows, '*and in vain do they worship me.*'

But what is this saying? Fasting is a human teaching, and the canons are human traditions; do those who teach these things worship God without cause? This should be understood to be the case as regards those who teach these things to the prejudice of God's commandments. *I will not level God with man* (Job 32:21). *We ought to obey God, rather than men* (Acts 5:29). Why? Because God cannot be deceived. *Offer sacrifice no more in vain* (Isa 1:13). And from this we have it that a man should make himself more aware of the transgression of a commandment than of the transgression of an ecclesiastical constitution.

1297. *And having called the multitudes to himself, he said to them.* Above, the Lord showed that the Pharisees, who were slandering, were unworthy to reproach the disciples because they were more bound up in sins than the disciples; but now, leaving them aside, he instructs others, that what was said above might be fulfilled, *you have hidden these things from the wise and prudent, and have revealed them to the little ones* (Matt 11:25). And

first, he instructs the crowds;
second, the disciples, at *then his disciples came*.

And concerning the first, he does two things:
first, he prepares them for listening;
second, he gives his teaching.

The second is at *it is not what goes into the mouth that defiles a man.*

1298. One should notice that to hear someone else, attention is required, which calls a man back to interior things, and gathers him together into himself. And he does this, when it says, *and having called the multitudes*, because we must be gathered together to him; *come to him and be enlightened* (Ps 33:6). The second thing necessary is diligence in hearing, so he says, *hear; a wise man will hear and will be wiser* (Prov 1:5). Also, understanding is required, hence he says, *and understand*; *understand, you senseless among the people: and, you fools, be wise at last* (Ps 93:8).

1299. Next, he sets out the highest teaching, which is the perfection of the moral life. Hence, notice that a thing can be changed from the outside, as water is heated by fire, or a thing can be changed from the inside, as a man is changed by sin. For however much he is moved exteriorly, it is not a sin unless a man consents interiorly; *out of the inner parts will a tempest come* (Job 37:9).

Unde primo ostendit quod non ab exterioribus, secundo quod ab interiori.

1300. Dicit ergo *non quod intrat in os coinquinat hominem*.

Contra, illud obiicitur quod habetur per veterem legem; habetur enim Lev. XI, quod multa cibaria prohibentur, unde homines fiebant immundi.

Respondet Augustinus contra Faustum dicens, quod aliquid dicitur immundum dupliciter. Uno modo secundum naturam suam: et sic nulla sunt immunda, secundum illud I ad Tim. IV, 4: *omnis creatura Dei bona est, et nihil reiiciendum quod cum gratiarum actione percipitur*. Item aliquid potest esse immundum secundum significationem. Et sic potest aliqua res esse signum immunditiae et munditiae: ut si accipiamus porcum et agnum in sua natura, utrumque est bonum; tamen sua significatione porcus significat immunditiam, agnus innocentiam: ideo quantum ad significationem unum est mundum, aliud immundum. Et quia ante adventum Christi erat tempus, in quo vivebant sub figuris, quia non adhuc patebat veritas, ideo illae observantiae erant servandae, et cadebant sub praecepto. Sed quia in adventu Christi veritas manifestabatur, cessabat figura; ideo et cetera.

1301. Sed iterum restat alia quaestio, quia habetur Act. XV, 20, quod apostoli praeceperunt, quod conversi abstinerent a suffocato et sanguine. Ergo videtur quod veritate manente, debeant teneri illae observantiae.

Antiqui dixerunt quod istud ad litteram intelligendum est, quod adhuc ab istis abstinendum est, quia immunda sunt. Sed hoc nihil est, quia contradicit auctoritati Apostoli ad Titum I, 15: *omnia munda mundis*. Aliqui dixerunt quod istud partim ad litteram intelligendum est, partim moraliter: quod enim dicitur de fornicatione, illud ad litteram prohibuerunt; quod autem a sanguine, hoc intelligendum est, quod sanguis innoxius non effunderetur; quod vero dicitur de suffocato, sic intelligendum erat, ut nullus alii calumniam inferret.

Sed non debet sic intelligi, quamvis sit expositio vera. Versabatur enim quaestio, utrum gentiles conversi tenerentur ad ista quae prohibuerunt apostoli. Ideo oportet intelligi secundum quod Iudaeis erat consuetum.

Ideo aliter dicendum est, quod apostoli aliquid considerabant, et prohibebant, vel quia secundum se illicitum, vel quia occasio scandali; unde fornicationem quasi illicitam prohibuerunt; sanguinem autem ne scandalum aliis facerent, ut scilicet scandalum tolleretur. Et hoc sonant verba Apostoli I ad Cor. VIII, 9: *videte autem ne haec licentia vestra offendiculum fiat infirmis*.

Hence first, he shows that a man is not made unclean by exterior things; second, that he is made unclean by interior things.

1300. He says then, *it is not what goes into the mouth that defiles a man*.

Against this is objected what is said by the old law; for it is written in Leviticus that many foods are forbidden, hence men became unclean through them (Lev 11).

Augustine responds, speaking against Faustus, that something is called unclean in two ways. In one way, according to its own nature: and in this way nothing is unclean, according to *for every creature of God is good, and nothing to be rejected that is received with thanksgiving* (1 Tim 4:4). Likewise, something can be unclean according to its signification. And in this way, something can be a sign of uncleanness and of cleanness; just as, if we take a pig and a lamb in their own natures, both are good, yet by its signification the pig signifies uncleanness, and the lamb cleanness. For this reason, as regards signification one is clean, the other unclean. And because before Christ's coming was the time in which they lived under figures, since the truth was not yet clear, therefore those observances were to be kept, and fell under commandment. But since the truth was manifested in Christ's coming, the figures ceased.

1301. But again another question remains, because it is written that the apostles commanded that the converts abstain from suffocated animals and from blood (Acts 15:20). Therefore it seems that, with the truth remaining, these observances should be held.

The ancients said that this was to be understood literally, because it was still necessary to abstain from these things, since they were unclean. But this amounts to nothing, because it contradicts the authority of the Apostle: *all things are clean to the clean* (Titus 1:15). Some said that this was to be understood partly literally, partly morally: for what is said about fornication, that they forbade literally; but what is said about blood should be understood to mean that harmless blood should not be poured out; while what is said about a suffocated animal was to be understood to mean that no one should bring slander on others.

But it should not be understood this way, however true the explanation is. The question discussed was whether the gentile converts were bound to those things which the apostles forbade. Therefore, one must understand it according as was customary with the Jews.

Therefore, one should say otherwise, that the apostles considered something, and forbade it, either because it was unlawful in itself or because it was an occasion of scandal. Hence they forbade fornication as unlawful; but they forbade blood lest they give scandal to others, that is, to remove scandal. And this harmonizes with the words of the Apostle: *but take heed lest perhaps this your liberty become a stumblingblock to the weak* (1 Cor 8:9).

Item si obiicitur: ponatur quod aliquis in Quadragesima comedat carnes, nonne coinquinatur? Dicendum quod non ex cibo, sed ex violatione praecepti; Rom. XIV, 17: *regnum Dei non est esca et potus*.

1302. Sed quod procedit ex ore, hoc coinquinat hominem. Hic videtur tangere solum peccata quae ex ore procedunt, et haec coinquinant; Lc. XIX, 22: *ex ore tuo te iudico, serve nequam*. Et supra VII, 2: **ex ore tuo iudicaberis**.

Sed dicendum, quod proprium officium oris est dicere. Est autem duplex dicere, exterius ore corporali, et interius ore mentis, de quo Ps. XIII, 1: *dixit insipiens in corde suo: non est Deus*. Sic ergo per 'os' potest intelligi os cordis, scilicet mens hominis, et sic omne peccatum est ex ore; quia numquam est peccatum nisi ex proposito mentis. Sic ergo **quod procedit ex ore**, scilicet cordis, **hoc coinquinat**, quia peccatum adeo est voluntarium, quod si non sit voluntarium, non est peccatum.

1303. Tunc accedentes discipuli eius et cetera. Hic instruit de scandalo vitando, et de principali quaestione, ibi **respondens autem Petrus**.

Circa primum duo.

Primo ponitur quaestio discipulorum;

secundo Christi responsio.

1304. Hic intelligendum quod Pharisaei et discipuli audierunt hoc verbum, in quo intelligebant, quod omnes suas traditiones subverteret, non autem praecepta Domini; ideo abominantes nihil dixerunt, sed turbationem habuerunt: ideo discipuli dixerunt **scis quia Pharisaei, audito verbo hoc, scandalizati sunt?**

1305. Hoc verbum 'scandalum,' frequenter invenitur in Scripturis; unde videndum quid significet.

Scandalum in Graeco idem est quod offendiculum, ut lapis in via; unde offendiculum dicitur, ubi est occasio ruinae. Sed aliquando aliquis scandalizat active, aliquando passive. Active scandalum dicitur, quando est aliquod factum, quod est non solum in se malum, sed etiam aliis offendiculum: ideo 'scandalum' dicitur dictum, vel factum minus rectum praebens occasionem ruinae. Et non dicit 'cogitatum,' quia oportet quod sit patens. Item non dicit 'malum,' sed minus rectum, quia oportet quod habeat speciem mali; I Thess. V, 22: *ab omni specie mali abstinete vos*. Item est scandalum passivum, ut si aliquis bonum verbum dicat, vel oret, alius scandalizetur, et accipit sibi occasionem ruinae: unde dominus non scandalizavit, sed ipsi ceperunt occasionem. Unde dixerunt discipuli sui, quod Pharisaei inde ceperunt scandalum, et hoc praenunciatum erat per Is. VIII, 14: *et erit vobis*

Likewise, if it is objected: suppose that someone eats meat in Lent; would he not be defiled? One should say that he would be defiled not by the food, but by the violation of a commandment; *for the kingdom of God is not meat and drink* (Rom 14:17).

1302. But what comes out of the mouth, this defiles a man. Here he seems to touch only on the sins which proceed from the mouth, and these defile a man; *out of your own mouth I judge you, you wicked servant* (Luke 19:22). And above, *for with what judgment you judge, you will be judged* (Matt 7:2).

But one should say that the proper function of the mouth is to speak. Now there are two ways of speaking: exteriorly, with a bodily mouth, and interiorly with the mouth of the mind, about which the Psalm says, *the fool has said in his heart: there is no God* (Ps 13:1). So in this way, one can understand by 'mouth' the mouth of the heart, namely the mind of a man, and thus every sin is from the mouth; because there is never sin except from the mind's intention. So in this way **what comes out of the mouth**, namely the heart, **this defiles a man**, because it is a sin to the degree it is voluntary, because if it is not voluntary, it is not a sin.

1303. Then his disciples came. Here he gives instruction about avoiding scandal, and about the principal question, at **and Peter answering**.

Concerning the first, two things:

first, the disciples' question is set down;

second, Christ's response.

1304. Here one should understand that the Pharisees and the disciples heard this saying, in which they understood that he overturned all their traditions, but they did not hear the Lord's precepts; so they said nothing, abhorring him, but were disturbed. For this reason, the disciples said, **do you know that the Pharisees, when they heard this word, were scandalized?**

1305. This word 'scandal' is found frequently in the Scriptures; hence one should see what it signifies.

In Greek, a scandal is the same thing as a stumbling block, like a rock on the road; hence it is called a stumbling block where there is an occasion of ruin. But sometimes a person scandalizes actively, and sometimes passively. It is called active scandal when it is something done, which is not only bad in itself, but also a stumbling block to others. Therefore a 'scandal' names a saying or deed less right which presents the occasion of ruin. And this definition does not say 'thought,' because a scandal has to be evident. Likewise, it does not say 'bad,' but less right, because it must have the appearance of evil; *from all appearance of evil refrain yourselves* (1 Thess 5:22). There is also passive scandal, as when someone speaks a good word, or prays, and another is scandalized, but he himself seized the occasion. Hence his disciples said that the Pharisees took scandal from it, and this was foretold by Isaiah: *and he will be a*

in sanctificationem, in lapidem autem offensionis, et in petram scandali.

1306. At ille respondens ait. Hic ponitur responsio Domini, et ostendit eorum scandalum contemnendum

primo quia alieni a Deo;

secundo quia nocivi hominibus, ibi **sinite illos: caeci sunt et duces caecorum**.

1307. Dicit ergo *at ille respondens ait: omnis plantatio quam non plantavit Pater meus caelestis, eradicabitur*. Ex verbis istis illi qui posuerunt duas naturas, voluerunt confirmare errorem suum, quia malam naturam a malo Deo dixerunt, bonam a bono; unde dicunt: si aliquis de mala creatione sit, etsi videatur facere bona, non potest perseverare. Sed non est sic: nam, ut dicit Hieronymus, contrarium habetur Ier. II, 21: *ego te plantavi vineam electam, omne semen verum; quomodo ergo conversa es in amaritudinem?* Hoc ergo patet, quod non est a Deo. Sic ergo conversa est per istam plantationem non natura; sed aliquid superveniens intelligitur, et hoc est perversa voluntas; unde natura semper remanet, sed voluntas perversa eradicatur.

Unde potest ista plantatio intelligi de traditione hominum, quae est eradicanda, si sit contra Deum; sed traditio quae est a Deo, numquam est eradicanda. Unde **omnis plantatio**, idest traditio quae non est a Deo Patre meo, **eradicabitur**. Et hoc habetur Act. V, v. 39 de Gamaliele qui dixit: *si fuerit hoc a Deo, non poteritis contradicere*.

Hoc patet etiam in omnibus. Videbis aliquem qui bona opera facit fundata in caritate, ad Eph. III, 17: *in caritate radicati et fundati*: et haec non possunt eradicari. Sed alia quae non habent bonum fundamentum, ut dare eleemosynam propter vanitatem, eradicantur; unde Eccli. XIV, 20: *omne opus corruptibile in fine deficiet, et qui facit illud, corruet in illo*. Unde sic intelligendum est Sap. IV, 3: *adulterinae plantationes non dabunt radices altas*.

Contra hoc habetur I ad Cor. III, 6, ubi dicit Paulus: *ego plantavi, Apollo rigavit*. Ergo Paulus eradicabitur. Dico, quod Paulus non plantavit ut principalis, sed ut minister.

1308. Sequitur **sinite illos, caeci sunt**. Hic ostendit scandalum eorum contemnendum, quia nocivi sunt hominibus. Et primo docet contemnendum; secundo praesumptionem eorum; tertio nocumentum.

Circa primum: dicitis quod ita scandalizentur, **sinite eos**, et non curetis.

Sed numquid non est curandum de scandalo? Nonne Dominus ut vitaret scandalum, misit Petrum ad mare, ut solveret tributum?

sanctification to you. But for a stone of stumbling, and for a rock of offense to the two houses of Israel (Isa 8:14).

1306. But he answered and said. Here the Lord's response is set down, and he shows that their scandal should be despised:

first, because it is unconnected with God;

second, because it is harmful to men, at **leave them alone; they are blind and leaders of the blind**.

1307. It says then, **but he answered and said: every plant which my heavenly Father has not planted, will be rooted up**. From these words, those who posited two natures wished to confirm their error, because they said that a bad nature was created by a bad god, and a good nature by a good god. Hence they say: if someone is of the bad creation, even if he seems to do good things he cannot persevere. But this is not so; for, as Jerome says, the contrary is written in Jeremiah, *yet I planted you a chosen vineyard, all true seed: how then are you turned unto me into that which is good for nothing, O strange vineyard?* (Jer 2:21). So this is clear, that it is not from God. So it was changed in this way by the plant itself, not by nature; but something is understood as coming over it, and this is corrupted will. Hence the nature always remains, but the corrupted will is rooted up.

Hence this plant can be understood as the tradition of men, which is to be rooted up if it is against God; but the tradition which is from God will never be rooted up. Hence, **every plant**, i.e., tradition, which is not from God, my Father, **will be rooted up**. And this is said in Acts by Gamaliel, who said, *but if it is of God, you cannot overthrow it* (Acts 5:39).

This is also clear in all things. You will see some who do good works founded in charity, *being rooted and founded in charity* (Eph 3:17): and these cannot be rooted up. But others, who do not have a good foundation, as those who give alms on account of vanity, are rooted up; hence, *every work that is corruptible will fail in the end: and the worker thereof will go with it* (Sir 14:20). Hence it should be understood in this way: *the slip of an adulterer will not take deep root, nor any fast foundation* (Wis 4:3).

Against this it is written, where Paul says, *I have planted, Apollo watered* (1 Cor 3:6). Therefore Paul will be rooted up. I say that Paul did not plant as the principal agent, but as a minister.

1308. There follows **leave them alone; they are blind**. Here he shows that their scandal is to be despised, because it is harmful to men. And first, he teaches that it is to be despised; second, about their presumption; third, about the harm.

Concerning the first: you say that they are scandalized in this way; **leave them alone**, and do not care.

But should not one care about scandal? Did not the Lord send Peter to the sea, that he might pay the tribute, to avoid scandal?

Dicendum quod scandalum aliquando oritur ex veritate; unde illud vitandum est scandalum quod potest vitari sine praeiudicio veritatis, vitae, vel doctrinae, vel iustitiae. Unde iudex non debet dimittere iudicium, si aliquis inde scandalizatur. Sed tamen distinguendum, quia aliqui scandalizantur ex infirmitate, aliqui ex certa malitia. Scandalum pusillorum vitandum est, veritate servata; et tamen potest homo differre, vel remittere. Sed si ex malitia, non: et sic isti scandalizantur. Unde si non ex malitia scandalizarentur, non dixisset Dominus *sinite illos*, sed potius, *instruite eos*. Ad Titum III, 10: *haereticum hominem post secundam monitionem devita*; Ier. LI, 9: *curavimus Babylonem, et non est curata*.

1309. Et quare *caeci sunt*? Spiritualiter caeci sunt ignorantes; Is. LVI, 10: *speculatores eius omnes caeci*. Et quia ex certa malitia, non solum sunt caeci, sed etiam *duces caecorum*, et magistri, Iob XIX, 4: *si ignoravi, mecum erit ignorantia mea*. Quod sint duces caecorum, hoc est bonum; sed quod caeci, hoc est malum. *Si caecus caeco ducatum praestet, ambo in foveam cadunt*. Iob. XL, 8: *absconde eos in pulvere*, scilicet quantum ad corpus.

1310. *Respondens autem Petrus*. Instruit eos hic de principali quaestione;

ubi tria facit: quia

primo ponitur petitio Petri;

secundo increpatio;

tertio doctrina.

Secunda ibi *at ille dixit: adhuc et vos sine intellectu estis?* Tertia ibi *non intelligitis* et cetera.

1311. Dicit ergo *respondens autem Petrus dixit ei: edissere nobis parabolam hanc*. Petrus consuetus erat audire parabolas multas ab eo; ideo credebat, quod loqueretur parabolice: vel quia Petrus nutritus erat in observantiis legalibus, sicut dixit in actibus apostolorum cap. X, 14: *absit a me, domine, numquam coinquinatum intravit in os meum*: ideo credebat, quod ad litteram non diceret, sed parabolice. Prov. I, 6: *animadvertet parabolam, et interpretationem, et verba sapientum, et aenigmata eorum*.

1312. *At ille dixit: adhuc et vos sine intellectu estis?* Dominus enim omnibus in Petro respondit, qui pro omnibus loquebatur. Hic reprehendit eos. Sed quare? Una ratio est, quam ponit Hieronymus, quia quod palam dictum est, parabolice dictum putant. Sicut enim reprehendendus est, qui manifestat occulta, sic e converso, qui occultat manifesta; Ps. XXXI, 9: *nolite fieri sicut equus et mulus, in quibus non est intellectus* et cetera. Alia ratio

One should say that scandal sometimes arises from the truth; hence, that scandal should be avoided which can be avoided without prejudice to the truth, to life, to doctrine, or to justice. Hence the judge should not give up judging if someone is scandalized by it. But nevertheless one must distinguish, because some are scandalized out of weakness, and some out of certain malice. The scandal of little ones should be avoided, the truth being preserved; and yet a man can put something off, or mitigate it. But not if it is out of malice: and these Pharisees are scandalized in this way. Hence if they were not scandalized out of malice, the Lord would not have said, **leave them alone**, but rather, **instruct them**. It is written: *a man who is a heretic, after the first and second admonition, avoid* (Titus 3:10); *we would have cured Babylon, but she is not healed* (Jer 51:9).

1309. And why **they are blind**? The spiritually blind are those who are ignorant; *his watchmen are all blind* (Isa 56:10). And because they are so out of certain malice, they are not only blind, but also **leaders of the blind**, and teachers, *for if I have been ignorant, my ignorance will be with me* (Job 19:4). The fact that they are leaders of the blind is good; but that they are blind, this is an evil. **And if the blind lead the blind, both will fall into the pit**. *Hide them in the dust together* (Job 40:8), namely as regards the body.

1310. **And Peter answering, said to him**. He gives instruction here about the principal question.

Here he does three things, for

first, Peter's question is set down;

second, a rebuke;

third, the teaching.

The second is at **but he said: are you also still without understanding?** The third, at **do you not understand**.

1311. **And Peter answering, said to him: expound this parable**. Peter was accustomed to hear parables from him; therefore he believed that he would speak in a parable; or because Peter was brought up in legal observances, as he said in Acts, *far be it from me; for I never did eat anything that is common and unclean* (Acts 10:14). For this reason, he believed that he did not speak literally, but in a parable. *He will understand a parable, and the interpretation, the words of the wise, and their mysterious sayings* (Prov 1:6).

1312. **But he said: are you also still without understanding?** For the Lord responded to all the disciples in Peter, who spoke for all. Here he reproaches him. But why? One reason, which Jerome sets out, is that what was spoken plainly he thought to be spoken in a parable. For just as he who discloses hidden things should be reproached, so, conversely, he who hides manifest things should be reproached; *do not become like the horse and the mule, who*

have no understanding (Ps 31:9). Another reason is Chrysostom's, that he seemed to be zealous for the Jews, since he was brought up in the teachings of the law; so he seemed to be saddened by this.

1313. Next, he explains. And

first, he explains what he had said, namely *it is not what goes into the mouth that defiles a man*;

second, according to what he had said, namely *but what comes out of the mouth, this defiles a man*;

third, he draws the intended conclusion.

1314. He says then, *do you not understand, that whatever enters into the mouth, goes into the belly, and is cast out in private?* And why does the Lord speak this way? Chrysostom says that he speaks to them as to those familiar with the observances of the law. Now, it was the law's intention that when food was in the mouth undigested, it was unclean; but when it was digested, it was clean. Hence it always says in the law, *he . . . will be unclean until evening*. Therefore, let us suppose that these observances should be kept: they still do not render a man unclean, except for a time. Hence what passes on cannot make them unclean. Or in another way. Nothing can make the soul unclean which does not touch it. But food does not touch the soul; and this is the sign: that it *goes into the belly, and is cast out in private*.

1315. But, as Jerome says, some object against this, saying that the Lord was ignorant of natural science, because the whole of the food is not cast out.

Hence certain men, wishing to understand it in this way, that the whole is cast out, would have it that nothing is changed into human nature, but what is received from Adam is simply multiplied, and this will rise at the last day. Hence what is from food, according to them, will not rise. Hence also craftsmen put lead with gold, that the lead may be consumed, and the gold preserved. In this way, foods provide resistance, lest the natural heat consume that which is from the power of nature.

But this seems impossible, because nothing can become greater except through rarefaction, because to be rarefied is nothing else than to take on a greater quantity. Also, man has the sensitive and nutritive powers in common with the animals, and the vegetative power in common with plants. But it is in this way that these grow and are nourished by nourishment.

1316. So why does he say that it is *cast out in private*?

Jerome says that it is not understood only as unclean excess, but rather however it comes about, whether through excrement, or in some other way. And this is also in accord with the Philosopher, because although it remains according to species, yet according to matter it flows on, just as a fire remains in species, but the matter is consumed.

Potest etiam sic dici *omne quod intrat in os, in ventrem vadit*, aliquid: unde aliquando in Scriptura totum pro parte sumitur.

1317. *Quae autem procedunt de ore*: iam dictum est, quod per os intelligitur mens. *De corde exeunt, et ea coinquinant hominem*: quia peccata cordis sunt cogitationes et affectus; Is. I, 16: *auferte malum cogitationum vestrarum ab oculis meis*. Item ponit peccata quae sunt contra praecepta secundae tabulae *homicidia, adulteria, fornicationes, furta*. Item peccata oris contra proximum *falsa testimonia; blasphemiae*, contra praecepta primae tabulae. Unde *haec sunt, quae coinquinant hominem*, quia haec a mente procedunt.

1318. *Non lotis autem manibus manducare, non coinquinat hominem*. Hic concludit, et ponit hanc conclusionem, ut principali intentioni respondeat. Item quia discipuli non erant intelligentes, ideo concludit quod contra traditionem solum dicebatur.

It can also be said this way: *whatever enters into the mouth, goes into the belly*, something of it: hence sometimes in the Scriptures, the whole is taken for the part.

1317. *But the things which proceed forth from the mouth*: it was already said that by the mouth is understood the mind. *Come forth from the heart, and those things defile a man*, because the sins of the heart are thoughts and affections; *take away the evil of your devices from my eyes* (Isa 1:16). He also sets down the sins which are against the commandments of the second tablet: *murders, adulteries, fornications, thefts*. Likewise, the sins of the mouth against neighbor: *false testimonies*. *Blasphemies*, against the commandments of the first tablet. Hence, *these are the things that defile a man*, because these come forth from the mind.

1318. *But to eat with unwashed hands does not defile a man*. Here he concludes, and sets out this conclusion, to respond to the principal intention. Also, since the disciples did not understand, he concludes that he spoke only against tradition.

Lecture 2

15:21 Et egressus inde Iesus secessit in partes Tyri et Sidonis. [n. 1320]

15:22 Et ecce mulier Chananaea a finibus illis egressa, clamavit dicens ei: miserere mei, Domine, Fili David; filia mea male a daemonio vexatur. [n. 1321]

15:23 Qui non respondit ei verbum. Et accedentes discipuli eius rogabant eum, dicentes: dimitte eam, quia clamat post nos. [n. 1323]

15:24 Ipse autem respondens ait: non sum missus nisi ad oves quae perierunt domus Israel. [n. 1326]

15:25 At illa venit, et adoravit eum dicens: Domine, adiuva me. [n. 1328]

15:26 Qui respondens ait: non est bonum sumere panem filiorum, et mittere canibus. [n. 1329]

15:27 At illa dixit: etiam, Domine; nam et catelli edunt de micis, quae cadunt de mensa dominorum suorum. [n. 1330]

15:28 Tunc respondens Iesus ait illi: O mulier, magna est fides tua, fiat tibi sicut vis. Et sanata est filia illius ex illa hora. [n. 1331]

15:21 Καὶ ἐξελθὼν ἐκεῖθεν ὁ Ἰησοῦς ἀνεχώρησεν εἰς τὰ μέρη Τύρου καὶ Σιδῶνος.

15:22 καὶ ἰδοὺ γυνὴ Χαναναία ἀπὸ τῶν ὁρίων ἐκείνων ἐξελθοῦσα ἔκραζεν λέγουσα· ἐλέησόν με, κύριε υἱὸς Δαυίδ· ἡ θυγάτηρ μου κακῶς δαιμονίζεται.

15:23 ὁ δὲ οὐκ ἀπεκρίθη αὐτῇ λόγον. καὶ προσελθόντες οἱ μαθηταὶ αὐτοῦ ἠρώτουν αὐτὸν λέγοντες· ἀπόλυσον αὐτήν, ὅτι κράζει ὄπισθεν ἡμῶν.

15:24 ὁ δὲ ἀποκριθεὶς εἶπεν· οὐκ ἀπεστάλην εἰ μὴ εἰς τὰ πρόβατα τὰ ἀπολωλότα οἴκου Ἰσραήλ.

15:25 ἡ δὲ ἐλθοῦσα προσεκύνει αὐτῷ λέγουσα· κύριε, βοήθει μοι.

15:26 ὁ δὲ ἀποκριθεὶς εἶπεν· οὐκ ἔστιν καλὸν λαβεῖν τὸν ἄρτον τῶν τέκνων καὶ βαλεῖν τοῖς κυναρίοις.

15:27 ἡ δὲ εἶπεν· ναὶ κύριε, καὶ γὰρ τὰ κυνάρια ἐσθίει ἀπὸ τῶν ψιχίων τῶν πιπτόντων ἀπὸ τῆς τραπέζης τῶν κυρίων αὐτῶν.

15:28 τότε ἀποκριθεὶς ὁ Ἰησοῦς εἶπεν αὐτῇ· ὦ γύναι, μεγάλη σου ἡ πίστις· γενηθήτω σοι ὡς θέλεις. καὶ ἰάθη ἡ θυγάτηρ αὐτῆς ἀπὸ τῆς ὥρας ἐκείνης.

15:21 And Jesus went away from there and retired to the coasts of Tyre and Sidon. [n. 1320]

15:22 And behold, a woman of Canaan who was from those coasts, came and cried out, saying to him: have mercy on me O Lord, Son of David; my daughter is grievously troubled by a devil. [n. 1321]

15:23 He answered her not a word. And his disciples came and petitioned him saying: send her away, for she cries after us. [n. 1323]

15:24 He however, answering, said: I was not sent except to the lost sheep of the house of Israel. [n. 1326]

15:25 But she came and adored him, saying: Lord, help me. [n. 1328]

15:26 Answering, he said: it is not good to take the bread of the children, and give it to the dogs. [n. 1329]

15:27 But she said: yes Lord; but the whelps also eat the crumbs that fall from the table of their masters. [n. 1330]

15:28 Then Jesus answering, said to her: O woman, great is your faith; let be it done for you as you will. And her daughter was cured from that hour. [n. 1331]

1319. Supra ostensa est sufficientia eius doctrinae, quia observantiam legis non requirit; hic ostendit quod non coarctatur ad unum populum, sed etiam ad salutem gentilium sufficit.

Ostenditur autem triplex effectus in gentilibus.
Primo in liberatione a potestate daemonis;
secundo ab infirmitatibus peccatorum;
tertio in spirituali refectione.

Secunda ibi *et cum transisset inde Iesus venit secus Mare Galilaeae*; tertia ibi *Iesus autem, convocatis discipulis suis, dixit*.

Ostenditur ergo liberatio a potestate daemonum, quia mulierem obsessam a diabolo liberavit.
Primo locus describitur;
secundo instantia mulieris;
tertio exauditio.

1319. Above, the sufficiency of his teaching was shown, because it does not require the observance of the law; here he shows that it is not limited to one people, but also suffices for the salvation of the gentiles.

And three effects on the gentiles are pointed out:
first, in liberation from the power of demons;
second, from the weakness of sins;
third, in spiritual refreshment.

The second is at **and when Jesus had gone away from there, he came near the Sea of Galilee** (Matt 15:29); the third, at **and Jesus called together his disciples, and said** (Matt 15:32).

So liberation from the power of demons is shown, for he freed the woman possessed by the devil.
First, the place is described;
second, the woman's insistence;
third, the response.

Secunda ibi *et ecce mulier Chananaea* et cetera. Tertia ibi *tunc respondens Iesus ait illi* et cetera.

1320. Dicit ergo *et egressus venit in partes Tyri et Sidonis*. Tyrus et Sidon sunt duae civitates gentilium. Quia a Iudaeis repellebatur, ideo ad gentes secessit, secundum illud Act. XIII, 46: *vobis oportebat primum loqui regnum Dei; sed quoniam repellitis illud et indignos vos iudicatis aeternae vitae, ecce convertimur ad gentes*. Et primo ostendit Dominus eminere conversionem observatorum legis; secundo transitum ad gentes, quod significatum fuit Act. X, 15, ubi dicitur quod cum Petrus esset apud Cornelium, vidit linteum etc. et dictum est ei: *quod Deus purificat, tu ne immundum dixeris* et cetera.

1321. *Et ecce mulier*. Hic ponitur instantia mulieris. Circa cuius petitionem tria significantur.

Primo pietas;

secundo fides;

tertio humilitas: et haec necessaria sunt ad impetrandum.

Secunda ibi *at illa venit et adoravit eum*; tertia ibi *at illa dixit, etiam, Domine*.

Primo ponitur interpellatio;

secundo adiutorium discipulorum, ibi *et accedentes discipuli eius rogabant eum*.

Circa primum

primo ponitur pietas mulieris;

secundo taciturnitas Christi, ibi *qui non respondit ei verbum*.

1322. Dicit ergo *et ecce mulier Chananaea*.

Sex possumus notare. Primo conversio petentis; Eccli. XVIII, 23: *ante orationem praepara animam tuam, et noli esse quasi homo qui tentat Deum*. Praeparat enim animam quando a vitiis se mundat; Is. I, 15: *cum multiplicaveritis orationes, non exaudiam vos; manus enim vestrae sanguine plenae sunt*. Et hoc designatur per hoc nomen **Chananaea**, quae idem est quod 'mutata'; Ps. LXXVI, 11: *haec est mutatio dexterae Excelsi*. Item qui convertitur, debet non solum vitare peccatum, sed etiam occasionem peccati; Eccli. XXI, v. 2: *quasi a facie colubri, fuge peccatum*. Secundo notanda est devotio, quia clamabat. Clamor magnum affectum designat; Ps. CXIX, v. 1: *ad Dominum, cum tribularer, clamavi*. Tertio notatur pietas, quia alienam miseriam suam reputabat, unde dicit *miserere mei*, et hoc est magna misericordia; Iob XXX, 25: *flebam super eum qui afflictus erat, et compatiebatur anima mea pauperi*. Item tangitur humilitas, quia petiit ex confidentia misericordiae Dei; Dan. IX, 4: *custodiens pactum et misericordiam diligentibus te, et custodientibus mandata tua*. Quarto tangitur fides, quae necessaria est ad petitionem; Iac. I, 6: *postulet autem in fide nihil haesitans*. Item confitetur divinam

The second is at *and behold, a woman of Canaan*. The third, at *then Jesus answering, said to her*.

1320. It says then, *and Jesus went away from there, and retired to the coasts of Tyre and Sidon*. Tyre and Sidon are two cities of the gentiles. Since he was driven away by the Jews, he turned to the gentiles, in accord with, *to you it behoved us first to speak the word of God: but because you reject it, and judge yourselves unworthy of eternal life, behold we turn to the gentiles* (Acts 13:46). And first, the Lord shows that the conversion of those who observe the law is preeminent; second, the going over to the gentiles, which was signified, where it says that when Peter was with Cornelius, he saw a linen cloth (Acts 10:15). And it was said to him, *that which God has cleansed, do not call common*.

1321. And behold, a woman. Here the woman's insistence is set down, concerning whose petition three things are signified:

first, piety;

second, faith;

third, humility; and these things are necessary for obtaining what one seeks.

The second is at *but she came and adored him*; the third, at *but she said: yes, Lord*.

First, the interruption is set down;

second, the disciples' help, at *and his disciples came and petitioned him*.

Concerning the first,

first, the woman's piety is set down;

second, Christ's silence, at *who answered her not a word*.

1322. It says then, *and behold, a woman of Canaan*.

We can notice six things. First, the conversion of the one asking; *before prayer prepare your soul: and do not be as a man who tempts God* (Sir 18:23). For a man prepares his soul when he cleanses himself of vices; *and when you multiply prayer, I will not hear: for your hands are full of blood* (Isa 1:15). And this is indicated by the name **Canaan**, which is the same as 'changed'; *this is the change of the right hand of the Most High* (Ps 76:11). Likewise, he who is converted should not only avoid sin, but even the occasion of sin; *flee from sins as from the face of a serpent* (Sir 21:2). Second, one should notice her devotion, for she was crying out. A great cry indicates emotion; *in my trouble I cried to the Lord* (Ps 119:1). Third, piety is noted, because she considered another's misery as her own; hence she says, **have mercy on me**. And this is great compassion; *I have wept for him who was afflicted, and my soul had compassion on the poor* (Job 30:25). Also, humility is touched upon, because she begged out of confidence in the mercy of God; *who keep the covenant, and mercy to those who love you, and keep your commandments* (Dan 9:4). Fourth, faith is touched upon, which is necessary for a petition; *but let him ask in faith, nothing wavering* (Jas 1:6). Also, she confesses the

naturam in eo, in hoc quod dicit **Domine**; Ps. XCIX, 3: *scitote, quoniam Dominus ipse est Deus*. Item humanam **Fili David**, qui ex semine David; ad Rom. I, v. 3: *qui factus est ei ex semine David secundum carnem*. Item expositio propriae necessitatis. **Filia mea male**, idest graviter, **a daemonio vexatur**. Et potest esse typus totius Ecclesiae gentilium, vel cuiuslibet pro conscientia, quae a Daemonio vexatur, cum contra conscientiam operatur; Lc. VI, 18: *et qui vexabantur a spiritibus immundis, curabantur*. Et dicit **male**, in quo aggravat peccatum; II Paralip. ult.: *peccavi, Domine, peccavi, et iniquitatem meam agnosco, ne simul perdas me cum iniquitatibus meis*.

1323. Consequenter ponitur taciturnitas Christi **qui non respondit ei verbum**. Sed hoc videtur mirabile quod fons pietatis tacuit.

Et assignatur triplex ratio. Prima ne videretur ire contra illud quod supra dixerat: **in viam gentium ne abieritis**. Ideo prompte noluit exaudire; nihilominus tamen quia multum institit, accepit quod petivit. Ideo datur intelligi quod propter instantiam petitionis impetratur quod supra legem est: erat enim de lege, quod soli Iudaei salvarentur; sed ista per instantiam suam impetravit quod erat supra legem.

Secunda ratio est, ut magis cresceret devotio. Hab. I, 2: *usquequo clamabo, et non exaudies, vociferabor ad te vim patiens, et non salvabis? Quare ostendisti mihi iniquitatem et dolorem, videre praedam et iniustitiam contra me?*

Tertia ratio, ut daret occasionem discipulis, ut et ipsi intercederent pro ea: quia quantumcumque sit aliquis bonus, indiget tamen orationibus aliorum.

1324. Statim sequitur intercessio discipulorum. Et

primo ponitur eorum petitio;
secundo Christi responsio.

1325. Dicit ergo **et accedentes discipuli eius rogabant eum**. Et quare accesserunt? Una ratio est, quia nesciebant quare tantum retardabat; secunda, moti erant misericordia; item, non poterant pati mulieris importunitatem; Lc. XI, 8: *si perseveraverit pulsans, dico vobis, et si non dabit illi surgens, eo quod amicus eius sit, propter improbitatem tamen eius surget, et dabit illi quotquot habet necessarios*. Discipuli non dicunt *sana eam*, sed **dimitte eam**; idest dicas ei: *nihil faciam tibi*. Et iste est modus loquendi: quoniam cum intendimus unum, dicitur contrarium.

Sed obiicitur, quia Marci VII, 25 dicitur quod ingressa est in domum, et ibi petiit. Quid est ergo quod hic dicitur **quia clamat post nos**? Augustinus dicit quod sine

divine nature in him, in that she calls him **Lord**; *know that the Lord is God* (Ps 99:3). Also, the human nature, **Son of David**, he who is of the seed of David; *who was made to him of the seed of David, according to the flesh* (Rom 1:3). Also, an explanation of the particular necessity: **my daughter is grievously**, i.e., gravely, **troubled by a devil**. And this can be a type of the whole Church of the gentiles, or of anyone on account of a conscience which is troubled by an unclean spirit, when he acts contrary to conscience. *And those who were troubled with unclean spirits, were cured* (Luke 6:18). And she says, **grievously**, in which she magnifies the sin; *I have sinned, O Lord, I have sinned, and I know my iniquity . . . do not destroy me with my iniquities!* (cf. 2 Sam 24:10).

1323. Next, Christ's silence is set down: **he answered her not a word**. But this seems astonishing, that the fount of goodness remained silent.

And three reasons are given. First, lest he seem to go against what he had said above: **do not go into the way of the gentiles** (Matt 10:5). For this reason, he did not want to hear her promptly; yet nonetheless because she insisted greatly, he accepted what she asked. Therefore, one is given to understand that what is beyond the law is obtained through insistence in prayer: for it was in the law that only the Jews would be saved; but this woman, by her insistence, obtained something which was beyond the law.

The second reason is so that her devotion would increase. *How long, O Lord, will I cry, and you will not hear? Will I cry out to you suffering violence, and you will not save? Why have you shown me iniquity and grievance, to see rapine and injustice before me?* (Hab 1:2–3).

The third reason, to give an occasion to the disciples to intercede for her, because however good someone is, he still needs the prayers of others.

1324. There follows immediately the disciples' intercession. And

first, their petition is set down;
second, Christ's response.

1325. It says then, **and his disciples came and petitioned him**. And why did they come? One reason is that they did not know why he delayed so much; second, they were moved by pity; also, they could not bear the woman's relentlessness. *Yet if he shall continue knocking, I say to you, although he will not rise and give him, because he is his friend; yet, because of his importunity, he will rise, and give him as many as he needs* (Luke 11:8). The disciples do not say, *heal her*, but **send her away**; i.e., say to her, *I will do nothing for you*. And this is a manner of speaking, for when we intend one thing, the contrary is said.

But it is objected that Mark says that she came into the house, and begged there (Mark 8:25). Why is it then that it says here, **for she cries after us**? Augustine says that

dubio primo in domo fuit, et ibi dixit *miserere mei*, et tunc recessit Iesus: et illa sequuta est eum.

1326. Tunc sequitur responsio Christi *ipse autem respondens* et cetera. Satis videbatur mulier pietatem ostendisse, sed haec videbatur naturalis, ideo Dominus exigebat professionem fidei. Ideo abiiciebat eam, et dixit *non sum missus nisi ad oves quae perierunt domus Israel*. Hebraeorum erat peculiaris, unde dicebant: *nos autem populus eius et oves pascuae eius*. Et illae oves perierant, quia abducti erant per diversas observantias; unde supra IX, 26: *videns turbas misertus est eis, quia erant vexati et iacentes sicut oves non habentes pastorem*; Ps. CXVIII, v. 176: *erravi sicut ovis quae periit*.

1327. Sed quid est quod dicit *non sum missus nisi ad oves quae perierunt domus Israel*? Nonne habetur Is. XLIX, 6: *dedi te in lucem gentium, ut sis salus mea usque ad extremum terrae*? Ergo non solum ad Iudaeos missus est, sed et ad gentes.

Dicendum quod ad omnes missus est, ut omnes in unum congregaret, sed missus est primo ad Iudaeos, ut Iudaeos ad gentes transferret; Rom. XV, 8: *dico autem Christum Iesum ministrum fuisse circumcisionis propter veritatem Dei, ad confirmandas promissiones patrum*.

1328. *At illa venit, et adoravit*, unde ingerit se. Et primo ponitur professio istius; secundo responsio.

Ponitur professio, quia Deum recognovit, quia eum adoravit. Licet enim haberet repulsus apostolorum, tamen ingessit se, et adoravit. In hoc Deum recognoscit; Deut. VIII, v. 19: *Dominum Deum tuum adorabis, et illi soli servies*; Ps. LXV, 4: *omnis terra adoret te, Deus* et cetera. *Adiuva me*. Non dicit, *ora pro me*, sed, tu *adiuva me*, quia potes; Ps. CXX, 2: *auxilium meum a Domino qui fecit caelum et terram* et cetera.

1329. *Qui respondens dixit: non est bonum sumere panem filiorum, et mittere canibus*. Hoc additur ad probandum humilitatem, quia iam constabat satis de fide, ostendens excellentiam Iudaeorum ad gentes: tunc enim probatur humilitas, quando patitur quod exprobretur gens sua; unde dicit *non est bonum* et cetera. Iudaei vocabantur *filii*, unde: *filios enutrivi et exaltavi; ipsi autem spreverunt me*: quia ipsi instructi erant in mandatis Dei, Io. X, 34. Panis est doctrina; Eccli. XV, 3: *cibavit eos pane vitae et intellectus*. Panis iste potest dici miracula domini, vel documenta legis. Hic ergo panis fidelibus, scilicet Iudaeis, debetur. *Non est ergo bonum sumere panem filiorum*, idest Iudaeorum, qui iamdiu sunt filii, *et mittere canibus*, scilicet gentilibus: quia sicut canis est animal immundum, sic gentes. Unde supra VII, 6: *nolite sanctum dare canibus*. Unde non adhuc

without doubt it first happened in the house, and there she said, *have mercy on me*, and then Jesus withdrew, and she followed him.

1326. Then there follows Christ's response: *he, however, answering, said*. It seemed enough that the woman showed piety, but this seemed natural, so the Lord required a profession of faith. For this reason, he went away from her, and said, *I was not sent except to the lost sheep of the house of Israel*. He was the Hebrews' own, hence they said, *we are his people and the sheep of his pasture* (Ps 99:3). And those sheep had perished, because they were led away by different observances; hence above, *and seeing the multitudes, he had compassion on them: because they were distressed, and lying like sheep that have no shepherd* (Matt 9:36). *I have gone astray like a sheep that is lost* (Ps 118:176).

1327. But why does he say, *I was not sent except to the lost sheep of the house of Israel*? Is it not written in Isaiah, *behold, I have given you to be the light of the gentiles, that you may be my salvation even to the farthest part of the earth*? (Isa 49:6). Therefore, he was not only sent to the Jews, but also to the gentiles.

One should say that he was sent to all, so that he might gather all into one; but he was sent first to the Jews, so that he might carry the Jews over to the gentiles. *For I say that Christ Jesus was minister of the circumcision for the truth of God, to confirm the promises made unto the fathers* (Rom 15:8).

1328. *But she came and adored him*; hence she thrusts herself in. And first, this woman's profession is set down; second, the response.

The profession is set down, for she acknowledged God, since she adored him. For although she had the apostles pushing her away, yet she thrust herself in, and adored. By this, she acknowledged God; *you shall fear the Lord your God, and shall serve him only* (Deut. 6:13); *let all the earth adore you* (Ps 65:4). **Lord, help me**. She does not say, *pray for me*, but **help me**, because you can; *my help is from the Lord, who made heaven and earth* (Ps 120:2).

1329. *Answering, he said: it is not good to take the bread of the children, and give it to the dogs*. Since enough was established concerning faith, this is added to test her humility, showing the excellence of the Jews over the gentiles. For humility is tested when what reproaches one's race is suffered, hence he says, *it is not good to take the bread of children*. The Jews are called **children**, hence, *I have brought up children, and exalted them: but they have despised me* (Isa 1:2). For they were instructed in the commandments of God (John 10:34). The bread is teaching; *with the bread of life and understanding, she shall feed him* (Sir 15:3). Therefore, this bread should be given to the faithful, namely to the Jews. Therefore, *it is not good to take the bread of the children*, i.e., the Jews, who were already children for a long time, *and give it to the dogs*, namely to the gentiles, because just as a dog is an unclean animal, so

the gentiles. Hence above, ***do not give that which is holy to dogs*** (Matt 7:6). For they had not yet completely rejected him, but, as Jerome says, it is fitting that the Jews be called dogs, according to the Psalm, *many dogs have encompassed me* (Ps 21:17). And, *now we . . . are the children* (Gal 4:28).

1330. *At illa dixit: etiam, Domine*. Hic tangitur mira humilitas mulieris, et sapientia. Visus est contumeliam inferre genti suae, sed humilitatis est, quod concedit contumeliam dictam. Unde dicit ***etiam, Domine***.

Item maior ostenditur humilitas, quia ipse Dominus dixerat ***canes***, sed ista dixit ***catellos***; unde dicit ***nam et catelli edunt de micis***. Item Dominus vocaverat filios Iudaeos, sed ista dominos: unde dicit ***quae cadunt de mensa dominorum***. Et humiliter ita scivit compellere Dominum; quasi dicat, non peto, Domine, quod tot beneficia conferas nobis, quot Iudaeis, sed de micis des nobis; Eccli. c. XXXV, 21: *oratio humiliantis se penetrat caelos*. Et Ps. ci, 18: *respexit in orationem humilium*.

1331. Ideo Dominus exaudivit ***tunc respondens Iesus ait illi*** et cetera. Et tria facit. Primo ponitur eius commendatio; secundo exauditio; tertio effectus.

Quando se humiliat, dicit ***magna est fides tua***. Magna, quia magna credit. Item propter rectitudinem; Iac. I, 6: *postulet autem in fide nihil haesitans*. Item magna propter fervorem. Unde ***si habueritis fidem sicut granum sinapis, dicetis monti huic: transi hinc illuc, et transibit***.

Ideo sequitur exauditio ***fiat tibi sicut vis***; Ps. CXLIV, 19: *voluntatem timentium se faciet*.

Sequitur effectus ***et sanata est filia eius ex illa hora***. Unde principio, Gen. I, 3, dixit, *fiat lux, et facta est lux*: sic et hic, ***fiat tibi***; illud enim verbum fuit verbum aeternum; Eccle. VIII, 4: *sermo eius potestate plenus est*.

1330. *But she said: yes, Lord*. Here the woman's marvelous humility and wisdom are touched upon. He seemed to cast an insult on her race, but it belongs to humility that she concedes the insult spoken. Hence she says, ***yes, Lord***.

Likewise a greater humility is shown, because the Lord had said ***dogs***, but this woman said, ***whelps***; hence she says, ***but the whelps also eat of the crumbs***. Also, the Lord had called the Jews ***children***, but this woman calls them ***masters***: hence she says, ***that fall from the table of their masters***. And in this way, humbly, she knew how to compel the Lord; as though to say, I do not ask, Lord, that you bestow on us as many benefits as on the Jews, but give to us from the crumbs; *the prayer of him who humbles himself, will pierce the clouds* (Sir 35:21). And, *he has had regard to the prayer of the humble* (Ps 101:18).

1331. For this reason, the Lord responded: ***then Jesus answering, said to her***. And he does three things. First, his commendation is set down; second, the response; third, the effect.

While she humiliates herself, he says, ***great is your faith***. Great, because she believes great things. Also, because of uprightness; *let him ask in faith, nothing wavering* (Jas 1:6). Hence, ***if you have faith as a grain of mustard seed, you would say to this mountain: remove from here, and it would be removed*** (Matt 17:20).

So there follows the response: ***let it be done for you as you will***; *he will do the will of those who fear him* (Ps 144:19).

There follows the effect: ***and her daughter was cured from that hour***. Hence in the beginning, he said, *let there be light. And light was made* (Gen 1:3); so also here, ***let it be done to you***. For that word was an eternal word; *his word is full of power* (Eccl 8:4).

Lecture 3

15:29 Et cum transisset inde Iesus, venit secus Mare Galilaeae, et ascendens in montem sedebat ibi. [n. 1333]

15:30 Et accesserunt ad eum turbae multae, habentes secum mutos, caecos, claudos, debiles, et alios multos; et proiecerunt eos ad pedes eius, et curavit eos, [n. 1334]

15:31 ita ut turbae mirarentur videntes mutos loquentes, claudos ambulantes, caecos videntes: et magnificabant Deum Israel. [n. 1337]

15:32 Iesus autem convocatis discipulis suis, dixit: misereor turbae, quia triduo iam perseverant mecum, et non habent quod manducent; et dimittere eos ieiunos nolo, ne deficiant in via. [n. 1338]

15:33 Et dicunt ei discipuli: unde ergo nobis in deserto panes tantos, ut saturemus turbam tantam? [n. 1344]

15:34 Et ait illis Iesus: quot panes habetis? At illi dixerunt: septem, et paucos pisciculos. [n. 1345]

15:35 Et praecepit turbae, ut discumberent super terram. [n. 1346]

15:36 Et accipiens septem panes et pisces, et gratias agens fregit, et dedit discipulis, et discipuli dederunt populo, [n. 1347]

15:37 et comederunt omnes, et saturati sunt. Et quod superfuit de fragmentis, tulerunt septem sportas plenas. [n. 1348]

15:38 Erant autem qui manducaverant quatuor millia hominum, extra parvulos et mulieres. [n. 1350]

15:29 Καὶ μεταβὰς ἐκεῖθεν ὁ Ἰησοῦς ἦλθεν παρὰ τὴν θάλασσαν τῆς Γαλιλαίας, καὶ ἀναβὰς εἰς τὸ ὄρος ἐκάθητο ἐκεῖ.

15:30 καὶ προσῆλθον αὐτῷ ὄχλοι πολλοὶ ἔχοντες μεθ᾽ ἑαυτῶν χωλούς, τυφλούς, κυλλούς, κωφούς, καὶ ἑτέρους πολλοὺς καὶ ἔρριψαν αὐτοὺς παρὰ τοὺς πόδας αὐτοῦ, καὶ ἐθεράπευσεν αὐτούς·

15:31 ὥστε τὸν ὄχλον θαυμάσαι βλέποντας κωφοὺς λαλοῦντας, κυλλοὺς ὑγιεῖς καὶ χωλοὺς περιπατοῦντας καὶ τυφλοὺς βλέποντας· καὶ ἐδόξασαν τὸν θεὸν Ἰσραήλ.

15:32 Ὁ δὲ Ἰησοῦς προσκαλεσάμενος τοὺς μαθητὰς αὐτοῦ εἶπεν· σπλαγχνίζομαι ἐπὶ τὸν ὄχλον, ὅτι ἤδη ἡμέραι τρεῖς προσμένουσίν μοι καὶ οὐκ ἔχουσιν τί φάγωσιν· καὶ ἀπολῦσαι αὐτοὺς νήστεις οὐ θέλω, μήποτε ἐκλυθῶσιν ἐν τῇ ὁδῷ.

15:33 καὶ λέγουσιν αὐτῷ οἱ μαθηταί· πόθεν ἡμῖν ἐν ἐρημίᾳ ἄρτοι τοσοῦτοι ὥστε χορτάσαι ὄχλον τοσοῦτον;

15:34 καὶ λέγει αὐτοῖς ὁ Ἰησοῦς· πόσους ἄρτους ἔχετε; οἱ δὲ εἶπαν· ἑπτὰ καὶ ὀλίγα ἰχθύδια.

15:35 καὶ παραγγείλας τῷ ὄχλῳ ἀναπεσεῖν ἐπὶ τὴν γῆν

15:36 ἔλαβεν τοὺς ἑπτὰ ἄρτους καὶ τοὺς ἰχθύας καὶ εὐχαριστήσας ἔκλασεν καὶ ἐδίδου τοῖς μαθηταῖς, οἱ δὲ μαθηταὶ τοῖς ὄχλοις.

15:37 καὶ ἔφαγον πάντες καὶ ἐχορτάσθησαν. καὶ τὸ περισσεῦον τῶν κλασμάτων ἦραν ἑπτὰ σπυρίδας πλήρεις.

15:38 οἱ δὲ ἐσθίοντες ἦσαν τετρακισχίλιοι ἄνδρες χωρὶς γυναικῶν καὶ παιδίων.

15:29 And when Jesus had gone away from there, he came near the Sea of Galilee. And going up into a mountain, he sat there. [n. 1333]

15:30 And there came to him great multitudes, having with them the dumb, the blind, the lame, the feeble, and many others, and they laid them down at his feet, and he healed them, [n. 1334]

15:31 so that the multitudes marvelled seeing the dumb speak, the lame walk, and the blind see, and they glorified the God of Israel. [n. 1337]

15:32 And Jesus called together his disciples, and said: I have compassion on the multitudes, because they have been with me now three days, and have nothing to eat, and I will not send them away fasting, lest they faint on the way. [n. 1338]

15:33 And the disciples say to him: where are we to find so many loaves in the desert in order to fill so great a multitude? [n. 1344]

15:34 And Jesus said to them: how many loaves do you have? But they said: seven, and a few little fish. [n. 1345]

15:35 And he commanded the multitude to sit down upon the ground. [n. 1346]

15:36 And taking the seven loaves and the fish, and giving thanks, he broke, and gave to his disciples, and the disciples gave them to the people. [n. 1347]

15:37 And they all ate, and were filled. And they collected seven baskets full of what remained of the fragments. [n. 1348]

15:38 And those who ate were four thousand men, beside children and women. [n. 1350]

15:39 Et dimissa turba, ascendit in naviculam, et venit in fines Magedan. [n. 1353]	**15:39** Καὶ ἀπολύσας τοὺς ὄχλους ἐνέβη εἰς τὸ πλοῖον καὶ ἦλθεν εἰς τὰ ὅρια Μαγαδάν.	**15:39** And having dismissed the multitude, he went up into a boat, and came into the coasts of Magedan. [n. 1353]

1332. Supra confirmata doctrina evangelica per liberationem gentilium a potestate daemonum per virtutem Christi, nunc confirmat per liberationem ab infirmitatibus spiritualibus per hoc quod multos curavit.

Et tria facit.
Primo ponitur locus;
secundo oblatio;
tertio liberatio.

Secunda ibi *et accesserunt ad eum turbae multae* etc.; tertia ibi *et curavit eos*.

1333. Describitur primo locus in generali, quia *cum transisset*, scilicet de regione gentilium, *venit iuxta mare*, quod erat in Iudaea, quod aliquando vocatur Genesareth, aliquando Mare Galilaeae. Per hoc quod revertitur ad Iudaeos, significatur quia reliquiae Israel salvabuntur; ad Rom. XI, 5: *sic ergo et in hoc tempore reliquiae secundum electionem gratiae Dei salvae factae sunt*.

Deinde describitur locus in speciali, dicens *et ascendens in montem sedebat*. Per montem significatur altitudo verbi; Ps. XXXV, 7: *iustitia tua sicut montes Dei*. Sed Iesus non stabat, sed sedebat, quia nisi descendisset, non cognovissemus, secundum illud Ps. CXLIII, v. 5: *Domine, inclina caelos tuos et descende*. Item per montem altitudo gloriae, ut habetur Gen. XIX, 17: *in monte salvum te fac* etc., ad significandum quod ibi est vera quies, non hic; ad Hebr. XIII, 14: *non habemus hic manentem civitatem, sed futuram inquirimus*, idest futuram expectamus.

1334. Sequitur oblatio *et accesserunt ad eum turbae multae* et cetera. Et primo ponitur quantum ad multitudinem turbarum; secundo quantum ad oblationem infirmorum; tertio quantum ad modum.

Circa primum *tunc accesserunt ad eum turbae multae*; Ps. LXXXV, 9: *omnes gentes quascumque fecisti, venient, et adorabunt coram te, Domine*.

1335. Et non accesserunt vacui, quia *secum habentes mutos, caecos, claudos* et cetera. Et in hoc significatur quod qui convertuntur ad Dominum, debent offerre alios Domino: et hoc est quod dicit *habentes mutos, caecos, claudos et debiles*.

'Debilis' Latine significat defectum virtutis, sed Graece dicitur qui habet manum debilem: sicut enim 'claudus' dicitur qui in pedibus laesus est, sic 'debilis' qui manum aridam habet.

Per istos significantur diversa genera morborum spiritualium. Per mutos significantur illi, qui Deum laudare

1332. Above, the evangelical teaching was confirmed by the liberation of the gentiles from demons' power through the power of Christ; now he confirms it by liberation from spiritual weaknesses, by the fact that he healed many people.

And he does three things:
first, the place is set down;
second, the presentation;
third, the liberation.

The second is at *and there came to him great multitudes*; the third, at *and he healed them*.

1333. First, the place is described in general, since *when Jesus had gone away from there*, namely from the region of the gentiles, *he came near the sea* which was in Judea, which is sometimes called Gennesaret, sometimes the Sea of Galilee. The fact that he returned to the Jews signifies that a remnant of Israel will be saved; *even so then at this present time also, there is a remnant saved according to the election of grace* (Rom 11:5).

Then the place is described in particular, saying, *and going up into a mountain, he sat there*. The mountain signifies loftiness of word; *your justice is as the mountains of God* (Ps 35:7). But Jesus did not stand, but sat, because unless he had come down, we would not have known him, following *Lord, bow down your heavens and descend* (Ps 143:5). Also, the mountain signifies the loftiness of glory, as is had from *save yourself in the mountain, lest you be also consumed* (Gen 19:17), to signify that true rest is found in that place, not here. *For we have not here a lasting city, but we seek one that is to come* (Heb 13:14), i.e., we await the one to come.

1334. There follows the presentation: *and there came to him great multitudes*. And it is set down first, as regards the greatness of the crowds; second, as regards the presentation of the sick; third, as regards the manner of the presentation.

Concerning the first, *and there came to him great multitudes*; *all the nations you have made shall come and adore before you, O Lord* (Ps 85:9).

1335. And they had not come empty handed, for *having with them the dumb, the blind, the lame*. And in this is signified that those who are converted to the Lord should offer others to the Lord; and this is what it says, *having with them the dumb, the blind, the lame, the feeble*.

'Feeble' signifies a defect in power in Latin, but in Greek it means one who has a feeble hand: for as 'lame' means one who is wounded in the feet, so 'feeble' means one who has a withered hand.

These signify the various kinds of spiritual illnesses. The mute signify those who cannot praise God, about whom

Isaiah says, *dumb dogs not able to bark* (Isa 56:10). The lame mean those who never walk firmly toward the good, but are suddenly converted toward evil; *how long do you halt between two sides? If the Lord is God, follow him* (1 Kgs 18:21). The blind signify unbelievers, who are deprived of the light of faith; *we looked for light, and behold darkness* (Isa 59:9). The feeble, those who have a withered hand, signify those who have a feeble heart; *my strength is dried up like a potsherd* (Ps 21:16).

And many others. They showed great faith by this, for they brought not only themselves, but others.

1336. They show their devotion by their manner of presentation: for sometimes they ask that he lay his hands on them, as above (Matt 9), and sometimes that he might touch the edge of his garment to them, as above in the same place (Matt 9; 14). But now it was enough to place them at his feet. And by this, mystically, we are given to understand that we should not subject to ourselves the sinners whom we convert, in accord with what is said, *let a man so account of us as of the ministers of Christ, and the dispensers of the mysteries of God* (1 Cor 4:1).

1337. There follows concerning the healing. And first, the healing is set down; second, the wonderment; third, the effect.

It says then, **and he healed them**; *he sent his word, and healed them: and delivered them from their destructions* (Ps 106:20). And in another place, *who forgives all your iniquities: who heals all your diseases* (Ps 102:3). And there follows the admiration: **so that the multitudes marvelled seeing the dumb speak**. Here the effect is set down. This was predicted: *then will the eyes of the blind be opened, and the ears of the deaf will be unstopped* (Isa 35:5); and, *wonderful are your works* (Ps 138:14).

But it is asked: why is no mention made of the feeble? Because there was no opposite act to which it could correspond.

But consider that some blasphemed when they saw miracles, as is said above (Matt 14), but these praised God greatly; hence, **and they glorified the God of Israel**.

1338. And Jesus called together his disciples. Here Christ's teaching is shown to be praiseworthy by the refreshment of the good. And

first, the motive is set down;
second, the matter;
third, the distribution;
fourth, the refreshment.

The second is at **and the disciples say to him**; the third, at **and he commanded the multitude to sit down upon the ground**; the fourth, at **and they all ate, and were filled**.

1339. One should notice that this motive is set down after the foregoing things, because the sick cannot eat, since *their soul abhorred all manner of meat* (Ps 106:18). Therefore it was necessary that before they should eat, they be healed:

spiritualibus. Augustinus: *palato infirmo poena est panis, qui sano est amabilis et cetera.* Et ideo Dominus post sanationem cibat.

Et notandum quod primo convocat discipulos ut reddat attentos, ut sint memores miraculi. Item ut det exemplum nobis quod quantumcumque sit homo magnus, debet se comportare minoribus; Eccli. III, 20: *quanto maior es, humilia te in omnibus.*

1340. Unde **convocatis discipulis suis, dixit: misereor turbae** et cetera. Hoc fuit motivum, unde ostendit humanitatem convenientem divinitati. Misericordia est passio, quia misericors est 'miserum cor habens,' qui reputat alienam miseriam suam. Sed misericordia maxime Deo convenit; Ps. CII, 8: *miserator et misericors Dominus, longanimis et multum misericors.* Et quam reputat ut suam, repellere debet ut suam. Unde Dominus inquantum repellit miseriam, dicitur misericors.

Sed ponitur motivum miserendi triplex.
Primo ponit perseverantiam;
secundo inopiam;
tertio periculum imminens.

1341. Primo ponitur perseverantia, cum dicitur **quia triduo iam perseverant mecum**. Ex quo potestis cognoscere quod qui cum Christo perseverant, pane suo reficiuntur: quia *qui perseveraverit usque in finem, hic salvus erit.*

Per **triduum** potestis intelligere confessionem sanctae Trinitatis; unde infra ult., 19: *euntes in universum mundum, baptizate in nomine Patris, et Filii, et Spiritus Sancti.* Vel triplicem actum, scilicet cordis, oris et operis. Item triplex tempus saeculi, scilicet tempus legis naturae, legis Mosaicae, et legis gratiae et gloriae in fine. Ps. XVI, 15: *satiabor, cum apparuerit gloria tua.* Vel per triduum, triduum mortis Christi. Unde illi triduo sustinent dominum, qui conformarunt se morti Christi; Osee VI, 3: *vivificabit nos post triduum, et in die tertia suscitabit nos.* Unde per mortem Christi expectamus iustificationem. Ad Gal. ult., 17: *semper mortificationem Iesu in corpore nostro portantes.*

1342. Secundum quod tangitur est inopia; unde dicit **non habent quid manducent**. Sed quare per triduum expectavit? Ne possent calumniari, quia refecti essent cibo, quem secum portaverant.

Secundum mysterium, illorum miseretur qui suam miseriam cognoscunt; Apoc. III, 17: *nescit quia miser es, et miserabilis, et pauper, et caecus, et nudus et cetera.*

so it is also in spiritual matters. Augustine: *to the sick palate, bread is punishment, which to the healthy is delightful.* And for this reason, the Lord feeds after the healing.

And one should note that he first calls the disciples together in order to make them attentive, so that they would remember the miracle. Likewise, that he might give them an example, that however great a man may be, he should associate himself with the lesser; *the greater you are, the more humble yourself in all things* (Sir 3:20).

1340. Hence, **and Jesus called together his disciples, and said: I have compassion on the multitudes**. This was the motive, by which he shows his humanity coming together with his divinity. Compassion is a suffering, because *misericors* is 'having a suffering heart,' which considers another's misery its own. But compassion belongs most of all to God; *the Lord is compassionate and merciful: longsuffering and plenteous in mercy* (Ps 102:8). And what is reckoned as one's own, ought to be repelled as one's own. Hence the Lord, insofar as he repels suffering, is said to be merciful.

But a threefold motive for compassion is set down:
first, their perseverance is set down;
second, their poverty;
third, the imminent danger.

1341. First, perseverance is set down, when it says, **because they have been with me now three days**. From this you can know that they who persevere with Christ are refreshed with his own bread, for **but he who will persevere to the end, he will be saved** (Matt 24:13).

By the **three days**, you can understand the confession of the holy Trinity; hence below, **going therefore, teach all nations, baptizing them in the name of the Father, and of the Son, and of the Holy Spirit** (Matt 28:19). Or the threefold act, namely of heart, of mouth, and of deed. Also, the threefold time of the age, namely the time of the natural law, the time of the Mosaic law, and the time of the law of grace and glory in the end. *I will be satisfied when your glory appears* (Ps 16:15). Or by the three days, the three days of Christ's death. Hence those endure with Christ for three days who conform themselves to Christ's death. *He will revive us after three days, and on the third day he will raise us up* (Hos 6:3). Hence we await justification through Christ's death. *Always bearing about in our body the mortification of Jesus* (Gal 6:17).

1342. The second thing touched upon is their poverty; hence he says, **and have nothing to eat**. But why did he wait for three days? Lest they be able to slander him because they were refreshed by food which they had carried with them.

According to a mystery, he has compassion on those who know their own misery; *and know not, that you are wretched, and miserable, and poor, and blind, and naked* (Rev 3:17).

1343. Tertium est periculum *et dimittere eos ieiunos nolo, ne deficiant in via*. Deficiunt enim in via qui verbo Dei non reficiuntur; Deut. VIII, 3: *non in solo pane vivit homo, sed in omni verbo, quod procedit de ore Dei*; Eccli. XV, 3: *cibavit eum pane vitae et intellectus*.

1344. *Et dicunt ei discipuli* et cetera. Hic ponitur materia. Et primo, quomodo dedit; secundo, quanta materia aderat.

Unde dicit *et dicunt: unde ergo in deserto panes tantos?* Hic tarditas et oblivio discipulorum reprehenditur, quia supra Dominus satiaverat ex quinque panibus quinque millia. Unde ex tarditate et oblivione reprehenduntur.

Secundum mysterium, in hoc gratia Dei et misericordia significatur, qui indignis mysteria sua revelat, et per eos sacramenta ministrat; Ier. I, 6: *nescio loqui, Domine, quia puer sum*. Cui dominus: *noli dicere, quia puer ego sum*; Ex. IV, 10: *impeditioris sum linguae, et tardioris* et cetera. Is. III, 7: *nam sum mendicus, et in domo mea non est panis, nolite me constituere principem populi*.

1345. Deinde ponitur quanta materia aderat; unde *ait illis Iesus; quot panes habetis?* Et non petiit ut ignorans, sed ut miraculum ostenderetur. Unde et paucos pisciculos, supra, in alio miraculo, commemorari fecit. Et dicitur, quod quinque panes habebant, et duos pisces, in quibus doctrina legis significabatur; et illi panes erant hordeacei; hic sunt septem, et non dicuntur hordeacei; in quibus significatur lex nova septiformi gratia Dei informata. Item in illa duo tantum fuerant pisces, in hac autem multi pisciculi. *Vos elegit Deus pauperes in mundo, divites in fide*. Et in Ps. VIII, 9: *volucres caeli et pisces maris, qui perambulant semitas maris*, idest huius mundi.

1346. *Et praecepit turbae ut discumberent super terram*. Hic ponitur dispositio. Et primo disponit; secundo materiam accipit; tertio gratias agit, et frangit, et distribuit.

Dicit ergo *et praecepit*. In alia refectione habetur quod fecit *super foenum recumbere*. Per foenum temporalia significantur; unde Is. XL, 6: *omnis caro foenum, et omnis gloria eius quasi flos agri*. Unde in veteri lege erat fundamentum super temporalia, in nova solum super stabilitatem gloriae; Eccle. I, 4: *terra autem in aeternum stat*. Vel per foenum significatur, quod super temporalia debemus sedere. Unde possessio non prohibetur, sed dilectio, sive affectio; I Ioan. II, 15: *nolite diligere ea, quae in mundo sunt*.

1347. *Et accipiens septem panes*: in quo significatur quod quidquid de spiritualibus administratum est aliis, primo fuit in Christo; unde Act. I, 1: *coepit Iesus*

1343. Third is the danger: *and I will not send them away fasting, lest they faint in the way*. For those faint on the road who are not refreshed with the word of God; *not in bread alone does man live, but in every word that proceeds from the mouth of God* (Deut 8:3). *With the bread of life and understanding, she will feed him* (Sir 15:3).

1344. *And the disciples say to him*. Here the matter is set down. And first, how he gave; second, how much matter was present.

Hence it says, *and the disciples say to him: where are we to find so many loaves?* Here the disciples' slowness and forgetfulness is reproached, because above the Lord had satisfied five thousand out of five loaves. Hence they are reproached for slowness and forgetfulness.

According to a mystery, this signifies the grace and compassion of God, who reveals his mysteries to the unworthy, and through them administers the sacraments; *Lord God: I do not know how to speak, for I am a child*. To which the Lord said: *say not: I am a child* (Jer 1:6). *I have more impediment and slowness of tongue* (Exod 4:10). *I am no healer, and in my house there is no bread, nor clothing: make me not ruler of the people* (Isa 3:7).

1345. Then is set down how much matter was present; hence, *and Jesus said to them: how many loaves do you have?* And he did not ask as though he were ignorant, but to show a miracle. Hence he also caused the small fish in the other miracle above to be remembered. And it says that they had five loaves and two fishes (Matt 14:17), which signified the teachings of the law; and those loaves were barley loaves. Here there are seven, and they are not called barley loaves. These things signify the new law, shaped by the sevenfold grace of God. Likewise, in the previous miracle there were only two fish, but in this one many little fish. *Has not God chosen the poor in this world, rich in faith?* (Jas 2:5). And, *the birds of the air, and the fishes of the sea, that pass through the paths of the sea* (Ps 8:9), i.e., of this world.

1346. *And he commanded the multitude to sit down upon the ground*. Here the arrangement is set down. And first, he arranges; second, he takes the matter; third, he gives thanks, and breaks, and distributes.

It says then, *he commanded*. In the other refreshment, it says that he made them *sit down on the grass* (Matt 14:19). The grass signifies temporal things; hence, *all flesh is grass, and all the glory thereof as the flower of the field* (Isa 40:6). Hence in the old law there was a foundation upon temporal things; in the new, only upon the stability of glory; *the earth stands for ever* (Eccl 1:4). Or the grass signifies that we should sit above temporal things. Hence possession is not forbidden, but rather delight, or affection; *love not the world, nor the things which are in the world* (1 John 2:15).

1347. *And taking the seven loaves*, which signifies that whatever spiritual things are administered to others were first in Christ; hence, *Jesus began to do and to teach*

facere et docere. Omnia spiritualia in eo fuerunt. Unde Ioan. III, 34: *non dedit ei Deus Spiritum ad mensuram*.

Et gratias agens fregit, et dedit discipulis: unde dedit nobis exemplum ut gratias agamus; I ad Thess. V, 18: *in omnibus gratias agentes*. Deinde quia non omnibus omnia, ut habetur I ad Cor. ult. Item I ad Cor. XII, 4: *divisiones gratiarum sunt*.

Consequenter sequitur ordinata distributio, quia *et dedit discipulis, et discipuli dederunt populo*. Primo discipulis, qui erant mediatores; Deut. V, 5: *ego sequester et medius fui inter Deum et vos in tempore illo, ut annuntiarem vobis verba eius* et cetera. Et I ad Cor. IV, v. 5: *sic nos existimet homo, ut ministros Christi et dispensatores mysteriorum Dei*.

1348. Consequenter ponit quoad plenitudinem refectionis ex abundantia reliquiarum, et ex numero manducantium. *Et comederunt omnes*. Posset aliquis dicere, quod de pauco pane possunt multi accipere, ita quod quilibet parum; sed non sic, immo *saturati sunt*; unde usque ad saturitatem manducaverunt; Ps. LXXVII, 29: *manducaverunt, et saturati sunt omnes*. Item multae fuerunt reliquiae, quia tulerunt septem sportas.

1349. Sed quare, cum pauciores panes fuissent, plures reliquiae remanserunt, cum scilicet saturaverit quinque millia de quinque panibus?

Potest dici, quod idem sunt, vel plus, septem sportae quam duodecim cophini. Chrysostomus dicit quod diversa fecit miracula, et modo diverso, ut discipuli magis memores essent. In primo miraculo tot fuerunt reliquiae quot apostoli. Hic autem secundum numerum panum, in quo significatur quod spirituales homines refici debent septiformi gratia Dei; I ad Cor. II, 14: *animalis enim homo non percipit ea quae Dei sunt*.

1350. Sequitur numerus comedentium *erant autem qui manducaverunt, quatuor millia hominum*. Supra fuerunt quinque millia, quia vacabant quinque sensibus; vel propter quinque libros Moysi; hic autem quatuor propter quatuor virtutes cardinales, vel propter quatuor evangelistas.

Extra parvulos et mulieres. Sed quare excipiuntur isti? Quia imperfecti et infirmi a vera doctrina excluduntur; ad Eph. IV, 13: *donec occurramus omnes in virum perfectum* et cetera.

(Acts 1:1). All spiritual things were in him. Hence, *God does not give the Spirit by measure* (John 3:34).

And giving thanks, he broke, and gave to his disciples: hence he gave us an example, that we might give thanks; *in all things give thanks* (1 Thess 5:18). Then because not all things are for all men (1 Cor 16). Also, *now there are diversities of graces* (1 Cor 12:4).

Next, there follows the ordered distribution: **and gave to his disciples, and the disciples gave them to the people**. First to the disciples, who were mediators; *I was the mediator and stood between the Lord and you at that time, to show you his words* (Deut 5:5). And, *let a man so account of us as of the ministers of Christ, and the dispensers of the mysteries of God* (1 Cor 4:5).

1348. Next the plenitude of the refreshment is set down, from the abundance of leftovers, and from the number of those eating. **And they all ate, and were filled**. Someone might say that many could take from a little bread, so that each one took only a little; but it was not so, but rather they were filled. Hence they ate until they were filled; *so they did eat, and were filled exceedingly* (Ps 77:29). Also, there were many leftovers, because they took up seven baskets.

1349. But why did more leftovers remain when there were fewer loaves, namely when he satisfied the five thousand with five loaves?

It can be said that seven baskets is as much or more than twelve hand-baskets. Chrysostom says that he worked different miracles, and in different ways, so that the disciples would remember better. In the first miracle there were as many left-overs as there were apostles. But here it was according to the number of loaves, which signifies that spiritual men should be refreshed by the sevenfold grace of God; *but the sensual man perceives not these things that are of the Spirit of God* (1 Cor 2:14).

1350. There follows the number of those who ate: **and those who ate were four thousand men**. Above, there were five thousand, because they were free from the five senses, or on account of the five books of Moses (Matt 14); but here four, on account of the four cardinal virtues, or on account of the four evangelists.

Beside children and women. But why are they not included? Because the imperfect and the weak are excluded from the true teaching; *until we all meet into the unity of faith, and of the knowledge of the Son of God* (Eph 4:13).

Chapter 16

Lecture 1

16:1 Et accesserunt ad eum Pharisaei et Sadducaei tentantes, et rogaverunt eum, ut signum de caelo ostenderet eis. [n. 1354]

16:2 At ille respondens ait illis: facto vespere dicitis: serenum erit, rubicundum est enim caelum: [n. 1356]

16:3 et mane: hodie tempestas: rutilat enim triste caelum. Faciem ergo caeli diiudicare nostis, signa autem temporum non potestis scire? [n. 1356]

16:4 Generatio mala et adultera signum quaerit, et signum non dabitur ei, nisi signum Ionae prophetae. Et, relictis illis, abiit. [n. 1360]

16:5 Et cum venissent discipuli eius trans fretum, obliti sunt panes accipere. [n. 1363]

16:6 Qui dixit illis: intuemini et cavete a fermento Pharisaeorum et Sadducaeorum. [n. 1364]

16:7 At illi cogitabant intra se dicentes: quia panes non accepimus? [n. 1365]

16:8 Sciens autem Iesus dixit: quid cogitatis inter vos modicae fidei, quia panes non habetis? [n. 1366]

16:9 Nondum intellegitis, neque recordamini quinque panum et quinque milium hominum, et quot cophinos sumpsistis? [n. 1366]

16:10 Neque septem panum, et quattuor milium hominum, et quot sportas sumpsistis? [n. 1366]

16:1 Καὶ προσελθόντες οἱ Φαρισαῖοι καὶ Σαδδουκαῖοι πειράζοντες ἐπηρώτησαν αὐτὸν σημεῖον ἐκ τοῦ οὐρανοῦ ἐπιδεῖξαι αὐτοῖς.

16:2 ὁ δὲ ἀποκριθεὶς εἶπεν αὐτοῖς· [ὀψίας γενομένης λέγετε· εὐδία, πυρράζει γὰρ ὁ οὐρανός·

16:3 καὶ πρωΐ· σήμερον χειμών, πυρράζει γὰρ στυγνάζων ὁ οὐρανός. τὸ μὲν πρόσωπον τοῦ οὐρανοῦ γινώσκετε διακρίνειν, τὰ δὲ σημεῖα τῶν καιρῶν οὐ δύνασθε;]

16:4 γενεὰ πονηρὰ καὶ μοιχαλὶς σημεῖον ἐπιζητεῖ, καὶ σημεῖον οὐ δοθήσεται αὐτῇ εἰ μὴ τὸ σημεῖον Ἰωνᾶ. καὶ καταλιπὼν αὐτοὺς ἀπῆλθεν.

16:5 Καὶ ἐλθόντες οἱ μαθηταὶ εἰς τὸ πέραν ἐπελάθοντο ἄρτους λαβεῖν.

16:6 ὁ δὲ Ἰησοῦς εἶπεν αὐτοῖς· ὁρᾶτε καὶ προσέχετε ἀπὸ τῆς ζύμης τῶν Φαρισαίων καὶ Σαδδουκαίων.

16:7 οἱ δὲ διελογίζοντο ἐν ἑαυτοῖς λέγοντες ὅτι ἄρτους οὐκ ἐλάβομεν.

16:8 γνοὺς δὲ ὁ Ἰησοῦς εἶπεν· τί διαλογίζεσθε ἐν ἑαυτοῖς, ὀλιγόπιστοι, ὅτι ἄρτους οὐκ ἔχετε;

16:9 οὔπω νοεῖτε, οὐδὲ μνημονεύετε τοὺς πέντε ἄρτους τῶν πεντακισχιλίων καὶ πόσους κοφίνους ἐλάβετε;

16:10 οὐδὲ τοὺς ἑπτὰ ἄρτους τῶν τετρακισχιλίων καὶ πόσας σπυρίδας ἐλάβετε;

16:1 And there came to him the Pharisees and Sadducees to tempt him, and they asked him to show them a sign from heaven. [n. 1354]

16:2 But he answered and said to them: when it is evening, you say: it will be fair weather, for the sky is red. [n. 1356]

16:3 And in the morning: today there will be a storm, for the sky is red and lowering. You know then how to discern the face of the sky; can you not know the signs of the times? [n. 1356]

16:4 A wicked and adulterous generation seeks after a sign, and a sign will not be given to it, except the sign of Jonah the prophet. And he left them, and went away. [n. 1360]

16:5 And when his disciples had crossed over the water, they had forgotten to take bread. [n. 1363]

16:6 He said to them: take heed and beware of the leaven of the Pharisees and Sadducees. [n. 1364]

16:7 But they thought within themselves, saying: because we have taken no bread. [n. 1365]

16:8 And Jesus knowing it, said: why do you think within yourselves, O you of little faith, that you have no bread? [n. 1366]

16:9 Do you not yet understand, do you neither remember the five loaves among five thousand men, and how many baskets you took up? [n. 1366]

16:10 Nor the seven loaves among four thousand men, and how many baskets you took up? [n. 1366]

16:11 Quare non intellegitis, quia non de pane dixi vobis: cavete a fermento Pharisaeorum et Sadducaeorum? [n. 1366]	**16:11** πῶς οὐ νοεῖτε ὅτι οὐ περὶ ἄρτων εἶπον ὑμῖν; προσέχετε δὲ ἀπὸ τῆς ζύμης τῶν Φαρισαίων καὶ Σαδδουκαίων.	**16:11** Why do you not understand that it was not concerning bread that I said to you: beware of the leaven of the Pharisees and Sadducees? [n. 1366]
16:12 Tunc intellexerunt, quia non dixerit cavendum a fermento panum, sed a doctrina Pharisaeorum et Sadducaeorum. [n. 1367]	**16:12** τότε συνῆκαν ὅτι οὐκ εἶπεν προσέχειν ἀπὸ τῆς ζύμης τῶν ἄρτων ἀλλὰ ἀπὸ τῆς διδαχῆς τῶν Φαρισαίων καὶ Σαδδουκαίων.	**16:12** Then they understood that he said not that they should beware of the leaven of bread, but of the doctrine of the Pharisees and Sadducees. [n. 1367]

1351. Supra Dominus ostendit sufficientiam evangelicae doctrinae, quia nec observantiis legalibus indiget, item quia non solum uni populo est necessaria, hic ostendit puritatem et excellentiam.

Primo ostendit eam puram servandam ab omni traditione;

secundo per altitudinem fidei omnes opiniones humanas transvolare, ibi **venit Iesus in partes Caesareae Philippi**.

Circa primum

primo describitur calumniosa tentatio;

secundo confutat;

tertio cavendum docet.

Secunda ibi **at ille respondens ait illis** etc.; tertia ibi **et cum venissent discipuli eius trans fretum** et cetera.

Circa primum

primo commemorat locum;

secundo ponitur tentativa interrogatio.

1352. Notandum quod sicut supra quando paverat de quinque panibus turbas, dimisit, et sic hic.

In hoc primo datur exemplum praedicatoribus quando non se ingerant, sed revertantur; Iob XXXIX, 5 de onagro: *quis dimisit onagrum liberum, et vincula eius quis solvit?* et cetera.

1353. Ascendit in naviculam, ne sequeretur eum turba. Unde ponitur impedimentum quare non posset eum sequi. Unde **ascendit in naviculam**, idest in mentem quae agitatur fluctibus huius mundi, Sap. XIV, 3: *quoniam dedisti in mari viam, et inter fluctus semitam*, ostendens quod debet ibi intrare, ut ibi requiescat. **Et venit in fines Magedan**. Magedan 'poma' interpretatur et per hunc locum Sacra Scriptura significatur, ubi poma simul cum aliis fructibus crescunt; Cant. VI, 10: *descendi ut viderem poma convallium*.

1354. Sequitur tentativa interrogatio **et accesserunt Pharisaei et Sadducaei tentantes, et rogaverunt eum**. Eccli. XIX, 23: *est qui nequiter se humiliat, et interiora eius plena sunt dolo*. **Ut signum de caelo ostenderet eis**.

1351. Above, the Lord showed the sufficiency of the evangelical teaching, because it does not need the legal observances, and also because it is necessary for not only one people; here he shows its purity and excellence.

First, he shows that it should be kept pure from every tradition;

second, that it flies across all human opinions by the loftiness of faith, at **and Jesus came into the regions of Cesarea Philippi** (Matt 16:13).

Concerning the first,

first, the slanderous temptation is described;

second, he refutes it;

third, he teaches that it should be avoided.

The second is at **but he answered and said to them**; the third, at **and when his disciples had crossed over the water**.

Concerning the first,

first, he recalls the place;

second, the tempters' question is set down.

1352. One should notice that just as above, when he sent the crowds away after he had fed them from the five loaves, so also here.

In this first an example is given to preachers, that they not thrust themselves in, but turn back; concerning a wild ass: *who has sent out the wild ass free, and who has loosed his bonds?* (Job 39:5).

1353. He went up into a boat (Matt 15:39), lest the crowd should follow him. Hence an impediment is set up, which is why they could not follow him. Hence, **he went up into a boat**, i.e., into the mind which is tossed about with the waves of this world, *you have made a way even in the sea, and a most sure path among the waves* (Wis 14:3), showing that one should enter there, and there find rest. **And came into the coasts of Magedan**. Magedan is interpreted 'apple,' and this place signifies the Holy Scriptures, where the apple grows together with the other fruits; *I went down into the garden of nuts, to see the apples of the valleys* (Song 6:10).

1354. There follows the tempters' question: **and there came to him the Pharisees and Sadducees to tempt him: and they asked him**. *There is one that humbles himself wickedly, and his interior is full of deceit* (Sir 19:23). **To show**

Et petierunt signum de caelo. Habetur Io. VI, 49: *patres vestri manducaverunt manna in deserto*, unde panem de caelo dedit eis. Et I Cor. I, v. 22: *Iudaei signa petunt*. Et in Ps. LXXIII, v. 9: *signa nostra non vidimus* et cetera.

1355. Tunc reprehendit eos, et primo de ignavia ad credendum divina. Si enim aliquis defectum habet ex natura sensuum, excusationem habet; sed cum habet sapientiam in terrenis, et ignaviam in spiritualibus, reprehendendus est; Sap. XIII, 1: *vani sunt omnes filii hominum, in quibus non est scientia Dei*. Et

primo ostendit solertiam in terrenis;
secundo ignaviam in spiritualibus.

1356. Dicit ergo *at ille respondens ait: vespere facto* et cetera. Hoc habet sensum litteralem et mysticum.

Litteralem, quia ex aliqua dispositione poterant cognoscere signum serenitatis. **Dicitis: serenum erit: rubicundum est enim caelum**. Item tempestatis, quia dicitis **hodie erit tempestas: rutilat enim triste caelum**, quia tristitiam designat. Quando enim aer est turbidus, non sunt homines ita laeti. Rubedo enim serotina est signum serenitatis. Ratio est, secundum Philosophum, ex diffusione radiorum solis super vapores. Quando enim vapores sunt multi, tunc radii non possunt penetrare, et tunc fit color niger in aere; quando vero subtiles, penetrant. Sed quando quod est igneum dominatur, tunc apparet color rubeus, ut apparet in flamma, quia cum magis elevatur, magis apparet rubedo in ea. Ideo significatur quod vapores non sunt multi, et significatur serenitas. Sed cum mane aliquando resolvitur in rorem, vel in pluviam, est signum tempestatis.

1357. Secundum mysterium per vespere significatur passio Christi. Vespere sol occidit, sic Christus vespere mundi passus est; Mal. III, 2: *quis poterit cogitare diem adventus eius, et quis stabit ad videndum eum? Ipse enim quasi ignis conflans*; Ps. XXIX, 6: *ad vesperum demorabitur fletus, et ad matutinum laetitia*. Unde rutilans apparuit in vespere, et significavit tranquillitatem; Tob. III, v. 22: *post tempestatem tranquillitatem facis, et post lacrimationem et fletum exultationem infundis*. In resurrectione, quae per mane significatur, apparuit rubedo in martyribus, et significat tempestatem peccatoribus. Vel per mane significatur mane diei iudicii, quem praecedet rubor; Ps. XCVI, 3: *ignis ante ipsum praecedet*.

Unde estis instructi in istis terrenis.

1358. *Faciem caeli diiudicare nostis, signa autem temporum non potestis scire?* Duo sunt tempora: unum respondet adventui primo, aliud adventui secundo. Quaedam signa praecesserunt primum adventum; Is. XLV, v. 8: *rorate, caeli, desuper, et nubes pluant iustum: aperiatur terra, et germinet salvatorem* et cetera. Et cap. XLV, 15: *vere tu es Deus absconditus*. Sed in fine Deus

them a sign from heaven. And they ask for a sign from heaven. It is written in John, *your fathers ate manna in the desert* (John 6:49), hence he gave them bread from heaven. And, *the Jews require signs* (1 Cor 1:22). And, *our signs we have not seen* (Ps 73:9).

1355. Then he reproaches them, and first, for laziness in believing divine things. For if someone has a defect from the nature of the senses, he has an excuse; but when he has wisdom in earthly things, and laziness in spiritual things, he is to be reproached. *But all men are vain, in whom there is not the knowledge of God* (Wis 13:1). And

first, he points out their cleverness in earthly things;
second, their laziness in spiritual things.

1356. It says then, **but he answered and said to them: when it is evening**. This has a literal sense, and a mystical one.

The literal, that from a certain arrangement they could recognize the sign of fair weather. **You say, it will be fair weather, for the sky is red**. Likewise of a storm, for you say, **today there will be a storm, for the sky is red and lowering**, since it indicates sorrow. For when the air is disturbed, men are not joyful. For redness in the evening is a sign of fair weather. The reason, according to the Philosopher, is the diffusion of the sun's rays over the vapors. For when there are many vapors, then the rays cannot penetrate, and then the air becomes black; but when the vapors are thin, they penetrate. But when what is fiery dominates, then the color red appears, as it appears in flames, because when it is more lifted up, the red appears in it more. Therefore it indicates that there are not many vapors, and indicates fair weather. But when it is resolved into dew or rain in the morning, it is a sign of a storm.

1357. According to a mystery, the evening signifies Christ's passion. The sun dies in the evening, and in the same way, Christ suffered in the evening of the world; *and who will be able to think of the day of his coming? And who will stand to see him? For he is like a refining fire* (Mal 3:2); *in the evening weeping will have place, and in the morning gladness* (Ps 29:6). Hence the reddening sky appears in the evening, and indicates tranquillity; *after a storm you make a calm, and after tears and weeping you pour in joyfulness* (Tob 3:22). In the resurrection, which is signified by the morning, redness appears in the martyrs, and indicates a storm for sinners. Or, by the morning is signified the morning of the day of judgment, which redness precedes; *a fire will go before him* (Ps 96:3).

Hence you are learned in earthly things.

1358. *You know then how to discern the face of the sky; can you not know the signs of the times?* There are two times: one corresponds to the first coming, the other to the second coming. Certain signs preceded the first coming; *drop down dew, you heavens, from above, and let the clouds rain the just: let the earth be opened, and bud forth a savior* (Isa 45:8). And, *verily you are a hidden God* (Isa 45:15). But

manifeste veniet, et non apparebunt signa de caelo. Sed non est tempus.

Vel aliter. **Faciem caeli diiudicare nostis** etc., quasi dicat, vos quaeritis signum adventus. Superfluum est signum petere, ubi sunt multa signa. Supra XI, 5: **caeci vident, claudi ambulant, leprosi mundantur** et cetera. Hoc signum dederat Is. XXXV, 4: *ipse dominus veniet, et salvabit nos; tunc aperientur oculi caecorum* et cetera.

1359. Quidam ex auctoritate ista arguunt, quod debemus satagere ad cognoscendum secundum adventum.

Augustinus autem exponit de primo adventu. Primus certissimus est, quia est ad salutem, salus per fidem, fides per cognitionem; ideo necessarium est ut agnoscatur. Sed secundus est ad remunerandum; ideo occultatur, ut homines magis sint sollicti.

1360. Deinde denegat signum petitum; unde dicitur **generatio mala et adultera signum quaerit**. Dicitur autem **generatio mala**, quia recedit a Deo: malum enim est per recessum a Deo. *Dereliquit Deum factorem suum, et recessit a Deo salutari suo*, ut habetur Deut. XXXII, 15. Sed **adultera**, quia alii se copulavit; Ps. XXVI: *si derelinquam te in vita mea*; Is. LV, 7: *derelinquat impius viam suam, et vir iniquus cogitationes suas*. **Signum petit**, et non debet habere, quia **signum non dabitur ei, nisi signum Ionae**, quia **sicut Ionas in ventre ceti fuit tribus diebus et tribus noctibus, ita** etc.; ut supra XII habitum est.

1361. Sed quare magis ponit signum resurrectionis quam aliud signum?

Dicendum, quod per resurrectionem nobis salus advenit; Rom. X, 9: *si credideris in corde tuo quod Christus resurrexit, salvus eris*, quia resurgendo vitam reparavit, quia per resurrectionem Christi resurgemus. Ideo istud signum datum est fidelibus, et omnia alia retorquentur ad istud, quia scilicet resuscitavit Lazarum et cetera. Unde istis non est datum aliud signum. Discipulis autem suis dedit signum de caelo, cum ostendit eis gloriam suam, ut habetur infra XVII. Sic ergo ostendit eorum ignaviam.

Sequitur pars, in qua confutat facto discedendo ab eis. **Et relictis illis, abiit**; non enim habitat cum malignis; Sap. I, 3: *separat se a perversis*.

1362. Postquam confutavit, docet eos vitari. Et

primo ponitur occasio;
secundo doctrina;
tertio malus intellectus discipulorum;
quarto reprehensio;
quinto effectus.

in the end, God will come manifestly, and there will not appear signs from heaven. But it is not the time.

Or in another way. **You know then how to discern the face of the sky**, as though to say, you seek a sign of the coming. It is superfluous to ask for a sign where there are many signs. Above, **the blind see, the lame walk, the lepers are cleansed** (Matt 11:5). He had given this sign, *God himself will come and will save you. Then will the eyes of the blind be opened* (Isa 35:4–5).

1359. Some argue from this authority that we should bustle about to know of the second coming.

But Augustine explains it as about the first coming. The first coming is most certain, because it is for salvation, salvation through faith, faith through knowledge; therefore it is necessary that it be known. But the second coming is for giving rewards; therefore it is hidden, so that men may be more concerned.

1360. Then he denies the sign asked; hence it says, **a wicked and adulterous generation seeks after a sign**. And it says, **a wicked generation**, because it draws back from God: for it is wicked through drawing back from God. *He forsook God who made him, and departed from God his savior* (Deut 32:15). But **adulterous**, because it joined itself to others; *if I abandon you in my life* (Ps 26); *let the wicked forsake his way, and the unjust man his thoughts* (Isa 55:7). **Seeks after a sign**, and should not have it, for **a sign will not be given to it, except the sign of Jonas the prophet**, for **as Jonas was in the whale's belly for three days and three nights: so will the Son of man be in the heart of the earth** (Matt 12:40).

1361. But why does he set down the sign of the resurrection rather than another sign?

One should say that salvation comes to us through the resurrection; *for if you . . . believe in your heart that God has raised him up from the dead, you shall be saved* (Rom 10:9), because he renewed life by rising again, since we rise again through Christ's resurrection. For this reason, this sign is given to the faithful, and all other signs are referred back to it, namely that he reawakened Lazarus and so forth. Hence to these no other sign is given. But to his disciples he gave a sign from heaven, when he showed them his glory (Matt 17). So then he pointed out their laziness.

There follows the part in which he refutes them by deed, by withdrawing from them. **And he left them, and went away**, for he does not dwell with the spiteful; *for perverse thoughts separate from God* (Wis 1:3).

1362. After he refuted them, he teaches the disciples to avoid them. And

first, the occasion is set down;
second, the teaching;
third, the disciples' bad understanding;
fourth, a reproach;
fifth, the effect.

1363. Dicit *et cum venissent discipuli eius trans fretum* et cetera. In hoc admirari debemus mentes discipulorum, quia non solent homines oblivisci nisi eorum de quibus parum curant: unde cum obliti essent panes, parum curabant de eis, sed solum de spiritualibus.

1364. *Quia dixit: intuemini, et cavete* et cetera. Hic ponitur doctrina. Per fermentum intelligit doctrinam corruptam; unde non intelligit doctrinam legis, sed traditiones Pharisaeorum, quae vocantur fermentum, quia sicut ex modico fermento totum corrumpitur, sic ex modico errore tota vita corrumpitur, sicut de via a qua parum homo recedit, postmodum elongatur: unde Philosophus in I *Coeli* dicit quod parvus error in principio, magnus fit in fine. Spiritualis intellectus est panis, non fermentum. Unde per panem vera doctrina intelligitur; Eccli. XV, v. 3: *cibavit eum pane vitae et intellectus*.

Unde dicitur **intuemini, et cavete**, quia falsa doctrina est periculosa. Dum enim manet fides in homine, non est periculum; sed quando fundamentum ablatum est, non est spes. Ps. CXXXVI, 7: *exinanite, exinanite usque ad fundamentum in ea*. Fundamentum est fides; ad Titum ult., 10: *haereticum hominem post primam et secundam admonitionem devita*. Quia falsa doctrina habet colorem, ideo dicit **intuemini**, idest diligenter considerate; Prov. IV, 25: *oculi tui recta videant, et palpebrae tuae praecedant gressus tuos*.

1365. Consequenter ponitur intellectus discipulorum: *at illi cogitabant* et cetera. Quia enim supra septem sportas fragmentorum acceperant, et non secum tulerant, credebant quod diceret, non accepistis panes; sed nolo quod a Pharisaeis accipiatis panes, quia animales erant, *et animalis homo non percipit quae Dei sunt*, I Cor. II, 14.

1366. In isto intellectu in duobus poterant reprehendi.

Primo, quia non intelligebant; item in eo quod de virtute Dei diffidebant. De primo non reprehendit eos, sed de secundo.

Dicit ergo *quid cogitatis inter vos modicae fidei, quia panes non habetis?* Quasi dicat, intelligitis carnaliter quod spiritualiter debetis intelligere. **Non recordamini quinque panum, et quinque millia hominum, et quot cophinos sumpsistis?** Nonne ergo qui tot pavi, possum vos pascere? *Quare non intelligitis, quia non de pane dixi vobis*, scilicet materiali, sed potius spirituali; qui panis doctrina dicitur in Io. VI, 64: *verba quae locutus sum vobis, spiritus et vita sunt*.

1367. *Tunc intellexerunt* et cetera. Hic ponitur correctio. Unde correcti sunt ex sermone eius;

1363. It says, *and when his disciples had crossed over the water*. In this, we should wonder at the disciples' minds, because men are only accustomed to forget those things which they care little about; so since they forgot bread, they cared little about it, but only about spiritual things.

1364. *He said to them: take heed and beware*. Here the teaching is set down. By leaven one understands corrupt teaching; hence one does not take it to mean the teaching of the law, but the traditions of the Pharisees, which are called leaven because, just as the whole is corrupted by a little bit of leaven, so a whole life is corrupted by a little bit of error, just as a man who withdraws a little way from a road is later separated a long way off. Hence the Philosopher says, in *On the Heavens* (Bk I), that a small error in the beginning becomes large in the end. Spiritual understanding is bread, not leaven. Hence by bread is meant true teaching; *with the bread of life and understanding, she shall feed him* (Sir 15:3).

Hence it says, *take heed and beware*, because false teaching is dangerous. For when a man remains in the faith, there is no danger; but when the foundation is taken away, there is no hope. *Raze it, raze it, even to the foundation thereof* (Ps 136:7). The foundation is faith; *a man that is a heretic, after the first and second admonition, avoid* (Titus 3:10). Because false teaching has a deceptive appearance, he says, *take heed*, i.e., consider diligently; *let your eyes look straight on, and let your eyelids go before your steps* (Prov 4:25).

1365. Next, the disciples' understanding is set down: *but they thought within themselves*. For since they had taken up seven baskets of fragments above, and had not brought them along, they thought that he said, you have not brought bread, but I do not want you to take bread from the Pharisees, because they are animals, and *the sensual man perceives not these things that are of the Spirit of God* (1 Cor 2:14).

1366. They could be reproached for two things in this understanding.

First, because they did not understand; likewise, for the fact that they lacked confidence in God's power. He does not reproach them for the first, but for the second.

He says then, *why do you think within yourselves, O you of little faith, that you have no bread?* As though to say, you understand carnally what you ought to understand spiritually. **Do you not yet understand, do you neither remember the five loaves among five thousand men, and how many baskets you took up?** So could not he who fed so many feed you? *Why do you not understand that it was not concerning bread that I said to you*, namely material bread, but rather spiritual; which bread is called teaching, *the words that I have spoken to you, are spirit and life* (John 6:64).

1367. *Then they understood*. Here the correction is set down. Hence they were corrected by his word; *the*

Ps. CXVIII, 130: *declaratio sermonum tuorum illuminat, et intellectum dat parvulis.*

declaration of your words gives light: and gives understanding to little ones (Ps 118:130).

Lecture 2

16:13 Venit autem Iesus in partes Caesareae Philippi, et interrogabat discipulos suos dicens: quem dicunt homines esse Filium hominis? [n. 1369]

16:14 At illi dixerunt: alii Ioannem Baptistam, alii autem Eliam, alii vero Ieremiam, aut unum ex prophetis. [n. 1371]

16:15 Dicit illis Iesus: vos autem quem me esse dicitis? [n. 1372]

16:16 Respondens Simon Petrus dixit: tu es Christus Filius Dei vivi. [n. 1374]

16:17 Respondens autem Iesus dixit ei: beatus es, Simon Bariona, quia caro et sanguis non revelavit tibi, sed Pater meus qui in caelis est. [n. 1376]

16:18 Et ego dico tibi, quia tu es Petrus, et super hanc petram aedificabo Ecclesiam meam, et portae inferi non praevalebunt adversus eam. [n. 1381]

16:19 Et tibi dabo claves regni caelorum. Et quodcumque ligaveris super terram erit ligatum et in caelis, et quodcumque solveris super terram erit solutum et in caelis. [n. 1386]

16:13 Ἐλθὼν δὲ ὁ Ἰησοῦς εἰς τὰ μέρη Καισαρείας τῆς Φιλίππου ἠρώτα τοὺς μαθητὰς αὐτοῦ λέγων· τίνα λέγουσιν οἱ ἄνθρωποι εἶναι τὸν υἱὸν τοῦ ἀνθρώπου;

16:14 οἱ δὲ εἶπαν· οἱ μὲν Ἰωάννην τὸν βαπτιστήν, ἄλλοι δὲ Ἠλίαν, ἕτεροι δὲ Ἰερεμίαν ἢ ἕνα τῶν προφητῶν.

16:15 λέγει αὐτοῖς· ὑμεῖς δὲ τίνα με λέγετε εἶναι;

16:16 ἀποκριθεὶς δὲ Σίμων Πέτρος εἶπεν· σὺ εἶ ὁ χριστὸς ὁ υἱὸς τοῦ θεοῦ τοῦ ζῶντος.

16:17 ἀποκριθεὶς δὲ ὁ Ἰησοῦς εἶπεν αὐτῷ· μακάριος εἶ, Σίμων Βαριωνᾶ, ὅτι σὰρξ καὶ αἷμα οὐκ ἀπεκάλυψέν σοι ἀλλ' ὁ πατήρ μου ὁ ἐν τοῖς οὐρανοῖς.

16:18 κἀγὼ δέ σοι λέγω ὅτι σὺ εἶ Πέτρος, καὶ ἐπὶ ταύτῃ τῇ πέτρᾳ οἰκοδομήσω μου τὴν ἐκκλησίαν καὶ πύλαι ᾅδου οὐ κατισχύσουσιν αὐτῆς.

16:19 δώσω σοι τὰς κλεῖδας τῆς βασιλείας τῶν οὐρανῶν, καὶ ὃ ἐὰν δήσῃς ἐπὶ τῆς γῆς ἔσται δεδεμένον ἐν τοῖς οὐρανοῖς, καὶ ὃ ἐὰν λύσῃς ἐπὶ τῆς γῆς ἔσται λελυμένον ἐν τοῖς οὐρανοῖς.

16:13 And Jesus came into the regions of Cesarea Philippi and he asked his disciples, saying: who do men say that the Son of man is? [n. 1369]

16:14 But they said: some John the Baptist, and others Elijah, and others Jeremiah, or one of the prophets. [n. 1371]

16:15 Jesus says to them: but who do you say that I am? [n. 1372]

16:16 Simon Peter answered and said: you are the Christ, the Son of the living God. [n. 1374]

16:17 And Jesus answering, said to him: blessed are you, Simon Bar-Jonah, because flesh and blood have not revealed this to you, but my Father who is in heaven. [n. 1376]

16:18 And I say to you that you are Peter; and upon this rock I will build my Church, and the gates of hell will not prevail against it. [n. 1381]

16:19 And I will give to you the keys of the kingdom of heaven. And whatever you bind on earth will be bound also in heaven, and whatever you loose on earth will be loosed also in heaven. [n. 1386]

1368. Supra Dominus docuit doctrinam evangelicam conservandam puram a fermento Iudaeorum, hic autem docet eminentiam doctrinae. Et

primo quantum ad fidem utriusque naturae, scilicet deitatis et humanitatis;

secundo quantum ad fidem passionis, ibi *exinde coepit Iesus ostendere discipulis suis* etc.;

tertio quantum ad fidem iudiciariae potestatis, ibi *Filius enim hominis venturus est in gloria Patris sui*.

Circa primum

primo exquiritur opinio turbarum de Christo;

secundo fides discipulorum, ibi *vos autem quem me esse dicitis?*

Circa primum

primo ponitur locus;

secundo interrogatio Christi, ibi *quem dicunt homines esse Filium hominis?*

1368. Above, the Lord taught that the evangelical teaching is to be preserved pure from the leaven of the Jews; and here he teaches the loftiness of the teaching. And

first, as regards faith in both natures, namely the deity and the humanity;

second, as regards faith in the passion, at *from that time, Jesus began to show to his disciples* (Matt 16:20);

third, as regards faith in the judiciary power, at *for the Son of man will come in the glory of his Father* (Matt 16:27).

Concerning the first,

first, the crowds' opinion about Christ is sought out;

second, the disciples' faith, at *but who do you say that I am?*

Concerning the first,

first, the place is set down;

second, Christ's questioning, at *who do men say that the Son of man is?*

tertio responsio Petri, ibi *at illi dixerunt* et cetera.

1369. Dicit ergo *venit autem Iesus in partes Caesareae Philippi* et non solum hoc, sed addidit *Philippi*, quia duae Caesareae fuerunt, scilicet Caesarea Traconis, ubi missus est Petrus ad Cornelium; alia haec quae dicitur aliter Paneas. Prima ab Herode constituta est in honorem Caesaris Augusti, istam construxit Philippus in honorem Tiberii.

Sed quare fecit hic istam quaestionem Dominus? Dicendum, quod haec civitas in finibus Iudaeorum erat sita; ideo antequam de fide petere vellet, a Iudaeis eos extraxit. Similiter habetur quod Dominus educens Iudaeos de Aegypto, non eduxit eos per sata Philisthinorum, ut habetur Ex. XIII, 17.

1370. Consequenter ponitur interrogatio *et interrogabat discipulos suos* et cetera. Sapiens quando interrogat, docet, ut dicit Hieronymus. Unde in multis instruimur, ut simus solliciti quid de nobis dicatur: ut si malum, quod corrigamus; si bonum, ut conservemus et multiplicemus. Unde *curam habe de bono nomine; hoc enim magis permanebit tibi, quam mille thesauri pretiosi et magni*, Eccli. XLI, 15. Unde Christus interrogavit quid de ipso diceretur. Item qui divinitatem cognoscunt, dicuntur dii, Ps. LXXXI, 6: *ego dixi, dii estis*, hi vero qui humanitatem, dicuntur homines; unde dicitur *quem dicunt homines esse Filium hominis?* Sed, ut dicit Hilarius, Christus solum homo videbatur: ideo voluit quod cognoscerent quod esset aliud quam simplex homo. Unde ipse ex hoc dat intelligere, aliud esse in eo. Item ostenditur humilitas Christi, quia se hominis Filium confitetur, secundum illud supra XI, v. 29: *discite a me, quia mitis sum et humilis corde*.

1371. Consequenter ponitur opinio turbarum *at illi dixerunt: alii Ioannem Baptistam* et cetera. Diversi de Christo senserunt diversa. Pharisaei blasphemabant Christum, sed turbae prophetam dicebant; unde Lc. VII, 16: *propheta magnus surrexit in nobis* et cetera. Dicebant eum Ioannem ratione auctoritatis, quia Ioannes poenitentiam praedicabat; supra cap. III, 2: *agite poenitentiam, appropinquavit regnum caelorum*. Ideo credebant ipsum esse Ioannem, quia similiter Christus incipiebat *agite poenitentiam, appropinquavit regnum caelorum*, ut supra IV, 17.

Item habebant in reverentia Eliam Prophetam; Mal. ult., 5: *ecce ego mittam Eliam prophetam, antequam veniat dies Domini magnus et horribilis*. Unde credebant esse Eliam propter potestatem sermonis et virtutem praedicationis; Eccli. XLVIII, 1: *et surrexit Elias Propheta quasi ignis, quia verbum ipsius quasi facula ardebat*. Et de Christo dicitur supra VII, 29, quod *erat docens tamquam potestatem habens*.

Item propter eminentiam vitae credebant eum esse Ieremiam, de quo Dominus ait: *antequam te formarem*

third, Peter's response, at *but they said*.

1369. It says then, *and Jesus came into the quarters of Cesarea Philippi*; and not only this, but he added *Philippi*, because there were two Cesareas, namely Cesarea Traconis, where Peter was sent to Cornelius, and this other one, which is otherwise called Paneas. The first was established by Herod, in honor of Caesar Augustus; Philip constructed this one in honor of Tiberius.

But why did the Lord ask this question here? One should say that this city was situated on the borders of the Jews; so before he wished to ask for faith, he took them out from the Jews. A similar thing is written, that the Lord, when he was leading the Jews from Egypt, did not lead them through the land of the Philistines (Exod 13:17).

1370. Next, the questioning is set down: *and he asked his disciples*. When the wise man asks, he teaches, as Jerome says. Hence we are instructed in many places that we should be concerned about what is said about us: so that if it is bad, we may correct it, and if it is good, we may preserve and multiply it. Hence, *take care of a good name: for this will continue with you, more than a thousand treasures precious and great* (Sir 41:15). Hence Christ asked what was said about him. Likewise, those who know the divinity are called gods, *I have said: you are gods* (Ps 81:6), but those who know the humanity are called men; hence he says, *who do men say that the Son of man is?* But, as Hilary says, Christ seemed to be only a man, so he willed that they should know that he was something other than a simple man. Hence he himself gives one to understand by this that there is something else in him. Also, Christ's humility is shown, because he confesses himself to be the Son of man, in accord with that above, *learn from me, because I am meek, and humble of heart* (Matt 11:29).

1371. Next, the crowds' opinion is set down: *but they said: some John the Baptist*. Different ones felt different things about Christ. The Pharisees blasphemed Christ, but the crowds said he was a prophet; hence, *a great prophet is risen up among us* (Luke 7:16). For they called him John by reason of authority, since John preached penance; *do penance: for the kingdom of heaven is at hand* (Matt 3:2). So they thought he was John, since Christ began in a similar way: *do penance, for the kingdom of heaven is at hand* (Matt 4:17).

Likewise, they held Elijah the Prophet in reverence; *behold I will send you Elijah the prophet, before the coming of the great and dreadful day of the Lord* (Mal 4:5). Hence they thought him to be Elijah, because of the power of his word and the virtue of his preaching; *and Elijah the Prophet stood up, as a fire, and his word burnt like a torch* (Sir 48:1). And it is said of Christ, above, that *he taught as one who has power* (Matt 7:29).

Also, on account of loftiness of life, they thought him to be Jeremiah, of whom the Lord said, *before I formed you in*

in utero, novi te, et antequam exires de ventre, sanctificavi te, Ier. I, 5. Et ibid. XL habetur, quia honoratus erat gentibus. Sic in reverentia ab extraneis Christus habebatur; a Iudaeis vero blasphemabatur: ideo Ieremiae comparabant eum.

Sed quomodo Eliam dicebant? Quia habetur IV regum II, 11 quod raptus est, et quod adhuc viveret, et erat promissus Iudaeis ad salutem, ut habetur Mal. ult., 5. Quia quidam posuerunt transcorporationem: et ideo secundum hanc opinionem posset esse, quod anima Eliae intrasset aliud corpus.

1372. *Dicit eis Iesus: vos autem quem me esse dicitis?* Hic exquiritur fides discipulorum. Et

primo ponitur interrogatio;
secundo responsio;
tertio approbatio.

Secunda ibi *respondens Petrus*; tertia ibi *respondens autem Iesus* et cetera.

1373. *Dicit eis Iesus: vos autem quem me esse dicitis?* Quasi dicat: ita dicunt turbae; sed quia magis est vobis commissum, ideo magis a vobis exigitur. Vidistis miracula, ideo magis debetis opinari.

Sed quare petiit? Nonne sciebat? Immo sciebat, sed volebat quod mererentur ex confessione; Rom. X, 10: *corde creditur ad iustitiam, ore autem confessio fit ad salutem*. Unde magis sunt meritoria, quanto magis sequestrata, et quasi turbis infima scientibus, maiora non respondeant, ideo et cetera.

1374. *Respondens autem Petrus dixit: tu es Christus Filius Dei vivi*. Ipse respondet pro se, et pro aliis; sed ipse frequentius respondet, et in hoc perfecta fides tangitur, quia tangitur fides humanitatis. *Tu es Christus*, idest unctus. Et constat quod unctus est oleo Spiritus Sancti. Unctio non convenit ei secundum divinitatem, quia ab ipsa procedit, sed secundum humanitatem. Hoc ergo dicit, ut humanitatem Christi aliter aestiment quam turbae.

Quaeritur autem quare prophetam eum dicebant. Ungebatur propheta, ut habetur de Eliseo. Ungebantur reges, ut habetur de Saule; item sacerdotes, ut habetur in Levitico. Et omnia haec in nomine *Christi* importantur: quia et rex dicitur, ut Ierem. XXIII, 5: *regnabit rex, et sapiens erit*. Item sacerdos; Ps. CIX, 4: *tu es sacerdos in aeternum secundum ordinem Melchisedech*. Item propheta: *prophetam suscitabit Deus de gente tua, et de fratribus tuis* etc., Deut. XVIII, 15.

1375. Item non solum confessus est humanitatem, sed testudine penetrata, usque ad divinitatem transcendit dicens *tu es Filius Dei*. Alii enim dicebant eum

the bowels of your mother, I knew you: and before you came forth out of the womb, I sanctified you (Jer 1:5). And in the same book, it says that he was honored among the gentiles (Jer 40). In this same way, Christ was held in reverence by outsiders, but was blasphemed by the Jews. So they compared him to Jeremiah.

But how did they call him Elijah? Because it is said that he was taken up, and that he was still alive (2 Kgs 2:11), and was promised to the Jews for salvation (Mal 4:5). For some posited transcorporation, and so according to this opinion it could have been that Elijah's soul entered another body.

1372. *Jesus says to them: but who do you say that I am?* Here the disciples' faith is sought out. And

first, the questioning is set down;
second, the response;
third, the approval.

The second is at *Simon Peter answered*; the third, at *and Jesus answering*.

1373. *Jesus says to them: but who do you say that I am?* as though to say: so the crowds say, but since more is entrusted to you, more is required of you. You have seen miracles, so you should suppose more.

But why did he ask? Did not he know? Indeed he knew, but he willed that they should merit by confession; *for with the heart, we believe unto justice; but with the mouth, confession is made unto salvation* (Rom 10:10). For things are more meritorious the more they are separated off, and, as it were, the greater things are not suited to the crowd, which knows the lowest things.

1374. *Simon Peter answered and said: you are the Christ, the Son of the living God*. He responds for himself and for the others; but he himself responds more frequently, and in this response perfect faith is touched upon, for faith in the humanity is touched upon. *You are the Christ*, i.e., the anointed one. And it is agreed that he is anointed with the oil of the Holy Spirit. Anointing does not belong to him according to the divinity, because it proceeds from it, but according to the humanity. So he says this that they might regard the humanity of Christ in a way different from the crowds.

But it is asked why they called him a prophet. A prophet was anointed, as is written of Elisha. Kings were anointed, as is written of Saul. Likewise, priests, as is written in Leviticus. And all these things are brought in by the name *Christ*. For he is called a king, as in Jeremiah, *a king will reign, and will be wise* (Jer 23:5). Also a priest: *you are a priest forever according to the order of Melchisedech* (Ps 109:4). And also a prophet: *the Lord your God will raise up to you a prophet of your nation and of your brethren like unto me* (Deut 18:15).

1375. And Peter did not just confess the humanity, but piercing through the outer shell, he climbed up even to the divinity, saying, *you are . . . the Son of the living God*. For

blasphemum; unde Io. X, 33: *non de bono opere lapidamus te, sed de blasphemia, quia homo cum sis, facis teipsum Deum*. Sed iste Filium Dei recognoscit.

Et dicit *vivi*, ad excludendum errorem gentilium, qui quosdam homines mortuos dicebant deos, ut Iovem etc., ut habetur Sap. cap. XIII, 2 ss. Item quidam elementa et cetera mortua, ut terram, ignem etc., ut habetur Sap. XIII; sed iste *Filium Dei vivi* dicit.

Sed sciendum, quod cum dicitur *Deus vivus*, et homo vivus, de homine dicitur per participationem vitae; sed de Deo dicitur, quia fons vitae; Ps. XXXV, 10: *apud te est fons vitae*. Et in Io. XIV, 6: *ego sum via, veritas et vita*.

1376. *Respondens Iesus* et cetera. Hic

primo approbat confessionem eius;

secundo mandat tacendam, ibi **tunc praecepit discipulis suis ut nemini dicerent, quod ipse esset Iesus Christus**.

Circa primum

primo approbat istam confessionem per commendationem confitentis;

secundo per remunerationem, ibi **et ego dico tibi quia tu es Petrus** et cetera.

1377. Unde dicit *respondit Iesus: beatus es, Simon Bariona*. 'Bar' idem est quod 'filius'; 'Ionas' idem quod 'columba': suo nomine. Unde **Bariona**, idest filius columbae.

Et videtur respondere responsio Christi confessioni Petri. Quia confessus erat eum filium Dei, Iesus autem dicit eum Filium columbae, scilicet Spiritus Sancti, quia haec confessio non potuit fieri nisi a Spiritu Sancto. Sed creditur quod primo dicebatur **Bar-Iona**, idest Ioannis filius, sed per corruptionem Scripturae ita dictum est.

1378. Sed quid est? Numquid alii non confessi sunt Filium Dei? Immo legitur de Nathanaele Io. I, 49. Item illi qui in navi, supra IX. Quare ergo hic beatificatur Petrus, et non alii?

Quia alii filium adoptivum confessi sunt, hic autem Filium naturalem; ideo hic prae ceteris beatificatur, quia primus confessus est divinitatem.

Origenes dicit: *videtur quod ante non confessus fuerit*. Sed quomodo misit eos praedicare?

Respondet quod a principio non praedicabant ipsum esse Christum, sed poenitentiam praedicabant. Item potest esse quod praedicabant Christum; sed hic primo ipsum esse Filium Dei. Ergo hic specialiter remunerat.

others said that he blasphemed; hence *not for a good work do we stone you, but for blasphemy; and because that you, being a man, make yourself God* (John 10:33). But this man recognized the Son of God.

And he says, **living**, to exclude the error of the gentiles, who called certain dead men gods, such as Jove (Wis 13:2). Likewise, some held as gods the elements and other dead things, like earth, fire, etc. (Wis 13); but this man calls him **the Son of the living God**.

But one should know that when he is called **the living God** and a living man, living is said of the man through participation in life, but it is said of God because he is the fount of life. *For with you is the fountain of life* (Ps 35:10). And, *I am the way, and the truth, and the life* (John 14:6).

1376. *And Jesus answering*. Here

first, he approves his confession;

second, he commands silence, at **then he commanded his disciples, that they should tell no one that he was Jesus the Christ** (Matt 16:20).

Concerning the first,

first, he approves this confession by praising the one who confessed;

second, by a reward, at **and I say to you that you are Peter and upon this rock I will build my Church**.

1377. Hence it says, *and Jesus answering, said to him: blessed are you, Simon Bar-Jonah*. 'Bar' is the same as 'son'; 'Jona' is the same as 'dove,' his name. Hence **Bar-Jonah**, i.e., son of the dove.

And Christ's response seems to correspond to Peter's confession. For he had confessed him to be the Son of God, and Jesus calls him the son of the dove, namely of the Holy Spirit, for this confession could only have come about by the Holy Spirit. But it is thought that it was said **Bar-Jonah** at first, i.e., son of John, but then was said in this way by a corruption of the Scripture.

1378. But what is this? Did not others confess him to be the Son of God? Indeed, it is written of Nathaniel (John 1:49). Likewise, those who were in the boat, above (Matt 9). Why then is Peter blessed here, and not the others?

Because the others confessed him to be an adoptive son, but this man confessed him to be the natural Son; therefore this one is blessed before the others, because he first confessed the divinity.

Origen says, *it seems that it had not been confessed before*. But how did he send them to preach?

He responds that they did not preach that he was the Christ from the beginning, but preached penance. Also, it could be that they preached Christ, but this man first confessed that he was the Son of God. Therefore he rewards this man especially.

1379. *Beatus es, Simon* etc., quia beatitudo est in cognitione; Io. XVII, 3: *haec est vita aeterna ut cognoscant te solum verum Deum*.

Sed duplex est cognitio: una quae est per naturalem rationem, alia quae supra rationem. Prima non facit beatitudinem, quia dubia est: unde non satiat intellectum; sed beatitudo debet satisfacere appetitui naturali, et hoc habebitur in patria; Is. LXIV, 4: *oculus non vidit, nec auris audivit quae praeparavit dominus diligentibus se*. Ergo in hac vita, quanto aliquis magis potest percipere de hac cognitione, magis est beatus; Prov. III, v. 13: *beatus qui invenit sapientiam*. Unde dicit **beatus es**, quia incipis esse beatus.

1380. *Quia caro et sanguis non revelavit tibi*. Hoc potest exponi ita quod caro et sanguis sumantur pro amicis carnalibus; ad Gal. I, 16: *continuo non acquievi carni et sanguini*. Unde **caro et sanguis non revelavit tibi**, idest non habuisti ex traditione Iudaeorum, sed ex revelatione Dei. Item in Christo erat caro, et sanguis, et divinitas; ideo quia Petrus non respexit ad carnem et sanguinem, ei dicitur **beatus es**, quia non iudicas secundum quod caro et sanguis revelat, sed secundum quod Pater meus. Vel non habes ex naturali industria, sed ex Patre meo. *Nemo enim cognovit Filium nisi Pater*, Lc. cap. X, 22. Illius enim est manifestare, cuius est cognoscere. Unde nemo novit nisi cui pater voluerit revelare; Dan. II, 28: *est Deus in caelo revelans mysteria*.

1381. *Et ego dico tibi, quia tu es Petrus* et cetera. Hic dat confessionis remunerationem. Confessus erat humanitatem et divinitatem, ideo dat Dominus remunerationem.

Primo dat nomen;
secundo potestatem.
Circa primum
primo dat nomen;
secundo nominis rationem, ibi **et super hanc petram aedificabo Ecclesiam meam**.

1382. Et ad hoc venit in hunc mundum ut ecclesiam fundaret. Is. XXVIII, 16: *ecce ego ponam in fundamento Sion lapidem probatum angularem pretiosum, in fundamento fundatum*. Iste signatum est per lapidem quem supposuit Iacob capiti, et unxit, ut habetur Gen. XXVIII, 18. Iste lapis est Christus, et ab ista unctione omnes dicti sunt Christiani; unde non solum dicimur Christiani a Christo, sed a petra. Ideo specialiter imponit nomen: **tu es Petrus**, a petra quae est Christus. Licet secundum Augustinum videatur quod modo non fuerit

1379. *Blessed are you, Simon*, because he is blessed in knowledge; *now this is eternal life: that they may know you, the only true God* (John 17:3).

But there are two kinds of knowledge: there is one which comes through natural reason, and another which is above reason. The first does not make for blessedness, because there is doubt, and hence it does not satisfy the intellect; but blessedness should satisfy the natural appetite, and this shall be had in the homeland. *The eye has not seen, O God, besides you, what things you have prepared for those who wait for you* (Isa 64:4). Therefore in this life, someone is more blessed to the degree that he is more able to perceive of this knowledge; *blessed is the man who finds wisdom* (Prov 3:13). Hence he says, **blessed are you**, because you begin to be blessed.

1380. *Because flesh and blood have not revealed this to you*. This can be explained in such a way that flesh and blood are taken for carnal friends; *immediately I condescended not to flesh and blood* (Gal 1:16). Hence **flesh and blood has not revealed this to you**, i.e., you did not get it from the Jews' traditions, but from God's revelation. Likewise, in Christ there was flesh and blood and divinity; therefore, since Peter did not focus on the flesh and blood, it is said to him, **blessed are you**, because you do not judge according as flesh and blood reveal, but according as my Father reveals. Or, you do not have this knowledge from natural diligence, but from my Father. For *no one knows who the Son is, except the Father* (Luke 10:22). For it is his to reveal, whose it is to know. Hence no one knows the Son except the one to whom the Father wills to reveal him; *but there is a God in heaven who reveals mysteries* (Dan 2:28).

1381. *And I say to you that you are Peter*. Here he gives a reward for the confession. He had confessed the humanity and the divinity, so the Lord gives a reward.

First, he gives a name;
second, a power.
Concerning the first,
first, he gives a name;
second, the reason for the name, at **and upon this rock I will build my Church**.

1382. And I came into the world for this, to found a church. *Behold I will lay a stone in the foundations of Zion, a tried stone, a corner stone, a precious stone, founded in the foundation* (Isa 28:16). This was signified by the stone which Jacob put beneath his head and oiled (Gen 28:18). This stone is Christ, and from this anointing all are called Christians; hence we are not only called Christians from Christ, but from the rock. For this reason, he specially imposes a name: **you are Peter**, from the rock which is Christ. Although, according to Augustine, it might seem that it was

impositum, sed a principio; Io. I, 42: *tu vocaberis Cephas*. Vel potest dici quod tunc fuit promissum, hic datum.

1383. In huius signum rei, **super hanc petram aedificabo Ecclesiam meam**. Proprietas petrae est, quod ponatur in fundamento; item, ut det firmitatem. Supra VII, 24: *similis est homini qui aedificat domum suam super petram*.

Unde potest exponi de Christo: *et super hanc petram*, idest Christum, ut sit fundamentum, et ut fundata firmamentum recipiat. Augustinus in libro *Retract*. dicit, quod multipliciter exposuit, et reliquit audientibus ut acciperent quam vellent. Vel ut demonstret ly **hanc petram** Christum; I ad Cor. X, 4: *petra autem erat Christus*. Et alibi, I ad Cor. III, v. 11: *fundamentum aliud nemo potest ponere nisi id quod positum est, quod est Christus Iesus*.

Alia expositio: **super hanc petram**, idest super te petram, quia a me petra trahes tu quod sis petra. Et sicut ego sum petra, ita super te petram aedificabo et cetera.

1384. Sed quid est? Est ne Christus et Petrus fundamentum?

Dicendum quod Christus secundum se, sed Petrus inquantum habet confessionem Christi, inquantum vicarius eius. Ad Ephes. II, 20: *superaedificati super fundamentum apostolorum et prophetarum ipso summo angulari lapide Christo Iesu* et cetera. Apoc. XXI, 4: *fundamenta civitatis duodecim, et in ipsis duodecim nomina apostolorum et Agni*. Ideo Christus secundum se est fundamentum, sed apostoli non secundum se, sed per concessionem Christi, et auctoritatem datam a Christo; Ps. cap. LXXXVI, 1: *fundamenta eius in montibus sanctis*. Sed specialiter Petri domus, quae est fundata super petram, non diruetur, ut supra VII, 25. Sic ista impugnari potest, expugnari non potest.

1385. *Et portae inferi non praevalebunt adversus eam*. Ier. I, 19: *bellabunt adversum te, et non praevalebunt*.

Et qui sunt portae inferi? Haeretici: quia sicut per portam intratur in domum, sic per istos intratur in infernum. Item tyranni, daemones, peccata. Et quamvis aliae Ecclesiae vituperari possint per haereticos, Ecclesia tamen Romana non fuit ab haereticis depravata quia supra petram erat fundata. Unde in Constantinopoli fuerunt haeretici, et labor apostolorum amissus erat; sola Petri Ecclesia inviolata permansit. Unde Lc. XXII, 32: *ego rogavi pro te, Petre, ut non deficiat fides tua*. Et hoc non solum refertur ad Ecclesiam Petri, sed ad fidem Petri, et ad totam occidentalem Ecclesiam. Unde credo quod occidentales maiorem reverentiam debent Petro, quam aliis apostolis.

not imposed now, but from the beginning: *you will be called Cephas* (John 1:42). Or it can be said that it was promised then, and given here.

1383. As a sign of this thing, **upon this rock I will build my Church**. It is a property of the rock that it is placed in the foundation; also, that it gives firmness. Above, *everyone therefore who hears these my words, and does them, shall be likened to a wise man that built his house upon a rock* (Matt 7:24).

Hence it can be explained as about Christ: *and upon this rock*, i.e., on Christ, that he might be the foundation, and that the thing founded might receive a support. Augustine says in the book of *Retractions* that he explained it in many ways, and left it to the hearers to accept what they would. Or, to demonstrate that **this rock** means Christ: *and the rock was Christ* (1 Cor 10:4). And in another place, *for other foundation no man can lay, but that which is laid; which is Christ Jesus* (1 Cor 3:11).

Another explanation: **upon this rock**, i.e., upon you, Peter, because from me, the rock, you receive that you are a rock. And just as I am a rock, so upon you, Peter, I will build my Church.

1384. But what is this? Are both Christ and Peter the foundation?

One should say that Christ is the foundation through himself, but Peter insofar as he holds the confession of Christ, insofar as he is his vicar. *Built upon the foundation of the apostles and prophets, Jesus Christ himself being the chief corner stone* (Eph 2:20). *And the wall of the city had twelve foundations, and in them, the twelve names of the twelve apostles of the Lamb* (Rev 21:14). So Christ is the foundation through himself, but the apostles are the foundation not through themselves, but by Christ's permission, and by the authority given by Christ; *the foundations thereof are in the holy mountains* (Ps 86:1). But especially Peter's house, which is founded upon the rock, shall not be destroyed (Matt 7:25). Thus it can be attacked, but cannot be conquered.

1385. *And the gates of hell will not prevail against it*. *And they will fight against you, and will not prevail* (Jer 1:19).

And who are the gates of hell? Heretics, because just as one enters into a house through a gate, so one enters into hell through these. Also tyrants, demons, sins. And although other churches can be reproached for heretics, yet the Roman church was not corrupted by heretics, because it was founded upon the rock. Hence there were heretics in Constantinople, and the apostles' labor was lost; only Peter's church remained inviolate. Hence, *but I have prayed for you, that your faith fail not* (Luke 22:32). And this does not only refer to Peter's church, but to Peter's faith, and to the whole western church. Hence I believe that those in the west owe more reverence to Peter than to the other apostles.

1386. *Et tibi dabo claves regni caelorum.* Hic ponitur secundum donum quod Petro dedit Christus secundum humanitatem. Fundavit enim Ecclesiam in terris, et Petrum vicarium suum instituit, ut introduceret in caelum; ad Hebr. X, 19: *habentes fiduciam in introitu sanctorum in sanguine Christi.* Unde Christus vicarium suum Petrum instituit, ut introduceret in caelum, unde illud ministerium dedit, unde claves dedit. Clavis enim introducit: unde Petrus habet ministerium introducendi.

Et duo facit.
Primo claves committit;
secundo usum docet *et quodcumque ligaveris super terram, erit ligatum et in caelis* et cetera.

1387. Sed videamus quae sunt claves. Domus quando est serata impedit introitum; clavis vero removet impedimentum. Regnum caelorum habebat impedimentum, sed non ex parte sua; Apoc. IV, 1: *vidi, et ecce ostium apertum*; sed impedimentum erat ex parte nostra, scilicet peccatum, quia *nihil coinquinatum intrabit in illam.* Ista impedimenta removit Christus per suam passionem, quia *lavit nos a peccatis nostris in sanguine suo,* Apoc. I, 5. Et hanc communicavit ut per ministerium peccata tollerentur, quod expletur per virtutem sanguinis Christi: unde sacramenta virtutem habent a virtute passionis Christi. Unde dabo tibi ministerium et cetera. Is. cap. XXII, 22: *dabo super te claves David.*

Sed dicit *tibi dabo*; nondum enim erant fabricatae; res autem non potest dari antequam sit. Fabricandae autem hae erant in passione; unde in passione fuit eorum efficacia. Unde hic promisit, sed post passionem dedit, cum dixit: *pasce oves meas.*

1388. Sed quare dicit *claves*? Quia absolvere est removere obstaculum. Duo enim sunt, quia duo requiruntur, potestas et scientia.

Sed quid est? Numquid non aliqui sacerdotes sunt, qui non habent scientiam? Intelligatis quod habent scientiam, quia nullus clavem scientiae habet nisi sacerdos. Non dicitur hic scientia habitus intellectus etc., sed dicitur auctoritas discernendi. Unde est aliquis iudex, qui non habet scientiam primo modo, et tamen habet scientiam secundo modo, quia habet auctoritatem; aliquis autem habet scientiam primo modo, et non secundo modo, quia non habet auctoritatem. Unde scientia hic dicitur auctoritas discernendi, et sacerdos quilibet hanc habet ut discernat in absolvendo.

1389. Consequenter ponit usum clavium *quodcumque ligaveris super terram, erit ligatum et in caelis*. Sed videtur quod inconvenienter ponatur, quia usus clavis non est ligare, sed aperire.

Dico quod clavium conveniens iste usus est. Ipsum enim caelum apertum est; Apoc. cap. IV, 1: *vidi ostium*

1386. *And I will give to you the keys of the kingdom of heaven.* Here is set down the second gift which Christ, according to his humanity, gave to Peter. For he founded a Church on earth, and established Peter as his vicar, that he might lead into heaven; *having therefore, brethren, a confidence in the entering into the holies by the blood of Christ* (Heb 10:19). For Christ established Peter as his vicar, that he might lead others into heaven, for which reason he gave him that ministry; hence he gave the keys. For keys lead one in; hence Peter has the ministry of leading in.

And he does two things:
first, he entrusts the keys;
second, he teaches their use: *and whatever you bind on earth will be bound also in heaven.*

1387. But let us see what the keys are. When a house is locked, it obstructs entry; but a key removes the obstacle. The kingdom of heaven had an obstacle, but not on its own part; *I looked, and behold a door was opened in heaven* (Rev 4:1), but the obstacle was on our part, namely, sin, because *there shall not enter into it anything defiled* (Rev 21:27). Christ removed this impediment by his passion, because *he washed us from our sins in his blood* (Rev 1:5). And he communicated this so that sins might be removed through a ministry, which is completed by the strength of Christ's blood. Hence the sacraments have strength from the strength of Christ's passion. Hence I will give to you a ministry. *And I will lay the key of the house of David upon his shoulder: and he will open, and none will shut: and he will shut, and none will open* (Isa 22:22).

But he says, *I will give to you*, for the keys were not yet made; and a thing cannot be given before it exists. Now, they were made in the passion, hence their efficacy came in the passion. Hence he promised them here, but gave them after the passion, when he said, *feed my sheep* (John 21:17).

1388. But why does he say *keys*? Because to absolve is to remove an obstacle. For there are two keys, since two things are required, power and knowledge.

But what is this? Are there not some priests who do not have knowledge? Understand that they have knowledge, because no one has the key of knowledge except priests. Knowledge here does not mean a habit of the intellect, but the authority of discerning. Hence there is a judge who does not have knowledge in the first way, and yet has knowledge in the second way, because he has authority; and there is someone who has knowledge in the first way, and not the second way, because he has no authority. Hence knowledge here means the authority of discerning, and any priest has this, so he may discern in absolving.

1389. Next, he sets down the use of the keys: *and whatever you bind on earth will be bound also in heaven.* But it seems that this is set down unfittingly, because a key is not used to bind, but to open.

I say that this is a fitting use of a key. For heaven itself is open: *I looked, and behold a door was opened in heaven*

apertum. Unde non est necessarium ut aperiatur; sed ligatus qui debet introire, oportet quod solvatur.

1390. Sed hic vitandi sunt aliqui errores. Primus tangitur in Glossa, quia quidam usurpaverunt quod possent omnes, quos vellent, absolvere, et introducere in regnum caelorum. Sed hoc non potest stare, quia solius Dei est immutare voluntates.

Alius error est, quod sacerdos non ligat, sed ostendit esse absolutum. Sed istud derogat virtuti sacramenti, eo quod sacramenta novae legis efficiunt quod figurant; sacramenta vero veteris legis non. Unde si nihil efficeret, non esset sacramentum novae legis.

Tertio aliqui dicunt quod in peccato sunt tria: culpa, et reatus, et poena. A duobus absolvitur homo per se per contritionem; sed quando homo ab his absolutus est, remanet obligatus ad poenam temporalem, quam per se tollere et evitare homo non sufficit; ideo dantur claves, quae minuunt aliquid de ista poena, et ligant quantum ad poenam aliquam.

Tamen videtur mihi, quod hoc non sit bene dictum, quia sacramentum novae legis dat gratiam, sed gratia non ordinatur contra poenam, sed contra culpam. Unde dico quod sic est in sacramento isto confessionis, sicut in sacramento baptismi, quod habet virtutem spiritualem instrumentalem, secundum quam mundat a culpa. Unde Augustinus: *quae est virtus aquae, ut carnem abluat, et culpam tollat?* Sic dico quod in sacerdote est quaedam vis spiritualis instrumentalis, a qua dicitur minister, et sic ministerialiter operatur remissionem, sicut aqua baptismi.

1391. Sed hic facit difficultatem, quia modo solum pueri veniunt ad baptismum: et si accedat adultus, aut venit fictus, aut non: fictus venit, quando sine innovatione mentis, et tunc non remittitur culpa; non fictus venit, quando cum proposito confessionis, unde requiritur gratia, sive propositum conversionis, et istud est ex gratia. Gratia autem tollit culpam. Unde in sacramento baptismi veniens adultus, si praeparat se, recipit remissionem culpae. Sic in sacramento poenitentiae, ad quod soli adulti accedunt, non est contritus, nisi habeat in proposito se subiicere discretioni et iudicio sacerdotis. Si non est contritus, non consequitur effectum, sicut nec in Baptismo. Sed potest accidere, quod aliquis accedit non totaliter contritus, qui virtute gratiae collatae in sacramento perfecto efficitur contritus; ideo intelligendum est: **quodcumque solveris**, idest si ministerium absolutionis adhibes. Et dicit **quodcumque**, quia non solam culpam, sed poenam. **Solutum erit in caelis**, idest habebitur tamquam absolutum in caelis, sicut est de baptismo: unde debet dicere sacerdos, *ego te absolvo*, sicut *ego te baptizo*.

(Rev 4:1). Hence it is not necessary that it be opened; rather, the bond of him who should enter must be loosed.

1390. But here some errors should be avoided. The first is touched upon in the Gloss, for some have claimed that anyone who wished could absolve, and lead others into the kingdom of heaven. But this cannot stand, because it belongs to God alone to change desires.

Another error is that the priest does not bind, but merely points out that a sin is absolved. But this takes away from the strength of the sacrament, because the sacraments of the new law effect what they figure; but the sacraments of the old law did not. Hence if it effected nothing, it would not be a sacrament of the new law.

Third, some say that there are three things in sin: guilt, liability, and punishment. A man is absolved *per se* from two of these by contrition; but when a man is absolved from these, he remains bound to a temporal punishment, which a man cannot take away and avoid of himself. Therefore the keys are given, which reduce something of this punishment, and bind as regards some punishment.

Yet it seems to me that this is not well said, because a sacrament of the new law gives grace, and grace is not ordered against punishment but against guilt. Hence I say that in the sacrament of confession, just as in the sacrament of baptism, there is a spiritual, instrumental strength, according to which it cleanses from guilt. Hence Augustine: *what is water's strength, that it washes off the body and takes away guilt?* Thus I say that in a priest there is a certain spiritual, instrumental strength, from which he is called a 'minister,' and thus he works the remission of sins ministerially, just as water works baptism.

1391. But here a difficulty arises, because at the present time only children come to baptism. And if an adult were to approach, he would come either falsely, or not: he would come falsely if he came without a renewal of the mind, and then guilt would not be remitted; he would not come falsely if he came with the intention of confession. Hence grace is required, or the intention of conversion, which is from grace. Now, grace takes away guilt. Hence in the sacrament of baptism, when an adult comes, if he prepares himself, he receives the remission of guilt. Thus in the sacrament of penance, to which only adults come, a man is not contrite unless he has the intention of subjecting himself to the discretion and judgment of a priest. If he is not contrite, the effect will not follow, just as neither in baptism. But it can happen that someone approaches not entirely contrite, and is made contrite by virtue of the grace received in the perfect sacrament; therefore one should understand, **whatever you loose**, i.e., if you use the ministry of absolution. And he says, **whatever** because not only guilt, but punishment is loosed. **Will be loosed also in heaven**, i.e., it will be held as loosed in heaven, just as it is with baptism. Hence the priest should say, *I absolve you*, just as he says, *I baptize you*.

1392. Sed potest quis quaerere qualiter ligat.

Sciendum quod sacerdos minister est Dei, et actio ministri dependet ab actu Domini: unde eo modo quo Dominus ligat et solvit, sic sacerdos ministerialiter. Solvit Deus infundendo gratiam, ligat non infundendo: sic sacerdos solvit sacramento, ministrando sacramentum, ligat vero non adhibendo.

Aliter dicitur, quod per caelos praesens Ecclesia designatur; unde **quodcumque ligaveris**, excommunicatione, **vel solveris**, erit solutum vel ligatum, quoad administrationem sacramentorum Ecclesiae. Unde volunt, quod ista administratio, haec ligatio et absolutio sit super terram, ita quod non se extendat ad mortuos.

Sed hoc reprobatur, quia non solum se extendit ad vivos, sed etiam ad mortuos: unde si ad utrumque referatur, sensus est: **quodcumque ligaveris super terram**, tunc dico existens super terram, **erit ligatum et in caelis**.

1393. Sed est alia quaestio, quia alibi habetur, Io. XX, 23: *quorum remiseritis peccata, remittentur eis*; hic vero solum hoc dicit Petro.

Dicendum quod immediate dedit Petro; alii vero a Petro recipiunt; ideo ne credantur ista solum dici Petro, dicit: *quorum remiseritis* et cetera. Et hac ratione Papa, qui est loco sancti Petri, habet plenariam potestatem, alii vero ab ipso.

1392. But someone can ask how he binds.

One should know that the priest is a minister of God, and the action of the minister depends on the Lord's action. Hence in the same way the Lord binds and looses, so the priests do ministerially. The Lord looses by pouring in grace, and binds by not pouring in: in the same way, the priest looses by the sacrament, by administering the sacrament, but binds by not giving it.

In another way, it is said that the present Church is designated by the heavens; hence **whatever you bind** by excommunication, or **loose**, will be loosed or bound as regards the administration of the Church's sacraments. Hence they would have it that this administration, this binding and loosing, is on earth, so that it does not extend to the dead.

But this is refuted, because it extends not only to the living, but even to the dead. Hence if it is referred to both, the sense is: **whatever you bind upon earth**, at that time, I say, being on earth, **will be bound also in heaven**.

1393. But there is another question, because it is written in another place, *whose sins you forgive, they are forgiven them* (John 20:23), but here he says this only to Peter.

One should say that he gave it to Peter immediately, but the others receive from Peter. For this reason, lest they believe that this is said only to Peter, he says, *whose sins you forgive* (John 20:23). And for this reason the Pope, who is in the place of holy Peter, has full power, but the others have power from him.

Lecture 3

16:20 Tunc praecepit discipulis suis, ut nemini dicerent, quia ipse esset Iesus Christus. [n. 1394]

16:21 Exinde coepit Iesus ostendere discipulis suis, quia oporteret eum ire Ierosolymam, et multa pati a senioribus, et scribis, et principibus sacerdotum, et occidi, et tertia die resurgere. [n. 1396]

16:22 Et assumens eum Petrus, coepit increpare illum, dicens: absit a te, Domine, non erit tibi hoc. [n. 1401]

16:23 Qui conversus dixit Petro: vade post me, satana, scandalum es mihi, quia non sapis ea quae Dei sunt, sed ea quae hominum. [n. 1403]

16:24 Tunc Iesus dixit discipulis suis: si quis vult post me venire, abneget semetipsum, et tollat crucem suam, et sequatur me. [n. 1407]

16:25 Qui enim voluerit animam suam salvam facere, perdet eam: qui autem perdiderit animam suam propter me, inveniet eam. [n. 1411]

16:26 Quid enim prodest homini si mundum universum lucretur, animae vero suae detrimentum patiatur? Aut quam dabit homo commutationem pro anima sua? [n. 1412]

16:27 Filius enim hominis venturus est in gloria Patris sui cum angelis suis, et tunc reddet unicuique secundum opera eius. [n. 1415]

16:28 Amen dico vobis, sunt quidam de hic stantibus, qui non gustabunt mortem, donec videant Filium hominis venientem in regno suo. [n. 1416]

16:20 τότε διεστείλατο τοῖς μαθηταῖς ἵνα μηδενὶ εἴπωσιν ὅτι αὐτός ἐστιν ὁ χριστός.

16:21 Ἀπὸ τότε ἤρξατο ὁ Ἰησοῦς δεικνύειν τοῖς μαθηταῖς αὐτοῦ ὅτι δεῖ αὐτὸν εἰς Ἱεροσόλυμα ἀπελθεῖν καὶ πολλὰ παθεῖν ἀπὸ τῶν πρεσβυτέρων καὶ ἀρχιερέων καὶ γραμματέων καὶ ἀποκτανθῆναι καὶ τῇ τρίτῃ ἡμέρᾳ ἐγερθῆναι.

16:22 καὶ προσλαβόμενος αὐτὸν ὁ Πέτρος ἤρξατο ἐπιτιμᾶν αὐτῷ λέγων· ἵλεώς σοι, κύριε· οὐ μὴ ἔσται σοι τοῦτο.

16:23 ὁ δὲ στραφεὶς εἶπεν τῷ Πέτρῳ· ὕπαγε ὀπίσω μου, σατανᾶ· σκάνδαλον εἶ ἐμοῦ, ὅτι οὐ φρονεῖς τὰ τοῦ θεοῦ ἀλλὰ τὰ τῶν ἀνθρώπων.

16:24 Τότε ὁ Ἰησοῦς εἶπεν τοῖς μαθηταῖς αὐτοῦ· εἴ τις θέλει ὀπίσω μου ἐλθεῖν, ἀπαρνησάσθω ἑαυτὸν καὶ ἀράτω τὸν σταυρὸν αὐτοῦ καὶ ἀκολουθείτω μοι.

16:25 ὃς γὰρ ἐὰν θέλῃ τὴν ψυχὴν αὐτοῦ σῶσαι ἀπολέσει αὐτήν· ὃς δ' ἂν ἀπολέσῃ τὴν ψυχὴν αὐτοῦ ἕνεκεν ἐμοῦ εὑρήσει αὐτήν.

16:26 τί γὰρ ὠφεληθήσεται ἄνθρωπος ἐὰν τὸν κόσμον ὅλον κερδήσῃ τὴν δὲ ψυχὴν αὐτοῦ ζημιωθῇ; ἢ τί δώσει ἄνθρωπος ἀντάλλαγμα τῆς ψυχῆς αὐτοῦ;

16:27 μέλλει γὰρ ὁ υἱὸς τοῦ ἀνθρώπου ἔρχεσθαι ἐν τῇ δόξῃ τοῦ πατρὸς αὐτοῦ μετὰ τῶν ἀγγέλων αὐτοῦ, καὶ τότε ἀποδώσει ἑκάστῳ κατὰ τὴν πρᾶξιν αὐτοῦ.

16:28 ἀμὴν λέγω ὑμῖν ὅτι εἰσίν τινες τῶν ὧδε ἑστώτων οἵτινες οὐ μὴ γεύσωνται θανάτου ἕως ἂν ἴδωσιν τὸν υἱὸν τοῦ ἀνθρώπου ἐρχόμενον ἐν τῇ βασιλείᾳ αὐτοῦ.

16:20 Then he commanded his disciples, that they should tell no one that he was Jesus the Christ. [n. 1394]

16:21 From that time, Jesus began to show to his disciples that he must go to Jerusalem, and suffer many things from the elders and scribes and chief priests, and be put to death, and on the third day rise again. [n. 1396]

16:22 And Peter taking him, began to rebuke him, saying: Lord, let it be far from you, this will not happen to you. [n. 1401]

16:23 Turning, he said to Peter: go behind me, satan, you are a scandal to me: because you do not understand the things that are of God, but the things that are of men. [n. 1403]

16:24 Then Jesus said to his disciples: if any man wants to come after me, let him deny himself, and take up his cross, and follow me. [n. 1407]

16:25 For he who would save his life, will lose it and he who would lose his life for my sake, will find it. [n. 1411]

16:26 For what does it profit a man, if he gain the whole world, and suffer the loss of his own soul? Or what exchange will a man give for his soul? [n. 1412]

16:27 For the Son of man will come in the glory of his Father with his angels and then he will render to every man according to his works. [n. 1415]

16:28 Amen I say to you, there are some of them who stand here, who will not taste death, till they see the Son of man coming in his kingdom. [n. 1416]

1394. Supra posita est confessio Petri de divinitate Christi, hic mandat taciturnitatem ad tempus, ne scilicet dicerent quod ipse esset Christus.

1394. Above, Peter's confession of Christ's divinity was set down; here he commands silence for a time, lest they should say that he is the Christ.

But here a question arises. Since, above, the Lord had sent the disciples to preach the kingdom of God, how does he forbid it here?

According to the surface of the letter, it can be said that he did not instruct them above that they should announce the Christ, but the kingdom of God. But since announcing the kingdom of God includes in itself announcing the Christ, then he seems to forbid here what he commanded above.

Jerome says that he does not forbid what he had preached before, because before he had commanded that Jesus be preached, while here he forbids them to call him the Christ: for Christ is a name of dignity, Jesus the name of the savior. Hence above, *and you will call his name Jesus* (Matt 1:21). Origen responds that the apostles spoke before about Christ, as of a great man; but he wished them to be silent about the Christ, so that he might appear more to them afterward, just as sometimes he gives them teaching beforehand, that they may have time for discernment.

Or one should say that this, *and going, preach* (Matt 10:7), should not be referred to the time before the passion, but after. Hence it touches there on the fact that they will be dragged before kings and governors, and this was not done before the passion.

1395. But why did the Lord command that this should be left unmentioned? For it was going to happen that people would see him suffering, and often when men perceive that some great man is confounded, they are incited more to scandal.

Chrysostom says: *if what is planted is rooted out, it cannot be re-planted as quickly. Hence if the faith had been planted, and then had been rooted up in the passion, afterward it would not have been planted as quickly.* Hence many things should not be said for the sake of avoiding scandal. And that this is the cause is clear, because he immediately announces his passion; hence there is added next:

1396. *From that time, Jesus began to show to his disciples that he must go to Jerusalem, and suffer many things*. And concerning this, he does three things:

first, he foretells the passion;

second, he convicts a disciple, at *turning, he said to Peter*.

third, he teaches the faith, at *then Jesus said to his disciples*.

And concerning the first, two things. For

first, he foretells the passion;

second, the resurrection, at *and on the third day rise again*.

And concerning the first, he touches upon the place, the agents, and the consummation.

1397. It says then, *from that time, Jesus began to show to his disciples*. He spoke of the passion here, and twice later on (Matt 17; 20).

Sed ante hoc tempus non praenuntiaverat. Sed quare modo coepit? Quia apostolis manifestavit. Sed quare non ante? Quia si antequam fides esset confirmata in eis, praenuntiasset passionem, forte dimisissent eum: sed nunc verum Deum credebant, ideo et cetera.

Et dicit **ostendere**, non *dicere* quia haec dicuntur quae manifestantur visibiliter, ostenduntur quae intelliguntur; ideo Iudaeis *dicebat*, discipulis *ostendebat*; Lucae ult., 26: *nonne oportuit Christum pati, et sic intrare in gloriam suam?*

1398. Unde quod dicit **oportet**, tangit locum.

Et quare Ierosolymam? Tangit rationem. Sed quod dicit Ierosolymam, prima ratio est, quia ibi erat templum Dei, ubi fiebant sacrificia. Sacrificia autem veteris legis fuerunt figura istius sacrificii, quod fuit in ara crucis; ideo voluit quod ubi erat figura, pateret veritas; Ephes. V, 2: *et tradidit semetipsum sacrificium, et oblationem, et hostiam Deo in odorem suavitatis* et cetera. Alia ratio est, quia prophetae passi sunt in Ierusalem, ut infra cap. XXIII, 37: ***Ierusalem, Ierusalem, quae occidis prophetas, et lapidas eos, qui ad te missi sunt***. Voluit igitur ibi pati ad ostendendum, quod mors eorum fuit signum passionis Christi. Item Ierusalem dicitur 'visio pacis'; sed ipsa passio pacifica fuit; ad Col. cap. I, 20: *pacificans quae in caelis et quae in terris sunt*. Item ut per istam viam esset nobis via ad Ierusalem supernam; ad Gal. IV, v. 26: *illa autem quae sursum est Ierusalem mater nostra, libera est*.

1399. Sed a quibus? ***A senioribus***. Et hoc est quia eis procurantibus passus est. Ille facit rem, cuius auctoritate fit; unde magis eum interfecerunt, quam milites.

Unde per hoc malitia populi significatur, quia qui videntur meliores, inveniuntur deteriores. Aliquis enim retrahitur a peccato propter aetatem, aliquis propter scientiam, aliquis propter dignitatem; tamen aetas eos non retraxit, quia ***a senioribus***; non scientia, quia ***a scribis***; non dignitas, quia ***a principibus sacerdotum***; Ier. V, 5: *ibo ad optimates, et loquar eis: ipsi enim cognoverunt viam domini et iudicium Dei sui. Et ecce magis hi confregerunt iugum*.

Item quaedam abiectio et humiliatio fuit, quia quando aliquis patitur a plebeis, non est magnum; sed quando a sapientibus, et ab his, qui boni videntur, magna est abiectio; unde Io. XVIII, 35: *gens tua et principes tradiderunt te mihi*.

1400. Item passus est usque ad mortem, ideo dicit ***et occidi***; Act. X, 39: *quem occiderunt suspendentes in ligno*; Dan. IX, v. 26: *occidetur Christus, et non erit eius populus, qui eum negaturus est*.

But before this time he had not foretold it. But why does he begin now? Because he has manifested himself to the apostles. But why not before? Because if he had foretold the passion before faith was well established in them, perhaps they would have abandoned him; but now they believed that he was the true God.

And it says, **to show**, not *to tell*, because things that are told are manifested visibly, while things that are shown are understood. For this reason he told the Jews, and showed the disciples; *ought not Christ to have suffered these things, and so to enter into his glory?* (Luke 24:26).

1398. Hence what he says, **he must**, touches upon the place.

And why Jerusalem? He touches upon the reason. But the first reason he says Jerusalem is that God's temple was there, where the sacrifices were made. Now, the sacrifices of the old law were figures of this sacrifice, which was made on the altar of the cross; therefore he willed that where the figures were, there the truth should stand open. *Christ also has loved us, and has delivered himself for us, an oblation and a sacrifice to God for an odour of sweetness* (Eph 5:2). Another reason is that the prophets suffered in Jerusalem, as below, ***Jerusalem, Jerusalem, you who kill the prophets and stone those who are sent to you*** (Matt 23:37). Therefore he willed to suffer there to show that their death was a sign of Christ's passion. Also, Jerusalem means 'vision of peace'; but the passion itself was peace-making. *And through him to reconcile all things unto himself, making peace through the blood of his cross, both as to the things that are on earth, and the things that are in heaven* (Col 1:20). *But that Jerusalem, which is above, is free: which is our mother* (Gal 4:26).

1399. But from whom? ***From the elders***. And this is because he suffered by their contrivance. The man by whose authority a thing is done, does that thing; hence they killed him more than the soldiers.

Hence this signifies the people's malice, because those who seem better are found to be worse. For some are held back from sin because of age, some because of knowledge, some because of dignity; yet age did not hold them back, ***from the elders***, nor knowledge, ***and scribes***, nor dignity, ***and chief priests***. *I will go therefore to the great men, and I will speak to them: for they have known the way of the Lord, the judgment of their God: and behold these have together broken the yoke more* (Jer 5:5).

Also, this caused a certain abjection and humiliation, for when someone suffers at the hand of the common people, it is no great thing; but when at the hand of the wise, and those who seem good, the humiliation is great. Hence, *your own nation, and the chief priests, have delivered you up to me* (John 18:35).

1400. Likewise, he suffered even unto death, so he says, ***and be put to death***; *whom they killed, hanging him upon a tree* (Acts 10:39); *Christ will be slain: and the people that will deny him will not be his* (Dan 9:26).

Sed adiungitur gaudium resurrectionis *et tertia die resurgere*; Os. VI, 3: *tertia die resuscitabit nos*.

1401. *Et assumens eum Petrus coepit increpare illum*. Hic increpat discipulum obviantem. Et

primo ponitur obviatio;

secundo responsio Christi, ibi *qui conversus dixit Petro* et cetera.

1402. *Et assumens*, vel in aspectu, vel ad se sumens, ne videretur praesumptuosus, quando Dominum ante alios reprehenderet, dixit *absit a te, Domine: non erit tibi hoc*. Dominus collaudaverat eius confessionem, et dederat ei potestatem, quia eum Filium Dei esse cognoverat, ideo putabat, quod si occideretur, quod fides sua frustraretur, et quod non esset Deus; et ideo increpavit eum. Habebat in corde, quod Filius Dei erat, et non advertebat, quod Deus non est increpandus, ut dicitur Iob XV, 3: *arguis eum, qui non est tibi aequalis, et loqueris quod tibi non expedit*. Sed servabat adhuc aliquam fidem divinitatis, quia in Marco habetur, *propitius sis tibi, Domine, et noli te tradere in mortem*.

1403. *Qui conversus dixit, vade retro post me, satana*. Hic ponitur responsio. Hunc locum sic exponit Hilarius: diabolus videns, quod ipse nuntiaverat passionem suam, et cognoscens testimonia prophetarum, incitavit Petrum ad hoc ut dissuaderet. Ideo videns Dominus, quod non suo instinctu loqueretur, increpavit eum, ideo dixit Petro *vade post me*: ita quod sit ibi punctus. Et ad satanam dixit *satana, scandalum es mihi*. Hieronymus dicit, quod non credit, quod instinctu diaboli locutus sit Petrus, sed pietatis affectu; unde ignoranter dixit.

Unde tria facit, quia

primo ponitur admonitio;

secundo increpatio;

tertio causae assignatio.

1404. Admonitio, quia *vade*, Petre. Unde est eadem sententia, quae dicta est supra diabolo, *vade retro, satana*. Vel *vade post me*, sequere me. 'Satanas' est idem quod 'adversarius'. Unde qui consilio divino contradicit, satanas dicitur. *Scandalum mihi es*; idest vis impedire meum propositum.

Sed nonne diligentibus Deum non est scandalum? Origenes dicit, quod perfectis non est scandalum. Unde non scandalizantur. Sed potest aliquis eis ponere scandalum. Unde Petrus scandalum assumpsit, sed Christus non. Vel sic, quia reputat scandalum membrorum esse suum. Unde Paulus: *quis scandalizatur, et ego non scandalizor?* Quia ergo posset aliis scandalum esse, dixit *scandalum mihi es*, non propter me, sed propter membra mea.

But the joy of the resurrection is joined to it: *and on the third day rise again*; *on the third day he will raise us up, and we will live in his sight* (Hos 6:3).

1401. *And Peter taking him, began to rebuke him*. Here he rebukes a disciple opposing him. And

first, the opposition is set down;

second, Christ's response, at *turning, he said to Peter*.

1402. *Taking him*, either in his gaze, or taking him to himself, lest he seem presumptuous when the Lord reprehended him in front of the others, he said, *Lord, let it be far from you, this will not happen to you*. The Lord had praised his confession highly, and had given him power, because he had known him to be the Son of God; for this reason he thought that if he were killed, his faith would be frustrated, and that he would not be God, and therefore he rebuked him. He held in his heart that he was the Son of God, and did not attend to the fact that God is not to be rebuked, as it says, *you reprove him by words, who is not equal to you, and you speak that which is not good for you* (Job 15:3). But he still kept some faith in the divinity, for it is written in Mark: *be merciful to yourself, Lord, and do not wish to hand yourself over to death*.

1403. *Turning, he said to Peter: go behind me, satan*. Here the response is set down. Hilary explains this place thus: the devil, seeing that he had announced his passion, and knowing the testimony of the prophets, incited Peter to advise against it. So the Lord, seeing that he did not speak on his own instigation, reproached him, for which reason he said, *go behind me*, so that he might be pricked there. And to satan he said, *satan, you are a scandal to me*. Jerome says that he does not believe Peter spoke on the devil's instigation, but out of the affection of piety; hence he spoke ignorantly.

Hence he does three things, for

first, the warning is set down;

second, the rebuke;

third, the giving of the cause.

1404. The warning, *go*. Hence it is the same sentence which was said above to the devil, *begone, satan* (Matt 4:10). Or *go behind me*, i.e., follow me. 'Satan' is the same as 'adversary.' Hence he who contradicts the divine counsel is called satan. *You are a scandal to me*; i.e., you wish to impede my intention.

But surely there is no scandal for those who love God? Origen says that there is no scandal for the perfect. Hence they are not scandalized. But someone can set up a scandal for them. Hence Peter took scandal, but not Christ. Or in this way, that he considered it to be a scandal to his members. Hence Paul, *who is scandalized, and I am not on fire?* (2 Cor 11:29). So since it could be a scandal to others, he said, *you are a scandal to me*, not on my account, but on account of my members.

1405. Sed quid est? Supra dixerat *tu es Petrus, et super hanc petram aedificabo Ecclesiam meam*; hic autem appellat eum *satanam*.

Hieronymus dicit quod quae promiserat Dominus, nondum habebat. Sed quia in futurum haec habebat, ideo potuit propter haec eum vocare satanam. Chrysostomus dicit quod voluit ostendere, quid homo potuit per se, et quid ex gratia Dei: quia supra ex gratia Dei recognovit Christi divinitatem; sed ubi retraxit Deus suam gratiam, apparuit humanitas et defectus, intantum quod satanam appellaret eum: ita Dominus vult aliquando viros perfectos cadere, ut suam humanitatem cognoscant.

Et quod ita debeat intelligi, satis concordat illud quod sequitur.

1406. Unde dat causam *quia non sapis quae Dei sunt*. Prius enim dixerat, *tu es Filius Dei*, ibi sapiebat secundum divinitatem; hic vero sapit quod hominis est; I ad Cor. II, 14: *animalis enim homo non percipit quae Dei sunt*. Prov. XIII, 16: *qui fatuus est aperiet stultitiam*. Petrus refugit carnis mortem, sed Spiritus Dei non; unde Io. cap. XV, 13: *maiorem caritatem nemo habet, ut animam suam ponat quis pro amicis suis*.

1407. *Tunc Iesus dixit discipulis suis*. Hic exhortatur ad passionis imitationem. Et

primo ponit exhortationem;

secundo rationem;

tertio confirmat.

Secunda ibi *qui voluerit animam suam salvam facere, perdet eam*; tertia ibi *quid prodest homini si mundum universum lucretur* et cetera.

1408. Ita Petrus volebat impedire passionem, sed ipse invitat eos dicens *si quis vult venire post me, abneget semetipsum, et tollat crucem suam, et sequatur me*; quasi dicat: oportet quod sitis parati ad passionem Christi imitandam. Imitantur speciali modo martyres corporaliter, sed spiritualiter spirituales homines, spiritualiter pro Christo morientes. Unde potest legi de cruce corporali.

Chrysostomus: *sic ergo cum dixit, Petre, vade post me, intelligatis quod soli Petro dixerit: cum vero dixit, qui vult venire* etc., omnes homines vult venire ad se.

Et dicit *vult*, quia magis trahitur qui voluntarie trahitur, quam qui violenter; Ps. LIII, v. 8: *voluntarie sacrificabo tibi*. Ideo tria dicit: quod *abneget*, quod *tollat crucem*, quod *sequatur me*.

1409. Chrysostomus dicit quod loquitur per similitudinem. Si haberes filium, et videres eum male tractari,

1405. But what is this? Above he had said, *you are Peter; and upon this rock I will build my Church* (Matt 16:18); but here he calls him *satan*.

Jerome says that he did not yet have what the Lord had promised. But since he would have these things in the future, for this reason he could call him satan on account of these things. Chrysostom says that he wished to show what a man is able to do by himself, and what he is able to do by the grace of God, since above, by the grace of God, he recognized Christ's divinity; but when God withdrew his grace, his humanity and weakness appeared, to the point that he called him satan. In this way, the Lord sometimes wills perfect men to fall, that they may know their own humanity.

And that it should be understood this way harmonizes well enough with what follows.

1406. Hence he gives the cause: *because you do not understand the things that are of God*. For he had said first, *you are the Christ, the Son of the living God* (Matt 16:16); there he understood according to the divinity, but here he understands what is of man. *But the sensual man perceives not these things that are of the Spirit of God* (1 Cor 2:14). *He who is a fool, lays open his folly* (Prov 13:16). Peter fled from bodily death, but the Spirit of God did not; *greater love than this no man has, that a man lay down his life for his friends* (John 15:13).

1407. *Then Jesus said to his disciples*. Here he urges them to the imitation of his passion. And

first, he sets out the exhortation;

second, the reason;

third, he confirms it.

The second is at *for he who would save his life, will lose it*; the third, at *for what does it profit a man, if he gain the whole world*.

1408. So Peter wished to impede the passion, but he invites them, saying, *if any man wants to come after me, let him deny himself, and take up his cross, and follow me*, as though to say, it is necessary that you be prepared to imitate Christ's passion. Martyrs imitate it in a special way, bodily, but spiritual men imitate it spiritually, dying spiritually for Christ. Hence it can be read as about the bodily cross.

Chrysostom: *so then, when he said, Peter, go behind me, understand that he spoke only to Peter; but when he said, if any man wants to come after me, he wishes all men to come after him*.

And he says, *wants to*, because the one who is drawn voluntarily is drawn more than the one who is drawn violently; *I will freely sacrifice to you* (Ps 53:8). Therefore he says three things, that he should *deny himself*, that he should *take up his cross*, and that he should *follow me*.

1409. Chrysostom says that he speaks by way of a likeness. If you had a son, and you saw him treated badly, if

si non curares, tu abnegares; sic si vis passionem Domini sequi, oportet quod abneges te, et pro nihilo te reputes; Ps. XXXVII, 15: *et factus sum sicut homo non audiens, et non habens in ore suo redargutiones.* Et Prov. XXIII, 35: *verberaverunt me, et non dolui; traxerunt me, et non sensi.* **Et tollat crucem suam, et sequatur me**: quod paratus sit pati crucem, sive mori morte acerbissima et turpissima; Sap. cap. II, 20: *morte turpissima condemnemus eum.* Unde homo debet esse paratus pati quamcumque mortem propter Deum. Pati propter sua scelera est turpe: sed propter Deum, non. Unde I Petr. IV, 15: *nemo patiatur ut homicida, aut fur, aut maledicus, aut alienorum appetitor. Si autem ut Christianus, non erubescat: glorificet autem Deum in isto nomine.*

1410. Secundum Gregorium intelligitur de mortificatione spirituali. Est enim abnegatio sui ipsius tripliciter. Primo quando abnegat statum peccati praecedentis; Rom. VI, 11: *existimate vos mortuos peccato.* Item si non est in peccato, et transferret se ad statum perfectum; ad Phil. III, 12: *si quo modo occurram ad resurrectionem quae est ex mortuis, non quod iam acceperim, aut iam perfectus sim: sequor autem si quo modo comprehendam, in quo et comprehensus sum a Christo Iesu.* Item qui proprium affectum abnegat; ad Gal. II, 19: *ego autem per legem legi mortuus sum ut Deo vivam: Christo confixus sum cruci.* Et II ad Cor. V, 14: *si unus mortuus est, et omnes mortui sunt.*

Tollat crucem. 'Crux' a 'cruciatu' dicitur. Spiritualiter cruciatur, cuius mens cruciatur propter proximi compassionem, ut Apostolus Rom. XII, 15: *flere cum flentibus.* Cruciatur similiter quis per poenitentiam; ad Gal. cap. V, 24: *qui Christi sunt, carnem suam crucifixerunt cum vitiis et concupiscentiis.* **Et sequatur me**. Multi compatiuntur, sed Deum non sequuntur. Qui compatitur, et in peccato est, non sequitur, quia venit Christus peccata destruere. Item si affligis te propter vanam gloriam, Deum non sequeris; supra VI, 16: *cum ieiunatis, nolite fieri sicut hypocritae tristes: exterminant enim facies suas, ut appareant hominibus ieiunantes* et cetera.

1411. Qui enim voluerit animam suam salvam facere perdet eam. Hic redditur ratio suae admonitionis, et est ratio a magnitudine retributionis. Et hoc dupliciter potest legi. Est enim duplex salus; salus scilicet animae, et haec est iustorum; salus corporis, et haec omnium, etiam iumentorum; Ps. XXXV, 7: *homines et iumenta salvabis, Domine.*

Unde dicamus qui voluerit animam suam salvam facere, vitam corporalem non abnegando non tollerando crucem, **perdet eam**. Supra dixit **qui vult**, hic **qui voluerit**. Unde sicut illud dupliciter interpretari poterat, similiter istud. **Qui voluerit animam suam**, quae est principium vitae corporalis, **salvam facere**, scilicet quod

you did not care, you would deny him; in the same way, if you wish to follow the Lord's passion, you must deny yourself, and consider yourself as nothing. *And I became as a man who hears not: and who has no reproofs in his mouth* (Ps 37:15). And, *they have beaten me, but I was not sensible of pain: they drew me, and I felt not* (Prov 23:35). **And take up his cross, and follow me**: for let him be prepared to suffer the cross, or to die a most bitter and shameful death; *let us condemn him to a most shameful death* (Wis 2:20). Hence a man should be prepared to suffer any death whatever for God's sake. To suffer for one's own sins is shameful, but to suffer for God's sake is not. Hence, *but let none of you suffer as a murderer, or a thief, or a railer, or a coveter of other men's things. But if as a Christian, let him not be ashamed, but let him glorify God in that name* (1 Pet 4:15–16).

1410. According to Gregory, it is understood as about spiritual mortification. For there are three denials of oneself. First, when one denies the preceding state of sin; *so do you also reckon, that you are dead to sin* (Rom 6:11). Likewise, if a man is not in sin, and carries himself over to the perfect state; *not as though I had already attained, or were already perfect; but I follow after, if I may by any means apprehend, wherein I am also apprehended by Christ Jesus* (Phil 3:12). Likewise, he who denies his own particular affection; *for I, through the law, am dead to the law, that I may live to God: with Christ I am nailed to the cross* (Gal 2:19). And, *if one died for all, then all were dead* (2 Cor 5:14).

Take up his cross. 'Cross' derives from 'crucify.' He is spiritually crucified whose mind is tormented out of compassion for a neighbor, as the Apostle says, *weep with those who weep* (Rom 12:15). Similarly, one is tortured by penance; *and they who are Christ's, have crucified their flesh, with the vices and concupiscences* (Gal 5:24). **And follow me**. Many have compassion, but do not follow God. One who has compassion and is in sin is not following, because Christ came to destroy sins. Likewise, if you afflict yourself for the sake of vainglory, you are not following God; above, *and when you fast, be not as the hypocrites, sad. For they disfigure their faces, that they may appear unto men to fast* (Matt 6:16).

1411. For he who would save his life, will lose it. Here he gives a reason for his warning, and it is a reason drawn from the greatness of the recompense. And this can be read in two ways. For there are two kinds of health, namely health of the soul, and this belongs to the just; and health of the body, and this belongs to all, even to beasts of burden. *Men and beasts you will preserve, O Lord* (Ps 35:7).

Hence let us say, he who would save his soul, while not denying his bodily life and not bearing the cross, **will lose it**. He said above, *if any man wants to*, but here **he who would**. Hence just as what he said above could be interpreted in two ways, similarly what he says here. **He who would save his life**, which is the principle of bodily life, namely

non occidatur, vel quod non compatiatur, **perdet eam**. Ps. LXXII, 27: *perdes omnes qui fornicantur abs te*. **Qui autem perdiderit**, vel tradendo in mortem, vel abnegando delectationes, **propter me, inveniet eam**; Eccli. LI, 35: *modicum laboravi, et inveni multam requiem*.

Vel sic. **Qui voluerit animam suam salvam facere**, et illam ad salutem aeternam ducere, Is. LI, 6: *salus mea in sempiternum erit*, **perdet eam**, vel sustinendo mortem, vel abnegando carnalia. **Qui autem perdiderit propter me**, scilicet qui carnalia desideria dimiserit, **inveniet eam**, scilicet vitam; II Cor. cap. XIII, 4: *nam et nos infirmi sumus in illo, sed vivemus cum eo*.

1412. Quid enim prodest homini si universum mundum lucretur, animae autem suae detrimentum patiatur? Hic confirmat per rationem. Posset aliquis dicere: non curo; magis volo vitam hanc praesentem quam aliam. Et hoc excludit. Primo per vitam illam inaestimabilem; secundo per damnum animae irrecompensabile.

1413. Dicit ergo **quid prodest** etc., idest quid proficiunt tibi ista temporalia, si animam perdis? Naturale est homini quod magis diligit finem quam ea quae sunt ad finem, ut corpus quam divitias. Unde naturale est quod omnia exponuntur pro salute corporis. Si contrarium fiat, perversitas est passionis. Sic et naturale est plus animam diligere quam corpus; unde sapiens est qui magis vellet corporaliter pati, quam sustinere confusionem magnam. Si ergo ita est, magis debet optare salutem animae quam corporis, etiam si totum mundum posset habere. Sed **quid prodest homini si universum mundum lucretur, animae vero suae detrimentum patiatur?** Quasi dicat: inaestimabile damnum est animae detrimentum.

1414. Item posset dicere: si habeo et perdo, potero recuperare: ideo excludit dominus **aut quam dabit homo commutationem pro anima sua?** Quasi dicat, nullam. Prov. VI, 35: *non accipiet pro redemptione dona plurima*.

Sed numquid non potest redimi? Dan. IV, v. 24: *peccata tua eleemosynis redime*. Dicendum quod hic loquitur quantum ad perfectam perditionem, quia non posset recuperare, nisi primo invenisset; sed quando est contritus, reinvenit. Gregorius aliter: *duplex est tempus Ecclesiae, prosperitatis et adversitatis: in adversitate adversa, in prosperitate prospera*.

1415. Filius autem hominis venturus est in gloria Patris sui. Hic agit de iudiciaria potestate. Et primo ponitur iudiciaria potestas; secundo tacitae obiectioni respondet.

Forte tu dices: ad quid sequar et tollam crucem? et cetera. Quia iudicium Filii hominis est, et potestas. Io. V, 27: *potestatem dedit ei iudicium facere, quia Filius*

he who shall will that he not be killed, or that he not suffer with his neighbor, **will lose it**. *For behold they who go far from you will perish* (Ps 72:27). But **he who would lose his life for my sake**, either by handing it over to death or by denying pleasures to it, **will find it**. *Behold with your eyes how I have labored a little, and have found much rest to myself* (Sir 51:35).

Or in this way. **For he who would save his life**, and lead it to eternal salvation, for *my salvation will be forever* (Isa 51:6), **will lose it**, either by enduring death or by denying bodily things. **And he who would lose his life for my sake**, namely he who will abandon carnal desires, **will find it**, namely life; *for we also are weak in him: but we shall live with him* (2 Cor 13:4).

1412. For what does it profit a man, if he gain the whole world, and suffer the loss of his own soul? Here he confirms what he said with a reason. Someone could say: I do not care; I want this present life more than the other life. And he excludes this. First, through that inestimable life; second, through the non-repayable loss of the soul.

1413. He says then, **for what does it profit**, i.e., what do these temporal things profit you, if you lose your soul? It is natural to man that he loves the end more than those things which are directed to the end, as he loves his body more than riches. Hence it is natural that he abandons all things for the health of the body. If the contrary happens, it is a perversion of the passion. In the same way it is also natural to love the soul more than the body; hence the wise man is he who wills rather to suffer bodily than to endure a great confusion. If then this is so, one should rather choose the soul's salvation than the body's, even if one could have the whole world. But **what does it profit a man, if he gain the whole world, and suffer the loss of his own soul?** As though to say, the loss of the soul is an inestimable injury.

1414. Likewise someone could say: if I have and I lose, I will be able to regain. So the Lord excludes this: **or what exchange will a man give for his soul?** as though to say, nothing. *Nor will he accept for satisfaction ever so many gifts* (Prov 6:35).

But is it unable to be redeemed? *Redeem your sins with alms* (Dan 4:24). One should say that he speaks here as regards complete loss, because one would not be able to regain unless one had first found; but when one is contrite, he re-finds. Gregory interprets it another way: *there are two times for the Church, the time of prosperity and the time of adversity: in adversity by adverse things, in prosperity by favorable things*.

1415. For the Son of man shall come in the glory of his Father. Here he treats of his judiciary power. And first, the judiciary power is set down; second, he responds to an unmentioned objection.

Perhaps you say: why should I follow, and take up the cross? Because judgment and power belong to the Son of man. *He has given him power to do judgment, because he is*

hominis est. Non doleas ergo quod patiatur, *quia venturus est in gloria*. Non doleas, quod reprobetur a senioribus, quia *venturus est in gloria Patris sui*: nec quod ante multos, quia *cum angelis suis*; Phil. II, 11: *omnis lingua confiteatur, quia Dominus Iesus Christus in gloria est Dei Patris*. Et infra XXV, 31: *cum autem venerit Filius hominis in maiestate sua, et omnes angeli cum eo, tunc sedebit super sedem maiestatis suae* et cetera. Tunc *reddet*, et restituet, *unicuique secundum opera sua*.

1416. Deinde respondet tacitae obiectioni *amen dico vobis*; quasi dicat: dixi vobis quod venturus est Filius hominis et cetera. Sed nolite mirari. Quare? Volo vobis ostendere, quia **sunt quidam de hic stantibus, qui non gustabunt mortem**. Peccatores absorbentur morte, sed iusti gustant mortem. Isti autem erant Petrus, Ioannes et Iacobus. **Donec videant Filium hominis venientem in regno suo**. Hoc fuit signum gloriae futurae. Eos autem non nominavit propter invidiam aliorum. Potuissent autem habere invidiam, quia magis his, quam aliis. Item propter importunitatem, quia importuni essent si nihil eis ostenderet.

Aliter potest dici, quod regnum Dei est Ecclesia: ideo est aliquis qui non gustabit mortem, sicut Ioannes, *donec videat Filium hominis venientem in regno suo*; idest donec dilatetur Ecclesia, quia tantum vixit, quod vidit Ecclesiam dilatari, et multas Ecclesias aedificari.

the Son of man (John 5:27). Therefore, do not sorrow because he suffers, for he *will come in the glory*. Do not sorrow because he is rejected by the elders, for he *will come in the glory of his Father*. Neither sorrow because this will happen in front of many, for he will come *with his angels*; *and that every tongue should confess that the Lord Jesus Christ is in the glory of God the Father* (Phil 2:11). And below, *and when the Son of man will come in his majesty, and all the angels with him, then will he sit upon the seat of his majesty* (Matt 25:31). *Then he will render* and restore *to every man according to his works*.

1416. Then he responds to an unmentioned objection: *amen I say to you*, as though to say, I said to you that the Son of man will come. But do not be astonished. Why? I wish to show you, for *there are some of them who stand here, who will not taste death*. Sinners are swallowed up by death, but the just *taste* death. Now, these men were Peter, John, and James. **Till they see the Son of man coming in his kingdom**. This was a sign of future glory. But he did not name them, lest the others be jealous. And they could have been jealous, since he gave more to these than to the others. Also, lest they pester him, because they would have pestered him if he did not show them anything.

In another way, it can be said that the kingdom of God is the Church. So there is someone who *will not taste death*, like John, *till they see the Son of man coming in his kingdom*, i.e., until the Church is widespread, for he lived so long that he saw the Church widespread, and many churches built.

Chapter 17

Lecture 1

¹⁷:¹ Et post dies sex asumpsit Iesus Petrum, et Iacobum, et Ioannem fratrem eius, et ducit illos in montem excelsum seorsum, [n. 1418]

¹⁷:² et transfiguratus est ante eos. Et resplenduit facies eius sicut sol, vestimenta autem eius facta sunt alba sicut nix. [n. 1421]

¹⁷:³ Et ecce apparuit illis Moyses et Elias cum eo loquentes. [n. 1428]

¹⁷:⁴ Respondens autem Petrus dixit ad Iesum: Domine, bonum est nos hic esse: si vis, faciamus hic tria tabernacula, tibi unum, et Moysi unum, et Eliae unum. [n. 1430]

¹⁷:⁵ Adhuc eo loquente, ecce nubes lucida obumbravit eos. Et ecce vox de nube dicens. Hic est Filius meus dilectus, in quo mihi bene complacui; ipsum audite. [n. 1433]

¹⁷:⁶ Et audientes discipuli ceciderunt in faciem suam, et timuerunt valde. [n. 1439]

¹⁷:⁷ Et accessit Iesus, et tetigit eos, dixitque eis: surgite, et nolite timere. [n. 1442]

¹⁷:⁸ Levantes autem oculos suos neminem viderunt nisi solum Iesum. [n. 1443]

¹⁷:⁹ Et descendentibus illis de monte, praecepit eis Iesus dicens: nemini dixeritis visionem, donec Filius hominis a mortuis resurgat. [n. 1444]

¹⁷:¹⁰ Et interrogaverunt eum discipuli dicentes: quid ergo scribae dicunt, quod Eliam oporteat primum venire? [n. 1445]

¹⁷:¹ Καὶ μεθ' ἡμέρας ἓξ παραλαμβάνει ὁ Ἰησοῦς τὸν Πέτρον καὶ Ἰάκωβον καὶ Ἰωάννην τὸν ἀδελφὸν αὐτοῦ καὶ ἀναφέρει αὐτοὺς εἰς ὄρος ὑψηλὸν κατ' ἰδίαν.

¹⁷:² καὶ μετεμορφώθη ἔμπροσθεν αὐτῶν, καὶ ἔλαμψεν τὸ πρόσωπον αὐτοῦ ὡς ὁ ἥλιος, τὰ δὲ ἱμάτια αὐτοῦ ἐγένετο λευκὰ ὡς τὸ φῶς.

¹⁷:³ καὶ ἰδοὺ ὤφθη αὐτοῖς Μωϋσῆς καὶ Ἠλίας συλλαλοῦντες μετ' αὐτοῦ.

¹⁷:⁴ ἀποκριθεὶς δὲ ὁ Πέτρος εἶπεν τῷ Ἰησοῦ· κύριε, καλόν ἐστιν ἡμᾶς ὧδε εἶναι· εἰ θέλεις, ποιήσω ὧδε τρεῖς σκηνάς, σοὶ μίαν καὶ Μωϋσεῖ μίαν καὶ Ἠλίᾳ μίαν.

¹⁷:⁵ ἔτι αὐτοῦ λαλοῦντος ἰδοὺ νεφέλη φωτεινὴ ἐπεσκίασεν αὐτούς, καὶ ἰδοὺ φωνὴ ἐκ τῆς νεφέλης λέγουσα· οὗτός ἐστιν ὁ υἱός μου ὁ ἀγαπητός, ἐν ᾧ εὐδόκησα· ἀκούετε αὐτοῦ.

¹⁷:⁶ καὶ ἀκούσαντες οἱ μαθηταὶ ἔπεσαν ἐπὶ πρόσωπον αὐτῶν καὶ ἐφοβήθησαν σφόδρα.

¹⁷:⁷ καὶ προσῆλθεν ὁ Ἰησοῦς καὶ ἁψάμενος αὐτῶν εἶπεν· ἐγέρθητε καὶ μὴ φοβεῖσθε.

¹⁷:⁸ ἐπάραντες δὲ τοὺς ὀφθαλμοὺς αὐτῶν οὐδένα εἶδον εἰ μὴ αὐτὸν Ἰησοῦν μόνον.

¹⁷:⁹ Καὶ καταβαινόντων αὐτῶν ἐκ τοῦ ὄρους ἐνετείλατο αὐτοῖς ὁ Ἰησοῦς λέγων· μηδενὶ εἴπητε τὸ ὅραμα ἕως οὗ ὁ υἱὸς τοῦ ἀνθρώπου ἐκ νεκρῶν ἐγερθῇ.

¹⁷:¹⁰ Καὶ ἐπηρώτησαν αὐτὸν οἱ μαθηταὶ λέγοντες· τί οὖν οἱ γραμματεῖς λέγουσιν ὅτι Ἠλίαν δεῖ ἐλθεῖν πρῶτον;

¹⁷:¹ And after six days, Jesus took with him Peter and James, and John his brother, and brought them up into a high mountain, apart; [n. 1418]

¹⁷:² and he was transfigured before them. And his face shone as the sun and his garments became white as snow. [n. 1421]

¹⁷:³ And behold there appeared to them Moses and Elijah talking with him. [n. 1428]

¹⁷:⁴ And Peter answering, said to Jesus: Lord, it is good for us to be here; if you wish, let us make here three tents, one for you, and one for Moses, and one for Elijah. [n. 1430]

¹⁷:⁵ And as he was still speaking, behold a bright cloud overshadowed them. And behold a voice out of the cloud, saying: this is my beloved Son, in whom I am well pleased: hear him. [n. 1433]

¹⁷:⁶ And hearing this, the disciples fell upon their face, and were very much afraid. [n. 1439]

¹⁷:⁷ And Jesus came and touched them, and said to them: arise, and fear not. [n. 1442]

¹⁷:⁸ And lifting up their eyes, they saw no one but only Jesus. [n. 1443]

¹⁷:⁹ And as they came down from the mountain, Jesus charged them, saying: tell to no one the vision, till the Son of man is risen from the dead. [n. 1444]

¹⁷:¹⁰ And his disciples asked him, saying: why then do the scribes say that Elijah must come first? [n. 1445]

17:11 At ille respondens ait eis: Elias quidem venturus est, et restituet omnia. [n. 1447]

17:12 Dico autem vobis, quia Elias iam venit, et non cognoverunt eum, sed fecerunt in eo quaecumque voluerunt. Sic et Filius hominis passurus est ab eis. [n. 1448]

17:13 Tunc intellexerunt discipuli, quia de Ioanne Baptista dixisset eis. [n. 1452]

17:11 ὁ δὲ ἀποκριθεὶς εἶπεν· Ἠλίας μὲν ἔρχεται καὶ ἀποκαταστήσει πάντα·

17:12 λέγω δὲ ὑμῖν ὅτι Ἠλίας ἤδη ἦλθεν, καὶ οὐκ ἐπέγνωσαν αὐτὸν ἀλλὰ ἐποίησαν ἐν αὐτῷ ὅσα ἠθέλησαν· οὕτως καὶ ὁ υἱὸς τοῦ ἀνθρώπου μέλλει πάσχειν ὑπ᾽ αὐτῶν.

17:13 τότε συνῆκαν οἱ μαθηταὶ ὅτι περὶ Ἰωάννου τοῦ βαπτιστοῦ εἶπεν αὐτοῖς.

17:11 But answering he said to them: Elijah indeed will come, and restore all things. [n. 1447]

17:12 But I say to you, that Elijah has already come, and they did not know him, but have done to him whatever they wished. So also will the Son of man suffer from them. [n. 1448]

17:13 Then the disciples understood that he had spoken to them of John the Baptist. [n. 1452]

1417. In parte praecedenti ostendit virtutem doctrinae evangelicae etc., hic ostenditur finis, qui est gloria futura:

et circa hoc duo facit.

Primo ostendit quomodo demonstrata est in transfiguratione;

secundo quomodo perveniri possit ad eam, in XVIII cap. *in illa hora* et cetera.

Circa primum duo.

Primo demonstratur futura gloria;

secundo praecipit celationem;

tertio ponit dubitationem.

Secunda ibi *et descendentibus illis de monte* etc., tertia ibi *et interrogaverunt eum discipuli* et cetera.

Circa primum tria.

Primo ponuntur circumstantiae transfigurationis;

secundo transfiguratio;

tertio effectus.

Secunda ibi *et transfiguratus est ante eos*; tertia ibi *et audientes discipuli ceciderunt in faciem suam*.

Ponit autem tres circumstantias, scilicet tempus; discipulos; locum.

1418. Tempus ponit, cum dicit *post dies sex*.

Sed hic est quaestio litteralis, quare statim cum dixit: *sunt quidam de hic stantibus* etc. non statim transfiguratus est. Solvit Chrysostomus. Primo ut accenderet desiderium apostolorum; secundo ut mitigaret invidiam eorum, quia forte post verbum istud turbati fuerunt.

Sed quid est quod hic habetur *post sex dies*, in Luca habetur, *post octo dies*?

Planum est quod Lucas numerat diem quo dixit, et diem transfigurationis; Matthaeus vero dies solum intermedios; ideo, remoto primo et ultimo, non remanent nisi sex dies. Per sex dies significantur sex aetates, post quas speramus venire ad gloriam futuram. Item in sex

1417. In the preceding part, he showed the power of the evangelical teaching; here the end is shown, which is future glory.

And concerning this he does two things:

first, he shows how it was revealed in the transfiguration;

second, how one can arrive at it, at *at that hour* (Matt 18:1).

Concerning the first, two things:

first, the future glory is revealed;

second, he commands that a secret be kept;

third, a doubt is set down.

The second is at *and as they came down from the mountain*; the third, at *and his disciples asked him*.

Concerning the first, three things:

first, the circumstances of the transfiguration are set down;

second, the transfiguration;

third, the effect.

The second is at *and he was transfigured before them*; the third, at *and hearing this, the disciples fell upon their face*.

And he sets down three circumstances, namely the time; the disciples; the place.

1418. He sets down the time, when he says, *and after six days*.

But there is a literal question here, namely why he was not transfigured right away when he said, *there are some of them who stand here, who will not taste death, till they see the Son of man coming in his kingdom* (Matt 16:28). Chrysostom solves it. First, to arouse the apostles' desire; second, to mitigate their envy, because perhaps they had been troubled after this word.

But why does it say here, *and after six days*, while in Luke it says, *eight days after these words*? (Luke 9:28).

It is clear that Luke counted the day on which he said it, and the day of the transfiguration; but Matthew only counted the days in between; and so, with the first and last days removed, there remained only six days. The six days signify the six ages, after which we hope to come to future

glory. Likewise, he perfected his work in six days, and so the Lord wished to show himself after six days, because unless we are lifted up to God above all the creatures which the Lord created in those six days, we cannot arrive at the kingdom of God.

1419. Likewise, ***Jesus took with him Peter and James, and John***. Why not all? To indicate that not all who are called, arrive; hence below, ***for many are called, but few chosen*** (Matt 20:16). And why three only? To indicate that no one shall arrive except in the faith of the Trinity. *He who believes and is baptized, will be saved* (Mark 16:16). But why these men rather than the others? The reason is that Peter was more fervent; John, because he had been specially loved; likewise James, because he was especially a warrior against the adversaries of the faith; hence Herod killed him first, since he thought to do something great for the Jews: *and he killed James* (Acts 12:2), and there follows, *seeing that it pleased the Jews* (Acts 12:3).

1420. ***And brought them up into a high mountain apart***. Why on a mountain? To indicate that no one is led to contemplation but he who goes up onto a mountain, as in Genesis, about Lot: *save yourself in the mountain* (Gen 19:17).

And he says, **high**, because of the loftiness of contemplation. *It will be exalted above the hills, and all nations will flow unto it. And many people will go, and say: come and let us go up to the mountain of the Lord* (Isa 2:2–3). For that loftiness of glory will be above every loftiness of knowledge and virtue.

Likewise **apart**, because they separated themselves from those who are evil. Below, ***he will separate them one from another, as the shepherd separates the sheep from the goats*** (Matt 25:32).

1421. There follows the transfiguration: ***and he was transfigured before them***. And

first, the transfiguration is set down;

second, the testimony, at ***and as he was still speaking***.

Concerning the first,

he sets down the transfiguration;

second, the manner;

third, Peter's wonderment.

1422. He says then, ***and he was transfigured***, i.e., he changed his figure, ***before them***. To be transfigured is the same as to be changed from one's own figure, as it is written that *satan transforms himself into an angel of light* (2 Cor 11:14). So it is no marvel if the just shall be transfigured into a figure of glory; and so he was transfigured, because he laid aside what is his own.

Some have said that he assumed another body, which is false; but whoever is changed in figure, in his exterior appearance, is called transfigured, just as when someone is healthy and ruddy and then becomes sick and pallid,

dicitur transfiguratus; sic Christus, quia in alia forma quam appareret, apparuit, quia corpus eius non erat lucidum, sed tantum claritatem accepit, ideo dicitur **transfiguratus**.

1423. Ideo sequitur *et resplenduit facies eius sicut sol*; ubi tangitur modus. Et

primo demonstratur quantum ad claritatem faciei;
secundo quantum ad nitorem vestium;
tertio quantum ad testimonium.

1424. Dicit ergo *et resplenduit facies eius sicut sol*. Hic futuram gloriam revelavit, ubi erunt corpora clara et splendentia. Et haec claritas non erat ab essentia, sed ex claritate interioris animae plenae caritate; Is. c. LVIII, 8: *tunc erumpet quasi mane lumen tuum*, et sequitur, *et gloria Domini colliget te*. Unde erat quaedam refulgentia in corpore. Anima enim Christi videbat Deum, et super omnem claritatem a principio suae conceptionis; Io. I, 14: *vidimus gloriam eius*.

1425. Si ergo in beatis aliis derivatur claritas ab anima ad corpus, quare non in Christo qui Deus erat et homo?

Dicendum quod quia Deus erat, ordo humanae naturae erat in sua potestate. Hic autem est ordo quod partes sibi communicent, ut laeso corpore, compassio sit in anima, et ex anima afficiatur corpus. Sed hic ordo subiectus erat Christo. Unde ita perfectum erat gaudium in parte superiori quod non egrediebatur extra: unde et perfecte erat viator, et perfecte comprehensor. Unde quando volebat, non fiebat reflexus, sed quando volebat, reflexus fuit, et apparuit splendidus.

1426. Sed nonne dos fuit in Christo? Quidam dicunt quod sic, et quod omnes dotes accepit in via: dotem subtilitatis in nativitate, agilitatis in undarum calcatione, claritatis hic, impassibilitatis in administrando sacramentum altaris.

Ego autem hoc non credo, quia dos est quaedam proprietas ipsius gloriae. Unde quod super mare ambulavit, quod resplenduit, totum fuit ex virtute divina, quia dos gloriae repugnat viatori, sed habuit aliquam similitudinem, quia *resplenduit facies eius sicut sol*; Apoc. I, 16: *facies eius sicut sol refulget in virtute sua*.

Sed potest obiici, quia iusti fulgebunt sicut sol. Ergo splendor Christi maior non erit aliis.

Dico quod sic. Sed quia in his sensibilibus non est clarius cui possit comparari; ideo soli comparatur.

1427. *Vestimenta autem eius facta sunt alba sicut nix*. Hic de vestimentis. Hoc apparet quod non fuit per

and thus is called transfigured. In the same way Christ was transfigured, because he appeared in another form than the one in which he was appearing before, since his body was not luminescent, but only took on a brightness; this is why he is called **transfigured**.

1423. So there follows *and his face shone as the sun*; here the manner is touched upon. And

first, it is described as regards the brightness of his face;
second, as regards the brightness of his clothing;
third, as regards the testimony.

1424. It says then, *and his face shone as the sun*. Here he revealed the future glory, where bodies will be brilliant and splendid. And this brilliance was not from the essence, but from the brilliance of the interior soul, full of charity; *then will your light break forth as the morning*, and there follows *and the glory of the Lord will gather you up* (Isa 58:8). Hence there was a certain splendor in his body. For Christ's soul was seeing God, and beyond all brilliance, from the beginning of his conception; *and we saw his glory* (John 1:14).

1425. If then, in the blessed, a brilliance descends from the soul to the body, why not in Christ, who was God and man?

One should say that since he was God, the order of human nature was in his power. But the order is that the parts communicate among themselves, so that when the body is wounded, the soul suffers together with it, and the body is affected by the soul. But here the order was subject to Christ. Hence the joy in the superior part was perfect in such a way that it did not go out from the superior part: hence he was both perfectly a *viator*, and perfectly a *comprehensor*. Hence when he wished, there was no reflection, but when he wished, there was a reflection, and he appeared resplendent.

1426. But did not Christ have the gifts? Some say that this is so, and that he received all the gifts *in via*: the gift of subtility at his birth, of agility when he walked on the waves, brilliance here, and impassibility when he administered the sacrament of the altar.

But I do not believe this, because a gift is a certain property of glory itself. Hence that he walked on the sea, that he was resplendent, all happened by the divine power, since the gift of glory is incompatible with a *viator*; but he had a certain likeness to a glorified body, since **his face shone as the sun**. *And his face was as the sun shines in his power* (Rev 1:16).

But it can be objected that the just will shine like the sun. Therefore Christ's splendor will not be greater than others' splendor.

I say that it will be. But since there is nothing more brilliant among sensible things to compare him to, he is compared to the sun.

1427. *And his garments became white as snow*. Here he treats of the clothing. It is clear that this was not due to

mutationem Christi, nec per dotem, quia vestimenta non sunt perceptiva dotis. Per vestimenta significantur sancti; Is. XLIX, 18: *vivo ego, dicit Dominus, quia his omnibus sicut ornamento vestieris*.

Et dicit **facta sunt alba sicut nix**. Nix habet candorem et frigiditatem, sic sancti habent candorem gloriae; Sap. III, 7: *fulgebunt iusti et tamquam scintillae in arundineto discurrent* et cetera. Item habebunt refrigerium ab ardore concupiscentiae; in Ps. LXVII, 15: *nive dealbabuntur in Selmon*. Vel per vestimenta intelligitur littera Sacrae Scripturae.

1428. *Et ecce apparuerunt illis Moyses et Elias*. Et quare apparuerunt? Chrysostomus assignat rationes. Prima ratio est ad confirmandum fidem discipulorum. Quaesierat supra: **quem dicunt homines esse filium hominis?** et cetera. Et dixerunt: **alii Eliam** et cetera. Ut vero ostenderet differentiam sui ad illos, ideo voluit eos adducere; Ps. LXXXV, v. 8: *non est similis tui in diis, Domine* et cetera. Secunda ratio est ad confutandum Iudaeos. Dicebant enim quod erat transgressor legis; item dicebant quod erat blasphemator, ut habetur Io. X, 33: *de bono opere non lapidamus te, sed de blasphemia*. Ideo quia Elias omnibus prophetis sanctior fuit, et Moyses legislator; coram Moyse et Elia ostendit, quia non erat Deo contrarius, nec transgressor legis. Tertia ratio est, ut ostendat se iudicem vivorum et mortuorum, quia Elias vivus erat, Moyses mortuus. Quarta ratio est ad certificationem Petri; quia Petrus increpaverat Dominum de morte, ideo ostendit quod non sunt increpandi qui exponunt se morti, invocando istos duos; quia Elias morti se exposuit coram Iezabel, similiter Moyses exposuit se propter legem. Quinta ratio est, quia duo erant in eo quod voluit ostendere in his duobus, scilicet mansuetudo, quam ostendit in Moyse, exemplum zeli Dei, quem ostendit in Elia, de quo dicitur quod *surrexit Elias quasi ignis, et verbum ipsius quasi facula ardebat*. Sexta ratio assignatur in Glossa, quia omnis lex et prophetae testimonium dixerunt Christo. Unde Lc. XXIV, 44: *omnia oportet impleri de me quae sunt in lege et prophetis*.

1429. Sed tunc est quaestio. De Elia non est mirum si ibi fuit, quia est vivus; sed de Moyse est quaestio quomodo ibi erat.

Quidam dixerunt quod angelus fuit ibi loco ipsius. Sed hoc nihil est, quia Moyses fuit ibi in anima solum. Sed qualiter visus est? Dicendum, quod sicut angeli videntur.

1430. Sequitur affectus Petri **respondens autem Petrus dixit** et cetera. Et possumus exponere torquendo ad carnalitatem, vel ad devotionem.

Chrysostomus retorquet ad carnalitatem. Supra Christus dixerat se passurum, et Petrus increpaverat

a change in Christ, nor due to one of the gifts, since clothes do not receive the gifts. Clothing signifies the saints; *I live, says the Lord, you will be clothed with all these as with an ornament* (Isa 49:18).

And it says, **and his garments became white as snow**. Snow has radiance and coldness, as the saints have the radiance of glory; *the just will shine, and will run to and fro like sparks among the reeds* (Wis 3:7). Likewise, the fire of concupiscence is cooled in them; *they will be whited with snow in Selmon* (Ps 67:15). Or by clothing is understood the letter of Sacred Scripture.

1428. *And behold there appeared to them Moses and Elijah*. And why did they appear? Chrysostom gives reasons. The first reason is to confirm the disciples' faith. He had asked above, **who do men say that the Son of man is?** (Matt 16:13). And they said, **some Elijah**. But so that he might make clear the difference between himself and them, he willed to bring them; *there is none among the gods like unto you, O Lord* (Ps 85:8). The second reason is to refute the Jews. For they said that he was a transgressor of the law; they also said that he was a blasphemer: *not for a good work do we stone you, but for blasphemy* (John 10:33). So since Elijah was holier than all the prophets, and Moses was a legislator, he made clear in the presence of Moses and Elijah that he was not contrary to God, nor a transgressor of the law. The third reason is to show that he is the judge of the living and the dead, because Elijah was living, Moses dead. The fourth reason is to assure Peter. For Peter had reproached the Lord about death, so by calling these two in, he showed that those who expose themselves to death are not to be reproached; for Elijah exposed himself to death before Jezabel, and Moses similarly exposed himself for the sake of the law. The fifth reason is because there were two things in him which he wished to point out in these two, namely meekness, which he pointed out in Moses, and an example of zeal for God, which he pointed out in Elijah, of whom it is said in Sirach that *Elijah the Prophet stood up, as a fire, and his word burnt like a torch* (Sir 48:1). The sixth reason is given in the Gloss, that all the law and the prophets gave witness to Christ. Hence, *all things must be fulfilled, which are written in the law of Moses, and in the prophets* (Luke 24:44).

1429. But then there is a question. It is no marvel if Elijah was there, because he was alive; but there is a question about Moses, how he was there.

Some say that an angel was there in his place. But this amounts to nothing, because Moses was there in soul only. But how was he seen? One should say that he was seen just as angels are seen.

1430. There follows Peter's affection: **and Peter answering, said**. And we can explain this either by referring it to carnality, or to devotion.

Chrysostom refers it to carnality. Above, Christ had said that he was going to suffer, and Peter had reproached him,

when he rebuked him. Hence Moses and Elijah appeared, speaking of his passion; so when Peter heard them refer to the passion, he could not listen. Now, he did not wish to set himself against them, so he thought that if he were to remain there, he would avoid death. Therefore, lest they leave quickly, he said, *let us make here three tents*.

And why did he say, *one for Moses, and one for Elijah*? Since he saw that Jesus was inclined toward death, he wanted these men to impede his death. Of Elijah it is written that when the king sent fifty men, he made fire come down from heaven (2 Kgs 1:10). Likewise, it is written of Moses that when a quarrel arose in the tabernacle, a cloud descended (Num 12:10). So he thought that a cloud could be gotten through Moses, and fire through Elijah.

1431. But others refer it to Peter's devotion. And in accord with this, he does two things: first, he touches upon the affection; second, the advice, at *if you wish*.

He says then, *Lord, it is good for us to be here*. Out of an exceedingly great fervor, when he saw the glory, he was so affected that he wanted never to be parted from it, God willing.

And what will it be like for those who shall be in perfect glory? For, being in that beatitude, they will never want to be parted; *but it is good for me to adhere to my God* (Ps 72:28).

1432. Second, he gives counsel, and as Luke says, *not knowing what he said* (Luke 9:33); hence he says, *if you wish, let us make here three tents*, since we should submit our will to the divine will, as above, *your will be done* (Matt 6:10).

Hence Peter spoke well in that, but badly in this, because he thought that he could have glory without death, which is contrary to: *for we know, if our earthly house of this habitation be dissolved, that we have a building of God, a house not made with hands, eternal in heaven* (2 Cor 5:1). Also, because he thought that the glory of the saints is in this world, while it is not here, but in heaven; above, *be glad and rejoice, for your reward is very great in heaven* (Matt 5:12). Also, because he thought that they needed houses; but they had no need of houses here, but had houses in heaven: *behold the tabernacle of God with men* (Rev 21:3). Also, because he wished three tents to be built, for one is enough for the Father and the Son and the Holy Spirit. Also, because he compared Christ to the others, which he should not have done; *I will not level God with man* (Job 32:21). Peter, all have one tent, which is faith.

1433. There follows the testimony: *and as he was still speaking, behold a bright cloud overshadowed them*. Peter spoke foolishly, so he was unworthy of a response. He wanted a material testimony, so the Lord willed to make it clear that the saints have no need. Likewise, he willed to show himself through a cloud; *his power is in the clouds* (Ps 67:35). But sometimes a brilliant cloud appears, sometimes a dark

nubes tenebrosa; Ex. XIX, 18 dicitur quod apparuit nubes caliginis; sed hic apparet lucida, quia significat consolationem gloriae, quia tunc protegentur ab omni aestu; Apoc. XXI, 4: *absterget Deus omnem lacrimam ab oculis sanctorum, et mors ultra non erit, neque luctus, neque clamor, neque dolor erit ultra, quoniam prima abierunt.*

1434. Sequitur testimonium ex voce Patris; unde *et vox de nube dicens* et cetera. Sed quare de nube? Ad significandum quod est vox Patris. Dominus habitat in nube.

1435. *Hic est Filius meus dilectus, in quo mihi bene complacui.* Tangitur Christi dignitas ex proprietate filiationis, ex perfectione dilectionis, et ex conformitate operationis. Unde dicit **hic est**, quasi singularis Filius. Alii sunt filii per adoptionem, Ps. LXXXI, 6: *ego dixi: dii estis, et filii Excelsi omnes,* sed iste est verus Filius, scilicet singulariter, ut I Io. V, 20: *Filius Dei venit, et dedit nobis sensum, ut cognoscamus verum Deum.*

1436. Item, aliter, **dilectus**. Dilectio nostra est ex bonitate creaturae. Non enim est res bona, quia diligo eam, sed quia res bona est, diligo eam. Sed dilectio Dei est causa bonitatis rerum. Et sicut Deus perfudit bonitatem in creaturis per creationem, sic in Filio per generationem, quia totam Filio communicat bonitatem; unde creaturae benedicuntur per participationem, sed Filio totum dedit; Io. III, 35: *Pater diligit Filium, et omnia posuit in manibus eius.* Unde ipse Amor procedit a Patre diligente Filium, et a Filio diligente Patrem.

1437. Sed contingit quod alicui datur aliquid, et non bene utitur datis, ideo non datori complacet; sed Deus dedit isti plenitudinem, et bene usus est eis; ideo sibi complacuit; unde dicit *in quo mihi bene complacui*. Idem habetur supra XII, 18: *in quo mihi complacui* et *in quo requiescit animus meus*.

Quia ergo talis est *ipsum audite*. Unde insinuat eum datum doctorem omnium; Deut. c. XVIII, 15: *prophetam suscitabit Dominus de gente vestra, ipsum sicut me audite.* Vel *ipsum audite*, non Moysen, non Eliam, nisi secundum quod Christum docent, vel doctrinam Christi.

1438. Notate quod Christus habuit testimonium de caelo a Patre, de inferno a Moyse, et ab Elia de paradiso, a discipulis de terra: *ut in nomine Iesu omne genu flectatur caelestium, terrestrium et infernorum*, Phil. II, 10.

Item notandum quod duplex est regeneratio: una in baptismo, alia quando ab omni inquinamento spiritus mundabimur. Unde in baptismo designatus est Iesus per columbam, quae est animal simplex, ad designandum

cloud. In Exodus, it says that a darksome cloud appeared (Exod 19:18); but here a shining one appeared, because it signifies the consolation of glory, since then they will be protected from all agitation. *And God will wipe away all tears from their eyes: and death will be no more, nor mourning, nor crying, nor sorrow will be any more, for the former things are passed away* (Rev 21:4).

1434. There follows a testimony from the voice of the Father; hence *and behold, a voice out of the cloud, saying*. But why from the cloud? To indicate that it is the voice of the Father. The Lord dwells in a cloud.

1435. *This is my beloved Son, in whom I am well pleased*. Christ's dignity is touched upon based on the property of sonship, the perfection of love, and the likeness of operation. Hence he says, *this is*, as it were, the unique Son. Others are sons through adoption; *I have said: you are gods and all of you the sons of the Most High* (Ps 81:6), but this one is the true Son, that is, uniquely, as John says, *the Son of God is come: and he has given us understanding that we may know the true God* (1 John 5:20).

1436. Also, in another way, **beloved**. Our love is based on a creature's goodness. For a thing is not good because I love it, but rather I love a thing because it is good. But God's love is the cause of goodness in things. And as God poured out goodness in creatures through creation, so in the Son through generation, since he communicates his entire goodness to the Son. Hence creatures are blessed by participation, but he gave the entire goodness to the Son; *the Father loves the Son: and he has given all things into his hand* (John 3:35). Hence Love itself proceeds from the Father loving the Son, and from the Son loving the Father.

1437. But it can happen that something is given to someone, and he does not use well what was given, and so does not please the one who gave it. But God gave the fullness of his goodness to this one, and he used it well. Therefore he was well pleased, and hence he says, *in whom I am well pleased*. The same thing is written above, *in whom I am well pleased* (Matt 3:17), and *in whom my soul has been well pleased* (Matt 12:18).

Therefore, because he is such, **hear him**. Hence he insinuates that he was given as a teacher for all; *the Lord your God will raise up to you a prophet of your nation and of your brethren like unto me: him you shall hear* (Deut 18:15). Or *hear him*: not Moses or Elijah, except according as they teach Christ, or Christ's teaching.

1438. Notice that Christ had testimony from heaven by the Father, from hell by Moses, from paradise by Elijah, and from earth by the disciples: *that in the name of Jesus every knee should bow, of those that are in heaven, on earth, and under the earth* (Phil 2:10).

Also, one should note that there are two regenerations: one in baptism, the other when we shall be cleansed from every unclean spirit. Hence in baptism, Jesus was pointed out by a dove, which is a simple animal, to indicate

simplicitatem: est etiam animal foecundum, ad designandum aliam regenerationem. Apparuit in nube lucida, ad designandum claritatem et extinctionem omnis concupiscentiae; Is. IV, 5: *et creabit Dominus super omnem locum montis Sion, et ubi invocatus est, nubem per diem, et fumum et splendorem ignis flammantis per noctem.*

1439. Et audientes discipuli ceciderunt in faciem suam, et timuerunt. Posita transfiguratione, hic ponitur effectus in discipulis. Et

primo ponitur timor;
secundo confortatio Christi contra timorem;
tertio effectus.

Secunda ibi *et accessit Iesus* etc.; tertia ibi **levantes autem oculos suos neminem viderunt**.

1440. Dicit ergo *et audientes*. Audierunt vocem Patris de nube, sicut dicitur II Petr. I, 18: *hanc vocem audivimus, cum essemus in monte.*

Et ponit signum timoris, quia **ceciderunt in faciem suam**.

Sequitur timor *et timuerunt valde*. Sed quare timuerunt? Ponit Hieronymus tres rationes. Prima, quia cognoverunt se errasse, sicut dicitur de Adam Gen. III, 10: *Domine, audivi vocem tuam, et timui, quia nudus eram.* Item quia nube erant involuti, cognoverunt maiestatis divinae praesentiam; Ex. c. XIII, 21: *Dominus autem praecedebat eos ad ostendendam viam per diem in columna nubis* et cetera. Et naturale est quod unusquisque ex eo quod non consuevit, stupescat. Item propter vocem de nube; Deut. V, 26: *quid est omnis caro ut audiat vocem Dei viventis?* Et ex hoc fortitudo eorum defecit, quia ceciderunt in faciem suam.

1441. Sed notandum quod aliter cadunt impii, aliter sancti. Impii cadunt retrorsum, ut habetur I Reg. IV, 18 de Heli, qui cum audisset rumores de arca Domini, cecidit de sella, et, fracta cervice, expiravit. Sed sancti in facies suas; Apoc. VII, 11: *qui ceciderunt in facies suas*. Et ratio est, quia non videmus quod retro est. Eccle. II, 14: *sapientis oculi in capite eius*.

1442. Consequenter ponitur confortatio Christi. Et confortat eos facto et verbo: facto, contra timorem et casum: contra timorem, per eius praesentiam, quia **accessit Iesus**. Ps. XXII, 4: *non timebo mala, quoniam tu mecum es.* Et supra XIV, 27: *ego sum, nolite timere.* Item confortat per contactum, quia *dat lasso virtutem*, Is. XL, v. 29, et in Daniele legitur: *manus eius tetigit me et erexit*; unde dicit *et tetigit eos*. Item confortat contra casum; unde, **dixitque eis: surgite**. Eph. V, 14: *surge qui dormis, et exurge a mortuis, et illuminabit te Christus.* Item contra

1439. And hearing this, the disciples fell upon their face, and were very much afraid. The transfiguration having been set down, here its effect on the disciples is set down. And

first, their fear is set down;
second, Christ's comfort against their fear;
third, the effect.

The second is at **and Jesus came**; the third, at **and lifting up their eyes, they saw no one**.

1440. He says then, **and the disciples hearing**. They heard the voice of the Father from the cloud, as is said in Peter, *and this voice we heard brought from heaven, when we were with him in the holy mount* (2 Pet 1:18).

And he sets down a sign of their fear, that the disciples **fell upon their face**.

There follows the fear: **and were very much afraid**. But why were they afraid? Jerome sets out three reasons. First, because they knew that they had erred, as is said of Adam: *I heard your voice in paradise; and I was afraid, because I was naked* (Gen 3:10). Also, since they were wrapped in the cloud, they were aware of the presence of the divine majesty; *and the Lord went before them to show the way by day in a pillar of a cloud* (Exod 13:21). And it is natural that anyone be astounded by what he is not accustomed to. Also, on account of the voice from the cloud; *what is all flesh, that it should hear the voice of the living God?* (Deut 5:26). And because of this their courage failed, for they fell down on their faces.

1441. But one should note that the impious fall down in one way, the saints in another. The impious fall back, as is written of Heli, who when he had heard rumors about the Lord's ark, fell from a chair and died of a broken neck (1 Sam 4:18). But the saints fall on their faces: *they fell down before the throne upon their faces* (Rev 7:11). And the reason is that we do not see what is behind. *The eyes of a wise man are in his head* (Eccl 2:14).

1442. Next, Christ's comforting is set down. And he comforts them by deed and by word. By deed, against fear and falling. Against fear by his presence: **Jesus came**. *I will fear no evils, for you are with me* (Ps 22:4). And above, **it is I, fear not** (Matt 14:27). Likewise, he comforts through contact, for *it is he who gives strength to the weary* (Isa 40:29); *and behold a hand touched me, and lifted me up upon my knees* (Dan 10:10); hence it says, **and touched them**. Likewise, he comforts them against falling; hence **and said to them: arise**. *Rise you who sleep, and arise from the dead: and*

timorem **nolite timere**. Timor ille erat pusillanimitas, et illi qui surgunt a peccato, timorem deponunt, quia *perfecta caritas foras mittit timorem*, I Io. IV, 18.

1443. Consequenter sequitur effectus confortationis **levantes autem oculos suos neminem viderunt nisi solum Iesum**. Et iste est effectus confortationis divinae, quia a Christo confortati non vident nisi Iesum, nec in ullo gaudent vel confortantur nisi in ipso; ad Phil. I, 21: *mihi vivere Christus est, et mori lucrum*. Item **neminem viderunt nisi solum Iesum**, quia recedente umbra legis, et doctrina prophetarum, quae per Moysen et Eliam designantur, sola doctrina Christi tenetur.

Vel, secundum aliam litteram, *solus remansit*, ne vox videretur esse prolata ad Moysen vel Eliam. Unde ipsis non apparentibus certum fuit quod ad eum vox prolata fuit.

1444. Consequenter ponitur mandatum de differenda huius visionis revelatione; unde dicit **et descendentibus illis de monte praecepit Iesus dicens: nemini dixeritis visionem**.

Sed quae est ratio? Triplex est. Prima, quia, ut dicit Hieronymus, futurum erat quod Christus pateretur, et quod Iudaei scandalizarentur; I ad Cor. I, 23: *Iudaeis quidem scandalum*: ideo si audissent istud, magis scandalizati fuissent, unde reputassent nihil fuisse. Unde magis essent tardi ad credendum resurrectionem.

Remigius sic exponit: quia si nuntiasset, numquam implevisset quod desiderabat, et sic frustratus esset suo desiderio; quia habetur Lc. XXII, 15: *desiderio desideravi hoc Pascha manducare vobiscum*.

Hilarius exponit sic: quia spiritualem gloriam non decebat nuntiari nisi per viros spirituales; sed ipsi nondum erant spirituales; Io. VII, 39: *nondum erat eis Spiritus datus*.

1445. Et interrogaverunt eum et cetera. In parte ista satisfacit petitioni discipulorum. Et

    primo ponitur petitio;

    secundo responsio;

    tertio effectus.

Secunda ibi **at ille respondens** etc.; tertia ibi **tunc intellexerunt** et cetera.

1446. Apostoli videntes eum transformari, credebant quod ex tunc inciperet regnare. Intellexerant enim quod Elias debebat prius venire, Mal. ult., 5. Et quia eum viderant, credebant quod iam venisset, et appropinquaret regnum eius, ut habetur Mal. cap. ult., 1: *ecce enim dies veniet* et cetera. Et ibid., 5: *mittam vobis Eliam Prophetam antequam veniat dies Domini magnus et horribilis*

Christ will enlighten you (Eph 5:14). Likewise, against fear: **and fear not**. This fear was pusillanimity, and those who rise from sin put off fear, because *perfect charity casts out fear* (1 John 4:18).

1443. Next, there follows the effect of the comforting: **and lifting up their eyes, they saw no one except Jesus**. And this is the effect of the divine comforting, that those comforted by Christ see no one but Jesus, nor do they rejoice or take comfort in any but him; *for to me, to live is Christ; and to die is gain* (Phil 1:21). Likewise, **they lifting up their eyes saw no one but only Jesus** because when one withdraws from the shadows of the law, and from the teachings of the prophets, which are indicated by Moses and Elijah, one holds only the teaching of Christ.

Or, according to another letter, he was *the only one remaining* lest it seem that the voice was speaking about Moses or Elijah. Hence when these two did not appear, it was certain that the voice was speaking about Jesus.

1444. Next is set down the command about delaying the revelation of this vision. Hence he says, **and as they came down from the mountain, Jesus charged them, saying: tell no one the vision**.

But for what reason? There are three reasons. First because, as Jerome says, it was going to happen that Christ would suffer, and that the Jews would be scandalized; *unto the Jews indeed a stumblingblock* (1 Cor 1:23). Therefore, if they had heard this, they would have been more scandalized, and hence they would have considered it to be nothing. Then they would have been more slow to believe in the resurrection.

Remigius explains it this way: because if he had told of it, what he desired would never have been fulfilled, and thus his own desire would have been frustrated, for it is written: *with desire I have desired to eat this Pasch with you* (Luke 22:15).

Hilary explains it this way: because spiritual glory would have been fittingly described only by spiritual men; but they were not yet spiritual. *As yet the Spirit was not given* (John 7:39).

1445. And his disciples asked him. In this part he satisfies the disciples' request. And

    first, the request is set down;

    second, the response;

    third, the effect.

The second is at **and his disciples asked him**; the third, at **then the disciples understood**.

1446. When the apostles saw him transformed, they thought that he would begin to reign from that moment. For they had understood that Elijah was supposed to come first (Mal. 4:5). And since they had seen him, they thought that he had already come, and his kingdom had drawn near: *for behold the day shall come* (Mal 4:1). And *behold I will send you Elijah the Prophet, before the coming of the*

et cetera. Sed istud nesciebant ex Scriptura, quia simplices erant, sed sciebant ex dictis scribarum. Unde dicunt **quid ergo scribae dicunt quod Eliam oportet primum venire?** Scribae, qui ex lege noverant, ita dicebant, sed pervertebant Scripturam.

Est enim duplex adventus Christi, scilicet gloriae: et de hoc adventu intelligitur quod Elias praecedet illum; sed est alius adventus in carne: unde ipsi pervertentes exponebant de isto.

1447. Huic dubitationi Dominus satisfacit. Et primo tangit adventum futurum; secundo praeteritum. Unde dicit **at ille respondens ait illi: Elias quidem venturus est**. Unde de duplici Elia loquitur, quia de Elia in propria persona venturo: et hic venturus est ad annuntiandum viam iustitiae **et restituet omnia**, et convertet corda hominum ad Christum, convertet Iudaeos ad fidem patriarcharum qui habuerunt fidem de Christo, quia, ut habetur Rom. XI, 25, *caecitas ex parte contigit in Israel, donec plenitudo gentium intraret, et sic omnis Israel salvus fiet*.

Augustinus aliter exponit **restituet omnia**, quia veniente Antichristo omnes seducentur; sed mortuo Antichristo omnes restituentur ad fidem per praedicationem Eliae.

Origenes sic: **restituet**, quia si aliquis debet quod non solvit, debet restituere. Sed quilibet debitor est mortis; et quia Elias nondum est mortuus, cum veniet, restituet omnia, et reddet debitum mortis.

1448. Additur de alio Elia **dico autem vobis, quia Elias iam venit**. Quis est iste? Ioannes Baptista, non quod ipse sit in persona, sicut habetur Io. I, 21, cum petebatur ab eo, *Elias es tu? Respondit, non*. Sed in spiritu et virtute: quia sicut Elias secundi adventus erit praecursor, ita Ioannes primi adventus. Item sicut Elias contradicebat Iezabel, sic Ioannes Herodiadi: et sicut Elias fuit eremi cultor, sic Ioannes. Unde de ipso dicitur Lc. I, 7: *ipse praecedet eum in spiritu et virtute Eliae*. In spiritu: non quia transeat spiritus Eliae in Ioannem, ut aliqui posuerunt, sed eamdem virtutem habebit.

1449. Et non cognoverunt eum, idest non approbaverunt, ut habetur infra XXI, 25, ubi quaesivit Dominus si baptismus Ioannis est de caelo vel de terra, quia, si de caelo dixissent, credere debuissent. **Sed fecerunt in eo quaecumque voluerunt**, quia eum male tractaverunt, non secundum quod iustitia exigebat, sed incarceraverunt eum. Simile habetur de Ieremia Eccli. XLIX, 9: *nam male tractaverunt eum, qui a ventre matris consecratus est propheta*.

great and dreadful day of the Lord (Mal 4:5). But they did not know this from Scripture, since they were simple, but rather they knew about it from the sayings of the scribes. Hence they say, **why then do the scribes say that Elijah must come first?** The scribes, who knew about it from the law, spoke thus, but corrupted the Scripture.

For there are two comings of Christ, namely the coming in glory, and about this coming it is understood that Elijah goes before him; but there is another coming in the flesh. Hence these men, corrupting the Scripture, explained it as about this coming.

1447. The Lord satisfies this doubt. And first, he touches upon the future coming; second, the past. Hence it says, **But answering, he said to them: Elijah indeed will come**. Hence he speaks of a double Elijah, for he speaks of the Elijah to come in his own person. And this one will come to announce the way of justice **and restore all things**, and he will convert the hearts of men to Christ, he will convert the Jews to the faith of the Patriarchs who had faith in Christ: *blindness in part has happened in Israel, until the fullness of the gentiles should come in and so all Israel should be saved* (Rom 11:25–26).

Augustine explains it another way: **he will restore all things**, because when the Antichrist comes he will seduce all, but when the Antichrist is dead all will be restored to faith by Elijah's preaching.

Origen, in this way: **he will restore**, because if someone owes what he has not paid back, he should restore it. But anyone is a debtor to death; and since Elijah is not yet dead, when he comes he will restore all things, and repay the debt of death.

1448. There is added, about the other Elijah, **but I say to you, that Elijah has already come**. Who is this one? John the Baptist, not that he is Elijah in person, as is said in John, when it was asked of him, *are you Elijah? And he said: I am not* (John 1:21). But he is Elijah in spirit and power, for just as Elijah will be the precursor to the second coming, so John was the precursor to the first coming. Likewise, just as Elijah spoke against Jezabel, so John spoke against Herodias. And as Elijah was a desert dweller, so was John. Hence it is said of him, *and he will go before him in the spirit and power of Elijah* (Luke 1:17). In spirit: not because Elijah's spirit will pass over into John, as some have held, but because he will have the same power.

1449. And they did not know him, i.e., they did not approve him, as is written below (Matt 21:25), where the Lord asked if John's baptism is from heaven or from earth, because if they said from heaven, they should have believed. **But have done to him whatever they wished**, because they treated him badly, not according as justice demanded, but rather they imprisoned him. Something similar is written about Jeremiah, *for they treated him evil, who was consecrated a prophet from his mother's womb* (Sir 49:9).

1450. *Sic et Filius hominis passurus est ab eis.* Ioannes praecursor fuit Christi quantum ad nativitatem, quia sicut Ioannes ex muliere veteri et sterili supra naturam, sic Christus ex virgine supra naturam. Item in praedicatione, quia incepit praedicare. *Agite poenitentiam*, sic et Christus. Item quantum ad baptismum; ideo requirebatur quod esset praecursor quantum ad passionem, quia sicut ipse propter iustitiam occisus est, sic et Christus. Unde *sic Filius hominis passurus est ab eis*.

1451. Sed a quibus *eis*? Videtur quod non ab eis a quibus Ioannes, quia Ioannes ab Herode, Christus a scribis.

Sed potest dici quod ab eisdem, quia Ioannes ab Herode et Iudaeis consentientibus, sed Christus a scribis, consentiente Herode. Unde in partibus illis erat, et oblatus fuit ei; Ps. II, 2: *astiterunt reges terrae, et principes convenerunt in unum adversus Dominum, et adversus Christum eius*.

Vel *sic passurus est ab eis*, ita quod ly *eis* faciat simplicem relationem, quia omnes sunt in una generatione, a quibus passus est Ioannes et Christus.

1452. Consequenter ponitur effectus huius responsionis *tunc intellexerunt discipuli quia de Ioanne Baptista dixisset eis*. *Tunc*: cum Dominus locutus est eis. *Declaratio sermonum tuorum illuminat, et intellectum dat parvulis*, Ps. CXVIII, 130.

1450. *So also will the Son of man suffer from them.* John was Christ's precursor as regards birth, because just as John was born from an old and sterile woman, beyond nature, so Christ was born from a virgin, beyond nature. Likewise in preaching, because he began to preach, *do penance* (Matt 3:2); so also did Christ. Likewise, as regards baptism. Therefore, it was required that he be the precursor as regards the passion, because just as he was killed for the sake of justice, so also was Christ. Hence, *so also will the Son of man suffer from them*.

1451. But from whom? *From them*? It seems that Jesus did not suffer from those by whom John suffered, because John suffered from Herod, and Christ from the scribes.

But one can say that it was from the same ones, because John suffered from Herod and with the Jews giving consent, while Christ suffered from the scribes, with Herod giving consent. For they were in that region, and he was presented to him; *the kings of the earth stood up, and the princes met together, against the Lord and against his Christ* (Ps 2:2).

Or, *so also will the Son of man suffer from them*, such that the *from them* expresses a simple relation, since all those from whom John and Christ suffered are in one generation.

1452. Next, the effect of this response is set down: *then the disciples understood that he had spoken to them of John the Baptist*. *Then*: that is, when the Lord had spoken to them. *The declaration of your words gives light: and gives understanding to little ones* (Ps 118:130).

Lecture 2

17:14 Et cum venisset ad turbam, accessit ad eum homo genibus provolutus ante eum, [n. 1453]

17:15 et dicens: Domine, miserere filio meo, quia lunaticus est, et male patitur: nam saepe cadit in ignem, et crebro in aquam. [n. 1457]

17:16 Et obtuli eum discipulis tuis, et non potuerunt curare eum. [n. 1460]

17:17 Respondens Iesus ait: O generatio incredula et perversa, quousque ero vobiscum? Usquequo patiar vos? Afferte huc illum ad me. [n. 1461]

17:18 Et increpavit illum Iesus, et exiit ab eo daemonium, et curatus est puer ex illa hora. [n. 1463]

17:19 Tunc accesserunt discipuli ad Iesum secreto, et dixerunt: quare nos non potuimus eiicere illum? [n. 1464]

17:20 Dicit illis Iesus: propter incredulitatem vestram. Amen quippe dico vobis, si habueritis fidem sicut granum synapis, dicetis monti huic: transi hinc, et transibit; et nihil impossibile erit vobis. [n. 1466]

17:21 Hoc autem genus non eiicitur nisi per orationem et ieiunium. [n. 1472]

17:22 Conversantibus autem eis in Galilaea, dixit illis Iesus: Filius hominis tradendus est in manus hominum, [n. 1473]

17:23 et occident eum, et tertio die resurget. Et contristati sunt vehementer. [n. 1474]

17:24 Et cum venissent Capharnaum, accesserunt, qui didrachma accipiebant, ad Petrum, et dixerunt ei: magister vester non solvit didrachma? [n. 1476]

17:14 Καὶ ἐλθόντων πρὸς τὸν ὄχλον προσῆλθεν αὐτῷ ἄνθρωπος γονυπετῶν αὐτὸν

17:15 καὶ λέγων· κύριε, ἐλέησόν μου τὸν υἱόν, ὅτι σεληνιάζεται καὶ κακῶς πάσχει· πολλάκις γὰρ πίπτει εἰς τὸ πῦρ καὶ πολλάκις εἰς τὸ ὕδωρ.

17:16 καὶ προσήνεγκα αὐτὸν τοῖς μαθηταῖς σου, καὶ οὐκ ἠδυνήθησαν αὐτὸν θεραπεῦσαι.

17:17 ἀποκριθεὶς δὲ ὁ Ἰησοῦς εἶπεν· ὦ γενεὰ ἄπιστος καὶ διεστραμμένη, ἕως πότε μεθ' ὑμῶν ἔσομαι; ἕως πότε ἀνέξομαι ὑμῶν; φέρετέ μοι αὐτὸν ὧδε.

17:18 καὶ ἐπετίμησεν αὐτῷ ὁ Ἰησοῦς καὶ ἐξῆλθεν ἀπ' αὐτοῦ τὸ δαιμόνιον καὶ ἐθεραπεύθη ὁ παῖς ἀπὸ τῆς ὥρας ἐκείνης.

17:19 Τότε προσελθόντες οἱ μαθηταὶ τῷ Ἰησοῦ κατ' ἰδίαν εἶπον· διὰ τί ἡμεῖς οὐκ ἠδυνήθημεν ἐκβαλεῖν αὐτό;

17:20 ὁ δὲ λέγει αὐτοῖς· διὰ τὴν ὀλιγοπιστίαν ὑμῶν· ἀμὴν γὰρ λέγω ὑμῖν, ἐὰν ἔχητε πίστιν ὡς κόκκον σινάπεως, ἐρεῖτε τῷ ὄρει τούτῳ· μετάβα ἔνθεν ἐκεῖ, καὶ μεταβήσεται· καὶ οὐδὲν ἀδυνατήσει ὑμῖν.

17:21 [τοῦτο δὲ τὸ γένος οὐκ ἐκπορεύεται εἰ μὴ ἐν προσευχῇ καὶ νηστείᾳ.]

17:22 Συστρεφομένων δὲ αὐτῶν ἐν τῇ Γαλιλαίᾳ εἶπεν αὐτοῖς ὁ Ἰησοῦς· μέλλει ὁ υἱὸς τοῦ ἀνθρώπου παραδίδοσθαι εἰς χεῖρας ἀνθρώπων,

17:23 καὶ ἀποκτενοῦσιν αὐτόν, καὶ τῇ τρίτῃ ἡμέρᾳ ἐγερθήσεται. καὶ ἐλυπήθησαν σφόδρα.

17:24 Ἐλθόντων δὲ αὐτῶν εἰς Καφαρναοὺμ προσῆλθον οἱ τὰ δίδραχμα λαμβάνοντες τῷ Πέτρῳ καὶ εἶπαν· ὁ διδάσκαλος ὑμῶν οὐ τελεῖ [τὰ] δίδραχμα;

17:14 And when he had come to the multitude, there came to him a man, falling down on his knees before him, [n. 1453]

17:15 saying: Lord, have pity on my son, for he is a lunatic, and suffers much, for he falls often into the fire, and often into the water. [n. 1457]

17:16 And I brought him to your disciples, and they could not cure him. [n. 1460]

17:17 Then Jesus answered and said: O unbelieving and perverse generation, how long will I be with you? How long will I suffer you? Bring him here to me. [n. 1461]

17:18 And Jesus rebuked him, and the devil went out of him, and the child was cured from that hour. [n. 1463]

17:19 Then the disciples came to Jesus secretly, and said: why could we not cast him out? [n. 1464]

17:20 Jesus said to them: because of your unbelief. For, amen I say to you, if you have faith as a grain of mustard seed, you would say to this mountain: remove from here, and it would be removed; and nothing will be impossible to you. [n. 1466]

17:21 But this kind is not cast out except by prayer and fasting. [n. 1472]

17:22 And when they gathered together in Galilee, Jesus said to them: the Son of man will be betrayed into the hands of men; [n. 1473]

17:23 and they will kill him, and the third day he will rise again. And they were troubled exceedingly. [n. 1474]

17:24 And when they had come to Capernaum, those who received the didrachmas came to Peter and said to him: does not your master pay the didrachmas? [n. 1476]

17:25 Ait: etiam. Et cum intrasset domum, praevenit eum Iesus dicens: quid tibi videtur, Simon? Reges terrae a quibus accipiunt tributum, vel censum: a filiis suis, an ab alienis? [n. 1478]

17:25 λέγει· ναί. καὶ ἐλθόντα εἰς τὴν οἰκίαν προέφθασεν αὐτὸν ὁ Ἰησοῦς λέγων· τί σοι δοκεῖ, Σίμων; οἱ βασιλεῖς τῆς γῆς ἀπὸ τίνων λαμβάνουσιν τέλη ἢ κῆνσον; ἀπὸ τῶν υἱῶν αὐτῶν ἢ ἀπὸ τῶν ἀλλοτρίων;

17:25 He said: yes. And when he had come into the house, Jesus prevented him, saying: what does it seem to you, Simon? The kings of the earth, from whom do they receive tribute or custom? From their own children, or from strangers? [n. 1478]

17:26 Et ille dixit: ab alienis. Dixit illi Iesus: ergo liberi sunt filii. [n. 1478]

17:26 εἰπόντος δέ· ἀπὸ τῶν ἀλλοτρίων, ἔφη αὐτῷ ὁ Ἰησοῦς· ἄρα γε ἐλεύθεροί εἰσιν οἱ υἱοί.

17:26 And he said: from strangers. Jesus said to him: then the children are free. [n. 1478]

17:27 Ut autem non scandalizemus eos, vade ad mare, et mitte hamum, et eum piscem qui primus ascenderit, tolle et, aperto ore eius, invenies staterem, illum sumens, da eis pro me et te. [n. 1481]

17:27 ἵνα δὲ μὴ σκανδαλίσωμεν αὐτούς, πορευθεὶς εἰς θάλασσαν βάλε ἄγκιστρον καὶ τὸν ἀναβάντα πρῶτον ἰχθὺν ἆρον, καὶ ἀνοίξας τὸ στόμα αὐτοῦ εὑρήσεις στατῆρα· ἐκεῖνον λαβὼν δὸς αὐτοῖς ἀντὶ ἐμοῦ καὶ σοῦ.

17:27 But that we may not scandalize them, go to the sea, and cast in a hook, and that fish which comes up first, take, and when you have opened its mouth, you will find a stater; take that, and give it to them for me and you. [n. 1481]

1453. *Et cum venisset* hic praenuntiat tranquillitatem gloriae, quae impugnatur per oppressionem daemonum, et turbationem hominum. Et

primo praenuntiat primam cessare per curationem lunatici;

secundo secundam.

Et circa primum

primo ponitur curatio lunatici;

secundo praenuntiat passionem, ibi *conversantibus autem eis in Galilaea* etc.,

tertio de solutione tributi, ibi *et cum venisset Capharnaum* et cetera.

Circa primum

primo sanat;

satisfacit dubitationi, ibi *dixit illis Iesus* et cetera.

Circa primum facit duo.

Primo ponitur petitio patris;

secundo satisfactio, ibi *afferte huc illum ad me*.

Circa primum tria facit. Quia

primo ponitur tempus;

secundo indicatio infirmi;

tertio petitio.

1454. Tempus ponitur, cum dicit *et cum venisset ad turbam*. Petrus allectus dulcedine gloriae, semper vellet esse in monte; sed Christus ex caritate quam habuit ad turbas, quia *caritas non quaerit quae sua sunt*, voluit descendere de monte, ut turbae haberent accessum ad eum.

Unde cum venisset *accessit ad eum homo genibus provolutus*. Si non descendisset, non venisset ad eum homo ille. Et accessit humiliter, quia *genibus provolutus*, quia *exaudit Deus orationem humilium*, Ps. ci, 18. Per istum genus humanum potest significari. Phil. II, 10:

1453. *And when he had come*. Here he foretells the tranquility of glory, which is attacked by the oppression of demons, and the disturbance of men. And

first, he foretells that the first will cease, through the healing of the lunatic;

second, the second.

And concerning the first,

first, the healing of the lunatic is set down;

second, he foretells the passion, at *and when they gathered together in Galilee*;

third, about paying the tribute, at *and when they had come to Capernaum*.

Concerning the first,

first, he heals;

second, he satisfies doubt, at *Jesus said to them*.

Concerning the first, he does two things:

first, the father's petition is set down;

second, the satisfaction, at *bring him here to me*.

Concerning the first, he does three things:

first, the time is set down;

second, the sick one is made known;

third, the petition.

1454. The time is set down when it says, *and when he had come to the multitude*. Peter, drawn by the sweetness of glory, would have remained on the mountain always; but Christ willed to come down from the mountain so the crowds could have access to him, out of the charity which he had toward the crowds, since *charity does not seek what is her own* (1 Cor 13:5).

Hence when he had come, *there came to him a man falling down on his knees*. If he had not come down, this man would not have come to him. And he came humbly, *falling down on his knees*, because *the Lord hears the prayer of the humble* (Ps 101:18). This man can signify the human race.

ut in nomine Iesu omne genu flectatur caelestium, terrestrium et infernorum et cetera.

1456. Deinde ponitur petitio. Non petit, sed infirmitatem exponit: sufficit enim misericordi miseriam exponere.

Primo exponit infirmitatem;
secundo accidentia;
tertio quod remedium non inveniebat.

1457. Dicit ergo **Domine, miserere filio meo, quia lunaticus est**.

Notandum quod multi pro se rogant, ut supra de muliere habente fluxum sanguinis: aliquando aliquis pro alio rogat, ut hic: aliquando vero aliquem curat non rogatus, sicut in spirituali infirmitate, ut habetur de publicano Lc. XVIII, 12 s., aliquando vero ad petitionem alterius aliquis curatur, ut habetur Iacobi ult., 16: *orate pro invicem ut salvemini*, aliquando sine oratione, ut in conversione Pauli, Act. IX, 4 ss.

1458. Sed quid est quod dicitur quod lunaticus est? Lunaticus proprie est qui secundum statum lunae alienatur. Sed videtur quod iste non esset lunaticus, sed daemoniacus, quia infra habetur, quod exivit daemonium ab eo.

Potest dici quod non est verbum Evangelistae, sed patris decepti, qui credebat eum esse lunaticum. Vel quia supra IV, 24 habetur quod lunaticos curavit, et isti erant daemoniaci.

Aliqui dicunt, ut aliqui medici, quod non erant alienati a daemone, sed ex mala complexione, vel corporis dispositione, et hoc quia crescente luna crescit omne humidum. Sic, cum cerebrum humidissimum sit, luna patiente defectum, defectum patitur et ipsum cerebrum: et ita tales deficientes patiuntur luna deficiente.

Sed hoc est contra fidem, quia expresse Scriptura dicit eos daemoniacos: et hoc patet, quia ex spiritu loquuntur, quia multi ignorantes patiuntur sic, et tamen loquuntur de Scripturis.

Ideo dicendum quod spiritus maligni intendunt multipliciter insidiari hominibus, et infamare volunt eos: ideo aliqui daemones inducunt infirmitates et vexationes secundum quod vident impressionem stellarum ad hoc convenientem, ut inducant homines ad errorem, ut credant quod solum ex influentia stellarum accidat eis ut male patiantur.

1459. *Et male patitur*. Hic ponuntur accidentia. In qualibet infirmitate sunt diversi status; quia quidam habent febrem magis gravem, alii magis debilem, sic etiam iste multum gravabatur. **Quia saepe cadit in ignem, et crebro in aquam**: ideo in magno erat periculo. Unde notandum quod Dominus non retrahit manum suam in periculis. Unde iam esset mortuus, nisi Deus manum

That in the name of Jesus every knee should bow, of those that are in heaven, on earth, and under the earth (Phil 2:10).

1456. Then the petition is set down. He does not ask, but rather explains the illness, for it is enough to explain a misery to the compassionate.

First, he explains the illness;
second, what happens;
third, that he did not find a remedy.

1457. He says then, **Lord, have pity on my son, for he is a lunatic**.

One should note that many ask on their own behalf, as above, with the woman who had a flow of blood. Sometimes, someone asks on behalf of another, as here, while sometimes he cures someone unasked, as in spiritual infirmity, as is written about the publican (Luke 18:13). Indeed, sometimes someone is cured at another's request, as is said in James, *pray one for another, that you may be saved* (Jas 5:16). Sometimes, without prayer, as in Paul's conversion (Acts 9:4).

1458. But why is it said that he is a lunatic? A lunatic, properly speaking, is one who goes mad according to the position of the moon. But it seems that this man was not a lunatic, but rather demon-possessed, because it says below that a demon went out of him.

It can be said that this is not the Evangelist's word, but the deceived father's word, who thought that he was a lunatic. Or because above it is written that he cured lunatics, and these were demon-possessed (Matt 4:24).

Some say, as some doctors do, that they were not made mad by a demon, but by a bad composition of the humors, or by the disposition of the body, and this is because when the moon grows, every moisture increases. Thus, since the brain is most moist, when the moon suffers a decrease, a decrease is suffered in the brain itself: and so the sort of people who decrease suffer when the moon decreases.

But this is against the faith, because Scripture expressly calls them demon-possessed. And this is clear, because they speak from a spirit, because many who are ignorant suffer in this way, and yet speak about the Scriptures.

Therefore one should say that the evil spirits aim to ensnare men in many ways, and they want to defame them. For this reason, some demons induce infirmities and vexations according as they see the thrust of the stars cooperating toward this, to lead men into error, that they might believe that they suffer badly merely from the influence of the stars.

1459. *And suffers much*. Here the things that happen are set down. In any infirmity there are different conditions. For some have a heavier fever, others are weaker; so also this one was heavily burdened. **For he falls often into the fire, and often into the water**. So he was in great danger. Hence one should notice that the Lord does not withdraw his hand in times of danger. Hence the man would already

suam extendisset, ut de Iob legitur II, 6: *quamvis satan eum multum cruciaret, tamen praecepit ei Dominus ut in animam manum non mitteret*.

Per istum significatur ratio instabilis, de quo in Eccli. XXVII, 12: *stultus ut luna mutatur*.

Et cadit quandoque in ignem, scilicet irae; Deut. XXXII, 22: *ignis succensus est in furore meo, et ardebit usque ad inferni novissima*. **Crebro in aquam**, scilicet cupiditatis. *Effusus es sicut aqua ne crescas*, Gen. XLIX, 4.

1460. Obtuli discipulis tuis, et non potuerunt curare eum. Hic tangitur nequitia istius, quia voluit accusare discipulos; unde Eccli. XI, 33: *qui in electis ponit maculam*.

1461. Unde Dominus increpat **respondens Iesus ait: generatio incredula et perversa**. Unde ponitur responsio:

et duo facit.

Primo increpat vitium;

secundo exhibet beneficium.

1462. Dicit ergo **respondens Iesus** et cetera. Iste volebat diffamare discipulos ad turbas, et etiam Iesum, quod non haberet istam potestatem, et multi in hoc consentiebant; ideo Christus invehitur contra totam gentem, et arguit eos infidelitate, dicens **generatio incredula**, quia hoc non erat propter impotentiam discipulorum, sed propter incredulitatem eorum. Item de perversitate, **et perversa** quia culpam suam apostolis imponebant; Deut. XXXII, 5: *generatio prava atque perversa, haeccine reddis Domino, popule stulte et insipiens?*

Quousque ero vobiscum? Et duo Christus proponit. Primo eorum impoenitentiam; secundo divinam patientiam, quia non est conveniens societas iusti ad iniustum; Eccli. c. XIII, 21: *sicut communicat lupus agno, sic peccator iusto*; II Cor. VI, 15: *quare conventio Christi ad Belial?* Unde vult dicere: mea societate potimini, et tamen mihi et discipulis meis detrahere non cessatis. Et, sicut dicit Hieronymus, Dominus hoc non dicit ut iratus, sed loquitur ad modum medici, qui venit ad infirmum, qui non vult servare mandata sua, qui dicit: quamdiu visitabo te qui non vis servare mandata mea?

Ideo dat exemplum praelatis, quod licet eis contrarientur homines, tamen beneficia conferant, sicut ipse, qui istius filium curavit, qui sibi et discipulis detrahebat.

1463. Unde dicit **afferte huc illum ad me**. Et primo ponitur curandi modus; secundo effectus.

Primo ponitur actor, scilicet Christus; unde dicit: **afferte eum ad me**. Homines multipliciter peccant. Quidam ex ignorantia, quidam ex infirmitate, quidam ex

have been dead if God had not extended his hand, as is written of Job: *however much Satan tortured him, still the Lord commanded him that he not lay a hand on his soul* (Job 2:6).

This signifies an unstable reason, about which it says *a fool is changed as the moon* (Sir 27:12).

And he falls often into the fire, namely wrath; *a fire is kindled in my wrath, and shall burn even to the lowest hell* (Deut 32:22). **Often into the water**, namely desire. *You are poured out as water, you do not grow* (Gen 49:4).

1460. And I brought him to your disciples, and they could not cure him. Here this man's wickedness is touched upon, for he wanted to accuse the disciples; hence, *for he lies in wait and turns good into evil, and on the elect he will lay a blot* (Sir 11:33).

1461. Hence the Lord reproaches him: **then Jesus answered and said: O unbelieving and perverse generation**. Hence the response is set down.

And he does two things:

first, he reproaches vice;

second, he grants a benefit.

1462. It says then, **then Jesus answered**. This man wanted to defame the disciples to the crowds, and even to defame Jesus, by saying that he did not have this power; and many were conspiring together in this. So Christ inveighs against the whole nation, and accuses them of disbelief, saying, **O unbelieving . . . generation**, because this was not due to the disciples' lack of power, but to their own disbelief. Likewise, he accuses them of perversity, **and perverse**, because they laid their own fault on the apostles; *they are a wicked and perverse generation. Is this the return you make to the Lord, O foolish and senseless people?* (Deut 32:5–6).

How long will I be with you? And Christ sets out two things. First, their impenitence; second, the divine patience, for there is no fitting fellowship of the just with the unjust; *if the wolf will at any time have fellowship with the lamb, so the sinner with the just* (Sir 13:21). *And what concord has Christ with Belial?* (2 Cor 6:15). Hence he wishes to say, you seize onto my fellowship, and yet you never cease to slander me and my disciples. And, as Jerome says, the Lord does not say this as though me were angry, but rather speaks in the manner of a doctor who comes to a sick person who will not obey his orders, and says: how long will I visit you, who do not want to obey my orders?

So he gives an example to prelates that, even though men be against them, still they should grant benefits, as he himself did by healing the son of this man, who was slandering him and the disciples.

1463. Hence he says, **bring him here to me**. And first, the manner of the healing is set down; second, the effect.

First, the one acting is set down, namely Christ; hence he says, **bring him here to me**. Men sin in many ways. Some out of ignorance, some out of weakness, some out of

malitia. Qui ex ignorantia, per hominem instrui potest; qui ex infirmitate, scilicet ille qui per incontinentiam peccat, qui de peccato dolet, et deducitur passionibus, iste non per quemcumque potest sanari, sed necessarium est quod adducatur ad Iesum, qui sanat omnes infirmitates nostras. Et haec est via, quia *increpavit eum*, quia per peccatum suum hoc ei acciderat; Prov. VI, 2: *illaqueatus es verbis oris tui, et captus propriis sermonibus*. Vel *increpavit eum*, scilicet daemonem.

Sequitur effectus *et exivit ab eo daemonium, et curatus est puer ex illa hora*, quia *ipse dixit, et facta sunt*, Ps. CXLVIII, 5.

1464. *Tunc accesserunt discipuli ad Iesum secreto* et cetera. Supra Dominus curavit lunaticum, hic satisfacit quaestioni discipulorum. Et

primo ponitur quaestio;

secundo responsio, ibi *dixit illis Iesus* et cetera.

1465. Ad hoc autem quod petitionem intelligatis, scire debetis quod supra X, 8 dominus dederat potestatem eis eiiciendi Daemonia, unde dubitabant ne gratiam datam propter culpam amisissent: ideo *accesserunt ad Iesum* et cetera.

Sed quare secreto? Non propter verecundiam, sed quia magnum audire debebant, et secreta omnibus dici non debebant; supra c. XIII, 11: *vobis datum est nosse mysteria regni caelorum, illis autem non est datum*.

1466. *Dixit eis Iesus*. Hic respondet. Et

primo satisfacit;

secundo proponit generale documentum, ibi *hoc autem genus non eiicitur nisi per orationem et ieiunium*.

Circa primum

primo quaestioni respondet, et

secundo responsionem manifestat, ibi *amen quippe dico vobis* et cetera.

1467. Quaesierant *quare non potuimus eiicere illum?* Dominus respondet: *propter incredulitatem vestram*. Ubi considerandum est quod antequam Spiritum Sanctum recepissent in tanta plenitudine, qua *repleti sunt omnes Spiritu Sancto*, Act. II, 4 aliqua infirma patiebantur; unde dominus eos redarguit Lc. ult., 25: *O stulti et tardi corde ad credendum*. Nec mirum, quia dum Dominus fuit in monte, illi qui praecipui fuerant in fide, scilicet Petrus, Iacobus et Ioannes, absentes erant: debilitas enim fidei est causa non faciendi miracula, quia miraculorum operatio est ab omnipotentia, quia fides innititur omnipotentiae; unde ubi est infirmitas fidei, est defectus miraculorum. Unde habetur supra XIII, 58 quod in patria sua non fecit Christus nisi pauca miracula propter eorum incredulitatem. Aliquando fiunt miracula propter exigentiam petentis, ut Sup. XV, v. 22 ss. habetur de muliere Chananaea, aliquando ad manifestandum sanctitatem

malice. The one who sins out of ignorance can be instructed by a man; the one who sins out of weakness, namely the one who sins through incontinence, who sorrows over sin, and is drawn by the passions, this one cannot be healed by just anyone, rather it is necessary that he be led to Jesus, who heals all our infirmities. And this is the path, for *Jesus rebuked him*, because this had happened to him through his own sin; *you are ensnared with the words of your mouth, and caught with your own words* (Prov 6:2). Or *Jesus rebuked him*, namely the demon.

There follows the effect: *and the devil went out of him, and the child was cured from that hour*, for *he spoke, and they were made* (Ps 148:5).

1464. *Then came the disciples to Jesus secretly*. Above, the Lord healed the lunatic; here he satisfies the disciples' questions. And

first, the question is set out;

second, the response, at *Jesus said to them*.

1465. Now, in order for you to understand the question, you should know that above, the Lord had given them the power of casting out demons (Matt 10:8). Hence they were uncertain whether they had lost the grace given because of guilt. So *then came the disciples to Jesus secretly*.

But why in secret? Not because of shame, but because they were supposed to hear something great, and secret things should not be spoken to all; above, *because it is given to you to know the mysteries of the kingdom of heaven: but it is not given to them* (Matt 13:11).

1466. *Jesus said to them*. Here he responds. And

first, he satisfies;

second, he sets out a general teaching, at *but this kind is not cast out except by prayer and fasting*.

Concerning the first,

first, he responds to the question, and

second, he manifests the response, at *amen I say to you*.

1467. They had asked, *why could not we cast him out?* The Lord responds: *because of your unbelief*. Here one should consider that before they had received the Holy Spirit in such fullness as that with which *they were all filled with the Holy Spirit* (Acts 2:4), they suffered from some weakness; hence the Lord reproached them, *O foolish, and slow of heart to believe.* (Luke 24:25). Nor is it a marvel, because when the Lord was on the mountain, those who were foremost in faith, namely Peter, James, and John, were absent. For weakness of faith is a reason why miracles are not worked, since the working of miracles comes from omnipotence, since faith rests on omnipotence. Hence where there is a weakness of faith, there is a lack of miracles. Hence it says above, that Christ worked only a few miracles in his own land on account of their unbelief (Matt 13:58). Sometimes, miracles happen because of the need of the one who asks, as is said above about the Canaanite woman

alicuius sancti: et hoc habetur IV Reg. XIII, 20 s., ubi dicitur quod cum latrunculi Syriae venissent in terram Israel, eiecerunt corpus mortuum iuxta Eliseum, et revixit, non quia meruisset mortuus, sed ad manifestationem sanctitatis Elisei.

1468. *Amen quippe dico vobis, si habueritis fidem sicut granum synapis* et cetera. Hic manifestat suam responsionem.

Et ponitur quaedam conditionalis, cuius antecedens est *si habueritis fidem* etc., consequens est *dicetis monti huic: transi et transibit*. Aliqui dicunt quod fides comparata grano synapis sit parva fides; quasi dicat: si habueritis aliquam fidem, dicetis et cetera. Sed hoc improbat Hieronymus, quia dicit Apostolus: *si habuero omnem fidem, ita ut montes transferam*. Unde perfecta fides requiritur ad translationem montium.

1469. Per hoc quod dicit *sicut granum synapis*, triplex perfectio designatur fidei. Invenimus enim in grano fervorem, foecunditatem, parvitatem.

Granum antequam conteratur, nullum fervorem habere videtur; cum conteritur, fervere incipit: sic homo fidelis, antequam probetur, despicabilis videtur quando vero atteritur, tunc apparet eius sanctitas. I Petr. I, v. 7: *modicum nunc si contristari oportet, ut probatio fidei vestrae multo pretiosior sit auro, quod per ignem probatur*.

Item invenimus in grano foecunditatem supra XIII, quod quamvis sit parvum, crescit in segetem magnam, ita quod volucres caeli habitant ibi. Ad Hebr. II, ubi narrantur opera fidei, et sequitur: *sancti per fidem vicerunt regna* et cetera.

Item invenimus parvitatem, et potest per hoc designari humilitas fidei. Tunc enim agnoscitur quis humilis in fide, quando acquiescit sermonibus Dei; I ad Tim. VI, 3: *si quis non acquiescit sermonibus Dei, superbus est*. Sic, e contrario, qui acquiescit sermonibus, humilis est.

Vult ergo dicere *si habueritis fidem*, et si fidem ferventem, indeficientem, in operibus foecundam, si parvam et humilem, *dicetis monti huic: transi, et transibit*.

1470. Hic est quaestio, quam movent infideles. Non invenitur quod apostoli unquam hoc fecerint.

Respondet Chrysostomus: *et si non invenitur de apostolis, invenitur tamen de apostolicis viris*. Legitur enim in libro *Dialogorum* beati Gregorii quod cum quidam vellet construere ecclesiam, non habens locum ad aedificandum, praecepit monti quod cederet ei, et cessit. Vel forte fecerunt, sed non est scriptum. Vel potest dici quod si non fecerunt, non fuit propter impossibilitatem, sed

(Matt 15:22). Sometimes they happen to manifest the sanctity of some saint, as is written, where it says that when the robbers of Syria had come into the land of Israel, they cast out a dead body next to Elisha, and it revived, not because the dead man had merited it, but to manifest Elisha's sanctity (2 Kgs 13:20).

1468. *For, amen I say to you, if you have faith as a grain of mustard seed*. Here he manifests his response.

And a certain conditional statement is set out, whose antecedent is *if you have faith*. The consequent is *you would say to this mountain: remove from here, and it would be removed*. Some say that faith compared to a grain of mustard would be a small faith, as though to say: if you have some faith, you shall say this. But Jerome disproves this, because the Apostle says, *if I should have all faith, so that I could remove mountains* (1 Cor 13:2). Hence perfect faith is required for moving a mountain.

1469. By the fact that he says, *as a grain of mustard*, the threefold perfection of faith is indicated. For we find in a grain fervor, fertility, and littleness.

Before a grain is crushed, it seems to have no fervor; when it is ground, it begins to ferment. In the same way, before a faithful man is tested he seems despicable, but when he is ground, then his sanctity appears. *If now you must be for a little time made sorrowful in diverse temptations: that the trial of your faith, much more precious than gold which is tried by the fire, may be found unto praise and glory and honor at the appearing of Jesus Christ* (1 Pet 1:6–7).

Likewise, we find fertility in a grain. Above, Jesus says that although it is little, it grows into a great harvest, such that the birds of the sky dwell there (Matt 13:32). As in Hebrews, where the works of faith are recounted; and there follows: *who by faith conquered kingdoms* (Heb 11:33).

Likewise, we find littleness, and this can point to the humility of faith. For someone is known to be humble in faith when he agrees with God's words; *if any man teach otherwise, and consent not to the sound words of our Lord Jesus Christ, and to that doctrine which is according to godliness, he is proud* (1 Tim 6:3–4). Thus, going the other way, he who agrees with God's words is humble.

So he wishes to say, *if you have faith*, and if it is a fervent faith, lacking in nothing, fertile in works, if it is small and humble, *you would say to this mountain: remove from here, and it would be removed*.

1470. Here is a question, which is raised by unbelievers. We do not find that the apostles ever did this.

Chrysostom responds: *even if it is not reported about the apostles, yet it is reported about apostolic men*. For it is written in blessed Gregory's book of *Dialogues* that when a certain man wished to construct a church, not having a place to build, he commanded the mountain to withdraw from there, and it withdrew. Or perhaps they did this, but it is not written. Or it can be said that if they did not do this, it

was not because it was impossible, but because the occasion did not present itself. For miracles are sometimes worked out of necessity, and sometimes for utility; and since it was not necessary, they did not do it.

Or, the mountain stands for the devil. **Remove from here**, i.e., from this body, **and it would be removed**. Or, according to Augustine, it is understood as about the spirit of pride.

1471. And nothing will be impossible to you. And what is this? Were they omnipotent? No, because only the one who can do all things by his own power is truly omnipotent; but these did not work by their own power, but as a king commands in one way, and his servant in another, for the king commands in his own name, the servant in the name of the king.

1472. But this kind of demon, the **this** does not indicate just the lunatic's kind, but every kind of demon, **is not cast out except by prayer and fasting**. Chrysostom says that to the degree that the soul is more lifted up, to that degree it is more terrible to demons; for Christ himself is terrible to the demons, hence those who are joined to Christ are terrible to them. But the lifting up of the mind is impeded by the heaviness of the body, is impeded by intemperance and drunkenness. Hence: *and take heed to yourselves, lest perhaps your hearts be overcharged with surfeiting and drunkenness* (Luke 21:34). Hence the one who is weighed down by drunkenness cannot have a mind lifted up to God. Therefore, fasting is required for lifting up the mind; hence, *prayer is good with fasting* (Tob 12:8). Likewise, *and I set my face to the Lord my God, to pray and make supplication with fasting, and sackcloth, and ashes* (Dan 9:3). Therefore, as Origen says, in order to drive out a spirit, one should not pursue feasting, but prayers and fasting. Or, the lunatic indicates the instability of the body, or the one who is carried along by different desires. The sort of man who often falls into fire and water is only cured in fasting and prayer. *For the flesh lusts against the spirit: and the spirit against the flesh* (Gal 5:17).

So it is necessary that you weaken the body, and strengthen the spirit. But the spirit is strengthened through prayer, since prayer is the ascent of the mind into God; but the flesh is weakened through fasting. Or because the spirit does not cease to lust against the flesh, good works, which are signified by prayer, are required, and abstinence from evil, which is signified by fasting.

1473. And when they gathered together in Galilee. Above, the tranquility of glory was represented by liberation from the power of demons. This liberation is completed by Christ's death; *that, through death, he might destroy him who had the empire of death, that is to say, the devil: and might deliver them, who through the fear of death were all their lifetime subject to servitude* (Heb 2:14–15).

For this reason, he immediately adds something about the prediction of the passion. And

primo ponitur praenuntiatio;

secundo effectus, ibi *et contristati sunt vehementer*.

1474. Dominus noster ante praenuntiaverat passionem suam, et modo etiam, et in sequenti. Et quare toties? Quia quae praevidentur, minus commovent; ideo quia futurum erat quod discipuli scandalizarentur in morte Domini, ideo voluit eis saepe praenuntiare, ut minus scandalizarentur. Sed semper addit aliquid. Prius tetigit de occisione, sed non de traditione; hic vero tangit de traditione, dicens *Filius hominis tradetur*.

Et recte dicit *Filius hominis*, quia etsi ille qui traditur, sit Dominus gloriae, tamen secundum quod filius hominis traditur. Unde Augustinus: *licet aliqua dicantur de Filio Dei et Filio hominis, tamen distinguitur, quia infirma de humana natura dicuntur, stabilia de natura divina*.

Sed non dicit a quibus traditus est. Quia tradidit se; ad Gal. II, 20: *qui tradidit semetipsum pro me*. Traditus est a Patre, *qui proprio Filio non pepercit, sed pro nobis omnibus tradidit illum*, Rom. VIII, 32. Item traditus est a Iuda; supra X, 4: *qui et tradidit eum*. Item a daemonibus: Io. XIII, habetur quod diabolus posuit in cor ut traderet eum Iudas. Et Sap. II, 12: *venite, occidamus iustum*.

Et tertia die resurget. Osee VI, 3: *vivificabit nos post duos dies, in die tertia suscitabit nos, et vivemus in conspectu eius*.

1475. Sequitur effectus *et contristati sunt*. Attendebant et mortem, et resurrectionem, sed non videbant utilitatem. Io. XVI, 6: *quia haec locutus sum vobis, tristitia implevit cor vestrum*.

1476. *Et cum venissent Capharnaum*. Completa tranquillitate gloriae, ponit solutionem tributi; Is. XIV, 4: *quievit tributum*; Iob III, 19: *servus liber est a domino suo*.

Unde tria facit.
Primo ponit exactionem tributi;
secundo libertatem filiorum;
tertio solutionem tributi.

1477. Dicit *et cum intrasset* et cetera. Didrachma duplex drachma dicitur. Unde quilibet Iudaeus debebat quolibet anno duplex drachma.

Sed unde erat illud tributum? Quidam dicunt quod ex lege Ex. XIII, quod propter hoc quod dominus occiderat primogenita Aegypti, ideo statuit quod omnia primogenita essent sua, et quod filii redimerentur. Post praecepit quod ad servitium Levitae praepararentur. Et

first, the prediction is set down;

second, the effect, at *and they were troubled exceedingly*.

1474. Our Lord had announced his passion before, and now again, and in what follows. And why so many times? Because things which are foreseen move one less; therefore, since it was going to happen that the disciples would be scandalized at the Lord's death, he wished to predict it to them often, that they might be scandalized less. But he always adds something. Before, he mentioned the killing, but not the handing over; while here he mentions the handing over, saying, *the Son of man will be betrayed into the hands of men*.

And rightly does he say, *the Son of man*, because although the one who is handed over is the Lord of glory, yet he is handed over according as he is a son of man. Hence Augustine: *although some things are said of the Son of God and the Son of man, yet a distinction is made, because weak things are said of the human nature, and enduring things of the divine*.

But he does not say by whom he was handed over. For he handed himself over; *and delivered himself for me* (Gal 2:20). He was handed over by the Father, who *spared not even his own Son, but delivered him up for us all* (Rom. 8:32). Likewise, he was handed over by Judas; above, *who also betrayed him* (Matt 10:4). Likewise, by the demons: John says that the devil put in the heart of Judas that he should hand him over (John 13:2). And, *let us therefore lie in wait for the just* (Wis 2:12).

And the third day he will rise again. He will revive us after two days: on the third day he will raise us up, and we will live in his sight (Hos 6:3).

1475. There follows the effect: *and they were troubled exceedingly*. They were aware of both the death and the resurrection, but they did not see their usefulness. *But because I have spoken these things to you, sorrow has filled your heart* (John 16:6).

1476. *And when they had come to Capernaum*. Having completed the tranquility of glory, he sets out the paying of the tribute; *the tribute has ceased* (Isa 14:4); *the servant is free from his master* (Job 3:19).

Hence he does three things:
first, he sets out the demanding of the tribute;
second, the liberty of the sons;
third, the paying of the tribute.

1477. It says, *and when they had come*. A *didrachma* means a double drachma. Hence each Jew was supposed to pay two drachmas every year.

But where was this tribute from? Some say that it was from the law (Exod 13), that since the Lord had killed the first-born males of Egypt, he decreed that all the first-born were his, and that the sons should be redeemed. Later, he commanded that they should be prepared for the service

post mandavit quod numerarentur Levitae. Et inventi sunt plures primogeniti quam Levitae. Tunc praecepit quod pro redemptione solveretur pretium. Hieronymus dicit quod non ex lege Dei, sed imperatoris: Iudaea nuper tributaria erat Romanorum, ut pro capite censum solveret. Et hoc videtur verius, quia infra dicitur: *reges terrae a quibus accipiunt tributum?* Ideo loquitur de tributo imperiali.

Sed quare in Capharnaum? Quia a quocumque recipiebatur in civitate sua, sed Capharnaum erat civitas principalis Galilaeae.

1478. Sed quia Christum in reverentiam habebant, ideo non accedunt ad eum, sed ad Petrum; et non petierunt eum nisi cum mansuetudine: *magister vester non solvit didrachma?* Deinde ponitur Petri responsio *et ait: etiam*; idest, verum est quod non solvit. Chrysostomus dicit quod ne inquietaretur dixit *etiam*, solvit.

Sequitur Christi interrogatio, deinde Petri responsio.

In interrogatione duo sunt consideranda, scilicet quod non expavit denuntiationem eius, quia cum esset in tali statu, ad quamdam indignitatem tenebatur; et aliqui sunt ita dispositi, quod cum vident aliquod infirmum in magno, statim scandalizantur. Ne ergo scandalizentur, ideo *praevenit*, ideo cum infirmitate apposuit aliquod magnum, scilicet, quod absens sciret quod dictum erat Petro. *Omnia nuda et aperta sunt oculis eius*, ad Hebr. IV, 13: item notandum quod Petro iudicium committit, quia frequentius et loquebatur dicens *quid tibi videtur, Simon?* Iob XII, 11: *nonne auris verba diiudicat? Reges terrae a quibus accipiunt tributum, vel censum?*

Differentia est inter tributum et censum: tributum enim de agris et vineis; census autem de capite datur. Unde in signum suae subiectionis debet aliquid homo subiectus; et hoc census dicitur. Ex hoc vult argumentari, quod cum filii regum non solvunt tributum, quod ipse non tenetur: ipse enim est Rex regum, per quem omnes regnant. Item, secundum carnem, erat ex semine regio. *Qui factus est ex semine David secundum carnem*, Rom. c. I, 3. Chrysostomus dicit, quod ex hoc possumus considerare, quod sit Filius naturalis quia prius dicitur qui naturalis est.

At ille dixit: ab alienis.

1479. Deinde ponitur Christi responsio, quia reges filiis suis parcunt. Is. III, 15: *quare populum meum atteritis, et facies pauperum commolitis?* Iustum enim videtur. Qui enim praesidet, curam debet habere de subditis; ideo ei servire debent subditi sicut membra corpori. Sicut enim membra corporis ex sibi proprio serviunt toti corpori, sic quilibet subditus ex propriis bonis debet servire communitati.

of the Levites. And later he commanded that the Levites be numbered. And there were found more first-born than Levites. Then he commanded that a price be paid for their redemption. Jerome says that this was not from God's law, but from the Emperor's: Judea was at that time a tributary of the Romans, and paid a tax per head. And this seems more true, because it says below, *the kings of the earth, from whom do they receive tribute or custom?* (Matt 17:25). Therefore he speaks of the imperial tribute.

But why in Capernaum? Because it was taken from each person in his own city, and Capernaum was the principal city of Galilee.

1478. But since they held Christ in reverence, they did not approach him, but Peter; and they only asked him with meekness: *does not your master pay the didrachmas?* Then Peter's response is set down: *he said: yes*, i.e., it is true that he does not pay it. Chrysostom says that, lest he be harassed, he said, *yes*, he does pay it.

There follows Christ's questioning, then Peter's response.

There are two things to be considered in the questioning, namely that he was not afraid of being denounced, for while he was in such a state, he was bound to a certain indignity; and there are some who are so disposed that when they see something weak in a great man, they are immediately scandalized. For this reason, lest they be scandalized, *Jesus prevented him*, so that next to the weakness he placed something great, namely that he knew what Peter had said while he was not there. *All things are naked and open to his eyes* (Heb 4:13). Also, one should notice that he entrusts judgment to Peter, since he spoke more frequently, saying, *what does it seem to you, Simon? Does not the ear discern words? The kings of the earth, of whom do they receive tribute or custom?* (Job 12:11).

There is a difference between tribute and custom, for a tribute is from the fields and the vines, while a custom is given from a person. For as a sign of his subjection, the man who is subjected should give something; and this is called a custom. From this he wanted to argue that since the sons of the king do not pay tribute, he himself is not bound: for he is the King of kings, through whom all reign. Likewise, according to the flesh, he was from royal seed. *Who was made to him of the seed of David, according to the flesh* (Rom 1:3). Chrysostom says that we can note from this that he is a natural Son, because the one who is natural is said first.

And he said: from strangers.

1479. Then Christ's response is set down, that the kings spare their own children. *Why do you consume my people, and grind the faces of the poor?* (Isa 3:15). For it seems just. For the one who governs has the care of those under him; therefore those under him should serve him like members of the body. For just as the members of the body serve the whole body out of what is their own, so anyone subject should serve the community out of his own goods.

Ideo concludit Dominus *ergo filii liberi*. Origenes: *uno modo sic*. Ergo filii regum terrae sunt liberi, sed filii Dei sunt liberi apud Deum.

1480. Sed quid facit hoc ad propositum? Aut loquitur secundum carnem de filiis, et sic ipse non erat filius secundum carnem; si secundum spiritum, tunc omnes Christiani erunt liberi. Sed hoc est contra Apostolum, *reddite omnibus debita, cui tributum tributum*.

Dico quod istud veritatem habebat de illo qui per naturam erat Filius. Ille enim vere erat liber. Sed liberi secundum spiritum eo modo habent libertatem quo filiationem per conformitatem ad Christum, qui *est primogenitus in multis fratribus*, Rom. VIII, 29. Inquantum conformes primogenito liberi sunt. Ad Phil. III, 21: *qui reformabit corpus humilitatis nostrae configuratum corpori claritatis suae*.

1481. *Ut autem non scandalizemus eos* et cetera. Verum est quod dominus liber est, sed quia formam servi accepit, ut habetur ad Phil. II, ideo non recusavit solvere, et in hoc dedit exemplum humilitatis.

Et in hac solutione tria laudanda et admiranda notantur. Primo eius mansuetudo, unde ipse est mitis, secundum quod ipse testatur supra XI, 29: ***discite a me, quia mitis sum et humilis corde***. Ille proprie dicitur mitis qui nullum vult offendere; I ad Cor. X, v. 32: *sine offensione estote Iudaeis, et gentibus, et Ecclesiae Dei*.

Sed contra hoc obiicitur. Supra XV, 12 habetur quod discipuli dixerunt: ***Domine, scis quia Iudaei scandalizantur in verbo isto?*** Et Dominus dixit: ***sinite eos, caeci sunt et duces caecorum***. Non curavit tunc de scandalo, hic vero curat. Unde dicendum quod scandalum aliquando oritur ex veritate; et tunc non est curandum: aliquando ex infirmitate, vel ignorantia; et tale est curandum. Sed si ipse non solvisset, scandalum eorum ex ignorantia esset, quia ipsi Deum non cognoscebant.

1482. Item admiranda est paupertas Christi, quia ita pauper fuit quod non habuit unde solveret; II Cor. VIII, 9: *qui cum dives esset, egenus factus est, ut illius inopia vos divites essetis*.

Potest quis obiicere: nonne loculos habebat? Verum est, sed omnia data erant in usus pauperum. Rapinam arbitrabatur quod erat ad usus pauperum in alios usus expendere. Chrysostomus dicit quod solvit, ut dum solveret tributum, ex una parte ostenderet eius potentiam, ex altera parte mysterium.

Vade ad mare, et mitte hamum, et eum piscem, qui primus ascenderit, tolle, et aperto ore eius, invenies staterem. In statere illo erat imago Caesaris: et significat diabolum qui nihil habebat in eo, Io. XIV, 30: *venit*

So the Lord concludes, ***then the children are free***. Origen: *this is so in one way*. Therefore, the sons of the earthly king are free, but the sons of God are free in the presence of God.

1480. But how is this to the point? Either he speaks about children according to the flesh, and in this way he was not a son according to the flesh; if according to the spirit, then all Christians are free. But this is against the Apostle: *render therefore to all men their dues. Tribute, to whom tribute is due: custom, to whom custom* (Rom 13:7).

I say that this holds true concerning the one who was a Son by nature. For he was truly free. But the children according to the spirit have freedom in the same way as they have sonship, by conformity to Christ, who is *the firstborn amongst many brethren* (Rom 8:29). Insofar as they are like the firstborn, they are free. *Who will reform the body of our lowness, made like to the body of his glory* (Phil 3:21).

1481. ***But that we may not scandalize them***. It is true that the Lord is free, but since he took on the form of a slave, as is written (Phil 2:7), he did not refuse to pay, and by this he gave an example of humility.

And in this payment there are noted three things to be praised and admired. First, his meekness, for he is meek, according as he himself testifies above, ***learn from me, because I am meek, and humble of heart*** (Matt 11:29). He is properly called meek who wishes to offend no one; *be without offense to the Jews, and to the gentiles, and to the Church of God* (1 Cor 10:32).

But it is objected against this: above, it is written that the disciples said, ***do you know that the Pharisees, when they heard this word, were scandalized?*** (Matt 15:12). And the Lord said, ***leave them alone: they are blind, and leaders of the blind***. He did not care then about scandal, but here he cares. Hence one should say that sometimes scandal arises from the truth, and then one should not care; sometimes it arises from weakness, or ignorance, and one should care about this kind of scandal. But if he had not paid, their scandal would have been from ignorance, because they did not know he was God.

1482. Likewise, Christ's poverty is to be admired, because he was so poor that he did not have anything to pay with; *being rich he became poor, for your sakes; that through his poverty you might be rich* (2 Cor 8:9).

Someone could object: did he not have a money-box? This is true, but it was all given for the use of the poor. He judged it robbery to spend on some other use what was for the use of the poor. Chrysostom says that he paid so that when he paid the tribute he might show on the one side his power, on the other side a mystery.

Go to the sea, and cast in a hook, and that fish which comes up first, take, and when you have opened its mouth, you will find a stater. The image of Caesar was on that stater, and it signifies the devil, who had nothing in him; *for*

the prince of this world comes, and in me he has not any thing (John 14:30). Therefore since he had nothing of his own, he did not wish to pay from his own money.

1483. Likewise, his providence; so he says that we should be amazed at how he could know that right away he would come across a fish which had a stater in its mouth. And if it was not there, but he created it from nothing, it was a marvel; but if he led the fish to the hook, it showed a tremendous providence.

By this fish which first came to the hook is understood the first martyr, blessed Stephen. It had a stater in its mouth, which was worth a didrachma, and double; and it signifies Stephen himself, who saw the very divinity and humanity. Or it can be understood as Adam.

Likewise notice that if someone often speaks of riches and of money, he has a stater in his mouth; hence the one who converts such a man gets the fish which has a stater in its mouth.

1484. Also, humility is indicated. Hence, **take that, and give it to them for me and you**. And the fact that he paid the tribute for Peter and for himself signifies that by Christ's passion, he would acquire for himself the glory of the resurrection; *for which cause God also has exalted him* (Phil 2:9). Peter and the others are redeemed from punishment and guilt. Or in another way: because he suffered for himself, that he might acquire the glory of the resurrection for his body, and for the people, that he might wash them from sins. For he *washed us from our sins in his own blood* (Rev 1:5).

Chapter 18

Lecture 1

¹⁸:¹ In illa hora accesserunt discipuli ad Iesum, dicentes: quis putas, maior est in regno caelorum? [n. 1486]

¹⁸:² Et advocans Iesus parvulum, statuit eum in medio eorum, [n. 1488]

¹⁸:³ et dixit: amen dico vobis, nisi conversi fueritis, et efficiamini sicut parvuli, non intrabitis in regnum caeluli. [n. 1488]

¹⁸:⁴ Quicumque ergo humiliaverit se sicut parvulus iste, hic est maior in regno caelorum. [n. 1488]

¹⁸:⁵ Et qui susceperit unum parvulum talem in nomine meo, me suscipit. [n. 1490]

¹⁸:⁶ Qui autem scandalizaverit unum de pusillis istis, qui in me credunt, expedit ei ut suspendatur mola asinaria in collo eius, et demergatur in profundum maris. [n. 1492]

¹⁸:⁷ Vae mundo a scandalis! Necesse est enim ut veniant scandala. Verumtamen vae homini illi, per quem scandalum venit. [n. 1496]

¹⁸:⁸ Si autem manus tua, vel pes tuus scandalizat te, abscide eum, et proiice abs te. Bonum tibi est ad vitam ingredi debilem vel claudum, quam duas manus vel duos pedes habentem mitti in ignem aeternum. [n. 1500]

¹⁸:⁹ Et si oculus tuus scandalizat te, erue eum, et proiice abs te. Bonum tibi est unum oculum habentem in vitam intrare, quam duos oculos habentem mitti in gehennam ignis. [n. 1500]

¹⁸:¹ Ἐν ἐκείνῃ τῇ ὥρᾳ προσῆλθον οἱ μαθηταὶ τῷ Ἰησοῦ λέγοντες· τίς ἄρα μείζων ἐστὶν ἐν τῇ βασιλείᾳ τῶν οὐρανῶν;

¹⁸:² καὶ προσκαλεσάμενος παιδίον ἔστησεν αὐτὸ ἐν μέσῳ αὐτῶν

¹⁸:³ καὶ εἶπεν· ἀμὴν λέγω ὑμῖν, ἐὰν μὴ στραφῆτε καὶ γένησθε ὡς τὰ παιδία, οὐ μὴ εἰσέλθητε εἰς τὴν βασιλείαν τῶν οὐρανῶν.

¹⁸:⁴ ὅστις οὖν ταπεινώσει ἑαυτὸν ὡς τὸ παιδίον τοῦτο, οὗτός ἐστιν ὁ μείζων ἐν τῇ βασιλείᾳ τῶν οὐρανῶν.

¹⁸:⁵ καὶ ὃς ἐὰν δέξηται ἓν παιδίον τοιοῦτο ἐπὶ τῷ ὀνόματί μου, ἐμὲ δέχεται.

¹⁸:⁶ Ὃς δ' ἂν σκανδαλίσῃ ἕνα τῶν μικρῶν τούτων τῶν πιστευόντων εἰς ἐμέ, συμφέρει αὐτῷ ἵνα κρεμασθῇ μύλος ὀνικὸς περὶ τὸν τράχηλον αὐτοῦ καὶ καταποντισθῇ ἐν τῷ πελάγει τῆς θαλάσσης.

¹⁸:⁷ Οὐαὶ τῷ κόσμῳ ἀπὸ τῶν σκανδάλων· ἀνάγκη γὰρ ἐλθεῖν τὰ σκάνδαλα, πλὴν οὐαὶ τῷ ἀνθρώπῳ δι' οὗ τὸ σκάνδαλον ἔρχεται.

¹⁸:⁸ Εἰ δὲ ἡ χείρ σου ἢ ὁ πούς σου σκανδαλίζει σε, ἔκκοψον αὐτὸν καὶ βάλε ἀπὸ σοῦ· καλόν σοί ἐστιν εἰσελθεῖν εἰς τὴν ζωὴν κυλλὸν ἢ χωλὸν ἢ δύο χεῖρας ἢ δύο πόδας ἔχοντα βληθῆναι εἰς τὸ πῦρ τὸ αἰώνιον.

¹⁸:⁹ καὶ εἰ ὁ ὀφθαλμός σου σκανδαλίζει σε, ἔξελε αὐτὸν καὶ βάλε ἀπὸ σοῦ· καλόν σοί ἐστιν μονόφθαλμον εἰς τὴν ζωὴν εἰσελθεῖν ἢ δύο ὀφθαλμοὺς ἔχοντα βληθῆναι εἰς τὴν γέενναν τοῦ πυρός.

¹⁸:¹ At that hour the disciples came to Jesus, saying: who do you think is the greater in the kingdom of heaven? [n. 1486]

¹⁸:² And Jesus, calling to him a little child, set him in the midst of them, [n. 1488]

¹⁸:³ and said: amen I say to you, unless you be converted, and become like little children, you will not enter into the kingdom of heaven. [n. 1488]

¹⁸:⁴ Whoever therefore will humble himself as this little child, he is greater in the kingdom of heaven. [n. 1488]

¹⁸:⁵ And he who will receive one such little child in my name, receives me. [n. 1490]

¹⁸:⁶ But he who will scandalize one of these little ones who believes in me, it would be better for him that a millstone of an ass were hung about his neck, and he were drowned in the depth of the sea. [n. 1492]

¹⁸:⁷ Woe to the world because of scandals. For it is necessary that scandals come, but nevertheless, woe to that man by whom the scandal comes. [n. 1496]

¹⁸:⁸ And if your hand, or your foot scandalize you, cut it off, and cast it from you. It is better for you to go into life maimed or lame, than having two hands or two feet, to be cast into everlasting fire. [n. 1500]

¹⁸:⁹ And if your eye scandalize you, pluck it out, and cast it from you. It is better for you, having one eye, to enter into life, than having two eyes to be cast into hell fire. [n. 1500]

18:10 Videte ne contemnatis unum ex his pusillis. Dico enim vobis, quia angeli eorum in caelis semper vident faciem Patris mei, qui in caelis est. [n. 1501]

18:10 Ὁρᾶτε μὴ καταφρονήσητε ἑνὸς τῶν μικρῶν τούτων· λέγω γὰρ ὑμῖν ὅτι οἱ ἄγγελοι αὐτῶν ἐν οὐρανοῖς διὰ παντὸς βλέπουσι τὸ πρόσωπον τοῦ πατρός μου τοῦ ἐν οὐρανοῖς.

18:10 See that you do not despise one of these little ones, for I say to you, that their angels in heaven always see the face of my Father who is in heaven. [n. 1501]

18:11 Venit enim Filius hominis salvare quod perierat. [n. 1508]

18:11 ἦλθε γὰρ ὁ υἱὸς τοῦ ἀνθρώπου σῶσαι τὸ ἀπολωλός.

18:11 For the Son of man came to save that which was lost. [n. 1508]

1485. Supra Dominus monstravit futuram gloriam in sua transfiguratione, hic de profectione ad illam gloriam agit.

Et dividitur in duo, quia
primo docet quomodo perveniendum est ad eam;
secundo reprehenduntur quidam inordinate petentes excellentiam in gloria, quae incipit in XX cap.

Circa primum
primo docet quomodo perveniendum est ad illam gloriam per viam communem;
secundo quomodo per viam perfectionis, quod incipit cap. XIX.

Primo quia per humilitatem pervenitur ad gloriam; ideo primo ostendit humilitatis modum;
secundo prohibet inferre scandalum, ibi *qui autem scandalizaverit unum de pusillis istis* etc.,
tertio docet quod illatum est dimittendum, ibi *si autem manus tua vel pes tuus scandalizat te, abscinde eum, et proiice abs te.*

Circa primum
ponitur interrogatio discipulorum;
secundo responsio Christi.

1486. Occasio interrogationis sumitur ex hoc quod dictum est Petro, quod iret ad mare, et staterem inventum in pisce solveret pro ipso, et pro Petro; unde videbatur eum aliis praetulisse. Et quia erant adhuc infirmi, ideo aliquem zelum et invidiae motum passi sunt.

Sed videte quod quando duxit tres solum in montem, non ita moti sunt, sicut hic, cum solum praefert. Unde quaerebant *quis putas maior est in regno caelorum?* Cum non per maioritatem perveniatur, sed per spiritum humilitatis; ad Phil. II, 3: *in humilitate superiores sibi invicem arbitrantes* et cetera.

In ista petitione est hoc imitandum, quod non erant cupidi de terrestribus, sed de caelestibus; II Cor. IV, 18: *non contemplantibus nobis quae videntur, sed quae non videntur* et cetera.

1487. Sed quid est? Nonne quaerenda est excellentia in regno caelorum?

Dicendum quod habere eminentiam in regno caelorum est dupliciter. Aut ita quod reputemus nos idoneos;

1485. Above, the Lord revealed the future glory in his transfiguration; here he treats of the progress toward that glory.

And it is divided into two parts, for
first, he teaches how one should arrive at it;
second, certain ones who were inordinately asking for excellence in glory are reproached, which begins in chapter twenty.

Concerning the first,
first, he teaches how one is to arrive at that glory by the common way;
second, how one is to arrive by the way of perfection, which begins in chapter nineteen.

First, since one arrives at glory through humility, first he shows humility's way;
second, he forbids one to cause scandal, at *but he who will scandalize one of these little ones*;
third, he teaches that what introduces scandal should be given up, at *and if your hand, or your foot scandalize you, cut it off, and cast it from you.*

Concerning the first,
the disciples' questioning is set down;
second, Christ's response.

1486. The occasion for the questioning is taken from what was said to Peter, that he should go to the sea, and having found a stater in a fish, he should pay for him and for Peter; hence he seemed to prefer him to the others. And since they were still weak, they suffered some movement of zeal and envy.

But see that when he took the three along onto the mountain, they were not moved as they are here, since he preferred only one. Hence they were asking, *who do you think is the greater in the kingdom of heaven?* while one does not arrive by being greater, but by the spirit of humility; *in humility, let each esteem others better than themselves* (Phil 2:3).

In this question there is this to be imitated, that they were not desirous of earthly things, but of heavenly things; *while we look not at the things which are seen, but at the things which are not seen* (2 Cor 4:18).

1487. But what is this? Ought not one to seek excellence in the kingdom of heaven?

It should be said that there are two ways of having eminence in the kingdom of heaven. Either in such a way that

et hoc est superbia et contra apostolum, Phil. II, 3: *in humilitate superiores sibi invicem arbitrantes* et cetera. Sed appetere maiorem gratiam, ut maior nobis sit gloria, non est malum, ut I ad Cor. XII, 31: *aemulamini charismata meliora*. Item apostoli sciebant quod in gloria erant diversae mansiones, sicut *stella differt a stella in claritate*; ideo quaerebant, quia credebant unum maiorem alio: contra haereticos aliquos qui contrarium posuerunt.

1488. Consequenter ponitur responsio Christi, et ponit factum Christi et dictum; unde dicit **et advocans Iesus parvulum**.

Quis sit iste parvulus, exponitur tripliciter. Chrysostomus exponit vere parvulum, quia passionibus erat immunis, ut exemplum humilitatis praeberet, ut infra cap. XIX, 14: *sinite parvulos venire ad me*. Et dicitur quod iste fuit Beatus Martialis.

Aliter exponitur, quod Christus se parvulum reputans, statuit se in medio dicens **nisi efficiamini sicut parvulus iste, non intrabitis in regnum caelorum**. Lc. XX, 27: *ego sum in medio vestrum sicut qui ministrat*.

Aliter. Quia per parvulum intelligitur Spiritus Sanctus, qui facit parvulos, quia est Spiritus humilitatis; Ez. XXXVI, 27: *ponam Spiritum meum in medio vestri*.

Item notandum est verbum Domini. Et primo tangit necessitatem; secundo efficaciam.

1489. Dicit **amen dico vobis, nisi conversi fueritis**, ab ista scilicet elatione immunes; Zach. I, 3: *convertimini ad me* etc., **et efficiamini ut parvulus iste**, non aetate, sed simplicitate; I ad Cor. XIV, 20: *nolite parvuli effici sensibus, sed malitia parvuli estote*.

Multae sunt conditiones parvulorum. Non magna appetunt; Rom. XII, 10: *non alta sapientes*. Sunt immunes a concupiscentia; supra V, 28: *qui viderit mulierem ad concupiscendum eam, iam moechatus est eam in corde suo*. Et talem concupiscentiam non habent pueri. Item non recordantur inimicitiae.

1490. Unde **nisi efficiamini sicut parvulus iste**, scilicet imitatores proprietatum parvulorum, **non intrabitis in regnum caelorum**. Nullus enim intrabit nisi humilis; *humiles spiritu suscipiet gloria*, Prov. XXIX, 23. Vel **non intrabitis in regnum caelorum**, idest in doctrinam Evangelii, sicut infra XXI, 43: *auferetur a vobis regnum Dei, et dabitur genti facienti fructus eius*.

Introitus enim est per fidem; unde **nisi efficiamini**, et si non credideritis **sicut parvuli, non intrabitis in regnum caelorum**, quia Marci ult., 16: *qui non crediderit,*

we consider ourselves suitable, and this is pride and against the Apostle, *in humility, let each esteem others better than themselves* (Phil 2:3). But to desire greater grace that glory may be greater for us is not evil: *be zealous for the better gifts* (1 Cor 12:31). Likewise, the apostles knew that there were different dwelling places in glory, just as *star differs from star in brilliance* (1 Cor 15:41); so they were asking because they believed that one is greater than another in heaven, against some heretics who have held the contrary.

1488. Next, Christ's response is set down, and he sets down Christ's deed and word; hence he says, **and Jesus, calling to him a little child**.

Who is this little child? It is explained in three ways. Chrysostom explains him as truly a child, since he was free from passions, that he might present an example of humility, as below: *allow the little children, and do not forbid thm to come to me* (Matt 19:14). And it is said that this child was Blessed Martial.

It is explained in another way, that Christ, considering himself a little child, stood himself in their midst, saying, **unless you be converted, and become like little children, you will not enter into the kingdom of heaven**. *But I am in the midst of you, as he who serves* (Luke 22:27).

In another way, that by the little child is understood the Holy Spirit, who makes little children, because he is the Spirit of humility; *and I will put my Spirit in the midst of you* (Ezek 36:27).

One should also note the Lord's word. And first, he touches upon the necessity; second, the effectiveness.

1489. Amen I say to you, unless you be converted, i.e., be free from this vanity; *turn to me* (Zech 1:3), **and become like little children**, not in age, but in simplicity; *brethren, do not become children in sense: but in malice be children* (1 Cor 14:20).

There are many qualities of little children. They do not desire great things; *not minding high things* (Rom 12:10). They are free from concupiscence; above: **whoever will look on a woman to lust after her, has already committed adultery with her in her heart** (Matt 5:28). And children do not have this sort of concupiscence. Likewise, they do not remember enmities.

1490. Hence **unless you . . . become like little children**, i.e., imitators of the properties of children, **you will not enter into the kingdom of heaven**. No one but the humble will enter; *glory will uphold the humble of spirit* (Prov 29:23). Or, **you will not enter into the kingdom of heaven**, i.e., into the teaching of the Gospel, as below, **the kingdom of God will be taken from you, and will be given to a nation yielding the fruits** (Matt 21:43).

For the entry is through faith; hence **unless you become**, and if you do not believe **like little children, you will not enter into the kingdom of heaven**, because *he who believes*

condemnabitur. Prov. XXIX, 23: *humilem spiritu suscipiet gloria.*

Et qui susceperit unum parvulum talem, idest, quicumque est imitator puerilis innocentiae, hic maior est, quia quanto humilior, tanto altior: quia *qui se humiliat, exaltabitur,* Lc. XVIII, 14.

1491. Sed potest esse quaestio: videtur enim quod hoc non sit verum, quia perfectio est in caritate; ergo ubi maior caritas, ibi maior perfectio.

Dicendum, quod caritatem necessario comitatur humilitas. Et potestis hoc videre si consideretis, quis sit humilis. Sicut enim in superbia sunt duo, affectus inordinatus, et aestimatio inordinata de se: ita, e contrario, est in humilitate, quia propriam excellentiam non curat, item non reputat se dignum. Istud de necessitate sequitur ad caritatem. Omnis homo cupit excellentiam quam diligit. Ergo quanto magis habet homo de humilitate, tanto magis diligit Deum, et magis excellentiam sui contemnit, et tanto minus sibi attribuit: sic quanto homo plus habet de caritate, habet etiam magis de humilitate.

Et qui susceperit unum parvulum talem, me suscipit.

1492. Ex quo parvuli sunt tam idonei, non sunt scandalizandi; unde **et qui scandalizaverit** et cetera. Et

primo ostendit quod non sunt scandalizandi propter poenam;

secundo propter divinam providentiam.

Secunda, **videte ne contemnatis unum ex his pusillis**.

Primo dicit quod non est inferendum scandalum pusillis;

secundo quod non est negligenter vitandum, ibi **si autem manus tua** et cetera. Et

primo ponit poenam in speciali;

secundo in generali, ibi **vae mundo a scandalis** et cetera.

1493. Videndum quod duplex est poena, scilicet poena damni, et poena sensus. Utramque tangit **qui susceperit unum talem**, non propter ipsum, sed propter me, **me suscipit**. Sequitur **qui autem scandalizaverit unum de pusillis istis** et cetera.

Si sit talis, constat quod maior est. Et quomodo qui maior est scandalizabitur? Perfecti enim non scandalizantur. Chrysostomus dicit quod scandalizare idem est quod iniuriam inferre, et haec potest perfecto et imperfecto inferri. Origenes dicit quod aliqui sunt effecti parvuli, aliqui in fieri: illi qui effecti sunt parvuli, sunt illi qui ad perfectionem pervenerunt, hi non possunt scandalizari; illi qui sunt in fieri, quia imperfecti sunt, possunt scandalizari, sicut sunt qui conversi sunt de novo.

not will be condemned (Mark 16:16). *Glory will uphold the humble of spirit* (Prov 29:23).

And he who will receive one such little child, i.e., whoever is an imitator of childlike innocence, he is the greater, because to the degree that one is more humble, to that degree one is higher, for *he who humbles himself, will be exalted* (Luke 18:14).

1491. But there can be a question. For it seems that this is not true, since perfection lies in charity; therefore where there is greater charity, there is greater perfection.

One should say that humility is necessarily joined with charity. And you can see this if you consider who is humble. For as there are two things in pride, namely inordinate affection and an inordinate estimation of self, so it is in humility, the other way around. For the humble man does not care about his own excellence, and does not consider himself worthy. This necessarily follows on charity. Every man desires the excellence which he loves. Therefore, the more a man has of humility, the more he loves God; and the more he despises his own excellence, the more also he attributes less to himself. Thus the more a man has of charity, the more he has also of humility.

And he who will receive one such little child in my name, receives me.

1492. Because the little ones are so suitable, they should not be scandalized; hence, **but he who will scandalize**. And

first, he shows that the little ones should not be scandalized on account of the punishment;

second, on account of divine providence.

The second is at **see that you do not despise one of these little ones**.

First, he says that scandal is not to be inflicted on the little ones;

second, that it is not to be avoided carelessly, at **and if your hand**.

And first, he sets out the punishment in particular;

second, in general, at **woe to the world because of scandals**.

1493. One should see that punishment is twofold, namely the punishment of the damned, and the punishment of the senses. He touches upon both: **and he who will receive one such little child**, not for his own sake, but for my sake, **receives me**. There follows **but he who will scandalize one of these little ones**.

If he is such a man, it is agreed that he is greater. And how will the one who is greater be scandalized? For the perfect are not scandalized. Chrysostom says that to scandalize is the same as to cause injury, and this can be done to the perfect and the imperfect. Origen says that some have been made little children, while others are in progress. Those who have been made little children are those who have arrived at perfection, and these cannot be scandalized; those who are in progress, since they are imperfect, can be

scandalized, as those who are newly converted. Jerome says that although they are not scandalized, nevertheless someone can scandalize them, because there is active scandal and passive scandal. The Lord seems to touch upon all the apostles, and he touches especially upon Judas, as below, *you will all be scandalized* (Matt 26:31).

Hieronymus dicit quod licet non scandalizentur, aliquis tamen potest eos scandalizare, quia est scandalum activum et passivum. Dominus videtur tangere omnes apostolos, et specialiter Iudam tangit, sicut infra XXVI, 31: *omnes vos scandalum patiemini* et cetera.

1494. Et quae est haec poena? ***Expedit ei ut suspendatur mola asinaria in collo eius***. Item, sicut dicit Hieronymus, loquitur Dominus secundum modum Palaestinorum, qui non habebant molendina in aqua, sed habebant molendina cum equis. Unde mola asinaria dicitur quam equus vel asinus ducere potest.

Et demergatur in profundum maris. Et haec erat poena quae inferebatur ei qui furtum fecerat: quia mola huiusmodi suspendebatur in collo eius, et proiiciebatur in mare. Quod etiam in Beato Clemente factum est, licet non quia fur esset et cetera. Unde dignus est poena aeterna. Unde melius est quamcumque poenam temporalem sustinere in praesenti, quam sustinere poenam aeternam; ad Hebr. X, 31: *horrendum est enim incidere in manus Dei viventis*; et Dan. XIII, 23: *melius est mihi absque opere incidere in manus hominum, quam peccare in conspectu Domini*.

1495. Aliter mystice: et hoc tripliciter. Uno modo, per molam caecitas gentilium intelligitur, quia animalia quae ponuntur ad ducendum hanc molam, sunt caeca: Iudic. c. XVI, 21 scribitur, quod eruerunt oculos Samsoni, et fecerunt eum molere. Unde expediret Iudaeis, quod numquam vidissent Christum, et essent proiecti in profundum maris, idest in profundum infidelitatis. Unde II Petr. II, 21: *melius enim erat illis non cognoscere viam iustitiae, quam post agnitionem retrorsum converti*.

Aliter per molam asinariam intelligitur vita activa. Et contingit quod aliquis ad vitam contemplativam transit, et cum est ibi, scandalizat contemplationem, quia non sapit sibi; ideo expedit sibi *ut suspendatur mola asinaria in collo eius, et proiiciatur in profundum maris*, idest in profundum causarum temporalium.

Augustinus dicit sic: *expedit*, idest congruit, et est poena congrua ei *ut mola*, idest cupiditas saeculi, quia qui scandalizat cupidus est, *suspendatur in collo*, idest in affectu, et *demergatur in profundum*, scilicet cupiditatum.

1496. *Vae mundo a scandalis*. Posita poena in speciali, ponitur in generali. Et tria facit.

Primo praenuntiat in generali;
secundo subiungit necessitatem;

1494. And what is this punishment? ***It would be better for him that the millstone of an ass were hung about his neck***. And as Jerome says, the Lord speaks in the manner of the Palestinians, who did not turn millstones in water, but turned millstones with horses. Hence he speaks of a millstone which a horse or a mule could carry.

And he were drowned in the depth of the sea. And this was the punishment which was inflicted on someone who committed theft, for a stone of this sort was tied around his neck, and he was cast into the sea. This was also done to Blessed Clement, although he was not a thief. Hence he is worthy of eternal punishment. Hence it is better to undergo any temporal punishment in the present than to undergo an eternal punishment; *it is a fearful thing to fall into the hands of the living God* (Heb 10:31); and, *but it is better for me to fall into your hands without doing it, than to sin in the sight of the Lord* (Dan 13:23).

1495. In another way, it is interpreted mystically, and this is threefold. In one way, by the stone is understood the blindness of the gentiles, since the animals which are appointed to bear this stone are blinded: it is written that they plucked out the eyes of Samson and made him grind (Judg 16:21). Hence it was expedient for the Jews that they had never seen Christ and had been cast into the depth of the sea, i.e., into the depth of unbelief. Hence, *for it had been better for them not to have known the way of justice, than after they have known it, to turn back from that holy commandment which was delivered to them* (2 Pet 2:21).

In another way, by the ass's millstone is understood the active life. And it happens that someone crosses over to the contemplative life, and while he is there, he scandalizes contemplation, because he does not understand himself; therefore it is expedient for him ***that the millstone of an ass were hung about his neck, and he were drowned in the depth of the sea***, i.e., into the depth of temporal affairs.

Augustine speaks this way: ***it would be better***, i.e., *it is fitting, and it is a punishment fitting for him* ***that the millstone***, *i.e., the desire for the world, because he who scandalizes is desirous*, ***were hung about his neck***, *i.e., in his affections*, ***and he were drowned in the depth***, *namely of desires*.

1496. *Woe to the world because of scandals*. The punishment in particular being set out, the punishment in general is set out. And he does three things:

first, he foretells it in general;
second, he adds the necessity;

tertio tollit excusationem, quia illis qui scandalizant, expedit ut suspendatur mola asinaria in collo eorum et cetera.

1497. *Vae mundo a scandalis*. Per mundum intelliguntur mundi amatores, quia quantum aliquis coniungitur mundo, tanto magis scandalum patitur; unde Dominus: *in me pacem habebitis, in mundo pressuram*, Io. XVI, 33. *Vae mundo* et amatoribus mundi.

1498. *Necesse est enim ut veniant scandala*. Quidam haeretici crediderunt quod esset necessitas absoluta quod peccata contingerent, et ex praescientia divina et ex natura stellarum induceretur necessitas. Sed hoc est falsum, quia Deo imputaretur, qui est auctor naturae.

Chrysostomus dicit quod necesse est quod ita eveniat, ut necessitas divinae providentiae sit necessitas conditionata. Unde necessarium est quod si praevidit istum peccaturum, peccabit, sed non sequitur quod necessario peccet.

Origenes dicit quod necessitas praesupponit malitiam daemonum et infirmitatem hominum: unde *necesse est quod veniant scandala*, quia necesse est quod diabolus homines decipiat, et homo ei obediat. Et ita ex suppositione malitiae diaboli et infirmitatis hominum accidit haec necessitas.

Alii exponunt *necesse est*, idest utile, quia per scandala probantur homines; I Cor. c. XI, 19: *nam oportet haereses esse, ut qui probati sunt, manifesti fiant in nobis*.

Vel secundum Haymonem loquitur de scandalo crucis; I Cor. v. I, 23: *nos praedicamus Christum crucifixum, Iudaeis quidem scandalum, gentibus autem stultitiam*.

1499. Sed obiicitur: si necesse est, ergo immunes sunt a peccato, cum ita sit necesse evenire.

Non dico quod hoc sit necesse necessitate absoluta; quia *vae homini illi per quem scandalum venit*. Unde licet daemones instigent, tamen imputatur ei ad poenam; Rom. c. VI, 13: *neque exhibeatis membra vestra arma iniquitatis peccato*. Specialiter dicitur de Iuda qui tradidit illum.

Tu dicis quod *vae homini illi per quem scandalum venit*; unde non est pusillis inferendum scandalum. Et quamvis non debeat inferri, tamen non debent esse negligentes in vitando scandalum; immo aliquis potest vitare per aliquod utile ad actionem, vel cognitionem, vel supportationem.

1500. Unde ponit sub similitudinem membrorum corporis *si autem manus tua vel pes tuus scandalizat te, abscinde eum et proiice abs te*. Non tamen intelligatis

1497. Woe to the world because of scandals. The world means those who love the world, because to the degree that someone is attached to the world, to that degree he suffers more scandal; hence the Lord says, *in the world you will have distress: but have confidence, I have overcome the world* (John 16:33). **Woe to the world**, and to those who love the world.

1498. For it must needs be that scandals come. Some heretics have thought that there is an absolute necessity that sins happen, and that necessity is introduced by both the divine foreknowledge and the nature of the stars. But this is false, because it would be attributed to God, who is the author of nature.

Chrysostom says that it is necessary that it happen this way, as the necessity of divine providence is a conditioned necessity. Hence it is necessary that if he foresees that this man will sin, he will sin, but it does not follow that he sins out of necessity.

Origen says that the necessity presupposes the demon's malice and men's weakness. Hence, *it is necessary that scandals come*, because it is necessary that the devil deceive men and men obey him. And so this necessity comes about on the supposition of the devil's malice and men's weakness.

Others explain it this way: *it is necessary*, i.e., it is useful, because men are tested by scandals; *for there must be also heresies: that they also, who are approved, may be made manifest among you* (1 Cor 11:19).

Or according to Haymo, he speaks of the scandal of the cross; *but we preach Christ crucified, unto the Jews indeed a stumblingblock, and unto the gentiles foolishness* (1 Cor 1:23).

1499. But it is objected: if it is necessary, then they are free of sin, since it must happen this way.

I do not say that this is necessary with an absolute necessity, for *nevertheless, woe to that man by whom the scandal comes*. Hence although the demons incite him, nevertheless it is attributed to him for punishment; *neither yield your members as instruments of iniquity unto sin* (Rom 6:13). It is spoken especially of Judas, who handed him over.

You say, *woe to that man by whom the scandal comes*; hence scandal should not be inflicted on the little ones. And although it should not be inflicted, nevertheless they should not be careless in avoiding scandal; quite the contrary, one can avoid scandal through something useful for action, or knowledge, or support.

1500. Hence he sets this out under the likeness of the members of the body: *and if your hand, or your foot scandalize you, cut it off, and cast it from you*. Yet do not think

quod debeant abscindi membra corporis, sed per membra intelliguntur amici et proximi. Est enim homo homini necessarius ad operandum, ad supportandum, ad docendum. Quod corrigit in agendis, est manus: quod supportat, est pes; unde Iob XXIX, 15: *oculus fui caeco, et pes claudo*. Unde **si manus tua**, idest ille qui dirigit operationem tuam, **vel pes**, idest ille qui sustentat te, **scandalizat te**, idest occasio peccati est tibi, **abscinde eum et proiice abs te**.

Et reddit causam bonum est tibi etc., quia melius est quodcumque malum temporale pati, quam mereri poenam aeternam.

Item aliquis est tibi necessarius ad docendum, unde est tibi oculus; unde **et si oculus tuus scandalizat te, erue eum**. Et reddit causam: **melius est tibi** et cetera.

Vel potest referri ad totam Ecclesiam, quia oculi sunt praelati, manus diaconi, pes homines simplices. Unde magis est deponendus praelatus, vel diaconus abscindendus, quam Ecclesia scandalizetur.

Vel per oculum accipitur contemplatio, per manum operatio, per pedem processio; unde si vides quod haec contemplatio, vel operatio, vel processio sit tibi occasio peccati, **abscinde eam, et proiice abs te**.

1501. Videte ne contemnatis unum ex pusillis istis. Supra docuerat vitare scandalum propter poenam, hic autem docet vitare ex consideratione divinae providentiae:

et circa hoc duo facit.

Primo proponit;

secundo rationem assignat, ibi **dico enim vobis** et cetera.

1502. Ita dixit quod **qui scandalizaverit unum ex his pusillis, expedit ei ut suspendatur mola asinaria in collo eius** etc., **videte ne contemnatis**: parvitas enim cito facit ad contemptum. *Ecce parvulum in gentibus dedi te, contemptibilem inter homines*, Ier. XLIX, 15.

Sed quaeritur de quibus pusillis hic loquitur. Dicendum de pusillis qui pusilli sunt reputatione hominum, sed magni apud Deum: isti sunt amici Dei; Lc. X, 16: *qui vos spernit, me spernit*.

Sed contra hoc obiicitur, quia tales non scandalizantur, nec pereunt, et tamen habetur infra in hoc cap. quod **venit Filius hominis salvare quod perierat**.

Dicendum, sicut solvit Origenes, quod per **parvulos** intelliguntur humiles, qui perfecti sunt; et tales non scandalizantur, et tamen interdum deficiunt. Vel quamvis non scandalizentur omnes, tamen aliquis scandalizatur. Secundum Hieronymum intelligitur de parvulis in

that you should cut off the members of your body, but by the members are understood friends and neighbors. For man is necessary for man, for working, for support, for teaching. The one that corrects in action is the hand; the one that supports is the foot. Hence, *I was an eye to the blind, and a foot to the lame* (Job 29:15). Hence, **if your hand**, i.e., the one who directs your working, or **your foot**, i.e., the one who supports you, **scandalize you**, i.e., is an occasion of sin for you, **cut it off, and cast it from you**.

And he gives the cause: **it is better for you**, because it is better to suffer any temporal evil whatsoever than to merit eternal punishment.

Likewise, someone is necessary to you for teaching; hence he is an eye for you. Hence **if your eye scandalize you, pluck it out**. And he gives the cause: **it is better for you, having one eye, to enter into life**.

Or it can be referred to the whole Church, because the eyes are the prelates, the hands the deacons, the feet the simple men. Hence one should rather depose a prelate, or cut off a deacon, than permit the Church to be scandalized.

Or by the eye is understood contemplation, by the hand work, by the foot progress; hence if you see that this contemplation, or work, or progress is an occasion of sin for you, **cut it off, and cast it from you**.

1501. See that you do not despise one of these little ones. Above, he had taught the apostles to avoid scandal on account of the punishment; now here he teaches them to avoid it out of consideration of divine providence.

And concerning this he does two things:

first, he sets it out;

second, he gives the reason, at **for I say to you that their angels in heaven always see the face of my Father who is in heaven**.

1502. Thus he said that **he who will scandalize one of these little ones who believe in me, it would be better for him that the millstone of an ass were hung about his neck . . . See that you do not despise one of these little ones**, for littleness quickly leads one to contempt. *For behold I have made thee a little one among the nations, despicable among men* (Jer 49:15).

But it is asked, which little ones does he speak of here? One should say, he speaks of the little ones who are little in the consideration of men, but great with God: these are God's friends. *He who despises you, despises me* (Luke 10:16).

But it is objected against this that such ones are not scandalized, nor are they lost, and yet it says below, that **the Son of man came to save that which was lost**.

One should say, as Origen solves it, that by **little ones** are understood the humble, who are perfect; and such men are not scandalized, and yet once in a while they fall. Or although not all are scandalized, yet some one is scandalized. According to Jerome, it is understood of those who are little

in Christ, as of those newly converted to Christ. And then it connects with what came before.

1503. Thus it was said that the part which scandalizes should be cut off, and then the very little, and the infirm, and sinners, although they should not be scandalized, yet they should not be despised. *For I say to you, that their angels in heaven always see the face of my Father who is in heaven*. Here a reason is given based on divine providence:

first, as regards the ministry of the angels;

second, as regards Christ's ministry, at *for the Son of man came to save that which was lost*.

1504. Thus it was said, do not despise them, because those for whom the Lord has such care are not to be despised. *For I say to you, that their angels*. Why *their*? Because they are assigned to their protection. For, as Jerome says, there is an angel assigned to each man for his protection; *for he has given his angels charge over you; to keep you in all your ways* (Ps 90:11); *are they not all ministering spirits, sent to minister for them, who will receive the inheritance of salvation?* (Heb 1:14). These angels have the role of bringing and announcing divine things to us. Likewise, they carry our prayers to God and present them; *and the smoke of the incense of the prayers of the saints ascended up before God from the hand of the angel* (Rev 8:4). Hence if the Lord provides for them so generously that he wills them to be served by angels, they are not to be despised; it is said of the widow that her tears ascend from the cheek even to heaven (Sir 35:18). Or *their angels*, because they are their fellow-citizens, since there is one society of angels and of men. Hence they are fellow-citizens of the heavenly city. Hence their dignity is so great, for *their angels in heaven always see the face of my Father who is in heaven*.

1505. And here four things can be pointed out. Continuity of vision, since they *always see*. Someone could say that since they are sometimes sent into service, they do not always see God's face, and for this reason he says, *always*.

Likewise, their sublimity of vision is recorded. We see something of the highest things, but in a certain obscurity, and through creatures, as is said, *for the invisible things of him, from the creation of the world, are clearly seen* (Rom 1:20). But the angels see in a certain loftiness; hence he says, *in heaven*.

Likewise, clear vision is noted. For *we see now through a glass in a dark manner; but then face to face* (1 Cor 13:12). It should not be said that he has a bodily face, but it says *face*, i.e., the open vision of him. For when someone is seen in a mirror, he is not seen with open vision; but when he is seen in the face, then he is seen openly. Thus God is seen in a mirror when he is seen through creatures; but when in himself, and through himself, then vision will be *face to face*.

Chrysostom says that a certain excelling pleasure is noted, for these are perfect men: if angels are their ministers, it

administratores eorum, denotatur esse quaedam maior iucunditas eorum, quam angelorum. Unde vident eum assistentem sibi. Unde non solum visio est dos, sed etiam comprehensio; ad Phil. III, 12: *sequor autem si quo modo comprehendam*.

1506. Sed quare dicit **Patris mei, qui in caelis est**? Ad excludendum errorem eorum qui ponebant angelos, idest daemones. Unde dicebant quod angeli in caelo sunt, daemones in medio, et ideo sunt medii, et administratores nostri. Ideo ad hoc excludendum dicit **semper vident faciem Patris mei, qui in caelis est**.

Item alia ratio est ad promovendum nostrum desiderium, quia si ipsi vident, et nos videbimus, hoc enim sperare debemus.

1507. Sed ne videatur esse parum quod angeli ad custodiam hominum deputati sunt, probat hoc etiam per ministerium Christi. Et

primo hoc probat;

secundo adducit similitudinem.

1508. Dicit ergo quod pusilli non sunt contemnendi, quia **Filius hominis venit salvare quod perierat**. I ad Tim. I, 15: *Christus Iesus venit in hunc mundum peccatores salvos facere*. Supra I, 21: **ipse enim salvum faciet populum suum a peccatis eorum**.

is indicated that a certain greater pleasure is theirs than is the angels'. Hence they see him taking a position for himself. Hence not only is the vision a gift, but also comprehension; *I follow after, if I may by any means apprehend* (Phil 3:12).

1506. But why does he say, *of my Father who is in heaven*? To exclude the error of those who set down **angels** to mean demons. Hence they said that angels are in heaven and demons in the middle, so they are mediators, and our ministers. So to exclude this, he says they **always see the face of my Father who is in heaven**.

Likewise, another reason is to arouse our desires, for if they see, we also shall see, for we should hope for this.

1507. But lest it seem to be a little thing that angels are assigned to the protection of men, he also proves this through the ministry of the Christ. And

first, he proves this;

second, he applies a likeness.

1508. He says then that the very little should not be despised, **for the Son of man came to save that which was lost**. *Christ Jesus came into this world to save sinners* (1 Tim 1:15). Above, **for he will save his people from their sins** (Matt 1:21).

Lecture 2

18:12 Quid vobis videtur? Si fuerint alicui centum oves, et erraverit una ex eis, nonne relinquet nonaginta novem in montibus, et vadit quaerere eam quae erravit? [n. 1509]

18:13 Et si contigerit ut inveniat eam, amen dico vobis, quia gaudet super eam magis quam super nonaginta novem, quae non erraverunt. [n. 1512]

18:14 Sic non est voluntas ante Patrem vestrum qui in caelis est, ut pereat unus de pusillis istis. [n. 1513]

18:15 Si autem peccaverit in te frater tuus, vade, et corripe eum inter te et ipsum solum. Si te audierit, lucratus eris fratrem tuum. [n. 1514]

18:16 Si autem non te audierit, adhibe tecum adhuc unum vel duos, ut in ore duorum vel trium testium stet omne verbum. [n. 1520]

18:17 Quod si non audierit eos, dic Ecclesiae. Si autem Ecclesiam non audierit, sit tibi sicut ethnicus et publicanus. [n. 1521]

18:18 Amen dico vobis, quaecumque alligaveritis super terram, erunt ligata et in caelo: et quaecumque solveritis super terram, erunt soluta et in caelo. [n. 1524]

18:19 Iterum dico vobis, quia si duo ex vobis consenserint super terram, de omni re quacumque petierint, fiet illis a Patre meo, qui in caelis est. [n. 1525]

18:20 Ubi enim sunt duo, vel tres congregati in nomine meo, ibi sum in medio eorum. [n. 1527]

18:21 Tunc accedens Petrus ad eum, dixit: Domine, quotiens peccabit in me frater meus, et dimittam ei? Usque septies? [n. 1528]

18:12 Τί ὑμῖν δοκεῖ; ἐὰν γένηταί τινι ἀνθρώπῳ ἑκατὸν πρόβατα καὶ πλανηθῇ ἓν ἐξ αὐτῶν, οὐχὶ ἀφήσει τὰ ἐνενήκοντα ἐννέα ἐπὶ τὰ ὄρη καὶ πορευθεὶς ζητεῖ τὸ πλανώμενον;

18:13 καὶ ἐὰν γένηται εὑρεῖν αὐτό, ἀμὴν λέγω ὑμῖν ὅτι χαίρει ἐπ᾽ αὐτῷ μᾶλλον ἢ ἐπὶ τοῖς ἐνενήκοντα ἐννέα τοῖς μὴ πεπλανημένοις.

18:14 οὕτως οὐκ ἔστιν θέλημα ἔμπροσθεν τοῦ πατρὸς ὑμῶν τοῦ ἐν οὐρανοῖς ἵνα ἀπόληται ἓν τῶν μικρῶν τούτων.

18:15 Ἐὰν δὲ ἁμαρτήσῃ [εἰς σὲ] ὁ ἀδελφός σου, ὕπαγε ἔλεγξον αὐτὸν μεταξὺ σοῦ καὶ αὐτοῦ μόνου. ἐάν σου ἀκούσῃ, ἐκέρδησας τὸν ἀδελφόν σου·

18:16 ἐὰν δὲ μὴ ἀκούσῃ, παράλαβε μετὰ σοῦ ἔτι ἕνα ἢ δύο, ἵνα ἐπὶ στόματος δύο μαρτύρων ἢ τριῶν σταθῇ πᾶν ῥῆμα·

18:17 ἐὰν δὲ παρακούσῃ αὐτῶν, εἰπὲ τῇ ἐκκλησίᾳ· ἐὰν δὲ καὶ τῆς ἐκκλησίας παρακούσῃ, ἔστω σοι ὥσπερ ὁ ἐθνικὸς καὶ ὁ τελώνης.

18:18 Ἀμὴν λέγω ὑμῖν· ὅσα ἐὰν δήσητε ἐπὶ τῆς γῆς ἔσται δεδεμένα ἐν οὐρανῷ, καὶ ὅσα ἐὰν λύσητε ἐπὶ τῆς γῆς ἔσται λελυμένα ἐν οὐρανῷ.

18:19 Πάλιν [ἀμὴν] λέγω ὑμῖν ὅτι ἐὰν δύο συμφωνήσωσιν ἐξ ὑμῶν ἐπὶ τῆς γῆς περὶ παντὸς πράγματος οὗ ἐὰν αἰτήσωνται, γενήσεται αὐτοῖς παρὰ τοῦ πατρός μου τοῦ ἐν οὐρανοῖς.

18:20 οὗ γάρ εἰσιν δύο ἢ τρεῖς συνηγμένοι εἰς τὸ ἐμὸν ὄνομα, ἐκεῖ εἰμι ἐν μέσῳ αὐτῶν.

18:21 Τότε προσελθὼν ὁ Πέτρος εἶπεν αὐτῷ· κύριε, ποσάκις ἁμαρτήσει εἰς ἐμὲ ὁ ἀδελφός μου καὶ ἀφήσω αὐτῷ; ἕως ἑπτάκις;

18:12 What think you? If a man has a hundred sheep, and one of them were to go astray, does he not leave the ninety-nine in the mountains, and go to seek that which has gone astray? [n. 1509]

18:13 And if it be that he finds it, amen I say to you, he rejoices more for that, than for the ninety-nine that did not go astray. [n. 1512]

18:14 Even so it is not the will of your Father, who is in heaven, that one of these little ones should perish. [n. 1513]

18:15 But if your brother should offend you, go and rebuke him between you and him alone. If he hears you, you will gain your brother. [n. 1514]

18:16 And if he will not hear you, take with you one or two more, that in the mouth of two or three witnesses every word may stand. [n. 1520]

18:17 And if he does not hear them, tell the Church. And if he does not hear the Church, let him be to you as a heathen and publican. [n. 1521]

18:18 Amen I say to you, whatever you will bind upon earth, will be bound also in heaven; and whatever you will loose upon earth, will be loosed also in heaven. [n. 1524]

18:19 Again I say to you, that if two of you should consent upon earth, concerning anything, whatever they will ask, it will be done to them by my Father who is in heaven. [n. 1525]

18:20 For where there are two or three gathered together in my name, there am I in the midst of them. [n. 1527]

18:21 Then Peter came to him and said: Lord, how often will my brother offend against me, and I forgive him? Till seven times? [n. 1528]

| 18:22 Dicit illi Iesus: non dico tibi usque septies, sed usque septuagies septies. [n. 1530] | 18:22 λέγει αὐτῷ ὁ Ἰησοῦς· οὐ λέγω σοι ἕως ἑπτάκις ἀλλὰ ἕως ἑβδομηκοντάκις ἑπτά. | 18:22 Jesus said to him: I do not say to you, till seven times; but till seventy times seven times. [n. 1530] |

1509. *Quid vobis videtur?* Hic ponitur similitudo. Et primo ponitur diligens inquisitio;

secundo gaudium de inventa ove.

1510. Unde dicit *quid vobis videtur?* Ita dictum est, quod *Filius hominis venit salvare quod perierat*, quia pastor quaerit ovem perditam. *Si alicui fuerint centum oves*. Per centenarium universitas rationalis creaturae significatur: nonaginta novem idem est numerus qui novem, sed solum multiplicatus, quia novem multiplicata per decem faciunt nonaginta; qui numerus, scilicet novem, deficit a denario in unitate; unde per istas oves omnes rationales creaturas significat; Io. X, 27: *oves meae vocem meam audiunt*; in Ps. XCIV, v. 7: *nos autem populus eius et oves pascuae eius*.

Per ovem quae erravit, significatur humanum genus. Et quare significavit per ovem quae erravit? Quia per unum hominem omnes erraverunt; I Petr. II, 25: *eratis sicut oves errantes*.

1511. *Nonne relinquit nonaginta novem in montibus?* Non est littera *in deserto*, sed *in montibus*, sicut habetur in Graeco.

Hoc tripliciter exponitur. Primo quia istae nonaginta novem significant Angelos qui relicti sunt in montibus, idest in caelestibus; Ezech. c. XXXIV, 13: *pascam eos in montibus Israel*. Vel per nonaginta novem significantur iusti, per ovem perditam peccatores; et sic reliquit in montibus, idest in altitudine iustitiae; Ps. XXXV, 7: *iustitiae tuae sicut montes Dei*. Vel per nonaginta novem superbi, per ovem humiles: unde *nonne relinquit nonaginta novem in montibus*, idest in superbia sua, *et vadit quaerere eam, quae erravit?* Ps. CXVIII, v. 176: *erravi sicut ovis quae periit, require servum tuum, domine*.

1512. Consequenter agitur de gaudio *et si contigerit quod inveniat eam* et cetera. Hic etiam triplex ratio potest assignari. Quod Dominus gaudet de bonis, habetur Soph. III, v. 17: *gaudebit super te Deus tuus in laetitia*. Si per nonaginta significentur angeli, per ovem homo, plana est ratio, quia dignus erat homo reparatione; ad Hebr. II, 16: *nusquam angelos apprehendit, sed semen Abrahae apprehendit*. Si per nonaginta intelligamus iustos, similiter plana est ratio, quia dux plus diligit militem, qui cadit in bello, et post viriliter pugnat semper, quam illum qui numquam cecidit, et semper tepide pugnat. Sic, cum aliquis peccavit, et post fortiter resurgit, et semper viriliter se habet, plus eum diligit; II ad Cor. VII, 9: *gaudeo quia contristati estis ad poenitentiam*; ideo plus gaudet Dominus de eo etc., cum maioris est zeli. Tamen non est extendendum ad omnes, quia potest habere iustus tantum zelum quod plus placet Deo, quam

1509. *What think you?* Here a likeness is set out. And first, the diligent search is set out;

second, the joy over the sheep which was found.

1510. Hence he says, *what think you?* So it was said, that *the Son of man came to save that which was lost* (Matt 18:11) because the shepherd seeks the sheep that has been lost. *If a man has a hundred sheep*. The hundred signifies the universality of rational creatures. Ninety-nine is the same number as nine, only multiplied, for nine multiplied by ten makes ninety. This number, namely nine, falls short of ten in unity. Hence by these sheep he signifies all rational creatures. *My sheep hear my voice* (John 10:27); *we are his people and the sheep of his pasture* (Ps 99:3).

The sheep which went astray signifies the human race. And why does he signify the human race by a sheep which went astray? Because through one man all men have gone astray; *for you were as sheep going astray* (1 Pet 2:25).

1511. *Does he not leave the ninety-nine in the mountains?* The text is not *in the desert*, but *in the mountains*, as is had in the Greek.

And this is explained in three ways. First, that these ninety-nine signify angels who were left in the mountains, i.e., in the heavens; *I will feed them in the mountains of Israel* (Ezek 34:13). Or, ninety-nine signify the just, and the lost sheep sinners. And thus he left them in the mountains, i.e., in the loftiness of justice; *your justice is as the mountains of God* (Ps 35:7). Or the ninety-nine signify the proud, the one sheep the humble; hence *does he not leave the ninety-nine in the mountains*, i.e., in their pride, *and go to seek that which has gone astray?* I have gone astray like a sheep that is lost: seek your servant (Ps 118:176).

1512. Next, he treats of the joy: *and if it be that he finds it*. Here also, three reasons can be given. That the Lord rejoices over the good is said in *he will rejoice over you with gladness* (Zeph 3:17). If the angels are signified by the ninety-nine, and man by the sheep, the reason is plain, for man was worthy of reparation; *for no where does he take hold of the angels: but of the seed of Abraham he takes hold* (Heb 2:16). If we take the ninety-nine to mean the just, the reason is similarly plain, for a leader loves a soldier who falls in battle after fighting manfully more than one who has never fallen and always fights half-heartedly. In the same way, when someone has sinned, and afterward rises up again strongly, and always carries himself manfully, he loves him more; *now I am glad . . . because you were made sorrowful unto penance* (2 Cor 7:9); therefore the Lord rejoices more over the one, since his zeal is greater. Yet it should not be extended to every case, because the just

in poenitente. Secundum etiam tertiam expositionem patet ratio, quia plus gaudet de eo, qui recognoscit peccatum, ut patet de publicano et Pharisaeo.

1513. Concludit ergo *sic non est voluntas ante Patrem vestrum qui in caelis est, ut pereat unus de pusillis istis*. Minus dicit, et plus significat, quia voluntas eius est ut salventur; I Tim. II, 4: *qui vult omnes homines salvos fieri*. Si enim non vellet, non mitteret angelos. Ez. XVIII, 23: *numquid voluntatis meae est mors impii? Dicit Dominus*.

1514. *Si ergo peccaverit in te frater tuus* et cetera. Hic agitur de scandalo dimittendo. Et

primo ponitur ordo;

secundo numerus, ibi *tunc accedens Petrus ad eum* et cetera.

Circa primum tria.

Primo ponit secretam admonitionem;

secundo testimonium, ibi *si autem non te audierit* etc.,

tertio Annuntiationem, ibi *quod si non audierit eos, dic Ecclesiae*.

Circa primum

primo dat suum documentum;

secundo assignat rationem dati, ibi *si autem te audierit, lucratus eris fratrem tuum*.

1515. Ita dixi quod non sunt contemnendi pusilli, sed quid faciendum est si aliquis scandalizat? Hic docet. *Si autem peccaverit in te frater tuus, vade, et corripe eum inter te et ipsum solum*.

Notate primo quod dicit *peccaverit*: unde loquitur de peccato perpetrato. Unde aliter procedendum est in peccato perpetrato, aliter in perpetrando, quia perpetratum non potest esse non perpetratum; unde in perpetrando est operam dare quod non fiat; Is. c. LVIII, 6: *dissolve colligationes impietatis, solve fasciculos deprimentes* et cetera. Unde in perpetrando non oportet quod servetur talis ordo, in perpetrato oportet.

Item dicit *in te*. Glossa: si iniuriam vel contumeliam intulerit tibi. Unde vult dicere quod peccatum factum contra nos, remittamus; sed peccatum quod fit contra Deum, nos remittere non possumus, ut dicit Glossa. I Reg. II, 25: *qui peccaverit contra Deum, quis orabit pro eo?*

Item debes praecipue curare iniurias factas ab eo, qui tecum est in eadem societate; de aliis etiam habenda est cura, sed non tanta. I Cor. V, 12: *quid nobis de eis qui foris sunt iudicare?*

man can have so much zeal that he pleases God more than he would in penance. The reason is plain according to the third explanation as well, because he rejoices more over the one who acknowledges sin, as is clear with the publican and the Pharisee.

1513. So he concludes: *even so it is not the will of your Father, who is in heaven, that one of these little ones should perish*. He says less and signifies more, because his will is that they should be saved; *who will have all men to be saved* (1 Tim 2:4). For if he did not will it, he would not send angels. *Is it my will that a sinner should die, says the Lord God* (Ezek 18:23).

1514. *But if your brother should offend you*. Here he treats of scandal which needs to be sent away. And

first, the order is set down;

second, the number, at *then came Peter to him*.

Concerning the first, three things:

first, he sets out the secret rebuke;

second, the witness, at *and if he does not hear you*;

third, the declaration, at *and if he does not hear them: tell the Church*.

Concerning the first,

first, he gives his instruction;

second, he gives a reason, at *if he hears you, you will gain your brother*.

1515. Thus he said that very little ones are not to be despised, but what should be done if someone is scandalizing them? Here he teaches. *But if your brother offends against you, go, and rebuke him between you and him alone*.

Notice first that he says, *should offend*: he is speaking of a sin which has been committed. Hence one should proceed in one way with a sin which has been committed, and another way with a sin which is yet to be committed, because what has been committed cannot be not committed; hence in the case of a sin which is yet to be committed, one should make sure it does not happen. *Loose the bands of wickedness, undo the bundles that oppress* (Isa 58:6). Hence it is not necessary to follow such an order in the case of a sin which is yet to be committed, but in the case of a sin committed it is necessary.

Likewise, he says, *offend you*. The Gloss: *if he has inflicted an injury or slander on you*. Hence he wished to say that we should forgive a sin committed against us; but we cannot forgive a sin which is committed against God, as the Gloss says. *If a man should sin against the Lord, who will pray for him?* (1 Sam 2:25).

Likewise, you should attend first of all to the injuries done by him who is with you in one society; one should pay attention to the others, but not so much. *For what have I to do to judge them that are without?* (1 Cor 5:12).

1516. *Vade et corripe eum inter te et ipsum solum.* Dominus discipulos ad perfectam sollicitudinem et correctionem ducit. Supra V, 23 Dominus dixerat, quod si aliquis offenderet fratrem, quod relinqueret munus ante altare etc., hic autem plus procedit, quia non solum ille qui laesit, sed qui laesus est: unde *si peccaverit in te, vade* etc.; Ps. CXIX, 7: *cum his, qui oderunt pacem, erant pacificus*. Et numquid primo remittes? Non; sed primo debes corripere: unde non iubet cuique dimittere, sed poenitenti.

Item dicit *corripe*, non *increpa*, vel *exaspera*: et breviter ostende. Si cognoscit, tunc debes dimittere; unde, *instruite eos in spiritu lenitatis*, ad Gal. VI, 1.

1517. Sed numquid peccat qui hanc correctionem dimittit? Augustinus: *si non corripis, peior factus es tacendo, quam ille peccando.*

Sed, cum hoc sit verum quod omnes corripere teneantur, diceret aliquis quod solis praelatis convenit ex officio, aliis vero ex caritate. Aliquando Dominus permittit bonos cum malis puniri. Quare? Quia non corripuerunt malos. Tamen dicit Augustinus quod aliquando debemus desistere, si times ne propter correctionem istam non emendentur, sed deteriores reddantur. Item si times ne inducat persecutionem Ecclesiae, non peccas. Si vero desistis, ne laedaris in temporalibus, ne molestia tibi accidat, vel huiusmodi, peccas; Prov. IX, 8: *argue sapientem, et diliget te*.

1518. *Corripe eum inter te et ipsum solum.* Et quare? Quia ista correctio fit ex caritate; caritas autem est amor Dei et proximi. Si amas, debes salutem eius diligere.

Sed in hoc duo sunt attendenda, scilicet conscientia et bona fama. Si vis ergo eum salvare, debes famam suam salvare; hoc autem facies corrigendo inter te et ipsum. Si ante omnes corripis, famam eius tollis: tamen conscientia praeponenda est famae. Tamen frequenter accidit quod quando homo videt publicari peccatum suum, ita fit effrons quod omni peccato se exponit; Ier. II, 20: *sub omni ligno frondoso tu prosternebaris, meretrix*; Eccli. IV, 25: *est confusio peccatum adducens*.

Sed contra hoc obiicitur quod habetur I Tim. V, 20: *peccantem coram omnibus argue*. Et hoc est verum si publice delinquatur. Est enim aliquis peccans publice, et tunc publice increpandus est: et aliquis secretus, et tunc secreto est increpandus; et hoc patet, quia dicit Augustinus, quod si te solo sciente peccaverit *corripe eum inter te et ipsum solum*.

1519. Quod *si te audierit lucratus es fratrem tuum*. Ad quid hoc dicit? Propter tria. Ut scias quo fine debeas corripere: quia si propter teipsum corripis, nihil facis,

1516. *Go, and rebuke him between you and him alone*. The Lord leads the disciples to perfect solicitude and correction. Above, the Lord had said that if someone has offended a brother, he should leave his gift before the altar (Matt 5:23). But here he goes further, because not only the one who wounds, but he who is wounded should go: hence if he *should offend you, go*. *With those who hated peace I was peaceable* (Ps 119:7). And should you forgive first? No, but first you should correct. Hence he does not order you to forgive everybody, but the penitent.

Likewise, he says, *rebuke*, not *upbraid*, or *irritate*; and make it clear briefly. If he acknowledges his sin, then you should forgive him; hence, *instruct such a one in the spirit of meekness* (Gal 6:1).

1517. But is it a sin to neglect this rebuke? Augustine: *if you do not rebuke, you are made worse by keeping silent than that man by sinning*.

But, since it is true that all are bound to rebuke those who sin, some would say that it belongs only to prelates by office, but to others in charity. Sometimes the Lord permits the good to be punished with the bad. Why? Because they did not rebuke the bad. Yet Augustine says that sometimes we should leave off, if you fear that they are not improved by this correction, but made worse. Also if you fear lest he bring a persecution on the Church, you do not sin. But if you leave off lest you be injured in temporal things, lest some molestation happen to you, or some such thing, you sin; *rebuke a wise man, and he will love you* (Prov 9:8).

1518. *Rebuke him between you and him alone*. And why? Because this correction comes from charity, and charity is the love of God and of neighbor. If you love, you should choose that he be saved.

But in this matter, there are two things one should keep in mind, namely conscience and good reputation. So if you wish to save him, you should save his reputation; and you do this by correcting him between the two of you. If you correct him in front of everyone, you take away his reputation. Nevertheless, conscience is to be placed before reputation. Yet it frequently happens that when a man sees his sin made public, he becomes so bold that he exposes himself to every sin; *under every green tree you prostituted yourself* (Jer 2:20); *for there is a shame that brings sin* (Sir 4:25).

But it is objected against this that Timothy says, *those who sin reprove before all* (1 Tim 5:20). And this is true if the wrong is committed publicly. For there is someone who sins publicly, and then he should be publicly rebuked; and there is someone who sins in secret, and then he should be rebuked in secret. And this is clear, for Augustine says that if you alone know that he has sinned, *rebuke him between you and him alone*.

1519. *If he hears you, you will gain your brother*. To what purpose does he say this? For three things. That you may know what your end should be when you rebuke: for

quia ubi privata est emenda, non est correctio meritoria; sed si propter Deum, tunc valet. Item hoc est ad quod debes intendere, scilicet menti fratris inserere correctionem et doctrinam. Item posset aliquis dicere, quod perdere fratrem suum non esset iustum. Sed si ita esset, non dixisset *lucratus es fratrem tuum*. Item *lucratus es*, quia ipse est commembrum tuum: et sicut membrum membro compatitur, sic et tu fratri tuo. Item *lucratus*, quia tibi ipsi lucraris salutem; Iac. IV, 11: *qui iudicat fratrem suum, detrahit legi, et iudicat legem*; unde ibid. V, 20: *qui converti fecerit peccatorem ab errore viae suae, liberat animam eius a morte, et operit multitudinem peccatorum*.

1520. *Si autem te non audierit, adhibe tecum unum vel duos*. Hic inducit testimonium *adhibe unum vel duos* et cetera. Deut. c. XIX, 15: *in ore duorum vel trium testium stet omne verbum*.

Sed hic est quaestio: quare statim non inducit testes? Dicendum quod sic debet mundari conscientia, quod non laedatur fama: unde si primo et per se potest, bene quidem; si non, tunc advocet testes. Et Hieronymus dicit quod unum primo, et post duos. Et quare? Ut sint testes correctionis factae, quia si ulterius procedit, non est tibi imputandum. Hieronymus dicit quod etiam ad aliud, ut scilicet convincat de peccato: quia aliqui sunt ita pertinaces, quod non recognoscunt, ideo debes testes adducere, ut convincas eum de facto. Vel forte iterabit iniuriam. Vel, secundum Augustinum, ad convincendum eum.

Sed contra hoc videtur esse quod Augustinus dicit quod antequam duobus ostendat, debet ostendere praeposito, et hoc est ostendere Ecclesiae. Ergo videtur pervertere ordinem.

Dico quod potest ostendi praelato, vel ordine iudiciario, vel ut personae privatae. Intendit ergo Augustinus quod debet ostendi praeposito primo ut personae privatae, ut tamquam persona privata det operam correctioni.

1521. Unde dicit *si eos non audierit, dic Ecclesiae*. Hic ponitur denuntiatio. Et

primo denuntiat;
secundo ponitur sententia;
tertio efficacia.

Secunda ibi *si autem Ecclesiam non audierit* etc.; tertia ibi *amen dico vobis* et cetera.

1522. Dicit *si autem non audierit eos, dic Ecclesiae*, idest toti multitudini, ut confundatur, ut qui noluit sine confusione corripi, cum confusione corripiatur. *Est enim confusio adducens peccatum, et est confusio adducens gloriam et gratiam*, Eccli. IV, 25. Vel *Ecclesiae*, idest

if you rebuke for your own sake, you do nothing, for where something private needs amending, there is no meritorious correction; but if it is for God, then it avails. Also, this is what you should aim at, namely to sow rebuke and teaching in the mind of a brother. Likewise, someone could say that to lose one's brother would not be just. But if this were so, he would not have said, *you will gain your brother*. Likewise, *you will gain*, because he is your co-member: and just as one member suffers with another, so also you suffer with your brother. Also, *you will gain*, because you gain salvation for yourself; *he who judges his brother, detracts the law, and judges the law* (Jas 4:11); hence, *he who causes a sinner to be converted from the error of his way, will save his soul from death, and will cover a multitude of sins* (Jas 5:20).

1520. *And if he does not hear you, take with you one or two more*. Here he brings in a witness: *take with you one or two more*. *In the mouth of two or three witnesses every word will stand* (Deut 19:15).

But here there is a question: why does not one bring in witnesses immediately? One should say that he should cleanse his conscience, lest a reputation be injured. Hence if he can do it first and on his own, well indeed; if not, then let him summon witnesses. And Jerome says that he should bring one at first, and later two. And why? That there may be witnesses of the correction made, because if he proceeds further, it should not be attributed to you. Jerome says that one should do this also for another reason, namely that one may convince the man of his sin: for there are some men so obstinate that they do not acknowledge their sins, so you should bring in witnesses that you may convince him of the deed. Or perhaps he will repeat the injury. Or, according to Augustine, to convince him.

But against this, it seems that Augustine says that before he reveals it to two witnesses, he should reveal it to the one in charge, and this is to reveal it to the Church. There Augustine seems to subvert the order.

I say that it can be revealed to the prelate, either in the judicial order, or as a private person. So Augustine meant that one should reveal it to the one in charge first as a private person, so that as a private person he may render the service of correction.

1521. From there he says, *and if he does not hear them, tell the Church*. Here the denunciation is set out. And

first, he denounces;
second, the sentence is set out;
third, the efficacy.

The second is at *and if he does not hear the Church*; the third, at *amen I say to you*.

1522. He says, *and if he does not hear them: tell the Church*, i.e., the whole multitude, that he may be confounded, so that he who would not be rebuked without shame, may be rebuked with shame. *For there is a shame that brings sin, and there is a shame that brings glory and*

iudicibus, ut corrigatur; Deut. XXI, 18: *si aliquis habeat filium contumacem et protervum, qui non audierit patris ac matris imperium, et coercitus audire contempserit, apprehendent eum, et ducent ad seniores civitatis illius, et ad portam iudicii* et cetera.

1523. Deinde additur poena *si Ecclesiam non audierit, sit tibi sicut ethnicus et publicanus*. Ethnici sunt gentiles et infideles; publicani, qui tributa recipiunt, qui sunt publici peccatores. Unde quasi separati excommunicentur per sententiam Ecclesiae, quia Ecclesiam non audierunt. Unde pro sola contumacia potest homo excommunicari.

1524. *Amen dico vobis* et cetera. Hic ponitur efficacia huius sententiae. Quia posset aliquis dicere: quid curo ego si Ecclesiae dicatur, et sim excommunicatus? Ideo ostendit efficaciam istam *amen dico vobis, quaecumque alligaveritis super terram, erunt ligata et in caelo: et quaecumque solveritis super terram, erunt soluta et in caelo*. Supra dicta sunt Petro haec; hic autem dicitur toti Ecclesiae. Et dicitur *alligare*, vel quia non solvit, vel quia excommunicat.

Origenes dicit quod hic dicit *in caelo* cum autem Petro locutus est, dixit *in caelis*, ad designandum quod Petrus habet universalem potestatem. Hic autem dicit *in caelo*, quia universalis non est eis potestas, sed in aliquo loco, quia Petro universalem potestatem dedit.

1525. *Iterum dico vobis* et cetera. Hic ponit efficaciam orationis. Et

primo hoc facit;

secundo rationem dat, ibi *ubi enim sunt duo* et cetera.

1526. Dicit *iterum dico vobis* et cetera.

Sed contra potes obiicere, quia multa petimus, quae non obtinemus. Hoc contingit primo propter indignitatem petentium; unde dicit *duo ex vobis*, scilicet, qui secundum Evangelium vivitis. Iac. IV, 3: *petitis, et non accipitis, eo quod male petatis*. Item quia non consentiunt, quia non habent vinculum pacis: impossibile est enim preces multorum non exaudiri, si ex multis orationibus fiat quasi una; II Cor. I, 11: *ut ex multarum personis facierum eius, quae in nobis est, donationis per multos gratiae agantur pro nobis*. Item quia quaedam petunt quae non expediunt eis ad salutem: petitio enim debet esse de re utili infra XX, 22: *nescitis quid petatis*.

Fiet illis a Patre meo, qui est in caelis, idest in altis: vel *in caelis*, idest in nobis.

1527. *Ubi enim sunt duo vel tres congregati in nomine meo, ibi sum in medio eorum*; congregatione

grace (Sir 4:25). Or *the Church*, i.e., to the judges, that he may be corrected; *if a man have a stubborn and unruly son, who will not hear the commandments of his father or mother, and being corrected, slights obedience: they shall take him and bring him to the ancients of his city, and to the gate of judgment* (Deut 21:18–19).

1523. Then the punishment is added: *and if he does not hear the Church, let him be to you as the heathen and publican*. The heathen are the gentiles and unbelievers; the publicans are those who take up the tributes, who are public sinners. Hence, as though separated, let them be excommunicated by the sentence of the Church, because they did not listen to the Church. Hence a man can only be excommunicated for stubbornness.

1524. *Amen I say to you*. Here the efficacy of this sentence is set out. For someone could say: what do I care if it is told to the Church, and I am excommunicated? So he reveals the efficacy: *amen I say to you, whatever you will bind upon earth, will be bound also in heaven; and whatever you will loose upon earth, will be loosed also in heaven*. Above this was said to Peter; but here it is said to the whole Church. And it says, *bind*, either because the Church does not loose, or because she excommunicates.

Origen says that he says here, *in heaven*, while when he spoke to Peter he said, *in the heavens* (Matt 16:18), to indicate that Peter has a universal power. But here he says, *in heaven*, because universal power is not given to them, but rather power in some place, for he gave universal power to Peter.

1525. *Again I say to you*. Here he sets out the efficacy of prayers. And

first, he does this;

second, he gives a reason, at *for where there are two*.

1526. He says, *again I say to you*.

But you can object that we ask for many things which we do not get. This happens first because of the unworthiness of those asking; hence he says, *two of you*, namely, of you who live according to the Gospel. *You ask, and receive not; because you ask amiss* (Jas 4:3). Also, because they do not agree, since they do not have the bond of peace: for it is impossible that the prayers of many not be heard if there comes out of many prayers as it were one prayer; *you helping withal in prayer for us: that for this gift obtained for us, by the means of many persons, thanks may be given by many in our behalf* (2 Cor 1:11). Likewise, because some pray for things which are not expedient for salvation: for a prayer should be for useful things; below, *you do not know what you ask* (Matt 20:22).

It will be done to them by my Father who is in heaven, i.e., in the highest, or *in heaven*, i.e., in us.

1527. *For where there are two or three gathered together in my name, there am I in the midst of them*; in the

sanctorum, non terrenorum. Ps. CX, 1: *in consilio iustorum et congregatione, magna opera Domini*. **Ubi ergo duo vel tres**. Caritas non est in uno, sed in pluribus; unde I Io. IV, 16: *qui manet in caritate, in Deo manet, et Deus in eo*. Ideo **ego sum in medio eorum**.

1528. Tunc accedens Petrus dixit ad eum: Domine, quoties peccabit in me frater meus, et dimittam ei? Supra docuit quo ordine sit dimittendum, quia post correctionem et emendam, hic agit de numero quoties sit dimittendum.

Primo ergo ponitur Petri interrogatio;

secundo Christi responsio;

tertio adhibetur similitudo.

Secunda ibi **dicit illi Iesus** etc.; tertia ibi **assimilatum est regnum caelorum**.

1529. Dicit ergo **tunc accedens**. **Tunc**, scilicet audito hoc verbo *si peccaverit in te frater tuus* etc., tunc motus fuit Petrus an semel, an pluries dimitteret, et dixit **quoties peccaverit in me frater meus** etc., **nonne dimittam usque septies** quasi dicat: usque septies, infirmitatis est, sed plus malitiae. Ideo petiit si dimitteret **usque septies**. Item sciebat illud, quod dictum est IV Reg. V, 10, quod Eliseus praecepit Naaman, quod septies lavaret se in Iordane; ideo cogitavit quod septies dimittere deberet.

1530. Dicit ei Iesus: non dico tibi septies, sed septuagies septies. Uno modo potest teneri hoc, quod dicit **septies**, aggregative, ut sit sensus: non septies, sed septuaginta vicibus. Vel potest teneri multiplicative, ita quod septem vicibus septuaginta: et sic exponit Hieronymus.

Secundum primam expositionem, quae est Augustini, datur intelligi quod totum debemus condonare, sicut Christus omnia condonavit. Ad Col. III, 13: *donantes vobismetipsis, si quis adversus aliquem habet querelam, sicut et Dominus donavit nobis, ita et vos*. Vel potest dici, quod ponitur numerus finitus pro infinito, sicut in Psalmis: *verbum quod mandavit in mille generationes*.

Secundum Hieronymum, eadem est causa; tamen additur ratio numeri. Per sex enim perfectio significatur, per centenarium, qui multiplicatur per denarium, decalogus significatur. Primus numerus, qui a denario recedit, est undecimus. Et quia per sex universitas significatur, ideo universitas peccatorum significatur; quasi dicat: omnia quaecumque frater tuus peccaverit contra te, dimitte ei. Unde secundum Hieronymum videtur, quod velit dicere, quod plus remittere potest, quam ipse possit offendere.

congregation of the holy, not of the earthly. *In the council of the just: and in the congregation, great are the works of the Lord* (Ps 110:1). Therefore, **where there are two or three**. Charity is not in one, but in many; hence, *he who abides in charity, abides in God, and God in him* (1 John 4:16). Therefore, **there am I in the midst of them**.

1528. Then Peter came to him and said: Lord, how often will my brother offend against me, and I forgive him? Above, he taught in what order one should forgive, that it is after correction and emendation; here he treats of the number of times one should forgive.

First, then, Peter's question is set down;

second, Christ's response;

third, a likeness is applied.

The second is at **Jesus says to him**; the third, at **therefore the kingdom of heaven is likened**.

1529. He says then, **then came Peter**. **Then**, that is, having heard this word: *but if your brother should offend you*, then Peter was moved to ask whether he should forgive once, or many times, and he said, **how often will my brother offend against me, and I forgive him? Till seven times?** As though to say: up to seven times is due to weakness, but more than that is due to malice. For this reason, he asked if he should forgive **till seven times**. Also, he knew what was said, that Elisha commanded Naaman to wash in the Jordan seven times (2 Kgs 5:10), so he thought that he should forgive seven times.

1530. Jesus says to him: I do not say to you, till seven times; but till seventy times seven times. In one way, this can be taken so that he says **seven times** collectively, so that the sense is this: not seven times, but on seventy occasions. Or it can be taken multiplicatively, so that it means seven occasions of seventy, and Jerome explains it in this way.

According to the first explanation, which is Augustine's, one is given to understand that we should pardon the whole, just as Christ pardoned all things. *Bearing with one another, and forgiving one another, if any have a complaint against another: even as the Lord has forgiven you, so do you also* (Col 3:13). Or it can be said that a finite number is set down for an infinite, as in the Psalm, *the word which he commanded to a thousand generations* (Ps 104:8).

According to Jerome the cause is the same; yet a reason is added for the number. For perfection is signified by six; the decalogue is signified by one hundred, which is multiplied by ten. The first number which moves away from ten is eleven. And since universality is signified by six, therefore the universality of sins is signified, as though to say: all things whatever your brother has sinned against you, forgive him. Hence according to Jerome he seems, or he wishes to say that one can forgive more than he is able to do wrong.

Lecture 3

18:23 Ideo assimilatum est regnum caelorum homini regi, qui voluit rationem ponere cum servis suis. [n. 1531]

18:24 Et cum coepisset rationem ponere oblatus est ei unus, qui debebat decem milia talenta. [n. 1533]

18:25 Cum autem non haberet unde redderet, iussit eum dominus venumdari, et uxorem eius, et filios, et omnia quae habebat, et reddi. [n. 1534]

18:26 Procidens autem servus ille orabat eum, dicens: patientiam habe in me, et omnia reddam tibi. [n. 1535]

18:27 Misertus autem dominus servi illius, dimisit eum, et debitum dimisit ei. [n. 1536]

18:28 Egressus autem servus ille invenit unum de conservis suis, qui debebat ei centum denarios, et tenens suffocabat eum, dicens: redde quod debes. [n. 1537]

18:29 Et procidens conservus eius rogabat eum, dicens: patientiam habe in me, et omnia reddam tibi. [n. 1537]

18:30 Ille autem noluit, sed abiit, et misit eum in carcerem, donec redderet debitum. [n. 1537]

18:31 Videntes autem conservi eius quae fiebant, contristati sunt valde, et venerunt, et narraverunt domino suo omnia quae facta fuerant. [n. 1538]

18:32 Tunc vocavit illum dominus suus, et ait illi: serve nequam, omne debitum dimisi tibi, quoniam rogasti me: [n. 1540]

18:33 nonne ergo oportuit et te misereri conservi tui, sicut et ego tui misertus sum? [n. 1540]

18:23 Διὰ τοῦτο ὡμοιώθη ἡ βασιλεία τῶν οὐρανῶν ἀνθρώπῳ βασιλεῖ, ὃς ἠθέλησεν συνᾶραι λόγον μετὰ τῶν δούλων αὐτοῦ.

18:24 ἀρξαμένου δὲ αὐτοῦ συναίρειν προσηνέχθη αὐτῷ εἷς ὀφειλέτης μυρίων ταλάντων.

18:25 μὴ ἔχοντος δὲ αὐτοῦ ἀποδοῦναι ἐκέλευσεν αὐτὸν ὁ κύριος πραθῆναι καὶ τὴν γυναῖκα καὶ τὰ τέκνα καὶ πάντα ὅσα ἔχει, καὶ ἀποδοθῆναι.

18:26 πεσὼν οὖν ὁ δοῦλος προσεκύνει αὐτῷ λέγων· μακροθύμησον ἐπ' ἐμοί, καὶ πάντα ἀποδώσω σοι.

18:27 σπλαγχνισθεὶς δὲ ὁ κύριος τοῦ δούλου ἐκείνου ἀπέλυσεν αὐτὸν καὶ τὸ δάνειον ἀφῆκεν αὐτῷ.

18:28 ἐξελθὼν δὲ ὁ δοῦλος ἐκεῖνος εὗρεν ἕνα τῶν συνδούλων αὐτοῦ, ὃς ὤφειλεν αὐτῷ ἑκατὸν δηνάρια, καὶ κρατήσας αὐτὸν ἔπνιγεν λέγων· ἀπόδος εἴ τι ὀφείλεις.

18:29 πεσὼν οὖν ὁ σύνδουλος αὐτοῦ παρεκάλει αὐτὸν λέγων· μακροθύμησον ἐπ' ἐμοί, καὶ ἀποδώσω σοι.

18:30 ὁ δὲ οὐκ ἤθελεν ἀλλὰ ἀπελθὼν ἔβαλεν αὐτὸν εἰς φυλακὴν ἕως ἀποδῷ τὸ ὀφειλόμενον.

18:31 ἰδόντες οὖν οἱ σύνδουλοι αὐτοῦ τὰ γενόμενα ἐλυπήθησαν σφόδρα καὶ ἐλθόντες διεσάφησαν τῷ κυρίῳ ἑαυτῶν πάντα τὰ γενόμενα.

18:32 τότε προσκαλεσάμενος αὐτὸν ὁ κύριος αὐτοῦ λέγει αὐτῷ· δοῦλε πονηρέ, πᾶσαν τὴν ὀφειλὴν ἐκείνην ἀφῆκά σοι, ἐπεὶ παρεκάλεσάς με·

18:33 οὐκ ἔδει καὶ σὲ ἐλεῆσαι τὸν σύνδουλόν σου, ὡς κἀγὼ σὲ ἠλέησα;

18:23 Therefore the kingdom of heaven is likened to a king of men, who wished to take an account of his servants. [n. 1531]

18:24 And when he had begun to take the account, one was brought to him, who owed him ten thousand talents. [n. 1533]

18:25 And as he had nothing with which to pay it, his lord commanded that he should be sold, and his wife and children and all that he had, and the payment be made. [n. 1534]

18:26 But that servant, falling down, begged him, saying: have patience with me and I will pay you all. [n. 1535]

18:27 And the lord of that servant, being moved with pity, let him go and forgave him the debt. [n. 1536]

18:28 But when that servant had gone out, he found one of his fellow servants who owed him a hundred pence, and laying hold of him, he throttled him, saying: pay what you owe. [n. 1537]

18:29 And his fellow servant, falling down, begged him, saying: have patience with me, and I will pay you all. [n. 1537]

18:30 And he would not, but went and cast him into prison, till he paid the debt. [n. 1537]

18:31 Now his fellow servants, seeing what was done, were very grieved, and they came and told their lord all that was done. [n. 1538]

18:32 Then his lord called him, and said to him: you wicked servant, I forgave you all the debt, because you begged me, [n. 1540]

18:33 should you not then have had compassion also on your fellow servant, even as I had compassion on you? [n. 1540]

18:34 Et iratus dominus eius tradidit eum tortoribus, quoadusque redderet universum debitum. [n. 1541]	18:34 καὶ ὀργισθεὶς ὁ κύριος αὐτοῦ παρέδωκεν αὐτὸν τοῖς βασανισταῖς ἕως οὗ ἀποδῷ πᾶν τὸ ὀφειλόμενον.	18:34 And his lord, being angry, delivered him to the torturers until he paid all the debt. [n. 1541]
18:35 Sic et Pater meus caelestis faciet vobis, si non remiseritis unusquisque fratri suo de cordibus vestris. [n. 1542]	18:35 οὕτως καὶ ὁ πατήρ μου ὁ οὐράνιος ποιήσει ὑμῖν, ἐὰν μὴ ἀφῆτε ἕκαστος τῷ ἀδελφῷ αὐτοῦ ἀπὸ τῶν καρδιῶν ὑμῶν.	18:35 So also will my heavenly Father do to you, if every one of you does not forgive his brother from your hearts. [n. 1542]

1531. *Ideo assimilatum est*, et cetera. Hic ponitur similitudo, et tria facit.

Primo innuitur divina misericordia;

secundo tangitur ingratitudo, ibi *egressus autem servus ille* etc.,

tertio ingratitudinis poena, ibi *videntes autem conservi eius* et cetera.

Circa primum

primo ponitur examinatio debitorum;

secundo *magnitudo debiti*, ibi *et cum coepisset rationem ponere, oblatus est ei unus qui debebat ei decem millia talenta*;

tertio iustitia exigendi, ibi *cum autem non haberet unde redderet* etc.,

quarto debiti remissio, ibi *misertus autem dominus servi illius* et cetera.

1532. Dicit ergo: quia semper debetis esse parati ad remittendum, ideo debetis hanc similitudinem intelligere: *regnum caelorum* est lex regni: ipsum verbum Dei est iustitia et veritas; I ad Cor. I, 30: *qui factus est nobis sapientia, et iustitia, et sanctificatio, et redemptio*. Istud ergo assimilatum est homini Regi, quando *Verbum caro factum est*. Vel per regnum praesens Ecclesia designatur, ut supra XIII, 41: *colligent de regno eius omnia scandala*. Et bene dicitur *regnum*, si consideremus omnia quae sunt in regno.

In regno est rex, servi, et huiusmodi. *Homini regi*. Iste rex est Deus, sive intelligatur de Patre, sive de Filio, sive de Spiritu Sancto. *Qui voluit ponere rationem cum servis suis*. Per servos Domini intelliguntur praelati Ecclesiae, quibus commissa est cura animarum. Lc. XII, 42: *fidelis servus et prudens, quem constituit dominus super familiam suam*.

Quid est ergo *rationem ponere* de commissis, nisi quod obligant se ut rationem reddant? Ad Hebr. XIII, 17: *ipsi pervigilant quasi rationem pro animabus vestris reddituri*. Quia etiam unicuique anima sua commissa est, ideo quilibet potest dici servus; unde Iob I, 8: *numquid considerasti servum meum Iob? et cetera*. Unde positus est quilibet ut reddat rationem de omnibus: nam etiam de quolibet verbo otioso oportet reddere rationem, supra XII, 36.

1531. *Therefore the kingdom of heaven is likened to a king*. Here a likeness is set out; and he does three things:

first, the divine mercy is alluded to;

second, ingratitude is touched upon, at *but when that servant had gone out*;

third, the punishment of ingratitude, at *now his fellow servants, seeing what was done*.

Concerning the first,

first, the examination of debts is set out;

second, the magnitude of the debt, at *and when he had begun to take the account, one was brought to him, who owed him ten thousand talents*;

third, the justice of requiring payment, at *and as he had nothing with which to pay it*;

fourth, the forgiving of the debt, at *and the lord of that servant, being moved with pity*.

1532. He says then: since you should always be prepared to forgive, then you should understand this likeness: *the kingdom of heaven* is the law of the king; the very word of God is justice and truth. *Who of God has made unto us wisdom, and justice, and sanctification, and redemption* (1 Cor 1:30). Therefore, this is likened to a man who is King, when *the Word was made flesh* (John 1:14). Or, the kingdom indicates the present Church, as above, *and they will gather out of his kingdom all scandals* (Matt 13:41). And well is it named a *kingdom*, if we consider all the things which are in a kingdom.

In a kingdom there are the king, the servants, and so on. *A king of men*. This king is God, whether it be understood of the Father, or of the Son, or of the Holy Spirit. *Who wished to take an account of his servants*. By the Lord's servants are understood the prelates of the Church, to whom the care of souls is entrusted. *The faithful and wise steward, whom his lord sets over his family* (Luke 12:42).

So what is it to *take an account* of the things entrusted except that they bind themselves to give an account? *For they watch as being to render an account of your souls* (Heb 13:17). And since to each man his own soul is entrusted, then anyone can be called a servant; hence, *have you considered my servant Job?* (Job 1:8). Hence anyone is set down here, that he may give an account of everything; for one must even give an account for any idle word, above (Matt 12:36).

1533. *Et cum coepisset ponere rationem.* Finis huius rationis erit in die iudicii; principium, quando primo inducit aliquam tribulationem. I Petr. IV, 19: *itaque et hi qui patiuntur secundum voluntatem Dei, fideli Creatori commendent animas suas.* Ez. IX, v. 6: *a sanctuario meo incipite.* Item tangitur diligens examinatio meritorum. Thren. III, v. 40: *scrutemur vias nostras*, per quod intelligitur examinatio conscientiarum.

Et in ista examinatione *oblatus est ei servus, qui debebat decem millia talenta.* Si ad praelatos referimus haec talenta, peccata subditorum intelligimus: quia quoties peccat subditus per negligentiam suam, efficitur debitor talentorum. Unde dicitur III Reg. XX, v. 39: *erit anima tua pro anima sua.* Vel potest dici, quod mille est numerus perfectus, quia est cubicus. Item per decem intelligitur numerus decalogi. Item per talentum gravitas peccati. Zach. V, 7: *et ecce talentum plumbi portabatur* et cetera. Unde significatur homo habens multitudinem maximorum criminum; unde quando Deus vult ponere rationem, et examinare conscientiam suam, invenit massam criminum. I Paralip. ult.: *peccavi super arenam maris.*

Cum autem fit haec examinatio debiti, petuntur tria. Primo significatur causa examinationis, vel causa poenae; secundo describitur poena; tertio fructus poenae.

1534. Aliquis punitur quando ex seipso non habet unde satisfaciat, unde dicit *cum autem non haberet unde redderet*, cum totum quod habet, non sufficit. Unde Michaeae VI, 6: *quid dignum offeram Domino?* et cetera. Ideo *cum non haberet unde redderet, iussit eum dominus eius venumdari* etc., quia cum Dominus facit rationem cum homine, et non habet homo unde solvat, et considerat iustitiam Dei, quae est poena, iubet quod venumdetur. Quando venumdatur, pretium peccati est poena: pretium est quod aliquis accipit pro eo: et sic venumdatur, quando poena infligitur. Is. l, 1: *in iniquitatibus vestris venumdati estis.* *Et uxorem, et filios.* De uxore generat filios. Filii autem sunt opera, uxor concupiscentia, vel radix peccati. *Et omnia quae habebat*, quae sunt Dei dona. Osee II, 8: *dedi ei frumentum, et vinum, et oleum, et argentum multiplicavi ei, et aurum* et cetera. Punitur ergo pro uxore, et filiis, et donis sibi datis. Sap. XIV, 9: *similiter autem odio sunt Deo impius et impietas eius.* Ps. CVIII, v. 9: *fiant filii eius orphani, et uxor eius vidua.*

1535. *Procidens autem servus ille rogabat eum, dicens.* Hic ponitur misericordia domini. Et primo ponitur

1533. *And when he had begun to take the account.* The end of this account will be on the day of judgment; the beginning, when he first introduces a tribulation. *Wherefore let them also who suffer according to the will of God, commend their souls in good deeds to the faithful Creator* (1 Pet 4:19). *Utterly destroy old and young, maidens, children and women: but upon whomever you see Thau, kill him not, and begin at my sanctuary* (Ezek 9:6). Likewise, the diligent examination of merits is touched upon; *let us search our ways* (Lam 3:40), which means the examination of conscience.

And in this examination, *one was brought to him, who owed him ten thousand talents.* If we refer these talents to the prelates, we understand the sins of those who are under them: for as often as those under him sin through his negligence, he is made a debtor who owes talents. Hence it says, *your life shall be for his life* (1 Kgs 20:39). Or it can be said that one thousand is a perfect number, because it is cubic. Likewise, by ten is understood the number of the decalogue. And by a talent is understood a sin's gravity. *And behold a talent of lead was carried, and behold a woman sitting in the midst of the vessel. And he said: this is wickedness* (Zech 5:7–8). Hence it signifies a man who has a multitude of the greatest crimes; hence when God wishes to take an account, and to examine his conscience, he finds a great mass of crimes. *For the sins I have committed are more in number than the sand of the sea* (1 Chr 21:8).

And when this examination of debt takes place, three things are set down: first, the cause of the examination is indicated, or the cause of punishment; second, the punishment is described; third, the fruit of the punishment.

1534. Someone is punished when he does not have of himself what he needs to make satisfaction; hence it says, *and as he had nothing with which to pay it*, since the whole of what he has is not enough. Hence, *what shall I offer to the Lord that is worthy?* (Mic 6:6). *And as he had nothing with which to pay it, his lord commanded that he should be sold*, since when the Lord takes account with a man, and the man has nothing to pay with, and he considers God's justice and considers what the punishment is, he commands that he be sold. When he is sold, the reward of sin is punishment: a reward is what someone receives for something. And thus he is sold when punishment is inflicted. *Behold you are sold for your iniquities* (Isa 50:1). *And his wife and children.* He begets children from his wife. Now, the children are works, the wife concupiscence, or the root of sin. *And all that he had*, which are the gifts of God. *I gave her corn and wine, and oil, and multiplied her silver, and gold* (Hos 2:8). Therefore, he is punished for his wife, and children, and for the gifts given to him. *But to God the wicked and his wickedness are hateful alike* (Wis 14:9). *May his children be fatherless, and his wife a widow* (Ps 108:9).

1535. *But that servant, falling down, begged him, saying.* Here the lord's mercy is set out. And first, that which

provocativum misericordiae: quod enim multum provocat misericordiam, est oratio. Unde quando homo sentit se in periculo, debet recurrere ad orationem. Eccli. XXI, 1: *fili, peccasti non adiicias ultra, sed et de pristinis deprecare, ut tibi dimittantur.*

Commendatur autem huius humilitas; item commendatur discretio; item commendatur iustitia. Humilitas, quia **procidens**. Ps. ci, 18: *respexit dominus in orationem humilium.* Unde **rogabat eum**. Origenes scribit, *orabat eum.*

Item tangitur discretio eius, quia non petiit totum sibi dimitti debitum, sed tantum petiit tempus; unde dicit: **patientiam habe in me** idest, da mihi tempus, ut possim satisfacere. Sic petebat Iob X, 20: *dimitte me paululum, ut plangam dolorem meum.* Item tangitur iustitia: **et omnia reddam tibi**. Ps. l, 21: *tunc imponent super altare tuum vitulos.*

1536. Item ponitur miseratio domini relaxantis **misertus autem dominus servi illius, dimisit eum, et debitum dimisit ei**. Unde dolor poenitentis non causat remissionem, sed misericordia Domini; unde ad Rom. IX, v. 26: *non est currentis, sed miserentis Dei*. **Misertus autem dominus** et cetera. Notate, quod Dominus plura dat, quam homo audeat petere: ut in illa oratione dicitur: *qui merita supplicum excedis et vota.* Unde **dimisit eum**, idest absolvit, **et debitum**, peccati, **dimisit**. Potest enim esse tanta contritio quod totum dimittat.

1537. Sequitur ingratitudo **egressus, autem servus ille** etc., et ponuntur quinque quae aggravant ingratitudinem eius. Primo enim aggravatur ex tempore, quia si post novem vel decem annos accidisset, non esset mirum; sed quia eodem die deliquit, ingratus efficitur; sicut de peccatore, qui quando sunt dimissa eius peccata, in eodem die ad peccata regreditur. Unde dicitur **egressus**, Iac. I, 24: *consideravit enim se, et abiit, et statim oblitus est qualis fuerit.* Item ex simulatione, quoniam in consideratione domini humilis fuit, sed egressus statim ostendit qualis esset. III regum XXII, 22: *egrediar, et ero spiritus mendax in ore omnium prophetarum eius.* Item ostenditur ex cognatione, quoniam **invenit unum de conservis suis.** Eccli. XXVIII, 3: *homo homini servat iram, et a Deo petit medelam.* Item ex parvitate debiti, quia **debebat centum denarios**; unde in numero erat differentia, quia ipse decem millia: in pondere, quia ille denarios, et ipse talenta. Unde peccata quae in Deum committuntur, sunt et plura et gravia magis quam peccata quae in hominem, quae levia sunt, quia ex infirmitate; unde differens ibi est gravitas, sicut inter talenta et denarios. Gravius enim esset regem percutere, quam unum famulum. Item designatur crudelitas in exigendo, quia **tenebat eum**, quia

calls forth mercy is set out: for what calls forth mercy is prayer. Hence when a man sees himself in danger, he should run back to prayer. *My son, have you sinned? Do so no more: but for your former sins also pray that they may be forgiven you* (Sir 21:1).

And this man's humility is commended; likewise his discretion is commended; also, his justice is commended. Humility, **falling down**; *he has had regard to the prayer of the humble* (Ps 101:18). Hence, **begged him**. Origen writes, *prayed him.*

Likewise, his discretion is touched upon, because he did not beg that the whole debt be forgiven him, but only begged for time; hence he says, **have patience with me**, i.e., give me time, so I can make satisfaction. Job prayed in the same way, *suffer me, therefore, that I may lament my sorrow a little* (Job 10:20). Likewise, justice is touched upon: **and I will pay you all**. *Then will they lay calves upon your altar* (Ps 50:21).

1536. Likewise, the mercy of the lenient lord is set down: **and the lord of that servant, being moved with pity, let him go and forgave him the debt**. Hence the penitent's sorrow does not cause forgiveness, but rather the Lord's mercy; hence, *so then it is not of him who wills, nor of him who runs, but of God who shows mercy* (Rom 9:16). **And the lord . . . being moved with pity**. Notice that the Lord gives more than a man dares to ask; as it is said in the prayer, *you who far exceed the merits and wishes of those who plead.* Hence he **let him go**, i.e., absolved him, **and forgave him the debt**, i.e., sins. For there can be such great contrition that he forgives the whole.

1537. There follows the ingratitude: **but when that servant had gone out**, and five things are set down which make his ingratitude worse. For first, it is made worse by the time, for if this had happened after nine or ten years it would be no marvel; but since he offended on the same day, he is made ungrateful, as with a sinner who, when his sins are forgiven, returns to his sins on the same day. Hence it says, **gone out**; *for he beheld himself, and went his way, and presently forgot what manner of man he was* (Jas 1:24). Likewise by pretense, because he was humble in the lord's gaze, but when he went out he immediately showed what sort of man he was. *I will go forth, and be a lying spirit in the mouth of all his prophets* (1 Kgs 22:22). Likewise, it is shown by knowledge, because **he found one of his fellow servants**. *Man to man reserves anger, and does he seek remedy of God?* (Sir 28:3). Likewise, by the smallness of the debt: **that owed him a hundred pence**. Hence there was a difference in number, for he himself owed ten thousands; in weight, because that man owed pence, and this man talents. Hence the sins which are committed against God are both more numerous and heavier than the sins which are committed against man, which are light, since they arise from weakness. Hence there is a difference in heaviness, just as there is a difference in heaviness between talents and pence.

trahebat in causam, et vexabat eum et *suffocabat eum*, et respirare non dimittebat.

Item ex crudelitate, quia noluit remittere. Unde primo ponitur supplicatio debitoris; secundo crudelitas ipsius, ibi *ille autem noluit* et cetera. Notandum quod omnia, quae ille servus fecit domino, iste fecit ei; unde *procidens rogabat*. Supra dicitur *orabat*, hic *rogabat*, quia supra reddebat honorem, qui debetur Deo; hic autem tangit honorem, qui debetur homini: ideo dicit *rogabat*. Sed nihil valuit ei; unde dicitur *ille autem noluit*. Prov. XII, 10: *viscera impiorum crudelia*. *Et misit eum in carcerem*, idest in tribulationem, *donec redderet debitum*, idest ad hoc, ut redderet debitum. Prov. VI, 34: *ira et furor viri non parcent in die vindictae*.

1538. *Videntes autem conservi eius*. Hic tanguntur quatuor.

Primo ponitur reprobatio istius peccati;

secundo obiurgatio peccati ex parte Dei, ibi *tunc vocavit illum dominus suus*;

tertio poena, *et iratus dominus eius tradidit eum tortoribus*;

quarto applicatur similitudo, ibi *sic et Pater meus caelestis faciet vobis* et cetera.

1539. Dicit ergo *videntes autem conservi eius* et cetera. Videmus enim, quod si patiatur unum membrum, compatiuntur alia; unde videntes hominem affligi, compatiuntur ei naturaliter. Ps. CXVIII, 158: *vidi praevaricantes, et tabescebam*. Unde *contristati sunt*. *Gaudere cum gaudentibus flere cum flentibus*, ad Rom. XII, 15. *Et venerunt, et nuntiaverunt domino suo*, idest divinam iustitiam imploraverunt. *Desiderium pauperum exaudivit dominus, praeparationes cordis eorum audivit auris tua*, Ps. X, 17.

1540. Consequenter ponitur obiurgatio *tunc vocavit eum dominus suus* et cetera. Vocat Dominus per mortem. Iob XIX, 16: *vocabis me, et ego respondebo tibi*. *Et ait illi*. Primo exprobrat malitiam; secundo beneficium collatum; tertio commemorat quod debuit facere.

Dicit ergo *serve nequam*. Superius cum deberet ei, non dixit ei opprobrium; sed nunc cum facere debuit quod non fecit, dixit, *serve nequam*; quia quod homo peccet, hoc humanum est; sed si perseveret, hoc diabolicum est. *Omne debitum dimisi tibi*. Hic exprobrat beneficium illatum, quod supra non fecerat, *numquid non oportuit et te misereri conservi tui?* Quasi dicat: tu recepisti magna, et non vis impendere parva?

For it would be more grave to strike a king than a member of one's family. Likewise, cruelty in demanding is indicated: *and laying hold of him*, since he dragged him into a lawsuit, and troubled him and *throttled him*, and did not let him breathe.

Likewise, by cruelty, because he would not let up. Hence first, the debtor's pleading is set down; second, his cruelty, at *and he would not, but went and cast him into prison*. One should notice that everything this servant did for the lord, this man did for him; hence *falling down, begged him*. Above it says *prayed*, here *begged*, because above he rendered the honor which is owed to God, but here he touches upon the honor which is owed to man; for this reason, it says, *besought*. But it did him no good, hence it says, *and he would not*. *The bowels of the wicked are cruel* (Prov 12:10). *But went and cast him into prison*, i.e., into affliction, *till he paid the debt*, i.e., for this purpose, that he would pay the debt. *Because the jealousy and rage of the husband will not spare in the day of revenge* (Prov 6:34).

1538. *Now his fellow servants, seeing what was done*. Here four things are touched upon:

first, the denunciation of this man's sin is set down;

second, the reproach of the sin on God's part, at *then his lord called him*;

third, the punishment, *and his lord, being angry, delivered him to the torturers*;

fourth, the likeness is applied, at *so also will my heavenly Father do to you*.

1539. He says then, *now his fellow servants, seeing what was done*. For we see that if one member suffers, the others suffer with it; hence seeing the man afflicted, they naturally suffered with him. *I beheld the transgressors, and I pined away* (Ps 118:158). Hence they *were very grieved*. *Rejoice with those who rejoice; weep with those who weep* (Rom 12:15). *And they came and told their lord*, i.e., they appealed to the divine justice. *The Lord has heard the desire of the poor: your ear has heard the preparation of their heart* (Ps 9:38).

1540. Next, the reproach is set down: *then his lord called him*. The Lord calls through death. *You shall call me, and I will answer you* (Job 14:14–15). *And said to him*. First, he upbraids his malice; second, the benefits received; third, he calls to mind what he should have done.

He says then, *you wicked servant*. Above, when he owed him money, he did not speak insults to him. But now, since he should have done what he did not do, he said, *you wicked servant*; for that a man should sin is human, but if he perseveres, this is diabolical. *I forgave you all the debt*. Here he upbraids him for benefits received, which above he had not given. *Should you not then have had compassion also on your fellow servant?* as though to say, you have received great things, and do you not want to grant little things?

1541. *Et iratus dominus* et cetera. Et primo agit de poena, per quam fit separatio a Deo. Quando supra dominus iussit venumdari, non dixit quod esset iratus, quia monitiones non sunt ex divina iustitia, sed ex misericordia; sed obiurgatio est ex ira Dei. Prov. XIX, v. 12: *sicut fremitus leonis, ita et ira regis.* Secundo quia subiicitur daemonibus; unde **tradidit eum tortoribus**. Eccli. XXXIII, 14: *reddet illis secundum iudicium suum.* Item tangitur poenae perpetuitas, **quoadusque redderet universum debitum**; et hoc erit in infinitum. Si enim poena cessare non debet, donec fiat satisfacio debiti, et nullus sine gratia potest satisfacere, qui decedit sine caritate, non poterit satisfacere.

1542. *Sic et Pater meus caelestis faciet vobis.* Hic adaptat similitudinem. Pater est Deus, sicut supra VI, 9: **Pater noster, qui es in caelis. Faciet vobis**; idest non remittet peccata vestra, **nisi remiseritis unusquisque fratri suo de cordibus vestris**.

Hic videtur innuere, quod peccata dimissa redeant, sicut vult Origenes, quod dimissa redeunt in aliquibus, sicut in apostasia. Item si dolet poenituisse. Sed hoc non videtur, eo quod remissio efficaciam habet a sacramentis: ideo peccata et manifesta et occulta remittuntur; dicuntur autem redire per ingratitudinem.

1541. *And his lord, being angry.* And first, he treats of the punishment, by which separation from God comes about. Above, when the lord commanded that he be sold, he did not say that he was angry, because warnings are not from divine justice, but from mercy, while reproach is from God's anger. *As the roaring of a lion, so also is the anger of a king* (Prov 19:12). Second, because he is subjected to the demons; hence he **delivered him to the torturers**. *He will render to him according to his judgment* (Sir 33:14). Also, the everlastingness of the punishment is touched upon: **until he paid all the debt**, and this will be forever. For if the punishment should not cease until satisfaction is made for the debt, and no one can give satisfaction without grace, then the one who passes away without charity will not be able to give satisfaction.

1542. *So also will my heavenly Father do to you.* Here he applies the likeness. The Father is God, as above, **our Father who art in heaven** (Matt 6:9). **Will . . . do to you**, i.e., he shall not forgive your sins, **if every one of you does not forgive his brother from your hearts**.

Here he seems to imply that they pay for forgiven sins, just as Origen would have it that they pay for forgiven sins in some cases, as in the case of apostasy. Similarly, if a man is sorry that he repented. But this does not seem true, because the forgiveness has efficacy from the sacraments; for this reason, both manifest and hidden sins are forgiven. However, they are said to pay through ingratitude.

Chapter 19

Lecture 1

¹⁹:¹ Et factum est cum consummasset Iesus sermones istos, migravit a Galilaea, et venit in fines Iudaeae trans Iordanem, [n. 1544]

¹⁹:² et secutae sunt eum turbae multae, et curavit eos ibi. [n. 1546]

¹⁹:³ Et accesserunt ad eum Pharisaei tentantes eum, et dicentes: si licet homini dimittere uxorem suam quacumque ex causa? [n. 1547]

¹⁹:⁴ Qui respondens ait eis: non legistis, quia qui fecit ab initio, masculum et foeminam fecit eos? [n. 1548]

¹⁹:⁵ Et dixit: *propter hoc dimittet homo patrem et matrem, et adhaerebit uxori suae, et erunt duo in carne una.* [n. 1552]

¹⁹:⁶ Itaque iam non sunt duo, sed una caro. Quod ergo Deus coniunxit, homo non separet. [n. 1553]

¹⁹:⁷ Dicunt illi: quid ergo Moyses mandavit dari libellum repudii, et dimittere? [n. 1555]

¹⁹:⁸ Ait illis: quoniam Moyses ad duritiam cordis vestri permisit vobis dimittere uxores vestras: ab initio autem non fuit sic. [n. 1556]

¹⁹:⁹ Dico autem vobis, quia quicumque dimiserit uxorem suam, nisi ob fornicationem, et aliam duxerit, moechatur; et qui dimissam duxerit, moechatur. [n. 1558]

¹⁹:¹⁰ Dicunt ei discipuli eius: si ita est causa homini cum uxore, non expedit nubere. [n. 1562]

¹⁹:¹ Καὶ ἐγένετο ὅτε ἐτέλεσεν ὁ Ἰησοῦς τοὺς λόγους τούτους, μετῆρεν ἀπὸ τῆς Γαλιλαίας καὶ ἦλθεν εἰς τὰ ὅρια τῆς Ἰουδαίας πέραν τοῦ Ἰορδάνου.

¹⁹:² καὶ ἠκολούθησαν αὐτῷ ὄχλοι πολλοί, καὶ ἐθεράπευσεν αὐτοὺς ἐκεῖ.

¹⁹:³ Καὶ προσῆλθον αὐτῷ Φαρισαῖοι πειράζοντες αὐτὸν καὶ λέγοντες· εἰ ἔξεστιν ἀνθρώπῳ ἀπολῦσαι τὴν γυναῖκα αὐτοῦ κατὰ πᾶσαν αἰτίαν;

¹⁹:⁴ ὁ δὲ ἀποκριθεὶς εἶπεν· οὐκ ἀνέγνωτε ὅτι ὁ κτίσας ἀπ' ἀρχῆς ἄρσεν καὶ θῆλυ ἐποίησεν αὐτούς;

¹⁹:⁵ καὶ εἶπεν· ἕνεκα τούτου καταλείψει ἄνθρωπος τὸν πατέρα καὶ τὴν μητέρα καὶ κολληθήσεται τῇ γυναικὶ αὐτοῦ, καὶ ἔσονται οἱ δύο εἰς σάρκα μίαν.

¹⁹:⁶ ὥστε οὐκέτι εἰσὶν δύο ἀλλὰ σὰρξ μία. ὃ οὖν ὁ θεὸς συνέζευξεν ἄνθρωπος μὴ χωριζέτω.

¹⁹:⁷ λέγουσιν αὐτῷ· τί οὖν Μωϋσῆς ἐνετείλατο δοῦναι βιβλίον ἀποστασίου καὶ ἀπολῦσαι [αὐτήν];

¹⁹:⁸ λέγει αὐτοῖς ὅτι Μωϋσῆς πρὸς τὴν σκληροκαρδίαν ὑμῶν ἐπέτρεψεν ὑμῖν ἀπολῦσαι τὰς γυναῖκας ὑμῶν, ἀπ' ἀρχῆς δὲ οὐ γέγονεν οὕτως.

¹⁹:⁹ λέγω δὲ ὑμῖν ὅτι ὃς ἂν ἀπολύσῃ τὴν γυναῖκα αὐτοῦ μὴ ἐπὶ πορνείᾳ καὶ γαμήσῃ ἄλλην μοιχᾶται [καὶ ὁ ἀπολελυμένην γαμήσας μοιχᾶται].

¹⁹:¹⁰ Λέγουσιν αὐτῷ οἱ μαθηταὶ [αὐτοῦ]· εἰ οὕτως ἐστὶν ἡ αἰτία τοῦ ἀνθρώπου μετὰ τῆς γυναικός, οὐ συμφέρει γαμῆσαι.

¹⁹:¹ And it came to pass when Jesus had finished these words, that he departed from Galilee, and came into the coasts of Judea, beyond Jordan. [n. 1544]

¹⁹:² And great multitudes followed him, and he healed them there. [n. 1546]

¹⁹:³ And there came to him the Pharisees tempting him, and saying: is it lawful for a man to put away his wife for every cause? [n. 1547]

¹⁹:⁴ Answering, he said to them: have you not read, that he who made man from the beginning, made them male and female? [n. 1548]

¹⁹:⁵ And said: *for this cause will a man leave father and mother, and will cleave to his wife, and they two will be in one flesh.* [n. 1552]

¹⁹:⁶ Therefore, now they are not two, but one flesh. What therefore God has joined together, let no man put asunder. [n. 1553]

¹⁹:⁷ They say to him: why then did Moses command to give a bill of divorce, and to put away? [n. 1555]

¹⁹:⁸ He said to them: because Moses by reason of the hardness of your heart permitted you to put away your wives, but from the beginning it was not so. [n. 1556]

¹⁹:⁹ And I say to you, that whoever puts away his wife, unless it be for fornication, and marries another, commits adultery; and he who marries her who is put away, commits adultery. [n. 1558]

¹⁹:¹⁰ His disciples say to him: if the case of a man with his wife is so, it is not expedient to marry. [n. 1562]

^{19:11} Qui dixit illis: non omnes capiunt verbum istud, sed quibus datum est. [n. 1564]

^{19:12} Sunt enim eunuchi, qui de matris utero sic nati sunt: et sunt eunuchi, qui facti sunt ab hominibus: et sunt eunuchi, qui seipsos castraverunt propter regnum caelorum. Qui potest capere, capiat. [n. 1566]

^{19:13} Tunc oblati sunt ei parvuli, ut manus eis imponeret, et oraret; discipuli autem increpabant eos. [n. 1573]

^{19:14} Iesus vero ait eis: sinite parvulos, et nolite eos prohibere ad me venire; talium est enim regnum caelorum. [n. 1577]

^{19:15} Et cum imposuisset eis manus, abiit inde. [n. 1578]

^{19:16} Et ecce unus accedens ait illi: Magister bone, quid boni faciam, ut habeam vitam aeternam? [n. 1579]

^{19:17} Qui dixit ei: quid me interrogas de bono? Unus est bonus, Deus. Si autem vis ad vitam ingredi, serva mandata. [n. 1581]

^{19:18} Dicit illi: quae? Iesus autem dixit: *non homicidium facies, non adulterabis, non facies furtum, non falsum testimonium dices*, [n. 1584]

^{19:19} *honora patrem et matrem et diliges proximum tuum sicut teipsum.* [n. 1584]

^{19:20} Dicit illi adolescens: omnia haec custodivi a iuventute mea, quid adhuc mihi deest? [n. 1586]

^{19:21} Ait illi Iesus: si vis perfectus esse, vade, vende omnia quae habes, et da pauperibus, et habebis thesaurum in caelo, et veni, sequere me. [n. 1589]

^{19:22} Cum audisset autem adolescens verbum, abiit tristis: erat enim habens multas possessiones. [n. 1599]

^{19:11} ὁ δὲ εἶπεν αὐτοῖς· οὐ πάντες χωροῦσιν τὸν λόγον [τοῦτον] ἀλλ' οἷς δέδοται.

^{19:12} εἰσὶν γὰρ εὐνοῦχοι οἵτινες ἐκ κοιλίας μητρὸς ἐγεννήθησαν οὕτως, καὶ εἰσὶν εὐνοῦχοι οἵτινες εὐνουχίσθησαν ὑπὸ τῶν ἀνθρώπων, καὶ εἰσὶν εὐνοῦχοι οἵτινες εὐνούχισαν ἑαυτοὺς διὰ τὴν βασιλείαν τῶν οὐρανῶν. ὁ δυνάμενος χωρεῖν χωρείτω.

^{19:13} Τότε προσηνέχθησαν αὐτῷ παιδία ἵνα τὰς χεῖρας ἐπιθῇ αὐτοῖς καὶ προσεύξηται· οἱ δὲ μαθηταὶ ἐπετίμησαν αὐτοῖς.

^{19:14} ὁ δὲ Ἰησοῦς εἶπεν· ἄφετε τὰ παιδία καὶ μὴ κωλύετε αὐτὰ ἐλθεῖν πρός με, τῶν γὰρ τοιούτων ἐστὶν ἡ βασιλεία τῶν οὐρανῶν.

^{19:15} καὶ ἐπιθεὶς τὰς χεῖρας αὐτοῖς ἐπορεύθη ἐκεῖθεν.

^{19:16} Καὶ ἰδοὺ εἷς προσελθὼν αὐτῷ εἶπεν· διδάσκαλε, τί ἀγαθὸν ποιήσω ἵνα σχῶ ζωὴν αἰώνιον;

^{19:17} ὁ δὲ εἶπεν αὐτῷ· τί με ἐρωτᾷς περὶ τοῦ ἀγαθοῦ; εἷς ἐστιν ὁ ἀγαθός· εἰ δὲ θέλεις εἰς τὴν ζωὴν εἰσελθεῖν, τήρησον τὰς ἐντολάς.

^{19:18} λέγει αὐτῷ· ποίας; ὁ δὲ Ἰησοῦς εἶπεν· τὸ οὐ φονεύσεις, οὐ μοιχεύσεις, οὐ κλέψεις, οὐ ψευδομαρτυρήσεις,

^{19:19} τίμα τὸν πατέρα καὶ τὴν μητέρα, καὶ ἀγαπήσεις τὸν πλησίον σου ὡς σεαυτόν.

^{19:20} λέγει αὐτῷ ὁ νεανίσκος· πάντα ταῦτα ἐφύλαξα· τί ἔτι ὑστερῶ;

^{19:21} ἔφη αὐτῷ ὁ Ἰησοῦς· εἰ θέλεις τέλειος εἶναι, ὕπαγε πώλησόν σου τὰ ὑπάρχοντα καὶ δὸς [τοῖς] πτωχοῖς, καὶ ἕξεις θησαυρὸν ἐν οὐρανοῖς, καὶ δεῦρο ἀκολούθει μοι.

^{19:22} ἀκούσας δὲ ὁ νεανίσκος τὸν λόγον ἀπῆλθεν λυπούμενος· ἦν γὰρ ἔχων κτήματα πολλά.

^{19:11} He said to them: all men do not take this word, but they to whom it is given. [n. 1564]

^{19:12} For there are eunuchs, who were born so from their mother's womb, and there are eunuchs, who were made so by men, and there are eunuchs, who have made themselves eunuchs for the kingdom of heaven. He who can take, let him take it. [n. 1566]

^{19:13} Then little children were presented to him, that he should impose hands upon them and pray. And the disciples rebuked them. [n. 1573]

^{19:14} But Jesus said to them: allow the little children, and do not forbid them to come to me, for the kingdom of heaven is for such. [n. 1577]

^{19:15} And when he had imposed hands upon them, he departed from there. [n. 1578]

^{19:16} And behold one came and said to him: good Master, what good should I do that I may have life everlasting? [n. 1579]

^{19:17} He said to him: why do you ask me concerning good? One is good, God. But if you wish to enter into life, keep the commandments. [n. 1581]

^{19:18} He said to him: which? And Jesus said: *do not murder, do not commit adultery, do not steal, do not bear false witness*. [n. 1584]

^{19:19} *Honor your father and your mother and, love your neighbor as yourself.* [n. 1584]

^{19:20} The young man said to him: all these I have kept from my youth, what is still wanting to me? [n. 1586]

^{19:21} Jesus said to him: if you will be perfect, go sell what you have, and give to the poor, and you will have treasure in heaven, and come follow me. [n. 1589]

^{19:22} And when the young man had heard this word, he went away sad, for he had great possessions. [n. 1599]

19:23 Iesus autem dixit discipulis suis: amen dico vobis, quia dives difficile intrabit in regnum caelorum. [n. 1600]

19:24 Et iterum dico vobis: facilius est camelum per foramen acus transire, quam divitem intrare in regnum caelorum. [n. 1602]

19:25 Auditis autem his, discipuli mirabantur valde, dicentes: quis ergo poterit salvus esse? [n. 1603]

19:26 Aspiciens autem Iesus dixit illis: apud homines hoc impossibile est; apud Deum autem omnia possibilia sunt. [n. 1605]

19:27 Tunc respondens Petrus dixit ei: ecce nos reliquimus omnia, et secuti sumus te, quid ergo erit nobis? [n. 1607]

19:28 Iesus autem dixit illis: amen dico vobis, quod vos qui secuti estis me, in regeneratione, cum sederit Filius hominis in sede maiestatis suae, sedebitis et vos super sedes duodecim, iudicantes duodecim tribus Israel. [n. 1609]

19:29 Et omnis qui reliquit domum, vel fratres, aut sorores, aut patrem, aut matrem, aut uxorem, aut filios, aut agros propter nomen meum, centuplum accipiet, vitam aeternam possidebit. [n. 1616]

19:30 Multi autem erunt primi novissimi, et novissimi primi [n. 1619]

19:23 Ὁ δὲ Ἰησοῦς εἶπεν τοῖς μαθηταῖς αὐτοῦ· ἀμὴν λέγω ὑμῖν ὅτι πλούσιος δυσκόλως εἰσελεύσεται εἰς τὴν βασιλείαν τῶν οὐρανῶν.

19:24 πάλιν δὲ λέγω ὑμῖν, εὐκοπώτερόν ἐστιν κάμηλον διὰ τρυπήματος ῥαφίδος διελθεῖν ἢ πλούσιον εἰσελθεῖν εἰς τὴν βασιλείαν τοῦ θεοῦ.

19:25 ἀκούσαντες δὲ οἱ μαθηταὶ ἐξεπλήσσοντο σφόδρα λέγοντες· τίς ἄρα δύναται σωθῆναι;

19:26 ἐμβλέψας δὲ ὁ Ἰησοῦς εἶπεν αὐτοῖς· παρὰ ἀνθρώποις τοῦτο ἀδύνατόν ἐστιν, παρὰ δὲ θεῷ πάντα δυνατά.

19:27 Τότε ἀποκριθεὶς ὁ Πέτρος εἶπεν αὐτῷ· ἰδοὺ ἡμεῖς ἀφήκαμεν πάντα καὶ ἠκολουθήσαμέν σοι· τί ἄρα ἔσται ἡμῖν;

19:28 ὁ δὲ Ἰησοῦς εἶπεν αὐτοῖς· ἀμὴν λέγω ὑμῖν ὅτι ὑμεῖς οἱ ἀκολουθήσαντές μοι ἐν τῇ παλιγγενεσίᾳ, ὅταν καθίσῃ ὁ υἱὸς τοῦ ἀνθρώπου ἐπὶ θρόνου δόξης αὐτοῦ, καθήσεσθε καὶ ὑμεῖς ἐπὶ δώδεκα θρόνους κρίνοντες τὰς δώδεκα φυλὰς τοῦ Ἰσραήλ.

19:29 καὶ πᾶς ὅστις ἀφῆκεν οἰκίας ἢ ἀδελφοὺς ἢ ἀδελφὰς ἢ πατέρα ἢ μητέρα ἢ τέκνα ἢ ἀγροὺς ἕνεκεν τοῦ ὀνόματός μου, ἑκατονταπλασίονα λήμψεται καὶ ζωὴν αἰώνιον κληρονομήσει.

19:30 πολλοὶ δὲ ἔσονται πρῶτοι ἔσχατοι καὶ ἔσχατοι πρῶτοι.

19:23 Then Jesus said to his disciples: amen, I say to you, that a rich man will hardly enter into the kingdom of heaven. [n. 1600]

19:24 And again I say to you: it is easier for a camel to pass through the eye of a needle, than for a rich man to enter into the kingdom of heaven. [n. 1602]

19:25 And when they had heard this, the disciples wondered very much, saying: who then can be saved? [n. 1603]

19:26 And Jesus looking, said to them: with men this is impossible, but with God all things are possible. [n. 1605]

19:27 Then Peter answering, said to him: behold we have left all things, and have followed you; what therefore will we have? [n. 1607]

19:28 And Jesus said to them: amen, I say to you, that you, who have followed me, in the regeneration, when the Son of man will sit on the seat of his majesty, you also will sit on twelve seats judging the twelve tribes of Israel. [n. 1609]

19:29 And every one who has left house, or brethren, or sisters, or father, or mother, or wife, or children, or lands for my name's sake, will receive a hundredfold, and will possess life everlasting. [n. 1616]

19:30 And many who are first, will be last, and the last will be first. [n. 1619]

1543. Supra ostensum est quomodo veniendum est ad vitam aeternam per communem viam; hic docet quomodo veniendum est per viam perfectionis, quae tangitur quantum ad duo: quantum ad continentiam, et quantum ad paupertatem voluntariam.

    Circa primum duo facit.
    Primo agit de adventu;
    secundo de continentia, ibi **dicunt ei discipuli eius** et cetera.

    Circa primum tria facit.
    Primo ponitur tentatio Pharisaeorum;
    secundo solutio Christi;
    tertio obiectio contra solutionem.

1543. Above, it was shown how one comes to eternal life by the common way; here he teaches how one comes by the way of perfection, which is touched upon with regard to two things: with regard to abstinence, and with regard to voluntary poverty.

    Concerning the first, he does two things:
    first, he treats of the coming;
    second, of abstinence, at **his disciples say to him**.

    Concerning the first, he does three things.
    First, the Pharisees' temptation is set out;
    second, Christ's solution;
    third, an objection against the solution.

Secunda *qui respondens ait eis*; tertia *quid ergo Moyses mandavit dari libellum repudii?*

Circa primum tria:
primo describitur locus;
secundo occasio ad tentandum;
tertio tentatio.

1544. Dicit ergo *et factum est*, quia dictum eius est factum. *Ipse enim dixit, et facta sunt: ipse mandavit, et creata sunt*, Ps. XXXII, 9. ***Cum consummasset sermones istos***, scilicet de vitando scandalum, ***migravit a Galilaea in fines Iudaeae trans Iordanem***. Iudaea aliquando sumitur pro tota terra, quam habitant Iudaei: aliquando pro terra, quae in dotem tribus Iudae cessit, et sic dividitur contra alias, et sic hic accipitur. Oportebat enim transire per Iudaeam, qui volebat ire in Ierusalem, quae erat in tribu Beniamin in finibus Iudaeae.

1545. Sed quare migravit a Galilaea? Propter tria. Ut daret praedicatoribus exemplum, quod non est solum in uno loco praedicandum, sed in multis; unde Lc. IV, 43: *quia aliis civitatibus oportet me evangelizare regnum Dei*. Item quia iam imminebat tempus passionis, ideo accedere volebat ad locum ubi pati debebat. Ad Eph. V, 2: *tradidit semetipsum pro nobis oblationem et hostiam Deo in odorem suavitatis* et cetera. Vel voluit redire ad Iudaeos, ut significaret quod in fine convertetur ad convertendum Iudaeos.

1546. ***Et secutae sunt eum turbae***. Signum est devotionis turbarum, quia secutae sunt eum, sicut filii patrem peregrinantem. Io. X, 27: *oves meae vocem meam audiunt* ***et curavit eos***. Osee I, 2: *percutiet et sanabit nos*. Aliquando Dominus curabat, aliquando signa faciebat. Signa ut confortaret, in Act. c. I, 1: *coepit Iesus facere et docere*.

Posset aliquis credere, quia transivit ad Iudaeos, quod dereliquerit gentes; ideo ad designandum, quod non dereliquit, dicit ***secutae sunt eum turbae***, idest ad salutem, *quia cum essent oleaster, inserti sunt et facti sunt olivae*, ad Rom. XI, 17. Vel quod sunt secutae trans Iordanem, significatur quod per baptismum peccata remittuntur.

1547. ***Et accesserunt ad eum Pharisaei tentantes***. Et in hoc reprehenduntur: quia cum turbae sequerentur, Pharisaei insidiabantur. Ier. V, 5: *ibo ad optimates, et loquar eis*.

Unde accesserunt dicentes ***si licet homini dimittere uxorem suam quacumque ex causa?*** Apparet in istis primo malitiosa astutia, quia venerunt ad Christum, ut Christo calumniam inferrent; quia aut diceret quod esset dimittenda, aut non. Si diceret quod sic, videretur

The second is at **answering, he said to them**; the third, **why then did Moses command to give a bill of divorce?**

Concerning the first, three things:
first, the place is described;
second, the occasion for tempting;
third, the temptation.

1544. He says then, **and it came to pass**, because his words are done. *For he spoke and they were made: he commanded and they were created* (Ps 32:9). **And it came to pass when Jesus had finished these words**, namely about avoiding scandal, **that he departed from Galilee, and came into the coasts of Judea, beyond Jordan**. Judea sometimes means the whole land which the Jews occupy, and sometimes the land which fell to the lot of the tribes of Judah, and in this way it is divided against the others, and this is what it means here. For he who wished to go to Jerusalem, which was in the tribe of Benjamin, in the borders of Judea, had to pass through Judea.

1545. But why did he depart from Galilee? For three reasons. To give an example to preachers that one should not preach only in one place, but in many; hence, *to other cities also I must preach the kingdom of God* (Luke 4:43). Also, because the time of the passion was already drawing near, and so he wished to approach the place where he ought to suffer. *And has delivered himself for us, an oblation and a sacrifice to God for an odour of sweetness* (Eph 5:2). Or he wished to return to the Jews, to signify that in the end he will turn to converting the Jews.

1546. And great multitudes followed him. It is a sign of the crowds' devotion that they followed him, like children following a wandering father. *My sheep hear my voice* (John 10:27). **And he healed them**. *He will strike, and he will cure us* (Hos 6:2). Sometimes the Lord healed, sometimes he worked signs. He worked signs to strengthen; *Jesus began to do and to teach* (Acts 1:1).

Someone could think that, since he crossed over to the Jews, he abandoned the gentiles. So to indicate that he did not abandon the gentiles, it says, **great multitudes followed him**, i.e., to salvation, *because when they were a wild-olive tree, they were ingrafted, and were made olives* (Rom 11:17). Or that they followed him across the Jordan signifies that sins are forgiven through baptism.

1547. And there came to him the Pharisees tempting him. And in this they are reproached, because while the crowds followed, the Pharisees plotted. *I will go therefore to the great men, and I will speak to them: for they have known the way of the Lord, the judgment of their God: and behold these have together broken the yoke more* (Jer 5:5).

Hence they approached, saying, **is it lawful for a man to put away his wife for every cause?** There appears in these words first malicious cunning, because they came to Christ to bring slander on Christ: for either he would say that she is to be sent away, or not. If he said that she was, he would

sibi contrarius, quia ipse erat praedicator castitatis. Si diceret quod non, accusabimus eum, quia hoc est contra Moysen legislatorem. Sicut dicit Chrysostomus, arguuntur, de incontinentia, quia si aliquis libenter audiat loqui de separatione uxori incontinens est. Unde quia isti de divortio loquebantur, ostendebant se incontinentes. Dominus dederat causam propter quam dimitteretur, scilicet propter turpitudinem; sed isti non solum ex hac causa petebant, sed utrum ex quacumque causa. Unde volebant habere potestatem liberam dimittendi uxorem.

1548. Ideo sequitur responsio *qui respondens ait eis*. Dominus dat optimum modum respondendi: quia quando quaerit aliquis ut addiscat, statim dicenda est veritas; sed ei qui quaerit ut calumnietur, non statim dicenda est veritas, sed primo dicenda sunt aliqua quae negari non possunt. Ideo primo Dominus interrogat de lege; unde

primo assumit verba Scripturae;

secundo dicit, quomodo ad propositum facit;

tertio principale propositum concludit.

Et circa primum tria facit.

Primo ostendit societatem maris et foeminae, quam Deus instituit;

secundo affectum quem indidit;

tertio modum quo coniunxit.

1549. Intendit probare quod coniunctio maris et foeminae est a Deo instituta. *Non legistis quod qui fecit hominem, ab initio masculum et foeminam fecit eos?* Hoc enim legitur Gen. I, 27: *et creavit Deus hominem ad imaginem et similitudinem suam*. Non est hoc intelligendum, ut aliqui intellexerunt quod primo fecerit hominem masculum, et post foeminam, et post separavit eos; sed primo fecit unum hominem, et in illo fecit unde fieret mulier.

1550. Sed quare voluit Dominus sic fieri, scilicet ex viro et muliere multitudinem hominum? Respondeo, ut significatur quod forma matrimonii ex Deo esset. Item ut magis se diligerent.

Sed tunc quaerit Chrysostomus, quare non semper sic facit, ut simul nascatur vir et mulier. Respondet, quia si ita esset, videretur necessitas utendi matrimonio. Et quia Dominus vult esse licitum uti matrimonio, vel non uti, et non esse necessarium, primo creavit masculum et foeminam, ad significandum quod licitum erat matrimonium; post, vero ut sine muliere nasceretur masculus, et e converso, ut liberam habeant facultatem et utendi matrimonio, et non utendi.

1551. Secundum hoc excluditur duplex error. Quidam enim dicebant matrimonium non esse a Deo: et

seem contrary to himself, because he himself was a preacher of chastity. If he said that she was not, we will accuse him, because this is against Moses the lawgiver. As Chrysostom says, they are convicted of lack of restraint, because if someone freely hears talk about separation from a wife, he is lacking in restraint. Hence since these men were speaking of divorce, they showed themselves to be incontinent. The Lord had given the cause for which she should be sent away, namely for baseness; but these men were asking not only if she could be sent away for this cause, but whether she could be sent away for any cause whatever. Hence they wished to have the free power of sending away a wife.

1548. So there follows the response: *answering, he said to them*. The Lord gives the very best manner of responding. For when someone asks in order to learn, the truth should be spoken right away; but the truth should not be spoken right away to him who asks in order to slander, but first, something which they cannot deny should be said. So first, the Lord asks about the law; hence

first, he takes up the words of Scripture;

second, he says how this relates the matter at hand;

third, he concludes the principal thing intended.

And concerning the first, he does three things:

first, he points out the society of male and female, which God established;

second, the affection imparted;

third, the manner in which he conjoined them.

1549. He intends to prove that the union of male and female is established by God. *Have you not read, that he who made man from the beginning, made them male and female?* For this is written: *and God created man to his own image* (Gen 1:27). This should not be understood, as some have understood it, that first he made man male, and afterwards female, and later separated them; but first he made one man, and in that one he made that from which the woman would come.

1550. But why did the Lord will it to happen this way, namely that a multitude of men should arise from a man and a woman? I respond, to signify that the form of matrimony was from God. Likewise, that they might love one another more.

But then Chrysostom asks why he does not always do it this way, that a man and a woman might be born at the same time. He responds that if it were so, it would seem necessary to enter matrimony. And since the Lord willed it to be lawful to enter matrimony or not to enter, and that it not be necessary, first he created male and female, to signify that matrimony was lawful, but afterward he willed that a male be born without a woman, and vice versa, that they might have the free opportunity both of entering matrimony and of not entering.

1551. In accord with this, two errors are excluded. For some said that matrimony is not from God. And he

excludes this, for if he made them male and female, and it is agreed that he made nothing in vain, then neither did he make something of these in vain, and they could be for nothing other than the society of matrimony. Others said that if man had not sinned, God would not have made the female, but rather men would have been multiplied in another way; but this amounts to nothing, because they were created before the sin. And he says male and female in the singular, that one might have one.

1552. *'For this cause will a man leave father and mother.'* Here the affection which he imparted is set out. **And he said.** Who said? The one who made them. But this does not seem true, because it seems that Adam said it.

Augustine says that the Lord sent a deep sleep into Adam, and took one of his ribs. This deep sleep was ecstasy; hence he revealed there many good things. Hence the Lord also revealed to him what is said here. Hence above, it was said, *for it is not you who speak, but the Spirit of your Father who speaks in you* (Matt 10:20). Since therefore Adam spoke, with God ruling over him, then it is said that God spoke: hence, *a man leaves his father who raised him* (Ezra 2:4).

1553. *'And will cleave to his wife.'*

What is the reason? Brother and sister are born from one parent, and they separate themselves; but husband and wife are born from different parents, and yet do not separate themselves.

Chrysostom says that this is by divine ordination. Also, every cause naturally has a tendency toward its effect, as the sap from the root toward the branches; hence fathers love children more than the other way around. For this reason, man and wife, although they are from different parents, are yet united in one effect.

'And they two will be in one flesh.' Jerome: *namely in the flesh of the offspring*. And this is the fruit of matrimony. Chrysostom explains: *'in one flesh'*, i.e., in one carnal affection, just as unity comes about in spiritual affection, as in Acts, *and the multitude of believers had but one heart and one soul* (Acts 4:32). Or *'they two will be in one flesh'*, i.e., in one carnal work. The Philosopher says that a man and a woman are always related in this work in such a way that, just as the active power and the passive are always conjoined in the effect, so action and passion are conjoined in this action. **Therefore, now they are not two, but one flesh.**

1554. Then he concludes the thing principally intended: **what therefore God has joined together, let no man put asunder**, because it was done by the will of God. If it is from God, a man cannot separate them, because if God conjoined, only God may separate. For the separation can come from God or from man: and this either for the sake of pleasure, or that one may have some other, and this is no use. Or it can come about by mutual consent, that one may serve God more freely, and in this way it is from God.

1555. *Dicunt illi: quid ergo Moyses mandavit dari libellum repudii et dimittere?* Hic ponitur obiectio eorum contra generalem legem: aperiunt enim quod erat in mente. *Quid ergo Moyses mandavit dari libellum repudii et dimittere?* Non mandavit Moyses dimittere, sed indirecte prohibere voluit, quia Moyses voluit quod non dimitteretur, nisi daretur libellus repudii. Et hoc magis pertinebat ad prohibitionem, quia libellus non fiebat nisi per manum communem; unde remittebat ad sapientes, ut viderent si haberent causam, quare deberent dimittere eas.

1556. *Et ait illis.* Hic obiectioni respondet. Et primo ponit responsionem; secundo confirmationem quia Dominus probat non esse dimittendam ex auctoritate Dei quae maior est; ideo contra Dei auctoritatem non est auctoritas Moysi.

Sed contra. Nonne Dominus dedit legem per Moysen?

Videte, sicut dicit Apostolus I ad Cor. VII, 25: *de virginibus praeceptum Domini non habeo, consilium autem do.* Unde aliquando dicebat quod a Domino acceperat, aliquando ex industria sibi inspirata: sic et Moyses. Istud autem permisit, non quod audisset a Domino, sed ab inspiratione divina, non tamen auctoritate firmata.

1557. *Ad duritiam cordis vestri permisit vobis dimittere uxores vestras.* Ipsi dixerant quod Moyses mandavit; sed non mandavit, sed permisit. De duritia eorum habetur Act. VII, 51: *dura cervice, et incircumcisis cordibus et auribus, vos semper Spiritui Sancto restitistis.*

Hic solet esse quaestio, utrum illi peccent mortaliter, qui uxores dimittunt.

Quidam dixerunt quod dimittentes peccabant mortaliter. Permissio enim quatuor modis accipitur. Dicitur permitti aliquid, quando contrarium non praecipitur, ut minus bonum permittitur, quia maius bonum non praecipitur, ut Apostolus dicit I Cor. VII, 6: *secundum indulgentiam dico vobis.* Item quandoque per privationem prohibitionis; et sic peccata venialia sunt permissa. Quandoque autem per privationem impedimenti: et sic omnia mala, quae fiunt in praesenti, dicuntur aliquando etiam 'permissa,' quia poena non adhibetur. Ideo Iudaeis quaedam permissa fuerunt, quae erant mortalia peccata, quia poena non fuit eis inflicta.

Sed istud habet locum in mundanis rebus: sic enim videmus, quod secundum leges humanas non punitur fornicatio simplex; unde si lex vetus solum inspiciat ad vitam praesentem, sic solutio est bona. Sed quia quamvis secundum corticem ad vitam pertineat praesentem, tamen secundum medullam pertinet etiam ad vitam aeternam Ex. XV, 25: *dedi eis praecepta mea*; et Dominus

1555. *They say to him: why then did Moses command to give a bill of divorce, and to put away?* Here is set out their objection against the general law; for they disclose what was in their mind. *Why then did Moses command to give a bill of divorce, and to put away?* Moses did not command them to put away their wives, but rather he wished to restrain it, for Moses wished that she not be sent away unless she be given a bill of divorce. And this pertained more to restraint, because a bill was only given by the common hand; hence he left it to the wise men to see if they had a reason why they should send her away.

1556. *He said to them.* Here he responds to the objection. And first, he sets out the response; second, a confirmation, for the Lord proves that she is not to be sent away from the authority of God, which is greater; therefore the authority of Moses is not against the authority of God.

But against this: did not the Lord give the law through Moses?

See, as the Apostle says, *now concerning virgins, I have no commandment of the Lord; but I give counsel* (1 Cor 7:25). Hence sometimes he spoke what he had received from the Lord, and sometimes, out of diligence, what was inspired in him: so also Moses. And he permitted this, not because he had heard from the Lord, but by divine inspiration, yet not with firm authority.

1557. *Because Moses by reason of the hardness of your heart permitted you to put away your wives.* These men had said that Moses commanded it; but he did not command it, but rather permitted it. About their hardness it says, *you stiffnecked and uncircumcised in heart and ears, you always resist the Holy Spirit* (Acts 7:51).

Here there is usually a question, whether those who send away their wives sin mortally.

Some have said that those who sent them away sinned mortally. Something is said to be permitted when the contrary is not commanded, as a lesser good is permitted because the greater good is not commanded, as the Apostle says, *but I speak this by indulgence, not by commandment* (1 Cor 7:6). Sometimes also through lack of a prohibition; and in this way, venial sins are permitted. But sometimes through lack of an impediment, and in this way all the evil things which happen in the present are also sometimes called 'permitted,' because no punishment is applied. Therefore, certain things had been permitted to the Jews which were mortal sins, because no punishment was inflicted on them.

But this holds true only in earthly affairs. For in this way we see that simple fornication is not punished according to human laws; hence if the old law looked only to the present life, then the solution is good. But since, although according to its outer shell it pertains to the present life, yet according to its inner kernel it pertains also to eternal life: *and I gave them my statutes* (Ezek 20:11); and the Lord says the same

dicit iuveni, infra eodem: *si vis ad vitam ingredi, serva mandata* ideo dicunt alii quod male provisum esset populo illi, si quod esset peccatum ignoraret, cum tamen scriptum sit, Is. LVIII, 1: *nuntia populo peccata eorum*. Ideo dicit Chrysostomus, quod a peccato abstulit peccati culpam. Et licet inordinatum quid esset, noluit tamen quod eis imputaretur ad culpam, ut Dominus Osee praecepit, ut faceret filios fornicationis: unde permissio non fuit ex praecepto, sed ad vitandum maius malum.

Ab initio autem non fuit sic. Unde actuale fuit, non ab initio institutum: unde post multos annos nullus dimisit uxorem.

1558. *Dico autem vobis* et cetera. Hic inducit legem.

Primo pro viro;
secundo pro muliere.

1559. Dicit ergo *quicumque dimiserit uxorem suam* et cetera. Sed excipitur fornicatio.

Sed videte quod duplex est fornicatio, scilicet corporalis et spiritualis. Unde propter utrumque potest dimittere, ut habetur I ad Cor. VII, 11: *si unus infidelis, alter fidelis, potest dimittere fidelis infidelem*.

Notandum, quod per nullum impedimentum sequens potest dissolvi vinculum matrimonii, quia significat unionem Christi et Ecclesiae: unde cum unio Christi et Ecclesiae dissolvi non possit, nec unio matrimonii. Sed propter fornicationem potest a consortio separari, et non debet eam secum retinere, ne videatur esse conscius turpitudinis; sed pro aliis turpitudinibus non potest, ut pro ebrietate. Item si vult hominem inducere ad infidelitatem, potest dimittere eam.

Sed quare fit mentio magis de fornicatione corporali, quam de spirituali? Quia est contra fidem matrimonii: et fidem frangenti fides non est servanda. Alia ratio est quam ponit Origenes, quia supra V, 32 dixit Dominus *qui dimiserit uxorem, excepta causa fornicationis, facit eam moechari*, et ideo dat ei occasionem moechandi; sed postquam ipsa peccavit, non dat ei occasionem moechandi, ideo post potest dimittere, non ante.

1560. *Et qui aliam duxerit, moechatur*. Sed quare non, nisi aliam ducat? Quia eadem res per ea quae solvitur, ligatur. Unde quando homo habet uxorem separatam, et non aliam, adhuc spes remanet quod uniri possint, vel per consimile peccatum, vel per animorum consensum; sed quando aliam duxit, tunc cor totaliter separavit, et assensum ab ea.

thing to the young man, below: *but if you wish to enter into life, keep the commandments*. For this reason, others say that this people would be badly provided for if it did not know what was a sin, while yet it is written, *cry, cease not, lift up your voice like a trumpet, and show my people their wicked doings* (Isa 58:1). So Chrysostom says that he took from the sin the guilt of sin. And although it was something disordered, yet he did not will that it be reckoned to them as guilt, just as the Lord commanded Hosea to have children of fornication (Hos 1:2). Hence the permission was not by commandment, but for avoiding a greater evil.

But from the beginning it was not so. Hence it was practical, not established from the beginning. Hence for many years, no one sent his wife away.

1558. *And I say to you, that whoever puts away his wife*. Here he brings in the law.

First, for a man;
second, for a woman.

1559. He says then, *whoever puts away his wife*. But fornication is excepted.

But see that there are two kinds of fornication, i.e., bodily and spiritual. Hence one can put away one's wife on account of either: *if one is an unbeliever, the other a believer, the believer can put away the unbeliever* (1 Cor 7:11).

One should note that the bond of matrimony cannot be dissolved by any impediment coming afterward, because it signifies the union of Christ and the Church; hence because the union of Christ and the Church cannot be dissolved, neither can the union of matrimony. But a partnership can be divided on account of fornication, and a man should not retain her with him, lest he seem to be an accomplice in her baseness; but the partnership cannot be divided for other basenesses, as for drunkenness. Likewise, if she wishes to lead a man into unbelief, he can put her away.

But why is bodily fornication mentioned more than spiritual? Because it is against the faith of matrimony, and the faith of one who breaks faith is not to be preserved. Another reason is what Origen sets down, for above, the Lord said, *whoever will put away his wife, except for the cause of fornication, makes her commit adultery* (Matt 5:32), and so gives her an occasion of committing adultery; but after she herself has sinned, he does not give her an occasion of committing adultery. Therefore he can put her away afterward, but not before.

1560. *And marries another, commits adultery*. But why does he not commit adultery unless he marries another? Because the same is bound by the things through which it is dissolved. Hence when a man is separated from his wife, and does not have another, there still remains hope that they can be united, either through a similar sin, or through the consent of souls; but when he marries another, then the heart entirely separates, and sets itself away from her.

Alia ratio, quia si praeter fornicationem posset dimittere uxorem suam, aliquando accideret quod homo imponeret uxori suae crimen, ut ab ea separaretur, et alii coniungeretur; ideo Dominus voluit quod non haberet aliam. Unde expresse prohibet, quod non habeat homo diversas uxores, quia, una dimissa, et alia accepta, moechatur.

1561. *Et qui dimissam duxerit, moechatur.* Hic ponit legem quantum ad mulierem: unde non vult quod uxor dimissa habeat virum.

Sed quare prohibet viro ne contrahat cum ea, et non mulieri? Respondeo, quod mulieres magis ad malum praecipites sunt. Ier. III, 3: *frons mulieris meretricis facta est tibi.* Ideo per istam prohibitionem praecipitaretur ad mala maiora. Ideo praecipit viro, quod non contrahat, non autem prohibet mulieri.

Sed quid? Nonne licebat ei, quae repudiata erat, accipere alium? Dicunt quidam quod non, quia adhuc manebat vinculum: et inducunt illud quod habetur Deut. XXIV, quod non poterit reverti ad priorem, quia polluta est; sed nisi peccasset, redire posset. Alii dicunt quod poterat alteri nubere, sed non isti, quia si posset ad eum redire, facilius repudiaret eam.

Quid ergo dicis, quod polluta est? Dico quod est polluta isti, quia ad eum redire non potest. Vel potest intelligi de immunditia legis, quia sacerdos non poterat eam habere.

1562. *Dixerunt ei discipuli: si ita est causa hominis cum uxore, non expedit nubere.* Postquam Dominus egit de insolutione matrimonii, hic tractat de perfectione continentium:

et circa hoc duo facit.

Primo ponit sententiam discipulorum;

secundo sententiam Christi, ibi *qui dixit illis* et cetera.

1563. Dicit ergo *dixerunt discipuli: si ita est causa hominis cum uxore, non expedit nubere.* Moti sunt ad hoc dicendum, quia audierant quod non poterat uxor dimitti nisi ob unam causam, cum tamen multae aliae causae reddant matrimonium onerosum, ut aliqua immunditia, ut lepra et huiusmodi; ita quod impleatur illud quod in Eccli. XXV, v. 23 dicitur: *commorari leoni et urso melius est quam cum muliere nequam.* Item multam affert sollicitudinem; I Cor. VII, 34: *si virgo nubat, cogitat quae sunt mundi.* Ideo ex hoc arguunt quod expedit cuilibet homini non nubere; ideo Dominus temperat, quia contingit esse aliquid melius dupliciter: vel simpliciter, vel secundum quid; sic continere aliquibus competit,

Another reason is that if in addition to fornication one could put away his wife, it would sometimes happen that a man would bring a charge against his wife in order to be separated from her, and joined to another. For this reason, the Lord willed that he not have another. Hence he expressly forbids that a man should have different wives, because, having put one away and taken another, he commits adultery.

1561. *And he who marries her who is put away, commits adultery.* Here he sets out the law as regards the woman: hence he does not will that a wife who has been put away should have a husband.

But why does he forbid a man to marry her, and not forbid the woman to marry? I respond that women are more prone toward evil. *You had a harlot's forehead* (Jer 3:3). Therefore she would be hastened on toward greater evil by this prohibition. So he commands the man that he not marry, but does not forbid the woman.

But why? Was it not lawful for her who had been rejected to take another? Some say that it was not, because the bond still remained. And they bring in that which is written: that she could not return to her prior husband, because she was defiled; but if she had not sinned, she could go back (Deut 24). Others say that she was able to marry another, but not this man, because if she could return to him, he would reject her more easily.

So why do you say that she was defiled? I say that she is defiled for this man, because she cannot go back to him. Or it can be understood as about the uncleanness of the law, because the priest could not have her.

1562. *His disciples say to him: if the case of a man with his wife is so, it is not expedient to marry.* After the Lord treated of the indissolubility of matrimony, here he treats of the perfection of abstinence.

And concerning this he does two things:

first, he sets out the disciples' thought;

second, Christ's thought, at *he said to them: all men do not take this word.*

1563. *His disciples say to him: if the case of a man with his wife is so, it is not expedient to marry.* They were moved to say this because they had heard that a man could not put away a wife except for one cause, while yet many other causes render matrimony burdensome, such as some uncleanness, like leprosy and suchlike; so that it is fulfilled which is said: *it will be more agreeable to abide with a lion and a dragon, than to dwell with a wicked woman* (Sir 25:23). Likewise, it introduces anxiety; *but she who is married thinks on the things of the world* (1 Cor 7:34). Therefore, they argued from this that it is expedient for any man not to marry. So the Lord tempers this conclusion, because something can be better in two ways: either simply,

aliquibus non: quia, ut dicit Apostolus I ad Cor. VII, 9, *melius est nubere, quam uri*.

1564. *Qui dixit illis* approbat sententiam discipulorum. Et

primo dictis;

secundo factis, ibi *tunc oblati sunt ei parvuli*. Et

primo approbat continentiam;

secundo assignat differentias continentium ibi *sunt enim eunuchi* etc.;

tertio difficultatem, ibi *qui potest capere capiat*.

1565. Dicit ergo *qui dixit illis: non omnes capiunt istud verbum*. Ita dicitis quod non expedit nubere: verum est aliquibus, sed non est verum quoad omnes, quia non omnes, habent tantam virtutem, quod abstineant; *sed quibus datum est*, quia aliquibus datum est non ex proprio facto, sed dono gratiae. Sap. c. VIII, 21: *scivi quod aliter non possum esse continens, nisi Deus det*. Quod enim homo in carne vivat praeter carnem, non hominis est, sed Dei; I ad Cor. VII, 7: *volo omnes homines esse sicut meipsum, sed unusquisque proprium donum habet ex Deo, alius quidem sic, alius vero sic*.

1566. Et quia possent credere quod omnes continere possent, ideo dicit *sunt enim eunuchi* et cetera. Unde distinguit, quod est continentia in aliquibus ex natura, aliquando ex violentia, aliquando ex voluntate. Ideo tria genera eunuchorum tangit: quia quidam per naturam *qui a matris utero sic nati sunt*. Sicut aliqui monstruose nascuntur propter defectum manus, sic et aliqui sine genitalibus: et hoc ex Dei providentia, quia si omnia secundum communem cursum naturae acciderent, attribueretur totum naturae, et non divinae providentiae; unde Sap. VIII, 8: *signa et monstra scit antequam fiant*.

1567. Item quidam per violentiam, ut illi qui castrantur a tyrannis vel barbaris, vel qui castrantur propter custodiam mulierum. *Qui sunt facti ab hominibus*, quos scilicet vel crudelitas hominum castravit, vel conservantia mulierum. Et hoc dicit Hieronymus quod scit, quia pueri acciperentur, et castrarentur, et ponerentur in domo Nabuchodonosor.

1568. Quidam vero voluntate, ut dicit *et sunt eunuchi, qui castraverunt seipsos propter regnum caelorum*. Quidam male intellexerunt verbum istud, dicentes scindenda esse genitalia, et leguntur hoc quidam fecisse, de quibus dicitur fuisse Origenes. Sed istud reprobatum est, et separari debent a clero, capit. ex parte, et capitul. significavit, extra de corp. Vit.

Unde datur occasio errori Manichaeorum, qui creaturam corporalem dixerunt esse causam mali. Item

or in a certain respect. Thus to abstain belongs to some and not to others; for, as the Apostle says, *for it is better to marry than to be burnt* (1 Cor 7:9).

1564. *He said to them*. He approves the disciples' thought. And

first, in words;

second, in deeds, at *then little children were presented to him*.

And first, he approves abstinence;

second, he gives the differences of abstinence, at *for there are eunuchs*;

third, the difficulty, at *he who can take, let him take it*.

1565. It says then *he said to them: all men do not take this word*. Thus you say that it is not expedient to marry. This is true for some, but it is not true with regard to all, because not all have such great virtue that they may abstain, *but they to whom it is given*, because to some it is given not from their own deed, but by the gift of grace. *And as I knew that I could not otherwise be continent, except God gave it* (Wis 8:21). For that a man in the flesh should live beyond the flesh is not of man, but of God; *for I would that all men were even as myself: but every one has his proper gift from God; one after this manner, and another after that* (1 Cor 7:7).

1566. And because they could think that all can abstain, he says, *for there are eunuchs*. Hence he makes the distinction that there is abstinence in some by nature, sometimes by violence, and sometimes by will. Therefore he touches upon three kinds of eunuchs. For some are eunuchs by nature, *who were born so from their mother's womb*. As some are born monstrously, because of a defect of the hand, so also some are born without genitals. And this is from God's providence, because if all things happened according to the common course of nature, the whole would be attributed to nature, and not to divine providence; hence, *she knows signs and monsters before they are done* (Wis 8:8).

1567. Likewise, there are some who are eunuchs by violence, such as those who are castrated by tyrants or barbarians, or who are castrated for the sake of guarding women. *Who were made so by men*, namely those whom either the cruelty of men or the preservation of women has castrated. And Jerome says that he knows this, because boys were taken and castrated, and placed in the house of Nabuchodonosor.

1568. But some are eunuchs by will, as he says: *and there are eunuchs, who have made themselves eunuchs for the kingdom of heaven*. Some have understood these words in a bad way, saying that the genitals should be cut off, and it is written that some have done this, of whom one is said to have been Origen. But this should be reproved, and should be kept out of the clergy (*Decrees*, I, 20, 3).

From this an occasion is given for the error of the Manichees, who said that the bodily creation is the cause of evil.

datur occasio errori gentilium, quia quidam in sacrificiis suis eunuchantur. Item hoc factum non est in utilitatem, quia tales, etsi actum non habent, a concupiscentia tamen non sunt immunes. Unde Eccli. XX, v. 2. *Concupiscentia spadonis devirginabit iuvenculam*. Ideo melius est quod homo sibi fraenum imponat, quam membrum abscindat, ut malas cogitationes et desideria refraenet. Is. I, 16: *auferte malas cogitationes a cordibus vestris*.

1569. Qui castraverunt seipsos, continuae castitati se dederunt, et hoc **propter regnum caelorum**. Aliquando enim membrum per actum intelligitur, ut supra c. XVIII, 9: *si oculus tuus scandalizat te, erue eum, et proiice abs te*. Sic hic membra genitalia pro actu accipiuntur. Unde ille se castrat, qui castitati se dedicat. Vel, secundum Hieronymum, quod continentiam servantes sic nati sunt frigiditate, scilicet naturae, ita quod non moventur ad actum illum. Unde dicuntur eunuchi propter actum eunuchorum, quem habent propter naturam quam ex utero habent. Quia aliqui habent aliquam dispositionem ad aliquam virtutem naturaliter, sicut Iob ad misericordiam, qui dicit cap. XXXI, 18: *ab infantia mecum crevit miseratio*. Quidam vero ex voluntate, vel propter simulationem; vel doctus ab haereticis, est factus ab hominibus. II Tim. III, 5: *habentes quidem speciem pietatis, virtutem autem eius abnegantes*. Quidam vero propter praemium vitae aeternae.

Primi duo, scilicet qui vel naturaliter, vel violenter castrantur, non habent meritum vitae aeternae, sed solum tertii.

Sed numquid est verum de primis, quod non mereantur? Dico quod merentur quantum ad voluntatem, licet non mereantur quantum ad actum; quia licet non possint facere, possunt tamen velle posse facere.

1570. Qui potest capere capiat. Posita differentia continentiae, hic ponitur exhortatio, ut dicit Hieronymus. Facit Dominus sicut facit dux in exercitu, qui quando est capienda civitas, dicit: qui intrabit civitatem, dabitur ei hoc, vel illud, sicut dicit David Ioab. Sic **qui potest capere** et continere, **capiat**, et non retrahat se. Apostolus I Cor. XII, v. 31: *aemulamini charismata meliora*.

1571. Sed quid est quod dicit? Nonne tenetur quisque ad virginitatem servandam? Videtur quod sic, quia homo ad meliora tenetur.

Dicendum, quod non est praeceptum, sed consilium, sicut dicit Apostolus I ad Cor. c. VII, 25: *de virginibus praeceptum Domini non habeo, consilium autem do*.

Sed quid est? Nonne tenetur homo ad meliora? Dico quod distinguendum est, quod melius est quantum ad actum, vel quantum ad affectum. Non tenetur ad meliora quoad actum, sed quoad affectum, quia omnis regula

Likewise, an occasion is given for the error of the gentiles, because some are made eunuchs in their sacrifices. Likewise, this is not useful when done, because such men, even though they do not have the act, still they are not free from concupiscence. Hence, *the lust of an eunuch shall devour a young maiden* (Sir 20:2). Therefore it is better that a man impose restraint on himself than that he cut off a member to restrain evil thoughts and desires. *Remove the evil thoughts from your hearts* (Isa 1:16).

1569. Who have made themselves eunuchs, who have given themselves continually to chastity, and this **for the kingdom of heaven**. For sometimes, a member is understood by its action, as above, **and if your eye scandalize you, pluck it out, and cast it from you** (Matt 18:9). In the same way, the genital members are taken here for their action. Hence that man castrates himself who dedicates himself to chastity. Or, according to Jerome, because those who keep abstinence are born that way, with a frigidity, namely of nature, such that they are not moved to that act. Hence they are called eunuchs on account of the act of eunuchs, which they have on account of the nature which they have from the womb. For some men naturally have a disposition toward some particular virtue, as Job toward mercy, who says, *for from my infancy mercy grew up with me* (Job 31:18). But some are disposed toward a virtue by their will, or for the sake of pretense or the one taught by heretics; they are made so by men. *Having an appearance indeed of godliness, but denying the power thereof* (2 Tim 3:5). But some, for the sake of the reward of eternal life.

The first two, namely those who are castrated naturally or violently, do not have the merit of eternal life, but only the third.

But is it true of the first ones, that they do not merit? I say that they merit as regards the will, although they do not merit as regards the act; for although they cannot act, yet they can wish they could act.

1570. He who can take, let him take it. The differences of abstinence being set down, here an exhortation is set down, as Jerome says. The Lord does as a leader in the army does who, when a city is to be taken, says: I will give this or that to the one who shall enter the city, as David said to Joab. Thus, **he who can take** and abstain, **let him take it**, and not draw himself back. The Apostle: *but be zealous for the better gifts* (1 Cor 12:31).

1571. But why does he say this? Is not everyone bound to preserve virginity? It seems so, because a man is bound to what is better.

One should say that it is not a commandment, but a counsel, as the Apostle says, *now concerning virgins, I have no commandment of the Lord; but I give counsel* (1 Cor 7:25).

But what is this? Is not a man bound to what is better? I say that one should distinguish what is better with regard to the act, and what is better with regard to disposition. One is not bound to what is better as regards act, but as regards

et omnis actus determinatur ad finitum et certum: et si tenetur ad melius, tenetur ad incertum. Unde quantum ad actus exteriores, quia non tenetur ad incertum, non tenetur ad meliora; sed quantum ad affectum, tenetur ad meliora. Unde qui non semper vellet esse melior, non posset sine contemptu velle.

1572. Sed quid est quod dicit *qui potest capere capiat*? Aut enim potentia naturali; et sic nullus potest: aut potentia gratiae; et sic quilibet potest, quia dicitur Lc. XI, v. 9: *petite et accipietis*. Item gratia Dei omnia potest.

Dico quod ly *potest* includit potestatem voluntatis: est enim voluntas firma et infirma. Constat autem quod homo cum habet voluntatem firmam, non timet multos impulsus; sed quando non, ex facili impulsu labitur. Unde *qui potest* per firmitatem voluntatis *capere, capiat*, et non a natura, sed a Deo. Unde qui hoc a Deo habet, consulimus quod hoc capiat et contineat. Vel *qui potest* secundum opportunitatem temporis, vel conditionis temporis, ut Abraham: unde caelibatus Ioannis non praefertur coniugio Abrahae. Item secundum conditionem; quia qui coniugatus est, non potest continere; unde excluduntur vel ratione temporis, vel conditionis.

1573. *Tunc oblati sunt ei parvuli*. Hic ostendit quod dixit, facto. Et

primo ponitur parvulorum oblatio;
secundo zelus discipulorum;
tertio satisfactio Christi.

Secunda ibi *discipuli autem increpabant eos*; tertia ibi *Iesus autem ait eis* et cetera.

1574. Dicit ergo *tunc oblati sunt ei parvuli*. Dominus commendaverat castitatem, et quia in parvulis est castitas et puritas, ideo videntes quod puritas placeret ei, obtulerunt ei parvulos *ut manus eis imponeret, et oraret*.

Notandum quod consuetudo erat quod pueri offerebantur antiquis, et benedicebant, et orabant, in signum quod benedictio est a Deo. Item experti quod tactum haberet salutarem, quia leprosum curaverat et multos alios, ideo et cetera. Item parvulos offerebant, quia credebant quod qui tangeretur ab eo, de caetero a daemonibus non infestaretur; ideo Ecclesia accepit in consuetudinem, quod parvulis exhibeantur sacramenta Ecclesiae, ut magis confirmentur.

1575. *Discipuli autem increpabant eos*. Hic tangitur zelus discipulorum. Sed quare increpabant? Quia credebant eum ut verum hominem fatigari ex frequentia hominum; ideo volentes parcere labori eius et cetera. Alia ratio, quia magnam opinionem habebant de Christo;

disposition, because every rule and every act is determined to something limited and certain; and if one is bound to the better thing, one is bound to what is uncertain. Hence with regard to the exterior act, since one is not bound to what is uncertain, one is not bound to the better thing; but with regard to disposition, one is bound to the better thing. Hence he who does not always will to be better is unable to will without contempt.

1572. But why does he say, *he who can take, let him take it*? For it is either by a natural power, and thus no one can; or it is by the power of grace, and thus anyone can, since it says, *ask, and it will be given you* (Luke 11:9). Likewise, the grace of God can do all things.

I say that this *can* includes the power of the will: for there is a firm will, and a weak will. Now, it is agreed that when a man has a firm will, he is not afraid of many impulses, but when he does not have a firm will, he falls from an easy impulse. Hence *he who can* by firmness of will *take, let him take it*, and not from nature, but from God. Hence he who has this from God, we consider that he may receive and abstain. Or, *he who can* according to the opportuneness of the time, or of condition, as with Abraham: hence John's celibacy is not preferred to Abraham's marriage. Likewise, according to condition, because the one who is married cannot abstain; hence they are excluded either by reason of time or of condition.

1573. *Then little children were presented to him*. Here he shows what he said by deed. And

first, the offering of the little children is set out;
second, the disciples' zeal;
third, Christ satisfies.

The second is at *and the disciples rebuked them*; the third, at *but Jesus said to them: allow the little children*.

1574. It says then, *then little children were presented to him*. The Lord had commended chastity, and since there is chastity and purity in little children, then, seeing that purity would please him, they presented little children to him *that he should impose hands upon them and pray*.

One should note that it was customary that children were offered to the elderly, and the elderly blessed them, and prayed, as a sign that blessing is from God. Also, they knew from experience that his touch carried salvation, because he had cured the leper and many others. They also offered the little children because they believed that the one who was touched by him would not be disturbed by demons in the future. Hence the Church received it as a custom that the sacraments of the Church are presented to little children, that they might be more strengthened.

1575. *And the disciples rebuked them*. Here the disciples' zeal is touched upon. But why did they rebuke them? Because they thought that he, as a true man, was tired out by a large attendance of men; for this reason, wishing to spare his labor, etc. Another reason, because they had a

ideo videbatur eis quod inhonestum erat quod parvuli accederent ad eum. Origenes: *quia per hoc significatur, quod in Ecclesia sunt quidam parvuli rudes. Per discipulos perfecti significantur; unde tales dedignantur cum vident parvulos, scilicet istos rudes, venire ad Christum, ignorantes quod omnes homines vult salvos fieri*. Apostolus, Rom. I, 14: *Graecis et barbaris debitor sum*.

1576. Consequenter utrisque satisfacit. Et

primo zelo iustitiae;

secundo satisfacit devotioni offerentium.

1577. Dicit ergo **sinite parvulos venire ad me**, idest humiles, sive paucos; I ad Cor. XIV, 20: *nolite parvuli esse sensibus, sed malitia parvuli estote*. **Et nolite prohibere**, scilicet paucos propter innocentiam. Non enim sunt prohibendi imperfecti venire ad perfectionem. **Talium est enim regnum caelorum**. Dicit **talium**, non *horum*, scilicet qui ita sunt puri per innocentiam. Supra XVIII, 3: *nisi efficiamini sicut parvulus iste, non intrabitis in regnum caelorum*. Iob XXII, 29: *qui humiliatus fuerit, erit in gloria*.

1578. Consequenter devotioni satisfacit **cum imposuisset eis manus**. Per quod virtutes confortat. Is. XL, 29: *qui dat lasso virtutem*.

Abiit inde. Aliquando Christus apponit manus, et non **abiit inde**: aliquando apponit, et **abiit**, quia aliqui ita fortes sunt, quod non retrocedunt. Et vocavit Petrum et Andream, et mansit cum eis, Io. I, 38 ss. Quia igitur isti adhuc imperfecti erant, nec habiles ad sequendum, ideo **abiit inde**.

1579. Et ecce unus accedens et cetera. Hic agit de perfectione paupertatis; et quia duplex est via, via communis, et specialis, ut est continentia: via prima est via salutis, secunda perfectionis: ideo

primo de prima,

secundo de secunda.

Et

primo ponitur interrogatio;

secundo Christi responsio;

tertio responsionis expositio.

1580. Interrogatio ponitur **et ecce unus accedens ait illi: Magister bone**.

De isto diversa est opinio, quia Hieronymus dicit quod erat perversus corde: et hoc patet, quia abiit tristis; unde si bono corde accessisset, non abiisset tristis. Chrysostomus dicit quod a passione avaritiae detinebatur; ideo ferre non potuit: et hoc patet, quia non causa

great opinion of Christ, so it seemed to them that it was disrespectful for little children to approach him. Origen: *because by this is signified that there are in the Church certain little, unrefined ones. The perfect are signified by the disciples. Hence such men are disdainful when they see the little ones, namely the unrefined ones, come to Christ, not knowing that he wishes all men to be saved*. The Apostle: *to the Greeks and to the barbarians, to the wise and to the unwise, I am a debtor* (Rom 1:14).

1576. Next, he satisfies both. And

first, the zeal for justice;

second, he satisfies the devotion of those offering the children.

1577. He says then, **allow the little children to come to me**, i.e., the humble, or the little; *brethren, do not become children in sense: but in malice be children* (1 Cor 14:20). **And do not forbid them**, namely those who are little through innocence. For the imperfect should not be forbidden to come to perfection. **For the kingdom of heaven is for such**. He says, **for such**, not *of these*, namely those who are children this way through innocence. Above, **unless you be converted, and become like little children, you will not enter into the kingdom of heaven** (Matt 18:3). *For he who has been humbled, shall be in glory* (Job 22:29).

1578. Next, he satisfies their devotion: **and when he had imposed hands upon them**, through which he supports their strength. *It is he who gives strength to the weary* (Isa 40:29).

He departed from there. Sometimes Christ lays a hand on and does not **depart from there**; sometimes he lays a hand on and does **depart**, because some are so steadfast that they do not fall away. And he called Peter and Andrew, and remained with them (John 1:38). Therefore, since they were still imperfect, nor suited for following him, **he departed from there**.

1579. And behold one came. Here he treats of the perfection of poverty, and that there are two ways, the common way and the special way, as is abstinence. The first way is the way of salvation, the second the way of perfection. Therefore,

first, he treats of the first;

second, of the second.

And

first, a questioning is set down;

second, Christ's response;

third, an explanation of the response.

1580. The questioning is set down: **and behold one came and said to him: good Master**.

There are different opinions about this man, for Jerome says that he was corrupt at heart; and this is clear, because he went away sad. Hence if he had approached with a good heart, he would not have gone away sad. Chrysostom says that he was hindered by the passion of avarice; therefore he

tentandi venit; quia quando aliqui veniebant ad Iesum causa tentandi, Dominus semper respondebat eorum malitiae: *ut quid me tentatis?* Vel huiusmodi; sed nullum ponit hic. Unde patet, quod non tentator erat, sed imperfectus, qui ad Deum accedebat, ut perficeretur; Ps. XXXIII, 6: *accedite ad eum et illuminamini*.

Magister bone et cetera. Vocat eum Magistrum, quasi scientem: talis enim debet esse magister, qui sciat. Item vocat bonum: de ratione boni est se communicare; unde Sap. VII, 13: *sine invidia communico*. Ipse enim vere bonus est; Ps. CXVIII, 68: *bonus es tu, et in bonitate tua doce me iustificationes tuas*. **Quid boni faciam, ut habeam vitam aeternam?** Audierat multa de vita aeterna. Bene audierat, Ps. XXXVI, 27: *declina a malo, et fac bonum*; sed in lege non audierat promitti vitam aeternam, sed temporalia tantum. Is. I, 19: *bona terrae comedetis*.

1581. *Qui dicit ei, quid me interrogas?* Hic ponit responsionem. Primo respondet, ut in Marco habetur, *quid me dicis bonum?* Hic autem **quid me interrogas?** Utrumque potest intelligi.

Sed quod Matthaeus dicit **quid me interrogas?** Non habet calumniam; secundum vero id quod dicit Marcus, assumpserunt Ariani errorem, dicentes quod Pater est bonus per essentiam, Filius per participationem; ideo ponebant Filium inaequalem Patri.

Sed notandum quod dicit: **unus est bonus Deus**. Sed nomine Dei Pater, et Filius, et Spiritus Sanctus intelligitur: unde ab hoc excluditur alia creatura, quia non per essentiam bona est.

1582. Sed quare respondet sic? Dicit Hieronymus quod respondet ad mentem ipsius, qui illam bonitatem commendabat, quae solet esse in homine; quia magis adhaerebant traditionibus hominum quam Dei, sicut supra XV, 6 dicitur: **irritum fecistis mandatum Dei propter traditiones vestras**. Ideo reprehendit eum, quia petebat ab eo tamquam ab homine bono, non autem tamquam a Deo.

Sed quid est quod dicit **quid me interrogas de bono?** Hoc dicit tamquam cognoscens eius affectum, quia non habebat animum ad obediendum bono, et omne bonum temporale est imperfectum et umbra respectu boni divini; Is. LXIV, 6: *omnes iustitiae vestrae tamquam pannus menstruatae*. Unde omnia ista bona sunt a Deo; ideo si vis habere ea, pete ab eo: ipse enim solus est bonus; Ps. CXXXV, v. 1: *confitemini Domino, quoniam bonus*. Ideo recurre ad Deum.

1583. *Si vis ad vitam ingredi, serva mandata*. Quidam enim habent vitam imperfectam, quidam perfectam et quidam totaliter extra vitam sunt, ut qui in peccato

could not bear the Lord's words. And this is clear, because he did not come in order to tempt the Lord; for when men came to Jesus to tempt him, the Lord always responded to their malice by saying, *why do you tempt me?* or something of the kind; but he sets down nothing of that sort here. Hence it is clear that the one who approached God that he might be made perfect was not a tempter, but imperfect. *Come to him and be enlightened* (Ps 33:6).

Good Master, what good should I do. He calls him Master, as though one who knows: for a master should be the sort of man who knows. Likewise, he called him good: it belongs to the notion of the good to communicate itself; hence, *which I have learned without guile, and communicate without envy* (Wis 7:13). For he is truly good; *you are good; and in your goodness teach me your justifications* (Ps 118:68). **What good should I do that I may have life everlasting?** He had heard many things about eternal life. He had heard well, *decline from evil and do good* (Ps 36:27); but in the law he had not heard that eternal life was promised, but temporal things only. *You shall eat the good things of the land* (Isa 1:19).

1581. *He said to him: why do you ask me?* Here he sets out the response. First, he responds, as is had in Mark, *why do you call me good?* (Mark 10:18). But here, **why do you ask me?** It can be understood either way.

But what Matthew says, **why do you ask me?** does not have a wrong interpretation; but following what Mark says, the Arians took up an error, saying that the Father is good by essence, and the Son by participation; therefore, they posited that the Son is not equal to the Father.

But one should notice that he says, **one is good, God**. But the name of God indicates the Father, and the Son, and the Holy Spirit. Hence other creatures are excluded, because they are not good by essence.

1582. But why does he respond this way? Jerome says that he responds to his mind, for he commended that goodness which is usually in men; for they clung more to the traditions of men than of God, as it says above, **you have made void the commandment of God for the sake of your tradition** (Matt 15:6). For this reason, he reproached him, because he asked of him as though of a good man, but not as though of God.

But why does he say, **why do you ask me concerning good?** He says this as though aware of his emotions, that his soul was not ready to submit to the good, and every temporal good is imperfect and a shadow with respect to the divine good; *and all our justices as the rag of a menstruous woman* (Isa 64:6). Hence all these good things are from God, so if you wish to have them, ask of him; for he alone is good; *praise the Lord, for he is good* (Ps 135:1). Therefore, have recourse to God.

1583. *But if you wish to enter into life, keep the commandments*. For some have imperfect life, some perfect life, and some are entirely outside of life, such as those

sunt, vel infideles, quia *iustus ex fide vivit*, Hebr. X, 38. Quidam igitur habent vitam inchoatam et imperfectam, ut iusti in hoc mundo; illi vero perfectam, qui iam sunt in vita aeterna; unde *si vis ad vitam ingredi, serva mandata*, quia introducitur homo per mandata. Ez. XX, 11: *dedi eis mandata mea, et iudicia mea ostendi eis.*

Sed numquid mandata sufficiebant ad salutem? Dico quod non, nisi ex fide Mediatoris, et caritate; unde Apostolus ad Gal. II, 21: *si ex lege est iustitia, ergo frustra mortuus est Christus.* Item Prov. VII, 2: *serva mandata mea, et vives.*

1584. *Dicit illi, quae?* Sequitur responsionis expositio, in qua mandata replicat. Et primo ponit mandata; secundo radicem, ibi *'diliges proximum tuum sicut teipsum.'*

Dicit ergo *Iesus autem dixit: 'non homicidium facies'* et cetera. Et quare non facit mentionem de mandatis primae tabulae? Quia pronum videbat ad dilectionem Dei, ideo non fuit necesse. Item haec sunt praevia ad dilectionem. Et primo ponit negativum; secundo affirmativum. Primo incipit a maiori *'non homicidium facies'*, quod est contra vitam in actu; *'non adulterabis'*, quod est contra vitam in potentia; *'non furtum facies'*, quod est contra bona personae; *'non falsum testimonium dices'*, quod est contra personam. Item affirmativum ponit: *'honora patrem.'*

1585. Deinde ponit radicem *'diliges proximum tuum sicut teipsum.'* Rom. XIII, 8: *qui diligit proximum, legem implevit.*

1586. *Dicit ei adolescens: omnia haec custodivi a iuventute mea.* Postquam Dominus tradtdit doctrinam communis salutis, hic tradit doctrinam perfectionis. Et

primo tradit doctrinam;
secundo necessitatem huius doctrinae;
tertio praemium observationis.

Secunda ibi *Iesus autem dixit discipulis suis*; tertia ibi *respondens Petrus* etc. Et

primo ponitur occasio doctrinae dandae;
secundo promulgatio;
tertio effectus.

Secunda ibi *dicit ei Jesus* etc.; tertia ibi *cum audisset adolescens verbum, abiit tristis.*

Occasio promulgandi hanc doctrinam est petitio adolescentis. Et

primo confitetur se observatorem legalium;
secundo petit quae sit perfectio, ad quam pervenire possit, ibi *quid adhuc mihi deest?*

1587. Dicit ergo *omnia haec custodivi a iuventute mea*; et dicit *omnia*, quia non sufficit unum facere tantum, nisi omnia serventur; Jacob. II, 10: *qui offenderit*

who are in sin, or unbelievers, for *my just man lives by faith* (Heb 10:38). So some have a beginning and imperfect life, as do the just in this world; but those who are in eternal life have perfect life; hence, *if you wish to enter into life, keep the commandments*, because a man is brought in through the commandments. *And I gave them my statutes, and I showed them my judgments, which if a man do, he will live in them* (Ezek 20:11).

But were the commandments enough for salvation? I say not, except on the basis of faith in the Mediator, and charity; hence the Apostle: *for if justice be by the law, then Christ died in vain* (Gal 2:21). Also, *keep my commandments, and you shall live* (Prov 7:2).

1584. *He said to him: which?* There follows the explanation of the response, in which he repeats the commandments. And first, he sets out the commandments; second, the root, at *'love your neighbor as yourself.'*

It says then, *and Jesus said: 'do not murder.'* And why did not he mention the commandments of the first tablet? Because he seemed inclined toward the love of God, so it was not necessary. Also, these commandments lead the way toward love. And first, he sets out the negative; second, the affirmative. First, he begins from what is greater: *'do not murder'*, which is against an actual life; *'do not commit adultery'*, which is against a potential life; *'do not steal'*, which is against a person's goods; *'do not bear false witness'*, which is against a person. Likewise, sets out an affirmative: *'honor your father.'*

1585. Then he sets out the root: *'love your neighbor as yourself.'* For he who loves his neighbor, has fulfilled the law (Rom 13:8).

1586. *The young man said to him: all these I have kept from my youth*. After the Lord handed down the teaching on common salvation, here he hands down the teaching on perfection. And

first, he hands down the teaching;
second, the necessity of this teaching;
third, the reward of observing it.

The second is at *then Jesus said to his disciples*; the third, at *then Peter answering, said to him: behold*. And

first, the occasion for giving this teaching is set out;
second, the proclamation;
third, the effect.

The second is at *Jesus says to him*; the third, at *and when the young man had heard this word, he went away sad*.

The occasion for proclaiming this teaching is the young man's question. And

first, he professes to be an observer of the law;
second, he asks what perfection he can come to, at *what is still wanting to me?*

1587. He says then, *all these I have kept from my youth*; and he says *all*, because it is not enough to do only one, if all are not kept; *and whosoever shall keep the whole law, but*

in uno, factus est omnium reus. Item dicit **a iuventute**; Prov. XXII, 6: *adolescens iuxta viam suam, et cum senuerit, non recedet ab ea.* Unde conveniebat ei quod dicitur Iob xxiii, 12: *a via labiorum non recessi.*

Utrum autem verum dixerit, est quaestio. Hieronymus dicit quod mentitus est: quod patet, quia ante hoc immediate praecedit, **'diliges proximum tuum sicut teipsum.'** Si sic dilexisset, non abiisset tristis, cum Dominus dixit **vade, et vende omnia quae habes, et da pauperibus**. Chrysostomus dicit quod verum dixit quod legalia servaverat; et confirmatur per illud quod habetur in Marco x, 21, quod cum intuitus esset eum Jesus, dilexit eum; quod non fecisset, nisi bonus esset.

Est enim duplex via. Una sufficiens ad salutem; et haec est dilectio Dei et proximi cum sui beneficio, sine suo gravamine, secundum quod habetur I Cor. VIII, 3: *qui diligit Deum, cognitus est ab eo*; et hanc servaverat. Alia est perfectionis, ut diligere proximum cum sui detrimento; et hanc non servaverat; ideo cum nuntiata fuit ei **abiit tristis**.

1588. Prima non fuit contentus; ideo petiit **quid mihi deest adhuc?** Quilibet tenetur facere hanc quaestionem, secundum quod dicitur Ps. XXXVII, 5: *Notum fac mihi, Domine, finem meum, et numerum dierum meorum quis est, ut sciam quid desit mihi.* Ipse enim solus scit quid desit nobis. *Imperfectum meum viderunt oculi tui*, Ps. cxxxviii, 16.

1589. Dicit ei Jesus: si vis perfectos esse, vade etc.
Primo ponitur studium;
secundo via;
tertio, quia difficilis, ponitur praemium;
quarto consummatio perfectionis.

1590. Dicit ergo **si vis perfectos esse, vade, et vende omnia quae habes, et da pauperibus**. Debemus enim niti ad perfectionem; Hebr. vr, 1: *intermittentes inchoationis Christi sermonem, ad perfectum feramur.*

Sed quaerit Origenes: *Perfectio legis est dilectio; sed dixerat* **'diliges proximum tuum sicut teipsum'**, *quare ergo dixit* **si vis perfectus esse**, *cum iam perfectos esset?*

Dicunt quidam quod in quibusdam libris non ponitur illud **'diliges proximum tuum sicut teipsum.'** Et hoc patet, quia in Marco non ponitur. Aliter potest dici quod illud dixit, sed non hoc ordine, quia in Evangelio Nazaraeorum ita est, Dominus dixit, **'non homicidium facies'** etc. usque ad illud de dilectione. Et post sequitur, **haec omnia** etc, et deinde sequitur, **'diliges proximum'** etc.

Tamen plana est solutio, quia duplex est dilectio proximi, scilicet dilectio secundum viam communem, et dilectio perfectionis.

offend in one point, is become guilty of all (Jas 2:10). Likewise, he says, **from my youth**; *a young man according to his way, even when he is old he will not depart from it* (Prov 22:6). Hence what is said in Job is fitting to him: *I have not departed from the commandments of his lips* (Job 23:12).

But whether he spoke the truth is a question. Jerome says that he lied: which is clear, because immediately before this came **'love your neighbor as yourself.'** If he had loved in this way, he would not have gone away sad, since the Lord said, **go sell what you have, and give to the poor**. Chrysostom says that he spoke the truth, that he had kept the legal commandments; and this is confirmed by what is said in Mark, that when Jesus had looked upon him, he loved him, which he would not have done unless he had been good (Mark 10:21).

For there are two ways. One, sufficient for salvation; and this is the love of God and of neighbor with one's own benefit, without burden to self, according to what is said, *but if any love God, the same is known by him* (1 Cor 8:3); and this he had kept. The other is the way of perfection, to love neighbor with one's own detriment; and this he had not kept. For this reason, when it was told him, **he went away sad**.

1588. He was not content with the first things, so he asked: **what is still wanting to me?** Everyone is bound to ask this question, according to what is said, *O Lord, make me know my end. And what is the number of my days: that I may know what is wanting to me* (Ps 38:5). For he alone knows what is lacking to us. *Your eyes saw my imperfect being* (Ps 138:16).

1589. Jesus says to him: if you will be perfect, go.
First, zeal is set down;
second, the way;
third, because of the difficulty, the reward is set down;
fourth, the consummation of perfection.

1590. He says then, **if you will be perfect, go sell what you have, and give to the poor**. For we should strive toward perfection; *wherefore leaving the word of the beginning of Christ, let us go on to things more perfect* (Heb 6:1).

But Origen asks: *the perfection of the law is love; but he had said,* **'love your neighbor as yourself'**; *why then did he say,* **if you will be perfect**, *when he was already perfect?*

Some say that **'love your neighbor as yourself'** is not set down in some books. And this is clear, because it is not set down in Mark. In another way, it can be said that he said this, but not in this order, because it is this way in the Gospel of the Nazarenes: the Lord said, **'do not murder'**, up to the part about love. And after that follows, **all these, I have kept**. And then there follows, **'love your neighbor.'**

Yet the solution is plain, that there are two ways of loving one's neighbor, namely love according to the common way, and the love of perfection.

1591. Unde dicit **vade, et vende omnia** etc., non partem, sicut fecerunt Ananias et Saphira, ut habetur in Act. v, 2. **Et da pauperibus**, non divitibus. I ad Cor. xiii, 3: *si distribuero facultates meas in cibos pauperum.* Ps. cxi, 9: *dispersit, dedit pauperibus.* Et non uni, sed pluribus.

1592. Sed quid est? Nonne statim tali esset perfectos? Videtur quid non, quia adhuc passiones sunt in eo; ergo non est perfectus in virtute.

Origenes dicit quod statim perfectos est, sicut illi perfecti sunt quibus bona sua distribuit. II ad Cor. VIII, 14: *vestra abundantia inopiam illorum suppleat; et illorum abundantia inopiae vestrae sit supplemento.* Unde perfectio illorum transit in illum, sicut qui recipit prophetam in nomine prophetae, mercedem prophetae accipiet etc. supra x, 41. Unde via perfectionis non est **vade et vende omnia quae habes**; sed tantum hoc quod sequitur **et da pauperibus**.

Alia responsio est **si vis perfectus esse**, non quod statim sis perfectus, sed quoddam principium habebis perfectionis, quia exoneratus istis, poteris facilius contemplari caelestia. Augustinus dicit quod vigiliae et huiusmodi sunt instrumenta perfectionis; sed in hoc quod sequitur est perfectio **et sequere me**. Unde supra IV, 20: Petrus et Andreas, relictis omnibus, **secuti sunt eum**. Et sic etiam Matthaeus supra IX, 9. Sed cum dimittis haec omnia, melior usus est dare pauperibus, et in hoc considerandus est proximus.

1593. Unde si non est in illis perfectio, in quo consistit?

Dicendum quod in perfectione caritatis; Col. III, 14: *super omnia caritatem habentes, quae est vinculum perfectionis.* Unde dilectio Dei est perfectio, sed dimissio rerum est via ad perfectionem. Et quomodo? Augustinus in libro LXXXIII Quaest. dicit quod *augmentum caritatis est diminutio cupiditatis; perfectio caritatis, nulla cupiditas.* Ille ergo perfectus est in caritate, qui diligit Deum usque ad contemptum sui et suorum. Unde difficile et quasi impossibile est quod aliquis possideat divitias, quin eis alliciatur: et hoc patet de Gregorio, de quo legitur, quod cum cogitasset melius se famulaturum Christo sub specie saeculari, coeperunt contra eum tot succrescere, ut non iam specie tantum, sed etiam mente retineretur. Ideo nihil est quod animum tam liberum faciat sicut quod non occupetur circa divitias: et haec est via perfectionis. Unde aliud est esse perfectum, et habere statum perfectionis. Quicumque habet caritatem perfectam usque ad contemptum sui et suorum, perfectionem habet.

1594. Status perfectionis duplex est, praelatorum et religiosorum; sed aequivoce, quia status religiosorum est ad acquirendum perfectionem; unde isti dictum est: **si**

1591. Hence he says, **go sell what you have**, not a part, as Ananias and Saphira did (Acts 5:2). **And give to the poor**, not to the rich. *And if I should distribute all my goods to feed the poor* (1 Cor 13:3). *He has distributed, he has given to the poor* (Ps 111:9). And not to one, but to many.

1592. But what is this? Would such a man be perfect immediately? It seems not, because there are still passions in him; therefore he is not perfect in virtue.

Origen says that he is immediately perfect, just as those to whom he distributes his goods are perfect. *Let your abundance supply their want, that their abundance also may supply your want* (2 Cor 8:14). Hence their perfection passes over into him, just as he who receives a prophet in the name of a prophet receives a prophet's reward (Matt 10:41). Hence the way of perfection is not **go sell what you have**, but only that which follows: **and give to the poor**.

Another response is that **if you will be perfect**, not that you will be perfect right away, but you will have a certain principle of perfection, because being unburdened of these things, you will be able to contemplate heavenly things more easily. Augustine says that vigils and suchlike are instruments of perfection; but perfection is in what follows: **and come follow me**. Hence above, Peter and Andrew left everything and **followed him** (Matt 4:20). And Matthew also, in the same way (Matt 9:9). But when you abandon all these things, the better use is to give to the poor, and in this one's neighbor should be considered.

1593. Hence if perfection is not in these things, in what does it consist?

One should say that it consists in the perfection of charity; *but above all these things have charity, which is the bond of perfection* (Col 3:14). Hence the love of God is perfection, but the abandonment of things is the way toward perfection. And how? Augustine says, in the book of *83 Questions*, that *the growth of charity is the diminution of greed, and the perfection of charity is no greed.* Therefore, that man is perfect in charity who loves God even to the contempt of self and of his own things. Hence it is difficult and as though impossible that someone should possess riches without being gently drawn by them. And this is clear concerning Gregory, of whom it is written that, when he had thought it better that he serve Christ under a secular appearance, they began to grow up against him so much that he was hindered by them not only in appearance, but in mind also. Therefore, there is nothing that makes the soul so free as not being occupied with riches: and this is the way of perfection. Hence it is one thing to be perfect, and another thing to have the state of perfection. Whoever has perfect charity even to the contempt of himself and his things has perfection.

1594. The state of perfection is twofold, that of prelates and that of religious; but equivocally, because the state of the religious is for acquiring perfection. Hence it was said

vis esse perfectus, et si vis ad perfectionis statum venire. Status autem praelationis non est ad acquirendum sibi, sed ad habitam communicandam: unde Dominus, Io. ult., 17, dixit Petro: *Petre, si diligis me, pasce oves meas*; et non dixit *si vis perfectus esse* etc.

Unde talis est differentia inter perfectionem religiosorum et praelatorum, qualis inter discipulum et magistrum. Unde discipulo dicitur: si vis addiscere, intra scholas ut addiscas. Magistro dicitur: lege, et perfice. Unde securior est status religiosorum, quia ignorantia non imputatur eis sicut praelato. Unde sicut ridiculum esset magistro quod nihil sciret, sic etc.

Sed dato quod uterque faciat quantum ad eum pertinet, et bene utatur officio suo, dico quod non est comparatio, nisi sicut inter discipulum et magistrum: unde in statu perfectiori est praelatus, etiam si des Eliam, vel quemcumque.

1595. Sed est quaestio: Si praelatus est perfectus, nonne tenetur omnia vendere?

Dico quod istud sequeretur, si in hoc quod est *vade, et vende omnia quae habes*, esset perfectio; sed non est, sed est via et praeambulum ad acquirendum perfectionem; ideo non oportet quod vendat ea quae habet. Sed quia hoc raro contingit, quod quis perfectionem cum divitiis habeat, ab eo qui venit ad perfectionem, relinquenda sunt omnia; ideo dat Dominus quod facilius est. Unde si praelatus esset idoneus, et curam bene ministraret, dico quod esset perfectior; sicut aliquis potest dicere: Volo intrare scholas ut addiscam, sed praesumptuosum est dicere, cum nihil sciat, velle se esse magistrum. Unde Augustinus *de Civit. Dei*: *status superior, sine quo populus regi non potest, etsi decenter administretur, indecenter tamen appetitur*.

Item est aliud esse praelatum, et in statu praelati.

1596. Numquid in statu perfectionis sunt sacerdotes plebei, vel curati?

Dico quod non sunt in statu, quia non faciunt statum. Omnis status cum solemnitate datur, ut ordo episcopatus et religio. Cum autem datur plebania, non datur cum solemnitate, unde statum non habent perfectionis: quod patet, quia aliquibus committitur cura et administratio, et si non sit promotus, potest dimittere et uxorari, et aliquando factus est religiosus. Episcopus autem non dimitteret episcopatum, nisi de licentia superioris; curatus potest intrando religionem. Si autem esset in statu perfection, iam caderet a statu, et sic peccaret: unde perfectionem potest habere secundum actum, sed non statum; quia non datur status, nisi cum solemnitate.

to this man, *if you will be perfect*, and if you wish to come to the state of perfection. But the prelate's state is not for acquiring perfection for himself, but for communicating what he has. Hence the Lord said to Peter, *Simon, son of John, do you love me? Feed my sheep* (John 21:17); and he did not say, *if you will be perfect*.

Hence the difference between the perfection of a religious and of a prelate is like the difference between a disciple and a teacher. Hence to the disciple it is said: if you wish to learn, enter a school that you may learn. To the teacher it is said: lecture, and perfect. Hence the state of the religious is more secure, because ignorance is not imputed to them as it is to a prelate. Hence just as it would be ridiculous for a teacher not to know anything, so likewise a prelate.

But given that each performs as much as pertains to him and uses his office well, I say that there is no comparison, just as there is no comparison between a disciple and a teacher. Hence in state, a prelate is more perfect, even if you bring up Elijah, or whomever.

1595. But there is a question: if a prelate is more perfect, is he not obliged to sell all that he has?

I say that this would follow if *go sell what you have* were perfection; but it is not, but rather is a way and a preamble for acquiring perfection. Therefore it is not necessary that he sell all that he has. But since it rarely happens that someone has perfection along with riches, he who comes to perfection should relinquish everything. So the Lord gives what is easier. Hence if a prelate were able, and tended well to his responsibility, I say that it would be more perfect. Just as someone can say: I wish to enter school that I may learn; but it is presumptuous for someone to say, while he knows nothing, I wish to be a teacher. Hence Augustine, in *The City of God*: *the state is higher, without which the people cannot be ruled, and though becomingly conducted, it is unbecomingly desired*.

Likewise, it is one thing to be a prelate, and another thing to be in the state of a prelate.

1596. Are priests of the common people or curates in the state of perfection?

I say that they are not in the state, because they do not make the state. Every state is given with solemnity, as the episcopal or religious orders. But when the simple priesthood is given, it is not given with solemnity; hence they do not have the state of perfection. Which is evident, because if a duty and administration is entrusted to someone, and he is not promoted, he can abandon it and take a wife, and sometimes is made a religious. But a bishop may not abandon a bishopric without the permission of a superior; the curate can abandon his position by entering religion. But if he were in the state of perfection, he would then fall from the state, and thus would sin: hence he can have perfection according to action, but not according to state, because the state is only given with solemnity.

1597. *Vade* ergo *et vende omnia quae habes, et da pauperibus*, quia per istud magnum habebis praemium, quia praemium respondet merito. *Et habebis thesaurum in caelo*. In thesauro duo sunt, stabilitas et abundantia. *Habebis thesaurum* et abundantiam spiritualium. Ps. CXI, 3: *gloria et divitiae in domo eius*. Is. XXXIII, 6: *et erit fides in temporibus tuis, divitiae salutis, sapientia et scientia*.

1598. *Et veni, sequere me*. Hic est finis perfectionis. Unde illi sunt perfecti, qui toto corde sequuntur Deum. Unde Gen. xvn, v. 1: *ambula coram me, et esto perfectus*. *Et sequere me*, idest imitare vita Christi; unde supra XVI, 24: *si quis vult venire post me, abneget semetipsum*. Imitatio enim est in sollicitudine praedicandi, docendi, curam habendi. Unde Chrysostomus: *dictum est Petro, 'sequere me,' scilicet in suscipiendo curam totius mundi*. Iob XXIII, 11: *vestigia eius custodivit pes meus*.

1599. *Cum autem audisset adolescens verbum, abiit tristis*. Ostenditur affectus, quia *abiit tristis*. Hoc accidit cum desideramus aliquid, et non possumus, habere ut optamus; unde iste desiderabat perfectionem, et audivit quid per hoc debebat habere. Et quia cupidus erat, *abiit tristis*.

Et quare? *Erat enim habens multas possessiones*. Augustinus: *ille qui dimisit voluntatem habendi, est magni meriti, quia imputatur ei quod habere potuit; sed maioris meriti est dimittere quod iam acquisivit, quia difficilius est quod evellantur quae iam sunt unita, quam quae non sunt unita*. Et hoc patet, quia iste, qui habebat, separari non poterat.

1600. *Iesus autem dixit discipulis suis*. Hic ponitur ratio praedictae doctrlnae. Et

primo assignatur ratio;

secundo satisfacit admirationi discipulorum, ibi *auditis autem his, discipuli mirabantur valde*.

1601. Dicit ergo *Iesus autem dixit discipulis suis* etc. Occasio dicendi verbum istud fuit, quia ille *abiit tristis*, quia dixerat, *vade, vende quae habes* etc. *Quia difficile dives intrabit in regnum caelorum*: non dicit impossibile.

Et dicit *dives*, non qui habet divitias: quia quidam habent, et non amant eas, quidam autem habent, et amant, et confidunt in eis. Hi qui habent, et non amant, possunt ingredi in regnum caelorum. Si enim hoc non essct, non diceret Paulus 1 ad Tim. VI, 17: *divitibus huius saeculi praecipe non sublime sapere, neque sperare in incerto divitiarum*. Sed qui habet et amat, *difficile est* etc. Supra XIII, 22: *sollicitudo saeculi huius, et fallacia divitiarum suffocant verbum*. Prov. c. XXVIII, 20: *qui festinat ditari non erit innocens*. Eccli. XXXI, 8: *beatus*

1597. So *go sell what you have, and give to the poor*, because by this you shall have a great reward, since the reward corresponds to the merit. *And you will have treasure in heaven*. There are two things in a treasure: stability and abundance. *You will have treasure* and an abundance of spiritual things. *Glory and wealth will be in his house* (Ps 111:3). *And there will be faith in your times: riches of salvation, wisdom and knowledge* (Isa 33:6).

1598. *And come follow me*. Here is the end of perfection. Hence those are perfect who follow God with their whole heart. Hence *walk before me, and be perfect* (Gen 17:1). *And come follow me*, i.e., imitate the life of Christ; hence above, *if any man wants to come after me, let him deny himself* (Matt 16:24). For the imitation is solicitude for preaching, teaching, and having care. Hence Chrysostom: *it was said to Peter, 'follow me,' namely in undertaking the care of the whole world*. As it is written: *my foot has followed his steps* (Job 23:11).

1599. *And when the young man had heard this word, he went away sad*. The emotion is shown: *he went away sad*. This happens when we desire something and cannot have it as we wish; hence this man desired perfection, and heard what he should have through this. And because he was greedy, *he went away sad*.

And why? *For he had great possessions*. Augustine: *he who gave up the will to have things has great merit, because it is attributed to him that could have had; but it is of greater merit to give up what he has already acquired, because it is more difficult to uproot things which are already united with him, than to uproot things which are not so united*. And this is clear, for this man, who had many things, was unable to be separated from them.

1600. *Then Jesus said to his disciples*. Here the reason for the aforesaid teaching is set out. And

first, he gives the reason;

second, he satisfies the wonderment of the disciples, at *and when they had heard this, the disciples wondered very much*.

1601. It says, *then Jesus said to his disciples*. The occasion for speaking this word was that the man *went away sad* because he had said, *go sell what you have*. Now he says, *a rich man will hardly enter into the kingdom of heaven*: he does not say it is impossible.

And he says, *a rich man*, not one who has riches. For some men have riches and do not love them, while some have and love and place hope in them. These who have and do not love can enter into the kingdom of heaven. For if this were not so, Paul would not have said, *charge the rich of this world not to be highminded, nor to trust in the uncertainty of riches* (1 Tim 6:17). But he who has and loves riches **will hardly enter into the kingdom of heaven**. Above, *the care of this world and the deceitfulness of riches chokes up the word* (Matt 13:22). *He who makes haste to be rich, will*

not be innocent (Prov 28:20). *Blessed is the rich man who is found without blemish: and who has not gone after gold* (Sir 31:8). But this is difficult, so there follows: *who is he, and we will praise him? For he has done wonderful things in his life* (Sir 31:9).

1602. He adds something which seems to pertain to impossibility; hence he says, *and again I say to you: it is easier for a camel to pass through the eye of a needle, than for a rich man to enter into the kingdom of heaven*.

Above, the Lord had said that the rich man would enter into the kingdom of heaven with difficulty; here, that it is impossible, just as it is impossible that a camel pass through the eye of a needle. Hence take it that it is difficult for a rich man who has riches and does not love them, but it is impossible for the one who loves and places hope in them to enter into the kingdom of heaven. For that a camel cannot enter through the eye of a needle, this is from nature; but that a rich man who loves riches cannot enter into the kingdom of heaven, this is from the divine justice. But all things could be overturned before the divine justice could be changed.

Others, as Jerome: *impossibility is not indicated, but difficulty*. It is found in a certain Gloss, whose author is unknown, that there was a certain gate in Jerusalem which was called 'the eye of the needle,' through which camels carrying burdens could not pass. In this way, a rich man cannot enter into the kingdom of heaven unless he unburden himself of affection for riches. But it is easier for a camel to be unburdened than for a rich man to lay aside this affection.

Chrysostom explains it mystically: the camel signifies the gentiles, who are burdened with the sin of idolatry, and the rich men signify the Jews; and Christ is the needle, and the passion is the eye of the needle. Hence it was easier for the gentile people to pass through the passion of Christ than the Jews, because they could only come by giving up the ceremonies of the law, and this they did not do. Hence it was asked of a demon what is the heavier sin, and he said: to have something from another's belongings. To which it was responded: you are lying! Oh, but indeed, he says, for I often lose other sinners, but these I do not lose.

Or thus: *it is easier for a camel*, as by the rich man we understand the proud man; by the camel Christ, by the eye of the needle Christ's passion; therefore, it was easier for the camel to pass through the eye of the needle than for the proud man to be humbled.

1603. *And when they had heard this, the disciples wondered very much, saying: who then can be saved?* Above, the Lord gave the reason for his teaching; here he satisfies the disciples' wonderment. And

first, the wonderment is set out;

second, the satisfaction, at *and Jesus looking, said to them*.

1604. Dicit ergo *auditis autem his, discipuli mirabantur valde, dicentes: Quis poterit salvus esse?*

Sed hic est quaestio litteralis. Cum plures sint pauperes quam divites, et divites difficile sit salvari, quomodo dicunt *quis poterit salvus esse?*

Respondetur quod intellexerunt quod intelligeret etiam de pauperibus qui sunt divites voluntate; quia plures sunt pauperes, qui voluntate sunt divites. Item ipsi iam erant effecti solliciti pro toto mundo: ideo ingruebat eis illa sollicitudo, quae habetur II ad Cor. XI, 28, ut solliciti erant rectores omnium creaturarum.

1605. *Aspiciens autem Iesus dixit eis: apud homines hoc impossibile est* etc. Hic satisfacit admirationi dicens: *apud homines hoc impossibile est, apud Deum autem omnia possibilia*.

Sed quid est quod dicit? Videtur enim quod periit liberum arbitrium, si impossibile est apud homines. Verum est quod homo a se habet ut possit peccare; sed resurgere, et opera salutis facere, hoc non habet a se sine auxilio gratiae Dei: ipse enim Deus est qui ista potest. Ad Rom. IX, 6: *non est currentis, nec volentis, sed miserentis Dei*. Unde Iob c. XLII, 1: *scio quod omnia pates, et apud te non est impossibile*. Unde secundum potentiam humanam impossibile est hominem salvum fieri, quia potentia humana non immutat voluntatem; sed solius Dei est immutare eam, sicut habetur Phil. 11, 13: *qui operatur in nobis velle et perficere*.

1606. Consequenter determinat de praemio perfectorum. Et

    primo ponitur interrogatio;

    secundo responsio, ibi *Iesus autem dixit illis*.

1607. Petrus audierat paupertatem laudari, et audierat: *vade, et vende omnia quae habes, et da pauperibus*. Audierat etiam quod *difficile est divites intrare in regnum caelorum*, ideo reputabat Petrus magnum fecisse, quia omnia dimiserat; unde dicit *tunc respondens Petrus dixit ei: ecce nos reliquimus omnia*. Et quia non solum illud audierat, *vade, et vende*, sed ulterius, *et sequere me* etc.; ideo addit Petrus *et secuti sumus te*. Relinquere omnia non facit perfectionem, sed relinquere omnia et sequi Christum, quia multi philosophi reliquerunt omnia. Sed reliquerat Petrus navem et rete. Sed Petrus magis de affectu suo laudatur quam de eo quod reliquit, quia ita prona voluntate dimisit, quod etiam totum dimisisset, si habuisset. Item sciebat quod Christus sciebat suam voluntatem, ideo dicit *ecce nos* etc.

Per quod dedit exemplum, quod non reputentur pauca dimisisse qui dimiserunt quod habebant, etiamsi pauca haberent.

1604. It says then, *and when they had heard this, the disciples wondered very much, saying: who then can be saved?*

But here there is a literal question. Since there are more poor men than rich men, and rich men are saved with difficulty, how can they say, *who then can be saved?*

It is responded that they had understood that he meant it even of the poor who are rich in desire; for there are many poor men who are rich in desire. Also, they were already made solicitous for the whole world: so that solicitude was coming over them (2 Cor 11:28), as they were the rulers of all creatures.

1605. *And Jesus looking, said to them: with men this is impossible*. Here he satisfies their wonderment, saying: *with men this is impossible, but with God all things are possible*.

But why does he say this? For it seems that he destroys free will, if it is impossible with men. It is true that man has from himself that he can sin; but to rise again, and do the works of salvation, this he does not have from himself without the help of God's grace: for God is the one who can accomplish these things. *So then it is not of him who wills, nor of him who runs, but of God who shows mercy* (Rom 9:16). Hence, *I know that you can do all things, and no thought is hid from you* (Job 42:2). Hence according to human power it is impossible that a man be saved; because human power does not change the will, but it belongs only to God to change it, as is written, *for it is God who works in you, both to will and to accomplish* (Phil 2:13).

1606. Next, he determines about the reward of the perfect. And

    first, a question is set down;

    second, the response, at *and Jesus said to them*.

1607. Peter had heard poverty be praised, and he had heard *go sell what you have, and give to the poor*. He had also heard that *a rich man will hardly enter into the kingdom of heaven*. For this reason, Peter considered that he had done a great thing, because he had left everything; hence it says, *then Peter answering, said to him: behold we have left all things*. And since he had heard not only *go sell*, but beyond that, *and come follow me*, Peter added, *and have followed you*. To leave everything does not make for perfection, but to leave everything and follow Christ, because many philosophers have left everything. But Peter had left a boat and a net! But Peter is praised more for his affection than for what he left, because he left his possessions with a will so inclined that he would also have left it all if he had had more. Also, he knew that Christ knew his will, so he said, *behold, we have left all things*.

By which he gave an example, that those who have left what they had should not be considered to have left little, even if they had little.

1608. And Jerome says that to leave possessions does not make for perfection, but to follow the Lord. And one follows God in many ways. With the mind, through contemplation; *we will know, and we will follow on, that we may know the Lord* (Hos 6:3). Hence those follow God who have God before their eyes, and know God by way of contemplation. Likewise, one follows the Lord by observing the commandments; *my sheep hear my voice: and I know them, and they follow me* (John 10:27). Likewise, through imitation of his works; *my foot has followed his steps* (Job 23:11). Likewise, through contempt of self and of one's own; above, **if any man wants to come after me, let him deny himself, and take up his cross, and follow me** (Matt 16:24). Likewise through purity of mind and body; *these are they who were not defiled with women: for they are virgins. These follow the Lamb wherever he goes* (Rev 14:4). Voluntary poverty disposes one to this following.

1609. *And Jesus said to them: amen, I say to you*. Here he treats of the reward of perfection. And

first, he sets out the reward of the apostles' perfection;

second, the reward of others' perfection;

third, he excludes a certain objection.

The second is at *and every one who has left house, or brethren*; the third, at *and many who are first, will be last*.

1610. He says then, *amen I say to you*. For since he willed that what he had said be certain, he professes to have spoken the truth, by saying, *amen*. And to show that perfection is not in *go sell what you have*, but in *follow me*, he says that *you, who have followed me, in the regeneration . . . also will sit on twelve seats*.

There are two regenerations. One is of the spirit, which comes about through grace in baptism, about which Peter says, *who according to his great mercy has regenerated us unto a lively hope* (1 Pet 1:3). Likewise, there is a regeneration of the body, for just as the spirit is regenerated by grace, so also in the resurrection he will revive our bodies. *Who will reform the body of our lowness, made like to the body of his glory* (Phil 3:21).

Some explain this as about the first regeneration, and punctuate it this way: *you who have followed me in the regeneration*, i.e., you have been regenerated by grace, *will sit*.

Chrysostom explains it the same way, but he does not punctuate it that way; hence he says that he promised them a reward in the present, this way: *you who have followed me . . . will sit*. The present Church is the faith of Christ. In the Church there are different states of men. And although all the virtues are necessary for salvation, yet one man is more praiseworthy in the act of one virtue than another: one in faith, another in chastity, another in charity. And just as it is in the various faithful, so it is also in the apostles, because Peter was the most fervent zealot for the faith, but John was strong in chastity, and so with the others. Thus those who are fervent in faith are seats of Peter, those who

Christi, quia omnes virtutes fuerunt in eo; ideo promisit eis quod ipsi essent futuri pastores Ecclesiae.

Aliter, secundum Augustinum, accipitur de regeneratione, scilicet pro resurrectione *amen dico vobis in regeneratione*, idest in resurrectione, cum revocabuntur secundum corpus et animam, *sedebitis*, scilicet in sede maiestatis, idest iudiciariam potestatem habebitis, *iudicantes duodecim tribus Israel*, quia sicut dedit Deus Filio iudicium, sic et datur his qui secuti sunt eum.

1611. Sed quid est quod dicit *super tribus Israel*? Numquid alios non iudicabunt? Quare ergo plus dicit *super duodecim tribus Israel*? Intelligitur tota plebs fidelium totius mundi, quia intravit gentilitas in pinguedinem olivae, et facta est concors promissionis factae patribus. Illi autem qui sunt infideles, non iudicabuntur: nam dicit Gregorius quod quidam damnantur, et non iudicantur, ut infideles: quidam autem damnantur, et iudicantur, ut qui crediderunt et perversi fuerunt. Et, ut ponit Hieronymus, aliter condemnantur hostes, aliter qui in fide permansit; quia hostes condemnantur absentes, alii vero praesentes. Ideo iudicabitis duodecim tribus Israel. Quia apostoli conversati sunt cum Iudaeis; ideo dicitur quod iudicabunt duodecim tribus.

Et quomodo? Comparatione, quia eos monuerant. Possent dicere: *quomodo crederemus quod tu esses Deus, qui eras mortaliter vivens inter nos?* etc. Sed dicet Dominus: *vos eratis sapientes in lege, et non credidistis; isti erant piscatores, et crediderunt*.

1612. Chrysostomus quaerit quid magnum datum sit apostolis. Nonne hoc datum etiam est Ninivitis et reginae austri? supra XII, 41.

Dicit Chrysostomus quod ipse modus ostendit auctoritatem iudicandi esse datam apostolis, quia iudicantes auctoritate iudicant sedendo, advocati et accusatores condemnant stando; ideo ad designandum quod apostoli iudicabunt auctoritate, dicit *sedebitis*; de Ninivitis vero dicit *viri Ninivitae surgent in iudicio cum generatione ista, et condemnabunt eam*.

1613. Sed hic est quaestio, quia aliqui damnabuntur et non iudicabuntur: sic aliqui salvabuntur et non iudicabuntur, ut apostoli et apostolici viri; alii vero salvandi iudicabuntur, et merita eorum discutientur. Et qualiter iudicabunt?

Dicunt aliqui per comparationem. Sed hoc non sufficit, quia sic etiam regina austri iudicabit. Quidam dicunt quod per iudicium Christi Sed hoc non sufficit, quia sic omnes sancti approbabunt. Ps. LVII, 11: *laetabitur iustus cum viderit vindictam*. Item dicunt quidam

are fervent in chastity are seats of John, and so with the others. But all are seats of Christ, because all the virtues were in him; therefore he promised them that they would be future pastors of the Church.

In another way, according to Augustine, it is taken as about the regeneration, namely for the resurrection: *amen I say to you . . . in the regeneration*, i.e., in the resurrection, when they will be called back in body and soul, *you also will sit*, namely in the seat of majesty, i.e., you will have the judiciary power, *judging the twelve tribes of Israel*, because just as God gave judgment to the Son, so also it is given to those who have followed him.

1611. But why does he say, *judging the twelve tribes of Israel*? Will they not judge others? Why then does he say rather, *the twelve tribes of Israel*? The whole people of the faithful of the whole world is understood, because the gentility entered into the fatness of the olive tree, and was made a partner in the promises made to the fathers (Rom 11:17). But they will not judge those who are infidels: for Gregory says that some are damned and are not judged, as the infidels; but some are damned and are judged, as those who have believed and were corrupted. And, as Jerome sets out, the enemies are condemned in one way, those who remained in the faith in another way; for the enemies are condemned while absent, but the others are condemned while present. Therefore you will judge the twelve tribes of Israel. Since the apostles passed their lives with the Jews, then it is said that they will judge the twelve tribes.

And how? By comparison, because they warned them. They could say: *how could we believe that you are God, you who lived among us as a mortal?* But the Lord will say: *you were wise in the law, and you did not believe; they were fishermen, and they believed*.

1612. Chrysostom asks what great thing is given to the apostles. Was not this also given to the Ninivites and to the queen of the south (Matt 12:41)?

Chrysostom says that the manner of judging itself shows that the authority of judging was given to the apostles, because those who judge with authority judge sitting down, while those advocates and accusers condemn while standing up; therefore, to indicate that the apostles shall judge with authority, he says, *you also will sit*. But about the Ninivites he says, *the men of Niniveh will rise in judgment with this generation, and will condemn it* (Matt 12:41).

1613. But here there is a question, because some will be damned and will not be judged; in the same way, some will be saved and will not be judged, such as the apostles and the apostolic men; but others to be saved will be judged, and their merits will be examined. And how will they judge?

Some say that they will judge by comparison. But this is not enough, because even the queen of the south will judge in this way. Some say that they will judge through Christ's judgment. But this is not enough, because all the saints will approve in this way. *The just will rejoice when he will see the*

per quamdam venerabilem iustitiam, quia elevabuntur iusti in aera Christo obviam, et erunt assessores Christi. Sed hoc etiam non sufficit, quia dicit *sedebitis* et *vos iudicantes*. Dicunt quidam quod iudicabunt sicut liber iudicat: iudicat enim, quia ibi scriptae sunt leges, quae illum iudicant; sicut corda apostolorum et iustorum, qui custodierunt mandata Dei, erunt liber eos condemnans. *Mortui iudicati sunt, libris apertis*, Apoc. xx. v. 12. Sed plus est, quia aliud exercebunt. Unde in Ps. cxux, 6: *gladii ancipites in manibus eorum*.

Quomodo ergo iudicabunt? Videte. Erit iudicium mentale, quia virtute divina fiet quod singulis ad memoriam omnia peccata sua reducantur. Unde deceptus fuit Lactantius qui ponit resurrectionem fieri ante iudicium per mille annos. Istud ergo erit mentale iudicium, quia per virtutem divinam reducentur ad memoriam ea, quae fecit unusquisque. Sed non est inconveniens quod aliquis recipiat ab aliquo lumen aliquod, quia angeli a Deo recipiunt, et homines ab angelis; ideo non est mirum quod homines illuminentur ab apostolis qui pleni erunt; ideo non solum iudicabunt, sed etiam quoddam lumen ab eis alii iusti recipient. Sed differenter Christus et apostoli, quia Christus auctoritate, illi vero sicut promulgatores: sicut lex per angelos data est, sic et executio iudicii fiet per angelos, quia ecce angeli dicuntur, Iob XXXVI, 6: *pauperibua iudicium dabitur*, qui iustitiam secuti sunt, et omnia dimiserunt.

1614. Et quare iudicabunt? Una ratio, quia peccata de mundo sunt. Unde illi qui debent iudicare, qebent esse de extra mundum, et tales sunt apostoli et apostolici viri; unde Io. xv, 9: *elegi vos de mundo*. Item dicit Philosophus quod virtuosus est iudex omnium hominum, sicut gustus omnium gustabilium. Sicut ergo qui vult aliquid gustare, dat ad gustandum ei qui habet gustum sanum: sic cum virtuosus habeat gustum sanum, ideo ipse regula est omnium actuum; ideo perfecti viri ut regula iudicabunt.

Item alia ratio, quia sunt alieni a mundo, ideo magis ferventer sequuntur Christum. Isti ergo debent magis iudicare, quia de rebus contemplandis incalescunt; Ps. XXXVIII, 4: *concaluit cor meum intra me, et in meditatione mea exardescet ignis*. Ideo etiam quia magis assueti, sunt magis ferventes. Item quia erant pauperes et magis abiecti, sed meritum abiectionis est exaltatio; ideo exaltabuntur. Ideo dicit *sedebitis iudicantes* etc.

revenge (Ps 57:11). Likewise, some say that the apostles will judge through a certain venerable justice, because the just will be raised up in the air to meet Christ, and they will be Christ's counselors. But even this is not enough, because he says, *you also will sit* and *judging*. Some say that they will judge as a book judges: for it judges, since laws which judge one are written in it; as the hearts of the apostles and the just, who will have kept God's commandments, will be a book condemning them. *And the dead were judged with books open* (Rev 20:12). But it is more, because they will administer something else. Hence, *and two-edged swords in their hands* (Ps 149:6).

So how will they judge? Attend. There will be a mental judgment, for it will come about by the divine power that for each man all his sins will be brought back to memory. Hence Lactantius was deceived: he held that the resurrection would happen one thousand years before the judgment. So it will be a mental judgment, because by the divine power those things which each man has done will be brought back to memory. But it is not unfitting that someone should receive some light from someone, since the angels receive light from God, and men from angels; therefore, it is no marvel that men shall be enlightened by the apostles, who will be full. Therefore, they will not only judge, but also the other just men will receive a certain light from them. But Christ and the apostles will judge in different ways, because Christ will judge with authority, but they as promulgators; as the law was given through angels, so also the execution of judgment will come about through angels, for behold, those are called angels, *he gives judgment to the poor* (Job 36:6), who have followed after justice and have left everything.

1614. And why will they judge? One reason, because sins are from the world. Hence those who should judge should be from outside the world, and such were the apostles and the apostolic men; hence, *I have chosen you out of the world* (John 15:19). Likewise, the Philosopher says that the virtuous man is the judge of all men, as taste is the judge of all tastable things. So just as he who wishes to taste something gives it to someone who has a healthy sense of taste for tasting, so, since the virtuous man has a healthy sense of taste, he himself is the measure of all actions. Therefore perfect men will judge as measures.

Likewise another reason: since they are foreign to the world, they follow Christ more fervently. Therefore, these men should judge, because they are more heated about the things to be considered. *My heart grew hot within me: and in my meditation a fire shall flame out* (Ps 38:4). For this reason also, since they are more familiar, they are more fervent. Likewise also, because they were poor men and more downcast, but the reward of being downcast is exaltation; therefore they will be exalted. For this reason, he says, *you also will sit on twelve seats judging*.

1615. Sed numquid Judas iudicabit? Non, quia istae promissiones semper sunt sub conditione; ideo Dominus dicit *vos qui secuti estis me* etc. Unde qui secutus fuerit, et perseveraverit, iudicabit etc.

Sed si isti iudicant, quid faciet Paulus? Si iam sedes plenae sunt, ubi ergo Paulus? Augustinus dicit quod per duodecim significatur universitas, quae per septem volvitur. Numerus ergo duodenus fit ex multitudine septem, quia septenarius numerus consistit ex tribus et quatuor, et ter quatuor sunt duodecim, vel quater tria; ideo per istum numerum significatur universitas electorum.

1616. *Et omnis qui reliquerit domum vel fratres* etc. Posito praemio apostolorum, hic ponitur aliorum: et sunt hic quaestiones. Prima quare apostolis nihil temporale promisit, aliis vero aliquod temporale, quia *centuplum accipiet* etc. Et hoc patet, quia in Marco x, 30 habetur quod centuplum in praesenti.

Secundum Chrysostomum promissum fuit apostolis aliquod temporale, quia iudicium in Ecclesia Dei, ut prius dictum est. Vel aliter, quia allicitur unusquisque secundum illud ad quod afficitur. Unde qui dimisit mundum et ea quae sunt in mundo, non alliciunt eum ea quae sunt in mundo; sed alii, qui alligati sunt rebus saecularibus, alliciuntur per eas. Ideo apostolis, quia totum dimiserant, nihil temporale promisit; sed aliis, quia habent affectum ad temporalia; ideo apostolis iudicium promisit. Vel, secundum Origenem, quod dictum est, *in regeneratione*, hoc est praemium eorum, qui omnia reliquerunt propter Christum.

Sed posset aliquis dicere: nolo omnia propter te dimittere, sed dimittam unam domum, vel unum agrum etc. Dico quod st aliquid relinquis, aliquid habebis; sed si omnia, iudex eris.

1617. Sed est alia quaestio. Dixit *domum*, et de hoc non est dubium; sed dicit *patrem aut matrem* etc. Qui iubet dimitti patrem aut matrem, iubet peccatum. Item ipse praecepit quod non dimittatur uxor, quod honorentur parentes.

Dicendum quod in istis duo considerantur. Naturalis affinitas; et haec non est contemnenda, sed bene faciendum est eis si indigent. Aliquando vero retrahunt a servitio Dei: unde tunc sunt sicut membrum scandalizans et tunc abscindendum est illud membrum; et ideo praecepit haec relinquere. Item alia ratio, quia Dominus praevidit tempus futurae persecutionis, quod insurgeret frater contra fratrem; ideo vult hominem separari ab eis.

1618. Alia quaestio est cum dicit *centuplum accipiet* etc., quomodo intelligatur.

1615. But will Judas judge? No, because these promises are always under a condition; for this reason the Lord says, *you, who have followed me, in the regeneration*. Hence he who will have followed, and persevered, will judge.

But if these men will judge, what will Paul do? If the seats are already full, then where will Paul sit? Augustine says that universality is signified by twelve, which is unfolded by seven. The number twelve comes from the multitude seven, because the number seven consists of three and four, and three fours are twelve, or four threes; so by this number the universality of the elect is signified.

1616. *And every one who has left house, or brethren*. The apostles' reward being set out, here is set out the others' reward. And there are questions here. First, why did he promise nothing temporal to the apostles, but to the others something temporal? For they *will receive a hundredfold*. And this is clear, because in Mark, it says that the hundredfold is in the present (Mark 10:30).

According to Chrysostom, something temporal had been promised to the apostles, namely judgment in God's Church, as was said before. Or in another way, the things which are in the world do not entice him who has left the world and the things which are in the world; but the others, who are bound to secular things, are drawn by those things. Therefore he promised nothing temporal to the apostles, who had left all; but he promised something temporal to the others, since they had an affection for temporal things. For this reason, he promised judgment to the apostles. Or, according to Origen, what was said before, *in the regeneration*, this is the reward of those who have left all for Christ's sake.

But someone could say: I do not want to leave all things for your sake, but I will leave one house, or one field. I say that if you relinquish something, you will have something; but if you relinquish all things, you will be a judge.

1617. But there is another question. He said, *house*, and there is no doubt about this; but he says, *father, or mother, or wife, or children*. He who orders father or mother to be abandoned, orders a sin. Likewise, he himself commanded that a wife not be sent away, and that parents should be honored.

One should say that in these matters two things are considered: natural affinity, and this is not to be despised, but one should do well for them if they are in need. But sometimes they draw one back from God's service: hence then they are like a member which scandalizes, and then that member should be cut off. And for this reason he commanded them to leave these. Likewise another reason, because the Lord foresaw the time of the future persecution, that brother would rise up against brother, so he willed that men be separated from them.

1618. Another question is when he says, *will receive a hundredfold*, how it is understood.

Quidam dixerunt quod sancti resurgent ante iudicium per mille annos, et tunc Christus habebit regnum completum: et tunc qui dimisit domum, habebit centuplum. Hieronymus improbat, quia non habebit centum patres etc. Item turpitudo significatur, quia non habebit centum uxores.

Ideo dicit Augustinus quod intelligitur quoad spiritualia. Unde *non elegit Dominus pauperes in hoc mundo et haeredes regni*: unde intelligitur gratia Dei, quae ponderat omni eo quod dimittis, et in infinitum; ideo ponit finitum pro infinito. Unde **centuplum accipiet**, idest aliquid quod valet centuplum.

Origenes dicit quod etiam ad litteram est intelligendum. Tu dimittis agrum, ex providentia Dei erit quod invenies multos ad servitium tuum; unde conveniet eis illud II Cor. VI, 10: *tamquam nihil habentes, et omnia possidentes*. Item fratres invenies, idest omnes viros spirituales. Item praeter hanc vitam aeternam; Io. x, 27: *oves meae vocem meam cudiunt, et ego cognosco eas, et sequuntur me, et ego vitam aeternam do eis*.

1619. Consequenter introducit incidens **multi autem erunt primi novissimi, et novissimi primi**. Illi qui relinquunt aliquid propter Christum, vel omnia, st negligenter vivant, habebuntne istud praemium?

Dico quod non, quia imperfecte assumpserunt, et non erunt primi, sed novissimi. Vel aliter, quia possent dicere **vos qui reliquistis omnia** etc. iudicabimus sic. Qui per superbiam elati erant primi, sunt novissimi. Origenes dicit quod potest intelligi de his qui veniunt ad Christum, et tepide, vivunt; post veniunt alii ferventes, et fervore suo transcendunt alios. Vel **primos** vocat qui ex Christianis nati sunt, qui novissimi facti sunt respectu aliorum qui fuerunt ex gentibus vel Iudaeis. Vel potest referri ad homines, vel angelos; quia qui primi sunt in ordine angelorum, facti sunt novissimi per culpam; et novissimi, idest homines, fient primi et superiores.

Some have said that the saints will rise one thousand years before the judgment, and then Christ will have complete rule. And then he who has left a home, will have a hundred. Jerome disproves this, because they will not have one hundred fathers, etc. Likewise, baseness is indicated, because they will not have one hundred wives.

So Augustine says that it is understood with regard to spiritual things. Hence, *has not God chosen the poor in this world . . . and heirs of the kingdom?* (Jas. 2:5): hence the grace of God is understood, which outweighs all that you have left, and infinitely. So he sets down the finite for the infinite. Hence they **will receive a hundredfold**, i.e., something which is worth a hundred.

Origen says that it should also be understood literally. You have left a field, and it will be, by God's providence, that you will find many at your service; hence, it can be applied to them: *as having nothing, and possessing all things* (2 Cor 6:10). Likewise, you will find brothers, i.e., every spiritual man. Likewise, beyond this, eternal life; *my sheep hear my voice: and I know them, and they follow me and I give them eternal life* (John 10:27).

1619. Next, cutting in, he brings in, **and many who are first, will be last: and the last will be first**. Those who leave something for Christ's sake, or all things, if they live negligently, will they have this reward?

I say not, because they received imperfectly, and they will not be first, but last. Or in another way, because they could say: **we have left all things**, thus we will judge. Those who were first, lifted up by pride, are last. Origen says that it can be understood of those who come to Christ, and live tepidly; afterward come others who are fervent, and by their fervor they transcend the others. Or, the **first** means those who are born from Christians, who were born last with respect to others who were born from the gentiles or the Jews. Or it can be referred to men and angels: for those who are first in the order of angels are made last through guilt; and the last, i.e., men, shall be made first, and higher.

Chapter 20

Lecture 1

20:1 Simile est regnum caelorum homini patrifamilias, qui exiit primo mane conducere operarios in vineam suam. [n. 1621]

20:2 Conventione autem facta cum operariis ex denario diurno, misit eos in vineam suam. [n. 1627]

20:3 Et egressus circa horam tertiam vidit alios stantes in foro otiosos, [n. 1628]

20:4 et dixit illis: ite et vos in vineam meam, et quod iustum fuerit, dabo vobis. [n. 1630]

20:5 Illi autem abierunt. Iterum autem exiit circa horam sextam et nonam, et fecit similiter. [n. 1631]

20:6 Circa undecimam vero exiit, et invenit alios stantes, et dicit illis: quid hic statis tota die otiosi? [n. 1632]

20:7 Dicunt ei: quia nemo nos conduxit. Dicit illis: ite et vos in vineam meam. [n. 1634]

20:8 Cum sero autem factum esset, dicit dominus vineae procuratori suo: voca operarios, et redde illis mercedem, incipiens a novissimis usque ad primos. [n. 1635]

20:9 Cum venissent ergo qui circa undecimam horam venerant, acceperunt singulos denarios. [n. 1639]

20:10 Venientes autem et primi arbitrati sunt quod plus essent accepturi; acceperunt autem et ipsi singulos denarios. [n. 1639]

20:1 Ὁμοία γάρ ἐστιν ἡ βασιλεία τῶν οὐρανῶν ἀνθρώπῳ οἰκοδεσπότῃ, ὅστις ἐξῆλθεν ἅμα πρωῒ μισθώσασθαι ἐργάτας εἰς τὸν ἀμπελῶνα αὐτοῦ.

20:2 συμφωνήσας δὲ μετὰ τῶν ἐργατῶν ἐκ δηναρίου τὴν ἡμέραν ἀπέστειλεν αὐτοὺς εἰς τὸν ἀμπελῶνα αὐτοῦ.

20:3 καὶ ἐξελθὼν περὶ τρίτην ὥραν εἶδεν ἄλλους ἑστῶτας ἐν τῇ ἀγορᾷ ἀργοὺς

20:4 καὶ ἐκείνοις εἶπεν· ὑπάγετε καὶ ὑμεῖς εἰς τὸν ἀμπελῶνα, καὶ ὃ ἐὰν ᾖ δίκαιον δώσω ὑμῖν.

20:5 οἱ δὲ ἀπῆλθον. πάλιν [δὲ] ἐξελθὼν περὶ ἕκτην καὶ ἐνάτην ὥραν ἐποίησεν ὡσαύτως.

20:6 περὶ δὲ τὴν ἑνδεκάτην ἐξελθὼν εὗρεν ἄλλους ἑστῶτας καὶ λέγει αὐτοῖς· τί ὧδε ἑστήκατε ὅλην τὴν ἡμέραν ἀργοί;

20:7 λέγουσιν αὐτῷ· ὅτι οὐδεὶς ἡμᾶς ἐμισθώσατο. λέγει αὐτοῖς· ὑπάγετε καὶ ὑμεῖς εἰς τὸν ἀμπελῶνα.

20:8 ὀψίας δὲ γενομένης λέγει ὁ κύριος τοῦ ἀμπελῶνος τῷ ἐπιτρόπῳ αὐτοῦ· κάλεσον τοὺς ἐργάτας καὶ ἀπόδος αὐτοῖς τὸν μισθὸν ἀρξάμενος ἀπὸ τῶν ἐσχάτων ἕως τῶν πρώτων.

20:9 καὶ ἐλθόντες οἱ περὶ τὴν ἑνδεκάτην ὥραν ἔλαβον ἀνὰ δηνάριον.

20:10 καὶ ἐλθόντες οἱ πρῶτοι ἐνόμισαν ὅτι πλεῖον λήμψονται· καὶ ἔλαβον [τὸ] ἀνὰ δηνάριον καὶ αὐτοί.

20:1 The kingdom of heaven is like a householder, who went out early in the morning to hire laborers into his vineyard. [n. 1621]

20:2 And having agreed with the laborers for a denarius a day, he sent them into his vineyard. [n. 1627]

20:3 And going about the third hour, he saw others standing in the market place idle. [n. 1628]

20:4 And he said to them: you also go into my vineyard, and I will give you what will be just. [n. 1630]

20:5 And they went their way. And again he went out about the sixth and the ninth hour, and did in like manner. [n. 1631]

20:6 But about the eleventh hour he went out and found others standing, and he said to them: why do you stand here all the day idle? [n. 1632]

20:7 They say to him: because no man has hired us. He said to them: you also go into my vineyard. [n. 1634]

20:8 And when evening had come, the lord of the vineyard said to his steward: call the laborers and pay them their hire, beginning from the last even to the first. [n. 1635]

20:9 When therefore those had come, who came about the eleventh hour, each man received a denarius. [n. 1639]

20:10 But when the first also came, they thought that they should receive more, and they also each received a denarius. [n. 1639]

²⁰:¹¹ Et accipientes murmurabant adversus patremfamilias, [n. 1641]	²⁰:¹¹ λαβόντες δὲ ἐγόγγυζον κατὰ τοῦ οἰκοδεσπότου	²⁰:¹¹ And receiving it they murmured against the master of the house, [n. 1641]
²⁰:¹² dicentes: hi novissimi una hora fecerunt, et pares illos nobis fecisti, qui portavimus pondus diei et aestus? [n. 1641]	²⁰:¹² λέγοντες· οὗτοι οἱ ἔσχατοι μίαν ὥραν ἐποίησαν, καὶ ἴσους ἡμῖν αὐτοὺς ἐποίησας τοῖς βαστάσασι τὸ βάρος τῆς ἡμέρας καὶ τὸν καύσωνα.	²⁰:¹² saying: these last have worked only one hour, and you have made them equal to us, who have borne the burden of the day and the heats. [n. 1641]
²⁰:¹³ At ille respondens uni eorum dixit: amice, non facio tibi iniuriam. Nonne ex denario convenisti mecum? [n. 1643]	²⁰:¹³ ὁ δὲ ἀποκριθεὶς ἑνὶ αὐτῶν εἶπεν· ἑταῖρε, οὐκ ἀδικῶ σε· οὐχὶ δηναρίου συνεφώνησάς μοι;	²⁰:¹³ But answering he said to one of them: friend, I do you no wrong, did you not agree with me for a denarius? [n. 1643]
²⁰:¹⁴ Tolle quod tuum est, et vade. Volo autem et huic novissimo dare sicut et tibi. [n. 1644]	²⁰:¹⁴ ἆρον τὸ σὸν καὶ ὕπαγε. θέλω δὲ τούτῳ τῷ ἐσχάτῳ δοῦναι ὡς καὶ σοί·	²⁰:¹⁴ Take what is yours and go your way; I will also give to this last even as to you. [n. 1644]
²⁰:¹⁵ Aut non licet mihi quod volo facere? An oculus tuus nequam est quia ego bonus sum? [n. 1645]	²⁰:¹⁵ [ἢ] οὐκ ἔξεστίν μοι ὃ θέλω ποιῆσαι ἐν τοῖς ἐμοῖς; ἢ ὁ ὀφθαλμός σου πονηρός ἐστιν ὅτι ἐγὼ ἀγαθός εἰμι;	²⁰:¹⁵ Or is it not lawful for me to do what I will? Is your eye evil, because I am good? [n. 1645]
²⁰:¹⁶ Sic erunt novissimi primi, et primi novissimi. Multi enim sunt vocati, pauci autem electi. [n. 1647]	²⁰:¹⁶ οὕτως ἔσονται οἱ ἔσχατοι πρῶτοι καὶ οἱ πρῶτοι ἔσχατοι.	²⁰:¹⁶ So will the last be first, and the first last. For many are called, but few chosen. [n. 1647]

1620. Supra Dominus egit de perventione ad regnum per viam communis salutis, et per viam perfectionis; et quia quidam credunt indebite pervenire, ideo repelluntur. Et

primo illi qui intendunt venire propter temporis antiquitatem;

secundo qui propter carnis originem. Secunda ibi *et ascendens Iesus Ierosolymam* et cetera.

Primum ergo proponitur sub parabola patrisfamilias et conductorum.

Primo ponit parabolam;

secundo concludit id ad quod prodest parabola, ibi *sic erunt novissimi primi, et primi novissimi*.

Parabola duas habet partes.

Primo agit de conductione;

secundo de remuneratione. Secunda ibi *cum sero autem factum esset* et cetera.

Circa primum ponuntur quatuor conductiones, quae sunt invitationes operariorum ad operandum.

Secunda ibi *et egressus circa horam tertiam* et cetera.

Tertia ibi *iterum autem exiit circa horam sextam* et cetera.

Quarta ibi *circa undecimam vero exiit*.

Circa primum tria tangit.

Primo tangitur conducens;

secundo ponuntur conducti;

1620. Above the Lord treated of arrival at the kingdom through the way of common salvation, and through the way of perfection; and since certain ones thought to arrive undeservedly, they are driven away. And

first, those who intend to arrive owing to temporal oldness;

second, those who intend to arrive owing to carnal origin. The second is at *and Jesus going up to Jerusalem* (Matt 20:17).

First then, it is proposed under the parable of the head of a household and the hired workers:

first, he sets out the parable;

second, he concludes that for which the parable is useful, at *so will the last be first, and the first last*.

The parable has two parts:

first, he treats of the hiring;

second, of the payment. The second is at *and when evening had come*.

Concerning the first, four hirings are set down, which are invitations of the workers to work:

the second is at *and going about the third hour*.

The third is at *and again he went out about the sixth and the ninth hour*.

The fourth is at *but about the eleventh hour he went out*.

Concerning the first, he touches upon three things:

first, the one hiring is touched upon;

second, those hired are set out;

tertio modus conducendi.

Secunda ibi *qui exiit primo mane conducere operarios*. Tertia ibi *conventione autem facta* et cetera.

1621. Iste paterfamilias Deus est, cuius familia est totus orbis, sed specialiter creatura rationalis: et dicitur paterfamilias ex similitudine gubernationis; Sap. XIV, 3: *tu autem, Pater, gubernas omnia sapientia*.

1622. *Qui exiit primo mane conducere operarios in vineam suam*. Hic agit de conductis. Primo quaeritur quae sit vinea, qui operarii, quare conducti.

1623. Quid sit vinea ista. Secundum Chrysostomum iustitia est, et quot virtutes producit, tot palmites emittit; Cant. VIII, 12: *vinea mea coram me est*. Gregorius: *per vinea significatur sancta Ecclesia*. Is. V, 7: *vinea Domini exercituum domus Israel est*. Et diversi palmites.

1624. Operarii vero sunt qui ab Adam descenderunt, unde omnes homines; Gen. II, v. 15: *posuit Dominus Adam in paradiso ut operaretur et custodiret illum*. Debet enim unusquisque operari iustitiam, et excolere eam, et habere curam de proximo; Eccli. cap. XVII, 12: *Deus mandavit unicuique de proximo suo*. Similiter praelati sunt operarii; Is. LXI, 3: *et vocabuntur in ea fortes iustitiae, plantatio Domini ad glorificandum*.

1625. Dicuntur autem 'conducti', qui pro merito operari debent, et quasi mercenarii; Iob VII, 1: *militia est vita hominis super terram, et sicut mercenarii dies eius*. Sicut enim mercenarius non statim accipit mercedem, sed expectat, sic nos in vita ista. Sed ad hoc quod sit bonus mercenarius, oportet quod laboret ad commodum domini sui: sic si laboremus in vinea Ecclesiae, totum referre ad Deum debemus. Unde I Cor. X, 31: *omnia ad gloriam domini facite*. Item primo excolit, et post comedit: et sic oportet quod primo excolamus et praeparemus aliorum salutem, post temporalia quaeramus; Sup. cap. VI, 33: ***primum quaerite regnum Dei, et omnia haec adiicientur vobis***; Lc. XVII, 8: *praecinge te, et ministra mihi, donec manducem et bibam, et post haec tu manducabis et bibes*. Item tertio requiritur quod tota die occupetur in labore: sic cultor vineae domini modicum tempus expendat in his quae ad ipsum pertinent, sed necessarium est quod expendamus totum tempus in servitio Dei; I ad Cor. XV, 58: *abundantes in opere Domini semper*. Item verecundatur apparere coram Domino nisi bene fecerit, sic etiam non debet hic apparere coram Domino nisi cum opere bono; Exod. XXIII et XXXIV, 20: *non apparebis coram me vacuus*.

third, the manner of the hiring.

The second is at *who went out early in the morning to hire laborers*. The third is at *and having agreed with the laborers*.

1621. This head of the household is God, whose family is the whole world, but in a special way the rational creatures; and he is called the head of a household based on the likeness of governance. *But your providence, O Father, governs it* (Wis 14:3).

1622. *Who went out early in the morning to hire laborers into his vineyard*. Here he treats of those hired. First is sought what the vineyard is, who the workers are, and why they were hired.

1623. What is this vineyard? According to Chrysostom, it is justice, and it sends out as many shoots as it produces virtues; *my vineyard is before me* (Song 8:12). Gregory: *by the vineyard is signified the holy Church*. And it is written: *for the vineyard of the Lord of hosts is the house of Israel* (Isa 5:7). And the various shoots.

1624. Now the workers are those who are descended from Adam, hence all men; *and the Lord God took man, and put him into the paradise for pleasure, to dress it, and keep it* (Gen 2:15). For each man should work justice, and cultivate it, and have care for his neighbor; *and he gave to every one of them commandment concerning his neighbor* (Sir 17:12). Similarly, prelates are the workers; *and they will be called in it the mighty ones of justice, the planting of the Lord to glorify him* (Isa 61:3).

1625. Those are called 'hired' who should work for a reward, wage workers, as it were; *the life of man upon earth is a warfare, and his days are like the days of a hireling* (Job 7:1). For just as a wage worker does not receive a reward immediately, but expects one, so we do in this life. But to be a good wage worker, he must labor for his lord's benefit; thus if we labor in the vineyard of the Church, we should return the whole thing to God. Hence, *do all to the glory of God* (1 Cor 10:31). Likewise, he first cultivates, and he eats later: and thus it is necessary that we first cultivate and prepare the salvation of others, and afterward seek temporal things. Above, ***seek you therefore first the kingdom of God . . . and all these things will be added unto you*** (Matt 6:33); *gird yourself, and serve me, while I eat and drink, and afterwards you shall eat and drink* (Luke 17:8). Likewise third, it is required that he be occupied with labor the whole day: thus the cultivator of a lord's vineyard spends a small amount of time on the things which pertain to it, but we must spend all our time in the service of God; *always abounding in the work of the Lord* (1 Cor 15:58). Likewise, one is ashamed to appear before a lord unless one has done well; so also, this one should not appear before the Lord except with a good work. *You will not appear empty before me* (Exod 23:15; 34:20).

1626. But let us see what the ***morning*** is. The time of this world is one day; *for a thousand years in your sight are as yesterday, which is past* (Ps 89:4). The various hours are the various ages. The first is from Adam to Noah, and in that time the Lord admonished them, both through messengers and through apparitions, to walk into the vineyard of justice. Or it can be said that a man's whole life is one day. The morning of this day is boyhood. For verdant boyhood is like grass; hence some are called from boyhood, as Jeremiah, Daniel, and John the Baptist were called from boyhood. And for this reason he says, ***who went out early in the morning***.

1627. Next, he determines concerning the mode of hiring; hence he says, ***and having agreed with the laborers for a denarius a day***. This denarius signifies eternal life, because this denarius was worth ten of the usual denarii. Also, the likeness of the king was imprinted on it. Hence what this denarius signifies consists in the observance of the decalogue; above, ***but if you wish to enter into life, keep the commandments*** (Matt 19:17). Likewise, it has the likeness of God; *when he appears, we will be like to him* (1 John 3:2).

1628. Next he treats of the second hiring: ***and going about the third hour***. If we take the one day as the whole of time, as the first hour signifies the time from Adam to Noah, so the second is from Noah to Abraham. Before the promises were made concerning the Christ, he warned many men at that time through angels, and had many men also who warned others. But if we take the one day as the life of one man, the third hour is adolescence, for just as the sun begins to grow warm, so in adolescence the sun of intelligence begins to shine. Likewise, it begins then to be warm; *for the sun rose with a burning heat* (Jas 1:11).

1629. And he found them ***in the market place*** and ***idle***. This marketplace is the present life. Now, a market place denotes a place in which there are quarrels; that place is called a market place in which there is selling and buying, and it signifies the present life, which is full of quarrels, of buying and selling. *The whole world is seated in wickedness* (1 John 5:9). And these men were idle, because they had already lost a part of their life: for not only those who do bad things are called idle, but also those who do not do good. And just as the idle do not obtain the end, so neither these men. The end of man is life eternal; therefore, he who works in the way he should will have it, if he has not been idle; *idleness has taught much evil* (Sir 33:29).

1630. *And he said to them: you also go into my vineyard*. For God repays according to justice; *and the Lord will reward every one according to his justice* (1 Sam 26:23). He did not agree with these men on a denarius. Why did he with the first, and not with these? The reason is according as it is referred to the age of the world. Since Adam was going to sin, he could be excused if he had not known his reward; but he knew, because he tasted. Likewise, the truth is made known more to those who have better senses. Therefore,

innotuit. Sed cum aliis non convenit, quia semper plus quam promittat solvit. Is. LXIV, 4 et I Cor. II, 9: *oculus non vidit absque te, quae praeparasti diligentibus te*.

Item primi conducti fuerunt ad totam diem. Ergo totam mercedem debent habere; ideo promittitur eis denarius diurnus, qui erit plena merces. Sed aliter non dat totam Deo; ideo non convenit cum eo, quia poterat esse quod ferventius operabitur, et sic magis retribuetur; vel ita negligenter, quod non merebitur. Ideo dicit ***et quod iustum fuerit dabo vobis***, quia si recuperent tempus amissum, habebunt mercedem plenam; I ad Cor. III, 13: *uniuscuiusque opus manifestum erit, dies Domini declarabit*. Item primos invitavit ad eundum, sed isti spontanee iverunt; quia in pueris non est discretio, ideo si faciant aliquod bonum, plus videtur esse a Spiritu Sancto, quam a discretione; sed in adolescentia homo movetur proprio consilio. Item de primis dicitur quod misit eos; de istis quod spontanee iverunt.

1631. ***Iterum autem exiit circa horam sextam et nonam***. Secundum quod dies dicitur saeculum, sic hora sexta fuit ab Abraham usque ad David, et nona a David usque ad Christum.

Sed quare coniungit duas horas? Quia tunc fuit populus distinctus, scilicet Iudaicus et gentilis. Unde potest dici quod hora sexta est iuventus, quia sicut in medio die est sol in sui perfectione, sic homo in iuventute. Nona autem hora est senectus: et coniungit istas duas, quia idem est modus vivendi in utraque.

1632. ***Circa vero undecimam horam exiit***. Ponitur quarta conductio: et tria facit.

Primo reprehendit;
secundo excusat;
tertio invitantur.

Secunda ibi ***dicunt ei: quia nemo nos conduxit***. Tertia ibi ***ite et vos in vineam meam***.

1633. Dicit ergo ***circa undecimam vero horam exiit***. Nona hora est tempus Christi. Unde I Io. II, 18 dicitur: *filioli, novissima hora est*. Et ad Hebr. I, 1: *olim loquens Deus patribus in prophetis, novissime diebus istis locutus est nobis in Filio*. Is. LII, v. 6: *ecce ego qui loquebar, adsum*. Vel potest dici senium, sive decrepita aetas, quia quidam in peccato perdurant usque ad aetatem decrepitam. Ps. LXXXIX, 6: *vespere decidat, induret et arescat*.

Et invenit alios stantes. Alios invenit in foro, istos non. Ratio est, secundum Philosophum, quia differentia est inter adolescentes et senes, quia adolescentes toti

since Adam had better senses, it was more truly known to him. But he did not make an agreement with the others, because he always returns more than he promises. *The eye has not seen, O God, besides you, what things you have prepared for those who wait for you* (Isa 64:4; 1 Cor 2:9).

Likewise, the first had been hired for the whole day. Therefore they should have the whole reward; so the day's denarius is promised to them, which will be a full reward. But otherwise one does not give the whole to God; so he does not make an agreement with him, because it could be that he will work more fervently, and thus more will be repaid; or he could work so negligently that it will not be deserved. For this reason he says, ***and I will give you what will be just***, because if they regain the lost time, they will have the full reward. *Every man's work will be manifest; for the day of the Lord will declare it* (1 Cor 3:13). Likewise, he invited the first ones to the same thing, but these men went spontaneously. For there is no discretion in boys, so if they do something good, it seems to be more from the Holy Spirit than from discretion; but in adolescence a man is moved by his own counsel. Similarly, it is said of the first ones that he sent them; of these, that they went spontaneously.

1631. ***And again he went out about the sixth and the ninth hour***. According as the day means the whole of time, the sixth hour was from Abraham to David, and the ninth from David to Christ.

But why did he put two hours together? Because then there was a distinct people, namely the Jewish and the gentile. Hence it can be said that the sixth hour is the age of youth, for just as the sun is in its perfection at midday, so is a man in the age of youth. But the ninth hour is old age: and these two are joined, because the manner of living is the same in both.

1632. ***But about the eleventh hour he went out***. The fourth hiring is set down: and he does three things:

first, he reproaches;
second, he excuses;
third, he invites.

The second is at ***they say to him: because no man has hired us***. The third, at ***you also go into my vineyard***.

1633. He says then, ***about the eleventh hour he went out***. The ninth hour is the time of Christ. Hence it says, *little children, it is the last hour* (1 John 2:18). And, *God . . . spoke in times past to the fathers by the prophets, last of all, in these days has spoken to us by his Son* (Heb 1:1–2). *I myself that spoke, behold I am here* (Isa 52:6). Or it can be called old age, or the decrepit age, because some persist in sin even to a decrepit age. *In the evening he will fall, grow dry, and wither* (Ps 89:6).

And found others standing. He found the others in the marketplace, but not these. The reason, in accordance with the Philosopher, is that there is a difference between

sunt in spe, senes non in spe, sed in memoriis. Unde illi in foro inveniuntur primi quasi volentes acquirere; isti autem inveniuntur stantes, quasi non volentes acquirere, sed acquisitum observare. Item vidit primos, et non increpavit; istos autem vidit, et increpavit, quia primo adhuc infirmi sunt, et dominantur passiones in eis, ideo excusandi sunt, quod non expendunt tempus in servitio Dei: sed senes abundant sensibus, ideo ipsos increpat, **quid hic statis tota die otiosi?** Prov. XII, 11: *qui sectatur otium, stultissimus est*; et XXVIII, 19: *qui sectatur otium, implebitur egestate*.

1634. Sequitur eorum excusatio **dicunt ei: quia nemo nos conduxit**. Si referamus ad statum saeculi, sic isti significant gentilem populum, qui non serviunt Deo, sed idolis. Sed excusantur, quia prophetas non habuerunt sicut Iudaei; unde Ps. CXLVII, 20: *non fecit taliter omni nationi, et iudicia sua non manifestavit eis*. Vel secundum quod refertur ad aetatem hominis, significatur quod quibusdam non datur occasio revertendi ad Deum usque ad senium. Et ratio est, quia omnia tempus habent. Vel potest contingere ex dispensatione divina, quia *diligentibus Deum omnia cooperantur in bonum*, Rom. VIII, 28. Unde novit Dominus quod si ante vocasset eos, non stetissent. Tunc ergo conducuntur, quando consentiunt, et efficaciter magis resurgunt; unde dicit **ite et vos in vineam meam**. Unde licet sint decrepiti, *vult* tamen *omnes salvos fieri*, I ad Tim. II, 4. Item primis praemium promisit, istis non, quia illis debebatur, quia mane servierunt ei; istis autem debetur ex sola misericordia. Sap. IV, 13: *consummatus in brevi complevit tempora multa*.

1635. Cum sero factum esset et cetera. Hic agit de remuneratione. Et ponitur

primo remuneratio;
secundo murmuratio;
tertio responsio.
Circa primum duo facit.
Primo ponitur tempus;
secundo persona committens;
tertio persona cui committitur.

1636. Tempus ponitur **cum sero factum esset** et cetera. Et potest intelligi vel de fine aetatis, vel de fine saeculi. Ps. XXIX, 6: *ad vesperum demorabitur fletus*, quia deficit lux mundi. Et dicitur **sero**, quia in mundo isto fiet iudicium.

1637. Dixit dominus vineae procuratori suo. Dominus est tota Trinitas.

adolescents and old men, for adolescents are entirely in hope, old men in memories. Hence those in the marketplace are found first, as though wanting to obtain; but these are found standing about, as though not wanting to obtain, but to observe what has been obtained. Likewise, he saw the first ones and did not reproach them, but he saw these and reproached them, because at first they were still weak, and the passions in them dominated, so they were to be excused for not spending their time in God's service; but the old abound with thoughts, so he reproaches them: **why do you stand here all the day idle?** *He who pursues idleness is very foolish* (Prov 12:11); and, *he who follows idleness will be filled with poverty* (Prov 28:19).

1634. There follows their being excused: **they say to him: because no man has hired us**. If we refer it to the state of an age, these men signify the gentile people, who do not serve God, but idols. But they are excused, because they did not have prophets like the Jews; hence, *he has not done in like manner to every nation: and his judgments he has not made manifest to them* (Ps 147:9). Or, according as it is referred to the lifetime of a man, it signifies that the occasion for turning back to God is not given to certain men until old age. And the reason is that they have all the time. Or it can happen by divine dispensation, since *to those who love God, all things work together unto good* (Rom 8:28). Hence the Lord knew that if he had called them before, they would not have stood. So they are hired at the time when they consent, and they arise more efficaciously; hence he says, **you also go into my vineyard**. Hence although they are decrepit, nevertheless he *will have all men to be saved* (1 Tim 2:4). Likewise, he promised a reward to the first ones, but not to these, because it was owed to those, since they served him in the morning, but it was owed to these only out of mercy. *Being made perfect in a short space, he fulfilled a long time* (Wis 4:13).

1635. And when evening had come. Here he treats of the repayment. And

first, the repayment is set down;
second, the murmuring;
third, the response.
Concerning the first, he does two things:
first, the time is set down;
second, the person assigning;
third, the persons to whom it is assigned.

1636. The time is set down: **and when evening had come**. And it can be understood either of the end of a life span, or of the end of the ages. *In the evening weeping will have place* (Ps 29:6), because the light of the world fails. And it says **evening**, because judgment will come about in that world.

1637. The lord of the vineyard said to his steward. The lord is the whole Trinity.

1638. *Dixit procuratori*, idest Christo. Et datur ei potestas resuscitandi, potestas iudicandi, et tangitur ordo iudicii.

Tangitur potestas *voca operarios*, idest mortuos resuscita; Io. V, 28: *omnes qui in monumentis sunt, audient vocem Filii Dei*.

Potestas iudicandi *redde illis mercedem*, idest sis iudex; unde dat potestatem iudicandi; Io. V, 27: *dedit ei iudicium facere, quia Filius hominis est*.

Consequenter tangitur ordo *incipiens a novissimis usque ad primos*. Et hoc potest retorqueri ad aetatem saeculi.

Incipiens a novissimis, scilicet ab his qui sacramentis imbuti sunt. Unde maior gratia eis data est, quam primis; Ephes. III, 5: *aliis generationibus non est agnitum, sicut nunc revelatum est sanctis apostolis eius*. Unde abundantius collata fuit eis, licet aliqua persona in Veteri Testamento habuerit quoad aliquid maiorem gratiam; Io. VII, 39: *nondum erat Spiritus datus, quia Iesus nondum erat glorificatus*, non quia non datus fuerit Spiritus Sanctus, sed quia tunc abundantius.

Vel potest retorqueri ad aetatem hominis, quia qui in decrepita sunt aetate, citius moriuntur, et citius remunerantur. Vel potest esse quod ex fervore recuperent rem prius amissam, ut legitur de latrone. Quantum ad utrumque dicit Chrysostomus, quod illud homo facit liberalius quod facit ex misericordia, quam quod alio modo; ideo designatur quaedam gratificatio et gaudium; Lc. XV, 10: *gaudium est in caelo super uno peccatore poenitentiam agente*.

1639. Deinde sequitur executio *cum venissent qui circa undecimam horam venerunt*, vel Christiani, vel homines in decrepita aetate receperunt singulos denarios. Apostolus I Cor. cap. III, 8: *quilibet propriam mercedem accipiet secundum suum laborem*.

Venientes autem et primi, non retorqueatis ad tempus saeculi, quia Iudaei, *arbitrati sunt quod plus essent accepturi*, eo quod plus habebant in alio saeculo. *Acceperunt autem et illi singulos denarios*, quia singulas stolas habuerunt.

1640. Sed quid est? Nonne omnes aequaliter habebunt gloriam?

Dico quod quantum ad aliquid erit par retributio, quantum ad aliquid non: quia beatitudo potest considerari quantum ad obiectum, et sic est una omnium beatitudo; vel quantum ad participationem obiecti, et sic non omnes aeque participabunt, quia non ita clare videbunt; Io. XIV, 2: *in domo Patris mei mansiones multae sunt*. Et est simile sicut si multi vadant ad aquam, et unus ferat maius vas quam alter: fluvius totum se exponit, non

1638. *Said to his steward*, i.e., to Christ. And to him is given the power of resuscitating and the power of judging; and the order of judgment is touched upon.

The power is touched upon: *call the laborers*, i.e., resuscitate the dead; *all who are in the graves will hear the voice of the Son of God* (John 5:28).

The power of judging: *pay them their hire*, i.e., be the judge, hence he gives the power of judging; *and he has given him power to do judgment, because he is the Son of man* (John 5:27).

Next, the order is touched upon: *beginning from the last even to the first*. And this can be referred to the age of the world.

Beginning from the last, namely from those who are immersed in the sacraments. Hence a greater gift is given to them than to the first; *which in other generations was not known to the sons of men, as it is now revealed to his holy apostles* (Eph 3:5). Hence it was given more abundantly to them, although some person in the Old Testament may have had a greater grace in some respect; *for as yet the Spirit was not given, because Jesus was not yet glorified* (John 7:39), not that the Holy Spirit was not given, but rather he was not given more abundantly at that time.

Or it can be referred to the life span of a man, for those who are decrepit in age die more quickly, and are rewarded more quickly. Or it could be that, from fervor, they recovered a thing previously lost, as is written of the thief. With regard to both, Chrysostom says that a man does more freely what he does out of pity than what he does in another way; for this reason, a certain joy and show of kindness is designated. *There will be joy before the angels of God upon one sinner doing penance* (Luke 15:10).

1639. Then there follows the execution of the command: *when therefore they had come, who came about the eleventh hour*, either Christians or men in decrepit old age, *each man received a denarius*. The Apostle: *and every man will receive his own reward, according to his own labor* (1 Cor 3:8).

But when the first also came, and do not refer to the time of ages, for they were Jews, *they thought that they should receive more*, from the fact that they had more in another age. *And they also each received a denarius*, because they had a robe apiece.

1640. But what is this? Will all have glory equally?

I say that there will be an equal repayment in a certain respect, but in a certain respect not. For beatitude can be considered as regards the object, and in this way there is one beatitude for all; or it can be considered as regards participation in the object, and in this way not all will participate equally, because they will not see thus clearly; *in my Father's house there are many mansions* (John 14:2). And it is as if many men go to water, and one carries more than

tamen omnes deferunt aequaliter; sic qui animam habet caritate magis dilatatam, magis accipiet et cetera. Eccli. XI, 24: *benedictio Dei in mercedem iusti festinat, et in honore veloci processus illius fructificat.*

1641. *Et accipientes murmurabant adversus patremfamilias dicentes: hi novissimi una hora fecerunt* et cetera. Supra posita est remuneratio, hic ponitur quorumdam murmuratio.

Sed hic est quaestio duplex, quia dicit quod accipientes singulos denarios murmurabant. Per denarium intelligitur vita aeterna. Est ne credendum quod accepta remuneratione aliquis murmuret? Non enim videtur, quia tunc esset ibi peccatum, ut habetur I ad Cor. X, 10: *neque murmuraveritis.*

Chrysostomus dicit quod non est vis facienda in eo quod dicitur, sed propter quod dicitur. Unde intelligendum est quod tanta erit remuneratio, quod si possibile esset, murmurarent. Vel potest intelligi in mundo isto. Gregorius dicit quod ista numeratio nihil aliud est quam remunerationem differri, quia sancti qui ultimo venerunt statim receperunt praemium, sed primi diu expectaverunt; unde II ad Cor. VI, 13: *eandem habentes remunerationem tamquam filiis dico, dilatamini et vos* et cetera. Unde illi murmurant, quia statim non acceperunt; isti autem non, quia statim.

Hilarius et Hieronymus dicunt sic: aliquando Scriptura loquitur de toto numero populi, aliquando ex persona bonorum, aliquando malorum, ut dicitur Ier. XXVI, 8 quod *omnis populus insurrexit in eum, et omnis populus liberavit.* Hic accipitur omnis populus pro parte populi. Sic in primo tempore aliqui fuerunt boni, et non omnes; ideo attribuitur aliquid ratione bonorum, aliquid ratione malorum, non quod tunc, sed ante murmurabant, quia populus Iudaeorum murmuravit contra gentilem, quod aequaretur ei.

1642. Est et alia quaestio. Quid est quod dicit **qui portavimus pondus diei et aestus**? Quia non portaverunt, nisi quantum vixerunt, et moderni similiter. Quid ergo est quod dicitur?

Tripliciter respondetur. Prima responsio est, quod spes quae differtur, affligit animam. Aliqui in principio mundi fuerunt qui portaverunt pondus, quia sciverunt suam retributionem differri; ideo dicuntur portasse pondus diei. Vel potest referri ad Iudaeos, qui portaverunt pondera legis, de quo pondere dicit Petrus Act. XV, 10: *hoc est onus quod nec nos, nec patres nostri portare potuimus.* Gentiles autem tale pondus non portaverunt, quia legi subiecti non fuerunt. Vel, secundum Gregorium,

another: the river puts forth its whole self, yet not all carry equally. In this way, he who has a soul more enlarged with charity will accept more. *The blessing of God makes haste to reward the just, and in a swift hour his blessing bears fruit* (Sir 11:24).

1641. *And receiving it they murmured against the master of the house, saying: these last have worked only one hour.* The repayment was set out above; here certain ones' murmuring is set down.

But there are two questions here, because he says that those receiving a denarius each were murmuring. By the denarius is understood eternal life. Should one believe that someone would murmur after receiving the reward? For it seems not, since then it would be a sin, as is said, *neither do you murmur: as some of them murmured, and were destroyed by the destroyer* (1 Cor 10:10).

Chrysostom says that what is said does not have the force of something to be done, but rather the reason why it is said. Hence one should understand that the repayment will be so great that, if it were possible, they would murmur. Or it can be understood as in this world. Gregory says that this murmuring is nothing other than putting off the repayment, because the saints who come last receive the reward immediately, but the first ones have been waiting for a long time; hence, *but having the same recompense, I speak as to my children, you also be enlarged* (2 Cor 6:13). Hence those murmured, because they did not receive immediately; but these did not murmur, because they received immediately.

Hilary and Jerome speak this way: sometimes Scripture speaks of the whole number of the people, sometimes in the person of the good, sometimes in the person of the bad, as it says in Jeremiah that *all the people rose up against him,* and *all the people freed him* (Jer 26:8). Here all the people is taken for a part of the people. Thus in the first time some were good, and not all; and so one thing is attributed by reason of the good, another by reason of the bad; not that they murmured at that time, but before, for the people of the Jews murmured against the gentiles, that they were made equal to them.

1642. And there is another question. Why does he say, **who have borne the burden of the day and the heats**? For they only bore it to the extent that they were troubled, and similarly with the recent ones. So what is it that is said?

One may respond in three ways. The first response is that hope which is delayed afflicts the soul. There were some in the beginning of the world who bore the weight, since they knew that their repayment was delayed; for this reason they are said to have borne the weight of the day. Or it can be referred to the Jews, who bore the weight of the law, about which weight Peter says, *why do you tempt God to put a yoke upon the necks of the disciples, which neither our fathers nor we have been able to bear?* (Acts 15:10). But

quia primi homines longiori tempore vixerunt, unde vivebant nongentis annis, ideo gravius pondus tulerunt.

1643. *At ille respondens uni illorum dixit.* Hic ponitur reprehensio. Et

primo ostendit suam iustitiam, et suam misericordiam:

secundo remunerationis aequitatem.

1644. Circa primum tria. Primo negat iniustitiam; secundo inducit pactum; tertio inducit retributionem factam.

Dicit ergo *at ille respondens uni illorum*; et adde, *et omnibus*, quia omnes unam causam habebant, *dixit, amice*. Amicum vocat, quia ipsum ad se traxerat. Deut. IV, 37: *elegit semen eorum post eos*. *Non facio tibi iniuriam*, quia quod meum est, do isti, non quod tuum est, ideo non facio tibi iniuriam. Iob VIII, 3: *numquid Omnipotens subvertit iudicium?*

Deinde commemorat pactum *nonne ex denario convenisti mecum?* Idest pro salute consequenda. Gen. XV, 1: *ego Dominus merces tua magna nimis*.

Tolle quod tuum est, idest quod ex promissione mea habes, *et vade*, in gloriam, II ad Tim. I, 12: *scio cui credidi, et certus sum, quia potens est depositum meum servare in illum diem*. Quidam exponunt sic: *tolle quod tuum est*, idest damnationem pro murmure, *et vade*, in ignem aeternum. Sed hoc non potest esse, quia dicit quod acceperunt singulos denarios.

1645. Consequenter ponit misericordiam impensam dicens *volo autem et huic novissimo dare sicut et tibi*. Et circa hoc duo facit. Primo ponit misericordiam; secundo facultatem miserendi.

Volo autem huic novissimo, idest gentili dare *sicut et tibi*. Ad Rom. III, 9: *quid ergo? Praecedimus? Nequaquam*.

Sed possent isti dicere, *tu non potes*. Immo dicit *aut non licet mihi quod volo facere?* Quia licet unicuique facere voluntatem suam de suo. Si enim esset debitor alterius, non liceret ei facere, similiter si esset sub altero; sed ipse est dominus, ideo potest plus dare. Balivus enim non potest dare aliquid, nisi secundum merita; rex autem potest sine meritis; sic Deus, qui est omnium Dominus, potest, Ps. CXIII, 11: *omnia quaecumque voluit fecit*; ad Rom. IX, 19: *voluntati eius quis resistit?*

1646. Hic notandum quod in eo quod ex misericordia datur, non est acceptio personarum, quia de eo quod pure meum est, possum dare cui volo absque acceptione personae. Unde dicit *an oculus tuus nequam est, quia ego bonus sum?* Constat quod murmur praecedens non

the gentiles did not bear such a weight, since they were not subject to the law. Or, according to Gregory, that the first men were troubled for a longer time, since they lived nine hundred years, and for this reason bore a heavier weight.

1643. *But answering he said to one of them.* Here the reproach is set down. And

first, he shows his justice, and his mercy;

second, the equity of the repayment.

1644. Concerning the first, he does three things: first, he denies injustice; second, he brings in the agreement; third, he brings in the repayment made.

It says then, *but answering he said to one of them*, and add, *and to all*, since they all had one complaint, *speak, friend*. He calls him a friend, because he had drawn him to himself. *He loved your fathers, and chose their seed after them* (Deut 4:37). *I do you no wrong*, because I give to these men what is mine, not what is yours, so I do you no injury. *Does the Almighty overthrow that which is just?* (Job 8:3).

Then he reminds him of the agreement: *did you not agree with me for a denarius*, i.e., on the salvation to be obtained. *I am your protector, and your reward exceedingly great* (Gen 15:1).

Take what is yours, i.e., what you have from my promise, *and go*, into glory; *I know whom I have believed, and I am certain that he is able to keep that which I have committed unto him, against that day* (2 Tim 1:12). Some men expound it this way: *take what is yours*, i.e., damnation for murmuring, *and go*, into eternal fire. But this cannot be, because he says that they each receive a denarius.

1645. Next, he sets out the mercy bestowed, saying, *I will also give to this last even as to you*. And concerning this, he does two things: first, he sets out the mercy; second, the faculty of showing mercy.

I will also give to this last, i.e., give to the gentile, *even as to you*. What then? Do we excel them? No, not so (Rom 3:9).

But these men could say, *you cannot do that*. On the contrary, he says, *or is it not lawful for me to do what I will?* For it is permitted for any man to do his own will with regard to what is his. For if he were another's debtor, it would not be permitted for him to do his own will, and similarly if he were under another; but he himself is the lord, so he can give more. For a magistrate can only give according to merit, but a king can give without merit. Thus God, who is the Lord of all, is able to give; *he has done all things whatsoever that he willed* (Ps 113:11); *who resists his will?* (Rom 9:19).

1646. Here one should note that there is no acceptance of persons in that which is given out of mercy, for of that which is entirely mine, I can give to whomever I want without acceptance of persons. Hence he says, *is your eye evil, because I am good?* It is agreed that the preceding murmur

fuit ex defectu domini, sed ex misericordia alii impensa, ideo ex misericordia et bonitate; sed 'nequam' est proprie qui de bonitate dolet. Ideo dicit **an oculus tuus nequam est, quia ego bonus sum?** Eo quod circa te iustitiam ostendi, circa alterum misericordiam? Constat autem istud esse ex bonitate. Et supra VI, 22: *si oculus tuus fuerit simplex, totum corpus tuum lucidum erit.* De bonitate Domini in Ps. LXXII, v. 1: *quam bonus Israel Deus his qui recto sunt corde.*

1647. *Sic erant novissimi primi, et primi novissimi.* Hic concludit id pro quo tota parabola inducta est. Et

primo ponit conclusionem;
secundo removet falsam opinionem.

1648. Dicit *sic erunt novissimi primi*. Dupliciter potest legi secundum Chrysostomum; idest novissimi primis aequabuntur, ita quod non erit differentia; et hoc respondet huic quod dictum est quod singuli receperunt singulos denarios, nec erit differentia secundum tempus. Vel aliter, idest illi qui sunt novissimi, erunt primi; Deut. XXVIII, 44: *advena erit super te, et erit in caput, tu in caudam.* Vel aliqui qui erant primi, propter negligentiam fient novissimi: et hoc praecedenti respondet, quia inceperunt a novissimis.

1649. Sed posset aliquis dicere: *nonne omnes primi salvabuntur?*

Dicit: **multi sunt vocati, pauci vero electi**, quia qui fide credunt, omnes vocati sunt; sed illi electi, qui bona opera faciunt, et isti sunt pauci, ut supra VII, 14: *arcta est via, quae ducit ad vitam, et pauci sunt qui inveniunt eam.*

was not about a defect in the lord, but about mercy bestowed on others, and so about mercy and goodness; but he is properly 'evil' who sorrows over goodness. Therefore he says, **is your eye evil, because I am good**, because of the fact that I showed justice with respect to you, and mercy with respect to others? But it is agreed that this is out of goodness. And above, *if your eye be sound, your whole body will be lightsome* (Matt 6:22). Concerning the Lord's goodness, it says in the Psalm, *how good is God to Israel, to those who are of a right heart!* (Ps 72:1).

1647. *So will the last be first, and the first last.* Here he concludes to that for which the whole parable was introduced. And

first, he sets out the conclusion;
second, he removes a false opinion.

1648. He says, *so will the last be first*. It can be read in two ways, according to Chrysostom: i.e., the last will be made equal to the first, such that there will be no difference; and this corresponds to what was said, that each one receives a denarius apiece, nor will there be a difference according to time. Or in another way, i.e., those who are last will be first; *he will be as the head, and you will be the tail* (Deut 28:44). Or, those who were first will become last, on account of negligence; and this corresponds to the preceding, because they began from the last.

1649. But someone could say, *will all the first be saved?*

He says, **many are called, but few chosen**, because all those who believe by faith are called; but those are chosen who do good works, and these are few, as above, *how narrow is the gate, and strait is the way that leads to life: and few there are who find it!* (Matt 7:14).

Lecture 2

20:17 Et ascendens Iesus Ierosolymam, assumpsit duodecim discipulos secreto, et ait illis: [n. 1651]

20:18 ecce ascendimus Ierosolymam, et Filius hominis tradetur principibus sacerdotum et scribis, et condemnabunt eum morte, [n. 1651]

20:19 et tradent eum gentibus ad illudendum, et flagellandum, et crucifigendum, et tertia die resurget. [n. 1652]

20:20 Tunc accessit ad eum mater filiorum Zebedaei cum filiis suis, adorans, et petens aliquid ab eo. [n. 1654]

20:21 Qui dixit ei: quid vis? Ait illi: dic ut sedeant hi duo filii mei, unus ad dexteram tuam, et unus ad sinistram in regno tuo. [n. 1656]

20:22 Respondens autem Iesus dixit: nescitis quid petatis. Potestis bibere calicem, quem ego bibiturus sum? Dicunt ei: possumus. [n. 1657]

20:23 Ait illis: calicem quidem meum bibetis, sedere autem ad dexteram meam, vel sinistram non est meum dare vobis, sed quibus paratum est a Patre meo. [n. 1660]

20:24 Et audientes decem indignati sunt de duobus fratribus. [n. 1662]

20:25 Iesus autem vocavit eos ad se, et ait: scitis quia principes gentium dominantur eorum, et qui maiores sunt, potestatem exercent in eos? [n. 1665]

20:26 Non ita erit inter vos: sed quicumque voluerit inter vos maior fieri, sit vester minister: [n. 1668]

20:27 et qui voluerit inter vos primus esse, erit vester servus. [n. 1669]

20:17 Καὶ ἀναβαίνων ὁ Ἰησοῦς εἰς Ἱεροσόλυμα παρέλαβεν τοὺς δώδεκα [μαθητὰς] κατ' ἰδίαν καὶ ἐν τῇ ὁδῷ εἶπεν αὐτοῖς·

20:18 ἰδοὺ ἀναβαίνομεν εἰς Ἱεροσόλυμα, καὶ ὁ υἱὸς τοῦ ἀνθρώπου παραδοθήσεται τοῖς ἀρχιερεῦσιν καὶ γραμματεῦσιν, καὶ κατακρινοῦσιν αὐτὸν θανάτῳ

20:19 καὶ παραδώσουσιν αὐτὸν τοῖς ἔθνεσιν εἰς τὸ ἐμπαῖξαι καὶ μαστιγῶσαι καὶ σταυρῶσαι, καὶ τῇ τρίτῃ ἡμέρᾳ ἐγερθήσεται.

20:20 Τότε προσῆλθεν αὐτῷ ἡ μήτηρ τῶν υἱῶν Ζεβεδαίου μετὰ τῶν υἱῶν αὐτῆς προσκυνοῦσα καὶ αἰτοῦσά τι ἀπ' αὐτοῦ.

20:21 ὁ δὲ εἶπεν αὐτῇ· τί θέλεις; λέγει αὐτῷ· εἰπὲ ἵνα καθίσωσιν οὗτοι οἱ δύο υἱοί μου εἷς ἐκ δεξιῶν σου καὶ εἷς ἐξ εὐωνύμων σου ἐν τῇ βασιλείᾳ σου.

20:22 ἀποκριθεὶς δὲ ὁ Ἰησοῦς εἶπεν· οὐκ οἴδατε τί αἰτεῖσθε. δύνασθε πιεῖν τὸ ποτήριον ὃ ἐγὼ μέλλω πίνειν; λέγουσιν αὐτῷ· δυνάμεθα.

20:23 λέγει αὐτοῖς· τὸ μὲν ποτήριόν μου πίεσθε, τὸ δὲ καθίσαι ἐκ δεξιῶν μου καὶ ἐξ εὐωνύμων οὐκ ἔστιν ἐμὸν [τοῦτο] δοῦναι, ἀλλ' οἷς ἡτοίμασται ὑπὸ τοῦ πατρός μου.

20:24 Καὶ ἀκούσαντες οἱ δέκα ἠγανάκτησαν περὶ τῶν δύο ἀδελφῶν.

20:25 ὁ δὲ Ἰησοῦς προσκαλεσάμενος αὐτοὺς εἶπεν· οἴδατε ὅτι οἱ ἄρχοντες τῶν ἐθνῶν κατακυριεύουσιν αὐτῶν καὶ οἱ μεγάλοι κατεξουσιάζουσιν αὐτῶν.

20:26 οὐχ οὕτως ἔσται ἐν ὑμῖν, ἀλλ' ὃς ἐὰν θέλῃ ἐν ὑμῖν μέγας γενέσθαι ἔσται ὑμῶν διάκονος,

20:27 καὶ ὃς ἂν θέλῃ ἐν ὑμῖν εἶναι πρῶτος ἔσται ὑμῶν δοῦλος·

20:17 And Jesus going up to Jerusalem, took the twelve disciples apart, and said to them: [n. 1651]

20:18 behold we go up to Jerusalem, and the Son of man will be betrayed to the chief priests and the scribes, and they will condemn him to death, [n. 1651]

20:19 and will deliver him to the gentiles to be mocked, and scourged, and crucified, and on the third day he will rise again. [n. 1652]

20:20 Then the mother of the sons of Zebedee came to him with her sons, adoring and asking something of him. [n. 1654]

20:21 He said to her: what do you wish? She said to him: say that these my two sons may sit, the one on your right hand, and the other on your left, in your kingdom. [n. 1656]

20:22 And Jesus answering, said: you do not know what you ask. Can you drink the chalice that I will drink? They say to him: we can. [n. 1657]

20:23 He said to them: my chalice indeed you will drink; but to sit on my right or left hand, is not mine to give to you, but to those for whom it is prepared by my Father. [n. 1660]

20:24 And the ten hearing it, were moved with indignation against the two brothers. [n. 1662]

20:25 But Jesus called them to him, and said: you know that the princes of the gentiles lord it over them; and those who are the greater, exercise power upon them. [n. 1665]

20:26 It will not be so among you, but whoever wishes to be the greater among you, let him be your minister, [n. 1668]

20:27 and he who wishes to be first among you, will be your servant. [n. 1669]

20:28 Sicut Filius hominis non venit ministrari, sed ministrare, et dare animam suam redemptionem pro multis. [n. 1670]	20:28 ὥσπερ ὁ υἱὸς τοῦ ἀνθρώπου οὐκ ἦλθεν διακονηθῆναι ἀλλὰ διακονῆσαι καὶ δοῦναι τὴν ψυχὴν αὐτοῦ λύτρον ἀντὶ πολλῶν.	20:28 Even as the Son of man has not come to be ministered to, but to minister, and to give his life as a redemption for many. [n. 1670]
20:29 Et egredientibus illis ab Iericho, secuta est eum turba multa. [n. 1671]	20:29 Καὶ ἐκπορευομένων αὐτῶν ἀπὸ Ἰεριχὼ ἠκολούθησεν αὐτῷ ὄχλος πολύς.	20:29 And when they went out from Jericho, a great multitude followed him. [n. 1671]
20:30 Et ecce duo caeci sedentes secus viam audierunt quia Iesus transiret, et clamaverunt dicentes: Domine, miserere nostri, Fili David. [n. 1673]	20:30 καὶ ἰδοὺ δύο τυφλοὶ καθήμενοι παρὰ τὴν ὁδὸν ἀκούσαντες ὅτι Ἰησοῦς παράγει, ἔκραξαν λέγοντες· ἐλέησον ἡμᾶς, [κύριε,] υἱὸς Δαυίδ.	20:30 And behold, two blind men sitting by the way side, heard that Jesus passed by, and they cried out, saying: O Lord, Son of David, have mercy on us. [n. 1673]
20:31 Turba autem increpabat eos ut tacerent. At illi magis clamabant dicentes: Domine, miserere nostri, Fili David. [n. 1676]	20:31 ὁ δὲ ὄχλος ἐπετίμησεν αὐτοῖς ἵνα σιωπήσωσιν· οἱ δὲ μεῖζον ἔκραξαν λέγοντες· ἐλέησον ἡμᾶς, κύριε, υἱὸς Δαυίδ.	20:31 And the multitude rebuked them, that they should hold their peace. But they cried out the more, saying: O Lord, Son of David, have mercy on us. [n. 1676]
20:32 Et stetit Iesus, et vocavit eos, et ait: quid vultis ut faciam vobis? [n. 1677]	20:32 καὶ στὰς ὁ Ἰησοῦς ἐφώνησεν αὐτοὺς καὶ εἶπεν· τί θέλετε ποιήσω ὑμῖν;	20:32 And Jesus stood, and called them, and said: what do you wish that I do to you? [n. 1677]
20:33 Dicunt illi: Domine, ut aperiantur oculi nostri. [n. 1678]	20:33 λέγουσιν αὐτῷ· κύριε, ἵνα ἀνοιγῶσιν οἱ ὀφθαλμοὶ ἡμῶν.	20:33 They say to him: Lord, that our eyes be opened. [n. 1678]
20:34 Misertus autem eorum Iesus tetigit oculos eorum. Et confestim viderunt, et secuti sunt eum. [n. 1679]	20:34 σπλαγχνισθεὶς δὲ ὁ Ἰησοῦς ἥψατο τῶν ὀμμάτων αὐτῶν, καὶ εὐθέως ἀνέβλεψαν καὶ ἠκολούθησαν αὐτῷ.	20:34 And Jesus having compassion on them, touched their eyes. And immediately they saw, and followed him. [n. 1679]

1650. In parte praecedenti repulit Dominus intendentes venire ad gloriam propter temporis antiquitatem, hic repellit eum, qui intendit venire propter carnis originem.

Primo ergo ponitur occasio petitionis;

secundo petitio;

tertio responsio.

Occasio fuit denuntiatio passionis Christi. Et

primo denuntiat locum;

secundo passionem;

tertio resurrectionem.

1651. Dicit *et ascendens Iesus Ierosolymam* et cetera. Supra XIX, 1 dictum est, quod relicta Galilaea venit in Iudaeam, et non statim ascendit Ierosolymam, sed postmodum imminente passione; unde dicit *et ascendens*, idest cum erat in promptu ascendendi. Ierosolyma erat locus altus.

Assumpsit duodecim discipulos secreto et cetera. Et quare dicit *secreto*? Propter duo. Primo quia magna eis ostendere volebat, ideo omnibus non erant communicanda; Sup. XIII, 11: *vobis datum est nosse mysterium regni caelorum*. Item propter vitandum scandalum, quia viri qui nondum perfecti erant, aversi fuissent ab eo, si

1650. In the preceding part, the Lord drove away those intending to arrive at glory due to temporal oldness; here he drives away the one who intends to arrive due to carnal origin.

First, then, the occasion for the request is set down;

second, the request;

third, the response.

The occasion was the declaration of Christ's passion. And

first, he declares the place;

second, the passion;

third, the resurrection.

1651. It says, *and Jesus going up to Jerusalem*. Above, it was said that having left Galilee he came into Judea, and did not go up immediately to Jerusalem, but rather went up after a while, as his passion drew near (Matt 19:1); hence it says, *and Jesus going up*, i.e., when he was ready to go up. Jerusalem was a high place.

Took the twelve disciples apart. And why does it say *apart*? For two reasons. First, because he wished to show them great things, so they were not to be communicated to all; *it is given to you to know the mysteries of the kingdom of heaven* (Matt 13:11). Again, for the sake of avoiding scandal, because men who were not yet perfect would have

audissent mortem eius; mulieres provocatae fuissent ad lacrimas. Item sciendum quod Iudas nondum malum conceperat; ideo Dominus eum a societate non repulit.

Et ait illis: ecce ascendimus Ierosolymam et cetera. Hic notatur firmitas sui propositi, unde ***ecce***, idest sum in eodem proposito, et in eadem voluntate, quia non mutor; Eccli. XXVII, v. 12: *stultus ut luna mutatur, sapiens autem in sapientia manet sicut sol.* Item propria voluntate; Is. LIII, 7: *oblatus est, quia ipse voluit*.

Tangit locum, quia ***Ierosolymam***; Lc. XIII, v. 33: *non capit prophetam perire extra Ierusalem.* Et quare? Quia erat locus legalis et sacerdotalis: et utrumque conveniebat Christo; quia sicut sacerdos verus debebat immolare pro populo, sic et Christus hostiam obtulit pro mundo. Item per passionem regnum acquisivit. Item ***Ierosolyma*** interpretatur 'visio pacis'; ad Col. I, 20: *pacificans per sanguinem crucis eius sive quae in terris, sive quae in caelis sunt*.

1652. Consequenter praenuntiatur passio. Et frequenter commemoravit suam passionem, ut eam reduceret ad memoriam.

Et tangit tria ad passionem pertinentia, quia passus est a discipulo traditionem ***et Filius hominis tradetur***, scilicet a discipulo. De ista traditione habetur infra XXVII, 10 et in Ps. XL, 10: *qui edebat panes meos, magnificavit super me supplantationem.* Item a principibus sacerdotum et scribis condemnationem; unde ***et condemnabunt eum morte***; Iob XXXIV, 17: *quomodo tu eum, qui iustus est, in tantum condemnas?* Sap. II, 20: *morte turpissima condemnemus eum.* ***Et tradent eum gentibus***, quia Iudaei in manus gentium eum tradiderunt; unde dixit Pilatus: *gens tua et pontifices tui tradiderunt te mihi*.

Et tria tangit quae fecerunt ei, contra tria quae maxime appetunt homines, scilicet honorem, quietem et vitam. Contra honorem, illusus est; unde dicit ***ad illudendum***; Ier. XX, v. 7: *factus sum in derisum tota die*; et in Ps. XXXVII, 12: *amici mei et proximi mei adversum me appropinquaverunt et steterunt.* Contra quietem, flagellatus est; unde ***ad flagellandum***; Is. l, 6: *faciem meam dedi percutientibus, et genas meas vellentibus.* Item contra tertium, occisus; unde ***et crucifigendum***; ad Phil. II, 8: *Christus factus est pro nobis obediens usque ad mortem, mortem autem crucis.*

1653. Deinde agit de resurrectione ***et tertia die resurget***. Hoc autem fecit Deus Pater; unde Act. II, 24: *quem Deus suscitavit, solutis doloribus Inferni, iuxta quod impossibile erat teneri illum ab eo.* ***Et tertia die***. Secundum Augustinum significatum est quod suum simplum

been turned away by it if they had heard of his death; women would have been provoked to tears. Again, one should know that Judas had not yet conceived evil, so the Lord did not drive him away from the fellowship.

And said to them: behold we go up to Jerusalem. Here the firmness of his intention is indicated; hence, ***behold***, i.e., I am of the same intention, and of the same will, for I am not changed; *a holy man continues in wisdom as the sun: but a fool is changed as the moon* (Sir 27:12). Again, by his own will; *he was offered because it was his own will* (Isa 53:7).

He touches upon the place: ***Jerusalem***; *it cannot be that a prophet perish, out of Jerusalem* (Luke 13:33). And why? Because it was the place of the law and the priesthood, and both belonged to Christ. For as a true priest had to sacrifice for the people, so also Christ offered a victim for the world. Again, by the passion he acquired a kingdom. Again, ***Jerusalem*** is interpreted as 'vision of peace'; *making peace through the blood of his cross, both as to the things that are on earth, and the things that are in heaven* (Col 1:20).

1652. Next, the passion is foretold. And he frequently recalled his passion, in order to drive it into their memory.

And he touches upon three things pertaining to the passion. For he suffered being handed over by a disciple: ***and the Son of man will be betrayed***, namely by a disciple. Below, it speaks of this handing over (Matt 27:10), and in the Psalm, it says, *for even the man of peace, in whom I trusted, who ate my bread, has greatly supplanted me* (Ps 40:10). Likewise, he suffered condemnation by the chief among the priests and the scribes; hence ***and they will condemn him to death***. *And how do you so far condemn him who is just?* (Job 34:17). *Let us condemn him to a most shameful death* (Wis 2:20). ***And will deliver him to the gentiles***, for the Jews handed him over into the hands of the gentiles; hence Pilate said, *your own nation, and the chief priests, have delivered you up to me* (John 18:35).

And he touches upon three things which they did to him, against three things which men most desire, namely honor, rest, and life. Against honor, he was mocked; hence he says, ***to be mocked***. *I am become a laughing-stock all the day* (Jer 20:7); and, *my friends and my neighbours have drawn near, and stood against Me* (Ps 37:12). Contrary to rest, he was scourged, hence, ***and scourged***; *I have given my body to the strikers, and my cheeks to those who plucked them* (Isa 50:6). Likewise, contrary to the third, he was killed; hence ***and crucified***. *He humbled himself, becoming obedient unto death, even to the death of the cross* (Phil 2:8).

1653. Next he treats of the resurrection: ***and on the third day he will rise again***. Now, God the Father did this, hence, *whom God has raised up, having loosed the sorrows of hell, as it was impossible that he should be held by it* (Acts 2:24). ***And on the third day***. According to Augustine, it signifies that

1654. Tunc accessit ad eum mater filiorum Zebedaei. Hic ponitur petitio occasionata. Et

primo ponitur petitio in generali;
secundo explicatur, ibi *at illi* et cetera.

1655. Dicit ergo *tunc accessit ad eum mater filiorum Zebedaei*. Filii isti fuerunt Ioannes et Iacobus, mater eorum fuit Salome: unde Salome nomen est mulieris. In Marco habetur quod filii petierunt, hic habetur quod mater; sed verum est quod mater petiit inducta a filiis. *Adorans*, quia cum humilitate petiit: sciebat enim quod semper Deo placet humilis deprecatio; Ps. ci, 18: *respexit in orationem humilium*. Et Iudith IX, 1: *et prosternens se Domino, clamabat ad Dominum*. **Et petens aliquid, dari ab eo**: idest rogo te ut des id quod volo: et haec petitio non est admittenda, et qui hoc concedit, fatue concedit. Legitur de Herode, quod istud concessit filiae Herodiadis, et non revocavit. Salomon autem matri concessit; sed quia sapiens fuit, incautum promissum revocavit. Ideo Christus sapientior his noluit concedere nisi exprimeretur; supra XII, 42: *et ecce plusquam Salomon hic*.

1656. Ideo sequitur explicatio petitionis *et ait illi: dic ut sedeant hi duo filii mei, unus ad dexteram tuam, et unus ad sinistram, in regno tuo*.

Sed est quaestio, unde haec mulier hoc conceperat. Audierat de passione et resurrectione, unde aliquid carnale conceperat, quod statim cum gloria deberet esse in Ierusalem; ideo petere voluit filiis suis eminentiam. Item audierat quod duodecim erant iudicaturi; ideo praeponere suos volebat, unde ad litteram intelligebat.

Et sciendum quod Iacobus et Ioannes magis honorabantur a Christo post Petrum; ideo Petrum voluerunt excludere.

Aliter dicit Chrysostomus, quod ista petiit aliquid spirituale, et in hoc fuit laudanda, quia matres plus petunt temporale quam spirituale; unde mater si videat filium peccantem, non tantum dolet, quantum si videt infirmantem. Unde per dexteram spiritualia significantur, terrena per sinistram. Vel possumus intelligere per dexteram et sinistram activam vitam et contemplativam; ideo petit istos perfici in utraque vita; Cant. c. II, 6: *laeva eius sub capite meo, et dextera illius amplexabitur me*.

1657. Respondens autem Iesus dixit. Hic ponitur responsio;

1654. Then the mother of the sons of Zebedee came to him with her sons. Here the request occasioned is set down. And

first, the request is set down in general;
second, it is explained, at **who said to her**: **what do you wish?**

1655. It says then, **then the mother of the sons of Zebedee came to him**. These sons were John and James, and their mother was Salome; hence the woman's name is Salome. In Mark, it says that the sons asked, while here it says that the mother asked, but the truth is that the mother asked, being prompted by the sons (Mark 10:35). *Adoring*, because she asked with humility, for she knew that a humble prayer is always pleasing to God; *he has had regard to the prayer of the humble* (Ps 101:18). And, *falling down prostrate before the Lord, she cried to the Lord* (Judg 9:1). **And asking something of him**, i.e., I ask you that you should give what I wish; and this request should not be granted, and the one who grants this grants it foolishly. It is written of Herod that he granted this to the daughter of Herodias, and did not take it back. Now, Solomon granted this to his mother, but because he was a wise man, he took back the reckless promise. For this reason Christ, wiser than these men, did not wish to grant it unless it were expressed; above, **and behold one greater than Solomon is here** (Matt 12:24).

1656. So there follows an explanation of the request: **say that these my two sons may sit, the one on your right hand, and the other on your left, in your kingdom**.

But there is a question: where did this woman get this question from? She had heard about the passion and resurrection, hence she had thought of something carnal, that he should be in Jerusalem with glory right away. So she wanted to request the eminence of her sons. Likewise, she had heard that the twelve were to be judges, so she wished to set her own sons forward; hence she understood it literally.

And one should know that James and John were honored more by Christ, after Peter; for this reason, they wished to exclude Peter.

Chrysostom says otherwise, that this woman requested something spiritual, and was to be praised for it, for mothers ask rather for temporal things than spiritual; hence if a mother should see her son sinning, she would not sorrow as much as if she saw him sick. Hence spiritual things are signified by the right, earthly things by the left. Or we can understand by the right and left the active life and the contemplative life; so she asked that her sons be perfected in either life. *His left hand is under my head, and his right hand will embrace me* (Song 2:6).

1657. And Jesus answering, said. Here the response is set down;

deinde murmur aliorum, ibi *et audientes decem indignati sunt de duobus fratribus*.

Et circa primum tria facit.
Primo increpat eorum stultitiam;
secundo examinat eorum promptitudinem, ibi *potestis bibere calicem quem ego bibiturus sum?*
Tertio repellit petitionem, ibi *sedere autem ad dexteram meam, vel sinistram, non est meum dare vobis*.

1658. Sed quid est? Ipsi non petebant, sed mater. Novit Dominus quod illa petebat inducta ab illis, ideo eis respondet, sicut supra XVI, 23 dixerat Dominus Petro: *nescis quid dicis*.

Nescitis quid petatis; quasi dicat: temporalia non debetis petere, sed excellentiam spiritualem. Vel si intelligerent spirituale, petebant quod super omnem creaturam haberent eminentiam, quia sedere a dextris nulli creaturae convenit, ut habetur ad Hebr. I, 13: *ad quem angelorum dixit aliquando: sede a dextris meis?* Unde sedere a dextris excedit omnem creaturam.

Vel aliter, secundum Hilarium: *nescitis quid petatis*; quia iam concessi vobis quod petitis, quia dictum est supra XIX, 28: *sedebitis super sedes duodecim* et cetera. Vel aliter: *nescitis*, quia vocavi vos ad dexteram, et vos petitis quod unus sit ad sinistram? Vel diabolus sicut per mulierem ad sinistram traxerat hominem, volebat istos per mulierem reducere ad sinistram; sed hoc non potuit, ex quo salus per mulierem facta est. Vel *nescitis* quia de praemio contenditis sine merito praecedente. Ideo considerare debetis, quod ad praemium non venitur nisi per meritum; ideo volo vos primo examinare si potestis pati et cetera.

1659. Unde dicit *potestis bibere calicem, quem ego bibiturus sum?* Hic examinat eos, et provocat eos ad passionem leviter, quia passionem nominat **calicem**. De isto dicitur in Ps. CXV, 13: *calicem salutaris accipiam*; et sequitur: *pretiosa in conspectu Domini mors sanctorum eius*. Et dicitur calix, quia inebriat. Item dicit *quem ego bibiturus sum*; I Petr. II, 21: *Christus passus est pro nobis, vobis relinquens exemplum ut sequamini vestigia eius*.

Dicunt ei: possumus. Et quare sic respondent? Propter tria. Primo ex amore ad Christum, quia ita adhaerebant Christo, quod mors eos ab ipso separare non posset, sicut dixit Petrus infra XXVI, 35: *et si oportuerit me mori tecum, non te negabo*.

Item ex ignorantia, quia vires suas non considerabant, quia quibus aliquando ante factum videtur leve, in ipso actu deficiunt.

then the murmuring of the others, at *and the ten hearing it, were moved with indignation against the two brothers*.

And concerning the first, he does three things:
first, he reproaches their foolishness;
second, he examines their readiness, at *can you drink the chalice that I will drink?*
Third, he repels the request, at *but to sit on my right or left hand, is not mine to give to you*.

1658. But what is this? They did not ask, but the mother. The Lord knew that the woman was asking at their prompting, so he responds to them, as above, the Lord had said to Peter, *you do not know what you say* (Matt 16:23).

You do not know what you ask, as though to say: you should not ask for temporal things, but for spiritual excellence. Or if they were thinking of spiritual things, they were asking that they should have eminence over every creature, because to sit at the right hand does not belong to any creature, as is said, *but to which of the angels said he at any time: sit on my right hand?* (Heb 1:13). Hence to sit at the right is above every creature.

Or in another way, according to Hilary: **you do not know what you ask**, for I have already granted you what you ask, for it was said above, *you also will sit on twelve seats* (Matt 19:28). Or in another way, **you do not know**, for I have called you to the right hand, and do you ask that one should sit at the left? Or the devil, just as he had drawn the man to the left hand through a woman, wished to lead these men back to the left through a woman. But he could not do this, he from whom salvation was accomplished through a woman. Or, **you do not know**, for you fight over a reward without preceding merit. So you should consider that one only obtains a reward through merit; therefore I want you first to consider whether you are able to suffer.

1659. Hence he says, *can you drink the chalice that I will drink?* Here he examines them, and incites them lightly toward the passion, for he calls the passion a **chalice**. It says of this, *I will take the chalice of salvation* (Ps 115:4), and there follows: *precious in the sight of the Lord is the death of his saints*. And it is called a chalice because it inebriates. Likewise he says, *that I will drink*; *Christ also suffered for us, leaving you an example that you should follow his steps* (1 Pet 2:21).

They say to him: we can. And why do they respond this way? For three reasons. First, out of love toward Christ, for they were clinging to Christ such that death could not separate them from him, as Peter said below, *even if I must die with you, I will not deny you* (Matt 26:35).

Likewise out of ignorance, since they were not considering their own abilities, for sometimes those to whom it seems easy before the deed fail in the act itself.

Item dixerunt ex cupiditate assequendi quod petierant. Unde credebant statim assequi quod petebant, ideo statim concedunt **possumus** hoc ex cupiditate.

1660. Consequenter repellit petitionem. Et primo futuram passionem praenuntiat; secundo respondet ad petitionem.

Dicit ergo **calicem meum bibetis**. Sed quid est? Verum est quod Iacobus bibit; unde in Act. XII, 2: *occidit autem Iacobum fratrem Ioannis gladio*. Sed Ioannes est mortuus sine calice passionis. Sed dicendum quod non bibit usque ad mortem, sed flagellatus fuit, in oleo positus, et relegatus. Item multas poenas passus est, et sic non fuit immunis a potu calicis.

1661. Sedere autem ad dexteram. Hic respondet ad petitionem gloriae. Si dixisset dominus: *dabo vobis*, tristati essent alii. Si negasset, ipsi effecti essent tristes; ideo **dixit sedere autem ad dexteram meam, vel sinistram, non est meum dare vobis; sed quibus paratum est a Patre meo.**

Ex hoc loco argumentati sunt Ariani, quod non est aequalis dignitas Patris et Filii. Hieronymus et alii exponunt quod ipse dat cum Patre. Unde vult dicere **non est meum dare vobis**, quasi dicat: eminentia dignitatis non datur personae, sed merito, et hoc secundum praedestinationem divinam. I Cor. II, 9: *oculus non vidit, nec auris audivit, nec in cor hominis ascendit quae praeparavit Deus diligentibus se*. Io. XIV, 3: *si abiero, et paravero vobis locum* et cetera. Unde ex quo parat Pater, et ipse.

Vel **non est meum dare vobis**, sine meritis, sed personis ex merito acquirentibus, sed meum ex praedestinatione, quae est mihi a Patre meo.

Et Augustinus sic: Salome erat soror matris Christi: et quia credebant impetrare per personam magis coniunctam, ideo credebant quod deberet eis dare, quia coniuncti ei erant secundum carnem. Sed in ipso in una persona erant duae naturae; unde dicit **non est meum**, scilicet secundum potestatem quam habeo a Patre, ideo dabo secundum quod disposuit Pater meus.

1662. Audientes decem indignati sunt de duobus fratribus. Supra Dominus repressit indiscretam petitionem discipulorum; hic ponit indignationem aliorum. Et

primo ponitur indignatio;
secundo reprimitur verbo;
tertio facto.

Secunda ibi *Iesus autem vocavit eos ad se, et ait*; tertia ibi *sicut Filius hominis non venit ministrari, sed ministrare*.

Likewise, they spoke out of a desire to obtain what they had requested. Hence they were thinking to obtain what they requested right away, so right away they conceded **we can**, out of eagerness.

1660. Next he repels the request. And first, he foretells future suffering; second, he responds to the request.

He says then, **my chalice indeed you will drink**. But what is this? It is true that James drank the chalice; hence, *and he killed James, the brother of John, with the sword* (Acts 12:2). But John died without the chalice of suffering. But one should say that while he did not drink the chalice even unto death, nevertheless he was scourged, and thrown in boiling oil, and exiled. He also suffered many punishments, and thus was not exempt from the chalice's draught.

1661. But to sit on my right. Here he responds to the request for glory. If the Lord had said, *I will give it to you*, the others would have been saddened. If he had denied it, they themselves would have been made sad. For this reason he said, **but to sit on my right or left hand, is not mine to give to you, but to those for whom it is prepared by my Father.**

The Arians argue from this passage that the Father's dignity and the Son's are not equal. Jerome and others explain that he himself gives with the Father. Hence he wanted to say, **is not mine to give to you**, as though to say: eminence of dignity is not given to a person, but for merit, and this according to the divine predestination. *That eye has not seen, nor ear heard, neither has it entered into the heart of man, what things God has prepared for those who love him* (1 Cor 2:9). *And if I will go, and prepare a place for you* (John 14:3). Hence by the fact that the Father prepares, he himself also prepares.

Or, **is not mine to give to you**, without merits, but to persons who acquire it by merit, but it is mine by predestination, which is given to me from my Father.

And Augustine, this way: Salome was the sister of Christ's mother, and since they were hoping to obtain what they desired through a person more connected, they thought that he should give it to them, since they were joined to him according to the flesh. But in him, in one person, there were two natures; hence he says it **is not mine**, namely according to the power which I have from the Father, therefore I will give according as my Father has arranged.

1662. And the ten hearing it, were moved with indignation against the two brothers. Above, the Lord repressed an indiscrete request from disciples; here he sets out the indignation of the others. And

first, the indignation is set out;
second, it is repressed by word;
third, by deed.

The second is at **but Jesus called them to him, and said**; the third, at **even as the Son of man has not come to be ministered to, but to minister**.

1663. Considerandum quod sicut ex quadam elatione duo fratres superiores esse volebant, sic ex quadam elatione isti indignati sunt. Prov. I, 10: *inter superbos semper sunt iurgia*.

Sed quare *de duobus fratribus*? Quia non ipsi petierunt, sed mater. Sed intellexerunt discipuli ex verbis Domini quod mater petierat ad vocem eorum.

Sed quare non ante sunt indignati? Dicit Chrysostomus quod reverebantur Magistrum, unde expectabant sententiam Domini; sed quando audierunt Magistrum reprehendentem, tunc indignati sunt.

1664. Consequenter reprehendit eos. Et
primo ponit in medium exemplum gentilium;
secundo docet exemplum non esse sequendum, ibi *scitis quia principes gentium dominantur eorum*;
tertio ponit quod est imitandum, ibi *non ita erit inter vos*.

1665. Dicit ergo *Iesus autem vocavit eos*, dans humilitatis exemplum. Supra XI, 29: *discite a me, quia mitis sum et humilis corde*.

Et ait: scitis quia principes gentium dominantur eorum. Apud Iudaeos gentiles abominabiles erant, ut habetur supra XVIII, 17: *sit tibi sicut ethnicus et publicanus*.

1666. Unde horrorem incutit *principes gentium dominantur eorum*, ut notetur quod hoc exemplum non est imitandum.

Sed notandum quod duplex est praeeminentia, scilicet dignitatis et potestatis: et utramque tangit cum dicit *principes gentium dominantur eorum* et cetera. Illi sunt principes qui ex officio praesunt.

1667. Sed quid est? Numquid dominari est malum?
Dominari aliquando dicitur pro praeesse; et sic non accipitur hic: aliquando prout correlative se habet ad 'servum,' unde idem est quod serviliter sibi servum subiicere; et sic sumitur hic. Principes enim instituti sunt ad hoc ut bonum procurent subditis; si vero volunt eos in servitutem redigere, tunc abutuntur, quia utuntur liberis ut servis: liber enim est qui est causa sui, servus qui causa alterius. Et quia hoc consuetum est apud gentiles, et adhuc est apud aliquos, ideo dicit *principes gentium dominantur eorum*, idest in servitutem redigunt subditos. Ez. XXII, 27: *principes tui in medio eius quasi lupi rapaces*.

Item aliqui habent eminentiam non in dignitate, sed in potestate, ut aliqui nobiles. Et consuetum est quod qui potestatem habent, non utuntur ad beneficium, sed *potestatem exercent in eos*, scilicet ad opprimendum, non ad iustitiam.

1663. One should consider that, just as the two brothers wished to be higher out of a certain vainglory, so these men were indignant out of a certain vainglory. *Among the proud there are always contentions* (Prov 13:10).

But why were they indignant over the two brothers? For they themselves had not asked, but the mother. But the disciples understood from the Lord's words that the mother had asked as their voice.

But why were they not indignant before? Chrysostom says that they respected the Teacher, hence they were waiting for the Lord's judgment; but when they heard the Teacher's reproach, then they were indignant.

1664. Next, he reproaches them. And
first, he sets in their midst the example of the gentiles;
second, he teaches that this example should not be followed, at *you know that the princes of the gentiles lord it over them*;
third, he sets out what should be imitated, at *it will not be so among you*.

1665. It says then, *but Jesus called them to him*, giving an example of humility. Above, *learn from me, because I am meek, and humble of heart* (Matt 11:29).

And said: you know that the princes of the gentiles lord it over them. Among the Jews, the gentiles were detestable, as is said above, *let him be to you as the heathen and publican* (Matt 18:17).

1666. Hence he instills horror: *the princes of the gentiles lord it over them*, so it may be noted that this example should not be imitated.

But one should note that there are two kinds of preeminence, namely the preeminence of dignity and the preeminence of power; and he touches upon both when he says, *the princes of the gentiles lord it over them*. Princes are those who have power by office.

1667. But what is this? Is it evil to rule?
Sometimes *lord it over* means to be in control, and it is not taken here in this way. Sometimes *lord it over* is taken as a correlative to 'slave,' so it is the same as to subject a slave to oneself in a servile manner; and it is taken here in this way. For princes are established so that they may attend to the good of those subjected; but if they wish to reduce them to slavery, then they misuse their power, for they treat free men as slaves. For a free man is one who is for himself, while a slave is one who is for another. And since this was the custom among the gentiles, and still is among some, he says, *the princes of the gentiles lord it over them*, i.e., reduce their subjects to slavery. *Her princes in the midst of her, are like wolves ravening the prey to shed blood* (Ezek 22:27).

Again, some have eminence not in dignity, but in power, as do some nobles. And it is common that those who have power do not use it for benefit, but *lord it over them*, i.e., namely for oppression, not for justice.

1668. Sed Dominus illam consuetudinem non vult in Ecclesia sua; ideo dicit *non ita erit inter vos*, idest non debet aliquis esse inter vos quasi dominativus; I Petr. V, 3: *neque ut dominantes in cleris*.

Sed quicumque. Contra haec duo facit duo, *sed quicumque voluerit inter vos maior fieri*; et istud refertur ad secundum dictum scilicet *et qui maiores sunt potestatem exercent inter eos*; idest sic desideret quis habere praesidentiam in Ecclesia Spiritus Sancti, ut sit sicut *minister*; I Petr. IV, 10: *unusquisque sicut accepit gratiam in alterutrum illam administrantes, sicut boni dispensatores*, ut quantum plus habebis, plus in utilibus expendas. Ideo *qui voluerit maior fieri inter vos*, idest in Ecclesia, *fiat ut minister*, idest ministret in necessitate aliorum.

1669. Quantum autem ad id quod dicitur *principes gentium dominantur eorum*; dicit: *et quicumque voluerit inter vos primus esse, erit vester servus*; idest, si aliquis desiderat habere primatum in Ecclesia, sciat quod illud non est habere dominium, sed servitutem. Servi enim est quod totum se ad servitium domini impendat: sic praelati Ecclesiae totum quicquid habent, quicquid sunt, subditis debent; I ad Cor. IX, 19: *cum essem liber ex omnibus, omnium me servum feci*; II ad Cor. IV, 5: *nos autem servos vestros per Iesum*. Unde secundum Chrysostomum miserum est. Ita ergo dictum est, quod non est agendum secundum consuetudinem gentilium.

1670. Quia ergo possent dicere, *quid sequemur?* Dicit, *sequimini me*: et ostendit se ministrum dicens *sicut filius hominis non venit ministrari, sed ministrare*.

Sed contra. Nonne habetur supra IV, 11, quod *accesserunt Angeli et ministrabant ei*? Unde Io. XII, 2 dicitur quod *Martha ministrabat*. Dico quod licet ministratum fuerit ei, non tamen ad hoc venit. Sed ad quid? Ut ipse ministraret, idest abundantiam gloriae aliis impenderet. Apostolus Rom. XV, 8: *dico autem Christum Iesum ministrum fuisse circumcisionis*. Et in Lc. XXII, 27: *ego sum in medio vestrum sicut qui ministrat*.

Sed dices: est ne servus, cum sit princeps? Ita. 'Servus' enim dicitur qui accipitur in pretium: et ipse fecit se pretium, et dedit se redemptionem pro multis; unde venit *ministrare, et dare animam suam*, idest vitam corporalem, *redemptionem pro multis*. Non dicit *pro omnibus*, quia quantum ad sufficientiam, pro omnibus; quantum vero ad efficientiam, pro multis, scilicet pro electis. Unde Io. XV, 13: *maiorem caritatem nemo habet ut animam suam ponat quis pro amicis suis*. Ier. XII, 7: *dedi dilectam animam meam in manibus inimicorum eius*.

1671. *Et egredientibus illis ab Iericho secuta est eum turba multa*. Repressa est indignatio discipulorum

1668. But the Lord does not want this custom in his Church, so he says, *it will not be so among you*, i.e., no one should be as it were domineering among you; *neither as lording it over the clergy* (1 Pet 5:3).

But whoever. Against this he does two things, *but whoever wishes to be greater among you*, and this is referred to the second thing said, namely *and those who are the greater, exercise power upon them*, that is, if someone should desire to preside over the Church of the Holy Spirit, that he should be as a *minister*. *As every man has received grace, ministering the same one to another: as good stewards* (1 Pet 4:10), that to the extent that you have more, you may expend more on useful things. Therefore, *whoever wishes to be greater among you*, i.e., in the Church, *let him be your minister*, i.e., let him minister to the necessities of others.

1669. And with respect to what was said, *the princes of the gentiles lord it over them*, he says: *and he who wishes to be first among you, will be your servant*, i.e., if someone desires to have the first place, let him know that this is not to have lordship, but servitude. For it belongs to a servant that he devote his whole self to the service of a lord: thus the prelates of the Church should give whatever they have, whatever they are, to those under them. *For whereas I was free as to all, I made myself the servant of all* (1 Cor 9:19); *ourselves your servants through Jesus* (2 Cor 4:5). Hence according to Chrysostom, it is miserable. Thus, therefore, it was said that one should not act according to the custom of the gentiles.

1670. So since they could say, *what example will we follow?* He says: *follow me*. And he shows himself a servant, saying, *even as the Son of man has not come to be ministered to, but to minister*.

On the contrary, does it not say above, that *the angels approached and ministered to him* (Matt 4:11)? Hence John says that *Martha ministered to him* (John 12:2). I say that, although he was ministered to, yet he did not come for this. But for what did he come? That he himself might minister, i.e., bestow the abundance of glory on others. The Apostle: *for I say that Christ Jesus was minister of the circumcision for the truth of God* (Rom 15:8). And, *but I am in the midst of you, as he who serves* (Luke 22:27).

But you say: is he a servant, while he is a ruler? Yes. For 'servant' names one who is received as a reward, and he himself made himself a reward, and gave himself as a redemption for many; hence he came *to minister, and to give his life*, i.e., bodily life, *as a redemption for many*. He does not say *for all*, because as regards sufficiency it was for all, but as regards efficacy it was for many, namely for the elect. Hence, *greater love than this no man has, that a man lay down his life for his friends* (John 15:13). *I have given my dear soul into the land of her enemies* (Jer 12:7).

1671. *And when they went out from Jericho, a great multitude followed him*. The indignation of the disciples

verbo, hic reprimit facto, ministerium in aliquos exercendo. Et

    primo ponitur devotio aliorum;

    secundo Christi miseratio, ibi *et stetit Iesus, et vocavit eos*.

    Circa primum

    primo ponitur devotio turbae;

    secundo caecorum, ibi *ecce duo caeci* et cetera.

1672. Dicit ergo *et egredientibus illis ab Iericho*, secutae sunt eum turbae multae; quia multi sequebantur, ideo erat Dominus sollicitus, sicut multa seges est sollicitudo colligentis. Sed secundum mysterium Iericho 'defectus' dicitur, et significat defectum mundi. Unde nisi venisset Dominus ad istos defectus, homines non venissent ad eum. Unde secutae sunt eum turbae, quasi oves eius; Io. X, 27: *oves meae vocem meam audiunt, et sequuntur me*.

1673. Sequitur devotio caecorum *et ecce duo caeci* et cetera. Et

    primo ponitur devotio.

    Secundo constantia, ibi *turba autem increpabat eos ut tacerent*.

1674. Sed hic est quaestio, quia in Lc. XVIII, 35 legitur, quod unus caecus fuit tantum qui occurrit ei, et hic dicitur quod duo, qui domino exeunte de Iericho occurrerunt ei in exitu. Sed Marcus convenit cum Luca, quod erat tantum unus, et ita Matthaeus discrepat ab utroque.

Augustinus dicit quod iste caecus, de quo Lucas scribit, fuit alius ab his, quia occurrit ei antequam intraret Iericho. Sed Marcus et Matthaeus dicunt quod egrediente de Iericho; sed quod Marcus non dixerit duo, sicut Matthaeus, ratio est, quia unus erat magis notus et famosus, et propter famam miraculum erat magis famosum. Et hoc patet, quia nominat eum quod vocatur Barthimaeus, et non nominantur in Scriptura nisi homines multum noti.

1675. Per istos caecos significantur duo populi, scilicet populus Iudaeorum et populus gentilium, qui sedebant secus viam, quae est Christus. Is. XXX, 21: *haec est via, ambulate per eam*. Vel significantur conversi ex utroque populo, qui sedent secus viam, idest Christum; Io. XIV, 6: *ego sum via, veritas et vita*. Audierunt per praedicationem, quod transiret secundum naturam humanam Iesus, ut mortem subiret, ut curaret infirmos, ideo *exclamaverunt dicentes: Domine, miserere nostri Fili David*. Causa exauditionis non fuit altitudo vocis, sed fervor devotionis. Ps. CXIX, 1: *ad Dominum cum tribularer clamavi, et exaudivit me*. Item fatentur ipsum esse Deum et hominem: Deum, quia dicunt: **Domine**. Ps. XCIX, 3: *scitote quoniam Dominus ipse est Deus*. Et petunt quod est proprium Deo, scilicet *miserere nostri*.

was repressed by word; here he represses it by deed, exercising a ministry to others. And

    first, the others' devotion is set out;

    second, Christ's compassion, at *and Jesus stood, and called them*.

    Concerning the first,

    first, the crowd's devotion is set out;

    second, the blind men's devotion, at *and behold, two blind men*.

1672. It says then, *and when they went out from Jericho, a great multitude followed him*; since many were following, the Lord was solicitous, just as a great harvest is the gatherer's solicitude. But according to a mystery, Jericho means 'revolt,' and signifies the world's revolt. Hence unless the Lord had come to these revolts, men would not have come to him. Hence the crowds followed him, as though his sheep; *my sheep hear my voice: and I know them, and they follow me* (John 10:27).

1673. There follows the devotion of the blind men: *and behold, two blind men*. And

    first, devotion is set out;

    second, constancy, at *and the multitude rebuked them, that they should hold their peace*.

1674. But there is a question here, because in Luke it is written that there was only one blind man who ran to meet him (Luke 18:35), and here it says that there were two who, as the Lord was coming out of Jericho, ran to meet him. But Mark agrees with Luke, that there was only one (Mark 10:46), and so Matthew differs from both.

Augustine says that the blind man of whom Luke writes was someone other than these men, because he ran to meet him before he was entering Jericho. But Mark and Matthew say that it was as he was leaving Jericho. But the reason that Mark does not say two men, as Matthew does, is because one was more known and famous, and owing to his fame the miracle was more famous. And this is clear, because he names him who is called Bartimaeus, and only well-known men are named in Scripture.

1675. These blind men signify two peoples, namely the people of the Jews and the people of the gentiles, who were sitting beside the way, which is Christ. *This is the way, walk in it* (Isa 30:21). Or they signify those converted from either people, who are sitting beside the way, i.e., Christ; *I am the way, and the truth, and the life* (John 14:6). They had heard through preaching that Jesus was passing by according to human nature, that he might undergo death and cure the sick, so *they cried out, saying: O Lord, Son of David, have mercy on us*. The reason they were heard was not highness of voice, but fervor of devotion. *In my trouble I cried to the Lord: and he heard me* (Ps 119:1). Likewise, they confessed him to be God and man: God, for they say **Lord**; *know that the Lord is God* (Ps 99:3). And they ask what is proper to God, namely **have mercy on us**. *His tender mercies are over*

Ps. CXLIV, v. 9: *miserationes eius super omnia opera eius*. Item dicunt eum ex semine David: et in hoc confitentur humanitatem.

1676. Consequenter ponitur constantia eorum. Et primo ponitur impedimentum; secundo constantia.

Dicit ergo **turba autem increpabat eos ut facerent**, ut possibile erat, quia in ista turba aliqui erant qui venerabantur Christum, et hi increpabant eos, quia vile reputabant quod viles personae ad tantum virum accederent. Illi vero qui Christo derogabant, increpabant, quia audiebant id quod audire nolebant: dolebant enim quod vocabant eum Filium David. Ier. XXIII, 5: *suscitabo David servum meum*.

Mystice significatur quod aliqui excaecati per peccatum, clamant ad Dominum **miserere nostri**. Sed turba cogitationum carnalium et hominum carnalium increpant eos venire ad Christum. Iob XX, 2: *ideo cogitationes variae succedunt sibi, et mens in diversa rapitur*. Sed homo contra hoc debet esse constans et viriliter pugnare et laborare, sicut docet Apostolus II ad Tim. II, 3: *labora sicut bonus miles Christi Iesu*.

Sed verbum Dei non alligatur verbis hominum; et ideo sequitur **at illi magis ac magis clamabant**.

1677. Et stetit Iesus. Hic ponitur misericordia Domini, et ostenditur, quia stetit. Et quare stetit? Quia via lapidosa erat et cavernosa; ideo stare voluit, quia si procederent, forte laedi possent. Secundum mysterium, quia veniendo in mundum commovit ad petendum, sed salutem dedit stando. Unde per incarnationem homines promoventur, sed per eum docentem et perseverantem sanantur.

Sequitur **vocavit eos**. Sed quare vocavit? Ut alii facerent eis viam; et significat illos quos Dominus vocat per praedestinationem. Ad Rom. VIII, 29: *quos praescivit et praedestinavit*. Item exquirit voluntatem **quid vultis ut faciam vobis?** Non petiit ut ipse sciret, sed ut daret intelligere quod pie petentibus satisfecit. Ps. CXLIV, 19: *voluntatem timentium se faciet*.

1678. Dicunt illi: Domine, ut aperiantur oculi nostri. Et hoc est iustum, ut quilibet peccator hoc petat. Ps. CXVIII, 18: *revela oculos meos, et considerabo mirabilia tua*. Et alibi Ps. XII, 4: *illumina oculos meos*. Confitebantur Deum, dicendo **Domine**, et hominem, vocando **Filium David**.

1679. Ideo **misertus est eorum**. Omnia enim ex sua misericordia facit. Thren. III, v. 22: *misericordia Domini est, quod non sumus consumpti*. **Tetigit oculos eorum, et confestim viderunt**. In hoc quod tetigit oculos eorum et confestim viderunt, tangitur humanitas et divinitas Christi: quod enim tetigit, opus fuit humanitatis; sed

all his works (Ps 144:9). Likewise, they claim him to be from the seed of David, and in this they confess his humanity.

1676. Next, their constancy is set down. And first, an impediment is set out; second, their constancy.

It says then, **and the multitude rebuked them, that they should hold their peace**, as was possible, for there were some in the crowd who held Christ in reverence, and these rebuked them, because they considered it base that base persons should draw near to such a man. Indeed, those who were Christ's detractors were rebuking them, because they were hearing what they did not want to hear; for they were grieved that they were calling him the Son of David. *I will raise up to David a just branch* (Jer 23:5).

Mystically it is signified that some men blinded by sin cry out to the Lord, **have mercy on us**. But a crowd of carnal thoughts and carnal men rebuke them for coming to Christ. *Therefore various thoughts succeed one another in me, and my mind is hurried away to different things* (Job 20:2). But a man should be firm against this, and fight and labor like a man, as the Apostle teaches, *labor as a good soldier of Christ Jesus* (2 Tim 2:3).

But the word of God is not bound by the words of men, and for this reason there follows, **but they cried out the more**.

1677. And Jesus stood. Here the Lord's mercy is set out, and is shown, for he stood. And why did he stand? Because the road was rocky and full of hollows, so he wished to stand, for if they went forward they might be injured. According to a mystery, because by coming into the world he moved us to ask, but he gave salvation by standing. Hence men are moved forward by the incarnation, but are healed by his teaching and perseverance.

There follows **called them**. But why did he call? That the others might make way for them, and this signifies those whom the Lord calls through predestination. *For whom he foreknew, he also predestined* (Rom 8:29). Again, he seeks out their will: **what do you wish that I do to you?** He does not ask so he himself may know, but that he may give one to understand that he satisfies those who ask piously. *He will do the will of those who fear him* (Ps 144:19).

1678. They say to him: Lord, that our eyes be opened. And this is just, that any sinner should ask this. *Open my eyes: and I will consider the wondrous things of your law* (Ps 118:18). And in another place, *enlighten my eyes* (Ps 12:4). They confessed God by saying, **Lord**, and man by calling, **Son of David**.

1679. Therefore, **he had compassion on them**. For he works all things out of his mercy. *The mercies of the Lord that we are not consumed* (Lam 3:22). He **touched their eyes. And immediately they saw**. The humanity and divinity of Christ are touched upon in the fact that he touched their eyes and they saw at once: for that he touched was a

quod statim illuminavit, fuit opus divinitatis. Ipse Dominus tangit per gratiam, sed illuminat per gloriam; Ps. CXLIII, 5: *tange montes, et fumigabunt*.

Sequitur *et secuti sunt eum*. Unde non fuerunt ingrati. Multi enim antequam habeant beneficium, sequuntur Dominum, sed accepto beneficio dimittunt eum, contra illud Eccli. XXIII, 38: *magna est gloria sequi Dominum*.

work of the humanity, but that he illumined immediately was a work of the divinity. The Lord touches through grace, but illumines through glory; *touch the mountains and they will smoke* (Ps 143:5).

There follows *and followed him*. Hence they were not ungrateful. For many follow the Lord before they receive a benefit, but leave him when the benefit is received, contrary to *it is great glory to follow the Lord* (Sir 23:38).

Chapter 21

Lecture 1

²¹:¹ Et cum appropinquassent Ierosolymis, et venissent Bethphage ad Montem Oliveti, tunc Iesus misit duos discipulos, [n. 1681]

²¹:² dicens eis: ite in castellum quod contra vos est, et statim invenietis asinam alligatam, et pullum cum ea; solvite et adducite mihi. [n. 1685]

²¹:³ Et, si quis vobis aliquid dixerit, dicite quia Dominus his opus habet, et confestim dimittet eos. [n. 1686]

²¹:⁴ Hoc autem factum est, ut adimpleretur quod dictum est per prophetam dicentem: [n. 1688]

²¹:⁵ *dicite filiae Sion: ecce rex tuus venit tibi mansuetus, et sedens super asinam, et pullum filium subiugalis.* [n. 1689]

²¹:⁶ Euntes autem discipuli fecerunt sicut praecepit illis Iesus, [n. 1690]

²¹:⁷ et adduxerunt asinam et pullum, et imposuerunt super eos vestimenta sua, et eum desuper sedere fecerunt. [n. 1690]

²¹:⁸ Plurima autem turba straverunt vestimenta sua in via. Alii autem caedebant ramos de arboribus, et sternebant in via. [n. 1691]

²¹:⁹ Turbae autem quae praecedebant, et quae sequebantur, clamabant dicentes: hosanna Filio David: benedictus qui venit est in nomine Domini: hosanna in altissimis. [n. 1693]

²¹:¹⁰ Et cum intrasset Ierosolymam, commota est universa civitas dicens: quis est hic? [n. 1694]

²¹:¹ Καὶ ὅτε ἤγγισαν εἰς Ἱεροσόλυμα καὶ ἦλθον εἰς Βηθφαγὴ εἰς τὸ ὄρος τῶν ἐλαιῶν, τότε Ἰησοῦς ἀπέστειλεν δύο μαθητὰς

²¹:² λέγων αὐτοῖς· πορεύεσθε εἰς τὴν κώμην τὴν κατέναντι ὑμῶν, καὶ εὐθέως εὑρήσετε ὄνον δεδεμένην καὶ πῶλον μετ' αὐτῆς· λύσαντες ἀγάγετέ μοι.

²¹:³ καὶ ἐάν τις ὑμῖν εἴπῃ τι, ἐρεῖτε ὅτι ὁ κύριος αὐτῶν χρείαν ἔχει· εὐθὺς δὲ ἀποστελεῖ αὐτούς.

²¹:⁴ τοῦτο δὲ γέγονεν ἵνα πληρωθῇ τὸ ῥηθὲν διὰ τοῦ προφήτου λέγοντος·

²¹:⁵ εἴπατε τῇ θυγατρὶ Σιών· ἰδοὺ ὁ βασιλεύς σου ἔρχεταί σοι πραΰς καὶ ἐπιβεβηκὼς ἐπὶ ὄνον καὶ ἐπὶ πῶλον υἱὸν ὑποζυγίου.

²¹:⁶ πορευθέντες δὲ οἱ μαθηταὶ καὶ ποιήσαντες καθὼς συνέταξεν αὐτοῖς ὁ Ἰησοῦς

²¹:⁷ ἤγαγον τὴν ὄνον καὶ τὸν πῶλον καὶ ἐπέθηκαν ἐπ' αὐτῶν τὰ ἱμάτια, καὶ ἐπεκάθισεν ἐπάνω αὐτῶν.

²¹:⁸ ὁ δὲ πλεῖστος ὄχλος ἔστρωσαν ἑαυτῶν τὰ ἱμάτια ἐν τῇ ὁδῷ, ἄλλοι δὲ ἔκοπτον κλάδους ἀπὸ τῶν δένδρων καὶ ἐστρώννυον ἐν τῇ ὁδῷ.

²¹:⁹ οἱ δὲ ὄχλοι οἱ προάγοντες αὐτὸν καὶ οἱ ἀκολουθοῦντες ἔκραζον λέγοντες· ὡσαννὰ τῷ υἱῷ Δαυίδ· εὐλογημένος ὁ ἐρχόμενος ἐν ὀνόματι κυρίου· ὡσαννὰ ἐν τοῖς ὑψίστοις.

²¹:¹⁰ Καὶ εἰσελθόντος αὐτοῦ εἰς Ἱεροσόλυμα ἐσείσθη πᾶσα ἡ πόλις λέγουσα· τίς ἐστιν οὗτος;

²¹:¹ And when they drew near to Jerusalem, and had come to Bethphage, unto Mount Olivet, then Jesus sent two disciples, [n. 1681]

²¹:² saying to them: go into the village that is over against you, and immediately you will find an ass tied, and a colt with her; loose them and bring them to me. [n. 1685]

²¹:³ And if any man will say anything to you, say that the Lord has need of them, and immediately he will let them go. [n. 1686]

²¹:⁴ Now all this was done that it might be fulfilled what was spoken by the prophet, saying: [n. 1688]

²¹:⁵ *tell the daughter of Zion: behold your king comes to you, meek, and sitting upon an ass, and a colt the foal of her that is used to the yoke.* [n. 1689]

²¹:⁶ And going, the disciples did as Jesus commanded them. [n. 1690]

²¹:⁷ And they brought the ass and the colt, and laid their garments on them, and made him sit on them. [n. 1690]

²¹:⁸ And a very great multitude spread their garments on the way, and others cut boughs from the trees, and strewed them in the way. [n. 1691]

²¹:⁹ And the multitudes that went before and that followed, cried, saying: hosanna to the Son of David, blessed is he who comes in the name of the Lord, hosanna in the highest. [n. 1693]

²¹:¹⁰ And when he had come into Jerusalem, the whole city was moved, saying: who is this? [n. 1694]

21:11 Populi autem dicebant: hic est Iesus propheta a Nazareth Galilaeae. [n. 1694]

21:12 Et intravit Iesus in templum Dei, et eiiciebat omnes vendentes et ementes in templo, et mensas nummulariorum et cathedras vendentium columbas evertit. [n. 1695]

21:13 Et dicit eis: scriptum est: *domus mea, domus orationis vocabitur*; vos autem fecistis illam speluncam latronum. [n. 1700]

21:14 Et accesserunt ad eum caeci et claudi in templo, et sanavit eos. [n. 1701]

21:15 Videntes autem principes sacerdotum et scribae mirabilia quae fecit, et pueros clamantes in templo, et dicentes, hosanna Filio David, indignati sunt, [n. 1702]

21:16 et dixerunt ei: audis quid isti dicunt? Iesus autem dicit eis: utique. Numquam legistis, quia *ex ore infantium et lactantium perfecisti laudem*? [n. 1704]

21:17 Et relictis illis abiit foras extra civitatem in Bethaniam, ibique mansit. [n. 1708]

21:18 Mane autem revertens in civitatem esuriit, [n. 1710]

21:19 et videns fici arborem unam secus viam, venit ad eam, et nihil invenit in ea nisi folia tantum; et ait illi: numquam ex te fructus nascatur in sempiternum. Et arefacta est continuo ficulnea. [n. 1712]

21:20 Et videntes discipuli mirati sunt dicentes: quomodo continuo aruit? [n. 1715]

21:21 Respondens autem Iesus ait eis: amen dico vobis, si habueritis fidem, et non haesitaveritis, non solum de ficulnea facietis, sed et si monti huic dixeritis: tolle, et iacta te in mare, fiet. [n. 1717]

21:11 οἱ δὲ ὄχλοι ἔλεγον· οὗτός ἐστιν ὁ προφήτης Ἰησοῦς ὁ ἀπὸ Ναζαρὲθ τῆς Γαλιλαίας.

21:12 Καὶ εἰσῆλθεν Ἰησοῦς εἰς τὸ ἱερὸν καὶ ἐξέβαλεν πάντας τοὺς πωλοῦντας καὶ ἀγοράζοντας ἐν τῷ ἱερῷ, καὶ τὰς τραπέζας τῶν κολλυβιστῶν κατέστρεψεν καὶ τὰς καθέδρας τῶν πωλούντων τὰς περιστεράς,

21:13 καὶ λέγει αὐτοῖς· γέγραπται· ὁ οἶκός μου οἶκος προσευχῆς κληθήσεται, ὑμεῖς δὲ αὐτὸν ποιεῖτε σπήλαιον λῃστῶν.

21:14 καὶ προσῆλθον αὐτῷ τυφλοὶ καὶ χωλοὶ ἐν τῷ ἱερῷ, καὶ ἐθεράπευσεν αὐτούς.

21:15 ἰδόντες δὲ οἱ ἀρχιερεῖς καὶ οἱ γραμματεῖς τὰ θαυμάσια ἃ ἐποίησεν καὶ τοὺς παῖδας τοὺς κράζοντας ἐν τῷ ἱερῷ καὶ λέγοντας· ὡσαννὰ τῷ υἱῷ Δαυίδ, ἠγανάκτησαν

21:16 καὶ εἶπαν αὐτῷ· ἀκούεις τί οὗτοι λέγουσιν; ὁ δὲ Ἰησοῦς λέγει αὐτοῖς· ναί. οὐδέποτε ἀνέγνωτε ὅτι ἐκ στόματος νηπίων καὶ θηλαζόντων κατηρτίσω αἶνον;

21:17 καὶ καταλιπὼν αὐτοὺς ἐξῆλθεν ἔξω τῆς πόλεως εἰς Βηθανίαν καὶ ηὐλίσθη ἐκεῖ.

21:18 Πρωῒ δὲ ἐπανάγων εἰς τὴν πόλιν ἐπείνασεν.

21:19 καὶ ἰδὼν συκῆν μίαν ἐπὶ τῆς ὁδοῦ ἦλθεν ἐπ' αὐτὴν καὶ οὐδὲν εὗρεν ἐν αὐτῇ εἰ μὴ φύλλα μόνον, καὶ λέγει αὐτῇ· μηκέτι ἐκ σοῦ καρπὸς γένηται εἰς τὸν αἰῶνα. καὶ ἐξηράνθη παραχρῆμα ἡ συκῆ.

21:20 Καὶ ἰδόντες οἱ μαθηταὶ ἐθαύμασαν λέγοντες· πῶς παραχρῆμα ἐξηράνθη ἡ συκῆ;

21:21 ἀποκριθεὶς δὲ ὁ Ἰησοῦς εἶπεν αὐτοῖς· ἀμὴν λέγω ὑμῖν, ἐὰν ἔχητε πίστιν καὶ μὴ διακριθῆτε, οὐ μόνον τὸ τῆς συκῆς ποιήσετε, ἀλλὰ κἂν τῷ ὄρει τούτῳ εἴπητε· ἄρθητι καὶ βλήθητι εἰς τὴν θάλασσαν, γενήσεται·

21:11 And the people said: this is Jesus the prophet, from Nazareth of Galilee. [n. 1694]

21:12 And Jesus went into the temple of God, and cast out all those who sold and bought in the temple, and overthrew the tables of the money changers, and the chairs of those who sold doves. [n. 1695]

21:13 And he said to them: it is written, *my house will be called the house of prayer*; but you have made it a den of thieves. [n. 1700]

21:14 And there came to him the blind and the lame in the temple; and he healed them. [n. 1701]

21:15 And the chief priests and scribes, seeing the wonderful things that he did, and the children crying in the temple, and saying: hosanna to the Son of David; were moved with indignation, [n. 1702]

21:16 and said to him: do you hear what they say? And Jesus said to them: yes, have you never read: *out of the mouth of infants and of sucklings you have perfected praise*? [n. 1704]

21:17 And leaving them, he went out of the city into Bethania, and remained there. [n. 1708]

21:18 And in the morning, returning into the city, he was hungry. [n. 1710]

21:19 And seeing a certain fig tree by the way side, he came to it, and found nothing on it but leaves only, and he said to it: may no fruit grow on you from now on and forever. And immediately the fig tree withered away. [n. 1712]

21:20 And the disciples seeing it wondered, saying: how is it presently withered away? [n. 1715]

21:21 And Jesus answering, said to them: amen, I say to you, if you have faith, and do not stagger, not only this, of the fig tree, will you do, but also if you say to this mountain: take up and cast yourself into the sea, it will be done. [n. 1717]

| 21:22 Et omnia quaecumque petieritis in oratione credentes, accipietis. [n. 1719] | 21:22 καὶ πάντα ὅσα ἂν αἰτήσητε ἐν τῇ προσευχῇ πιστεύοντες λήμψεσθε. | 21:22 And all things whatever that you ask in prayer, believing, you will receive. [n. 1719] |

1680. Supra divisum est Evangelium Matthaei in tres partes, in prima ponit introitum Christi in mundum usque ad tertium capitulum; secundo de processu in mundo; in tertia de egressu. Completis igitur duabus primis partibus, hic agitur de tertia.

Et dividitur: quia
primo agitur de quibusdam praeambulis;
secundo de passione Christi, et hoc XXVI capitulo.
Et
primo ponitur provocatio persecutorum;
secundo confortatio discipulorum, et hoc XXIV.
Confortaverat discipulos praedicens futura. Inde provocati fuerunt quidam per eius gloriam, cui invidebant; de hoc agitur in isto capitulo. Aliqui per eius scientiam, et de hoc XXII capitulo.
Prima dividitur in duas. Quia
primo agitur de gloria Christi;
secundo de persecutorum indignatione, ibi **videntes autem principes sacerdotum et scribae** et cetera.
Circa primum tria.
Primo ponitur gloria Christi quae fuit in via exhibita;
secundo quae in civitate;
tertio de ea quam potestative accepit de templo.

Secunda ibi **et cum intrasset Ierosolymam** et cetera. Tertia ibi **et intravit Iesus in templum Dei**.
In via a duobus ei gloria impensa fuit, scilicet per discipulos, et per ministerium turbarum.
Secunda ibi **plurima autem turba straverunt vestimenta sua in via**.
Et circa primum tria.
Primo ponit mandatum de ministerio;
secundo ponitur ratio;
tertio mandati executio.
Secunda ibi **hoc autem totum factum est** etc.; tertia ibi **euntes autem discipuli** et cetera.

Circa primum tria.
Primo ponitur locus;
secundo personae quibus fit;
tertio mandatum.

1681. Locus ponitur cum dicit **et cum appropinquassent Ierosolymis** et cetera. Paulatim Evangelista narravit accessum Christi ad Ierusalem. Primo narravit quomodo a Galilaea venerat, et quomodo per Iericho, et quomodo ibi caecos illuminaverat, qui erant in confinibus. Post dicit **cum appropinquassent Ierosolymis,**

1680. Above, the Gospel of Matthew was divided into three parts: in the first he set forth the entrance of Christ into the world, up to the third chapter; second, concerning his progress in the world; in the third, concerning his departure. Therefore, the first two parts being finished, here the third is treated.

And it is divided: for
first, he treats of certain preparatory things;
second, of Christ's passion (Matt 26).

First, the provocation of the persecutors is set out;
second, the strengthening of the disciples (Matt 24).
He had strengthened the disciples by foretelling the future. From there, certain men were provoked by his glory, which they envied; this is treated in this chapter. Some were provoked by his knowledge (Matt 22).
The first is divided into two. For
first, he treats of Christ's glory;
second, of the persecutors' indignation, at **and the chief priests and scribes, seeing**.
Concerning the first, three things:
first is set out Christ's glory, which was displayed on the road;
second, that which was displayed in the city;
third, of those things which he took by force from the temple.

The second is at **and when he had come into Jerusalem**. The third, at **and Jesus went into the temple of God**.
On the road, glory was given him by two, namely by the disciples and by the crowds' service.
The second is at **and a very great multitude spread their garments on the way**.
And concerning the first, three things:
first, he sets out a command about the service;
second, the reason is given;
third, the command is carried out.
The second is at **now all this was done, that it might be fulfilled**; the third, at **and going, the disciples did as Jesus commanded them**.

Concerning the first, three things:
first, the place is set down;
second, the persons through whom it came about;
third, the command.

1681. The place is set down when it says, **and when they drew near to Jerusalem**. The Evangelist describes Christ's approach to Jerusalem step by step. First, he describes how he had come from Galilee, and through Jericho, and how there he had illumined the blind men who were in the region. After that, he says, **and when they drew near**

to Jerusalem, and had come to Bethphage, unto Mount Olivet. And it is called this because there are many olive trees there, and it is about a thousand paces from Jerusalem. Bethphage was a priestly village, for the priests served the temple through the week: and on the Sabbath day, when the priest left the temple, he would come up to there, since he was only supposed to travel a thousand paces. Those also who went to the temple on the Sabbath day would withdraw from there. Or, Bethphage is the same as 'home of the jaw,' because the jaw of the sacrifice was the priest's portion.

1682. Morally, Jerusalem is interpreted as 'vision of peace,' and signifies the society of the good. *Jerusalem, which is built as a city, which is compact together* (Ps 121:3). Hence, desiring to draw near to Jerusalem, he came through Bethphage, and through the house of confession. *For, with the heart, we believe unto justice; but, with the mouth, confession is made unto salvation* (Rom 10:10). Bethphage is situated on the Mount of Olives, where there is an abundance of oil. *My beloved, a son of oil, had a vineyard on a hill* (Isa 5:1). Oil signifies mercy, which has the property of gladdening. *That he may make the face cheerful with oil* (Ps 103:15). In this way, mercy makes glad: *God loves a cheerful giver* (2 Cor 9:7). Similarly, oil is good for lighting an oil lamp. The Lord commanded that the clearest oil be offered to him. Similarly, it is useful for healing sorrows; and it signifies the grace of the Holy Spirit, which heals. Hence it says in Luke that the Samaritan poured out oil and wine (Luke 10:34).

1683. *Then Jesus sent two disciples, saying to them*; and it signifies the sending of the apostles into this world. *As the Father has sent me, I also send you* (John 20:21). But two, to signify charity, which is established between two at the least. Hence in another place, *he sent them two and two* (Luke 10:1). Or it signifies the active and the contemplative life. Or the two orders of those who preach, namely of the Jews and of the gentiles. Hence the Apostle: *for he who wrought in Peter to the apostleship of the circumcision, wrought in me also among the gentiles* (Gal 2:8). Or the two who were supposed to be sent to the gentiles, namely Peter and Philip.

1684. And he does three things:
first, he entrusts the saving mission to them;
second, he gives a command about the salvation;
third, about those who object.

1685. He says then, *go into the village that is over against you*. Literally, there was a certain village which was opposite them, to signify the world into which the Lord sent them. *Go into the whole world, and preach the Gospel to every creature* (Mark 16:15). And this world will be against them. *I have chosen you out of the world, therefore the world hates you* (John 15:19).

So he says, *go into the village that is over against you*. He commands one thing and foretells another. He commands *go into the village*; he foretells, *and immediately*

cum ea. Alii non faciunt mentionem de asina. Utrumque invenerunt.

Moraliter per asinam et pullum significantur homines brutaliter viventes, quia quantum ad hoc similes sunt bestiis; Ps. XLVIII, v. 13: *homo cum in honore esset, non intellexit: comparatus est iumentis insipientibus, et similis factus est illis*. Per asinam significatur Iudaea, per pullum populus gentilis.

Et quare per asinam significatur populus Iudaicus? Quia triplex est proprietas asini. Primo quia est animal stultum, unde dicitur 'asinus', idest insensatus. Sic homo insensatus est relinquens legem Domini. Deut. XXXII, 6: *popule stulte et insipiens*. Item est oneribus deputatus, sic populus Iudaicus oneribus legis est gravatus, ut dixit Petrus Act. XV, 10: *hoc est onus quod nec nos, nec patres nostri ferre potuerunt*. Item asinus est animal ignobile; sic illi ignobiles dicuntur, qui contemnunt mandata Domini. Sed ligatam, vinculis scilicet ignorantiae. Sap. XVII, 17: *una enim catena tenebrarum omnes erant ligati*. Item erant ligati vinculo peccati. Prov. V, 22: *iniquitates suae capiunt impium*.

1686. *Solvite et adducite mihi*. Hic inducit populi salvationem. Solvite a vinculis ignorantiae per doctrinam. Ps. CVI, 14: *eduxit eos de tenebris et umbra mortis*. Item solvite a vinculis peccatorum; unde Petro dixit supra XVI, 19. ***Quodcumque solveris super terram, erit solutum et in caelis***. Et in Ps. XXXI, 1: *beati quorum remissae sunt iniquitates, et quorum tecta sunt peccata*. Unde isti populum convertentes adduxerunt ad Iesum. I ad Cor. I, 13: *numquid Paulus crucifixus est*? Is. LXVI, 19: *annuntiabunt gloriam meam in gentibus*. Sed, sicut dicit Apostolus ad Titum I, 9, oportet episcopum habere doctrinam, *ut sit potens exhortari in doctrina sana*: unde quod dicit **solvite**, hoc ad doctrinam pertinet; quod vero sequitur *et si quis aliquid vobis dixerit* etc., ad potestatem pertinet.

1687. Unde *si quis dixerit*, contradicendo, idest si quis voluerit contradicere, **dicetis quia Dominus his opus habet, et confestim dimittet eos**. In hoc ostenditur virtus Christi, quia non propter apostolos dimisissent, nisi hoc fieret opere Christi invisibiliter cor immutantis. Unde dabat intelligere quod ipse erat Deus, quia solius Dei est immutare cor; unde cor hominis in manu eius. Item, quia dicit **confestim**, dat intelligere quod sicut illi statim dimittebant, ipsi etiam statim dimitterent. Vel ad litteram, quia parum tenebit, et statim dimittet, quia solum indiget ad diem.

Sed quaestio est secundum mysticam expositionem. Nonne dicitur, bonorum nostrorum non indiget? Dico quod non indiget nisi ad nostram necessitatem, et ad

you will find an ass tied, and a colt with her. The others make no mention of the ass. They found both.

Morally, the ass and the colt signify men living bestially, for in this respect they are like the beasts; *and man when he was in honor did not understand; he is compared to senseless beasts, and is become like to them* (Ps 48:13). The ass signifies Judea, the colt, the gentile peoples.

And why is the Jewish people signified by an ass? Because the ass has three properties. First, it is a stupid animal, hence it is called 'ass,' i.e., senseless. Thus a man is senseless when he abandons the law of the Lord. Likewise, it is assigned to burdens, and thus the Jewish people was weighed down with the burden of the law, as Peter said, *a yoke upon the necks of the disciples, which neither our fathers nor we have been able to bear* (Acts 15:10). Likewise, the ass is an ignoble animal; in this way, those who despise the Lord's commands are called ignoble. But bound, namely with the bond of ignorance. *For they were all bound together with one chain of darkness* (Wis 17:17). Likewise, they were bound by the bond of sin. *His own iniquities catch the wicked* (Prov 5:22).

1686. *Loose them and bring them to me*. Here he brings in the salvation of the people. Loose them from the bonds of ignorance by teaching. *And he brought them out of darkness, and the shadow of death* (Ps 106:14). Likewise, loose them from the bonds of sins; hence he said to Peter above, ***and whatever you bind upon earth will be bound also in heaven*** (Matt 16:19). And, *blessed are they whose iniquities are forgiven, and whose sins are covered* (Ps 31:1). Hence these men, converting the people, led them to Jesus. *Was Paul then crucified for you?* (1 Cor 1:13). *And they will declare my glory to the gentiles* (Isa 66:19). But, as the Apostle says to Titus, a bishop must have teaching, *that he may be able to exhort in sound doctrine* (Titus 1:9): hence what he says here, **loose**, pertains to teaching, while what follows, ***and if any man will say anything to you***, pertains to power.

1687. Hence, ***if any man will say anything***, objecting, i.e., if anyone wishes to contradict you, ***say that the Lord has need of them, and immediately he will let them go***. And this shows Christ's power, since they would not have let them go for the apostles' sake, unless this had happened through Christ's working, invisibly changing the heart. Hence he let it be understood that he himself was God, for only God can change the heart; hence the heart of man is in his hand. Likewise, since he says, ***immediately***, he lets it be understood that just as those men sent away immediately, so they themselves would send away immediately. Or literally, because the Lord will only keep them for a little while, and send them away immediately, because he only needs them for the day.

But there is a question, according to the mystical exposition. Is it not said that he has no need of our goods? I say that he has no need, unless on account of our necessity and

suam gloriam. Ioel II, 32: *quicumque invocaverit nomen Domini, salvus erit. Omne quod invocat nomen meum.*

1688. Hoc autem totum factum est et cetera. Hic ponitur ratio mandati. Ne crederet aliquis quod hoc factum esset sine ratione, ideo rationem ostendit: **ut adimpleretur quod dictum est per prophetam** et cetera. Istud dicit per Zachariam cap. IX, 9. Sed ly *ut* non tenetur causaliter, sed consecutive. Non enim facit quia propheta dixerat, sed potius e converso: finis enim prophetiae est Christus.

1689. 'Dicite filiae Sion' et cetera. Annuntiate filiae Sion, haec dicitur plebs Ierusalem quae subiecta erat monti Sion. Item significatur tota Ecclesia, quia Sion 'specula' interpretatur. *Annuntiate studia eius inter gentes*, Ps. IX, 12. Praenuntiatur dignitas **'ecce rex tuus.'** Isti Iudaei diu passi fuerant tyrannos, unde expectabant regem, sicut dictum est Ier. c. XXIII, 5. *regnabit rex et sapiens erit.*

Et ponit quatuor, quae dignitatem regis commendant; consequenter quatuor, quae in tyrannis inveniuntur. Primo affinitas, quia magis afficitur homo ad magis coniunctos. Deut. c. XVII, 15: *non poteris super te facere regem, nisi sit frater tuus.* Unde dicit **'ecce rex tuus.'** Idest de gente tua. Sed quandoque reges degenerant in tyrannos, quia quaerunt utilitatem suam, quod est contra morem regis; ideo dicitur **'venit tibi'**, idest ad utilitatem tuam. Hab. III, 13: *egressus es in salutem cum Christo tuo.* **'Mansuetus.'** Mansuetudo pertinet ad regem, quia infligere poenam ferocitatis est. Prov. XX, 28: *misericordia et iustitia custodiunt regem.* Ideo David a populo dilectus fuit, quia mansuetus fuit. Item requiritur humilitas, quia Dominus superbos respuit; ideo dicit **'sedens super asinam.'** Supra XI, 29: **discite a me, quia mitis sum et humilis corde.**

1690. Euntes autem discipuli fecerunt sicut praecepit illis Iesus. Postquam positum est mandatum, hic ponitur executio mandati.

Et primo in generali **euntes discipuli**. Ecce datur obedientiae mandatum. Ex. XXIX, 35: *omnia quae praecepit Dominus faciemus.*

Deinde in speciali **et adduxerunt asinam et pullum**. Per hoc significatur quod converterunt et Iudaeos, et gentiles, ut habetur ad Rom. I, 14: *Graecis ac barbaris, sapientibus et insipientibus debitor sum.* **Et imposuerunt super eos vestimenta sua**. Vestimenta sunt virtutes eorum. Ad Col. III, 12: *induite vos ergo sicut electi Dei sancti et dilecti, viscera misericordiae.* Vestimenta imposuerunt, quia in exemplum aliis fuerunt, ut dicitur ad Phil. c. III, 17: *imitatores mei estote, fratres, et observate eos, qui ita ambulant, sicut habetis formam nostram.* **Et**

for his glory. *Everyone who calls upon the name of the Lord will be saved* (Joel 2:32). *And everyone who calls upon my name, I have created him for my glory* (Isa 43:7).

1688. Now all this was done that it might be fulfilled. Here the reason for the command is set down. Lest someone should think that this was done without reason, he shows the reason: **that it might be fulfilled what was spoken by the prophet**. It is through Zechariah that he says this (Zech 9:9). But **that it might** is not taken causally, but consecutively. For he does not act because the prophet had spoken, but rather the other way around: for the end of prophecy is Christ.

1689. 'Tell the daughter of Zion.' Announce to the daughter of Zion, that is, the people of Jerusalem, which was subjected to Mount Zion. Likewise, the whole Church is signified, for Zion is interpreted as 'watchtower.' *Declare his ways among the gentiles* (Ps 9:12). Dignity is foretold: **'behold your king.'** Those Jews had suffered tyrants for a long time, and so they were hoping for a king, as is said in Jeremiah, *a king will reign, and will be wise* (Jer 23:5).

And he sets down four things which commend the dignity of the king; next, four things which are found in tyrants. First, close relation, because a man has more affection for those more closely connected with him. *You may not make a man of another nation king, who is not your brother* (Deut 17:15). Hence he says, **'behold your king'**, i.e., from your people. But sometimes kings corrupt into tyrants, because they seek their own gain, which is contrary to the natural disposition of a king; for this reason it says, **'comes to you'**, i.e., for your gain. *You went forth for salvation with your Christ* (Hab 3:13). **'Meek.'** Meekness pertains to a king, because inflicting punishment belongs to fierceness. *Mercy and truth preserve the king* (Prov 20:28). This is why the people loved David, because he was meek. Likewise, humility is required, because the Lord rejects the proud; for this reason, he says, **'sitting upon an ass.'** Above, **learn from me, because I am meek, and humble of heart** (Matt 11:29).

1690. And going, the disciples did as Jesus commanded them. After the command was set out, here the execution of the command is set out.

And first, in general: **and going, the disciples did**. Behold, a command is given for obedience. *All that the Lord has spoken, we will do* (Exod 19:8).

Then in particular: **and they brought the ass and the colt.** By this is signified that they converted both the Jews and the gentiles: *to the Greeks and to the barbarians, to the wise and to the unwise, I am a debtor* (Rom 1:14). **And laid their garments upon them**. The garments are their virtues. *Put on therefore, as the elect of God, holy, and beloved, the bowels of mercy* (Col 3:12). They laid their garments on them because they were made examples for others, as is said, *be followers of me, brethren, and observe them who walk so as you have our model* (Phil 3:17). **And made him**

eum desuper sedere fecerunt. Secundum litteram dicitur quod super utrumque, quia super corda Iudaeorum et gentilium.

1691. *Plurima autem turba straverunt vestimenta sua in via*. Postquam determinavit de ministerio discipulorum, determinat de gloria turbarum. Et

primo de gloria, quam exhibent ei in opere;

secundo quam exhibent ei verbo, ibi *turbae autem . . . clamabant*.

1692. Et primo *straverunt vestimenta*; secundo *ramos de arboribus*. Et quare? Ad faciendum ei honorem, sicut magnis hominibus venientibus sternitur via. Item, quia via erat lapidosa, ideo ne laederetur, sternebant.

Secundum mysterium, discipuli straverunt vestimenta super asinam, quae significant virtutes, quas a Deo acceperunt, et istas communicaverunt gentilibus et Iudaeis. Sed vestimenta turbae sunt legalia quae propter Christum sunt dispersa. Ad Phil. III, 7: *quae fuerunt mihi lucra, haec arbitratus sum propter Christum detrimenta*. Item per vestimenta, corpora. Apoc. III, 4: *habes paucos in Sardis qui custodierunt vestimenta sua*. Illi ergo qui in via straverunt vestimenta, fuerunt primi martyres. Rom. XII, 19: *non defendentes vosmetipsos, carissimi; sed date locum irae*.

Alii caedebant ramis de arboribus. Isti sunt rami qui fructificare debebant, per quos significantur sancti patres. Ille ergo ramos abscindit, qui eos ad Christum convertit. Ps. I, 3: *et erit tamquam lignum quod plantatum est secus decursus aquarum*.

1693. *Turbae autem quae praecedebant, et quae sequebantur clamabant*. Hic ponitur honor exhibitus ei verbo. Sed a quibus? A praecedentibus et sequentibus, scilicet ab his, qui ante adventum fuerunt et post; et utrique petunt salutem, et habent a Christo. II ad Cor. VI, 13: *eamdem habentes remunerationem*. Turbae autem salutem petebant; unde **clamabant dicentes: hosanna Filio David** et cetera. Haec salus incipitur in praesenti, et perficietur in futuro. Sup. I, 21: *ipse enim salvum faciet populum suum a peccatis eorum*. Unde dicebant, **hosanna** et cetera. Multi dicunt quod significat redemptionem. Sed idem est quod 'obsecro salve': 'anna' affectum dicit obsecrantis. Ps. XI, 2: *salvum me fac*. Et istam petunt a Filio David. Ita scriptum est Ier. XXIII, 5: *suscitabo David germen iustum*, et sequitur, *in diebus illis salvabitur Iuda*. Et poterit hoc facere, quia Filius David? Non, sed quia **venit in nomine Domini**. Quare? Quia venit confitens Dominum. Io. V, v. 43: *ego veni in nomine Patris mei, et non suscepistis me*. Est ergo una salus, liberatio a peccatis. Is. XXXV, 4: *ipse veniet, et salvabit nos*. Item alia salus, per quam liberantur ab omni poena. Is. LI, 8: *salus autem mea in sempiternum erit, et iustitia mea non*

sit on them. Literally, it says on top of both, because he sits over the hearts of the Jews and of the gentiles.

1691. *And a very great multitude spread their garments on the way*. After he has explained the disciples' service, he explains the crowds' glory. And

first, concerning the glory which they showed him in deed;

second, the glory which they showed him in word, at *and the multitudes . . . cried*.

1692. And first they **spread their garments**; second, they **cut boughs from the trees**. And why? To give him honor, as the road is spread for a great man who is coming. Likewise, because the road was rocky, so they were spreading garments and tree branches lest he be hurt.

According to a mystery, the disciples spread garments over the ass, which signify the virtues which they had received from God, and they imparted these to the gentiles and the Jews. But the crowd's garments are the things of the law which are scattered for Christ's sake. *But the things that were gain to me, the same I have counted loss for Christ* (Phil 3:7). Likewise, the garments signify bodies. *But you have a few names in Sardis, which have not defiled their garments* (Rev 3:14). Therefore those who spread garments in the way were the first martyrs. *Do not revenge yourselves, my dearly beloved; but give place unto wrath* (Rom 12:19).

Others cut boughs from the trees. These are the boughs which ought to bear fruit, which signify the holy fathers. He therefore cuts off the boughs who converts them to Christ. *And he shall be like a tree which is planted near the running waters* (Ps 1:3).

1693. *And the multitudes that went before and that followed, cried*. Here the honor shown to him by word is set out. But who showed him honor? Those going before and those following after, namely those who were before and after his coming; and both beg for salvation, and they have it from Christ. *Having the same recompense* (2 Cor 6:13). Now, the crowds were begging for salvation; hence they **cried, saying: hosanna to the Son of David**. This salvation is begun in the present, and will be perfected in the future. *He will save his people from their sins* (Matt 1:21). Hence they said, **hosanna**. Many say that it signifies redemption. But it is the same as 'I seek salvation': 'anna' bespeaks the disposition of one who implores. *Save me, O Lord* (Ps 11:2). And they ask this of the Son of David. Thus it is written, *I will raise up to David a just branch* (Jer 23:5–6) and there follows, *in those days shall Judah be saved*. And will he be able to do this because he is the Son of David? No, but because **he comes in the name of the Lord**. Why? Because he comes confessing the Lord. *I have come in the name of my Father, and you do not receive* (John 5:43). Therefore one salvation is liberation from sins. *God himself will come and will save you* (Isa 35:4). Similarly, there is another salvation

deficiet. Et hoc **in excelsis**, idest, des primo salutem in terris, et postea in caelis.

1694. *Et cum intrasset Ierosolymam* et cetera. Hic agitur de gloria ei exhibita in civitate. Et primo ponitur admiratio turbarum *et commota est universa civitas*, idest admirata. Is. LX, 5: *tunc videbis, et afflues, et mirabitur, et dilatabitur cor tuum*. Ps. LIX, 4: *commovisti terram, et conturbasti eam*. **Dicens: quis est hic?** Et non est mirum si isti mirantur, quia etiam Angeli mirati sunt in sua ascensione dicentes: *quis est hic qui venit de Edom, tinctis vestibus de Bosra?* Is. LXIII, v. 1.

Ponitur responsio *populi autem dicebant, hic est Iesus propheta a Nazareth Galilaeae*. 'Propheta' actum denuntiationis significat. *A Nazareth*, quia ibi nutritus erat, et inde magis notus, et ideo dicebatur Nazaraenus.

1695. *Et intravit Iesus in templum Dei, et eiecit ementes et vendentes*. Supra ostendit Evangelista gloriam quae Christo exhibita est in via, et quae in civitate, nunc autem de gloria quantum ad ea quae facta sunt in templo. Et tria sunt gesta in templo, quae pertinent ad gloriam Christi. Quia primo purgavit templum; secundo infirmos curavit; tertio ora infantium aperuit. De istis per ordinem determinat Evangelista.

Circa primum
primo ponitur visitatio templi;
secundo purgatio;
tertio reprehensio Iudaeorum.

Secunda ibi *et eiiciebat omnes vendentes et ementes*; tertia ibi *dixit eis* et cetera.

1696. Dicit ergo *et intravit Iesus in templum Dei* et cetera.

Sed quare intrans civitatem, statim venit ad templum? Una ratio, quia venerat ut hostia immolanda; ideo primo venit ad locum immolationis, et iste erat dies statutus in quo agnus praesentari debebat, ut legitur Ex. XII, v. 6 quod luna decima debebat agnus praesentari, qui debebat occidi quartadecima luna. Sed occisus est in die Iovis in sero. Ergo oblatio fieri debuit in ramis palmarum.

Secunda ratio, quia ostendit se esse Filium reverendi Patris, ut reverentiam Patri exhiberet, venit ad domum Patris sui. Mal. I, 6: *si ego pater, ubi honor meus?* Et in hoc datur nobis religionis exemplum, ut cum in civitatem aliquam venimus, quod primo templum adeamus. Ps. V, 8: *adorabo ad templum sanctum tuum*.

by which we are freed from every punishment. *But my salvation will be forever, and my justice from generation to generation* (Isa 51:8). And this is **in the highest**, i.e., may you give the first salvation on earth, and afterward in heaven.

1694. *And when he had come into Jerusalem*. Here the glory shown to him in the city is treated. And first, the wonderment of the crowds: **the whole city was moved**, i.e., wondered. *Then you will see, and abound, and your heart will wonder and be enlarged* (Isa 60:5). *You have moved the earth, and have troubled it* (Ps 59:4). **Saying: who is this?** And it is no marvel if they marveled, for even the angels marveled at his ascension, saying, *who is this that comes from Edom, with dyed garments from Bosra?* (Isa 63:1).

The response is set down: *and the people said: this is Jesus the prophet, from Nazareth of Galilee*. 'Prophet' signifies the act of declaration. *From Nazareth*, because he was raised there, and from there became more known, and it is for this reason that he was called a Nazarene.

1695. *And Jesus went into the temple of God, and cast out all those who sold and bought in the temple*. Above, the Evangelist set out the glory which was shown to Christ in the way, and in the city; now he treats of glory with regard to those things which happened in the temple. And three things were done in the temple which pertain to Christ's glory. For first, he purged the temple; second, he cured the sick; third, he opened the mouths of the speechless. The Evangelist explains these things in order.

Concerning the first,
first, the visitation of the temple is set down;
second, the purging;
third, the reproach of the Jews.

The second is at *and cast out all those who sold and bought in the temple*; the third, at *and he said to them: it is written*.

1696. It says then, *and Jesus went into the temple of God*.

But why, as he entered the city, did he come immediately to the temple? One reason is because he had come as a victim to be sacrificed; for this reason, he came first to the place for sacrificing, and this was the established day on which the lamb was supposed to be presented, as it is written, that on the tenth day of the month the Passover lamb was to be presented, which was to be killed on the fourteenth day of the month (Exod 12:3–6). But it was killed on the day of Jove, in the evening. Therefore the sacrifice was supposed to be made in boughs of palm trees.

A second reason is because he showed himself to be the Son of a Father who should be revered; that he might show reverence to the Father, he came to his Father's house. *If then I am a father, where is my honor?* (Mal 1:6). And in this an example of religion is given to us, that when we come into some city, we should first go to the temple. *I will worship towards your holy temple* (Ps 5:8).

Item egit ut bonus medicus, qui primo obviat causae morbi. Unde aegritudo et causa corruptionis spiritualis a templo procedit, quia si sacerdos est corruptus, de facili corrumpetur populus; ideo primo adivit templum, ut curationem adhiberet primo circa templum. Ez. IX, 6: *a sanctuario meo incipite*.

1697. Ad intellectum istorum debetis intelligere, ut legitur Ex. XXIII, 15 quod omnes filii Israel semel in anno habebant comparere coram Domino, et non debebant apparere vacui, sed debebant offerre oblationes suas. Et ita erat quod illi qui de prope habitabant, adducebant secum animalia sua, ut sic lucrarentur. Item, quia aliqui non habebant pecuniam, ideo habebant nummularios qui accommodarent non habentibus, ut sic non possent se excusare ab oblatione. Sed quia prohibitum erat, quod non accommodarent ad usuram, ideo usuram non recipiebant, sed munuscula quae *coliba* dicuntur, scilicet uvas passas, vel huiusmodi. Item quia aliqui erant pauperes, qui non poterant habere animalia grossa, nec eis credebatur, ideo habebant ministros qui vendebant columbas et turtures, ne alicui deficeret oblatio. Unde Dominus non reprehendebat oblationes, sed cupiditatem eorum.

Dicit ergo *et eiiciebat ementes et vendentes*, ad litteram. Vendentes erant ministri sacerdotum. Item habebant nummularios: ideo *mensas nummulariorum evertit, et cathedras vendentium columbas*, idest sedilia in quibus sedebant.

1698. Mystice in templo, idest in Ecclesia, sunt qui lucris temporalibus inhiant, qui de Ecclesia eiiciuntur: quia *qui volunt divites fieri, incidunt in tentationem et in laqueum diaboli*, I ad Tim. VI, 9. Nummularii possunt dici diaconi, quibus datur administratio temporalium, ut habetur Act. VI, 2. Unde cum officium dispensationis retorquent ad quaestum, debent eiici de Ecclesia. Per columbam intelligitur Spiritus Sanctus; unde vendentes columbas sunt praelati vendentes dona spiritualia, ut ordinem, vel huiusmodi. Act. VIII, 20: *pecunia tua tecum sit in perditionem*.

Item potest exponi quod unusquisque est templum Dei. I ad Cor. III, 16: *nescitis quia templum Dei estis vos?* Unde debet unusquisque expellere a se venditionem et emptionem, ut non serviat Deo propter divitias; item avaritiam, quae per nummularios; item simoniae pravitatem, evellere etiam appetitum simoniae a corde, qui per cathedras significatur.

1699. Sed hic est quaestio litteralis, quia habetur in Io. II, 14 ss. quod ante traditionem Ioannis factum fuit istud miraculum; hic autem habetur, quod imminente passione. Dicit Augustinus quod bis factum est istud miraculum; ideo magis sunt culpabiles, cum alias reprehensi fuissent.

Likewise, he acted as a good doctor, who first confronts the cause of the illness. Hence the sickness and cause of spiritual corruption proceeds from the temple, for if a priest is corrupt, the people is easily corrupted; for this reason he went first to the temple, that he might first apply treatment with regard to the temple. *Begin at my sanctuary* (Ezek 9:6).

1697. To understand these things, you should understand, as is written, that all the children of Israel had to gather before the Lord at one time of the year, and they were not supposed to appear empty-handed, but were to offer their sacrifices (Exod 23:15). And so it was that those who lived nearby brought their own animals with them, so as to make a profit. Similarly, since some did not have money, they had money-changers who would accommodate those who did not have money, so that they could not excuse themselves in this way from the obligation of offering sacrifice. But since it was forbidden that they should exchange money with interest, they did not take interest but rather a little gift which they called a *coliba*, namely raisins or some such thing. Similarly, since there were some poor men who could neither own nor borrow large animals, for this reason they had attendants who sold pigeons and doves, lest someone fail in his obligation. Hence the Lord did not reproach the sacrifices, but their greed.

So it says, *and cast out all those who sold and bought*, literally. Those who bought were the priests' attendants. Likewise they had money changers, so he *overthrew the tables of the money changers, and the chairs of those who sold doves*, i.e., the seats on which they sat.

1698. Mystically, in the temple, i.e., in the Church, there are those who covet temporal profits, who are cast out of the Church: for *they who wish to become rich, fall into temptation, and into the snare of the devil* (1 Tim 6:9). The money changers can be called deacons, to whom is given the administration of temporal things, as is said (Acts 6:2). Hence when they turn the office of stewardship to gain, they should be cast out of the Church. By the dove is understood the Holy Spirit; hence those selling doves are the prelates who sell spiritual gifts, such as holy orders. *Keep your money to yourself, to perish with you* (Acts 8:20).

Similarly, it can be explained that each man is the temple of God. *Do you not know, that you are the temple of God?* (1 Cor 3:16). Hence each man should cast out from himself buying and selling, that he may not serve God for the sake of riches; likewise greed, which is signified by the money-changers; likewise the depravity of simony, to tear the appetite of simony out of his heart, which is signified by the chairs.

1699. But there is a literal question here, because it says in John, that he worked this miracle before John was handed over (John 2:14); but here it says just before the passion. Augustine says that this miracle was done twice; therefore they are the more culpable, since the others had been reproached.

Item cum esset homo despectibilis et humilis, quomodo hoc potuit facere contra voluntatem sacerdotum et magnorum? Hieronymus dicit quod hoc est unum maximum miraculum quod Dominus fecerit, et quod virtus quaedam radiabat a vultu suo, per quam terrebat homines quando volebat.

1700. *Et dixit eis: scriptum est* etc., hic reprehendit eos. Et primo in hoc quod pertinet ad dignitatem templi; secundo per hoc quod pertinet ad usum.

Scriptum est, scilicet Is. LVI, 7, *'domus mea domus orationis est.'* Expositio huius habetur III Reg. VIII, 27, ubi dicitur, *cum caeli caelorum capere te non possunt, quanto magis domus haec quam aedificavi tibi?* Unde non dicitur domus Domini, quia ibi corporaliter inhabitet, sed quia locus est deputatus ad orandum Deum. Sicut aliquis dominus habet locum ubi petitiones recipit et exaudit, sic templum est locus ubi Dominus vota fidelium audit. Ecclesia nostra specialiter dicitur domus, quia ibi habitat corporaliter in sacramento Christus Deus. Ps. CXLVII, 20: *non fecit taliter omni nationi.* Unde Augustinus in *Regula*: *in oratorio nihil aliud fiat, nisi ad quod deputatum est.*

Consequenter reprehendit eos quantum ad usum ***vos autem fecistis eam speluncam latronum***: quia ea quae religionis sunt, in quaestum convertunt, et latrones in speluncis latitant, ut spolient transeuntes, et sibi acquirant quod non est suum.

1701. *Accesserunt autem ad eum caeci et claudi.* Hic ponitur quod ad gloriam Christi pertinet quantum ad infirmorum curationem. Caeci vero, qui in templo sunt, significant eos, qui excaecati sunt per ignorantiam. Is. LIX, 10: *palpavimus sicut caeci parietem.* 'Claudi' dicuntur, qui per vias ambulant iniquorum. III Reg. XVII, 28: *ut quid claudicatis in duas partes?* Et isti accedunt ad Christum in templo, et sanat eos. Et congruit huic facto locus, per quod significatur quod morbi spirituales non curantur nisi in Ecclesia. Facto ostendit, quia pueri clamaverunt, supra, ***benedictus qui venit in nomine Domini***. Is. XXXV, 4: *ecce Dominus veniet, et salvabit nos; tunc aperientur oculi eorum.*

1702. Sequitur indignatio sacerdotum, unde dicit ***videntes autem principes sacerdotum et scribae ... indignati sunt***. De talibus dicitur II ad Tim. III, 13: *semper proficiunt in peius.* Et
    primo ponitur reprehensio;
    secundo inquisitio;
    tertio responsio.
    Circa primum tria.
    Primo ponitur causa indignationis;
    secundo ponitur indignatio;
    tertio ponitur confutatio.

Similarly, since he was an unobtrusive and humble man, how could he do this against the will of the priests and the great? Jerome says that this was the one greatest miracle that the Lord worked, and that a certain power radiated from his will, through which he terrified men when he wished.

1700. *And he said to them: it is written.* Here he reproaches them. And first, with regard to the dignity of the temple; second, with regard to its use.

It is written, namely in Isaiah, *'my house will be called the house of prayer'* (Isa 56:7). The explanation of this is found where it says, *for if heaven, and the heavens of heavens cannot contain you, how much less this house which I have built?* (1 Kgs 8:27). Hence it is not called the house of the Lord because he dwells there bodily, but because it is the designated place for praying to God. As a lord has a place where he receives and hears requests, so the temple is the place where the Lord hears the prayers of the faithful. Our Church is called a house in a special way, because Christ God dwells there bodily in the sacrament. *He has not done in like manner to every nation* (Ps 147:9). Hence Augustine in the *Regula*: *let nothing happen in the oratory except that to which it is assigned.*

Next, he reproaches them with regard to their use of it: ***but you have made it a den of thieves***. For those things which belong to religion, they have turned to profit, and thieves hide in caves to rob those going by, and acquire for themselves that which is not their own.

1701. *And there came to him the blind and the lame.* Here is set down what pertains to Christ's glory with regard to the healing of the sick. Now, the blind who were in the temple signify those who were blinded by ignorance. *We have groped for the wall, and like the blind we have groped as if we had no eyes* (Isa 59:10). Those are called 'lame' who walk on the ways of iniquities. *How long do you halt between two sides?* (1 Kgs 18:21). And these approached Christ in the temple, and he healed them. And the place was fitting for this deed, which signifies that spiritual illnesses are only cured in the Church. He reveals by deed, for the children cried out, above, ***blessed is he who comes in the name of the Lord***. *Behold your God will bring the revenge of recompense: God himself will come and will save you* (Isa 35:4).

1702. There follows the priests' indignation; hence it says, ***and the chief priests and scribes, seeing ... were moved with indignation***. It says about such men that they *will grow worse and worse* (2 Tim 3:13). And
    first, the reproach is set out;
    second, a questioning;
    third, the response.
    Concerning the first, three things:
    first, the cause of the indignation is given;
    second, the indignation is set out;
    third, the refutation is set out.

1703. Unde *videntes mirabilia quae fecit*, scilicet caecos illuminari etc., et non minus fuit quod ementes et vendentes eiecit. Hoc enim videntes dicebant ad eum conversi, *mirabilia testimonia tua, ideo scrutata est ea anima mea*, Ps. CXVIII, 129. Item videntes *pueros clamantes hosanna* etc., debebant moveri ad reverentiam. Supra XI, 15: *abscondisti ea a sapientibus et prudentibus, et revelasti ea parvulis*. Mc. IV, 12: *ut videntes non videant*.

1704. Unde isti pueri laudabant, sed isti sapientes indignati sunt et dixerunt ei *audis quid isti dicunt?* Quasi dicerent, non est iustum quod homo purus sustineat laudari ut Deus. Act. XII, 22 s. quia Herodes sustinuit ut honoraretur ut Deus, ideo percussus est ab Angelo, et consumptus vermibus expiravit: in quo datur nobis exemplum quod si laudamur supra nos, quod non debemus sustinere. Sed ipse non poterat laudari supra se, quia ipse Deus erat.

1705. Sequitur reprobatio. Et
primo reprobantur verbo;
secundo facto.

1706. *Iesus autem dixit eis, utique*. Dominus valde sapienter respondet. Intendebant quod si reprimeret pueros, quod ipsi haberent propositum: si non, haberent accusationem erga eum. Sed Dominus ita sapienter respondet, quod nec pueros reprobavit, nec ipsi habuerunt unde calumniari possent.

Unde dixit *utique* audio, sed nihil contra me dicunt. Sed David dicit *'ex ore infantium et lactentium perfecisti laudem.'* Non dicit *dixisti* sed *'perfecisti'*, quia quod tales pueri laudant Deum, hoc est ex divina inspiratione, *quia Dei perfecta sunt opera*, Deut. XXXII, 4. Unde non ex industria, sed a Spiritu Sancto. Sap. X, 21: *qui linguas infantium facit disertas*.

1707. Sed quomodo dicit *'infantes'*, quia tales non possunt loqui: ergo nec laudare? Dico quod non dicuntur *'infantes'* propter aetatem, sed propter simplicitatem, quia a malitia immunes. Apostolus I Cor. XIV, 20: *nolite pueri effici sensibus, sed malitia parvuli estote*. Item *'lactentes'* dicuntur, quia a miraculis commovebantur: in miraculis commoveri est quidem ut lac, quia lac absque difficultate bibitur, sic isti cum dulcedine per miraculum adducuntur ad fidem. Ad Hebr. V, 12: *facti estis quibus lacte opus est, non solido cibo*.

1708. *Et relictis illis abiit foras extra civitatem in Bethaniam*. Hic confutat facto. Et
primo facto quod fit circa se;
secundo facto quod fit circa ficulneam.

1703. Hence, *seeing the wonderful things that he did*, namely to enlighten the blind, and not less was that he cast out those buying and selling. For seeing this, those turned toward him were saying, *your testimonies are wonderful: therefore my soul has sought them* (Ps 118:129). Likewise, seeing *the children crying out and saying, hosanna*, they should have been moved to reverence: above, *you have hidden these things from the wise and prudent, and have revealed them to the little ones* (Matt 11:25). *That seeing they may see, and not perceive* (Mark 4:12).

1704. Hence the children were praising, but the wise men were indignant, and said to him, *do you hear what these say?* As though to say, it is not just that a mere man should endure to be praised as God. Because Herod permitted men to honor him as a god, he was struck by an angel, and died, consumed by worms (Acts 12:22); in which there is given to us an example, that if we are praised above ourselves, we should not put up with it. But he could not have been praised beyond himself, because he himself was God.

1705. There follows the condemnation. And
first, they are condemned by word;
second, by deed.

1706. *And Jesus said to them: yes*. The Lord responds very wisely. Their plan was that if he restrained the children, they would have what they wanted; if not, they would have an accusation against him. But the Lord responds wisely, such that he neither rebukes the children, nor gives them something by which to falsely accuse them.

Hence he said, *yes*, I hear, but they do not say anything against me. But David says, *'out of the mouth of infants and of sucklings you have perfected praise.'* He does not say, *you have said*, but *'you have perfected'*, for that such children praise God is from divine inspiration, for *the works of God are perfect* (Deut 32:4). Hence not by human industry do they praise God, but by the Holy Spirit. *For wisdom opened the mouth of the dumb, and made the tongues of infants eloquent* (Wis 10:21).

1707. But how can he say *'infants'*, since such are not able to speak, and therefore neither to praise? I say that they are not called *'infants'* on account of age, but on account of simplicity, because they are immune from malice. The Apostle: *brethren, do not become children in sense: but in malice be children* (1 Cor 14:20). Similarly, they are called *'sucklings'*, because they were stirred by the miracles: to be stirred in miracles is indeed as milk, because milk is drunk without difficulty, and in the same way these are led to faith with sweetness through the miracle. *You have become such as have need of milk, and not of strong meat* (Heb 5:12).

1708. *And leaving them, he went out of the city into Bethania*. Here he refutes them by deed. And
first, by a deed he does with regard to himself;
second, by a deed he does with regard to a fig tree.

1709. Dicit ergo quod *relictis illis, abiit foras*. Et derelictio illa fuit signum, quod ipsi derelinquerent eum. Ier. LI, 9: *curavimus Babylonem, et non est sanata*. Et *transit in Bethaniam*, in domum obedientiae: ibi enim moratur Iesus, ad Rom. VI. *Et mansit ibi*, quia in obedientibus sibi manet. Act. V, 29: *obedire oportet Deo magis quam hominibus*. Et non solum in Bethaniam, sed in quemcumque obedientem. Unde Io. XIV, v. 15: *si quis diligit me, sermonem meum servabit*, et sequitur, *et mansionem apud eum faciemus*.

1710. *Mane autem revertens in civitatem esuriit*. Hic ponitur confutatio sub quodam figurali facto. Et

primo ponitur factum;
secundo discipulorum admiratio.
Circa primum
primo ponitur occasio miraculi faciendi;
secundo sterilitas arboris;
tertio maledictio;
quarto effectus.

1711. Dicit ergo *mane revertens in civitatem esuriit*. Per hoc significatur sollicitudo, quam habebat de salute Iudaeorum. Unde mane venit sicut operarius sollicitus de diaeta sua, sicut supra XX, 1, quod *simile est regnum caelorum patrifamilias, qui exiit primo mane conducere operarios in vineam suam*.

Esuriit, et corporaliter et spiritualiter, quia semper desiderat facere voluntatem Patris; Io. IV, 34: *meus cibus est ut faciam voluntatem eius, qui misit me*. Item corporaliter. Sed quomodo? Cum esset Deus, omnia in potestate sua habebat, unde quando volebat, ieiunabat; unde supra IV, 2: *ieiunavit quadraginta diebus et quadraginta noctibus*; sed, quando voluit *esuriit*.

1712. *Et videns fici arborem*. Sed quare magis in ficu hoc miraculum fecit? Quia arbor humidissima est. Unde quod statim aruit, evidentissimum fuit miraculum. Et significat Iudaeam propter duo: tum quia ficus profert grossos, qui citius maturescunt, et isti fuerunt apostoli, qui maiores fuerunt. Item fructus iste sub una cortice multa habet grana, sicut sub una lege fuerunt multi. Et ista erat *secus viam*, idest Christum, quia in expectatione fuit, et non voluit ad viam venire: ipse enim est via; Io. XIV, 6: *ego sum via, veritas et vita*; et Is. XXXVI, 21: *haec via, ambulate per eam*. *Venit ad eam*. In Marco habetur quod venit ad videndum si aliquid inveniret.

Sed quid est? Tunc non erat tempus ficuum. Dicendum quod aliquando Scriptura aliquid ponit, non quod ita sit, sed propter aliquem effectum: unde non venit ut

1709. It says then that *and leaving them, he went out*. And that abandonment was a sign that they themselves would abandon him. *Let us forsake her, and let us go every man to his own land* (Jer 51:9). And *he went out of the city into Bethania*, into the house of obedience: for there Jesus stayed (Rom 6). *And he remained there* because he remains in those obedient to him. *We ought to obey God, rather than men* (Acts 5:29). And not only in Bethania, but in any obedient one whomsoever. Hence, *if any one love me, he will keep my word*, and there follows *and we will come to him, and will make our abode with him* (John 14:23).

1710. *And in the morning, returning into the city, he was hungry*. Here the refutation is set forth under a certain figurative deed. And

first, the deed is set out;
second, the disciples' wonderment.
Concerning the first,
first, the occasion for working the miracle is set out;
second, the barrenness of the tree;
third, the curse;
fourth, the effect.

1711. It says then, *and in the morning, returning into the city, he was hungry*. This indicates the solicitude which he had for the salvation of the Jews. Hence he came in the morning, like a worker solicitous for his regimen, as above, *the kingdom of heaven is like a householder, who went out early in the morning to hire laborers into his vineyard* (Matt 20:1).

He was hungry, both bodily and spiritually, for he always desires to do the will of the Father; *my meat is to do the will of him who sent me* (John 4:34). Likewise bodily. But how? Since he was God, he had all things in his power; hence when he wished, he fasted. Hence above, *he had fasted forty days and forty nights* (Matt 4:2); but, when he wished, *he hungered*.

1712. *And seeing a certain fig tree*. But why did he work this miracle on a fig tree, rather than on something else? Because this tree is the moistest. Hence that it was immediately dried up was the most obvious miracle. And it signifies the Jews, for two reasons. For the fig tree bears *grossos*, which mature more quickly, and these were the apostles, who were greater. Likewise, this fruit has many seeds under one outer covering, just as there were many under one law. And this tree was *by the way side*, i.e., by Christ, because it was in expectation, and did not want to come to the way: for he himself is the way; *I am the way, and the truth, and the life* (John 14:6); and, *this is the way, walk in it* (Isa 30:21). *He came to it*. In Mark, it says that he came to see whether he would find anything (Mark 11:13).

But why is this? It was not then the time for figs. One should say that sometimes the Scriptures set something down, not because it is that way, but on account of some effect: hence he did not come that he might find, but he came

Venit ad eam, quando visitavit Iudaeam. Lc. I, 78: *visitavit nos oriens ex alto*. Ista habet folia, scilicet observantias legales; sed non fructum. Sic aliqui quamdam speciem honestatis habent, licet interius mali et perversi sint.

1713. Sequitur maledictio ***et ait illi: numquam ex te fructus nascatur***. Videtur quod iniuste egerit, quia non erat tempus ficuum. Item videtur quod intulerit iniuriam possessori: vide quod sicut verba Domini sunt quaedam figura, sic facta. Aliquando Dominus vult manifestare suam doctrinam, et tunc manifestat eam in hominibus; aliquando suam potentiam punitricem, et tunc manifestat eam in aliis. Unde exercuit ibi potestatem, ut ostenderet quod Iudaea sterilis futura esset, sicut habetur Rom. XI. Sic aliquando contingit quod aliqui mali interius, exterius autem virentes, siccantur a Domino ne alios corrumpant. II ad Tim. III, 8: *homines corrupti mente, et reprobi circa fidem, sed ultra non proficient*. Lc. XIII, 7: *ecce tres anni sunt ex quo venio quaerens fructum in ficulnea hac, et non invenio. Abscinde eam*.

1714. Sequitur effectus ***et arefacta est continuo ficulnea***. Ps. XXI, 16: *aruit tamquam testa virtus mea*, quia in tempore discipulorum Iudaismus aruit, et post legalia aruerunt crescente Evangelio. *Et ipsi facti sunt abominabiles, terra fructifera versa est in amaritudinem a malitia inhabitantium in ea*, Ps. CVI, 34.

1715. ***Et videntes discipuli mirati sunt***. Hic
primo ponitur admiratio;
secundo admirationis satisfactio.

1716. Dicit ***et videntes discipuli mirati sunt***. Sicut mirantur homines quando videtur animus bonus, et cito arescit, sic isti mirantur quomodo tam cito aruit.

1717. ***Respondens autem Iesus*** et cetera. Hic satisfacit. Et primo ostendens virtutem fidei: unde dicit ***amen dico vobis***. Supra eamdem sententiam posuit, sed hic exponit; unde dicit ***si habueritis fidem, et non haesitaveritis***; quare fides firma debet esse sine haesitatione; Iac. I, 6: *postulet autem in fide nihil haesitans*. ***Non solum de ficulnea facietis***: ipse enim per fidem inhabitat in homine, et operatur in homine; ideo sicut ipse facit et ille in quo habitat. ***Si dixeritis monti huic, tolle et iacta te in mare, fiet***.

Quidam dicunt quod numquam factum est. Dicit Hieronymus quod multa fecerunt apostoli quae scripta non sunt. Item si non legitur ab eis factum, legitur ab aliis viris apostolicis fuisse factum, ut de quodam

He came to it when he visited the Jews. *The orient from on high has visited us* (Luke 1:78). It had leaves, namely the legal observances, but not fruit. In the same way, some have a certain appearance of honor, although interiorly they are bad and perverse.

1713. There follows the curse: ***he said to it: may no fruit grow on you from now on and forever***. It seems that he acted unjustly, since it was not the time for figs. Likewise, it seems that he inflicted an injury on the owner. See that, just as the Lord's words are certain figures, so are his deeds. Sometimes the Lord wills to manifest his teaching, and then he manifests it in men; sometimes he wills to manifest his power to punish, and then he manifests it in other things. Hence he exercised his power there, to show that the Jews were going to be barren (Rom 11). In the same way, it sometimes happens that some who are interiorly evil, but exteriorly green, are dried up by the Lord, lest they corrupt others. *Men corrupted in mind, reprobate concerning the faith. But they will proceed no farther; for their folly will be manifest to all men* (2 Tim 3:8–9). *Behold, for these three years I come seeking fruit on this fig tree, and I find none. Cut it down therefore* (Luke 13:7).

1714. There follows the effect: ***and immediately the fig tree withered away***. *My strength is dried up like a potsherd* (Ps 21:16), for Judaism dried up in the time of the disciples, and afterwards the things of the law dried up as the Gospel grew. And they themselves were made abominable: *a fruitful land into barrenness, for the wickedness of them that dwell therein* (Ps 106:34).

1715. ***And the disciples seeing it wondered***. Here
first, the wonderment is set out;
second, the satisfaction of the wonderment.

1716. It says, ***and the disciples seeing it wondered***. As men marvel when a soul seems good and suddenly dries up, so these men marveled at how suddenly it dried up.

1717. ***And Jesus answering, said to them: amen, I say to you***. Here he satisfies their wonderment. And first, showing the power of faith; hence he says, ***amen, I say to you, if you have faith***. He had set out the same thought above, but here he explains; hence he says, ***if you have faith, and do not stagger***; wherefore faith should be firm, without hesitation: *but let him ask in faith, nothing wavering* (Jas 1:6). ***Not only this, of the fig tree, will you do***, for he himself dwells in a man through faith, and works in a man, so just as he himself works, the one in whom he dwells also works. ***But also if you say to this mountain, take up and cast yourself into the sea, it will be done***.

Some say that this was never done. Jerome says that the apostles did many things which were not written down. Also, although it is not written that they did it, it is written that other apostolic men have done it, as is told of a certain

Gregorius narrat, ut dictum est supra. Item Dominus non dixit quod fieret, sed quod posset, si necessitas esset; sed necessitas non se obtulit.

1718. Spiritualiter per montem intelligimus diabolum. Unde *si* diabolo *dixeritis iacta te in mare*, idest in infernum, *ita fiet*. Vel *in mare*, idest in malos homines. Vel per mare superbia. Ps. LXXXIX, 2: *antequam montes fierent, aut formaretur terra et orbis, a saeculo et usque in saeculum tu es Deus*. Unde *si dixeritis*, superbo, *tolle*, a iustis, *et iacta te in mare*, idest in malos homines.

Vel per montem Christus, unde *si dixeritis monti huic*, idest Christo, *tolle te*, scilicet a Iudaeis, *et iacta te in mare*, idest in gentiles, qui sunt mare per turbulentiam. Act. XIII, 46: *quia indignos vos reputastis aeternae vitae, ecce convertimur ad gentes*.

1719. Item tangit fidei virtutem quantum ad orationem; *quia quaecumque petieritis in orationes credentes, accipietis*; supra II, 7: *petite et accipietis*.

Gregory, as was said above. Also, the Lord did not say that it would happen, but that it could, if it were necessary; but the necessity did not present itself.

1718. Spiritually, by the mountain we understand the devil. Hence *if you say* to the devil *cast yourself into the sea*, i.e., into hell, *it will be done*. Or, *into the sea*, i.e., into evil men. Or by the sea is understood pride. *Before the mountains were made, or the earth and the world was formed; from eternity and to eternity you are God* (Ps 89:2). Hence *if you say* to a proud man *take up* from the just *and cast yourself into the sea*, i.e., into evil men.

Or by the mountain is understood Christ, hence *if you say to this mountain*, i.e., to Christ, *take up*, namely from the Jews, *and cast yourself into the sea*, i.e., into the gentiles, who are a sea by turbulence. *Because you reject it, and judge yourselves unworthy of eternal life, behold we turn to the gentiles* (Acts 13:46).

1719. Likewise, he touches upon the power of faith with regard to prayer, for *all things whatever that you ask in prayer, believing, you will receive*; above, *ask, and it will be given to you* (Matt 7:7).

Lecture 2

21:23 Et cum venisset in templum, accesserunt ad eum principes sacerdotum et seniores populi dicentes: in qua potestate haec facis? Et quis tibi dedit hanc potestatem? [n. 1720]

21:24 Respondens Iesus dixit eis: interrogabo vos et ego unum sermonem, quem si dixeritis mihi, et ego vobis dicam in qua potestate haec facio. [n. 1722]

21:25 Baptismus Ioannis unde erat: e caelo, an ex hominibus? At illi cogitabant inter se dicentes: [n. 1722]

21:26 Si autem dixerimus: ex hominibus, timemus turbam; omnes enim habent Ioannem sicut prophetam. [n. 1723]

21:27 Et respondentes Iesu dixerunt: nescimus. Ait illis et ipse: nec ego dico vobis in qua potestate haec facio. [n. 1723]

21:28 Quid autem vobis videtur? Homo quidam habebat duos filios, et accedens ad primum dixit: fili, vade hodie operare in vineam meam. [n. 1724]

21:29 Ille autem respondens ait: nolo. Postea autem poenitentia motus abiit. [n. 1727]

21:30 Accedens autem ad alterum dixit similiter. At ille respondens ait: eo, domine, et non ivit. [n. 1728]

21:31 Quis ex duobus fecit voluntatem patris? Dicunt ei: primus. Dicit illis Iesus: amen dico vobis, quia publicani et meretrices praecedent vos in regno Dei. [n. 1729]

21:23 Καὶ ἐλθόντος αὐτοῦ εἰς τὸ ἱερὸν προσῆλθον αὐτῷ διδάσκοντι οἱ ἀρχιερεῖς καὶ οἱ πρεσβύτεροι τοῦ λαοῦ λέγοντες· ἐν ποίᾳ ἐξουσίᾳ ταῦτα ποιεῖς; καὶ τίς σοι ἔδωκεν τὴν ἐξουσίαν ταύτην;

21:24 ἀποκριθεὶς δὲ ὁ Ἰησοῦς εἶπεν αὐτοῖς· ἐρωτήσω ὑμᾶς κἀγὼ λόγον ἕνα, ὃν ἐὰν εἴπητέ μοι κἀγὼ ὑμῖν ἐρῶ ἐν ποίᾳ ἐξουσίᾳ ταῦτα ποιῶ·

21:25 τὸ βάπτισμα τὸ Ἰωάννου πόθεν ἦν; ἐξ οὐρανοῦ ἢ ἐξ ἀνθρώπων; οἱ δὲ διελογίζοντο ἐν ἑαυτοῖς λέγοντες· ἐὰν εἴπωμεν· ἐξ οὐρανοῦ, ἐρεῖ ἡμῖν· διὰ τί οὖν οὐκ ἐπιστεύσατε αὐτῷ;

21:26 ἐὰν δὲ εἴπωμεν· ἐξ ἀνθρώπων, φοβούμεθα τὸν ὄχλον, πάντες γὰρ ὡς προφήτην ἔχουσιν τὸν Ἰωάννην.

21:27 καὶ ἀποκριθέντες τῷ Ἰησοῦ εἶπαν· οὐκ οἴδαμεν. ἔφη αὐτοῖς καὶ αὐτός· οὐδὲ ἐγὼ λέγω ὑμῖν ἐν ποίᾳ ἐξουσίᾳ ταῦτα ποιῶ.

21:28 Τί δὲ ὑμῖν δοκεῖ; ἄνθρωπος εἶχεν τέκνα δύο. καὶ προσελθὼν τῷ πρώτῳ εἶπεν· τέκνον, ὕπαγε σήμερον ἐργάζου ἐν τῷ ἀμπελῶνι.

21:29 ὁ δὲ ἀποκριθεὶς εἶπεν· οὐ θέλω, ὕστερον δὲ μεταμεληθεὶς ἀπῆλθεν.

21:30 προσελθὼν δὲ τῷ ἑτέρῳ εἶπεν ὡσαύτως. ὁ δὲ ἀποκριθεὶς εἶπεν· ἐγώ, κύριε, καὶ οὐκ ἀπῆλθεν.

21:31 τίς ἐκ τῶν δύο ἐποίησεν τὸ θέλημα τοῦ πατρός; λέγουσιν· ὁ πρῶτος. λέγει αὐτοῖς ὁ Ἰησοῦς· ἀμὴν λέγω ὑμῖν ὅτι οἱ τελῶναι καὶ αἱ πόρναι προάγουσιν ὑμᾶς εἰς τὴν βασιλείαν τοῦ θεοῦ.

21:23 And when he had come into the temple, there came to him, as he was teaching, the chief priests and elders of the people, saying: by what authority do you do these things? And who has given you this authority? [n. 1720]

21:24 Jesus answering, said to them: I also will ask you one word, which if you will tell me, I will also tell you by what authority I do these things. [n. 1722]

21:25 The baptism of John, where was it from? From heaven or from men? But they thought within themselves, saying: if we say: from heaven, he will say to us: why then did you not believe him? [n. 1722]

21:26 But if we say: from men, we are afraid of the multitude, for all held John as a prophet. [n. 1723]

21:27 And answering Jesus, they said: we do not know. He also said to them: neither do I tell you by what authority I do these things. [n. 1723]

21:28 But what think you? A certain man had two sons, and coming to the first, he said: son, go work today in my vineyard. [n. 1724]

21:29 And answering, he said: I will not. But afterwards, being moved with repentance, he went. [n. 1727]

21:30 And coming to the other, he said in like manner. And answering, he said: I go sir; and he did not go. [n. 1728]

21:31 Which of the two did the father's will? They say to him: the first. Jesus said to them: amen I say to you, that the publicans and the harlots will go into the kingdom of God before you. [n. 1729]

21:32 Venit enim ad vos Ioannes in via iustitiae, et non credidistis ei: publicani autem et meretrices crediderunt ei: vos autem videntes, nec poenitentiam habuistis postea ut crederetis ei. [n. 1732]

21:33 Aliam parabolam audite: homo erat paterfamilias, qui plantavit vineam, et sepem circumdedit ei, et fodit in ea torcular, et aedificavit turrim, et locavit eam agricolis, et peregre profectus est. [n. 1733]

21:34 Cum autem tempus fructuum appropinquasset, misit servos suos ad agricolas, ut acciperent fructus eius. [n. 1737]

21:35 Et agricolae, apprehensis servis eius, alium ceciderunt, alium occiderunt, alium vero lapidaverunt. [n. 1739]

21:36 Iterum misit alios servos plures prioribus, et fecerunt illis similiter. [n. 1740]

21:37 Novissime autem misit ad eos filium suum, dicens: verebuntur forte filium meum. [n. 1741]

21:38 Agricolae autem videntes filium, dixerunt intra se: hic est haeres; venite, occidamus eum, et habebimus haereditatem eius. [n. 1743]

21:39 Et apprehensum eum eiecerunt extra vineam, et occiderunt. [n. 1745]

21:40 Cum ergo venerit dominus vineae, quid faciet agricolis illis? [n. 1746]

21:41 Aiunt illi: malos male perdet, et vineam locabit aliis agricolis, qui reddant ei fructum temporibus suis. [n. 1746]

21:42 Dicit illis Iesus: numquam legistis in Scripturis: *Lapidem quem reprobaverunt aedificantes, hic factus est in caput anguli? A Domino factum est istud, et est mirabile in oculis nostris*? [n. 1748]

21:32 ἦλθεν γὰρ Ἰωάννης πρὸς ὑμᾶς ἐν ὁδῷ δικαιοσύνης, καὶ οὐκ ἐπιστεύσατε αὐτῷ, οἱ δὲ τελῶναι καὶ αἱ πόρναι ἐπίστευσαν αὐτῷ· ὑμεῖς δὲ ἰδόντες οὐδὲ μετεμελήθητε ὕστερον τοῦ πιστεῦσαι αὐτῷ.

21:33 Ἄλλην παραβολὴν ἀκούσατε. ἄνθρωπος ἦν οἰκοδεσπότης ὅστις ἐφύτευσεν ἀμπελῶνα καὶ φραγμὸν αὐτῷ περιέθηκεν καὶ ὤρυξεν ἐν αὐτῷ ληνὸν καὶ ᾠκοδόμησεν πύργον καὶ ἐξέδετο αὐτὸν γεωργοῖς καὶ ἀπεδήμησεν.

21:34 ὅτε δὲ ἤγγισεν ὁ καιρὸς τῶν καρπῶν, ἀπέστειλεν τοὺς δούλους αὐτοῦ πρὸς τοὺς γεωργοὺς λαβεῖν τοὺς καρποὺς αὐτοῦ.

21:35 καὶ λαβόντες οἱ γεωργοὶ τοὺς δούλους αὐτοῦ ὃν μὲν ἔδειραν, ὃν δὲ ἀπέκτειναν, ὃν δὲ ἐλιθοβόλησαν.

21:36 πάλιν ἀπέστειλεν ἄλλους δούλους πλείονας τῶν πρώτων, καὶ ἐποίησαν αὐτοῖς ὡσαύτως.

21:37 ὕστερον δὲ ἀπέστειλεν πρὸς αὐτοὺς τὸν υἱὸν αὐτοῦ λέγων· ἐντραπήσονται τὸν υἱόν μου.

21:38 οἱ δὲ γεωργοὶ ἰδόντες τὸν υἱὸν εἶπον ἐν ἑαυτοῖς· οὗτός ἐστιν ὁ κληρονόμος· δεῦτε ἀποκτείνωμεν αὐτὸν καὶ σχῶμεν τὴν κληρονομίαν αὐτοῦ,

21:39 καὶ λαβόντες αὐτὸν ἐξέβαλον ἔξω τοῦ ἀμπελῶνος καὶ ἀπέκτειναν.

21:40 ὅταν οὖν ἔλθῃ ὁ κύριος τοῦ ἀμπελῶνος, τί ποιήσει τοῖς γεωργοῖς ἐκείνοις;

21:41 λέγουσιν αὐτῷ· κακοὺς κακῶς ἀπολέσει αὐτοὺς καὶ τὸν ἀμπελῶνα ἐκδώσεται ἄλλοις γεωργοῖς, οἵτινες ἀποδώσουσιν αὐτῷ τοὺς καρποὺς ἐν τοῖς καιροῖς αὐτῶν.

21:42 Λέγει αὐτοῖς ὁ Ἰησοῦς· οὐδέποτε ἀνέγνωτε ἐν ταῖς γραφαῖς· λίθον ὃν ἀπεδοκίμασαν οἱ οἰκοδομοῦντες, οὗτος ἐγενήθη εἰς κεφαλὴν γωνίας· παρὰ κυρίου ἐγένετο αὕτη καὶ ἔστιν θαυμαστὴ ἐν ὀφθαλμοῖς ἡμῶν;

21:32 For John came to you in the way of justice, and you did not believe him. But the publicans and the harlots believed him, but you, seeing it, did not even afterwards repent, that you might believe him. [n. 1732]

21:33 Hear another parable. There was a man, a householder, who planted a vineyard, and made a hedge around it, and dug in it a press, and built a tower, and let it out to husbandmen, and went into a strange country. [n. 1733]

21:34 And when the time of the fruits drew near, he sent his servants to the husbandmen, that they might receive the fruits from it. [n. 1737]

21:35 And the husbandmen, laying hands on his servants, beat one, and killed another, and stoned another. [n. 1739]

21:36 Again he sent other servants more than the former; and they did to them in the same manner. [n. 1740]

21:37 And last of all he sent to them his son, saying: perhaps they will reverence my son. [n. 1741]

21:38 But the husbandmen seeing the son, said among themselves: this is the heir; come, let us kill him, and we will have his inheritance. [n. 1743]

21:39 And taking him, they cast him out of the vineyard, and killed him. [n. 1745]

21:40 Therefore when the lord of the vineyard comes, what will he do to those husbandmen? [n. 1746]

21:41 They say to him: he will bring those evil men to an evil end; and will let out his vineyard to other husbandmen, who will render him the fruit in due season. [n. 1746]

21:42 Jesus said to them: have you never read in the Scriptures: *the stone which the builders rejected, the same has become the head of the corner. By the Lord this has been done; and it is wonderful in our eyes*? [n. 1748]

21:43 Ideo dico vobis, quia auferetur a vobis regnum Dei, et dabitur genti facienti fructus eius. [n. 1750]	21:43 διὰ τοῦτο λέγω ὑμῖν ὅτι ἀρθήσεται ἀφ' ὑμῶν ἡ βασιλεία τοῦ θεοῦ καὶ δοθήσεται ἔθνει ποιοῦντι τοὺς καρποὺς αὐτῆς.	21:43 Therefore I say to you, that the kingdom of God will be taken from you, and will be given to a nation yielding its fruits. [n. 1750]
21:44 Et qui ceciderit super lapidem istum, confringetur: super quem vero ceciderit, conteret eum. [n. 1751]	21:44 [καὶ ὁ πεσὼν ἐπὶ τὸν λίθον τοῦτον συνθλασθήσεται· ἐφ' ὃν δ' ἂν πέσῃ λικμήσει αὐτόν.]	21:44 And whoever will fall on this stone, will be broken, but on whomever it will fall, it will grind him to powder. [n. 1751]
21:45 Et cum audissent principes sacerdotum et Pharisaei parabolas eius, cognoverunt quod de ipsis diceret: [n. 1752]	21:45 Καὶ ἀκούσαντες οἱ ἀρχιερεῖς καὶ οἱ Φαρισαῖοι τὰς παραβολὰς αὐτοῦ ἔγνωσαν ὅτι περὶ αὐτῶν λέγει·	21:45 And when the chief priests and Pharisees had heard his parables, they knew that he had spoken of them. [n. 1752]
21:46 et quaerentes eum tenere, timuerunt turbas, quoniam sicut prophetam eum habebant. [n. 1752]	21:46 καὶ ζητοῦντες αὐτὸν κρατῆσαι ἐφοβήθησαν τοὺς ὄχλους, ἐπεὶ εἰς προφήτην αὐτὸν εἶχον.	21:46 And seeking to lay hands on him, they feared the multitudes: because they held him as a prophet. [n. 1752]

1720. *Et cum venisset*. Hic reprehendunt inquirendo. Et

primo ponitur inquisitio;

secundo confutatio, ibi *respondens Iesus dixit eis*.

Circa primum duo. Et primo ponuntur interrogationes; secundo Christi responsiones. Et

primo ponitur interrogatio Iudaeorum;

secundo Christi, ibi *respondens autem Iesus dixit eis: interrogabo vos* et cetera.

1721. Dicunt ergo *in qua potestate haec facis?* Ipse eiecerat ementes et vendentes de templo, item fecit miracula: ideo petunt in qua potestate haec faciat. Chrysostomus dicit quod in mundo erat duplex potestas, scilicet regia et sacerdotalis: unde quantum ad primum petunt: unde profiteris hanc potestatem habere? Item quantum ad secundum: quis dedit tibi hanc potestatem? Habes ne a sacerdote vel a Deo? Sic enim erat quod filii succedebant sacerdotibus in potestate. Quis dedit tibi? Non habes hoc a Caesare, non a sacerdote. Unde Chrysostomus: *omnis homo, qualis est opinio de aliquo apud eum, talem eum existimat*. Ideo quia ipsi non habebant opinionem bonam de Christo, ideo et cetera.

Vel ad factum miraculorum potest retorqueri. Est potestas Dei et potestas diaboli. Iob XLI, v. 24: *non est potestas in terris, qua huic valeat comparari*. Unde *in qua potestate hoc facis?* Dei, an diaboli? Sed Origenes obiicit quod si in potestate diaboli faceret, non diceret. Ideo aliter exponit, quia dicit quod potestas Dei multiplex est, quaedam in generali, multae in speciali, ut quaedam ad hoc, quaedam ad illud. Unde petunt in qua potestate, idest in quo gradu potestatis, ut de prophetis. Quidam enim habuerunt unam potestatem, quidam aliam.

1720. *And when he had come*. Here they reproach by inquiring. And

first, the question is set out;

second, the refutation, at ***Jesus answering, said to them***.

Concerning the first, two things: first, the questions are set out; second, Christ's responses. And

first, the Jews' questioning;

second, Christ's, at ***Jesus answering, said to them: I also will ask you***.

1721. They say therefore, **by what authority do you do these things?** He had cast those buying and selling out of the temple, and likewise he worked miracles; so they ask in what power he does these things. Chrysostom says that there were two powers in the world, namely the kingly and the priestly: hence with regard to the first they ask, from where do you claim to have this power? Likewise with regard to the second, who has given you this power? Do you not have it from a priest or from God? For this was how sons succeeded the priests in power. Who has given it to you? You do not have it from Caesar, nor from a priest. Hence Chrysostom: *as the opinion is about someone with him, such every man supposes him to be*. So, these men did not have a good opinion of Christ.

Or it can be referred to the working of the miracles. There is the power of God and the power of the devil. *There is no power upon earth that can be compared with him* (Job 41:24). Hence in what power do you do this? The power of God, or of the devil? But Origen objects that, if he were working in the power of the devil, he would not say so. So it should be explained in another way, for he says that the powers of God are many, some in general, many in particular, as certain ones for this, certain ones for that. Hence they ask in what power, i.e., in what step of power, as was the case with the prophets. For certain ones had one power, other ones another.

1722. Secundum Chrysostomum quando aliquis interrogat ut discat, tunc ei respondenda est veritas; sed quando ut tentet, tunc reprehendendus est et confutandus. Sic Dominus, quia sciebat quod tentabant, dixit *interrogabo vos et ego unum sermonem. Baptismus Ioannis unde erat: e caelo, an ex hominibus?* baptizavit Petrus, nec dicitur baptismus Petri, et baptizavit Ioannes, et dicitur baptismus Ioannis, quia in baptismo Ioannis totum factum erat hominis; sed in baptismo Petri remittebantur peccata, quod per hominem fieri non poterat. Io. I, 33: *ille super quem videris Spiritum descendentem, et manentem super eum, ille est qui baptizat in Spiritu Sancto.* Licet enim Ioannes baptizaret, non tamen a se; unde Io. I, 33: *ipse qui me misit baptizare in aqua, dixit mihi* et cetera.

1723. Consequenter agitur de responsionibus. Et primo de responsione Iudaeorum; secundo Christi.

Verum est quod minores crediderunt, sed Pharisaei indignati sunt; ideo si dicerent quod ex hominibus, sequeretur eorum confusio. Item *omnes habebant Ioannem sicut prophetam*; supra XI, 7: *quid existis in desertum videre?* et cetera. *Et respondens dixerunt: nescimus.* Mentiuntur. Ps. XXVI, 12: *mentita est iniquitas sibi.*

Consequenter ponitur responsio Christi *nec ego dico vobis*. In quo habetur exemplum, quod qui non vult dicere quod scit, quod Dominus abscondit alia ab eo; unde Sap. VII, v. 13: *sine fictione didici, et sine invidia communico.*

1724. *Quid autem vobis videtur? Homo quidam habebat duos filios* et cetera. Supra Dominus inquisitionem repressit sua interrogatione, hic inquirentes redarguit. Et

primo de inobedientia;

secundo de malitia, et hoc secundum duas parabolas, quarum secunda aliam exponit et declarat.

Circa primum duo.
Primo ponit parabolam;
secundo expositionem, ibi *dicit illis Iesus* et cetera.

Circa primum tria.
Primo committit audientibus iudicium;
secundo narrat factum;
tertio requirit sententiam.

1725. Dicit *quid vobis videtur?* Magnum est testimonium pro eo quod iudicium adversariis committit. Iob VI, 29: *respondete, obsecro absque contentione, et quod iustum est, iudicate.*

1726. Deinde proponit factum *homo quidam habebat duos filios*. Iste homo Deus est; duo filii sunt duo populi. Eccli. XXXIII, v. 15: *intuere in omnia opera Altissimi, duo contra duo, unum contra unum.* Vel duo genera

1722. According to Chrysostom, when someone asks so as to learn, then one should respond to him with the truth; but when he asks so as to test, then he should be reproached and refuted. Thus the Lord, since he knew that they were testing, said, *I also will ask you one word . . . the baptism of John, where was it from? From heaven or from men?* Peter baptized, nor is it called the baptism of Peter, but John baptized, and it is called the baptism of John; this is because in the baptism of John the whole thing was from man, while in the baptism of Peter sins were remitted, which cannot come about through a man. *He upon whom you shall see the Spirit descending, and remaining upon him, he it is who baptizes with the Holy Spirit* (John 1:33). For although John baptized, yet not from himself; hence, *he who sent me to baptize with water, said to me* (John 1:33).

1723. Next, the responses are treated. And first, the Jews' response; second, Christ's.

It is true that those who were lesser believed, but the Pharisees were indignant; so if they said that it was from men, their refutation would follow. Likewise, *all held John as a prophet*; above, *what did you go out into the desert to see?* Thus, *and answering Jesus, they said: we do not know* (Matt 11:7). They lie. *Iniquity has lied to itself* (Ps 26:12).

Next, Christ's response is set out: *neither do I tell you by what authority I do these things*. In which an example is had, that when someone does not wish to say what he knows, the Lord hides other things from him; hence *which I have learned without guile, and communicate without envy, and her riches I hide not* (Wis 7:13).

1724. *But what think you? A certain man had two sons.* Above, the Lord repressed the questioning with his own inquiry; here he refutes those who question him. And

first, concerning disobedience;

second, concerning malice, and this according to two parables, of which the second explains and reveals the other.

Concerning the first, two things:
first, he sets out a parable;
second, the explanation, at *Jesus said to them: amen I say to you, that the publicans*.

Concerning the first, three things:
first, he entrusts judgment to those listening;
second, he describes a deed;
third, he seeks a judgment.

1725. He says, *but what think you?* It is a great witness for him that he entrusts judgment to his adversaries. *Answer, I beseech you, without contention: and speaking that which is just, judge* (Job 6:29).

1726. Then he sets out a deed: *a certain man had two sons*. This man is God; the two sons are two peoples. *And so look upon all the works of the Most High. Two and two, and one against another* (Sir 33:15). Or two kinds of man,

hominum, iusti et peccatores. Non dicuntur iusti quicumque, sed qui profitentur se iustos; et peccatores non quicumque, sed qui poenitentiam agunt. Vel isti duo filii sunt clerici et laici.

1727. Agitur ergo de obedientia. Et primo ponitur mandatum; secundo recusatio; tertio impletio.

Et accedens ad primum. Primus est populus gentilium qui incepit a Noe, sicut populus Iudaeorum ab Abraham. Item primus dicitur gens laicorum, quia clerici sunt propter laicos ad informandum eos. Unde accessit ad primum, idest ad populum gentilem per internam inspirationem, vel per manifestationem Angelorum. *Dixit fili, vade operare hodie in vineam*. Vinea Dei iustitia est. *Operare* ergo *in vinea*, idest opera fac iustitiae. Et dicit *hodie*, quasi per totum tempus vitae tuae. Et quando dixit? Quando interius inspiravit dando lumen rationis. Ps. IV, 6: *multi dicunt: quis ostendit nobis bona? Signatum est super nos lumen vultus tui, Domine*.

Consequenter ponitur recusatio. *Ille autem respondens ait, nolo*. Hoc nihil aliud est quam contemnere mandata Dei. Iob XXI, 14: *scientiam viarum tuarum nolumus*.

Post sequitur adimpletio: *postea autem poenitentia motus, abiit*. Ier. XXXI, 19: *postquam convertisti me, egi poenitentiam*.

1728. Sequitur inobedientia secundi: et primo ponitur mandatum secundo transgressio.

Dicit *accedens ad alterum* hoc est Iudaicum populum, vel ad clerum, vel qui iustos se dicunt, *dixit similiter. At ille respondens ait: eo, domine*. Profitetur iustitiam se servaturum; unde dicit populus Iudaicus: *omnia quaecumque praeceperit Dominus, faciemus*. Sic etiam dicunt clerici et quicumque religiosi. Unde promisit ire. *Et non ivit*. Mal. II, 8: *vos autem recessistis de via, et scandalizastis plurimos, irritum fecistis pactum, dicit Dominus exercituum*.

1729. Tunc expedit sententiam: *quis ex duobus voluntatem fecit patris?* Primus non promisit, sed fecit; secundus promisit, sed non fecit. Quis ex istis fecit voluntatem patris? Respondent et *dicunt ei: primus*, quia *melius est non vovere, quam post votum promissa non reddere*, Eccl. V, 4. Et II Petr. II, 21: *melius est viam veritatis non agnoscere, quam post agnitionem retrorsum abire*; est enim ibi duplex peccatum: peccatum inobedientiae et transgressio voti.

1730. Consequenter adaptat parabolam. Et
  primo ponit praeeminentiam gentilium ad Iudaeos, vel laicorum ad clericos;
  secundo rationem assignat.

the just and sinners. Not just anyone is called just, but those who profess to be just; and not anyone is called a sinner, but those who do penance. Or these two sons are clerics and laymen.

1727. He treats therefore of obedience. And first, a command is imposed; second, a refusal; third, a fulfillment.

And coming to the first. The first is the people of the gentiles who began from Noah, just as the people of the Jews began from Abraham. Likewise, the first is called the people of the laity, for the clerics are for the sake of laymen, to form them. Hence he came to the first, i.e., to the gentile people through internal inspiration, or through the manifestation of angels. *He said: son, go work today in my vineyard*. The vineyard of God is justice. *Work* therefore *in my vineyard*, i.e., do works of justice. And he says *today*, as it were through the whole time of your life. And when did he speak? When he interiorly inspired by giving the light of reason. *Many say, who shows us good things? The light of your countenance O Lord, is signed upon us* (Ps 4:6–7).

Next, the refusal is set down: *and he answering, said: I will not*. This is nothing other than to despise God's command. *We do not desire the knowledge of your ways* (Job 21:14).

Afterwards there follows the fulfillment: *but afterwards, being moved with repentance, he went*. *For after you converted me, I did penance* (Jer 31:19).

1728. There follows the disobedience of the second: and first, the command is set out; second, the transgression.

He says, *and coming to the other*, which is the people of the Jews, or to the clerics or those who call themselves just, *he said in like manner. And answering, he said: I go sir*. He claims that he will keep justice; hence the people of the Jews says, *all things that the Lord has spoken we will do* (Exod 23:7) So also the clerics say, and any religious. Hence he promised to go. *And he did not go*. *But you have departed out of the way, and have caused many to stumble at the law: you have made void the covenant of Levi, says the Lord of hosts* (Mal 2:8).

1729. Then he obtains a judgment: *which of the two did the father's will?* The first did not promise, but did it; the second promised, but did not do it. Which of these did the father's will? They respond: *they say to him: the first*, because *it is much better not to vow, than after a vow not to perform the things promised* (Eccl 5:4) And, *for it had been better for them not to have known the way of justice, than after they have known it, to turn back* (2 Pet 2:21). For there are two kinds of sin: the sin of disobedience and the transgression of a vow.

1730. Next he applies the parable. And
  first, he sets out the excellence of the gentiles over the Jews, or of laymen over clerics;
  second, he gives the reason.

1731. Dicit illis *amen dico vobis, quod publicani et meretrices praecedent vos in regno Dei*. Simile dictum est supra XX, 16: *et erunt novissimi primi*.

Chrysostomus quaerit, quare magis ponit publicanos et meretrices quam alios. Respondet quod per publicanos intelligit peccatores. Peccatum publicanorum est avaritia, quia cum tributa recipiunt, multa sibi acquirunt, et ultra quam commissum sit sibi, rapiunt. Sed peccatum hominum est avaritia, peccatum mulierum est luxuria, cum sint otiosae, et multa mala docuit otiositas. Ez. XVI, 49: *haec fuit iniquitas Sodomae, abundantia panis et otium*.

Praecedent vos in regno Dei, idest magis appropinquant ad regnum; supra c. XII, 41: *viri Ninivitae praecedent vos* et cetera.

1732. Sequitur ratio. Et primo dicit quod Iudaei inobedientes fuerunt; secundo quod publicani obedierunt; tertio quod non secuti sunt eum.

Dicit *venit Ioannes ad vos in via iustitiae*, quia in iustitiae viam duxit. Vel *in via iustitiae*, quia viam iustitiae observavit, scilicet viam poenitentiae, *et non credidistis*. Dicebant enim ei: *Elias es tu?* Et cum dixisset non dixerunt: *quid ergo baptizas?* *Publicani autem et meretrices crediderunt ei*. Et hoc habetur supra cap. III, quod venerunt ad Ioannem ut baptizarentur. *Vos autem videntes*, alios scilicet converti et implere quod mandaverat, *nec poenitentiam habuistis, ut postea crederetis ei*. Ille enim est pessimus, qui de facto suo non poenitet. Ier. VIII, 6: *nullus est qui agat poenitentiam de peccato suo dicens: quid feci?*

1733. *Aliam parabolam audite*. Dominus interrogaverat de baptismo, et noluerunt respondere, modo autem occulte interrogat, ut non percipiant; ideo disserit parabolam, et facit duo.

Primo ponit parabolam;

secundo exquirit eorum sententiam, ibi *cum ergo venerit dominus vineae, quid faciet agricolis illis?*

Circa primum tria.

Primo ponitur beneficium exhibitum;

secundo ponitur requisitio recompensationis, ibi *cum autem tempus fructuum appropinquasset* etc.;

tertio ponit ingratitudinem, ibi *et agricolae, apprehensis servis eius* et cetera.

Circa primum tria.

Primo ponitur plantatio vineae;

secundo eius ornatio;

tertio eius locatio.

1734. Dicit ergo *homo erat paterfamilias qui plantavit vineam* et cetera. Simile ponitur Is. V, 1, ubi dicitur: *vinea facta est dilecto meo in cornu filio olei*. Hic autem dicit quod paterfamilias plantat vineam. Dicunt

1731. He says to them, *amen I say to you, that the publicans and the harlots will go into the kingdom of God before you*. A similar thing was said above, *so will the last be first, and the first last* (Matt 20:16).

Chrysostom asks why he sets down publicans and harlots rather than others. He responds that by publicans he means sinners. The publicans' sin is avarice, because when they receive the tax, they acquire many things for themselves, and seize more than what is entrusted to them. But the sin of men is avarice; the sin of women is luxury, since they are idle, and *idleness has taught much evil* (Sir 33:29). *This was the iniquity of Sodom, abundance of bread and leisure* (Ezek 16:49).

Will go into the kingdom of God before you, i.e., approach nearer to the kingdom; above, *the men of Niniveh go before you* (Matt 12:41).

1732. There follows the reason. And first, he says that the Jews were disobedient; second, that the publicans obeyed; third, that they have not followed him.

He says, *for John came to you in the way of justice*, for he led men into the way of justice, namely the way of penance, *and you did not believe*. For they said to him, *are you Elijah?* And when he had said *I am not*, they said, *why then do you baptize?* (John 1:21). *But the publicans and the harlots believed him*. And this is said above, that they came to John and were being baptized (Matt 3). *But you, seeing it*, namely seeing others be converted and fulfill what he had commanded, *did not even afterwards repent, that you might believe him*. For the worst of men is he who does not repent of his deed. *There is none who does penance for his sin, saying: what have I done?* (Jer 8:6).

1733. *Hear another parable*. The Lord had asked about the baptism, and they did not want to answer; but now he asks in a hidden way, so they would not perceive, and so he sets out a parable. And he does two things:

first, he sets out the parable;

second, he seeks their judgment, at *therefore when the lord of the vineyard comes, what will he do to those husbandmen?*

Concerning the first, three things:

first, the benefit shown is set out;

second, the request for recompense is set out, at *and when the time of the fruits drew near*;

third, he sets out the ingratitude, at *and the husbandmen, laying hands on his servants*.

Concerning the first, three things:

first, the planting of the vineyard is set out;

second, its adornment;

third, its allocation.

1734. He says then, *there was a man, a householder, who planted a vineyard*. A similar thing is set out in Isaiah: *my beloved had a vineyard on a hill in a fruitful place.* (Isa 5:1). But here it says that the householder plants the

aliqui quod ibi invehitur contra vineam; unde dicit: *quid ultra debui facere vineae meae?* Hic autem contra agricolas. Ideo dupliciter exponitur secundum Hieronymum et Chrysostomum. Vinea dicitur populus Iudaicus; Is. V, 7: *vinea Domini domus Israel est*. Quod contra agricolas, quia quantum ad praesens huius malitia non processit ex populo, sed ex principibus; Io. VII, 48: *numquid aliqui ex principibus crediderunt in eum?* Ideo non contra vineam. Haec vinea non est domus Israel, sed iustitia Dei, quae occulte tradita est in Sacra Scriptura; unde dicit *homo erat paterfamilias qui plantavit vineam*, idest populum Iudaicum; Ps. LXXIX, 9: *vineam de Aegypto transtulisti*. Vel iustitiam posuit in doctrina legis.

1735. *Et sepem circumdedit ei*, ad protectionem vineae, unde quae ponuntur ad custodiam, sive sint orationes sanctorum, vel custodia angelorum dicuntur sepes; unde Osee c. II, 6: *sepiam viam tuam spinis*. Si autem vinea dicatur iustitia, sepe dicit occulta verba Scripturae. Secundum enim mysticum intellectum occulta Scripturae non sunt pandenda cuilibet, quia non est sanctum dandum canibus, supra VII, 6.

Et fodit in ea torcular. Torcular ponitur, ut exprimatur vinum caritatis. Si intelligatur per vineam Iudaicus populus, intelligitur per torcular altare holocaustorum. Item intelliguntur martyres, qui pro fide sanguinem fuderunt, Is. LXIII, 3: *torcular calcavi solus*. Vel potest etiam intelligi ordo prophetarum, in quibus vinum sapientiae est expressum. Vel potest dici profunditas Sacrae Scripturae. Item totus fructus vineae congregatur in torculari: sic quicquid potest animus, totum debet congregare ad laudem Dei.

Et aedificavit turrim. Per turrim templum intelligitur. Michaeae IV, 8: *et tu turris nebulosa gregis, usque ad te veniet potestas prima*. Vel cognitio Dei, Prov. XVIII, 10: *turris fortissima nomen Domini*.

1736. Consequenter de locatione *et locavit eam agricolis*, idest super certa mercede constituit. Agricolae sunt Moyses et Aaron, qui gubernaculum habuerunt. Iob XXXI, 39: *si afflixi animam agricolarum eius*. Gregorius: *qui praeponuntur populo*. **Profectus est peregre**, Dominus, non mutando locum, sed hominem in suo arbitrio relinquendo. Eccli. c. XV, 14: *Deus ab initio creavit hominem, et reliquit eum in manu consilii sui*, idest suo arbitrio dimisit. Unde dicitur peregre proficisci, quando non ad quamcumque culpam poenam infligit. Vel non

vine. Some say that there he inveighs against the vine; hence he says, *what is there that I ought to do more to my vineyard?* But here he inveighs against the farmers. For this reason, it is explained in two ways, according to Jerome and Chrysostom. The Jewish people is called the vine; *for the vineyard of the Lord of hosts is the house of Israel* (Isa 5:7). This is against the farmers, because as far as the present is concerned, its malice does not come from the people, but from the leaders; *has any one of the rulers believed in him, or of the Pharisees?* (John 7:48). So this parable is not against the vine. This vine is not the house of Israel, but the justice of God, which is handed down in a hidden way in the Sacred Scriptures; hence he says, **there was a man, a householder, who planted a vineyard**, i.e., the Jewish people; *you have brought a vineyard out of Egypt* (Ps 79:9). Or, he placed justice in the teachings of the law.

1735. And made a hedge round about it, for the protection of the vine; hence those things which are set up for protection, whether the prayers of the saints, or the protection of the angels, are called hedges; hence *wherefore behold I will hedge up your way with thorns* (Hos 2:6). But if the vine means justice, then by the hedge he means the hidden words of Scripture. For according to a mystical understanding, the hidden things of Scripture should not be opened up for just anyone, because one should not give what is holy to dogs (Matt 7:6).

And dug in it a press. A press is set up, so that the wine of charity may be pressed out. If the vine is taken as the Jewish people, the press is understood as the altar of holocausts. Likewise it is understood as the martyrs, who poured out their blood for the faith; *I have trodden the winepress alone* (Isa 63:3). Or as the order of prophets, in which the wine of wisdom is pressed out. Or it can mean the profundity of Sacred Scripture. Likewise, the whole fruit of the vine is gathered together in the press: thus whatever the soul is capable of, the whole should be gathered together to the praise of God.

And built a tower. By the tower is understood the temple. *And you, O cloudy tower of the flock, of the daughter of Zion, unto you will it come: yea the first power will come* (Mic 4:8). Or, the knowledge of God; *the name of the Lord is a strong tower* (Prov 18:10).

1736. Next, of the allocation; and he **let it out to husbandmen**, i.e., arranges a contract with a specified reward. The husbandmen are Moses and Aaron, who had the governance. *If I have eaten the fruits thereof without money, and have afflicted the soul of the tillers thereof* (Job 31:39). Gregory: *those who are set over the people*. The Lord **went into a strange country**, not by changing place, but by leaving man in his own judgment. *God made man from the beginning, and left him in the hand of his own counsel* (Sir 15:14), i.e., left him to his own judgment. Hence he is said to depart to

1737. *Cum autem tempus fructuum appropinquasset*. Quicumque facit aliquem fructum, expectat beneficium: et sic Dominus expectat ut reddatur ei beneficium ad suam gloriam. Quantum ad unum hominem fructus non est in pueritia, sed in plena aetate, unde cum venit ad adolescentiam, tunc petit fructus: sic cum populus fuit plantatus, et lex data, petiit fructum, et non cognoverunt eum. Ier. VIII, 7: *milvus in caelo cognovit tempus suum; populus autem meus non cognovit iudicium Domini*. **Misit servos suos**, idest prophetas, **ad agricolas**, idest ad Iudaeos, **ut acciperent fructus eius**, idest ut inducerent homines ad bene agendum. Infra c. XXVIII, 34: *misi ad vos prophetas, sapientes et scribas, et ex illis occidetis* et cetera.

1738. Post hoc agitur de malitia. Et

primo quantum ad primos;
secundo quantum ad secundos;
tertio quantum ad tertios.

1739. *Et agricolae, acceptis servis eius, alium ceciderunt*, ut Michaeam, **alium occiderunt**, ut Isaiam, **alium lapidaverunt**, ut Naboth. Hebr. XI, 37: *lapidati sunt, secti sunt, in occisione gladii mortui sunt*.

1740. *Iterum misit alios*. Item singulariter misit prophetas, ut Moysen, et Aaron, et alios; sed post tempore David misit multos cuneos prophetarum. Vult enim Dominus pugnare misericordiam suam contra malitiam eorum. Unde **et fecerunt eis similiter**. Deut. c. XXXI, 27: *vos semper contentiose contra Dominum egistis*.

1741. Sequitur tertio **novissime autem misit ad eos filium suum** etc., quod fuit malitiae consummatae. Et tria facit.

Primo ponitur misericordia Domini;
secundo malitia eorum;
tertio executio pravi propositi.

1742. *Novissime autem misit ad eos filium suum*. Ad Hebr. I, 1: *multifarie multisque modis olim Deus loquens patribus in prophetis, novissime locutus est nobis in Filio*. **Misit ad eos filium suum dicens: forte verebuntur filium meum**.

Sed quid est quod dicit **forte**? Numquid ignorabat ipse? Hieronymus dicit quod iste modus loquendi dubius significat libertatem arbitrii, ut ostenderet quid futuri essent, quia *qui non honorificat Filium, non honorificat Patrem*. Vel dicit sic, quia aliqui reveriti sunt eum.

1743. Consequenter ponitur propositum malitiae. Et primo ponitur requisitio; secundo propositum; tertio malitia.

1737. *And when the time of the fruits drew near*. Whoever produces fruit expects a benefit; thus the Lord expects that a benefit be rendered to him to his glory. In the case of one man, the fruit is not in boyhood, but at maturity; hence when he comes to adolescence, then he asks for the fruit. Thus when the people was planted, and the law given, he asked for fruit, and they did not know him. *The kite in the air has known her time: the turtle, and the swallow, and the stork have observed the time of their coming: but my people have not known the judgment of the Lord* (Jer 8:7). **He sent his servants**, i.e., the prophets, **to the husbandmen**, i.e., to the Jews, **that they might receive the fruits thereof**, i.e., that they might lead men to acting well. Below, **behold I send to you prophets, and wise men, and scribes: and some of them you will put to death** (Matt 23:34).

1738. After this, he treats of malice. And

first, with regard to the first ones;
second, with regard to the second ones;
third, with regard to the third ones.

1739. *And the husbandmen laying hands on his servants, beat one*, like Michaeas, **and killed another**, like Isaiah, **and stoned another**, like Naboth. *They were stoned, they were cut asunder, they were tempted, they were put to death by the sword* (Heb 11:37).

1740. *Again he sent other servants*. Similarly, he sent the prophets one by one, such as Moses, and Aaron, and the others; but after the time of David he sent many battalions of prophets. For the Lord wishes to set his mercy to fight against their malice. Hence, **and they did to them in the same manner**. *You have always been rebellious against the Lord* (Deut 31:27).

1741. There follows the third act of malice: **and last of all he sent to them his son**, which pertained to complete malice. And he does three things:

first, the Lord's mercy is set out;
second, their malice;
third, the execution of their perverse intention.

1742. *And last of all he sent to them his son*. God, who, *at sundry times and in diverse manners, spoke in times past to the fathers by the prophets, last of all, in these days has spoken to us by his Son* (Heb 1:1–2). The householder **sent to them his son, saying: perhaps they will reverence my son**.

By why does he say **perhaps**? Did he not know? Jerome says that this doubtful way of speaking indicates freedom of judgment, to show what was to happen, because *he who does not honor the Son, does not honor the Father* (John 5:23). Or he speaks this way because some did reverence him.

1743. Next he sets out the evil intention. And first, the request is set out; second, the intention; third, the malice.

Agricolae autem videntes filium dixerunt intra se: hic est haeres; venite, occidamus eum, et habebimus haereditatem eius; ipse enim Filius vere haeres est Patris, quia quod petit obtinet. Ps. II, 8: *postula a me, et dabo tibi gentes haereditatem tuam.* Item est haeres, quia quaecumque habet Pater, habet et ipse: non enim dicitur haeres sicut aliquis alius qui decedente patre habet haereditatem, sed quia semper quod est Patris, ipsius etiam est.

Sed contra: *si cognovissent, numquam Dominum gloriae crucifixissent* I Cor. II, 8. Verum est si cognovissent vere, sed cognoverunt per coniecturam.

1744. Sequitur propositum *venite, occidamus eum.* Sap. II, 20: *morte turpissima condemnemus eum.* Et quod est propositum? *Habebimus haereditatem eius.* Sciebant enim ex lege quod debebat dominari super Iudaicum populum. Unde timebant ne imponeret super eos iugum legis, et traditiones eorum destrueret. Ideo noluerunt pati iugum Christi, unde passi sunt iugum Romanorum. Unde Io. XI, 48: *ne forte veniant Romani, et tollant locum nostrum et gentem.*

1745. Consequenter ponitur executio *et apprehensum eum eiecerunt extra vineam, et occiderunt*, quia extra portam civitatis crucifixerunt eum, et sic quasi alienum a vinea occiderunt. Is. LIII, 7: *quasi ovis ad occisionem ductus est* et cetera. Quod eum extra vineam eiecerunt habetur in Io., quod quicumque confiteretur nomen Christi, neret extra synagogam.

1746. Consequenter requirit eorum sententiam *cum ergo venerit dominus vineae, quid faciet agricolis illis?* Ita subtiliter petit Dominus ut iudicent contra se, sicut Nathan fecit David, quando peccavit cum Bersabee.

Ponitur sententia *malos male perdet*, idest perditione in praesenti et futuro. Et dicunt *male*, idest acerbe. Supra VII, 2: *in ea mensura qua mensi fueritis, remetietur vobis.* Sap. VI, 7: *potentes potenter tormenta patientur. Malos male perdet, et vineam suam*, idest populum suum, *locabit aliis agricolis*, idest apostolis, *qui reddant ei fructum temporibus suis.* Ps. I, 3: *et erit tamquam lignum, quod plantatum est secus decursus aquarum, quod fructum suum dabit in tempore suo.* Iob XXXIV, 24: *conteret multos et innumerabiles, et stare faciet alios pro eis.*

1747. Et hic est quaestio, quare in Marco Dominus respondit hic Iudaei.

Solutio. Dico quod primo dixit Dominus, postea ipsi dixerunt.

Item Lc. habetur, quod cum Dominus hoc diceret, ipsi dixerunt, *absit*.

But the husbandmen seeing the son, said among themselves: this is the heir; come, let us kill him, and we will have his inheritance; for the Son is truly the heir of the Father, because he obtains what he asks. *Ask of me, and I will give you the gentiles for your inheritance* (Ps 2:8). Likewise he is the heir because whatever the Father has, he himself has: for he is not called an heir like some other who has the inheritance by being descended from the father, but because always what is the Father's is also his own.

On the contrary: *if they had known it, they would never have crucified the Lord of glory* (1 Cor 2:8). It is true, if they had truly known, but they know only by conjecture.

1744. There follows the intention: *come, let us kill him. Let us condemn him to a most shameful death* (Wis 2:20). And what is the intention? *We will have his inheritance.* For they knew from the law that he was supposed to rule over the Jewish people. Hence they feared lest he should impose on them the yoke of law, and destroy their traditions. For this reason they were unwilling to suffer the yoke of Christ; hence they suffered the yoke of the Romans. Hence, *and the Romans will come, and take away our place and nation* (John 11:48).

1745. Next, the execution of their intention is set down: *And taking him, they cast him out of the vineyard, and killed him*, because they crucified him outside the gate of the city, and thus they killed him as though a foreigner to the vineyard. *He will be led as a sheep to the slaughter* (Isa 53:7). That they cast him out of the vineyard is found in John, for whoever confessed the name of Christ would be put out of the synagogue (John 9:22).

1746. Next he seeks their judgment: *therefore when the lord of the vineyard comes, what will he do to those husbandmen?* The Lord asks in this subtle way so they will pass judgment on themselves, just as Nathan did to David when he sinned with Bethsabee.

The judgment is set out: *he will bring those evil men to an evil end*, i.e., with perdition in the present and the future. And they say, *to an evil end*, i.e., harshly. Above, *with what measure you measure out, it will be measured to you again* (Matt 7:2). *The mighty will be mightily tormented* (Wis 6:7). *He will bring those evil men to an evil end; and will let out his vineyard*, i.e., his people, *to other husbandmen*, i.e., the apostles, *who will render him the fruit in due season. And he will be like a tree which is planted near the running waters, which will bring forth its fruit, in due season* (Ps 1:3). *He will break in pieces many and innumerable, and will make others to stand in their stead* (Job 34:24).

1747. And here there is a question, why in Mark the Lord responds here to the Jews (Mark 12:9).

Solution: I say that first the Lord spoke, and afterwards they themselves spoke.

Likewise in Luke, it says that when the Lord said this, they said, *God forbid* (Luke 20:16).

Responsio vera est, quia primo ipsi dixerunt, post intelligentes quod contra eos esset, dixerunt *absit*. Item verum est quod principes dixerunt. Et quamvis perciperent quod contra eos esset, non contradicebant, sed populus dixit *absit*.

1748. *Dicit illi Iesus*. Hic ponitur confirmatio. Et

primo ponitur auctoritas;
secundo expositio.

1749. Dicit **numquam legistis in Scripturis**, istud legitur in Ps. CXVII, 22: *'lapidem, quem reprobaverunt aedificantes, hic factus est in caput anguli'*? Et ponit quatuor.

Primo ponit reprobationem; secundo dignitatem; tertio causam; quarto admirationem.

Dicit **'lapidem'** et cetera. Lapis Christus est, qui dicitur lapis ex multis similitudinibus. Is. c. XXVIII, 16: *ecce ego ponam in fundamentis Sion lapidem angularem* et cetera. Aedificantes sunt apostoli. *Unusquisque videat quomodo aedificet*. Unde **'ille lapis quem reprobaverunt'**, idest eiecerunt, **'hic factus est'**, idest constitutus, **'in caput anguli'**, idest in caput Iudaeorum et gentilium. Unde ipse factus est caput Ecclesiae. Sed possent dicere: ipse fecit se caput; ideo dicit **'a Domino factum est istud.'** Ps. CXVII, 16: *dextera domini fecit virtutem* et cetera. Et qualis est ista exaltatio? **'Et est mirabile in oculis nostris'**; Habac. I, 5: *aspicite in gentibus, et videte, et admiramini, et obstupescite: quia opus factum est in diebus vestris, quod nemo credet cum narrabitur*. Tanta enim fuit dignitas, quod non factum fuisset, nisi gratia Dei hoc fecisset. Ad Eph. II, 8: *gratia estis salvati a Christo*.

1750. Consequenter exponit; et ponit duas conclusiones. Primo quod dictum est de parabola; secundo sumitur de hoc quod dictum est in auctoritate.

Dicitur ergo **ideo dico vobis quod auferetur a vobis regnum**, idest Sacra Scriptura, quia amittetis intellectum Sacrae Scripturae. Io. XII, 40: *excaecavit oculos eorum, et induravit cor eorum, ut non videant oculis, et non intelligant corde, et convertantur, et sanem eos*. Vel praelationem super Ecclesiam fidelium, quia translata est gloria eorum. **Et dabitur genti facienti fructum eius**. Is. LV, v. 4: *ecce testem populis dedi eum, ducem ac praeceptorem gentibus. Ecce gentem quam nesciebas, vocabis, et gentes quae te non cognoverunt, ad te current*.

Sed quomodo datus est eis? Superius dictum est quod locavit, hic autem quod datur. Quia cum non facit

The true response is that first they themselves spoke, and understanding afterwards that it was against them, they said, *God forbid*. Likewise, it is true that the leaders spoke. And although they saw that it was against them, they did not speak out against it, but the people said, *God forbid*.

1748. *Jesus says to them*. Here a confirmation is set down. And

first, an authority is set out;
second, the explanation.

1749. He says, **have you never read in the Scriptures: *'the stone which the builders rejected, the same has become the head of the corner'*?** (Ps 117:22). And he sets out four things.

First, he sets out the condemnation; second, the dignity; third, the cause; fourth, the wonderment.

He says, **'the stone which the builders rejected.'** Christ is the stone, who is called a stone by reason of many similarities. *Behold I will lay a stone in the foundations of Zion, a tried stone, a cornerstone* (Isa 28:16). Those who build are the apostles. *But let every man take heed how he builds thereupon* (1 Cor 3:10). Hence, **'the stone which the builders rejected'**, i.e., cast out, here **'has become'**, i.e., is established, **'the head of the corner'**, i.e., into the head of the Jews and the gentiles. Hence he himself has been made the head of the Church. But someone could say, he himself made himself head; this is the reason he says: **'by the Lord this has been done.'** *The right hand of the Lord has wrought strength: the right hand of the Lord has exalted me* (Ps 117:16). And what sort of exaltation is this? **'And it is wonderful in our eyes'**; *behold among the nations, and see: wonder, and be astonished: for a work is done in your days, which no man will believe when it shall be told* (Hab 1:5). For so great was his dignity that this would not have been done unless the grace of God had done it. *For by grace you are saved through faith* (Eph 2:8).

1750. Next, he explains; and he sets out two conclusions. First, what was said about the parable; the second is taken from what was said in the authority.

It says then, **therefore I say to you, that the kingdom of God will be taken from you**, i.e., the Sacred Scriptures, because you have abandoned the understanding of Sacred Scripture. *He has blinded their eyes, and hardened their heart, that they should not see with their eyes, nor understand with their heart, and be converted, and I should heal them* (John 12:40). Or the prelateship over the Church of the faithful, because their glory is transferred. **And will be given to a nation yielding its fruits**. *Behold I have given him for a witness to the people, for a leader and a master to the gentiles. Behold you will call a nation, which you do not know: and the nations that did not know you will run to you* (Isa 55:4–5).

But how is it given to them? It was said further up that he allocated it, but here that it is given. For when it does not

fructum, dicitur conductus, sive mercenarius; sed cum datur, tunc fructum facit.

1751. Ponit duplicem poenam *et qui ceciderit super lapidem istum, confringetur*. Exponitur secundum Hieronymum, sic: ille cadit super lapidem Christum, qui fidem tenet de eo, idest de Christo, sed cadit per peccatum quod contra eum facit. Ideo peccatores cadunt, quia non habent caritatem. *Super quem vero ceciderit, conteret eum*. Cadit autem Christus super infidelibus.

Haec est differentia, quia quando vas cadit super lapidem, non confringitur vas propter lapidem, sed propter modum casus, secundum quod magis cadit ab alto; sed quando lapis cadit supra vas, confringit illud secundum magnitudinem lapidis. Sic homo cum cadit super lapidem Christum, tunc confringitur secundum magnitudinem peccati; quando vero fit infidelis, totaliter conteritur. Vel aliquis cadit super lapidem, quando proprio arbitrio peccat; sed tunc scilicet lapis super eum cadit, quando Christus punit eum, et tunc totus comminuitur. Ps. XVII, 43: *comminuam eos sicut pulverem ante faciem venti*.

1752. Sequitur tempus malitiae *et cum audissent, cognoverunt quod de ipsis diceret*.

Et sequitur malitia *et volentes eum tenere, timuerunt turbas, quia sicut prophetam eum habebant*. Et planum est.

yield fruit it is called a hireling, or a wage-worker; but when it is given, then it yields fruit.

1751. He sets out a twofold punishment: *and whoever will fall on this stone, will be broken*. This is explained according to Jerome thus: he falls on the rock of Christ who holds to the faith concerning it, i.e., concerning Christ, but falls through a sin which he commits against him. Hence sinners fall, because they do not have charity. *But on whomever it will fall, it will grind him to powder*. And Christ falls upon the unfaithful.

There is this difference, that when a vase falls on a rock, the vase is not broken to pieces because of the rock, but because of the way it fell, according as it falls harder from a greater height; but when a rock falls on a vase, it smashes it according to the magnitude of the rock. Thus when a man falls on the rock of Christ, then he is broken to pieces according to the magnitude of his sin; but when he becomes unfaithful, he is totally crushed. Or, someone falls on the rock when he sins by his own judgment; but then the rock falls on him when Christ punishes him, and then the whole thing is pulverized. *And I shall beat them as small as the dust before the wind* (Ps 17:43).

1752. There follows the time of the malice: *and when the chief priests and Pharisees had heard his parables, they knew that he spoke of them*.

And there follows the malice: *and seeking to lay hands on him, they feared the multitudes, because they held him as a prophet*. And this is clear.

Chapter 22

Lecture 1

²²:¹ Et respondens Iesus dixit iterum in parabolis, eis dicens: [n. 1754]

²²:² simile factum est regnum caelorum homini regi, qui fecit nuptias filio suo, [n. 1754]

²²:³ et misit servos suos vocare invitatos ad nuptias, et nolebant venire. [n. 1758]

²²:⁴ Iterum misit alios servos dicens: dicite invitatis: ecce prandium meum paravi, tauri mei et altilia occisa sunt, et omnia parata, venite ad nuptias. [n. 1759]

²²:⁵ Illi autem neglexerunt, et abierunt, alius in villam suam, alius vero ad negotiationem suam; [n. 1762]

²²:⁶ reliqui vero tenuerunt servos eius, et contumeliis affectos occiderunt. [n. 1763]

²²:⁷ Rex autem cum audisset, iratus est: et missis exercitibus suis perdidit homicidas illos, et civitatem illorum succendit. [n. 1764]

²²:⁸ Tunc ait servis suis: nuptiae quidem paratae sunt, sed qui invitati erant, non fuerunt digni. [n. 1766]

²²:⁹ Ite ergo ad exitus viarum, et quoscumque inveneritis, vocate ad nuptias. [n. 1767]

²²:¹⁰ Et egressi servi eius in vias, congregaverunt omnes quos invenerunt, malos et bonos; et impletae sunt nuptiae discumbentium. [n. 1768]

²²:¹ Καὶ ἀποκριθεὶς ὁ Ἰησοῦς πάλιν εἶπεν ἐν παραβολαῖς αὐτοῖς λέγων·

²²:² ὡμοιώθη ἡ βασιλεία τῶν οὐρανῶν ἀνθρώπῳ βασιλεῖ, ὅστις ἐποίησεν γάμους τῷ υἱῷ αὐτοῦ.

²²:³ καὶ ἀπέστειλεν τοὺς δούλους αὐτοῦ καλέσαι τοὺς κεκλημένους εἰς τοὺς γάμους, καὶ οὐκ ἤθελον ἐλθεῖν.

²²:⁴ πάλιν ἀπέστειλεν ἄλλους δούλους λέγων· εἴπατε τοῖς κεκλημένοις· ἰδοὺ τὸ ἄριστόν μου ἡτοίμακα, οἱ ταῦροί μου καὶ τὰ σιτιστὰ τεθυμένα καὶ πάντα ἕτοιμα· δεῦτε εἰς τοὺς γάμους.

²²:⁵ οἱ δὲ ἀμελήσαντες ἀπῆλθον, ὃς μὲν εἰς τὸν ἴδιον ἀγρόν, ὃς δὲ ἐπὶ τὴν ἐμπορίαν αὐτοῦ·

²²:⁶ οἱ δὲ λοιποὶ κρατήσαντες τοὺς δούλους αὐτοῦ ὕβρισαν καὶ ἀπέκτειναν.

²²:⁷ ὁ δὲ βασιλεὺς ὠργίσθη καὶ πέμψας τὰ στρατεύματα αὐτοῦ ἀπώλεσεν τοὺς φονεῖς ἐκείνους καὶ τὴν πόλιν αὐτῶν ἐνέπρησεν.

²²:⁸ τότε λέγει τοῖς δούλοις αὐτοῦ· ὁ μὲν γάμος ἕτοιμός ἐστιν, οἱ δὲ κεκλημένοι οὐκ ἦσαν ἄξιοι·

²²:⁹ πορεύεσθε οὖν ἐπὶ τὰς διεξόδους τῶν ὁδῶν καὶ ὅσους ἐὰν εὕρητε καλέσατε εἰς τοὺς γάμους.

²²:¹⁰ καὶ ἐξελθόντες οἱ δοῦλοι ἐκεῖνοι εἰς τὰς ὁδοὺς συνήγαγον πάντας οὓς εὗρον, πονηρούς τε καὶ ἀγαθούς· καὶ ἐπλήσθη ὁ γάμος ἀνακειμένων.

²²:¹ And Jesus answering, spoke again in parables to them, saying: [n. 1754]

²²:² the kingdom of heaven is likened to a man, a king, who made a marriage for his son. [n. 1754]

²²:³ And he sent his servants, to call those who were invited to the marriage; and they would not come. [n. 1758]

²²:⁴ Again he sent other servants, saying: tell those who were invited: behold, I have prepared my dinner; my bulls and fatlings are killed, and all things are ready: come to the marriage. [n. 1759]

²²:⁵ But they neglected, and went their ways, one to his farm, and another to his merchandise. [n. 1762]

²²:⁶ And the rest laid hands on his servants, and having treated them contumeliously, put them to death. [n. 1763]

²²:⁷ But when the king had heard of it, he was angry, and sending his armies, he destroyed those murderers, and burnt their city. [n. 1764]

²²:⁸ Then he said to his servants: the marriage indeed is ready, but those who were invited were not worthy. [n. 1766]

²²:⁹ Go therefore into the offroads of the ways; and as many as you will find, call to the marriage. [n. 1767]

²²:¹⁰ And his servants, going out into the ways, gathered together all whom they found, both bad and good, and the marriage was filled with guests. [n. 1768]

22:11 Intravit autem rex ut videret discumbentes, et vidit ibi hominem non vestitum veste nuptiali, [n. 1769]	22:11 εἰσελθὼν δὲ ὁ βασιλεὺς θεάσασθαι τοὺς ἀνακειμένους εἶδεν ἐκεῖ ἄνθρωπον οὐκ ἐνδεδυμένον ἔνδυμα γάμου,	22:11 And the king went in to see the guests, and he saw there a man who was not wearing a wedding garment. [n. 1769]
22:12 et ait illi: amice quomodo huc intrasti non habens vestem nuptialem? At ille obmutuit. [n. 1771]	22:12 καὶ λέγει αὐτῷ· ἑταῖρε, πῶς εἰσῆλθες ὧδε μὴ ἔχων ἔνδυμα γάμου; ὁ δὲ ἐφιμώθη.	22:12 And he said to him: friend, how did you come in here not having on a wedding garment? But he was silent. [n. 1771]
22:13 Tunc dixit rex ministris: ligatis pedibus eius et manibus, mittite eum in tenebras exteriores; ibi erit fletus et stridor dentium. [n. 1773]	22:13 τότε ὁ βασιλεὺς εἶπεν τοῖς διακόνοις· δήσαντες αὐτοῦ πόδας καὶ χεῖρας ἐκβάλετε αὐτὸν εἰς τὸ σκότος τὸ ἐξώτερον· ἐκεῖ ἔσται ὁ κλαυθμὸς καὶ ὁ βρυγμὸς τῶν ὀδόντων.	22:13 Then the king said to the waiters: bind his hands and feet, and cast him into the exterior darkness: there will there be weeping and gnashing of teeth. [n. 1773]
22:14 Multi autem sunt vocati, pauci vero electi. [n. 1775]	22:14 πολλοὶ γάρ εἰσιν κλητοί, ὀλίγοι δὲ ἐκλεκτοί.	22:14 For many are called, but few are chosen. [n. 1775]

1753. Dictum est supra quod Christi persecutores provocati sunt ad occidendum eum tribus de causis: ex eius gloria, ex eius sapientia qua confutabat eos, ex eius iustitia qua arguebat eos. Qualiter autem provocati sunt ex gloria Christi, dictum est; nunc autem dicendum qualiter ex sapientia. Et

primo inquantum eorum damnationem praemonstrat;

secundo inquantum disputando confutat, ibi *tunc abeuntes Pharisaei consilium inierunt ut caperent eum in sermone*.

In ista parabola, in qua determinatur de reprobatione Iudaeorum et vocatione gentium,

primo ponitur instructio nuptiarum;

secundo de vocatione Iudaeorum et recusatione;

tertio de vocatione gentium.

Secunda ibi *et misit servos suos vocare invitatos*; tertia ibi *tunc ait servis suis* et cetera.

1754. Dicit ergo *et respondens Iesus dixit*. Cui respondit? Non est dictum quod alicui loqueretur. Sed eum tenere volebant, ideo non verbis, sed malitiae eorum respondit, ideo *in parabolis dicit eis: simile est regnum caelorum homini regi qui fecit nuptias filio suo*.

Hic ponitur parabola de nuptiis, et similis parabola ponitur Lc. XIV, 16. Et non videtur eadem secundum Gregorium, quia ibi fit mentio de coena, hic de nuptiis. Item nullus exclusus est ab illa coena, hic autem est aliquis exclusus. Unde alia est parabola. Per illam convivium caeleste intelligitur, per istam convivium quod fit in terra. Et ideo illud dicitur coena, quia ab eo nullus excluditur, ab isto aliquis excluditur.

1753. It was said above that Christ's persecutors were provoked to kill him by three things: by his glory, by the wisdom with which he refuted them, and by the justice with which he accused them. Moreover, it has been said how they were provoked by Christ's glory; but now it must be said how they were provoked by his wisdom. And

first, insofar as he shows beforehand their condemnation;

second, insofar as he refutes them in argument, at *then the Pharisees, going out, consulted among themselves how to ensnare him in his speech*.

In this parable, in which he explains about the rejection of the Jews and the calling of the gentiles,

first, the preparation for the marriage is set out;

second, the calling of the Jews and their refusal;

third, the calling of the gentiles.

The second is at *and he sent his servants, to call those who were invited to the marriage*; the third, at *then he said to his servants: the marriage indeed is ready*.

1754. It says then, *and Jesus answering, spoke*. To whom does he respond? It is not said that he spoke to anyone. But they wanted to lay hands on him, and so he responds, not to their words, but to their malice, and for this reason he spoke to them in parables: *the kingdom of heaven is likened to a man, a king, who made a marriage for his son*.

Here the parable of the marriage is set out, and a similar parable is set out elsewhere (Luke 14:16). And it does not seem to be the same parable, according to Gregory, because there a dinner is mentioned, here a wedding. Likewise, no one is excluded from that dinner, but here someone is excluded. Hence it is another parable. By this one is understood the heavenly banquet, by that one the banquet which happens on earth. And therefore that one is called a feast, because no one is excluded from it, while from this one someone is excluded.

It can be said, according to some, that it is the same parable, because in ancient times lunch and dinner were called the same thing, because men were accustomed to eat only up to the ninth hour. Or it can be said that Luke says what Matthew leaves unmentioned.

But I believe it is another.

1755. Concerning this one, let us see who this man the king is. And it is said that he is God, and the person of the Father is understood, because he speaks of **his son**.

But why does he say, *a man, a king*? The reason is, as Origen says, that a king is named from 'ruling.' But we are not able, nor are we capable of his rule according as he is, but he rules us according to our mode. *As the eagle enticing her young to fly* (Deut 32:11). And for this reason it says, *a man, a king*, because he rules us in a human mode. But when we see him as he is, then he will be a king, because then he will rule according to himself. Hence the Apostle, *we see now through a glass in a dark manner; but then face to face* (1 Cor 13:12).

He says, *the kingdom of heaven is likened to a man, a king*. For just as in a kingdom there are many parts, for there is the king, the kingdom, and those who serve, so it is in this kingdom; therefore it is *likened to a man, a king, who made a marriage for his son*. The son is Christ, of whom, *that we may know the true God, and may be in his true Son. This is the true God and life eternal* (1 John 5:20).

1756. What is this marriage? It can be explained in four ways. First, through the unity of the human nature with the divine; that human nature might be the bride, the womb of the Virgin became the bridal chamber. *He, as a bridegroom coming out of his bride chamber* (Ps 18:6). And this explanation is somewhat dubious, because it could be thought that the person of the Father is not other than the person of the Son.

Hence it can be said that this bridegroom is the Word incarnate; the bride, the Church; hence the Apostle: *this is a great sacrament; but I speak in Christ and in the Church* (Eph 5:32). Likewise, the marriage of the Word himself to our soul. For the soul becomes a partaker of God's glory through faith, and in this way our marriage comes about. *And I will espouse you to me in faith* (Hos 2:20). Likewise, there will be a marriage in the common resurrection. And Christ is the way of this resurrection; *I am the way* (John 14:6). There will be a marriage at that time, when our mortal body is swallowed up by life (2 Cor 5:4).

But if we speak according to Gregory, it must be explained as about the present, according as the Church is espoused to Christ, and our soul to God by faith.

1757. There follows the calling of the Jews. And
first, a twofold calling is set out;
second, the excuse, at **but they neglected, and went their ways**.

Concerning the first, he does two things according to the two callings.

1758. Hence he says, **and he sent his servants, to call those who were invited**. And according to what Origen says, there are two texts there, because some texts have **his servant**, while some have **his servants**.

If the text is **servant**, in this way three things should be considered. First, the invitation; second, the calling; and third, the other invitation. Therefore, the Jews had been invited in the patriarchs; hence it was said to Abraham, *and in your seed will all the nations of the earth be blessed* (Gen 22:18). *To Abraham were the promises made and to his seed* (Gal 3:16). First, Moses was sent. *But it is not so with my servant Moses who is most faithful in all my house* (Num 12:7). And there follows, *why then were you not afraid to speak ill of my servant Moses?* **And they would not come**. *While I am yet living, and going in with you, you have always been rebellious against the Lord* (Deut 31:27).

The second calling is through the prophets, of whom Amos says, *for the Lord God does nothing without revealing his secret to his servants the prophets* (Amos 3:7).

Or the text can be **servants**, and then the first ones signify the prophets, against whom the Jews were always rebels; *you always resist the Holy Spirit* (Acts 7:51). The second ones signify the apostles, to whom it was said above, **do not go into the way of the gentiles** (Matt 10:5). Or by the first prophets, the first apostles; by the second, the successors of the apostles.

1759. Again he sent other servants. Here the other invitation is set out.

And an increase of kindness is set out on the part of the one inviting, and an increase of malice on the part of the ones excusing themselves.

1760. In the first calling, nothing was promised; but in this one he makes a promise, because he says, **tell those who were invited: behold, I have prepared my dinner**. This dinner is spiritual refreshment; *she has slain her victims, mingled her wine, and set forth her table. She has sent her maids to invite to the tower* (Prov 9:2–3).

My bulls and fatlings are killed. And this can be explained, according to Origen, as the disposing of God's wisdom. **Bulls** name strong reasons; *he has taught me, with a strong arm* (Isa 8:11). **Fatlings** name, as it were, the well fed. **Fatlings** properly name fattened birds, which are fed and made fat, and they signify delicate senses, and they become fattened when they are increased by the sacred senses by which the soul is fattened; *let my soul be filled as with marrow and fatness* (Ps 62:6). For whatever is necessary is found in Sacred Scripture. Therefore, **all things are ready**. *The law of the Lord is unspotted, converting souls* (Ps 18:8). This is the invitation of wisdom: *come, eat my bread, and drink the wine which I have mingled for you* (Prov 9:5).

1761. Or, it signifies spiritual refreshment, and the bulls signify the examples of the saints, which the Lord prepared

praeparavit in exemplum; Iac. V, 10: *accipite in exemplum exitus mali, et longanimitatis, et laboris, et patientiae, prophetas*. Unde tribulationes sanctorum ponit in exemplum.

Secundum Gregorium, per tauros significantur patres Veteris Testamenti, quia taurus ferit cornibus, et in tempore patrum semper quaerebatur vindicta, et praecipiebatur oculum dari pro oculo. Per altilia patres Novi Testamenti, qui omnia dimiserunt pro Christo, et impinguantur Sapientia Dei, occisi propter Deum, et utrique occisi sunt. **Omnia parata sunt, venite ad nuptias**. Passus est Christus, aperuit caelos, misit apostolos. Vel per tauros intelliguntur sacerdotes Veteris Testamenti, quia taurus est animal immolatitium; per altilia prophetae qui impinguati sunt Sapientia Dei.

1762. **Sed illi**, scilicet indurati in malitia, **neglexerunt**. Quidam dimittunt ex negligentia, quidam autem ex malitia, qui persequuntur praedicatores; unde dicit **illi autem neglexerunt**. Et quae fuit causa? Quia **abierunt unus in vineam suam, alius ad negotiationem suam**. Videbantur habere iustam causam exterius, sed Dominus non recipit, quia nulla temporalia debent detinere de veniendo ad Deum.

Secundum Hilarium, per hoc quod dicit, **in vineam suam**, significat appetitum humanae gloriae; Io. XII, 43: *dilexerunt magis gloriam hominum quam gloriam Dei*; Ier. c. V, 4: *ego autem dixit: forsitan pauperes sunt et stulti, ignorantes Viam domini et iudicium Dei sui*. Per hoc quod dicit **alius in negotiationem suam**, signatur appetitus avaritiae; Ier. VI, 13: *a maiori usque ad minorem omnes avaritiae student*.

Secundum Chrysostomum quidam habent occupationem laborando propriis manibus, alii in negotiationem, idest in proprium officium suum.

1763. Sequitur **reliqui vero tenuerunt servos suos**, idest apostolos, **et contumeliis affectos occiderunt**, quia multos occiderunt ex Veteri et Novo Testamento. Unde infra XXIII, v. 34: *mitto ad vos sapientes et Scribas, et ex illis occidetis* et cetera. Et non facit hic mentionem de morte sua, sed solum discipulorum quia satis superius fecerat mentionem.

1764. Tunc sequitur punitio eorum **rex vero cum audisset, iratus est** et cetera. Supra posuit poenam spiritualem, hic autem ponit temporalem; unde supra dicebatur **homini regi**, hic autem dicitur **rex**, quia nomen 'hominis' ad pietatem pertinere videtur, 'regis' vero ad punitionem; ideo hic solum dicitur **rex**; Sap. XIV, 17: *hos quos in palam homines honorare non poterant propter hoc quod longe essent, a longinquo figura eorum allata, evidentem imaginem regis, quem honorare volebant,*

as an example; *take, my brethren, for an example of suffering evil, of labor and patience, the prophets, who spoke in the name of the Lord* (Jas 5:10). Hence he sets out the saints' afflictions as an example.

According to Gregory, the bulls signify the fathers of the Old Testament, because a bull strikes blows with horns, and in the time of the fathers vengeance was always sought, and it was commanded that an eye be given for an eye. The fatlings indicate the fathers of the New Testament, who left everything for Christ, and are fattened with the Wisdom of God, killed for God's sake, and both are killed. ***All things are ready: come to the marriage***. Christ has suffered, has opened the heavens, has sent the apostles. Or by the bulls are understood the priests of the Old Testament, because the bull is an animal of sacrifice; by the fatlings are understood the prophets who were fattened by the Wisdom of God.

1762. ***But they***, namely those hardened in malice, ***neglected***. Some wander away out of negligence, and others out of malice, namely those who persecute the preachers; hence it says, ***but they neglected***. And what was the cause? Because they ***went their ways, one to his farm, and another to his merchandise***. Exteriorly, they seemed to have a just cause, but the Lord does not accept it, because no temporal things should hold one back from coming to God.

According to Hilary, by saying, ***his farm***, he indicates the appetite for human glory; *for they loved the glory of men more than the glory of God* (John 12:43); *but I said: perhaps these are poor and foolish, that do not know the way of the Lord, the judgment of their God* (Jer 5:4). By saying, ***another to his merchandise***, he indicates the appetite of greed; *for from the least of them even to the greatest, all are given to covetousness* (Jer 6:13).

According to Chrysostom, some have employment in working with their hands, others in business, i.e., in their proper duties.

1763. There follows, ***and the rest laid hands on his servants***, i.e., the apostles, ***and having treated them contumeliously, put them to death***, because they killed many from the Old and the New Testaments. Hence below, *therefore behold I send to you prophets, and wise men, and scribes: and some of them you will put to death* (Matt 23:34). And he does not mention his own death here, but only the deaths of the disciples, because he had sufficiently mentioned his own death above.

1764. Then there follows their punishment: ***but when the king had heard of it, he was angry***. Above he set out a spiritual punishment, but here he sets out a temporal one; hence above it said, ***a man, a king***, but here it says, ***the king***, because the name 'man' seems to pertain to piety, but the name 'king' to punishment, and so it says here only, ***the king***. And those whom men could not honor in presence, because they dwelt far off, they brought their resemblance from afar, and made an express image of the king whom they had a

fecerunt: ut illum qui aberat tamquam praesentem colerent sua sollicitudine.

Rex autem iratus. Notandum quod quando ira attribuitur Deo, non commotionem significat, sed vindictam: quia irati punire solent, unde ira punitio vocatur. Quod est notandum contra haereticos, quia solent obiicere Deum Veteris Testamenti non esse bonum, quia praecepit punitiones et cetera.

Unde **missis exercitibus suis perdidit homicidas illos**. Exercitus sunt spiritus angelici, vel cives Romani qui sub Tito et Vespasiano occiderunt multos; Ps. XXIII, 1: *domini est terra, et plenitudo eius*. **Et civitates illorum succendit**, quia combustae sunt; Is. I, 7: *civitates vestras ignis comburet*. Vel potest mystice intelligi, scilicet corpora eorum, vel congregationes haereticorum.

1765. Sequitur vocatio gentium, et ponitur examinatio.

Et tria facit.

Primo ponitur mandatum;

secundo executio;

tertio effectus.

Secunda ibi *et egressi servi eius* etc.; tertia ibi *et impletae sunt nuptiae discumbentium*.

Circa primum duo facit.

Primo assignat rationem praecepti;

secundo ponit praeceptum.

1766. Dicit ergo **tunc ait servis suis: nuptiae quidem paratae sunt, sed qui invitati erant non fuerunt digni**.

Nuptiae quidem praeparatae sunt, idest Filius incarnatus est, secundum illud Is. V, v. 4: *quid ultra potui facere tibi, vinea mea?* **Sed qui fuerant invitati, indigni fuerunt**, idest, indignos se reddiderunt. Et quomodo? Sicut dicitur ad Rom. X, 3: *ignorantes Dei iustitiam, et suam volentes statuere, iustitiae Dei non sunt subiecti*; et Act. c. XIII, 46: *sed quoniam repellitis illud, et indignos vos iudicastis vitae aeternae, ideo convertimur ad gentes*. Unde per delictum Iudaeorum salus facta est gentibus; Apoc. III, v. 11: *tene quod habes, ne alter accipiat coronam tuam*.

1767. Sequitur mandatum *ite ergo ad exitus viarum* et cetera. Per **vias** intelliguntur diversa dogmata, quia ista sunt viae quaedam, quae ducunt nos ad veritatem. Gentiles sunt in exitibus dogmatum. Unde **ite ad exitus viarum**, idest ad illos qui haerent erroneis dogmatibus.

Vel aliter. Is. IX, 2: *populus qui ambulabat in tenebris, vidit lucem*. Unde per vias intelliguntur actiones bonae, de quibus Prov. c. IV, 27: *vias quae a dextris sunt, novit Dominus*; per **exitus**, quaecumque possunt concurrere ad actiones. **Et quoscumque inveneritis, vocate ad**

mind to honor: that by this their diligence, they might honor as present, him that was absent (Wis 14:17).

He was angry. One should note that when anger is attributed to God, it does not signify agitation, but vengeance: for usually those who are angry punish, so punishment is called anger. This is to be noted against heretics, who often object that the God of the Old Testament is not good, because he commands punishments.

Hence, **sending his armies, he destroyed those murderers**. The armies are the angelic spirits, or the Roman citizens who killed many under Titus and Vespasian; *the earth is the Lord's and the fullness thereof* (Ps 23:1). **And burnt their city**, because they were burned; *your cities are burnt with fire* (Isa 1:7). Or it can be understood mystically, namely their bodies, or the communities of heretics.

1765. There follows the calling of the gentiles, and an examination is set out.

And he does three things:

first, a command is set out;

second, the execution of the command;

third, the effect.

The second is at **and his servants going out into the ways**; the third, at **and the marriage was filled with guests**.

Concerning the first, he does two things:

first, he gives the reason for the command;

second, he sets out the command.

1766. He says therefore, **then he said to his servants: the marriage indeed is ready, but those who were invited were not worthy**.

The marriage indeed is ready, i.e., the Son is incarnate, in accord with, *what is there that I ought to do more to my vineyard, that I have not done to it?* (Isa 5:4) **But those who were invited were not worthy**, i.e., have rendered themselves unworthy. And how? As is said in Romans, *for they, not knowing the justice of God, and seeking to establish their own, have not submitted themselves to the justice of God* (Rom 10:3); and *because you reject it, and judge yourselves unworthy of eternal life, behold we turn to the gentiles* (Acts 13:46). Hence through the Jews' fault, salvation was brought to the gentiles; *behold, I come quickly: hold fast that which you have, that no man take your crown* (Rev 3:11).

1767. There follows the command: **go therefore into the offroads of the ways**. By the **ways** are understood various doctrines, because these are certain ways which lead us to the truth. The gentiles are in the offroads of doctrines. Hence, **go therefore into the offroads of the ways**, i.e., to those who hold to erroneous doctrines.

Or in another way. *The people that walked in darkness, have seen a great light* (Isa 9:2). Hence by the ways are understood good actions: *for the Lord knows the ways that are on the right hand* (Prov 4:27); by the **offroads** are understood all those who can engage in actions. **And as many**

nuptias. Unde infra ult., 19: *ite, docete omnes gentes* et cetera.

1768. Sequitur executio *et egressi servi eius in vias, congregaverunt omnes*; Marci ult., 20: *illi autem profecti praedicaverunt ubique, Domino cooperante*.

Sed quid est quod dicit **bonos et malos**? Potest dici quod illos, qui primo mali, et post boni. Vel potest dici, cum dicit **bonos et malos**, quod loquitur comparative, quod inter illos aliqui sunt boni secundum virtutes civiles. Vel **bonos et malos**, quia postquam congregati fuerint, commiscentur boni et mali.

Et impletae sunt nuptiae discumbentium, idest fidelibus. Supra XIII, 48 simile ponitur, *quam cum impleta esset, educentes, et secus littus sedentes, elegerunt bonos in vasa sua, malos autem foras miserunt*.

1769. *Intravit autem rex* et cetera. Hic ponitur examinatio congregatorum. Et

primo ponitur examinans;

secundo examinatio;

tertio condemnatio.

1770. Examinans intravit. Intrat enim quando exercet iudicium super eos; Gen. c. XVIII, 21: *intrabo, et videbo*: et hoc in finali iudicio; item in morte; item quando imminent tribulationes Ecclesiae.

Sed quis est examinatus? *Vidit hominem non habentem vestem nuptialem*. Quae est ista vestis? Christus. Qui sumus Christi, Christum induamus. Apostolus Rom. XIII, 14: *induimini Dominum Iesum Christum*. Quidam enim induunt Christum per sacramentum; Gal. III, 27: *quicumque in Christo baptizati estis, Christum induistis*. Quidam sunt in Christo per caritatem et amorem; Col. III, 15: *super omnia autem caritatem habete, quod est vinculum perfectionis. Et pax Christi exultet in cordibus vestris, in qua et vocati estis in uno corpore*. Item per mortis rememorationem. Item per operum conformitatem; ad Rom. XIII, 14: *induimini Dominum Iesum Christum*.

Habere ergo vestem nuptialem est induere Christum per operationem bonam, per conversationem sanctam, per caritatem veram; et si unum deficiat, malum.

1771. Tunc sequitur examinatio. Deinde dicit qualiter defecit.

Dicit ergo *amice*. Amicum vocat per fidem, vel quia ipse amavit eum. Vel potest dici quod ubicumque vocat aliquem amicum, improperando dicit: unde improperat amorem quo amavit eum. *Quomodo huc intrasti non habens vestem nuptialem?*

Sed posset dicere aliquis: qua occasione punivit illum, quia vocavit bonos et malos? Sed noluit quod mali

as you will find, call to the marriage. Hence below, *going therefore, teach all nations* (Matt 28:19).

1768. There follows the execution of the command: *and his servants going out into the ways, gathered together all whom they found*; *but going forth they preached everywhere: the Lord working withal* (Mark 16:20).

But why does he say, **bad and good**? It could be said that the **bad** refers to those who first were bad, and afterwards good. Or it can be said that when he says, **bad and good**, he speaks comparatively, because among them some are good according to public virtue. Or **bad and good**, because after they had been gathered, the good and the bad were mixed together.

And the marriage was filled with guests, i.e., the faithful. Above, a similar thing is set out: *which, when it was filled, they drew out, and sitting by the shore, they put the good into vessels, but the bad they threw out* (Matt 13:48).

1769. *And the king went in to see the guests*. Here the examination of those gathered is set down. And

first, the one examining is set down;

second, the examination;

third, a condemnation.

1770. The one examining entered. For he enters when he exercises judgment over them; *I will go down and see* (Gen 18:21); and this in the final judgment; likewise in death; also, when afflictions threaten the Church.

But who is the one examined? *He saw there a man who was not wearing a wedding garment*. What is this garment? Christ. We who are Christ's, let us put on Christ. The Apostle: *but put on the Lord Jesus Christ* (Rom 13:14). For some put on Christ through the sacrament; *for as many of you as have been baptized in Christ, have put on Christ* (Gal 3:27). Some are in Christ through charity and love; *but above all these things have charity, which is the bond of perfection: and let the peace of Christ rejoice in your hearts, wherein also you are called in one body* (Col 3:14–15). Also through the remembrance of death. Also through likeness of works; *but put on the Lord Jesus Christ* (Rom 13:14).

Therefore, to have a wedding garment is to put on Christ through good works, through a holy life, through true charity; and if one of these is lacking, it is bad.

1771. There follows the examination. Then he says how he failed.

He says therefore, *friend*. He calls him a friend through faith, or because he himself loved him. Or it can be said that where he calls someone a friend, he speaks by way of reproach: hence he reproaches the love by which he loved him. *How did you come in here not having on a wedding garment?*

But someone could say: on what pretext did he punish him, since he called the good and the bad? But he did not

venirent, nisi pararent se et disponerent se, ut essent boni.

1772. Deinde sequitur qualiter defecit. Unde sequitur **at ille obmutuit**, quia non potest habere sufficientem rationem peccator, quare vestem nuptialem contempsit; Iob IX, v. 3: *si voluerit contendere eum eo, non poterit respondere ei*.

1773. Et concludit sententia parabolae. Ponitur poena duplex, poena damni et poena sensus. Nam in mundo tripliciter perficitur: per intellectum cogitando, per affectum tendendo in summum bonum, item per actum; ideo tripliciter punitur.

Unde **dixit rex ministris: ligatis manibus et pedibus eius, mittite eum in tenebras exteriores**. Per pedes intelliguntur affectus. Mali in mundo isto pedes habent, sed non ligatos, quia possunt fieri boni; sed post ligabuntur, quia post redire non poterunt; Eccl. IX, 10: *quodcumque potest facere manus tua, instanter operare, quia nec opus, nec ratio, nec scientia erunt apud inferos quo tu properas*. Item modo potest homo proficere in cogitando veritates, sed tunc non; ideo dicitur **mittite eum in tenebras exteriores**. Modo enim aliqui peccatores non sunt tenebrosi quantum ad cognitionem exteriorem, licet quoad cognitionem interiorem; sed tunc habebunt tenebras exteriores. Vel, ad litteram, quia non solum quoad animam, sed quoad corpus, quia separabuntur a societate sanctorum.

1774. Tunc sequitur poena sensus **ibi erit fletus et stridor dentium**. Fletus procedit ex tristitia, stridor ex ira. In Act. VII, v. 54: *stridebant dentibus in eum*. Aliqui flent pro peccatis, et humiliantur, et mundantur. Ibi erit tristitia, sed non ad humilitatem, sed vertetur in iram. Item stridor propter impatientiam, quia *superbia eorum qui te oderunt, ascendit semper*, Ps. LXXIII, 23. Vel potest dici in resurrectione, quia non solum in anima, sed etiam in corpore punientur; vel quia calorem et frigora patientur; Iob XXIV, 19: *transibunt ab aquis nivium ad calorem nimium*.

1775. Deinde concludit **multi sunt vocati, pauci vero electi**, quia quidam nolunt venire, quidam non habent vestem nuptialem. Unde supra VII, 14: **arcta est via quae ducit ad vitam, et pauci sunt qui inveniunt eam**.

will that the bad should come unless they prepared themselves and disposed themselves to be good.

1772. Next there follows how he failed. Hence there follows, **but he was silent**, because a sinner cannot have a sufficient reason why he has scorned a wedding garment; *if he will contend with him, he cannot answer him one for a thousand* (Job 9:3).

1773. And the judgment of the parable concludes. A twofold punishment is set out, the punishment of the damned and the punishment of the senses. For in the world a thing can be perfected in three ways: through the intellect, by thinking; through affection, by tending to the highest good; and through action; therefore it is punished in three ways.

Hence, **bind his hands and feet, and cast him into the exterior darkness**. By the feet are understood the affections. The wicked in this world have feet, but not bound, because they are able to become good; but afterwards they are bound, because they cannot come back. *Whatever your hand is able to do, do it earnestly: for neither work, nor reason, nor wisdom, nor knowledge will be in hell, to which you are hastening* (Eccl 9:10). Likewise, now a man can make progress in knowing the truth, but not then; for this reason it says, **cast him into the exterior darkness**. For now some sinners are not darkened with regard to exterior knowledge, although they are with respect to interior; but then they will have exterior darkness. Or, literally, because they will be cast out not only as regards the soul, but as regards the body, because they will be separated from the society of the saints.

1774. Then there follows the punishment of the senses: **there will be weeping and gnashing of teeth**. Weeping comes from sorrow, gnashing of teeth from anger. *They gnashed with their teeth at him* (Acts 7:54). Some weep over sins, and are humiliated, and are cleansed. There will be sorrow, but not unto humility, but it will be turned into anger. Likewise gnashing of teeth, on account of lack of ability to endure the suffering, because *the pride of those who hate you ascends continually* (Ps 73:23). Or it can be said in the resurrection, because they will suffer not only in soul, but also in body; or because they will suffer heat and cold; *let him pass from the snow waters to excessive heat* (Job 24:19).

1775. Then he concludes: **for many are called, but few are chosen**, for some do not wish to come, and some do not have a wedding garment. Hence above, **how narrow is the gate, and strait is the way that leads to life: and few there are who find it!** (Matt 7:14).

Lecture 2

22:15 Tunc abeuntes pharisaei consilium inierunt ut caperent eum in sermone. [n. 1777]

22:16 Et mittunt ei discipulos suos cum Herodianis dicentes: Magister, scimus quia verax es, et viam Dei in veritate doces, et non est tibi cura de aliquo: non enim respicis personam hominum. [n. 1778]

22:17 Dic ergo nobis quid tibi videatur. Licet censum dare Caesari, aut non? [n. 1785]

22:18 Cognita autem Iesus nequitia eorum ait: quid me temptatis, hypocritae? [n. 1786]

22:19 Ostendite mihi numisma censsus. At illi obtulerunt ei denarium. [n. 1787]

22:20 Et ait illis Iesus: cuius est imago haec et suprascriptio? [n. 1787]

22:21 Dicunt ei: Caesaris. Tunc ait illis: reddite ergo quae sunt Caesaris Caesari, et quae sunt Dei Deo. [n. 1788]

22:22 Et audientes mirati sunt, et relicto eo abierunt. [n. 1789]

22:15 Τότε πορευθέντες οἱ Φαρισαῖοι συμβούλιον ἔλαβον ὅπως αὐτὸν παγιδεύσωσιν ἐν λόγῳ.

22:16 καὶ ἀποστέλλουσιν αὐτῷ τοὺς μαθητὰς αὐτῶν μετὰ τῶν Ἡρῳδιανῶν λέγοντες· διδάσκαλε, οἴδαμεν ὅτι ἀληθὴς εἶ καὶ τὴν ὁδὸν τοῦ θεοῦ ἐν ἀληθείᾳ διδάσκεις καὶ οὐ μέλει σοι περὶ οὐδενός· οὐ γὰρ βλέπεις εἰς πρόσωπον ἀνθρώπων,

22:17 εἰπὲ οὖν ἡμῖν τί σοι δοκεῖ· ἔξεστιν δοῦναι κῆνσον Καίσαρι ἢ οὔ;

22:18 γνοὺς δὲ ὁ Ἰησοῦς τὴν πονηρίαν αὐτῶν εἶπεν· τί με πειράζετε, ὑποκριταί;

22:19 ἐπιδείξατέ μοι τὸ νόμισμα τοῦ κήνσου. οἱ δὲ προσήνεγκαν αὐτῷ δηνάριον.

22:20 καὶ λέγει αὐτοῖς· τίνος ἡ εἰκὼν αὕτη καὶ ἡ ἐπιγραφή;

22:21 λέγουσιν αὐτῷ· Καίσαρος. τότε λέγει αὐτοῖς· ἀπόδοτε οὖν τὰ Καίσαρος Καίσαρι καὶ τὰ τοῦ θεοῦ τῷ θεῷ.

22:22 καὶ ἀκούσαντες ἐθαύμασαν, καὶ ἀφέντες αὐτὸν ἀπῆλθαν.

22:15 Then the Pharisees, going out, consulted among themselves how to ensnare him in his speech. [n. 1777]

22:16 And they sent to him their disciples with the Herodians, saying: Master, we know that you are a true speaker, and teach the way of God in truth, and do not care for any man: for you do not regard the person of men. [n. 1778]

22:17 Tell us therefore what you think, is it lawful to give tribute to Caesar, or not? [n. 1785]

22:18 But Jesus, knowing their wickedness, said: why do you tempt me, you hypocrites? [n. 1786]

22:19 Show me the coin of the tribute. And they offered him a denarius. [n. 1787]

22:20 And Jesus said to them: whose image and inscription is this? [n. 1787]

22:21 They say to him: Caesar's. Then he said to them: render therefore to Caesar the things that are Caesar's, and to God, the things that are God's. [n. 1788]

22:22 And hearing this they wondered, and leaving him, went their ways. [n. 1789]

1776. Supra Dominus confutavit Pharisaeos per parabolam; secundo hic manifestat disputando. Et

primo respondendo;
secundo obiiciendo, ibi *congregatis autem Pharisaeis, interrogavit* et cetera.
Et respondet Dominus triplici quaestioni.
Primo de solutione tributi;
secundo de resurrectione;
tertio de lege.
Secunda ibi *in illo die accesserunt ad eum Sadducaei*; tertia ibi *Pharisaei autem audientes* et cetera.

Circa primum tria facit.
Primo ponitur interrogatio;
secundo responsio;
tertio effectus.

1776. Above the Lord refuted the Pharisees by a parable; here next he makes clear his conclusion by disputing. And

first, by responding;
second, by objecting, at *and while the Pharisees were gathered together, Jesus asked them* (Matt 22:41).
And the Lord responds to three questions:
first, about the payment of the tribute;
second, about the resurrection;
third, about the law.
The second is at *that day there came to him the Sadducees* (Matt 22:23), the third, at *but the Pharisees hearing that he had silenced the Sadducees* (Matt 22:34).

Concerning the first, he does three things:
first, the questioning is set out;
second, the response;
third, the effect.

Secunda ibi *cognita autem Iesus nequitia eorum*; tertia ibi *et audientes mirati sunt*.

In ista interrogatione tria sunt consideranda.

Primo interrogantium intentio;
secundo ministri interrogantes;
tertio interrogatio;

1777. Intentio interrogantium aperitur cum dicitur *abeuntes inierunt*, idest inter se, *consilium*, scilicet stultum fecerunt, *ut Iesum caperent in sermone*. Et hoc erat stultum, quia ipse erat Verbum Dei, et Verbum Dei non est comprehensibile; Eccli. XLIII, 29: *multa loquimur, et deficimus in verbis*. Fuit autem consilium impium; Ps. I, 1: *beatus vir qui non abiit in consilio impiorum, et in via peccatorum non stetit*. Et Genes, penult., 6: *in consilium eorum non veniat anima mea*.

1778. Ministri describuntur cum dicit *et mittunt discipulos suos cum Herodianis*. Sed quare non iverunt? Ratio est, quia dolose interrogare voluerunt: unde si ivissent, non haberet locum dolus; sed ipsi etiam discipuli erant; Eccli. X, 2: *secundum iudicem populi, sic et ministri eius*.

1779. Cum Herodianis. Qui sunt isti Herodiani? Secundum quod in Luca tangitur, sub Herode facta est Iudaea tributaria Romanis. Iste filius Antipatris alienigenae constitutus est rex a Romanis; ideo voluit compellere Iudaeos reddere censum Romanis. Unde **Herodiani**, idest famuli deputati ad colligendum institutionem Herodis. Sed iste iam mortuus erat, et dimisit tres filios. Unus Herodes, et iste erat tunc praesens, sicut dicitur in Lc. c. XXII, quod fuit etiam in morte Domini: ideo facile fuit quod famuli sui irent cum aliis.

1780. Sed quare iverunt cum Herodianis? Una ratio, quia Herodiani zelabant pro imperatore. Ideo discipuli Pharisaeorum secum duxerunt eos, ut si diceret quod esset solvendum tributum, accusarent eum ad Phariseos: si diceret quod non, tunc Herodiani caperent eum. Item isti non cognoscebantur, ideo credebant quod non perciperet; unde faciebant contra illud Ps. XXV, 4: *non sedi in consilio vanitatis et cum iniqua agentibus non introibo*.

Vel aliter, quia cum Iudaea facta esset tributaria Romanis, divisi sunt, quia quidam dicebant quod plebs Deo dedicata non debebat esse homini tributaria; alii vero dicebant, quod quia pro pace militabat omnium, quod omnes debebant Caesari dare tributum. Ideo illi qui dicebant solvi tributa Caesari, dicebantur Herodiani.

The second is at *but Jesus, knowing their wickedness*; the third, at *and hearing this they wondered*.

In this questioning there are three things to be considered:
first, the intention of those questioning;
second, the accomplices questioning;
third, the questioning.

1777. The intention of those questioning is revealed when it says, *then the Pharisees, going out, consulted*, that is, *among themselves*, namely they did something stupid, *how to ensnare him in his speech*. And this was stupid, because he was the Word of God, and the Word of God cannot be grasped; *we will say much, and yet will want words: but the sum of our words is, he is all* (Sir 43:29). And it was an impious counsel; *blessed is the man who has not walked in the counsel of the ungodly, nor stood in the way of sinners* (Ps 1:1). And *do not let my soul go into their counsel* (Gen 49:6).

1778. The accomplices are described when he says, *and they sent to him their disciples with the Herodians*. But why did they not go? The reason is that they wished to question him deceitfully: hence if they had gone, deceit would have had no place; but these were also disciples. *As the judge of the people is himself, so also are his ministers* (Sir 10:2).

1779. With the Herodians. Who are these Herodians? According as it is touched upon in Luke, Judea was made a tributary to the Romans under Herod. That son of Antipater the foreigner was made king by the Romans; therefore he wanted to force the Jews to pay the census to the Romans. Hence, *the Herodians*, i.e., the servants assigned to collect the established tax for Herod. But he was dead then, and he left three sons. One was Herod, and this one was present at the time, as is said in Luke, who was there also at the Lord's death (Luke 22). It was for this reason that his servants went willingly with the others.

1780. But why did they go with the Herodians? One reason is that the Herodians were zealous for the emperor. So the disciples of the Pharisees brought them with them so that if he said that the tribute should be paid they would accuse him to the Pharisees; if he said that it should not, then the Herodians would take him. Likewise, these were not known, so they thought that he would not perceive the trap; hence they acted against the Psalm: *I have not sat with the council of vanity: neither will I go in with the doers of unjust things* (Ps 25:4).

Or in another way, because when Judea was made a tributary to the Romans, they were divided, for some said that the people dedicated to God should not be tributary to man; but others said that since they were fighting for the peace of all, all should give tribute to Caesar. So those who said the tribute should be paid to Caesar were called Herodians.

1781. Positis ministris, ponitur interrogatio. Et

primo ponitur adulatio;
secundo interrogatio, ibi **dic quid tibi videtur**.

Homines mali ab adulatione incipiunt. *Loquuntur bona, mala autem in cordibus suis*, Ps. XXIII, 3.

Et primo commendant personam; secundo doctrinam; tertio constantiam.

Personam commendant ex auctoritate et virtute.

1782. Ex auctoritate cum dicunt **Magister**. Et licet mentirentur secundum cor suum, quia non eum magistrum putabant, sed seductorem, ut habetur infra XXVII, 63: **recordati sumus quod seductor ille dixit, quia die tertia resurgam** etc. tamen in veritate erat magister, ut infra: *unus est Magister vester* et cetera. Item, **scimus quia verax es**. Verax est qui veritatem loquitur; et hoc est proprium Dei, et eius qui Deo coniunctus est; Ps. CXV, 11: *ego dixi in excessu meo: omnis homo mendax*; Rom. III, 4: *est autem Deus verax, omnis autem homo mendax*. Christus autem est Deo coniunctus per unionem, et ideo verax est. Et sic commendatur ab auctoritate.

1783. Deinde a virtute **et viam Dei in veritate doces**. Primo oportet quod sciat quae doceat; Sap. VII, 13: *quam sine fictione didici, et sine invidia communico*. Item aliqui docent, sed non utilia; sed iste docet utilia, scilicet viam Dei; Is. XLVIII, 17: *ego sum Deus tuus docens te utilia*. Item aliqui docent quae Dei sunt, sed non in veritate, ut haeretici; iste autem docet in veritate. De isto in Ps. XXIV, 4: *vias tuas, Domine, demonstra mihi, et semitas tuas edoce me. Dirige me in veritate tua* et cetera.

1784. Item commendant de constantia; unde dicunt **non est tibi cura de aliquo**, non praetermittis timore alicuius quod debes dicere vel facere; Is. LI, 12: *quis tu ut timeas ab homine mortali?* Et quare? **Non enim respicis personam hominum**, scilicet contra Deum. Ille enim accipit personam qui, ratione hominis, dimittit dicere veritatem quam debet dicere; Deut. I, 17: *non accipietis personam cuiusquam*.

Et videte qualiter malitiosi erant. Quaestio habebat duo membra, scilicet quod non solverent, ad honorem Dei pertinebat; quod solverent, ad favorem hominum. Unde voluerunt quod favorem Dei quaereret, et viam Dei doceret: et sic si diceret quod non, quod magis volebant, statim caperetur ab Herodianis.

1781. The accomplices being set down, the questioning is set down. And

first, flattery is set out;
second, the questioning, at **tell us therefore what you think**.

Wicked men begin from flattery. *Who speak peace with their neighbor, but evils are in their hearts* (Ps 27:3).

And first, they commend the person; second, the teaching; third, his constancy.

They commend the person on authority and virtue.

1782. On authority when they say, **Master**. And although they were lying in their heart, since they did not consider him a teacher but a seducer, as is said below, **Lord, we have remembered, that that seducer said, while he was yet alive: after three days I will rise again** (Matt 27:63), yet he was in truth a teacher, as below: *for one is your Master* (Matt 23:8). Likewise, **we know that you are a true speaker**. A truthful man is one who speaks the truth; and this is proper to God, and to him who is connected to God; *I said in my excess: every man is a liar* (Ps 115:2); *God is true; and every man a liar* (Rom 3:4). But Christ is connected to God through union, and so he is truthful. And thus he is commended on authority.

1783. Next on virtue: **and teach the way of God in truth**. First, it is necessary that one know what he teaches; *which I have learned without guile, and communicate without envy* (Wis 7:13). Likewise there are some who teach, but not useful things; but this one teaches useful things, namely the way of God; *I am the Lord your God who teach you profitable things* (Isa 48:17). Likewise there are some who teach the things of God, but not in truth, like heretics; but this one teaches in truth. Of this one it says, *show, O Lord, your ways to me, and teach me your paths. Direct me in your truth* (Ps 24:4–5).

1784. Similarly, they commend him for constancy; hence they say, **and do not care for any man**, i.e., you do not omit what you should say or do for fear of anyone; *who are you, that you should be afraid of a mortal man?* (Isa 51:12). And why? **For you do not regard the person of men**, namely against God. For that man attends to the person who, on account of a man, foregoes to speak a truth which he should speak; *neither will you respect any man's person* (Deut 1:17).

And see how malicious they were. The question had two sides, namely that they would not pay, which pertained to the honor of God; and that they would pay, which pertained to the favor of men. Hence they wanted him to seek the favor of God, and teach the way of God; and thus if he should say that the tribute should not be paid, which is what they preferred, he would be taken immediately by the Herodians.

1785. Sequitur interrogatio *dic ergo nobis . . . licet ne censum dare Caesari, aut non?* Census erat tributum quod pro capite dabatur.

1786. Sequitur responsio *cognita autem Iesus malitia eorum ait.* Et primo respondet ad mentem eorum; secundo ad verba, ibi *reddite*.

Quia hominis est respondere ad verba, Dei autem respondere ad mentem, ideo quia Christus erat Deus et homo, ideo ad utrumque respondet. *Scrutans corda et renes Deus*, Ps. VII, 10.

Hypocritae. Et bene dicit hypocritas, quia hypocritae sunt proprie qui aliud in ore habent, aliud in corde. *Quid me tentatis?* Hoc enim erat prohibitum Deut. VI, 16: *non tentabis Dominum Deum tuum*. Item isti blande allocuti sunt Christum; Christus autem aspere respondit, quia respondit ad cor eorum, non ad verba. Item datur nobis exemplum, quod non debemus adulatoribus credere; Prov. XXIX, 12: *princeps qui libenter audit verba mendacii, omnes ministros suos habet impios*.

1787. Item quando vult, aliquid respondere, non potest melius confutare opponentem, quam secundum verba sua.

Unde primo ponit quaestionem; secundo ex responsione elicit veritatem. Et primo quaerit de numismate; secundo de forma: sensibiliter enim volebat ostendere intentum; Prov. XIV, 6: *doctrina prudentum facilis*.

Dicit *ostendite mihi numisma census*, idest denarium qui pro censu datur. Iste denarius valet decem usuales, et quilibet solvit unum denarium.

Deinde quaerit de forma *cuius est imago haec et superscriptio?* In qualibet enim denarii publici forma ponitur inscriptio, sic erat in isto. Dicunt, *Caesaris*: intelligatis non Caesaris Augusti, sed Tiberii Caesaris. Et debetis intelligere, quod Dominus interrogabat non erat ex ignorantia, sed potius ex dispensatione. Bene erat tantae aetatis, et tantum inter homines conversatus fuerat, quod bene noverat formam denarii, sed petiit ad significationem.

1788. Consequenter concludit veritatem *reddite ergo quae sunt Caesaris Caesari, et quae sunt Dei Deo*; quasi dicat: vos estis Dei et Caesaris, et habetis in usu vestro et quae Dei sunt et quae Caesaris. Habetis divitias naturales a Deo, scilicet panem et vinum, et de his date Deo: habetis ista artificialia, ut denarios, a Caesare, et haec Caesari reddite.

Mystice sic: nos habemus animam quae est ad imaginem Dei, ideo eam Deo reddere debemus; secundum ea quae a mundo habemus, pacem cum mundo habere debemus. Etiam sancti viri hic elevati a mundo, quia tamen in mundo cum aliis conversantur, debent pacem requirere Babylonis, ut habetur Baruch I, 10 ss. Et hoc

1785. There follows the questioning: *tell us therefore . . . is it lawful to give tribute to Caesar, or not?* The census was the tribute which was given per head.

1786. There follows the response: *but Jesus, knowing their wickedness, said*. And first, he responds to their mind; second, to the words, at *render*.

For to respond to words is of man, but to respond to the mind is of God; so, since Christ was God and man, for this reason he responds to both. *The searcher of hearts and reins is God* (Ps 7:10).

You hypocrites. And well does he say, *hypocrites*, for hypocrites are properly those who have one thing in the mouth and another in the heart. *Why do you tempt me?* For this was forbidden: *you will not tempt the Lord your God* (Deut 6:16). Likewise, they spoke flatteringly to Christ, but Christ responded harshly, because he responded to their heart, not to their words. Likewise, an example is given to us, that we should not believe flatterers; *a prince who gladly hears lying words, has all his servants wicked* (Prov 29:12).

1787. Likewise, when a man wishes to answer something, he cannot refute his opponent better than according to his own words.

Hence first he sets out a question; second, he draws forth the truth from the response. And first, he asks about the coin; second, about the figure: for he wished to show his meaning sensibly; *the learning of the wise is easy* (Prov 14:6).

He says, *show me the coin of the tribute*, i.e., the denarius which is given for the census. This denarius is worth ten usuales, and each man paid one denarius.

Next he asks about the figure: *whose image and inscription is this?* For on each denarius of the state a figure and inscription is placed, and so it was on this one. They say, *Caesar's*. Understand, not Caesar Augustus's, but Caesar Tiberius's. And you should understand that the Lord did not ask out of ignorance, but rather with a plan. He was old enough and had lived among men enough that he knew well the figure of the denarius, but he asked to make a point.

1788. Next he concludes the truth: *render therefore to Caesar the things that are Caesar's, and to God, the things that are God's*, as though to say: you are God's and Caesar's, and you have in your use both things which are God's and things which are Caesar's. You have natural riches from God, namely bread and wine, and give of these to God; you have these artificial things, like the denarius, from Caesar, and these things render to Caesar.

Mystically, thus: we have a soul which is made to the image of God, and therefore we should render it to God; with regard to the things which we have from the world, we should have peace with the world. Even holy men, who are raised here above the world, since nevertheless they associate with others in the world, should seek the peace of Babylon (Bar 1:10). And this is what all things that are of

est quod omnia quae sunt carnis, quae sunt mundi, vel hominum cum quibus conversantur, reddant Deo.

1789. Sequitur effectus *et audientes mirati sunt, et relicto eo abierunt*. Mirum fuit, quia statim, sapientia sua visa, debuissent esse conversi; sed non potuerunt capere, et recesserunt; Ps. CXXXVIII, 6: *mirabilis facta est scientia tua ex me, confortata est, et non potero ad eam*.

the flesh, of the world, or of the men with whom they deal, render to God.

1789. There follows the effect: ***and hearing this they wondered, and leaving him, went their ways***. It was astonishing, for having seen his wisdom they should have been converted immediately; but they were unable to understand, and withdrew; *your knowledge has become wonderful to me: it is high, and I cannot reach to it* (Ps 138:6).

Lecture 3

22:23 In illo die accesserunt ad eum Sadducaei, qui dicunt non esse resurrectionem, et interrogaverunt eum [n. 1790]

22:24 dicentes: Magister, Moyses dixit: *si quis mortuus fuerit, non habens filium, ut ducat frater eius uxorem illius, et suscitet semen fratri suo.* [n. 1793]

22:25 Erant autem apud nos septem fratres, et primus uxore ducta defunctus est, et non habens semen reliquit uxorem suam fratri suo. [n. 1794]

22:26 Similiter secundus et tertius usque ad septimum. [n. 1794]

22:27 Novissime autem omnium et mulier defuncta est. [n. 1794]

22:28 In resurrectione ergo cuius erit de septem uxor? Omnes enim habuerunt ea. [n. 1795]

22:29 Respondens autem Iesus ait illis: erratis nescientes Scripturas, neque virtutem Dei. [n. 1797]

22:30 In resurrectione enim neque nubent, neque nubentur, sed erunt sicut angeli Dei in caelo. [n. 1798]

22:31 De resurrectione autem mortuorum non legistis quod dictum est a Deo dicente vobis: [n. 1802]

22:32 *ego sum Deus Abraham, et Deus Isaac, et Deus Iacob?* Non est Deus mortuorum, sed viventium. [n. 1802]

22:33 Et audientes turbae mirabantur in doctrina eius. [n. 1805]

22:23 Ἐν ἐκείνῃ τῇ ἡμέρᾳ προσῆλθον αὐτῷ Σαδδουκαῖοι, λέγοντες μὴ εἶναι ἀνάστασιν, καὶ ἐπηρώτησαν αὐτὸν

22:24 λέγοντες· διδάσκαλε, Μωϋσῆς εἶπεν· ἐάν τις ἀποθάνῃ μὴ ἔχων τέκνα, ἐπιγαμβρεύσει ὁ ἀδελφὸς αὐτοῦ τὴν γυναῖκα αὐτοῦ καὶ ἀναστήσει σπέρμα τῷ ἀδελφῷ αὐτοῦ.

22:25 ἦσαν δὲ παρ' ἡμῖν ἑπτὰ ἀδελφοί· καὶ ὁ πρῶτος γήμας ἐτελεύτησεν, καὶ μὴ ἔχων σπέρμα ἀφῆκεν τὴν γυναῖκα αὐτοῦ τῷ ἀδελφῷ αὐτοῦ·

22:26 ὁμοίως καὶ ὁ δεύτερος καὶ ὁ τρίτος ἕως τῶν ἑπτά.

22:27 ὕστερον δὲ πάντων ἀπέθανεν ἡ γυνή.

22:28 ἐν τῇ ἀναστάσει οὖν τίνος τῶν ἑπτὰ ἔσται γυνή; πάντες γὰρ ἔσχον αὐτήν·

22:29 ἀποκριθεὶς δὲ ὁ Ἰησοῦς εἶπεν αὐτοῖς· πλανᾶσθε μὴ εἰδότες τὰς γραφὰς μηδὲ τὴν δύναμιν τοῦ θεοῦ·

22:30 ἐν γὰρ τῇ ἀναστάσει οὔτε γαμοῦσιν οὔτε γαμίζονται, ἀλλ' ὡς ἄγγελοι ἐν τῷ οὐρανῷ εἰσιν.

22:31 περὶ δὲ τῆς ἀναστάσεως τῶν νεκρῶν οὐκ ἀνέγνωτε τὸ ῥηθὲν ὑμῖν ὑπὸ τοῦ θεοῦ λέγοντος·

22:32 ἐγώ εἰμι ὁ θεὸς Ἀβραὰμ καὶ ὁ θεὸς Ἰσαὰκ καὶ ὁ θεὸς Ἰακώβ; οὐκ ἔστιν [ὁ] θεὸς νεκρῶν ἀλλὰ ζώντων.

22:33 καὶ ἀκούσαντες οἱ ὄχλοι ἐξεπλήσσοντο ἐπὶ τῇ διδαχῇ αὐτοῦ.

22:23 That day there came to him the Sadducees, who say there is no resurrection, and they asked him, [n. 1790]

22:24 saying: Master, Moses said: *if a man die having no son, his brother shall marry his wife, and raise up issue to his brother.* [n. 1793]

22:25 Now there were with us seven brothers: and the first having married a wife, died; and not having issue, left his wife to his brother. [n. 1794]

22:26 In like manner the second, and the third, and so on to the seventh. [n. 1794]

22:27 And last of all the woman died also. [n. 1794]

22:28 At the resurrection therefore whose wife of the seven will she be? For they all had her. [n. 1795]

22:29 And Jesus answering, said to them: you err, not knowing the Scriptures, nor the power of God. [n. 1797]

22:30 For in the resurrection they will neither marry nor be married; but will be as the angels of God in heaven. [n. 1798]

22:31 And concerning the resurrection of the dead, have you not read what was spoken by God, saying to you: [n. 1802]

22:32 *I am the God of Abraham, and the God of Isaac, and the God of Jacob?* He is not the God of the dead, but of the living. [n. 1802]

22:33 And the multitudes hearing it, were in admiration at his doctrine. [n. 1805]

1790. *In illo die.* Hic ponitur secunda interrogatio, et tria facit.

    Primo ponitur interrogatio;
    secundo responsio;
    tertio effectus.

1790. *That day.* Here the second questioning is set down, and he does three things:

    first, the questioning is set out;
    second, the response;
    third, the effect.

Secunda ibi *respondens autem Iesus* etc.; tertia ibi *et audientes turbae mirabantur*.

Circa primum
primo ponitur dispositio et conditio interrogantis;

secundo interrogatio.

1791. Dicit ergo *in die illo*. Et quare in die illo? Non sine ratione, quia cum viderunt illos confusos, non sine praesumptione quaesierunt eum. Sed, secundum Chrysostomum, concordati erant ad invicem quod caperent eum in sermone, et quilibet volebat honorem victoriae: ideo illis confusis isti accedere voluerunt; Iob XIX, 12: *venerunt latrones eius, et fecerunt sibi viam per me*.

Duae enim erant sectae: Pharisaei, idest 'divisi', et Sadducaei, idest 'iusti'. Et hi errabant in dogmatibus, quia non recipiebant prophetias, nec credebant resurrectionem. Item credebant quod mortuo corpore totus homo moreretur: et hoc est quod dicit *qui dicunt non esse resurrectionem*.

1792. Sequitur interrogatio. Et
primo ponit legem;
secundo casum;
tertio interrogationem.

1793. Dicunt ergo *et interrogaverunt eum dicentes: magister, Moyses dicit: 'si quis mortuus fuerit non habens filium'* et cetera. Deut. XXV, 5 s. Quae fuit causa legis? Populus carnalis fuit. Unde nil nisi temporalia quaerebat. Lex ergo illa promisit.

Manifestum enim est, quod homo non potest durare in se, ideo consolatio est ei quod maneat in suo simili, scilicet in filio; et hoc natura desiderat, ut quod non potest in se salvari, salvetur in suo simili. Unde contingebat quod aliquis sine filio moreretur, ideo subvenit huic casui Moyses secundum hanc legem, ut frater suus haberet uxorem suam. Nec ponebatur extraneus, qui nihil pertineret ad eum; item non haberet tantam curam de domo et familia sicut frater: et hoc est quod dicit *et suscitaret semen fratri suo*, idest generet filium qui habeat haereditatem illius.

1794. Posita lege, ponunt casum *erant apud nos septem fratres, et primus, uxore ducta, defunctus est, et non habens semen reliquit uxorem suam fratri suo* et cetera. Potest esse quod talis casus accidit, vel quod ipsi confinxerunt. Tamen secundum Augustinum per septem fratres homines mali signantur, qui in septem aetatibus moriuntur sine fructu. Apost. Rom. VI, 21: *quem fructum habetis, vel habuistis, in his, in quibus nunc erubescitis?* Ista mulier est mundana conversatio; Ps. ci, 27: *ipsi peribunt, tu autem permanebis, et omnes sicut vestimentum veterascent*.

The second is at *and Jesus answering, said to them: you err*; the third, at *and the multitudes hearing it, were in admiration*.

Concerning the first,
first, the disposition and condition of those questioning is set out;

second, the questioning.

1791. It says then, *that day*. And why does he specify on that day? Not without reason, for since they saw the others perplexed, not without presumption did they question him. But, according to Chrysostom, they had agreed with one another that they would capture him in his words, and each one desired the honor of victory: so when those were perplexed these wished to approach. *His troops have come together, and have made themselves a way by me* (Job 19:12).

For there were two sects: the Pharisees, i.e., 'the separated,' and the Sadducees, i.e., 'the just ones.' And these men, i.e., the Sadducees, erred in their teachings, because they did not accept the prophets, nor did they believe in the resurrection. Likewise, they thought that when the body died the whole man died; and this is why it says, *who say there is no resurrection*.

1792. There follows the questioning. And
first, the law is set out;
second, the situation;
third, the questioning.

1793. They speak therefore, and *asked him, saying: Master, Moses said: 'if a man die having no son'* (Deut 25:5). What was the reason for the law? The people were carnal. Hence they sought nothing but temporal things. Therefore the law promised those things.

For it is evident that a man cannot endure in himself, so it is a consolation to him that he remain in his like, namely in a son; and nature desires this, that what cannot be preserved in itself be preserved in its like. Hence it happened that someone died without a son, so Moses brought aid to this misfortune through this law, that his brother should have his wife. Nor was an outsider set down, who would not pertain to him at all; nor would he have only the care of the house and family, like a brother: and this is why it says, *and raise up issue to his brother*, i.e., he would beget a son who would have his inheritance.

1794. The law being set down, they set out the situation: *now there were with us seven brothers: and the first having married a wife, died; and not having issue, left his wife to his brother*. It could be that such a case happened, or that they made it up. Yet according to Augustine, the seven brothers signify evil men, who die in the seven ages without fruit. The Apostle: *what fruit therefore had you then in those things, of which you are now ashamed?* (Rom 6:21). This woman is worldly living; *they will perish but you remain: and all of them will grow old like a garment* (Ps 101:27).

1795. Unde quaerunt: omnes mortui sunt, *et omnes eam habuerunt: cuius uxor erit in resurrectione*, quia omnium esse non poterit? Ista opinio non est bona, et est contra Pharisaeos, quia credebant quod resurrectio debet esse quantum ad hanc vitam, quod quisque rehabeat uxorem suam et possessionem suam et cetera. Unde dicunt *cuius erit uxor?* Quia non potest esse uxor omnium. Ista opinio reprobatur in Iob VII, 10: *non revertetur in domum suam*. Unde non resurget ad eumdem modum vivendi.

1796. Sequitur responsio. Et

primo ostendit errorem et causam;

secundo insinuat veritatem.

1797. Unde dicit *respondens Iesus ait: erratis*, idest erroneam opinionem habetis; Sap. II, 21: *cogitaverunt, et erraverunt; excaecavit enim eos malitia eorum*.

Et quae est causa erroris? *Nescientes Scripturas*. Unde non meditabantur in mandatis Dei; Ps. CXVIII, 100: *super senes intellexi, quia mandata tua quaesivi*. Unde qui meditatur in mandatis Dei, potest vitare errores; unde Io. V, 39: *scrutamini Scripturas*. Isti autem non scrutabantur, ideo errabant, sicut faciunt aliqui qui male intelligunt. Item aliqui nescientes *virtutem Dei*, volentes virtutem Dei metiri secundum inferiora; ad Rom. I, 20: *invisibilia Dei a creatura mundi per ea quae facta sunt intellecta conspiciuntur*.

1798. *In resurrectione neque nubent, neque nubentur*. Manifestat propositum. Et quia duo dixerat, scilicet quod nesciebant Scripturas, nec virtutem Dei, ideo

primo declarat quod virtutem Dei ignorabant;

secundo quod Scripturas.

Et cum primo dixerit de Scripturis, quare hoc secundo declaratur? Chrysostomus respondet, quia cum aliquis disputat cum aliquo qui errat ex malitia, primo debet allegare auctoritatem; quando cum eo qui ex ignorantia, primo debet proponere rationem, et post auctoritatem. Sic facit Dominus.

1799. Primo rationem proponit; unde dicit *in resurrectione neque nubent, neque nubentur*. Primum, secundum litteram, verum est. *Neque nubent* etc., quia tunc non erit necessarium sicut nunc est. Hieronymus: *aliter accipitur 'nubere' secundum Latinum, aliter secundum Graecum, quia proprie 'nubere' secundum Latinum mulierum est: unde dicitur esse neutrum passivum; sed secundum Graecum viri nubent, idest ducunt uxores, mulieres nubentur, non nubent*. Ideo dicit, **non nubent**, viri; **nec nubentur**, mulieres. Cum enim nuptiae sint

1795. Hence they ask: all died; *at the resurrection therefore whose wife of the seven will she be?* Since she cannot be the wife of all of them. *For they all had her*. This idea is not good, and is against the Pharisees, because they thought that the resurrection should be with regard to this life, that each one would have his own wife and his own possessions. Hence they say, *whose wife of the seven will she be?* Since she cannot be the wife of them all. This idea is refuted: *nor will he return any more into his house* (Job 7:10). They will not rise again to the same manner of living.

1796. There follows the response. And

first, he shows the error and its cause;

second, he insinuates the truth.

1797. Hence it says, *and Jesus answering, said to them: you err*, i.e., you have an erroneous opinion; *these things they thought, and were deceived: for their own malice blinded them* (Wis 2:21).

And what is the cause of the error? *Not knowing the Scriptures*. Hence they did not meditate on the commands of God; *I have had understanding above ancients: because I have sought your commandments* (Ps 118:100). Hence those who meditate on God's command can avoid errors; *search the Scriptures* (John 5:39). But these men did not examine them, so they erred, as do men who understand badly. Likewise some, not knowing *the power of God*, wishing to measure the power of God according to lower things; *for the invisible things of him, from the creation of the world, are clearly seen, being understood by the things that are made* (Rom 1:20).

1798. *For in the resurrection they will neither marry nor be married*. He manifests the proposition. And since he had said two things, namely that they did not know the Scriptures, nor the power of God, for this reason

first, he shows that they were ignorant of the power of God;

second, that they were ignorant of the Scriptures.

And since he had mentioned the Scriptures first, why does he prove it second? Chrysostom replies that when disputing with someone who errs out of malice, one should first put forward an authority; when disputing with one who errs out of ignorance, one should first set forth an argument, and afterwards an authority. This is what the Lord does.

1799. First, he sets forth the reason; hence he says, *for in the resurrection they will neither marry nor be married*. The first thing, taken literally, is true. *Neither marry*, because then it will not be necessary as it is now. Jerome: 'to marry' is taken in one way in Latin and another way in Greek, for 'to marry' in Latin is proper to a woman; hence it is said to be neuter passive. But in Greek, men marry, i.e., lead women, while women are married, but do not marry. This is why he says, *neither marry*, the men, *nor be married*, the women. For since marriage is for the procreation of

ad prolis procreationem, ut conservetur homo in esse in suo simili, qui non potest in seipso conservari, ideo cum resurrectio fiat ad immortalitatem, tunc non erunt necessariae nuptiae. Ideo isti errabant, et virtutem Dei ignorabant. *Sed sunt sicut angeli in caelo*. Ille status est status praemii, et finis istius vitae. Iob XIV, 14: *putas ne homo mortuus rursum vivat? Cunctis diebus quibus nunc milito, expecto donec veniat immutatio mea*; et illa immutatio erat praemium. Vita illa erit refulgentium intellectu.

1800. Sed quare erunt similes angelis? Quia erunt immunes a passionibus; quia nunc homo habet intellectum adnexum sensibus, et in hoc excedunt angeli, sed tunc depurabitur, ideo similes erunt angelis: II Reg. XIV, 17: *sicut enim angelus Domini, sic et dominus meus rex, ut nec benedictione, nec maledictione moveatur*. Unde qui habent animum a passionibus elevatum, similes sunt angelis. Passiones autem quae magis faciunt homines bestiales, sunt passiones venereorum, quae exercentur per coniugium; ideo tunc nec nubent, nec nubentur.

1801. Item quidam dixerunt quod non omnes resurgent, sed solum homines. Sed hoc Augustinus destruit dicens quod sexus resurget; sexus autem non salvatur in homine solum. Hanc opinionem tollit, cum dicit **nec nubent, nec nubentur**. Ex quo datur intelligi quod uterque sexus, sed **nec nubent, nec nubentur**.

1802. *De resurrectione autem mortuorum* et cetera. Postquam ostendit quod ignorabant virtutem Dei, hic ostendit quod ignorabant Scripturas. Unde **non legistis quod dictum est a Domino dicente vobis: 'ego sum Deus Abraham, Isaac et Iacob'?** Hoc scribitur Ex. III, 6.

Sed quaerit Hieronymus, cum aliae auctoritates sint magis expressae de resurrectione, ut habetur Is. VI et Ez. XXXIII et Dan. XII, quare istam quae ambigua est posuit? Respondet quod non recipiebant prophetas, sed quinque libros Moysi.

1803. Et quomodo facit ad propositum? Dicit, *'ego sum Deus Abraham, Deus Isaac et Deus Iacob.'* Deus dicitur aliquorum in colendo eum. Isti ergo colunt eum. Sed colere Deum non est mortuorum, sed viventium. Ergo Abraham, Isaac et Iacob vivunt; sed non secundum corpus: ergo secundum animam.

Sed quid valet hoc ad resurrectionem? Valet, quia isti dicebant animam non esse; ipse autem ostendit animam remanere: et si anima remanet, ergo et resurrectio, quia naturaliter anima inclinatur ad corpus.

offspring, so that man, who cannot be preserved in himself, may be preserved in being in his like, for this reason when the resurrection unto immortality happens, then marriage will not be necessary. So those men erred, and did not know the power of God. ***But will be as the angels of God in heaven***. That state is the state of reward, and the end of this life. *Will man who is dead, do you think, live again? All the days in which I am now in warfare, I expect until my change come* (Job 14:14); and that change was a reward. That life will belong to those who shine brightly in intellect.

1800. But why will they be like the angels? Because they will be immune to passions; for now man has an intellect bound to the passions, and in this respect he goes beyond the angels; but then it will be purified, so they will be like the angels. *For even as an angel of God, so is my lord the king, that he is neither moved with blessing nor cursing* (2 Kgs 14:17). Hence those who have a soul raised above the passions are like the angels. Moreover, the passions which make a man more beastlike are the sexual passions, which are exercised through marriage; for this reason they will then neither marry nor be married.

1801. Again, some said that not all will rise, but only men. But Augustine refutes this, saying that the sexes will rise, since the sexes are not preserved in man alone. This opinion is also removed when he says ***they neither marry nor are given in marriage***. From which we are given to understand that both sexes rise, but that ***they neither marry nor are given in marriage***.

1802. ***And concerning the resurrection of the dead***. After he showed that they did not know the power of God, here he shows that they did not know the Scriptures. Hence ***have you not read what was spoken by God, saying to you: 'I am the God of Abraham, and the God of Isaac, and the God of Jacob'?*** (Exod 3:6).

But Jerome asks, since other authorities are more explicit about the resurrection (Isa 6; Ezek 33; Dan 12), why did he present this one which is uncertain? He responds that they did not accept the prophets, but the five books of Moses.

1803. And how does it relate to his intention? He says, ***'I am the God of Abraham, and the God of Isaac, and the God of Jacob.'*** He is called the God 'of' some in their worshipping him. Therefore these men worship him. But to worship God does not belong to the dead, but to the living. Therefore Abraham, Isaac, and Jacob are alive; but not as regards the body: therefore they are alive as regards the soul.

But how does this suffice for proving the resurrection? It suffices because these men said that the soul is not; but he has shown that the soul remains. And if the soul remains, therefore there is also a resurrection, because the soul naturally inclines to the body.

1804. Sed quid est quod dicit, quod ***non est Deus mortuorum***? Verum est secundum corpus. Est tamen etiam Deus mortuorum, quia vivunt secundum spiritum; Rom. c. XIV, 8: *sive vivimus, sive morimur, Domini sumus*. Item est contra haereticos qui damnant patres Veteris Testamenti, quia hic dicit quod vivunt secundum animam. Item dicit singulariter, quia in aliis gentibus quilibet deum suum habebat. *Audi, Israel: Dominus Deus tuus unus est*, Deut. VI, 4.

1805. Sequitur effectus, quia mirabantur ***et audientes turbae mirabantur in doctrina eius***. Ps. CXVIII, 129: *mirabilia testimonia tua, Domine* et cetera.

1804. But why does he say that ***he is not the God of the dead***? It is true as regards the body. Yet he is also the God of the dead because they live according to the spirit; *therefore, whether we live, or whether we die, we are the Lord's* (Rom 14:8). Likewise, it is against the heretics who condemn the fathers of the Old Testament, because here he says that they live according to the spirit. Likewise he speaks in the singular, because in other nations any given god had his own. *Hear, O Israel, the Lord our God is one Lord* (Deut 6:4).

1805. There follows the effect, that they marveled: ***and the multitudes hearing it, were in admiration at his doctrine***. *Your testimonies are wonderful* (Ps 118:129).

Lecture 4

²²:³⁴ Pharisaei autem audientes quod silentium imposuisset Sadducaeis, convenerunt in unum; [n. 1807]

²²:³⁵ et interrogavit eum unus ex eis legis doctor tentans eum: [n. 1809]

²²:³⁶ Magister, quod est mandatum magnum in lege? [n. 1811]

²²:³⁷ Ait illi Iesus: *diliges Dominum Deum tuum ex toto corde tuo, et in tota anima tua, et in tota mente tua.* [n. 1812]

²²:³⁸ Hoc est maximum et primum mandatum. [n. 1815]

²²:³⁹ Secundum autem simile est huic: *diliges proximum tuum sicut teipsum.* [n. 1816]

²²:⁴⁰ In his duobus mandatis universa lex pendet, et prophetae. [n. 1820]

²²:⁴¹ Congregatis autem Pharisaeis, interrogavit eos Iesus [n. 1821]

²²:⁴² dicens: quid vobis videtur de Christo, cuius filius est? Dicunt ei: David. [n. 1822]

²²:⁴³ Ait illis: quomodo ergo David in spiritu vocat eum Dominum dicens: [n. 1824]

²²:⁴⁴ *dixit Dominus Domino meo, sede a dextris meis, donec ponam inimicos tuos scabellum pedum tuorum?* [n. 1824]

²²:⁴⁵ Si ergo David vocat eum Dominum, quomodo filius eius est? [n. 1829]

²²:⁴⁶ Et nemo poterat ei respondere verbum, neque ausus fuit quisquam ex illa die eum amplius interrogare. [n. 1830]

²²:³⁴ Οἱ δὲ Φαρισαῖοι ἀκούσαντες ὅτι ἐφίμωσεν τοὺς Σαδδουκαίους συνήχθησαν ἐπὶ τὸ αὐτό,

²²:³⁵ καὶ ἐπηρώτησεν εἷς ἐξ αὐτῶν [νομικὸς] πειράζων αὐτόν·

²²:³⁶ διδάσκαλε, ποία ἐντολὴ μεγάλη ἐν τῷ νόμῳ;

²²:³⁷ ὁ δὲ ἔφη αὐτῷ· ἀγαπήσεις κύριον τὸν θεόν σου ἐν ὅλῃ τῇ καρδίᾳ σου καὶ ἐν ὅλῃ τῇ ψυχῇ σου καὶ ἐν ὅλῃ τῇ διανοίᾳ σου·

²²:³⁸ αὕτη ἐστὶν ἡ μεγάλη καὶ πρώτη ἐντολή.

²²:³⁹ δευτέρα δὲ ὁμοία αὐτῇ· ἀγαπήσεις τὸν πλησίον σου ὡς σεαυτόν.

²²:⁴⁰ ἐν ταύταις ταῖς δυσὶν ἐντολαῖς ὅλος ὁ νόμος κρέμαται καὶ οἱ προφῆται.

²²:⁴¹ Συνηγμένων δὲ τῶν Φαρισαίων ἐπηρώτησεν αὐτοὺς ὁ Ἰησοῦς

²²:⁴² λέγων· τί ὑμῖν δοκεῖ περὶ τοῦ χριστοῦ; τίνος υἱός ἐστιν; λέγουσιν αὐτῷ· τοῦ Δαυίδ.

²²:⁴³ λέγει αὐτοῖς· πῶς οὖν Δαυὶδ ἐν πνεύματι καλεῖ αὐτὸν κύριον λέγων·

²²:⁴⁴ εἶπεν κύριος τῷ κυρίῳ μου· κάθου ἐκ δεξιῶν μου, ἕως ἂν θῶ τοὺς ἐχθρούς σου ὑποκάτω τῶν ποδῶν σου;

²²:⁴⁵ εἰ οὖν Δαυὶδ καλεῖ αὐτὸν κύριον, πῶς υἱὸς αὐτοῦ ἐστιν;

²²:⁴⁶ καὶ οὐδεὶς ἐδύνατο ἀποκριθῆναι αὐτῷ λόγον οὐδὲ ἐτόλμησέν τις ἀπ' ἐκείνης τῆς ἡμέρας ἐπερωτῆσαι αὐτὸν οὐκέτι.

²²:³⁴ But the Pharisees, hearing that he had silenced the Sadducees, came together; [n. 1807]

²²:³⁵ and one of them, a doctor of the law, asked him, tempting him: [n. 1809]

²²:³⁶ Master, which is the greatest commandment in the law? [n. 1811]

²²:³⁷ Jesus said to him: *you shall love the Lord your God with your whole heart, and with your whole soul, and with your whole mind.* [n. 1812]

²²:³⁸ This is the greatest and the first commandment. [n. 1815]

²²:³⁹ And the second is similar to this: *you shall love your neighbor as yourself.* [n. 1816]

²²:⁴⁰ On these two commandments depends the whole law and the prophets. [n. 1820]

²²:⁴¹ And while the Pharisees were gathered together, Jesus asked them, [n. 1821]

²²:⁴² saying: what do you think of the Christ? Whose son is he? They say to him: David's. [n. 1822]

²²:⁴³ He said to them: how then does David in spirit call him Lord, saying: [n. 1824]

²²:⁴⁴ *the Lord said to my Lord, sit on my right hand, until I make your enemies your footstool?* [n. 1824]

²²:⁴⁵ If David then calls him Lord, how is he his son? [n. 1829]

²²:⁴⁶ And no man was able to answer him a word; neither did any man dare from that day forth to ask him any more questions. [n. 1830]

1806. Supra Dominus respondit quaestioni factae de solutione tributi, quaestioni etiam de resurrectione; hic autem respondet quaestioni de comparatione mandatorum divinorum: et duo facit. Quia

1806. Above, the Lord responded to a question about the payment of the tribute, and to a question about the resurrection; and here he responds to a question about the comparison of the divine commands. And he does two things:

primo ponitur interrogatio;
secundo responsio, ibi **ait illis Iesus** et cetera.

Circa primum duo facit.
Primo describit nequitiam interrogantium;
secundo interrogationem, ibi **Magister, quod est mandatum magnum in lege?**

Nequitiam describit quantum ad tria.
Primo quantum ad impudentiam;
secundo quantum ad excogitatam malitiam;
tertio quantum ad fraudulentiam.

1807. Quantum ad impudentiam, cum dicitur **audientes quod silentium imposuisset**. Iam confutaverat Pharisaeorum discipulos et Sadducaeos, unde ex hoc satis poterant ei credere et erubescere. Unde Chrysostomus: livor et ira impudentiam nutriunt et causant. Sed isti non propter hoc dimiserunt, quin adhuc interrogaverunt eum; Is. LVI, 11: *canes impudentissimi nescierunt saturitatem*. Et significatur quod quamvis hoc audirent, non tamen siluerunt. Aliquis servat silentium sponte, et hoc est prudentis. Item aliquis servat, quia imponitur ei silentium, et hoc est imprudentis; Eccli. XX, 6: *est tacens, non habens sensum loquelae; et est tacens, sciens tempus aptum*; Eccl. III, 7: *est tempus tacendi, est tempus loquendi*.

1808. Item tangitur excogitata malitia, quia, ut melius convincant eum, simul congregantur; Ps. II, 2: *principes convenerunt in unum adversus Dominum*. **Convenerunt in unum**. Potest dici quod Pharisaei et Sadducaei convenerunt, quamvis in sectis differrent, tamen in unum ad tentandum Dominum. Vel Pharisaei convenerunt in unum adversus Dominum.

1809. Item fraudulentia significatur, quia cum in multitudine essent congregati, noluerunt quod omnes interrogarent, sed unus; ut si ille vinceretur, alii non confutarentur, et si iste vinceret, omnes in eo gloriarentur. **Et interrogavit eum unus ex eis legis doctor tentans eum**, quia non animo addiscendi; Iob c. XVI, 11: *aperuerunt in me ora sua, et exprobrantes percusserunt maxillam meam*.

1810. Hic potest esse obiectio litteralis, quia Marcus dicit quod Dominus *intuitus eum dixit: non longe es a regno Dei*. Et quomodo hic dicitur quod tentat eum?

Solvit Augustinus, quia primo venit causa tentandi, sed cum Christus satisfaceret ei, consensit ei. Et ideo quod tentavit eum, debet referri ad principium; quod non longe est a regno Dei, debet retorqueri ad finem. Et

first, the questioning is set down;
second, the response, at **Jesus said to him**: *'you shall love the Lord your God.'*

Concerning the first, he does two things:
first, he describes the wickedness of those questioning;
second, the questioning, at **Master, which is the greatest commandment in the law?**

He describes the wickedness as regards three things:
first, as regards shamelessness;
second, as regards premeditated malice;
third, as regards dishonesty.

1807. As regards shamelessness, when it says, **but the Pharisees, hearing that he had silenced the Sadducees**. He had already suppressed the Pharisees' disciples and the Sadducees, hence from this they were well enough able to believe in him and to be ashamed. Hence Chrysostom: *envy and anger feed and cause shamelessness*. But these men did not give up on this account, but rather they still interrogated him; *and meet impudent dogs, they never had enough* (Isa 56:11). And it indicates that however much they heard, they would still not be silent. Some keep silence freely, and this belongs to the prudent man. Likewise, some keep silence because silence is imposed on them, and this belongs to the imprudent man; *there is one who holds his peace, because he knows not what to say: and there is another who holds his peace, knowing the proper time* (Sir 20:6). *A time to keep silence, and a time to speak* (Eccl 3:7).

1808. Likewise their premeditated malice is touched upon, because, so that they might better overthrow him, they all came together at once; *the princes met together, against the Lord and against his Christ* (Ps 2:2). They **came together**. It can be said the Pharisees and the Sadducees came together, although they differed in sects, yet were one for testing the Lord. Or, the Pharisees came together as one against the Lord.

1809. Likewise dishonesty is indicated, because while they were gathered together in a crowd, they did not wish that all should ask, but one, so that if that one man were conquered, the others would not be suppressed, and if that one did conquer, all might glory in him. **And one of them, a doctor of the law, asked him, tempting him**, because he did not ask with a mind for learning; *they have opened their mouths upon me, and reproaching me they have struck me on the cheek* (Job 16:11).

1810. Here a literal objection could arise, because Mark says that the Lord, having looked at him, said: *you are not far from the kingdom of God* (Mark 12:34). So why is it said here that he tests him?

Augustine resolves it, for he first came for the purpose of testing, but when Christ satisfied him, he consented to him. And therefore that he tested him should be referred to the beginning; that he is not far from the kingdom of God

sic non fuit mirum si verba Domini animum eius mutaverunt.

1811. Sciendum autem quod aliqui tentant eo quod non sunt certi, quia, secundum quod dicit sapiens Eccli. XIX, 4, *qui cito credit, levis est corde*. Iste cum multa audisset de Christo, voluit experiri si talis esset: et haec tentatio non esset mala. Unde dicit **Magister, quod est mandatum magnum in lege?**

Haec tamen quaestio videbatur calumniosa et praesumptuosa: calumniosa, quia omnia mandata Dei sunt magna; Prov. VI, 23: *mandata lucerna, et lex lux*. Item indeterminate quaesivit, quia omnia sunt magna, ut si responderet de uno, obiiceret de alio. Item fuit praesumptuosa, quia non deberet de magno quaerere qui minimum non implevit; Iob XV, 12: *quid te elevat cor tuum, et quasi magna cogitans, attonitos habes oculos?* Et poterat esse quod esset controversia super hac quaestione inter eos, quia aliqui dicebant salutem esse in aliquibus exterioribus; unde Is. XXIX, 13: *populus hic labiis me honorat, cor autem eorum longe est a me*. Sed respondet Dominus, quod solum est in interioribus.

1812. Unde sequitur responsio **ait Iesus ei: 'diliges Dominum tuum'** et cetera. Et non solum respondet ad quaestionem propositam, sed veritatem docet. Et

primo docet quod sit primum;
secundo quod ei est simile;
tertio rationem assignat.

Secunda ibi **secundum autem simile est huic** et cetera. Tertia ibi **in his duobus mandatis universa lex pendet et prophetae**.

1813. Dicit ergo **'diliges Dominum Deum tuum'** et cetera. Istud scribitur Deut. VI, 5. Item Dominus per Moysen dicit Deut. X, 14: *numquid Dominus petit a te, nisi ut timeas et diligas eum?* Ergo duo praecipit, timorem scilicet et dilectionem.

Et quare non respondet Dominus de timore, sicut de dilectione? Dicendum quod quidam timent Deum, qui timent pati ab eo, ut qui timent poenam Gehennae, vel qui timent amittere aliquid quod habent a Deo; et hic est timor servilis, quia illud diligit in quo timet puniri. Alius est, qui ipsum Deum timet propter se, qui timet eum offendere; et talis timor est ex amore, et ex hoc timet, quod amat; ergo principium est amor; I Io. c. IV, 16: *Deus caritas est, et qui manet in caritate, in Deo manet, et Deus in eo*. Et ideo dicit **'diliges Dominum'**; non *timeas*, quia Deus diligendus est sicut primum diligibile, quia ipse finis primus est, sed quaecumque alia diliguntur propter finem. Qui ergo diligit Deum ut finem, diligit in toto corde; Ioel II, 12: *convertimini ad me in toto corde*

should be referred to the end. Thus it was not a marvel if the Lord's words changed his soul.

1811. But one should know that a man tests because he is not certain, for, in accord with what the wise man says, *he who is hasty to give credit, is light of heart* (Sir 19:4). Since this man had heard many things about Christ, he wished to test whether he was such a one; and this testing is not bad. Hence he says, **Master, which is the greatest commandment in the law?**

Yet this question seems crafty and presumptuous. Crafty, because all the commands of God are great; *the commandment is a lamp, and the law a light* (Prov 6:23). Likewise he asked in an indeterminate way, since they are all great, so that if he responded about one, he could object about another. Likewise it was presumptuous, because he who does not fulfill the least should not ask about what is great; *why does your heart elevate you, and why do you stare with your eyes, as if they were thinking great things?* (Job 15:12). And it could be that there was a controversy among them about this question, because some said that salvation is in certain exterior things; hence, *with their lips glorify me, but their heart is far from me* (Isa 29:13). But the Lord responds that it is only in interior things.

1812. Hence there follows the response: **Jesus said to him: 'you shall love the Lord your God.'** And he not only responds to the question proposed, but teaches the truth. And

first, he teaches which is the first;
second, what is like it;
third, he gives the reason.

The second is at **and the second is similar to this**; the third, at **on these two commandments depends the whole law and the prophets**

1813. He says therefore, **'you shall love the Lord your God'** (Deut 6:5). Likewise, the Lord says through Moses, *and now, Israel, what does the Lord your God require of you, but that you fear the Lord your God . . . and love him?* (Deut 10:12). So he commands two things, namely fear and love.

And why does the Lord not respond about fear, as about love? It should be said that some fear God who fear to be hurt by him, as those who fear the punishment of Gehenna, or those who fear to lose something they have from God; and this is servile fear, because he loves that in which he fears being punished. There is another who fears God himself on account of himself, who fears to offend him; and such fear is from love, and he fears because he loves. Therefore the principle is love; *God is charity: and he who abides in charity, abides in God, and God in him* (1 John 4:16). And for this reason he says, **'you shall love the Lord'**, not *you shall fear*, because God is to be loved as the first lovable thing, since he himself is the first end, while any other things are loved for the sake of the end. Therefore he who

vestro. Et quantumcumque nitamini, non poteritis eum comprehendere, quia Deus maior est toto corde.

1814. Sed quid est quod dicit *'ex toto corde tuo, et ex tota anima tua, et in tota mente tua'*? Chrysostomus exponit sic: quia in dilectione sunt duo: unum quod est principium; secundum quod est dilectionis effectus et sequela dilectionis. Principium dilectionis est duplex. Dilectio enim potest fieri ex passione, et ex iudicio rationis: ex passione, cum nescit homo vivere sine eo quod diligit; ex ratione, secundum quod diligit ut ratio dictat. Dicit ergo quod ille ex toto corde diligit, qui diligit carnaliter; ille ex anima, qui ex iudicio rationis. Et nos Deum utroque modo debemus diligere: carnaliter, ut cor carnaliter afficiatur circa Deum; unde in Ps. LXXXIII, 3: *cor meum et caro mea exultaverunt in Deum vivum.* Tertium est sequela dilectionis, quia illud quod diligo, libenter video, libenter de eo cogito, libenter facio quod ei placet; Io. XIV, 23: *qui diligit me, sermones meos servabit*; et totum refero in ipsum; Ps. LXXXIII, 2: *quam dilecta tabernacula tua, Domine virtutum. Concupiscit et deficit anima mea in atria Domini.* Et possumus addere illud quod Marcus addit, *et in omni fortitudine tua*, quia qui Deum diligit, totum se transfert in illum, et fortitudinem expendit in ipsum.

Augustinus sic distinguit inter cor et animam et mentem, secundum tria quae procedunt ex ipsis. De corde exeunt cogitationes, ut habetur supra XV, 19, ex anima vita procedit, ex mente scientia et intelligentia. Unde quod dicit *'ex toto corde'*, intelligendum est ut omnes cogitationes in ipsum referamus; quod *'ex tota anima'*, quod tota vita; quod *'ex tota mente'*, ut tota scientia referatur in eum, idest ut scientiam captives in obsequium eius; II Cor. X, 5: *in captivitatem redigentes omnem intellectum in obsequium Christi.*

Magistralis quaedam Glossa exponit quod anima est imago Dei secundum suas potentias, secundum memoriam, intelligentiam et voluntatem, ita quod illud quod dicitur *'ex corde'*, ad intelligentiam referatur; quod dicitur *'ex anima'*, ad voluntatem; quod *'ex mente'*, ad memoriam, ita ut perfecte Deo vivatur.

Origenes sic exponit: *'diliges Deum ex tota anima'*, ita ut sis paratus animam tuam ponere pro eo si necesse est; Io. XIII, 37: *animam meam ponam pro te.*

Sed differentia est inter mentem et cor. 'Mens' enim dicitur a 'metiendo'; 'cor' sumitur pro simplicitate intellectus; 'mens' vero quoad prolationem, quia per sermonem metitur intellectus, sive cogitatio: unde vult dicere

loves God as the end, loves with his whole heart; *be converted to me with all your heart* (Joel 2:12). And however much you struggle, you will not be able to completely grasp him, because God is greater than the whole heart.

1814. But why does he say, *'with your whole heart, and with your whole soul, and with your whole mind'*? Chrysostom explains it this way: there are two things in love, one which is the beginning, and a second which is an effect of love and a consequence of love. There are two principles of love. For love can arise from passion, and from the judgment of reason: from passion, when a man does not know how to live without that which he loves; from reason, inasmuch as he loves as reason dictates. He says therefore that he who loves bodily loves with the whole heart; he who loves out of the judgment of reason loves with the soul. And we should love God both ways: bodily, as the heart is moved bodily concerning God; hence, *my heart and my flesh have rejoiced in the living God* (Ps 83:3). Third, there is a consequence of love, because that which I love, I freely behold, I freely think on it, I freely do what pleases it; *if any one love me, he will keep my word* (John 14:23); and I refer the whole to it; *how lovely are your tabernacles, O Lord of hosts! My soul longs and faints for the courts of the Lord* (Ps 83:2–3). And we can add what Mark adds, *and with the whole strength* (Mark 12:33), because he who loves God, transfers his whole self into him, and expends his strength on him.

Augustine distinguishes between the heart and the soul and the mind according to the three things which come from them. From the heart come thoughts, as is said above (Matt 15:19); from the soul comes life; from the mind, knowledge and intelligence. Hence when he says, *'with your whole heart'*, it should be understood that we should refer all our thoughts to him; when he says, *'with your whole soul'*, that we should refer our whole life to him; when he says, *'with your whole mind'*, that the whole of knowledge should be referred to him, i.e., that you should lay hold of knowledge in his service. *Bringing into captivity every understanding unto the obedience of Christ* (2 Cor 10:5).

A certain magisterial Gloss explains that the soul is the image of God according to its powers, according to memory, understanding, and will, so that when it says, *'with your whole heart'*, it is referred to the understanding; when it says, *'with your whole soul'*, to the will; when *'with your whole mind'*, to the memory, such that one lives perfectly for God.

Origen explains it this way: *'you shall love the Lord your God . . . with your whole soul'* such that you are prepared to lay down your soul for him if it is necessary; *I will lay down my life for you* (John 13:37).

But there is a difference between the mind and the heart. For 'mind' is derived from 'measuring'; 'heart' is used for simplicity of understanding, but 'mind' with regard to enlargement, because understanding or thought is measured

quod in locutionibus et in meditationibus Deum totaliter diligamus.

1815. Hic posito, subdit *hoc est primum et maximum mandatum*. Maximum capacitate: istud enim est, in quo omnia continentur, quia in isto dilectio proximi continetur, secundum quod I Io. IV, 21 dicitur: *qui diligit Deum, diligit et fratrem suum*; et ideo maximum. Item primum origine, maximum dignitate et capacitate. Non primum in Scriptura, quia in Scriptura primum mandatum fuit, *Dominus Deus tuus Deus unus est*, Deut. VI, 4. Et quare? Quia omnis inclinatio appetitivae virtutis est in amore: ideo habemus mandatum quod colamus Deum in dilectione; ad Rom. XIII, 10: *plenitudo legis dilectio est*; ad Eph. III, 17: *in caritate radicati et fundati*.

1816. Secundo, ponit secundum mandatum *secundum autem simile huic est: 'diliges proximum tuum sicut teipsum.'* Voluit significare quod in mandatis est ordo. Et quae est causa? Constat quod mandata sunt de actibus virtutum; virtutes autem habent ordinem, quia una dependet ab alia, et sicut virtutes, sic et mandata.

1817. Sed quare dicit quod est simile primo? Quia quando diligitur homo, cum homo sit ad similitudinem Dei, diligitur Deus in illo; ideo simile est primo mandato, quod est de dilectione Dei.

1818. Sed quid intelligit nomine *'proximi'*, cum dicit *'diliges proximum'*? Istud satis signatur in parabola Lc. X, 36, ubi quaeritur, *quis tibi videtur, quod fuerit eius proximus?* Et respondetur, *qui fecit misericordiam in eum*. Unde qui debet facere misericordiam nobis, vel nos ipsi, sub nomine *'proximi'* continetur. Sed non est aliqua rationalis creatura, cui non debeamus misereri, et e converso: et ideo sub nomine *'proximi'* continetur homo et angelus.

1819. Et quod dicit *'sicut teipsum'*, non intelligitur *quantum teipsum*, quia hoc esset contra ordinem caritatis; sed *'sicut teipsum'*, idest eo fine quo teipsum, vel eo modo quo teipsum. Eo fine, quia te non debes diligere propter te, sed propter Deum, sic etiam proximum. Apostolus I Cor. X, 31: *omnia in gloriam Dei facite*. Item in eo quod teipsum diligis, diligis te in eo in quo vis tibi bonum, et tale bonum, quod sit secundum te et legem Dei, et hoc est bonum iustitiae. Sic etiam et proximo debes optare bonam iustitiam; unde debes eum diligere, vel quia iustus est, vel quia iustus fit. Item debes eum diligere eo modo quo teipsum, quia cum dico diligo istum, dico volo bonum ei. Unde actus dilectionis cadit super duo: vel super ipsum qui bonus est, vel super ipsum bonum, quod volo sibi; unde diligo istum, quia volo ipsum esse bonum mihi. Unde aliquis diligit bona temporalia, quia scit ea bona esse sibi; aliqui vero diligunt aliquid,

by words. Hence he wished to say that we should love God entirely in speech and in meditation.

1815. This being set out, he adds, ***this is the greatest and the first commandment***. The greatest in comprehension: for this is the one in which all are contained, because the love of neighbor is contained in this, according as is said in John, *he who loves God, loves also his brother* (1 John 4:21); and so it is the greatest. Likewise it is the first in origin, the greatest in dignity and comprehension. Not the first in Scripture, because in Scripture the first commandment was, *the Lord our God is one Lord* (Deut 6:4). And why? Because every inclination of the appetitive power is in love, so we have a commandment that we should worship God in love; *love therefore is the fulfilling of the law* (Rom 13:10); *rooted and founded in charity* (Eph 3:17).

1816. Second, he sets out the second commandment: ***and the second is similar to this: 'you shall love your neighbor as yourself.'*** He wished to indicate that there is an order in the commandments. And what is the reason? It is agreed that the commandments are about acts of virtue; but the virtues have an order, since one depends on another, and as are the virtues, so also are the commandments.

1817. But why does he say that it is like the first? Because when a man is loved, since man is made to the likeness of God, God is loved in him; for this reason it is like the first commandment, which is about the love of God.

1818. But what does he understand by the name *'neighbor'*, when he says, *'you shall love your neighbor'*? This is sufficiently indicated in the parable, where it is asked, *which of these three, in your opinion, was neighbor to him?* (Luke 10:36). And it is responded, *he who showed mercy to him*. Hence the one who should show mercy to us, or we to him, is contained under the name *'neighbor.'* But there is no rational creature to whom we should not show mercy, and vice versa; and therefore under the name *'neighbor'* are contained man and angel.

1819. And when he says, *'as yourself'*, it should not be understood to mean *as much as yourself*, for this would be against the order of charity, but *'as yourself'*, i.e., for the same end as yourself, or in the same way as yourself. For the same end, because you should not love yourself for your own sake, but for God's sake; so also your neighbor. The Apostle: *do all to the glory of God* (1 Cor 10:31). Likewise by the fact that you love yourself, you love yourself in that in which you will good to yourself, and such a good as is in accord with you and with the law of God, and this is the good of righteousness. So also you should choose the good of righteousness for your neighbor; hence you should love him either because he is righteous, or that he may be righteous. Likewise you should love him in the same way as yourself, because when I say, I love this man, I say I will good to him. Hence the act of love falls upon two things: either on the one who is good, or on that good which I will to myself; hence I love this man, because I will him to be

quia bonum est in se: sic debes diligere teipsum, et etiam proximum.

1820. Consequenter assignat rationem quare ista duo sint maxima mandata *in his duobus mandatis universa lex pendet, et prophetae*. Tota doctrina legis et prophetarum dependet ab his. Finis in appetibilibus se habet ut principium in speculativis: procedit enim scientia a principiis ad conclusiones, et sic tota scientia ex principiis iudicatur, sicut et in omnibus operabilibus totum dependet a fine. Quia ergo dilectio est finis; I ad Tim. c. I, 5: *finis praecepti est caritas*; ideo ab istis dependent omnia alia, et haec est expositio Augustini.

Origenes sic exponit: *in his*, idest in observantia istorum, dependet intellectus legis et prophetarum, quia qui haec observat, meretur intelligentiam legis et prophetarum; Eccli. II, 10: *qui timetis Dominum, diligite illum, et illuminabuntur corda vestra*. Ps. CXVIII, 104: *a mandatis tuis intellexi, propterea odivi omnem viam iniquitatis*.

1821. *Congregatis autem Pharisaeis interrogavit eos Iesus*. Postquam responderat eis, ipse voluit obiicere: et facit duo.

Primo ponitur interrogatio;
secundo eius effectus, ibi *nemo poterat ei respondere verbum*.
Circa primum
primo proponit interrogationem;
secundo responsionem;
tertio obiicit contra.

1822. Dicit ergo *congregatis autem Pharisaeis, interrogavit eos Iesus*. Congregati autem erant ad tentandum; unde ponit interrogationem *quid vobis videtur de Christo, cuius filius est?* Haec quaestio difficillima erat et congrua.

Difficillima, quia habetur Is. LIII, 8: *generationem eius quis enarrabit?*

Erat etiam congrua, quia habebant opinionem, quod esset purus homo, et non credebant ipsum esse Deum, quia sic non tentarent eum, quia scriptum est Deut. VI, 16: *non tentabis Dominum Deum tuum*. Ideo ut ostendat se Deum dicit *quid vobis videtur de Christo?*

1823. Sequitur responsio *dicunt ei: David*. Christi enim erat duplex generatio: una secundum carnem, alia secundum divinitatem, secundum quam est Filius Dei Patris, de qua dicitur Ps. II, 7: *Dominus dixit ad me: Filius meus es tu* et cetera. Ideo ipsi respondent de generatione secundum carnem, cum dicunt *David*. Ier. XXIII, 5: *suscitabo David germen iustum*. Et ad Rom. I, 3: *qui factus*

good for me. So some love temporal goods because they know that those goods are for them; but some love a thing because it is good in itself. And you should love yourself in this way, and also your neighbor.

1820. Next he gives the reason why these two are the greatest commandments: *on these two commandments depends the whole law and the prophets*. The teaching of the law and the prophets depends on these. The end in appetible things stand as do the principles in speculative matters: for science proceeds from principles to conclusions, and in this way the whole science is judged from the principles, just as in all doable things the whole thing depends on the end. Since therefore love is of the end: *now the end of the commandment is charity* (1 Tim 1:5), therefore on these depend all the others, and this is Augustine's explanation.

Origen explains it this way: *on these*, i.e., on the observance of these, depends the understanding of the law and the prophets, because the one who observes these merits understanding of the law and the prophets; *you who fear the Lord, love him, and your hearts will be enlightened* (Sir 2:10). *By your commandments I have had understanding: therefore have I hated every way of iniquity* (Ps 118:104).

1821. *And while the Pharisees were gathered together, Jesus asked them*. After he had responded to them, he wished to pose an objection himself: and he does two things:
first, the questioning is set down;
second, its effect, at *and no man was able to answer him a word*.
Concerning the first,
first, he sets forth the question;
second, the response;
third, he objects against the contrary.

1822. It says therefore, *and while the Pharisees were gathered together, Jesus asked them*. They were gathered together to test him; hence he poses the question: *what do you think of the Christ? Whose son is he?* This question was most difficult, and fitting.

Most difficult, because it says, *who will declare his generation?* (Isa 53:8).

It was also fitting, because they had the opinion that he was a mere man, and they did not believe that he was God, for then they would not have tested him, since it is written, *you shall not tempt the Lord your God* (Deut 6:16). So to show that he was God he says, *what do you think of the Christ?*

1823. There follows the response: *they say to him: David's*. For Christ had two generations: one according to the flesh, and another according to the divinity, according to which he is the Son of God the Father, about which the Psalm says, *the Lord has said to me: you are my Son* (Ps 2:7). So these men respond concerning the generation according to the flesh, when they say, *David's*. *I will raise up to*

est ei ex semine David secundum carnem. Et isti insufficienter responderunt, quia insufficienter cognoscebant eum.

1824. Tunc obiicit ut eis det intelligere aliam generationem *quomodo ergo David in spiritu vocat eum Dominum, dicens: 'dixit Dominus Domino meo: sede a dextris meis'?* Ps. CIX, 1. Habetur in lege quod pater maior est filio. Non ergo filius dominus est patris. Ergo vel Christus non est Filius David, vel in eo est aliquid maius David, cum vocet eum Dominum. Sed forte dicerent quod David fuit deceptus: quod removet, quia *in spiritu* hoc dicit, unde *Spiritu Sancto Dei locuti sunt homines*, II Petri I, 21.

1825. Possumus autem tria videre in auctoritate ista Psalmi. Primo praeeminentiam ad sanctos, aequalitatem ad Patrem, et dominium super rebelles.

Praeeminentiam ad sanctos, cum dicit *'dixit Dominus Domino meo.'* *'Dominus'*, scilicet Pater, *'Domino'*, scilicet Filio: ipse enim Filius habet dominium super omnes sanctos: nullus enim sanctus illuminatur nisi a lumine vero: ipse autem est lumen verum; Io. I, 4: *vita erat lux hominum*. Si ergo ipse est, cuius participatione omnes sancti lumen recipiunt, praeeminentiam habet ad omnes sanctos in eo quod dicitur: *tecum principium in die virtutis tuae, in splendoribus sanctorum* etc.; unde ipse originaliter est splendor omnium sanctorum.

1826. Item aequalitas Patris tangitur, cum dicitur *'sede a dextris meis'*: non quod sint sedes locales, sed metaphorice, quia honorabilior locus est sedere a dextris. Dicere enim est emittere verbum. Quod ergo dixit Dominus *'sede a dextris meis'* quid est aliud, nisi quod generando me Verbum, dedit mihi potestatem, aequalitatem et auctoritatem? Potest etiam exponi de temporalibus, idest in potioribus bonis, sed non est ad propositum. Dominus enim semper videtur a dextris, ut in Marc. ult., 5: *viderunt iuvenem sedentem a dextris*. Et Stephanus, Act. VII, 55, *vidit Iesum sedentem a dextris virtutis Dei*.

1827. Et quid fiet de inimicis eius? Ei omnes subiicientur; unde subdit *'donec ponam inimicos tuos scabellum pedum tuorum.'* Isti vel sunt penitus infideles, vel hi qui noluerunt obedire et subesse; unde istos ponet *'scabellum pedum tuorum.'* Scabellum enim est quod ponitur sub pedibus; illud autem quod est sub pedibus totaliter ei subiicitur, non autem illud quod est in manu. Quidam ponuntur scabellum ad punitionem, quidam ad salutem: ad punitionem, qui nolunt facere eius voluntatem; ad salutem, qui faciunt eius voluntatem.

Sed obiiciunt Ariani: ergo non est aequalis Patri.

Dico quod legitur utrumque, et quod subiicitur Patri, et quod est aequalis Patri; I ad Cor. XV, 25: *oportet*

David a just branch (Jer 23:5). And, *who was made to him of the seed of David, according to the flesh* (Rom 1:3). And they responded insufficiently, because they knew him insufficiently.

1824. Then he objects, that he may give them to understand the other generation: *how then does David in spirit call him Lord, saying: 'the Lord said to my Lord, sit on my right hand, until I make your enemies your footstool'?* (Ps 109:1). It says in the law that father is greater than son. Therefore a son is not the lord of his father. Therefore either Christ is not the son of David, or in him is something greater than David, since he calls him Lord. But perhaps they would say that David was deceived; which possibility he removes, because he says this, *in spirit*, hence, *the holy men of God spoke, inspired by the Holy Spirit* (2 Pet 1:21).

1825. And we can see three things in this quotation from the Psalm: preeminence over the saints, equality with the Father, and lordship over rebels.

Preeminence over the saints, when he says, *'the Lord said to my Lord.'* *'The Lord'*, namely the Father, *'to my Lord'*, namely the Son: for the Son has dominion over all the saints. For no saint is enlightened unless by the true light; but he himself is the true light; *the life was the light of men* (John 1:4). If therefore he is the one participation with whom all the saints receive, he has preeminence over all the saints in what is said, *with you is the principality in the day of your strength: in the brightness of the saints* (Ps 109:3). Hence he himself as origin is the splendor of all the saints.

1826. Likewise equality with the Father is touched upon, when it says, *'sit on my right hand'* not that there are physically located seats, but metaphorically, because the more honorable place is to sit at the right hand. For to speak is to send forth a word. Therefore when the Lord says, *'sit on my right hand'*, what else is it but, by generating me the Word, he gave me power, equality, and authority? It can also be explained as about temporal things, i.e., in more powerful goods, but this is irrelevant. For the Lord is always seen on the right hand, as in Mark, *they saw a young man sitting on the right side* (Mark 16:5). And Stephen *saw Jesus sitting at the right hand of the power of God* (Acts 7:55).

1827. And what will happen to his enemies? They will all be subjected to him; hence he adds: *'until I make your enemies your footstool.'* These are either the thoroughly unfaithful, or those who would not obey and be subject; hence he will make those *'your footstool.'* For a footstool is what is placed under the feet; but that which is under the feet is entirely subjected to him, not however that which is in the hand. Some are made a footstool for punishment, others for salvation: for punishment, those who do not want to do his will; for salvation, those who do his will.

But the Arians object: therefore he is not equal to the Father.

I say that both things are written, both that he is subjected to the Father and that he is equal to the Father; *for*

autem illum regnare, donec ponat inimicos sub pedibus. Item Christus sibi omnia subiiciet; Phil. III, 21: *reformabit corpus humilitatis nostrae configuratum corpori claritatis suae.* Unde illud dicit ad demonstrandum unitatem potestatis: unde omnia quae potest Pater, eadem potest et Filius.

1828. Sed quid est quod dicit *'donec ponam inimicos tuos scabellum pedum tuorum'*? Ergo videtur quod postquam supposuerit inimicos, quod ultra non sedebit a dextris.

Dicendum quod *'donec'* aliquando importat tempus determinatum, aliquando infinitum. Hic vero importat infinitum.

Sed diceret aliquis: nonne multi rebellant Christo?

Ita, verum est quod multi rebellant, et ideo poterat esse dubium de tempore quando multi rebellarent: ideo voluit Christus exprimere.

1829. *Si ergo David vocat eum Dominum, quomodo filius eius est?* Ergo Dominus est et filius, quia filius est secundum carnem, quia ab ipso traxit originem, et Dominus secundum divinitatem.

1830. *Et nemo poterat respondere ei verbum.* Hic ponitur effectus, et est duplex, quia Christus fuit respondens et opponens. Quia opponens: *nemo poterat respondere*; Iob IX, 3: *si voluerit contendere cum eo, non poterit ei respondere unum pro mille.* Item quia in respondendo confutaverat eos, ideo sequitur *nec ausus fuit quisquam ex illa die eum amplius interrogare.* Ideo potestis videre, quod isti non interrogabant ut eos doceret, sed ut eum tentarent; Deut. XXXII, 7: *interroga Patrem tuum et annuntiabit tibi.*

he must reign, until he has put all his enemies under his feet (1 Cor 15:25). Likewise, Christ will subject all things to himself; *who will reform the body of our lowness, made like to the body of his glory* (Phil 3:21). Hence he says this to show the unity of power: so everything which the Father can do, the Son can do as well.

1828. But why does he say, *'until I make your enemies your footstool'*? Therefore it seems that after he has subjected the enemies, he will no longer sit at the right hand.

One should say that *'until'* sometimes implies a determinate time, and sometimes an infinite. But here it implies an infinite.

But someone would say: do not many rebel against Christ?

Yes, it is true that many rebel, and so there could be a doubt about the time when many were rebelling: it is for this reason that Christ wished to make a statement.

1829. *If David then calls him Lord, how is he his son?* Therefore the Lord is both son, because he is David's son according to the flesh, since he took his origin from him, and Lord, according to the divinity.

1830. *And no man was able to answer him a word.* Here the effect is set down, and it is twofold, because Christ was both responding and opposing. Because he was responding: *and no man was able to answer him a word*; *if he will contend with him, he cannot answer him one for a thousand* (Job 9:3). Likewise, because by responding he confounded them, there follows, *neither did any man dare from that day forth to ask him any more questions.* So you can see that they were not questioning that he might teach them, but that they might test him; *ask your Father, and he will declare to you* (Deut 32:7).

Chapter 23

Lecture 1

²³:¹ Tunc Iesus locutus est ad turbas et ad discipulos suos, [n. 1832]

²³:² dicens: super cathedram Moysi sederunt scribae et Pharisaei. [n. 1832]

²³:³ Omnia ergo quaecumque dixerint vobis, servate et facite; secundum opera vero eorum nolite facere: dicunt enim, et non faciunt. [n. 1835]

²³:⁴ Alligant autem opera gravia et importabilia, et imponunt in humeros hominum: digito autem suo nolunt ea movere. [n. 1840]

²³:⁵ Omnia vero opera sua faciunt ut videantur ab hominibus: dilatant enim phylacteria sua, et magnificant fimbrias. [n. 1841]

²³:⁶ Amant autem primos recubitus in coenis et primas cathedras in synagogis, [n. 1845]

²³:⁷ et salutationes in foro, et vocari ab hominibus Rabbi. [n. 1845]

²³:⁸ Vos autem nolite vocari Rabbi: unus enim est Magister vester, omnes autem vos fratres estis. [n. 1846]

²³:⁹ Et patrem nolite vocare vobis super terram: unus enim est Pater vester qui in caelis est. [n. 1851]

²³:¹⁰ Nec vocemini magistri, quia Magister vester unus est Christus. [n. 1852]

²³:¹¹ Qui maior est vestrum, erit minister vester. [n. 1853]

²³:¹² Qui autem se exaltaverit, humiliabitur; et qui se humiliaverit, exaltabitur. [n. 1855]

²³:¹ Τότε ὁ Ἰησοῦς ἐλάλησεν τοῖς ὄχλοις καὶ τοῖς μαθηταῖς αὐτοῦ

²³:² λέγων· ἐπὶ τῆς Μωϋσέως καθέδρας ἐκάθισαν οἱ γραμματεῖς καὶ οἱ Φαρισαῖοι.

²³:³ πάντα οὖν ὅσα ἐὰν εἴπωσιν ὑμῖν ποιήσατε καὶ τηρεῖτε, κατὰ δὲ τὰ ἔργα αὐτῶν μὴ ποιεῖτε· λέγουσιν γὰρ καὶ οὐ ποιοῦσιν.

²³:⁴ δεσμεύουσιν δὲ φορτία βαρέα [καὶ δυσβάστακτα] καὶ ἐπιτιθέασιν ἐπὶ τοὺς ὤμους τῶν ἀνθρώπων, αὐτοὶ δὲ τῷ δακτύλῳ αὐτῶν οὐ θέλουσιν κινῆσαι αὐτά.

²³:⁵ πάντα δὲ τὰ ἔργα αὐτῶν ποιοῦσιν πρὸς τὸ θεαθῆναι τοῖς ἀνθρώποις· πλατύνουσιν γὰρ τὰ φυλακτήρια αὐτῶν καὶ μεγαλύνουσιν τὰ κράσπεδα,

²³:⁶ φιλοῦσιν δὲ τὴν πρωτοκλισίαν ἐν τοῖς δείπνοις καὶ τὰς πρωτοκαθεδρίας ἐν ταῖς συναγωγαῖς

²³:⁷ καὶ τοὺς ἀσπασμοὺς ἐν ταῖς ἀγοραῖς καὶ καλεῖσθαι ὑπὸ τῶν ἀνθρώπων ῥαββί.

²³:⁸ Ὑμεῖς δὲ μὴ κληθῆτε ῥαββί· εἷς γάρ ἐστιν ὑμῶν ὁ διδάσκαλος, πάντες δὲ ὑμεῖς ἀδελφοί ἐστε.

²³:⁹ καὶ πατέρα μὴ καλέσητε ὑμῶν ἐπὶ τῆς γῆς, εἷς γάρ ἐστιν ὑμῶν ὁ πατὴρ ὁ οὐράνιος.

²³:¹⁰ μηδὲ κληθῆτε καθηγηταί, ὅτι καθηγητὴς ὑμῶν ἐστιν εἷς ὁ Χριστός.

²³:¹¹ ὁ δὲ μείζων ὑμῶν ἔσται ὑμῶν διάκονος.

²³:¹² ὅστις δὲ ὑψώσει ἑαυτὸν ταπεινωθήσεται καὶ ὅστις ταπεινώσει ἑαυτὸν ὑψωθήσεται.

²³:¹ Then Jesus spoke to the multitudes and to his disciples, [n. 1832]

²³:² saying: the scribes and the Pharisees have sat on the chair of Moses. [n. 1832]

²³:³ Therefore, all things whatever that they will say to you, observe and do, but according to their works, do not; for they say, and do not. [n. 1835]

²³:⁴ For they bind heavy and insupportable burdens, and lay them on men's shoulders; but with a finger of their own they will not move them. [n. 1840]

²³:⁵ And all their works they do in order to be seen by men. For they make their phylacteries broad, and enlarge their fringes. [n. 1841]

²³:⁶ And they love the first places at feasts, and the first chairs in the synagogues, [n. 1845]

²³:⁷ and salutations in the market place, and to be called by men, Rabbi. [n. 1845]

²³:⁸ But you, do not be called Rabbi. For one is your Master; and you are all brethren. [n. 1846]

²³:⁹ And call none your father upon earth; for one is your Father, who is in heaven. [n. 1851]

²³:¹⁰ Neither be called masters; for one is your Master, Christ. [n. 1852]

²³:¹¹ He who is the greatest among you will be your servant. [n. 1853]

²³:¹² And whoever will exalt himself will be humbled: and he who will humble himself will be exalted. [n. 1855]

1831. Supra ostensum est quomodo Pharisaei et scribae provocati sunt ex gloria Christi, et etiam ex sapientia eius, qua colliserat eos, nunc autem ostendit quomodo ex iustitia qua eos arguebat: et duo facit.

Primo instruit aliquos;

secundo redarguit. Secunda ibi *vae autem vobis, scribae et Pharisaei*.

Circa primum duo facit.

Primo ostendit eorum dignitatem;

secundo aperit eorum intentionem in usu auctoritatis, ibi *omnia opera sua faciunt ut videantur ab hominibus*.

Circa primum tria facit.

Primo commendat eorum auctoritatem;

secundo docet exhibere obedientiam cum cautela;

tertio assignat rationem.

Secunda ibi *omnia ergo quaecumque dixerint vobis, servate et facite* etc.; tertia ibi *dicunt enim et non faciunt*.

1832. Dicit ergo *tunc Iesus locutus est ad turbas* et cetera. Ita continuandum est. Dominus intantum eos confutavit, quod nec interrogare audebant, nec respondere sciebant. Sed, secundum quod dicit Chrysostomus, inutilis est sermo qui redarguit et non instruit: ideo convertit se ad turbas et ad discipulos suos, ut eos instruat.

Sciendum autem quod quidam audiunt eum ut discipuli, quidam ut turbae: ut discipuli, qui veritatem percipiunt mente; Io. VIII, 31: *si manseritis in sermone meo, vere discipuli mei eritis*. Ut turbae, qui veritatem mente apprehendere non possunt. Ideo quandoque convertit sua verba ad turbas, quandoque ad discipulos, quandoque ad utrosque; et diversimode: quia ad discipulos alta dicendo, ut habetur Io. XV, 15: *quaecumque audivi a Patre meo, nota feci vobis*. Quandoque vero ad turbas profert parabolas, sicut habetur supra. Utrisque autem loquitur de necessitate salutis, et talia sunt haec verba.

Super cathedram Moysi sederunt scribae et Pharisaei. Cathedra proprie est magistrorum; et ideo illi super cathedram dicuntur sedere, qui sunt successores Moysi; Eccli. XXIV, v. 33: *legem mandavit Moyses in praeceptis iustitiarum*. Unde illi qui Moysis legem docebant, sedebant super cathedram Moysi. Et in lege continebantur quaedam ad fidem pertinentia, et quaedam ad bonos mores. Ad fidem pertinentia erant ea, in quibus praefigurabatur Christus; unde ipse dicit, Io. V, 46: *si crederetis Moysi, crederetis forsitan et mihi*. Item continebantur

1831. It was shown above how the Pharisees and the scribes were provoked by Christ's glory, and also by his wisdom, with which he crushed them; and now he shows how they were provoked by the justice with which he accused them; and he does two things:

first, he teaches some things;

second, he refutes some things. The second is at *but woe to you scribes and Pharisees* (Matt 23:13).

Concerning the first, he does two things:

first, he sets forth their dignity;

second, he reveals their intention in the use of authority, at *and all their works they do in order to be seen by men*.

Concerning the first, he does three things:

first, he commends their authority;

second, he teaches the crowds to show obedience with caution;

third, he gives the reason.

The second is at *therefore all things whatever they will say to you, observe and do*; the third, at *for they say, and do not*.

1832. It says therefore, *then Jesus spoke to the multitudes*. It should be continued in the following way. The Lord confounded them so greatly that they neither dared to ask questions nor knew how to respond. But, in accordance with what Chrysostom says, a speech which refutes and does not instruct is useless; so he turns himself toward the crowds and toward his disciples, and instructs them.

But one should know that some men hear him as disciples, others as the crowds: as disciples, those who perceive truth with the mind; *if you continue in my word, you will be my disciples indeed* (John 8:31). As the crowds, those who cannot grasp truth with the mind. For this reason, sometimes he turned his words toward the crowds, sometimes toward the disciples, and sometimes toward both; and in different ways, for to the disciples by speaking high things, as is said in John, *all things whatever I have heard of my Father, I have made known to you* (John 15:15). But sometimes, toward the crowds, he sets out parables, as is said above. But he speaks to both about the necessity of salvation, and such are these words.

The scribes and the Pharisees have sat on the chair of Moses. A chair properly belongs to teachers, and for this reason those who are the successors of Moses are said to sit on a chair; *Moses commanded a law in the precepts of justices* (Sir 24:33). Hence those who taught the law of Moses sat on the chair of Moses. And in the law there were contained some things pertaining to faith, and some things pertaining to good behavior. Those pertaining to faith were the things in which Christ was prefigured; hence he says, *for if you believed Moses, you would perhaps believe me also*

praecepta moralia; Eccli. cap. XXIV, 33: *legem mandavit Moyses in praeceptis iustitiarum*.

1833. Sed notandum quod supra cathedram sedent et scribae, et Pharisaei, et discipuli Christi: scribae qui solam litteram considerant; Pharisaei qui aliquantulum de sensu suo interiori; discipuli Christi qui totum perpendunt: et non dicuntur discipuli Moysi, sed Christi; Lc. ult., 27: *incipiens a lege et prophetis interpretabatur illis in omnibus Scripturis, quae de ipso erant*.

1834. Tunc monet eos ad obedientiam cum cautela; et facit duo.

Primo hortatur ad obediendum;

secundo ad cavendum.

1835. *Omnia quaecumque dixerint vobis, servate*, scilicet in corde, *et facite*, in opere; Deut. XVII, 9: *venies ad sacerdotes Levitici generis, et ad iudicem*; et post: *et facies quaecumque dixerint*; et sequitur: *sequerisque sententiam eorum*. Et Apostolus: *obedite praepositis vestris*. Et hoc est contra Manichaeos qui dicebant legem veterem non esse bonam. Et patet quod sit bona, quia Dominus praecepit eam servari.

1836. Sed potest quis obiicere: ergo debemus legalia observare, quod est contra doctrinam apostolorum, Act. XV, 29.

Sciendum quod semper auctoritas servanda est legislatoris secundum intentionem eius; sed legislator aliqua dicit ut semper servanda, et talia semper debent servari; aliqua vero dicit quae sunt vel ut umbra, ut habetur ad Col. II, 17: *quae sunt umbra futurorum*. Moralia ergo sunt mandata secundum intentionem legislatoris, ut semper serventur; sed legalia pro tempore tantum, scilicet pro tempore ante Christum. Unde ante tempus illud debent servari, post non: quia qui servaret, iniuriam Christo faceret. Et ponit Augustinus exemplum. Si diceret aliquis: ego comedam cras, haec vox est signum huius rei; et si postquam comedisset, diceret illud idem, non bene diceret. Sic cum ista legalia essent signa Christi venturi, postquam Christus venit, qui servaret ea, non bene servaret. Unde **omnia quae dixerint vobis**, secundum intentionem legislatoris, *facite*.

1837. *Secundum vero opera eorum nolite facere*. Hic docet cautelam. Debetis scire quod praelatus praeficitur, ut doceat non solum doctrina, sed etiam vita. Et debemus nos ei concordare quantum ad ea quae docet, quia, secundum quod dicitur ad Gal. I, 9, *si quis evangelizat vobis praeter id quod accepistis, anathema sit*. Similiter etiam debemus ei conformari in vita. Debet enim esse vita eius nobis in exemplum, sicut vita Christi: unde

(John 5:46). Likewise the moral precepts were contained in the law; *Moses commanded a law in the precepts of justices* (Sir 24:33).

1833. But one should note that on the chair sit both the scribes and the Pharisees, and the disciples of Christ: the scribes, who consider only the letter; the Pharisees, who consider a small part of its interior sense; the disciples of Christ, who ponder the whole. And they are not called disciples of Moses, but of Christ; *and beginning at Moses and all the prophets, he expounded to them in all the Scriptures, the things that were concerning him* (Luke 24:27).

1834. Then he warns them to obey with caution; and he does two things:

first, he exhorts to obedience;

second, to caution.

1835. *Observe*, namely in the heart, *and do* in deed *whatever they will say to you*; *and you will come to the priests of the Levitical race, and to the judge* (Deut 17:9–11), and afterwards, *and you will do whatever they will say*, and there follows, *and you will follow their sentence*. And the Apostle: *obey your prelates* (Heb 13:17). And this is against the Manichees, who said that the old law is not good. And it is clear that it is good, because the Lord commanded that it be preserved.

1836. But someone could object: so we should keep the legal observances, which is against the teaching of the apostles (Acts 15:29).

One should know that the authority of a lawgiver should always be preserved according to his intention; but a legislator says some things to be kept always, and such things should always be kept; but he says some things which are like shadows, as is said, *which are a shadow of things to come* (Col 2:17). Therefore the moral precepts are commanded, according to the intention of the legislator, that they may be kept always; but the legal observances are commanded for a time only, namely for the time before Christ. Hence before that time they should be kept, afterwards not: for those who would keep them do injury to Christ. And Augustine sets out an example. If someone should say, I will eat tomorrow, these words are a sign of this thing; and if he were to say the same thing after having eaten, he would not speak well. In this way since those legal observances were signs of the Christ to come, after Christ has come those who would keep them do not keep them well. Hence, *therefore all things whatever they will say to you, observe and do*, according to the intention of the lawgiver.

1837. *But according to their works, do not*. Here he teaches caution. You should know that a prelate is put in command that he may teach, not only by teaching, but also by his life. And we should pattern ourselves to him as regards the things he teaches, because, as is said, *if any one preach to you a gospel, besides that which you have received, let him be anathema* (Gal 1:9). Similarly, we should also be conformed to him in life. For his life should be an example

I Cor. IV, 16: *imitatores mei estote, sicut et ego Christi*. Isti vero non dissonant a doctrina, sed a vita; ideo doctrina eorum est attendenda, sed vita cavenda.

1838. *Dicunt enim, et non faciunt*. Hic assignat rationem. Et

primo ponit rationem;

secundo exponit, ibi ***alligant autem onera gravia*** et cetera.

1839. Tu dicis ***quaecumque dixerint vobis, facite*** quia dicunt: vos debetis benefacere, sed ***non faciunt***; et ideo non debetis facere secundum opera eorum, quia qui doces non furandum, furaris; Ps. XLIX, 16: *peccatori enim dixit Deus: quare tu enarras iustitias meas, et assumis testamentum meum per os tuum?*

1840. *Alligant enim onera gravia et importabilia* et cetera. Dominus enim vult exaggerare malitiam eorum ***quia dicunt, et non faciunt***. Si simpliciter dicerent et non facerent, adhuc istud tolerabile esset; sed non sufficit illis, quia adiiciunt praeceptis Dei gravissima onera. Et ideo notatur praesumptio eorum, quia alligant alia onera super onera a Deo imposita, quia faciunt novas observantias, sicut habetur in Mc. VII, 2, quod prohibebant comedere panem, nisi frequenter lavarentur manus; contra illud Is. LVIII, 6: *dissolve colligationes impietatis, solve fasciculos deprimentes*. Item notatur crudelitas eorum qui imponunt onera, contra illud I Io. cap. V, 3: *quia mandata Dei levia sunt*. ***Iugum enim meum suave est, et onus meum leve***, supra XI, 30. Item notatur eorum indiscretio, quia si forti grave imponerent, non esset magnum; sed debilibus imponunt onera importabilia: illud enim non potest portari quod superat vires portantis. In Act. XV, v. 10: *hoc est onus quod nec nos, nec patres nostri portare potuimus*. Item notatur eorum nimia severitas, quia si imponerent onus, et darent indulgentiam, adhuc sufficeret; sed ex quadam violentia praecipiunt.

Imponunt in humeros hominum, unde excedunt in dicendo. Item excedunt in non faciendo, quia sunt aliqui homines, qui non volunt perficere totum, tamen volunt aliquid perficere. Item sunt aliqui qui etsi nolunt facere aliquid difficile, volunt tamen aliquid leve. Item aliqui sunt qui etsi non faciunt, habent tamen voluntatem faciendi.

Sed qui nihil istorum vult, in malitia superexcedit; unde dicit ***digito autem suo nolunt ea movere***; unde non solum non faciebant, sed nolebant ea saltem ***digito suo movere***, idest non inchoare. Item nec etiam levia facere, quae per digitum significantur. Ideo debetis facere quae docent, sed non sequendi sunt quoad opera, quia nec minimum faciunt. Chrysostomus dicit: *tales sunt qui magna dicunt, et parva faciunt; tales sunt similes*

for us, as is the life of Christ; hence, *be followers of me, as I also am of Christ* (1 Cor 4:16). Truly, these men do not disagree by doctrine, but by their life; so their doctrine should be heeded, but their life avoided.

1838. *For they say, and do not*. Here he gives the reason. And

first, he sets out the reason;

second, he explains it, at ***for they bind heavy and insupportable burdens***.

1839. You say, ***whatever that they will say to you, observe and do***, because they say to do good, but ***they say, and do not***; and for this reason you should not act according to their works, because you, who teach that one should not steal, steal. *But to the sinner God has said: why do you declare my justices, and take my covenant in your mouth?* (Ps 49:16)

1840. *For they bind heavy and insupportable burdens*. For the Lord wishes to magnify their malice, because ***they say, and do not***. If they simply said and did not do, this would still be tolerable; but this is not enough for them, for they add the heaviest burdens to God's precepts. And so their presumption is noted, for they bind other burdens beyond the burdens imposed by God, for they make new observances (Mark 7:2), that they forbade one to eat bread without frequent washing of hands, contrary to, *loose the bands of wickedness, undo the bundles that oppress* (Isa 58:6). Likewise, there is noted the cruelty of those who impose burdens, contrary to, *his commandments are not heavy* (1 John 5:3). ***For my yoke is easy and my burden light*** (Matt 11:30). Likewise, their indiscretion is noted, because if they imposed a heavy burden on a strong man it would be no great thing; but they impose unbearable burdens on the weak: for that which exceeds the powers of the one bearing it cannot be carried. *Which neither our fathers nor we have been able to bear* (Acts 15:10). Likewise, their excessive severity is noted, because if they imposed a burden and were lenient, it would yet be enough; but they command out of a certain violence.

They ***lay them on men's shoulders***, hence they are excessive in speaking. Likewise, they are excessive in not doing, because there are some men who do not want to accomplish the whole job, yet want to accomplish something. Likewise there are some who, although they do not want to do something difficult, yet want something light. Likewise there are some who, although they do nothing, yet they have the desire for doing.

But those who do not will any of these things go beyond excess in malice; hence he says, ***but with a finger of their own they will not move them***. Hence, not only do they not do, but they do not wish at the very least to move ***a finger of their own***, that is, they do not wish to begin. Likewise not even to do easy things, which are signified by the finger. Therefore you should do what they teach, but they should not be followed with regard to works, because they do not

exactoribus tributorum, qui aliis magna faciunt solvere plusquam tributa exigant, ipsi autem sui nihil solvunt. Non te videam magna docentem, sed parva facientem. Unde magis parcet tibi Dominus, si declinas ad misericordiam, quam ad severitatem.

1841. **Omnia vero opera sua faciunt ut videantur ab hominibus**. Hic intentionem proponit: et facit duo.

Primo aperit eorum intentionem;
secundo monet discipulos ad eorum vitationem. Et primo intentionem proponit;
secundo exponit, ibi **dilatant enim phylacteria sua** et cetera.

1842. Quae est ratio quare dicunt, et non faciunt? Quia sunt incorrigibiles. Causa autem quare homo sit difficilis ad corrigendum vel incorrigibilis, est quaerere gloriam propriam. Unde Chrysostomus: *tolle gloriam inanem de clero, et sine labore alia omnia vitia resecabis.* Unde ab isto incipit dicens: **omnia vero opera sua faciunt, ut videantur ab hominibus**; Io. XII, 43: *dilexerunt gloriam hominum magis quam gloriam Dei.* Unde dicit **omnia vero opera sua faciunt**, quia non solum unum, sed **omnia ut videantur ab hominibus**, contra illud quod dicitur supra VI, 16: *nolite fieri sicut hypocritae.* Nolite ergo assimilari eis.

1843. Sequitur expositio: **dilatant enim phylacteria sua** et cetera. Et facit duo.

Primo dicit quod faciunt;
secundo quod requirunt **amant enim primos recubitus in coenis** et cetera.

1844. Quid faciunt? Onerosa non faciunt, sed aliqua quae exterius patent, bene faciunt; unde Bernardus: *portant vestes sanctitatis, et hoc non est onerosum, quod ostendebant in phylacteriis et in fimbriis.* Dicitur enim Deut. VI, 8: *ligabis ea in manu tua, et ante oculos tuos. In manu*, idest in completione operis, et *ante oculos tuos*, idest in consideratione tua. Ideo isti volentes gloriam, ut viderentur zelatores mandatorum Dei, scribebant mandata in schedula, et ponebant ante oculos, et illud phylacteria vocabant, et dilatabant magis ista, ut magis viderentur ab hominibus; unde dicitur **dilatant enim phylacteria sua**. Item de fimbriis legitur Num. XV, 38, quod praecepit Dominus ut facerent fimbrias, quia voluit ut discerneretur populus Iudaicus ab aliis populis. Et isti ut magis ostenderent se religiosos, magnificabant fimbrias, et alligabant spinas, ut viderentur se pungere, ut recordarentur se esse Iudaeos. Non ergo exhibent nisi

even do the slightest things. Chrysostom says: *they are the sort who say great things, and do little; such men are similar to those who collect the tributes, who make others pay large sums beyond what the tribute requires, but they themselves pay nothing. I will not see you teaching great things, but doing little. Hence the Lord will spare you more if you incline toward mercy than if you incline toward severity.*

1841. **And all their works they do in order to be seen by men**. Here he sets forth their intention; and he does two things:

first, he reveals their intention;
second, he warns the disciples to avoid them. And first, he sets forth the intention;
second, he explains, at **for they make their phylacteries broad**.

1842. What is the reason why they talk and do not do? Because they are incorrigible. And the reason why a man is difficult to correct, or incorrigible, is that he seeks his own glory. Hence Chrysostom: *take away vainglory from a cleric, and you will cut off all other vices without labor.* Hence he begins from this, saying, **and all their works they do in order to be seen by men**; *for they loved the glory of men more than the glory of God* (John 12:43). Hence he says, **all their works they do**, because they do not only one, but all, **in order to be seen by men**, contrary to what is said above, *do not be like the hypocrites* (Matt 6:16). Therefore, do not be made like to them.

1843. There follows the explanation: **for they make their phylacteries broad**. And he does two things:

first, he says what they do;
second, what they seek: for **they love the first places at feasts**.

1844. What do they do? They do not do burdensome things, but they do well some things which are exteriorly evident; hence Bernard: *they carry the garments of holiness, and this is not burdensome, which they showed in the phylacteries and in fringes.* For it says, *and you will bind them as a sign on your hand, and they will be and will move between your eyes* (Deut 6:8). *On your hand*, i.e., in the completion of works, and *between your eyes*, i.e., in your contemplation. So these men, desiring glory, that they might seem to be zealous for the commands of God, wrote the commandments on little pieces of paper and placed them before their eyes, and they called this a phylactery, and they made these things wider, that they might be better seen by men; hence it says, **for they make their phylacteries broad**. Likewise, it says about fringes that the Lord commanded that they make fringes, because he desired that the Jewish people be marked off from the other peoples (Num 15:38). And these

exteriora; supra VII, 15: ***veniunt ad vos in vestimentis ovium***.

men, the better to show that they were religious, made the fringes large, and bound on thorns, that they might be seen to prick themselves, that they might remember that they are Jews. So they showed nothing but exterior things; ***they come to you in the clothing of sheep*** (Matt 7:15).

1845. Et quid requirunt? ***Ut videantur ab hominibus***. Haec autem gloria in tribus ostenditur. In primatu, in reverentia exhibita, et in laude nominis; qui enim quaerit gloriam, quaerit unum istorum, vel omnia.

Isti autem quaerebant primatum in loco sacro et in loco communi; unde in loco communi dicit ***amant autem primos recubitus in coenis***. Volebant enim sedere in capite mensarum, contra illud Lc. XIV, 8: *cum invitatus fueris ad nuptias, recumbe in novissimo loco*. Et dicit ***amant***, quia non reprehenditur auctoritas, sed inordinatus appetitus. Quidam enim sunt in primo loco corporaliter, qui tamen in corde sedent in novissimo; et e converso aliquis sedet in novissimo loco, ut dicatur, *vide, ille est humilis, et sic* etc., sed in primo, corde, quia inde quaerit gloriam.

Item quaerunt primatum in loco sacro, quia in Ecclesia; unde dicit ***et primas cathedras in synagogis***, contra illud Eccli. VII, 4: *noli quaerere ab homine ducatum, neque a rege cathedram honoris*.

Item appetunt reverentiam, unde dicit ***et salutationes in foro***, idest ut salutentur et honorentur ab hominibus, ut amoveatur capucium coram ipsis, et flectantur genua ante eos; et appetunt ***vocari ab hominibus Rabbi***, idest quod laudentur ut magistri. Origenes refert istud ad illos, qui dignitates appetunt in ecclesiis: est enim quaedam dignitas archidiaconorum, diaconorum, sacerdotum, episcoporum. Diaconi sunt ut praesint mensis, Act. cap. VI, 2 ss. Unde illi appetunt primos recubitus, qui appetunt locum diaconorum. Item cathedra proprie sacerdotum est; ideo illi amant cathedras qui amant locum sacerdotum. Qui autem debent esse magistri, sunt proprie episcopi; unde illi volunt vocari Rabbi, qui amant esse episcopi.

1846. *Vos autem nolite vocari Rabbi*. In parte ista arcet ab imitatione gloriae;

secundo invitat ad humilitatem, ibi ***qui maior est vestrum, erit minister vester***.

Notandum autem quod qui primatum habet, habet instruere et gubernare; quorum primum est proprium magistri, secundum patrum.

Et ideo

primo prohibet inanem gloriam quantum ad utrumque;

secundum ibi ***et patrem nolite vocare vobis super terram***.

Circa primum
primo ponit documentum;
secundo rationem assignat.

1845. And what do they seek? ***To be seen by men***. And this glory is shown in three things. In the first place, in reverence shown, and in the praise of a name. For those who seek glory seek one of these, or all of them.

And these men sought the first place in the holy place and in the common place; hence in the common place, he says, ***they love the first places at feasts***. For they wanted to sit at the head of the table, contrary to, *when you are invited to a wedding, do not sit down in the first place* (Luke 14:8). And he says, ***they love***, because their authority is not reproached, but their inordinate appetite. For some are in the first place bodily, who nevertheless sit in the last place in their heart; and, vice versa, some sit in the last place, that it may be said, *look, this man is humble, and thus*, but in the first place in their heart, because they seek glory from there.

Likewise they seek the first place in the holy place, in the Church; hence he says, ***and the first chairs in the synagogues***, contrary to, *seek not of the Lord a pre-eminence, nor of the king the seat of honor* (Sir 7:4).

Likewise, they desire reverence, hence he says, ***and salutations in the market place***, i.e., to be greeted and honored by men, and to have hats taken off in their presence, and knees bent before them; and they desire ***to be called by men, rabbi***, i.e., to be praised as teachers. Origen applies this to those who desire dignities in the churches: for there is the dignity of the archdeacons, of the deacons, of the priests, of the bishops. There are deacons so that they may be in charge of the tables (Acts 6:2). Hence those desire the first places who desire the place of deacons. Likewise a chair properly belongs to priests; so those love chairs who love the place of priests. And properly, those who should be teachers are the bishops; hence those desire to be called rabbi who love to be bishops.

1846. *But you, do not be called Rabbi*. In this part he wards men away from the imitation of glory;

second, he invites them to humility, at ***he who is the greatest among you will be your servant***.

And one should note that those who have the first place must instruct and govern; of which the first is proper to teachers, the second to fathers.

And therefore,
first, he forbids vainglory with respect to both;

the second is at ***and call none your father upon earth***.

Concerning the first,
first, he sets out the lesson;
second, he gives the reason.

1847. Dicit ergo *vos autem nolite vocari Rabbi*; contra quod est illud I Tim. V, 17: *qui bene praesunt presbyteri, duplici honore digni habeantur, maxime qui laborant in verbo et doctrina*. Potest dici *nolite*, idest non ambiatis.

1848. Et subiungit rationem *unus est enim Magister vester* etc. scilicet Deus; Ps. LXXXIV, 9: *audiam quid loquatur in me Dominus Deus*.

Sed quid vult dicere? Dicendum quod ille proprie dicitur magister, qui doctrinam habet a se, non ille qui traditam ab alio aliis dispergit. Et sic solum unus est magister, scilicet Deus, qui proprie doctrinam habet; sed ministerio multi sunt magistri. Si quaeris auctoritatem, quaeris quae Dei sunt; sed si ministerium, quaeris quod humilitatis est; unde subditur *qui maior est vestrum, erit minister vester*, idest reputabit se ministrum. Chrysostomus dicit quod sicut unus est Deus per naturam, multi per participationem, sic etiam unus magister est naturaliter, multi ministerialiter.

1849. Sed quomodo potest homo scire quod a se non habeat doctrinam? Patet quia sic esset in eius voluntate dare doctrinam cui vellet, sed non potest, immo solius Dei est, qui interius cor illuminat. Et est exemplum manifestum in sanitate, quia medicus sanat, quia aliqua exterius ministrat; sed natura principaliter sanat, medicus vero quaedam adiumenta ministrat; et sanat medicus sicut natura, reducendo scilicet ad medium. Sic est de scientia, quia principium est nobis a natura, scilicet intellectus; unus qui docet, adhibet quaedam auxilia doctrinae, sicut medicus ad sanitatem, sed solus Deus operatur in intellectu. Unde *unus est Magister vester*, unde non debetis vocari magistri.

1850. Item ostendit quod non ament auctoritatem patris: *vos autem omnes fratres estis*, et hoc ostendit ex aequali conditione. In magisterio non fecit differentiam in qualitate conditionis, sed in paternitate conditionem apponit, unde dicit *vos omnes fratres estis*, quia a me patre; Mal. ult., 5: *ecce ego mittam vobis Eliam prophetam*; et post: *et convertet cor patrum ad filios, et cor filiorum ad patres eorum*. Item estis filii mei per regenerationem; I Petr. I, 3: *qui regeneravit nos in spem vivam per resurrectionem Iesu Christi*. Unde unus non habet auctoritatem super alium.

1851. Et sequitur *et patrem nolite vocare vobis super terram*: quia enim estis filii Patris superni, ideo non debetis habere patrem in terris. Ille proprie dicitur patrem habere in terris, qui haereditatem quaerit in terris; et ille habet Patrem in caelis, qui haereditatem quaerit

1847. He says therefore, *but you, do not be called Rabbi*; contrary to what is said, *let the priests who rule well be esteemed worthy of double honor: especially they who labor in the word and doctrine* (1 Tim 5:17). It can be said, *do not*, i.e., do not solicit it.

1848. And he adds the reason: *for one is your Master*, namely God; *I will hear what the Lord God will speak in me* (Ps 84:9).

But what does he wish to say? It is said that he is properly called a master, or teacher, who has the teaching from himself, and not he who passes on to others what is handed down by another. And thus only one is the teacher, namely God, who properly has doctrine; but by service, many are teachers. If you seek authority, you seek what is God's, but if you seek service, you seek what belongs to humility; hence he adds, *he who is the greatest among you will be your servant*, i.e., will consider himself a servant. Chrysostom says that just as God is one by nature and many by participation, so also there is one teacher naturally, and many ministerially.

1849. But can a man know that he does not have the teaching from himself? It is plain, because then it would be in his will to give teaching to whom he would; but he cannot, rather it belongs only to God, who interiorly illuminates the heart. And there is a clear example in health, for a doctor heals, since he administers certain things exteriorly, but nature is the principal healer, while the doctor administers certain aids; and the doctor heals like nature, namely by leading things back to a mean. So it is with knowledge, because the beginning is in us by nature, namely the intellect. One who teaches supplies certain aids to teaching, just as a doctor does toward health, but only God works in the intellect. Hence, *one is your Master*, so you should not be called teachers.

1850. Likewise, he shows that they should not love the authority of a father: *and you are all brethren*, and this shows his point from equality of condition. In teaching authority he makes no distinction in quality of condition, but in fatherhood he assigns a condition, hence he says, *you are all brethren*, because you are from me as from a father; *behold I will send you Elijah the prophet* (Mal 4:5), and afterward, *and he will turn the heart of the fathers to the children, and the heart of the children to their fathers*. Likewise, you are my sons through regeneration; *who according to his great mercy has regenerated us unto a lively hope, by the resurrection of Jesus Christ from the dead* (1 Pet 1:3). Hence one does not have authority over another.

1851. And there follows: *and call none your father upon earth*, for since you are children of a heavenly Father, you should not have a father on earth. He is properly said to have a father on earth who seeks an inheritance on earth; and he has a Father in heaven who seeks an inheritance in

in caelis; I Petr. I, 4: *qui regeneravit nos in haereditatem incorruptibilem, et incontaminatam, et immarcescibilem, conservatam in caelis.*

Quare ergo in monasteriis maiores dicuntur patres? Dicendum quod est quantum ad auctoritatem; Ephes. III, 4: *potestis intelligere prudentiam meam in ministerio Christi* et cetera.

Unus enim est Pater vester. Supra VI, 9: **Pater noster qui es in caelis**.

1852. Item **nec vocemini magistri, quia Magister vester unus est: Christus**. Unde Christus magisterium sibi attribuit, quia Christus Verbum est; et ideo ipsius est docere, quia nullus docet nisi per verbum. Item est magister quantum ad naturam humanam, quia missus est ut doceret; Io. I, 18: *Deum nemo vidit umquam. Unigenitus qui est in sinu Patris, ille nobis enarravit.* Item ibid. XIII, 13: *vos vocatis me Magister et Domine.*

1853. **Qui maior est vestrum, erit minister vester**. Postquam retraxit a superbia, hortatur ad humilitatem. Et

primo ponit hortationem;
secundo assignat rationem.

1854. Et hoc potest sic continuari. Chrysostomus: *vos non debetis patres vocari, nec magistri; unde hoc non debetis ambire, sed magis humilitatem.* Unde **qui maior est vestrum, erit minister vester**, idest debet se exhibere ministrum. Unde I Cor. IV, 1: *sic nos existimet homo ut ministros Christi.*

Vel aliter. Ita dixerat **nolite vocari Rabbi**, unde dicerent ei: vis quod non sit praelatio in terra? Dicit Dominus: hoc non volo, sed volo quod **qui maior est vestrum sit minister**, idest non se existimet ut superiorem, sed ut ministrum; II Cor. IV, 5: *nos autem servos vestros per Iesum.* Et hoc est quod dicitur Lc. XXII, 27: *quis maior est, qui ministrat, an qui recumbit?* et cetera.

1855. Deinde assignat rationem **qui autem se exaltaverit, humiliabitur, et qui se humiliaverit, exaltabitur**. Unde in cantico Virginis Lc. I, 52: *deposuit potentes de sede, et exaltavit humiles.*

heaven; *unto an inheritance incorruptible, and undefiled, and that cannot fade, reserved in heaven for you* (1 Pet 1:4).

Why then are the greater men called fathers in monasteries? One should say that it is as regards authority; *as you reading, may understand my knowledge in the mystery of Christ (Eph 3:4).*

For one is your Father. As above: **our Father who art in heaven** (Matt 6:9).

1852. Likewise, **neither be called masters; for one is your Master, Christ**. Hence Christ attributes teacherhood to himself, for Christ is the Word; and so it belongs to him to teach, for no one teaches except through a word. Likewise, he is a teacher with regard to his human nature, because he was sent that he might teach; *no man has seen God at any time: the only begotten Son who is in the bosom of the Father, he has declared him* (John 1:18). Likewise, *you call me Master, and Lord* (John 13:13).

1853. **He who is the greatest among you will be your servant**. After he has withdrawn them from pride, he exhorts them to humility. And

first, he sets out the exhortation;
second, he gives the reason.

1854. And this can be continued in this way. Chrysostom: *you should not be called fathers, nor teachers; hence you should not solicit this, but rather humility.* Hence, **he who is the greatest among you will be your servant**, i.e., should present himself as a servant. Hence, *let a man so account of us as of the ministers of Christ* (1 Cor 4:1).

Or in another way. He had spoken thus: **do not be called Rabbi**, hence they would say to him: do you want that there be no prelateship on earth? The Lord says: I do not want this, rather I want that **he who is the greatest among you will be your servant**, i.e., should not present himself as superior, but as a servant; *ourselves your servants through Jesus* (2 Cor 4:5). And this is what is said in Luke, *for who is greater, he who sits at table, or he who serves?* (Luke 22:27).

1855. Then he gives the reason: **and whoever will exalt himself will be humbled: and he who will humble himself will be exalted**. Hence in the canticle of the Virgin, *he has put down the mighty from their seat, and has exalted the humble* (Luke 1:52).

Lecture 2

23:13 Vae autem vobis, scribae et Pharisaei hypocritae, quia clauditis regnum caelorum ante homines. Vos enim non intratis, nec introeuntes sinitis intrare. [n. 1858]

23:14 Vae vobis, scribae et Pharisaei hypocritae, quia comeditis domos viduarum, orationes longas orantes; propter hoc amplius accipietis iudicium. [n. 1859]

23:15 Vae vobis, scribae et Pharisaei hypocritae, quia circuitis mare et aridam, ut faciatis unum proselytum, et cum fuerit factus, facitis eum filium gehennae duplo quam vos. [n. 1861]

23:16 Vae vobis, duces caeci, qui dicitis: quicumque iuraverit per templum, nihil est: qui autem iuraverit in auro templi, debitor est. [n. 1863]

23:17 Stulti et caeci; quid enim maius est, aurum, an templum quod sanctificat aurum? [n. 1865]

23:18 Et quicumque iuraverit in altari, nihil est: quicumque autem iuraverit in dono quod est super illud, debet. [n. 1866]

23:19 Caeci; quid enim maius est, donum, an altare quod sanctificat donum? [n. 1867]

23:20 Qui ergo iurat in altare, iurat in eo et in omnibus quae super illud sunt. [n. 1867]

23:21 Et qui iuraverit in templo, iurat in illo et in eo qui habitat in ipso. [n. 1867]

23:22 Et qui iurat in caelo, iurat in throno Dei et in eo qui sedet super eum. [n. 1867]

23:13 Οὐαὶ δὲ ὑμῖν, γραμματεῖς καὶ Φαρισαῖοι ὑποκριταί, ὅτι κλείετε τὴν βασιλείαν τῶν οὐρανῶν ἔμπροσθεν τῶν ἀνθρώπων· ὑμεῖς γὰρ οὐκ εἰσέρχεσθε οὐδὲ τοὺς εἰσερχομένους ἀφίετε εἰσελθεῖν.

23:14 [Οὐαὶ δέ ὑμῖν, γραμματεῖς καὶ Φαρισαῖοι ὑποκριταί, ὅτι κατεσθίετε τὰς οἰκίας τῶν χηρῶν, καὶ προφάσει μακρὰ προσευχόμενοι· διὰ τοῦτο λήψεσθε περισσότερον κρίμα.]

23:15 Οὐαὶ ὑμῖν, γραμματεῖς καὶ Φαρισαῖοι ὑποκριταί, ὅτι περιάγετε τὴν θάλασσαν καὶ τὴν ξηρὰν ποιῆσαι ἕνα προσήλυτον, καὶ ὅταν γένηται ποιεῖτε αὐτὸν υἱὸν γεέννης διπλότερον ὑμῶν.

23:16 Οὐαὶ ὑμῖν, ὁδηγοὶ τυφλοὶ οἱ λέγοντες· ὅς ἂν ὀμόσῃ ἐν τῷ ναῷ, οὐδέν ἐστιν· ὃς δ' ἂν ὀμόσῃ ἐν τῷ χρυσῷ τοῦ ναοῦ, ὀφείλει.

23:17 μωροὶ καὶ τυφλοί, τίς γὰρ μείζων ἐστίν, ὁ χρυσὸς ἢ ὁ ναὸς ὁ ἁγιάσας τὸν χρυσόν;

23:18 καί· ὃς ἂν ὀμόσῃ ἐν τῷ θυσιαστηρίῳ, οὐδέν ἐστιν· ὃς δ' ἂν ὀμόσῃ ἐν τῷ δώρῳ τῷ ἐπάνω αὐτοῦ, ὀφείλει.

23:19 τυφλοί, τί γὰρ μεῖζον, τὸ δῶρον ἢ τὸ θυσιαστήριον τὸ ἁγιάζον τὸ δῶρον;

23:20 ὁ οὖν ὀμόσας ἐν τῷ θυσιαστηρίῳ ὀμνύει ἐν αὐτῷ καὶ ἐν πᾶσι τοῖς ἐπάνω αὐτοῦ·

23:21 καὶ ὁ ὀμόσας ἐν τῷ ναῷ ὀμνύει ἐν αὐτῷ καὶ ἐν τῷ κατοικοῦντι αὐτόν,

23:22 καὶ ὁ ὀμόσας ἐν τῷ οὐρανῷ ὀμνύει ἐν τῷ θρόνῳ τοῦ θεοῦ καὶ ἐν τῷ καθημένῳ ἐπάνω αὐτοῦ.

23:13 But woe to you scribes and Pharisees, hypocrites; because you shut the kingdom of heaven against men, for you yourselves do not enter in; and those who are going in, you do not suffer to enter. [n. 1858]

23:14 Woe to you scribes and Pharisees, hypocrites; because you devour the houses of widows, praying long prayers. For this you will receive the greater judgment. [n. 1859]

23:15 Woe to you scribes and Pharisees, hypocrites; because you go round about the sea and the land to make one proselyte; and when he is made, you make him the child of hell twofold more than yourselves. [n. 1861]

23:16 Woe to you blind guides, who say: whoever will swear by the temple, it is nothing; but he who will swear by the gold of the temple, is a debtor. [n. 1863]

23:17 You foolish and blind; for which is greater, the gold, or the temple that sanctifies the gold? [n. 1865]

23:18 And whoever will swear by the altar, it is nothing; but whoever will swear by the gift that is upon it, is a debtor. [n. 1866]

23:19 You blind; for which is greater, the gift, or the altar that sanctifies the gift? [n. 1867]

23:20 He therefore who swears by the altar, swears by it, and by all things that are upon it: [n. 1867]

23:21 And whoever will swear by temple, swears by it, and by him who dwells in it. [n. 1867]

23:22 And he who swears by heaven, swears by the throne of God, and by him who is seated there. [n. 1867]

23:23 Vae vobis, scribae et Pharisaei hypocritae quia decimatis mentham, et anethum, et cyminum, et reliquistis quae graviora sunt legis, iudicium, et misericordiam, et fidem. Haec oportuit facere, et illa non omittere. [n. 1869]

23:24 Duces caeci excolantes culicem, camelum autem glutientes. [n. 1873]

23:25 Vae vobis scribae et Pharisaei hypocritae, quia mundatis quod deforis est calicis et paropsidis; intus autem pleni sunt rapina et immunditia. [n. 1874]

23:26 Pharisaee caece, munda prius quod intus est calicis et paropsidis, ut fiat, et id quod deforis est, mundum. [n. 1877]

23:27 Vae vobis, scribae et Pharisaei hypocritae, quia similes estis sepulchris dealbatis, quae a foris parent hominibus speciosa, intus vero plena sunt ossibus mortuorum et omni spurcitia. [n. 1878]

23:28 Sic et vos a foris quidem paretis hominibus iusti, intus autem pleni estis hypocrisi et iniquitate. [n. 1880]

23:29 Vae vobis, scribae et Pharisaei hypocritae, qui aedificatis sepulchra prophetarum, et ornatis monumenta iustorum, [n. 1881]

23:30 et dicitis: si fuissemus in diebus patrum nostrorum, non essemus socii eorum in sanguine prophetarum. [n. 1884]

23:31 Itaque testimonio estis vobismetipsis, quia filii estis eorum, qui prophetas occiderunt. [n. 1886]

23:32 Et vos implete mensuram patrum vestrorum. [n. 1887]

23:33 Serpentes, genimina viperarum, quomodo fugietis a iudicio gehennae? [n. 1889]

23:23 Οὐαὶ ὑμῖν, γραμματεῖς καὶ Φαρισαῖοι ὑποκριταί, ὅτι ἀποδεκατοῦτε τὸ ἡδύοσμον καὶ τὸ ἄνηθον καὶ τὸ κύμινον καὶ ἀφήκατε τὰ βαρύτερα τοῦ νόμου, τὴν κρίσιν καὶ τὸ ἔλεος καὶ τὴν πίστιν· ταῦτα [δὲ] ἔδει ποιῆσαι κἀκεῖνα μὴ ἀφιέναι.

23:24 ὁδηγοὶ τυφλοί, οἱ διϋλίζοντες τὸν κώνωπα, τὴν δὲ κάμηλον καταπίνοντες.

23:25 Οὐαὶ ὑμῖν, γραμματεῖς καὶ Φαρισαῖοι ὑποκριταί, ὅτι καθαρίζετε τὸ ἔξωθεν τοῦ ποτηρίου καὶ τῆς παροψίδος, ἔσωθεν δὲ γέμουσιν ἐξ ἁρπαγῆς καὶ ἀκρασίας.

23:26 Φαρισαῖε τυφλέ, καθάρισον πρῶτον τὸ ἐντὸς τοῦ ποτηρίου, ἵνα γένηται καὶ τὸ ἐκτὸς αὐτοῦ καθαρόν.

23:27 Οὐαὶ ὑμῖν, γραμματεῖς καὶ Φαρισαῖοι ὑποκριταί, ὅτι παρομοιάζετε τάφοις κεκονιαμένοις, οἵτινες ἔξωθεν μὲν φαίνονται ὡραῖοι, ἔσωθεν δὲ γέμουσιν ὀστέων νεκρῶν καὶ πάσης ἀκαθαρσίας.

23:28 οὕτως καὶ ὑμεῖς ἔξωθεν μὲν φαίνεσθε τοῖς ἀνθρώποις δίκαιοι, ἔσωθεν δέ ἐστε μεστοὶ ὑποκρίσεως καὶ ἀνομίας.

23:29 Οὐαὶ ὑμῖν, γραμματεῖς καὶ Φαρισαῖοι ὑποκριταί, ὅτι οἰκοδομεῖτε τοὺς τάφους τῶν προφητῶν καὶ κοσμεῖτε τὰ μνημεῖα τῶν δικαίων,

23:30 καὶ λέγετε· εἰ ἤμεθα ἐν ταῖς ἡμέραις τῶν πατέρων ἡμῶν, οὐκ ἂν ἤμεθα αὐτῶν κοινωνοὶ ἐν τῷ αἵματι τῶν προφητῶν.

23:31 ὥστε μαρτυρεῖτε ἑαυτοῖς ὅτι υἱοί ἐστε τῶν φονευσάντων τοὺς προφήτας.

23:32 καὶ ὑμεῖς πληρώσατε τὸ μέτρον τῶν πατέρων ὑμῶν.

23:33 ὄφεις, γεννήματα ἐχιδνῶν, πῶς φύγητε ἀπὸ τῆς κρίσεως τῆς γεέννης;

23:23 Woe to you scribes and Pharisees, hypocrites; because you tithe the mint, and anise, and cummin, and have left the weightier things of the law: judgment, and mercy, and faith. These things you ought to have done, and not to leave those undone. [n. 1869]

23:24 Blind guides, who strain out a gnat, and swallow a camel. [n. 1873]

23:25 Woe to you scribes and Pharisees, hypocrites; because you make clean the outside of the cup and of the dish, but within you are full of rapine and uncleanness. [n. 1874]

23:26 You blind Pharisee, first make clean the inside of the cup and of the dish, that the outside may become clean. [n. 1877]

23:27 Woe to you scribes and Pharisees, hypocrites; because you are like whitened sepulchres, which outwardly appear beautiful to men, but within are full of dead men's bones, and of all filthiness. [n. 1878]

23:28 So you also outwardly indeed appear just to men; but inwardly you are full of hypocrisy and iniquity. [n. 1880]

23:29 Woe to you scribes and Pharisees, hypocrites; who build the sepulchres of the prophets, and adorn the monuments of the just, [n. 1881]

23:30 and say: if we had been in the days of our fathers, we would not have been partakers with them in the blood of the prophets. [n. 1884]

23:31 Therefore you are witnesses against yourselves, that you are the sons of those who killed the prophets. [n. 1886]

23:32 Fill up then the measure of your fathers. [n. 1887]

23:33 You serpents, generation of vipers, how will you flee from the judgment of hell? [n. 1889]

1856. Postquam instruxit discipulos et turbas de cautela quam habere debebant super doctrina Iudaeorum, hic convertit sermonem ad scribas, increpando eos.

Primo increpat de simulatione religionis, cum irreligiosi essent;

secundo de simulatione puritatis, cum impuri essent;

tertio de simulatione pietatis, cum impii essent. Secunda ibi *vae vobis, scribae et Pharisaei hypocritae, qui mundatis quod deforis est calicis* et cetera. Tertia ibi *vae vobis qui aedificatis sepulcra prophetarum* et cetera.

In his quae ad religionem spectant, quaedam a sacerdotibus debentur populo, quaedam e converso.

Primo ergo ponit malitiam eorum in his quae a sacerdotibus;

secundo in his quae a populo, ibi *vae qui dicit: quicumque iuraverit* et cetera.

Sacerdos debet subdito iam converso aliquid, et aliquid non converso. Non converso, ut convertat ipsum; converso doctrinam; Mal. cap. II, 7: *labia sacerdotis docent sapientiam*. Item debet ei suffragia; ad Hebr. V, v. 1: *omnis namque pontifex ex hominibus assumptus, pro hominibus constituitur in his quae sunt ad Deum*. Et isti mala agebant in utroque; unde

primo arguit eos de primo;

secundo de secundo, ibi *vae vobis qui comeditis domos viduarum* et cetera.

1857. In istis omnibus increpationibus designat se esse Filium eius, qui veterem legem dedit. Deut. XXVI, et XXVIII dantur maledictiones eis qui in lege non permanserint, et post dantur benedictiones. Sed quia venerat ut solveret maledicta legis, ideo primo datae sunt superius benedictiones, ubi dictum est, *beati pauperes, beati mites* et cetera. Circa finem vero suae doctrinae dat maledictionem. Ideo male reprehendunt, qui reprehendunt veterem legem propter hoc quod ibi continebantur maledictiones, quia sicut in veteri lege, ita et in nova. Sicut enim in lege non maledicebantur nisi qui legem praeteribant, sic nec hic; Prov. III, 11: *disciplinam Domini non abiicias*.

1858. Sed quid est quod dicit *qui clauditis regnum caelorum ante homines*? Regnum caelorum dicitur beatitudo vitae aeternae; supra V, 20: *nisi abundaverit iustitia vestra plusquam scribarum et Pharisaeorum, non intrabitis in regnum caelorum*. Item Sacra Scriptura dicitur regnum; supra XXI, 43: *auferetur a vobis regnum Dei*, idest intellectus Sacrae Scripturae. Ad utrumque regnum Christus ostium est; Io. X, 9: *ego sum*

1856. After he had instructed the disciples and the crowds about the caution which they should have regarding the teaching of the Jews, here he turns his words toward the scribes, by rebuking them.

First, he rebukes them about the pretense of religion, while they were irreligious;

second, about the pretense of purity, while they were impure;

third, about the pretense of piety, while they were impious. The second is at *woe to you scribes and Pharisees, hypocrites; because you make clean the outside of the cup*. The third, at *woe to you scribes and Pharisees, hypocrites; who build the sepulchres of the prophets*.

In those things which pertain to religion, some things are owed by the priests to the people, and some things the other way around.

First, therefore, he sets out their malice in those which are owed by the priests;

second, in those which are owed by the people, at *woe to you blind guides, who say: whoever will swear by the temple*.

A priest owes one thing to the subject already converted, and another thing to the unconverted. To the unconverted he owes that he convert him; to the converted he owes teaching; *for the lips of the priest will keep knowledge* (Mal 2:7). Likewise, he owes intercession; *for every high priest taken from among men, is ordained for men in the things that appertain to God* (Heb 5:1). And these men did evil things in both; hence

first, he accuses them of the first;

second, of the second, at *woe to you scribes and Pharisees, hypocrites; because you devour the houses of widows*.

1857. In all these reproaches he points to himself as the Son of him who gave the old law. In Deuteronomy, there are curses given to those who would not persevere in the law, and after that are given blessings (Deut 26, 28). But since he had come to unbind the curses of the law, first there were blessings given above, at *blessed are the poor in spirit* (Matt 5:3). But near the end of his teaching he gives a curse. So they reproach badly who reproach the old law because curses are contained in it, for just as it is in the old law, so it is in the new. For just as in the law only those who transgressed were cursed, so also here; *my son, do not reject the correction of the Lord* (Prov 3:11).

1858. But why does he say, *you shut the kingdom of heaven against men*? The beatitude of eternal life is called the kingdom of heaven; above, *unless your justice abound more than that of the scribes and Pharisees, you will not enter into the kingdom of heaven* (Matt 5:20). Likewise, Sacred Scripture is called a kingdom; above, *the kingdom of God will be taken from you* (Matt 21:43), i.e., the understanding of Sacred Scripture. To either kingdom, Christ is

ostium. Per me si quis introierit, salvabitur, et ingredietur et egredietur, et pascua inveniet. Quid est ergo claudere regnum, nisi quod isti claudebant per malam doctrinam et malam vitam? Non clauditur nisi quod apertum est. Doctrinae de Christo apertae erant, sed isti claudebant, quia obscuras eas faciebant. Habetur Is. XXXV, 5: *dominus ipse veniet, et salvabit nos. Tunc aperientur oculi caecorum, et aures surdorum patebunt*. Quando Dominus faciebat ista miracula, aperta erat haec Scriptura, sed ipsi claudebant dicentes, *in Beelzebub principe daemoniorum eiicit daemonia*, Lc. XI, 15. Item ipsi claudebant per malam vitam, quando per malum exemplum inducebant ad peccandum; Ps. I, 1: *beatus vir qui non abiit in consilio impiorum, et in via peccatorum non stetit, et in cathedra pestilentiae non sedit*. Ille proprie in cathedra pestilentiae sedet, qui officium docendi accipit, et per malam vitam populum corrumpit. Per iniustam etiam sententiam iudex hominem perimit, tamen iniustam sententiam in vanum proiicit. Data est enim potestas ligandi et solvendi ad aedificationem, non ad destructionem. Unde potest eis dici **vae vobis ... quia clauditis regnum caelorum ante homines**. Item quicumque impedit introitum ad regnum, non est dubium quin male agat; unde sequitur **vos enim non intratis, nec introeuntes sinitis intrare**, idest alios converti. Unde Mal. II, 8: *recessistis a via, et scandalizastis plurimos*.

1859. Vae vobis ... qui comeditis domos viduarum, orationes longas orantes. Hoc est secundum vae, in quo tangitur simulatio quantum ad orationem.

Et primo arguit de voracitate, cum dicit **qui comeditis domos viduarum**, quia quicquid faciebant, totum ad gulam retorquebant, ita quod eis convenit illud II Mc. VI, 4, quod totum templum luxuriis et comessationibus erat plenum.

Domos viduarum, idest facultates viduarum. Sed quare magis domos viduarum quam aliorum? Ratio est, quia magis intendunt seducere mulieres, quia viri sapientiores sunt et discretiores, nec ita cito decipiuntur. Item mulieres habent affectum magis proclivem ad largiendum; I ad Tim. II, 10: *sed quod decet mulieres, promittentes pietatem per bona opera*.

Item **domos viduarum**, quia mulier quae habet virum, habet eum ut caput et ut consiliarium, ideo non ita decipitur. Item coniugata non habet potestatem domus suae, sed vidua habet; ideo magis potest dare quam coniugata, et ideo magis faciebant quaestum circa eas, quam circa alias, cum magis esset eis dandum; unde bene convenit eis illud Ps. XCIII, 6: *viduam et advenam interfecerunt*.

Et hoc in oratione. **Orationes longas orantes**, propter simulationem sanctitatis: et sic retorquebant orationem ad quaestum, et quaestum ad gloriam.

the door; *I am the door. By me, if any man enter in, he will be saved: and he will go in, and go out, and will find pastures* (John 10:9). What therefore is shutting the kingdom except that these men were shutting it through bad teaching and a bad life? Only that which is opened can be shut. The teachings about Christ were open, but these men were shutting them, because they made them obscure. *Then will the eyes of the blind be opened, and the ears of the deaf will be unstopped* (Isa 35:5). When the Lord was working this miracle, this Scripture was opened, but they were shutting it, saying, *he casts out devils by Beelzebub, the prince of devils* (Luke 11:15). Likewise, they were shutting the kingdom through a bad life, when by bad example they led men into sinning; *blessed is the man who has not walked in the counsel of the ungodly, nor stood in the way of sinners, nor sat in the chair of pestilence* (Ps 1:1). He properly sits in the chair of pestilence who accepts the duty of teaching and corrupts the people through a bad life. A judge also destroys a man by an unjust judgment, yet he hands down an unjust judgment to no end. For the power of binding and loosing is given for building up, not for pulling down. Hence it can be said to him, **but woe to you ... because you shut the kingdom of heaven against men**. Likewise, anyone who impedes entrance into the kingdom undoubtedly acts badly; hence there follows, **for you yourselves do not enter in; and those who are going in, you do not suffer to enter**, i.e., others to be converted. Hence, *but you have departed out of the way, and have caused many to stumble at the law* (Mal 2:8).

1859. Woe to you ... because you devour the houses of widows, praying long prayers. This is the second woe, in which pretense is touched upon as regards prayer.

And first, he accuses them of voraciousness, when he says, **you devour the houses of widows**, because whatever they did, they turned the whole thing to gluttony, such that Maccabees applies to them: *the temple was full of the riot and revellings of the gentiles* (2 Macc 6:4).

The houses of widows, i.e., widows' supplies. But why the houses of widows more than others? The reason is that they aimed more at seducing women, because men are wiser and more discerning, nor are they deceived as quickly. Likewise, women have an affection more prone to generous giving; *but as it becomes women professing godliness, with good works* (1 Tim 2:10).

Likewise, **the houses of widows**, because a woman who has a man has him as head and counselor, so that way she is not deceived. Likewise, a married woman does not have her house at her own disposal, but a widow does; so she is more able to give than a married woman, and so they made more profit among them than among the others, since there was more to be given to them. Hence the Psalm befits them well: *they have slain the widow and the stranger* (Ps 93:6).

And this in prayer. **Praying long prayers**, owing to the pretense of sanctity: and thus they were turning prayer to profit, and profit to glory.

1860. Unde reprehendi poterant, quia gulosi, quia depraedatores, item quia simulabant sanctitatem; et ideo sequitur *et propter hoc amplius accipietis iudicium*, idest amplius peccatis. Et quare? Quia si aliquis rapit per arma diaboli, peccat; et si per arma Dei, peccat dupliciter, quia peccat contra Deum, et contra proximum. Vel *amplius* etc., quia accipitis ab eis, quibus debebatis dare. Vel *amplius*, sicut habetur Lc. cap. XII, 47: *servus sciens voluntatem Domini, et non faciens, vapulabit plagis multis*.

1861. *Vae vobis, scribae et Pharisaei hypocritae, qui circuitis mare et aridam, ut faciatis unum proselytum*. Et hoc dupliciter exponitur, ut referatur ad tempus post Christum, et ante Christum.

Si ad tempus post, sic loquitur futura et praesentia. Praevidit enim quod per totum mundum Iudaei essent dispergendi, et quod converterent ad legem suam, et perverterent a Christo quos possent. Et ideo dicitur *circuitis mare et aridam* et cetera. Dicuntur proselyti qui convertuntur a gentibus ad fidem eorum, vel a Christianis; et quia praevidebat istos aliquos ad fidem suam conversuros de Christianis, ideo hoc dicit. Et dicit *unum* quia paucissimi conversi sunt. Ideo intrarunt illam maledictionem, quae habetur Os. IX, 10: *quasi uvas in deserto inveni Israel*. *Et cum factus fuerit*, scilicet Iudaeus, *facitis eum filium gehennae duplo quam vos*: quia est primo gentilis et post Iudaeus, et tunc habet duplicia peccata, scilicet gentilitatis et Iudaeorum, quia cum sit Iudaeus, fit particeps occisionis Christi; si autem fuerit Christianus, et post Iudaeus, efficitur in duplo peior, quia maculat donum Spiritus Sancti, quod acceperat in sacramentis. Item particeps fit peccatorum Iudaeorum; Io. VIII, 44: *vos ex patre diabolo estis*.

1862. Potest etiam referri ad tempus ante Christum, quia ante Christum convertebant aliquos ad fidem suam. Et hoc patet, quia quilibet diligit magis se quam alium; ergo si converterent alios propter salutem animae, magis deberent de sui ipsius salute curare, sed non curabant. Sed hoc faciebant totum propter quaestum, quia volebant quod oblationes augmentarentur; unde futilis erat doctrina eorum. *Et cum factus fuerit, facitis eum filium gehennae duplo quam vos*; quia primo convertebatur ad Iudaismum et scandalizabatur, et sic post iterato convertebatur. Unde II Petr. II, 21: *melius est viam iustitiae non agnoscere, quam post agnitam regredi*. Item aliter. Antequam esset Iudaeus, abstinebat a malis, saltem propter laudem hominum, sed post, non: unde ad Rom. II, v. 14: *cum enim gentes, quae legem non habent, naturaliter ea*

1860. Hence they could be reproached for gluttony, for plundering, and because they pretended sanctity; and so there follows, *for this you will receive the greater judgment*, i.e., you sin more. And why? Because if someone pillages using the devil's weapons, he sins; if using God's weapons, he sins doubly, because he sins against God and against his neighbor. Or *greater*, because you take from them what you should have given. Or *greater*, as is said, *and that servant who knew the will of his lord, and did not prepare himself, and did not according to his will, will be beaten with many stripes* (Luke 12:47).

1861. *Woe to you scribes and Pharisees, hypocrites; because you go round about the sea and the land to make one proselyte*. And this is explained in two ways, according as it is referred to the time after Christ or to the time before Christ.

If to the time after, in this way he speaks of future things as present things. For he foresaw that the Jews would be scattered through the whole world, and that they would convert others to their law, and would turn aside from Christ those whom they could. And for this reason it says, *you go round about the sea and the land*. Those are called proselytes who are converted to their faith from the gentiles or from Christians; and since he foresaw that they would convert some from Christians to their own faith, he says this. And he says, *one*, because only a very few were converted. So they enter that curse which is found in Hosea, *I found Israel like grapes in the desert* (Hos 9:10). *And when he is made* a Jew *you make him the child of hell twofold more than yourselves*: for he is first a gentile and then a Jew, and then he has a double sin, namely that of the gentiles and that of the Jews, for since he is a Jew, he becomes a partaker in the killing of Christ; but if he is a Christian and then a Jew, he is made worse twice over, for he dishonors the gift of the Holy Spirit, which he had received in the sacraments. Likewise, he becomes a partaker in the sins of the Jews; *you are of your father the devil* (John 8:44).

1862. It can also be referred to the time before Christ, because before Christ they were converting some men to their faith. And this is clear, because any man loves himself more than another; therefore if they converted others for the sake of saving a soul, all the more should they have taken care for the salvation of their own, but they did not take care. But they did this whole thing for profit, because they wanted to increase the offerings; hence their teaching was futile. *And when he is made, you make him the child of hell twofold more than yourselves*; for first he was converted to Judaism and then was scandalized, and thus afterward was converted again. Hence, *for it had been better for them not to have known the way of justice, than after they have known it, to turn back* (2 Pet 2:21). Similarly, in another way. Before he was a Jew he refrained from evil things, at least for

quae legis sunt faciunt, eiusmodi legem non habentes ipsi sibi sunt lex. Unde accipiebant exemplum a malis.

1863. *Vae vobis, duces caeci.* In hoc ostendit quomodo sunt simulatores sanctitatis in his quae praelatis debentur. Et

primo de oblationibus;

secundo de decimis, ibi *vae vobis . . . qui decimatis mentham* et cetera.

Videte: primo ponit traditionem eorum; secundo arguit tribus rationibus.

Prima pars, ubi ponitur traditio cum ratione, habet duas partes. Secunda ibi *et quicumque iuraverit in altari* et cetera.

Isti totam religionem trahebant ad quaestum, ut traherent homines ad offerendum. In templo erat multum aurum positum: unde dicebant quod si aliquis iuraret per templum, nihil debebat; sed qui iurabat per aurum, obligabat se ad tantum pro quo iurabat.

Item secunda traditio erat, quod erat ibi altare et offerebantur multa super altare; unde dicebant quod qui iurabat per altare, nihil solvebat, qui autem per oblationem, obligabat se ad valorem oblationis. Et quare? Ut lucrarentur ex poenis, et ut elevarent per sanctitatem oblationem, et ut incitarentur homines ad magis offerendum.

Et primo ponit primam partem; secundo secundam.

Circa primum duo facit.

Primo proponit traditionem;

secundo improbationem, ibi *stulti et caeci* et cetera.

1864. Dicit ergo *vae vobis, duces caeci* et cetera. Idem habetur supra XV, 14: *caeci sunt et duces caecorum*; Is. LVI, 10: *speculatores eius caeci omnes*. *Qui dicitis, quicumque iuraverit per templum Dei, nihil est*, quia impossibile est quod iste aliud templum faciat; *qui autem iuraverit in auro templi*, idest per aurum, *debitor est*, scilicet illius auri.

1865. Consequenter ponit improbationem *stulti et caeci; quid enim maius est, aurum, an templum quod sanctificat aurum?* Constat quod illud quod est in templo, ratione templi sanctum est, unde qui aliquid in templo furatur, sacrilegium committit: unde maius est iurare per templum, quam per aurum. Chrysostomus: *contra quosdam qui dicunt quod iurare per Deum, nihil est.* Unde qui iurant per Deum, credunt nihil iurare; sed cum iurant per sancta Dei Evangelia, credunt magnum esse. Unde potest eis dici: quid maius est, Deus vel Evangelium? Constat quod Deus. Et hoc verum est simpliciter; secus cum aliqua circumstantia additur, quae aggravat peccatum. Quia qui iurat per sancta Evangelia Dei,

the sake of the praise of men, but not afterwards: hence, *for when the gentiles, who do not have the law, do by nature those things that are of the law; these not having the law are a law to themselves* (Rom 2:14). Hence they took example from the evil.

1863. *Woe to you, blind guides.* In this he shows how they are pretenders of sanctity in those things which are owed to prelates:

first, concerning offerings;

second, concerning the tithe, at *woe to you . . . you tithe mint*.

Observe: first, he sets out their tradition; second, he convicts them with three arguments.

The first part, where the tradition is set out with an argument, has two parts. The second is at *and whoever will swear by the altar*.

These men turned the whole of religion to profit, to draw men in to make offerings. There was much gold placed in the temple: hence they said that if someone swore by the temple, he owed nothing; but whoever swore by the gold obligated himself to as much as he swore.

Likewise there was a second tradition, for there was an altar there and many things were offered on the altar. Hence they said that whoever swore by the altar paid nothing, but whoever swore by the offering, bound himself to the fulfillment of the offering. And why? That they might profit by the penalties, and that they might elevate the offerings by sanctity, and that men might be urged on to offering more.

And first, he sets out the first part; second, the second.

Concerning the first, he does two things:

first, he sets forth the tradition;

second, a refutation, at *you foolish and blind*.

1864. He says therefore, *woe to you, blind guides.* The same thing is said above, *they are blind, and leaders of the blind* (Matt 15:14); *his watchmen are all blind* (Isa 56:10). *Who say: whoever will swear by the temple, it is nothing*, because it is impossible that this man build another temple; *but he who will swear by the gold of the temple*, i.e., by gold, *is a debtor*, namely of that gold.

1865. Next he sets out a refutation: *you foolish and blind; for which is greater, the gold, or the temple that sanctifies the gold?* It is agreed that what is in the temple is holy by reason of the temple, hence someone who steals something in the temple commits a sacrilege: hence it is greater to swear by the temple than by the gold. Chrysostom: *against certain men who say that to swear by God is nothing.* Hence those who swear by God believe that they swear nothing; but when they swear by the holy Gospel of God, they think it a great thing. Hence it can be said to them: which is greater, God or the Gospel? It is agreed that God is greater. And this is true simply speaking; it is otherwise when some circumstance is added, which aggravates the sin. For he who swears by the holy Gospel of

iuravit cum quadam deliberatione et solemnitate, et ideo gravius peccat.

1866. Deinde ponit secundam partem traditionis *et quicumque iuraverit in altari, nihil est: qui autem iuraverit in dono quod est super illud, debet*.

1867. Tunc ponit reprobationem *caeci, quid maius est, donum an altare quod sanctificat donum?* Non enim sanctificatur donum nisi per altare.

Qui ergo iuraverit in altari, iurat in eo et in omnibus quae super illud sunt. Hic ponit aliam rationem. Templum continet aurum, et non e converso: similiter altare continet donum, et non e converso. Unde qui iurat per templum, iurat per aurum quod est in templo: et qui iurat in altari, idest per altare, iurat per id quod est in eo.

Item sequitur alia ratio *et qui iuraverit in templo, iurat in illo et in eo qui habitat in ipso*. Isti dicebant: *qui iurat in templo, nihil iurat*. Sed ipse vult ostendere quod qui iurat per templum, iurat per Deum, quia non iurat per templum nisi sanctificatum, et non est sanctificatum nisi Deo. Ergo qui iurat per templum, iurat per Deum.

Deinde ponitur alia ratio *et qui iurat in caelo*, idest per caelum, non iurat per eum, nisi quia thronus Dei, et quia manifestatur ibi potentia Dei; unde *qui in caelo iurat, iurat in throno Dei, et in eo qui sedet super eum*. Ps. X, 5: *Deus in templo sancto suo, Dominus in caelo sedes eius*. Et istud inducitur ibi secundum similitudinem.

1868. Sed mystice, secundum Origenem, facit mentionem de templo, de auro et de altari, in quibus significatur vita contemplativa et gloriosa. Per aurum contemplativa significatur, per quod significatur subtilis sensus excogitatus ipsius Scripturae: quia quantumcumque videatur rationabilis, nihil est nisi sit in templo, idest nisi confirmetur in Sacra Scriptura. Per altare signatur cor, in quo debet esse ignis devotionis; Lev. VI, 12: *ignis in altari meo non deficiet*. Per oblationes servitia et oblationes, quae nisi a corde sancto, vel ab altari sancto exeant, non possunt valere; Sup. VI, 22: *si oculus tuus fuerit simplex, totum corpus tuum lucidum erit*. Per thronum vita gloriosa signatur: ibi Deus est qui est excedens universa.

Vel per altare et templum intelligimus Christum: ipse enim se nominat templum; Io. II, v. 19: *solvite templum hoc, et in tribus diebus reaedificabo illud*. Item dicitur altare; ad Hebr. ult., 10: *habemus altare, de quo edere non habent potestatem qui in tabernaculo deserviunt*. Unde quicquid boni facimus, nisi sit in templo hoc, idest Christo, sanctificatum, non valet; unde totum contemptibile est nisi referatur ad Christum.

God swears with a certain deliberation and solemnity, and so sins more seriously.

1866. Hence he sets out the second part of the tradition: *and whoever will swear by the altar, it is nothing; but whoever will swear by the gift that is upon it, is a debtor*.

1867. Next he sets out a condemnation: *you blind: for which is greater, the gift, or the altar that sanctifies the gift?* For the gift is only made holy by the altar.

He therefore who swears by the altar, swears by it, and by all things that are upon it. Here he sets out another argument. The temple contains the gold, and not the other way around: similarly, the altar contains the gift, and not the other way around. Hence he who swears by the temple, swears by the gold which is in the temple; and he who swears on the altar, swears by that which is on it.

And there follows another argument: *and whoever will swear by the temple, swears by it, and by him who dwells in it*. These men said, *whoever will swear by the temple, it is nothing*. But he wishes to show that he who swears by the temple, swears by God, because he only swears by the temple as it is sanctified, and it is only sanctified by God. Therefore he who swears by the temple, swears by God.

Then another argument is set out: *and he who swears by heaven*, only swears by it because it is the throne of God, and because God's power is manifested there; hence, *and he who swears by heaven, swears by the throne of God, and by him who is seated there*. *The Lord is in his holy temple, the Lord's throne is in heaven* (Ps 10:5). And this is introduced by way of likeness.

1868. But mystically, according to Origen, he mentions the temple, the gold, and the altar, which things signify the contemplative and the glorious life. The contemplative is signified by the gold, which signifies the subtle thought-out sense of Scripture itself: for however reasonable it may seem, it is nothing unless it is in the temple, i.e., unless it is confirmed in Sacred Scripture. The altar signifies the heart, which should have in it the fire of devotion; *this is the perpetual fire which will never go out on the altar* (Lev 6:13). The offerings signify services and offerings which cannot do any good unless they proceed from a holy heart, or from a holy altar; above, *if your eye be sound, your whole body will be lightsome* (Matt 6:22). The glorious life is signified by the throne: God is there, who exceeds the universe.

Or, by the altar and the temple we understand Christ: for he called himself the temple; *destroy this temple, and in three days I will raise it up* (John 2:19). Likewise, he is called the altar; *we have an altar, whereof they have no power to eat who serve the tabernacle* (Heb 13:10). Hence whatever good we do, unless it is sanctified in this temple, i.e., Christ, it does no good; hence the whole thing is contemptible unless it is referred to Christ.

1869. *Vae vobis, scribae et Pharisaei hypocritae, qui decimatis mentham, et anethum, et cyminum.* Hic reprehendit eos de decimis; et tria facit.

Primo ponitur eorum consuetudinem;

secundo inducit doctrinam;

tertio ponit quamdam similitudinem.

Secunda ibi **haec oportuit facere**; tertia ibi **duces caeci excolantes culicem** et cetera.

1870. Unde dicit *vae vobis, scribae et Pharisaei*, et superaddit *hypocritae*, quia principalis intentio erat simulatio, *qui decimatis mentham, anethum et cyminum.* Potest intelligi, vel decimas datis, vel qui decimas exigitis; unde plurimi erant sacerdotes et Levitae, ad quos pertinebant decimas exigere quae eis debebantur, ut habetur Num. XVIII, v. 21 et Deut. XIV, 22, ideo diligentissimi erant ad exigendum, ideo usque ad minima exigebant, ut de cymino et anetho.

Et reliquistis quae graviora sunt legis, iudicium, misericordiam et fidem. Quaedam enim debebantur sacerdotibus propter se, ut decimae ex quibus debebant vivere; ad quaedam vero tenebantur propter Deum, ut facere iudicium et misericordiam; unde Dominus ab eis ista requirebat, scilicet iudicium et misericordiam; Ps. c, 1: *misericordiam et iudicium cantabo tibi, Domine.* Item vult fidem propter gloriam suam. Unde illa ad quae tenebantur propter Deum, non curabant, unde dicit: *et reliquistis quae graviora sunt legis, iudicium, et misericordiam, et fidem.*

Sed de decimis, ad quae tenebantur propter se, bene curabant, secundum illud Phil. c. II, 21: *omnes quaerunt quae sua sunt, non Dei.* E contrario facit caritas, quae *non quaerit quae sua sunt*, sed quae Iesu Christi, I Cor. XIII, 5.

Item potest dici vae vobis, qui decimas datis, quia datis de minimis, de mentha, et cymino, et huiusmodi, et hoc ut appareatis religiosi; sed de interioribus non curatis, quia nec misericordiam, nec iudicium, nec fidem diligitis; supra XII, 7: *si sciretis quid est, 'misericordiam volo, et non sacrificium,' numquam condemnassetis innocentes.*

Origenes dicit quod per mentham et cyminum etc. possunt quaedam intelligi, quae ad honestatem religionis pertinent. Unde misericordia, iudicium et fides sunt sicut cibi, alia vero minima sunt sicut condimentum. Unde sicut faciebant maiorem vim in condimento suo in parando cibum, quam in cibo, sic et isti magis faciebant vim in hoc quod flecteretur genu coram eis, quam in eis quae ad Deum pertinebant.

1871. *Haec oportuit facere, et illa non omittere.* Quia dixerat, *vae vobis, qui decimatis*, posset aliquis dicere quod prohiberet Dominus dare decimas, ideo dicit quod immo, cum dicit *haec oportuit facere, et illa non omittere*; quasi dicat: non peccatis in istis, sed in omittendo

1869. *Woe to you scribes and Pharisees, hypocrites; because you tithe mint, and anise, and cummin.* Here he reproaches them about the tithe; and he does three things:

first, their custom is set out;

second, he introduces a teaching;

third, he sets out a certain likeness.

The second is at **these things you ought to have done**; the third, at **blind guides, who strain out a gnat**.

1870. Hence he says, *woe to you scribes and Pharisees*, and he adds, *hypocrites*, because their principal intention was pretense, *because you tithe mint, and anise, and cummin.* It can either be understood as you give tithes or as you who weigh tithes; many were priests and Levites, to whom it pertained to weigh the tithes which were owed to them (Num 18:21: Deut 14:22), so they were most diligent at weighing, even down to the least things, like cummin and anise.

And have left the weightier things of the law: judgment, and mercy, and faith. For some things were owed to the priests for their sake, as the tithes from which they were to live; but to some things they were bound for God's sake, as to render judgment and mercy; hence the Lord requires these things of them, namely judgment and mercy: *mercy and judgment I will sing to you, O Lord* (Ps 100:1). Likewise, he wills faith for the sake of his own glory. Hence they took no care for those things to which they were bound for God's sake, so he says, *and have left the weightier things of the law: judgment, and mercy, and faith.*

But they cared well for the tithe, to which they were bound for their own sakes, in accordance with, *for all seek the things that are their own; not the things that are Jesus Christ's* (Phil 2:21). To the contrary is charity, which *seeks not her own* (1 Cor 13:5), but what is Jesus Christ's.

Similarly it can be said, woe to you who give tithes, because you give of the least things, of mint, and cummin, and suchlike, and you do this to appear religious; but you take no care of interior things, for you love neither mercy, nor judgment, nor faith; above, *and if you knew what this means: 'I desire mercy, and not sacrifice,' you would never have condemned the innocent* (Matt 12:7).

Origen says that mint and cummin and so on can be taken to mean certain things which pertain to the honor of religion. Hence mercy, judgment, and faith are like food, while the others are least, like spices. Hence, just as they put greater stress on their spice in preparing food than on the food, so also these men put a greater stress on the knee being bent before them than on those things which pertain to God.

1871. *These things you ought to have done, and not to leave those undone.* Since he had said, *woe to you . . . because you tithe*, someone could say that the Lord forbade the giving of tithes; for this reason he speaks to the contrary, when he says, *these things you ought to have done,*

ea ad quae magis tenemini. Ideo et *haec oportuit facere*, idest decimas exigere, *et illa*, scilicet iudicium, iustitiam et fidem, *non omittere*.

1872. Sed hic potest esse quaestio de decimis. Videtur Dominus ponere necessitatem solvendi decimas; unde in toto Novo Testamento non ita expresse fit mentio sicut hic. Sed numquid ex praecepto legis habetur? Non: quia in lege quaedam moralia continentur, quaedam caeremonialia, quaedam iudicialia. Moralia per omne tempus servanda sunt, et ab omnibus; caeremonialia a certis hominibus, et certis temporibus, ut circumcisio, et haec erant solum in figura; item quaedam iudicialia, ut si quis furaretur ovem, reddat quadruplum. Ideo quaeritur de decimis, utrum decimae sint praeceptum morale. Et videtur quod non, quia moralia sunt de lege naturali. Illud autem solum est de lege naturali, quod ratio naturalis suadet. Sed non plus suadet dare decimam, quam nonam vel undecimam et cetera. Ergo non est de iure naturali. Item, si decimae sint caerimoniales, ergo peccant qui solvunt eas.

Ad hoc dixerunt, qui ante nos fuerunt, quod quaedam sunt pure moralia, quaedam pure caeremonialia, quaedam habent aliquid de morali et aliquid de caerimoniali. *Non occides*, pure morale est. Similiter, *Dominum Deum tuum adorabis* et cetera. Si dicas: quartadecima luna ad vesperam offeres agnum, istud pure caerimoniale est. Sed si dicitur: memento quod diem Sabbati sanctifices, aliquid habet naturale, vel morale, et aliquid caerimoniale. Morale, scilicet quod ratio naturalis suggerit, scilicet quod habeat aliquod tempus, ad quod vacat, vel in quo vacet ad orandum Deum. Sed quod die Sabbati, vel Dominico etc., iudiciale est. Unde dicunt quod praeceptum de decimis partim caeremoniale est, partim morale. Sunt enim ad sustentationem pauperum et eorum qui vacant servitio Dei, vel praedicationi: qui enim servit communitati, convenit ei de communitate vivere, et hoc est de iure naturali; sed quod decimam partem, hoc est caeremoniale.

Sed numquid tenentur modo? Dico quod determinatio ad quemlibet principem qui habet potestatem legem constituendi, pertinet; unde in potestate Ecclesiae est constituere vel decimam, vel nonam, vel huiusmodi. Unde tenentur, non quia sit de iure naturali, sed ex constitutione Ecclesiae.

1873. *Duces caeci excolantes culicem, camelum autem glutientes*. In parte ista ponit similitudinem; unde dicit *excolantes culicem*. Qui excolat, cum difficultate transglutit. Unde vult dicere quod magnam curam ponunt in minimis, et parvam in magnis. Vel per culicem peccata minima intelliguntur, per camelum grandia,

and not to leave those undone, as though to say, you do not sin in these things, but in omitting those things to which you are more bound. So, *these things you ought to have done*, i.e., to exact the tithes, *and not to leave those*, namely judgment, justice, and faith, *undone*.

1872. But here there is a question about the tithe. The Lord seems to lay down the necessity of paying tithes; hence in the whole New Testament it is not mentioned so expressly as here. But is this gotten from a precept of the law? No: for the law contains some things pertaining to morality, some ceremonial things, and some judicial things. Those things pertaining to morality should be kept for all time, and by all; the ceremonial things should be kept by certain men, and at certain times, such as circumcision, and these were only in figure; likewise certain judicial things, such as if someone steals a sheep, he shall repay fourfold. So one may ask about the tithe whether tithes are a moral precept. And it seems not, because the things pertaining to morality are from the natural law. But only that which natural reason suggests is from the natural law. But reason does not suggest giving a tenth more than a ninth or an eleventh, etc. Therefore it is not of the natural law. Likewise, if the tithes were ceremonial, then those who pay them sin.

To this question those who were before us have said that some things are purely moral, some purely ceremonial, and some have something of the moral and something of the ceremonial. *You shall not kill* is purely moral. Similarly, *the Lord your God you shall adore*. If you say, on the fourteenth day of the month, in the evening, you shall offer a lamb, this is purely ceremonial. But if it is said: mind that you keep holy the Sabbath day, it has something natural, or moral, and something ceremonial. The moral, namely what natural reason suggests, that one have a certain time for which he is free, or in which he is free, for praying to God. But that it is the Sabbath day, or the Lord's day, is judicial. Hence they say that the commandment about tithes is partially ceremonial, partially moral. For they are for the support of the poor and of those who are free for the service of God, or for preaching: for it is fitting that he who serves a community live from the community, and this is from the natural law; but that it is a tenth part, this is ceremonial.

But are tithes binding now? I say that the determination pertains to any ruler who has the power of establishing law; hence it is in the power of the Church to establish either a tenth, or a ninth, or so on. Hence they are binding, not because they are from the natural law, but by the Church's establishing it.

1873. *Blind guides, who strain out a gnat, and swallow a camel*. In this part he sets out a likeness; hence he says, *who strain out a gnat*. He who strains out, swallows with difficulty. Hence he wishes to say that they put great care into little things, and little in great things. Or by a gnat are understood the smallest sins, and by a camel large ones,

unde faciunt vim in parvis peccatis; et hoc est quod dicit *camelum autem transglutientes*.

1874. *Vae vobis, scribae et Pharisaei, qui mundatis quod deforis est calicis et paropsidis*. Supra Dominus increpuit Pharisaeos de simulatione quam exterius praetendebant quam non habebant in corde, sed ad quaestum retorquebant; hic de simulatione puritatis quam exterius ostendebant.

Et hic primo quantum ad appetitum temporalium bonorum, vel quantum ad peccata carnalia: secundo quantum ad spiritualia.

Et primo agit de primo; secundo de secundo, ibi *vae vobis . . . quia similes estis sepulcris dealbatis*.

Circa primum duo facit.

Primo enim arguit eorum simulationem;

secundo proponit sacram doctrinam, ibi **Pharisaee caece** et cetera.

1875. Dicit ergo *vae vobis, scribae et Pharisaei hypocritae, qui mundatis quod deforis est calicis* et cetera. Notate quod istud potest intelligi dupliciter. Uno modo, quod sit locutio propria; et vult tangere morem Pharisaeorum, qui ponebant magnam curiositatem in mundando exteriora, ut habetur supra, quod servabant munditiam urceorum et vasorum; unde *vae vobis*, qui magnam sollicitudinem imponitis in mundando vasa, sed non corda. Unde sequitur *intus autem*, idest in corde, *pleni estis rapina et immunditia*.

Hieronymus vult quod sit figurativa locutio, unde vult quod intelligatur munditia omnis quae foris ostenditur. In paropside cibus ministratur, in calice potus. Homo autem paropsis dicitur; cibus autem in quo Deus delectatur, sunt bona opera quae facit; Io. IV, 34: *cibus meus est ut faciam voluntatem Patris mei*. Constat quod usus calicis et paropsidis non est in superficie exteriori, sed interiori. Ille ergo mundat calicem exterius, qui parat corpus suum exterius.

1876. Vos autem estis huiusmodi *intus autem pleni estis rapina et immunditia*. Et duo ponit, rapinam et immunditiam, quia duo sunt genera peccatorum: carnalia quae consummantur in delectatione carnis, ut gula et luxuria; alia quae in delectatione spiritus, ut superbia et avaritia, quia avaritia quantum ad obiectum se tenet cum peccato carnali; quantum ad completionem, quia completur in delectatione mentis, scilicet in cupiditate pecuniae, se tenet cum spirituali.

Unde reprehendit avaritiam, cum dicit *rapina*. Rapina autem proprie est quando accipitur alienum, sic proprie avarus detinet alienum: unde opponitur iustitiae; Is. III, 34: *rapina pauperum in domo vestra*. Item *pleni immunditia*, quantum ad gulam et luxuriam. Anima redditur impura per passionem, nulla autem passio ita deprimit rationem sicut gula et luxuria; Eph. V, 3:

hence they put a great stress on little sins; and this is why he says, *and swallow a camel*.

1874. *Woe to you scribes and Pharisees, hypocrites; because you make clean the outside of the cup and of the dish*. Above, the Lord reproached the Pharisees for pretense, because they pretended exteriorly what they did not have in the heart, but turned it to profit; here he reproaches them for the pretense of purity which they showed exteriorly.

And this first as regards the appetite for temporal goods, or as regards carnal sins; second, as regards spiritual things.

And first, he treats of the first; second, of the second, at *woe to you . . . because you are like whitened sepulchres*.

Concerning the first, he does two things:

first, he discloses their pretense;

second, he sets forward sacred teaching, at *you blind Pharisee, first make clean the inside*.

1875. He says therefore, *woe to you scribes and Pharisees, hypocrites; because you make clean the outside of the cup*. Note that this can be understood in two ways. One way, that it is a proper locution; and he wishes to touch upon the custom of the Pharisees, who put great diligence into exterior cleaning, as it is said above that they preserved cleanliness of jugs and vases; hence, *woe to you*, who impose a great solicitude about cleaning vases, but not hearts. Hence there follows, *but within*, i.e., in the heart, *you are full of rapine and uncleanness*.

Jerome would have it be a figurative locution, hence he would have it be understood of every cleanliness which is outwardly shown. Food is served in a dish, and drink in a cup. Moreover, a man is called a dish, and the food in which God delights are the good works which he does; *my food is to do the will of him who sent me* (John 4:34). It is agreed that the use of a cup and a dish is not in the exterior surface, but the interior. Therefore, that man cleans the cup exteriorly who exteriorly equips his body.

1876. And you are such men: *but within you are full of rapine and uncleanness*. And he sets out two things, rapine and uncleanness, because there are two kinds of sins: carnal sins, which are accomplished in the enjoyment of the flesh, such as gluttony and luxury; and others which are accomplished in the enjoyment of the spirit, such as pride and greed. For greed stands with carnal sin as regards its object; as regards its accomplishment, since it is accomplished in the enjoyment of the mind, namely in the desire of money, it stands with the spiritual.

Hence he reproaches greed when he says, *rapine*. Now, it is rapine in the proper sense when another's property is taken; thus the greedy man in the proper sense withholds another's property: hence it is opposed to justice. *The spoil of the poor is in your house* (Isa 3:14) Likewise, *full of . . . uncleanness* as regards gluttony and luxury. A soul is rendered impure through passion, and no passion so

fornicatio et immunditia, aut avaritia, nec nominetur in vobis, sicut decet sanctos.

1877. Tunc reducit ad sanam doctrinam **Pharisaee caece, munda prius quod intus est calicis et paropsidis**. Tota puritas exterior est a puritate interiori, ut habetur supra VI, 22: *si oculus tuus fuerit simplex, totum corpus tuum lucidum erit* et cetera. Ideo docet quod mundet cor, et sic erit totum mundum. Unde dicit **Pharisaee caece** et cetera. Sap. II, 21: *excaecavit eos malitia eorum. Munda quod interius est*, quia quodcumque fiat exterius, dummodo fiat ex bona voluntate, totum bonum est; Prov. IV, 23: *omni diligentia serva cor tuum*.

Item potest exponi de verbo hominis: unde illud quod interius est, potest intelligi intellectus Sacrae Scripturae, Eccli. XV, 3: *cibavit eum pane vitae et intellectus*, in quo propinatur sapientia. Panis sapientiae est verbum vitae. Unde quidam volunt ornare verbum exterius, et de sententia non curant. Et isti mundant quod deforis est.

1878. Vae vobis . . . quia similes estis sepulcris dealbatis. Hic arguit eos quantum ad peccata spiritualia. Et
primo ponit similitudinem;
secundo exponit.

1879. Sepulcrum dicitur ubi mortuum corpus quiescit. Mortua corpora sanctorum templum Dei sunt, in quibus Deus habitat; I Cor. III, 17: *templum Dei sanctum est, quod estis vos*. Corpus est habitaculum animae, et anima est thronus Dei: ita sicut corpus est habitaculum animae, ita anima Dei; Ps. X, 5: *Dominus in templo sancto suo* et cetera. Corpus vero peccatoris est sepulcrum, quia mortuum continet, quia anima per peccatum moritur; ideo mali sepulcrum dicuntur; Ps. XIII, 3: *sepulcrum patens est guttur eorum*.

In sepulcro est corpus mortuum intus, tantum aliquando exterius est aliqua imago, quae videtur in facie vivere; Apoc. III, 1: *nomen habes quod vivas, et mortuus es*. Et ideo dicit **quae foris apparent speciosa**, propter decorem exterius appositum, **intus autem plena sunt ossibus mortuorum et omni spurcitia**, idest omni putredine et omni immunditia.

1880. Post hoc exponit **sic et vos foris quidem apparetis hominibus iusti**, idest homines vos iudicant iustos, **intus autem pleni estis hypocrisi et iniquitate**. Comprehendit peccata carnalia, avaritiam et gulam, sicut dictum est supra, sub qua vanagloria continetur; Io. XII, 43: *dilexerunt magis gloriam suam quam Dei*. Item sub **iniquitate** omnia peccata spiritualia.

1881. Tunc cum dicit **vae vobis . . . qui aedificatis sepulcra prophetarum**, arguit eos de simulatione pietatis et duo facit.
Primo ponit simulationem eorum;

suppresses reason as gluttony and luxury; *but fornication, and all uncleanness, or covetousness, let it not so much as be named among you, as becomes saints* (Eph 5:3).

1877. Then he leads back to healthy teaching: **you blind Pharisee, first make clean the inside of the cup and of the dish**. The whole of exterior purity is from interior purity, as is said above, *if your eye be sound, your whole body will be lightsome* (Matt 6:22). So he teaches that one must clean the heart, and in this way the whole will be clean. Hence he says, **you blind Pharisee**. Their own malice blinded them (Wis 2:21). Clean what is interior, because whatever comes about exteriorly, provided that it come from a good will, the whole thing will be good; *with all watchfulness keep your heart* (Prov 4:23).

Similarly, it can be explained as about a man's word: hence that which is interior can be taken as the understanding of Sacred Scripture; *with the bread of life and understanding, she will feed him* (Sir 15:3). The bread of wisdom is the word of life. Hence some wish to decorate the exterior word, and take no care for thought. And these men clean what is outside.

1878. Woe to you . . . because you are like whitened sepulchres. Here he accuses them as regards spiritual sins. And
first, he sets out a likeness;
second, he explains.

1879. A sepulcher is where a dead body rests. The dead bodies of the saints are the temple of God, in which God dwells; *for the temple of God is holy, which you are* (1 Cor 3:17). The body is the dwelling place of the soul, and the soul is God's throne: so as the body is the dwelling place of the soul, so the soul is the dwelling place of God; *the Lord is in his holy temple* (Ps 10:5). But a sinner's body is a sepulcher, because it contains something dead, since the soul dies through sin. For this reason, the bad are called a sepulchre; *their throat is an open sepulchre* (Ps 13:3).

Inside a sepulcher there is a dead body; there is sometimes an image outside of such a size, which seems in appearance to live; *you have the name of being alive: and you are dead* (Rev 3:1). And so he says, **which outwardly appear beautiful to men** owing to the outward decoration put on it, **but within are full of dead men's bones, and of all filthiness**, i.e., every rottenness and every uncleanness.

1880. After this, he explains: **so you also outwardly indeed appear just to men**, i.e., men judge you to be just, **but inwardly you are full of hypocrisy and iniquity**. He encompasses the fleshly sins, greed and gluttony, as was said above, under which vainglory is contained; *for they loved the glory of men more than the glory of God* (John 12:43). Likewise under **iniquity** all spiritual sins are contained.

1881. Then when he says, **woe to you . . . who build the sepulchres of the prophets**, he accuses them of the pretense of piety; and he does two things:
first, he sets out their pretense;

secundo crudelitatem, ibi *itaque testimonio estis vobismetipsis* et cetera.

Item simulant dupliciter, factis et verbis. Unde

primo redarguit eos de factis;
secundo de verbis. Secunda ibi *et dicitis: si fuissemus* et cetera.

1882. Dicit ergo *vae vobis qui aedificatis sepulcra prophetarum*.

Sed quid est? Numquid ipsi male faciebant? Nonne nos hoc bene facimus, qui corpora sanctorum in capsis argenteis et aureis ponimus?

Dicunt aliqui quod non reprehenduntur de opere, sed de intentione, quia mala erat eorum intentio; faciebant enim ut memoria sceleris patrum suorum ad memoriam redigeretur hominum: unde consuetudo erat quod quando aliquod novum accidebat, quod fiebat aliquid ad memoriam illius. Unde volebant quod audacia parentum, quia ausi fuerunt interficere prophetas, esset in memoria omnium.

Sed haec expositio non consonat litterae. Ideo aliter dicendum quod non vituperantur propter hoc, sed quia non faciebant hoc nisi ut exterius ostenderent signa pietatis, sicut supra dicitur quod decimabant mentham et cyminum.

1883. Item *ornatis sepulcra iustorum*. Ornabant sepulcra, et tamen habebant animum ad interficiendum propter simulationem. Similiter, dicit Chrysostomus, est temporibus nostris, quod si aliquis faciat multa bona, ornet sepulcra, manum habeat largam, et huiusmodi; si in lapidibus aedificet, et intendat vanam gloriam, nec ambulet in viis Domini, non prodest ei.

1884. Item ostendebant verbo pietatem *et dicitis: si fuissemus in diebus patrum nostrorum, non essemus socii eorum in sanguine prophetarum*. Commune est quod in factis aliorum omnes sunt iudices austeri: unde si videmus aliquem peccantem, iudicamus grande peccatum, nostrum autem peccatum attenuamus; ideo isti filii malitiam patrum suorum cognoscebant, suam autem non; supra VII, 5: *eiice primo trabem de oculo tuo, et tunc videbis eiicere festucam de oculo fratris tui*.

1885. Tunc ponit crudelitatem eorum. Et primo in generali; secundo in speciali.

Et ponit poenam temporalem, ibi *ecce ego mitto ad vos prophetas, et sapientes, et scribas*.

Circa primum
primo describit originem;
secundo imitationem mali;
tertio minatur poenam.

1886. Dicit *itaque testimonio estis vobismetipsis, quia filii estis eorum qui prophetas occiderunt*.

second, their cruelty, at *therefore you are witnesses against yourselves*.

They also pretended in two ways, by deeds and by words. Hence

first, he refutes them concerning deeds;
second, concerning words. The second is at *and say: if we had been in the days of our fathers*.

1882. He says therefore, *woe to you . . . who build the sepulchres of the prophets*.

But why is this? Did they act badly? Do we not act well, when we place the bodies of the saints in silver and gold cases?

Some say that they are not reproached for the deed, but for their intention, because their intention was bad. For they acted so that the memory of their fathers' wickedness would be brought back to men's memory: hence it was customary that when something new happened, something would be made to its memory. Hence they wanted their parents' boldness, since they were bold to kill the prophets, to be in everyone's memory.

But this explanation does not agree with the text. So one should say otherwise, that they are not blamed for this, but because they only did this to show signs of piety exteriorly, as it is said above that they tithed mint and cumin.

1883. Likewise, they *adorn the monuments of the just*. They adorned the sepulchers, and yet they had a mind to kill for the sake of pretense. It is similar, Chrysostom says, in our times, that if someone were to do many good things, decorate sepulchers, have a generous hand, and so on, if he built in stones, and intended vainglory, and did not walk in the ways of the Lord, it would be no use to him.

1884. Likewise, they showed piety in word: *and say: if we had been in the days of our fathers, we would not have been partakers with them in the blood of the prophets*. It is common that all are harsh judges of the deeds of others: hence if we see someone sinning, we judge it to be a great sin, while we lessen our own sin. For this reason, these children knew their fathers' malice, but not their own; above, *first cast the beam out of your own eye, and then you will see to cast out the mote out of your brother's eye* (Matt 7:5).

1885. Then he sets out their cruelty. And first, in general; second, in particular.

And he sets out a temporal punishment, at *behold I send to you prophets, and wise men, and scribes* (Matt 23:34).

Concerning the first,
first, he describes the origin;
second, the imitation of evil;
third, he threatens punishment.

1886. He says, *therefore you are witnesses against yourselves, that you are the sons of those who killed the prophets*.

Sed quid mali erat eis, quia non erat in potestate eorum? Ideo videtur quod non debebat eis imputari.

Videte: aliquando filius non imitatur peccata patris, aliquando imitatur malitiam paternam. Si non sequitur malitiam paternam, non ei imputatur. Aliquando accidit quod habet bonum patrem et malam matrem, et e converso, et sequitur bonitatem patris, vel matris. Sed si uterque malus, raro accidit quin imitetur malitiam eorum. Et ratio est, quia filii malorum assuescunt malis a principio; et ei quod assuescunt in iuventute, fortius adhaerent, et ideo magis sunt proclives ad malum. Item parentes mali cum vident filios aliquod malum agere, non castigant eos; quare peccatum eorum aggravatur ita quod peccata parentum redundant in filios; Ex. XX, 5: *ego sum Deus zelotes vindicans peccata patrum in filios*. Ideo dicit **quia filii estis eorum**, qui habetis malitiam eorum; Sap. III, 12: *nequissimi filii eorum*.

1887. Unde estis filii per imitationem: et hoc est quod sequitur **implete mensuram patrum vestrorum**. Non est imperativum, sed nuntiativum: implete idest implebitis, quasi ut homo loqueretur, idest interficietis me; Io. c. XIII, 27: *quod facis fac citius*. Vel potest esse permissivum, idest, non impediemini per me; idest aliquando voluistis sed non permisi; de caetero non impediam. Ideo **implete mensuram patrum vestrorum**.

1888. Sed quid est quod dicit **implete**? Videndum quod omnia quae eveniunt, ex certo Dei iudicio eveniunt. Sed in illo Dei iudicio non statim solvitur poena, donec totaliter exaggeretur et veniat ad cumulum: unde quantum ad iudicium Dei non adhuc erat impleta culpa eorum. Unde interfecerunt prophetas, et non est adhuc impleta culpa, sed in me complebitur. Ideo **implete mensuram patrum vestrorum**. Is. XXVII, 8: *in mensura contra mensuram cum abiecta fuerit, iudicabis eam*. Vel **implete**. Patres peccaverunt, sed vos implete. Tunc aliquis implet, quando pervenit ad tantum quantum patres sui. Ideo patres vestri occiderunt prophetas, et vos implete.

Vel potest dici quod illi peccaverunt servos interficiendo, isti autem Filium interficiendo; unde impleverunt nequitiam patrum. Sed Dominus voluntarie se obtulit, et non se opposuit. Item non improperat eis peccatum suum, sed solum suorum, quia Boni Pastoris est ut iniuriam suorum reputet suam.

1889. Tunc subiungit de poena **serpentes, genimina viperarum** et cetera. Et videtur quod satis congrue loquitur de culpa. Serpens animal venenosum est, et occidit veneno suo: sic isti serpentes dicuntur, quia

But what evil was it for them, since it was not in their power? So it seems that it should not have been ascribed to them.

Observe: sometimes a child does not imitate the sins of his father, and sometimes he does imitate the father's malice. If he does not follow in the father's malice, it is not ascribed to him. Sometimes it happens that he has a good father and a bad mother, or the other way around, and he follows the goodness of the father or of the mother. But if both are bad, it almost always happens that he imitates their malice. And the reason is that the children of the evil grow accustomed to evil from the beginning; and they cling more strongly to that to which they become accustomed in youth, and so they are more prone to evil. Likewise, evil parents do not correct their children when they see them do something evil; for which reason their sin is increased, such that the sins of the parents overflow into the children. *I am the Lord your God, mighty, jealous, visiting the iniquity of the fathers upon the children* (Exod 20:5). For this reason he says, **that you are the sons of those**, you who have their malice; *their children wicked* (Wis 3:12).

1887. Hence you are children through imitation; and this is what follows: **fill up then the measure of your fathers**. It is not imperative, but declarative: **fill up**, i.e., you will fill up, as though he spoke as a man, i.e., you will kill me. *That which you do, do quickly* (John 13:27). Or it can be permissive, i.e., you will not be impeded by me, that is, sometimes you have wanted it but I have not permitted it; for the rest, I will not impede it. So, **fill up then the measure of your fathers**.

1888. But why does he say, **fill up**? One should see that everything which comes to pass, comes to pass by the certain judgment of God. But in that judgment of God, the penalty is not paid right away, until it is entirely enlarged and comes to a peak: hence as regards God's judgment their guilt was not yet filled up. Hence they killed the prophets, and their guilt is not yet filled up, but in me it will be completed. So, **fill up then the measure of your fathers**. *In measure against measure, when it will be cast off, you will judge it* (Isa 27:8). Or **fill up**: your fathers sinned, but you, fill it up. One fills up the measure of his fathers when he arrives at as much as his fathers. So, your fathers killed the prophets, and you, fill up their measure.

Or it can be said that those men sinned by killing the servants, but these by killing the Son; hence they fulfilled the wickedness of the fathers. But the Lord offered himself willingly, and did not set himself against their deeds. Likewise, he does not blame them for their own sin, but only for the sins of their fathers, since it belongs to the Good Shepherd to consider as his own the injury of those who are his.

1889. Then he adds, concerning the punishment, **you serpents, generation of vipers**. And it seems that he speaks fittingly enough about the guilt. The serpent is a poisonous animal, and kills with its venom: just so, these men

prophetas occiderunt. De vipera etiam dicitur quod pariendo moritur, unde foetus corrodit viscera matris: sic cum ipsi essent mali, vituperabant patres. Unde, vos tales, *quomodo effugietis iudicium gehennae?* Secundum iudicium hominum evaditis, sed secundum iudicium Dei quomodo evadetis? Unde oportet habere cor mundum. Iob XIX, 29: *fugite a facie gladii*.

are called serpents, because they killed the prophets. It is also said of the viper that it dies in giving birth, so the fetus gnaws up the inner organs of the mother. In the same way, since these men were bad, they disparaged their fathers. Hence, since you are such, **how will you flee from the judgment of hell?** According to the judgment of men you escape, but according to God's judgment, how will you escape? Hence one must have a clean heart. *Flee then from the face of the sword, for the sword is the revenger of iniquities: and know that there is judgment* (Job 19:29).

Lecture 3

²³:³⁴ Ideo dico vobis: ecce ego mitto ad vos prophetas, et sapientes, et scribas, ex illis occidetis, et crucifigetis, et ex eis flagellabitis in synagogis vestris, et persequemini de civitate in civitatem, [n. 1890]

²³:³⁵ ut veniat super vos omnis sanguis iustus, qui effusus est super terram, a sanguine Abel iusti usque ad sanguinem Zacchariae filii Barachiae, quem occidistis inter templum et altare. [n. 1894]

²³:³⁶ Amen dico vobis, venient haec omnia super generationem istam. [n. 1896]

²³:³⁷ Ierusalem, Ierusalem, quae occidis prophetas, et lapidas eos qui ad te missi sunt, quotiens volui congregare filios tuos, quemadmodum gallina congregat pullos suos sub alas, et noluisti? [n. 1897]

²³:³⁸ Ecce relinquitur vobis domus vestra deserta. [n. 1901]

²³:³⁹ Dico enim vobis, non me videbitis amodo, donec dicatis: benedictus qui venit in nomine Domini. [n. 1901]

²³:³⁴ Διὰ τοῦτο ἰδοὺ ἐγὼ ἀποστέλλω πρὸς ὑμᾶς προφήτας καὶ σοφοὺς καὶ γραμματεῖς· ἐξ αὐτῶν ἀποκτενεῖτε καὶ σταυρώσετε καὶ ἐξ αὐτῶν μαστιγώσετε ἐν ταῖς συναγωγαῖς ὑμῶν καὶ διώξετε ἀπὸ πόλεως εἰς πόλιν·

²³:³⁵ ὅπως ἔλθῃ ἐφ' ὑμᾶς πᾶν αἷμα δίκαιον ἐκχυννόμενον ἐπὶ τῆς γῆς ἀπὸ τοῦ αἵματος Ἄβελ τοῦ δικαίου ἕως τοῦ αἵματος Ζαχαρίου υἱοῦ Βαραχίου, ὃν ἐφονεύσατε μεταξὺ τοῦ ναοῦ καὶ τοῦ θυσιαστηρίου.

²³:³⁶ ἀμὴν λέγω ὑμῖν, ἥξει ταῦτα πάντα ἐπὶ τὴν γενεὰν ταύτην.

²³:³⁷ Ἰερουσαλὴμ Ἰερουσαλήμ, ἡ ἀποκτείνουσα τοὺς προφήτας καὶ λιθοβολοῦσα τοὺς ἀπεσταλμένους πρὸς αὐτήν, ποσάκις ἠθέλησα ἐπισυναγαγεῖν τὰ τέκνα σου, ὃν τρόπον ὄρνις ἐπισυνάγει τὰ νοσσία αὐτῆς ὑπὸ τὰς πτέρυγας, καὶ οὐκ ἠθελήσατε.

²³:³⁸ ἰδοὺ ἀφίεται ὑμῖν ὁ οἶκος ὑμῶν ἔρημος.

²³:³⁹ λέγω γὰρ ὑμῖν, οὐ μή με ἴδητε ἀπ' ἄρτι ἕως ἂν εἴπητε· εὐλογημένος ὁ ἐρχόμενος ἐν ὀνόματι κυρίου.

²³:³⁴ Therefore I say to you: behold I send to you prophets, and wise men, and scribes, and some of them you will put to death and crucify, and some you will scourge in your synagogues, and persecute from city to city, [n. 1890]

²³:³⁵ that upon you may come all the just blood that has been shed upon the earth, from the blood of Abel the just, even to the blood of Zacharias the son of Barachias, whom you killed between the temple and the altar. [n. 1894]

²³:³⁶ Amen I say to you, all these things will come upon this generation. [n. 1896]

²³:³⁷ Jerusalem, Jerusalem, you who kill the prophets and stone those who are sent to you, how often would I have gathered together your children, as the hen gathers her chickens under her wings, and you would not? [n. 1897]

²³:³⁸ Behold, your house will be left to you, desolate. [n. 1901]

²³:³⁹ For I say to you, you will not see me from now on till you say: blessed is he who comes in the name of the Lord. [n. 1901]

1890. *Ecce ego.* In parte ista ponit crudelitatem eorum, et addit poenam temporalem. Et

primo primum facit;
secundo poenam addit.
Et
primo ponit beneficium;
secundo culpam;
tertio magnitudinem poenae.

1891. Unde dicit *ecce ego mitto ad vos prophetas, et sapientes et scribas* et cetera. Et potest referri ad illud quod immediate sequitur, vel ad illud totum quod sequitur. Si ad totum, sic planiorem habet sensum. Ita dico quod estis impleturi, et quod estis serpentes et cetera. *Unde mitto ad vos prophetas, et sapientes, et scribas, et ex illis occidetis*, quia tales estis qui occidere consuevistis.

1890. *Therefore behold I send to you.* In this part he sets out their cruelty, and adds a temporal punishment. And

first, he does the first;
second, he adds the punishment.
And
first, he sets out a benefit;
second, a fault;
third, the greatness of the punishment.

1891. Hence he says, *therefore behold I send to you prophets, and wise men, and scribes.* And it can be referred to what immediately follows, or to the whole of what follows. If to the whole, then it has a clearer meaning. I say thus that you will fill up your father's measure, and that you are serpents, etc. Hence, *therefore behold I send to you prophets, and wise men, and scribes: and some of them you will put to death*, because you are the sort of men who are accustomed to kill.

Or in another way, such that it is referred to the whole. The Lord not only wills that judgment is just, but also that it appear just, that others may take example. Hence if someone has a good intention, the Lord rewards him for the good intention, and from there gives the will to execute the good work; thus on the other hand when someone has a bad intention, and is full of bad will, in accord with what it is written, *I will hedge up your way with thorns* (Hos 2:6), he arouses God's anger, and out of God's anger his malice is made manifest. ***Therefore behold I send to you prophets, and wise men, and scribes***; ***and you will kill***. And he says, ***behold***, because it is close at hand, because he sent the apostles; hence, *and you will be witnesses unto me in Jerusalem, and in all Judea, and Samaria, and even to the uttermost part of the earth* (Acts 1:8).

1892. But note that when he says, ***I send to you prophets, and wise men, and scribes***, he indicates different gifts of the Holy Spirit. *To some the gift of wisdom is given, to others, various kinds of tongues* (1 Cor 12:10). The apostles had all these gifts. They had the gift of prophecy in speaking the future; *I will pour out my Spirit upon all flesh: and your sons and your daughters will prophesy* (Joel 2:28). Likewise, the gift of wisdom, for they knew all things; *for I will give you a mouth and wisdom, which all your adversaries will not be able to resist and gainsay* (Luke 21:15). Likewise, they were scribes, because they had understanding of Scripture; *he opened their understanding, that they might understand the Scriptures* (Luke 24:45).

1893. And why did he predict this? That the disciples, thinking over what they had heard, might more easily bear it. Likewise, to establish their malice, because just as their fathers killed the prophets, so these men the apostles; hence, ***some of them you will put to death***, as it is said, that *Herod killed James the brother of John with the sword, seeing that it would please the Jews* (Acts 12:2). Others were crucified; hence, ***and crucify***. For this was the most vile death; this is why they killed Christ with this death, in accordance with, *let us condemn him to a most shameful death* (Wis 2:20). ***And some you will scourge***. Acts says that *after they had scourged them, they charged them that they should not speak at all in the name of Jesus* (Acts 5:40). ***And persecute***. This is clear, how they persecuted Paul. And above, *and when they will persecute you in this city, flee into another* (Matt 10:23).

1894. Last, the punishment is set out, which, since it seemed heavy, he confirms: ***amen I say to you, all these things will come upon this generation***.

He says, ***that upon you may come all the just blood that has been shed upon the earth, from the blood of Abel the just, even to the blood of Zacharias the son of Barachias***. It is known who this man Abel is, that he was killed by his brother Cain. But who this man Zacharias was is not known. It is written that there were three Zachariases. One was the son of Barachias, who was the eleventh among the

Alius pater Ioannis, et cuius fuerit filius non invenitur; sed dicit Chrysostomus quod fuit occisus propter Christum, quia in templo erat locus virginum, et cum sederet Virgo Maria in loco virginum, expellere voluerunt eam Iudaei a loco; quod prohibuit Zacharias eam defendens, et propter hoc occisus fuit. Alius dicitur filius Ioiadae, quem occidit Ioas in atrio templi, ideo *inter templum et altare*; unde concordat locus, sed nomen dissonat. Sed tamen dicit Hieronymus quod interpretatur 'benedictus Domini,' et designatur sanctitas patris eius Ioiadae sacerdotis. Et dicit quod ipse vidit Evangelium Nazarenorum, et ibi continebatur, *filius Ioiadae*.

1895. Sed quare sub isto Zacharia incipit, potest esse quaestio litteralis. Ratio autem videtur esse, quia etsi praecedentia magis frequentia, ista tamen inveniebantur in Scriptura. Vel aliter, quod Abel pastor, Ioiades sacerdos; ideo per istos duos significantur laici et clerici. Unde omnis poena pro occisione hominum veniet super vos. Vel aliter, quia quidam activi, quidam contemplativi; unde utrique signantur per istos.

1896. Sed *amen dico vobis, quod omnia venient super generationem istam*. Sed quomodo potest esse quod omnia veniant super generationem istam? Punitur ne unus pro alio? Ez. XVIII, 20: *filius non portabit iniquitatem patris*. Quomodo ergo super generationem istam?

Hieronymus solvit, quod consuetum est in Scriptura quod tota generatio bonorum pro una generatione sumitur, de qua in Ps. CXI, v. 2: *generatio rectorum benedicetur*. De generatione malorum supra XII, 39: *generatio mala signum quaerit*. Chrysostomus dicit sic: aliqui peccant, sed Deus non statim vindicat; unde in Ps. VII, 12: *numquid irascitur per singulos dies?* Aliqui vero numquam cum peccant corriguntur, sed in peius mutantur; II ad Tim. III, 13: *mali autem homines et seductores in peius proficient*; et tunc expectat Dominus donec compleatur malitia eorum. Unde isti, in quibus complebitur malitia, portant pondus totius quantum ad temporalem poenam, tamen quantum ad aeternam quilibet suam. Unde tanta erit quod videbitur quod pro omnibus patiantur; unde Ex. XXXII, 34, dicitur quod istud peccatum servetur usque in diem ultionis. Sicut fuit plenitudo bonorum his qui credunt in Christum, sic plenitudo malorum his qui occiderunt Christum; ideo dicit *venient omnia super generationem istam*.

1897. Sed quae est ista poena? Destructio civitatis Ierusalem. Et quoniam intendit loqui de excidio civitatis, ideo convertit se ad civitatem, dicens *Ierusalem, Ierusalem*. Et

prophets. But it cannot be understood as about this man, because there was no altar at that time. Another was the father of John, and whose son he was is unknown; but Chrysostom says that he was killed for the sake of Christ, because there was in the temple a place for virgins, and when the Virgin Mary sat in the virgins' place, the Jews wanted to expel her from the place, which Zacharias forbade, defending her, and he was killed because of this. Another Zacharias is called the son of Joiada, whom Joas killed in the court of the temple (2 Chr 24:20–22), and therefore *between the temple and the altar*; hence the place agrees, but the name disagrees. But Jerome says that the name Barachias means 'blessed by the Lord,' and indicates the holiness of his father Joiada the priest. And he says that he saw the Gospel of the Nazarenes, and it has there, *the son of Joiada*.

1895. But why he begins under this Zacharias can be a literal question. And the reason seems to be that, although the foregoing things were more frequent, yet these two men are found in Scripture. Or otherwise, because Abel was a shepherd and Joiada a priest, so these two signify laymen and clerics. Hence every punishment for the killing of men will come upon you. Or otherwise, because some are active and others contemplative; hence both are signified by these two men.

1896. But *amen I say to you, all these things will come upon this generation*. But how can it be that everything should come on that generation? Is one man punished for another? *The son will not bear the iniquity of the father* (Ezek 18:20). How then can all this come on this generation?

Jerome solves it, saying that it is a custom in Scripture that the whole generation of the good is taken for one generation, of which it says, *the generation of the righteous will be blessed* (Ps 111:2). About the generation of the bad, it says above, *an evil and adulterous generation seeks a sign* (Matt 12:39). Chrysostom speaks this way: some men sin, but God does not immediately punish them; hence, *is he angry every day?* (Ps 7:12). But some are never corrected when they sin, but grow worse and worse; *but evil men and seducers will grow worse and worse* (2 Tim 3:13); and then the Lord waits until their malice is complete. Hence these men, in whom malice will be completed, carry the weight of the whole as regards temporal punishment, yet as regards eternal punishment each man bears his own. Hence, what will be seen will be so great because it is suffered for all; hence Exodus says that this sin will be kept until the day of retribution (Exod 32:34). As there was a fullness of goods for those who believe in Christ, so a fullness of evils for those who killed Christ; so he says, *all these things will come upon this generation*.

1897. But what is this punishment? The destruction of the city of Jerusalem. And because he meant to speak about the overthrow of the city, he turned himself toward the city, saying, *Jerusalem, Jerusalem*. And

primo ponit delictum;
secundo commemorat beneficia;
tertio praenuntiat poenam.

Secunda ibi *quoties volui congregare filios tuos . . . et noluisti?* Tertia ibi *ecce relinquetur vobis domus vestra deserta.*

1898. Dicit ergo *Ierusalem, Ierusalem*; et designat ista geminatio affectum miserantis; unde dicitur Lc. XIX, 41, quod *videns civitatem flevit super eam. Quae occidis prophetas*; Act. VII, 52: *quem prophetarum non sunt persecuti patres vestri?* Et dicit, *quae occidis*, non quae occidisti, ideo adhuc in malitia perseverabant. Haec est illa Ierusalem, de qua habetur Ez. V, 6: *ista est Ierusalem, in medio gentium posui eam, et in circuitu eius terras, et contempsit iudicia mea.* Possent se excusare: *non habuimus qui diceret nobis*; ideo dicit *et lapidas eos qui ad te missi sunt*; unde misi prophetas et multa auxilia, et non cognovistis.

1899. *Quoties volui congregare filios tuos, quemadmodum gallina congregat pullos suos sub alas, et noluisti?* Designatur in hoc perpetuitas divinitatis eius, secundum quod ipse dicit, Io. VIII, 58: *antequam Abraham fieret, ego sum.* Unde ipse Christus misit prophetas, patriarchas et angelos. Quandocumque misit, *voluit congregare* et cetera. Illi congregantur qui ad dominum convertuntur, quia in eo uniuntur peccatores; disperguntur qui ab unitate separantur. Unde *volui congregare quemadmodum gallina congregat pullos suos sub alas*. Dicitur quod non est animal aliquod ita compatiens pullis sicut gallina. Gallina defendit a milvo, et vitam exponit pro eis, et congregat sub alas. Sic Christus compatitur nobis, *vere languores nostros ipse tulit*, Is. LIII, 4. Item milvo, idest Diabolo, se exposuit; Deut. XXXI, 27: *adhuc vivente me et ingrediente vobiscum, semper contentiose egistis contra dominum.*

1900. Sed contra. Dominus voluit, et isti noluerunt: ergo praevaluit mala voluntas eorum voluntati Dei.

Unde dicendum: quoties volui, feci, sed te invito, feci cum feci; unde tua voluntas impedivit quod non facerem. Vel quod misit prophetas signum fuit quod voluit congregare *et noluisti.*

1901. Tunc sequitur poena *ecce relinquetur vobis domus vestra deserta.* Totus populus honorabatur propter Ierusalem, et Ierusalem propter templum; ideo dicitur *relinquetur domus*, idest templum, vel habitatio; Ps. LXVIII, 26: *fiat habitatio eorum deserta.* Vel dicitur domus *deserta* quando caret proprio habitatore; Ps. X, 5:

first, he sets out the crime;
second, he remembers benefits;
third, he foretells the punishment.

The second is at *how often would I have gathered together your children . . . and you would not?* The third, at *behold, your house will be left to you, desolate.*

1898. He says therefore, *Jerusalem, Jerusalem*; and this repetition indicates the affection of one who feels compassion; hence Luke says that *seeing the city, he wept over it* (Luke 19:41). *You which kill the prophets*; *which of the prophets have not your fathers persecuted?* (Acts 7:52). And he says, *you which kill*, not you who have killed, because they were still persisting in malice. This is that Jerusalem of which it says, *this is Jerusalem, I have set her in the midst of the nations, and the countries round about her. And she has despised my judgments* (Ezek 5:5–6). They could excuse themselves: *we did not have anyone who spoke to us*; so he says, *and stones those who are sent to you*. Hence I sent prophets and many aids, and you did not acknowledge them.

1899. *How often would I have gathered together your children, as the hen gathers her chickens under her wings, and you would not?* In this is indicated the perpetuity of his divinity, in accordance with what he himself says, *before Abraham was made, I am* (John 8:58). Hence Christ himself sent the prophets, the patriarchs, and the angels. Whenever he sent someone, he would *have gathered together*. Those who are converted to the Lord are gathered together, for in him sinners are united; those who are separated from unity are dispersed. Hence, *I have gathered together your children, as the hen gathers her chickens under her wings*. It is said that there is no animal so compassionate to chicks as the hen. The hen defends them from the kite, and exposes her life for them, and gathers them under her wings. In the same way, Christ has pity on us: *surely he has borne our infirmities and carried our sorrows* (Isa 53:4). Likewise, he exposed himself to the kite, i.e., to the devil; *while I am yet living, and going in with you, you have always been rebellious against the Lord* (Deut 31:27).

1900. On the contrary. The Lord willed, and these men did not will: therefore their evil will was more powerful than God's will.

Hence it must be said: as often as I willed, I have done; but with you unwilling, I did as I did; hence your will set up an impediment so that I did not do it. Or, that he sent the prophets was a sign that he willed to gather together *and you would not*.

1901. Then there follows the punishment: *behold, your house will be left to you, desolate.* The whole people was honored because of Jerusalem, and Jerusalem because of the temple; this is why it says, *your house will be left*, i.e., the temple, or dwelling-place. *Let their habitation be made desolate* (Ps 68:26). Or, a house is called *desolate* when

Dominus in templo sancto suo. Unde dicitur relinquere per habitationem; ideo **non videbitis me amodo** etc., quia fui vobiscum per potentiam divinitatis, et post fui corporaliter, sed recedam a vobis. Sed iam **relinquetur domus vestra deserta et non me videbitis amodo**, nec corporaliter, scilicet post passionem, nec spiritualiter.

1902. Sed numquid est hoc verum quod nulli Iudaeorum viderunt eum, cum tamen multi conversi fuerint ad eum?

Ideo dicit **donec dicatis: benedictus qui venit in nomine Domini**, quia quando confitebimini, tunc videbitis per fidem. Vel aliter, designat occulte secundum adventum: videbant ipsum corpore, sed istam visionem non habebant usque ad secundum adventum, in quo poteritis dicere, et recognoscetis quod ego sum **benedictus qui venit in nomine Domini**.

it lacks its proper inhabitant; *the Lord is in his holy temple* (Ps 10:5). Hence, to leave is said through inhabitance; therefore, **you will not see me from now**, because I was with you by the power of the divinity, and afterwards I was with you bodily, but I will withdraw from you. But your house is already left deserted, **you will not see me henceforth**, neither bodily, namely after the passion, nor spiritually.

1902. But is it true that no Jews saw him, while yet many were converted to him?

For this reason he says, **till you say: blessed is he who comes in the name of the Lord**, for when you acknowledge me, then you will see by faith. Or in another way, he points to the second coming in a hidden way: they saw him in the body, but they did not have that vision until the second coming, in which you will be able to speak, and you will recognize that I am the **blessed . . . who comes in the name of the Lord**.

Chapter 24

Lecture 1

²⁴:¹ Et egressus Iesus de templo ibat. Et accesserunt discipuli eius, ut ostenderent ei aedificationes templi. [n. 1906]

²⁴:² Ipse autem respondens dixit illis: videtis haec omnia? Amen dico vobis, non relinquetur hic lapis super lapidem, qui non destruatur. [n. 1907]

²⁴:³ Sedente autem eo super Montem Oliveti, accesserunt ad eum discipuli secreto, dicentes: dic nobis, quando haec erunt, et quod signum adventus tui et consummationis saeculi? [n. 1908]

²⁴:⁴ Et respondens Iesus dixit eis: videte ne quis vos seducat. [n. 1911]

²⁴:⁵ Multi enim venient in nomine meo dicentes, ego sum Christus, et multos seducent. [n. 1911]

²⁴:⁶ Audituri autem estis praelia et opiniones praeliorum, videte ne turbemini: oportet enim haec fieri, sed nondum est finis. [n. 1912]

²⁴:⁷ Consurget enim gens in gentem, et regnum in regnum, et erunt pestilentiae, et fames, et terraemotus per loca. [n. 1914]

²⁴:⁸ Haec autem omnia initia sunt dolorum. [n. 1914]

²⁴:⁹ Tunc tradent vos in tribulationem, et occident vos, et eritis odio omnibus gentibus propter nomen meum. [n. 1915]

²⁴:¹⁰ Et tunc scandalizabuntur multi, et invicem tradent, et odio habebunt invicem. [n. 1917]

²⁴:¹ Καὶ ἐξελθὼν ὁ Ἰησοῦς ἀπὸ τοῦ ἱεροῦ ἐπορεύετο, καὶ προσῆλθον οἱ μαθηταὶ αὐτοῦ ἐπιδεῖξαι αὐτῷ τὰς οἰκοδομὰς τοῦ ἱεροῦ.

²⁴:² ὁ δὲ ἀποκριθεὶς εἶπεν αὐτοῖς· οὐ βλέπετε ταῦτα πάντα; ἀμὴν λέγω ὑμῖν, οὐ μὴ ἀφεθῇ ὧδε λίθος ἐπὶ λίθον ὃς οὐ καταλυθήσεται.

²⁴:³ Καθημένου δὲ αὐτοῦ ἐπὶ τοῦ ὄρους τῶν ἐλαιῶν προσῆλθον αὐτῷ οἱ μαθηταὶ κατ᾽ ἰδίαν λέγοντες· εἰπὲ ἡμῖν, πότε ταῦτα ἔσται καὶ τί τὸ σημεῖον τῆς σῆς παρουσίας καὶ συντελείας τοῦ αἰῶνος;

²⁴:⁴ Καὶ ἀποκριθεὶς ὁ Ἰησοῦς εἶπεν αὐτοῖς· βλέπετε μή τις ὑμᾶς πλανήσῃ·

²⁴:⁵ πολλοὶ γὰρ ἐλεύσονται ἐπὶ τῷ ὀνόματί μου λέγοντες· ἐγώ εἰμι ὁ χριστός, καὶ πολλοὺς πλανήσουσιν.

²⁴:⁶ μελλήσετε δὲ ἀκούειν πολέμους καὶ ἀκοὰς πολέμων· ὁρᾶτε μὴ θροεῖσθε· δεῖ γὰρ γενέσθαι, ἀλλ᾽ οὔπω ἐστὶν τὸ τέλος.

²⁴:⁷ ἐγερθήσεται γὰρ ἔθνος ἐπὶ ἔθνος καὶ βασιλεία ἐπὶ βασιλείαν καὶ ἔσονται λιμοὶ καὶ σεισμοὶ κατὰ τόπους·

²⁴:⁸ πάντα δὲ ταῦτα ἀρχὴ ὠδίνων.

²⁴:⁹ Τότε παραδώσουσιν ὑμᾶς εἰς θλῖψιν καὶ ἀποκτενοῦσιν ὑμᾶς, καὶ ἔσεσθε μισούμενοι ὑπὸ πάντων τῶν ἐθνῶν διὰ τὸ ὄνομά μου.

²⁴:¹⁰ καὶ τότε σκανδαλισθήσονται πολλοὶ καὶ ἀλλήλους παραδώσουσιν καὶ μισήσουσιν ἀλλήλους·

²⁴:¹ And Jesus having come out of the temple, went away. And his disciples came to show him the buildings of the temple. [n. 1906]

²⁴:² And he answering, said to them: do you see all these things? Amen I say to you there shall not be left here a stone upon a stone that will not be destroyed. [n. 1907]

²⁴:³ And when he was sitting on Mount Olivet, the disciples came to him privately, saying: tell us, when will these things be? And what will be the sign of your coming, and of the consummation of the world? [n. 1908]

²⁴:⁴ And Jesus answering, said to them: take heed that no man seduce you. [n. 1911]

²⁴:⁵ For many will come in my name saying, I am Christ, and they will seduce many. [n. 1911]

²⁴:⁶ And you will hear of wars and rumours of wars. See that you are not troubled. For these things must come to pass, but the end is not yet. [n. 1912]

²⁴:⁷ For nation will rise against nation, and kingdom against kingdom; and there will be pestilences, and famines, and earthquakes in places. [n. 1914]

²⁴:⁸ Now all these are the beginnings of sorrows. [n. 1914]

²⁴:⁹ Then they will deliver you up to be afflicted, and will put you to death, and you will be hated by all nations for my name's sake. [n. 1915]

²⁴:¹⁰ And then many will be scandalized, and will betray one another, and will hate one another. [n. 1917]

24:11 Et multi pseudoprophetae surgent, et seducent multos: [n. 1919]	**24:11** καὶ πολλοὶ ψευδοπροφῆται ἐγερθήσονται καὶ πλανήσουσιν πολλούς.	**24:11** And many false prophets will rise, and will seduce many. [n. 1919]
24:12 et quoniam abundabit iniquitas, refrigescet caritas multorum. [n. 1920]	**24:12** καὶ διὰ τὸ πληθυνθῆναι τὴν ἀνομίαν ψυγήσεται ἡ ἀγάπη τῶν πολλῶν.	**24:12** And because iniquity has abounded, the charity of many will grow cold. [n. 1920]
24:13 Qui autem perseveraverit usque in finem, hic salvus erit. [n. 1920]	**24:13** ὁ δὲ ὑπομείνας εἰς τέλος οὗτος σωθήσεται.	**24:13** But he who will persevere to the end, he will be saved. [n. 1920]
24:14 Et praedicabitur hoc evangelium regni in universo orbe in testimonium omnibus gentibus, et tunc veniet consummatio. [n. 1921]	**24:14** καὶ κηρυχθήσεται τοῦτο τὸ εὐαγγέλιον τῆς βασιλείας ἐν ὅλῃ τῇ οἰκουμένῃ εἰς μαρτύριον πᾶσιν τοῖς ἔθνεσιν, καὶ τότε ἥξει τὸ τέλος.	**24:14** And this gospel of the kingdom, will be preached in the whole world, for a testimony to all nations, and then will the consummation come. [n. 1921]

1903. Supra posita est multiplex provocatio Iudaeorum; nunc ponitur praeparatio per instructionem discipulorum Christi. Instruuntur autem de periculis. Et

primo ponitur interrogatio discipulorum;

secundo responsio Christi, ibi *et respondens Iesus dixit eis*.

Circa primum duo.

Primo ponitur occasio interrogationis;

secundo interrogatio, ibi *sedente autem eo super Montem Oliveti* et cetera.

1904. Occasio fuit duplex. Praenuntiatio destructionis templi, quam quidem praenuntiationem fecit facto et verbo, quia egressus est de templo. Supra cap. proximo. *Ecce relinquetur vobis domus vestra deserta*; et hoc ostendit, quia exivit; unde quia corporaliter exivit, ideo ostendit quia spiritualiter; Io. VIII, v. 59: *Iesus autem abscondit se, et exivit de templo*. Cum peccator non vult corrigi, exit dominus ab eo; Thren. I, 6: *egressus est a filia Sion omnis decor eius*.

1905. Tunc ponitur interrogatio, ibi *et accesserunt ad eum discipuli secreto, dicentes*;

secundo responsio, ibi *ipse autem respondens* et cetera.

1906. Ita *ibat*. Sed tunc *accesserunt discipuli, ut ostenderent aedificationes templi*, ut videret quam pulchra est domus, quam decora; unde in alio loco, scilicet Mc. XIII, 1, habetur: *vide quales lapides et quales structurae*.

Sed quaerit Origenes: nonne alias ibi fuerat, et nonne bene sciebat? Solvit quod non petebant ut eum docerent, vel quasi nesciret, sed ut remedium inveniret destructioni. Ita Christianus est templum Dei, ut habetur ad Phil. II, discipuli autem sunt intercessores, ne destruatur templum hoc.

1907. Tunc respondet Dominus: *videntur vobis ista magna?* Is. XXIII, 9: *Dominus exercituum cogitavit hoc ut detraheret superbiam omnis gloriae* et cetera. Unde

1903. Above, the manifold provocation of the Jews was set out; now the preparation of Christ's disciples through instruction. And they are in instructed about dangers:

first, the disciples' questioning is set down;

second, Christ's response, at *and Jesus answering, said to them*.

Concerning the first, two things:

first, the occasion of the questioning;

second, the questioning, at *and when he was sitting on Mount Olivet*.

1904. There was a twofold occasion. The prediction of the temple's destruction, which indeed he predicted by deed and by word, for he came out of the temple. Above, *behold, your house will be left to you, desolate* (Matt 23:38); and he demonstrates this, for he left. So since he left bodily, he showed that he left spiritually; *but Jesus hid himself, and went out of the temple* (John 8:59). When a sinner does not wish to be corrected, the Lord leaves him; *and from the daughter of Zion all her beauty is departed* (Lam 1:6).

1905. Then the questioning is set out, at *the disciples came to him privately, saying*;

second, the response, at *and Jesus answering, said to them*.

1906. Thus he *went away*. But then *his disciples came to show him the buildings of the temple*, that he might see how beautiful the house is, how splendid; hence in another place, namely Mark, it says: *behold what manner of stones and what buildings are here* (Mark 13:1).

But Origen asks: had he not been there before, and did not he know the temple well? He answers that they were not asking in order to teach him, or as though he did not know, but that he might find a remedy for the destruction. Thus Christ is God's temple, as is said, and the disciples are intercessors lest this temple be destroyed (Phil 2).

1907. Then the Lord responds: *do you see all these things? The Lord of hosts has designed it, to pull down the pride of all glory* (Isa 23:9). Hence he adds next, *amen I say*

subdit *amen dico vobis, non relinquetur hic lapis super lapidem*.

Estne hoc verum? Tempore Chrysostomi non adhuc totum evenerat, sed sperabatur quod veniret. Vel potest dici quod non vult dicere nisi quod destrueretur. Vel dicendum quod sicut secundum Dei provisionem aliquando restauratum est templum, sic secundum Dei provisionem, incipiente confirmatione legis novae, destructum est templum, ne sacrificia fiant in templo. Unde si non fuisset destructum, multi facti Christiani caeremonias facerent, et ad templum redirent: unde dispensatione divina factum est ut destructum sit. Et hoc habetur Lc. XXI, 6, ubi de templo dicitur: *venient dies, in quibus non relinquetur lapis super lapidem, qui non destruatur*. Sic etiam contingit quod aliquis aedificatus per bonas virtutes, si cadat per aliquod peccatum mortale, si negligens fuerit et non sollicitus, totaliter cadit et destruitur; Ps. CXXXVI, 7: *exinanite, exinanite usque ad fundamentum in ea*.

Unde vult dicere quod non solum templum, sed etiam pertinentia, quae erant umbra, ut habetur ad Hebr. X, 1: *umbram habens lex futurorum bonorum*.

1908. Posita occasione, ponitur interrogatio. Et debemus notare quod exivit et ivit ad Montem Oliveti, et significat Ecclesiam, in qua olivae uberes sunt plantatae; Ps. LI, 10: *ego sicut oliva fructifera*. Et inde instruit discipulos. Dixerat destruendum templum, ideo tria quaerunt. Primum de templo; secundum de adventu; tertium de fine saeculi. Unde dicunt **dic nobis quando haec erunt**, scilicet consummatio tuae comminationis; et de adventu tuo: *et quod signum adventus tui*; item de fine saeculi: *et consummationis saeculi*.

In Luca solum tangitur de una quaestione, scilicet de destructione Ierusalem, quia non credebant quod deberet destrui nisi post adventum secundum; unde dicebant, Act. I, 6: *si in tempore hoc restitues regnum Israel?* In Marco XIII, 3, dicitur quod solum miserunt Petrum, et Ioannem, et Iacobum, et Andream; quia isti primo vocati sunt, et magis habebant fiduciam accedendi ad eum.

In quo habemus exempla, quod illi qui diutius Deo adhaerent in contemplatione, sunt Deo magis familiares; Deut. XXXIII, 3: *et qui appropinquant pedibus eius, accipient de doctrina eius*.

1909. Isti discipuli quaesierunt de adventu, et iste duplex est. Ultimus, qui est ad iudicandum; et iste erit in consummatione saeculi. De isto habetis Act. I, 11: *quemadmodum vidistis eum ascendentem in caelum, ita veniet*. Alius est adventus confortans mentes hominum, ad quos venit spiritualiter. Infra **videbunt filium hominis**

to you there shall not be left here a stone upon a stone that will not be destroyed.

And is this true? In the time of Chrysostom it had not entirely come to pass, but it was hoped that it would come. Or it can be said that he meant to say only that it would be destroyed. Or one should say that just as in God's providence the temple was at one time restored, so also in God's providence, as the confirmation of the new law was beginning, the temple was destroyed, lest sacrifices be made in the temple. Hence if it had not been destroyed, many of those made Christians would have performed the ceremonies, and returned to the temple. So in the divine dispensation it happened that it was destroyed. And this is said, where it says about the temple, *the days will come in which there will not be left a stone upon a stone that will not be thrown down* (Luke 21:6). So also it happens that a man built up by good virtues, if he falls through some mortal sin, if he is negligent and not solicitous, falls entirely and is destroyed; *raze it, raze it, even to the foundation thereof* (Ps 136:7).

Hence he wishes to say that not only the temple would be destroyed, but also those things pertaining to the temple, which were shadows, as is said, *the law having a shadow of the good things to come* (Heb 10:1).

1908. The occasion being set down, the questioning is set down. And we should notice that he left and went to the Mount of Olives; and this signifies the Church, on which fertile olive trees are planted; *I, as a fruitful olive tree* (Ps 51:10). And then he instructed the disciples. He had said that the temple was to be destroyed, so they ask three things: first, about the temple; second about the coming; third, about the end of the age. Hence they say, **tell us when will these things be**, namely the consummation of your threats; and about your coming: **and what will be the sign of your coming**; likewise about the end of the age, **and of the consummation of the world?**

In Luke, only one question is touched upon, namely about the destruction of the temple, because they did not think that it should be destroyed until after the second coming (Luke 21:5); hence they said, *will you at this time restore again the kingdom to Israel?* (Acts 1:6). In Mark, it says that they sent only Peter and John and James and Andrew, because these were the first ones called, and had more confidence to approach him (Mark 13:3).

In which we have an example, that those who cling to God a long time in contemplation are more familiar with God; *and they who approach to his feet, will receive of his doctrine* (Deut 33:3).

1909. The disciples asked about the coming, and this is twofold. There is the last coming, which is for the sake of judging, and this will happen at the consummation of the age. About this you have, *this Jesus who is taken up from you into heaven, will so come, as you have seen him going into heaven* (Acts 1:11). The other is his coming as the one who

venientem in nubibus, idest in praedicatoribus, quia per praedicatores venit Deus in hominum mentes. Unde dubium est ad quid debet referri. Tamen dicit Augustinus quod totum debet referri ad adventum spiritualem. Aliqui vero quod ad secundum adventum. Quidam autem exponunt de destructione Ierusalem, et de ultimo adventu.

1910. Primo ergo respondet quantum ad destructionem;

secundo quantum ad secundum adventum, ibi ***sicut enim fulgur exit ab oriente***.

Circa primum duo.

Primo praenuntiat quae antecedentia sunt ad destructionem;

secundo ipsam destructionem, ibi ***cum ergo videritis 'abominationem desolationis'*** et cetera.

Ista praeambula erant et ex parte extraneorum, et eorum qui in Ecclesia continentur.

Primo ergo ex parte extraneorum;

secundo ex parte eorum qui sunt in Ecclesia, ibi ***et multi pseudoprophetae surgent, et seducent multos***.

Circa primum duo.

Primo praemittit pericula spiritualia;

secundo corporalia, ibi ***audituri enim estis praelia et opiniones praeliorum***.

1911. Dicit ergo: ita quaeritis de consummatione, tamen ante debetis esse solliciti de vobis, quod non decipiamini; ideo dicit ***videte ne quis vos seducat***. Ad Eph. V, 15: *videte itaque, fratres, quomodo caute ambuletis*. **Multi venient in nomine meo dicentes: ego sum Christus**. Aliquis venit ut missus a Christo, sic venerunt discipuli. Alii vero dicuntur venire in nomine Christi, qui dicunt se esse 'Christum', usurpantes sibi nomen quod non datur alii; Phil. II, 9: *datum est ei nomen, quod est super omne nomen*. Unde multi seductores venient, qui venient a seipsis; Christus autem non a seipso, sed a Deo; unde Io. VII, 28: *a meipso non veni*.

Licet autem hoc de antichristo specialiter dictum sit, tamen potest dici de multis aliis. Unde quia veritati non adhaeserunt, dati sunt erroribus. Et hoc accidit in Simone Mago, qui libros scripsit, et appellavit se librum Dei, Deum magnum, omnia Dei, et multos seduxit. Illorum enim est seduci qui divisi sunt in errores, quia *stultorum infinitus est numerus*, Eccle. I, 15. Unde veritas congregat, error autem dividit, et hoc est periculum. Potest etiam ad secundum adventum referri, ista enim accident circa diem iudicii.

1912. *Audituri enim estis praelia* et cetera. Hic primo ponit pericula; secundo confortat.

comforts the minds of men, to whom he comes spiritually. Below, ***they will see the Son of man coming in the clouds*** (Matt 24:30), i.e., in the preachers, for God comes into the minds of men through preachers. Hence it is uncertain to what it should be referred. Augustine says that the whole thing should be referred to the spiritual coming. But some say that it should be referred to the second coming, and some explain it as about the destruction of Jerusalem, and the last coming.

1910. First, therefore, he responds as regards the destruction;

second, as regards the second coming, at ***for as lightning comes out of the east*** (Matt 24:27).

Concerning the first, two things:

first, he foretells those things which come before the destruction;

second, the destruction itself, at ***when therefore you will see 'the abomination of desolation'*** (Matt 24:15).

These foregoing things were both on the part of outsiders and of those who are in the Church.

First, therefore, on the part of outsiders;

second, on the part of those who are in the Church, at ***and many false prophets will rise, and will seduce many***.

Concerning the first, two things:

first, he sends forth the spiritual dangers;

second, the bodily ones, at ***and you will hear of wars and rumours of wars***.

1911. He says then, you have asked about the consummation, but before that you should be solicitous for yourselves, that you may not be deceived; so he says, ***take heed that no man seduce you***. *See therefore, brethren, how you walk circumspectly* (Eph 5:15). **For many will come in my name saying: I am Christ**. Some come as sent by Christ, and the disciples came this way. But others are said to come in the name of Christ, who call themselves 'Christ,' usurping to themselves a name which is not given to any other; *and has given him a name which is above all names* (Phil 2:9). Hence many seducers will come, who will come of themselves; but Christ came, not of himself, but of God. Hence, *I am not come of myself* (John 7:28).

And although this is said particularly of the antichrist, yet it can be said of many others. Hence because they did not cling to the truth, they were given over to errors. And this happened with Simon Magus, who wrote books and called himself the book of God, great God, all things of God, and seduced many. For it belongs to those who are divided into errors to be seduced, for *the number of fools is infinite* (Eccl 1:15). Hence the truth gathers, while error divides, and this is a danger. It can also be referred to the second coming, for these things will happen near the day of judgment.

1912. *And you will hear of wars*. Here he first sets out the dangers; second, he gives comfort.

Dicit ergo: ita dictum est *videte ne quis vos seducat . . . quia audituri estis praelia* et cetera. Et hoc statim post passionem. Statim enim missi fuerunt in Iudaeam ab imperatore pessimi tyranni, qui mirabiliter eos gravabant, ita quod quasi ferre non possent. Unde *audituri estis praelia et opiniones praeliorum*, quia in praeliis multum valent opiniones; unde frequenter contingit quod pauci debellant multos; Ier. VIII, 16: *a Dan auditus est fremitus equorum eius, a voce hinnituum pugnatorum eius commota est omnis terra.*

1913. Et *videte*. Possent aliqui credere quod esset statim finis mundi; unde dicitur quod tanta fuit tribulatio, quod credebant finem mundi venisse, ideo dicit *videte ne turbemini. Oportet enim haec fieri, sed nondum finis*, quasi sit destructio Ierusalem, quia non fuit eius destructio post passionem usque ad quinquagesimum annum.

1914. Sed posset aliquis dicere: *tu dicis quod audituri sumus praelia, semper fuerunt praelia*. Respondet: *numquam vidistis talia*. *Consurget enim gens in gentem*, scilicet gens Romanorum contra gentem Iudaeorum *et regnum*, scilicet Romanorum contra regnum Iudaeorum. *Et erunt pestilentiae* et cetera.

Posset dicere: ista praelia a casu fiunt, et non ex Dei vindicta. Sed quod fiant a Dei vindicta hoc patet, quia non solum ista mala infligentur a populo, sed a Deo, quia *erunt pestilentiae*, quae ex corruptione aeris proveniunt, *et fames, et terraemotus per loca*. Et haec omnia acciderunt ante destructionem Ierusalem.

Diceret aliquis: omnia ista fuerunt a casu, et non fuerunt indicativa doloris: immo. Unde dicit *haec autem omnia initia dolorum*. Is. XIII, 8: *quasi parturientes dolebunt*. Sic exponit Chrysostomus.

Sed secundum quod refertur ad consummationem saeculi, sic exponit Origenes. Sic debemus considerare de mundo sicut de uno homine, quia cum tendit ad mortem, incipiunt debilitari virtutes vitales. Sic in ostensione universalis commutationis immittet Dominus aliquam particularem immutationem, ita quod non habebunt aliquam virtutem, et tunc *erunt pestilentiae*, quia corrumpetur aer qui servit nobis in duobus. Item corrumpetur terra, quae servit nobis in cibum, quia germinat herbas et grana, unde cibus nascitur, et haec debilitabitur ita quod erit fames in terra. Item terra sustentat nos, et contra hoc terra inquietabitur, unde fiet terraemotus. Prima duo universalia, sed hoc ultimum erit particulare, quia fiet *per loca*. Et quare non fiet universaliter per totum mundum? Ut homines videntes redeant ad cor et convertantur. Item contingit quod ex penuria rerum

He says then, *take heed that no man seduce you . . . you will hear of wars*. And this immediately after the passion. For immediately, terrible tyrants were sent into Judea by the emperor, who wondrously oppressed them, such that they were as though unable to bear it. Hence, *and you shall hear of wars and rumours of wars* because in wars rumors are powerful; hence it often happens that a few men vanquish many. *The snorting of his horse was heard from Dan, all the land was moved at the sound of the neighing of his warriors* (Jer 8:16).

1913. And *see*. Someone could think that the end of the world would come at once; hence it is said that so great was the affliction that they thought that the end of the world had come. So he says, *see that you are not troubled. For these things must come to pass, but the end is not yet*, as if it were the destruction of Jerusalem, because its destruction did not happen after the passion until the fiftieth year.

1914. But someone could say: *you say that wars will be heard of, while there have always been wars*. He responds: *you have never seen such wars*. *For nation shall rise against nation*, namely the Roman nation against the Jewish nation, *and kingdom*, namely the Romans', *against kingdom*, namely the Jews'. *And there will be pestilences*.

One might say: these wars happen by chance, and not by God's retribution. But it is clear that they happen by God's retribution, because these evils were not inflicted only by a people, but by God, for *there will be pestilences*, which come from the corruption of the air, *and famines, and earthquakes in places*. And all these things happened before the destruction of Jerusalem.

Someone might say: all these things happened by chance, and were not indicative of sorrow; on the contrary. Hence he says, *now all these are the beginnings of sorrows. They will be in pain as a woman in labor* (Isa 13:8). Chrysostom explains it this way.

But Origen explains it according as it is referred to the consummation of the age. Thus we should think of the world as one man, for when it tends toward death, the vital forces begin to be weakened. Thus in the revelation of universal upheaval, the Lord will send in a particular alteration, such that they will lack a particular power, and then *there will be pestilences*, because the air will be corrupted, which serves us in two ways. Likewise the earth will be corrupted, which serves us as regards food, for it sprouts forth the grasses and seeds from which food is made, and this will be weakened such that there will be famine in the land. Similarly, the earth upholds us, and against this the earth will be disturbed, from which there will come earthquakes. The first two universally, but this last one particularly, because it will come about *in places*. And why will it not happen universally, throughout the whole world? That men,

accidit fames, et tunc propter famem exurget gens contra gentem; et hoc poterit esse circa finem mundi.

Aliter tamen potest esse quod aliquando resurget gens contra gentem, non propter penuriam, sed propter vanam gloriam. Aliquando convenit propter iniustitias hominum. Aliquando propitiatur Deus, et coarctat malos angelos per bonos angelos, ut Ez. XIII, 5: *non ascendistis ex adverso, neque opposuistis murum pro domo Israel, ut staretis in praelio in die Domini.* Unde stat mundus per orationem bonorum. Et tunc, scilicet in fine mundi **refrigescet caritas**, et tunc erunt multa mala, quia tunc Angeli boni dimittent Daemones, qui habent nocere terrae et mari; ideo quia potestatem habent super terram et mare, commovebunt totam terram. Et quod hoc possunt, habetur Iob I, 7 ss.

Hieronymus dicit quod potest dici de adventu domini quo venit quotidie in Ecclesiam. Secundum enim quod haeretici impediunt ipsa bona ipsius Ecclesiae, tunc accidunt **pestilentiae** spirituales, **et fames**, scilicet indigentia boni documenti, Amos V, alias VII, **et terraemotus**, idest homines qui sunt solidi movebuntur.

1915. *Tunc tradent vos in tribulationem*. Tunc ponit quaedam praeambula, quae futura erant in Ecclesia. In Ecclesia futura erant prospera et adversa. Et

primo ponit adversa;
secundo prospera, ibi *et praedicabitur hoc Evangelium regni in universo orbe*.

Adversa autem nuntiat dupliciter, ab exterioribus et interioribus. Deut. XXXII, v. 25. *Foris vastabit eos gladius, et intus pavor.*

1916. Et tangit tria pericula: tribulationem, occisionem et odium.

Possent dicere: verum est quod mundus hoc patietur, sed quid ad nos? Immo, dicit. Et ideo dicit **vos**; quasi dicat, *non eritis immunes, sed tribulabimini*, ad litteram; II ad Cor. VI, 4: *in tribulationibus, in necessitatibus* et cetera. Item **occident vos**, sicut patuit quod occiderunt Stephanum et Iacobum: unde dicit Ps. XLIII, 22: *aestimati sumus sicut oves occisionis.* Item **eritis odio omnibus gentibus**, idest Iudaeis. Vel omnibus, qui diffusi sunt per universum mundum; supra V, 10: *beati qui tribulationem patiuntur propter iustitiam.* Et ponit consolationem, quia cum omnes patiantur, hoc patiemini **propter nomen meum**. Ier. XLV, 4: *ecce quos aedificavi, ego destruo*, et post: *et tu quaeris gaudia?*

Origenes dicit quod referendum est ad secundum adventum, quia ita erit universalis persecutio, quod

when they see, may return to their heart and be converted. Similarly, it happens that due to the scarcity of things a famine happens, and then on account of the famine a nation will rise against a nation; and this will be possible near the end of the world.

Yet in another way, it can be that sometimes nation will rise against nation not owing to scarcity, but for the sake of vainglory. Sometimes it comes together because of the injustices of men. Sometimes God is propitiated, and restricts the bad angels through the good angels, as, *you have not gone up to face the enemy, nor have you set up a wall for the house of Israel, to stand in battle in the day of the Lord* (Ezek 13:5). Hence the world stands through the prayers of the good. And then, namely at the end of the world, **the charity of many will grow cold**, and then there will be many evils, because at that time the good angels will unbind the demons, who have power to harm the earth and the sea. And because they have power over earth and sea, they will disturb the whole earth. And that this is possible is said in Job (Job 1:7).

Jerome says that it can be said of the Lord's coming by which he comes daily into the Church. For according as heretics obstruct the very goods of the Church herself, then spiritual **pestilences** happen, **and famines**, namely the lack of good example (Amos 5:7), and **earthquakes**, i.e., men who are solid will be moved.

1915. *Then will they deliver you up to be afflicted*. Then he sets out certain things which were to happen in the Church beforehand. In the Church there were favorable things and unfavorable. And

first, he sets out the unfavorable;
second, the favorable, at *and this gospel of the kingdom, will be preached in the whole world*.

And he describes the unfavorable things in two ways, from the outside and from the inside. *Without, the sword will lay them waste, and terror within* (Deut 32:25).

1916. And he touches on three dangers: affliction, killing, and hatred.

They could say: It is true that this world will suffer, but what is that to us? On the contrary, he says. And so he says, **you**, as though to say, *you will not be immune, but you will be afflicted*, literally; *in tribulation, in necessities* (2 Cor 6:4). Likewise, they **will put you to death**, as it was clear that they killed Stephen and James. Hence, *we are counted as sheep for the slaughter* (Ps 43:22). Likewise, **you will be hated by all nations**, i.e., by the Jews. Or by all those who are scattered through the whole world; above, *blessed are they who suffer persecution for justice' sake* (Matt 5:10). And he sets out a consolation, for when everything is suffered, you will suffer this **for my name's sake**. *Behold, them whom I have built, I do destroy* (Jer 45:4), and later, *and do you seek joys for yourself?*

Origen says that it should be referred to the second coming, because there will be such universal persecution

omnes mali persequentur bonos; et propter hoc dicit *tunc*. Consuetudo enim erat quod cum accidebant mala, dicebant hoc esse propter peccatum Christianorum. Unde insurgebant contra eos; unde **tunc tradent vos in tribulationem**.

1917. *Et tunc scandalizabuntur multi*. Hic ponit pericula ab interioribus. Est enim triplex scandalum quod patiemini, scilicet infirmorum, item mutuam laesionem, item debilitatem.

1918. Unde dicit **tunc scandalizabuntur multi**; quia etiam multum perfecti scandalizabuntur; unde supra XVIII, 7: *necesse est ut veniant scandala*. Unde etiam electi turbantur, cum vident scandala, unde dicebat Paulus II Cor. XI, 29: *quis scandalizatur, et ego non uror?*

1919. *Et invicem tradent*. Ex hoc patet tribulatio. Supra X, 21: **tradet autem frater fratrem in mortem** et cetera. Et non solum corporaliter, sed etiam spiritualiter, quia aliqui sunt principium erroris, et ex hoc sequetur quod **odio habebunt invicem**. *Et multi pseudoprophetae surgent et seducent multos*. Tales sunt qui in Ecclesia multos seducunt; II Petr. II, 1: *fuerunt et pseudoprophetae in populo*. Item I Io. II, 18: *antichristi multi facti sunt. Ex nobis prodierunt, sed non erant ex nobis*. Unde haec mala accident, quod fratres corrumpent, quod **multos seducent**.

1920. Item tertium, quia non tantum hoc facient sed etiam corrumpent, unde deficient: **quoniam abundabit iniquitas, refrigescet caritas multorum**. Apoc. II, 4: *sed habeo adversum te pauca, quia caritatem tuam pristinam reliquisti*. Potest dici refrigescere, quia cum vident alios relinquentes caritatem, et ipsi refrigerantur, licet non penitus pereat; et in multis, sed non in omnibus, quia semper fuit fervida in apostolis; Rom. VIII, 35: *quis separabit nos a caritate Christi? Tribulatio, an angustia, an fames, an nuditas, an periculum, an persecutio, an gladius?* Unde ita erit in multis, sed non in omnibus, quia **qui perseveraverit usque in finem**, scilicet praesentis vitae, **hic salvus erit**. Idem habetur supra X, 22.

1921. *Et praedicabitur hoc Evangelium regni in universo mundo*. Supra Dominus praedixit adversa in Ecclesia futura; nunc autem praedicit prospera, quia apostoli qui ex Iudaeis nati erant, aemulabantur carnem suam; Rom. IX, 2: *tristitia mihi est magna, et continuus dolor cordi meo*; ideo ad eorum consolationem, quia multo plures erant vocandi ad fidem, dicit: **praedicabitur hoc Evangelium regni in universo orbe**. Ipse enim incipiens praedicationem dixit: **poenitentiam agite: appropinquabit enim regnum caelorum**. Hoc autem **praedicabitur in universo orbe**: non enim lex nova determinata est uni populo, sicut lex vetus. Marc. ult., 15: *praedicate Evangelium omni creaturae*.

that evil men will persecute the good; and this is why he says, **then**. For it was customary that when bad things happened, they said it was owing to the sin of Christians. So they rose up against them; hence, **then will they deliver you up to be afflicted**.

1917. *And then will many be scandalized*. Here he sets out the dangers from within. For there are three scandals which you will suffer, namely that of the weak, and mutual injury, and feebleness.

1918. Hence he says, **then will many be scandalized**, because even many of the perfect shall be scandalized; hence above, *it must needs be that scandals come* (Matt 18:7). Hence even the elect are disturbed when they see scandals, so that Paul said, *who is scandalized, and I am not on fire?* (2 Cor 11:29)

1919. *And will betray one another*. From this, the affliction is clear. Above, **the brother also will deliver up the brother to death** (Matt 10:21). And not only bodily, but even spiritually, for some are the beginning of error, and from this it follows that they **will hate one another**. Such are those who seduce many in the Church; *but there were also false prophets among the people* (2 Pet 2:1). Likewise, *there are become many antichrists . . . they went out from us, but they were not of us* (1 John 2:18–19). Hence these evils will happen, that they will corrupt brothers, that they will **seduce many**.

1920. Likewise the third, because they not only will do this, but they will also corrupt, so that they fail: **and because iniquity has abounded, the charity of many will grow cold**. *But I have somewhat against you, because you have left your first charity* (Rev 2:4). It can be said to grow cold because when they see others abandoning charity, they too are made cold, although it does not entirely wither away; and in many, but not in all, because it was always fervent in the apostles. *Who then will separate us from the love of Christ? Will tribulation? or distress? or famine? or nakedness? or danger? or persecution? or the sword?* (Rom 8:35). So it will be that way in many, but not in all, because **he that will persevere to the end**, namely of the present life, **he will be saved**. The same thing is said above (Matt 10:22).

1921. *And this gospel of the kingdom, will be preached in the whole world*. Above, the Lord foretold the unfavorable things to happen in the Church; but now he foretells favorable things, for the apostles, who were born from the Jews, imitated his body; *that I have great sadness, and continual sorrow in my heart* (Rom 9:2); so for their consolation, since many more were to be called to the faith, he says, **this gospel of the kingdom, will be preached in the whole world**. For he himself, beginning the preaching, said, **do penance, for the kingdom of heaven is at hand** (Matt 3:2; 4:17). And **this gospel of the kingdom, will be preached in the whole world**: for the new law is not limited to one people, as was the old law. *Go into the whole world, and preach the gospel to every creature* (Mark 16:15).

1922. And Chrysostom says that this was fulfilled before the destruction of the city Jerusalem, and he proves this through the Apostle, where the Apostle says, *yes, verily, their sound has gone forth into all the earth* (Rom 10:18). Therefore, the diffusion of the gospel teaching will be seen throughout the world. Likewise through another authority which is found in Colossians: *the gospel, which is come unto you, as also it is in the whole world, and brings forth fruit* (Col 1:5–6). And it is no marvel, since one apostle, namely Paul, so widened the area reached by the gospel that he reached Rome and Spain; by which what is said in Isaiah is fulfilled, *you have sent your messengers far off* (Isa 57:9). And for this reason Chrysostom says that Christ's power should be wondered at in this, for in a space of less than forty years his teaching so grew that it filled the whole world; so he says well, **and this gospel of the kingdom, will be preached in the whole world**. But will all believe? No, but some will, some will not. And the fact that some will believe will be a witness against those who will not believe, as Jerome says. **For a testimony to all nations**; *we have received grace and apostleship for obedience to the faith, in all nations* (Rom 1:5), so that they are inexcusable.

And then, namely when all nations believe, **will the consummation come**, i.e., the destruction of Jerusalem. And what is said can be understood as about this: *now is an end come upon you, and I will send my wrath upon you* (Ezek 7:3). For he gave signs, he made known the Gospel, and they would not believe; so it happened to them as is said, *I will not receive a gift of your hand* (Mal 1:10).

1923. Augustine would have it that it should not be referred to the consummation of Jerusalem, but of the world; hence he says, **will be preached**, namely before the end of the world, **a testimony to all nations**, because not all will believe; **and then will the consummation come**, i.e., the end of the world. And this is one sign, that until the preaching of the gospel is made known throughout the whole world, the end will not come. Now, it had not yet come, as Augustine says, to certain barbarians in Africa. And he responds to the Psalm, *their sound has gone forth into all the earth* (Ps 18:5), that the past is set down for the future. And to what is written, he says that it was not yet fully bearing fruit, but was just beginning (Col 1:6).

And a distinction can be made in this way, that the diffusion of the gospel can be understood in two ways: either with regard to report only, and in this way it was completed before the destruction of the city, for although some had not received it, nevertheless there was no nation to which the report had not come; but if diffusion is understood with the effect, then what Augustine says is true, that it had not yet come to all the nations.

Lecture 2

24:15 Cum ergo videritis *abominationem desolationis*, quae dicta est a Daniele propheta, stantem in loco sancto, qui legit intellegat. [n. 1925]

24:16 Tunc qui in Iudaea sunt, fugiant ad montes; [n. 1926]

24:17 et qui in tecto, non descendat tollere aliquid de domo sua; [n. 1929]

24:18 et qui in agro, non revertatur tollere tunicam suam. [n. 1929]

24:19 Vae autem praegnatibus et nutrientibus in illis diebus. [n. 1931]

24:20 Orate autem ut non fiat fuga vestra hieme, vel Sabbato: [n. 1932]

24:21 erit enim tunc tribulatio magna, qualis non fuit ab initio mundi usque modo, neque fiet. [n. 1934]

24:22 Et nisi breviati fuissent dies illi, non fieret salva omnis caro; sed propter electos breviabuntur dies illi. [n. 1935]

24:15 Ὅταν οὖν ἴδητε τὸ βδέλυγμα τῆς ἐρημώσεως τὸ ῥηθὲν διὰ Δανιὴλ τοῦ προφήτου ἑστὸς ἐν τόπῳ ἁγίῳ, ὁ ἀναγινώσκων νοείτω,

24:16 τότε οἱ ἐν τῇ Ἰουδαίᾳ φευγέτωσαν εἰς τὰ ὄρη,

24:17 ὁ ἐπὶ τοῦ δώματος μὴ καταβάτω ἆραι τὰ ἐκ τῆς οἰκίας αὐτοῦ,

24:18 καὶ ὁ ἐν τῷ ἀγρῷ μὴ ἐπιστρεψάτω ὀπίσω ἆραι τὸ ἱμάτιον αὐτοῦ.

24:19 οὐαὶ δὲ ταῖς ἐν γαστρὶ ἐχούσαις καὶ ταῖς θηλαζούσαις ἐν ἐκείναις ταῖς ἡμέραις.

24:20 προσεύχεσθε δὲ ἵνα μὴ γένηται ἡ φυγὴ ὑμῶν χειμῶνος μηδὲ σαββάτῳ.

24:21 ἔσται γὰρ τότε θλῖψις μεγάλη οἵα οὐ γέγονεν ἀπ' ἀρχῆς κόσμου ἕως τοῦ νῦν οὐδ' οὐ μὴ γένηται.

24:22 καὶ εἰ μὴ ἐκολοβώθησαν αἱ ἡμέραι ἐκεῖναι, οὐκ ἂν ἐσώθη πᾶσα σάρξ· διὰ δὲ τοὺς ἐκλεκτοὺς κολοβωθήσονται αἱ ἡμέραι ἐκεῖναι.

24:15 When therefore you will see *the abomination of desolation*, which was spoken of by Daniel the prophet, standing in the holy place: he that reads let him understand. [n. 1925]

24:16 Then those who are in Judea, let them flee to the mountains; [n. 1926]

24:17 and he who is on the housetop, let him not come down to take anything out of his house; [n. 1929]

24:18 and he who is in the field, let him not go back to take his coat. [n. 1929]

24:19 And woe to those who are with child, and who give suck in those days. [n. 1931]

24:20 But pray that your flight may not be in the winter, or on the Sabbath. [n. 1932]

24:21 For there will be great tribulation then, such as has not been from the beginning of the world till now, neither will there be. [n. 1934]

24:22 And unless those days had been shortened, no flesh would be saved; but for the sake of the elect those days will be shortened. [n. 1935]

1924. Iam destructionem posuit, in parte ista ponit quod veniet consummatio: et ponit quaedam praeambula. Et

primo ponit prophetiam;

secundo admonitionem, ibi *tunc qui in Iudaea sunt, fugiant ad montes*;

tertio rationem admonitionis, ibi *erit enim tunc tribulatio magna*.

1925. Ita dixit *veniet consummatio, cum ergo videritis 'abominationem desolationis'* et cetera. Quid est quod vocat '*abominationem*'? Potest dici quod abominatio dicitur exercitus Romanorum, et dicuntur '*abominationes desolationis*', quia fuerunt desolatores terrae. Vel per abominationes idola: et de duplici idolo potest dici. Legitur quod Pilatus introduxit aquilam in templum, quod erat signum Romanorum, quod Iudaei 'abominationem' dicebant. Unde tunc cum videritis idolum positum in loco sancto, tunc potestis cognoscere impletionem prophetiae Danielis de destructione Ierusalem. Vel potest dici quod Ierusalem destructa fuit dupliciter.

1924. He already set out the destruction; in this part, he sets out that the consummation will come. And he sets out certain preambles:

first, he sets out a prophecy;

second, a warning, at *then those who are in Judea, let them flee to the mountains*;

third, the reason for the warning, at *for there will be great tribulation then*.

1925. He spoke thus: *the consummation will come. When therefore you will see the 'abomination of desolation.'* What is this thing he calls '*the abomination*'? It can be said that the Roman army is called the abomination, and they are called '*the abomination of desolation*' because they were desolators of the earth. Or by abominations are understood idols: and it can be said of an idol in two ways. It is written that Pilate brought an eagle into the temple, which was the sign of the Romans, which the Jews called an 'abomination'. So at the time when you see an idol set up in the holy place, then you will be able to know the fulfillment of the prophecy of Daniel about the destruction of

Primo a Tito et Vespasiano, et tunc combustum fuit templum, et tunc adhuc dimissi fuerunt aliqui. Postmodum adhuc aliqui rebellaverunt, et tunc Adrianus, qui successit Traiano, destruxit penitus, et dedit legem quod nullus Iudaeus ibi de caetero habitaret, et vocavit civitatem nomine suo; item posuit in sacro loco idolum. Unde illud idolum, quod posuit Adrianus, potest dici 'abominatio'; unde *cum hoc videritis* et cetera. De hac deiectione satis habetur Thren. II.

Qui legit intelligat. Et quare hoc dicit? Quia in illa prophetia Danielis multa dicuntur de passione Christi. Sunt enim haec verba observanda; unde ibi dicitur: *occidetur Christus . . . et erit in templo abominatio desolationis, et usque ad consummationem et finem perseverabit desolatio.* Unde *qui videt, intelligat* quod talia acciderunt.

1926. *Tunc qui in Iudaea sunt fugiant ad montes.* Ponit admonitionem utilem. Et

primo ponit eam;

secundo excludit impedimenta fugae.

Quaedam enim sunt impedimenta evitabilia, quaedam inevitabilia.

1927. Dicit *tunc qui in Iudaea sunt, fugiant ad montes.* *Tunc,* scilicet in tempore Vespasiani. Tunc temporis quidam dictus Agrippa dominabatur in montibus, et iste obediebat Romanis, nec rebellabat eis: unde cum aliae gentes haberent guerram, iste et gens sua in pace erat. Unde ex Dei providentia admoniti fuerunt fideles qui erant in Iudaea quod recederent et irent ad regnum istius Agrippae, et sic fecerunt: unde *tunc qui in Iudaea sunt,* scilicet fideles, *fugiant in montes*; Zach. II, 6: *fugite a terra Aquilonis* et cetera.

1928. Tunc removet impedimenta fugae. Et quia quaedam impedimenta sunt evitabilia, quaedam non, ideo primo ponit pericula evitabilia; secundo inevitabilia, ibi *vae praegnantibus* et cetera.

Quae sunt vitabilia, sunt negotia terrenorum: et istorum quaedam accidunt in civitate, quaedam extra; ideo utrumque ponit. Secundum ibi *et qui in agro, non revertatur tollere tunicam suam.*

1929. Dicit ergo *et qui in tecto, non descendat tollere aliquid de domo sua*; idest quicumque habitat in civitate, etiam si in domo, non revertatur tollere et cetera. Item et *qui in agro non revertatur,* in domum, *tollere tunicam suam,* scilicet quaecumque sint necessaria, quia cuncta quae habet homo, dabit pro anima sua. Et quare hoc dicit? Quia imminente festo Paschae convenerunt multi in Ierusalem: quod sciens Titus obsedit civitatem, cum ita

Jerusalem. Or it can be said that Jerusalem was destroyed in two ways. First, by Titus and Vespasian, and at that time the temple was burned, and some were still left then. Afterwards, some still rebelled, and then Adrianus, who succeeded Trajan, destroyed it thoroughly, and made a law that no Jew of those remaining could live there, and called the city by his own name; likewise, he set up an idol in the holy place. Hence that idol, which Adrianus set up, can be called the 'abomination'; so, **when therefore you will see 'the abomination of desolation'**. Enough is said about this degradation in Lamentations (Lam 2).

He that reads let him understand. And why does he say this? Because many things are said in that prophecy of Daniel about Christ's passion. For these words should be kept; hence it says there, *Christ will be slain . . . and there will be in the temple 'the abomination of desolation': and the desolation will continue even to the consummation, and to the end* (Dan 9:26–27). Hence, *he that reads let him understand* that such things have happened.

1926. *Then those who are in Judea, let them flee to the mountains.* He sets out a useful warning. And

first, he sets it out;

second, he excludes obstacles to flight.

For there are some avoidable obstacles, some unavoidable.

1927. He says, *then those who are in Judea, let them flee to the mountains.* *Then,* namely in the time of Vespasian. At that time a certain man named Agrippa ruled in the mountains, and this man was obedient to the Romans, and did not rebel against them. So while the other nations were having conflict, he and his nation were in peace. Hence by God's providence the faithful who were in Judea were warned that they should withdraw and go to the kingdom of this man Agrippa, and so they did. Hence, *then those who are in Judea,* namely the faithful, *let them flee to the mountains*; *O, O flee out of the land of the north* (Zech 2:6).

1928. Then he removes obstacles to flight. And since some obstacles are avoidable, some not, he sets out first the avoidable dangers; second, the unavoidable, at *and woe to those who are with child.*

Those which are avoidable are worldly occupations: and of these, some happen in the city, some outside, so he sets out both. The second is at *and he who is in the field, let him not go back to take his coat.*

1929. He says therefore, *and he who is on the housetop, let him not come down to take any thing out of his house,* i.e., whoever lives in the city, even if he is at home, let him not turn back to take. Likewise, *and he who is in the field, let him not go back* home *to take his coat,* namely whatever things are necessary, because a man will give everything he has for his life. And why does he say this? Because when the feast of the Passover is at hand, many people come together into Jerusalem. Titus, knowing this, besieged the city while they were gathered together this way. Hence he wishes to

essent congregati. Unde vult dicere: *ita cito accidet istud malum, quod non poterit aliquis sibi cavere.*

1930. Item ponit impedimenta inevitabilia. Et quia erant quaedam inevitabilia virtute hominum et simpliciter, quaedam licet inevitabilia, tamen virtute Dei vitabilia; ideo primo de primo; secundo de secundo, ibi **orate** et cetera.

1931. Illud quod cum est, nullo modo vitari potest, est onus filiorum. Quamvis enim posset alicui dici: salva animam tuam, posset dicere: quomodo possum dimittere filium? Ideo hoc exponit: **vae praegnantibus et nutrientibus**, quia tales non poterant fugere, quia nec illis erat dicendum quod abortum procurarent, nec nutrientibus ut filios occiderent; et sic impletur quod dicitur Lc. XXIII v. 29: *beata ubera quae non lactaverunt.*

1932. Item alia sunt impedimenta ubi non potest homo ponere remedium nisi per Deum. Aliquod enim tempus est ineptum vel per naturam, vel per legem: per naturam, ut tempus hiemale, quia tunc impeditur homo fugere propter asperitatem temporis. Item propter legem, ut si accidat in sabbato, quia Deus praecepit quod non irent ultra unum milliare. Et quia istud non est in potestate nostra, sed Dei, ideo **orate ne fiat fuga vestra in hieme, vel sabbato**, quia in talibus ad Deum solum est recurrendum. Unde Osee VI, v. 1: *venite et revertamur ad dominum, quia ipse cepit et salvabit nos.* **Orate quod non fiat in hieme**, quia impedit fugam naturaliter propter discrimen viae; **nec sabbato**, quia impedit secundum legem Dei.

Item notate quod dicit **sabbato**, in quo designat, quod in die festo fuerunt debite interfecti.

1933. Unde necessitas fugiendi? Ex magnitudine tribulationis. Unde

primo ponit tribulationem et magnitudinem tribulationis;

secundo ponit causam, ibi **et nisi breviati fuissent dies illi** et cetera.

1934. Dicit ergo **erit enim tunc tribulatio magna qualis non fuit ab initio mundi**. Et hoc satis potest perpendere qui legit historiam Iosephi, quod multi fame mortui sunt. Item erant seditiones in civitate, ita quod ipsi se invicem interficiebant: unde cum Titus, qui erat mitissimus, vellet eis parcere, ipsi nolebant. Item erant latrones inter eos qui interficiebant multos. Et quaedam mulier comedit filium suum. Unde fuit talis tribulatio, qualis numquam visa est. Et hoc dicit Lucas XXI, 23 s.: *erit tribulatio et cadent in ore gladii.*

Sed numquid erit maior in tempore antichristi? Sic; sed non erit inter Iudaeos. Et quaerit Chrysostomus

say: *this evil will happen so quickly that a man will not be able to take precautions for himself.*

1930. Likewise, he sets out unavoidable obstacles. And because there were some obstacles unavoidable to human power and simply, and some which, although unavoidable, were yet avoidable by God's power, therefore first he speaks of the first, and second of the second, at **but pray that your flight**.

1931. That which, when it is, can in no way be avoided is the burden of children. For although one may say to someone: *save your life*, he could say: *how can I leave my child*? So he explains this: **and woe to those who are with child, and that give suck** because such were unable to flee, since it should not have been said to them that they should obtain an abortion, nor to those nursing that they should kill the children; and thus what is said in Luke is fulfilled, *blessed are . . . the paps that have not given suck* (Luke 23:29).

1932. Likewise there are other obstacles where a man can only find a remedy through God. For a certain time is unsuitable either by nature, or by law: by nature, as is winter time, because then a man is prevented from fleeing by the harshness of the season; likewise on account of law, as if it happens on the Sabbath, because God commanded that they should not travel further than a thousand paces. And because this is not in our power, but God's, therefore, *pray that your flight may not be in the winter, or on the sabbath*, because at such times one can only turn to God. Hence *come, and let us return to the Lord: for he has taken us, and he will heal us* (Hos 6:1–2). **Pray that your flight may not be in the winter**, because it naturally impedes flight owing to the hazard of the road, **or on the sabbath**, because it impedes flight according to God's law.

Likewise note that he says, **the sabbath**, in which he indicates that they were fatefully killed on a feast day.

1933. Where did the necessity of fleeing come from? From the greatness of the afflictions. So

first, he sets out the affliction and the greatness of the affliction;

second, he sets out the cause, at **and unless those days had been shortened**.

1934. *For there will be great tribulation then, such as has not been from the beginning of the world*. And this can be judged well enough by anyone who reads the history of Josephus, for many died by famine. Likewise, there were riots in the city, such that they were killing one another: hence when Titus, who was most meek, wished to spare them, they did not want it. Likewise there were robbers among them who killed many. And a certain woman ate her own child. So there was such an affliction as had never been seen. And Luke says this: *there will be great distress . . . and they will fall by the edge of the sword* (Luke 21:23).

But will it not be greater in the time of the antichrist? Yes, but it will not be among the Jews. And Chrysostom

1935. And since they could say that these things happened to them because of the sins of the Christians, he says that they did not; hence, **and unless those days had been shortened, no flesh would be saved**. Augustine says that some have explained it this way, that the days were made shorter at that time just as they were made longer in the time of Josue. But the Psalm contradicts this: *by your ordinance the day goes on* (Ps 118:91). So it can be said in two ways. First, that the days of the affliction were shortened first of all in number. Hence if that time had lasted, all would have been killed, for no one would have remained. And why? Because the Romans ruled the whole world, and the Jews were already scattered over the whole world, so if that time had lasted, they would have been killed everywhere on the earth.

Or, the days are called **shortened** when the evils are shortened. And why are they shortened? **For the sake of the elect**, not that God's word would perish. For many were converted from that people, and they prayed for the people that a seed might be left; *except the Lord of hosts had left us seed, we had been as Sodom* (Isa 1:9).

1936. Then Chrysostom sets out two considerations as to why this is said, for some disciples were there, and likewise John was alive afterwards. So he says that John does not mention this in his gospel because he wrote after it happened, so he would have said things that had already happened; but Matthew and Luke, who wrote beforehand, mention it, because at that time it was yet to happen. So he says that the miracle became manifest when the Romans fought the Jews, and almost the whole Jewish nation suffered the destruction, the miracle being that so few Jews were able to go through the whole world to convert almost the whole world, and this was the marvelous strength of Christ.

1937. Hilary explains that these words are referred to the end of the world. **When therefore you will see the 'abomination'**, this names the antichrist. *That you be not easily moved from your sense, nor be terrified, neither by spirit, nor by word . . . as if the day of the Lord were at hand. Let no man deceive you by any means* (2 Thess 2:2–3).

Then those who are in Judea, let them flee to the mountains; for the Jews will die away, so they will flee the land of the Jews and be converted to the mountains of Christianity. **And he who is on the housetop, let him not come down to take any thing out of his house**. He wishes to say that the perfect should not be moved from their perfection. So he touches on the contemplative life, which is signified by the

qui in agro, tangit vitam activam. Tales non revertantur ad pristinam vitam, sed maneant in suo proposito.

1938. Et quid per praegnantes? Homines graves peccatis. Homines nutrientes sunt homines imperfecti. Unde vult dicere: *quod vae hominibus oneratis peccatis, et non confirmatis*.

Secundum Augustinum praegnantes sunt qui concipiunt male agere; nutrientes, qui iam opere complent.

Et quid dicit **hieme** et **sabbato**? Per hiemem signatur tristitia, per sabbatum laetitia. Unde ne fiat in hieme per tristitiam absorbentem, vel sabbato per laetitiam animum elevantem. Vel per sabbatum otium bonae operationis, per hiemem refrigerationem caritatis. *Et nisi breviati fuissent dies illi*; quia parum durabit, et si duraret *non salva fieret omnis caro*, idest omnis carnalis.

1939. Item possunt referri ad adventum Christi per Ecclesiam; et sic dicit Origenes quod sicut verbum Evangelii divulgatum est adveniente ipso, sic falsa doctrina divulgabitur adveniente antichristo; et sicut Christus habuit suos prophetas, sic et antichristus. *Tunc qui in civitate fugiant ad montes*, perfectae iustitiae. Praegnantes dicuntur, qui adhuc percurrunt verbum salutis; nutrientes qui aliquid iam fecerunt. *Orate ergo* ut non impediantur per desidiam et torporem. *Erit tunc tribulatio magna*, quia erit perversio doctrinae Christianae per falsam doctrinam. *Et nisi essent dies breviati*, scilicet documento doctrinae, per additamenta verae doctrinae, *non fieret salva omnis caro*, idest omnes converterentur ad falsam doctrinam.

roof; hence such men should not withdraw from their contemplation. Likewise, **he who is in the field** touches on the active life. Such men should not turn back to their original life, but should endure in their intention.

1938. And what do the pregnant women signify? Men heavy with sins. Those who nurse are imperfect men. So he wishes to say: *woe to men burdened with sins, and not firmly based*.

According to Augustine, the pregnant ones are those who think to act badly; those nursing are those who have already completed the act.

And what does he call **winter** and **the sabbath**? The winter signifies sorrow, and the Sabbath, joy. So lest it happen in winter through absorbing sorrow, or on the Sabbath through joy lifting up the soul. Or the Sabbath signifies the leisure of good works, and the winter the cooling action of charity. **And unless those days had been shortened**, for they will last a very little while, and if they lasted, **no flesh would be saved**, i.e., no carnal man.

1939. Likewise, they can be referred to the coming of Christ through the Church; and thus Origen says that, just as the word of the gospel was made known by his coming, so false teaching will be spread abroad by the coming of the antichrist. And just as Christ had his prophets, so also the antichrist. **Then those who are in Judea, let them flee to the mountains** of perfect righteousness. Those are called pregnant who are still looking over the word of salvation; those are called nursing who have already done something. **Pray therefore** that they not be impeded by sloth and torpor. **For there will be great tribulation then**, for Christian teaching will be perverted by false teaching. **And unless those days had been shortened**, namely by the instruction of teaching, through the addition of true teaching, **no flesh would be saved**, i.e., all would be converted to false teaching.

Lecture 3

24:23 Tunc si quis vobis dixerit: ecce hic Christus, aut illic, nolite credere. [n. 1941]

24:24 Surgent enim pseudochristi et pseudoprophetae, et dabunt signa magna et prodigia, ita ut in errorem inducantur, si fieri potest, etiam electi. [n. 1942]

24:25 Ecce praedixi vobis. [n. 1948]

24:26 Si ergo dixerint vobis: ecce in deserto est, nolite exire; ecce in penetralibus, nolite credere. [n. 1949]

24:27 Sicut enim fulgur exit ab oriente, et paret usque in occidentem, ita erit et adventus Filii hominis. [n. 1953]

24:28 Ubicumque fuerit corpus, illic congregabuntur et aquilae. [n. 1955]

24:29 Statim autem, post tribulationem dierum illorum, sol obscurabitur, et luna non dabit lumen suum, et stellae cadent de caelo, et virtutes caelorum commovebuntur, [n. 1956]

24:30 et tunc parebit signum Filii hominis in caelo, et tunc plangent omnes tribus terrae, et videbunt Filium hominis venientem in nubibus caeli cum virtute multa et maiestate. [n. 1961]

24:31 Et mittet angelos suos cum tuba et voce magna, et congregabunt electos eius a quatuor ventis, a summis caelorum usque ad terminos eorum. [n. 1970]

24:32 Ab arbore autem fici discite parabolam: cum iam ramus eius tener fuerit, et folia nata, scitis quia prope est aestas: [n. 1975]

24:33 ita et vos cum videritis haec omnia, scitote quia prope est in ianuis. [n. 1978]

24:23 Τότε ἐάν τις ὑμῖν εἴπῃ· ἰδοὺ ὧδε ὁ χριστός, ἤ· ὧδε, μὴ πιστεύσητε·

24:24 ἐγερθήσονται γὰρ ψευδόχριστοι καὶ ψευδοπροφῆται καὶ δώσουσιν σημεῖα μεγάλα καὶ τέρατα ὥστε πλανῆσαι, εἰ δυνατόν, καὶ τοὺς ἐκλεκτούς.

24:25 ἰδοὺ προείρηκα ὑμῖν.

24:26 ἐὰν οὖν εἴπωσιν ὑμῖν· ἰδοὺ ἐν τῇ ἐρήμῳ ἐστίν, μὴ ἐξέλθητε· ἰδοὺ ἐν τοῖς ταμείοις, μὴ πιστεύσητε·

24:27 ὥσπερ γὰρ ἡ ἀστραπὴ ἐξέρχεται ἀπὸ ἀνατολῶν καὶ φαίνεται ἕως δυσμῶν, οὕτως ἔσται ἡ παρουσία τοῦ υἱοῦ τοῦ ἀνθρώπου·

24:28 ὅπου ἐὰν ᾖ τὸ πτῶμα, ἐκεῖ συναχθήσονται οἱ ἀετοί.

24:29 Εὐθέως δὲ μετὰ τὴν θλῖψιν τῶν ἡμερῶν ἐκείνων ὁ ἥλιος σκοτισθήσεται, καὶ ἡ σελήνη οὐ δώσει τὸ φέγγος αὐτῆς, καὶ οἱ ἀστέρες πεσοῦνται ἀπὸ τοῦ οὐρανοῦ, καὶ αἱ δυνάμεις τῶν οὐρανῶν σαλευθήσονται.

24:30 καὶ τότε φανήσεται τὸ σημεῖον τοῦ υἱοῦ τοῦ ἀνθρώπου ἐν οὐρανῷ, καὶ τότε κόψονται πᾶσαι αἱ φυλαὶ τῆς γῆς καὶ ὄψονται τὸν υἱὸν τοῦ ἀνθρώπου ἐρχόμενον ἐπὶ τῶν νεφελῶν τοῦ οὐρανοῦ μετὰ δυνάμεως καὶ δόξης πολλῆς·

24:31 καὶ ἀποστελεῖ τοὺς ἀγγέλους αὐτοῦ μετὰ σάλπιγγος μεγάλης, καὶ ἐπισυνάξουσιν τοὺς ἐκλεκτοὺς αὐτοῦ ἐκ τῶν τεσσάρων ἀνέμων ἀπ᾽ ἄκρων οὐρανῶν ἕως [τῶν] ἄκρων αὐτῶν.

24:32 Ἀπὸ δὲ τῆς συκῆς μάθετε τὴν παραβολήν· ὅταν ἤδη ὁ κλάδος αὐτῆς γένηται ἁπαλὸς καὶ τὰ φύλλα ἐκφύῃ, γινώσκετε ὅτι ἐγγὺς τὸ θέρος·

24:33 οὕτως καὶ ὑμεῖς, ὅταν ἴδητε πάντα ταῦτα, γινώσκετε ὅτι ἐγγύς ἐστιν ἐπὶ θύραις.

24:23 Then if any man will say to you: look, here is Christ, or there, do not believe him. [n. 1941]

24:24 For there will arise false Christs and false prophets, and will show great signs and wonders, so as to deceive (if possible) even the elect. [n. 1942]

24:25 Behold I have told it to you, beforehand. [n. 1948]

24:26 If therefore they will say to you: behold he is in the desert, do not go out: behold he is in the closets, believe it not. [n. 1949]

24:27 For as lightning comes out of the east, and appears even into the west; so will the coming of the Son of man be. [n. 1953]

24:28 Wherever the body will be, there will the eagles also be gathered together. [n. 1955]

24:29 And immediately after the tribulation of those days, the sun will be darkened and the moon will not give her light, and the stars will fall from heaven, and the powers of heaven will be moved, [n. 1956]

24:30 and then there will appear the sign of the Son of man in heaven; and then will all tribes of the earth mourn, and they will see the Son of man coming in the clouds of heaven with much power and majesty. [n. 1961]

24:31 And he will send his angels with a trumpet, and a great voice, and they will gather together his elect from the four winds, from the farthest parts of the heavens to the utmost bounds of them. [n. 1970]

24:32 And from the fig tree learn a parable: when its branch is now tender, and the leaves come out, you know that summer is close. [n. 1975]

24:33 So you also, when you will see all these things, know that it is close, even at the doors. [n. 1978]

24:34 Amen dico vobis, quia non praeteribit haec generatio donec omnia haec fiant. [n. 1979]

24:35 Caelum et terra transibunt, verba vero mea non praeteribunt. [n. 1980]

24:36 De die autem illa et hora nemo scit, neque angeli caelorum, nisi solus Pater. [n. 1981]

24:37 Sicut autem in diebus Noe, ita erit et adventus Filii hominis. [n. 1985]

24:38 Sicut enim erant in diebus ante diluvium comedentes et bibentes, nubentes et nuptui tradentes, usque ad eum diem quo intravit Noe in arcam, [n. 1987]

24:39 et non cognoverunt donec venit diluvium et tulit omnes: ita erit et adventus Filii hominis. [n. 1987]

24:40 Tunc duo erunt in agro, unus assumetur, et unus relinquetur. [n. 1989]

24:41 Duae molentes in mola: una assumetur, et una relinquetur. Duo in lecto: unus assumetur, et unus relinquetur. [n. 1989]

24:34 ἀμὴν λέγω ὑμῖν ὅτι οὐ μὴ παρέλθῃ ἡ γενεὰ αὕτη ἕως ἂν πάντα ταῦτα γένηται.

24:35 ὁ οὐρανὸς καὶ ἡ γῆ παρελεύσεται, οἱ δὲ λόγοι μου οὐ μὴ παρέλθωσιν.

24:36 Περὶ δὲ τῆς ἡμέρας ἐκείνης καὶ ὥρας οὐδεὶς οἶδεν, οὐδὲ οἱ ἄγγελοι τῶν οὐρανῶν οὐδὲ ὁ υἱός, εἰ μὴ ὁ πατὴρ μόνος.

24:37 Ὥσπερ γὰρ αἱ ἡμέραι τοῦ Νῶε, οὕτως ἔσται ἡ παρουσία τοῦ υἱοῦ τοῦ ἀνθρώπου.

24:38 ὡς γὰρ ἦσαν ἐν ταῖς ἡμέραις [ἐκείναις] ταῖς πρὸ τοῦ κατακλυσμοῦ τρώγοντες καὶ πίνοντες, γαμοῦντες καὶ γαμίζοντες, ἄχρι ἧς ἡμέρας εἰσῆλθεν Νῶε εἰς τὴν κιβωτόν,

24:39 καὶ οὐκ ἔγνωσαν ἕως ἦλθεν ὁ κατακλυσμὸς καὶ ἦρεν ἅπαντας, οὕτως ἔσται [καὶ] ἡ παρουσία τοῦ υἱοῦ τοῦ ἀνθρώπου.

24:40 τότε δύο ἔσονται ἐν τῷ ἀγρῷ, εἷς παραλαμβάνεται καὶ εἷς ἀφίεται·

24:41 δύο ἀλήθουσαι ἐν τῷ μύλῳ, μία παραλαμβάνεται καὶ μία ἀφίεται. [δύο ἐπὶ κλίνης μιᾶς, εἷς παραλαμβάνεται καὶ εἷς ἀφίεται.]

24:34 Amen I say to you, that this generation will not pass, till all these things will be done. [n. 1979]

24:35 Heaven and earth will pass, but my words will not pass. [n. 1980]

24:36 But of that day and hour no one knows, not the angels of heaven, but the Father alone. [n. 1981]

24:37 And as in the days of Noah, so will the coming of the Son of man also be. [n. 1985]

24:38 For as in the days before the flood, they were eating and drinking, marrying and giving in marriage, even until that day in which Noah entered into the ark, [n. 1987]

24:39 and they did not know till the flood came, and took them all away; so also will the coming of the Son of man be. [n. 1987]

24:40 Then two will be in the field; one will be taken, and one will be left. [n. 1989]

24:41 Two women will be grinding at the mill; one will be taken, and one will be left. Two will be in one bed; one will be taken, and one left. [n. 1989]

1940. Postquam Dominus respondit interrogationi discipulorum de destructione civitatis, hic incipit respondere his quae ad secundum adventum pertinent. Iste autem adventus est adventus ad iudicium: ideo dividitur, quia

primo proponit signa et modum veniendi;

secundo tractat de iudicio, infra XXV, 1 *simile est regnum caelorum decem virginibus*.

Circa primum duo facit.

Primo praemittit signa praecedentia Christi adventum;

secundo agit de ipso, ibi *et videbunt Filium hominis* et cetera.

Circa primum duo, quia duo praecedentia erunt,

primo ex parte hominum, et electorum;

secundo ex parte elementorum ibi *statim autem post tribulationem dierum illorum sol obscurabitur* et cetera.

Circa primum duo facit.

1940. After the Lord responded to the disciples' questions about the destruction of the city, here he begins to respond to those which pertain to the second coming. And this coming is a coming for judgment: so it is divided, for

first, he sets forth the signs and manner of the coming;

second, he treats of the judgment, below, **then will the kingdom of heaven be like ten virgins** (Matt 25:1).

Concerning the first, he does two things:

first, he sets out signs which precede Christ's coming;

second, he treats of himself, at **and they will see the Son of man coming**.

Concerning the first, two things, for two things will precede:

first, on the part of men, and of the elect;

second, on the part of the elements, at **immediately after the tribulation of those days, the sun will be darkened**.

Concerning the first, he does two things:

first, he sets out a certain warning;

second, the reason for this warning, at ***for there will arise false Christs and false prophets***.

1941. He says therefore, ***then if any man will say to you: look, here is Christ***.

One should note that this ***then*** does not name a determinate time, but an indistinct time, for this did not happen immediately after the destruction of Jerusalem, but is expected to happen at the end. A similar thing is said above (Matt 2), that the Lord lived in Nazareth, from which he is called a Nazarene, and there follows: ***in those dayes came John the Baptist preaching in the desert of Judea*** (Matt 3:1), not because he came then, because there were perhaps twenty years between the two times, so it is taken as an indistinct time. So it is here. For in the future many seducers will come, and they shall say that the antichrist is God. ***Then if any man will say to you: look, here is Christ, or there, do not believe him***. *That you be not easily moved from your sense, nor be terrified, neither by spirit, nor by word, nor by epistle, as sent from us, as if the day of the Lord were at hand* (2 Thess 2:2).

1942. Then when he says, ***for there will arise false Christs and false prophets***, he gives the reason for the warning. And

first, he sets out a reason from necessity;

second, from falsity of teaching, at ***for as lightning comes out of the east***.

Concerning the first, he does three things:

first, he introduces the seducers;

second, the violence of the seduction;

third, a warning.

1943. It says then, you say that there will be some who call themselves the Christ: but will there not be others? Yes, ***for there will arise false Christs***, i.e., those who call themselves Christs, and this happened before the destruction of Jerusalem; *as you have heard that antichrist comes, even now there are become many antichrists* (1 John 2:18).

And false prophets. For just as Christ had true prophets who foretold him, so the antichrist has false prophets; and this is what is said, *many false prophets are gone out into the world* (1 John 4:1).

1944. But will they work miracles and marvelous effects? Hence, ***and will show great signs and wonders***; *whose coming is according to the working of satan, in all power, and signs, and lying wonders* (2 Thess 2:9); *and I saw from the mouth of the dragon, and from the mouth of the beast, and from the mouth of the false prophet, three unclean spirits like frogs* (Rev 16:13).

1945. But there is a question: can demons work miracles?

One should say that they cannot, if miracle be taken properly, for properly a miracle is not that which comes about beyond the order of some particular cause, but when

ordinem totius creaturae, et hoc fit per solam virtutem divinam. Sed bene possibile est, quod creatura superior non contineatur in ordine creaturae inferioris; unde aliquid fit per virtutem superiorum, quod non fit per virtutem elementorum: sic in hominibus aliquis facit per artificium aliquid, quod mirum videtur aliis. Sic de daemonibus, quia subtilioris sunt intelligentiae; ideo sicut artifices aliqui aliquid faciunt quod videtur mirum aliis, sic et daemones aliqua faciunt naturaliter, quae videntur nobis mira.

1946. Sed quomodo fiet istud? Opinio fuit Avicennae quod natura corporalis obedit ad nutum intelligentis, unde ad apprehensionem immutatur corpus. Sed Augustinus istud amovet, quia non obedit ad nutum alicuius creaturae, sed solius Dei.

Ideo dicendum quod in rebus naturalibus sunt virtutes determinatae ad procreandum aliqua, ut ranas, et huiusmodi: istas virtutes noverunt melius daemones quam alii. Et hoc probat Augustinus, quia ignis qui descendit super oves Iob fuit naturalis. Potest enim excitare corpora, et congregare, ut faciant talia miracula. Illa vero miracula quae non procedunt ex virtute alicuius rei naturalis, haec non possunt facere, scilicet ut mortuus suscitetur. Unde talia non faciunt nisi in praestigiis, ut Simon Magus fecit movere caput. Unde ista quae non fiunt ex virtute naturae, non possunt; unde *dabunt signa magna*, idest, quae homines reputant magna.

1947. Sed quis erit effectus? *Ita ut in errorem inducantur, si fieri potest, etiam electi*. Et dicit Origenes quod sermo dictus est per exaggerationem, quia quicumque homo est in hac vita, si secundum se consideretur, seduci potest; tamen, comparando ad electionem Dei, ut sit sensus, electum seduci, hoc est impossibile. Ideo aggravando dicit quod tanta erit vis, quod nisi praeservarentur ex praedestinatione divina, seducerentur.

Vel dicendum quod non vere electi, sed electi secundum apparentiam; I ad Tim. I, 19: *quam quidam repellentes circa fidem naufragaverunt*; Is. XIX, 14: *dominus miscuit spiritum vertiginis in medio eius, et errare fecerunt Aegyptum*.

1948. *Ecce praedixi*, quia, secundum Gregorium, minus nocent iacula quae praevidentur: Amos III, 7: *non faciet dominus verbum, nisi revelaverit secretum suum*.

1949. Unde *si dixerint vobis: ecce in deserto est, nolite exire*. Posita necessitate in generali, ponit magis in speciali: *si dixerint vobis, ecce in deserto* et cetera.

Notandum quod vera doctrina fit in publico, supra X, 27: *quod dico vobis in occulto, dicite super tecta*, sed

something comes about beyond the order of all creation, and this only happens by the divine power. But it is quite possible that a higher creature not be contained in the order of a lower creature. So, for example, things come about through a higher power which do not come about through the power of the elements: thus among men one man does something through art which seems like a marvel to others. So it is with the demons, for their minds are more subtle, so just as some artisans do something which seems like a marvel to others, so also the demons do some things naturally which seem like marvels to us.

1946. But how does this happen? Avicenna's opinion was that a bodily nature obeys the command of an intelligent one, so that the body is changed to the perception. But Augustine rules this out, because it does not completely obey any creature, but only God.

Therefore one should say that there are powers in natural things which are determined toward producing certain things, such as frogs, and such; the demons know these powers better than others do. And Augustine proves this, because the fire which fell on the flocks of Job was natural (Job 1:16). For a demon can arouse bodies, and gather them together, so that they do these sorts of miracles. But a miracle which does not proceed from the power of some natural thing, this they cannot do, for example that the dead be raised. Hence they do such things only in illusions, as Simon Magus made a head move. So they are not capable of those things which do not come about by the power of nature; hence they *shall show great signs*, i.e., signs which men consider great.

1947. But what will be the effect? *So as to deceive (if possible) even the elect*. And Origen says that this is said by way of exaggeration, because any man who is in this life, if he be considered in himself, can be seduced; nevertheless, considering the election of God, so that the meaning would be 'to seduce the elect,' it is impossible. So he says by way of exaggeration that the strength of the seduction will be so great that unless they were preserved by divine predestination, they would be seduced.

Or, one should say that he means not the truly elect, but the elect according to appearances; *which some rejecting have made shipwreck concerning the faith* (1 Tim 1:19); *the Lord has mingled in the midst thereof the spirit of giddiness: and they have caused Egypt to err* (Isa 19:14).

1948. *Behold I have told it to you, beforehand*, because, according to Gregory, a spear which is seen beforehand does less harm; *for the Lord God does nothing without revealing his secret to his servants the prophets* (Amos 3:7).

1949. *If therefore they will say to you: behold he is in the desert, do not go out*. Having set out the necessity in general, he sets it out more particularly: *if therefore they will say to you: behold he is in the desert*.

Note that true teaching happens in public. Above, *that which you hear in the ear, preach upon the housetops*

falsa semper quaerit angulos, Prov. I, 20: *sapientia dat vocem in plateis.* Unde veritas est lumen, et quaerit in lumine videri: sed si fuerit perversum dogma, quaerit occulta. Prov. IX, 14: *sapientia sedet in foribus,* et sequitur *aquae furtivae dulciores sunt.* Unde desertus est locus occultus, quia caret hominibus, vel quia est interclusus; unde **si dixerint vobis, ecce in deserto est, nolite exire**.

1950. Et quid vult dicere? Isti infideles et haeretici, dum sunt fideles in societate vel congregatione non possunt decipere, sed nituntur quod a societate separentur, et tunc decipiunt; et hoc est quod vult dicere: **si dixerint vobis, ecce in deserto est, nolite exire**. Nolite a bona societate et congregatione separari. Item, **si in penetralibus**, quia semper intendunt locum secretum, nec doctrinam in publico audent dicere; unde Io. XVIII, v. 20: *ego palam locutus sum mundo.* **Nolite credere**, quia *qui cito credit, levis est corde*, Eccli. XIX, 4.

1951. Secundum Hieronymum potest retorqueri ad tempus ante destructionem: sed melius est ut retorqueatur ad finem. Item potest intelligi de seductione facta in Ecclesia. Pseudochristi dant documentum mendacii, et dicitur unum documentum, quia omnia in uno uniuntur: et quodlibet mendacium habet suos prophetas; unde dicunt: **hic est Christus, aut illic**; Ez. XIII, 6: *perseveraverunt confirmare sermonem*; et aliquando volunt confirmare per Scripturas apocryphas, aliquando per occultos sensus Scripturae. Quando per apocryphas, dicunt quod **in deserto** est; quando per occultos sensus, dicunt quod **in penetralibus**.

1952. Vel secundum Augustinum vera doctrina duo habet, quia et idem in omni loco et publice proferri debet, et ab istis deficit haeresis; unde dicit **hic est Christus**, idest in hac terra, et non in alia. Item, quia doctrina sua non est publica, ideo dicunt **in penetralibus** est; unde **nolite credere**.

1953. *Sicut enim fulgur exit ab oriente* et cetera. Hic aliam rationem assignat, quia falsum dicunt quod Christus veniet occultus, sed non est verum, immo veniet manifestus.

Et ponit duas rationes.
Unam ex manifestatione Christi,
aliam ex congregatione sanctorum.

1954. Dicit **nolite credere**, quod non veniat manifestus: *sicut enim fulgur exit ab oriente, et paret usque in occidentem, ita erit adventus Filii hominis*; Ps. XLIX, 3: *Deus manifeste veniet.*

(Matt 10:27), but false teaching always seeks the corners. *Wisdom preaches abroad, she utters her voice in the streets* (Prov 1:20). So truth is light, and seeks to be seen in the light, but if it is corrupt doctrine, it seeks what is hidden. *A foolish woman . . . sat at the door of her house* (Prov 9:14), and there follows, *stolen waters are sweeter*. Now a desert is a hidden place, since it lacks men, or because it is cut off, whence ***if therefore they will say to you: behold he is in the desert, do not go out***.

1950. And what does he want to say? Those who are unbelievers and heretics are unable to deceive while there are believers in the society or congregation, but they seek to be separated from society, and then they deceive. And this is what he wants to say: ***if therefore they will say to you: behold he is in the desert, do not go out***. Do not be separated from the society and congregation of good men. Similarly, if they claim he is ***in the closets***, because they always seek a hidden place, and do not dare to speak their teaching in public. Hence, *I have spoken openly to the world* (John 18:20), ***believe it not***, for *he who is hasty to give credit, is light of heart* (Sir 19:4).

1951. According to Jerome, it can be referred to the time before the destruction, but it is better that it be referred to the end. Likewise, it can be understood as about the seduction worked in the Church. The false Christs teach a lie, and it is called one teaching, because all are united in one: and any given lie has its prophets. Hence they say, ***here is Christ, or there***; *they see vain things, and they foretell lies, saying: The Lord says: whereas the Lord has not sent them: and they have persisted to confirm what they have said* (Ezek 13:6). And sometimes they wish to confirm their teaching through apocryphal Scriptures, sometimes through a hidden sense of Scripture. When through apocryphal Scriptures, they say that he is ***in the desert***; when through a hidden sense, they say that he is ***in the closets***.

1952. Or, according to Augustine, true teaching has two properties, for it should both be the same in every place and be set forth publicly, and heresy falls short of these two; hence it says, ***here is Christ***, i.e., in this land, and not in other lands. Similarly, since their teaching is not public, they say, ***behold he is in the closets***; hence, ***believe it not***.

1953. ***For as lightning comes out of the east***. Here he gives another reason, for they say something false, that Christ will be hidden when he comes. But it is not true; rather, he will be manifest.

And he sets out two reasons:
one from Christ's manifestation,
and another from the gathering together of the saints.

1954. He says, ***believe it not*** that he will not come manifest, ***for as lightning comes out of the east, and appears even into the west: so will the coming of the Son of man be***. *God will come manifestly* (Ps 49:3).

Sed numquid veniet sicut fulgur qui modo videtur hic, et post versus orientem? Ideo non intelligatis quod sic solum manifestetur in uno oriente, sed in omnibus.

Si velimus referre ad mysterium, fulgur est adventus veritatis. Nolite ergo quaerere occultum dogma, quia veritas manifestatur per totum mundum. Vel oriens principium, occidens finis. Unde veritas dogmatis semper habet concordantiam a principio usque ad finem: verum enim dogma totam Scripturam recipit. Quidam non recipiunt vetus testamentum, quidam non recipiunt prophetas, et ita non possent confirmari per alias Scripturas; sed vera doctrina a principio nascentis Ecclesiae usque ad finem habebit confirmationem; unde dicitur infra ult., 20: *ecce ego vobiscum sum omnibus diebus usque ad consummationem saeculi*.

1955. *Ubicumque fuerit corpus, ibi congregabuntur et aquilae*. Posset enim aliquis dicere: isti dicunt **hic est Christus, aut illic**, quomodo cognoscemus quando veniet? Ostendit autem quod non indigebit quaerere, quia manifestus fiet adventus eius, quandoquidem et alii congregabuntur. Et erit simile ei quod accidit, cum quidam petiit a domino suo multum celante consilium suum de movendo castra, et dixit: *quando movebis castra*? Et ille: *nonne audies tubam? Ad quid petis*? Sic dicitur hic: tu dicis quod erit hic, vel illic; scio quod **ubi fuerit corpus, illic congregabuntur et aquilae**.

Notate quod in Hebraeo habetur 'anathe', quod idem est quod 'cadaver', unde voluit signare passionem Christi, quia tunc veniet Christus ostendens signa passionis: et loquitur per similitudinem *ubi fuerit corpus* et cetera. I ad Thess. IV, 16: *occurremus in nubibus obviam Christo*. Sed quidam sunt aquilae, quidam vultures et corvi. Sed non dicit *vultures* vel *corvi*, sed **aquilae**, per quas sancti signantur. Is. XL, 31: *assument pennas ut aquilae, volabunt, et non deficient*. Sic, ut dicit Hieronymus, ubicumque fit memoria Christi passionis, viri sancti debent congregari per iugem memoriam passionis eius. Ad Hebr. X, 32: *memoramini pristinos dies, in quibus illuminati magnum certamen sustinuistis passionum*.

1956. Et quia non solum erunt haec manifesta per tribulationes, ideo ait: **statim autem post tribulationem dierum illorum sol obscurabitur** et cetera. Et agit de signis sumptis ab aliis rebus quae supra nos sunt. Et primo ponit signa; secundo effectus. Secunda ibi **et tunc plangent omnes tribus terrae**.

In his autem quae supra nos ostendit, triplex est ordo: corpora caelestia, angeli, Christus. Ad Eph. c. I, 21: *constituit eum super omnem potestatem et principatum* et cetera.

But will he come like the lightning which is seen, now here, and later toward the east? Therefore you should not understand that he will be manifested only in one east, but in all.

If we wish to refer it to a mystery, the lightning is the coming of truth. Therefore, do not seek hidden doctrine, because the truth is made manifest throughout the whole world. Or, the east is the beginning and the west the end, so truth of doctrine always has harmony from beginning to end: for true teaching accepts the whole Scripture. Some do not accept the Old Testament, and some do not accept the prophets, and thus they cannot be strengthened by the other Scriptures; but true teaching shall have confirmation from the beginning of the Church's arising all the way to the end. Hence it says below, **behold I am with you all days, even to the consummation of the world** (Matt 28:20).

1955. *Wherever the body will be, there will the eagles also be gathered together*. For someone could say: these men say, **here is Christ, or there**, how will we know when he comes? And he shows that one will not have to seek, because his coming will be manifest, since the others will also be gathered together. And it will be like what happened when a man asked his master, who was concealing his plan about moving the camp, many questions, and said: *when will you move the camp*? And the master said: *will you not hear the trumpet? Why are you asking*? In the same way it says here: you say that it will be here, or there; I know that **wherever the body will be, there will the eagles also be gathered together**.

Note that in Hebrew it says 'anathe,' which is the same as 'cadaver,' hence he wishes to indicate Christ's passion, for at that time Christ will come showing the signs of his passion; and he speaks by way of likeness, **wherever the body will be**. *Then we . . . will be taken up together with them in the clouds to meet Christ* (1 Thess 4:17). But some are eagles, some are vultures and ravens. But he does not say *vultures* or *ravens*, but **eagles**, through which the saints are indicated. *They will take wings as eagles, they will run and not be weary, they will walk and not faint* (Isa 40:31). Thus, as Jerome says, wherever the memory of Christ's passion takes place, holy men should be gathered together through the continual memory of his passion. *But call to mind the former days, wherein, being illuminated, you endured a great fight of afflictions* (Heb 10:32).

1956. And because these things will not only be manifest through afflictions, he says: **immediately after the tribulation of those days, the sun will be darkened**. And he treats of signs taken from other things, which are above us. And first, he sets out the signs; second, the effects. The second is at **and then will all tribes of the earth mourn**.

And in what he describes above us, there is a threefold order: the heavenly bodies, the angels, Christ. *He made him sit . . . over all powers and principalities* (Eph 1:21).

1957. Quantum ergo ad primum dicit *statim autem post tribulationem dierum illorum*, quando scilicet veniet antichristus. *Statim*, quia non diu post, quia multis esset in periculum; et hoc est contra illos qui fabulam ponunt de mille annis. *Sol obscurabitur, et luna non dabit lumen suum.* Et quid est? Hoc dictum habet sensum litteralem et mysticum. Secundum quod ad ultimum adventum refertur, habet sensum litteralem; secundum quod ad alium, mysticum.

1958. Sed videtur obiici quod dicit, quod *sol obscurabitur*, quia dicitur Is. XXX, v. 26: *et erit lux lunae sicut lux solis, et lux solis septempliciter.*

Unde ad hoc videndum debetis distinguere tria tempora: tempus ante adventum, tempus in adventu, et post adventum. Ante adventum Christi huiusmodi observationes fient, de quibus hic dicitur, et Ioel II, 31: *sol convertetur in tenebras, et luna in sanguinem, antequam veniat dies domini magnus et horribilis.* In Christi adventu non mutabantur secundum substantiam, sed secundum comparationem, quia tanta erit claritas Christi et sanctorum, quod nec apparebit claritas eorum; Is. XXIV, 23: *erubescet luna et confundetur sol.* Sed post diem iudicii augebitur claritas lunae et stellarum. Et tunc erit verum quod dicitur Is. XXX, 26, scilicet quod *solis lumen erit septempliciter sicut lumen septem dierum.*

1959. Sed videtur falsum quod dicitur, quod stellae cadent de caelo, quia una stella maior est tota terra.

Rabanus solvit per litteram Marci XIII, 25, quod *stellae erunt decidentes* in lumine, idest in lumine minoratae. Sed unde ista minoratio poterit esse? Ex duobus est quod lumen alicuius luminaris minoratur: vel in seipso, vel propter interpositum aliquod, ut si nubes interponatur, ut cum eclipsatur luna, minuitur lumen eius; unde dicit Origenes quod dupliciter potest intelligi. Primo quod hoc interpositum erit ignis, qui ante Christum praecedet, et consumet omnia usque ad medium spatium aeris, quantum scilicet elevatae sunt aquae diluvii, quem ignem sequetur multus fumus, ita quod tenebrabuntur luminaria caeli. Vel potest dici quod quidam tenebant, ista corpora esse corruptibilia; et sicut elementaria immutabuntur, ita et ista. De istis tribus habetur una auctoritas Apoc. VI, 12: *sol factus est niger tamquam saccus cilicinus, et luna tota facta est sicut sanguis, et stellae de caelo ceciderunt.*

Stellae cadent de caelo. Stellae de caelo videntur cadere quando suo lumine privantur. Sic ergo erit immutatio in corporibus caelestibus.

1960. Item in angelis; unde dicit *et virtutes caelorum movebuntur*, idest virtutes quae Deo ministrant. Et dicit

1957. Therefore, as regards the first, he says, *immediately after the tribulation of those days*, namely when the antichrist comes. *Immediately*, because it will not be long after, since many will be in danger; and this is against those who set forth the fable of the thousand years. *The sun will be darkened, and the moon will not give her light.* And what is this? This saying has a literal sense and a mystical one. According as it is referred to the last coming, it has a literal sense; according as it is referred to another coming, it has a mystical one.

1958. But there seems to be an objection to what he says, that the sun will be obscured, because it says, *and the light of the moon will be as the light of the sun, and the light of the sun will be sevenfold* (Isa 30:26).

So to understand this, you should distinguish between three times: the time before the coming, the time at the coming, and the time after the coming. Before the coming of Christ such appearances will happen as are spoken of here, and, *the sun will be turned into darkness, and the moon into blood: before the great and dreadful day of the Lord does come* (Joel 2:31). At Christ's coming they were not changed in substance, but by comparison, for Christ's brilliance will be so great that their brilliance will not be apparent; *and the moon will blush, and the sun will be ashamed* (Isa 24:23). But after the day of judgment, the brilliance of the moon and of the stars will be increased. And then what is said will be true, namely that *the light of the sun will be sevenfold, as the light of seven days* (Isa 30:26).

1959. But what is said seems false, that the stars will fall from heaven, because one star is bigger than the whole earth.

Rabanus solves this through the text of Mark, that *the stars of heaven will be falling* (Mark 13:25) in light, i.e., lessened in light. But what can this lessening come from? That the light of some luminous thing is lessened can happen in two ways: either in itself, or owing to something interposed, as when a cloud is interposed, or as when the moon is eclipsed, its light is lessened. Hence Origen says that it can be understood in two ways. First, that this thing interposed will be fire, which will come before Christ and consume all things, up to the middle space of the air, namely as high as the waters of the flood rose. This fire will be followed by a lot of smoke, such that the luminous bodies of heaven will be darkened. Or, what some have held can be said, that the bodies themselves are corruptible; and just as the elements will be changed, so these also. One authority is found for these three things, *the sun became black as sackcloth of hair: and the whole moon became as blood: and the stars from heaven fell upon the earth* (Rev 6:12-13).

And the stars will fall from heaven. The stars seem to fall from heaven when their light is taken away. So in this way there will be a change in the heavenly bodies.

1960. Likewise in the angels; hence he says, *and the powers of heaven will be moved*, i.e., the powers which

Augustinus quod omnia corpora administrantur per spiritum vitae; unde dicuntur moveri in effectu, quia in adventu domini cessabit motus caeli. Unde illae dicuntur moveri, quando illa quae ad suum officium pertinent, in alium statum mutantur. Vel angeli movebuntur non commotione timoris sed admirationis, quia admirabuntur virtutem Christi. Vel commovebuntur commotione gaudii super glorificatione sanctorum. De hoc potest accipi quod dicitur Iob c. XXVI, 11, quod *columnae caeli contremiscunt et pavent ad motum eius*.

1961. *Et tunc apparebit signum Filii hominis in caelo*. Hic ponitur signum filii hominis super angelos existentis. *Filii signum*, idest signum victoriae Christi; quia quando totus mundus innovabitur, signabitur quod obtinuit victoriam omnium per passionem suam, quod modo non apparet. Vel apparebit signum crucis, ad ostendendum quod tota ista gloria est per passionem eius. Item significabitur quod omnem iudiciariam potestatem acquisivit per passionem suam. Iob XXXVI, v. 29: *si voluerit nubes extendere quasi tentorium suum* et cetera. Et sequitur: *per haec enim iudicat populus*. Item apparebit ad confundendum malos qui Christum noluerunt sequi. Item signum crucis erit clarius quam sol.

1962. Sed quis erit effectus? *Tunc plangent omnes tribus terrae*, videntes tantam Christi potestatem quam despexerunt, et tantam sapientiam, cui non obedierunt, et tantam claritatem sanctorum; unde dicent illud quod dicitur Sap. V, 3: *hi sunt quos habuimus aliquando in derisum et in similitudinem improperii. Nos insensati vitam illorum aestimabamus insaniam et finem illorum sine honore. Ecce nunc quomodo computati sunt inter filios Dei, et inter sanctos sors illorum est*. Item tribus caeli, idest illi qui portaverunt imaginem caeli; Is. XL, 18: *cui similem fecistis Deum, aut quam imaginem ponetis ei?* Imputabunt sibi ipsis quod talia sustinent; Apoc. I, 7: *videbit eum omnis oculus, et qui eum pupugerunt, et plangent se super eum omnes fines terrae*. Et Zach. XII, 10: *aspicient ad me quem confixerunt, et plangent eum planctu quasi super unigenitum, et dolebunt super eum ut doleri solet in morte primogeniti*.

Haec est litteralis expositio.

1963. Sed si referatur ad secundum adventum, tunc tantum exponitur mystice. Origenes: *per solem diabolus signatur, per lunam antichristus*. De his dicitur Iob XXXI, v. 27: *si vidi solem cum fulgeret, et lunam incedentem clare, et laetatum est in abscondito cor meum*. Vidi, idest approbavi solem, idest ea quae videntur habere claritatem et sanctitatem, et qui virtutem, tunc apparebunt; I ad Cor. IV, 5: *illuminabit abscondita tenebrarum, et manifestabit consilia cordium*. Unde tota doctrina, tota claritas tunc apparebit, quia imago Christi apparebit in

minister to God. And Augustine says that all bodies are directed through a spirit of life: so they are said to be moved in effect, because at the Lord's coming the motion of the heavens will cease. So those powers are said to be moved when those things which pertain to their duty are changed to another state. Or, the angels will be moved, not with the stirring of fear but of wonder, because they will wonder at Christ's power. Or, they will be stirred with the stirring of joy over the glorification of the saints. And what is said in Job can be taken as about this, that *the pillars of heaven tremble, and dread at his beck* (Job 26:11).

1961. *And then will appear the sign of the Son of man in heaven*. Here a sign of the Son being over the angels is set out. *The sign of the Son*, i.e., the sign of Christ's victory, for when the whole world is renewed, it will be indicated that he has obtained victory over all things through his passion, which now is not apparent. Or, the sign of the cross will appear, to show that all this glory is through his passion. Likewise, it will be indicated that he has acquired every judicial power through his passion. *If he will spread out clouds as his tent* (Job 36:29), and there follows, *for by these he judges people*. Likewise, it will appear to confound evil men who were unwilling to follow Christ. Likewise, the sign of the cross will be more brilliant than the sun.

1962. But what will be the effect? *Then will all tribes of the earth mourn*, seeing Christ with such great power, whom they have despised, and such wisdom of him whom they have not obeyed, and the saints with such great brilliance; hence they will say what is said: *these are they, whom we had some time in derision, and for a parable of reproach. We fools esteemed their life madness, and their end without honor. Behold how they are numbered among the children of God, and their lot is among the saints* (Wis 5:3–5). Likewise the tribes of heaven, i.e., those who have born the image of heaven; *to whom then have you likened God? Or what image will you make for him?* (Isa 40:18). They will count it against their own selves that they suffer such things; *every eye will see him, and they also that pierced him. And all the tribes of the earth will bewail themselves because of him* (Rev 1:7). *And they will look upon me, whom they have pierced: and they will mourn for him as one mourns for an only son, and they will grieve over him, as the manner is to grieve for the death of the firstborn* (Zech 12:10).

This is the literal exposition.

1963. But if it is referred to the second coming, then only is it explained in a mystical way. Origen: *the devil is signified by the sun, the antichrist by the moon*. It says about this, *if I beheld the sun when it shined, and the moon going in brightness: and my heart in secret has rejoiced* (Job 31:26–27). *I beheld*, i.e., have approved, *the sun*, i.e., those things which seem to have brilliance and sanctity, and which seem to have virtue, will then be plain. *Who both will bring to light the hidden things of darkness, and will make manifest the counsels of the hearts* (1 Cor 4:5). Hence all teaching, all

brilliance will then be plain, for the image of Christ will be plain in all things. Or, the sun signifies the Church; hence the Church will seem not to shine, because of afflictions.

And why does he say, *after the tribulation*? Origen responds: both after and at the same time as.

Likewise *the stars*, i.e., those who seemed to shine before. *The powers of heaven*, i.e., the saints, *will be moved*.

1964. *And they will see the Son of man coming in the clouds of heaven*. Above, the Lord foretold what will happen before the second coming; but here he foretells the coming itself.

And concerning this he does three things:
first, he sets out his coming;
second, the certainty of the coming;
third, the uncertainty of the hour or day.

The second is at *and from the fig tree learn a parable*; the third, at *but of that day and hour no one knows*.

Concerning the first, he does two things:
first, he sets out the coming, or the appearance of the Son of man;
second, the gathering together of the saints to himself, at *and he will send his angels*.

1965. And notice that where he mentioned the coming, he set out two things, namely that the coming would be manifest, and that the saints would be gathered together; hence he said, *as lightning . . . so will the coming of the Son of man be*. And this is about the manifestation. Likewise he said, *wherever the body will be, there will the eagles also be gathered together*. And he wishes to explain these two things more. And how will he come? *And they will see the Son of man coming in the clouds of heaven*. And who shall see? All men, for he will come to pass judgment. For he has a human nature and a divine nature. According to the divine nature, he will be seen only by the clean of heart, in accord with what is said above, *blessed are the clean of heart: for they will see God* (Matt 5:8); but according to the human nature, even the evil will see him. *All flesh will see the salvation of God* (Luke 3:6). This is why they will see *the Son of man*, because the Son of man and of God is the same; but they will not see him as the Son of God, but as the Son of man. *And he has given him power to do judgment, because he is the Son of man* (John 5:27).

1966. But there can be a question as to whether both the good and the evil will see him in glorious appearance; and it seems that they will. And the reason is given, where the Lord, conversing with the prophet, says: *he will not see the glory of the Lord*. And the prophet responds: *Lord, let your hand be exalted, and let them not see*. To which the Lord responds, *let the envious people see, and be confounded* (Isa 26:10). So the good will see unto rejoicing, the evil unto torment and sorrow. For when someone fears being punished, the greater the judge against him appears, the more is he afflicted; thus to the degree that Christ appears more

signatur cum dicitur **venientem in nubibus caeli**. Et hoc respondet huic quod supra dixerat, quod *sicut fulgur . . . ita erit et adventus Filii hominis*. In fulgure duo sunt, splendor et terror. Splendor aliquam iucunditatem repraesentat, sed terror fit ex sono, et nubes ad refrigerium fit; Is. XVIII, 4: *et erit sicut nubes rorida in die messis*, quae tunc iucunda est. Item nubes habet obscuritatem, et quando spissa est, est terribilis propter fulgura et pluvias quae ex nubibus oriuntur; et hoc convenit terrori impiorum; Ps. XCVI, 2: *nubes et caligo in circuitu eius*.

1967. Item competit quod in nubibus veniat ad designandum divinitatem Christi, quia maiestas Dei apparuit in nube, Ex. XVI, v. 10; unde dicitur III regum VIII, 12: *dixit dominus quod habitaret in nebula*: ideo in nubibus veniet. Item competit ad ostendendum humanitatem eius; quia, sicut habetur Act. I, v. 9: *videntibus illis, elevatus est, et nubes suscepit eum ab oculis eorum*, et audierunt angelos dicentes: *quemadmodum vidistis eum euntem in caelum, sic veniet*. Ut ergo ostendatur quod sit ille idem qui in nube sublatus est, apparebit in nube.

Competit etiam ad significandum glorificationem. Quando enim transfiguratus est, apparuit nubes lucida, et tunc fuit una; sed tunc erunt plures, quia tunc solum tribus apparuit, sed tunc pluribus apparebit; Apoc. c. I, 7: *ecce veniet in nubibus, et videbit eum omnis oculus*.

1968. Et quid erunt istae nubes? Non erunt nisi quaedam claritates redundantes ex corpore Christi et aliorum sanctorum. Origenes dicit quod erunt angeli assumentes non solum intelligibiliter, sed veraciter ministrantes. In primo enim adventu venit humilis; Zach. IX, 9: *ecce rex tuus venit tibi mansuetus*. Sed post veniet **in nubibus caeli cum virtute multa et maiestate**. In primo enim adventu duo fuerunt: habuit enim infirmitatem et ignominiam. Infirmitatem, quia dicit apostolus, II ad Cor. XIII, 4: *crucifixus est ex infirmitate*. Ignominiam, secundum quod habetur Is. LII, 14: *sic inglorius erit inter viros aspectus eius, et forma eius inter filios hominum*.

1969. Consequenter ad haec duo, duo dicit. Consequenter ad infirmitatem, ponit virtutem, unde de ista dicitur: **data est mihi omnis potestas in caelo et in terra**, et haec data est ei per generationem, inquantum filius Dei. Sed ipse promeruit inquantum homo; et hoc manifestabitur quando omnes angeli et omnia elementa ministrabunt ei. Item contra ignominiam dicit veniet in **maiestate**, quasi iudex vivorum et mortuorum.

1970. Tunc veniet **et mittet angelos suos cum tuba et voce magna**. Hic agit de congregatione sanctorum; et tria ponit.

gloriously, to that degree the evil will be tormented more. And this is indicated when it says, **coming in the clouds of heaven**. And this corresponds to what he had said above, that *as lightning . . . so will the coming of the Son of man be*. There are two things in lightning, splendor and terror. The splendor presents a pleasure, but terror comes from the sound, and the clouds become cold; *as a cloud of dew in the day of harvest* (Isa 18:4), which is pleasant at that time. Likewise, a cloud has obscurity, and when it becomes thick, it is frightening because of the lightning and the rain which arises from clouds; and this conduces to the terror of the impious; *clouds and darkness are round about him* (Ps 96:2).

1967. Similarly, that he comes in the clouds works toward showing Christ's divinity, because God's majesty appeared in a cloud (Exod 16:10). Hence it says, *the Lord said that he would dwell in a cloud* (1 Kgs 8:12); for this reason, he will come in the clouds. Similarly, it works toward showing his humanity, for, as is said, *while they looked on, he was raised up: and a cloud received him out of their sight*, and they heard angels saying, *this Jesus who is taken up from you into heaven, will come, as you have seen him going into heaven* (Acts 1:9). Therefore, to show that he is the same one who was taken up in a cloud, he will appear in a cloud.

It works also toward indicating glorification. For when he was transfigured, a luminous cloud appeared; and then there was only one, because at that time he appeared to only three men, but then at the second coming he will appear to many; *behold, he comes with the clouds, and every eye will see him* (Rev 1:7).

1968. And what will these clouds be? They will be nothing but certain brilliances overflowing from the body of Christ and of the other saints. Origen says that they will be angels taking up not only intelligibly, but truly serving. For in the first coming, he came humbly; *behold your king will come to you, the just and savior: he is poor* (Zech 9:9). But later, he will come **in the clouds of heaven with much power and majesty**. For there were two things in the first coming: for he had weakness and dishonor. Weakness, for the Apostle says, *he was crucified through weakness* (2 Cor 13:4). Dishonor, in accord with what is said, *so will his visage be inglorious among men, and his form among the sons of men* (Isa 52:14).

1969. Corresponding to these two things, he says two things. Corresponding to weakness, he puts **power**, hence it says about this, **all power is given to me in heaven and in earth** (Matt 28:18), and this is given to him through generation, insofar as he is the Son of God. But he merited insofar as he is a man, and this will be made manifest when all the angels and all the elements serve him. Similarly, against dishonor he says that he will come in **majesty**, as the judge of the living and the dead.

1970. Then he will come **and he will send his angels with a trumpet, and a great voice**. Here he treats of the gathering together of the saints; and he sets out three things:

Primo ponit ministros;
secundo congregatos;
tertio unde congregantur.

1971. Ministri sunt angeli, ut habetur Ps. CII, 21: *ministri eius qui facitis voluntatem eius*. Sed dicit **cum voce magna et tuba**. In resurrectione triplex virtus operabitur. Primo virtus divina; secundario virtus humanitatis Christi, quia sua resurrectio est causa nostrae resurrectionis, ut dicit Apostolus I ad Cor. XV, 22: *sicut in Adam omnes mortui sumus, ita in Christo omnes resurgemus*. Item operabitur ibi virtus angelica ad quaedam praeambula, scilicet ad colligendos pulveres. Et haec tria tangit.

Virtutem angelicam, cum dicit **mittet angelos**; virtutem Dei, cum dicit **cum tuba**; virtutem humanitatis in hoc quod dicit **et in voce magna**. De ista habetur in Io. V, 25: *omnes qui audierint vocem Filii Dei, vivent*. Et oportebit quod illa vox sit magna, quia *dabit voci suae vocem virtutis*, Ps. LXVII, 34. Per tubam bene signatur divinitas, quia maior est vox tubae, quam vox humana; Apoc. c. XI, 12: *et audierunt vocem magnam de caelo dicentem eis, ascendite huc*. Et paulo post: *et septimus angelus tuba cecinit, et factae sunt voces magnae in caelo*.

1972. Et notate quod tuba satis ei congruit, quia Num. X, 2 mandavit Dominus Moysi duas tubas fieri; et clangebant tubis ad concilium, ad festa, ad pugnam, et ad commotionem castrorum. Et sic erit in iudicio; quia erit ibi concilium, idest adunatio omnium sanctorum, quia *non resurgent impii in iudicio, neque peccatores in concilio iustorum*, Ps. I, 5. Item erit tunc solemnitas sempiterna. Item erit ibi pugna contra malos, ut habetur Zach. ult., 14: *sed et Iudas pugnabit adversus Ierusalem*. Item erit ibi commotio castrorum, quia sancti transferentur ad vitam sanctorum; Zach. II, 11: *et applicabuntur gentes multae ad Dominum in die illa*. Item quidam modo congregantur, sed non omnes; sed tunc omnes; infra XXV, 32: **congregabuntur ante eum omnes gentes**. Hic congregantur solum electi, quia solum congregantur ut regnent cum ipso; Ps. XLIX, 5: *congregate illi sanctos eius*.

1973. Unde dicit **et congregabunt electos eius**. Sed unde congregabuntur? **A quatuor ventis caeli, a summis caelorum usque ad terminos eorum**. Venti caeli distinguuntur per quatuor partes mundi. Ab oriente provenit subsolanus; ab occidente Favonius; a septemtrione Boreas; a meridie Auster: et sub his omnes alii continentur; unde **a quattuor ventis caeli**, idest ab omnibus partibus mundi.

first, he sets out the ministers;
second, those gathered together;
third, where they are gathered from.

1971. The ministers are the angels, as is said, *you ministers of his that do his will* (Ps 102:21). But he says, **with a trumpet, and a great voice**. In the resurrection, three powers will be at work. First, the divine power; secondarily, the power of Christ's humanity, since his resurrection is the cause of our resurrection, as the Apostle says, *and as in Adam all die, so also in Christ all will be made alive* (1 Cor 15:22). Likewise, the angelic power will be at work there with regard to certain foregoing things, namely to collect the dust. And he touches on these three things.

He touches on the angelic power when he says, **he will send his angels**; the power of God, when he says, **with a trumpet**; the power of the humanity by the fact that he says, **and a great voice**. It says about these things, *the dead will hear the voice of the Son of God, and they who hear will live* (John 5:25). And that voice will necessarily be great, because *he will give to his voice the voice of power* (Ps 67:34). The divinity is well signified by the trumpet, because the voice of a trumpet is greater than a human voice; *and they heard a great voice from heaven, saying to them: come up here* (Rev 11:12). And a little later: *and the seventh angel sounded the trumpet: and there were great voices in heaven*.

1972. And note that the trumpet befits him well enough, for the Lord commanded Moses that two trumpets be made; and they made a great noise with the trumpets at gatherings, at feasts, at battle, and for stirring the camps (Num 10:2). And so it will be at the judgment, for there will be a gathering there, i.e., the uniting of all the saints, for *the wicked will not rise again in judgment: nor sinners in the council of the just* (Ps 1:5). Similarly, there will be then an eternal solemnity. Similarly, there will be there a battle against evil men, as is said, *and even Judah will fight against Jerusalem* (Zech 14:14). Likewise, there will be there a stirring of camps, because the saints will be carried over to the life of the saints; *and many nations shall be joined to the Lord in that day* (Zech 2:11). Similarly, some are gathered together now, but not all; but at that time all will be gathered; below, **and all nations will be gathered together before him** (Matt 25:32). Here only the elect are gathered together, because they only are gathered together to reign with him; *gather together his saints to him* (Ps 49:5).

1973. Hence he says, **and they will gather together his elect**. But where will they be gathered from? **From the four winds, from the farthest parts of the heavens to the utmost bounds of them**. The winds of heaven are distinguished by the four parts of the world. Subsolanus comes from the east; Favonius from the west; Boreas from the north; Auster from the south; and all the others are contained under these. Hence, **from the four winds**, i.e., from all parts of the world.

1974. Sequitur *a summis caelorum usque ad terminos eorum*. Istud potest dupliciter exponi.

Origenes dicit sic: *congregabuntur*. Posset aliquis dicere quod solum ista congregatio esset vivorum, et non mortuorum; quod removet ad ostendendum quod etiam mortui congregabuntur; ideo dicit *a summis caelorum* et cetera.

Scitis quod sancti ascendunt in caelos, et quidam sunt inferiores, quidam superiores, quia secundum modum meritorum erit modus praemii; unde hoc est quod dicit Augustinus, quod *a quatuor ventis*, hoc est propter corpora: quod *a summis caelorum*, hoc dicit propter animas.

Remigius dicit sic, et est in Glossa: *congregabo* et cetera. Posset aliquis credere quod solum esset congregatio ab extremis terrae; sed quid erit de meditullio terrae? Unde *usque ad terminos eorum*. Et vult dicere quod non solum fiet congregatio ab extremis terrae, sed a caelo, idest a meditullio mundi.

1975. *Ab arbore fici discite parabolam*. Hic docet de certitudine adventus sui. Magna dixerat, et a quibusdam incredibilia; modo tripliciter certificat.

Primo similitudine;
secundo assertione;
tertio ratione.

Secunda ibi *amen dico vobis* etc.; tertia ibi *caelum et terra* et cetera.

1976. Dicit ergo *ab arbore fici discite parabolam*. Dicit Chrysostomus: *quando vult Deus ostendere aliquid, semper inducit similitudinem naturalem*. Arbores in hieme vitam habent, tamen occulte, unde non producunt folia, neque fructus; sed in principio veris incipiunt pullulare, et tunc apparet vita. Sic etiam sancti modo non apparent, ut habetur ad Col. III, 3: *mortui estis, et vita vestra abscondita est cum Christo in Deo*; sed tunc vita sanctorum apparebit, eorum scilicet qui non seducentur tempore antichristi. Tunc veniet aestas, idest aeterna retributio; Ps. CXXV, 6: *euntes ibant et flebant mittentes semina sua*; et sequitur, *venientes autem venient cum exultatione portantes manipulos suos*.

1977. Unde dicit *ab arbore fici discite parabolam*. Per ficum signatur synagoga, de qua habetur Lc. XIII, 6: *arborem fici habebat quidam plantatam in vinea sua*.

Cum iam ramus eius tener fuerit et folia nata, scitis quia prope est aestas. Et hoc potest exponi sic: ramus tener antichristus est, cuius potestas parum durabit, et sicut folia multum adhaerent ei, tunc potestas eius manifestabitur. Vel potest exponi in bono. Per ramum virtus et fortitudo sanctorum. Quando Ecclesia incipiet

1974. *From the farthest parts of the heavens to the utmost bounds of them*. This can be explained in two ways.

Origen speaks thus: *they will gather*. Someone could say that this gathering would be only of the living, and not of the dead; which he prevents, showing that the dead will also be gathered, and so he says, *from the farthest parts of the heavens*.

You know that the saints ascend into heaven, and some are lower, some higher, because the manner of reward will be according to the manner of merits. So this is what Augustine says, that *from the four winds* is owing to the body; he says *from the farthest parts of the heavens* because of the souls.

Remigius speaks thus, and it is in the Gloss: *they will gather*. Someone might think that the gathering would be only from the extremes of the earth, but what about the middle region of the earth? Hence *to the utmost bounds of them*. And he wishes to say that the gathering will happen not only from the earth's extremes, but from heaven, i.e., from the middle region of the world.

1975. *And from the fig tree learn a parable*. Here he teaches about the certitude of his coming. He had said things tremendous, and unbelievable to many; now he confirms what he had said in three ways:

first, by a likeness;
second, by an assertion;
third, by a reason.

The second is at *amen I say to you*; the third, at *heaven and earth will pass*.

1976. He says then, *and from the fig tree learn a parable*. Chrysostom says: *when the Lord wishes to show something, he always brings in a natural likeness*. Trees have life in winter, yet in a hidden way, so that they produce neither leaves nor fruit; but in the beginning of spring they begin to send forth new growth, and then the life is apparent. So also the saints are not now apparent, as is said, *for you are dead; and your life is hid with Christ in God* (Col 3:3); but at that time the life of the saints will be apparent, namely of those who will not be seduced in the time of the antichrist. Then the summer will come, i.e., eternal repayment; *going they went and wept, casting their seeds*, and there follows, *but coming they will come with joyfulness, carrying their sheaves* (Ps 125:6).

1977. Hence he says, *and from the fig tree learn a parable*. The fig tree signifies the synagogue, about which Luke says, *a certain man had a fig tree planted in his vineyard* (Luke 13:6).

When its branch is now tender, and the leaves come forth, you know that summer is close. And this can be explained this way: the tender branch is the antichrist, whose power few shall endure; many will cling to him like leaves, and then his power will be made manifest. Or it can be explained as about the good. The branch signifies the virtue

finiri, virtus Christi et sanctorum apparebit qui sustinebunt eam; Cant. II, 13: *ficus protulit grossos suos*. **Ita et vos, cum videritis haec omnia**; idest cum videritis signa praecedentia evenire, **scitote quod prope est in ianuis**. Sicut dicitur aliquid esse prope, quando est in ianuis; Iac. V, v. 4: *ecce merces operariorum vestrorum quae defraudata est a vobis, clamat, et clamor eorum in aures domini Sabaoth introivit*.

1978. Notate quod Augustinus facit vim in hoc quod dicit **omnia**, cum dicit: **cum videritis haec omnia** et cetera. Supra dixerat quod Dominus prope est; sed quid est? Semper enim Dominus prope est. Ideo dicit: *si velimus, dicamus quod nihil pertinet ad finem mundi, sed ad adventum Christi per Ecclesiam; unde quod dictum est,* **videbunt Filium hominis venientem in nubibus**, idest in praedicatoribus, **cum virtute magna**, quoniam dat Dominus verbum evangelizantibus virtute multa; et tunc veniet cum **maiestate**, quoniam dant ei reverentiam.

Tamen secundum expositionem aliorum referre ad finem mundi possumus, et aliter dicere.

Secundum quod Augustinus exponit, dat intelligere aliquid quod prope est, idest aliqua esse signa quod prope est; unde quod dictum est, **videbunt** etc. refertur ad omnia supra dicta, scilicet ad signa, fulgura et terraemotus.

1979. Manifestavit ergo per similitudinem, nunc manifestat per assertionem, scilicet cum iuramento dicens **amen dico vobis**, idest infallibiliter verum est, **quia non praeteribit generatio haec donec omnia fiant**. Dicit Origenes: *quasi in promptu esset quod audietis*. Posset enim aliquis credere haec esse dicta de destructione Ierusalem, et quia tunc completa sunt ad destructionem, quia multi supervixerunt usque ad tempus illud, unde **non praeteribit generatio haec**, idest homines nunc viventes, **donec omnia fiant**.

Sed magnum esset omnia dicta ad destructionem Ierusalem referre: ideo aliter dicendum, quod omnes fideles sunt una generatio; Ps. XXIII, 6: *haec est generatio quaerentium Dominum*; et praemiserat quod *Domini est terra*. Unde vult dicere **non praeteribit generatio haec**, idest non cessabit fides Ecclesiae usque ad finem mundi, contra aliquos qui dicebant quod duraret usque ad tempus aliquod: quod Dominus redarguit dicens, infra ult., 20: *ecce ego vobiscum sum omnibus diebus usque ad consummationem saeculi*.

1980. Et tunc ponit rationem **caelum et terra transibunt, verba autem mea non transibunt**; quasi dicens: *facilius est caelum et terram transire, quam verba*; Is. c. XL, 8: *verbum autem meum manet in aeternum*. Et Ps. XXXII, 6: *verbo Domini caeli firmati sunt*. Unde verbum est causa caeli, et causa semper validior est suo

and fortitude of the saints. When the Church begins to be ended, the power of Christ and of the saints, which will sustain them, will be apparent; *the fig tree has put forth her green figs* (Song 2:13). **So you also, when you will see all these things**, i.e., when you see the preceding signs come to pass, **know that it is close, even at the doors**. As something is said to be near when it is in the doors; *behold the hire of the laborers, who have reaped down your fields, which by fraud has been kept back by you, cried: and the cry of them has entered into the ears of the Lord of Sabaoth* (Jas 5:4).

1978. Note that Augustine puts stress on the fact that he says, **all**, when he says, **when you will see all these things**. Above, the Lord had said that it is near; but what of it? For the Lord is always near. For this reason he says: *if we wish, let us say that nothing pertains to the end of the world, but to Christ's coming through the Church; hence what was said,* **they will see the Son of man coming in the clouds of heaven**, i.e., in preachers, **with much power**, because the Lord gives the word to those evangelizing with great power; and then he will come with **majesty**, because they give him reverence.

Yet according to the explanation of others, we can refer it to the end of the world, and say otherwise.

According as Augustine explains it, he gives one to understand that something is near, i.e., that certain things are a sign that it is near; hence when he says **they will see the Son of man**; it refers to everything said above, namely to the signs, the lightning, and the earthquakes.

1979. So he manifested it by a likeness; now he manifests it by an assertion, namely with an oath, saying, **amen I say to you**, i.e., it is infallibly true, **that this generation will not pass, till all these things will be done**. Origen says, *what you will hear is at hand, as it were*. For someone might think that these things were said about the destruction of Jerusalem, and that they are now fulfilled at the destruction, because many lived up to that time; hence, **this generation** i.e., the men now living, **shall not pass, till all these things will be done**.

But it would be enormous to refer everything said to the destruction of Jerusalem: so one should say otherwise, that all the faithful are one generation; *this is the generation of those who seek him* (Ps 23:6); and he had said before that *the earth is the Lord's* (Ps 23:1). Hence he wishes to say that **this generation will not pass**, i.e., the faith of the Church will not cease until the end of the world, contrary to some who said that it would endure up to a certain time; which the Lord refutes, saying below, **behold I am with you all days, even to the consummation of the world** (Matt 28:20).

1980. And then he sets out a reason: **heaven and earth will pass, but my words will not pass**, as though to say: *it is easier for heaven and earth to pass away than my words. But the word of our Lord endures for ever* (Isa 40:8). And, *by the word of the Lord the heavens were established* (Ps 32:6). Hence the word is the cause of heaven, and a cause is always

effectu, ideo et cetera. Et non dicitur quod caelum et terra transeant, quia esse desinant, sed quia transibunt in alium statum; Apoc. XXI, 1: *vidi caelum novum et terram novum*.

Secundum Origenem boni per caelum signantur, per terram mali; Is. I, 2: *audite, caeli, et auribus percipe, terra*. Utrique transibunt, boni in vitam aeternam, mali in ignem aeternum. Et quod dicitur Verbum Dei non praeteriri, non dicitur quod non transeat secundum substantiam verbi, sed secundum id cuius est: unde hoc, ut dicit Origenes, habet praeter alia, quia non praeteribit verbum domini. Verba autem Moysi et aliorum praetereunt; unde verba Moysi sunt signa praesentis Ecclesiae. Sed verba Christi praenuntiant statum vitae aeternae. Unde verba Moysi transeunt, idest quod promisit Moyses transit: quod Christus, non, quia promisit futuram gloriam, quae non transit. Item verbum Christi secundum quod est de terrenis et temporalibus, transit.

1981. *De die autem et hora illa nemo scit*. In parte autem ista determinat de incertitudine temporis.

Et circa hoc duo facit.

Primo ponit temporis incertitudinem;

secundo hortatur ad similitudinem;

tertio ostendit eventum futurum.

Secunda ibi *sicut in diebus Noe* etc.; tertia ibi *tunc duo erunt in agro*.

1982. Dicit quod *videbunt filium hominis*. Tu dicis indeterminate; dicas nobis determinate si est verum. *De die autem et hora nemo scit, neque Angeli caelorum*. Quod dicit de Angelis caelorum, manifestum est, et non habet magnam dubietatem, quia est cognitio naturalis in eis, et hoc non se extendit nisi ad ea quae secundum cursum naturae fiunt; iudicium autem non fiet nisi secundum voluntatem Dei. Item est alia cognitio gloriae, et sic tantum sciunt sicut quibus Dominus vult revelare, et istud sibi retinuit; Mal. c. III, 2: *ecce veniet Dominus, et quis poterit scire adventum eius?* I ad Thess. V, 2: *dies Domini sicut fur in nocte, ita veniet*.

1983. Sed est quaestio hic, secundum Hieronymum, quia dicit Marcus XIII, 26: *nec etiam Filius hominis*; ex quo videtur Arius suam haeresim confirmare, quia si pater scit quod nescit filius, ergo maior est eo. Ideo potest dici quod filius scit, et quod dies iudicii secundum aliquam rationem determinatus est, et quidquid determinatur a Deo, suo verbo aeterno determinatur; ideo impossibile est quin verbum sciat.

Sed quare dicitur nescire? Augustinus et Hieronymus dicunt quod consuetus modus loquendi est dicere nescire aliquid, quando non facit illud scire; sicut dicitur Gen. XXII, v. 12: *nunc cognovi quod timeas Deum*; idest,

more powerful than its effect. And he does not say that heaven and earth will pass away because they cease to be, but because they will pass over into another state; *and I saw a new heaven and a new earth* (Rev 21:1).

According to Origen, the good are signified by heaven, the evil by the earth; *hear, O heavens, and give ear, O earth* (Isa 1:2). Both will pass on, the good into eternal life, the evil into eternal fire. And when it says that the word of God will not pass, it does not say that it does not pass according to the substance of the word, but according to whose it is. Hence, as Origen says, it has this above the others, that the Lord's word will not pass. But the words of Moses and of others will pass; hence the words of Moses are signs of the present Church. But the words of Christ foretell the state of eternal life. Hence the words of Moses pass, i.e., what Moses promised passes; what Christ promised does not, because he promised the future glory, which does not pass. Similarly, the word of Christ does pass, according as it is about earthly and temporal things.

1981. *But of that day and hour no one knows*. And in this part he teaches about the uncertainty of the time.

And concerning this he does two things:

first, he sets out the uncertainty of the time;

second, he urges by a likeness;

third, he shows what will come to pass.

The second is at, *as in the days of Noah*; the third, at *then two will be in the field*.

1982. He says that they will see the Son of man. You speak indeterminately; speak to us determinately, if it is true. *But of that day and hour no one knows, not the angels of heaven*. What he says about the angels of heaven is clear, and has no great difficulty, because they have a natural knowledge, and this only extends to those things which happen in the course of nature; but the judgment will only happen by the will of God. Similarly, they have another knowledge, the knowledge of glory, and in this way they know just as much as the Lord wishes to reveal, and he has kept this thing to himself; *behold he comes, says the Lord of hosts. And who will be able to think of the day of his coming?* (Mal 3:2). *The day of the Lord will so come, as a thief in the night* (1 Thess 5:2).

1983. But there is a question here, according to Jerome, because Mark says, *nor the Son* (Mark 13:32), from which Arius seems to confirm his heresy, for if the Father knows what the Son does not know, then he is greater than him. So it can be said that the Son knows, and that the day of judgment is determined in accord with some reason, and whatever is determined by God is determined by his eternal Word; therefore the Word cannot but know.

But why is he said not to know? Augustine and Jerome say that it is a customary way of speaking to say one does not know something when he does not make it known; as it says, *now I know that you fear God* (Gen 22:12), i.e., I have

cognoscere feci; ideo dicitur Filius nescire, quia non facit scire.

Alio modo dicit Origenes quod Christus et Ecclesia sunt sicut caput et corpus, quia sicut caput et corpus sunt sicut una persona, ita Christus et Ecclesia. Sed Christus aliquando accipit formam Ecclesiae, ut in illo Ps. XXI, v. 2: *Deus, Deus meus, respice in me*, unde quod dicitur quod Christus non scit, intelligitur quod Ecclesia non scit: unde Dominus, Act. I, 7: *non est vestrum scire tempora vel momenta* et cetera.

1984. Notate quod dicit Augustinus quod ipse volebat ostendere ex quibusdam signis, quod adventus iudicii non possit sciri determinate, quia non determinat quodcumque tempus. Probatio dicit quod non possit sciri, quia sicut est in aetatibus hominis, ita est in aetatibus mundi. Unde sicut ultima aetas hominis non habet terminum certum, sed aliquando protenditur plusquam aliae, sic et de ultima parte mundi dici debet, quod non habet certum terminum, et poterit plus durare quam omnes aliae partes.

1985. *Sicut autem fuit in temporibus Noe, ita erit et adventus Filii hominis.* Supra Dominus posuit incertitudinem horae sui adventus; nunc autem adhibet similitudinem. Et

primo ponit eam;

secundo exponit, ibi *sicut enim erant in diebus ante diluvium* et cetera.

1986. Proponit autem similitudinem convenientem, quia dum loqueretur de fine mundi, quievit in fine mundi. Proponit ergo de alia similitudine. Legitur enim duplex consummatio. Una per aquam; II Petri II, 5: *et originali mundo non pepercit, sed octavum Noe iustitiae praeconem custodivit, diluvium mundo impiorum inducens*. Unde dicitur satis convenienter, quia prima consummatio fuit ad amputanda peccata carnalia; unde dicitur Gen. VI, 2: *videntes filii Dei filias hominum quod essent pulchrae, acceperunt sibi uxores ex omnibus quas elegerant*. Ideo contra ardorem huius concupiscentiae debuit esse consummatio per aquam. In fine autem mundi peccatum erit, quia refrigescet caritas, sicut supra dictum est, ideo ignis convenienter erit in poenam; unde dicit *sicut in tempore Noe*, scilicet quod finis fuit incertus, sicut habetur Gen. VI, 13: *finis universae carnis venit coram me*. Unde sicut illi qui adhaeserunt Noe, salvati fuerunt, sic in adventu Filii hominis, qui adhaerebunt Filio Christo, salvi fient.

1987. Secundo exponit istam similitudinem quantum ad incertitudinem *sicut enim erant in diebus ante diluvium comedentes et bibentes* et cetera. In verbis istis duo tangere videtur: unum scilicet desperationem de futuro adventu, et causam eius. Causa autem quod homo non speret futurum adventum, est, quia versatur in curis carnis, quoniam ambulat secundum eius

made it known. For this reason the Son is said not to know, because he does not make it known.

In another way, Origen says that Christ and the Church are as head and body, for just as the head and the body are as one person, so are Christ and the Church. But Christ sometimes takes on the form of the Church, *O God my God, look upon me: why have you forsaken me?* (Ps 21:2). Hence when it says that Christ does not know, it means that the Church does not know; hence the Lord says, *it is not for you to know the times or moments* (Acts 1:7).

1984. Note that Augustine says that he wished to show by certain signs that the coming of the judgment cannot be known determinately, because he does not determine any given time. The proof, he says, that it cannot be known is that, just as it is with the lifetime of a man, so it is with the lifetime of the world. So just as the last age of a man has no certain end, but sometimes is extended further than the others, so should it be said with regard to the last part of the world, that it has no certain end, and could endure longer than all the other parts.

1985. *And as in the days of Noah, so will also the coming of the Son of man be*. Above, the Lord set out the uncertainty of the hour of his coming; and now, he applies a likeness. And

first, he sets it out;

second, he explains, at *for as in the days before the flood*.

1986. And he sets out a fitting likeness, for when he was speaking of the end of the world, he rested in the end of the world. So he sets out another likeness. For two consummations have been written about. One, through water; *and spared not the original world, but preserved Noah, the eighth person, the preacher of justice, bringing in the flood upon the world of the ungodly* (2 Pet 2:5). So it is said fittingly enough that the first consummation was for cutting off carnal sins; hence it says, *the sons of God seeing the daughters of men, that they were fair, took themselves wives of all which they chose* (Gen 6:2). So against the fire of this concupiscence there ought to have been a consummation through water. But at the end of the world the sin will be that charity will grow cold, as was said above, and therefore the punishment will fittingly be fire; hence he says, *as in the days of Noah*, namely because the end was uncertain, as is said, *the end of all flesh is come before me* (Gen 6:13). Hence just as those who clung to Noah were saved, so in the coming of the Son of man those who cling to the Son, Christ, will be saved.

1987. Second, he explains this likeness as regards the uncertainty: *For as in the days before the flood, they were eating and drinking*. In these words two things seem to be touched upon: one is despair of the future coming, and the other is its cause. The reason that a man does not hope for the future coming is because he is focused on the care of the body, because he walks in accord with its desires; *you have*

concupiscentias; Iac. V, 5: *epulati estis super terram, et in luxuriis vestris enutristis corda vestra*. Ideo vacabunt lasciviae, quae duas habet partes, scilicet *in comessationibus et ebrietatibus, in cubilibus et impudicitiis*, ad Rom. XIII, 13.

Quantum ad primum dicit *comedentes et bibentes*: non quod comedere et bibere sit peccatum, sed ponere ibi finem suum est peccatum. Quantum ad secundum dicit *nubentes, et nuptui tradentes* et cetera.

Et sequitur *et non cognoverunt donec venit diluvium, et tulit omnes*, scilicet qui non adhaeserunt Noe, qui erat figura Christi. *Ita erit et adventus Filii hominis*.

1988. Sed habetur Lc. XXI, 26: *arescentibus hominibus prae timore*. Et supra hoc eodem habetur quod *sol obscurabitur*. Quomodo ergo securi erunt homines ut comedant et luxurientur?

Duplex est responsio. Dicit Hieronymus quod verum est quod circa tempora antichristi multae erunt tribulationes, et hoc ad probationem electorum; et post restituentur tranquillitati, et in illa tranquillitate mali vacabunt laetitiae. Unde Lucas loquitur secundum statum tribulationis; Matthaeus autem secundum tempus quod immediate praecedet adventum Dei.

Item aliter, quia quidam sunt boni, quidam mali. Et universaliter Ecclesia patietur tribulationem, et boni punientur a malis: unde dicitur supra X, 22: *odio eritis omnibus hominibus propter nomen meum*. Unde illi qui patientur, erunt boni; qui vero exercebunt huiusmodi tribulationes, erunt mali. Quod ergo dicitur hic *comedentes et bibentes* etc. intelligitur quoad malos; quod autem in Luca dicitur, *arescentibus hominibus prae timore*, hoc intelligitur quoad bonos. Vel sic: cum frequenter accidat quod boni emendantur per tribulationem, mali autem non, ideo mali arescent, boni autem non.

1989. *Tunc duo erunt in agro: unus assumetur, et alter relinquetur*. In parte ista ponit eventum huius incertitudinis. Et quis erit? Quia continget quod homines in uno officio assumpti, quod unus assumetur, et alter relinquetur. Et potest hoc exponi, secundum Chrysostomum, quod non velit aliud dicere, quam quod in omni conditione hominum et omni officio quidam erunt reprobi, quidam electi: qui boni, assumentur; qui mali, relinquentur. Quomodo? Sicut dictum est supra XIII, 41, quia venient angeli, et assument bonos, scilicet ad Christum. Item quidam sunt delitiose viventes, quidam vero quaedam officia exercentes. Item laborantium quaedam sunt officia ad homines pertinentia, quaedam ad mulieres; labor hominum est proprie in agris.

feasted upon earth: and in riotousness you have nourished your hearts (Jas 5:5). For this reason they will give themselves up to lasciviousness, which has two parts, namely *in rioting and drunkenness . . . in chambering and impurities* (Rom 13:13).

With regard to the first, he says, *eating and drinking*: not that to eat and drink is a sin, but to place your end there is a sin. With regard to the second, he says, *marrying and giving in marriage*.

And there follows, *and they did not know not till the flood came, and took them all away*, namely those who did not cling to Noah, who was a figure of Christ. *So also will the coming of the Son of man be*.

1988. But in Luke, it speaks of *men withering away for fear, and expectation of what will come upon the whole world* (Luke 21:26). And above this same passage it says that the sun will be hidden. So how will men be untroubled, so that they eat and indulge themselves?

There are two responses. Jerome says that it is true that around the time of the antichrist there will be many afflictions, and this for the testing of the elect; and afterward they will be restored to tranquility, and in that tranquility the evil will give themselves up to joy. Hence Luke speaks according to the state of the afflictions, but Matthew according to the time which will immediately precede God's coming.

Likewise in another way, because some are good and some evil. And universally, the Church will suffer affliction, and the good will be punished by the bad; hence it says above, *you will be hated by all men for my name's sake* (Matt 10:22). Hence those who suffer will be the good; but those who cause such afflictions will be the evil. So what is said here, *eating and drinking*, is understood as about the evil; and what is said in Luke, *men withering away for fear*, is understood as about the good. Or in this way, since it frequently happens that good men are improved by affliction, but not the evil, for this reason the evil will wither away but not the good.

1989. *Then two will be in the field: one will be taken, and one will be left*. In this part he sets out the outcome of this uncertainty. And what will it be? For it will happen that of men appointed to the same position, one will be taken, and the other left. And this can be expounded, according to Chrysostom, that he wishes to say nothing other than that in every condition of man and every position, some will be rejected, some chosen: those who are good will be taken; those who are evil will be left. How? As was said above (Matt 13:41), the angels will come and take up the good, namely to Christ. Likewise, some live a life of delights, while some carry out certain duties. Similarly, some duties of those who work pertain to men, some to women; the work of men is properly in the fields.

Tunc ergo *erunt duo in agro uno*, litteraliter scilicet laborantes, *unus assumetur*, tamquam electus, *alter relinquetur*, tamquam reprobus.

Item *duae erunt molentes in mola una: una assumetur, altera relinquetur*. Hoc est officium mulierum. Solebat esse quod mulieres molerent, et loquitur secundum consuetudinem terrae, ubi non est aqua; et nunc molitur cum equis, vel cum hominibus, sed tunc erat officium mulierum; Is. XLVII, 2: *tolle molam, et mole farinam*. Unde *duae* erunt molentes, idest exercentes officium suum. Et tunc, *una assumetur*, exponitur ut prius.

1990. Item, *duo in lecto uno: unus assumetur, et unus relinquetur*. Chrysostomus dicit quod divites non laborant, sed quiescunt; ideo assignantur per illos qui in lecto iacent; et de istis unus assumetur, et alter relinquetur.

1991. Potest etiam exponi allegorice, et haec est expositio Hilarii. Per agrum assignatur mundus, sicut supra dictum est. Per duos homines populus fidelium et infidelium. De istis unus assumetur, scilicet populus fidelium, alter relinquetur, scilicet infidelium. Item lex vetus per molam assignatur, quae gravis et ponderosa est; Act. XV, 10: *hoc est onus quod nec nos, nec patres nostri ferre potuimus* et cetera. Et eorum qui veterem legem recipiunt, aliqui recipiunt Christum, alii non. Omnes illi dicuntur in mola molere qui veterem legem recipiunt; et illi quidem assumuntur, qui veterem legem cum nova recipiunt; illi vero qui non, relinquuntur. Item, qui Christum recipiunt, sunt sicut iacentes in lecto, quia per lectum signatur memoria passionis, et de talibus quidam assumuntur, quidam relinquuntur: quidam enim conformant se passioni per bona opera, quidam non.

1992. Potest aliter exponi, ut ad tres status fidelium referatur; quia sunt tria genera hominum, quidam contemplativi, quidam praelati, quidam activi. Nullus status securus est, quin aliqui damnentur in statu aliquo. Status contemplationis per lectum significatur. De hoc in Cant. I, 15: *lectus noster floridus*; et tamen aliqui in hoc statu damnantur. Status activorum per molentes in mola signatur, quia ponderositatem habent, et sunt solliciti; Lc. X, v. 41: *Martha, Martha, sollicita es, et turbaris erga plurima*. Unde involvuntur in saecularibus: et ideo inter eos aliqui damnantur. Per agrum in quem homines exeunt ad laborandum, signantur praelati; Cant. VII, 11: *veni, dilecte mi, egrediamur in agrum*. Et in talibus quidam assumuntur, et quidam relinquuntur.

Then therefore **two will be in the field**, that is, literally working, **one will be taken**, as one chosen, **and one will be left**, as one rejected.

Similarly, **two women will be grinding at the mill: one will be taken, and one will be left**. This is the duty of women. It was customary that women would grind, and he speaks in accordance with the custom of a land where there is no water; and now grain is ground with horses, or with men, but at that time it was the duty of women. *Take a millstone and grind meal* (Isa 47:2). Hence, **two women**, i.e., carrying out their duty. And then, **one will be taken** is explained as before.

1990. Similarly, **two will be in one bed: one will be taken, and one left**. Chrysostom says that the rich do not labor, but rest; for this reason they are indicated by those who lie in bed, and of these one will be taken, and another left.

1991. It can also be explained allegorically, and this is Hilary's exposition. The field signifies the world, as was said above. The two men signify the peoples of the faithful and of the unfaithful. Of these, one will be taken, namely the people of the faithful, the other left, namely the people of the unfaithful. Likewise the millstone signifies the old law, which is heavy and burdensome; *which neither our fathers nor we have been able to bear* (Acts 15:10). And of those who accept the old law, some accept Christ, others not. All those who accept the old law are said to grind at the mill; and those who are taken up are those who accept the old law with the new; but those who do not, are left. Similarly, those who accept Christ are like those who lie in bed, because the bed signifies the memory of the passion, and of such men some are taken, some left: for some conform themselves to the passion through good works, some not.

1992. It can be explained in another way, as it is referred to the three states of the faithful: for there are three kinds of men, some contemplative, some prelates, and some active. No state is without care, but rather some are condemned in each state. The state of contemplation is signified by the bed. It says about this: *our bed is flourishing* (Song 1:15); and yet some in this state are condemned. The state of the active is signified by those grinding at the mill, because they have a burdensomeness, and are anxious; *Martha, Martha, you are careful and are troubled about many things* (Luke 10:41). Hence they are entangled in worldly things, and for this reason some among them are condemned. The prelates are signified by the field into which the men go out to work; *come, my beloved, let us go forth into the field* (Song 7:11). And from such men some are taken, and some left.

Lecture 4

24:42 Vigilate ergo, quia nescitis qua hora Dominus vester venturus sit. [n. 1994]

24:43 Illud autem scitote, quoniam si sciret paterfamilias qua hora fur venturus esset, vigilaret utique, et non sineret perfodi domum suam: [n. 1997]

24:44 ideo et vos estote parati, quia nescitis qua hora Filius hominis venturus est. [n. 1998]

24:45 Quis putas est fidelis servus et prudens, quem constituit dominus supra familiam suam, ut det illis cibum in tempore? [n. 1999]

24:46 Beatus ille servus, quem cum venerit dominus eius, invenerit sic facientem. [n. 2002]

24:47 Amen dico vobis, quoniam super omnia bona sua constituet eum. [n. 2003]

24:48 Si autem dixerit malus servus ille in corde suo: moram facit dominus meus venire, [n. 2004]

24:49 et coeperit percutere conservos suos, manducet autem et bibat cum ebriosis; [n. 2006]

24:50 veniet dominus servi illius in die qua non sperat, et hora qua ignorat: [n. 2007]

24:51 et dividet eum, partemque eius ponet cum hypocritis. Illic erit fletus et stridor dentium. [n. 2008]

24:42 Γρηγορεῖτε οὖν, ὅτι οὐκ οἴδατε ποίᾳ ἡμέρᾳ ὁ κύριος ὑμῶν ἔρχεται.

24:43 Ἐκεῖνο δὲ γινώσκετε ὅτι εἰ ᾔδει ὁ οἰκοδεσπότης ποίᾳ φυλακῇ ὁ κλέπτης ἔρχεται, ἐγρηγόρησεν ἂν καὶ οὐκ ἂν εἴασεν διορυχθῆναι τὴν οἰκίαν αὐτοῦ.

24:44 διὰ τοῦτο καὶ ὑμεῖς γίνεσθε ἕτοιμοι, ὅτι ᾗ οὐ δοκεῖτε ὥρᾳ ὁ υἱὸς τοῦ ἀνθρώπου ἔρχεται.

24:45 Τίς ἄρα ἐστὶν ὁ πιστὸς δοῦλος καὶ φρόνιμος ὃν κατέστησεν ὁ κύριος ἐπὶ τῆς οἰκετείας αὐτοῦ τοῦ δοῦναι αὐτοῖς τὴν τροφὴν ἐν καιρῷ;

24:46 μακάριος ὁ δοῦλος ἐκεῖνος ὃν ἐλθὼν ὁ κύριος αὐτοῦ εὑρήσει οὕτως ποιοῦντα·

24:47 ἀμὴν λέγω ὑμῖν ὅτι ἐπὶ πᾶσιν τοῖς ὑπάρχουσιν αὐτοῦ καταστήσει αὐτόν.

24:48 ἐὰν δὲ εἴπῃ ὁ κακὸς δοῦλος ἐκεῖνος ἐν τῇ καρδίᾳ αὐτοῦ· χρονίζει μου ὁ κύριος,

24:49 καὶ ἄρξηται τύπτειν τοὺς συνδούλους αὐτοῦ, ἐσθίῃ δὲ καὶ πίνῃ μετὰ τῶν μεθυόντων,

24:50 ἥξει ὁ κύριος τοῦ δούλου ἐκείνου ἐν ἡμέρᾳ ᾗ οὐ προσδοκᾷ καὶ ἐν ὥρᾳ ᾗ οὐ γινώσκει,

24:51 καὶ διχοτομήσει αὐτὸν καὶ τὸ μέρος αὐτοῦ μετὰ τῶν ὑποκριτῶν θήσει· ἐκεῖ ἔσται ὁ κλαυθμὸς καὶ ὁ βρυγμὸς τῶν ὀδόντων.

24:42 Watch therefore, because you do not know what hour your Lord will come. [n. 1994]

24:43 But know this, that if the master of the house knew at what hour the thief would come, he would certainly watch, and would not suffer his house to be broken into. [n. 1997]

24:44 Therefore, you also be ready, because you do not know at what hour the Son of man will come. [n. 1998]

24:45 Who, do you think, is a faithful and wise servant, he whom his lord has appointed over his family, to give them meat in season? [n. 1999]

24:46 Blessed is that servant, who, when his lord will come he will find doing so. [n. 2002]

24:47 Amen I say to you, he will place him over all his goods. [n. 2003]

24:48 But if that evil servant will say in his heart: my lord is long in coming, [n. 2004]

24:49 and will begin to strike his fellow servants, and will eat and drink with drunkards, [n. 2006]

24:50 the lord of that servant will come in a day that he hopes not, and at an hour that he knows not, [n. 2007]

24:51 and will separate him, and appoint his portion with the hypocrites. There will be weeping and gnashing of teeth. [n. 2008]

1993. Postquam Dominus posuit incertitudinem horae, monet ad vigilantiam. Et
  primo monet omnes;
  secundo specialiter praelatos, ibi *quis putas est fidelis servus et prudens?* et cetera.
    Circa primum tria facit.
    Primo proponit admonitionem;
    secundo similitudinem;
    tertio concludit propositum.
  Secunda ibi *illud autem scitote* etc.; tertia ibi *et vos estote parati* et cetera.

1993. After the Lord has set out the uncertainty of the hour, he warns men to vigilance. And
  first, he warns all men;
  second, prelates in particular, at *who, do you think, is a faithful and wise servant*.
    Concerning the first, he does three things:
    first, he sets out the warning;
    second, a likeness;
    third, he concludes what he intended.
  The second is at *but know this, that if the master*; the third, at *therefore you also be ready, because at what hour*.

1994. Dicit ergo: *ita dico quod dies est incertus, et nullus potest confidere de suo statu, quia de quolibet unus assumetur et alter relinquetur, ideo debetis esse diligentes et solliciti.* ***Vigilate ergo***. Et, ut dicit Hieronymus, ideo voluit dominus incertum ponere terminum, ut homo semper expectaret.

In tribus enim homo delinquit: quia vacant eius sensus, item quia vacat a motu, item iacet homo. Ideo ***vigilate***, ut sensus vestri eleventur per contemplationem; Cant. V, v. 2: *ego dormio, et cor meum vigilat*. Item ***vigilate***, ne in morte torpeatis: ille enim vigilat qui se exercet in operibus bonis; I Petr. ult., 8: *sobrii estote, et vigilate, quia adversarius vester diabolus tamquam leo rugiens circuit quaerens quem devoret.* Item ***vigilate***, ne iaceatis per negligentiam; Prov. VI, 9: *usquequo, piger, dormies?*

1995. Sed quid dicit? ***Quia nescitis qua hora dominus vester venturus sit***. Hoc dicebat apostolis, et non habetur alibi quod ita expresse se vocet ***Dominum***, sicut hic, et in Io. XIII, 13: *vos vocatis me Magister et Domine, et bene dicitis, sum etenim.*

1996. Sed posset aliquis dicere, quod Dominus loquebatur apostolis; apostoli autem non erant victuri usque ad finem mundi, quomodo ergo dicit ***vigilate, quia nescitis qua hora Dominus vester venturus sit?***

Dicit Augustinus quod istud necessarium est etiam apostolis, et eis qui ante nos erant, et nobis, quia Dominus venit dupliciter. In fine mundi veniet ad omnes generaliter; item venit ad unumquemque in fine suo, scilicet in morte; Io. XIV, 18: *non relinquam vos orphanos, veniam ad vos.*

Ergo duplex est adventus, in fine mundi et etiam in morte: et utrumque voluit esse incertum. Et isti adventus sibi respondent, quia talis invenitur quis in secundo, qualis fuerit in primo. Augustinus: *imparatum invenit illum mundi novissimus dies, quem imparatum invenit suus ultimus dies.* Item potest exponi de alio adventu, scilicet invisibili, quando venit in mentem; Iob IX, 11: *si venerit ad me, non percipiam.* Unde ad multos venit, et non percipiunt. Unde multum debetis vigilare, ut si pulsaverit, aperiatis ei; unde Apoc. III, 20: *ego sto ante ostium, et pulso: si quis aperuit mihi, intrabo ad eum, et coenabo cum illo.*

1997. ***Illud autem scitote, quod si sciret paterfamilias qua hora fur veniret, vigilaret illa hora, et non sineret perfodi domum suam***. Sed quia nescit qua hora, oportet quod tota nocte vigilet.

Quis est iste paterfamilias? Domus anima est. In ista debet homo quiescere; Sap. VIII, v. 16: *intrans in domum meam, idest in conscientiam meam, conquiescam cum*

1994. He says therefore: *I say thus that the day is uncertain, and no one can be confident on the basis of his state, for from any given state one will be taken and the other left; therefore you should be diligent, and solicitous.* ***Watch therefore***. And, as Jerome says, the Lord wished to set down an uncertain end of the world so that man would always be awaiting it.

For man falls short in three things: because his senses are idle, and because he rests from motion, and because a man lies down. Therefore, ***watch***, that your senses may be elevated through contemplation; *I sleep, and my heart watches* (Song 5:2). Likewise, ***watch***, lest you be sluggish in death: for the one who watches is the one who exercises himself in good works; *be sober and watch: because your adversary the devil, as a roaring lion, goes about seeking whom he may devour* (1 Pet 5:8). Likewise, ***watch***, lest you lie down through negligence; *how long will you sleep, O sluggard?* (Prov 6:9)

1995. But what is he saying? ***Because you do not know what hour your Lord will come***. He said this to the apostles, and there is nowhere else that he calls himself ***Lord*** so explicitly as here and, *you call me Master, and Lord; and you say well, for so I am* (John 13:13).

1996. But someone could say that the Lord was speaking to the apostles; but the apostles were not going to live to the end of the world, so why does he say, ***watch therefore, because you do not know what hour your Lord will come***?

Augustine says that this is necessary even for the apostles, and for those who were before us, and for us, because the Lord comes in two ways. At the end of the world he will come to all generally; likewise, he comes to each man at his own end, namely in death. *I will not leave you orphans, I will come to you* (John 14:18).

Therefore the coming is twofold, at the end of the world and also at death: and he wished both to be uncertain. And these comings correspond to one another, because a man is found at the second as he was at the first. Augustine: *the last day finds that man unprepared whom it finds unprepared at his own last day.* Likewise, it can be explained as about the other coming, namely the invisible one, when he comes into the mind; *if he come to me, I will not see him* (Job 9:11). So you should watch much, so that if he knocks, you may open to him; hence, *behold, I stand at the gate, and knock. If any man will hear my voice, and open to me the door, I will come in to him, and will sup with him, and he with me* (Rev 3:20).

1997. ***But know this, that if the master of the house knew at what hour the thief would come, he would certainly watch, and would not suffer his house to be broken into***. But since you do not know which hour, you must keep watch the whole night.

Who is this master of the house? The house is the soul. In it, a man should rest; *when I go into my house*, i.e., into my conscience, *I will repose myself with her* (Wis 8:16). The

illa. Paterfamilias ratio est: Prov. XX, 8: *rex qui sedet in solio, dissipat omne malum intuitu suo*. Aliquando fur perfodit domum suam. Fur est aliqua persuasio falsae doctrinae, vel tentatio aliqua. Et dicitur fur, sicut habetur Io. X, 1: *qui non intrat per ostium in ovile ovium, ille fur est et latro*. Ostium proprie dicitur naturalis cognitio, seu ius naturale. Quisquis ergo per rationem intrat, per ostium intrat; sed qui intrat per ostium concupiscentiae, vel irae, vel huiusmodi, est fur. Fures consueverunt in nocte venire. In Abdia 5: *si fures introissent ad te, si latrones per noctem, quomodo conticuisses?* Unde si de die veniant, non timentur. Sic quando homo est in contemplatione divinorum, tunc non venit tentatio; sed quando remisse se habet, tunc venit. Ideo bene dicit propheta, Ps. LXX, 9: *cum defecerit virtus mea, ne derelinquas me*. Unde debemus vigilare, quia nescimus quando veniet Dominus, scilicet ad iudicium.

Vel possumus referre ad diem mortis; I ad Thess. V, 3: *cum enim dixerint, pax et securitas, tunc repentinus eis superveniet interitus*.

1998. *Et vos estote parati, quia qua hora non putatis, Filius hominis venturus est*. Dicit Chrysostomus quod homines solliciti circa temporalia, vigilant de nocte. Et si pro temporalibus vigilant, multo magis vigilandum est pro spiritualibus; Apoc. III, 3: *si non vigilaveris, veniam ad te tamquam fur*.

1999. *Quis putas est fidelis servus et prudens quem constituit dominus super familiam suam?* Hic specialiter admonet ad vigilandum praelatos. Et

primo alliciendo praemiis;
secundo terrendo suppliciis.
Circa primum tria facit.
Primo ponit idoneitatem boni praelati;
secundo officium;
tertio praemium.

2000. Idoneitas est quod sit fidelis et prudens. In quolibet bono opere duo sunt necessaria: ut intentio constituatur in debito fine, item quod accipiat vias congruas ad illum finem; ideo in officio praelationis haec duo sunt necessaria. Primo quod figat intentionem in debito fine, quem quidam constituunt in seipsis, de quibus dicitur Ez. XXXIV, 2: *vae pastoribus qui pascunt se*; quia illi qui in recto fine intentionem constituunt, non intendunt quod sibi utile sit, sed quod multis, ut salvi fiant. Et hoc totum propter gloriam Dei recte operantur. Qui autem quaerit quod suum est, non. Unde oportet quod sit fidelis; I Cor. IV, 2: *iam quaeritur inter dispensatores, ut fidelis quis inveniatur*. Item debet esse prudens,

head of the house is reason: *the king, who sits on the throne of judgment, scatters away all evil with his look* (Prov 20:8). Sometimes, a thief breaks open his home. The thief is the persuasion of some false teaching, or a temptation. And it is called a thief, as is said, *he who enters not by the door into the sheepfold, but climbs up another way, the same is a thief and a robber* (John 10:1). The door properly names natural knowledge, or the natural law. So whoever enters in through reason, enters through the door; but he who enters through the door of concupiscence, or of anger, or of any such thing, is a thief. Thieves usually come at night. *If thieves had gone in to you, if robbers by night, how would you have held your peace?* (Abdia 5). Hence if they came in the day, they would not be feared. In the same way, when a man is in contemplation of divine things, then temptation does not come; but when he carries himself carelessly, then it comes. So the prophet speaks well, *when my strength will fail, do not forsake me* (Ps 70:9). Hence we should watch, because we do not know when the Lord will come, namely for judgment.

Or, we can refer it to the day of death; *for when they will say, peace and security; then will sudden destruction come upon them* (1 Thess 5:3).

1998. *Therefore you also be ready, because at what hour you know not the Son of man will come*. Chrysostom says that men who are solicitous about temporal things keep watch at night. And if they keep watch for temporal things, much more should watch be kept for spiritual things. *If then you will not watch, I will come to you as a thief* (Rev 3:3).

1999. *Who, do you think, is a faithful and wise servant, whom his lord has appointed over his family, to give them meat in season*. Here he warns the prelates in particular to keep watch. And

first, by enticing them with rewards;
second, by frightening them with punishments.
Concerning the first, he does three things:
first, he sets out the proper quality of a good prelate;
second, the duty;
third, the reward.

2000. The proper quality is that he be faithful and prudent. There are two things necessary in any given good work: that the intention be settled on a due end, and that one take fitting paths to that end. Therefore these two things are necessary in the office of a prelate. First, that he fix his intention on a due end, which some set up as themselves, of whom it says, *woe to the shepherds of Israel, who fed themselves* (Ezek 34:2); for the one who settles his intention on a right end does not intend to be useful to himself, but to many, that they may be saved. And all this is rightly worked for the sake of God's glory. But he who seeks what is his own does not work rightly. Hence he must be faithful; *here now it is required among the dispensers, that a man be*

quia potest esse quod aliquis quaerat gloriam Dei, sed non secundum scientiam. Praelati enim est corripere vitia. Posset ergo ita increpare, quod posset inducere in peccatum. Ideo oportet quod sit prudens. Sup. c. X, 16: *estote prudentes sicut serpentes*.

Et notate quod nominat servum, quia differentia est inter liberum et servum, quia omnis actio servi retorquetur in dominum, non liberi: sic omnis actio praelati referri debet in Deum. Sic Paulus vocabat se servum, cum dicebat, II Cor. IV, 5: *nos autem servos vestros per Iesum*.

Sed quare dicit **quis putas est fidelis servus et prudens?** Quia pauci sunt fideles; Phil. c. II, 21: *omnes enim quae sua sunt quaerunt, non quae Iesu Christi*; Prov. XX, 6: *virum autem fidelem quis inveniet?* Et si pauci fideles, pauciores et prudentes; ideo sic dicit dominus notans paucitatem.

2001. Deinde tangit eorum officium **quem constituit dominus super familiam suam**. Et tria agit. Primo agit de sui institutione super officium suum, cum dicit **quem constituit dominus**, non quod ipse procuret vel muneribus, vel precibus; ad Hebr. c. V, 4: *nullus assumat sibi honorem, sed qui vocatur a Deo sicut Aaron*. Deinde tangit super quod constitutus est, quia **super familiam suam**, scilicet super Ecclesiam suam, non super temporalia, secundum quod dicit Apostolus, II Tim. II, 4: *nemo militans Deo implicat se negotiis saecularibus*. Item oportet eum esse prudentem, ut vigilet circa Ecclesiam, non circa alia quae extra Ecclesiam sunt; I Cor. V, 12: *quia ad nos de his quae foris sunt?* Item tangit officium praelati **ut det illis cibum in tempore**: cibum scilicet doctrinae, boni exempli, et temporalis subsidii; ideo Dominus dicit Petro ter: *pasce... pasce... pasce oves meas*. Pasce verbo, pasce exemplo, pasce temporali subsidio habetur ultimo, sed tamen **in tempore**; Eccle. III, 1: *omnia tempus habent*. Item Io. XVI, 12: *multa habeo vobis dicere, sed non potestis portare modo*. Si enim vult dicere verba, quando non competit, perdit.

2002. Sequitur de praemio; et primo dicit quod est istud; secundo in quo sit.

Quod est praemium? Beatitudo; unde dicit, **beatus**, sive in morte, sive in fine mundi, **quem cum venerit dominus, invenerit sic facientem**, scilicet administrantem, ut dictum est. Ps. CXVIII, 1: *beati immaculati in via, qui ambulant in lege domini*.

2003. Et quare sunt beati? **Amen dico vobis, quoniam super omnia bona sua constituet eum**. Hoc tripliciter exponitur. Uno modo, ut ostendatur in quo consistat omnis beatitudo. Beatitudo enim in aliquo bono

found faithful (1 Cor 4:2). Likewise, he should be prudent, because it could be that someone would seek the glory of God, but not in accordance with knowledge. For it pertains to a prelate to correct vices. So he could rebuke in such a way as would lead men into sin. For this reason, he must be prudent. Above, **be therefore wise as serpents and simple as doves** (Matt 10:16).

And notice that he names him a servant, because the difference between a free man and a servant is that the servant's every action is referred to the master, but not the free man's: thus a prelate's every action should be referred to God. In this way Paul called himself a servant, when he said, *ourselves your servants through Jesus* (2 Cor 4:5).

But why does he say, **who, do you think, is a faithful and wise servant**? Because few are faithful; *for all seek the things that are their own; not the things that are Jesus Christ's* (Phil 2:21); *who will find a faithful man?* (Prov 20:6). And if there are few who are faithful, there are even fewer who are prudent. So the Lord speaks this way to point to the scarcity.

2001. Then he touches on their position: **whom his lord has appointed over his family**. And he does three things. First, he treats of his being established in his office, when he says, **whom his lord has appointed**, not that he himself obtains it by bribes or by requests; *neither does any man take the honor to himself, but he who is called by God, as Aaron was* (Heb 5:4). Then he touches on that over which he is set up, that it is **over his family**, namely over his Church, not over temporal things, in accordance with what the Apostle says, *no man, being a soldier to God, entangles himself with secular businesses* (2 Tim 2:4). Similarly, he must be prudent, that he might keep watch around the Church, not around other things which are outside the Church; *for what have I to do to judge them that are without?* (1 Cor 5:12). Likewise, he touches upon the duty of a prelate: **to give them meat in season**, namely the food of teaching, of good example, and temporal relief. For this reason the Lord says to Peter three times: *feed... feed... feed my sheep* (John 21:16–17). Feed by word, feed by example, feed by temporal relief is had last, but yet **in season**; *all things have their season* (Eccl 3:1). Likewise, *I have yet many things to say to you: but you cannot bear them now* (John 16:12). For if he wants to speak words when it is unsuitable, he wreaks destruction.

2002. There follows concerning the reward: and first, he says what it is; second, what it is in.

What is the reward? Beatitude; hence he says **blessed**, whether at death or at the end of the world, **whom when his lord will come he will find doing so**, namely administering, as was said. *Blessed are the undefiled in the way, who walk in the law of the Lord* (Ps 118:1).

2003. And why are they blessed? **Amen I say to you, he will place him over all his goods**. This is explained in three ways. In one way, to show what all beatitude consists in. For beatitude consists in some good; but all goods are God's. So

consistit; sed omnia bona Dei sunt. Numquid ergo in aliquo istorum est beatitudo? Beatitudo est in illo bono quod est super omnia bona: non enim est aliquis beatus, nisi in illo bono quod Deus est. Unde **super omnia bona sua constituet eum**, idest beatificabitur in illo, scilicet in Deo, qui est super omnia.

Secundo modo exponi potest quod hoc dicit ad ostendendum praeeminentiam, quam habebunt boni praelati. Lc. XII, 37 habetur quod *faciet eos discumbere*; sed hic habetur quod **super omnia bona sua constituet eum**; quia inter omnia praemia maximum est praemium boni praelati; supra V, 19: *qui fecerit et docuerit, hic magnus vocabitur*. Dan. XII, 3: *qui docti fuerint, erunt sicut splendor firmamenti, et qui ad iustitiam erudiunt plurimos, quasi stellae in perpetuas aeternitates*. Et hoc est **super omnia bona sua**, idest super omnia praemia sanctorum.

Tertio modo potest exponi per unionem ad Christum; quia sicut in hoc mundo non perveniet ad statum perfectionis, nisi qui sequitur vestigia Christi, sic nec tunc, nisi qui coniuncti fuerint Christo: et habebunt dominium super omnia, inquantum voluntas sua fit conformis voluntati divinae; Lc. XXII, 29: *et ego dispono vobis, sicut disposuit mihi pater meus regnum*. Et Apoc. II, 28: *qui vicerit, dabo ei stellam matutinam*.

2004. *Si autem dixerit malus ille servus in corde suo* et cetera. Postquam allexit ut sint vigilantes per praemia, hic terret per supplicia. Et

primo ponit culpam;

secundo poenam, ibi **veniet dominus** et cetera.

In culpa duo sunt, scilicet causa culpae, et ipsa culpa; et tamen utrumque culpa est.

2005. Causa culpae est desperatio de adventu *si dixerit: moram facit dominus meus venire*. Augustinus dicit quod aliquis posset dicere hoc nimio desiderio, et hoc demonstrabat qui dicebat: *quando veniam, et apparebo ante faciem Dei mei?* Aliquando dicitur propter desperationem de cito veniendo; Ez. XII, 22: *Fili hominis, quod est proverbium istud in terra Israel dicentium: in longum differentur dies, et peribit omnis visio? Non enim diu tardabit*. II Petr. c. III, 9: *non tardat Dominus promissionem suam*. Unde haec est radix omnium.

2006. Sed quae sunt quae consequuntur inde? Unum crudelitatis, aliud voluptatis. Quantum ad primum dicit **et coeperit percutere conservos suos**, quia reputat sibi subiectos ut servos, contra illud I Petr. V, 3: *sed voluntarie, neque dominantes in cleris*. Et non solum sufficit ei, sed etiam percutit et affligit; Mich. III, 10: *qui aedificatis Sion in sanguinibus*. Vel **percutiunt** fratres, quos servos reputant, malo exemplo. Item istud non sufficit eis, sed convertunt se ad voluptates. **Manducet autem et bibat**

then, is beatitude in some one of those goods? Beatitude is in that good which is over all goods: for there is no beatitude except in that good which is God. Hence, **he will place him over all his goods**, i.e., he will be blessed in that which is over all, namely in God.

In the second way, it can be explained that he says this to show the preeminence which good prelates will have. Luke says that *he will . . . make them sit down to meat* (Luke 12:37), but here it says that **he will place him over all his goods**; for among all rewards, the greatest is the reward of a good prelate. Above, *but he who will do and teach, he will be called great in the kingdom of heaven* (Matt 5:19). *But they that are learned will shine as the brightness of the firmament: and they who instruct many to justice, as stars for all eternity* (Dan 12:3). And this is **over all his goods**, i.e., above every reward of the saints.

In the third way, it can be explained through union with Christ. For just as in this world only those who follow in Christ's footsteps arrive at the state of perfection, so at that time only those who are conjoined to Christ. And they will have dominion over all things, insofar as their will is conformed to the divine will; *and I dispose to you, as my Father has disposed to me, a kingdom* (Luke 22:29). And, *and he who will overcome . . . I will give him the morning star* (Rev 2:28).

2004. **But if that evil servant will say in his heart**. After he has enticed them to vigilance with rewards, here he frightens them with punishments:

first, he sets out the crime;

second, the punishment, at **the lord of that servant will come**.

In the crime there are two things, namely the cause of crime, and the crime itself; and yet either one is a crime.

2005. The cause of the crime is despair of the coming: **but if that evil servant will say in his heart: my lord is long in coming**. Augustine says that someone could say this out of excessive desire, and the one who says, *when will I come and appear before the face of God?* (Ps 41:3) shows this. Sometimes it is said due to despair of his coming quickly; *Son of man, what is this proverb that you have in the land of Israel? Saying: the days will be prolonged, and every vision will fail* (Ezek 12:22). *The Lord delays not his promise* (2 Pet 3:9). Hence this is the root of it all.

2006. But what are the things which follow from it? One of cruelty, another of pleasure. With regard to the first, he says, **and will begin to strike his fellow servants**, because he considers them subjected to himself as servants, contrary to: *but voluntarily: neither as lording it over the clergy* (1 Pet 5:2–3). And this alone is not enough for him, but he even strikes and afflicts them; *you who build up Zion with blood* (Mic 3:10). Or they **strike** their brothers, whom they consider to be servants, with bad example. Likewise this is

cum ebriosis, idest habebit societatem cum voluptuosis, si ipse est voluptuosus.

2007. Et quid erit inde? Ponit iudicium. Primo enim ponit iudicium ex insperato; secundo poenam.

Dicit **veniet Dominus servi illius in die qua non sperat**; quia credit aliquando homo esse securus de longa vita, et tamen subito deficit; I ad Thess. V, 2: *dies Domini sicut fur veniet*; Is. XXX, 13: *subito dum non speratur, veniet contritio eius*.

2008. Et quid fiet inde? Sequitur triplex poena. **Et dividet eum**, non, ut dicit Hieronymus, ut dividat gladio, sed a societate bonorum; infra XXV, 32: **et separabit eos ab invicem, sicut pastor segregat oves ab hoedis**. Et haec est maxima poena. Dicit Origenes sic: in homine tria sunt: est anima, corpus, spirituale donum. Et haec in bonis praelatis non dividentur, sed in malis praelatis. Spirituale donum dividetur, quia accipiet spirituale donum quod eis dederat; corpus autem et anima mittentur in ignem.

Item alia poena est quod annumerabitur iniquis, unde dicit **partemque eius ponet cum hypocritis**. Hypocritae sunt simulatores qui unum profitentur, et aliud agunt: unde partem eius ponet cum talibus. Et sic accipitur Ps. X, 7: *sulphur et spiritus procellarum pars calicis eorum*.

Item adhuc ista non sufficit, sed erit alia poena, quia **ibi erit fletus et stridor dentium**. Iob XXIV, 19: *transibunt enim a frigore nivium ad calorem nimium*. Unde fletus ex fumo generatur, stridor dentium ex frigore. Dicit Origenes quod possumus hinc considerare quod male dicunt qui dicunt quod praelati mali non sunt praelati.

2009. Item notate quamdam similitudinem quam ponit Augustinus. Removeamus ab oculis illum servum de quo fit sermo, et ponamus tres servos, qui diligant adventum domini. Unus dicat: dominus meus cito veniet, et ideo vigilabo. Alius dicat: dominus tardabit, sed volo vigilare. Alter dicat: nescio quando veniet, et ideo volo vigilare. Quis istorum melius dicit? Respondet Augustinus quod primus male decipitur, quia si putat quod cito veniat, et postea tardat, est in periculo ne prae taedio dormiat. Secundus potest decipi, sed non est in periculo. Sed tertius bene facit, qui sub dubio semper expectat; ideo malum est determinare aliquod tempus.

not enough for them, but they turn themselves to pleasures: **and will eat and drink with drunkards**, i.e., he will keep company with sensual men, if he himself is sensual.

2007. And what will come from it? He sets out the judgment: first, he sets out the judgment of the lack of hope; second, the punishment.

He says: **the lord of that servant will come in a day that he hopes not**; for sometimes a man thinks he is sure to have a long life, and yet he suddenly perishes; *the day of the Lord will so come, as a thief in the night* (1 Thess 5:2); *the destruction thereof will come on a sudden, when it is not looked for* (Isa 30:13).

2008. And will happen from there? There follows a threefold punishment. **And will separate him**, as Jerome says, not that he divides him with a sword, but rather he divides him from the society of the good; below, **he will separate them one from another, as the shepherd separates the sheep from the goats** (Matt 25:32). And this is the greatest punishment. Origen speaks thus: There are three things in a man: there is the soul, the body, and the spiritual gift. And these are not divided in good prelates, but in bad prelates. The spiritual gift is divided, because he will take the gift which he had given to him; and the body and the soul will be cast into fire.

Similarly, another punishment is that he will counted among the wicked, hence he says, **and appoint his portion with the hypocrites**. Hypocrites are pretenders who profess one thing, and do another: hence he will place his portion with such men. And the Psalm is taken in this way: *fire and brimstone and storms of winds will be the portion of their cup* (Ps 10:7).

Likewise, even these things are not enough, but there will be another punishment, for **there will be weeping and gnashing of teeth**. *Let him pass from the snow waters to excessive heat, and his sin even to hell* (Job 24:19). Hence weeping is generated by the smoke, and gnashing of teeth by the coldness. Origen says that we can see from here that they speak badly who say that bad prelates are not prelates.

2009. Likewise, note a certain similarity which Augustine sets out. Let us set aside that servant about whom these words were spoken, and let us set out three servants who are eager for the Lord's coming. One says: my lord will come quickly, and for this reason I will keep watch. Another says: the lord will delay, but I wish to keep watch. The other says: I do not know when he will come, and for this reason I wish to keep watch. Which of them speaks better? Augustine responds that the first is badly deceived, because if he thinks that he will come quickly, and later he delays, he is in danger of sleeping out of boredom. The second can be deceived, but is not in danger. But the third does well, who is always expecting with uncertainty; therefore it is bad to settle on some time.

Chapter 25

Lecture 1

25:1 Tunc simile erit regnum caelorum decem virginibus, quae accipientes lampadas suas, exierunt obviam sponso et sponsae. [n. 2011]

25:2 Quinque autem ex eis erant fatuae et quinque prudentes. [n. 2015]

25:3 Sed quinque fatuae acceptis lampadibus non sumpserunt oleum secum. [n. 2016]

25:4 Prudentes vero acceperunt oleum in vasis suis cum lampadibus. [n. 2017]

25:5 Moram autem faciente sponso, dormitaverunt omnes, et dormierunt. [n. 2018]

25:6 Media autem nocte clamor factus est: ecce sponsus venit, exite obviam ei. [n. 2021]

25:7 Tunc surrexerunt omnes virgines illae, et ornaverunt lampades suas. [n. 2023]

25:8 Fatuae autem sapientibus dixerunt: date nobis de oleo vestro, quia lampades nostrae extinguuntur. [n. 2024]

25:9 Responderunt prudentes dicentes: ne forte non sufficiat nobis et vobis, ite potius ad vendentes, et emite vobis. [n. 2025]

25:10 Dum autem irent emere, venit sponsus, et quae paratae erant, intraverunt cum eo ad nuptias, et clausa est ianua. [n. 2027]

25:11 Novissime vero veniunt et reliquae virgines dicentes: domine, domine, aperi nobis. [n. 2030]

25:12 At ille respondens ait: amen dico vobis, nescio vos. [n. 2030]

25:1 Τότε ὁμοιωθήσεται ἡ βασιλεία τῶν οὐρανῶν δέκα παρθένοις, αἵτινες λαβοῦσαι τὰς λαμπάδας ἑαυτῶν ἐξῆλθον εἰς ὑπάντησιν τοῦ νυμφίου.

25:2 πέντε δὲ ἐξ αὐτῶν ἦσαν μωραὶ καὶ πέντε φρόνιμοι.

25:3 αἱ γὰρ μωραὶ λαβοῦσαι τὰς λαμπάδας αὐτῶν οὐκ ἔλαβον μεθ' ἑαυτῶν ἔλαιον.

25:4 αἱ δὲ φρόνιμοι ἔλαβον ἔλαιον ἐν τοῖς ἀγγείοις μετὰ τῶν λαμπάδων ἑαυτῶν.

25:5 χρονίζοντος δὲ τοῦ νυμφίου ἐνύσταξαν πᾶσαι καὶ ἐκάθευδον.

25:6 μέσης δὲ νυκτὸς κραυγὴ γέγονεν· ἰδοὺ ὁ νυμφίος, ἐξέρχεσθε εἰς ἀπάντησιν [αὐτοῦ].

25:7 τότε ἠγέρθησαν πᾶσαι αἱ παρθένοι ἐκεῖναι καὶ ἐκόσμησαν τὰς λαμπάδας ἑαυτῶν.

25:8 αἱ δὲ μωραὶ ταῖς φρονίμοις εἶπαν· δότε ἡμῖν ἐκ τοῦ ἐλαίου ὑμῶν, ὅτι αἱ λαμπάδες ἡμῶν σβέννυνται.

25:9 ἀπεκρίθησαν δὲ αἱ φρόνιμοι λέγουσαι· μήποτε οὐ μὴ ἀρκέσῃ ἡμῖν καὶ ὑμῖν· πορεύεσθε μᾶλλον πρὸς τοὺς πωλοῦντας καὶ ἀγοράσατε ἑαυταῖς.

25:10 ἀπερχομένων δὲ αὐτῶν ἀγοράσαι ἦλθεν ὁ νυμφίος, καὶ αἱ ἕτοιμοι εἰσῆλθον μετ' αὐτοῦ εἰς τοὺς γάμους καὶ ἐκλείσθη ἡ θύρα.

25:11 ὕστερον δὲ ἔρχονται καὶ αἱ λοιπαὶ παρθένοι λέγουσαι· κύριε κύριε, ἄνοιξον ἡμῖν.

25:12 ὁ δὲ ἀποκριθεὶς εἶπεν· ἀμὴν λέγω ὑμῖν, οὐκ οἶδα ὑμᾶς.

25:1 Then the kingdom of heaven will be like to ten virgins, who taking their lamps, went out to meet the bridegroom and the bride. [n. 2011]

25:2 And five of them were foolish, and five wise. [n. 2015]

25:3 But the five foolish, having taken their lamps, did not take oil with them. [n. 2016]

25:4 But the wise took oil in their vessels with the lamps. [n. 2017]

25:5 And the bridegroom being delayed, they all slumbered and slept. [n. 2018]

25:6 And at midnight a cry was made: behold the bridegroom comes, go out to meet him. [n. 2021]

25:7 Then all those virgins rose and trimmed their lamps. [n. 2023]

25:8 And the foolish said to the wise: give us some of your oil, for our lamps have gone out. [n. 2024]

25:9 The wise answered, saying: lest perhaps there is not enough for us and for you, go rather to those who sell, and buy for yourselves. [n. 2025]

25:10 Now while they went to buy, the bridegroom came, and those who were ready, went in with him to the marriage, and the door was shut. [n. 2027]

25:11 But at last the other virgins also came, saying: lord, lord, open to us. [n. 2030]

25:12 But he answering said: amen I say to you, I know you not. [n. 2030]

25:13 Vigilate itaque quia nescitis diem neque horam. [n. 2030]

25:13 γρηγορεῖτε οὖν, ὅτι οὐκ οἴδατε τὴν ἡμέραν οὐδὲ τὴν ὥραν.

25:13 Watch therefore, because you do not know the day nor the hour. [n. 2030]

2010. Supra actum est de adventu Domini ad iudicium, hic agitur de ipso iudicio: unde dividitur istud capitulum in duas partes.

In prima parte loquitur de iudicio per quasdam parabolas;

in secunda manifeste et explicite formam iudicii demonstrat, ibi *cum autem venerit* et cetera.

Circa primum duo facit.

Primo ponitur quaedam parabola, in qua aliqui excluduntur a regno propter defectum interiorem;

in secunda, quod quidam excluduntur propter negligentiam exterioris operationis, ibi *sicut enim homo peregre proficiscens* et cetera.

Prima est de virginibus, quae solent animos hominum exercere: et in hac tria consideranda sunt.

Primo ponitur praeparatio aliquorum se disponentium ut regnent cum Christo;

secundo ponitur excitatio ad iudicium;

tertio adventus iudicii.

Secunda ibi *media autem nocte* etc.; tertia ibi *dum autem irent* et cetera.

Circa primum

primo tangit studium praeparantium;

secundo eorum somnum, ibi *moram autem faciente* et cetera.

Circa primum duo facit.

Primo ponit quod est commune omnibus se praeparantibus;

secundo distinctionem in his, qui se praeparant, ibi *quinque autem* et cetera.

Circa primum quatuor considerantur communia quantum ad omnes: numerus; status; officium; et finis intentus.

2011. Numerus tangitur quod decem erant: *simile est regnum caelorum decem virginibus*.

Sed quare decem? Triplex ratio est. Una quidem, quia decem est numerus universitatis: in numerando procedimus usque ad decem, et post incipimus ad uno; unde per decem, per unum, et per centum universitas significatur.

Vel, secundum Hilarium, omnes obsistunt decem praeceptis observandis, vel obligantur ad ea.

Vel decem propter quinque sensus duplicatos. Sunt enim duplicati uno modo, secundum Gregorium, quia quinque sunt in viris, et quinque in mulieribus: et sic decem. Secundum Hieronymum, duplicantur secundum quod ad diversos sensus referuntur: sunt enim quidam sensus exteriores, et quidam interiores. De visu interiori

2010. Above, the Lord's coming for judgment was treated; here the judgment itself is treated. Hence this chapter is divided into two parts.

In the first part, he speaks of the judgment through certain parables;

in the second, he points out manifestly and explicitly the form of the judgment, at *when the Son of man will come*.

Concerning the first, he does two things:

first, a certain parable is set out, in which some are excluded from the kingdom owing to an interior defect;

in the second, some are excluded owing to the neglect of exterior works, at *for even as a man going into a far country* (Matt 25:14).

The first is about virgins, who are accustomed to train the souls of men: and in this, three things should be considered:

first, the preparation of some, who dispose themselves to reign with Christ, is set out;

second, the awakening for judgment;

third, the coming of the judge.

The second is at *and at midnight a cry*; the third, at *now while they went to buy*.

Concerning the first,

first, he touches upon the zeal of those who prepared;

second, their sleep, at *the bridegroom being delayed*.

Concerning the first, he does two things:

first, he sets out what is common to all those who prepare themselves;

second, the distinction among those who prepare themselves, at *and five of them were foolish*.

Concerning the first, four things common to all are considered: number; state; duty; and the end intended.

2011. The number is touched upon, that there were ten: *then will the kingdom of heaven be like to ten virgins*.

But why ten? There are three reasons. One, because ten is the number of universality: in numbering, we go forward up to ten, and then we begin at one; hence universality is signified by ten, by one, and by one hundred.

Or, according to Hilary, all resist the ten commandments which must be observed, or are obliged to them.

Or, there are ten owing to the five senses taken twice. For they are taken twice in one way according to Gregory, since there are five in men, and five in women, and thus ten. According to Jerome, they are taken twice according as they are referred to different senses, for there are some senses which are exterior, and some which are interior.

dicitur Io. IV, 12: *Deum nemo vidit umquam*. De gustu dicitur Ps. XXXIII, 9: *gustate et videte quoniam suavis est dominus*. De olfactu dicitur Cant. c. I, 3: *in odorem unguentorum tuorum currimus*. Et sic sunt omnes decem, qui ad iudicium veniunt.

2012. Status tangitur cum dicitur **virginibus**. Sed quare dicuntur virgines? Triplex est ratio. Secundum Chrysostomum intelligitur de his qui integritatem carnis servant. Sed quare magis facit mentionem de virginibus? Dicit quod supra XIX, 12 locutus est de virginibus, ubi dicit quod **sunt quidam eunuchi, qui seipsos castraverunt propter regnum caelorum. Qui potest capere capiat**. Ideo cum virginitas sit tantum bonum quod non cadit sub praecepto, sed sub consilio, secundum quod habetur I Cor. VII, 25: *de virginibus praeceptum non habeo, consilium autem do*, si isti damnantur, multo magis et alii.

Vel virgines dicuntur qui ab illecebris quinque sensuum abstinent. Secundum Hieronymum et Origenem virgines dicuntur fideles qui non admittunt corruptelam, secundum quod dicit Apostolus, II Cor. XI, 2: *despondi vos uni viro virginem castam exibere Christo*.

2013. Sequitur videre studium: **quae accipientes lampades suas**. Lampades sunt vasa luminis. Unde secundum Hilarium possumus intelligere animas illuminatas lumine fidei, quod in baptismo receperunt; Is. LVIII, v. 8: *tunc erumpet quasi mane lumen tuum*. Vel per lampades opera signantur, secundum Augustinum: opera enim vestra debent esse lucerna; supra V, 16: **sic luceat lux vestra coram hominibus, ut videant opera vestra bona, et glorificent patrem vestrum qui in caelis est**. Ergo accipere lampades est praeparare animam, vel disponere ad bona opera.

2014. Quartum quod ponitur est quod **exierunt obviam sponso et sponsae**. Quis est sponsus, et quae est sponsa? Dupliciter exponitur secundum duplex matrimonium. Unum divinitatis ad carnem, quod celebratum est in utero virginis; *ipse enim tamquam sponsus procedens de thalamo suo*, Ps. XVIII, 6. Sponsus ipse Filius est, sponsa humana natura; unde nihil aliud est exire obviam sponso et sponsae, nisi servire Christo.

Item est matrimonium Christi et Ecclesiae; Io. III, 29: *qui habet sponsam, sponsus est*. Ergo praeparantes lampades intendunt ut placeant sponso, idest Christo, et sponsae, idest Matri Ecclesiae. Et sic in istis conveniunt.

2015. Ponuntur etiam duo, in quibus discrepant, discrepant, in interiori discretione et exteriori sollicitudine.

Quantum ad primum dicit **quinque autem ex eis erant fatuae, et quinque prudentes**; Prov. X, 23: *sapientia*

About interior vision, it says, *no man has seen God at any time* (1 John 4:12). About taste, it says, *O taste, and see that the Lord is sweet* (Ps 33:9). Of smell, it says, *we will run after you to the odour of your ointments* (Song 1:3). And thus there are ten altogether who come to the judgment.

2012. The state is touched upon when it says, **virgins**. But why are they called virgins? There are three reasons. According to Chrysostom, it is understood of those who preserve the integrity of the body. But why does he make special mention of virgins? He says that above, he spoke of virgins, where he says that **there are eunuchs, who have made themselves eunuchs for the kingdom of heaven. He that can take, let him take it** (Matt 19:12). Therefore since virginity is such a great good that it does not fall under precept, but under counsel, in accord with what it says, *now concerning virgins . . . I give counsel* (1 Cor 7:25), if those are condemned, much more will others be as well.

Or, those are called virgins who withhold the five senses from enticements. According to Jerome and Origen, those are called faithful virgins who admit no seductive influence, in accordance with what the Apostle says, *for I have espoused you to one husband that I may present you as a chaste virgin to Christ* (2 Cor 11:2).

2013. There follows their zeal to see: **who, taking their lamps**. Lamps are vessels of light. Hence according to Hilary we can understand souls enlightened with the light of faith, which they received in baptism; *then will your light break forth as the morning* (Isa 58:8). Or, the lamps signify works, according to Augustine: for your works should be a lamp; above, **so let your light shine before men, that they may see your good works, and glorify your Father who is in heaven** (Matt 5:16). Therefore to take up a lamp is to prepare the soul, or to dispose it for good works.

2014. The fourth thing set out is that they **went out to meet the bridegroom and the bride**. Who is the bridegroom, and who is the bride? It is explained in two ways, in accordance with two marriages. One, the marriage of divinity to flesh, which was celebrated in the womb of a virgin; *he, as a bridegroom coming out of his bride chamber* (Ps 18:6). The bridegroom is the Son himself, the bride human nature; hence to go out to meet the bridegroom and the bride is nothing other than to serve Christ.

Likewise, there is the marriage of Christ and the Church; *he who has the bride, is the bridegroom* (John 3:29). Therefore those who prepare the lamps intend to please the bridegroom, i.e., Christ, and the bride, i.e., Mother Church. And thus they come together in these things.

2015. There are also two things set out in which they differ, namely interior discretion and exterior solicitude.

With regard to the first, he says, **and five of them were foolish, and five wise**; *wisdom is prudence to a man*

est viro prudentia. Ille prudens est qui quae facit, non vult pro nullo perdere. Ideo dictum est supra X, 16: *estote prudentes sicut serpentes*. Vel sic fatui sunt qui divertunt a Deo, vel per malam intentionem et non rectam, vel per falsam doctrinam; Prov. IX, 13: *mulier stulta, et clamosa, plenaque illecebris, et nihil omnino sciens, sedet in foribus domus suae*. Secundum Origenem, qui habet unam virtutem, habet omnes: unde non potest esse unus sensus ordinatus quin sint alii ordinati. Item sicut etiam dicitur Iacob II, 10, *qui delinquit in uno, factus est omnium reus*.

2016. Item discrepant quantum ad exteriorem sollicitudinem, quia *quinque fatuae acceptis lampadibus non sumpserunt oleum secum*. Omnes istae bene volebant habere lampades accensas, quia ipse qui lumen est, vult sibi servire cum lumine; sed lumen non potest nutriri sine oleo: stultus enim esset qui crederet servare lumen in lampade, et non poneret oleum.

2017. Per oleum quatuor significantur. Secundum Hieronymum per oleum significantur bona opera. Et quare? Fides est lumen animarum quo accenduntur lampades. Per bona opera fides nutritur; I ad Tim. I, 18: *hoc praeceptum commendo tibi, fili mi Timothee, secundum praecedentes in te prophetias, ut milites in illis bonam militiam, habens fidem et bonam conscientiam, quam quidam repellentes circa fidem naufragaverunt*. De isto potest accipi quod dicitur Prov. XXI, v. 20: *thesaurus desiderabilis, et oleum in habitaculo iusti, et imprudens homo dissipabit illud*.

Alio modo per oleum misericordia signatur: et sic dicit Chrysostomus. Unde habetur Lc. c. X, 34, quod *Samaritanus infudit vinum et oleum*. Per vinum severitas signatur, per oleum opus misericordiae. Vult ergo quod qui intendit continentiam servare, et non fecerit misericordiam, stultus est. Unde dicit Iac. II, v. 13: *iudicium sine misericordia ei, qui non fecerit misericordiam*.

Item per oleum signatur interior laetitia, de quo in Ps. CIII, 15: *ut exhilaret faciem in oleo*. Et alibi in Ps. XLIV, 8: *unxit te Deus oleo laetitiae*. Multi sunt qui exterius abstinent et quaerunt intus gaudium, scilicet conscientiae, et ibi habent secum oleum. Alii vero non quaerunt gaudium conscientiae, sed gloriam hominum, et isti non habent oleum.

Secundum Origenem per oleum sancta doctrina signatur; Cant. I, 2: *oleum effusum nomen tuum*. Oleum iustitiae rectam doctrinam signat; Ps. CXVIII, 11: *in corde meo abscondi eloquia tua*.

Unde virgines dicuntur qui continentiam servant, qui faciunt misericordiam, qui gaudium interius quaerunt, qui rectam doctrinam assumunt.

2018. Sequitur de somno repentino. Ponitur causa somni, et somnus.

(Prov 10:23). That one is prudent who does not wish what he does to perish for nothing. For this reason it was said above, **be therefore wise as serpents** (Matt 10:16). Or, those are foolish in this way who turn aside from God, either through an intention which is evil and not right, or through false teaching; *a foolish woman and clamorous, and full of allurements, and knowing nothing at all, sat at the door of her house* (Prov 9:13–14). According to Origen, he who has one virtue, has them all; hence one sense cannot be ordered unless the others are ordered. Likewise, as is also said, *and whosoever will keep the whole law, but offend in one point, is guilty of all* (Jas 2:10).

2016. Similarly, they differ with regard to exterior solicitude, for **the five foolish, having taken their lamps, did not take oil with them**. All these certainly wished to have lamps that were lit, because the one who is light, wishes to keep himself with light; but the light cannot be nourished without oil: for he would be a fool who thought to keep light in the lamp, and did not put in oil.

2017. Four things are signified by the oil. According to Jerome, the oil signifies good works. And why? Faith is the light of souls by which the lamps are lit. Faith is nourished by good works; *this precept I commend to you, O son Timothy; according to the prophecies going before on you, that you war in them a good warfare, having faith and a good conscience, which some rejecting have made shipwreck concerning the faith* (1 Tim 1:18–19). What is said in Proverbs can be taken as about this: *there is a treasure to be desired, and oil in the dwelling of the just: and the foolish man will spend it* (Prov 21:20).

In another way, the oil signifies mercy, and this is what Chrysostom says. Hence it says that the Samaritan poured in wine and oil (Luke 10:34). The wine signifies severity; oil, the work of mercy. Therefore, he would have it that the one who aims to preserve continence and does not show mercy is foolish. Hence James says, *for judgment without mercy to him who has not done mercy* (Jas 2:13).

Likewise, the oil signifies interior joy, about which it says, *that he may make the face cheerful with oil* (Ps 103:15). And in another place, *God has anointed you with the oil of gladness* (Ps 44:8). There are many who abstain exteriorly, and seek joy within, namely the joy of conscience, and they have oil with them there. But others do not seek the joy of conscience, but the glory of men, and these do not have oil.

According to Origen, the oil signifies holy teaching; *your name is as oil poured out* (Song 1:2). The oil of justice signifies right teaching; *your words have I hidden in my heart* (Ps 118:11).

Hence those are called virgins who preserve continence, who show mercy, who seek interior joy, who take up right teaching.

2018. There follows concerning the sudden sleep. The cause of the sleep is set out, and the sleep.

Causa somni est mora. Quando enim aliqui expectant aliquem, et maxime de nocte, cito dormiunt. Unde per hoc spatium signatur spatium inter adventum Christi in carne, et adventum ad iudicium; unde dicit **moram autem faciente sponso, dormitaverunt omnes, et dormierunt**. Secundum omnes expositores exponitur de morte.

Sed quare dicitur mors somnus? Hoc est propter spem resurrectionis. Sicut enim qui dormit, intendit evigilare, sic qui dormit morte, intendit resurgere; I Thess. IV, 12: *nolumus vos ignorare de dormientibus, ut non contristemini, sicut et caeteri, qui spem non habent*.

Sed quid est dormitio, et dormitatio? Exponit Gregorius: dormitatio est proprie via ad somnum; unde per dormitationem possumus intelligere longiorem vitam, per somnum mortem.

Secundum Origenem intelligitur de somno pigritiae; Prov. VI, 9: *usquequo, piger, dormies, quando consurges de somno tuo?*

2019. Unde **moram autem faciente sponso**, vel ad iudicium, vel ad mortem, **dormitaverunt omnes, et dormierunt**; vix enim sunt aliqui qui longo tempore vivant quin torpescant. Vel qui totaliter negligunt, **dormiunt**; qui vero aliquo modo aliqualiter desistunt a primo fervore, **dormitant**.

2020. Tunc sequitur excitatio; secundo effectus; tertio petitio fatuarum virginum; quarto responsio sapientum.

2021. Dicit ergo **media nocte clamor factus est; ecce sponsus venit**. De ista dicit Origenes aliter quam alii, et magis secundum litteram. Alii omnes exponunt excitationem istam referendo ad finale iudicium; et secundum hoc iste clamor erit tuba, vel vox Christi; I Thess. IV, 15: *quoniam ipse Dominus in iussu et in voce Archangeli, et in tuba Dei descendet de caelo*; I ad Cor. XV, v. 52: *canet tuba . . . et mortui qui in Christo sunt resurgent primi*.

Et quare **media nocte**? Dicit Hieronymus quod Hebraeus dicit quod sicut angelus in media nocte descendit ad interficiendum primogenita Aegypti, sic venturus est Dominus in media nocte. Unde solebat esse consuetudo apud eos, quod non dimittebatur populus usque ad mediam noctem. Augustinus dicit quod non est propter rationem temporis, sed solum est propter occultationem; I ad Thess. c. V, 2: *dies Domini sicut fur de nocte*.

2022. Sed quid est quod dicit **ecce sponsus venit, exite obviam ei?** Quia tunc omnes resurgent ei obviam; Io. V, 25: *venit hora, in qua omnes qui in monumentis sunt, audient vocem eius*; Amos IV, 12: *praepara te, Israel, in occursum Dei tui*. Origenes refert ad praesentem vitam. Et hoc quando homo detinetur inani gloria, et fit

The cause of sleep is delay. For when someone awaits someone, and most of all at night, he quickly falls asleep. Hence this interval signifies the interval between Christ's coming in the flesh and the coming for judgment; hence he says, **and the bridegroom being delayed, they all slumbered and slept**. According to all expositors, this is explained as about death.

But why is death called sleep? This is owing to the hope of the resurrection. For just as the one who sleeps intends to wake up, so the one who sleeps in death intends to rise again; *and we will not have you ignorant, brethren, concerning them that are asleep, that you be not sorrowful, even as others who have no hope* (1 Thess 4:13).

But what is drowsiness, and sleep? Gregory explains: drowsiness is properly the way toward sleep; hence by drowsiness we can understand a longer life; by sleep, death.

According to Origen, it is understood as about the sleep of laziness; *how long will you sleep, O sluggard? When will you rise out of your sleep?* (Prov 6:9).

2019. Hence, **and the bridegroom being delayed**, either for judgment, or for death, **they all slumbered and slept**; for there are scarcely any who live a long time and do not grow lazy. Or, those who are entirely negligent **slept**, while those who in some way fall a bit from their first fervor **slumbered**.

2020. Then there follows the awakening; second, the effect; third, the foolish virgins' request; fourth, the wise ones' response.

2021. He says therefore, **and at midnight a cry was made: behold the bridegroom comes**. Origen speaks about this differently from the others, and more according to the letter. All the others explain the awakening by referring to the final judgment; and according to this the cry will be the trumpet, or the voice of Christ; *for the Lord himself will come down from heaven with commandment, and with the voice of an archangel, and with the trumpet of God* (1 Thess 4:16); *the trumpet will sound. And the dead who are in Christ, will rise first* (1 Cor 15:52).

And why **at midnight**? Jerome says that a Hebrew says that just as the angel came down at midnight to kill the firstborn of Egypt, so the Lord will come at midnight. Hence it used to be the custom among them that the people would not disperse until midnight. Augustine says that it is not because of the nature of the time, but only because of the hiddenness; *the day of the Lord will so come, as a thief in the night* (1 Thess 5:2).

2022. But why does he say: **behold the bridegroom comes, go out to meet him**? Because at that time all shall rise to meet him; *the hour comes, wherein all who are in the graves will hear the voice of the Son of God* (John 5:28); *be prepared to meet your God, O Israel* (Amos 4:12). Origen refers it to the present life. And this happens when a man is

clamor per praedicatorem, vel per internam inspirationem; tunc revertitur ad Christum; Is. XL, 9: *exalta in fortitudine vocem tuam qui evangelizas Ierusalem*.

2023. Tunc sequitur effectus: ***tunc surrexerunt omnes virgines illae, et ornaverunt lampades suas***. Ad litteram, facto clamore per tubam, vel per vocem Christi, omnes resurgent. Unde Io. V, 25: *omnes enim qui in monumentis sunt, vocem eius audient*.

Sed quid fecerunt? ***Ornaverunt lampades suas***. Sed quid est hoc? Erit ne tempus? Dicendum, quod ornare lampades nihil aliud est quam dinumerare opera quae fecerunt, ut possint congruam rationem reddere. Unde habebunt sollicitudinem quando audient vocem Filii Dei, ut infra: ***quando vidimus te esurientem, et pavimus; sitientem, et dedimus tibi potum?*** et cetera.

Secundum Origenem est planior littera. Quia si ad praesentem vitam referatur, quando fit clamor per praedicatorem, vel internam inspirationem, tunc surgunt a negligentia, et tunc incipiunt surgere ad corrigendum facta sua.

2024. Tunc sequitur petitio fatuarum: ***fatuae autem sapientibus dixerunt: date nobis de oleo vestro, quia lampades nostrae extinguuntur***. Istae erant fatuae quoad aliquid et quoad aliquid non, quia aliquid habebant de lumine fidei; unde dicunt: ***quia lampades nostrae extinguuntur***. Si enim nihil haberent fidei, dicerent *extinctae sunt*, unde cognoscunt quod non possunt ignem sine oleo conservare.

Et quid est hoc dictum? Sive intelligatur per oleum opus misericordiae, sive iustitiae, idem est sensus, quia illi resurgentes, qui non habent haec opera in abundantia, petunt suos defectus suppleri per eos qui habuerunt magis abundanter. Sed hoc non poterit fieri, quia unicuique erunt sua necessaria; ad Gal. ult., 5: *onus suum unusquisque portabit*. Et quia videbant quod non poterat valere lumen fidei sine opere misericordiae, petebant ab aliis qui fecerant opera misericordiae.

Augustinus sic exponit. Consuetum est quod quando aliquis praeoccupatur in aliquo, solet recurrere ad illud in quo sperat; istae habebant exterius fiduciam, quia laudem aliorum quaerebant, unde dicunt: ***date nobis de oleo vestro***, idest de laude vestra, idest laudetis nos de opere nostro. Sed istud non valebit eis, secundum quod habetur ad Rom. c. II, 15: *testimonium reddente illis conscientia ipsorum*; Iob XVI, 20: *ecce enim in caelo est testis meus, et conscius meus in excelsis*. Unde confidunt in humano favore qui prodesse non potest.

Secundum Origenem contingit quod aliqui in rebus vanis expenderunt vitam suam: et cum recognoscunt,

held back by vainglory, and a cry is made through a preacher, or through an internal inspiration; then he turns back to Christ. *Lift up your voice with strength, you who bring good tidings to Jerusalem* (Isa 40:9).

2023. Then there follows the effect: ***then all those virgins arose and trimmed their lamps***. Literally, when the cry is made by the trumpet, or by Christ's voice, all will rise. Hence, *the hour comes, wherein all who are in the graves will hear the voice of the Son of God* (John 5:28).

But what did they do? ***They trimmed their lamps***. But why is this? Will there be time? One should say that to trim the lamps is nothing other than to enumerate the works which they did, that they may be fit to render an account. Hence they will have solicitude when they hear the voice of the Son of God, as below, ***Lord, when did we see you hungry, and fed you; thirsty, and gave you drink?*** (Matt 25:37).

According to Origen, the text is clearer. For if it is referred to the present life, when a cry is made through a preacher, or an internal inspiration, then they rise from negligence, and then they begin to rise to correct their deeds.

2024. Then there follows the foolish ones' request: ***and the foolish said to the wise: give us of your oil, for our lamps are gone out***. These virgins were foolish in one respect, and in another respect not, because they had something of the light of faith; hence they say, ***for our lamps are gone out***. For if they had no faith at all, they would say *have gone out*. So they know that they cannot preserve their fire without oil.

And what is this saying? Whether oil is taken to mean works of mercy, or of justice, the sense is the same, because when they arise, those who do not have these works in abundance ask that their own defects be supplied by those who had works more abundantly. But this will not be able to happen, because for each one his own works will be necessary; *for every one will bear his own burden* (Gal 6:5). And since they saw that their light could not do well without works of mercy, they begged from the others who had done works of mercy.

Augustine explains it this way. It is usually the case that when someone anticipates something, he is accustomed to run back to that in which he hopes; these had external assurance, because they sought the praise of others; hence they say, ***give us of your oil***, i.e., some of your praise, i.e., praise us for our works. But this will do them no good, according to what it says in Romans, *their conscience bearing witness to them* (Rom 2:15); *for behold my witness is in heaven, and he who knows my conscience is on high* (Job 16:20). Hence they confide in human favor, which cannot be of profit.

According to Origen, it happens that some men spend their life in vain things; and when they realize this, they run

recurrunt ad alios, et petunt orationes et beneficia eorum. Et in hoc non sunt fatui si incipiunt reverti ad Dominum.

2025. *Responderunt prudentes dicentes*. Hic ponitur responsio sapientum, et in ista responsione duo ponuntur. Et primo ponitur responsio repudiandi; item ponitur quoddam consilium, ibi *ite potius ad vendentes*.

Et quae est ratio? *Ne forte non sufficiat nobis et vobis*. Unde, quia oleum misericordiae, vel interius gaudium, vel exteriora opera non sufficiunt nobis et vobis, sicut dicitur I Petr. IV, 18: *si iustus vix salvabitur, impius et peccator ubi parebunt?* Et Apostolus Rom. VIII, 18: *non sunt condignae passiones huius temporis ad futuram gloriam quae revelabitur in nobis.* Et Is. LXIV, 6: *omnes iustitiae vestrae tamquam pannus menstruatae*.

Quia ergo non sufficit nobis et vobis, *ite potius ad vendentes et emite vobis*.

2026. Sed numquid erit tempus quod requirant sibi oleum? Ideo intelligendum quod istud magis dicitur per modum improperii quam per modum consilii; quasi dicerent: *debuissetis ivisse*.

Secundum Chrysostomum isti vendentes sunt pauperes, quia mercantur regnum; Lc. XVI, v. 9: *facite vobis amicos de mammona iniquitatis*; unde dicunt *ite*, idest ire debuissetis. Secundum Augustinum dicitur enim per modum improperii. Venditores olei sunt adulatores, unde videntes quod istae petunt auxilium, dicunt: *ite potius ad vendentes, et emite vobis*; quasi dicerent: *vos numquam quaesistis nisi oleum, idest laudem humanam, modo eatis ad mundum, et ematis illud testimonium quod semper quaesistis*.

Secundum Origenem plana est littera, quia vult quod totum in mundo isto contingat. Aliquando accidit quod peccator videt iustum, et petit quid debeat facere. Sed aliqui sunt ita sapientes quod sibi sufficit sapientia sua, sed non sufficit sibi et aliis. Unde tales dicunt illis, qui ab eis petunt consilium: non habemus tantum de doctrina spirituali quod possimus nobis et vobis sufficere; ideo ite ad doctores Ecclesiae, et ad sapientes qui vendent vobis. De ista habetis Is. LV, 1: *omnes sitientes venite ad aquas, et qui non habetis argentum, properate, emite, et comedite*.

Sed quomodo sine argento venditur? Dico quod sapientia venditur sine argento. Et quod est pretium eius? Quod homo libenter studeat, hoc est pretium sapientiae; Prov. II, v. 4: *si quaesieris eam quasi pecuniam, et sicut thesauros effoderis illam, tunc intelliges timorem, et scientiam Dei invenies*.

2027. *Dum autem irent emere, venit sponsus*. Dicit Augustinus quod quidam referunt istud ad statum praesentis vitae; sed non potest stare cum eo quod dicitur *et*

2025. *The wise answered, saying*. Here the wise ones' response is set out, and in this response two things are set out. And first, the refusal is set out; likewise, a certain counsel is set out, at *go rather to those who sell*.

And what is the reason? *Lest perhaps there be not enough for us and for you*. So, since the oil of mercy, or interior joy, or exterior works are not enough for us and for you, as is said, *and if the just man will scarcely be saved, where will the ungodly and the sinner appear?* (1 Pet 4:18). And the Apostle, *for I reckon that the sufferings of this time are not worthy to be compared with the glory to come, that will be revealed in us* (Rom 8:18). And, *all our justices as the rag of a menstruous woman* (Isa 64:6).

Since therefore there is not enough for us and for you, *go rather to those who sell, and buy for yourselves*.

2026. But will there be time for them to acquire oil for themselves? So one should understand that this is said rather in the manner of a rebuke than in the manner of a counsel; as though to say: *you should have gone*.

According to Chrysostom, these sellers are the poor, because they buy the kingdom; *make unto you friends of the mammon of iniquity* (Luke 16:9); hence they say, *go*, i.e., you were supposed to go. According to Augustine, it is said in the manner of a rebuke. The sellers of oil are the flatterers, hence, seeing that these foolish ones beg for help, they say: *go rather to those who sell, and buy for yourselves*, as though to say: *you never sought anything but oil*, i.e., human praise, *now go to the world and buy that testimony you have always sought*.

According to Origen, the text is more clear, for he would have it that all this happens in this world. It sometimes happens that a sinner sees a just man, and asks what he should do. But some are wise in such a way that their wisdom is enough for themselves, but is not enough for themselves and others. Hence such men say to those who ask their advice: we do not have so much spiritual teaching that we can suffice for us and for you, so go to the teachers of the Church, and to the wise men who will sell to you. About this, it says, *all you who thirst, come to the waters: and you who have no money make haste, buy, and eat* (Isa 55:1).

But how is it sold without money? I say that wisdom is sold without money. And what is its price? That a man freely study, this is the price of wisdom; *if you will seek her as money, and will dig for her as for a treasure: then will you understand the fear of the Lord, and will find the knowledge of God* (Prov 2:4-5).

2027. *Now while they went to buy, the bridegroom came*. Augustine says that some refer this to the state of the present life; but this cannot be reconciled with the fact that

clausa est ianua. Ideo Origenes etiam hoc exponit de futuro adventu. Et tria facit.

Primo ponitur adventus iudicis;

secundo receptio bonorum;

tertio exclusio malorum.

2028. Dicit ergo *dum irent emere venit sponsus*; idest dum haberent sollicitudinem quomodo excusarent se in iudicio, venit Dominus ad iudicium. Sed Origenes dicit quod quidam sunt qui venient ad consilium, vel ad sacerdotes, et cum deliberatione ut convertantur, et tunc in adventu moriuntur. Unde tunc venit sponsus, quando homo moritur.

Sed quid est quod hic dicitur, *veniente sponso*, cum supra dixerit, *exierunt obviam sponso et sponsae*? Ratio est, quia in iudicio sponsa, idest caro Christi, erit assumpta in glorificationem. Vel si referamus ad Ecclesiam, tunc perfecte ipsa unietur ipsi sponso per adhaesionem. Unde Apostolus I Cor. VI, 17: *qui adhaeret Deo, unus spiritus est cum illo*.

2029. Et sequitur *et quae paratae erant, intraverunt cum eo ad nuptias*. Istae nuptiae sunt regnum caelorum, de quo Apoc. c. XVII, 14: *quoniam Dominus dominorum est, et Rex regum, et qui cum illo sunt vocati, et electi, et fideles*. Et statim *clausa est ianua*, quia nulli postea aperietur. Modo autem aperitur; unde Ps. XXIII, 7: *attollite portas, principes, vestras*. Et Apoc. IV, 1: *post haec vidi, et ecce ostium apertum in caelo*. Sed tunc claudetur.

2030. Consequenter ponitur repulsio malorum: et dicuntur tria. Primo exprimitur negligentia, quia tarde veniunt; unde dicitur *novissime autem veniunt*. Unde signat eos qui tardam poenitentiam agunt; Sap. V, 3: *dicentes intra se, poenitentiam agentes, et prae angustia spiritus gementes*.

Desiderium tangitur cum dicunt: *domine, domine, aperi nobis*. Unde in hoc quod dicunt eum *dominum* dicunt aliquid per quod deberent impetrare. Per hoc autem quod geminant, signatur quod ex angustia petant; unde dicitur supra VII, 21: *non omnis qui dicit mihi, Domine, Domine, intrabit in regnum caelorum*. Desiderium autem eorum tangitur cum dicitur *aperi nobis*.

Sequitur repulsio: *at ille respondens ait: amen dico vobis, nescio vos*; idest non approbo vos. *Novit enim Dominus qui sunt eius*, II ad Tim. II, 19, sicut artifex nescit opus quod discordat ab arte sua.

Consequenter concludit: *vigilate itaque et orate quia nescitis diem neque horam*.

it says, *and the door was shut*. So even Origen explains this as about the future coming. And he does three things:

first, the coming of the judge is set out;

second, the acceptance of the good;

third, the exclusion of the evil.

2028. He says therefore, *now while they went to buy, the bridegroom came*; i.e., while they were being solicitous about how they would excuse themselves at the judgment, the Lord came for judgment. But Origen says that there are some who will come for advice, even to the priests, and with deliberation, in order to be converted, and then in coming they die. Hence the bridegroom comes at that point, when a man dies.

But why does it say, *the bridegroom came*, since he had said above that they *went out to meet the bridegroom and the bride*? The reason is that at the judgment the bride, i.e., the flesh of Christ, will be taken up unto glorification. Or if we refer it to the Church, she will then be perfectly united to the bridegroom through adherence. Hence the Apostle: *but he who is joined to the Lord, is one spirit* (1 Cor 6:17).

2029. And there follows: *and those who were ready, went in with him to the marriage*. This marriage is the kingdom of heaven, about which it says: *because he is Lord of lords, and King of kings, and they that are with him are called, and elect, and faithful* (Rev 17:14). And immediately *the door was shut*, because it will never afterwards be opened. But it is open at the present time; hence, *lift up your gates, O princes* (Ps 23:7). And, *after these things I looked, and behold a door was opened in heaven* (Rev 4:1). But at that time it will be closed.

2030. Next the rejection of the evil is set out; and three things are said. First, their negligence is expressed, because they came late; hence it says, *but at last the other virgins also came*. Hence it signifies those who do penance late; *saying within themselves, repenting, and groaning for anguish of spirit* (Wis 5:3).

Desire is touched upon when they say: *lord, lord, open to us*. Hence by the fact that they call him *lord*, they say something through which they were supposed to obtain their request. And the fact that they repeat the word *lord* signifies that they ask out of anguish; hence it says above, *not every one who says to me, Lord, Lord, will enter into the kingdom of heaven* (Matt 7:21). Further, their desire is touched upon when it says, *open to us*.

There follows the rejection: *but he answering said: amen I say to you, I know you not*; i.e., I do not approve you. For *the Lord knows who are his* (2 Tim 2:19), as an artisan does not know a work which is not in harmony with his art.

Next he concludes: *watch therefore, because you do not know the day nor the hour*.

Lecture 2

25:14 Sicut enim homo peregre proficiscens vocavit servos suos, et tradidit illis bona sua; [n. 2032]

25:15 et uni dedit quinque talenta, alii autem duo, alii vero unum, unicuique secundum propriam virtutem, et profectus est statim. [n. 2036]

25:16 Abiit autem qui quinque talenta acceperat, et operatus est in eis, et lucratus est alia quinque. [n. 2044]

25:17 Similiter qui duo acceperat, lucratus est alia duo. [n. 2046]

25:18 Qui autem unum acceperat, abiens fodit in terram, et abscondit pecuniam domini sui. [n. 2047]

25:19 Post multum vero temporis venit dominus servorum illorum, et posuit rationem cum eis. [n. 2048]

25:20 Et accedens qui quinque talenta acceperat, obtulit alia quinque talenta, dicens: domine, quinque talenta tradidisti mihi, ecce alia quinque superlucratus sum. [n. 2050]

25:21 Ait illi dominus eius: euge, serve bone et fidelis, quia super pauca fuisti fidelis, super multa te constituam: intra in gaudium domini tui. [n. 2052]

25:22 Accessit autem et qui duo talenta acceperat, et ait: domine, duo talenta tradidisti mihi, ecce alia duo lucratus sum. [n. 2055]

25:23 Ait illi dominus eius: euge, serve bone et fidelis, quia super pauca fuisti fidelis, supra multa te constituam: intra in gaudium domini tui [n. 2055]

25:14 Ὥσπερ γὰρ ἄνθρωπος ἀποδημῶν ἐκάλεσεν τοὺς ἰδίους δούλους καὶ παρέδωκεν αὐτοῖς τὰ ὑπάρχοντα αὐτοῦ,

25:15 καὶ ᾧ μὲν ἔδωκεν πέντε τάλαντα, ᾧ δὲ δύο, ᾧ δὲ ἕν, ἑκάστῳ κατὰ τὴν ἰδίαν δύναμιν, καὶ ἀπεδήμησεν. εὐθέως

25:16 πορευθεὶς ὁ τὰ πέντε τάλαντα λαβὼν ἠργάσατο ἐν αὐτοῖς καὶ ἐκέρδησεν ἄλλα πέντε·

25:17 ὡσαύτως ὁ τὰ δύο ἐκέρδησεν ἄλλα δύο.

25:18 ὁ δὲ τὸ ἓν λαβὼν ἀπελθὼν ὤρυξεν γῆν καὶ ἔκρυψεν τὸ ἀργύριον τοῦ κυρίου αὐτοῦ.

25:19 μετὰ δὲ πολὺν χρόνον ἔρχεται ὁ κύριος τῶν δούλων ἐκείνων καὶ συναίρει λόγον μετ' αὐτῶν.

25:20 καὶ προσελθὼν ὁ τὰ πέντε τάλαντα λαβὼν προσήνεγκεν ἄλλα πέντε τάλαντα λέγων· κύριε, πέντε τάλαντά μοι παρέδωκας· ἴδε ἄλλα πέντε τάλαντα ἐκέρδησα.

25:21 ἔφη αὐτῷ ὁ κύριος αὐτοῦ· εὖ, δοῦλε ἀγαθὲ καὶ πιστέ, ἐπὶ ὀλίγα ἦς πιστός, ἐπὶ πολλῶν σε καταστήσω· εἴσελθε εἰς τὴν χαρὰν τοῦ κυρίου σου.

25:22 προσελθὼν [δὲ] καὶ ὁ τὰ δύο τάλαντα εἶπεν· κύριε, δύο τάλαντά μοι παρέδωκας· ἴδε ἄλλα δύο τάλαντα ἐκέρδησα.

25:23 ἔφη αὐτῷ ὁ κύριος αὐτοῦ· εὖ, δοῦλε ἀγαθὲ καὶ πιστέ, ἐπὶ ὀλίγα ἦς πιστός, ἐπὶ πολλῶν σε καταστήσω· εἴσελθε εἰς τὴν χαρὰν τοῦ κυρίου σου.

25:14 For even as a man going into a far country, called his servants, and delivered to them his goods; [n. 2032]

25:15 and to one he gave five talents, and to another two, and to another one, to every one according to his proper ability, and immediately he took his journey. [n. 2036]

25:16 And he who had received the five talents, went his way, and worked with the same, and gained another five. [n. 2044]

25:17 And in like manner he who had received the two, gained another two. [n. 2046]

25:18 But he who had received the one, going his way, dug into the earth, and hid his lord's money. [n. 2047]

25:19 But after a long time the lord of those servants came, and reckoned with them. [n. 2048]

25:20 And he who had received the five talents coming, brought another five talents, saying: lord, you did deliver to me five talents, behold I have gained another five over and above. [n. 2050]

25:21 His lord said to him: well done, good and faithful servant, because you have been faithful over a few things, I will place you over many things: enter into the joy of your lord. [n. 2052]

25:22 And he also who had received the two talents came and said: lord, you delivered two talents to me, behold I have gained another two. [n. 2055]

25:23 His lord said to him: well done, good and faithful servant, because you have been faithful over a few things, I will place you over many things: enter into the joy of your lord. [n. 2055]

25:24 Accedens autem et qui unum talentum acceperat, ait: domine, scio quia homo durus es, metis ubi non seminasti et congregas ubi non sparsisti; [n. 2057]	25:24 προσελθὼν δὲ καὶ ὁ τὸ ἓν τάλαντον εἰληφὼς εἶπεν· κύριε, ἔγνων σε ὅτι σκληρὸς εἶ ἄνθρωπος, θερίζων ὅπου οὐκ ἔσπειρας καὶ συνάγων ὅθεν οὐ διεσκόρπισας,	25:24 But he who had received the one talent, came and said: lord, I know that you are a hard man; you reap where you have not sown, and gather where you have not scattered. [n. 2057]
25:25 et timens abii, et abscondi talentum tuum in terra. Ecce habes quod tuum est. [n. 2064]	25:25 καὶ φοβηθεὶς ἀπελθὼν ἔκρυψα τὸ τάλαντόν σου ἐν τῇ γῇ· ἴδε ἔχεις τὸ σόν.	25:25 And being afraid, I went and hid your talent in the earth. Behold here you have that which is yours. [n. 2064]
25:26 Respondens autem dominus eius dixit ei: serve male et piger, sciebas quia meto ubi non semino et congrego ubi non sparsi: [n. 2066]	25:26 ἀποκριθεὶς δὲ ὁ κύριος αὐτοῦ εἶπεν αὐτῷ· πονηρὲ δοῦλε καὶ ὀκνηρέ, ᾔδεις ὅτι θερίζω ὅπου οὐκ ἔσπειρα καὶ συνάγω ὅθεν οὐ διεσκόρπισα;	25:26 And his lord answering, said to him: wicked and slothful servant, you knew that I reap where I sow not, and gather where I have not scattered; [n. 2066]
25:27 oportuit ergo te mittere pecuniam meam nummulariis, et veniens ego recepissem utique quod meum est cum usura. [n. 2070]	25:27 ἔδει σε οὖν βαλεῖν τὰ ἀργύριά μου τοῖς τραπεζίταις, καὶ ἐλθὼν ἐγὼ ἐκομισάμην ἂν τὸ ἐμὸν σὺν τόκῳ.	25:27 therefore you should have committed my money to the bankers, and at my coming I would have received my own with usury. [n. 2070]
25:28 Tollite itaque ab eo talentum, et date ei qui habet decem talenta. [n. 2073]	25:28 ἄρατε οὖν ἀπ' αὐτοῦ τὸ τάλαντον καὶ δότε τῷ ἔχοντι τὰ δέκα τάλαντα·	25:28 Take away therefore, the talent from him, and give it to him who has ten talents. [n. 2073]
25:29 Omni enim habenti dabitur, et abundabit, ei autem qui non habet, et quod videtur habere, auferetur ab eo. [n. 2074]	25:29 τῷ γὰρ ἔχοντι παντὶ δοθήσεται καὶ περισσευθήσεται, τοῦ δὲ μὴ ἔχοντος καὶ ὃ ἔχει ἀρθήσεται ἀπ' αὐτοῦ.	25:29 For to every one who has will be given, and he will abound, but from him who has not, that also which he seemed to have will be taken away. [n. 2074]
25:30 Et inutilem servum eiicite in tenebras exteriores: illic erit fletus et stridor dentium. [n. 2075]	25:30 καὶ τὸν ἀχρεῖον δοῦλον ἐκβάλετε εἰς τὸ σκότος τὸ ἐξώτερον· ἐκεῖ ἔσται ὁ κλαυθμὸς καὶ ὁ βρυγμὸς τῶν ὀδόντων.	25:30 And cast the unprofitable servant out into the exterior darkness; there will be weeping and gnashing of teeth. [n. 2075]

2031. Supra posuit Dominus parabolam de iudicio, in qua reprobatur aliquis propter hoc quod bonum spirituale interius susceptum non conservat, hic vero ponit parabolam, in qua quis bona suscepta non multiplicat: unde dividitur. Quia

    primo de distributione donorum agit;
    secundo de usu eorum;
    tertio de iudicio utentium.

Secunda ibi *abiit autem qui quinque talenta acceperat* etc.; tertia ibi *post multum vero temporis* et cetera.

    Circa primum tria facit.
    Primo ponit necessitatem distribuendi;
    secundo distributionem;
    tertio recessum distribuentis.

2032. Necessitatem ostendit in hoc quod dicit *sicut enim homo peregre proficiscens vocavit servos suos, et tradidit illis bona sua*. Ubi debetis notare quod iste homo Christus est. Et possumus dicere quod peregre

2031. Above, the Lord set out a parable about the judgment in which someone is rejected owing to the fact that he does not preserve a spiritual good interiorly received; but here he sets out a parable in which someone does not multiply the goods received, whence it is divided. For

    first, he treats of the distribution of gifts;
    second, of their use;
    third, of the judgment of the users.

The second is at *and he who had received the five talents, went his way*; the third, at *but after a long time, the lord of those servants came*.

    Concerning the first, he does three things:
    first, he sets out the need for distributing the gifts;
    second, the distribution;
    third, the departure of the one distributing.

2032. He shows the need when he says: *for even as a man going into a far country, called his servants, and delivered to them his goods*. Here you should note that this man is Christ. And we can say that he went abroad in three

proficiscebatur tripliciter: quia pergebat in locum, qui quamvis sit sibi proprius per divinitatem, scilicet in caelum, tamen peregrinus erat secundum carnem, quia nulla caro ibi ascenderat. Unde Io. III, 13: *nemo ascendit in caelum, nisi qui descendit de caelo, Filius hominis qui est in caelo.*

Item proficiscebatur in caelum, quia in mundo peregrinus existens in caelum proficiscebatur; Ier. XIV, 8: *quare futurus es quasi colonus in terra, et quasi viator declinans ad manendum?*

Item potest intelligi spiritualiter: nunc enim peregrinatur a nobis, quoniam nos peregrinamur ab eo; II ad Cor. V, 6: *dum sumus in corpore peregrinamur a domino.* Quando autem videbimus eum, tunc non erimus sicut peregrini, sed sicut cives et domestici Dei.

2033. Et notandum quod, sicut dicit Origenes, ubi ponitur **sicut** debet iungi aliquid, nisi ponatur in similitudine, sicut habetur supra XXIV, 27: **sicut enim fulgor exit ab oriente, ita erit adventus Filii Dei**. Sed hic non ponitur in similitudine, et non ponitur postea aliud; propter hoc debet sic legi. Aliquis peregre proficiscens sicut homo, quia Christus et Deus et homo est. Unde secundum quod Deus, non peregrinatur, quia *omnia nuda et aperta sunt oculis eius*, ad Hebr. IV, 13. Peregre autem proficiscitur sicut homo; Io. I, 14: *vidimus eum tamquam unigenitum a Patre*, idest sicut unigenitum a Patre.

2034. Et hoc fuit necesse ex quo peregre proficisceretur, quod curam committeret de suis; et hoc facit cum dicit **vocavit servos suos et tradidit illis bona sua**. Et

primo tangitur liberalitas dantis;
secundo diversitas donorum;
item discretio dandi.

2035. Dantis liberalitas in duobus tangitur: eo quod praevenit eos quibus dedit, item eo quod abundanter dedit.

Eo quod praevenit, quia qui expectat dare, diminuit de liberalitate sua; non sic autem dominus; in Ps. XX, 4: *domine, praevenisti eum in benedictionibus dulcedinis.* Unde **vocavit servos suos**, non illi ipsum; unde Io. c. XV, 16: *non vos me elegistis, sed ego elegi vos*; Rom. VIII, 29: *quos praescivit, hos et praedestinavit.*

Item tangitur liberalitas, quia de suo: *dedit bona sua*, non aliena. Aliqui bene sunt liberales de alieno, sed non de suo; iste autem de suo. Unde de isto potest intelligi quod dicitur in Ps. LXVII, 19: *ascendisti in altum, cepisti captivitatem, dedisti dona hominibus.*

2036. Consequenter ponitur diversitas donorum: **et uni dedit quinque talenta, alii autem duo, alii vero**

ways: because he traveled in place, for although he is in the place proper to him through his divinity, namely in heaven, yet he is far off according to the flesh, because no flesh had ascended there. Hence, *and no man has ascended into heaven, but he who descended from heaven, the Son of man who is in heaven* (John 3:13).

Similarly, he departed into heaven because, being a foreigner in the world, he departed into heaven; *why will you be a stranger in the land, and as a wayfaring man turning in to lodge?* (Jer 14:8).

Likewise, it can be understood spiritually: for now he is absent from us, because we are absent from him; *while we are in the body, we are absent from the Lord* (2 Cor 5:6). But when we see him, then we will not be like foreigners, but like citizens and members of God's household.

2033. And one should note that, as Origen says, where **as** is set down, something should be joined to it, unless it is set out in a likeness, as is had above, **for as lightning comes out of the east, and appears even into the west: so will the coming of the Son of man be** (Matt 24:27). But here it is not set down in a likeness, and nothing is set down afterward; because of this, it should be read in this way: someone going abroad as a man, for Christ is both God and man. Hence according as he is God, he does not set out abroad, because *all things are naked and open to his eyes*, (Heb 4:13). But he goes abroad as a man; *and we saw his glory, the glory as it were of the only begotten of the Father* (John 1:14), i.e., as the only begotten of the Father.

2034. And because he was setting out abroad, it was necessary that he entrust the care of his own things to someone; and he does this when he says he **called his servants, and delivered to them his goods**. And

first, the liberality of the one giving is touched upon;
second, the diversity of the gifts;
likewise, the discretion of the giving.

2035. The liberality of the one giving is touched upon in two ways: by the fact that he preceded those to whom he gave, and likewise by the fact that he gave abundantly.

By the fact that he preceded, because the one who expects to give diminishes his liberality, but not so the Lord; *for you have prevented him with blessings of sweetness* (Ps 20:4). Hence he **called his servants**, not they him; hence, *you have not chosen me: but I have chosen you* (John 15:16); *for whom he foreknew, he also predestined* (Rom 8:29).

Similarly, his liberality is touched upon because it was from his own things: he gave his own goods, not another's. Some are quite liberal with another's goods, but not with their own; but this man was liberal with his own. Hence what is said in the Psalm can be understood as about this man: *you have ascended on high, you have led captivity captive; you have given gifts to men* (Ps 67:19).

2036. Next, the diversity of the gifts is set out: **and to one he gave five talents, and to another two, and to another**

unum. Omnes istos dividit per tres, in fructum trigesimum, sexagesimum, et centesimum; quia omnis multitudo dividitur in summum, et infimum, et medium.

Ista **talenta** sunt diversa dona gratiarum: sicut enim talentum pondus dicitur metalli, sic gratia pondus est quod inclinat ipsam animam; unde amor est pondus animae. Apostolus, I ad Cor. XII, 4: *divisiones gratiarum sunt*: unde ista dona dividuntur, ita quod non aequaliter dantur omnibus; ad Eph. IV, v. 7: *unicuique nostrum data est gratia secundum mensuram donationis Christi*. Et hoc est quod dicit: **uni dedit quinque talenta, alii autem duo, alii vero unum**.

Ista talenta sunt diversa dona gratiarum: sicut enim talentum pondus dicitur metalli, sic gratia pondus est quod inclinat ipsam animam; unde amor est pondus animae. Apostolus, I ad Cor. XII, 4: *divisiones gratiarum sunt*: unde ista dona dividuntur, ita quod non aequaliter dantur omnibus; ad Eph. IV, v. 7: *unicuique nostrum data est gratia secundum mensuram donationis Christi*. Et hoc est quod dicit: **uni dedit quinque talenta, alii autem duo, alii vero unum**.

2037. Et quae est ratio huius numeri? Possumus dicere quod aliquis ita superabundat, quod habet mensuram dupli; aliquis vero ita quod ultra duplum. Unde qui accipit duo, se habet ad illum qui unum, sicut proportio dupli: qui autem quinque, se habet ultra proportionem dupli. Unde vult dicere quod aliquis accipit quinque, qui accipit secundum mensuram incomparabilem.

Possumus etiam dicere quod ista dona sunt eloquia Dei, verba sapientiae: frequenter enim sapientia divitiis comparatur; Is. XXXIII, 6: *divitiae salutis sapientia*.

2038. Quid est quod dicit, quod **uni dedit quinque talenta, alii autem duo, alii vero unum**? Origenes dicit quod illi dedit quinque talenta, qui omnia quae in Scriptura dicuntur, ad spiritualem intellectum refert; unde dictum est supra: sicut sunt quinque sensus corporales, sic sunt quinque spirituales. Sic Dominus apostolis dedit. Lc. XXIV, v. 45 dicitur quod *aperuit eis sensum, ut intelligerent Scripturas*. Et in Daniele I, 17 dicitur quod *dedit Deus pueris intelligentiam in omni Scriptura*.

Qui autem sunt illi, qui duo accipiunt? Secundum Origenem dualitas numerus est materiae, unde omnis numerus est ex binario et unitate; unde binario attribuitur materia, unitati forma. Unde illi dicuntur duo recipere, qui minus recipiunt, quia nesciunt se in omnibus regere; sed aliquid habent in quo sciunt, quia sunt boni aedificatores, vel huiusmodi. Unde secundum Origenem plus accipit qui recipit unum, quam qui duo.

Secundum Gregorium et Hieronymum est e converso, quia per quinque talenta intelliguntur quinque

one. He divided all these things by three, into the fruit thirty-fold, sixty-fold, and a hundred-fold; for every multitude is divided into the highest, the least, and the in-between.

These **talents** are the diverse gifts of grace: for as a talent is a weight of metal, so grace is a weight which inclines the soul itself; hence love is the weight of the soul. The Apostle: *now there are diversities of graces* (1 Cor 12:4); hence these gifts are divided such that they are not given equally to all. *But to every one of us is given grace, according to the measure of the giving of Christ* (Eph 4:7). And this is what he says: **to one he gave five talents, and to another two, and to another one**.

These talents are the various gifts of grace: for as a weight of metal is said to be a talent, so is the weight of grace which inclines the soul; whence love is the weight of the soul. The Apostle says: *there are diversities of graces* (1 Cor 12:4), hence these gifts are divided and are thus not equally given to all. *Grace was given to each one of us according to the measure of the gifts of Christ* (Eph 4:7). And thus it is said, **to one he gave five talents, to another, however, two, but to another, one**.

2037. And what is the reason for this number? We can say that someone superabounds such that he has a double measure, but someone else such that he has more than double. Hence the one who receives two stands to the one who receives one in a double proportion; but the one who receives five stands in a proportion of more than double. Hence he wishes to say that he receives five who receives according to an incomparable measure.

We can also say that these gifts are the utterances of God, words of wisdom: for wisdom is frequently compared to gifts; *riches of salvation, wisdom and knowledge* (Isa 33:6).

2038. Why does he say that **to one he gave five talents, and to another two, and to another one**? Origen says that he gave five talents to the one who refers everything said in Scripture to a spiritual understanding; hence it was said above that just as there five bodily senses, so there are five spiritual senses. The Lord gave to the apostles in this way. Luke says that *he opened their understanding, that they might understand the Scriptures* (Luke 24:45). And it says that *God gave the children the understanding of all Scripture* (Dan 1:17).

But who are the ones who receive two? According to Origen, two is the number of matter, whence every number is made out of two and one. Hence to the two is attributed matter, to the one, form. So those are said to receive two who receive less, because they do not know how to rule themselves in all things; but they have something in which they know how, since they are good builders, or suchlike. Hence according to Origen, the one who receives one receives more than the one who receives two.

According to Gregory and Jerome it is the other way around, for by the five talents are understood the five senses:

sensus: unde ille recipit quinque talenta, qui gratiam a Deo recipit circa temporalia, circa quae operatio sensuum versatur. Per duo autem talenta intelliguntur sensus et intellectus. Per unum vero assignatur intellectus solum. Unde ille unum recipit, qui gratiam intellectus recipit, non gratiam operandi.

Secundum Hilarium, ille recipit quinque qui Christum invenit in quinque libris Moysi; ille autem duo, qui gratiam Novi et Veteris Testamenti veneratur, qui in Christo veneratur naturam divinam et humanam; unum autem recipit Iudaeus, qui in solis legalibus gloriatur.

2039. Deinde sequitur ratio: ***unicuique secundum propriam virtutem***. Si hoc referatur ad illud quod talenta sint eloquia, plana est expositio, quia debent dari secundum maiorem capacitatem; Io. XVI, 12: *multa habeo vobis dicere, quae non potestis portare modo*. Et Apostolus I Cor. III, 2: *tamquam parvulis in Christo lac potum dedi vobis, non escam*. Ideo magis subtilibus magis subtilia dedit.

2040. Si autem referamus ad bona gratiarum, sciendum quod quidam dixerunt, quod secundum bona naturalia daret bona gratuita. Unde secundum quod magis habet homo de bonis naturalibus, habet etiam de bonis gratuitis: et hoc verum fuit in angelis, at in hominibus non. Et quae est ratio? Quia in angelis una est natura spiritualis; ideo ad quod moventur, totaliter moventur secundum totalitatem virtutis. Ideo quantum valet conatus eorum, tantum capiunt. Sed homo est ex duabus contrariis naturis, quarum una retrahitur ab alia a suo corpore: unde non tantum datur ei nisi quantum homo cum isto bono naturali habet de studio.

2041. Item alius error fuit, qui dixit quod initium gratiae fuit a nobis.

Et contra hoc obiicit Augustinus per verbum Apostoli, II Cor. III, 5, qui dicit quod *non sufficientes sumus cogitare aliquid a nobis quasi ex nobis*. Sed quod est prius principium, quam cogitatio? Et si cogitatio a nobis non est, ergo nec operatio. Unde qui plus conatur plus habet de gratia; sed quod plus conetur, indiget altiori causa; Thren. V, 21: *converte nos ad te, et convertemur*.

2042. Si autem quaeris quare unus magis habet de gratia quam alter, dico quod huius rei est causa proxima, et causa prima: proxima est maior conatus istius quam illius; causa prima est electio divina; Eccli. XXXIII, 7: *quare dies diem superat, et lux lucem, et annus annum, et sol solem? A domini scientia separati sunt*. Et quae est ratio huius? Videte quod aliter est de agente universali et particulari. Agens particulare praesupponit sibi aliquid, et secundum hoc diversimode operatur, ut artifex aliam

hence he receives five talents who receives grace from God concerning temporal things, with which the operation of the senses is concerned. But by the two talents are understood the senses and the understanding, while one talent indicates the understanding alone. Hence he receives one, who receives the grace of understanding, but not the grace of working.

According to Hilary, that man receives five who finds Christ in the five books of Moses, and that man receives two who venerates the grace of the New and the Old Testament, who venerates in Christ the divine and human natures; and the Jews receive the one, who glory only in what pertains to the law.

2039. Next there follows the reason: ***to every one according to his proper ability***. If this is referred to the interpretation in which the talents are utterances, the explanation is clear, because they should be given according to the greater capacity; *I have yet many things to say to you: but you cannot bear them now* (John 16:12). And the Apostle, *I gave you milk to drink, not meat; for you were not able as yet* (1 Cor 3:2). So to the more subtle he gave more subtle teachings.

2040. But if we refer it to the goods of graces, one should know that some have said that he gave the gratuitous goods according to natural goods. Hence according as a man has more of natural goods, he also has more of gratuitous goods: and this was true among the angels, but not among men. And what is the reason? Because there is one spiritual nature in the angels, so toward whatever they are moved, they are moved entirely, according to the totality of their power. So they obtain as much as their effort avails. But a man is composed of two contrary natures, of which one is drawn back by the other, his own body: hence so much is given to a man only insofar as he has zeal along with this natural good.

2041. Likewise there was another error, which said that the beginning of grace was from us.

And Augustine objected against this through the Apostle's words, who says, *not that we are sufficient to think any thing of ourselves, as of ourselves* (2 Cor 3:5). But what principle is prior to thought? And if thought is not from ourselves, therefore neither is operation. Hence the one who tries more has more grace; but to try more requires a higher cause. *Convert us, O Lord, to you, and we will be converted* (Lam 5:21).

2042. But if you seek to know why one has more grace than another, I say that there is a proximate cause of this thing, and a first cause: the proximate cause is this man's effort being greater than that man's; the first cause is divine election. *Why does one day excel another, and one light another, and one year another year, when all come of the sun? By the knowledge of the Lord they were distinguished* (Sir 33:7). And what is the reason for this? Note that it is not the same with a universal agent as with a particular agent. A

formam dat uni materiae, et aliam alii. Sed si posset facere materiam, diceretur quod talis fecit talem materiam, ut induceret formam secundum voluntatem suam. Sic Dominus, cum sit Creator omnium, creavit istum, ut sic eum faceret. Unde intelligitur, ut intelligatur capacitas naturae cum conatu.

2043. Tunc ponitur recessus dantis cum dicit *et profectus est statim*. Et potest intelligi quod iste peregre proficiscebatur, quia cum apostolis dixisset: *accipite Spiritum Sanctum*, Io. ult., 22, et Petro dixisset, Io. c. XXI, 17: *pasces oves meas*, statim profectus est. Unde dicebat, Io. XIII, 33: *filioli, adhuc modicum vobiscum sum*, et statim ascendit.

Vel potest dici quod profectus est non recedendo, sed quia relinquit eos sub arbitrio, quia non compellit eos uti donis datis.

2044. *Abiit autem qui quinque talenta acceperat* et cetera. Hic ponitur de usu donorum, et hoc quantum ad tres servos. Et

primo quantum ad primum;
secundo quoad secundum;
tertio quoad tertium.

2045. Unde dicit *abiit autem qui quinque talenta acceperat*. Designatur hic profectus virtutis; Ps. LXXXIII, 8: *ibunt de virtute in virtutem*. Et hoc habetur Gen. XXVI, 13: *ibat crescens et proficiens*. Virtus enim proficit per exercitium operationis; nisi enim operetur, deficit. Et ideo dicit *operatus est*. Unde dicitur Prov. XIII, 4: *anima operantium impinguabitur*. *Et lucratus est alia quinque*. Et quomodo? Dupliciter proficit aliquis: uno modo in seipso, alio modo in alio. In se, si habeat intelligentiam Scripturarum, ita ut proficiat; si caritatem, ut proficiat aliis. Profectus est, ut proficiat in alio, ut quod accepit, communicet; I Petr. IV, 10: *unusquisque gratiam quam accepit, in alterutrum administrantes*.

Unde si quod accipis communicas, totidem lucraris. Unde dicit quod *superlucratus est alia quinque*; quia vix est quod aliquis conferat ad aliquem id quod non habet. I ad Cor. XI, 23: *ego enim accepi a Domino quod et tradidi vobis*. In eo autem quod habet, in eo proficit. Apostolus: *gratia eius in me vacua non fuit*.

Secundum Hilarium ille lucratur quinque, qui proficit in quinque libris Moysi, ut Christum lucretur.

2046. *Similiter qui duo acceperat*, scilicet qui proficit intellectu et operatione, *lucratus est alia duo*, idest praemiationem quoad utrumque. Vel *duo*, quia non solum proficit praedicando viris, sed etiam mulieribus,

2043. Then the departure of the one giving is set out, when he says, ***and immediately he took his journey***. And it can be understood that this man went abroad, for when he had said to the apostles, *receive the Holy Spirit* (John 20:22), and had said to Peter, *feed my sheep* (John 21:17), he immediately left. Hence he said, *little children, yet a little while I am with you* (John 13:33), and immediately ascended.

Or it can be said that he set out not by departing, but because he left them under their own judgment, because he does not compel them to use the gifts given.

2044. ***And he who had received the five talents***. Here the use of the gifts is set down, and this with regard to the three servants. And

first, with regard to the first;
second, as regards the second;
third, as regards the third.

2045. Hence he says, ***and he who had received the five talents***. The progress of virtue is indicated here; *they will go from virtue to virtue* (Ps 83:8). And this is found in Genesis, *he went on prospering and increasing* (Gen 26:13). For virtue progresses through the exercise of work; for unless it works, it fades away. And for this reason he says he ***worked***. Hence it says, *the soul of those who work, will be made fat* (Prov 13:4). ***And gained another five***. And how? Someone can profit in two ways: in one way, in himself; in another way, in another. In himself, if he has the understanding of the Scriptures, such that he profits; if he has charity, such that he profits others. He has profited so that he might profit in others, so that what he receives, he might communicate; *as every man has received grace, ministering the same one to another* (1 Pet 4:10).

Hence if you communicate what you receive, you gain just as much again. Hence he says that he ***gained another five***; for a man would scarcely bestow on another what he does not have. *For I have received of the Lord that which also I delivered unto you* (1 Cor 11:23). Moreover, he profits in that which he has. The Apostle: *and his grace in me has not been void* (1 Cor 15:10).

According to Hilary, that man gains five who makes profit in the five books of Moses, that he may gain Christ.

2046. ***And in like manner he who had received the two***, namely the one who profits by understanding and by work, ***gained another two***, i.e., a reward with regard to both. Or ***two***, because he not only profits by preaching to men, but

secundum Gregorium. Secundum Origenem, quod illud quod acceperat secundum rationem naturalium, ad intellectum referat.

2047. *Qui autem unum acceperat abiens fodit in terram* et cetera.

Quid autem est fodere in terram? Tripliciter exponitur secundum Gregorium. Ille thesaurum abscondit, qui donum acceptum abscondit in peccatis carnis, vel temporalibus: unde qui potest in temporalibus proficere, et convertit se ad terrena, abscondit pecuniam domini sui in terra. De talibus dicitur in Ps. XVI, 11: *oculos suos statuerunt declinare in terram*.

Secundum Origenem habet aliquis donum intellectus, et tamen vult religiose vivere, et sibi solum vivere, cum tamen multis possit proficere; iste abscondit in terra; Tob. XII, 7: *opera Dei revelare et confiteri honorificum est*. Talis enim pecunia est ad multiplicandum, non abscondendum. Hilarius: qui sunt qui recipiunt unum? Iudaei, qui puram litteram recipiunt. Isti abscondunt pecuniam in terra, idest in carne Christi, qui propter carnem non possunt credere ipsum esse Deum. Unde Apost., I Cor. I, 23: *nos autem praedicamus Christum Iesum, Iudaeis quidem scandalum, gentibus autem stultitiam*.

2048. *Post multum vero temporis venit dominus servorum illorum*. Hic agitur de iudicio. Et

primo ponitur ratio adventus iudicis;

secundo de iudicio, ibi *et posuit rationem cum eis*.

Notandum quod de operibus et donis debemus Deo reddere rationem; supra XII, 36: *de omni verbo, quod locuti fueritis, oportebit reddere rationem*. Et supra XVIII, 23: *simile est regnum caelorum homini, qui voluit ponere rationem cum servis suis*.

Et primo ponitur in speciali *et posuit rationem cum eis*, quia quilibet tenetur reddere rationem primo in sua morte, secundo in die iudicii, quando oportebit nos adstare ante tribunal Christi.

2049. Cum ergo dicit *post multum vero temporis venit dominus*, potest referri ad utrumque. Si enim ad diem iudicii, datur intelligi quod magna est mora inter adventum Christi et diem iudicii; contra illud quod crediderunt quidam tempore Apostoli; unde II ad Thess. II, 2: *non terreamini quasi instet dies domini*. Sed si ad diem mortis, dicit Origenes: *consideretis quod vix fuerit aliquis utilis in Ecclesia, qui parum vixerit*. Et hoc probat de Petro cui dixit Dominus, Io. XXI, v. 18: *cum autem senueris, extendes manum tuam, et alius te cinget*. Item de Paulo, qui adolescens fuit in sui conversione, et post factus est senex; unde ad Philemonem v. 9: *ut Paulus senex* et cetera. Unde cum dicitur *post multum vero temporis*, datur intelligi quod dat dominus longum

also to women, according to Gregory. According to Origen, because he refers to the understanding what he had received according to natural reason.

2047. *But he who had received the one, going his way dug into the earth*.

And what is it to dig into the earth? It is explained in three ways, according to Gregory. That man hides the treasure who hides a gift received in sins of the flesh, or in temporal things: hence he who is able to make profit in temporal things and turns himself toward earthly things, hides his lord's money in the ground. Of such men it says, *they have set their eyes bowing down to the earth* (Ps 16:11).

According to Origen, someone has the gift of understanding, and yet wishes to live religiously and to live only for himself, when nevertheless he could profit many; this man hides the gift in the earth; *it is . . . honorable to reveal and confess the works of God* (Tob 12:7). For such money is for multiplying, not for hiding. Hilary: who is it who receives the one? The Jews, who receive only the letter. They hide the money in the ground, i.e., in the flesh of Christ, for on account of the flesh they could not believe that he was God. Hence the Apostle, *but we preach Christ crucified, unto the Jews indeed a stumblingblock, and unto the gentiles foolishness* (1 Cor 1:23).

2048. *But after a long time the lord of those servants came*. Here he treats of the judgment. And

first, the reason for the coming of the judge;

second, about the judgment, at *and reckoned with them*.

One should notice that we must render to God an account of the works and gifts; above, *that every idle word that men shall speak, they shall render an account for it in the day of judgment* (Matt 12:36). And above, *therefore is the kingdom of heaven likened to a king, who would take an account of his servants* (Matt 18:23).

And first, it is set out in particular: *and reckoned with them*, because everyone is bound to render an account first at his own death, second on the day of judgment, when we will have to stand before the tribunal of Christ.

2049. So when he says, *but after a long time the lord of those servants came*, it can be referred to either. For if it is referred to the day of judgment, one is given to understand that the delay between Christ's coming and the day of judgment is great; contrary to what some thought in the time of the Apostle; hence, *nor be terrified . . . as if the day of the Lord were at hand* (2 Tim 2:2). But if it is referred to the day of death, Origen says: *consider that he who has not lived very long will hardly have been useful in the Church*. And what the Lord said to Peter proves this, *but when you will be old, you will stretch forth your hands, and another will gird you* (John 21:18). Likewise in the case of Paul, who was a young man at his conversion, and later grew old; hence, *Paul an old man* (Phlm 5:9). Hence when it says, *but after*

spatium ad bene agendum: et de hoc intelligitur quod dicitur Prov. c. III, 2: *longitudinem dierum, et annos vitae, et pacem apponet tibi*.

2050. *Et accedens qui quinque talenta acceperat, obtulit alia quinque* et cetera. Hic agitur de tribus servis. Et

primo de primo;
secundo de secundo;
tertio de tertio.
In primo duo facit.
Primo ponitur ratio reddita;
secundo remuneratio debita ibi *ait illi dominus eius* et cetera.

2051. Ex parte istius primo ponit securitatem, fidelitatem, humilitatem et strenuitatem, sive sollicitudinem.

Securitatem tangit, quia non expectavit quod Dominus vocaret eum, sed ingessit se; unde dicit *accedens*. Hanc securitatem habebat Paulus per sanguinem Christi; ad Hebr. X, 19: *habentes fiduciam in introitu sanctorum in sanguine Christi*; II Cor. III, 12: *habentes talem spem, multa fiducia utimur*.

Item notatur fidelitas, quia et *obtulit alia quinque*. Infidelis quidem esset, qui de bonis domini sui aliquid sibi attribueret: unde iste totum obtulit domino. Si ergo feceris aliquod bonum, si aliquem convertisti, et tibi attribuis, non Deo, non es fidelis; I Paral. XXIX, 14: *tua sunt omnia, et quae de manu tua accepimus, dedimus tibi*.

Item notatur humilitas confessionis doni, quia cognoscebat ab eo recepisse; I Cor. IV, v. 7: *quid habes quod non accepisti?* Unde iste confitetur donum dicens: *domine, quinque talenta tradidisti mihi* et cetera.

Item tangit strenuitatem sive sollicitudinem: *ecce alia quinque superlucratus sum*. Unde bene dicebat cum Apostolo: *gratia Dei in me vacua non fuit*.

2052. Sequitur remuneratio debita: et in ista facit quatuor. Quia primo ponitur congratulatio; secundo commendatio meritorum; tertio aequalitas iudicii; quarto magnitudo praemii.

Congratulatio tangitur, cum dicit *ait illi dominus eius: euge, serve bone et fidelis* et cetera. Unde dicitur Is. LXII, 5: *ecce gaudebit sponsus super sponsam, et gaudebit super te Dominus tuus*. Unde exultanti animo recipit eum, cum dicit *euge. Euge* vox est exultationis.

Sequitur commendatio. Et primo commendat de humilitate, cum dicit *serve*, quia recognoscebat se esse servum eius; Lc. XVII, 10: *cum omnia bene feceritis, dicite: servi inutiles sumus*. Item commendat eum de bonitate

a long time, one is given to understand that the Lord gives one a long space of time for the sake of doing well; and what is said is understood as about this: *for they will add to you length of days, and years of life and peace* (Prov 3:2).

2050. *And he who had received the five talents coming, brought another five talents*. Here the three servants are treated of. And

first, of the first;
second, of the second;
third, of the third.
In the first, he does two things:
first, the account rendered is set out;
second, the reward due, at *his lord said to him: well done*.

2051. On the part of this man, he sets out security, faithfulness, humility, and strenuous effort, or solicitude.

He touches upon security, because he did not expect that the Lord would call him, but brought himself in; hence he says, *coming*. Paul had this security through the blood of Christ; *having therefore, brethren, a confidence in the entering into the holies by the blood of Christ* (Heb 10:19); *having therefore such hope, we use much confidence* (2 Cor 3:12).

Likewise, fidelity is pointed out: *brought another five*. Indeed, the one who attributed something of his lord's to himself would be unfaithful, hence this man brought the whole amount to the lord. Therefore, if you do something good, if you convert someone, and you attribute it to yourself, not to God, you are not faithful; *all things are yours: and we have given you what we received of your hand* (1 Chr 29:14).

Likewise, the humility of the confession of a gift is pointed out, because he knew that he had received from him; *or what have you that you have not received?* (1 Cor 4:7). Hence this man confesses the gift, saying, *lord, you did deliver to me five talents*.

Likewise, he touches upon strenuous effort or solicitude: *behold I have gained another five over and above*. Hence he said well with the Apostle, *his grace in me has not been void* (1 Cor 15:10).

2052. There follows the reward due: and in this part he does four things. For first, the congratulation is set out; second, the commendation of merits; third, the equality of judgment; fourth, the greatness of the reward.

The congratulation is touched upon when he says, *his lord said to him: well done, good and faithful servant*. Hence it says, *and the bridegroom will rejoice over the bride, and your God will rejoice over you* (Isa 62:5). Hence he receives him with a joyful soul when he says: *well done. Well done* is a word of rejoicing.

There follows the commendation. And first, he commends him for humility, when he says, *servant*, for he recognized that he was his servant; *when you will have done all these things that are commanded you, say: we are*

per hoc quod dicit *bone*; quia proprie bonum est diffusivum sui; unde bonus multiplicavit bonitatem. Item a fidelitate, quia non sibi retinuit, sed domino obtulit; unde dicitur *et fidelis*; I Cor. IV, 2: *iam quaeritur inter dispensatores, ut fidelis quis inveniatur*. Et supra XXIV, 45: *quis putas est fidelis servus et prudens?* Unde approbat eum dicens *fidelis*. *Non enim qui seipsum commendat, ille probatus est, sed quem Deus commendat*, II Cor. X, 18.

Deinde ponit aequalitatem, ut praestet aequitatem iudicii, dicens: *quia super pauca fuisti fidelis supra multa te constituam*. Ista pauca sunt omnia quae sunt in vita ista, quia quasi nihil sunt in comparatione ad caelestia. Unde vult dicere: quia fuisti fidelis ratione bonorum, quae sunt praesentis vitae, *super multa te constituam*, idest dabo tibi spiritualia, quae sunt super omnia bona ista; Lc. c. XVI, 10: *qui fidelis est in minimo, et in maiore fidelis est*.

Sequitur magnitudo praemii: *intra in gaudium domini tui*. Gaudium enim est praemium; Io. XVI, 22: *videbo vos, et gaudebit cor vestrum*.

2053. Et posset dicere aliquis: *nonne visio est praemium, vel aliquod aliud bonum?* Dico quod si alia res dicatur praemium, gaudium tamen est finale praemium. Sicut possem dicere, quod est finis gravium locus inferior; item quiescere in illo loco, et illud est magis principale. Sic gaudium nihil aliud est quam quies animi in bono adepto; unde ratione finis dicitur gaudium praemium.

2054. Et quare dicit *intra in gaudium*, non *accipe*? Dicendum quod duplex est gaudium: de bonis exterioribus et de bonis interioribus; qui gaudet de bonis exterioribus, non intrat in gaudium, sed intrat gaudium in ipsum; qui autem gaudet de spiritualibus intrat in gaudium. Cant. c. I, 5: *introduxit me rex in cellaria sua*.

Vel aliter. Quod est in aliquo, continetur ab illo, et continens maius est. Quando ergo gaudium est de aliquo, quod minus est quam cor tuum, tunc gaudium intrat in cor tuum. Sed Deus maior est corde; ideo qui gaudet de Deo, intrat in gaudium.

Item intrat *in gaudium domini*, idest de Domino, quia Dominus veritas est. Unde nihil aliud est beatitudo, quam gaudium veritatis. Vel sic: *intra in gaudium domini tui*, idest de eo gaude quo gaudet, et de quo gaudet Dominus tuus, scilicet de fruitione suiipsius. Tunc ergo gaudet homo ut Dominus, cum fruitur ut Dominus; unde dicit Dominus apostolis: *statui vos ut edatis et*

unprofitable servants (Luke 17:10). Similarly, he commends him for goodness when he says, *good*; for properly the good is diffusive of itself, so the good man multiplied goodness. Likewise for fidelity, because he did not keep anything back for himself, but brought it to the lord; hence it says, *and faithful*. *Here now it is required among the dispensers, that a man be found faithful* (1 Cor 4:2). And above, *who, do you think, is a faithful and wise servant?* (Matt 24:45). Hence he approved of him, saying, *faithful*. *For not he who commends himself, is approved, but he, whom God commends* (2 Cor 10:18).

Next he sets out the equality, to show the equity of the judgment, saying: *because you have been faithful over a few things, I will place you over many things*. Those few things are all the things which are in this life, because they are as nothing in comparison to heavenly things. Hence he wishes to say: because you have been faithful with regard to the good things which belong to the present life, *I will place you over many things*, i.e., I will give you spiritual things, which are above all these goods; *he that is faithful in that which is least, is faithful also in that which is greater* (Luke 16:10).

There follows the greatness of the reward: *enter into the joy of your lord*. For joy is the reward; *I will see you again, and your heart will rejoice* (John 16:22).

2053. And someone could say: *is not vision the reward, or some other good?* I say that if something is called a reward, nevertheless joy is the final reward. Just as I could say that the lower place is the end of weight; likewise to rest in that place is the end, and that is more principal. Thus joy is nothing other than the soul's rest in the good obtained; hence by reason of the end, joy is called the reward.

2054. And why does he say, *enter into the joy*, not *accept*? One should say that there are two joys: joy over exterior goods and joy over interior goods. The one who rejoices over exterior goods does not enter into joy, but rather joy enters into him; but the one who rejoices over spiritual things enters into joy. *The king has brought me into his storerooms* (Song 1:3).

Or in another way: what is in something is contained by that thing, and the one containing is greater. When therefore the joy is over something which is less than your heart, then joy enters into your heart. But God is greater than the heart; therefore the one who rejoices over God enters into joy.

Likewise, he enters into *the joy of your lord*, i.e., over the Lord, because the Lord is truth. Hence beatitude is nothing other than the joy of truth. Or thus: *enter into the joy of your lord*, i.e., rejoice over that by which he rejoices, and over which your Lord rejoices, namely in the enjoyment of himself. So a man rejoices as the Lord does when he enjoys as the Lord does; hence the Lord says to the apostles, *and I dispose to you, as my Father has disposed to me,*

bibatis super mensam meam in regno meo, idest ut sitis beati in quo sum beatus.

2055. *Accessit autem et qui duo talenta acceperat*: supra actum est de iudicio quantum ad primum servum, qui quinque talenta acceperat; hic agitur de iudicio quantum ad secundum servum, qui duo talenta acceperat.

Quantum ad litteram nihil differt a primo, nec est aliquid dicendum nisi quod dictum est de primo; et ideo non oportet iterare, quia et iste eamdem commendationem et idem praemium recepit, sicut qui quinque talenta acceperat. In quo datur intelligi, secundum Origenem, quod qui parvum donum a Deo recipit, et bene utitur secundum posse suum, tantum accipit et meretur quantum qui magnum. Hoc enim solum requirit Dominus ab omni homine, quod ei serviat in toto corde suo, ut habetur Deut. VI, 5.

2056. Sed hoc potest habere dubietatem. Ponatur quod aliquis habeat magnam mensuram bonorum, alter parvam; si operatur iste secundum paucam caritatem quam accepit, tunc merebitur tantum quantum qui plus accepit: quod videtur quod non possit esse, quia sic mereretur tantum vel plus qui minus habet de caritate quam qui plus.

Et ideo distinguendum est, quia quaedam sunt bona quae perficiunt, et eliciunt actum voluntatis et inclinant; quaedam autem quae non. Donum quod inclinat voluntatem et elicit actum est caritas. Non potest ergo esse qui plus habet de caritate, quin maiori nixu utatur, et melius. Sed sunt alia dona quibus potest aliquis uti secundum maiorem et minorem caritatem, ut scientia et huiusmodi: in talibus qui maiori conatu utitur, quantum ad praemium magis meretur; unde dicitur Lc. XXI, 3 s., quod paupercula mulier plus misit in gazophilacium quam illi qui plus apposuerunt, quia usa est secundum totum posse suum.

2057. *Accedens autem et qui unum talentum acceperat, ait*. Hic determinatur de iudicio mali servi. Et
primo ponitur ratio;
secundo condemnatio quam suscepit, ibi *respondens autem dominus eius dixit ei*.
Mirabilem rationem proposuit.
Primo enim blasphemiam proposuit; inde negligentiam assumpsit;
tertio innocentiam conclusit. Et sic non poterat valere syllogismus.
Blasphemiam, cum dicit **domine, scio quod homo durus es**. Negligentiam, cum dicit **abii et abscondi talentum** et cetera. Innocentiam, cum dicit **ecce habes quod tuum est**.

2055. *And he also who had received the two talents came*: above, the judgment was treated with regard to the first servant, who had received the five talents; here the judgment is treated with regard to the second servant, who had received the two talents.

With regard to the letter of the text, he does not differ at all from the first, nor is anything to be said except what was said about the first; and so it is unnecessary to repeat, because this one also receives the same commendation and the same reward as the one who had received the five talents. In which one is given to understand, according to Origen, that the one who receives a small gift from the Lord, and uses it well according to his ability, receives and merits as much as the one who receives a greater gift. For the Lord requires only this from any man, that he serve him with his whole heart (Deut 6:5).

2056. But there can be a doubt about this. Suppose that someone has a great measure of good things, and another a small measure; if this man works according to the little charity which he received, then he will merit as much as the one who received more. It seems that this is not possible, because he thus merits more who has less of charity than he who has more.

And for this reason one should make a distinction, for there are certain goods which perfect and draw forth and incline the act of the will; there are others which do not. The gift which inclines the will and draws forth its act is charity. Therefore it is impossible that someone have more charity and not make a greater effort, and a better one. But there are other goods which one can make use of according to greater and lesser charity, such as knowledge and suchlike: in such things, the one who exerts a greater effort merits more as regards the reward. Hence it says that the poor woman cast more into the treasury than those who placed more in, because she acted according to her whole ability (Luke 21:3).

2057. *But he who had received the one talent, came and said*. Here the judgment of the bad servant is settled. And
first, the account is set out;
second, the condemnation which he receives, at *and his lord answering, said to him*.
He set out an amazing account:
for first, he set out a blasphemy; from there, he added negligence;
third, he concluded to his own innocence. And thus the syllogism cannot work.
Blasphemy, when he says **lord, I know that you are a hard man**. Negligence, when he says **I went and hid your talent**. Innocence, when he says **behold here you have that which is yours**.

2058. Et consideremus quod dicit quod *accessit*. Dictum est supra de illo qui quinque talenta acceperat quod accessit, idest fiduciam habuit; sed iste non accessit cum fiducia, sed per violentiam.

Vel aliter, quia aliqui in his quae male faciunt, videtur eis bene fecisse. Prov. XXVI, v. 16: *sapientior sibi piger videtur septem viris loquentibus sententias*. Unde visum fuit ei quod bene fecisset.

2059. Secundum Origenem, videtur aestimatio de Deo alicui sicut de homine duro, a quo se abstrahit aliquis propter duritiam. Eccli. IX, 18: *longe abesto ab homine potestatem habente occidendi*. Et ideo sicut qui cognoscit hominem durum, non vult ei servire, sic cogitant aliqui de Deo, quod sit homo durus.

Et secundum hoc iste servus habebat tres malas opiniones de Deo. Primo quod Deus non esset misericors; secundo quod ei aliquid accresceret a bonis nostris; tertio quod non omnia essent a Deo; et omnes istae opiniones procedebant ab una radice mala, quia cogitabat quod Deus esset quasi unus homo. Et hoc signatur cum dicit: **scio quod homo durus es**, idest aestimo te esse hominem; quod non est verum, ut habetur Num. XXIII, v. 19: *non est Deus ut homo*; Is. LV, 9: *sicut exaltantur caeli a terra, sic exaltatae sunt viae meae a viis vestris*. Et dicit, **durus**, quia homo durus non flectitur. Et dicitur de tali Iob XLI, 15: *cor eius indurabitur ut malleatoris incus*. Sed non sic est Dominus, quia *miserator et misericors Dominus*, Ps. CX, v. 4.

Duritia solet accidere ex avaritia; Prov. c. XXIX, 4: *rex iustus erigit terram, vir avarus destruet eam*; ideo ita aestimat quod sit durus, et ita avarus; et ideo attribuit ei quae sunt avari: **metis ubi non seminasti, et congregas ubi non sparsisti**, idest ita durus es quod aliena rapere non cessas; quod tamen falsum est; Iob XXXV, 7: *porro si iuste egeris, quid donabis ei, aut quid de manu tua accipiet?* Et in Ps. XV, 2: *bonorum meorum non eges*. Unde in hoc imponebat ei quod indigeret bonis nostris.

Tertium erat quod esset aliquod bonum, quod non esset a Deo; ut sunt aliqui qui ea quae habent de patrimonio, vel de studio, non dicuntur habere a Deo: et hoc est quod dicit **ubi non seminasti**; contra illud Iac. I, v. 17: *omne datum optimum, et omne donum perfectum desursum est, descendens a Patre luminum*.

2060. Item aliqui aestimantes ipsum esse durum, extrahunt se a servitio suo. Unde aliqui, qui possunt multum proficere, dicunt: *si audirem confessiones, et facerem praedicationes, fortassis male accideret mihi*: tales Deum durum reputant. Item aliqui dicunt: *si intrarem religionem, fortassis peccarem, et essem deterius*; isti reputant Deum durum, qui credunt si adhaeserint Deo quod

2058. And let us consider that he says that the servant *came*. It was said above about the one who had received the five talents that he came, i.e., he had confidence; but this man did not approach with confidence, but by violence.

Or in another way, because a man seems to himself to have done well in those things which he has done badly. *The sluggard is wiser in his own conceit, than seven men who speak sentences* (Prov 26:16). Hence it seemed to him that he had done well.

2059. According to Origen, God seems like a hard man to the one who withdraws himself because of hardness. *Keep far from the man who has power to kill* (Sir 9:18). And so just as the one who knows that a man is hard does not wish to serve him, so some think of God that he is a hard man.

And in accord with this, that servant had three evil opinions about God. First, that God would not be merciful; second, that something would be added to him by our goods; third, that not all things are from God; and all these opinions came from one evil root, for he thought that God was as if a mere man. And this is indicated when he says, **I know that you are a hard man**, i.e., I consider you to be a man; which is not true, as is had, *God is not a man*; (Num 23:19); *for as the heavens are exalted above the earth, so are my ways exalted above your ways* (Isa 55:9). And he says, **hard**, because a hard man is not persuaded. And Job says about such a man, *his heart shall be as hard as a stone, and as firm as a smith's anvil* (Job 41:15). But the Lord is not this way, *being a merciful and gracious Lord* (Ps 110:4).

Hardness often arises from greed; *a just king sets up the land: a covetous man will destroy* (Prov 29:4). For this reason, he considers him to be hard in this way, and greedy in this way, and so he attributed to him the things which belong to a greedy man: **you reap where you have not sown, and gather where you have not scattered**, i.e., you are so hard that you do not refrain from taking another's things; which yet is false: *and if you do justly, what will you give him, or what will he receive of your hand?* (Job 35:7). And, *you have no need of my goods* (Ps 15:2). Hence in this statement he imposed on him the idea that he needed our goods.

The third was that there was some good which was not from God, as there are some men who do not say that they have from God the things which they have by inheritance or by effort. And this is what he says: **where you have not sown**, contrary to: *every best gift, and every perfect gift, is from above, coming down from the Father of lights* (Jas 1:17).

2060. Likewise some, considering him to be hard, withdraw themselves from his service. Hence some, who are able to accomplish much, say: *if I heard confessions, and preached, perhaps something bad would happen to me*; such men consider God to be hard. Similarly, some say: *if I were to enter religion, perhaps I would sin, and would be worse off*; those men consider God to be hard, who think that if

deficiat eis. Tales sunt similes his qui desperant de Dei misericordia. Ista allegabat iste servus.

2061. Et tamen ista vera sunt, et habent fulcimentum ab auctoritate. Est enim durus cum peccatoribus, et benignus recurrentibus ad eum; Sap. XI, 11: *hos quidem tamquam pater monens probasti, illos autem tamquam rex durus interrogans condemnasti*; Thren. III, 25: *bonus est Dominus animae quaerenti eum*; II Paral. XXX, 18: *Dominus bonus propitiabitur cunctis, qui requirunt in toto corde Dominum Deum patrum suorum*. Ergo durus est cum peccatoribus, et misericors bonis. Et non est dubium quod timeri debet ne contemnatur; unde ad Hebr. X, 31: *horrendum est incidere in manus Dei viventis*. Sed inquantum est misericors, debemus sperare quod si se dat aliquis servitio suo, quod non cadet; et si ceciderit, resurget.

2062. Item quod dicit *metis ubi non seminasti*, licet falsum sit, tamen quoad aliquem sensum verum potest esse; quia non requirit propter se, sed propter nostram utilitatem; quia ipse metit gloriam suam quam non seminavit. Item *congregas ubi non sparsisti*. Qui enim metit, accipit in multitudine; ille autem qui congregat, ex multis recipit; sic vult Dominus quod sua gloria ex diversis hominibus crescat. Unde Apostolus, II ad Cor. I, 14: *gloria vestra sumus, sicut vos nostra, in die Domini nostri Iesu Christi*.

2063. Similiter quod dicit *metis ubi non seminasti*, quoad aliquid veritatem habet, quia homo seminat, et Deus colligit; Io. IV, 37: *alius est qui seminat, alius qui metit. Ego misi vos metere ubi non laborastis*. Homo enim seminat opera sua, et Deus metit ad gloriam suam; ad Gal. ult., 8: *quae seminaverit homo, haec et metet*. Et dominus dicit, Io. XIV, 3: *veniam et accipiam vos ad meipsum*. Si enim facis eleemosynam, tu seminas, et dominus metit, quia sibi fortasse reputat. Unde ipse dicit, infra in hoc cap.: *quod uni ex minimis meis fecistis, mihi fecistis*. Item sicut supra dictum est: *semen est verbum Dei*, unde aliquando colligit Deus fructus boni operis, ubi non est seminata praedicatio; Rom. II, 14: *homines qui legem non habent, ipsi sibi sunt lex*. Tertio modo quod quaedam mala fiunt ab homine, sicut mala carnis, ex quibus malum colligi debet. De quo ad Gal. ult., 8: *qui seminat in carne, de carne metet corruptionem*. Attamen Deus facit venire ad bonum aliquid, ut bonum iustitiae, humilitatis vel huiusmodi. Unde iste servus primo blasphemus fuit.

2064. Deinde tangitur negligentia sua *timens abii*; Ps. XIII, 5: *trepidaverunt timore, ubi non erat timor*. Verum est quod timendus est Deus, ut evitetur peccatum, secundum quod habetur Iob XXXI, 23: *semper enim quasi tumentes super me fluctus timui Deum*. Unde quod

2061. And yet these things are true, and have support from authority. For he is hard with sinners, and kind to those who run back to him; *for you did admonish and try them as a father: but the others, as a severe king, you did examine and condemn* (Wis 11:11); *the Lord is good to those who hope in him, to the soul who seeks him* (Lam 3:25); *the Lord who is good will show mercy, to all them, who with their whole heart, seek the Lord the God of their fathers* (2 Chr 30:18–19). Therefore he is hard with sinners, and merciful to the good. And there is no doubt that he should be feared, lest one be condemned; hence, *it is a fearful thing to fall into the hands of the living God* (Heb 10:31). But insofar as he is merciful, we should hope that if someone gives himself to his service, that he will not fall; and if he does fall, he will get up again.

2062. Likewise, what he says, *you reap where you have not sown*, although it is false, yet it can be true in some sense: for he does not make demands for his own sake, but for our gain; for he reaps his glory where he has not sown. Similarly, *and gather where you have not strewed*. For the one who reaps takes in a multitude, and the one who gathers receives from many; in this way the Lord wills that his glory arise from diverse men. Hence the Apostle: *we are your glory, as you also are ours, in the day of our Lord Jesus Christ* (2 Cor 1:14).

2063. Similarly, when he says, *you reap where you have not sown*, it has some truth in it, for man sows and God gathers; *it is one man who sows, and it is another who reaps. I have sent you to reap that in which you did not labor* (John 4:37). For a man sows his works, and God reaps to his own glory; *for what things a man will sow, those also will he reap* (Gal 6:8). And the Lord says, *I will come again, and will take you to myself* (John 14:3). For if you give alms, you sow, and the Lord reaps, for perhaps he imputes it to himself. Hence he himself says, below, *as long as you did it to one of these my least brethren, you did it to me* (Matt 25:40). Likewise, as was said above, *the seed is the word of God* (Luke 8:11), hence sometimes God collects the fruits of good works where preaching is not sown; *these having not the law are a law to themselves* (Rom 2:14). In a third way, because some evils are done by men, such as evils of the body, from which evil should be gathered. About which Galatians says, *for he who sows in his flesh, of the flesh also will reap corruption* (Gal 6:8). And yet God makes it come to something good, like the good of justice, humility, or some such. Hence this servant first blasphemed.

2064. Then his negligence is touched upon: *and being afraid I went*; *there have they trembled for fear, where there was no fear* (Ps 13:5). It is true that God should be feared, that sin may be avoided, in accordance with what is said, *I have always feared God as waves swelling over me*

non peccet homo, hoc debet facere ex amore, non timore. Ideo sequitur: *abscondi talentum tuum in terra*, quia ex timore, quia timor servilis multa mala facit.

2065. Tunc concludit *ecce habes quod tuum est*. Unde conservavit scientiam, et non multiplicavit. Et hoc non sufficit, quia oportet multiplicare; I ad Cor. IX, 16: *si non evangelizavero, non est mihi gloria*.

2066. *Respondens autem dominus eius dixit ei*. Hic ponitur condemnatio servi. Et sicut in aliis servis primo commendavit eos, deinde posuit aequitatem iudicii, et postea praemium; sic in isto,

primo vituperat eum;
secundo ponit aequitatem iudicii;
tertio poenam.
Secunda ibi *sciebas quia meto ubi non semino* etc.; tertia ibi *tollite itaque ab eo talentum*.

2067. Dicit ergo *serve male et piger*. Servum vocat, quia propter timorem dimisit, et servorum est timere serviliter. Et ideo ad Rom. VIII, 15: *non accepistis spiritum servitutis iterum in timore*. Item eum malum vocat, quia malum dixerat de domino suo; supra XII, 35: *malus homo de malo thesauro cordis sui profert mala*. Item vocat eum pigrum, quia operari noluit; Prov. XX, 4: *propter frigus piger arare noluit*, propter frigus scilicet timoris.

2068. *Sciebas quia meto ubi non semino* et cetera. Nunc arguit eum de culpa. Et
primo proponit quod sciebat;
secundo quid facere oportebat;
tertio quid inde sequeretur.

2069. Dicit ergo *sciebas quod meto ubi non semino*, et tamen non operabaris; quamvis habeatur Lc. XII, 47: *servus sciens voluntatem domini sui, et non faciens plagis vapulabit multis*. Item dixerat quod erat durus, et quod colligebat ubi non seminabat. Dominus bene confitetur quod ipse metit ubi non seminat; sed non confitetur quod sit durus, quia quod requirit ab homine, hoc non facit propter duritiam, sed propter misericordiam, ut bonum suum multiplicetur.

2070. *Oportuit ergo te pecuniam meam committere nummulariis*. Et sequitur: sicut tu dicis quod meto ubi non seminavi, et colligo ubi non sparsi. Sed quia haec facio, multo magis volo quod pecunia mea multiplicetur. Et loquitur secundum similitudinem illorum, qui pecuniam tradunt ad multiplicationem. Pecunia ista sunt verba Dei: unde in Graeco habetur 'argireon': per argentum enim, quod sonorum est, signatur verbum

(Job 31:23). Hence that a man does not sin, he should do out of love, not fear. For this reason there follows: *I went and hid your talent in the earth*, because he acted out of fear, for servile fear works many evils.

2065. Then he concludes: *behold here you have that which is yours*. Hence he preserved knowledge, and did not multiply it. And this is not enough, because one must multiply it; *for if I preach the Gospel, it is no glory to me* (1 Cor 9:16).

2066. *And his lord answering, said to him*. Here the servant's condemnation is set out. And just as with the other servants he first commended them, then set out the equity of the judgment, and afterwards the reward, so with this one:

first, he reproaches him;
second, he sets out the equity of the judgment;
third, the punishment.
The second is at *you knew that I reap where I sow not*; the third, at *take away therefore the talent from him*.

2067. He says therefore, *wicked and slothful servant*. He calls him a servant, because he gave up because of fear, and it belongs to servants to fear in a servile manner. And so, *for you have not received the spirit of bondage again in fear* (Rom 8:15). Likewise, he calls him wicked, because he had said a wicked thing about his lord; above, *an evil man out of an evil treasure brings forth evil things* (Matt 12:35). Likewise, he calls him slothful, because he did not want to work; *because of the cold the sluggard would not plough* (Prov 20:4), namely because of the cold of fear.

2068. *You knew that I reap where I sow not*. Now he convicts him of guilt. And
first, he sets out what he knew;
second, what he should have done;
third, what will follow from it.

2069. He says therefore, *you knew that I reap where I sow not*, and yet you did not work; while it says, *and that servant who knew the will of his lord, and prepared not himself, and did not according to his will, will be beaten with many stripes* (Luke 12:47). Similarly, he had said that he was hard, and that he collected where he did not sow. The lord indeed confesses that he reaps where he does not sow; but he does not confess that he is hard, because he does not demand what he demands from a man out of hardness, but out of mercy, that his good may be multiplied.

2070. *You should have committed my money to the bankers*. And it follows: just as you say, I reap where I have not sown, and gather where I have not scattered. But because I do these things, much more do I wish that my money be increased. And he speaks according to a likeness with those who trade money for increase. This money is the word of God: hence in Greek it has 'argireon', for the word of God is signified by silver, which is sonorous; *the words*

Dei; Ps. XI, 7: *eloquia domini eloquia casta, argentum igne examinatum.*

Nummularii possunt dici dupliciter, propter duplex officium, quia officium habent ut probent pecuniam utrum sit bona, item ut exhibita pecunia lucrentur. Secundum primum nummularii sunt auditores qui debent probare quod audiunt; Iob XII, 11: *nonne auris verba diiudicat?* Item illi qui multiplicant, ut apostoli, qui aliis dederunt donum spiritus sancti, constituendo episcopos et cetera. Ad Tit. c. I, 5: *huius gratia dimisi te Cretae, ut constituas per civitates presbyteros* et cetera.

2071. ***Et ego veniens recepissem utique quod meum est.*** Unde istud bonum sequeretur. Et quod est illud bonum? Triplex. Cum Dominus dat tibi intellectum, et tu studes ad operandum, multiplicas; Iac. I, 22: *estote factores verbi et non auditores tantum.* Item quando dat Dominus virtutem, et studes ad bene utendum; I Petr. II, 2: *quasi modo geniti infantes, rationabiles sine dolo lac concupiscite, ut in eo crescatis in salutem.* Item ut quod in te habes, aliis studeas impartiri.

2072. Consequenter ponit poenam, et circa hoc duo facit.

Primo ponit poenam damni;

secundo sensus.

Circa primum

primo ponit poenam damni;

secundo generalem sententiam, ibi ***omni enim habenti dabitur, et abundabit.***

2073. Dicit ergo ***tollite itaque ab eo talentum, et date ei qui habet decem talenta.*** Sicut dicit Gregorius, ille qui quinque talenta acceperat, est ille qui scientiam habet de terrenis, quae subiacent quinque sensibus; qui autem unum, est qui habet intellectum sine opere. Accidit ergo quod qui habet intellectum, exercitat se in illo; Ps. CXVIII, 104: *a mandatis tuis intellexi, propterea odivi omnem viam iniquitatis.* Aliquando e converso accidit quod aliquis habet donum intellectus, et occupat se in terrenis, et totum amittit; Apoc. III, 11: *tene quod habes ne alius accipiat coronam tuam.* Vel potest dici quod ille qui quinque talenta recipit, magis accepit: et secundum quod magis laboravit, magis accepit. Unde unus accepit talentum alterius, quia sanctus homo non solum gaudebit de suis bonis, sed de omnibus quae facta sunt per quoscumque, et ita accipiet coronam istius, et sic talentum eius.

2074. Consequenter ponitur generalis sententia ***omni enim habenti dabitur, et abundabit.***

Istud potest exponi quadrupliciter. Primo sic, secundum Gregorium: ab eo qui non habet, non posset aliquid auferri; sed contingit quod aliquis habet dona

of the Lord are pure words: as silver tried by the fire, purged from the earth, refined seven times (Ps 11:7).

Bankers can be said in two ways, owing to their two duties, for they have the duty of testing whether money is good, and of making a profit out of the money presented to them. In accordance with the first, the bankers are listeners, who should test what they hear; *does not the ear discern words?* (Job 12:11). Again, they are those who increase, like the apostles, who gave the gift of the Holy Spirit to others by establishing bishops. *For this cause I left you in Crete, that you . . . should ordain priests in every city* (Titus 1:5).

2071. ***And at my coming I should have received my own with usury.*** Hence this good would follow. And what is that good? Threefold. When the Lord gives you understanding, and you are zealous at working, you increase; *but be doers of the word, and not hearers only* (Jas 1:22). Likewise, when the Lord gives virtue, and you are zealous to use it well; *as newborn babes, desire the rational milk without guile, that thereby you may grow unto salvation* (1 Pet 2:2). Likewise, that you be zealous to impart to others what you have within yourself.

2072. Next he sets out the punishment, and concerning this he does two things:

first, he sets out the punishment of loss;

second, that of the senses;

Concerning the first,

first, he sets out the punishment of loss;

second, a general sentence, at ***for to every one who has will be given, and he will abound.***

2073. He says therefore, ***take away therefore the talent from him, and give it to him who has ten talents.*** As Gregory says, the one who had received five talents is the one who has knowledge of earthly things, which lie under the five senses; and the one who had received one talent is the one who has understanding without work. So it happens that the one who has understanding exercises himself in it; *by your commandments I have had understanding: therefore have I hated every way of iniquity* (Ps 118:104). Sometimes it happens the other way around: someone has the gift of understanding, and occupies himself with earthly things, and loses the whole thing; *hold fast that which you have, that no man take your crown* (Rev 3:11). Or it can be said that the one who receives the five talents receives more: and according as he has labored more, he receives more. Hence one receives another's talent, because a holy man will not only rejoice over his own goods, but over all those which are done by anyone, and thus he will receive that man's crown, and thus his talent.

2074. Next the general sentence is set out: ***for to every one who has will be given, and he will abound.***

This can be explained in four ways. First, this way, according to Gregory: nothing can be taken away from the one who has nothing; but it sometimes happens that

gratuita, et non habet caritatem; unde omnia auferentur ab eo, quia non habet ad sui utilitatem; I ad Cor. XIII, 1: *si linguis hominum loquar et angelorum, caritatem autem non habeam, factus sum velut aes sonans, aut cymbalum tinniens*. Unde si habeat homo caritatem, dantur ei multa bona, quia accipiet bonum alterius, quia gaudebit de bono alterius sicut de suo.

Chrysostomus exponit de doctrina: qui habet gratiam docendi, et non exercitat se, amittit illam. Alter, qui non habet, et exercitat se, acquirit eam, ita ut sit doctor.

Hieronymus exponit sic: aliquis habet ingenium, et dat se otio, efficitur rudis et hebes; aliquis autem non habet ingenium, et exercitat se, et acquirit ingenium. Et ita habenti studium datur scientia et ingenium; et non habenti, etiam illud quod habet, scilicet ingenium, auferetur ab eo. Item, secundum Hieronymum, exponitur de fide, quia habenti fidem dabitur gratia; ad Ephesios II, 8: *gratia estis salvati per fidem*. Unde qui non haberet fidem, etsi haberet alia, sine fide nihil valerent.

Hilarius autem exponit de populo Iudaeorum et gentilium, quia Iudaei videbantur habere legem Dei, et noluerunt obedire, unde facti sunt alieni; populus autem gentilium recepit quod non habebat, et intravit in benedictionem olivae.

2075. Consequenter agit de poena sensus. Duo autem sunt sensus, visus scilicet et tactus. Ideo ponit primo poenam visus; secundo tactus.

Cum dicit *et inutilem servum mittite in tenebras exteriores*. Et notate quod non punitur propter malum quod fecerit, sed propter bonum quod omisit; unde supra VII, 19: *omnis arbor quae non facit fructum bonum, excidetur*. Et alibi, Io. XV, 2: *omnem palmitem in me non ferentem fructum tollet eum*.

Et dicitur *servus inutilis*, quia bonum quod habet, non expendit in utilitatem aliorum: ut si intellectum habuit et non expendit in usum bonum, alios docendo; si pecuniam, et non exercuit opus misericordiae.

2076. *Mittite in tenebras exteriores*. Origenes dicit quod quidam ante eum dixerunt quod damnati a toto mundo eiicientur. Unde dicunt Infernum esse extra totum mundum. Et innitebantur illi quod dixit Iob XVIII, v. 18: *de orbe transfert eos Deus*. Ipse autem

someone has gratuitous gifts and does not have charity; hence everything will be taken away from him, because he does not have them unto his own gain. *If I speak with the tongues of men, and of angels, and have not charity, I am become as sounding brass, or a tinkling cymbal* (1 Cor 13:1). Hence if a man has charity, many good things will be given to him, because he will receive another's good, since he will rejoice over another's good as over his own.

Chrysostom explains it as about teaching: the one who has the grace of teaching and does not exercise himself, loses it. Another, who does not have this grace, and exercises himself, acquires it, such that he is a teacher.

Jerome explains it this way: someone has a natural disposition, and gives himself to leisure, and he is made coarse and blunt; but someone else does not have a natural disposition, and exercises himself, and acquires a disposition. And thus to the one who has zeal, knowledge is given, and the disposition; and from the one who does not have zeal, even what he has, namely the natural disposition, will be taken away from him. Likewise, according to Jerome, it is explained as about faith, for to the one who has faith, grace will be given; *for by grace you are saved through faith* (Eph 2:8). Hence the one who does not have faith, even if he were to have other things, without faith they would do no good.

And Hilary explains it as about the people of the Jews and of the gentiles, for the Jews seemed to have God's law, and did not obey, on account of which they were made foreigners; but the people of the gentiles received what they did not have, and entered into the blessing of the olive tree.

2075. Next, he treats of the punishment of the senses. Now, there are two senses, namely vision and touch. For this reason, he sets out first the punishment of vision, second the punishment of touch.

He says, *and the unprofitable servant cast out into the exterior darkness*. And notice that he is not punished for the bad which he did, but for the good which he omitted; hence above, *every tree that does not bring forth good fruit, will be cut down, and will be cast into the fire* (Matt 7:19). And in another place, *every branch in me, that bears not fruit, he will take away* (John 15:2).

And he is called an *unprofitable servant* because he does not spend the good he has for others' gain: as for example if he had understanding and did not spend it on a good use, by teaching others; or if he had money, and did not perform a work of mercy.

2076. *Cast . . . into the exterior darkness*. Origen says that some before him had said that the damned will be thrown entirely out of the world. Hence they say that hell is entirely outside the world. And they took support from what Job says, *he will drive him out of light into darkness,*

sic exponit: ***in tenebras***, quia ignorant; Ps. LXXXI, 5: *nescierunt, neque intellexerunt, in tenebris ambulant*.

2077. Et sequitur poena tactus ***illic erit fletus et stridor dentium***. Hoc est expositum supra c. XXIV.

and will remove him out of the world (Job 18:18). But he himself explained it this way: ***into the outer darkness***, because they are ignorant; *they have not known nor understood: they walk on in darkness* (Ps 81:5).

2077. And there follows the punishment of touch: ***there will be weeping and gnashing of teeth***. This was explained above, in chapter twenty-four.

Lecture 3

25:31 Cum autem venerit Filius hominis in maiestate sua, et omnes angeli cum eo, tunc sedebit super sedem maiestatis suae; [n. 2079]

25:32 et congregabuntur ante eum omnes gentes, et separabit eos ab invicem, sicut pastor segregat oves ab hoedis; [n. 2083]

25:33 et statuet oves quidem a dextris suis, hoedos autem a sinistris. [n. 2090]

25:34 Tunc dicet Rex his qui a dextris eius erunt: venite, benedicti Patris mei, possidete paratum vobis regnum a constitutione mundi. [n. 2091]

25:35 Esurivi enim, et dedistis mihi manducare; sitivi, et dedistis mihi bibere; hospes eram, et colligistis me; [n. 2096]

25:36 nudus, et operuistis me; infirmus, et visitastis me; in carcere eram, et venistis ad me. [n. 2101]

25:37 Tunc respondebunt ei iusti dicentes: Domine, quando te vidimus esurientem, et pavimus te? Sitientem et dedimus tibi potum? [n. 2098]

25:38 Quando autem te vidimus hospitem, et collegimus te? Aut nudum, et cooperuimus te? [n. 2102]

25:39 Aut quando te vidimus infirmum, aut in carcere, et venimus ad te? [n. 2102]

25:40 Et respondens Rex dicet illis: amen dico vobis, quamdiu fecistis uni de his fratribus meis minimis, mihi fecistis. [n. 2098]

25:41 Tunc dicet et his qui a sinistris erunt: discedite a me, maledicti, in ignem aeternum, qui paratus est diabolo et angelis eius: [n. 2106]

25:42 esurivi enim, et non dedistis mihi manducare: sitivi, et non dedistis mihi potum, [n. 2109]

25:31 Ὅταν δὲ ἔλθῃ ὁ υἱὸς τοῦ ἀνθρώπου ἐν τῇ δόξῃ αὐτοῦ καὶ πάντες οἱ ἄγγελοι μετ' αὐτοῦ, τότε καθίσει ἐπὶ θρόνου δόξης αὐτοῦ·

25:32 καὶ συναχθήσονται ἔμπροσθεν αὐτοῦ πάντα τὰ ἔθνη, καὶ ἀφορίσει αὐτοὺς ἀπ' ἀλλήλων, ὥσπερ ὁ ποιμὴν ἀφορίζει τὰ πρόβατα ἀπὸ τῶν ἐρίφων,

25:33 καὶ στήσει τὰ μὲν πρόβατα ἐκ δεξιῶν αὐτοῦ, τὰ δὲ ἐρίφια ἐξ εὐωνύμων.

25:34 τότε ἐρεῖ ὁ βασιλεὺς τοῖς ἐκ δεξιῶν αὐτοῦ· δεῦτε οἱ εὐλογημένοι τοῦ πατρός μου, κληρονομήσατε τὴν ἡτοιμασμένην ὑμῖν βασιλείαν ἀπὸ καταβολῆς κόσμου.

25:35 ἐπείνασα γὰρ καὶ ἐδώκατέ μοι φαγεῖν, ἐδίψησα καὶ ἐποτίσατέ με, ξένος ἤμην καὶ συνηγάγετέ με,

25:36 γυμνὸς καὶ περιεβάλετέ με, ἠσθένησα καὶ ἐπεσκέψασθέ με, ἐν φυλακῇ ἤμην καὶ ἤλθατε πρός με.

25:37 τότε ἀποκριθήσονται αὐτῷ οἱ δίκαιοι λέγοντες· κύριε, πότε σε εἴδομεν πεινῶντα καὶ ἐθρέψαμεν, ἢ διψῶντα καὶ ἐποτίσαμεν;

25:38 πότε δέ σε εἴδομεν ξένον καὶ συνηγάγομεν, ἢ γυμνὸν καὶ περιεβάλομεν;

25:39 πότε δέ σε εἴδομεν ἀσθενοῦντα ἢ ἐν φυλακῇ καὶ ἤλθομεν πρός σε;

25:40 καὶ ἀποκριθεὶς ὁ βασιλεὺς ἐρεῖ αὐτοῖς· ἀμὴν λέγω ὑμῖν, ἐφ' ὅσον ἐποιήσατε ἑνὶ τούτων τῶν ἀδελφῶν μου τῶν ἐλαχίστων, ἐμοὶ ἐποιήσατε.

25:41 τότε ἐρεῖ καὶ τοῖς ἐξ εὐωνύμων· πορεύεσθε ἀπ' ἐμοῦ [οἱ] κατηραμένοι εἰς τὸ πῦρ τὸ αἰώνιον τὸ ἡτοιμασμένον τῷ διαβόλῳ καὶ τοῖς ἀγγέλοις αὐτοῦ.

25:42 ἐπείνασα γὰρ καὶ οὐκ ἐδώκατέ μοι φαγεῖν, ἐδίψησα καὶ οὐκ ἐποτίσατέ με,

25:31 And when the Son of man will come in his majesty, and all the angels with him, then will he sit upon the seat of his majesty. [n. 2079]

25:32 And all nations will be gathered together before him, and he will separate them one from another, as the shepherd separates the sheep from the goats; [n. 2083]

25:33 and he will set the sheep on his right hand, but the goats on his left. [n. 2090]

25:34 Then the King will say to those who will be on his right hand: come, you blessed of my Father, possess the kingdom prepared for you from the foundation of the world. [n. 2091]

25:35 For I was hungry, and you gave me to eat; I was thirsty, and you gave me to drink; I was a stranger, and you took me in; [n. 2096]

25:36 naked, and you covered me; sick, and you visited me; I was in prison, and you came to me. [n. 2101]

25:37 Then the just will answer him, saying: Lord, when did we see you hungry, and feed you; thirsty, and gave you drink? [n. 2098]

25:38 And when did we see you a stranger, and take you in? Or naked, and covered you? [n. 2102]

25:39 Or when did we see you sick or in prison, and come to you? [n. 2102]

25:40 And the King answering, will say to them: amen I say to you, as long as you did it to one of these, my least brethren, you did it to me. [n. 2098]

25:41 Then he will say to those also who will be on his left hand: depart from me, you cursed, into the everlasting fire which was prepared for the devil and his angels. [n. 2106]

25:42 For I was hungry, and you gave me nothing to eat; I was thirsty, and you gave me no drink. [n. 2109]

25:43 hospes eram, et non collegistis me; nudus, et non operuistis me; infirmus, et in carcere, et non visitastis me. [n. 2109]	25:43 ξένος ἤμην καὶ οὐ συνηγάγετέ με, γυμνὸς καὶ οὐ περιεβάλετέ με, ἀσθενὴς καὶ ἐν φυλακῇ καὶ οὐκ ἐπεσκέψασθέ με.	25:43 I was a stranger, and you did not take me in; naked, and you did not cover me; sick and in prison, and you did not visit me. [n. 2109]
25:44 Tunc respondebunt et ipsi dicentes: Domine, quando te vidimus esurientem, aut sitientem, aut hospitem, aut nudum, aut infirmum, aut in carcere, et non ministravimus tibi? [n. 2110]	25:44 τότε ἀποκριθήσονται καὶ αὐτοὶ λέγοντες· κύριε, πότε σε εἴδομεν πεινῶντα ἢ διψῶντα ἢ ξένον ἢ γυμνὸν ἢ ἀσθενῆ ἢ ἐν φυλακῇ καὶ οὐ διηκονήσαμέν σοι;	25:44 Then they also will answer him, saying: Lord, when did we see you hungry, or thirsty, or a stranger, or naked, or sick, or in prison, and did not minister to you? [n. 2110]
25:45 Tunc respondebit illis dicens: amen dico vobis, quamdiu non fecistis uni de minoribus his, nec mihi fecistis. [n. 2111]	25:45 τότε ἀποκριθήσεται αὐτοῖς λέγων· ἀμὴν λέγω ὑμῖν, ἐφ᾽ ὅσον οὐκ ἐποιήσατε ἑνὶ τούτων τῶν ἐλαχίστων, οὐδὲ ἐμοὶ ἐποιήσατε.	25:45 Then he will answer them, saying: amen I say to you, as long as you did it not to one of these least, neither did you do it to me. [n. 2111]
25:46 Et ibunt hi in supplicium aeternum, iusti autem in vitam aeternam. [n. 2112]	25:46 καὶ ἀπελεύσονται οὗτοι εἰς κόλασιν αἰώνιον, οἱ δὲ δίκαιοι εἰς ζωὴν αἰώνιον.	25:46 And these will go into everlasting punishment, but the just, into life everlasting. [n. 2112]

2078. Supra Dominus praemisit diversas parabolas pertinentes ad iudicium; hic autem manifeste de suo iudicio agit:

et tria facit.

Primo agit de adventu iudicis;

secundo de congregatione iudicandorum;

tertio de iudicio.

Secunda ibi *et congregabuntur ante eum omnes gentes*; tertia ibi *et dicet Rex* et cetera.

Circa primum quatuor sunt consideranda.

Primo tangitur conditio iudicis venientis;

secundo dignitas;

tertio ministri;

quarto iudiciaria auctoritas.

2079. In hoc quod dicitur *cum venerit Filius hominis*, non est dubium quin idem sit Filius Dei.

Sed quare potius nominat Filium hominis quam Filium Dei? Una ratio est, quia inquantum Filius hominis iudicabit; Io. V, 27: *potestatem dedit ei iudicium facere, quia Filius hominis est*. Et hoc propter tria. Primo ut ab omnibus videatur: in forma enim divinitatis non poterit videri nisi a bonis, unde si ab omnibus videri debeat, debet videri in forma hominis. Apoc. I, 7: *videbit eum omnis oculus*. Item propter meritum Christi: hoc enim ipse meruit per suam passionem; ad Philipp. II, 8: *humiliavit semetipsum factus obediens usque ad mortem, mortem autem crucis; propter quod et Deus exaltavit illum*. Item ut appareat iudicaturus in forma in qua iudicatus fuit; Iob XVI, 22: *utinam sic iudicaretur vir cum Deo, quomodo iudicatur Filius hominis cum collega suo*. Item ex Dei clementia, ut homines ab homine iudicentur; ad

2078. Above, the Lord set out various parables pertaining to the judgment; now here he treats clearly about his judgment,

and he does three things:

first, he treats of the coming of the judge;

second, of the gathering together of those to be judged;

third, of the judgment.

The second is at *and all nations will be gathered together before him*; the third, at *then will the King say to those who will be on his right hand: come*.

Concerning the first, there are four things to be considered:

first, the condition of the judge's coming is touched upon;

second, his dignity;

third, the ministers;

fourth, his judicial authority.

2079. When it says, *and when the Son of man will come*, there is no doubt that the same is the Son of God.

But why does he name the Son of man rather than the Son of God? One reason is that he will judge insofar as he is the Son of man; *and he has given him power to do judgment, because he is the Son of man* (John 5:27). And this for three reasons. First, that he might be seen by all: for in the form of the divinity he will be visible only to the good, so if he should be seen by all, then he must be seen in the form of a man. *Every eye will see him* (Rev 1:7). Likewise, owing to Christ's merit: for he merited this by his passion; *he humbled himself, becoming obedient unto death, even to the death of the cross. For which cause God also has exalted him* (Phil 2:8–9). Likewise, that the one who is to judge might appear in the form in which he was judged; *and O that a man might so be judged with God, as the Son of man is judged with his companion* (Job 16:22). Likewise, out of

Hebr. IV, 15: *non habemus pontificem qui non possit compati infirmitatibus nostris*. Iste ergo erit Filius hominis.

2080. Et cuius erit dignitas? Veniet **in maiestate sua**; Lc. XXI, 27: *videbunt Filium hominis venientem in nube cum potestate magna et maiestate*. Sed quid per **maiestatem** potest intelligi? Dicendum quod divinitas, quia licet appareat in forma hominis, tamen apparebit cum divinitate. Unde Apostolus, I Thess. c. IV, 15: *Dominus in iussu et in voce archangeli, et in tuba Dei descendet de caelo*. Et de hoc dicitur etiam Act. IX. Vel **in maiestate**, idest in gloria, quia suum corpus erit gloriosum; et veniet cum societate gloriosa; unde supra XVI, 27: **Filius hominis venturus est cum gloria**.

2081. Et ideo subdit **et omnes angeli cum eo**. Hic agit de ministris. Et potest intelligi de caelestibus spiritibus; Ps. CIII, 4: *qui facit angelos suos spiritus*. Et quare veniet cum istis? Quia custodes sunt hominum; Ps. XC, 11: *angelis suis Deus mandavit de te*. Ideo aderunt tamquam testes, quia boni custodiam suam receperunt, mali autem non, sed repulerunt; Is. l, 7: *curavimus Babylonem, et non est sanata*.

Vel **omnes angeli**, idest praedicatores, vel doctores veritatis; Mal. II, 7: *labia sacerdotis custodiunt scientiam, et legem requirunt ex ore eius*. Istis competit iudiciaria potestas, ut dicit Augustinus. Is. III, 14: *Dominus ad iudicium veniet et omnes sancti eius cum eo*; Prov. ult., 23: *nobilis in portis vir eius, quando sederit cum senatoribus terrae*.

2082. Tunc sequitur iudiciaria potestas: **tunc sedebit super sedem maiestatis suae**. Non debemus intelligere secundum sedem corporalem; sed sedes eius homines sancti sunt et angeli. In eis sedebit, quia per eos iudicium exercebit. De hominibus dicitur supra c. XIX, 28 quod sedebunt **super sedes duodecim** et cetera. De angelis dicitur Col. I, 16: *sive throni, sive dominationes* etc. et in Ps. LXXIX, v. 3: *sedes super cherubim*; et Ps. IX, 5: *sedisti super thronum, qui iudicas iustitiam*.

2083. Consequenter ponitur congregatio; secundo divisio.

Dicit ergo **et congregabuntur omnes gentes**. Per gentes non solum gentes signantur, sed omnes homines qui nati sunt ab Adam usque ad finem mundi; II ad Cor. V, 10: *omnes nos manifestari oportet ante tribunal Christi, ut referat unusquisque quod gessit in corpore, sive bonum, sive malum*. Inter istos etiam parvuli nati, quia, etsi nihil habeant proprio merito, habent tamen aliquid,

God's clemency, that men might be judged by a man; *for we have not a high priest, who can not have compassion on our infirmities* (Heb 4:15). Therefore, this judge will be the Son of man.

2080. And whose will the dignity be? He will come **in his majesty**; *and then they shall see the Son of man coming in a cloud, with great power and majesty* (Luke 21:27). But what can be understood by **majesty**? One should say that it is the divinity, for although he appears in the form of a man, nevertheless he will appear with the divinity. Hence the Apostle, *for the Lord himself will come down from heaven with commandment, and with the voice of an archangel, and with the trumpet of God* (1 Thess 4:16). And Acts also speaks about this (Acts 9). Or, **in his majesty**, i.e., in glory, because his body will be glorious; and he will come with a glorious company; hence above, **for the Son of man will come in the glory of his Father** (Matt 16:27).

2081. And for this reason he adds next, **and all the angels with him**. Here he treats of the ministers. And it can be understood as about the heavenly spirits; *who makes your angels spirits* (Ps 103:4). And why will he come with them? Because they are the guardians of men; *he has given his angels charge over you; to keep you in all your ways* (Ps 90:11). So they will be present as though witnesses that the good have accepted their protection, and the wicked have not, but rejected it; *we would have cured Babylon, but she is not healed* (Jer 51:9).

Or, **all the angels**, i.e., the preachers, or teachers of truth; *for the lips of the priest will keep knowledge, and they will seek the law at his mouth: because he is the angel of the Lord of hosts* (Mal 2:7). Judicial power belongs to them, as Augustine says. *The Lord will enter into judgment, and all his saints with him* (Isa 3:14); *her husband is honorable in the gates, when he sits among the senators of the land* (Prov 31:23).

2082. Then there follows the judicial power: **then will he sit upon the seat of his majesty**. We should not understand this as a bodily seat; but the holy men and the angels are his seat. He will sit on them, for he will exercise judgment through them. It says about the men above, that they will **sit on twelve thrones** (Matt 19:28). It says about the angels: *whether thrones, or dominations, or principalities, or powers* (Col 1:16). And, *you who sit upon the cherubims* (Ps 79:2); and, *you have sat on the throne, who judge justice* (Ps 9:5).

2083. Next the gathering together is set out; second, the division.

He says therefore, **and all nations will be gathered together**. The nations indicate not only the nations, but all men who have been born from Adam to the end of the world; *for we must all be manifested before the judgment seat of Christ, that every one may receive the proper things of the body, according as he has done, whether it be good or evil* (2 Cor 5:10). Among them will also be the children that were newly born, because even though they have nothing

scilicet vel culpam ex peccato primi hominis, vel gratiam ex sacramento Christi.

2084. Unde notandum quod non omnes isti congregabuntur ad idem; sed erit quadruplex genus eorum qui comparebunt in iudicio. Quidam enim comparebunt ut iudicentur per discussionem meritorum; sed istorum quidam damnabuntur, quidam salvabuntur. Quidam vero ut sine discussione sententiam recipiant. Iudicari enim dupliciter dicitur: scilicet vel sententiam recipere, quia omnes vel praemiabuntur vel punientur, vel dicitur iudicari, per discussionem meritorum reddere rationem. Et haec discussio non erit necessaria omnibus, quia peccata et merita illorum praecipue discutientur, qui fuerunt coniuncti cum Christo per fidem: illi enim qui totaliter alieni sunt a Christo, non indigent discussione, secundum quod dicitur Io. III, 18: *qui non credit, iam iudicatus est*. Gregorius ponit exemplum: qui inimicum suum accipit in bello, non expectat iudicium, sed iam iudicatus est, sic et cetera. Item aliqui sunt qui nihil habent commune cum mundo, quia omnia dimiserunt propter Christum, et isti apparebunt ut iudices; unde supra XIX, 28: **vos qui secuti estis me, sedebitis super sedes duodecim tribus Israel**.

Qui sunt ergo qui iudicabuntur? Fideles qui implicati sunt saecularibus, quorum quidam sunt eis bene utentes, ut habetur I ad Tim. VI, 18: *divitibus praecipe bene agere, divites fieri in bonis operibus, facile tribuere, communicare* et cetera. Qui autem detinentur, et eis involvuntur, damnabuntur.

2085. Sed quae est necessitas? Nonne omnes in morte recipiunt quod meruerunt? Ad quid ergo iudicabuntur?

Notandum quod praemium quod iusto Dei iudicio datur hominibus, est duplex: primum est stola animae, et secundum stola corporis. Quantum ad stolam animae, in morte recipitur, sed tunc gloriam corporis simul recipient. Unde quantum ad animam omnes simul recipiunt corpora, sed quantum ad poenam, omnes simul damnabuntur; unde Is. XXIV, 22: *congregabuntur congregatione unius fascis*, quia unum sunt in peccato.

2086. Istam congregationem possumus intelligere congregationem localem, quia omnes congregabuntur in uno loco; Ioel III, 2: *congregabo omnes gentes, et deducam eas in vallem Iosaphat*; quia qui salvantur, per passionem Christi salvantur, et qui damnantur, per contemptum passionis eius damnantur; ideo ubi facta fuit passio Christi, ibi iudicium. Et intelligendum est quod boni in aere occurrent ei obviam, aliqui vero in terra manebunt. Secundum Origenem ista congregatio non erit localis, sed dispersi erunt, et in locis singulis congregabuntur; et hoc vult illud quod est dictum supra XXIV,

by their own merit, yet they have something, namely either guilt from the sin of the first man or grace from the sacrament of Christ.

2084. Hence one should note that they will not all be gathered together for the same thing; but there will be a fourfold grouping of those who will appear at the judgment. For some will appear to be judged by the examination of merits; but of these, some will be condemned, some saved. However, some receive a sentence without examination. For to be judged is said in two ways: namely either to receive a sentence, for all will either be rewarded or punished; or to be judged means to render an account by the examination of merits. And this examination will not be necessary for all, for principally the sins and merits of those who were conjoined with Christ through faith will be examined: for those who were entirely foreign to Christ need no examination, according to what is said, *but he who does not believe, is already judged* (John 3:18). Gregory gives an example: Just as someone who meets an enemy in war does not expect a judgment, but is already judged, so likewise. Likewise there are some who have nothing in common with the world, but have left all things for Christ, and these will appear as judges; hence above, **you, who have followed me . . . you also will sit on twelve seats judging the twelve tribes of Israel** (Matt 19:28).

So who are those who will be judged? The believers who have entangled themselves in worldly things, of whom some indeed have used them well, as is said, *charge the rich . . . to do good, to be rich in good works, to give easily, to communicate to others* (1 Tim 6:18). But those who are held back and wrapped up in them will be condemned.

2085. But what is the need? Do not all receive what they have merited at death? So why will they be judged?

Note that the reward which by God's just judgment is given to men is twofold: the first is the robe of the soul, the second the robe of the body. As regards the robe of the soul, it is received at death, but then they will receive the glory of the body as well. Hence as regards the soul, all receive the body together, but as regards punishment, all will be condemned together; hence, *and they will be gathered together as in the gathering of one bundle* (Isa 24:22), because they are one in sin.

2086. We can understand this gathering as a gathering in place, because all will be gathered together in one place; *I will gather together all nations, and will bring them down into the valley of Josaphat* (Joel 3:2); for those who are saved, are saved through Christ's passion, and those who are condemned, are condemned through contempt for his passion; for this reason, the judgment will happen there where Christ's passion happened. And one should understand that the good will fly up to meet him in the air, while the others will remain on the earth. According to Origen, this gathering will not be in a place, but rather they will be

27, quod *sicut fulgur exit ab oriente, et paret usque in occidentem, ita erit et adventus Filii hominis*, quia ubicumque erunt, erunt ibi praesentes. Unde vult quod erit congregatio spiritualis, quia modo quidam disperguntur ab eo, quidam se tenent cum eo; sed tunc omnes congregabuntur; Is. XL, 5: *videbit omnis caro salutare Dei nostri*.

2087. Tunc agit de separatione *et separabit eos ab invicem, sicut pastor segregat oves ab hoedis*. Et

primo ponitur secundum nomen;
secundo secundum situm, ibi *et statuet oves quidem a dextris* et cetera.

2088. Dicit ergo *et separabit eos ab invicem*.

Notate quod quamdiu mundus durat, mali sunt bonis permixti. Vix autem est aliqua societas, quin aliqui sint mali; Cant. II, 2: *sicut lilium inter spinas, sic amica mea inter filias*. Sed in illo iudicio mali erunt ad unam partem, boni ad aliam; Eccli. XXXV: *iudicabit inter oves et hoedos*.

2089. Sed quare bonos vocat *oves*? Hoc est propter quatuor. Invenimus enim in ovibus innocentiam, II regum XXIV, 17: *isti qui oves sunt, quid fecerunt?* Item patientiam; Is. LIII, 7: *tamquam ovis ad occisionem ducetur, et quasi agnus coram tondente se obmutescet, et non aperiet os suum*. Item Ps. XLIII, 22: *aestimati sumus sicut oves occisionis*. Item obedientiam, quia ad vocem pastoris congregantur; Io. X, 27: *oves meae vocem meam audiunt*. Item affluentiam fructuum: sicut ex ove plures fructus percipimus, sic multi sunt fructus bonorum; Ez. c. XXXIV, 3: *lac comedebatis, et lanis cooperiebamini*. Item per hoedos intelligit peccatores, quia est animal per praecipitia vadens, item ad coitum fervidum et contrarias habet proprietates, item pro peccato offerebatur.

2090. Consequenter ponitur divisio quoad situm *et statuet oves quidem a dextris, hoedos autem a sinistris*. Quid intelligitur per dexteram, et quid per sinistram? Potest dici quod ad litteram ita fiet, quod boni ad partem unam, et mali ad aliam constituentur. Vel quia dextera pars nobilior est, ideo qui sunt boni, situm habebunt nobiliorem, quia occurrent Christo in aere.

Origenes retorquet istud ad finalem remunerationem; quia qui intentionem suam direxerunt ad Deum, erunt a dextris, idest in remuneratione aeterna; Eccle. X, 2: *cor sapientis in dextera eius, et cor stulti in sinistra illius*. Item Prov. IV, 27: *vias quae a dextris sunt novit Dominus; perversae vero sunt, quae sunt a sinistris*.

dispersed, and will be gathered together into separate places; and he would have this be the meaning of what is said above, that *as lightning comes out of the east, and appears even into the west: so will the coming of the Son of man be* (Matt 24:27), because wherever they are, they will be present there. Hence he would have it that it will be a spiritual gathering, because now some are divided from him, some hold themselves with him; but then all will be gathered together; *all the ends of the earth will see the salvation of our God* (Isa 51:10).

2087. Then he treats of the separation: *and he will separate them one from another, as the shepherd separates the sheep from the goats*. And

first, it is set out according to name;
second, according to position, at *and he will set the sheep on his right hand*.

2088. He says therefore, *and he will separate them one from another*.

Note that as long as the world endures, the wicked are mixed together with the good. And there is scarcely any society without some who are bad; *as the lily among thorns, so is my love among the daughters* (Song 2:2). But at that judgment the wicked will be on one side, the good on another; *he will judge between the sheep and the goats* (Sir 35).

2089. But why does he call the good *sheep*? This is for four reasons. For we find innocence in sheep; *these that are the sheep, what have they done?* (2 Sam 24:17). Likewise patience; *he will be led as a sheep to the slaughter, and will be dumb as a lamb before his shearer, and he will not open his mouth* (Isa 53:7). Likewise *we are counted as sheep for the slaughter* (Ps 43:22). Likewise obedience, because they are gathered together at the shepherd's voice; *my sheep hear my voice* (John 10:27). Likewise abundance of fruits: as we gather many fruits from a sheep, so the fruits of the good are many; *you ate the milk, and you clothed yourselves with the wool* (Ezek 34:3). Likewise by the goats he means sinners, because it is an animal which rushes headlong, likewise is passionate for coitus, and has contrary properties, and was offered for sin.

2090. Next the division with regard to position is set out: *and he will set the sheep on his right hand, but the goats on his left*. What is understood by the right hand, and by the left hand? It can be said that it will happen this way literally, that the good will be set on one side, and the wicked on the other. Or since the right is the nobler side, then those who are good will have the nobler position, because they will fly up in the air to Christ.

Origen refers this to the final reward: for those who have directed their intention toward God will be on the right, i.e., in the eternal reward; *the heart of a wise man is in his right hand, and the heart of a fool is in his left hand* (Eccl 10:2). Similarly, *the Lord knows the ways which are on the right, but those are perverse which are on the left* (Prov 4:27).

2091. *Then the King will say to those who will be on his right hand*. Here he treats of the judgment. And

first, a sentence is made known with regard to the good;

second, with regard to the wicked;

third, he sets out the conclusion.

Concerning the first, he does three things:

first, the judgment is set out;

second, the wonderment of those who will be saved;

third, the satisfaction of their wonderment.

The second is at **then the just will answer him**; the third, at **and the King answering, will say to them**.

Concerning the first, he does two things:

firsts, he invites them to the reward;

second, he matches it to their merit.

2092. He says therefore, **then the King will say**. And he calls him a king because it belongs to a king to judge; *the king, who sits on the throne of judgment, scatters away all evil with his look* (Prov 20:8).

But there is a question: will it happen by a vocal judgment? Some say that it will be by word, and that he will hold judgment for a long time. And Lactantius says this, that it will go on for a thousand years; but this is not true. Rather, this should be referred to an interior speaking; and it leads to men's knowledge, for the good are deserving of glory, the wicked of punishment. Hence what those men will say will not be vocal, but according to an interior inspiration; and this is what Augustine says, that it will happen by the divine power that to each one will come to mind what he has done. And this is clear through the Apostle, *their conscience bearing witness to them, and their thoughts between themselves accusing, or also defending one another, in the day when God will judge the secrets of men by Jesus Christ* (Rom 2:15–16). So it should be referred to an interior speaking.

And he seems to touch on three things, for an invitation is set out, the reason for the judgment, and the reward itself.

2093. The invitation: *come, you blessed of my Father*.

But why does he say, *you blessed of my Father*? Because it will not be given to us according to our merit, but according as we are confirmed by Christ's merit; hence, *to him that will overcome, I will give to sit with me in my throne: as I also have overcome, and am set down with my Father in his throne* (Rev 3:21); *I dispose to you, as my Father has disposed to me, a kingdom* (Luke 22:29). I, insofar as I am a man, insofar as I enjoy the Word. Likewise as regards the body; *who will reform the body of our lowness, made like to the body of his glory* (Phil 3:21). *Come*, i.e., be conformed; *when he will appear, we will be like to him* (1 John 3:2).

But are not the good joined to God even now? I say that it is so through charity which is not full, and through the obscurity of faith; but then they will be gathered together in full charity, in faith which is not obscure; for now *the*

corrumpitur, aggravat animam, et terrena inhabitatio deprimit sensum multa cogitantem, Sap. IX, 15.

2094. Causa huius praemii est duplex: causa damnationis est ex homine, causa salutis ex Deo; Osee XIII, 9: *ex te perditio tua, Israel, ex me tantummodo auxilium tuum*. Unde causam salutis invenimus temporalem et aeternam; temporalis est appositio gloriae, et hoc tangitur, **venite, benedicti Patris mei**. Dicere suum est facere; unde Ps. XXXII, 9: *ipse dixit, et facta sunt*. Unde eius benedicere, est gratiam infundere, unde dicit **Patris**, quia non est ex nobis, sed ex Deo; Iac. c. I, 17: *omne datum optimum, et omne donum perfectum desursum est, descendens a Patre luminum*.

Item alia causa est Dei praedestinatio; et hoc notatur cum dicit **paratum vobis regnum**. Unde Apostolus ad Rom. VIII, 30: *quos praedestinavit, hos et vocavit*; Is. LXIV, v. 4: *oculus non vidit, nec auris audivit, quae praeparavit Deus diligentibus se*.

Et dicit **a constitutione mundi**. Sed quomodo est hoc? Nonne ipse elegit eos ab aeterno? *Ipse elegit nos ante mundi constitutionem*, ad Eph. I, 4. Et dicendum quod elegit ab aeterno, sed a constitutione mundi manifestavit.

2095. Sed quid est praemium illud, quod tangit **possidete paratum vobis regnum**? Et quod est istud regnum? Istud regnum est regnum caelorum; Ps. CXLIV, 13: *regnum tuum, domine, regnum omnium saeculorum*. Qui possidet Deum, possidet regnum; Apoc. V, 10: *et fecisti nos Deo nostro regnum et sacerdotes*.

Sed diceret aliquis: *nolo regnare, sufficit mihi quod non damner*. Hoc non potest esse. Vel eris rex et habebis regnum, vel eris damnatus.

Et dicit **possidete**, idest intrate in possessionem. Intrare autem in possessionem proprie convenit ei, qui ius habuit. Istud autem ius habuimus ex ordinatione divina; item ex acquisitione Christi, qui nobis hoc acquisivit; item ex gratia sua; Eph. I, 14: *qui est pignus haereditatis nostrae*. Item dicitur possessio, quae 'pacifice habetur'; unde plenarium dominium signatur. Modo habemus Deum, sed non quiete, quia inquietatur homo multis modis; sed tunc quieta erit possessio; I Petr. III, 9: *in hoc vocati estis, ut benedictionem haereditate possideatis*; supra XVIII, v. 29: *et vitam aeternam possidebit*.

2096. *Esurivi enim, et dedistis mihi manducare* et cetera. Supra posita est sententia de praemio, hic posita est de merito. Ex quo considerare debemus quod duplex est causa beatitudinis: una ex parte Dei, idest benedictio Dei; alia ex parte nostra, idest meritum quod est de libero arbitrio: non enim debent homines esse desides, sed

corruptible body is a load upon the soul, and the earthly habitation presses down the mind that muses upon many things (Wis 9:15).

2094. The cause of this reward is twofold: the cause of condemnation is from man, the cause of salvation from God; *destruction is your own, O Israel: your help is only in me* (Hos 13:9). Hence we find a temporal and an eternal cause of salvation. The temporal cause is the application of glory, and this is touched upon at **come, you blessed of my Father**. His saying is doing; hence, *for he spoke and they were made* (Ps 32:9). Hence his blessing is the infusing of grace. Hence he says, **of my Father**, because it is not from us, but from God; *every best gift, and every perfect gift, is from above, coming down from the Father of lights* (Jas 1:17).

Likewise the other cause is God's predestination; and this is pointed out when he says, **the kingdom prepared for you**. Hence the Apostle, *and whom he predestined, them he also called* (Rom 8:30); *eye has not seen, nor ear heard, neither has it entered into the heart of man, what things God has prepared for those who love him* (Isa 64:4).

And he says, **from the foundation of the world**. But how is this? Did he choose them from eternity? *He chose us in him before the foundation of the world* (Eph 1:4). And one should say that he chose from eternity, but he manifested his choice from the foundation of the world.

2095. But what is that reward, which he touches upon at **possess you the kingdom prepared for you**? And what is this kingdom? This kingdom is the kingdom of heaven; *your kingdom is a kingdom of all ages* (Ps 144:13). The one who possesses God, possesses the kingdom; *and has made us to our God a kingdom and priests* (Rev 5:10).

Someone may say: *I do not want to reign; it is enough for me that I not be condemned*. But this cannot be. Either you will be a king, and have a kingdom, or you will be condemned.

And he says, **possess**, i.e., enter into possession. Now, to enter into possession belongs properly to the one who has a right. And we have this right by divine ordinance; likewise, by Christ's acquisition, who acquired this for us; likewise by his grace; *who is the pledge of our inheritance* (Eph 1:14). Likewise, what is called a possession is that 'which is had peacefully'; hence it indicates the plenitude of dominion. We have God now, but not restfully, because a man is disquieted in many ways; but then there will be restful possession. *For unto this are you called, that you may inherit a blessing* (1 Pet 3:9); above, **and will possess life everlasting** (Matt 19:29).

2096. *For I was hungry, and you gave me to eat*. Above, the judgment about the reward was set out; here it is set out with regard to the merit. From this we should reflect that there are two causes of beatitude: one on God's part, i.e., God's blessing; another on our part, i.e., the merit which is from free will. For men should not be idle, but should cooperate with God's grace, as is said, *but by the grace of*

2097. But since there are many good merits, he only mentions the works of mercy. And some have taken an occasion for error from this, saying that men are only saved through works of mercy, or condemned through their omission, such that if someone were to commit many sins, and exercised himself in works of mercy, he would be saved, in accord with, *redeem your sins with alms, and your iniquities with works of mercy to the poor* (Dan 4:24); contrary to what is said, *they who do such things*, namely sins, *are worthy of death* (Rom 1:32). And, after an enumeration of bodily sins, it says, *they who do such things will not obtain the kingdom of God* (Gal 5:21). So that position should not be held.

But it could happen that someone abstains from sins, and repents, and in this way can be freed through almsgiving: for a man should begin giving alms with himself. *Have pity on your own soul, pleasing God* (Sir 30:24).

2098. And why does he mention these works rather than others?

One should say, according to Gregory, that he sets out these as the least: for if they do not do the things which nature dictates, much less will they do other things. And this is in harmony with the words of the Gospel, for those who are saved say, **when did we see you hungry**, as though to say: this is a little thing. And since they consider it to be rather little, the Lord exalts it the more, saying, **as long as you did it to one of these, my least brethren, you did it to me**.

Augustine says that everyone in the world sins, yet not everyone is condemned, but only those who do not repent or make satisfaction. But those who repent and promise satisfaction through works of mercy are saved.

Origen says that all good works are named under the works of mercy, or omitted owing to the omission of such works. And this is indicated, because alms are given not only to one's neighbor, but also to oneself: for if a man feeds the hungry, much more should he feed himself when he is hungry, and so on with the other works. Likewise, there is not only bodily almsgiving, but also spiritual; so whatever a man does, whether for his own good or for his neighbor's, it is all contained under 'work of mercy.' Hence all works are contained either under these or under the contrary.

There are seven works of mercy, but only six are touched upon. These seven are remembered by a verse:

visit, drink, feed, redeem, cover, take in, bury.

Now, burial is not touched upon here. But why? To exclude the error of certain men who said that souls do not gain rest until the body is buried. But this is not true, because the soul receives nothing from the body while it is separated.

2099. So he sets out six things which are given in time of need. And since there is a certain general need and a

specialis; primo agit de generali, secundo de speciali. Et quia quidam generaliter ab exteriori, quidam ad interiori, primo tangit defectus a parte interiori, secundo ab exteriori.

2100. Dicit ergo *esurivi, et dedistis mihi manducare*. Hoc habetur Isaiae LVIII, 7: *frange esurienti panem tuum*.

Sitivi, et dedistis mihi bibere, quia propter me dedistis proximo. Unde supra X, 42: *qui dederit calicem aquae frigidae uni ex minimis meis, non perdet mercedem suam*, de istis duobus Prov. XXV, 21: *si esurierit inimicus tuus, ciba illum: si sitierit, da ei aquam bibere*.

2101. Item sunt defectus ab exteriori, et hi sunt duo, scilicet a tegumento coniuncto et separato. Dicit ergo *hospes eram et collegistis me*. Ad Hebr. ult., 2: *hospitalitatem nolite oblivisci; per hanc enim latuerunt quidam angelis hospitio recepti*. Quantum ad tegumentum coniunctum dicit *nudus fui et operuistis me*; Iob XXXI, 19: *si despexi praetereuntem eo quod non haberet indumentum*: et sequitur, *si non benedixerunt mihi latera eius, et de velleribus ovium meorum calefactus est*; Is. LVIII, 7: *cum videris nudum, operi eum*.

Item quidam sunt particulares defectus; et horum quidam sunt naturales quidam ab exteriori. Defectus naturalis et ab intrinseco est infirmitas; unde dicit *infirmus, et visitastis me*. Quantum ad exteriorem defectum dicit *in carcere eram, et venistis ad me*. Et potest per carcerem intelligi quaelibet tribulatio; ad Hebr. X, 34: *nam et vinctis compassi estis*.

2102. *Tunc respondebunt iusti dicentes*. Hic ponitur responsio mentalis. Bonarum mentium est quod ea quae propter Deum faciunt, parva reputent; Lc. XVII, 10: *cum feceritis omnia quae praecepta sunt vobis, dicite, quia servi inutiles sumus*. Et ad Rom. c. VIII, 18: *existimo quod non sunt condignae passiones huius temporis ad futuram gloriam quae revelabitur in nobis*. Unde dicent quod ignorantes fecerunt, et haec dicent parva reputantes; unde *quando vidimus te esurientem et pavimus?* et cetera. Unde hoc dicent admirantes.

2103. *Et respondens Rex dicet illis*. Huic admirationi satisfacit, quia quando homo humiliat se et Deus exaltat hunc, quando homo se vilificat et Deus collaudat; unde *quamdiu fecistis uni de his fratribus meis minimis, mihi fecistis*; supra X, 40: *qui vos recipit, me recipit*, quia caput et membra sunt unum corpus.

certain particular need, first he treats of the general, second of the particular. And since there are some general exterior needs and some interior, first, he touches on the need on the part of the interior, second on the part of the exterior.

2100. He says therefore, *I was hungry, and you gave me to eat*. This is found, *deal your bread to the hungry* (Isa 58:7).

I was thirsty, and you gave me to drink, because for my sake you gave to your neighbor. Hence above, *and whoever will give to drink to one of these little ones a cup of cold water only in the name of a disciple, amen I say to you, he will not lose his reward* (Matt 10:42), and about these two, *if your enemy is hungry, give him to eat: if he thirsts, give him water to drink* (Prov 25:21).

2101. Likewise there are exterior needs, and there are two of these, namely covering which is conjoined and covering which is separate. He says therefore, *I was a stranger, and you took me in*. And hospitality do not forget; for by this some, being not aware of it, have entertained angels (Heb 13:2). As regards the conjoined covering, he says, *naked, and you covered me*; *if I have despised him that was perishing for want of clothing, and the poor man that had no covering* (Job 31:19), and there follows, *if his sides have not blessed me, and if he were not warmed with the fleece of my sheep* (Job 31:20); *when you will see one naked, cover him* (Isa 58:7).

Likewise there are certain particular needs; and of these some are natural, and some from the outside. A natural need, and one from the inside, is sickness; hence he says, *sick, and you visited me*. As regards the exterior need, he says, *I was in prison, and you came to me*. And the prison can be taken to mean any given affliction; *for you both had compassion on them that were in bands* (Heb 10:34).

2102. *Then the just will answer him, saying*. Here a mental response is set out. It belongs to the thoughts of the good that they consider the things they do for God's sake to be small; *when you will have done all these things that are commanded you, say: we are unprofitable servants* (Luke 17:10). And, *for I reckon that the sufferings of this time are not worthy to be compared with the glory to come, that will be revealed in us* (Rom 8:18). Hence they say that they acted in ignorance, and they speak, considering these things small; hence, *when did we see you hungry, and fed you?* So they speak in wonderment.

2103. *And the King answering, will say to them*. He satisfies this wonderment, for when a man humbles himself God also exalts him, and when a man cheapens himself God also praises him; hence, *as long as you did it to one of these, my least brethren, you did it to me*. Above, *he who receives you, receives me* (Matt 10:40), because the head and the members are one body.

And he says, **brethren**, because those are his brothers who do God's will; hence above, it says that *stretching forth his hand towards his disciples, he said: behold my mother and my brethren* (Matt 12:49).

In which one should note that one should give to those who are good; *give to the merciful and uphold not the sinner* (Sir 12:4).

2104. **And should one not give to a sinner?**

One should give, when he is in extreme need, but more and first to those who are just; for this reason he says, **my brethren**. For many come who are not brothers of God; hence, *and every spirit that dissolves Jesus, is not of God* (1 John 4:3). So all other things being equal, we should do better for those who are good; yet in a case of need one should give even to the evil in a time of necessity, not for the sake of aiding sin, but nature.

Are all the brothers of God? Yes; but some according to nature, and some according to grace. According to nature, all the good and the wicked: *in perils from false brethren* (2 Cor 11:26); according to grace, however, only the good: *that he might be the firstborn amongst many brethren* (Rom 8:29). And one should principally have pity on these and help them; hence the Apostle says, *therefore, while we have time, let us work good to all men, but especially to those who are of the household of the faith* (Gal 6:10).

2105. **But why does he call them least?** He says this as regards the common opinion. It is known that men who are small for God's sake are considered *least* (Jas 3). Likewise, they are least owing to humility; above, *you have hidden these things from the wise and prudent, and have revealed them to the little ones* (Matt 11:25). And he speaks about the least, because people could say: if I had done this for an equal, or for some of the great, I believe that it would be repaid. And so the Lord says that it is not only what is done for those who are greater, but also what is done for the imperfect; for this reason he says, **least**.

2106. ***Then he will say to those also who will be on his left hand***. Here the condemnation of the wicked is set out. And

first, the condemnation is set out;
second, their excuse;
third, a refutation.
And concerning the first,
first, he sets out the judgment;
second, the punishment.

2107. He says therefore, ***depart from me, you cursed***. This judgment differs from the first, for in the first he said, ***come, you blessed of my Father***; but here he does not say, *my Father's cursed ones*, because our blessing is from God, and our curse from ourselves. And Hebrews (Heb 5), as well as Deuteronomy, turns a curse into a blessing: *and he turned his cursing into your blessing* (Deut 23:5).

Item differentia est, quia supra dixit **possidete paratum vobis regnum** etc., hic autem dicit *ite in ignem aeternum qui paratus est diabolo et angelis eius*.

2108. Et quae est ratio? Dicit Origenes quod poenas non fecit propter homines, sed ipsi acquirunt sibi mortem manibus suis; Is. c. XXXI, 7: *in die illa abiiciet vir idola auri et argenti sui, quae fecerunt vobis manus vestrae*.

Sed potest aliquis dicere: nonne etiam fecit dominus diabolum bonum? Notate quod loquitur Dominus de praeparatione secundum quod manifestatur ab origine mundi. Sed diabolus ab initio peccavit: unde angelo, qui quantum ad naturam creatus est bonus, non paravit, sed peccato.

2109. *Esurivi*. Hic non est aliud dicendum nisi quod diversimode loquitur ad bonos et ad malos: quia supra dixit explicite unumquodque per se, hic multa coniungit; unde ***infirmus et in carcere***. Et quia coniungit ista duo, dicendum quod ad modum boni iudicis procedit qui invite condemnat, et large remunerat: unde verba remunerationis dilatat, verba condemnationis abbreviat.

2110. *Tunc respondebunt ei et ipsi*. Et notate quod sicut boni abbreviant bona, ita mali culpas; unde dicunt: ***Domine, quando vidimus te esurientem aut sitientem?*** et cetera. Totum simul dicunt; in quo datur intelligi quod non libenter discutiunt conscientias suas, contra illud Is. XLVI, 8: *redite, praevaricatores, ad cor*. Unde, cum oportet redire, redeunt ad valde breve.

2111. Tunc sequitur confutatio ***amen dico vobis: quamdiu non fecistis*** et cetera. Simile habetur Lc. X, 16: *qui vos spernit, me spernit*; Zach. II, 8: *qui tetigerit vos, tangit pupillam oculi mei*.

2112. *Et ibunt hi in supplicium aeternum* et cetera. Posita sententia, ponitur effectus.

Et ibunt hi in supplicium aeternum. Supra dixerat quod in ignem aeternum, quia stare posset quod esset ignis aeternus, et tamen non aeterne cruciaret; ideo dicit ***in supplicium***. ***Iusti autem in vitam aeternam***; Io. c. XVII, 3: *haec est vita aeterna, ut cognoscant te solum verum Deum, et quem misisti Iesum Christum*.

Quod autem sit supplicium aeternum habetur Dan. XII, 2: *multi de his qui dormiunt in pulvere, evigilabunt, alii in vitam aeternam, alii in opprobrium, ut videant semper*; Apoc. c. XX, 15: *missus est in stagnum ignis et sulphuris, ubi et bestia et pseudoprophetae cruciabuntur die ac nocte in saecula saeculorum*; Is. ult., 24: *vermis eorum non morietur, et ignis eorum non extinguetur*.

Likewise there is this difference, that above he said, ***possess the kingdom prepared for you***; while here he says, ***depart from me, you cursed, into everlasting fire which was prepared for the devil and his angels***.

2108. And what is the reason for this? Origen says that he does not make punishments for men, but they themselves acquire death for themselves with their own hands; *for in that day a man will cast away his idols of silver, and his idols of gold, which your hands have made for you to sin* (Isa 31:7).

But someone could say: did not the Lord make even the devil good? Note that the Lord speaks of preparation according as it is manifested by the origin of the world. But the devil has sinned from the beginning: hence he did not prepare the fire for an angel, who as regards the nature created is good, but for sin.

2109. *I was hungry*. Here there is nothing to say, except that he speaks to the good and to the wicked in different ways: for above he said each thing explicitly on its own, while here he joins many together; hence ***sick and in prison***. And since he joins those two, one should say that he proceeds in the manner of a good judge, who reluctantly condemns, and lavishly rewards. Hence he extends the words of reward, but cuts short the words of condemnation.

2110. *Then they also will answer him*. And note that just as the good lessen their good deeds, so the wicked lessen their guilt. Hence they say: ***Lord, when did we see you hungry, or thirsty?*** They say everything together; in which one is given to understand that they do not freely examine their consciences, contrary to, *return, you transgressors, to the heart* (Isa 46:8). Hence when they must return to the heart, they return very briefly.

2111. Then there follows the refutation: ***amen I say to you, as long as you did it not***. A similar thing is said in Luke, *he who despises you, despises me* (Luke 10:16); *for he who touches you, touches the apple of my eye* (Zech 2:8).

2112. *And these will go into everlasting punishment*. The judgment being set out, the effect is set out.

And these will go into everlasting punishment. He had said above that they would go into eternal fire, for it is possible that fire be eternal, and yet not eternally torment; for this reason he says, ***into punishment***. ***But the just, into life everlasting***; *now this is eternal life: that they may know you, the only true God, and Jesus Christ, whom you have sent* (John 17:3).

It says what the eternal punishment is: *and many of those who sleep in the dust of the earth, will awake: some unto life everlasting, and others unto reproach, to see it always* (Dan 12:2); *and the devil, who seduced them, was cast into the pool of fire and brimstone, where both the beast and the false prophet will be tormented day and night for ever and ever* (Rev 20:9–10); *their worm will not die, and their fire will not be quenched* (Isa 66:24).

2113. Quae est causa huius supplicii? Quidam, ut Origenes, voluerunt quod non esset aeternum supplicium. Unde ponunt quod omne supplicium terminatur. Unde dicit quia quod dictum est hic, dictum est propter exaggerationem. Sed Augustinus arguit: si hoc ita est, ergo quod dicitur quod iusti ibunt in vitam aeternam, similiter diceretur secundum exaggerationem. Sed hoc dicitur secundum diuturnitatem, ut etiam concedit Origenes. Et hoc est detestabile, quod in eadem Scriptura sit talis diversitas. Sed quod hoc non possit esse, patet sic: quia hoc exigit iustitia, ut culpae poena respondeat aequalis. *In qua enim mensura mensi fueritis remetietur vobis*, supra VII, 1.

2114. Sed quomodo post mortem tantam dilationem habebit supplicium aeternum?

Respondet Gregorius dicens quod Deus iudex est voluntatis, unde qui non retinuit voluntatem a peccato usque ad mortem, peccavit in suo aeterno; ideo dignum est quod Deus puniat in suo aeterno. Augustinus dicit sic: videmus quod poena debet esse aequalis culpae, et sic est etiam in iustitia humana, quod si quis peccat contra societatem civitatis, iudex non intendit mortem, nisi ut separet a societate civitatis perpetuo. Sed qui contra Deum, intendit excludere eum a societate caelestis curiae. Secundum Hilarium, culpae debetur poena, sed culpa non deletur nisi per caritatem; ergo quamdiu homo non habet caritatem, iustum est quod semper sit in poena. Ex quo ergo caritatem non habuit in hac vita, necesse est quod semper maneat in poena.

2115. Item obiicitur quod sancti orabunt, et ipsi exaudientur. Ergo et cetera.

Dicit Gregorius quod dum sunt in via sancti pro eis exaudiuntur, sed non post.

2116. Item obiicitur: Deus non delectatur in poena; quomodo ergo sine fine affliget?

Dicendum quod etsi non delectatur, tamen hoc facit ad iustitiam suam conservandam.

2113. What is the cause of this punishment? Some, like Origen, wanted that it not be eternal punishment. Hence they posit that every punishment has an end. So he says that what is said here is said by way of exaggeration. But Augustine argues: if this is so, it follows that when it says that the just will go into eternal life, it is similarly said by way of exaggeration. But this is said according to eternity, as even Origen concedes. And this is detestable, that there should be such a difference in the same Scripture. But that this cannot be is clear in this way: for justice requires that there be a punishment equal to the guilt. For *with what measure you measure out, it will be measured to you again*, above (Matt 7:2).

2114. But how will eternal punishment have such a duration after death?

Gregory responds, saying that God is the judge of the will, so whoever does not restrain his will from sin before death has sinned in his own eternity; therefore it is right that God should punish in his eternity. Augustine speaks thus: we see that the punishment should be equal to the guilt, and so it is in human justice as well, that if someone sins against the community of the city, the judge only intends his death to separate him forever from the community of the city. But God intends to exclude the one who sins against him from the community of the heavenly court. According to Hilary, a punishment is due to guilt, but guilt is only wiped out by charity; therefore, as long as a man does not have charity, it is just that he be always in punishment. Therefore, since he did not have charity in this life, it is necessary that he remain always in punishment.

2115. Likewise it is objected that the saints will pray, and they will be heard.

Gregory says that when the sinners are on the way, the saints are heard on their behalf, but not afterwards.

2116. Likewise it is objected: God does not delight in punishment; so how will he afflict without end?

One should say that even though he is not delighted, nevertheless he does this to preserve his justice.

Chapter 26

Lecture 1

26:1 Et factum est, cum consummasset Iesus sermones hos omnes, dixit discipulis suis. [n. 2118]

26:2 Scitis quia post biduum Pascha fiet, et Filius hominis tradetur, ut crucifigatur. [n. 2119]

26:3 Tunc congregati sunt principes sacerdotum et seniores populi in atrium principis sacerdotum, qui dicebatur Caiaphas, [n. 2122]

26:4 et consilium fecerunt, ut Iesum dolo tenerent et occiderent. [n. 2125]

26:5 Dicebant autem: non in die festo, ne forte tumultus fieret in populo. [n. 2126]

26:6 Cum autem esset Iesus in Bethania in domo Simonis leprosi, [n. 2127]

26:7 accessit ad eum mulier habens alabastrum unguenti pretiosi, et effudit super caput ipsius recumbentis. [n. 2129]

26:8 Videntes autem discipuli indignati sunt dicentes: ut quid perditio haec? [n. 2134]

26:9 Potuit enim istud venumdari multo, et dari pauperibus. [n. 2134]

26:10 Sciens autem Iesus, ait illis: quid molesti estis huic mulieri? Opus enim bonum operata est in me. [n. 2135]

26:11 Nam semper pauperes habebitis vobiscum: me autem non semper habebitis. [n. 2137]

26:12 Mittens enim haec unguentum hoc in corpus meum, ad sepeliendum me fecit. [n. 2138]

26:1 Καὶ ἐγένετο ὅτε ἐτέλεσεν ὁ Ἰησοῦς πάντας τοὺς λόγους τούτους, εἶπεν τοῖς μαθηταῖς αὐτοῦ·

26:2 οἴδατε ὅτι μετὰ δύο ἡμέρας τὸ πάσχα γίνεται, καὶ ὁ υἱὸς τοῦ ἀνθρώπου παραδίδοται εἰς τὸ σταυρωθῆναι.

26:3 Τότε συνήχθησαν οἱ ἀρχιερεῖς καὶ οἱ πρεσβύτεροι τοῦ λαοῦ εἰς τὴν αὐλὴν τοῦ ἀρχιερέως τοῦ λεγομένου Καϊάφα

26:4 καὶ συνεβουλεύσαντο ἵνα τὸν Ἰησοῦν δόλῳ κρατήσωσιν καὶ ἀποκτείνωσιν·

26:5 ἔλεγον δέ· μὴ ἐν τῇ ἑορτῇ, ἵνα μὴ θόρυβος γένηται ἐν τῷ λαῷ.

26:6 Τοῦ δὲ Ἰησοῦ γενομένου ἐν Βηθανίᾳ ἐν οἰκίᾳ Σίμωνος τοῦ λεπροῦ,

26:7 προσῆλθεν αὐτῷ γυνὴ ἔχουσα ἀλάβαστρον μύρου βαρυτίμου καὶ κατέχεεν ἐπὶ τῆς κεφαλῆς αὐτοῦ ἀνακειμένου.

26:8 ἰδόντες δὲ οἱ μαθηταὶ ἠγανάκτησαν λέγοντες· εἰς τί ἡ ἀπώλεια αὕτη;

26:9 ἐδύνατο γὰρ τοῦτο πραθῆναι πολλοῦ καὶ δοθῆναι πτωχοῖς.

26:10 γνοὺς δὲ ὁ Ἰησοῦς εἶπεν αὐτοῖς· τί κόπους παρέχετε τῇ γυναικί; ἔργον γὰρ καλὸν ἠργάσατο εἰς ἐμέ·

26:11 πάντοτε γὰρ τοὺς πτωχοὺς ἔχετε μεθ᾽ ἑαυτῶν, ἐμὲ δὲ οὐ πάντοτε ἔχετε·

26:12 βαλοῦσα γὰρ αὕτη τὸ μύρον τοῦτο ἐπὶ τοῦ σώματός μου πρὸς τὸ ἐνταφιάσαι με ἐποίησεν.

26:1 And it came to pass, when Jesus had ended all these words, he said to his disciples: [n. 2118]

26:2 you know that after two days there will be the Pasch, and the Son of man will be delivered up to be crucified. [n. 2119]

26:3 Then were gathered together the chief priests and ancients of the people into the court of the high priest, who was called Caiphas, [n. 2122]

26:4 and they consulted together, that by subtilty they might apprehend Jesus, and put him to death. [n. 2125]

26:5 But they said: not on the festival day, lest perhaps there should be a tumult among the people. [n. 2126]

26:6 And when Jesus was in Bethania, in the house of Simon the leper, [n. 2127]

26:7 there came to him a woman having an alabaster box of precious ointment, and poured it on his head as he was at table. [n. 2129]

26:8 And the disciples seeing it, were indignant, saying: to what purpose is this waste? [n. 2134]

26:9 For this might have been sold for much, and given to the poor. [n. 2134]

26:10 And Jesus knowing it, said to them: why do you trouble this woman? For she has wrought a good work upon me. [n. 2135]

26:11 For the poor you always have with you: but me you do not always have. [n. 2137]

26:12 For she, in pouring this ointment upon my body, has done it for my burial. [n. 2138]

26:13 Amen dico vobis, ubicumque praedicatum fuerit hoc Evangelium in toto mundo, dicetur et quod haec fecit in memoriam eius. [n. 2139]	**26:13** ἀμὴν λέγω ὑμῖν, ὅπου ἐὰν κηρυχθῇ τὸ εὐαγγέλιον τοῦτο ἐν ὅλῳ τῷ κόσμῳ, λαληθήσεται καὶ ὃ ἐποίησεν αὕτη εἰς μνημόσυνον αὐτῆς.	**26:13** Amen I say to you, wherever this Gospel will be preached in the whole world, that also which she has done, will be told in memory of her. [n. 2139]
26:14 Tunc abiit unus de duodecim, qui dicitur Iudas Scarioth, ad principes sacerdotum, [n. 2140]	**26:14** Τότε πορευθεὶς εἷς τῶν δώδεκα, ὁ λεγόμενος Ἰούδας Ἰσκαριώτης, πρὸς τοὺς ἀρχιερεῖς	**26:14** Then one of the twelve, who was called Judas Iscariot, went to the chief priests, [n. 2140]
26:15 et ait illis: quid vultis mihi dare, et ego vobis eum tradam? At illi constituerunt ei triginta argenteos. [n. 2145]	**26:15** εἶπεν· τί θέλετέ μοι δοῦναι, κἀγὼ ὑμῖν παραδώσω αὐτόν; οἱ δὲ ἔστησαν αὐτῷ τριάκοντα ἀργύρια.	**26:15** and said to them: what will you give me, and I will deliver him to you? But they appointed him thirty pieces of silver. [n. 2145]
26:16 Et exinde quaerebat opportunitatem ut eum traderet. [n. 2149]	**26:16** καὶ ἀπὸ τότε ἐζήτει εὐκαιρίαν ἵνα αὐτὸν παραδῷ.	**26:16** And from then on he sought an opportunity to betray him. [n. 2149]

2117. Postquam posuit Evangelista praeparatoria passionis, hic accedit ad passionem Christi;

et dividitur in duas partes: quia

primo narratur passio quantum ad ea quae facta sunt a Iudaeis;

secundo quantum ad ea quae a gentilibus XXVII, 1 *mane autem facto* et cetera.

Circa primum duo facit.

Primo ponitur praenuntiatio Dominicae passionis;

secundo narratur passio et ordo, ibi *tunc abiit* et cetera.

Praenuntiatur passio tripliciter: verbo Christi, consilio inimicorum, tertio facto et obsequio.

Secunda *tunc congregati sunt* etc.; tertia *cum autem esset Iesus* et cetera.

Circa primum primo ponit ordinem praenuntiationis, et ipsam praenuntiationem.

2118. Ordinem *et factum est cum consummasset*. Et dicit sic, quia ipse solus est qui consummare potest. Nos incipere possumus, sed non consummare, iuxta illud Eccle. IV: *multa dicimus, et deficimus*.

Item dicit *sermones hos*, scilicet quos a principio suae praedicationis dixerat, ex quo dixerat: *poenitentiam agite, appropinquavit enim regnum caelorum*. Vel sermones quos dixerat de praenuntiatione gloriae, quia passio fuit exaltatio gloriae; Phil. II, v. 9: *propter quod exaltavit illum Deus, et dedit illi nomen quod est super omne nomen, ut in nomine Iesu omne genu flectatur caelestium, terrestrium et Infernorum, et omnis lingua confiteatur, quia dominus Iesus Christus in gloria est Dei Patris*.

2117. After the Evangelist has set out those things preparatory to the passion, here he approaches Christ's passion;

and it is divided into two parts, for

first, the passion is described as regards those things done by the Jews;

second, as regards those things done by the gentiles, *and when morning came, all the chief priests* (Matt 27:1).

Concerning the first, he does two things:

first, a prediction of the Lord's passion is set down;

second, the passion and the order is described, at *then one of the twelve . . . went*.

The passion is foretold in three ways: by Christ's word, by the enemies' plan, and third by deed and service.

The second, *then were gathered together the chief priests and ancients*; the third, *when Jesus was in Bethania*.

Concerning the first, he sets out first the placement of the prediction, and then the prediction itself.

2118. The placement: *and it came to pass, when Jesus had ended*. And he speaks thus because he alone is able to complete his words. We can begin, but we cannot complete, according to, *we will say much, and yet will want words* (Sir 43:29).

Similarly, he says, *these words*, namely those which he had spoken from the beginning of his preaching, when he had said, *do penance, for the kingdom of heaven is at hand* (Matt 4:17). Or, the words which he had spoken about the prediction of glory, because the passion was an exaltation of glory; *for which cause God also has exalted him, and has given him a name which is above all names: that in the name of Jesus every knee should bow, of those that are in heaven, on earth, and under the earth: and that every tongue confess that the Lord Jesus Christ is in the glory of God the Father* (Phil 2:9–11).

Item non dicit solum **omnes**, sed **hos omnes**, quia omnia ad utilitatem credentium et fidei est locutus.

2119. Scitis quia post biduum Pascha fiet: in ista praenuntiatione non simpliciter praenuntiat, sed dicit, **post biduum Pascha fiet**: et hoc factum est ad designandum quod non quaecumque passio est passio Christi, sed quae signatur per paschale sacrificium.

Et dicit **post biduum**. Et secundum hoc debetis considerare, quod verba haec dicta fuerunt luna decima tertia, idest feria tertia, quia luna decima quinta celebrabatur Pascha. Sed habetur Io. XII, 1 quod Dominus venit in Bethaniam, et hoc in die sabbati; et alio die venit in Ierusalem, et ibi eiecit vendentes et ementes, et in die lunae rediit, et vidit ficum arentem cui maledixit. Et secundum Marcum in die Martis rediit, et tunc in illo die constituit omnes parabolas illas. Et illo die cum consummasset sermones hos, dixit: **scitis quia post biduum Pascha fiet**.

2120. Hoc nomen **Pascha**, secundum quod dicit Hieronymus, a 'pascendo' dicitur, sed proprie dicitur 'phase', quod est 'transitus'. Quadruplex autem est transitus, secundum quod Pascha quadrupliciter accipitur. Secundum historiam celebrata est Pascha, quando exterminator percussit primogenita Aegypti; tunc praecepit dominus quod manducarent *phase*, Ex. XII, 3. Item secundum allegoriam est transitus Christi per mortem; et de isto Io. XIII, 1: *sciens Iesus quod iam hora esset ut transiret de hoc mundo ad patrem* et cetera. Item est moralis, sive typicus, secundum quod de carnali conversatione transitur ad spiritualem; Eccli. XXIV, 26: *transite ad me omnes qui concupiscitis me*. Item transitus generalis est, secundum quod dicitur quod caelum et terra transibunt et cetera. Unde post duos dies, scilicet post doctrinam veteris et novae legis. Secundum Graecum dicitur a 'pasqui', quod est 'pasci'.

2121. Unde congrue sciens Christus quod transiret a mundo ad Patrem, dixit **et Filius hominis tradetur, ut crucifigatur**. Non dicit a quo tradetur, quia traditus est a Patre; Rom. VIII, 32: *qui proprio Filio non pepercit, sed pro nobis omnibus tradidit eum*. Item a seipso; ad Eph. V, 2: *dilexit nos, et tradidit semetipsum pro nobis* et cetera. Item a Iuda. Hic: **quid vultis mihi dare, et ego eum vobis tradam?** Item a Iudaeis Pilato; Io. XVIII, v. 35: *gens tua et pontifices tui tradiderunt te mihi*. Item a Pilato gentibus; unde dicitur Io. XIX, 16: *tradidit eum ad crucifigendum*.

2122. Tunc congregati sunt principes sacerdotum et cetera. In parte ista ponitur perversum consilium Pharisaeorum. Et

Similarly, he does not only say **all**, but **all these**, for everything was spoken for the usefulness of those who believe, and of faith.

2119. You know that after two days there will be the Pasch: In this prediction he does not simply predict, but says, **after two days will be the Pasch**; and this was done to indicate that Christ's passion is not just any passion, but the one which is signified by the paschal sacrifice.

And he says, **after two days**. And in this connection you should consider that these words were spoken on the thirteenth day of the month, i.e., the third feastday, because the Pasch was celebrated on the fifteenth day of the month. But it says in John that the Lord came to Bethania, and this was on the Sabbath day; and on another day he came into Jerusalem, and there he cast out the buyers and sellers, and on the next day of the month he returned, and saw the barren fig tree which he cursed (John 12:1). And according to Mark, he returned on the day of Mars, and then on that day he set out all those parables (Mark 11:18). And on that day, when he had completed all these words, he said: **you know that after two days there will be the Pasch**.

2120. This name **Pasch**, according to what Jerome says, is taken from 'feeding,' but is properly called 'Phase,' which is 'Passover.' Now the passover is fourfold, according as the Pasch is taken in four ways. According to history, the Pasch was celebrated when the destroyer struck the firstborn of Egypt; then the Lord commanded that they eat the *Phase* (Exod 12:11). Likewise, according to allegory, it is the 'passover' of Christ through death; and about this John says, *Jesus knowing that his hour was come, that he should pass out of this world to the Father* (John 13:1). Likewise it is moral, i.e., a type, according as one passes over from a carnal way of life to a spiritual way of life; *pass over to me, all you who desire me, and be filled with my fruits* (Sir 24:26). Likewise, it is a general passover, according as it is said that heaven and earth shall pass away, etc. Hence after two days, i.e., after the teaching of the Old and New Law. According to the Greek, it is said from 'pasqui,' which is 'to be fed'.

2121. Hence fittingly Christ, knowing that he would pass over from the world to the Father, said, **and the Son of man will be delivered up to be crucified**. He does not say by whom he will be handed over, because he was handed over by the Father; *he who spared not even his own Son, but delivered him up for us all* (Rom 8:32). Likewise, by himself; *Christ also has loved us, and has delivered himself for us* (Eph 5:2). Likewise, by Judas; here: **what will you give me, and I will deliver him unto you?** Likewise, by the Jews to Pilate; *your own nation, and the chief priests, have delivered you up to me* (John 18:35). Likewise, by Pilate to the gentiles; hence it says, *he delivered him to them to be crucified* (John 19:16).

2122. Then were gathered together the chief priests and ancients of the people. In this part the perverse plan of the Pharisees is set out. And

primo ponitur consilium de Christi passione;

secundo de dilatione, ibi *dicebant autem: non in die festo*.

2123. Circa primum notare possumus quod peccatum Iudaeorum aggravatur ex tempore, quia *tunc*, imminente paschali festivitate; Is. LVIII, 13: *si averteris a sabbato pedem tuum, facere voluntatem tuam in die sancto meo*. Sed, ut credo, non ad diem immediatum refertur, sed circa illud tempus, quia Io. XI, 13 habetur quod *collegerunt consilium et ex illa die cogitaverunt ut interficerent eum*. Et tunc dicitur quod recessit Iesus in regionem iuxta desertum. Unde non fuit hoc immediate factum. Vel potest dici quod bis fuit factum.

Item aggravatur ex multitudine; unde dicitur: *congregati sunt principes sacerdotum et seniores populi*; Is. I, 14: *solemnitates vestras odivit anima mea: ecce enim manus vestrae sanguine plenae sunt*.

Item ex conditione peccantium, quia erant de maioribus; unde dicitur, *principes sacerdotum*; Ier. V, 5: *ibo ad optimates, et loquar eis*; et post: *et ecce magis hi simul confregerunt iugum, ruperunt vincula*. Et Ps. II, 2: *astiterunt reges terrae, et principes convenerunt in unum adversus Dominum, et adversus Christum eius*.

Item ex loco, quia *in atrio principis sacerdotum*. Unde isti debebant alios cohibere a malitia, ipsi autem faciebant; Dan. XIII, 5: *a senioribus egressa est iniquitas*.

2124. Sed numquid erant multi principes? Praeceperat enim Dominus, quod esset unus solus summus sacerdos, sed non sufficiebat eis. Unde propter cupiditatem sacerdotium diviserant. Item iam amiserant, et a Romanis sacerdotium emebant. Vel vocat *principes* illos qui ante eum fuerant principes, et illum qui illius anni fuerat princeps.

2125. Item tangitur illud de quo consiliabantur *ut Iesum dolo tenerent*. Et hoc erat fatuum eum credere dolo tenere, qui omnia sciebat; Ier. IX, 8: *sagitta vulnerans lingua eorum, dolum locuta est*. **Dicebant autem: non in die festo**. Hic agitur de dilatione: et ponitur consilium, et ratio.

2126. *Dicebant autem: non in die festo*. Posset aliquis dicere quod hoc dicerent ex devotione, ideo hoc tollit dicens **ne forte tumultus fieret in populo**; sciebant enim quod multi habebant eum ut prophetam, quidam vero ut Christum: ideo dissensio erat in populo, sicut habetur Io. VII, 30 ss. et IX, 8 ss. Ideo timebant ne tollerent eum a manibus suis. Hoc isti cogitabant, sed aliud cogitabat Christus: unde illi duo cogitabant, scilicet quod eum volebant occidere, et quod non in die festo crucifigeretur,

first, the plan of Christ's passion is set out;

second, the plan of delay, at **but they said: not on the festival day**.

2123. Concerning the first, we can note that the Jews' sin is made worse by the time, because the Paschal festivity was then at hand; *if you turn away your foot from the sabbath, from doing your own will in my holy day* (Isa 58:13). But as I see it, it does not refer to that immediate day, but to a time around then, because John says that they took counsel and *from that day therefore they devised to put him to death* (John 11:53). And then it says that Jesus withdrew into a region near the desert. So this did not happen immediately. Or it can be said that it happened twice.

Likewise, it is made worse by the multitude; hence it says, **then were gathered together the chief priests and ancients of the people**; *My soul hates . . . your solemnities . . . for your hands are full of blood* (Isa 1:14–15).

Likewise, by the condition of those who sinned, because they were from among the great; hence it says, **the chief priests**; *I will go therefore to the great men, and I will speak to them*, and then, *and behold these have together broken the yoke more, and have burst the bonds* (Jer 5:5). And, *the kings of the earth stood up, and the princes met together, against the Lord and against his Christ* (Ps 2:2).

Likewise, by the place, for it was **into the court of the high priest**. While these men should have restrained others from malice, they themselves were doing it; *iniquity came out . . . from the ancient judges* (Dan 13:5).

2124. But were there many high priests? For the Lord had commanded that there should be only one high priest, but it was not enough for them. So out of greed, they had divided the high priesthood. Likewise, they had already lost it, and were buying the priesthood from the Romans. Or the evangelist calls **chief priests** both those who were high priests before him, and him who was the high priest that year.

2125. Likewise, he touches on that about which they took counsel: **And they consulted together, that by subtilty they might apprehend Jesus**. And this was silly, thinking to seize him by deceit, he who knew all things; *their tongue is a piercing arrow, it has spoken deceit* (Jer 9:8). **But they said: not on the festival day**. Here he treats of the delay: both the plan is set out, and the reason.

2126. *But they said: not on the festival day*. Someone could say that they said this out of devotion, so he removes this possibility, saying, **lest perhaps there should be a tumult among the people**; for they knew that men considered him a prophet, some indeed the Christ, so there was a disagreement among the people, as is said (John 7:30; 9:8). So they were afraid that the people would take him from their hands. They were thinking this, but Christ was thinking something else: hence they were thinking two things, namely that they wanted to kill him, and that he would not

ad significandum quod ista immolatio succedebat immolationi agni Paschalis.

2127. *Cum autem esset Iesus in Bethania*. Hic ponitur praenuntiatio per factum mulieris.

Et primo ponitur factum;
secundo reprehensio;
tertio excusatio.

Secunda ibi *videntes autem discipuli indignati sunt*; tertia ibi *sciens autem Iesus*.

Circa primum quatuor facit.
Primo locus describitur;
secundo persona;
tertio facultas;
quarto opus.

2128. Primo duplex locus ponitur, scilicet generalis et specialis.

Generalis, cum dicit *cum esset Iesus in Bethania*; specialis cum dicit *in domo Simonis leprosi*.

Notate quod tunc non erat leprosus, sed curatus fuerat a Christo, si enim esset, non remansisset Christus cum eo, cum esset illud prohibitum in lege: et tamen utrumque ad mysterium attinet. *Bethania* 'domus obedientiae' dicitur: unde per hoc significatur eius obedientia; Phil. II, 8: *factus est obediens usque ad mortem*. Ideo competit ei esse in domo leprosi; Is. LIII, 4: *et nos reputavimus eum ut leprosum*. Et ob hoc potius ibi venit. Alia ratio potest esse litteralis, scilicet ut illa haberet fiduciam veniendi ad Christum, quia iste erat cognatus Mariae, et curatus erat ab eo lepra corporali, et ipsa veniebat ut curaretur a lepra spirituali.

Et notandum quod nullus alius dicitur venire ad Christum pro salute spirituali, excepta ista; ideo laude digna fuit.

2129. *Accessit ad eum mulier*. Ecce persona. Matthaeus et Marcus dicunt hoc accidisse in eodem loco, Ioannes et Lucas non. Lucas enim loquitur de ista c. VII, v. 37, ss., et Ioannes XII, 3 ss.

Est ergo quorumdam opinio, ut fuit Origenis, quod fuerunt mulieres plures. Loquamur de primis duabus. Expresse dicit Hieronymus quod illa, de qua loquitur Lucas, non fuit soror Lazari, quia de illa dicitur quod pedes unxit, de ista dicitur quod pedes et caput. Ambrosius super Lucam dicit quod utrumque potest dici, quod sit eadem, vel diversa. Si dicimus quod eadem, possumus dicere: etsi eadem, non tamen eiusdem meriti: sed peccatrix non est ausa caput tangere, sed post habita fiducia caput unxit. Et Augustinus probat quod sit eadem, quia Io. XI, 5 antequam accedat ad istud factum, dicit: *erat autem Maria soror Lazari, quae unxit dominum unguento, et extersit pedes eius capillis suis*. Ideo videtur quod

be crucified on the festival day, to indicate that this immolation was following after the immolation of the Paschal lamb.

2127. *And when Jesus was in Bethania*. Here a prediction of Christ's death is set out through the deed of a woman.

And first, the deed is set out;
second, a reproach;
third, an excuse.

The second, at *the disciples seeing it, were indignant*; the third, at *Jesus knowing it*.

Concerning the first, he does four things:
first, the place is described;
second, the persons;
third, the means;
fourth, the deed.

2128. First, a twofold place is set out, namely general and particular.

General, when he says, *when Jesus was in Bethania*; particular, when he says, *in the house of Simon the leper*.

Note that he was not a leper at that time, but had been cured by Christ, for if he were, Christ would not have stayed with him, since that was forbidden in the law: and yet both relate to a mystery. *Bethania* means 'house of obedience': hence this signified his obedience; *he humbled himself, becoming obedient unto death* (Phil 2:8). For this reason, it was fitting that he be in a leper's house; *we have thought him as it were a leper* (Isa 53:4). There can be another reason, a literal one, namely that this woman had the confidence to come to Christ because this man was a relative of Mary, and had been cured by him of bodily leprosy, and she was coming to be cured from spiritual leprosy.

And one should notice that no one else is said to have come to Christ for spiritual health except this woman; for this reason, she was worthy of praise.

2129. *There came to him a woman*. Behold, the person. Matthew and Mark say that this happened in the same place, but not John and Luke. For Luke speaks about this woman (Luke 7:37), and John does as well (John 12:3).

Therefore some are of the opinion, as was Origen, that there was more than one woman. Let us speak about the first two. Jerome explicitly says that the woman about whom Luke speaks was not the sister of Lazarus, because it says about her that she anointed the feet, while it says about that woman that she anointed the feet and the head. Ambrose, commenting on Luke, says that both can be said, that she is the same, or different. If we say that she is the same, we can say: even though she is the same, yet she is not of the same merit: rather, the sinner did not dare to touch the head, but afterward, having confidence, anointed the head. And Augustine proves that she is the same, because, before she drew near for that deed, John says, *and Mary was she who anointed the Lord with ointment, and wiped his*

illa, de qua Lucas loquitur, sit eadem cum illa, quae est soror Lazari.

Origenes dicit quod non est eadem illa de qua Lucas loquitur, et illa de qua Ioannes loquitur. Et potest probari ratione temporis, quia illud legitur factum antequam iret in Ierusalem; hoc factum est cum dicit: *scitis, quia post biduum Pascha fiet*. Item ex loco, quia illa in domo Marthae, de qua in Ioanne; haec autem in domo Simonis. Item per hoc quod ibi pedes, hic caput ungit. Quartum est quod ibi Iudas dixit: *ut quid perditio haec?* Hic autem quod omnes discipuli. Augustinus dicit quod eadem mulier est, et respondet ad rationes Origenis. Ad primam dicit, quod Matthaeus non servat ordinem historiae, sed recitat, quia ex hoc casu assumpsit Iudas occasionem peccandi, cum vidit unguentum effundi. Quod obiicit de loco Augustinus non solvit. Potest tamen sic solvi: quia iste homo erat magnae auctoritatis, et potestatem habens, et domus una eorum, quia cognatus eius erat. Aliter quomodo verum esset quod dicitur quod *fecerunt ibi caenam . . . et Lazarus erat unus de discumbentibus?*

2130. *Accessit* ergo ***mulier habens alabastrum unguenti***. Alabastrum est genus marmoris, quod est translucens, et fiunt inde fenestrae. Et de ista petra fiebant quaedam vasa, ubi conservabantur unguenta, sicut modo fiunt de terra contrita, quia ex sui frigiditate erant conservativa; unde **alabastrum**, idest vas de alabastro plenum unguento. Et dicitur hic **pretiosi**, alibi quod *nardi pistici*. 'Pistis Graece', fidelis Latine. Unde pistici, idest non sophisticati.

2131. Consequenter effectus ponitur: ***et effudit super caput eius discumbentis***.

Sed hic quaestio duplex. Quomodo Christus sustinuit, quia videtur ad lasciviam pertinere? Ad hoc respondit Augustinus *de Doctrina Christiana*. Aliter existimatur in persona communi, aliter in persona prophetica: quia in persona communi secundum factum, sed in prophetica secundum suam significationem. In persona communi significaret lasciviam; in persona prophetica significationem.

Expositio allegorica: quia significat sepulturam Christi, quia antiquitus corpora solebant inungi. Marci XIV habetur quod praevenit corpus inungere in sepulturam. Item mystice unguentum significat quodcumque opus bonum. Istud autem opus dupliciter potest fieri, quia quoddam est quod non fit propter Deum, sed propter iustitiam naturalem, ut opus gentilis, et hoc est unguentum, sed non pretiosum. Si propter Deum, sic est

feet with her hair (John 11:2). So it seems that the woman about whom Luke speaks is the same as the woman who is the sister of Lazarus.

Origen says that the one about whom Luke speaks and the one about whom John speaks are not the same. And it can be proven by an argument from the time, because it is written that it was done before he came into Jerusalem; this was done when it says, *you know that after two days will be the Pasch*. Likewise, by the place, because the woman in John's account was in the home of Martha, while this woman was in the home of Simon. Likewise, by the fact that there she anointed the feet, here the head. The fourth argument is that Judas said, *Why was not this ointment sold for three hundred pence, and given to the poor?* (John 12:5) but here it says that all the disciples said it. Augustine says that it is the same woman, and responds to Origen's arguments. To the first, he says that Matthew does not observe the order of history, but tells the story here because Judas took occasion for the sin from this chance thing, when he saw the ointment poured out. Augustine does not answer his objection about the place, but it can be answered in this way: because that man had great authority and power, and their home was one, for he was his relative. Otherwise, how could what is said in John be true, that *they made him a supper there . . . but Lazarus was one of them who were at table?* (John 12:2).

2130. *There came* therefore ***a woman having an alabaster box of precious ointment***. Alabaster is a kind of marble which is transparent, and windows are made out of it. And a certain vessel was made out of this rock in which ointment was kept, such as now are made out of crushed earth, because they tended to conserve the ointment by their coldness. Hence, ***an alabaster***, i.e., a vessel made out of alabaster full of ointment. And here it is called ***precious***, in another place, *pure nard* (John 12:3). 'Pistis' in Greek, 'faithful' in Latin; hence, *pure*, i.e., unadulterated.

2131. Next, the effect is set out: ***and poured it on his head as he was at table***.

But here there are two questions: how did Christ put up with it, since it seems to be wantonness? Augustine responds to this in *On Christian Doctrine*. One must judge in one way with a common person, and in another way with a prophetic person: for in a common person one must judge according to the deed, but in a prophetic person according to its signification. In the case of a common person it would signify wantonness; in a prophetic person, a signification.

An allegorical explanation: because it signifies Christ's burial, since in ancient times bodies were customarily anointed. Mark says that she came beforehand to anoint his body for burial (Mark 14:8). Likewise, mystically the ointment signifies any good work. But that work can happen in two ways, for some works are not done for God's sake, but for the sake of natural justice, like the work of a gentile, and this is ointment, but not precious. If it is done for God's

pretiosum. Unde pedes ungit, quando bonum opus facit propter utilitatem proximi; sed quando ad gloriam Dei, tunc ungit caput.

2132. Sed quid est quod dicit Ioannes quod pedes, et Matthaeus quod caput? Augustinus dicit quod utrumque.

2133. Sed quid est quod dicit Marcus quod fregit alabastrum? Dicit Augustinus, quod sicut accidit aliquando, quod aliquis effundit sic, ut nihil remaneat, et post frangit: sic fecit ista, et effudit, et fregit. Vel si vult aliquis calumniari, potest dici quod primo pedes, deinde caput unxit.

2134. Tunc sequitur increpatio mulieris *videntes autem discipuli indignati sunt*. Sed hic opponitur, quia Io. XII dicitur quod solus Iudas dixit, iste quod omnes.

Duplex est responsio secundum Hieronymum: quia illud quod dicitur hic quod discipuli dixerunt, dicitur per synecdochem: *discipuli*, idest discipulus, et hic modus consuetus est in Scriptura; Hebr. XI, 37: *secti sunt*, quia unus sectus, scilicet nonnisi Isaias. Vel potest dici quod omnes, quia, secundum quod dicit Augustinus, Iudas omnes excitavit. Item, quod alii excitati propter inopiam pauperum, iste vero motus fuit propter avaritiam. Unde dicunt *ut quid perditio haec?*

Sed quare hoc dicebant? Audierant Dominum multum commendasse misericordiam; supra XIX, 21: *si vis perfectus esse, vade, et vende omnia quae habes, et da pauperibus*.

2135. *Sciens autem Iesus ait illis*. Hic ponitur excusatio mulieris: et duo facit.

Primo excusat et commendat;

secundo praemium eius tangit *amen dico vobis* et cetera. Et

primo excusat;

secundo obiectioni discipulorum respondet;

tertio exponit quod dixerat.

2136. Dicit ergo *quid molesti estis huic mulieri?* Dominus semper est advocatus huius mulieris, quia Lc. VII, 39 Pharisaeus accusabat eam de peccato, unde dicebat: *hic si esset propheta, sciret utique quae et qualis est mulier, quae tangit eum* etc., et Dominus excusavit eam per dilectionem. Item Lc. X, v. 40 etiam Martha accusabat eam de otio, et Dominus excusabat eam per contemplationem. Hic discipuli de unguenti effusione, et Dominus excusat eam ex devotione, dicens: *quid molesti estis huic mulieri?* Iob VI, 27: *super pupillum irruitis, et subvertere nitimini amicum vestrum*.

Opus bonum operata est in me; Prov. III, v. 27: *noli prohibere aliquem benefacere; si potes, tu ipse benefac*.

sake, in this way it is precious. Whence, someone anoints the feet when he does a good work for the benefit of his neighbor; but when for the glory of God, then he anoints the head.

2132. But why does John say that she anointed the feet (John 12:3), and Matthew that she anointed the head? Augustine says that she anointed both.

2133. But why does Mark say that she broke the alabaster? (Mark 14:3). Augustine says that, just as it sometimes happens that someone pours out so much that nothing remains and then breaks the container, so this woman did: she both poured out, and broke it. Or, if someone wishes to find fault with this, it can be said that first she anointed the feet, then the head.

2134. Then there follows the rebuke of the woman: *the disciples seeing it, were indignant*. But this is opposed to another account, because John says that only Judas spoke (John 12:4), while this gospel says that all did.

According to Jerome, there are two responses. For what it says here, that the disciples spoke, is said by way of synecdoche: *the disciples*, i.e., a disciple, and this manner of speaking is commonly used in Scripture; *they were cut asunder* (Heb 11:37), because one was sawn in two, namely none but Isaiah. Or, it can be said that all spoke because, according to what Augustine says, Judas incited them all. Likewise, it can be said that the others were aroused by the need of the poor, while this man was moved by greed. Hence they say, *to what purpose is this waste?*

But why did they say this? They had heard the Lord commend mercy many times; above, *if you will be perfect, go sell what you have, and give to the poor* (Matt 19:21).

2135. *And Jesus knowing it, said to them*. Here the woman's exoneration is set down: and he does two things:

first, he excuses and praises;

second, he touches upon her reward, *Amen, I say to you*. And

first, he excuses;

second, he responds to the disciples' objection;

third, he explains what he had said.

2136. He says therefore, *why do you trouble this woman?* The Lord is always this woman's advocate, for in Luke a Pharisee accused her of sin, and said, *this man, if he were a prophet, would know surely who and what manner of woman this is who touches him* (Luke 7:39), and the Lord excused her by love. Likewise, Martha also accused her of laziness, and the Lord excused her by contemplation (Luke 10:40). Here the disciples reproach her for pouring out the ointment, and the Lord excuses her by devotion, saying, *why do you trouble this woman? You rush in upon the fatherless, and you endeavour to overthrow your friend* (Job 6:27).

For she has wrought a good work upon me; do not withhold him from doing good, who is able. if you are able, do

Chrysostomus: *aliquando contingit quod aliquis facit bonum opus ex genere, et forte melius facere potuisset; unde aliter est agendum ante factum et post factum. Unde post factum de facto commendandus est; sed si veniret ante factum, consulendum esset ei quod faceret quod melius est. Unde credendum quod si a Domino petiisset ante consilium, dixisset ei quod daret pauperibus.*

2137. *Nam pauperes semper habebitis vobiscum* et cetera. Hic ponitur responsio ad obiectionem eorum, quia illi dicebant quod poterat dari pauperibus. *Me autem non semper habebitis*. Verum est secundum praesentiam corporalem, sed semper erit secundum praesentiam spiritualem. Unde dicit infra ult., 20: *ecce ego vobiscum sum omnibus diebus usque ad consummationem saeculi*.

2138. Et quid fecit? *Mittens autem hoc unguentum in corpus meum, ad sepeliendum me fecit*.

Sed quid est? Numquid intendit sepelire Christum? Non. Sed, sicut dicit Augustinus, Spiritus Sanctus sicut movet ad loquendum, ita aliquando ad operandum; unde scriptum est Rom. VIII, 14: *qui Spiritu Dei aguntur, non sunt sub lege*. Unde accidit quod a Spiritu Sancto instruatur aliquis ad aliquem sensum, quem non intendebat. Sic ista bonum opus intendebat, sed Spiritus Sanctus illud ordinabat ad sepulturam.

2139. Dicit *bonum opus operata est in me*. Posset aliquis dicere quod dare proximo esset bonum opus. Verum est, sed non tantum quod praedicetur per universum mundum; ideo subdit *amen dico vobis: ubicumque praedicatum fuerit hoc Evangelium in toto mundo, dicetur in memoriam eius*, idest in commendationem eius. Hieronymus dicit quod iste crucifigendus praenuntiat Evangelium narrandum in universo mundo, et tamen non erat adhuc divulgatum, cum Matthaeus scripsit.

Item notate, quod multi voluerunt divulgari nativitatem suam per universum mundum, et deleta est memoria eorum, factum tamen huius non est deletum; Prov. X, 7: *memoria iustorum cum laudibus*; et Ps. CXI, 7: *in memoria aeterna erunt iusti*.

2140. *Tunc abiit unus de duodecim*. Supra posuit triplicem praenuntiationem Dominicae passionis, hic intendit ad narrationem: et duo facit.

Primo praemittit praeparatoria;

secundo agit de ipsa passione, ibi *adhuc eo loquente* et cetera.

Sunt autem tria praeparatoria.

Primo ponitur tractatus proditionis;

secundo institutio communionis dominicae;

tertio de oratione Christi.

good yourself also (Prov 3:27). Chrysostom: *It sometimes happens that someone does a work which is good in genus, and perhaps he could have done better; hence one should act in one way before the deed, and in another way after the deed. After the deed, he should be commended for the deed; but if he should come to you before the deed, one should advise him that he do what is better. So one should think that if she had asked the Lord for advice beforehand, he would have told her to give to the poor.*

2137. *For the poor you have always with you*. Here the response to their objection is set out, for they said that it could have been given to the poor. *But me you have not always*. This is true regarding bodily presence, but as regards spiritual presence he will always be with us. Hence he says below, *behold I am with you all days, even to the consummation of the world* (Matt 28:20).

2138. And what did she do? *For she in pouring this ointment upon my body, has done it for my burial*.

But what is this? Did she intend to bury Christ? No. But, as Augustine says, just as the Holy Spirit moves one to speak, so sometimes he moves one to act; hence it is written, *for whoever are led by the Spirit of God, they are the sons of God* (Rom 8:14). Hence it sometimes happens that someone is instructed by the Holy Spirit to speak a meaning which he did not intend. In the same way, this woman intended a good work, but the Holy Spirit ordained it to the burial.

2139. He says, *she has wrought a good work upon me*. Someone might say that to give to one's neighbor would be a good work. This is true, but not so great that it will be preached throughout the whole world; for this reason he adds next, *Amen I say to you, wherever this gospel will be preached in the whole world, that also which she has done, will be told in memory of her*, i.e., to her praise. Jerome says that he, about to be crucified, foretold that the gospel would be recounted throughout the whole world, and yet it was not well known at the time when Matthew wrote.

Note also that many had wanted to make their birth well known throughout the whole world, and their memory was forgotten, yet this woman's deed was not forgotten; *the memory of the just is with praises* (Prov 10:7); and *the just will be in everlasting remembrance* (Ps 111:7).

2140. *Then went one of the twelve*. Above he set out the threefold prediction of the Lord's passion; here he intends to describe it: and he does two things:

first, he sets out preparatory things;

second, he treats of the passion itself, at *as he yet spoke*.

Now, there are three preparatory things:

first, the arrangement of the betrayal is set out;

second, the institution of the Lord's communion;

third, concerning Christ's prayer.

The second is at ***and on the first day of the Azymes*** (Matt 26:17); the third, at ***then Jesus came with them into a country place which is called Gethsemani*** (Matt 26:36).

Concerning the first, three things:
first, the person of the betrayer is described;
second, the arrangement of the betrayal;
third, the solicitude.

2141. It says therefore, ***then***. Understand that this does not refer to what is immediately before, for the woman with the alabaster is spoken of by way of transposition; but rather it is referred to what was said before, that ***were gathered together the chief priests and ancients of the people . . . that by subtilty they might apprehend Jesus, and put Him to death***.

Then went one of the twelve, who was called Judas Iscariot. And his person is described in three ways.

2142. By office, for he was one of the twelve, not only of the disciples, but of the twelve specially called; *have not I chosen you twelve; and one of you is a devil?* (John 6:71).

But why did he will to choose a future villain and betrayer? The first reason can be to indicate that he condemns or saves no one because of their predestination, but because of their present justice. For if he condemned a man because of his predestination, it would not be blamed on anyone. Likewise, to console men: for he knew that in the future many would be deceived in their choices, as happened to Philip, who chose Simon Magus; for this reason, the Lord permitted there to be a betrayer among the disciples. Another reason can be so that no one may be blamed if someone in the Church is wicked, since there was a wicked man in the first college.

2143. Likewise, the person of the betrayer is described by name: ***who was called Judas***. There were two called by this name among the disciples; yet one was bad, which signifies that some who profess God are good, and some bad. About the good, *Judea made his sanctuary* (Ps 113:2). About the bad, it says, *they profess that they know God: but in their works they deny him* (Titus 1:16).

2144. Likewise, he is described by homeland. ***Iscariot*** is a certain village, and is interpreted 'the memory of death,' because Judas's sin is held in memory. And what is said can be referred to it: *the sin of Judah is written with a pen of iron, with the point of a diamond* (Jer 17:1).

To the chief priests, who wished to kill Christ, forgetting what is said, *blessed is the man who has not walked in the counsel of the ungodly* (Ps 1:1). And Jacob says, *let not my soul go into their counsel* (Gen 49:6).

2145. *And said to them*. Here the arrangement of the betrayal is set out. And
first, the arrangement is set out;
second, the fulfillment.

Et
primo consideranda est cupiditas eius;
secundo praesumptio.

2146. Cupiditas, cum dicit *quid vultis mihi dare et ego eum vobis tradam?* Propter pecuniam omnem amicitiam contempsit; Eccli. X, 10: *nihil est iniquius, quam amare pecuniam; hic enim animam suam venalem habet.* Iste enim quia non refraenavit cupiditatem, incidit in proditionem. Quia enim vidit quod fraudatus erat pretio unguenti, ideo voluit recuperare in prodendo Christum.

2147. Item tangitur praesumptio, cum dicit *et ego eum vobis tradam*. Magna praesumptio fuit eum tradere, qui omnia sciebat. Item loquitur iste ut valde male sentiens de Deo, quia quando aliquis vult vendere rem quam diligit, imponit ei pretium; sed quando habet rem de qua vult se expedire, dicit: *date mihi quod placet*. Sic dicit iste: *quid vultis mihi dare?* Idest date quod vultis. *Pro nihilo habuerunt terram desiderabilem*, Ps. CV, 24.

2148. Et isti *constituerunt ei triginta argenteos*. Dicit Origenes quod simili modo faciunt qui pro temporali commodo Deum dimittunt. Habitat enim in nobis per fidem; sed tunc dimittimus quando nimis temporalibus adhaeremus; unde dixit: *at illi constituerunt ei triginta argenteos*.

Sed quare ita expressit? Quia ita significatum erat per illud Zac. XI, 12: *et appenderunt mercedem meam triginta argenteis*. Et non est dicendum quod Ioseph venditus fuit triginta denariis, sed Scriptura vult quod solum viginti argenteis, idest denariis.

Sed quid vult dicere quod triginta? Intelligendum est: iste numerus componitur ex quinque et sex, unde quinquies sex sunt triginta. Per quinque significantur quinque libri Moysi, vel temporalia quae subiecta sunt quinque sensibus; unde signatur quod post legem Moysi in sexta aetate fieret salus.

2149. *Et exinde quaerebat opportunitatem ut eum traderet*. Hic ponitur sollicitudo. Et quare hoc faciebat? Ut facilius et occultius facinus perpetraret, sicut est de peccantibus, quia *qui male agit, odit lucem*, Io. c. III, 20; et Iob XXIV, 15: *oculus adulteri observat caliginem*.

And
first, his greed should be considered;
second, his presumption.

2146. Greed, when he says, *what will you give me, and I will deliver him unto you?* For the sake of money he disregarded every friendship; *there is not a more wicked thing than to love money: for such a one sets even his own soul to sale* (Sir 10:10). For this man, since he did not restrain greed, fell into betrayal. For since he saw that he had been cheated of the price of the ointment, he wished to recover it by betraying Christ.

2147. Likewise presumption is touched upon, when he says, *I will deliver him unto you*. It was a great presumption to hand over him who knows all things. Likewise, he speaks as one who thinks very badly of God, for when someone wishes to sell a thing he loves, he sets a price on it; but when he has a thing from which he wishes to free himself, he says, *give me what pleases you*. So this man speaks: *what will you give me?* i.e., give what you want. *And they set at naught the desirable land* (Ps 105:24).

2148. *But they appointed him thirty pieces of silver*. Origen says that those who abandon God for a temporal benefit act in a similar way. For he dwells in us through faith; but we abandon him when we cling too much to temporal things; hence it said, *but they appointed him thirty pieces of silver*.

But why is he so explicit? Because it had been indicated this way: *and they weighed for my wages thirty pieces of silver* (Zech 11:12). And one should not say that Joseph was sold for thirty pieces of silver, but Scripture would have it that Joseph was sold for only twenty silver pieces, i.e., denarii (Gen 37:28).

But why does he want to say that it was thirty? One should understand: this number is composed of five and six, so that five sixes are thirty. The five signifies the five books of Moses, or the temporal things which fall under the five senses; hence it signifies that after the law of Moses salvation would come about in the sixth age.

2149. *And from then on he sought opportunity to betray him*. Here the solicitude is set down. And why did he do this? To commit the crime more easily and in a more hidden manner, as is often the case with those who are sinning, for, *everyone who does evil hates the light, and comes not to the light* (John 3:20); and, *the eye of the adulterer observes darkness, saying: no eye will see me* (Job 24:15).

Lecture 2

26:17 Prima autem die azymorum accesserunt discipuli ad Iesum, dicentes: ubi vis paremus tibi comedere Pascha? [n. 2151]

26:18 At Iesus dixit: ite in civitatem ad quendam, et dicite ei: magister dicit: tempus meum prope est, apud te facio Pascha cum discipulis meis. [n. 2154]

26:19 Et fecerunt discipuli sicut constituit illis Iesus, et paraverunt Pascha. [n. 2157]

26:20 Vespere autem facto, discumbebat cum duodecim discipulis suis. [n. 2158]

26:21 Et edentibus illis dixit: amen dico vobis, quia unus vestrum me traditurus est. [n. 2159]

26:22 Et contristati valde, coeperunt singuli dicere: numquid ego sum, Domine? [n. 2161]

26:23 At ipse respondens ait: qui intinguit mecum manum in paropside, hic me tradet. [n. 2162]

26:24 Filius quidem hominis vadit, sicut scriptum est de illo. Vae autem homini illi, per quem Filius hominis tradetur. Bonum erat ei si natus non fuisset homo ille. [n. 2164]

26:25 Respondens autem Iudas, qui tradidit eum, dixit: numquid ego sum, Rabbi? Ait illi: tu dixisti. [n. 2166]

26:17 Τῇ δὲ πρώτῃ τῶν ἀζύμων προσῆλθον οἱ μαθηταὶ τῷ Ἰησοῦ λέγοντες· ποῦ θέλεις ἑτοιμάσωμέν σοι φαγεῖν τὸ πάσχα;

26:18 ὁ δὲ εἶπεν· ὑπάγετε εἰς τὴν πόλιν πρὸς τὸν δεῖνα καὶ εἴπατε αὐτῷ· ὁ διδάσκαλος λέγει· ὁ καιρός μου ἐγγύς ἐστιν, πρὸς σὲ ποιῶ τὸ πάσχα μετὰ τῶν μαθητῶν μου.

26:19 καὶ ἐποίησαν οἱ μαθηταὶ ὡς συνέταξεν αὐτοῖς ὁ Ἰησοῦς καὶ ἡτοίμασαν τὸ πάσχα.

26:20 Ὀψίας δὲ γενομένης ἀνέκειτο μετὰ τῶν δώδεκα.

26:21 καὶ ἐσθιόντων αὐτῶν εἶπεν· ἀμὴν λέγω ὑμῖν ὅτι εἷς ἐξ ὑμῶν παραδώσει με.

26:22 καὶ λυπούμενοι σφόδρα ἤρξαντο λέγειν αὐτῷ εἷς ἕκαστος· μήτι ἐγώ εἰμι, κύριε;

26:23 ὁ δὲ ἀποκριθεὶς εἶπεν· ὁ ἐμβάψας μετ' ἐμοῦ τὴν χεῖρα ἐν τῷ τρυβλίῳ οὗτός με παραδώσει.

26:24 ὁ μὲν υἱὸς τοῦ ἀνθρώπου ὑπάγει καθὼς γέγραπται περὶ αὐτοῦ, οὐαὶ δὲ τῷ ἀνθρώπῳ ἐκείνῳ δι' οὗ ὁ υἱὸς τοῦ ἀνθρώπου παραδίδοται· καλὸν ἦν αὐτῷ εἰ οὐκ ἐγεννήθη ὁ ἄνθρωπος ἐκεῖνος.

26:25 ἀποκριθεὶς δὲ Ἰούδας ὁ παραδιδοὺς αὐτὸν εἶπεν· μήτι ἐγώ εἰμι, ῥαββί; λέγει αὐτῷ· σὺ εἶπας.

26:17 And on the first day of the azymes, the disciples came to Jesus, saying: where do you wish for us to prepare for you to eat the Pasch? [n. 2151]

26:18 But Jesus said: go into the city to a certain man, and say to him: the master said, my time is near at hand, with you I make the Pasch with my disciples. [n. 2154]

26:19 And the disciples did as Jesus appointed to them, and they prepared the Pasch. [n. 2157]

26:20 But when it was evening, he sat down with his twelve disciples. [n. 2158]

26:21 And while they were eating, he said: amen I say to you, that one of you is about to betray me. [n. 2159]

26:22 And they, being very troubled, began everyone to say: is it I, Lord? [n. 2161]

26:23 But he, answering, said: he who dips his hand with me in the dish, he will betray me. [n. 2162]

26:24 The Son of man indeed goes, as it is written of him, but woe to that man by whom the Son of man will be betrayed. It were better for him, if that man had not been born. [n. 2164]

26:25 And Judas that betrayed him, answering, said: is it I, Rabbi? He said to him: you have said it. [n. 2166]

2150. *Prima autem die* tunc agit de constitutione sacramenti, et quia nova succedunt veteribus, ut dicitur Lev. c. XXVI, 10: *novis supervenientibus vetera proiicietis*;
    primo agit de veteri;
    secundo de novo.
    Circa primum duo.
    Primo ponitur praeparatio Paschae;
    secundo ponitur praenuntiatio proditoris, ibi *edentibus illis dixit* et cetera.
    Et circa primum
        primo tempus designatur;
        secundo praeparatio convivii;

2150. *On the first day*. Next he treats of the institution of the sacrament, and since the new follows on the old, as is said, *new coming on, you will cast away the old* (Lev 26:10).
    first, he treats of the old;
    second, of the new.
    Concerning the first, two things:
    first, the preparation for the Pasch is set down;
    second, the prediction of the betrayer is set down, at *and while they were at supper*.
    And concerning the first,
        first, the time is designated;
        second, the preparation of the meal;

tertio institutio sacramenti.

2151. Dicit ergo *prima die azymorum*. Et hic potest esse obiectio, quia hic dies erat prima dies Paschae. Et videtur contra hoc quod dicitur in Io. XIII, 1: *ante diem festum Paschae* et cetera. Dicunt Graeci, Matthaeum, Lucam et Marcum errasse, et quod Ioannes correxit eos, quia fuit facta ante diem Paschae. Unde dicunt quod Dominus passus est decima quarta luna, et coenam fecit decima tertia. Unde dicunt quod Dominus confecit non in azymo, sed in fermentato. Et hoc nituntur confirmare plurimis argumentis. Primo quia dicitur Io. XVIII, 28 quod *non introierunt, ut non contaminarentur, sed manducarent Pascha*: et ita die passionis debebant comedere Pascha. Item alia ratio eorum, quia mulieres praeparaverunt aromata, ideo et cetera.

Sed hoc non potest stare, quia Dominus non fregit caeremonias: non enim invenitur quod praeveniretur Pascha, invenitur tamen quod prolongaretur. Et dato quod praeveniretur, hoc non est pro Graecis, quia scriptum est quod Pascha debebat comedi cum azymis et lactucis agrestibus. Si ergo aliter fecisset, contra legem fecisset. Ideo secundum quod tres evangelistae dicunt, hoc fuit factum decima quarta luna, et tunc erat necesse comedere Pascha.

Quid ergo respondendum ad id quod dicit Ioannes: *ante diem festum Paschae*? Dicendum quod consuetudo fuit quod incipiunt diem a vesperis, et sic dies Paschalis a vesperis, incipiebat. Et hoc habetur in Ex. XII, v. 18: *decima quarta luna ad vesperum celebrabitis Pascha*: et ex tunc non inveniebatur fermentatum in domibus Iudaeorum usque ad vigesimum primum diem. Unde si computamus a vespere quartae decimae lunae, praeparatio fuit facta ante diem Paschae, tamen erat decima quarta luna. Vocat ergo Ioannes diem illum azymorum, et diem Paschae decimam quintam lunam.

Quod tu dicis secundo, quod *non introierunt praetorium* etc., Chrysostomus sic solvit, et dicit quod Dominus non praetermisit aliquid de legalibus observantiis: unde Pascha comedit decima quarta luna. Sed isti principes inhiarunt ad interfectionem Christi propter quod distulerunt, et tunc non celebraverunt, et hoc contra legem suam. Vel per 'Pascha' intelliguntur panes azymi.

Quod dicunt de mulieribus, dicit Augustinus quod habebant multas solemnitates; sed Sabbatum solemnior erat solemnitas. Unde non licebat Sabbato praeparare cibaria, quod tamen licebat in aliis festis, sed in die Sabbati non. Ideo tunc ita accidit quod festivitas Paschae accidit in die Veneris, et sequebatur Sabbatum; ideo tunc

third, the institution of the sacrament.

2151. He says therefore, *and on the first day of the azymes*. And here there can be an objection, because this day was the first day of the Pasch. And it seems contrary to what is said, *before the festival day of the Pasch* (John 13:1). The Greeks say that Matthew, Luke (Luke 22:7), and Mark (Mark 14:12) were mistaken, and that John corrected them, because it happened before the day of the Pasch. Hence they say that the Lord suffered on the fourteenth day of the month, and had the supper on the thirteenth. So they say that the Lord prepared the meal not with unleavened bread, but with leavened. And they strive to confirm this with many arguments. First, because it says that *they went not into the hall, that they might not be defiled, but that they might eat the Pasch* (John 18:28); and thus they had to eat the Pasch on the day of the passion. Similarly, another of their arguments is that the women prepared spices.

But this cannot stand, for the Lord did not break the ceremonies: for nowhere is it found that the Pasch was anticipated, yet it is found that it was prolonged. And given that it was anticipated, this is not favorable to the Greeks, because it is written that the Pasch had to be eaten with unleavened bread and wild lettuce. If therefore he had done otherwise, he would have acted against the law. Therefore, in accordance with what the three evangelists say, this was done on the fourteenth day of the month, and at that time it was necessary to eat the Pasch.

What then should one respond to what John says: *before the festival day of the Pasch*? (John 13:1). One should say that it was customary that they began the day from the evening, and thus the Paschal day began from the evening. And this is found, *the fourteenth day of the month in the evening, you will eat unleavened bread* (Exod 12:18): and from that time no leavened bread was found in the homes of the Jews until the twenty-first day. Hence if we reckon from the evening of the fourteenth day of the month, the preparation was made before the day of the Pasch, yet it was the fourteenth day of the month. Therefore, John calls that day the day of unleavened bread, and calls the day of the Pasch the fifteenth day of the month.

As for what you say in the second place, that *they went not into the praetorium* (John 18:28), Chrysostom resolves it this way, and says that the Lord did not omit anything of the legal observances, hence he ate the Pasch on the fourteenth day of the month. But the chief priests yearned to kill Christ, for the sake of which they delayed, and did not celebrate the Pasch at that time, and this contrary to their own law. Or, by 'the Pasch' is meant the unleavened bread.

As for what they say about the women, Augustine says that they had many solemnities; but the Sabbath was more solemn than a solemnity. Hence it was not permitted to prepare food on the Sabbath, which nevertheless was permitted on the other feast days, but not on the Sabbath day. So it happened at that time that the festival of the Pasch fell

praeparaverunt, et in die Sabbati quieverunt. Ideo possumus dicere quod decima quarta luna celebravit Pascha.

2152. Sequitur sollicitudo discipulorum *accesserunt discipuli ad Iesum dicentes: ubi vis paremus tibi comedere Pascha?* Et

primo ponitur inquisitio;
secundo mandatum;
tertio impletio.

2153. Dicit *accesserunt discipuli eius*. Sed qui discipuli? Dicit Remigius quod ex obsequio Iudas, ut celaret proditionem suam. Tamen Leo Papa dicit quod etiam alii. *Ubi vis paremus tibi comedere Pascha?* Per hoc designatur quod Christus non habebat ibi domum, nec aliquis de societate; ideo signatur paupertas eius; unde supra VIII, 20: *Filius autem hominis non habet ubi reclinet caput suum*.

2154. *At ille dixit*. Hic ponitur mandatum. Et

primo denuntiat hospitem;
secundo passionem;
tertio exposcit locum ad convivandum.

2155. Dicit ergo *ite in civitatem ad quemdam*. Et notare debetis quod non erat hospitatus in civitate, sed in Bethania.

Sed quid est quod dicit *quemdam?* Dicit Augustinus quod Dominus aliquem certum nominavit; sed quia non erat necessarium nominare, Matthaeus praetermisit nominare. Chrysostomus dicit quod dicit *ite ad quemdam*, idest ad quemcumque, quia voluit ostendere suam virtutem, ut non turbarentur de passione. Ita enim erat divulgata fama eius quod iam sententiatum erat quod qui reciperet eum, fieret extra synagogam. Unde voluit dare intelligi quod non reciperet eum aliquis nisi immutaret cor eius; Prov. XXI, 1: *cor regis in manu Domini, et quocumque voluerit inclinabit illud*.

2156. *Et dicite ei* et cetera. Praenuntiat passionem ut non turbentur; unde dicit *tempus*, non quodcumque dicitur, sed determinatum a Patre. Secundum istum modum dicitur Io. VII, 6: *tempus meum nondum advenit, tempus autem vestrum semper est paratum*.

Apud te facio Pascha, idest celebrabo paschale convivium apud te. Et addit *cum discipulis meis*, ad denotandum quod non occulte, sed publice. Secundum Chrysostomum istud dixit, quia volebat quod praepararentur cibaria sufficientia et sibi, et discipulis.

Sed quid est quod ipse celebravit, et nos non debemus celebrare? Quia Io. XIII, 15 dicitur: *exemplum dedi vobis, ut quemadmodum ego feci, ita et vos faciatis*. Ad hoc respondet Augustinus, quod sicut Christus passus

on Friday, and the Sabbath followed; for this reason they prepared the spices then, and went seeking on the Sabbath day. Therefore we can say that he celebrated the Pasch on the fourteenth day of the month.

2152. There follows the disciples' solicitude: *the disciples came to Jesus, saying: where do you wish for us to prepare for you to eat the Pasch?* And

first, the questioning is set down;
second, the command;
third, the fulfillment.

2153. He says, *the disciples came*. But which disciples? Remigius says that Judas came out of obsequiousness, to conceal his betrayal. Yet Pope Leo says that others also came. *Where do you wish for us to prepare for you to eat the Pasch?* This indicates that Christ did not have a house there, nor someone of the society; which indicates his poverty. Hence above, *the Son of man has nowhere to lay his head* (Matt 8:20).

2154. *But Jesus said*. Here the command is set down. And

first, he foretells the host;
second, the passion;
third, he requests a place for having the meal.

2155. He says then, *go into the city to a certain man*. And you should notice that he had not been a guest in the city, but in Bethania.

But why does he say, *a certain man*? Augustine says that the Lord named some certain man; but since it was not necessary to name him, Matthew omits the name. Chrysostom says that he says, *go to a certain man*, i.e., to anyone at all, because he wished to show his power, that they might not be disturbed over the passion. For his reputation was so well known that it was already decided that anyone who received him would be put out of the synagogue. Hence he wished to give the disciples to understand that no one would receive him unless he changed his heart; *the heart of the king is in the hand of the Lord: wherever he will he will turn it* (Prov 21:1).

2156. *And say to him*. He foretells the passion so that they will not be disturbed; hence he speaks of the *time*, not whatever is said, but what has been determined by the Father. John says it in this manner, *my time is not yet come; but your time is always ready* (John 7:6).

With you I make the Pasch, i.e., I celebrate the Paschal meal with you. And he adds *with my disciples*, to designate that he would not celebrate secretly, but publicly. According to Chrysostom, he said this because he wanted them to prepare food enough for both himself and the disciples.

But why is it that he himself celebrated the Pasch, and we should not celebrate it? For John says, *I have given you an example, that as I have done to you, so you do also* (John 13:15). Augustine responds to this that, as Christ

est, ut a morte nos redimeret, sic legem voluit observare, ut nos a lege absolveret.

2157. Tunc sequitur executio *et fecerunt discipuli sicut praeceperat eis Iesus* et cetera. Similiter habetur Ex. XXIV, 3: *omnia verba quae praecepit Dominus faciemus*.

2158. Consequenter agitur de convivio *vespere autem facto discumbebat cum duodecim discipulis eius*. Et dicitur *vespere*, quia, sicut praecipitur Ex. XII, 18, *decima quarta luna ad vesperam celebrabitis Pascha*. Vel *vespere*, quia tendit ad occasum; Zach. c. XIV, 7: *et in tempore vesperi erit lux*. Vel signatur verus transitus Christi, scilicet finis: ad vesperum enim est finis diei.

2159. *Et edentibus illis dixit* et cetera. Hic ponitur de praenuntiatione proditoris. Et

primo designat ex societate;
secundo ex auctoritate;
tertio ex propria voce.

Secunda ibi *at ille respondens* etc., tertia ibi *tu dixisti*.

Et circa primum
primo ponitur praenuntiatio;
secundo effectus *et contristati sunt*.

2160. Unde dicit *et edentibus illis dixit: amen dico vobis quod unus vestrum me traditurus est*. *Amen dico*, affirmat, quia magnum dicebat, *quod unus vestrum*, quos elegi esse columnas Ecclesiae; Eccli. VI, 10: *est amicus socius mensae, et non permanet in die necessitatis*. Et in Ier. IX, 4: *in omni fratre tuo non habeas fiduciam*.

2161. Tunc sequitur effectus, et est duplex effectus, tristitia et dubitatio. Quantum ad tristitiam dicit *et contristati*. Et quare? Contristabantur de morte Christi, quia amarum erat eis carere tali duce, tali patrono. Item tristabantur de tali scelere quod erat futurum; Ier. IX, 1: *quis dabit oculis meis fontem lacrimarum?*

Tunc ponitur dubitatio *coeperunt singuli dicere*.

Sed quare dubitabant? Nonne unusquisque erat certus de se? Responsio: instructi erant discipuli, quia homines sunt cito proni ad peccatum; unde Apostolus, I Cor. X, 12: *qui stat, videat ne cadat*. Item dubitabant, quia magis ei credebant, quam propriae conscientiae. Simile est illud quod dicitur I Cor. IV, 4: *nihil mihi conscius sum, sed non tamen in hoc iustificatus sum*.

2162. *At ille respondens ait: qui intingit manum in paropside hic me tradet*. Hic ponitur praenuntiatio ex verbo prophetico. Et

primo ponit praenuntiationem propheticam;
secundo necessitatem passionis;
tertio poenam proditoris.

suffered to redeem us from death, so he willed to observe the law, to free us from the law.

2157. Then there follows the execution of the command: *and the disciples did as Jesus appointed to them*. A similar thing is found: *we will do all the words of the Lord, which he has spoken* (Exod 24:3).

2158. Next, he treats of the meal: *but when it was evening, he sat down with his twelve disciples*. And it says *evening* because, as is commanded, *the fourteenth day of the month in the evening, you will eat unleavened bread* (Exod 12:18). Or *evening*, because he approached his setting; *and in the time of the evening there will be light* (Zech 14:7). Or, it signifies Christ's true passing over, namely the end: for the end of the day is at evening.

2159. *And while they were eating, he said*. Here the prediction of the betrayer is set down. And

first, he designates the betrayer by company;
second, by authority;
third, by his own voice.

The second is at *but he answering, said*; the third, at *you have said it*.

And concerning the first,
first, the prediction is set down;
second, the effect, at *and they, being very troubled*.

2160. Hence it says, *and while they were eating, he said: amen I say to you, that one of you is about to betray me*. *Amen, I say*, he affirms what he says, because he said a great thing, *that one of you*, whom I chose to be the pillars of the Church; *and there is a friend a companion at the table, and he will not abide in the day of distress* (Sir 6:10). And, *let him not trust in any brother of his* (Jer 9:4).

2161. Then there follows the effect, and there are two effects, sorrow and doubt. As regards sorrow, it says, *and they, being very troubled*. And why? They were troubled over Christ's death, for it was bitter for them to lose such a leader, such a patron. Similarly, they sorrowed over such an evil which was to happen; *who will give . . . a fountain of tears to my eyes?* (Jer 9:1).

Then the doubt is set down: *began everyone to say*.

But why did they doubt? Was not each one certain about himself? The response: the disciples had been taught that men are quickly prone to sin; hence the Apostle, *wherefore he who thinks himself to stand, let him take heed lest he fall* (1 Cor 10:12). Again, they doubted because they believed him more than their own consciences. What is said in Corinthians is similar: *I am not conscious to myself of anything, yet am I not hereby justified* (1 Cor 4:4).

2162. *But he, answering, said: he who dips his hand with me in the dish, he will betray me*. Here the prediction by prophetic word is set down. And

first, he sets out the prophetic prediction;
second, the necessity of the passion;
third, the punishment of the betrayer.

2163. Dicit ergo *at ipse respondens ait*. De hoc potest intelligi illud Ps. XL, 10: *qui edebat panes meos magnificavit super me supplantationem*.

Qui intingit manum in paropside. Marcus dicit *in catino*. Paropsis dicitur vas quadrangulare, et dicitur quasi latera paria habens. Catinus dicitur vas fictile ad recipiendum liquores: unde in catino reponebantur liquores, in paropside sicca; unde poterat ibi esse utrumque. Vel dicebatur paropsis, sed ex officio catinus.

Et quid est quod dicit. *Qui intingit manum in paropside?* Dicendum quod consuetudo apud antiquos erat quod multi comedebant ex una scutella, et forte vas accipiebant. Unde omnes admirantes retraxerunt manum, praeter Iudam, ut magis excusaret se: et ideo erat verbum dubium, quia simul intingebat cum omnibus: ideo noluit eum detegere ne fieret magis peccator. Vel potest dici quod duo et duo sedebant, et istum secum posuerat, ut ipsum retraheret. Sed multi per amicitiam non retrahuntur.

2164. *Filius quidem hominis vadit sicut scriptum est de illo*. Quid est quod dicis, quod tu traderis? Dicit *Filius hominis vadit*, scilicet propria voluntate. *Oblatus est, quia ipse voluit*, sicut scriptum est Is. LIII, 7. Unde praedicta fuit passio a prophetis, ut habetur Lc. ult., 27: *et incipiens a Moyse, et omnibus prophetis interpretabatur illis in omnibus Scripturis, quae de ipso erant*. Et ita Filio hominis nihil nocet, quia fit quod ipse disposuit.

Sed dicet aliquis: *si vadit ex propria voluntate, ergo non est imputandum Iudae*. Dicendum quod immo, quia hoc mala voluntate faciebat, quod filius spontaneus agebat.

2165. Ideo sequitur poena *vae autem homini illi, per quem Filius hominis tradetur*. Sicut supra XVII, 7: *necesse est ut veniant scandala; vae autem homini illi per quem scandalum venit*. Et tangitur magnitudo poenae *bonum erat illi si natus non fuisset*. Ex hoc sequitur occasio erroris. Dicunt enim quidam quod non existenti non infertur poena, ideo dicunt quod melius est simpliciter non fuisse, quod est contra Apostolum ad Rom. IX. Unde, secundum Hieronymus, dicendum quod loquitur secundum communem modum loquendi, idest minus nocumentum, idest maius tormentum sentit, quam si natus non fuisset. Et ad hoc videtur facere quod dicitur Eccle. IV, 2: *laudavi magis mortuos quam viventes*.

Et hoc est contra Augustinum in libro *de Libero arbitrio*. Quod nihil est, non potest eligi. Item quod eligimus, est propinquius felicitati. Sed quod non est, non est propinquum felicitati.

2163. It says therefore, **but he, answering, said**. The Psalm can be understood as about this: *even the man of peace, in whom I trusted, who ate my bread, has greatly supplanted me* (Ps 40:10).

He who dips his hand with me in the dish. Mark says, *in the bowl* (Mark 14:20). A bowl is an earthenware vessel for holding liquids: hence liquids were placed in a bowl, and dry stuff in a dish; hence it could have been either one there. Or, it was called a dish, but was a bowl in function.

And why does he say, **he who dips his hand with me in the dish**? One should say that it was customary among the ancients that many ate from one saucer, and perhaps they took a vessel. Hence everyone withdrew their hands, being astonished, except Judas, that he might better excuse himself: and so it was an uncertain saying, since he was dipping at the same time as everyone. For he did not want to expose him, lest he should become even more of a sinner. Or it can be said that they were sitting two by two, and this one was with him, that he might draw him back. But many are not drawn back through friendship.

2164. **The Son of man indeed goes, as it is written of him**. What is this you are saying, that you will be betrayed? He says, **the Son of man indeed goes**, namely by his own will. *He was offered because it was his own will* (Isa 53:7). For the passion had been predicted by the prophets, as is said, *and beginning at Moses and all the prophets, he expounded to them in all the scriptures, the things that were concerning him* (Luke 24:27). And thus nothing harms the Son of man, because he himself ordains what comes to pass.

But someone will say: *if he went by his own will, then it should not be blamed on Judas*. One should say that rather he brought about with a bad will what the Son freely did.

2165. For this reason, the punishment comes next: **but woe to that man by whom the Son of man will be betrayed**. As above, *for it is necessary that scandals come: but nevertheless woe to that man by whom the scandal comes* (Matt 18:7). And he touches upon the magnitude of the punishment: **it were better for him, if that man had not been born**. From this arises an occasion of error. For some say that punishment is not inflicted on those who do not exist, and for this reason they say that it is better simply speaking not to have been, which is contrary to the Apostle (Rom 9). Hence, according to Jerome, one should say that he speaks according to the common way of speaking, i.e., it would have been a lesser harm, i.e., he feels a greater torment than if he had not been born. And what is said in Sirach seems to support this: *and I praised the dead rather than the living* (Sir 4:2).

And this is contrary to Augustine, in the book *On Free Will*. That which is nothing cannot be chosen. Similarly, we choose is what is closer to happiness. But what is not, is not closer to happiness.

Quid est ergo dicendum? Potest ne aliquis magis eligere non esse quam poenale esse? Ideo dicendum quod non esse dupliciter potest accipi: vel secundum se, vel per comparationem ad aliud. Secundum se dico quod non est eligibile, ut dicit Augustinus, sed per comparationem ad aliud est eligibile, ut dicit Hieronymus. Quia hoc non est aliquid in natura, sed secundum apprehensionem animae accipitur ut aliquid, ut non sedere. Sed electio accipitur ab eo quod est apprehensum: ideo carere malo accipitur ut bonum. Quando ergo eligit non propter se, sed inquantum exclusivum mali, sic eligit, ut dicit Philosophus.

Per hoc patet responsio ad secundum. Dicit ergo quod illud quod magis removet a malo, accipitur ut magis propinquum felicitati; unde homini febrienti carere febre videtur esse felicitatem, quia sub miseriis videtur non esse; unde melius est non esse quam sub miseriis esse.

2166. *Respondens autem Iudas qui tradidit eum, dixit: numquid ego sum, Rabbi?* Notandum quod simulatorie hoc dixit, unde quia tardavit quaerere, significavit quod erat tristis, sed simulavit. Item alii vocant ipsum **Dominum**, sed iste *Magistrum*. Utrumque tamen erat; Io. XIII, 13: *vos vocatis me Magister et Domine, et bene dicitis, sum etenim.*

Ait illi: tu dixisti. Notate mansuetudinem domini. Supra XI, 29: *discite a me, quia mitis sum et humilis corde*; et hoc ut nobis exemplum mansuetudinis daret; unde dicit **tu dixisti**, idest confessus es. Vel tu dicis ista, non assero ego, sed tu dicis. Unde non est verbum asserentis. Nolebat enim eum revelare; quasi dicat: *non assero, sed tu dicis.*

What then should be said? Could not someone choose non-being rather than a punitive being? Therefore one should say that not to be can be taken in two ways: either in itself, or in comparison to another. In itself, I say that it is not able to be chosen, as Augustine says; but in comparison to another it is able to be chosen, as Jerome says. For this is not something in nature, but is taken as something in the soul's perception, such as not to sit. But a choice is made from that which is perceived: for this reason, to lack an evil is taken as a good. Therefore, when a man chooses something not for its own sake, but insofar as it excludes an evil, then he chooses it, as the Philosopher says.

By this, the response to the second argument becomes clear. He says therefore that what is further removed from an evil is taken as closer to happiness; hence to a man with a fever, not to have a fever seems to be happiness, because it seems not to be in misery. Hence it is better not to be than to be in misery.

2166. *And Judas that betrayed him, answering, said: is it I, Rabbi?* One should notice that he said this in pretense; hence the fact that he delayed to ask signified that he was sorrowful, but he pretended. Also, the others called him **Lord**, but this man called him **Rabbi**. Yet he was both; *you call me Master, and Lord; and you say well, for so I am* (John 13:13).

He said to him: you have said it. Note the Lord's gentleness. Above, *learn of me, because I am meek, and humble of heart* (Matt 11:29). And he did this to give us an example of gentleness: hence he says, *you have said it*, i.e., you have confessed. Or, you say this thing; I do not assert it, but you say it. Hence it is not the word of one who asserts. For he did not want to expose him. It is as though he said, *I do not assert it, but you say it.*

Lecture 3

26:26 Coenantibus autem eis accepit Iesus panem, et benedixit, ac fregit, deditque discipulis suis, et ait: accipite, et comedite. Hoc est corpus meum. [n. 2168]

26:26 Ἐσθιόντων δὲ αὐτῶν λαβὼν ὁ Ἰησοῦς ἄρτον καὶ εὐλογήσας ἔκλασεν καὶ δοὺς τοῖς μαθηταῖς εἶπεν· λάβετε φάγετε, τοῦτό ἐστιν τὸ σῶμά μου.

26:26 And while they were at supper, Jesus took bread, and blessed, and broke, and gave to his disciples, and said: take, and eat. This is my body. [n. 2168]

2167. Supra posuit Evangelista celebrationem veteris Paschae; hic ponitur institutio sacramenti altaris. Et

primo instituitur sacramentum;

secundo praenuntiatur futurum scandalum discipulorum, ibi **tunc dixit illis Iesus: omnes vos scandalum patiemini**.

Primo duo facit.

Primo instituitur paschale sacramentum;

secundo hymnus gratiarum actionis, ibi **et hymno dicto exierunt in montem oliveti**.

Et circa primum duo facit.

Primo ponitur institutio sacramenti sub specie panis;

secundo sub specie vini, ibi **et accipiens calicem gratias egit** et cetera.

Circa primum

primo tangit facta Christi;

secundo verba, ibi **accipite et comedite; hoc est corpus meum**.

In factis quinque sunt notanda. Primo ponitur tempus; secundo designatur materia; tertio benedictio; quarto fractio; quinto communicatio, sive distributio.

2168. Tempus tangitur cum dicit **coenantibus autem eis** etc., idest dum essent in coenando, idest dum coenarent.

Et quare hoc constituit in ipsa coena, et non ante? Duplex est ratio. Quia voluit Dominus quod istud succederet veteri sacramento, sicut veritas figurae; ideo post constitutionem veteris sacramenti novum constituit; Lev. XXVI, 10: *novis supervenientibus vetera proiicietis*. Item propter aliud, quia voluit ut infigeretur memoriae: quae enim ultimo audiuntur, altius infiguntur memoriae. Thren. c. III, 19: *recordare paupertatis et transgressionis meae, absinthii et fellis*.

2169. Quare ergo constituit Ecclesia quod homines ieiuni istud sacramentum reciperent?

Dicendum quod hoc est ad reverentiam sacramenti: conveniens enim est quod ante cibum sumatur. Et hoc intelligendum est eodem die. Cum enim dies a media nocte incipiat, non debet recipere quicquam a media nocte usque ad perceptionem huius sacramenti.

2167. Above the Evangelist set down the celebration of the old Pasch; here he sets down the institution of the sacrament of the altar. And

first, the sacrament is instituted;

second, the disciples' future scandal is foretold, at **then Jesus said to them: you will all be scandalized** (Matt 26:31).

First, he does two things:

first, the paschal sacrament is instituted;

second, the hymn of thanksgiving, at **and a hymn being said, they went out to Mount Olivet** (Matt 26:30).

And concerning the first, he does two things:

first, he sets down the institution of the sacrament under the appearance of bread;

second, under the appearance of wine, at, **and taking the chalice, he gave thanks** (Matt 26:27).

Concerning the first,

first, he touches on Christ's deeds;

second, the words, at **take, and eat. This is my body**.

In the deeds, there are five things to be noticed: first, the time is set down; second, the matter is designated; third, the blessing; fourth, the breaking; fifth, the communication, or distribution.

2168. The time is touched upon when he says, **and while they were at supper**, i.e., while they were in the midst of eating, i.e., while they were eating.

And why did he establish this during the meal itself, and not before? There are two reasons. For the Lord willed that it take the place of the old sacrament as the truth takes the place of the figure; so after the establishment of the old sacrament, he establishes the new. *New coming on, you will cast away the old* (Lev 26:10). Likewise for another reason, for he wished to fix it in the memory: for the last thing heard is more profoundly fixed in the memory. *Remember my poverty, and transgression, the wormwood, and the gall* (Lam 3:19).

2169. Why then did the Church decree that men should receive this sacrament while fasting?

One should say that this is for reverence for the sacrament: for it is fitting that it be taken before food. And this should be understood as on the same day. For since the day begins from midnight, one should not take anything from midnight until the reception of this sacrament.

2170. Sed quaesierunt aliqui, si quodcumque intrat in os, solvat sumptionem sacramenti, ut si bibit aliquis aquam.

Intelligendum est quod duplex est ieiunium, scilicet ieiunium Ecclesiae, et ieiunium naturae. Ieiunium Ecclesiae non solvit potus aquae, sed ieiunium naturae solvit; quia etsi aqua per se non nutriat, cum aliis nutrit. Et debetis intelligere quod aquam recipit et potum, si aliquis lavet os, et transglutiat unam guttam casualiter. Non tamen propter hoc debet dimittere, immo computatur cum saliva. Similiter de cibo dico, quod si qui anisum comedit in sero, et remanserit aliquid in dentibus, si casu transglutiat, non propter hoc debet dimittere.

2171. Item aliqui conscientiam faciunt, quod si non dormiunt, non recipiant. Hoc non habet locum, quia non fuit de constitutione Ecclesiae. Unde non facit ad rem utrum dormiat, vel non dormiat.

2172. *Accepit Iesus panem* et cetera. Hic tangitur materia. Notandum quod istud sacramentum quantum ad aliquid veteri sacramento attinet, sicut veritas figurae. Sacramentum illud sumebatur ut cibus, quia mandatum erat quod comederent agnum: et istud, quod loco eius sumitur, debet sumi ut cibus. Et sicut ille erat vere cibus, ita et iste agnus; Io. VI, v. 56: *caro mea vere est cibus*. Unde falsa est illa opinio quae ponebat quod solum erat ibi Christus sub signo, quia si ita esset, quid plus haberet istud signum quam illud? Sed illud erat signum tantum; hoc autem est figura et veritas.

2173. Sed numquid est irreverentia, quia aliquis comedat corpus Domini?

Dicendum quod differt iste cibus ab aliis cibis, quia alii cibi convertuntur in corpus nostrum: unde si Christus ita converteretur, irreverentia esset. Sed non est sic, immo e converso, ut dicit Augustinus: *non tu me mutabis in te, sed tu mutaberis in me*. Unde illud sacramentum finis et perfectio omnium est sacramentorum. Et ratio est, quia esse quod est per essentiam, est finis et perfectio eorum quae per participationem: alia enim sacramenta Christum continent per participationem, in isto autem est Christus secundum substantiam. Ideo dicit Dionysius quod nullum est sacramentum quod non perficiatur in Eucharistia. Unde si adultus baptizetur, debet ei dari Eucharistia. Debet ergo sumi in cibo, ut veritas respondeat figurae.

2174. Et quare non sub specie propria? Una ratio est ratione meriti fidei, quia fides non habet meritum, ubi humana ratio praebet experimentum. Item ut parcatur

2170. But some have asked if one loses the reception of the sacrament if anything at all enters the mouth, as for instance if someone drinks water.

One should understand that there are two fasts, namely the fast of the Church and the fast of nature. Drinking water does not break the fast of the Church, but it does break the fast of nature; for although water does not nourish by itself, it does nourish with other things. And you should understand that if someone washes his mouth and accidentally swallows one drop, he receives water and drink. Yet he should not lose the reception of the sacrament on this account, but rather it is counted with his saliva. I say similarly, with regard to food, that if someone eats an herb in the evening, and something remains in his teeth, and he swallows it by chance, he should not lose the reception of the sacrament on this account.

2171. Similarly, some have made it a matter of conscience that if they do not sleep, they do not receive the sacrament. This has no place, because it was not decreed by the Church. Hence it makes no difference whether one sleeps or does not sleep.

2172. *Jesus took bread*. Here the material is touched upon. Note that this sacrament retains the old in a certain respect, as the truth retains the figure. That sacrament was taken as food, for it had been commanded that they should eat the lamb; and this sacrament, which takes its place, should be taken as food. And just as that one was truly food, so also this lamb; *for my flesh is meat indeed* (John 6:56). Hence the opinion which held that Christ was there only in sign is false, because if it were so, what more would this sign have than that one? But that one was a sign only, while this one is figure and truth.

2173. But is it an irreverence that someone should eat the Lord's body?

One should say that this food and other foods are different, because other foods are turned into our body; and if Christ were thus changed, it would be an irreverence. But it is not so, but rather the other way around, as Augustine says: *you will not change me into you, but you will be changed into me*. Hence this sacrament is the end and perfection of all the sacraments. And the reason is that being which is by essence is the end and perfection of those which are by participation: for the other sacraments contain Christ by participation, while Christ is in this one in substance. For this reason, Dionysius says that there is no sacrament which is not perfected in the Eucharist. Hence if an adult is baptized, the Eucharist should be given to him. It should, therefore, be taken in food, that the truth may correspond to the figure.

2174. And why not under his own appearance? One reason is for the sake of the merit of faith, because faith has no merit where human reason offers evidence. Likewise, that those who receive the sacrament might be spared,

sumentibus, quia non est consuetum quod caro humana comedatur. Item ut defendatur a derisionibus infidelium.

2175. Et quare sub tali specie? Quia voluit celebrari ab omnibus ubique terrarum: ideo voluit eis dare materiam, quae communis est omnibus. Communis autem cibus est panis, et communis potus hominum est vinum: unde panis et vinum sunt cibus principalis, alia potius quasi edulia. Item in aliis sacramentis in unctione non quodcumque oleum accipitur, sed commune, quod dicitur oleum ex multis olivis; sic unitas Ecclesiae ex multitudine fidelium.

Et sic patet quod nostra sacramenta magis sunt antiqua quam sacramenta veteris legis; quia sacramenta veteris legis habuerunt initium a Moyse et Aaron, sed sacramenta novae legis a Melchisedech, qui obtulit Abraham panem et vinum. Ideo dicitur Christus factus *sacerdos secundum ordinem Melchisedech*, Ps. CIX, 4.

2176. Consequenter agitur de benedictione; et haec benedictio refertur ad tria. Ad materiam, quia benedixit fructum terrae, in quo significatur quod maledictio Adae revocata est per Christum, quando dixit ei, Gen. c. III, 17: *maledicta terra in labore tuo . . . spinas et tribulos germinabit tibi*. Item refertur quantum ad illud quod continebatur in illo, scilicet Christum; supra XXI, 9: **benedictus qui venit in nomine Domini**. Item ad fructum sacramenti, quia per istum benedicuntur fideles, et transit a capite ad membra; Prov. X, 6: *benedictio Domini super caput iusti*.

2177. Deinde tangitur fractio **et fregit**: et tria significat. Primo significat mysterium futurae passionis, quia in passione perforata sunt membra, secundum illud Ps. XXI, 17: *foderunt manus meas et pedes meos, dinumeraverunt omnia ossa mea*. Et hoc factum est, quia ipse voluit; Is. LIII, 7: *oblatus est quia ipse voluit*. Item significatur quod frangatur ab unitate in multitudinem, unde significat incarnationem: quia, cum ipsum Dei Verbum simplex esset, venit in istam multitudinem, non relinquendo simplicitatem. Item signatur effectus quem in diversos intulit; quia, secundum Apostolum, I Cor. XII, 4, *divisiones gratiarum sunt, idem autem Spiritus*.

2178. Item ponitur distributio **dedit discipulis suis**; Eccli. XXIX, 33: *ex his quae in manu habes, ciba singulos*. Et dicit, **discipulis**, quia nulli non baptizato debet dari huiusmodi sacramentum. Sicut non conficeret sacerdos nisi consecratus, sic non debet alicui illud administrari nisi baptizato. Item non est dandum nisi fidelibus; immo infideles non debent admitti ad videndum istud sacramentum: unde in primitiva Ecclesia, quando multi erant

because it is not customary to eat human flesh. Likewise, that it might be defended against the mockery of unbelievers.

2175. And why under this sort of appearance? Because he wished it to be celebrated by all men everywhere on earth: so he wished to give them a matter which is common to all. Now men's common food is bread, and their common drink is wine: hence bread and wine are the principal food; the others are rather, so to speak, edible. Similarly in the other sacraments, not just any oil is used in anointing, but the common one which is called oil from many olives; even so, the unity of the Church is out of the multitude of the faithful.

And thus it is clear that our sacraments are older than the sacraments of the old law; for the sacraments of the old law had their beginning from Moses and Aaron, but the sacraments of the new law from Melchisedech, who brought bread and wine to Abraham. For this reason Christ is said to be made *a priest for ever according to the order of Melchisedech* (Ps 109:4).

2176. Next, he treats of the blessing; and this blessing is referred to three things. To the matter, because he blessed the fruit of the earth, which signifies that the curse of Adam was revoked through Christ, when he said to him, *cursed is the earth in your work . . . Thorns and thistles will it bring forth to you* (Gen 3:17–18). Likewise, it is referred to what was contained in it, namely Christ; above, **blessed is he who comes in the name of the Lord** (Matt 21:9). Likewise, to the fruit of the sacrament, because the faithful are blessed through it, and it passes from the head to the members; *the blessing of the Lord is upon the head of the just* (Prov 10:6).

2177. Then he touches upon the breaking: **and broke**; and it signifies three things. First, it signifies the mystery of his future passion, for his members were pierced in the passion, in accord with the Psalm, *they have pierced my hands and feet. They have numbered all my bones* (Ps 21:17–18). And this was done because he himself willed it; *he was offered because it was his own will* (Isa 53:7). Likewise, it signifies that he is broken from unity into multitude, hence it signifies the incarnation: for, while he was himself the simple Word of God, he came into this multitude, not abandoning his simplicity. Likewise, it signifies the effect which he brought to diverse men; for, according to the Apostle, *there are diversities of graces, but the same Spirit* (1 Cor 12:4).

2178. Likewise, the distribution is set down: **and gave to his disciples**; *give others to eat what you have in your hand* (Sir 29:33). And it says, **to his disciples**, because such a sacrament should not be given to anyone who is unbaptized. Just as only a consecrated priest confects the sacrament, so it should only be administered to the baptized. Similarly, it should only be given to the faithful; or rather, the unfaithful should not be let in to see this sacrament: hence in

catechumeni, recipiebantur in Ecclesia usque ad Evangelium, et tunc expellebantur.

2179. Item cum dicat quod *discipulis suis*, quaeritur utrum Iudas ibi fuerit. Omnes dicunt quod simul dedit omnibus, et etiam Iudae, et hoc ut eum sua benignitate a peccato revocaret. Item ut daret Ecclesiae documentum ut dum esset occultus peccator, quod non prohiberetur a receptione huius sacramenti: homines enim non habent iudicare de occultis. Hilarius hic dicit quod non fuit Iudas, quia iam exierat. Et vult probare per illud quod dicitur in Io. XIII, 25, cum petierunt discipuli: *quis est qui tradet te?* Quibus dixit: *cui tradidero buccellam intinctam*. Ideo ostendit quod iam exierat. Sed magis tenendum est quod alii dicunt.

2180. *Et ait: accipite, et comedite; hoc est corpus meum*. Hic ponuntur verba: et in istis verbis tria facit. Primo hortatur ad recipiendum; secundo ad comedendum; tertio denuntiat veritatem.

Dicit *accipite et comedite*. Et quod dicit *accipite*, ad spiritualem receptionem debet referri, quia non debet accipi nisi in fide et caritate; Io. VI, 55: *qui manducat carnem meam, et bibit sanguinem meum, in me manet, et ego in eo*.

Item inducit ad comestionem, *comedite*, non solum spiritualiter, sed etiam sacramentaliter; Cant. V, 1: *comedite, amici, et bibite*.

Item designat veritatem *hoc est corpus meum*. Forma sacramenti continetur in his verbis, quae sunt verba domini, quia in verbis domini sacramentum conficitur. Unde si verbum Eliae tantam virtutem habuit quod faceret ignem de caelo descendere, multo magis verbum Dei poterit transmutare unum corpus in aliud.

2181. Tunc quaeritur utrum virtus sit in verbis. Et non est dubium quod sic. Unde dicitur Ps. LXVII, 34: *dedit voci suae vocem virtutis*; Eccle. VIII, 4: *quia sermo eius potestate plenus est*. Unde sacerdos peragit in persona Christi, et non utitur verbis in persona propria, sed in persona Christi.

Sed quae est haec virtus? Quomodo tanta est virtus? Ideo dicunt aliqui quod nulla est ibi virtus, sed potestas Christi solum, quae ibi assistit. Et hoc non videtur, quia sacramenta novae legis efficiunt quod figurant.

Sed quam virtutem habuit? Dicendum quod est causa agens principalis, et haec virtutem habet in se manentem; item causa instrumentalis, et haec non operatur per virtutem in se manentem, sed ab alio transeuntem: unde sacramenta sunt causae, non sicut causae principales, sed instrumentales ab alio transeuntes.

the primitive Church, when there were many catechumens, they were received in the Church until the Gospel, and then they were put out.

2179. Likewise, when it says, *to his disciples*, it is asked whether Judas was there. All say that he gave at once to all, and even to Judas, and this was to call him back from sin by his kindness. Likewise, to give to the Church the doctrine that when someone is a hidden sinner he is not prevented from receiving this sacrament: for men do not have judgment over hidden things. Hilary says here that Judas was not present, because he had already left. And he would prove it by what is said, when the disciples asked, *Lord, who is it?* to whom he said, *he it is to whom I will reach bread dipped* (John 13:25). So he shows that he had already left. But one should rather hold what the others say.

2180. *And said: take and eat. This is my body.* Here the words are set down: and he does three things in these words: first, he exhorts them to receive; second, to eat; third, he declares the truth.

He says, *take and eat*. And when he says *take*, it should be referred to spiritual reception, because one should only take it in faith and charity; *he who eats my flesh, and drinks my blood, abides in me, and I in him* (John 6:57).

Likewise, he urges them to eating: *eat*, not only spiritually, but also sacramentally; *eat, O friends, and drink* (Song 5:1).

Likewise, he declares the truth: *this is my body*. The form of the sacrament is contained in these words, which are the words of the Lord, for the sacrament is confected in the words of the Lord. For if the words of Elijah had so much strength that he made fire come down from heaven, much more can the word of God transmute one body into another.

2181. At this point it is asked whether there is power in the words. And there is no doubt that there is. For it says, *behold he will give to his voice the voice of power* (Ps 67:34); *his word is full of power* (Sir 8:4). For the priest acts in the person of Christ, and does not use the words in his own person, but in the person of Christ.

But what is this power? How is there so great a power? For this reason, some say that there is no power there, but only the power of Christ, which gives assistance. And this does not seem true, because the sacraments of the new law effect what they signify.

But what power did it have? One should say that there is a principal agent cause, and this cause has the power abiding in itself; likewise there is an instrumental cause, and this cause does not work through a power abiding in itself, but through a transient power from another: hence the sacraments are causes, not as principal causes, but instrumental, transient causes.

2182. Sed tunc quaeritur quid est de facto: utrum istud *accipite et comedite* etc. sit de forma sacramenti.

Et dicendum quod solum illud *hoc est corpus meum*, est de forma sacramenti. Unde intelligendum quod aliter est de sacramento hoc et de aliis sacramentis, quia consecratio materiae aliquando est de necessitate sacramenti, aliquando non; ut in baptismo consecratio materiae non est de necessitate baptismi, sed in unctionibus nulla fit unctio, nisi oleum benedicatur. In aliis etiam sacramentis non percipitur sacramentum in benedictione, sed in infusione; quia oleum et aqua, cum sint inanimata, non continent gratiam: unde cum gratia sit finis sacramenti, non potest inferri nisi per susceptionem sacramenti. Sed in isto sacramento continetur ille qui est plenitudo gratiae; ideo non perficitur in nobis, sed in consecratione materiae. Unde dato quod nullus acciperet, non minus esset sacramentum: unde usus est consequens et non est de necessitate. Unde in aliis illud est de forma quod pertinet ad usum: istud non pertinet ad usum, sed ad materiae sanctitatem. Unde istud quod dicitur *accipite et comedite* quod pertinet ad usum, non est de forma.

2183. Item solet esse quaestio, utrum Dominus confecerit sub his verbis. Et videtur quod non: quia dicitur ibi *accepit panem, et benedixit*. Ergo videtur quod in benedictione consecraverit. Ideo dixerunt aliqui quod non consecravit primo verbis, sed spirituali virtute. Et hoc potuit facere propter virtutem excellentiae, quia poterat veritatem sacramenti sine sacramento tradere, quia virtutem suam non alligaverat sacramentis: unde hoc potuit facere per virtutem excellentiae.

Alii dicunt quod primo in occulto dixit, et post in publico.

Melius dicitur quod semel dixit, et non bis, et in his verbis consecravit. Unde debet ita legi quod illud quod dicitur *ait: accipite et comedite*, referatur ad praecedentia, unde, sic dicendo, dixit *hoc est corpus meum*.

2184. Hic quaeritur quid demonstret hoc pronomen *hoc*. Dixerunt quidam quod demonstrat non ad sensum, sed ad intellectum, quia non est nisi ad substantiam panis, et non est nisi ad significandum. Unde sensus est *hoc est corpus meum*, idest signatum per *hoc*, est *corpus meum*. Et hoc non potest stare, quia sacramenta novae legis efficiunt quod signant, ideo nihil aliud facit nisi quod signat: et signat corpus Christi, et sic solum est corpus Christi sub signo.

Alii dicunt quod ly *hoc* demonstrat ipsam substantiam corporis. Sed quomodo est hoc? Estne statim

2182. But next a question is asked about the deed: whether *take and eat* is of the form of the sacrament.

And one should say that only *this is my body* is of the form of the sacrament. Hence one should understand that with this sacrament it is different than with the other sacraments, for sometimes the consecration of the matter is necessary for the sacrament, and sometimes not, as in baptism the consecration of the matter is not necessary for baptism, while in unction there is no unction unless the oil is blessed. Also, in the other sacraments the sacrament is not obtained in the blessing, but in the application: because oil and water, which are inaminate, do not contain grace. For since grace is the end of the sacrament, it can only be had through the reception of the sacrament. But in this sacrament he who is the fullness of grace is contained; therefore it is not perfected in us, but in the consecration of the matter. Hence given that no one received it, it would be no less a sacrament, for its use is consequent and not necessary. Whence in others that which pertains to the use is of the form; this one does not pertain to the use, but to the sanctity of the matter. Hence when he says, *take and eat*, which pertains to its use, it is not of the form.

2183. Likewise, there is often the question whether the Lord confected the sacrament under these words. And it seems that he did not, for it says there he *took bread, and blessed*. Therefore it seems that he consecrated the sacrament in the blessing. For this reason, some have said that he did not consecrate first by the words, but by a spiritual power. And this could have been, owing to the power of excellence, for he could have given the truth of the sacrament without the sacrament, since he had not bound his power to the sacraments. Hence he could have done this through the power of excellence.

Others say that he spoke first in secret, and then in public.

It is better said that he spoke once, and not twice, and consecrated in these words. Hence it should be read in such a way that when it says, *and said: take and eat*, this is referred to what came before; hence, speaking in this way, he said, *this is my body*.

2184. Here it asked what this pronoun *this* points to. Some have said that it does not point to the thing sensed, but to the thing understood, because it is only to the substance of bread, and is only for signifying. Hence the meaning is *this is my body*, i.e., the thing signified through *this* is *my body*. And this cannot stand, because the sacraments of the new law effect what they signify, so it brings about nothing other than what it signifies: and it signifies the body of Christ, and in this way only is the body of Christ under a sign.

Others say that *this* points to the very substance of the body. But how is this? Is it immediately the body of Christ when he says *this*? It is agreed that it is not, for if the priest

corpus Christi cum dicit, **hoc?** Constat quod non, quia si moreretur sacerdos, non esset consecratum nisi expleret.

Ideo dicunt alii quod ly **hoc** retardat suam significationem, et demonstrat illud quod erit post prolationem istius verbi **meum**. Istud etiam non competit, quia sic idem videretur dicere, ac si diceret: *corpus meum est corpus meum*; et Deo non competit.

Alii dicunt quod verba proferuntur materialiter, non significative. Et hoc non potest stare, quia dicit Augustinus: *accedit verbum ad elementum, et fit sacramentum*.

Quid ergo? Dicendum quod recitative dicuntur, et simul recitative et significative. Quare? Quia ipse loquitur in persona Christi, et peragit ac si Christus esset praesens: aliter verba non accederent ad propriam materiam. Quid ergo? Dicendum quod aliter est in verbis sacramentalibus, et verbis aliis humanis: quia verbum humanum est solum significativum, sed divinum significativum et factivum. Unde verba sacramentalia habent virtutem a virtute divina. Unde simul dicit, et ex virtute divina facit. Ideo non solum est illud verbum significativum, sed etiam factivum. Et primo facit, secundo significat. In factione enim materiali ita est quod praeexistit aliquod commune in qualibet transmutatione, et illud commune est sub uno termino transmutationis, et in fine sub alio. Verbi gratia, ponatur quod de nigro fiat album; in ista transmutatione erat corpus, sed in principio erat sub nigredine, et post sub albedine. Unde quoad aliquid est simile, quoad hoc scilicet quod est aliquid commune; sed dissimile, quia non eodem modo; quia in aliis transmutationibus materialibus commune est subiectum, et differens forma; hic autem est contrarium, quia commune est accidens, differens est substantia. Unde substantia transmutatur, commune accidens manet.

Quid ergo demonstrat ly **hoc?** Dicendum quod sensus est: **hoc est corpus meum**, idest contentum sub accidente est corpus meum. Vel hoc fit quod contentum sub accidentibus sit corpus meum. Unde in fine posuit nomen, sed in principio pronomen, quod substantiam indeterminatam significat; sed per nomen forma determinata. Unde in principio non est forma, sed in fine.

2185. Sed quomodo est ibi corpus Christi? Una fuit opinio, quod simul cum corpore Christi substantia panis manebat. Unde quod dicit **hoc est corpus meum**, refertur ad corpus solum. Alii dicunt quod transit substantia panis in praeiacentem materiam, et advenit ibi corpus Christi, praeter hoc quod substantia panis transeat in corpus Christi.

Improbatur autem hoc sic. Quia sic videtur quod aliquid incipiat esse ubi non primo fuit, quod non potest esse nisi vel mutetur secundum locum, vel quod aliquid

were to die, it would not be consecrated unless he had finished.

For this reason, others say that ***this*** delays its signification, and points to that which will be after the pronunciation of the word ***my***. This is also unfitting, because this way he would seem to say the same thing, as though he said: *my body is my body*; and this does not befit God.

Others say that the words are brought forth materially, but not so as to signify. And this cannot stand, for Augustine says, *the words are added to the element, and the sacrament comes about*.

What then? One should say that they are spoken recitatively, both recitatively and at the same time significantly. Why? Because he speaks in the person of Christ, and acts as though Christ were present: otherwise, the words would not be added to the proper matter. What therefore? One should say that it is not the same with sacramental words as with other human words: for a human word is only significant, but a divine word is significant and effective. Hence sacramental words have power from the divine power. So he simultaneously speaks and acts by the divine power. Therefore the word is not only significant, but also effective. And it effects first, and signifies second. For in a material making there necessarily pre-exists something common in any given transmutation, and that common thing is under one terminus of the transmutation and in the end under another terminus. For example, suppose that a white thing comes to be from a black thing: in that transmutation there was a body, but at the beginning it was under blackness, and afterwards under whiteness. Hence in a certain respect it is similar, namely with respect to the fact that there is something common; but it is dissimilar, because not in the same way. For in other material transmutations the subject is common, and the form is different; but here it is the other way around, because the accident is common, while the substance is different. Hence the substance is transmuted, while the common accident remains.

What, therefore, does ***this*** point to? One should say that the sense is: ***this is my body***, i.e., the thing contained under the accident is my body. Or, it is coming about that what is contained under the accidents be my body. Hence he put a noun at the end, but at the beginning a pronoun, which signifies a substance indeterminately; while a noun signifies a determinate form.

2185. But how is the body of Christ there? One opinion was that the substance of the bread remained at the same time with the body of Christ. Hence when he says, ***this is my body***, it is referred to the body only. Others say that the substance of the bread turns into the pre-existing matter, and the body of Christ arrives there, contrary to this, that the substance of the bread changes into the body of Christ.

But this is disproved in this way. For thus it seems that something would begin to be where it was not at first, which cannot be unless either it changes place or something is

convertatur in ipsum. Sicut si dicatur: *hic non est ignis*, quod ergo post sit ibi, hoc non potest esse, nisi quod ibi aliunde apportetur, vel quod aliquid, quod ibi sit, in ignem mutetur. Sed secundum istam opinionem tollitur modus conversionis; ergo non est nisi mutatio localis. Sed impossibile est idem corpus esse in diversis locis; ideo et cetera.

Ideo aliter dicendum quod corpus incipit ibi esse, non per motum localem, sed per conversionem alterius in ipsum; et in hoc manet forma, et transit subiectum. Unde mutatur subiectum in subiectum, quod est principium individuationis, non propter hoc quod simul cum substantia panis sit corpus Christi, vel annihiletur substantia panis, sed per hoc quod transmutetur per conversionem in ipsum.

2186. Sed qualiter poterit esse in tam parvo loco?

Dicendum quod aliquid est ibi de vi sacramenti, et istud ibi principaliter est; aliquid vero per concomitantiam. Illud est ibi de vi sacramenti, in quod terminatur conversio. Et quia panis convertitur in corpus Christi, illud quod significatur, est corpus Christi, et non est sine anima, nec sine divinitate: nec tamen panis convertitur in animam, vel divinitatem, sed sunt ibi per concomitantiam. Unde si aliquis in triduo celebrasset, cum anima esset separata a corpore, non esset ibi anima. In pane enim duo sunt, substantia et accidentia: accidentia manent, substantia transit. Illud ergo ibi est principaliter, in quod terminatur transmutatio; sed terminatur in substantiam; ergo substantia est principaliter, sed accidentia per concomitantiam: dimensiones autem sunt accidentia. Nec corpus Christi in sacramento comparatur ad locum per dimensiones proprias, sed per dimensiones panis praeexistentes.

2187. Item *fregit*. Sed numquid in qualibet parte est totum corpus?

Dico quod sic. Et debetis intelligere quod dicitur aliter esse in loco, quam locatum in loco; quia locatum comparatur ad locum sub suis dimensionibus, sed non sic hic. Ideo notandum quod ubicumque est aliqua differentia quantitatis, non facit differentiam in substantia; sed si sit aliquod sequens quantitatem, dividitur secundum quantitatem. Sed anima non habet a quantitate suam totalitatem accipere, sed habet suam totalitatem in qualibet parte: unde corpus Christi non comparatur ad corpus illud secundum quantitatem, sed solum secundum substantiam. Ideo sicut anima est in qualibet parte corporis, sic Christus in qualibet parte hostiae.

turned into it. So if it be said, *there is no fire here*, then there can be no fire there afterwards unless either it is brought in from somewhere else, or something else which is there is changed into fire. But according to this opinion, the way of conversion is ruled out; therefore it is only a change in place. But it is impossible that the same body be in different places.

Therefore one should say otherwise, that the body begins to be there not through local motion, but through the conversion of another thing into it; and in this the form remains, and the subject passes. Hence subject is changed into subject, which is the principle of individuation, not because the body of Christ is present at the same time as the substance of the bread, or because the substance of the bread is annihilated, but because it is transmuted, through conversion into the very body of Christ.

2186. But how could it be in such a small place?

One should say that one thing is there by the strength of the sacrament, and that is there principally, while another thing is there through concomitance. That in which the conversion terminates is there by the strength of the sacrament. And since the bread is converted into the body of Christ, that which is signified, is the body of Christ, and it is neither without the soul nor without the divinity; nevertheless, the bread is not converted into the soul, or the divinity, but rather they are there through concomitance. So if someone had celebrated Mass during the three days when the soul was separated from the body, the soul would not have been there. For there are two things in bread, substance and accidents: the accidents remain while the substance passes away. Therefore, that in which the transmutation terminates is what is principally there; but it terminates in the substance; therefore the substance is there principally, but the accidents through concomitance. Now, dimensions are accidents. Nor is the body of Christ in the sacrament brought into relation to a place through its own dimensions, but through the preexisting dimensions of the bread.

2187. Similarly, he *broke* it. But is the whole body in any given part?

I say that it is. And you should understand that to be in a place is not the same as to be located in a place: for that which is located is brought into relation to a place under its own dimensions, but this is not the case here. Therefore one should note that a difference in quantity does not always cause a difference in substance; but if there is something which follows upon quantity, it is divided according to quantity. But the soul does not have to receive its totality from quantity, but has its totality in any given part: hence the body of Christ is not brought into relation to that body according to quantity, but only according to substance. Therefore, just as the soul is in any given part of the body, so Christ is in any given part of the host.

2188. Quid ergo erit de istis accidentibus? Dicendum quod manent absque subiecto ex virtute divina. Et quo modo potest hoc esse, cum accidentia dependeant a substantia? Dicendum quod Deus est principium essendi; unde potest producere effectum separatum a subiecto et sine principiis; ideo cum principium substantiae sit conservare accidentia in esse, potest Deus absque suis principiis conservare.

2189. Si quaeris utrum sit verum de omnibus accidentibus, dicendum quod omnia accidentia referuntur ad substantiam mediantibus dimensionibus, unde quodammodo individuantur; ideo dimensiones sunt sine subiecto, sed qualitas in dimensionibus est ut in subiecto. Unde sensus est **hoc**, idest contentum sub his accidentibus, quae accidentia manent in dimensionibus, quia substantia, quae primo suberat sub his accidentibus, mutatur in corpus Christi.

2188. What then of the accidents? One should say that they remain without a subject, by divine power. And how can this be, since accidents depend on substance? One should say that God is the principle of being; hence he can produce an effect separated from its subject and without its principles. Therefore, since the principle of substance is to preserve accidents in being, God can preserve them without their principles.

2189. If you ask whether this is true of all the accidents, one should say that all the accidents are related to the substance through the mediation of the dimensions, hence they are in a certain way individuated. Therefore, the dimensions are without a subject, but the quality is in the dimensions as in a subject. Hence the sense is **this**, i.e., the thing contained under these accidents, which accidents remain in the dimensions, since the substance, which at first was underlying these accidents, is changed into the body of Christ.

Lecture 4

26:27 Et accipiens calicem gratias egit, et dedit illis dicens: bibite ex hoc omnes. [n. 2191]

26:28 Hic est enim sanguis meus Novi Testamenti, qui pro multis effundetur in remissionem peccatorum. [n. 2200]

26:29 Dico autem vobis, non bibam amodo de hoc genimine vitis, usque in diem illum, cum illud bibam vobiscum novum in regno Patris mei. [n. 2203]

26:27 καὶ λαβὼν ποτήριον καὶ εὐχαριστήσας ἔδωκεν αὐτοῖς λέγων· πίετε ἐξ αὐτοῦ πάντες,

26:28 τοῦτο γάρ ἐστιν τὸ αἷμά μου τῆς διαθήκης τὸ περὶ πολλῶν ἐκχυννόμενον εἰς ἄφεσιν ἁμαρτιῶν.

26:29 λέγω δὲ ὑμῖν, οὐ μὴ πίω ἀπ' ἄρτι ἐκ τούτου τοῦ γενήματος τῆς ἀμπέλου ἕως τῆς ἡμέρας ἐκείνης ὅταν αὐτὸ πίνω μεθ' ὑμῶν καινὸν ἐν τῇ βασιλείᾳ τοῦ πατρός μου.

26:27 And taking the chalice, he gave thanks, and gave to them, saying: drink, all of you, of this. [n. 2191]

26:28 For this is my blood of the New Testament, which will be shed for many unto the remission of sins. [n. 2200]

26:29 And I say to you, from this time forward, I will not drink of this fruit of the vine, until that day when I will drink it with you new in the kingdom of my Father. [n. 2203]

2190. Supra actum est de institutione novi sacramenti quantum ad sacramentum corporis Domini, hic agitur de institutione eiusdem quantum ad sacramentum sanguinis:

et circa hoc duo facit.
Primo ponuntur facta Christi;
secundo dicta, ibi **bibite ex hoc omnes**.
Circa primum tria facta ponuntur.
Primo quod accepit calicem;
secundo quod gratias egit;
tertio quod discipulis dedit.

2191. Unde dicit *et accipiens calicem* etc.; per quod signatum est, quod non fuit institutum quod agatur sub una specie, sed sub duabus.

Et quae est ratio huius? Una ratio est, quia tria sunt in hoc sacramento: unum quod est sacramentum tantum, aliud quod est res tantum, aliud quod est sacramentum et res. Sacramentum tantum sunt species panis et vini, res tantum est effectus spiritualis, res et sacramentum est corpus contentum. Si ergo consideremus sacramentum tantum, sic bene competit ut corpus signetur sub specie panis, sanguis sub specie vini, quia signatur ut indicans refectionem spiritualem; sed refectio est proprie in cibo et potu, ideo et cetera. Item si sumatur ut res et sacramentum, ad hoc competit quod illud sacramentum est rememorativum Dominicae passionis. Et non potuit melius significare quam sic, ut significetur sanguis ut effusus et separatus a corpore. Item quantum ad id quod sumitur ut res tantum, quia sanguis pertinet ad animam, non quia sanguis sit anima, sed in sanguine vita conservatur: unde signatur quod cum illud sacramentum sit ad salutem fidelium, quod panis offertur pro salute corporis, sed sanguis pro salute animae. Prov. IX, 5: *venite, comedite panem meum, et bibite vinum quod miscui vobis,*

2190. Above, he treated of the institution of the new sacrament with regard to the sacrament of the Lord's body; here he treats of the institution of the same sacrament with regard to the sacrament of the blood.

And concerning this he does two things:
first, Christ's deeds are set down;
second, his words, at **drink, all of you, of this**.
Concerning the first, three deeds are set down:
first, that he took the chalice;
second, that he gave thanks;
third, that he gave to the disciples.

2191. Hence it says, **and taking the chalice**, which indicates that it was not instituted that the sacrament be done under one appearance, but under two.

And what is the reason for this? One reason is that there are three things in this sacrament: one which is a sacrament only, another which is a reality only, and another which is both sacrament and reality. The appearances of bread and wine are a sacrament only, the spiritual effect is a reality only, and the body contained is both reality and sacrament. If therefore we consider that which is a sacrament only, in this way it is quite fitting that the body be signified under the appearance of bread, and the blood under the appearance of wine, for it is signified as indicating spiritual refreshment; but refreshment is found properly in food and drink. Likewise, if it be taken as both reality and sacrament, it pertains to this that the sacrament is commemorative of the Lord's passion. And it could not signify better than in this way, that it signify the blood as poured out and separated from the body. It is likewise with regard to that which is taken as reality only, for the blood pertains to the soul, not because the blood is the soul, but because life is preserved in the blood. Hence it signifies that, since this sacrament is for the health of the faithful, the bread is offered

quia refectio ista est in pane et vino. Item alia ratio, quia totus Christus continetur in corpore.

2192. Quae est ergo necessitas quod sanguis per se? Ideo est accipiendum quod dictum est supra, quod aliud est ibi ex vi sacramenti directe, aliud ex naturali concomitantia. Sub panis specie continetur corpus Christi de vi sacramenti, sed sanguis per concomitantiam. In sanguine vero e converso, quia sanguis est de vi sacramenti, sed corpus per concomitantiam. Unde sanguine Christi effuso in terram, si fuisset celebratum, non fuisset sanguis nisi seorsum. Ideo quia haec non intellexerunt quidam, dixerunt quod formae istae continuantur. Unde dicunt quod cum consecratur corpus, non est ibi sanguis donec vinum fuerit consecratum. Sed hoc non est ita, quia si moreretur sacerdos antequam consecraret vinum, esset in hostia et corpus et sanguis.

2193. Item dicit **accipiens calicem**, et non dicit *accipiens vinum*, ideo quidam dixerunt quod debebat fieri in aqua. Et hoc excluditur, quia sequitur **non bibam de genimine vitis** et cetera. Secundo patet quod fuit vinum et aqua mixtum. Et huius ratio est ex parte sacramenti, quia celebrandum est ut Dominus instituit. Sed in terra calida consuetudo est quod non bibatur vinum sine aqua; ideo non est credendum quod in puro vino confecerit. Competit et contento, quia illud sacramentum est rememorativum Dominicae passionis; sed a latere Christi exivit sanguis et aqua, ut habetur Io. XIX, 34. Item ad significandum effectus, et hoc dupliciter: quia istud significat memoriam passionis Christi; ergo inducit in nos effectus passionis Christi. Effectus autem est duplex, abluere et redimere. Redemit nos per sanguinem suum; Apoc. V, v. 9: *redemisti nos Deo in sanguine tuo*. Item abluit sordes; Apoc. I, 5: *dilexit nos, et lavit nos a peccatis nostris in sanguine suo*. Et haec erant necessaria ut ablueret et redimeret. Et ablutio signatur per aquam, redemptio per vinum. Item per aquam populus; Apoc. XVII, 1: *aquae multae, populus multus*. Et per istud sacramentum populus unitur Christo; ideo per istam admixtionem signatur populus uniri Christo.

2194. Sed quid fit de illa aqua? Dicunt aliqui quod manet. Alii dicunt quod convertitur in vinum, quia cum ponatur parum, species mutatur, et ita totum est

for the health of the body, and the blood for the health of the soul. *Come, eat my bread, and drink the wine which I have mingled for you* (Prov 9:5), for this refreshment is with bread and wine. Likewise another reason, because the whole Christ is contained in the body.

2192. What need then is there that the blood be by itself? Hence one should consider what was said above, that one thing is there directly, by the strength of the sacrament, and another by a natural concomitance. The body of Christ is contained under the appearance of bread by the strength of the sacrament, and the blood by concomitance. But it is the other way around with the blood contained under the appearance of wine, for the blood is there by the strength of the sacrament, and the body by concomitance. Hence when the blood of Christ was poured out on the ground, if the sacrament had been celebrated, the blood would only have been present separately. So, since some had not understood this, they said that this form is continued. Hence they say that when the body is consecrated, the blood is not there until the wine has been consecrated. But this is not so, because if the priest were to die before he consecrated the wine, both the body and the blood would be present in the host.

2193. Likewise, it says, **taking the chalice**, and does not say, *taking the wine*, and because of this some have said that the sacrament should be performed with water. And this is ruled out, because there follows, **I will not drink of this fruit of the vine**. Second, it is clear that it was wine mixed with water. And one reason for this is on the side of the sacrament, for it was going to be celebrated as the Lord instituted. But it is customary in hot regions that wine is not drunk without water; so one should not believe that he confected the sacrament with pure wine. It also befits the thing contained, for this sacrament is commemorative of the Lord's passion; but from Christ's side flowed out blood and water, as is said in John (John 19:34). Likewise, to signify the effect of the sacrament, and this in two ways: for it signifies the memory of Christ's passion, so it produces in us the effect of Christ's passion. Now, there are two effects, to purify and to redeem. He redeemed us through his blood; *and has redeemed us to God, in your blood* (Rev 5:9). Similarly, he purified the unclean; *who has loved us, and washed us from our sins in his own blood* (Rev 1:5). And these things were necessary, that he should purify and redeem. And the purification is signified by the water, the redemption by the wine. Likewise, the water signifies the people; *many waters, a great people* (Rev 17:1). And through this sacrament, the people is united to Christ; so this mixing together of water and wine signifies that the people is united to Christ.

2194. But what happens to the water? Some say that it remains. Others say that it is turned into wine, because when a very little is put in, the species is changed, and thus

conversum; et ita pertinet ad mysterium, quia in hoc unitas ecclesiastica continetur.

2195. Item in hoc quod dicit *accipiens*, signatur quod voluntarie sustinuit passionem; unde in Psal. CXV, 13: *calicem salutaris accipiam, et nomen Domini invocabo*.

2196. Item *gratias egit*. Et de quo? De duobus, de signo et signato. De signo, quia de effectu; de signato, quia de passione. In quo signatur quod non solum de bonis gratias reddere debemus, sed etiam de malis et adversis; I ad Thess. V, 18: *in omnibus gratias agentes*; ad Rom. VIII, 28: *diligentibus Deum omnia cooperantur in bonum*. Item gratias egit de institutione huius sacramenti, quia virtute divina hoc faciebat; unde in Io. c. V, 30: *a meipso facio nihil*. Ideo gratias agit Deo Patri; Io. XI, 41: *gratias ago tibi, quoniam audisti me*. In quo datur nobis exemplum quod si Christus gratias egit, qui erat Patri aequalis, quod nos gratias agere debemus. Item gratias agit de effectu, quia effectus est salus totius mundi. Et hoc non poterat facere nisi ex divinitate; Io. VI, 64: *Spiritus est qui vivificat, caro autem non prodest quicquam*.

2197. Sequitur *et dedit*, ut sumerent in sacramento. Et per hoc significavit quod fructus suae passionis debebat per alios aliis ministrari. Unde apostoli possunt comparari pullis aquilae, de quibus dicitur Deut. XXXII, v. 11: *sicut aquila provocans pullos suos ad volandum, et super eos volitans*.

2198. Tunc iniungit usum. Et

primo ponit usum;

secundo verba consecrationis sanguinis;

tertio resurrectionem praenuntiat.

2199. Dicit ergo *bibite ex hoc omnes*; Cant. V, 1: *bibite et inebriamini, carissimi*. Unde signatur quod Christiani possunt communicare loco et tempore.

2200. *Hic est enim sanguis meus* et cetera. Haec sunt verba consecrationis. Et notate quod in his verbis est differentia cum his quibus utitur Ecclesia. Ecclesia addit: *hic est calix*. Item ubi dicit, ***Novi Testamenti***, Ecclesia addit *Novi et aeterni Testamenti*. Item ubi dicit ***qui pro multis***, Ecclesia addit *qui pro vobis* et cetera. Unde ergo Ecclesia habet istam formam? Dicendum quod, sicut dicit Dionysius, non fuit intentio Evangelistarum tradere formas sacramentorum, sed eas tamquam secretas servare; unde non intendebant nisi historiam narrare. Unde ergo habet Ecclesia? A constitutione apostolorum. Unde dixit Paulus I Cor. XI, 34: *caetera cum venero, disponam*.

the whole is converted; and in this way it has to do with a mystery, that the Church's unity is contained in this sacrament.

2195. Likewise, when it says ***taking***, it signifies that he endured the passion voluntarily; hence, *I will take the chalice of salvation; and I will call upon the name of the Lord* (Ps 115:4).

2196. Likewise, ***he gave thanks***. And for what? For the sign, and for the thing signified. For the sign, ***he gave thanks*** for the effect; for the thing signified, ***he gave thanks*** for the passion. Which indicates that we should not only give thanks for good things, but for evils and adversities as well; *in all things give thanks* (1 Thess 5:18); *to those who love God, all things work together unto good* (Rom 8:28). Likewise, he gave thanks for the institution of this sacrament, because he brought this about by the divine power; hence, *I cannot of myself do anything* (John 5:30). This is why he gives thanks to God the Father; *Father, I give you thanks that you have heard me* (John 11:41). Which gives us an example, that if Christ gave thanks, who was equal to the Father, we should give thanks. Likewise, he gives thanks for the effect, because the effect is the salvation of the whole world. And he could only have brought this about by the divinity; *it is the Spirit that quickens: the flesh profits nothing* (John 6:64).

2197. There follows, ***and gave***, that they might receive him in the sacrament. And by this he signified that the fruit of his passion should be ministered to others through others. Hence the apostles can be compared to an eagle's young, of whom it says, *as the eagle enticing her young to fly, and hovering over them* (Deut 32:11).

2198. Then he enjoins its use. And

first, he sets out the use;

second, the words of the consecration of the blood;

third, he foretells the resurrection.

2199. He says therefore, ***drink, all of you, of this***. *Drink, and be inebriated, my dearly beloved* (Song 5:1). Hence it is signified that Christians can communicate in time and place.

2200. ***For this is my blood***. These are the words of consecration. And notice that there is a difference between these words and those which the Church uses. The Church adds, *this is the chalice*. Likewise, where he says, ***of the new testament***, the Church adds, *of the new and eternal testament*. And where he says, ***for many***, the Church adds *for you*. So where does the Church get this form from? One should say that, as Dionysius says, the evangelists did not intend to hand down the forms of the sacraments, but kept them as secrets; hence they meant only to recount the history. So where does the Church get it from? From the apostles' ordinance. Hence Paul said, *and the rest I will set in order, when I come* (1 Cor 11:34).

2201. But there is a question: why does he say, ***this is my body*** (Matt 26:26), or ***this is my blood***? Why does he not say, *this is converted into a body*, or *into blood*? But there are two reasons. The first is that the forms of the sacraments should signify what they effect. What they effect is that the bread be changed into the body of Christ; but the ultimate effect is that the body comes to be, and so the ultimate effect is what should be signified. Therefore, what should be signified is that this is the body, and not that the bread is converted into the body.

2202. Now, in this form there is one thing similar to the old, and another thing dissimilar.

They are similar in that, as is written, when Moses had written the law, he sacrificed bulls, and took the blood, and said: *this is the blood of the covenant which the Lord has made with you* (Exod 24:8). Thus this blood was offered for the salvation of the people. Hebrews says, *the high priest alone, once a year: not without blood, which he offers for his own, and the people's ignorance* (Heb 9:7).

But a difference shows up with regard to four things. First, in the fact that that was the blood of bulls, and this the blood of Christ; therefore this blood is efficacious for the remission of sins. *For if the blood of goats and of oxen, and the ashes of an heifer being sprinkled, sanctify such as are defiled, to the cleansing of the flesh: how much more will the blood of Christ . . . cleanse our conscience from dead works, to serve the living God?* (Heb 9:13–14). Likewise, that blood was called the blood of the testament, but this is called the testament. Again, 'testament' is taken commonly and properly. Commonly, it is taken to mean any given deed, because it used to be that witnesses were brought in for everything done. 'Testament' is said properly when something is written at death, in accord with what the Apostle says, that a testament is confirmed at the death of the one who made it (Heb 9:16). Either way of speaking fits here, for a covenant was made there, and it was made with blood, for in ancient times when they made a covenant of peace, they showed blood, and this is why it was called *the blood of the covenant*. Similarly, according as it is said with reference to the dead, in this way there was a certain pact between God and men in the old and in the new law, but in different ways. For the first one, namely the old law, was about temporal things, as it is clear that he promised them the land of the Amorites; this is why it was old, for it did not renew men, but rather aged them. But this testament is about heavenly things, and about lofty things. Hence above, ***do penance, for the kingdom of heaven is at hand*** (Matt 4:17). This is why he says, ***of the New Testament***, while it was said, *this is the blood of the covenant which the Lord has made with you concerning all these words* (Exod 24:8). *I will make a new covenant with the house of Israel, and with the house of Judah* (Jer 31:31).

Item pro morte competit; quia per mortem Christi confirmata est repromissio.

Item alia differentia, quia ista addit **Novi et aeterni Testamenti**, quod potest referri vel ad haereditatem aeternam, vel ad Christum, qui aeternus est. Alia differentia est, quia in illa habetur: *quod pepigit vobiscum*; unde ad illos solum restrictum est illud testamentum; sed istud etiam ad gentes, Is. c. LII, 15: *ipse asperget*, scilicet sanguine suo, *gentes multas*. **Pro multis**, et pro omnibus, quia si consideretur sufficientia, *ipse est propitiatio pro peccatis nostris; non pro nostris autem tantum, sed et pro totius mundi*. Sed si consideremus effectum, non habet effectum nisi in his qui salvantur, et hoc ex culpa hominum. Sed Ecclesia addit, *pro vobis*, idest apostolis, quia ipsi ministri sunt huius sanguinis, et per istos derivatur ad gentes.

Item ponitur **in remissionem peccatorum**, quia ille non poterat remittere peccata.

2203. Dico autem. Hic ponitur consolatio, secundum Chrysostomum. Quia fecerat mentionem de effusione sanguinis, per quem signatur passio, ideo consolatur eos, et praenuntiat gloriam suam. Et potest quatuor modis exponi. Exponit sic Chrysostomus, quod Dominus praenuntiaverat passionem, ideo vult eos laetificare. **Non bibam amodo de genimine vitis**, idest de vino, **usque in diem illum** et cetera. Hoc **regnum** appellat regnum resurrectionis. Tunc accepit regnum novum, idest novo modo. Quod post biberit cum eis patet Act. X.

Sed quare dicitur **novo** modo? Quia ante aliter comedit, et post; quia ante comedit ex necessitate, sed post resurrectionem non propter necessitatem, sed ut demonstraret resurrectionis veritatem.

Hieronymus dicit sic, quod per vineam signatur populus Iudaeorum; Is. V, 7: *vinea Domini exercituum domus Israel est*; Ier. II, v. 21: *ego plantavi te vineam electam, omne semen verum*.

Dico autem vobis quod amodo non bibam, idest non gaudebit anima mea de populo isto, **usque in illum diem, cum illud bibam vobiscum novum in regno patris mei. Regnum** signat praesentem Ecclesiam; **novum**, idest innovatum per fidem, quia tunc convertentur, et tunc gaudebo cum eis. Multi enim sunt conversi, et multi convertentur.

Remigius exponit sic, et dicit quod hoc referendum est ad caeremonias Paschales, idest: non celebrabo de caetero huiusmodi caeremonias usque ad statum Ecclesiae, cum gaudebo de innovatione Ecclesiae.

Hence, *for this is my blood of the New Testament*, in which you should have confidence; *having therefore, brethren, a confidence . . . by the blood of Christ* (Heb 10:19). Likewise, it befits the meaning of testament regarding the dead; for the promise was confirmed through Christ's death.

Likewise there is another difference, for this adds **of the New and eternal Testament**, which can be referred either to the eternal inheritance, or to Christ, who is eternal. Another difference is that in that one it says, *which the Lord has made with you*; hence that testament was restricted to those only, but this testament is also with the nations; *he will sprinkle*, namely with his blood, *many nations* (Isa 52:15). **For many** and for all, because if its sufficiency is considered, *he is the propitiation for our sins: and not for ours only, but also for those of the whole world* (1 John 2:2). But if we consider the effect, it has effect only on those who are saved, and this is due to men's fault. But the Church adds *for you*, i.e., the apostles, because they are the ministers of this blood, and it passes on through them to the nations.

Likewise, there is set down **unto remission of sins**, because the blood of the Old Testament could not remit sins.

2203. And I say. Here a consolation is set down, according to Chrysostom. For he had mentioned his blood being poured out, by which he indicated the passion, and so he consoles them, and foretells his glory. And it can be explained in four ways. Chrysostom explains it this way, that the Lord had foretold the passion, and so wanted to cheer them. *From this time forward, I will not drink of this fruit of the vine*, i.e., of wine, *until that day*. This **kingdom** names the day of the resurrection. At that time he received a new kingdom, i.e., in a new way. That he drank with them afterward is clear (Acts 9).

But why does it say, in a **new** way? Because he ate differently before and after: for before he ate out of necessity, but after the resurrection he ate not out of necessity but to demonstrate the truth of the resurrection.

Jerome speaks this way, that the vine signifies the Jewish people; *for the vineyard of the Lord of hosts is the house of Israel* (Isa 5:7); *yet I planted you a chosen vineyard, all true seed* (Jer 2:21).

And I say to you, from this time forward, I will not drink of this fruit of the vine, i.e., my soul will not rejoice over this people, ***until that day when I will drink it with you new in the kingdom of my Father***. The kingdom signifies the present Church; **new**, i.e., renewed through faith, because then they will be converted, and then I will rejoice with them. For many have converted, and many will be converted.

Remigius explains it this way, and says that this should be referred to the Paschal ceremonies, that is: I will not celebrate the other ceremonies of this sort until the establishment of the Church, when I will rejoice over the renewal of the Church.

Augustinus sic: in hoc quod dicit **novum**, opponitur veteri. Vetustas autem duplex est: poenae et culpae, et haec derivata est ab Adam, ut habetur ad Rom. V, 12 ss. Christus autem vetustatem habuit poenae, non culpae. Unde suum simplum solvit nostrum duplum. Dicit ergo **non bibam**, de vetustate poenae, **usque**, etc., quia depositurus erat corpus istud, et assumpsit in resurrectione corpus glorificatum, et promittit apostolis quod ipsi etiam assument. Et signat quod non sunt diversae naturae, quia corpus quod assumet, erit eiusdem naturae, sed alterius gloriae.

Augustine, this way: when he says, **new**, it is opposed to the old. Now, there are two sorts of oldness: that of punishment, and that of guilt, and this is passed down from Adam, as is said (Rom 5:12). Now, Christ had the oldness of punishment, not of guilt. Hence his simple unbound our double. He says therefore, *I will not drink* of the oldness of punishment *until that day when I will drink it with you new*, because he was going to lay aside that body, and take up the body glorified in the resurrection, and he promised the apostles that they also would take up their bodies again. And this signifies that they are not of a different nature, because the body which he will take up will be of the same nature, but of a different glory.

Lecture 5

26:30 Et hymno dicto exierunt in Montem Oliveti. [n. 2205]

26:30 Καὶ ὑμνήσαντες ἐξῆλθον εἰς τὸ ὄρος τῶν ἐλαιῶν.

26:30 And a hymn having been said, they went out to Mount Olivet. [n. 2205]

26:31 Tunc dicit illis Iesus: omnes vos scandalum patiemini in me in ista nocte. Scriptum est enim: *percutiam pastorem, et dispergentur oves gregis.* [n. 2207]

26:31 Τότε λέγει αὐτοῖς ὁ Ἰησοῦς· πάντες ὑμεῖς σκανδαλισθήσεσθε ἐν ἐμοὶ ἐν τῇ νυκτὶ ταύτῃ, γέγραπται γάρ· πατάξω τὸν ποιμένα, καὶ διασκορπισθήσονται τὰ πρόβατα τῆς ποίμνης.

26:31 Then Jesus said to them: you will all be scandalized in me this night. For it is written: *I will strike the shepherd, and the sheep of the flock will be dispersed.* [n. 2207]

26:32 Postquam autem resurrexero, praecedam vos in Galilaeam. [n. 2210]

26:32 μετὰ δὲ τὸ ἐγερθῆναί με προάξω ὑμᾶς εἰς τὴν Γαλιλαίαν.

26:32 But after I will be risen again, I will go before you into Galilee. [n. 2210]

26:33 Respondens autem Petrus ait illi: et si omnes scandalizati fuerint in te, ego numquam scandalizabor. [n. 2212]

26:33 ἀποκριθεὶς δὲ ὁ Πέτρος εἶπεν αὐτῷ· εἰ πάντες σκανδαλισθήσονται ἐν σοί, ἐγὼ οὐδέποτε σκανδαλισθήσομαι.

26:33 And Peter answering, said to him: although all will be scandalized in you, I will never be scandalized. [n. 2212]

26:34 Ait illi Iesus: amen dico tibi, quia in hac nocte, antequam gallus cantet, ter me negabis. [n. 2213]

26:34 ἔφη αὐτῷ ὁ Ἰησοῦς· ἀμὴν λέγω σοι ὅτι ἐν ταύτῃ τῇ νυκτὶ πρὶν ἀλέκτορα φωνῆσαι τρὶς ἀπαρνήσῃ με.

26:34 Jesus said to him: amen I say to you, that in this night, before the cock crows, you will deny me three times. [n. 2213]

26:35 Ait illi Petrus: etiamsi oportuerit me mori tecum, non te negabo. Similiter et omnes discipuli dixerunt. [n. 2215]

26:35 λέγει αὐτῷ ὁ Πέτρος· κἂν δέῃ με σὺν σοὶ ἀποθανεῖν, οὐ μή σε ἀπαρνήσομαι. ὁμοίως καὶ πάντες οἱ μαθηταὶ εἶπαν.

26:35 Peter said to him: even if I must die with you, I will not deny you. And in like manner said all the disciples. [n. 2215]

26:36 Tunc venit Iesus cum illis in villam quae dicitur Gethsemani, et dixit discipulis suis: sedete hic, donec vadam illuc, et orem. [n. 2216]

26:36 Τότε ἔρχεται μετ᾽ αὐτῶν ὁ Ἰησοῦς εἰς χωρίον λεγόμενον Γεθσημανὶ καὶ λέγει τοῖς μαθηταῖς· καθίσατε αὐτοῦ ἕως [οὗ] ἀπελθὼν ἐκεῖ προσεύξωμαι.

26:36 Then Jesus came with them into a country place which is called Gethsemane; and he said to his disciples: sit here, till I go over there and pray. [n. 2216]

26:37 Et adsumpto Petro et duobus filiis Zebedaei, coepit contristari et moestus esse. [n. 2220]

26:37 καὶ παραλαβὼν τὸν Πέτρον καὶ τοὺς δύο υἱοὺς Ζεβεδαίου ἤρξατο λυπεῖσθαι καὶ ἀδημονεῖν.

26:37 And taking with him Peter and the two sons of Zebedee, he began to grow sorrowful and to be sad. [n. 2220]

26:38 Tunc ait illis: tristis est anima mea usque ad mortem. Sustinete hic, et vigilate mecum. [n. 2224]

26:38 τότε λέγει αὐτοῖς· περίλυπός ἐστιν ἡ ψυχή μου ἕως θανάτου· μείνατε ὧδε καὶ γρηγορεῖτε μετ᾽ ἐμοῦ.

26:38 Then he said to them: my soul is sorrowful even unto death: stay here, and watch with me. [n. 2224]

26:39 Et progressus pusillum, procidit in faciem suam orans, et dicens: pater mi, si possibile est transeat a me calix iste: verumtamen non sicut ego volo, sed sicut tu. [n. 2229]

26:39 καὶ προελθὼν μικρὸν ἔπεσεν ἐπὶ πρόσωπον αὐτοῦ προσευχόμενος καὶ λέγων· πάτερ μου, εἰ δυνατόν ἐστιν, παρελθάτω ἀπ᾽ ἐμοῦ τὸ ποτήριον τοῦτο· πλὴν οὐχ ὡς ἐγὼ θέλω ἀλλ᾽ ὡς σύ.

26:39 And going a little further, he fell upon his face, praying, and saying: my Father, if it be possible, let this chalice pass from me. Nevertheless not as I will, but as you will. [n. 2229]

26:40 Et venit ad discipulos suos et invenit eos dormientes, et dicit Petro: sic non potuistis una hora vigilare mecum? [n. 2233]

26:40 καὶ ἔρχεται πρὸς τοὺς μαθητὰς καὶ εὑρίσκει αὐτοὺς καθεύδοντας, καὶ λέγει τῷ Πέτρῳ· οὕτως οὐκ ἰσχύσατε μίαν ὥραν γρηγορῆσαι μετ᾽ ἐμοῦ;

26:40 And he came to his disciples, and found them asleep, and he said to Peter: what? Could you not watch one hour with me? [n. 2233]

²⁶:⁴¹ Vigilate, et orate, ut non intretis in tentationem: spiritus quidem promptus est, caro autem infirma. [n. 2236]

²⁶:⁴² Iterum secundo abiit, et oravit dicens: Pater mi, si non potest hic calix transire nisi bibam illum, fiat voluntas tua. [n. 2238]

²⁶:⁴³ Et venit iterum, et invenit eos dormientes: erant enim oculi eorum gravati. [n. 2240]

²⁶:⁴⁴ Et relictis illis, iterum abiit, et oravit tertio, eundem sermonem dicens. [n. 2241]

²⁶:⁴⁵ Tunc venit ad discipulos suos, et dicit illis: dormite iam, et requiescite. Ecce appropinquavit hora, et Filius hominis traditur in manus peccatorum. [n. 2243]

²⁶:⁴⁶ Surgite, eamus. Ecce appropinquavit qui me tradet. [n. 2246]

²⁶:⁴¹ γρηγορεῖτε καὶ προσεύχεσθε, ἵνα μὴ εἰσέλθητε εἰς πειρασμόν· τὸ μὲν πνεῦμα πρόθυμον ἡ δὲ σὰρξ ἀσθενής.

²⁶:⁴² πάλιν ἐκ δευτέρου ἀπελθὼν προσηύξατο λέγων· πάτερ μου, εἰ οὐ δύναται τοῦτο παρελθεῖν ἐὰν μὴ αὐτὸ πίω, γενηθήτω τὸ θέλημά σου.

²⁶:⁴³ καὶ ἐλθὼν πάλιν εὗρεν αὐτοὺς καθεύδοντας, ἦσαν γὰρ αὐτῶν οἱ ὀφθαλμοὶ βεβαρημένοι.

²⁶:⁴⁴ καὶ ἀφεὶς αὐτοὺς πάλιν ἀπελθὼν προσηύξατο ἐκ τρίτου τὸν αὐτὸν λόγον εἰπὼν πάλιν.

²⁶:⁴⁵ τότε ἔρχεται πρὸς τοὺς μαθητὰς καὶ λέγει αὐτοῖς· καθεύδετε [τὸ] λοιπὸν καὶ ἀναπαύεσθε· ἰδοὺ ἤγγικεν ἡ ὥρα καὶ ὁ υἱὸς τοῦ ἀνθρώπου παραδίδοται εἰς χεῖρας ἁμαρτωλῶν.

²⁶:⁴⁶ ἐγείρεσθε ἄγωμεν· ἰδοὺ ἤγγικεν ὁ παραδιδούς με.

²⁶:⁴¹ Watch and pray that you do not enter into temptation. The spirit indeed is willing, but the flesh is weak. [n. 2236]

²⁶:⁴² Again the second time, he went and prayed, saying: my Father, if this chalice may not pass away, but I must drink it, your will be done. [n. 2238]

²⁶:⁴³ And he came again and found them sleeping: for their eyes were heavy. [n. 2240]

²⁶:⁴⁴ And leaving them, he went again: and he prayed the third time, saying the same word. [n. 2241]

²⁶:⁴⁵ Then he came to his disciples, and said to them: sleep now and take your rest; behold the hour is at hand, and the Son of man will be betrayed into the hands of sinners. [n. 2243]

²⁶:⁴⁶ Rise, let us go: behold he is at hand who will betray me. [n. 2246]

2204. Posita institutione novi sacramenti, hic praenuntiatur futurum scandalum discipulorum. Et

primo praemittitur locus;

secundo praenuntiatio, ibi *et dixit illis*.

Et hoc competit praemissis, et ei quod sequitur. Unde cum utroque potest ordinari.

2205. Dicit ergo *et hymno dicto*. Per hoc exemplum duorum nobis dat; quia primo fuit coena et prandium materiale, post quod gratias debemus reddere, et Deum laudare; Ps. XXI, 27: *edent pauperes, et saturabuntur, et laudabunt Dominum qui requirunt eum*. Item post istud fuit coena sacramentalis, post quam etiam debemus gratias agere. Unde post illud, hymnum dixit. Unde illud quod post communionem dicitur in Missa, repraesentat istum hymnum; ideo fideles debent expectare usque ad finem Missae ut hymnum istum audiant. Et hoc est quod Io. XVII, 1 dicitur: *Pater, clarifica Filium tuum, ut Filius tuus clarificet te*.

2206. Et hoc dicto *exierunt in Montem Oliveti*. Mons enim Oliveti pinguedinem significat, quia olivae pingues sunt; unde spiritualem pinguedinem significat. In Gen. XLIX, 20: *pinguis panis eius*. Unde signat pinguedinem gratiae et gloriae caelestis in quam provehitur; Ps. LXVII, 16: *mons domini mons pinguis*. Oleum membra fessa quietat, dolorem mitigat, igni pabulum et claritatem praestat. Sic erit in illa gloria, quia amovebitur omnis labor, omnis dolor; omnis aderit claritas.

2204. The institution of the new sacrament having been set down, here the disciples' future scandal is foretold. And first, the place is described;

second, the prediction, at *then Jesus said to them*.

And this fits both with what came before and with what follows it, so it can be set in order with either.

2205. It says therefore, *and a hymn having been said*. By this he gives us an example: for first came the meal, and the material dinner, after which we should give thanks, and praise God; *the poor will eat and will be filled: and they will praise the Lord who seek him* (Ps 21:27). And after that was the sacramental meal, after which we should also give thanks. Hence after that, he said a hymn. Hence what is called the post communion prayer in the Mass represents this hymn; for this reason, the faithful should wait until the end of Mass, so they can hear this hymn. And this is what is said, *Father . . . glorify your Son, that your Son may glorify you* (John 17:1).

2206. And this having been said, **they went out to Mount Olivet**. For Mount Olivet signifies richness, for olives are rich; hence it signifies spiritual richness. *His bread shall be fat* (Gen 49:20). Hence it signifies the richness of grace and heavenly glory into which one is carried; *the mountain of God is a fat mountain* (Ps 67:16). Oil soothes weary members, eases sorrow, and provides fodder and brightness to fire. So will it be in that glory, because all labor will be taken away, and every sorrow; every brilliance will be there.

Item, quod dicit, **in Montem Oliveti**, convenit praenuntiationi futurae. Per oleum misericordia signatur: sicut enim supernatat aliis liquoribus, sic misericordia; Ps. CXLIV, 9: *miserationes eius super omnia opera eius*. Item in monte scandalum ostendit, ut misericordia signetur praevia. *Cum ceciderit iustus, non collidetur, quia dominus supponit manum suam*, Ps. XXXVI, 24.

2207. Tunc dicit ... omnes vos scandalum patiemini in me. Hic ponitur scandalum. Et

primo in generali;

secundo in speciali, ibi **respondens autem Petrus**.

Circa primum duo facit.

Primo praenuntiat;

secundo ne videatur fortuitum, auctoritatem inducit, ibi **scriptum est enim: 'percutiam pastorem et dispergentur oves.'**

2208. Et in isto verbo aggravatur peccatum discipulorum ex multis. Primo ex universitate, **omnes vos**; Is. I, 6: *a planta pedis usque ad verticem capitis non est in eo sanitas* et cetera. Item materia tangitur **scandalum patiemini in me**; I ad Cor. I, 23: *nos praedicamus Christum crucifixum, Iudaeis quidem scandalum*. Iudaei, quia non quaerebant nisi infirmitatem carnis, scandalum passi sunt. Item aggravatur peccatum appropinquatione temporis, quia post tantas monitiones, post sacramenti susceptionem. Unde iam obliti erant quae fecerat eis; unde bene comparati sunt viro consideranti vultum nativitatis suae in speculo: *consideravit enim se, et abiit, et statim oblitus est qualis fuerit*, Iac. I, 24. Item quia in nocte, quia *qui ebrii sunt, et qui dormiunt, in nocte dormiunt*, I ad Thess. c. V, 7: sic etiam qui scandalizantur.

2209. Tunc subiungit auctoritatem: **scriptum est enim: 'percutiam pastorem et dispergentur oves.'** Et scribitur Zac. XIII, 7, et dicitur ibi: *percute pastorem*, scilicet Christum, *et dispergentur oves*; hic autem dicitur *'percutiam'*, et satis convenienter, quia propheta desiderabat quod istud fieret, ideo dixit, *percute pastorem*; sed Christus in propria persona loquitur; et in isto die praenuntiat primo passionem Christi; secundo scandalum, cum dicit *'percutiam pastorem'*. Iste pastor est Christus; Io. X, 11: *ego sum pastor bonus*. Et I Petr. II, 25: *conversi estis ad pastorem et episcopum animarum vestrarum*. Et iste percussus est, quia Deus tradidit eum, quia *proprio filio non pepercit*, Rom. VIII, 32: et hoc propter peccata nostra; Is. LIII, 8: *propter scelus populi mei percussi eum*.

Item praenuntiat scandalum *'et dispergentur oves.'* Oves sunt fideles; Io. X, 27: *oves meae vocem meam audiunt*. Et sic Deus passus est ut dispergerentur, ut post congregaret; Ps. CXLVI, 2: *dispersiones Israel congregabit*.

Likewise, when it says, **to Mount Olivet**, this pertains to a prediction of the future. Oil signifies mercy: for just as it floats above other liquids, so it is with mercy; *his tender mercies are over all his works* (Ps 144:9). Similarly, he described the scandal on a mountain, to signify mercy leading the way. *When he will fall he will not be bruised, for the Lord puts his hand under him* (Ps 36:24).

2207. Then Jesus said to them: you will all be scandalized in me. Here the scandal is set down. And

first, in general;

second, in particular, at **and Peter answering, said**.

Concerning the first, he does two things:

first, he predicts;

second, lest it seem to be a chance happening, he brings in an authority, at **for it is written: 'I will strike the shepherd, and the sheep of the flock will be dispersed.'**

2208. And in these words, the disciples' sin is made worse by many things. First, by universality, **you ... all**; *from the sole of the foot unto the top of the head, there is no soundness therein* (Isa 1:6). Likewise, the matter is touched upon: **will ... be scandalized in me**; *we preach Christ crucified, unto the Jews indeed a scandal* (1 Cor 1:23). The Jews, since they sought only the weakness of the flesh, were scandalized. Likewise, the sin is made worse by the time's drawing near, because it was after so many warnings, and after the reception of the sacrament. For they had already forgotten what he had done for them; hence they are well compared to a man looking at his own face in a mirror: *he beheld himself, and went his way, and presently forgot what manner of man he was* (Jas 1:24). Likewise because it was at night, for *they that sleep, sleep in the night; and they that are drunk, are drunk in the night* (1 Thess 5:7); so also those who are scandalized.

2209. Then he adds an authority: **for it is written: 'I will strike the shepherd, and the sheep of the flock shall be dispersed.'** And this is written in Zechariah, and it says there, *strike the shepherd*, namely Christ, *and the sheep will be scattered* (Zech 13:7); but here it says, *'I will strike'*, and fittingly enough, for the prophet desired that this should come about, and this is why he said, *strike the shepherd*; but Christ speaks in his own person. And on that day he predicts first Christ's passion, second the scandal, when he says, *'I will strike the shepherd.'* This shepherd is Christ; *I am the good shepherd* (John 10:11). And, *you are now converted to the shepherd and bishop of your souls* (1 Pet 2:25). And he was struck, because God handed him over, for *he who spared not even his own Son* (Rom 8:32). And this was on account of our sins; *for the wickedness of my people have I struck him* (Isa 53:8).

Likewise, he predicts the scandal: *'and the sheep of the flock will be dispersed.'* The sheep are the faithful; *my sheep hear my voice* (John 10:27). And thus God suffered that they might be scattered, that afterward they might be

Io. X, 16: *alias oves habeo quae non sunt ex hoc ovili, et illas oportet me adducere.*

2210. Tunc praenuntiat gaudia resurrectionis *postquam autem resurrexero, praecedam vos in Galilaeam*; quia licet Pater resuscitaverit eum, sicut alibi dicitur, Act. II, v. 24: *quem Deus suscitavit, solutis doloribus inferni*, tamen propria virtute surrexit, quia virtus Patris est virtus Filii; II ad Cor. ult., 4: *sed si crucifixus est propter infirmitatem nostram, vivit tamen ex virtute Dei.* Item contra illud quod dixerat quod *dispergentur oves*, dicit *praecedam vos in Galilaeam*. Oves enim sequuntur pastorem: unde pastor congregat vocando eas nominatim; ideo dicit *praecedam*.

Vel potest referri ad illud quod dicit *postquam resurrexero*. Quia possent aliqui credere quod multum esset tempus usque ad resurrectionem suam, ideo dixit quod non multum, quia *praecedam vos in Galilaeam*. Consuetudo eius erat quod parum moraretur in Iudaea, sed cito transibat in Galilaeam. Vult ergo dicere: ante resurgam quam possitis venire in Galilaeam, ut ostenderet se esse illum, qui apparebit eis. Ideo satis potuerunt certificari. Item quod dicit quod praecedet, securitatem dat. Quia in Iudaea persecutionem patiebantur, ideo dicit quod praecedet in Galilaeam, ut removeat eos a timore.

Et dicit Chrysostomus quod non est intelligendum quod primo apparuerit in Galilaea: sed hic apparuit, sed non primo, immo in Ierusalem. Quare ergo magis dicit *in Galilaeam*? *Galilaea* interpretatur 'transmigratio': unde significatur quod per resurrectionem transibimus a vita mortali ad immortalem: et in ista nos praecessit, quia Christus est primitiae dormientium. Item signatur transmigratio discipulorum ad gentes: et in hoc Christus praecessit, corda movendo.

2211. *Respondens autem Petrus.* Hic ponitur praenuntiatio de scandalo Petri. Et

primo ponitur occasio;
secundo praenuntiatio;
tertio excusatio.

Secunda ibi *ait ei Iesus* etc.; tertia ibi *ait ei Petrus* et cetera.

2212. Hic est quaestio litteralis; quia videtur quod Petrus hoc dixerit postquam recessissent de coenaculo; sed Lucas XXII, 34-39 videtur dicere quod antequam recessissent, et huic consonat Ioannes XIII, 36-38.

Augustinus solvit quod Petrus hoc ter dixit, et sic concordant omnes etc., quia si consideremus narrationem, ex pluribus causis hoc dicit. Hic motus fuit ex hoc quod scandalum praenuntiavit. Lc. XXII, 32 dixerat Dominus: *ego pro te rogavi, Petre, ut non deficiat fides*

gathered together; *he will gather together the dispersed of Israel* (Ps 146:2). *And other sheep I have, that are not of this fold: them also I must bring* (John 10:16).

2210. Then he predicts the joy of the resurrection: *but after I will be risen again, I will go before you into Galilee*; for although the Father raised him up, as is said in another place, *whom God has raised up, having loosed the sorrows of hell* (Acts 2:24), yet he arose by his own power, because the Father's power is the Son's power; *for although he was crucified through weakness, yet he lives by the power of God* (2 Cor 13:4). Similarly, against what he had said, that *the sheep would be scattered*, he says, *I will go before you into Galilee*. For sheep follow the shepherd: hence the shepherd gathers them together by calling them by name (John 10:3). This is why he says, *I will go before*.

Or it can be referred to when he says, *after I will be risen again*. For some could think that there would be a long time before his resurrection, so he said that it would not be long, because *I will go before you into Galilee*. For his custom was that he would stay a little while in Judea, but quickly cross over into Galilee. So he wishes to say: I will rise before you can come into Galilee, that he might show that he is the one who will appear to them. So they were well enough able to be certain. Likewise, when he says that he will go before, it gives them security, for they suffered persecution in Judea. So he says that he will go before them into Galilee, to remove their fear.

And Chrysostom says that one should not understand this to mean that he first appeared in Galilee: he appeared there, but not first, but rather in Jerusalem. So why does he say rather *into Galilee*? *Galilee* means 'transmigration,' so it signifies that through the resurrection we will pass over from mortal life to immortal: and he went before us in this, because Christ is the first fruits of those who sleep (1 Cor 15:20). Also, it signifies the transmigration of the disciples to the gentiles: and Christ went before them in this, by moving hearts.

2211. *And Peter answering, said.* Here the prediction of Peter's scandal is set down. And

first, the occasion is set down;
second, the prediction;
third, an excuse.

The second is at *Jesus said to him: amen I say to you*; the third, at *Peter said to him: even if I must die*.

2212. Here there is a literal question, for it seems that Peter said this after they had left the upper room, but Luke seems to say that it was before they had left (Luke 22:34-39); and John agrees with this (John 13:36-38).

Augustine resolves it by saying that Peter said this three times, and all agree, for if we consider the story, he said this for more than one reason. Here he was moved by the fact that he predicted scandal. The Lord had said, *but I have prayed for you, that your faith fail not*, and then Peter said,

tua, et tunc dixit Petrus: *Domine, tecum paratus sum et in carcerem, et in mortem ire*. Sed in Io. dictum est alia de causa; quia Io. XIII, 33 dixit Dominus: *quo ego vado, vos non potestis venire modo*. Tunc dixit Petrus: *animam meam ponam pro te*. Ideo ter dixit; ideo potest esse quod bis dixerit in coenaculo, sed semel dixit extra, sicut hic dicitur. Et potest esse quod ex fervore dicebat, et non considerabat virtutes suas.

Tamen in tribus deliquit. Primo quia non plus Domino credidit quam sibi, cum tamen scriptum sit ad Rom. III, 4: *solus Deus verax, omnis homo mendax*. Item quia praetulit se aliis; unde dixit **et si omnes scandalizati fuerint in te, ego numquam scandalizabor**. Unde reputabat se aliis firmiorem; et incidit in illud quod dicitur Lc. XVIII, 11: *non sum sicut caeteri hominum* et cetera. Item quia attribuebat sibi quod non debebat, cum scriptum sit Io. XV, 5: *sine me nihil potestis facere*. Quia ergo arroganter locutus est, ideo magis permisit eum cadere. Et hoc facit Deus, quia multum odit Deus superbiam; Iob XL, 6: *et respiciens omnem arrogantem humiliat*.

2213. *Ait illi Iesus: amen dico tibi, quia in hac nocte antequam gallus cantet, ter me negabis*. Quia putare poteras quod dicerem comminatorie, ideo **dico tibi, amen**, idest corde tibi dico, quia **antequam gallus in hac nocte cantet, ter me negabis**. Et aggravatur eius culpa ex propinquitate temporis, quia **in hac nocte**. Item ex multitudine, quia **ter**: sicut ter praesumpserat, ita ter negavit post praesumptionem; Iob XXXI, 27: *si laetatum est in abscondito cor meum*.

2214. Sed quaestio est de hoc **antequam gallus cantet, ter me negabis**; quia in Mc. XIV, 30 habetur quod *antequam gallus bis vocem dederit*. Secundum Augustinum potest solvi quod secundum historiam verum est quod Marcus dicit. Et quod Matthaeus dicit, potest sic solvi, quod homo dicitur facere quando facit in proposito, sicut supra V, 28: **qui viderit mulierem ad concupiscendum eam, moechatus est eam in corde suo**. Sic Petrus in suo proposito negavit ter, vel etiam pluries; ex quo timorem concepit quod sufficiens erat ad negandum ter vel pluries; ideo dicit quod ter negavit quia iam conceperat se ter vel pluries negaturum. Unde Matthaeus dixit quod interius intendebat; sed Marcus quod exterius gessit.

Vel potest aliter dici quod quando dico: ego faciam istud infra tale tempus tunc non oportet quod in illo factum sit, sed sufficit quod inceptum fuerit. Unde quod dixit quod ter esset negaturus, non oportebat quod ante galli cantum completum esset, sed inchoatum.

2215. Sequitur excusatio Petri *ait ei Petrus* et cetera. Excusat se Petrus **quia si oportuerit me mori tecum, non**

Lord, I am ready to go with you, both into prison, and to death (Luke 22:32). But in John it was said for a different reason, for the Lord said, *where I go you cannot come; so I say to you now* (John 13:33). Then Peter said, *I will lay down my life for you*. Therefore he spoke three times; so it could be that he spoke twice in the upper room, but spoke once outside, as is said here. And it could be that he spoke out of fervor, and did not consider his own strength.

Yet he fell short in three things. First, because he did not believe the Lord more than himself, while yet it is written, *God is true; and every man a liar* (Rom 3:4). Again, because he put himself before the others; hence he said, **although all will be scandalized in you, I will never be scandalized**. So he considered himself stronger than the others, and fell into what is said, *I am not as the rest of men* (Luke 18:11). Again, because he attributed to himself what he should not have, since it is written, *without me you can do nothing* (John 15:5). Since therefore he spoke arrogantly, the Lord permitted him to fall more. And God did this because God greatly hates the proud; *behold every arrogant man, and humble him* (Job 40:6).

2213. *Jesus said to him: amen I say to you, that in this night before the cock crows, you will deny me three times*. For you could have thought that he spoke threateningly, so **Amen I say to you**, i.e., I speak to you with the heart, **that in this night before the cock crows, you will deny me three times**. And his guilt is made worse by the time's drawing near, because it was **this night**. Also, by number, **three**: just as he had been presumptuous three times, so he denied Christ three times after the presumption; *and my heart in secret has rejoiced* (Job 31:27).

2214. But there is a question about this **before the cock crows, you will deny me three times**, because it says, *before the cock crows twice* (Mark 14:30). According to Augustine, it can resolved by saying that according to history, what Mark says is true. And what Matthew says can be resolved in this way, that a man is said to do something when he does it in intention, as above, **whoever will look on a woman to lust after her, has already committed adultery with her in his heart** (Matt 5:28). Thus Peter in his intention denied the Lord three times, or even many times; for he had conceived a fear sufficient for denying three times or more; this is why it says he denied Christ three times, because he had already decided that he would deny three times or more. Hence Matthew said what he intended interiorly, but Mark what he did exteriorly.

Or in another way, it can be said that when I say: I will do this thing before such a time, it is not necessary that it be done at that time, but rather it is enough that it has begun. So when he said that he would deny him three times, it was not necessary that it be finished before the cock's crow, but only that it be started.

2215. There follows Peter's excuse: *Peter said to him*. Peter excuses himself: **even if I must die with you, I will not**

te negabo. Et tamen timuit, quia ad vocem ancillae negavit. Hieronymus dicit quod nescivit quid diceret, quia solus Christus moriturus erat, ut solus esset redemptor; Is. LXIII, 3: *torcular calcavi solus*.

Deinde ponit affirmationem, scilicet aliorum *similiter et omnes discipuli dixerunt*. Unde dixerunt sicut et Petrus; tamen alii meliorem causam habebant quam Petrus se excusandi, quia alii sine assertione.

2216. *Tunc venit Iesus in villam quae dicitur Gethsemani*. In ista parte ponitur praeparatio, quae est per orationem; et tria facit.

Primo proponitur propositum orandi;
secundo necessitas orandi;
tertio differentia.
Secunda ibi *et assumpto Petro* etc.; tertia ibi *et progressus pusillum procidit in faciem suam*.

Circa primum duo facit.
Primo ponitur locus;
secundo praenuntiat propositum *et dixit discipulis suis*.

2217. Dicit ergo *tunc venit Iesus in villam quae dicitur Gethsemani*. Contrarium videtur quod dicitur in Io. XVIII, 1, quod *egressus Iesus venit trans torrentem Cedron*. Unde notandum quod villa illa erat in pede Montis Oliveti, unde idem erat locus; et veniebat ibi post coenam quasi ad spatiandum.

2218. Tunc praenuntiat propositum orandi *et dixit discipulis suis: sedete hic donec vadam illuc, et orem*. Simile habetur Gen. XXII, 5: dixit Abraham ad pueros suos: *expectate hic cum asino, et ego et puer illuc usque properantes, postquam adoraverimus, revertemur ad vos*.

Sed hic movet Damascenus quaestionem. Oratio est ascensus in Deum, intellectus autem Christi coniunctus erat Deo, quomodo ergo indigebat Deus qui faciebat?

Unde dicatur quod ipse orabat non propter se, sed propter nostram utilitatem. Et haec duplex est, quia oravit ut daret nobis exemplum, ut in tribulatione recurramus ad Dominum; Ps. CXIX, 1: *ad Dominum cum tribularer clamavi*. Item ut ostenderet se esse ab alio, et quod ab alio habebat; unde dicit: *non potest Filius a seipso facere quidquam*. Et ibid. VIII, 28: *ego a meipso facio nihil*. Item ad excludendum errorem, quia dicebant aliqui quod non esset eadem virtus Patris et Filii; Io. VIII, 49: *ego honorifico Patrem meum*.

2219. Dat ergo exemplum orandi, et quomodo sit orandum. Prima enim conditio orationis est quia debet

deny you. And yet he was afraid, for he denied Christ at the voice of a maidservant. Jerome says that he knew not what he was saying, because Christ alone was going to die, that he alone might be the redeemer; *I have trodden the winepress alone* (Isa 63:3).

Next he sets down an affirmation, namely the others': *and in like manner said all the disciples*. Hence they spoke as Peter did; yet the others had better cause for excusing themselves than Peter, because the others excused themselves without an assertion.

2216. *Then Jesus came with them into a country place which is called Gethsemani*. In this part he sets down the preparation, which is through prayer; and he does three things:
first, the intention of praying is set down;
second, the need for prayer;
third, a difference.
The second is at *and taking with him Peter, and the two sons of Zebedee*; the third, at *and going a little further, he fell upon his face*.

Concerning the first, he does two things:
first, the place is set down;
second, he declares his intention: *and he said to his disciples*.

2217. It says therefore, *then Jesus came with them into a country place which is called Gethsemani*. What is said in John seems contrary, that *Jesus went forth . . . over the brook Cedron* (John 18:1). Hence one should note that this village was at the foot of Mount Olivet, so it was the same place; and he came there after the meal as though to take a walk.

2218. Then he declares his intention of praying: *and he said to his disciples: sit here, till I go over there and pray*. A similar thing is found in Genesis, *and he said to his young men: stay you here with the ass: I and the boy will go with speed as far as there, and after we have worshipped, will return to you* (Gen 22:5).

But here Damascene raises a question. Prayer is an ascent into God, but Christ's intellect was conjoined to God; how then was God, who did this, in need?

So let it be said that he did not pray for his own sake, but for our benefit. And this benefit is twofold, for he prayed in order to give us an example, that in affliction we may have recourse to the Lord; *in my trouble I cried to the Lord* (Ps 119:1). Likewise, to show that he was from another, and that he had everything from another; hence he says, *the Son cannot do any thing of himself* (John 5:19). And in the same book, *I do nothing of myself* (John 8:28). Likewise, to exclude an error, for some said that the Father's power and the Son's power are not the same; *I honor my Father, and you have dishonoured me* (John 8:49).

2219. Therefore he gives an example of praying, and how one should pray. For the first condition for prayer is

esse humilis oratio: quod signatur quia ivit in vallem; Iudith IX, v. 16: *humilium et mansuetorum semper tibi placuit deprecatio*. Item debet esse devota; unde in Gethsemani, scilicet in 'villa pinguedinis'; Ps. LXII, 6: *sicut adipe et pinguedine repleatur anima mea*. Item quod sit solitaria, sicut supra VI, 6: **intra in cubiculum tuum, et clauso ostio ora patrem tuum**.

2220. *Et assumpto Petro, et duobus filiis Zebedaei* et cetera. Hic praenuntiat necessitatem orationis: et haec erat tristitia. Et

primo ponit testes tristitiae;
secundo ostendit tristitiam;
tertio repellit.

Secunda ibi *coepit contristari et maestus esse*; tertia ibi *sustinete hic et vigilate mecum*.

2221. Dicit ergo *et assumpto Petro, et duobus filiis Zebedaei* et cetera. Tres secum assumpsit. Et quare istos prae aliis? Una ratio, quia isti firmiores erant, et quia omnes scandalizabat infirmitas, ideo magis istis infirmitatem suam voluit monstrare quam aliis. Item ostenderat eis gloriam; ideo volebat quod sicut viderant gloriam, ita viderent infirmitatem, ut cognoscerent quod nec infirmitas gloriam, nec gloria absorberet infirmitatem.

2222. Sequitur ostensio infirmitatis. Et primo facto; secundo verbo.

Et secundum hoc tria facit: quia
primo dicit secundum quae Christus tristatus est;
secundo quare tristatus est;
tertio quomodo tristatus sit.

2223. Quoad primum *coepit contristari et moestus esse*. Hic cavendi sunt duo errores; quia quidam dixerunt quod tristatus est secundum divinitatem: et hoc non potest esse, quia tristatus est quia passibilis erat, sed divinitas non erat passibilis. Item opinio Arianorum, alias Eunomii, erat quod in Christo non erat anima, sed Verbum loco animae. Et quare hoc dicebat? Ut omnia quae ad defectum pertinent, ad Verbum referrentur, ut ostenderetur minor Patre. Et hoc falsum est. Ideo passus est secundum quod pati potuit, idest secundum animam.

2224. *Tunc ait illis: tristis est anima mea usque ad mortem* et cetera. Non dicit: ego sum tristis, quia ego est ostensivum personae, sed non tristabatur inquantum Verbum, sed secundum animam, ideo excluditur error et Arii, et Apollinaris; item Manichaei, qui ponit eum non vere passum. Unde patet secundum quod tristatus est.

2225. Sed quare tristatus est? Diversa sunt verba sanctorum. Quia Hilarius et multi alii dixerunt quod non tristatus est propter se, nec propter mortem suam,

that it should be a humble prayer, which is indicated because he went into a valley; *the prayer of the humble and the meek has always pleased you* (Jude 9:16). Likewise, it should be devoted; hence he was in Gethsemani, namely in the 'valley of richness'; *let my soul be filled as with marrow and fatness* (Ps 62:6). Likewise, that it be solitary, as above, **enter into your chamber, and, having shut the door, pray to your Father in secret** (Matt 6:6).

2220. *And taking with him Peter and the two sons of Zebedee*. Here he declares the need for prayer: and this was sorrow. And

first, he sets down a witness of the sorrow;
second, he describes the sorrow;
third, he pushes back the disciples.

The second is at **he began to grow sorrowful and to be sad**; the third, at **stay you here, and watch with me**.

2221. It says therefore, **and taking with him Peter and the two sons of Zebedee**. He took three men with him. And why those rather than the others? One reason is because they were stronger, and since weakness scandalized all of them, he willed to show his weakness to these rather than to the others. Likewise, he had shown them glory; so he wished that, as they had seen glory, so they should see weakness, that they might know that neither did the weakness swallow up the glory, nor the glory the weakness.

2222. There follows the description of the weakness. And first, by deed; second, by word.

And in accord with this, he does three things, for
first, he says according to what things Christ sorrowed;
second, why he sorrowed;
third, how he sorrowed.

2223. With regard to the first, **he began to grow sorrowful and to be sad**. There are two errors to be avoided here. For some have said that he sorrowed according to the divinity; and this cannot be, because he sorrowed because he was passible, but the divinity was not passible. Also, the opinion of the Arians, and at another time the Eunomians, was that there was no soul in Christ, but the Word in place of a soul. And why did they say this? So that they could refer everything having to do with defect to the Word, to show that he was less than the Father. And this is false. Therefore he suffered according as he was able to suffer, i.e., according to his soul.

2224. **Then he said to them: my soul is sorrowful even unto death**. He does not say: *I am sorrowful*, because 'I' points to the person, but he did not sorrow insofar as he was the Word, but according to his soul; therefore the error of Arius and of Apollinaris is excluded; likewise the error of Manichaeus, who held that he did not truly suffer. Hence what he suffered according to is clear.

2225. But why did he sorrow? The sayings of the saints are different. For Hilary and many others have said that he did not sorrow on his own account, nor on account of his

sed propter scandalum discipulorum: et hoc vult probare per hoc quod assumpsit eos. Damascenus dicit quod tristabatur pro seipso. Et quare? Quia tristitia inest ex hoc quod caremus eo quod naturaliter amamus. Anima naturaliter vult uniri corpori, et istud fuit in anima Christi, quia comedit, et bibit, et esuriit. Ergo separatio erat contra naturale desiderium: ergo separari erat ei triste. Tamen possumus intelligere quod aliquid inest animae secundum se, et aliquid inest animae per comparationem ad aliud: sicut amara potio, secundum se considerata, dolorosa est, sed relata ad finem nostrae salutis, est causa gaudii. Sicut aliquid est rationis ut natura est, et aliquid rationis inquantum ratio: sic ista mors Christi erat materia tristitiae secundum quod considerabatur secundum se; sed secundum quod referebatur ad rationem, referendo ad finem, sic gaudebat. Ideo verba Hilarii et Hieronymi intelliguntur referendo ad finem.

2226. Item quaeritur quomodo tristitia cadit in Christo.

Ideo notandum quod quandoque tristitia accidit secundum passionem, aliquando secundum propassionem. Secundum passionem, quando aliquid patitur et immutatur: sed quando patitur, et non immutatur, tunc habet propassionem. Sed quandoque huiusmodi sunt in nobis, ita quod ratio immutatur, et tunc passiones sunt completae: quando autem ratio non immutatur, tunc est propassio. Sed in Christo numquam fuit ratio immutata; ideo fuit propassio, et non passio. Unde signanter dicit Evangelista *coepit tristari*. Item dicit Augustinus quod nos habemus tristitiam ut contractam, Christus autem ut assumptam: illud enim contrahitur quod nascendo per originem habetur, sed Christus assumpsit naturam nostram ut voluit; ideo non fuit necessitas quod passibilitatem acciperet, ut tristitiam, sed a voluntate. Item notandum quod dicit Damascenus, quia in nobis motus passionum praevenit rationem, quia aliquando est in nobis passio, et aliquando propassio; in Christo autem non fuit nisi propassio, et numquam fuit in Christo, quod motus insurgeret in inferioribus viribus animae, immo suberant totaliter inferiores vires rationi, et quando volebat, permittebat agere inferiores vires secundum quod eis erat naturale. Ideo alius Evangelista dixit quod *turbavit seipsum*, quia isti motus non potuissent accidisse nisi secundum quod voluit.

2227. *Tunc ait illis: tristis est anima mea usque ad mortem*. Notate quod dicit, *usque ad mortem*, per quam satisfaciam pro isto scandalo et pro aliis. Vel secundum aliam expositionem: non credatis quod in perpetuum debeat durare, quia quamdiu corpus erit passibile, et hoc est usque ad mortem, *tristis est anima mea*, et tunc glorificabitur.

death, but on account of the disciples' scandal: and he would prove this by the fact that he took them with him. Damascene says that he sorrowed for himself. And why? Because sorrow is present by the fact that we lack what we naturally love. The soul naturally desires to be united to the body, and this desire was in Christ's soul, for he ate, and drank, and hungered. Therefore the separation was contrary to natural desire: therefore to be separated was sorrowful for it. Yet we can understand that a thing can be present in the soul according to itself, and a thing can be present in the soul by comparison to another: just as a bitter drink, considered in itself, is sorrowful, but related to the end of our health, it is a cause of joy. As a thing can belong to reason as nature, and another thing can belong to reason insofar as it is reason, so Christ's death was a matter for sorrow according as it was considered in itself, but according as it was referred to reason, by referring it to the end, in this way he rejoiced. So the sayings of Hilary and Jerome are understood by referring to the end.

2226. Likewise, it is asked how sorrow occurred in Christ.

Therefore one should note that sometimes sorrow happens according to passion, sometimes according to propassion. According to passion, when a thing suffers and is changed; but when it suffers and is not changed, then it has propassion. But sometimes these sort of things are in us such that reason is changed, and then the passions are perfected: but when reason is not changed, then it is propassion. But in Christ, reason was never changed; therefore it was propassion, and not passion. Hence the evangelist says meaningfully, *he began to grow sorrowful*. Similarly, Augustine says that we have sorrow as imposed, but Christ as assumed: for that which is had through origin, by being born, is imposed, but Christ assumed our nature as he willed. Therefore it was not a necessity that he take on a passibility, such as sorrow, but voluntary. Likewise, one should note what Damascene says, that in us the motion of passion comes before reason, because sometimes passion is in us, sometimes propassion; but in Christ there was only propassion, and it never happened in Christ that a motion arose rebelliously in the lower powers of the soul, but on the contrary the lower powers were entirely subject to reason, and when he willed, he permitted the lower powers to act in accord with what was natural to them. This is why the other evangelist said that he *troubled himself* (John 11:33), because that motion could only have happened according as he willed it.

2227. *Then he said to them: my soul is sorrowful even unto death*. Note that he says, *even unto death*, through which I will satisfy for this scandal and for others. Or according to another explanation: do not think that it should endure forever, because as long as the body is passible, and this is until death, *my soul is sorrowful*, and then it will be glorified.

2228. Deinde excludit alios *sustinete hic, et vigilate mecum*.

2229. *Et progressus pusillum procidit in faciem suam orans et dicens*. Supra tetigit causam tristitiae, hic autem agit de ordine orationis Christi. Et quia ter oravit, ideo dividitur haec pars in tres partes secundum tres orationes.

Et circa primum duo facit.

Primo ponit orationem orantis;

secundo increpat discipulorum defectum, ibi *et venit ad discipulos* et cetera.

Et in prima

primo ponit conditionem orantis;

secundo tenorem orationis.

2230. Triplex autem conditio commendatur quia primo notat sollicitudinem, secundo humilitatem, tertio devotionem.

Sollicitudinem, quia *progressus pusillum*, quia etiam ab illis quos elegerat se separavit; supra VI, 6: *cum oraveris, intra in cubiculum tuum, et clauso ostio ora patrem tuum in abscondito*. Sed notate quod non multum, sed pusillum, ut notaret quod non longe est ab invocantibus eum; Ps. CXLIV, 18: *prope est Dominus omnibus invocantibus*. Item, ut viderent eum orantem, et formam acciperent.

Ideo sequitur humilitas *et procidit in faciem suam*, unde exemplum humilitatis ostendit. Et primo propter humilitatem communem, quia humilitas necessaria est ad orationem; Eccli. XXXV, 21: *oratio humiliantis se nubes penetrabit*. Item propter humilitatem specialem, scilicet Petri, quia dixerat: *si oportuerit me mori tecum, non te negabo*. Ideo Dominus procidit, ut signaret quod non debebat de sua virtute confidere; supra XI, 29: *discite a me, quia mitis sum et humilis corde*.

Item signatur conditio pietatis, sive devotionis, cum dicit *Pater mi*; necessarium enim est oranti ut ex devotione oret, unde dicitur *Pater mi*, quia ipse singulariter Filius, nos autem per adoptionem; Io. ult., 17: *ascendo ad Patrem meum et Patrem vestrum*; quasi *aliter meum et aliter vestrum*.

2231. Consequenter tenorem orationis subiungit: *si possibile est, transeat a me calix iste*. Ista oratio tripliciter potest exponi et quocumque modo exponatur, duo sunt consideranda.

Primo considerare debetis in communi quantum ad omnes, quia, secundum Damascenum, oratio est ascensus mentis in Deum: unde oratio est secundum mentem, vel secundum superiorem rationem; sed tamen infra Deum constitutam, supra tamen humanam naturam, vel sub divina voluntate. Quid ergo debet intelligi? Secundum quod est cum superior ratio descendit ad ista, inquantum decet, tamen quod semper subdatur rationi

2228. Then he excludes the others: *stay here, and watch with me*.

2229. *And going a little further, he fell upon his face, praying, and saying*. Above, he touched on the cause of the sorrow, and here he treats of the order of Christ's prayer. And since Christ prayed three times, this part is divided into three parts, according to the three prayers.

And concerning the first, he does two things:

first, he sets down the prayer of the one praying;

second, he reproaches the disciples' failure, at, *and he came to his disciples*.

And in the first,

first, he sets down the condition of the one praying;

second, the tenor of the prayer.

2230. Now, he points out three conditions, for first he notes solicitude, second humility, third devotion.

Solicitude, at *going a little further*, because he separated himself even from those whom he had chosen; above, *enter into your chamber, and, having shut the door, pray to your Father in secret* (Matt 6:6). But notice that he does not go much further, but a little, that one may notice that he is not far off from those who call upon him; *the Lord is near unto all those who call upon him* (Ps 144:18). Also, that they might see him praying, and receive the form.

So there follows humility: *he fell upon his face*, by which he showed an example of humility. And first, for the sake of common humility, for humility is necessary for prayer; *the prayer of him who humbles himself, will pierce the clouds* (Sir 35:21). Also for the sake of a particular humility, namely Peter's, because he had said, *even if I must die with you, I will not deny you*. So the Lord fell down, to signify that he should not confide in his own strength; above, *learn of me, because I am meek, and humble of heart* (Matt 11:29).

Likewise, the condition of piety or devotion is indicated, when he says, *my Father*. For it is necessary for one who prays that he pray out of devotion; hence it says, *my Father*, for he himself is a Son in a singular way, and we through adoption; *I ascend to my Father and to your Father* (John 20:17), as though to say, *mine in one way and yours in another*.

2231. Next he adds the tenor of the prayer: *if it be possible, let this chalice pass from me*. This prayer can be explained in three ways, and whatever way it is explained, there are two things to be considered.

You should consider the first thing in common with regard to all, for, according to Damascene, prayer is the ascent of the mind into God: hence prayer is according to the mind, or according to the higher reason; but although it holds a place below God, yet it is above human nature, or under the divine will. So what should be understood? Insofar as it is with the superior reason he descends to it, as far as is fitting, yet such that it is always subject to the divine

divinae; et hoc notatur cum dicitur ***verumtamen non sicut ego volo, sed sicut tu***; quia superior ratio sequitur voluntatem naturae, non tamen simpliciter, idest, si relata superiori, non repugnat. Unde vult dicere: volo quod impleatur quod volo si non repugnat tuae iustitiae, sed volo tuam iustitiam impleri.

Et in hoc docet exemplum qualiter affectiones debemus ordinare, quia ita debemus ordinare, quod non a regula divina dissonent. Unde non est grave quod aliquis, quod grave est naturae, refugit, dum tamen ordinet ad voluntatem divinam.

2232. Item potest exponi, secundum Chrysostomum et Origenem, ita quod per calicem significetur passio Christi, de quo in Ps. CXV, 13: *calicem salutaris accipiam*, et cetera. Constat quod Christus habuit naturalem hominis voluntatem; hoc autem est quod mortem refugiat: ideo, ut hominem se ostendat, petit transire calicem a se; et haec est ita naturalis, quod petitionem non amovit ab eo. Item dixit ***si possibile est, transeat calix***, idest passio: sed non absolute dico, sed si possibile. Et quia posset aliquis credere quod dubitaret an esset Deo possibile, ideo ostendit quod est possibile, quia *omnia tibi possibilia sunt*, Mc. XIV, 36.

Verumtamen non sicut ego volo, sed sicut tu, idest si congruit iustitiae tuae, volo; ideo dicit ***non sicut ego volo***. Unde duas tangit voluntates: unam quam habebat a Patre inquantum Deus; unam qua habebat cum Patre. Et in hoc confunditur error multorum. Item aliam voluntatem inquantum homo: et istam voluntatem in omnibus submittebat Patri; in hoc dans nobis exemplum, quod voluntatem nostram voluntati Dei submittamus; Io. VI, 38: *descendi de caelo non ut faciam voluntatem meam, sed voluntatem eius qui misit me*, Patris.

Secundum Hieronymum, non petebat simpliciter sed ut iste calix transiret. Videbat se passurum a Iudaeis; volebat igitur quod transiret, idest quod ita redimeret mundum, quod non esset delictum Iudaeorum; Rom. XI, 11: *delictum Iudaeorum salus est gentibus*.

Hilarius vero dicit sic: non rogat Dominus ut non moriatur, sed rogat ut calix in alios transeat; quasi dicat: *accipiam calicem cum fiducia. Rogo ut discipuli mei sine diffidentia accipiant*. Sed quare dicit ***si possibile est***? Quia hoc videtur contra naturam, quod mortem sine dolore accipiant. Unde vult dicere: *ego vellem alios non pati, si possibile esset; sed fiat sicut vis*, idest secundum tuam ordinationem.

2233. *Et venit ad discipulos suos*. Hic increpat discipulorum defectum. Et
    primo ponitur defectus;
    secundo increpatio;

reason; and this is pointed out when he says, ***nevertheless not as I will, but as you will***; for the higher reason follows the desire of nature, yet not simply, i.e., if is not incompatible as related to what is higher. Hence he wishes to say: I will that what I will be fulfilled if it is not incompatible with your justice, but I will that your justice be fulfilled.

And by this he teaches an example about how we should order affections, for we should so order them that they are not out of harmony with the divine rule. Hence it is not grave if someone flees what is grave for nature, while yet he orders it to the divine will.

2232. Likewise it can be explained, according to Chrysostom and Origen, such that Christ's passion is signified by the chalice, about which: *I will take the chalice of salvation* (Ps 115:4). It is agreed that Christ had the natural will of a man, and this is what is such as to flee from death: therefore, that he might show that he was a man, he asked that the chalice pass from him; and this is natural in such a way that the petition does not withdraw him from it. Similarly, he said, ***if it be possible, let this chalice pass***, i.e., the passion: but I do not speak absolutely, but if it is possible. And since someone might think that he doubted whether it was possible for God, he shows that it is possible, because *all things are possible to you* (Mark 14:36).

Nevertheless not as I will, but as you will, i.e., if it fits with your justice, I will it; this is why he says, ***not as I will***. Hence he touches on two wills: one which he had from the Father insofar as he is God, one which he had with the Father. And in this the error of many is refuted. Also, another will which he had insofar as he is man: and he submitted this will to the Father in all things, by this giving us an example, that we might submit our will to God's will; *I came down from heaven, not to do my own will, but the will of him who sent me* (John 6:38), the Father.

According to Jerome, he did not simply ask, but asked that this chalice might pass. He saw that he was about to suffer under the Jews, so he willed that it might pass, i.e., that he might redeem the world in such a way that it would not be the Jews' crime; *by their offense, salvation is come to the gentiles* (Rom 11:11).

But Hilary speaks this way: the Lord does not ask not to die, but asks that the chalice might pass on to others; as though to say: *I accept the chalice with confidence. I ask that my disciples may accept it with no lack of confidence.* But why does he say, ***if it be possible***? Because it seems contrary to nature that they should accept death without sorrow. Hence he wishes to say: *If it were possible, I would will that others not suffer; but let it be as you will*, i.e., according to your decree.

2233. *And he came to his disciples, and found them asleep*. Here he reproaches the disciples' failure. And
    first, the failure is set out;
    second, the reproach;

tertio admonitio;

quarto causa admonitionis.

2234. Cum orasset, ***venit ad discipulos et invenit eos dormientes***. Et istud habet rationem secundum litteram, quia iam pars noctis transierat, ideo somno erant gravati. Item causa erat, quia tristes erant, et tales facile subrepit somnus; Prov. XVII, 22: *spiritus tristis desiccat ossa*. Item signatur quod Christo ascendente pro nobis ad passionem, multi dormiere, sicut ***dormitaverunt omnes et dormierunt***, supra XXV, 5.

2235. ***Et dicit Petro: sic non potuistis una hora vigilare mecum?*** Sed quare magis dixit Petro? Ratio est quia Petrus magis se iactaverat quod assisteret ei in necessitatibus: ideo iam erat futurum praesagium casus sui. ***Non potuistis una hora vigilare mecum?*** Et quare est ratio quod omnibus postea dixit? Quia omnes promiserant cum Petro; unde dictum est supra: ***similiter autem et omnes dixerunt***.

2236. ***Vigilate et orate, ut non intretis in tentationem***. In ista parte subiungitur admonitio. Vos de vobis confiditis; sed vos debetis refugere ad suffragia orationis, unde ***orate ne intretis in tentationem***. Unde supra c. VI, 13 in oratione communi docet hoc petere: ***et ne nos inducas in tentationem***. Et praemittit vigilantiam ad praeparationem; Eccli. XVIII, 23: *ante orationem praepara animam tuam*, idest necessaria est prudentia; supra X, 16: *estote prudentes sicut serpentes*.

2237. ***Spiritus quidem promptus est, caro autem infirma***; quasi dicat: *quod promittis, ex promptitudine est spiritus; sed tamen non est necessaria oratio propter spiritum, sed propter carnem, quae infirma est*; ideo necessaria est vigilantia. Simile est quod Apostolus dicit, Rom. VIII, 10: *corpus quidem mortuum est propter peccatum, sed spiritus vivit propter iustificationem*.

Sed notandum quod omnium caro est infirma, sed non omnium spiritus est promptus. In malis siquidem sicut caro est infirma, ita et spiritus: e contrario in bonis, quia spiritum habent promptum, et ideo in resurrectione spiritus redit corpus promptum.

Vel potest esse duplex infirmitas. Una mala quae inclinat ad peccatum, secundum quod dicit Apostolus ad Rom. VII, 18: *non habitat in carne mea bonum*. Alia infirmitas bona, secundum quod carnalis deficit secundum promptitudinem, secundum quod dicitur in Cant. V, 8: *nunciate dilecto, quia amore langueo*. Et ex ista causa debet homo vigilare, sicut dicit Origenes, sicut qui habet magnum thesaurum, diligenter vigilat ut illud custodiat.

2238. ***Iterum secundo abiit, et oravit***. Hic secundo orat. Secundum Chrysostomum, ad hoc secundo orat ut firmius veritatem humanae naturae ostendat: unde in

third, a warning;

fourth, the reason for the warning.

2234. When he had prayed, ***he came to his disciples, and found them asleep***. And there is a literal reason for this, for a part of the night had already passed, so they were heavy with sleep. Another reason was that they were sorrowful, and sleep easily creeps over such men; *a sorrowful spirit dries up the bones* (Prov 17:22). Likewise, it signifies that as Christ went up to the passion for us, many slept, just as ***they all slumbered and slept***, above (Matt 25:5).

2235. ***And he said to Peter: what? Could you not watch one hour with me?*** But why did he speak especially to Peter? The reason is that Peter had boasted more of himself, that he would stay near him in his need: so there was already a presage of his fall. ***Could you not watch one hour with me?*** And why did he speak to everyone after that? Because they had all made promises along with Peter; for it said above, ***And in like manner said all the disciples***.

2236. ***Watch and pray that you do not enter into temptation***. In this part he adds a warning. You have confidence in yourselves; but you should flee to the intercessions of prayer; hence, ***pray that you do not enter into temptation***. For above, in the common prayer, he teaches all to pray this: ***and lead us not into temptation*** (Matt 6:13). And he puts watchfulness first, for preparation; *before prayer prepare your soul* (Sir 18:23), i.e., prudence is necessary; above, *therefore be wise as serpents* (Matt 10:16).

2237. ***The spirit indeed is willing, but the flesh is weak***; as though to say: *the spirit is ready to do what you promised, but still prayer is needed not on account of the spirit, but on account of the flesh, which is weak*; this is why watchfulness is necessary. A similar thing is what the Apostle says, *the body indeed is dead, because of sin; but the spirit lives, because of justification* (Rom 8:10).

But one should note that every man's flesh is weak, but not every man's spirit is ready. For indeed in the evil, just as the flesh is weak, so also the spirit: it is the other way around in the good, for they have a ready spirit, and this is why in the resurrection the spirit returns to a ready body.

Or, there can be two sorts of weakness. One, an evil weakness which inclines toward sin, as the Apostle says, *there dwells not . . . in my flesh, that which is good* (Rom 7:18). Another, a good weakness, according to which the body fails in readiness, as is said, *I adjure you, O daughters of Jerusalem, if you find my beloved, that you tell him that I languish with love* (Song 5:8). And for this reason a man should keep watch, as Origen says, as one who has a great treasure diligently watches, to guard it.

2238. ***Again the second time, he went and prayed***. Here he prays a second time. According to Chrysostom, he prays a second time to show more strongly the truth of the

Gen. XLI, v. 32: *quod secundo vidisti, firmitatis indicium est.*

2239. Quod autem dicit *si non potest hic calix transire, nisi bibam illum, fiat voluntas tua*, potest tripliciter exponi. Primo sic. Supra sub conditione petierat, hic autem quia fuit certificatus quod non poterat esse quin illum biberet, ideo petit ut fiat voluntas eius; quasi dicat: *si non potest esse quin transiturus sim ad gloriam immortalitatis*, quia mortalitas non erat contracta, sed assumpta: ideo sive pateretur, sive non, erat transiturus ad gloriam immortalitatis. Sed non poterat transire a se et a membris; unde si non biberet, non transiret a membris. Vult ergo dicere: *si non potest transire a me, et a membris, fiat voluntas tua*; Ps. XXXIX, 9: *ut facerem voluntatem tuam, Deus meus, volui.*

Secundo exponit sic Hieronymus: si non potest fieri quod veritas transeat ad gentes, nisi Iudaei excedant, *fiat voluntas tua*: eorum enim delicto salus gentibus facta est.

Hilarius sic exponit: si non potest fieri quod alii sancti bibant calicem passionis nisi exemplo meo, *fiat voluntas tua*; quia alii sancti ex passione Christi exemplum ceperunt. Vult ergo dicere: si non potest transire a me in discipulos, nisi ego bibam, ut fortiores efficiantur ad bibendum, *fiat voluntas tua*.

2240. Consequenter ponitur secunda dormitio discipulorum: *et venit iterum, et invenit eos dormientes: erat enim oculi eorum gravati*, somno, idest propter somnum, et propter tristitiam; Ps. XXX, 10: *turbatus est in ira oculus meus.*

2241. *Et relictis illis, iterum abiit, et oravit tertio.* Hic de tertia agit oratione: et duo facit.

Primo ponit ordinem;

secundo concessionem somni, ibi *tunc venit ad discipulos* et cetera.

2242. Dicit *et relictis illis, iterum abiit et oravit tertio, eumdem sermonem dicens.*

Sed quid signat quod ter oravit? Ter oravit ut nos a malis praesentibus, praeteritis et futuris liberaret.

Item ut orationem nostram doceret ad Patrem, et Filium, et Spiritum Sanctum dirigendam; unde in orationibus Ecclesiae semper dicitur: *gloria Patri, et Filio, et Spiritui Sancto.* Item ut trina oratione trinam Petri negationem liberaret; Lc. XXII, 32: *ego pro te rogavi, Petre, ut non deficiat fides tua.*

Item ter oravit contra tres timores. Est enim timor contra concupiscentiam; est enim triplex concupiscentia, curiositatis, superbiae et carnis, et ista triplex

human nature; hence, *and for that you did see the second time a dream pertaining to the same thing: it is a token of the certainty* (Gen 41:32).

2239. What he says, *if this chalice may not pass away, but I must drink it, your will be done*, can be explained in three ways. First, in this way. Above, he had prayed with a condition, but here, since it had been made certain that it could not be otherwise than that he drink it, he asks that his will be done; as though to say: *if it cannot be otherwise than that I will pass over to immortal glory*, for his mortality was not imposed, but assumed, so whether he suffered or not, he was going to pass over to immortal glory. But it could not have passed from himself and from his members; hence if he did not drink it, it would not pass from his members. He wishes therefore to say: *if it cannot pass from me, and from my members, your will be done*. That I should do your will: *O my God, I have desired it* (Ps 39:9).

Second, Jerome explains it this way: if it cannot come about that the truth passes to the gentiles unless the Jews trespass, *your will be done*; for their crime was made salvation for the gentiles.

Hilary explains it this way: if it cannot cannot come about that the other saints drink the chalice of the passion except by my example, *your will be done*; for the other saints took example from Christ's passion. He wishes therefore to say: if it cannot pass from me into the disciples unless I drink it, that they might be made stronger for drinking it, *your will be done*.

2240. Next the disciples' second sleep is set down: *and he came again and found them sleeping: for their eyes were heavy* with sleep, that is, owing to sleep, and owing to sorrow; *my eye is troubled with wrath* (Ps 30:10).

2241. *And leaving them, he went again: and he prayed the third time*. Here he treats of the third prayer: and he does two things:

first, he sets down the order;

second, the concession of sleep, at *then he came to his disciples*.

2242. It says, *and leaving them, he went again: and he prayed the third time, saying the same word*.

But what does it mean that he prayed three times? He prayed three times to free us from present, past, and future evils.

Also, to teach that our prayer should be directed to the Father, and to the Son, and to the Holy Spirit; hence it always says in the prayers of the Church: *glory be to the Father, and to the Son, and to the Holy Spirit*. Also, that by a triple prayer he might unloose Peter's triple denial; *but I have prayed for you, that your faith fail not* (Luke 22:32).

Likewise, he prayed three times against three fears. For fear is contrary to concupiscence; for concupiscence is threefold: of curiosity, of pride, and of the flesh, and these

tangitur I Io. c. II, 16: *omne quod est in mundo, aut est concupiscentia carnis, aut concupiscentia oculorum, aut superbia vitae*. Isti triplici concupiscentiae triplex timor respondet, scilicet: concupiscentiae carnis, timor doloris; concupiscentiae oculorum, timor paupertatis; concupiscentiae superbiae, timor opprobrii et ignominiae. Et haec passus est Christus, non quia indigeret, sed pro nobis.

2243. *Tunc venit ad discipulos suos, et dixit illis*. Et

primo indulget somno;
secundo excitat, ibi **surgite, eamus**.
Primo dat licentiam;
secundo causam assignat, ibi **ecce appropinquabit hora et filius hominis tradetur**.

2244. Christus prima vice invenit eos dormientes et increpavit eos; secundo invenit eos dormientes, et tacuit; tertio invenit eos dormientes, et somnum concessit. Quae est ratio? Ratio litteralis est quia praelatis datur forma correctionis; quia quando venit ad aliquem, et invenit dormientem, nescit si ex negligentia ei accidit, vel ex infirmitate. Et potest indulgere. Item quia post resurrectionem invenit dormientes, et eis exprobravit; Lc. XXIV, v. 25: *O stulti et tardi corde ad credendum*. Item visitavit post acceptum Spiritum Sanctum, et tunc nihil dixit, quia adhuc erant infirmi; quia adhuc legalia observabant, ut dicitur de Petro ad Gal. II, 11. Sed ultimo in suo adventu visitabit, et dimittet eos in quiete sancta et pacifica; Ps. IV, 9: *in pace in idipsum dormiam et requiescam*.

Secundum Augustinum, concedit eis, et supra negavit: sed alius est hic somnus, et supra. Quia est somnus aggravationis, et de hoc loquitur supra, unde dicitur v. 43: **erant oculi eorum gravati**, somno, et hoc est increpandum. Hic autem somnus est somnus quietis; et iste permittitur. Item est somnus propter turbationem; et hic prohibetur. De isto dicitur ad Ephes. V, 14: *surge qui dormis, et exurge a mortuis*. Aliquando enim est somnus propter quietem corporis, sed tamen anima vigilat: *ego dormio, et cor meum vigilat*, Cant. V, 2. Item, quia laboraturi erant, ideo oportebat quod quiescerent.

2245. Tunc causa assignat **ecce appropinquavit hora**. Non hoc habuit ex aliqua necessitate facere, sed ex ordinatione divina; Io. VII, 30: *quaerebant eum, et non poterant manus iniicere in eum, quia nondum venerat hora eius*. Sed haec hora venerat; Io. XIII, 1: *sciens Iesus quia venit hora eius, ut transeat ex hoc mundo ad patrem*.

Sed possent dicere: *si hora est ex ordinatione divina, ergo non peccant occidentes eum*. Ideo cum hoc ponit

three are touched on, *for all that is in the world, is the concupiscence of the flesh, and the concupiscence of the eyes, and the pride of life* (1 John 2:16). To these three concupiscences there correspond three fears, namely: to the concupiscence of the flesh, the fear of sorrow; to the concupiscence of the eyes, the fear of poverty; to the concupiscence of pride, the fear of reproach and disgrace. And Christ suffered these things not because he was in need, but on our behalf.

2243. *Then he came to his disciples, and said to them*. And

first, he concedes sleep;
second, he arouses, at **rise, let us go**.
First, he gives permission;
second, he gives the reason, at **behold the hour is at hand, and the Son of man will be betrayed into the hands of sinners**.

2244. The first time, Christ found them sleeping and reproached them; the second, he found them sleeping, and was silent; the third, he found them sleeping, and granted the sleep. What is the reason? A literal reason is that the form for correction is given to prelates, for when he comes to someone and finds him sleeping, he does not know whether it happened out of negligence or out of weakness. And he can concede it. Also, because after the resurrection he found them sleeping, and rebuked them; *O foolish, and slow of heart to believe* (Luke 24:25). Likewise, he visited them after the Holy Spirit was received, and then he said nothing, because they were as yet weak, because they as yet observed the things pertaining to the law, as is said about Peter (Gal 2:11). But last of all he will visit them at his coming, and he will leave them in holy and peaceful rest; *in peace in the same I will sleep, and I will rest* (Ps 4:9).

According to Augustine, he granted it to them, while above he denied it: but this sleep is different from the one above. For the one above is the sleep of heaviness, and this was spoken about above, for it says, **their eyes were heavy** with sleep, and this should be reproached. But here the sleep is the sleep of rest; and this is permitted. Likewise, there is a sleep owing to disturbance, and this is forbidden. It says about this, *rise you who sleep, and arise from the dead* (Eph 5:14). For sometimes sleep is owing to rest of the body, but yet the soul keeps watch: *I sleep, and my heart watches* (Song 5:2). Also, since they were about to labor, it was necessary that they rest.

2245. Then he gives the reason: **behold the hour is at hand**. He did not have to do this out of some necessity, but by the divine decree; *they sought therefore to apprehend him: and no man laid hands on him, because his hour was not yet come* (John 7:30). But this hour had come; *Jesus knowing that his hour was come, that he would pass out of this world to the Father* (John 13:1).

But they might say: *if the hour is by the divine decree, therefore those who kill him do not sin*. This is why along

with this he sets down the sin: **and the Son of man will be betrayed into the hands of sinners**, i.e., they are not doing this by the divine decree, but for the fulfillment of their own will. *I have given my dear soul into the hands of her enemies* (Jer 12:7).

2246. Then he sets down the rousing. And first, he sets it down; second, the need for it, at **behold**.

And when he says, **rise**, he shows his own readiness; hence John says that he went to them (John 18:4).

And why? **Behold he is at hand who will betray me**. He was near, not that Christ saw him with a bodily eye, but with the spirit, namely the eye of the divinity.

But why did he tell them, **rise**, when he had given them permission to sleep? Augustine resolves it, saying that he had spoken by way of rebuke, as though to say: *sleep as much as you want*, **behold the hour is at hand**. And Augustine says that this explanation would be sufficient, except that a better occurred to him; so he says otherwise, that they had slept for a little while, and when they had slept, he said, **rise, let us go**.

Lecture 6

26:47 Adhuc eo loquente, ecce Iudas unus de duodecim venit, et cum eo turba multa, cum gladiis et fustibus, a principibus sacerdotum et senioribus populi. [n. 2248]

26:48 Qui autem tradidit eum, dedit illis signum dicens: quemcumque osculatus fuero, ipse est, tenete eum. [n. 2251]

26:49 Et confestim accedens ad Iesum dixit: ave, Rabbi, et osculatus est eum. [n. 2252]

26:50 Dixitque illi Iesus: amice, ad quid venisti? Tunc accesserunt et manus iniecerunt in Iesum, et tenuerunt eum. [n. 2253]

26:51 Et ecce unus ex his qui erant cum Iesu, extendens manum exemit gladium suum, et percutiens servum principis sacerdotum amputavit auriculam eius. [n. 2256]

26:52 Tunc ait illi Iesus: converte gladium tuum in locum suum: omnes enim qui acceperint gladium, gladio peribunt. [n. 2257]

26:53 An putas quia non possum rogare Patrem meum, et exhibebit mihi modo plusquam duodecim legiones angelorum? [n. 2261]

26:54 Quomodo ergo implebuntur Scripturae, quia sic oportet fieri? [n. 2264]

26:55 In illa hora dixit Iesus turbis: tamquam ad latronem existis cum gladiis et fustibus comprehendere me. Quotidie apud vos sedebam docens in templo, et non me tenuistis. [n. 2265]

26:56 Hoc autem totum factum est, ut adimplerentur Scripturae prophetarum. Tunc discipuli omnes, relicto eo, fugerunt. [n. 2266]

26:47 Καὶ ἔτι αὐτοῦ λαλοῦντος ἰδοὺ Ἰούδας εἷς τῶν δώδεκα ἦλθεν καὶ μετ' αὐτοῦ ὄχλος πολὺς μετὰ μαχαιρῶν καὶ ξύλων ἀπὸ τῶν ἀρχιερέων καὶ πρεσβυτέρων τοῦ λαοῦ.

26:48 ὁ δὲ παραδιδοὺς αὐτὸν ἔδωκεν αὐτοῖς σημεῖον λέγων· ὃν ἂν φιλήσω αὐτός ἐστιν, κρατήσατε αὐτόν.

26:49 καὶ εὐθέως προσελθὼν τῷ Ἰησοῦ εἶπεν· χαῖρε, ῥαββί, καὶ κατεφίλησεν αὐτόν.

26:50 ὁ δὲ Ἰησοῦς εἶπεν αὐτῷ· ἑταῖρε, ἐφ' ὃ πάρει. τότε προσελθόντες ἐπέβαλον τὰς χεῖρας ἐπὶ τὸν Ἰησοῦν καὶ ἐκράτησαν αὐτόν.

26:51 Καὶ ἰδοὺ εἷς τῶν μετὰ Ἰησοῦ ἐκτείνας τὴν χεῖρα ἀπέσπασεν τὴν μάχαιραν αὐτοῦ καὶ πατάξας τὸν δοῦλον τοῦ ἀρχιερέως ἀφεῖλεν αὐτοῦ τὸ ὠτίον.

26:52 τότε λέγει αὐτῷ ὁ Ἰησοῦς· ἀπόστρεψον τὴν μάχαιράν σου εἰς τὸν τόπον αὐτῆς· πάντες γὰρ οἱ λαβόντες μάχαιραν ἐν μαχαίρῃ ἀπολοῦνται.

26:53 ἢ δοκεῖς ὅτι οὐ δύναμαι παρακαλέσαι τὸν πατέρα μου, καὶ παραστήσει μοι ἄρτι πλείω δώδεκα λεγιῶνας ἀγγέλων;

26:54 πῶς οὖν πληρωθῶσιν αἱ γραφαὶ ὅτι οὕτως δεῖ γενέσθαι;

26:55 Ἐν ἐκείνῃ τῇ ὥρᾳ εἶπεν ὁ Ἰησοῦς τοῖς ὄχλοις· ὡς ἐπὶ λῃστὴν ἐξήλθατε μετὰ μαχαιρῶν καὶ ξύλων συλλαβεῖν με; καθ' ἡμέραν ἐν τῷ ἱερῷ ἐκαθεζόμην διδάσκων καὶ οὐκ ἐκρατήσατέ με.

26:56 τοῦτο δὲ ὅλον γέγονεν ἵνα πληρωθῶσιν αἱ γραφαὶ τῶν προφητῶν. Τότε οἱ μαθηταὶ πάντες ἀφέντες αὐτὸν ἔφυγον.

26:47 As he was still speaking, behold Judas, one of the twelve, came, and with him a great multitude with swords and clubs, sent from the chief priests and the elders of the people. [n. 2248]

26:48 And he who betrayed him, gave them a sign, saying: whomever I will kiss, that is he, hold him fast. [n. 2251]

26:49 And coming to Jesus immediately, he said: hail, Rabbi. And he kissed him. [n. 2252]

26:50 And Jesus said to him: friend, for what have you come? Then they came up, and laid hands on Jesus, and held him. [n. 2253]

26:51 And behold one of those who were with Jesus, stretching out his hand, drew out his sword, and striking the servant of the high priest, cut off his ear. [n. 2256]

26:52 Then Jesus said to him: put your sword back into its place: for all who take the sword will perish with the sword. [n. 2257]

26:53 Do you think that I cannot ask my Father, and he will give me presently more than twelve legions of angels? [n. 2261]

26:54 How then will the Scriptures be fulfilled, that so it must be done? [n. 2264]

26:55 In that same hour Jesus said to the multitudes: you are come out as it were to a robber with swords and clubs to apprehend me. I sat with you daily, teaching in the temple, and you did not lay hands on me. [n. 2265]

26:56 Now all this was done, that the Scriptures of the prophets might be fulfilled. Then the disciples, all leaving him, fled. [n. 2266]

2247. Supra posita sunt praeparatoria ad passionem, scilicet institutio sacramenti et oratio Christi; hic autem

2247. Above, those things preparatory to the passion were set down, namely the institution of the sacrament and

ponit passionem quantum ad ea quae a Iudaeis sunt illata. Et

    primo ostendit quomodo capitur;
    secundo quomodo examinatur;
    tertio quomodo condemnatur.

Secunda ibi *principes* etc.; tertia ibi *tunc principes sacerdotum* et cetera.

    Circa primum tria facit.
    Primo agit de proditione;
    secundo de captione;
    tertio quomodo ductus est post captionem.

Secunda ibi *tunc accesserunt*; tertia ibi *at illi tenentes eum*, et cetera.

    Circa primum tria facit.
    Primo describit personam proditoris;
    secundo signum proditionis;
    tertio complementum.

Secunda ibi *qui autem tradidit* etc., tertia ibi *et confestim* et cetera.

Describit proditorem ex tribus. Primo ex nomine; secundo ex dignitate; tertio ex societate.

2248. Ex nomine *adhuc eo loquente, ecce Iudas* et cetera. *Loquente* scilicet verba haec, quibus eis fiduciam adhibebat, *ecce Iudas*, qui dicitur 'confitens.' Duo fuerunt Iudae, quorum unus est malus, alter bonus, ad signandum quod quidam confitentes in Ecclesia futuri erant boni, Rom. X, 10: *ore autem confessio fit ad salutem*, quidam futuri mali; ad Tit. I, 16: *confitentur se nosse Deum, factis autem negant*.

2249. Consequenter describitur ex dignitate *unus ex duodecim*, quia licet in tanta esset dignitate constitutus, in tantum tamen scelus cecidit. In quo datur exemplum quod nullus de statu suo debet confidere. Apostolus I Cor. X, 12: *qui stat, videat ne cadat*; Io. VI, 71: *nonne vos duodecim elegi, et unus ex vobis Diabolus est?*

Et quare eligit eum, cum sciret ipsum futurum malum? Ratio una est, ut daret exemplum praelatis, ut non desolarentur.

2250. Item describitur ex societate *et cum eo venit turba multa* et cetera. Sicut habuit crudelem animum, ita crudelem societatem, quia omne animal sibi simile appetit.

Et hoc describitur, quia *multa*. In hoc notatur quod erant stulti, stulti enim sunt in multitudine; Eccle. I, 15: *stultorum infinitus est numerus*. Et ipsi bene stulti erant, quia sapientiae contradicebant.

Item erant armati, quia *cum gladiis et fustibus*. Et quae est ratio? Origenes dicit quod multi credebant in eum, et ideo timebant ne eum turba ab eis raperet. Item, quia dicebant, supra XII, quod in Beelzebub daemonia

the prayer of Christ; and here he sets down the passion as regards those things inflicted by the Jews. And

    first, he shows how he is seized;
    second, how he is examined;
    third, how he is condemned.

The second is at **and the chief priests** (Matt 26:59); the third, at **then the high priest** (Matt 26:65).

Concerning the first, he does three things:
    first, he treats of the betrayal;
    second, of the seizing;
    third, how he was led after the seizing.

The second is at **then they came up**; the third, at **but they holding Jesus**.

Concerning the first, he does three things:
    first, he describes the person of the betrayer;
    second, the sign of betrayal;
    third, the completion.

The second is at **and he who betrayed him, gave them a sign**; the third, at **and immediately coming to Jesus**.

He describes the betrayer by three things: first, by name; second, by dignity; third, by company.

2248. By name: *as he was still speaking, behold Judas*. *Speaking* namely these words, by which he gave them courage, *behold Judas*, which means 'he who professes.' There were two Judases, of whom one is bad and one good, to signify that some of those who would profess belief within the Church were going to be good, *with the mouth, confession is made unto salvation* (Rom 10:10); some were going to be bad, *they profess that they know God: but in their works they deny him* (Titus 1:16).

2249. Next, he is described by dignity: *one of the twelve*, because although he had been set up in such great dignity, yet he fell into so great an evil. In which an example is given, that no one should place confidence in his state. The Apostle: *he who thinks himself to stand, let him take heed lest he fall* (1 Cor 10:12); *have not I chosen you twelve; and one of you is a devil?* (John 6:71).

And why did he choose him, when he knew that he was going to be evil? One reason is to give an example to prelates, that they may not be desolated.

2250. Likewise, he is described by company: *and with him a great multitude*. As he had a cruel soul, so he had a cruel company, for every animal desires its like.

And this is described: *great*. This indicates that they were foolish, for the foolish are in a multitude; *the number of fools is infinite* (Eccl 1:15). And these men were quite foolish, because they were speaking out against wisdom.

Likewise they were armed: *with swords and clubs*. And why is this? Origen says that many believed in him, and so they were afraid that a crowd might steal him away from them. Also, since they said (Matt 12) that he cast demons

eiiciebat; ideo ut nulla potestas tueretur eum, venerunt armati.

Item describitur ab auctoritate, quia **missi erant a principibus sacerdotum et senioribus populi**; unde instructi erant eorum auctoritate, ita ut nullus eis contradiceret, ut impletum sit quod dicitur in Ps. II, 2: *astiterunt reges terrae, et principes convenerunt in unum adversus Dominum, et adversus Christum eius.*

2251. Consequenter agitur de signo proditionis **qui autem tradidit eum, dedit eis signum, dicens** et cetera.

Sed hic est quaestio. Cum esset notus in Iudaea, quare petebant signum? Ratio duplex potest esse. Una, quia audierat Iudas quod Christus transfiguratus erat in monte, et credebat hoc esse factum arte magica; ideo praevenire voluit per osculi signum, antequam posset se transfigurare. Hanc expositionem ponit Hieronymus. Origenes autem dicit sic, quia sicut manna in deserto unicuique sapiebat id de quo opinabatur, sic Christus apparebat unicuique secundum quod habebat opinionem de ipso; ideo fuit necessarium quod signum daret. Dedit mirabile signum, quia **quemcumque osculatus fuero, ipse est, tenete eum**. Signum amicitiae fecit signum proditionis; Prov. XXVII, 6: *meliora sunt vulnera diligentis, quam fraudulenta oscula inimici.*

2252. Et confestim accedens ad Iesum dixit: ave, Rabbi, et osculatus est eum. Hic ponitur complementum proditionis. Et primo signa demonstravit; secundo coepit agere. Et ostendit primo dicto, cum dicit **ave, Rabbi**; secundo facto, **et osculatus est eum**. Simile habetur II Reg. X, 1, quod Ioab tenuit mentum Amasae, et interfecit eum.

Sed quare non venit statim ad eum, sed primo salutavit? Una ratio est propter reverentiam magistri. Item primo salutavit eum, quia timebat ne priusquam eum manifestaret, se primo posset transfigurare.

2253. Dixitque illi Iesus: amice, ad quid venisti? Et potest illico legi interrogative, vel remissive. Si interrogative, tunc potest legi quod per opprobrium dictum est, ac si dicat: *tu ostendis amicitiam per osculum, et venisti perdere me?* Secundum illud Ps. XXVII, 3: *loquuntur pacem in ore suo, mala autem in cordibus eorum.* Et dixit **amice**. Quoties amicum aliquem vocat, improperando loquitur. Unde dictum est supra XXII, 12: **amice, quomodo huc intrasti, non habens vestem nuptialem?** Et alibi c. XX, v. 13: **amice, non facio tibi iniuriam** et cetera. I Io. IV, 19: *non enim prius dileximus eum, sed ipse prior dilexit nos.*

Vel potest legi remissive, et non est verbum increpatorium, sed permissivum **amice, ad quid venisti**, secundum illud Io. XIII, v. 27: *quod facis, fac citius.* Et vocat eum amicum quantum est de se, quia *cum his qui*

out in Beelzebub, they came armed, so that no power might protect him.

Likewise, he is described by authority, for they had been sent *from the chief priests and the elders of the people*; for they had been given instructions by their authority, so that no one might speak against them, that what is said in the Psalm might be fulfilled: *the kings of the earth stood up, and the princes met together, against the Lord and against his Christ* (Ps 2:2).

2251. Next, he treats of the sign of betrayal: *and he who betrayed him, gave them a sign, saying.*

But here there is a question. Since he was known in Judea, why did they ask for a sign? There can be two reasons. One, because Judas had heard that Christ had been transfigured on the mount, and he thought that this was done by a magic art; so he wanted to prevent this by the sign of a kiss, before he could transfigure himself. Jerome posits this explanation. But Origen speaks this way, that just as the manna in the desert tasted to each man as he thought of it, so Christ appeared to each man in accord with his opinion of him; so it was necessary that he give a sign. He gave an amazing sign: *whomever I will kiss, that is he, hold him fast*. He made a sign of friendship into a sign of betrayal; *better are the wounds of a friend, than the deceitful kisses of an enemy* (Prov 27:6).

2252. And coming to Jesus immediately, he said: hail, Rabbi. And he kissed him. Here the completion of the betrayal is set down. And first, he gave a sign; second, he began to act. And he shows it first by word, when he says, *hail, Rabbi*; second, by deed, *and he kissed him*. A similar thing is found, that Joab held Amasa's chin and killed him (2 Sam 20:9).

But why did he not come to him immediately, but saluted him first? One reason is owing to reverence for a teacher. Also, he saluted him first because he feared that he would transfigure himself before he could point him out.

2253. And Jesus said to him: friend, for what have you come? And this can be read directly either interrogatively, or remissively. If interrogatively, then it can be understood as said by way of rebuke, as though to say: *you make a show of friendship with a kiss, and have you come to destroy me?* In accord with this, *who speak peace with their neighbor, but evils are in their hearts* (Ps 27:3). And he said, *friend*. Whenever he calls someone a friend, he speaks by way of reproach. Hence it was said above, *friend, how did you come in here not having on a wedding garment?* (Matt 22:12). And in another place, *friend, I do you no wrong* (Matt 20:13). *Not as though we had loved God, but because he has first loved us* (1 John 4:10).

Or, it can be read remissively, and in this way it is not a reproachful saying, but permissive: *friend, for what have you come?* in accord with, *that which you do, do quickly* (John 13:27). And he calls him a friend insofar as he is

oderunt pacem, eram pacificus, Ps. CXIX, v. 7. Et licet sciret eum osculaturum esse, tamen occurrit ei.

2254. At illi tenentes manus iniecerunt in Iesum. Nunc agitur de captione. Et

primo ponitur severitas captionis;

secundo testimonium

tertio reprehensio discipuli.

Circa primum tria facit. Quia

primo dicit quomodo ministri eum capiunt;

secundo quomodo quidam discipulus impedire volebat;

tertio quod Christus reprehendit eum.

2255. Dicit ergo **at illi tenentes iniecerunt manus in Iesum**. Is. I, 15: *manus vestrae sanguine plenae sunt*. Ipse enim tradidit se; Ier. XII, 7: *dedi dilectam animam meam in manibus inimicorum eius*.

2256. Tunc ponitur quomodo unus discipulus invasit invadentes **et ecce unus ex his qui erant cum Iesu, extendens manum exemit gladium suum**. Quis fuit iste? Dicendum quod Petrus. Unde sicut supra XVI, v. 22, voluit passionem Christi impedire, sic et hic. Unde habuit occasionem? Ex eo quod habetur Lc. XXII, 36, ubi dominus praecepit quod emant gladios, et hoc intelligentes crediderunt quod gladii essent necessarii; unde habebant cultellum ad incidendum agnum. Ideo Petrus habuit unum.

Percutiens servum principis sacerdotum, amputavit ei auriculam. Non credatis quod habuit tempus deliberationis quod auriculam amputaret; sed proiecit ictum, et cum vellet percutere eum ad mortem, accidit quod auriculam amputavit.

Nomen istius erat Malchus, qui interpretabatur 'rex.' Et signat abscissionem regni a populo Iudaico, et tamen factus est servus principum sacerdotum, idest Romanorum: huic Petrus abscidit auriculam. Per auriculam auditus signatur; et hic est duplex, scilicet dexter, per quem signatur vita aeterna; sinister, per quem temporalis. **Amputavit auriculam eius**, quia a populo Iudaeorum doctrinam spiritualium amputavit; et hoc factum fuit occasionaliter, quod gentes receperint dexteram, quia Petrus primo praedicavit gentilibus; et ita amputavit dexteram, trahendo gentiles ad fidem.

2257. Tunc ait illi Iesus: converte gladium tuum in locum suum. Hic ponitur reprehensio. Et

primo reprehendit Petrum;

secundo ministros **in illa hora dixit Iesus turbis** et cetera.

Et

primo ponit admonitionem,

secundo rationem admonitionis assignat **omnes enim qui acceperint gladium, gladio peribunt**.

from himself, for *with them who hated peace I was peaceable* (Ps 119:7). And although he knew that he was about to kiss him, yet he went to him.

2254. Then they came up, and laid hands on Jesus. Now he treats of the seizing. And

first, the severity of the seizing is set down;

second, a testimony;

third, the reproach of a disciple.

Concerning the first, he does three things:

first, he says how the emissaries seized him;

second, how a certain disciple wanted to prevent it;

third, how Christ reproached him.

2255. It says therefore, **then they came up, and laid hands on Jesus**. *Your hands are full of blood* (Isa 1:15). For he himself handed himself over; *I have given my dear soul into the hand of her enemies* (Jer 12:7).

2256. Then he sets down how one disciple attacked the attackers: **and behold one of those who were with Jesus, stretching out his hand, drew out his sword**. Who was this man? One should say that it was Peter. Hence as he wished to prevent Christ's passion above (Matt 16:22), so also here. What was the occasion for this? It was what is said, where the Lord commanded that they buy swords (Luke 22:36), and thinking on this, they believed that swords were necessary; hence they had a knife for killing the lamb. This is why Peter had one.

Striking the servant of the high priest, cut off his ear. Do not think that he had time to decide that he would cut off the ear; rather he struck a blow, and while he wanted to strike him dead, it happened that he cut off the ear.

This man's name was Malchus, which means 'king.' And it signifies the cutting off of the kingdom from the Jewish people, and yet it was made the servant of the high priest, i.e., of the Romans: Peter cut off this man's ear. The ear signifies hearing, and there are two, namely the right, which signifies eternal life, and the left, which signifies temporal life. He **cut off his ear**, because he cut off spiritual teaching from the Jewish people. This was done indirectly, because the gentiles received the right ear, for Peter first preached to the gentiles, and in this way he cut off the right ear, by drawing the gentiles to faith.

2257. Then Jesus said to him: put your sword back into its place. Here the reproach is set down. And

first, he reproaches Peter;

second, the emissaries, **in that same hour Jesus said to the multitudes**.

And

first, he sets out a warning;

second, he gives a reason for the warning, **for all who take the sword will perish with the sword**.

2258. Dicitur *tunc ait illi Iesus. Converte gladium tuum in locum suum*. Venerat ut voluntarie pateretur, ideo nolebat defendi. Et in hoc dabat exemplum ut martyres patientes pro Christo non defenderent se.

2259. Deinde rationem assignat: et
primo ex poena;
secundo ex voluntate Christi;
tertio ex auctoritate.

Secunda ibi *an putas quia non possum rogare Patrem meum* etc.; tertia ibi *quomodo ergo implebuntur Scripturae?*

2260. Primo mitigat ex terrore poenae dicens *omnes qui acceperint gladium, gladio peribunt*.

Sed movet quaestionem Augustinus, quia non omnes qui gladio feriunt, gladio pereunt, sed aliquando febre; ideo potest exponi tripliciter, secundum quod triplex est gladius: materialis, de quo in Ps. XXXVI, 14: *gladium evaginaverunt peccatores*. Item divinae sententiae, de quo Ier. XIX, 7: *subvertam eos gladio*. Item divini Verbi; Eph. VI, 17: *et gladium spiritus accipite, quod est Verbum Dei*. Potest ergo intelligi de omnibus istis. De gladio materiali, quia qui gladio perimit, gladio peribit, idest suo, non alieno. Unde Ps. XXXVI, 15: *gladius eorum intret in corda ipsorum*. Item potest exponi de gladio condemnationis, de quo habetur Gen. III, v. 24, quod Dominus gladium versatilem posuit ante Paradisum. Unde qui alios condemnant, divina sententia condemnabuntur. Vel aliqui propria auctoritate accipiunt quod non habent ab alio, et tales gladio pereunt.

2261. *An putas quod non possum rogare Patrem meum* et cetera. Hic assignat rationem ad mitigandum animum Petri, dans intelligere quod voluntarie patiebatur, et quod poterat effugere. Et quia videbat eum praesumentem, ideo dicit *non possum rogare Patrem meum?* Et non dicit, non possum vocare, vel adducere, sed *rogare*: dicit enim verba hominis, quia orare hominis est. *Et exhibebit mihi modo plusquam duodecim legiones angelorum?* Et istud dictum est secundum infirmitatem animi Petri. Ita Petrus se habebat, quod deberet eum defendere, et indigeret auxilio hominum; ideo vult dicere quod si auxilio hominum posset defendi, multo magis angelorum. Sed non erat necesse, quia magis angeli sustentantur per ipsum.

2262. Sed quid est quod dicit *duodecim legiones angelorum?* Dicendum quod societas apud Graecos dicitur 'phalanga,' apud Romanos 'legio,' et habebat sex millia

2258. It says, *then Jesus said to him: put your sword back into its place*. He had come so that he might voluntarily suffer, so he did not wish to be defended. And by this he gave an example, that the martyrs suffering for Christ should not defend themselves.

2259. Then he gives a reason; and
first, from a punishment;
second, from Christ's desire;
third, from an authority.

The second is at *do you think that I cannot ask my Father, and he will give me presently more than twelve legions of angels?* The third, at *how then will the Scriptures be fulfilled?*

2260. First, he calms him down by the fear of punishment, saying, *all who take the sword will perish with the sword*.

But Augustine raises a question, because not all who have carried a sword have perished by the sword, but sometimes they have perished by a fever. So it can be explained in three ways, according as there are three swords: the material sword, about which it says, *the wicked have drawn out the sword* (Ps 36:14). Also, the sword of divine judgment, about which it says, *I will destroy them with the sword* (Jer 19:7). Also, the sword of the divine Word; *and the sword of the Spirit (which is the Word of God)* (Eph 6:17). It can therefore be understood as about all these. As about the material sword, because those who destroy by the sword will perish by the sword, i.e., their own, not another's. Hence, *let their sword enter into their own hearts* (Ps 36:15). Likewise, it can be explained as about the sword of condemnation, about which it says that the Lord placed a sword turning every which way in front of paradise (Gen 3:24). For those who condemn others will be condemned by the divine judgment. Or, some men take up by their own authority what they do not have from another, and such men perish by the sword.

2261. *Do you think that I cannot ask my Father*. Here he gives a reason to calm Peter's soul, giving him to understand that he was suffering voluntarily, and that he could have fled. And since he saw him supposing that he was helpless, he says, *I cannot ask my Father?* And he does not say, that I am not able to call, or induce, but *ask*: for he speaks the words of a man, since to pray belongs to a man. *And he will give me presently more than twelve legions of angels?* And this was said in conformity with the weakness of Peter's soul. Peter considered himself such that he should defend him, and thought that he would need the help of men; so he wishes to say that if he could be defended by the help of men, much more could he be defended by the help of angels. But it was not necessary, because the angels are rather upheld by him.

2262. But why does he say, *twelve legions of angels?* One should say that among the Greeks a company is called a 'phalanx,' among the Romans a 'legion,' and it had six

hominum; unde duodecim legiones sunt septuaginta-duo millia, et tot sunt linguae hominum, sicut habetur ex Gen. XI. Unde vult dicere: si omnes homines insurgerent contra me, posset Dominus mittere contra quamlibet linguam mille Angelos: et si unus Angelus destruxit tot millia, ut patet Is. XXXVII, multo magis mille poterunt occidere unam linguam; Iob XXV, 3: *numquid est numerus militum eius?* Et Dan. VII, 10: *millia millium ministrabant ei, et decies millies centena millia assistebant ei.*

Remigius dicit sic: quicumque faciunt voluntatem Dei, possunt dici angeli, idest nuntii; Is. XVIII, 2: *ite, angeli veloces ad gentem convulsam et dilaceratam.* Quicumque enim obsequuntur Deo, angeli dicuntur; Ps. CIII, 4: *qui fecit angelos suos spiritus, et ministros suos ignem urentem.* Potest ergo per legionem intelligi legio Romanorum. Unde dominus posset adducere et provocare legiones Romanorum ad destruendos Iudaeos, sicut post sub Tito et Vespasiano factum fuit.

2263. Et isto loco destruxerunt quidam opinionem illorum, qui dicebant quod non poterat Dominus facere nisi quod facit; quia si poterat legiones convocare, quas non convocavit, constat quod potest facere multa quae non facit.

2264. *Quomodo ergo implebuntur Scripturae?* Hic ponitur tertia ratio, quare non debeat impedire: quia ita Scripturae dixerunt; et ideo sic oportet fieri. Et non dicit quae Scripturae, quia omnes prophetae dixerunt vel occulte, vel manifeste. Unde Lc. c. ult., 26: *nonne oportuit Christum pati, et ita intrare in gloriam suam?*

2265. *In illa hora dixit Iesus turbis.* In parte ista redarguit ministros: et duo facit. Primo commemorat factum; secundo irrationabilitatem facti, cum dicit ***quasi ad latronem existis cum gladiis et fustibus comprehendere me.*** Iob XVI, 10: *infremuit contra me dentibus,* quia exierunt ac si esset latro; sed ipsi magis veniebant ut latrones. Latro latet ut non capiatur; sed Christus offert se in manifesto. Et latrones si nocere volunt, non nocent in publico; sed Christus se offerebat. Unde dicit ***quotidie apud vos eram docens in templo, et non me tenuistis***; ideo venistis ut latrones. Ut enim daret opportunitatem, exivit civitatem. ***Quotidie apud vos eram docens in templo.*** Simile habetur Io. XVIII, 20: *in occulto locutus sum nihil.* Et dicit ***docens in templo.*** Haec erat consuetudo sua semper ut doceret in templo. ***Et non me tenuistis.*** Unde patet quod sicut latrones venistis.

2266. Consequenter ponitur testimonium ***hoc autem totum factum est, ut implerentur Scripturae prophetarum.*** Et non dicit quorum, quia quasi in omnibus habetur; Ps. XXI, 17: *foderunt manus meas et pedes*

thousand men. Hence twelve legions are seventy-two thousands, and that is how many languages of men there are, as is had from Genesis (Gen 11). Hence he wishes to say: if all men were to rise up against me, the Lord could send a thousand angels against each language; *is there any numbering of his soldiers?* (Job 25:3) and, *thousands of thousands ministered to him, and ten thousand times a hundred thousand stood before him* (Dan 7:10).

Remigius speaks this way: all those who do God's will can be called angels, i.e., messengers; *go, swift angels, to a nation rent and torn in pieces* (Isa 18:2). For all those who serve God are called angels; *who make your angels spirits: and your ministers a burning fire* (Ps 103:4). Therefore the legion can be understood as a legion of the Romans. Hence the Lord could have brought in and provoked legions of Romans to destroy the Jews, as was done later under Titus and Vespasian.

2263. And some have used this passage to destroy the opinion of those who said that the Lord could not have done anything but what he does; for if he could have called together legions which he did not call together, it follows that he can do many things which he does not do.

2264. *How then will the Scriptures be fulfilled?* Here a third reason is set down why he should not prevent it: for Scripture has spoken this way, and therefore it must happen this way. And he does not say which Scriptures, because all the prophets had said it either in a hidden way or manifestly. Hence, *ought not Christ to have suffered these things, and so to enter into his glory?* (Luke 24:26).

2265. *In that same hour Jesus said to the multitudes.* In this part he reproves the emissaries. And he does two things: first, he mentions the thing done; second, the irrationality of the thing done, when he says ***as it were to a robber with swords and clubs to apprehend me.*** *He has gnashed with his teeth upon me* (Job 16:10), because they had come out as though he were a robber; they themselves came much more like robbers. A robber hides so as not to be caught; but Christ presents himself openly. And robbers, if they wish to do harm, do no harm in public; but Christ offered himself. Hence he says, ***I sat daily with you, teaching in the temple, and you did not lay hands on me***; therefore you have come like robbers. For in order to give them an opportunity, he left the city. ***I sat daily with you, teaching in the temple.*** A similar thing is found in John, *in secret I have spoken nothing* (John 18:20). And he says, ***teaching in the temple.*** This was always his custom, that he would teach in the temple. ***And you laid not hands on me.*** Hence it is clear that you have come like robbers.

2266. Next a testimony is set down: ***now all this was done, that the Scriptures of the prophets might be fulfilled.*** And he does not say which ones, because it is found as it were in all; *they have pierced my hands and feet. They have*

meos, et dinumeraverunt omnia ossa mea. Et Is. LIII, 3: *reputavimus eum novissimum virorum, virum dolorum.* Et dicit *ut implerentur*. Ly *ut* potest teneri causative, et sic non tenetur hic: vel consecutive, et sic accipitur hic. Quia enim prophetae dixerunt, non accidit; sed ideo praedixerunt, quia accidere debebat. Unde sensus est ut adimpleretur, idest hoc facto adimpletum est quod per prophetas praedictum erat.

2267. ***Tunc discipuli omnes, relicto eo, fugerunt***; ita quod compleretur quod dicitur in Ps. XXXVII, 12: *dereliquerunt me amici mei et proximi mei.*

Sed quare non a principio dereliquerunt? Respondet Hieronymus: quia scriptum est Io. VII, 30, quod *quaerebant eum, et nemo misit in eum manum, quia nondum venerat hora eius.* Unde a principio credebant quod se liberare posset, et se defenderet; sed cum viderunt quod captus esset, et quod non vellet se defendere, fugerunt et dereliquerunt eum.

numbered all my bones (Ps 21:17–18). And, *the most abject of men, a man of sorrows* (Isa 53:3). And he says, **that the Scriptures of the prophets might be fulfilled**. This **that** can be taken causatively, and it is not taken this way here; or consecutively, and this is how it is taken here. For it did not happen because the prophets had spoken, but rather they predicted it for this reason, that it was to happen. Hence the meaning is: so that it is fulfilled, i.e., by this deed was fulfilled what had been predicted by the prophets.

2267. **Then the disciples, all leaving him, fled**; so that what is said in the Psalm was fulfilled, *my friends and my neighbours . . . stood afar off* (Ps 37:12).

But why did they not leave him at the beginning? Jerome responds: because it is written that *they sought therefore to apprehend him: and no man laid hands on him, because his hour was not yet come* (John 7:30). Hence at the beginning they thought that he could free himself, and defend himself, but when they had seen that he was captured, and that he did not wish to defend himself, they fled and left him.

Lecture 7

26:57 At illi tenentes Iesum, duxerunt ad Caiapham principem sacerdotum, ubi scribae et seniores convenerant. [n. 2268]

26:58 Petrus autem sequebatur eum a longe usque in atrium principis sacerdotum, et ingressus intro sedebat cum ministris, ut videret finem. [n. 2270]

26:59 Principes autem sacerdotum et omne concilium, quaerebant falsum testimonium contra Iesum, ut eum morti traderent; [n. 2273]

26:60 et non invenerunt, cum multi falsi testes accessissent. Novissime autem venerunt duo falsi testes, [n. 2274]

26:61 et dixerunt: hic dixit: possum destruere templum Dei, et post triduum reaedificare illud. [n. 2276]

26:62 Et surgens princeps sacerdotum ait illi: nihil respondes ad ea quae isti adversum te testificantur? [n. 2279]

26:63 Iesus autem tacebat. Et princeps sacerdotum ait illi: adiuro te per Deum vivum, ut dicas nobis, si tu es Christus Filius Dei. [n. 2280]

26:64 Dicit illi Iesus: tu dixisti. Verumtamen dico vobis: amodo videbitis Filium hominis sedentem a dextris virtutis Dei, et venientem in nubibus caeli. [n. 2282]

26:65 Tunc princeps sacerdotum scidit vestimenta sua, dicens: blasphemavit: quid adhuc egemus testibus? Ecce nunc audistis blasphemiam, [n. 2286]

26:66 quid vobis videtur? At illi respondentes dixerunt: reus est mortis. [n. 2288]

26:57 Οἱ δὲ κρατήσαντες τὸν Ἰησοῦν ἀπήγαγον πρὸς Καϊάφαν τὸν ἀρχιερέα, ὅπου οἱ γραμματεῖς καὶ οἱ πρεσβύτεροι συνήχθησαν.

26:58 ὁ δὲ Πέτρος ἠκολούθει αὐτῷ ἀπὸ μακρόθεν ἕως τῆς αὐλῆς τοῦ ἀρχιερέως καὶ εἰσελθὼν ἔσω ἐκάθητο μετὰ τῶν ὑπηρετῶν ἰδεῖν τὸ τέλος.

26:59 Οἱ δὲ ἀρχιερεῖς καὶ τὸ συνέδριον ὅλον ἐζήτουν ψευδομαρτυρίαν κατὰ τοῦ Ἰησοῦ ὅπως αὐτὸν θανατώσωσιν,

26:60 καὶ οὐχ εὗρον πολλῶν προσελθόντων ψευδομαρτύρων. ὕστερον δὲ προσελθόντες δύο

26:61 εἶπαν· οὗτος ἔφη· δύναμαι καταλῦσαι τὸν ναὸν τοῦ θεοῦ καὶ διὰ τριῶν ἡμερῶν οἰκοδομῆσαι.

26:62 καὶ ἀναστὰς ὁ ἀρχιερεὺς εἶπεν αὐτῷ· οὐδὲν ἀποκρίνῃ τί οὗτοί σου καταμαρτυροῦσιν;

26:63 ὁ δὲ Ἰησοῦς ἐσιώπα. καὶ ὁ ἀρχιερεὺς εἶπεν αὐτῷ· ἐξορκίζω σε κατὰ τοῦ θεοῦ τοῦ ζῶντος ἵνα ἡμῖν εἴπῃς εἰ σὺ εἶ ὁ χριστὸς ὁ υἱὸς τοῦ θεοῦ.

26:64 λέγει αὐτῷ ὁ Ἰησοῦς· σὺ εἶπας. πλὴν λέγω ὑμῖν· ἀπ᾿ ἄρτι ὄψεσθε τὸν υἱὸν τοῦ ἀνθρώπου καθήμενον ἐκ δεξιῶν τῆς δυνάμεως καὶ ἐρχόμενον ἐπὶ τῶν νεφελῶν τοῦ οὐρανοῦ.

26:65 τότε ὁ ἀρχιερεὺς διέρρηξεν τὰ ἱμάτια αὐτοῦ λέγων· ἐβλασφήμησεν· τί ἔτι χρείαν ἔχομεν μαρτύρων; ἴδε νῦν ἠκούσατε τὴν βλασφημίαν·

26:66 τί ὑμῖν δοκεῖ; οἱ δὲ ἀποκριθέντες εἶπαν· ἔνοχος θανάτου ἐστίν.

26:57 But they, holding Jesus, led him to Caiphas the high priest, where the scribes and the elders were assembled. [n. 2268]

26:58 And Peter followed him from far off, even to the court of the high priest. And going in, he sat with the servants, that he might see the end. [n. 2270]

26:59 And the chief priests and the whole council sought false witness against Jesus, that they might put him to death; [n. 2273]

26:60 and they found not, though many false witnesses had come in. And last of all there came two false witnesses: [n. 2274]

26:61 and they said: this man said, I am able to destroy the temple of God, and after three days to rebuild it. [n. 2276]

26:62 And the high priest rising up, said to him: do you answer nothing to the things which these witness against you? [n. 2279]

26:63 But Jesus held his peace. And the high priest said to him: I adjure you by the living God, that you tell us if you are the Christ, the Son of God. [n. 2280]

26:64 Jesus said to him: you have said it. Nevertheless I say to you, hereafter you will see the Son of man sitting on the right hand of the power of God, and coming in the clouds of heaven. [n. 2282]

26:65 Then the high priest rent his garments, saying: he has blasphemed; what further need have we of witnesses? Behold, now you have heard the blasphemy. [n. 2286]

26:66 What do you think? But answering, they said: he is guilty of death. [n. 2288]

²⁶:⁶⁷ Tunc expuerunt in faciem eius, et colaphis eum ceciderunt. Alii autem palmas in faciem ei dederunt [n. 2289]

²⁶:⁶⁸ dicentes: prophetiza nobis, Christe: quis est qui te percussit? [n. 2291]

²⁶:⁶⁹ Petrus vero sedebat foris in atrio. Et accessit ad eum una ancilla, dicens: et tu cum Iesu Galilaeo eras. [n. 2292]

²⁶:⁷⁰ At ille negavit coram omnibus dicens: nescio quid dicis. [n. 2293]

²⁶:⁷¹ Exeunte autem illo ianuam, vidit eum alia ancilla, et ait his qui erant ibi: et hic erat cum Iesu Nazareno. [n. 2294]

²⁶:⁷² Et iterum negavit cum iuramento: quia non novi hominem. [n. 2294]

²⁶:⁷³ Et post pusillum accesserunt qui stabant, et dixerunt Petro: vere et tu ex illis es: nam et loquella tua manifestum te facit. [n. 2295]

²⁶:⁷⁴ Tunc coepit detestari et iurare, quia non novisset hominem. Et continuo gallus cantavit. [n. 2297]

²⁶:⁷⁵ Et recordatus est Petrus verbi Iesu, quod dixerat: priusquam gallus cantet ter me negabis: et egressus foras flevit amare. [n. 2302]

²⁶:⁶⁷ Τότε ἐνέπτυσαν εἰς τὸ πρόσωπον αὐτοῦ καὶ ἐκολάφισαν αὐτόν, οἱ δὲ ἐράπισαν

²⁶:⁶⁸ λέγοντες· προφήτευσον ἡμῖν, χριστέ, τίς ἐστιν ὁ παίσας σε;

²⁶:⁶⁹ Ὁ δὲ Πέτρος ἐκάθητο ἔξω ἐν τῇ αὐλῇ· καὶ προσῆλθεν αὐτῷ μία παιδίσκη λέγουσα· καὶ σὺ ἦσθα μετὰ Ἰησοῦ τοῦ Γαλιλαίου.

²⁶:⁷⁰ ὁ δὲ ἠρνήσατο ἔμπροσθεν πάντων λέγων· οὐκ οἶδα τί λέγεις.

²⁶:⁷¹ ἐξελθόντα δὲ εἰς τὸν πυλῶνα εἶδεν αὐτὸν ἄλλη καὶ λέγει τοῖς ἐκεῖ· οὗτος ἦν μετὰ Ἰησοῦ τοῦ Ναζωραίου.

²⁶:⁷² καὶ πάλιν ἠρνήσατο μετὰ ὅρκου ὅτι οὐκ οἶδα τὸν ἄνθρωπον.

²⁶:⁷³ μετὰ μικρὸν δὲ προσελθόντες οἱ ἑστῶτες εἶπον τῷ Πέτρῳ· ἀληθῶς καὶ σὺ ἐξ αὐτῶν εἶ, καὶ γὰρ ἡ λαλιά σου δῆλόν σε ποιεῖ.

²⁶:⁷⁴ τότε ἤρξατο καταθεματίζειν καὶ ὀμνύειν ὅτι οὐκ οἶδα τὸν ἄνθρωπον. καὶ εὐθέως ἀλέκτωρ ἐφώνησεν.

²⁶:⁷⁵ καὶ ἐμνήσθη ὁ Πέτρος τοῦ ῥήματος Ἰησοῦ εἰρηκότος ὅτι πρὶν ἀλέκτορα φωνῆσαι τρὶς ἀπαρνήσῃ με· καὶ ἐξελθὼν ἔξω ἔκλαυσεν πικρῶς.

²⁶:⁶⁷ Then they spat in his face, and buffeted him; and others struck his face with the palms of their hands, [n. 2289]

²⁶:⁶⁸ saying: prophesy to us, O Christ, who is he that struck you? [n. 2291]

²⁶:⁶⁹ But Peter sat without in the court; and there came to him a servant maid, saying: you also were with Jesus the Galilean. [n. 2292]

²⁶:⁷⁰ But he denied before them all, saying: I do not know what you are saying. [n. 2293]

²⁶:⁷¹ And as he went out of the gate, another maid saw him, and she said to those who were there: this man also was with Jesus of Nazareth. [n. 2294]

²⁶:⁷² And again he denied with an oath: I do not know the man. [n. 2294]

²⁶:⁷³ And after a little while those came who stood by, and said to Peter: surely you also are one of them; for even your speech discovers you. [n. 2295]

²⁶:⁷⁴ Then he began to curse and to swear that he did not know the man. And immediately the cock crowed. [n. 2297]

²⁶:⁷⁵ And Peter remembered the word of Jesus which he had said: before the cock crow, you will deny me three times. And going out, he wept bitterly. [n. 2302]

2268. Supra actum est de captione Christi, nunc agitur quo sit ductus; et describitur locus et societas convenientium ad locum.

Dicit ergo *at illi*, scilicet qui tenuerunt eum, *duxerunt eum ad Caipham*. Iste Caiphas erat pontifex anni illius secundum Hieronymum, secundum quod habetur Io. XI, v. 49: *cum autem esset pontifex anni illius*. Iam enim sacerdotium non secundum legis praeceptum agebatur. Mandaverat Dominus quod Aaron et filii eius essent sacerdotes iure haereditario, ita quod mortuo uno remaneret alter sacerdos. Sed post, ambitione crescente, non potuerunt pati, sed subiecta Iudaea Romanis, iste Caiphas emerat sacerdotium a Iudaeis, emerat a Pilato;

2268. Above, he treated of the seizing of Christ; now he treats of how he was led. And he describes the place and the group which came together to the place.

It says therefore, *but they*, namely those who had seized him, *led him to Caiphas*. This Caiphas was the high priest that year according to Jerome, in accord with what is said in John, *being the high priest that year* (John 11:49). For at that time the priesthood was not handled according to the precept of the law. The Lord had commanded that Aaron and his sons should be the priests by right of inheritance, such that when one died another priest would remain. But later, as their ambition grew, they could not endure but, with Judea subjected to the Romans, this man Caiphas bought the

ideo iniquus erat princeps. Et non mirum si iniquus iudex, sive princeps, iniquum facit iudicium.

Et hoc convenit mysterio; quia sicut passio Christi erat oblatio veri sacrificii, sic et locus congruere debebat, ut Christus, qui est sacerdos in aeternum, in domo pontificis offerretur. *Caiphas* 'investigator' interpretatur, et potest referri ad malitiam, qua Christum condemnavit.

2269. Sed hic est quaestio, quia Io. c. XVIII, 13 dicitur quod primo ductus est ad Annam. Et hoc intelligendum est esse verum: convenerant enim ad domum Annae, et ibi congregati erant; et in hoc apparet malitia eorum, quia cum intenti esse deberent solemnitati, erant intenti malitiae, ita quod bene conveniebat eis quod dicitur Is. I, 14: *solemnitates vestras odivit anima mea*. Unde completum est quod dictum est Ps. II, 2: *convenerunt adversus Deum, et adversus Christum eius*.

2270. *Petrus autem sequebatur eum a longe*. Actum est de loco, hic agitur de Petro perveniente. Primo ducitur, deinde Petrus pervenit. Et tria facit: quia primo tangit modum; secundo quomodo sequens pervenerit.

Quod pervenerit, hoc erat fervoris; quod a longe, hoc erat timoris; unde significabatur quod in fide Petri fundata Ecclesia secutura erat Christum, tamen a longe; quia Christus passus est pro Ecclesia, non pro se; Petrus autem et Ecclesia passa est pro se.

Item tangitur locus, quia **usque in atrium principis sacerdotum**: non enim ausus est intrare domum, ne videretur esse de discipulis Iesu. Quomodo autem intravit, tacet Matthaeus, sed narrat Ioannes XVIII, 15, quia *discipulus quidam notus erat pontifici, et introduxit Petrum*.

2271. Sequitur societas *et ingressus intro sedebat cum ministris, ut videret finem*; et hoc faciebat vel ex curiositate, vel ex pietate. Et haec tria iam erant quaedam dispositiva ad casum Petri: quod a longe sequebatur, hoc disponebat, quia significabat quod non erat firmus; qui enim firmus est, debet appropinquare. Unde dicitur Iac. IV, 8: *appropinquate Deo, et appropinquabit vobis*. In domo enim est sedes Dei et Agni, ut habetur Apoc. ult., 3. In domo enim erat perfecta caritas. Unde Petrus non appropinquavit ad caritatem Christi.

Item non pervenerat ad malitiam Iudaeorum, ideo tepidus erat; ideo accidit ei id quod dicitur in Apoc. III, 16: *quia tepidus es, eiiciam te de ore meo*.

Item quia famuli mali. Eccli. X, 2: *secundum iudicem populi, sic et minister eius*. Et ideo non fuit mirum si priesthood from the Jews, and bought it from Pilate; so a wicked man was the ruler. And it is no marvel if a wicked judge, or a wicked ruler, should form a wicked judgment.

And this fits with a mystery, for just as Christ's passion was the oblation of a true sacrifice, so also the place should have been fitting, that Christ, who is a priest forever, might be offered in the house of the high priest. *Caiphas* means 'investigator,' and can be referred to the malice with which he condemned Christ.

2269. But here there is a question, because John says that he was led first to Annas (John 18:13). This should be understood to be true: for they had come together at the house of Annas, and were gathered there; and this shows their malice, for when they were supposed to be focused on the solemnity, they were focused on malice, such that what is said in Isaiah fits them well: *my soul hates your new moons, and your solemnities* (Isa 1:14). Hence what was said was fulfilled: *the princes met together, against the Lord and against his Christ* (Ps 2:2).

2270. *And Peter followed him from far off*. Having treated of the place, here he treats of Peter's arrival. First he is led, then Peter arrives. And he does three things: for first, he touches on the manner; second, how he arrived, following.

That he came was due to fervor; that he followed from a distance was due to fear; hence it signified that the Church, founded on Peter's faith, was going to follow Christ, yet from a distance: for Christ suffered for the Church, not for himself, while Peter and the Church suffered for themselves.

Likewise, the place is touched upon: *even to the court of the high priest*, for he did not dare to enter the house, lest he seem to be a disciple of Jesus. Matthew does not mention how he entered, but John says that *a certain disciple was known to the high priest, and brought Peter in* (John 18:15).

2271. There follows the group: *and going in, he sat with the servants, that he might see the end*. And he did this either out of curiosity or out of piety. And these three things were already certain dispositive factors toward Peter's fall: that he followed from a distance was dispositive, because it indicated that he was not firm, for one who is firm should draw near. Hence it says, *draw near to God, and he will draw near to you* (Jas 4:8). For in the house is the seat of God and of the Lamb, as is said (Rev. 22:3). For perfect charity was in the house. Hence Peter did not draw near to the charity of Christ.

Also, he had not arrived at the malice of the Jews, and so he was tepid; so what is said, happened to him: *but because you are lukewarm, and neither cold, nor hot, I will begin to vomit you out of my mouth* (Rev 3:16).

Also, because of the bad servants. *As the judge of the people is himself, so also are his ministers* (Sir 10:2). And

cecidit, quia in mala societate mansit. Quare Ps. XVII, 16: *cum sancto sanctus eris*.

2272. Tunc sequitur examinatio Christi. Et

primo per testes;

secundo per propriam confessionem, ibi ***et surgens princeps sacerdotum ait illi*** et cetera.

Circa primum tria facit.

Primo designatur perversum studium principum;

secundo defectum;

tertio falsum testimonium.

2273. Dicit ergo ***principes autem sacerdotum quaerebant falsum testimonium contra Iesum, ut eum morti traderent***.

Sed est quaestio, quare non sine testimonio eum morti tradebant. Una causa est, quia hypocritae quaerunt quod videtur esse bonum, sed veritatem non quaerunt: sic isti quaerebant ut viderentur non a se facere, unde contra legem faciebant; Ex. XX, 16: *non loquaris contra proximum tuum falsum testimonium*. Si non licet loqui, nec quaerere. Alia ratio erat, quia non habebant auctoritatem occidendi, et ideo quaerebant ut ipsum tradere possent principi.

2274. ***Et non invenerunt, cum tamen multi falsi testes accessissent***. Ecce defectus, in quo designatur innocentia Christi, ut posset dicere: *ego in innocentia mea ingressus sum*. Semper enim insidiati sunt Christo, sed non invenerunt aliquid mali. Unde implevit illud quod habetur I Petr. II, v. 15: *benefacientes obmutescere faciatis imprudentium hominum ignorantiam*.

2275. Tunc sequitur falsum testimonium ***novissime autem venerunt duo falsi testes, et dixerunt***.

Sed hic est quaestio, quare dicantur ***falsi testes***: quia manifestum est Christum dixisse, Io. II, 19. Secundum Hieronymum, non solum falsus dicitur qui dicit quod nescit, sed qui dictum ad falsum refert intellectum.

2276. ***Hic dixit: possum destruere templum Dei, et post triduum reaedificare illud***. Sed non intelligebat de templo materiali, sed de templo corporis sui. Item non solum est falsum testimonium quoad sensum, sed quoad vocem, quia dixerat: ***solvite templum hoc***; et non dixit: *possum solvere templum Dei*; quasi dicat: *vos Iudaei solvite templum, idest Christum, et post triduum resuscitabo illud*. Non dixit: *et post triduum reaedificabo*; quia reaedificare magis ad materiale templum pertinet, sed excitare magis ad corpus. Unde falsi testes erant tam ratione vocis, quam ratione significationis.

therefore it was not a marvel if he fell, since he stayed in bad company. For which reason it says, *with the holy, you will be holy* (Ps 17:26).

2272. Then there follows the examination of Christ. And

first, through witnesses;

second, through his own confession, at ***and the high priest rising up***.

Concerning the first, he does three things:

first, the chief priests' corrupt pursuit is described;

second, the failure;

third, false testimony.

2273. It says therefore, ***and the chief priests and the whole council sought false witness against Jesus, that they might put him to death***.

But there is a question, why they did not put him to death without testimony. One reason is that hypocrites seek what seems to be good, but do not seek the truth: thus these men sought to seem like they were not acting of themselves, whence they acted against the law; *you shall not bear false witness against your neighbor* (Exod 20:16). If one is not permitted to speak it, neither is one permitted to seek it. Another reason was that they did not have the authority to kill, and so they sought to be able to hand him over to the ruler.

2274. ***And they found not, though many false witnesses had come in***. Behold, the failure, by which Christ's innocence is indicated, so that he could say, *I have walked in my innocence* (Ps 25:1). For they were always plotting against Christ, but did not find anything bad. Hence he fulfilled what is said: *that by doing well you may put to silence the ignorance of foolish men* (1 Pet 2:15).

2275. Then there follows the false testimony: ***and last of all there came two false witnesses: and they said***.

But there is a question here, why they are called ***false witnesses***, for it is clear that Christ said these things (John 2:19). According to Jerome, not only is he called false who says what he does not know, but also he who refers the thing said to a false understanding of it.

2276. ***This man said, I am able to destroy the temple of God, and after three days to rebuild it***. But he did not understand this as about the material temple, but as about the temple of his own body. Also, it is not only false testimony as regards the meaning, but as regards the words spoken, for he had said: ***destroy this temple***, and he did not say, *I am able to destroy the temple of God*, as though to say: *you Jews, destroy the temple, i.e., Christ, and after three days I will raise it up*. He did not say, *and after three days to rebuild it*, because to rebuild pertains more to a material temple, but to raise up pertains more to the body. Hence they were false witnesses both by reason of what was said, and by reason of its meaning.

2277. Item est quaestio. Quare non accusant eum de violatione Sabbati?

Respondet Chrysostomus quod quia saepe accusaverunt eum de hoc, et semper excusaverat se, et excusationem confirmaverat miraculis; ideo cogitabant quod non valeret eis. Item iudex non erat Iudaeus, ideo sciebant quod non reciperet hanc accusationem.

2278. Tunc sequitur examinatio per propriam confessionem. Et

primo ponitur interrogatio quantum ad testificationem;

secundo quoad principale. Secunda ibi *et princeps sacerdotum ait illi* et cetera.

2279. Dicit ergo *surgens princeps sacerdotum ait illi: nihil respondes ad ea quae isti adversum te testificantur?* Quod surrexit, fuit ex impatientia et furore, audiens quod Christus non convincebatur: et quod dicit, *nihil respondes* etc., non dicit ut excusaret eum, sed ut caperet eum in sermone; Is. XXXII, v. 6: *stultus fatua loquetur, et cor eius faciet iniquitatem.*

2280. *Iesus autem tacebat.* Sed quare tacebat? Propter tria. Ut doceret nos cautelam: sciebat enim quod quicquid ille diceret, totum ad calumniam referrent; et in tali casu coram insidiatoribus est tacendum; Ps. XXXVIII, 2: *posui ori custodiam, cum consisteret peccator adversum me.* Alia ratio erat, quia tunc non erat tempus docendi, sed patientiam habendi: et ita completum est quod dicitur Is. c. LIII, 7: *quasi agnus coram tondente se obmutescet, et non aperit os suum.* Tertia ratio est ut doceret nos constantiam, quando aliquis de aliquo accusatur iniuste; Is. LI, 7: *opprobrium hominum ne metuatis.*

2281. Tunc sequitur quaestio de principali *princeps autem sacerdotum ait illi: adiuro te per Deum vivum, ut dicas mihi, si tu es Christus Filius Dei.* Et primo ponitur inquisitio; secundo Domini responsio.

Videns princeps quod non posset capere, adiuravit eum: et hoc ut in sermone caperet. Et hoc habetur Io. X, 24: *usquequo animam nostram tollis? Si tu es Christus, dic nobis palam.* Apud enim Iudaeos pro magno habebatur adiurare: adiurare enim est ad iuramentum cogere. Sicut enim Christiani non debent iurare nisi ex necessitate, sic nec debent uti adiuratione, sed loco adiurationis debent uti oratione.

2282. Tunc sequitur responsio *dixit illi Iesus: tu dixisti.* Notate quod cum aliquid fuit contra eum, tacuit; sed statim cum adiurata fuit potestas patris, respondet. Unde gloriam patris semper quaesivit; Io. VIII, 50: *ego gloriam meam non quaero.* Et circa hoc primo ponit responsionem; secundo manifestationem.

2277. Again there is a question. Why do they not accuse him of violation of the Sabbath?

Chrysostom responds that they had often accused him of this, and he had always exonerated himself, and confirmed the exhonoration with miracles; so they thought it would do them no good. Also, the judge was not a Jew, so they knew that he would not accept this accusation.

2278. Then there follows the examination by his own confession. And

first, he sets down the questioning as regards the testimony;

second, as regards the main issue at hand. The second is at, *and the high priest said to him*.

2279. It says therefore, *and the high priest rising up, said to him: do you answer nothing to the things which these witness against you?* That he arose was due to impatience and fury, hearing that Christ was not convicted. And when he says, *do you answer nothing*, he does not speak to exonerate him, but to catch him in his words; *for the fool will speak foolish things, and his heart will work iniquity* (Isa 32:6).

2280. *But Jesus held his peace.* But why was he silent? For three reasons. To teach us caution: for he knew that whatever he might say, the whole thing would be used for a false accusation; and in such a case one should be silent before the treacherous. *I have set guard to my mouth, when the sinner stood against me* (Ps 38:2). Another reason was that then was not the time for teaching, but for having patience: and so what is said was fulfilled, *he will be led as a sheep to the slaughter, and will be dumb as a lamb before his shearer, and he will not open his mouth* (Isa 53:7). A third reason is to teach us constancy when someone accuses us unjustly of something; *fear not the reproach of men* (Isa 51:7).

2281. Then there follows a question from the chief priest: *and the high priest said to him: I adjure you by the living God, that you tell us if you are the Christ, the Son of God.* And first, the questioning is set down; second, the Lord's response.

The chief priest, seeing that he could not catch him, adjured him: and this was to catch him in his words. And this is found, *how long do you hold our souls in suspense? If you are the Christ, tell us plainly* (John 10:24). For to adjure was considered a great thing among the Jews: for to adjure is to force an oath. For just as Christians should only take an oath out of necessity, so they should not use adjuration, but should use a request instead of adjuration.

2282. Then there follows the response: *Jesus said to him: you have said it.* Note that when something was done against him, he was silent, but when the power of the Father was adjured, he responds at once. For he always sought the Father's glory; *I seek not my own glory* (John 8:50). And concerning this, first he sets out a response; second, a manifestation.

Dicit ergo *dixit illi Iesus: tu dixisti*, potest exponi ut Christus non asserat, sed relinquat in dubio; supra VII, 6: *nolite sanctum dare canibus*. Vel potest assertive legi: *tu dixisti*, idest verum est; et patet, quia dicitur in Mc. XIV, 62: *ego sum*.

Tunc evidentiam ostendit *verumtamen dico vobis: amodo videbitis Filium hominis sedentem a dextris virtutis Dei*. Et vult evidenter ostendere quod ipse sit Filius Dei, secundum duas auctoritates. Una est in Ps. CIX, 1: *dixit Dominus Domino meo: sede a dextris meis*. Et per hanc ostenderat supra XXII, 42–46 quod Christus erat Filius Dei. Alia est Daniel VII, 7: *aspiciebam in visione noctis; et ecce cum nubibus caeli quasi Filius hominis veniebat* et cetera. Ita, dico, dicit, scilicet *tu dixisti*; sed non nosti veritatem. Attende, quia veritas manifestabitur, quia *videbitis Filium hominis sedentem a dextris virtutis Dei*.

2283. Quia dixit *sedentem a dextris*, exponit Chrysostomus quod sessio a dextris signat dignitatem regiam; Is. IX, 7: *super solium David, et super regnum eius sedebit*. Vel sedere a dextris est esse in plena beatitudine virtutis, vel in bonis potioribus: dextera enim nobilior pars est; ideo maiorem dignitatem significat, non quia maiorem habeat potestatem, sed aequalem; infra ult., v. 18: *data est mihi omnis potestas in caelo et in terra*. Item de eius potestate dicit: *venientem in nubibus caeli*.

2284. Sed quid est quod dicit *amodo videbitis?* et cetera. Notandum quod id quod dicit *in nubibus*, potest referri ad adventum ultimum, vel quotidianum. Adventus ultimus erit in nube; Act. I, 11: *quemadmodum vidistis eum euntem in caelum*; et supra XXIV dicitur quod *veniet in nubibus*. Alio modo potest exponi de adventu quotidiano, de quo Iob c. IX, 11: *si venerit ad me, non videbo eum*. Et iste adventus est in nubibus, idest in apostolis et sacris doctoribus. De istis dicitur Is. c. LX, 8: *qui sunt isti, qui ut nubes volant?* Isti dicuntur nubes, quia in altum ascendunt. Item nubes foecundae sunt. Primum pertinet ad altitudinem vitae, secundum ad foecunditatem doctrinae. Et sunt nubes caeli, idest caelestes, quia portaverunt imaginem caelestem.

2285. Sed quid est *amodo videbitis?* Idest statim post passionem aliquos convertit ad fidem, alios per operum evidentiam. Unde aliqui conversi sunt propter eorum fidem, quidam propter bonam operationem. Item si referatur ad ultimum adventum, dicit Origenes: *totum tempus mundi comparatum ad aeternitatem nihil est, sicut unum momentum*. Ps. LXXXIX, 4: *mille anni ante oculos tuos sicut dies hesterna, quae praeteriit*. Ideo dicit *amodo*, quia nihil est tempus usque ad iudicium respectu aeternitatis. Verumtamen postquam a me recideritis, non

It says therefore, *Jesus said to him: you have said it*. It can be explained such that Christ does not assert anything, but leaves it in doubt; above, *do not give that which is holy to dogs* (Matt 7:6). Or, it can be read assertively: *you have said it*, i.e., it is true; and it is clear, because it says, *I am* (Mark 14:26).

Then he offers evidence: *nevertheless I say to you, hereafter you will see the Son of man sitting on the right hand of the power of God*. And he wishes to show plainly that he is the Son of God, according to two authorities. One is, *the Lord said to my Lord: sit at my right hand* (Ps 109:1). And by this he had shown above (Matt 22:42–46), that Christ was the Son of God. The other is, *I beheld therefore in the vision of the night, and lo, one like the son of man came with the clouds of heaven* (Dan 7:13). Thus, I say, he says, namely *you have said it*; but you have not known the truth. Pay attention, because the truth will be manifested, for *you will see the Son of man sitting on the right hand of the power of God*.

2283. Because he said, *sitting on the right hand*, Chrysostom explains that to sit at the right hand signifies kingly dignity; *he will sit upon the throne of David, and upon his kingdom* (Isa 9:7). Or, to sit at the right hand is to be in the full beatitude of power, or in the more powerful goods: for the right hand is the nobler part, so it signifies a greater dignity, not because he has a greater power, but an equal one; below, *all power is given to me in heaven and in earth* (Matt 28:18). He also says about his power: *coming in the clouds of heaven*.

2284. But why does he say, *hereafter you will see*? Note that when he says, *in the clouds*, it can be referred to the last coming, or to the daily coming. The last coming will be on a cloud; *this Jesus who is taken up from you into heaven, will so come, as you have seen him going into heaven* (Acts 1:11); and above (Matt 24), it says that he will come in clouds. In another way, it can be explained as about the daily coming, about which it says, *if he come to me, I will not see him* (Job 9:11). And this coming is in the clouds, i.e., in the apostles and holy doctors. It says about this, *who are these, that fly as clouds?* (Isa 60:8). They are called clouds because they go up on the heights. Likewise, clouds are fruitful. The first pertains to loftiness of life, the second to fruitfulness of doctrine. And they are the clouds of heaven, i.e., heavenly, because they bear the heavenly image.

2285. But what is *hereafter you will see*? That is, immediately after the passion he converted some to the faith, others through the evidence of works. Hence some were converted owing to their faith, some owing to a good work. Also, if it is referred to the last coming, Origen says: *the whole time of the world, compared to eternity, is nothing, is as one moment*. For it is written, *for a thousand years in your sight are as yesterday, which is past* (Ps 89:4). This is why he says, *hereafter*, because the time until the judgment is nothing with regard to eternity. Nevertheless, after you

restat nisi quod manifeste me cognoscetis, quia veniam in nubibus caeli. Et tunc cognoscetis me esse Filium hominis. Similis modus loquendi habetur supra c. XXIII, 39: *non me videbitis amodo, donec dicatis: benedictus qui venit in nomine Domini.*

2286. *Tunc princeps sacerdotum scidit vestimenta tua.* Hic ponitur condemnatio. Et
  primo ponitur quomodo condemnatur;
  secundo quomodo a discipulo negatur.
  Et
  primo agit de condemnatione;
  secundo de delusione.
  Circa primum duo facit. Quia
  primo princeps eum condemnat;
  secundo exquirit sententiam.

2287. Condemnans autem ostendit culpam et facto, et verbo: facto, quia *scidit vestimenta sua*. Eodem furore scidit vestimenta sua, quo paulo ante surrexit de sede sua: consuetum enim erat quod qui audiebant blasphemiam scindebant vestimenta sua in signum quod non poterant audire. Verum quod haec duo fecit, aliquid significabatur: quod surrexit de solio, ostendebat quod amitteret sacerdotium; et quod scidit vestimenta sua, significabat quod transferri debebat; ad Hebr. VII, 12: *translato sacerdotio, necesse est quod translatio legis fiat.* Vestis Christi non fuit scissa; Io. XIX, 24: *non dividamus eam, sed sortiamur de illa, cuius sit.* Unde significabat abolitionem. Et hoc signatur I Reg. XV, 28: *scidit dominus regnum Israel a te hodie.* Sic scissum est a Iudaeis, et datum est membris Christi.

Tunc imponit culpam *blasphemavit*, quia hoc dixerat, reputabat eum blasphemum; unde Io. X, 33: *de bono opere non lapidamus te, sed de blasphemia, quia homo cum sis, filium Dei te facis*; et tali debebatur mors.

Tunc manifestat culpam *quid adhuc indigemus testibus?*

2288. Tunc exquirit sententiam *quid vobis videtur? At illi respondentes dixerunt: reus est mortis*, secundum iudicium legis. Et hoc esset verum, si esset blasphemus; sed non erat, ideo male iudicant, quia auctorem vitae morti condemnant; I Cor. XV, 22: *sicut enim mors per Adam in omnes homines, sic et vita per Iesum.*

2289. *Tunc expuerunt in faciem eius* et cetera. Post condemnationem Christi agitur de illusione. Et satis convenienter, quia Christus peccata nostra tulit, ut Is. LXII. Homo autem per peccatum in mortem est traditus, quando dictum est ei, Gen. II, 17: *quacumque hora comederitis, morte moriemini.* Item proprium honorem amisit, quia *homo cum in honore esset, non intellexit, comparatus est iumentis insipientibus*, Ps. XLVIII, 13.

have fallen away from me, there is nothing left but that you know me manifestly, because I will come on the clouds of heaven. And then you will know that I am the Son of man. A similar way of speaking is found above, *you will not see me from now on, till you say: blessed is he who comes in the name of the Lord* (Matt 23:39).

2286. *Then the high priest rent his garments.* Here the condemnation is set down. And
  first, how he is condemned is set down;
  second, how he is denied by a disciple.
  And
  first, he treats of the condemnation;
  second, of the ridiculing.
  Concerning the first, he does two things:
  first, the chief priest condemns him;
  second, he seeks a judgment.

2287. However, the one condemning expressed Christ's guilt both by deed and by word: by deed, because he **rent his garments**. He tore his garments in the same fury in which a little while before he rose from his seat, for it was customary that one who heard blasphemy tore his garments as a sign that he could not bear to hear it. The fact that he did these two things signified something: that he rose from the throne showed that he lost the priesthood; and that he tore his garments signified that it had to be passed on. *For the priesthood being translated, it is necessary that a translation also be made of the law* (Heb 7:12). Christ's garments were not torn; *let us not cut it, but let us cast lots for it, whose it shall be* (John 19:24). Hence it signified abolition. And this is indicated: *the Lord has rent the kingdom of Israel from you this day* (1 Sam 15:28). Thus it was cut off from the Jews, and was given to the members of Christ.

Then he imputes guilt: **he has blasphemed**. Because he had said this, he considered him a blasphemer; hence, *for a good work we do not stone you, but for blasphemy; and because you, being a man, make yourself God* (John 10:33); and such a man deserves to die.

Then he manifests the guilt: **what further need have we of witnesses?**

2288. Then he seeks a judgment: **what do you think? But answering, they said: he is guilty of death**, according to the judgment of the law. And this would be true, if he were a blasphemer; but he was not, so they judge badly, for they condemn to death the author of life; *and as in Adam all die, so also in Christ all will be made alive* (1 Cor 15:22).

2289. **Then they spat in his face**. After the condemnation of Christ, he treats of the ridiculing. And fittingly enough, for Christ bore our sins (Isa 53). Moreover, through sin man was handed over to death, when it was said to him, *for in whatever day you eat of it, you will die the death* (Gen 2:17). Likewise, he lost honor, for *man when he was in honor did not understand; he is compared to senseless beasts, and is become like to them* (Ps 48:13).

Et ideo Christus redemptor mortem et opprobria primo facto sustinuit; secundo verbo, ibi **prophetiza nobis, Christe**.

In prima conspuitur, et colaphis caeditur; in secunda in facie percutitur.

2290. Quantum ad primum dicitur **tunc expuerunt in faciem eius, et colaphis eum ceciderunt**; secundum quod habetur ex verbis, istud fiebat in signum mandati Dei contempti, unde habetur Deut. XXV, 5 ss. si aliquis nolebat accipere uxorem fratris, quod conspuebant in faciem suam. Item propter contemptum mandati paterni: sic de Maria sorore Moysi. Unde expuebant in faciem eius, quia blasphemum reputabant; Is. c. l, 6: *faciem meam non averti ab increpantibus et conspuentibus in me*. Item *colaphis caedebant*, ad modum ebrii vel stulti; Is. c. LIII, 3: *vidimus eum novissimum virorum*, idest ita despectus videbatur ac si esset novissimus omnium virorum. **Alii autem palmas in faciem dederunt**, in irreverentiam; Thren. III, v. 30: *dabit percutienti se maxillam*. Mystice, secundum Augustinum, adhuc hoc aliqui faciunt: quia spuere in faciem nihil aliud est quam contemnere praesentiam gratiae Christi; ad Hebr. X, 29: *quanto magis putatis maiora mereri supplicia, qui Filium Dei conculcaverit, et sanguinem testamenti pollutum duxerit, in quo sanctificatus est, et Spiritui gratiae contumeliam fecerit?* Sed proprie colaphizat, qui caput manui supponit: et tales sunt qui magis dignitatem suam inquirunt, quam Christi honorem. De talibus dicitur quod *dilexerunt homines magis tenebras quam lucem*. Illi autem qui faciem percutiunt, sunt illi qui quodammodo praesentiam eius demoliri contendunt, ut sunt Iudaei. De his Is. XXX, 11: *cesset a facie nostra Sanctus Israel*.

2291. Tunc improperia ingerunt verbo **prophetiza nobis, Christe: quis est qui te percussit?** Et hoc dicebant illudendo, quia nullus eorum pro propheta eum habebat; et non erat necessarium: infamia enim eorum manifesta erat. Unde hoc noluit dicere; Iob XVI, v. 11: *et exprobrantes percusserunt maxillam meam*.

2292. Petrus autem sedebat foris. Hic agitur de negatione Petri. Lucas XXII, 55 autem alio ordine refert, quia primo ponit negationem Petri, quam illusionem Christi; Matthaeus autem e contrario. Et non est contrarietas, quia dum illuderetur, simul factum est; ideo non refert si ante vel post ponatur.

Et notandum quod cum ducebatur, non negat; sed quando illuditur, negat, ad significandum quod quidam magis timent opprobria quam verbera, contra illud Is. LI, 7: *nolite timere opprobria hominum et blasphemias eorum nolite metuere*.

And this is why Christ the redeemer endured death and reproach, first by deed; second by word, at **prophesy to us, O Christ**.

In the first he is spat upon, and struck with blows; in the second, he is struck in the face.

2290. With regard to the first, it says, **then they spat in his face, and buffeted him**; according to what is had from the words, this was done as a sign of contempt of God's commandment, for it says that if anyone would not receive the wife of a brother, they spat in his face (Deut 25:5). Also, owing to contempt of the commandment of a father: so it was said about Mary the sister of Moses (Num 12:14). Hence they spat in his face because they considered him a blasphemer; *I have not turned away my face from those who rebuked me, and spit upon me* (Isa 50:6). Likewise, they hit him, in the manner of a man drunk or foolish; *the most abject of men* (Isa 53:3), i.e., he seemed despised as though he were the most abject of all men. **And others struck his face with the palms of their hands**, in irreverence; *he will give his cheek to him who strikes him* (Lam 3:30). Mystically, according to Augustine, some do this even now: for to spit in his face is nothing other than to despise the presence of Christ's grace; *how much more, do you think he deserves worse punishments, who has trodden under foot the Son of God, and has esteemed the blood of the testament unclean, by which he was sanctified, and has offered an affront to the Spirit of grace?* (Heb 10:29). But he properly strikes a blow who subjects the head to the hand: and such are those who seek their own dignity more than Christ's honor. About such men it is said, that *men loved darkness rather than the light* (John 3:19). And the ones who strike his face are those who in a certain way strive to remove his presence, as are the Jews. Of these Isaiah says, *let the Holy One of Israel cease from before us* (Isa 30:11).

2291. Then they inflict taunts by word: **prophesy to us, O Christ, who is he that struck you?** And they said this by way of ridicule, because none of them took him for a prophet; and it was not necessary for Christ to prophesy, for their irreverent speech was plain. So he did not wish to speak; *reproaching me they have struck me on the cheek* (Job 16:11).

2292. But Peter sat without in the court. Here he treats of Peter's denial. Luke reports another order, for he puts Peter's denial before the mockery of Christ (Luke 22:25), but Matthew the other way around. And there is no conflict, because while he was being mocked this was done at the same time; so it makes no difference whether it be placed before or after.

And one should notice that when Christ was led away, he did not deny him; but when he is mocked, he denies him, to signify that some fear reproach more than lashes, contrary to: *fear not the reproach of men, and be not afraid of their blasphemies* (Isa 51:7).

Et circa hoc
primo ponitur negatio;
secundo poenitentia Petri *et continuo gallus cantavit; et recordatus est Petrus verbi Iesu*.
Prima dividitur in tres, secundum tres negationes.

Secunda ibi *exeunte autem illo ianuam* etc.; tertia ibi *et post pusillum accesserunt qui stabant* et cetera.

2293. Et primo ponitur locus, secundo occasio, tertio negatio.

Dicit ergo *Petrus autem sedebat foris*, scilicet extra locum ubi Christus patiebatur: illi enim qui a Christo se elongant, cito confunduntur; Ier. XVII, 13: *domine, omnes qui te derelinquunt, confundentur*. E contrario in Ps. XXXIII, 6: *accedite ad eum, et illuminamini et facies vestrae non confundentur*. Qui enim est extra passionem Christi, de facili labitur.

Tunc ponitur excitativum ad denegandum *et accessit ad eum una ancilla dicens: et tu cum Iesu Galilaeo eras*. Et convenit casus Petri casui primi hominis; Eccli. XXV, 33: *a muliere initium peccati*. Sic Petrus ad vocem mulieris Christum negavit; in quo Dominus praesumptionem eius humiliare voluit, quia non ad vocem viri, sed mulieris. *Et tu cum Iesu Nazareno eras*. Hoc solebat ei esse gloriosum, sed modo est ei terribile, et ideo negavit *at ille negavit coram omnibus dicens: nescio quid dicis*.

Si volumus aggravare culpam Petri, possumus aggravare ex tribus. Aggravatur, quia statim ad modicum terrorem negavit; Lev. XXVI, v. 36: *terrebit eos sonitus folii volantis*. Item quia non erubuit coram omnibus. Item ex mendacio, quia dixit *nescio quid dicis*, et *non novi hominem*; contra illud Eccli. IV, 24: *ne confundaris dicere verum*.

2294. *Exeunte autem illo ianuam, vidit eum alia ancilla et ait his qui erant ibi: et hic erat cum Iesu Nazareno. Et iterum negavit*. Hic ponitur secunda negatio. Et primo tangitur locus; secundo incitativum; tertio negatio.

Quantum ad historiam, secundum Marcum c. XIV, 66 post primam negationem gallus cantavit, et tunc exivit ianuam, et vidit eum ancilla, et negavit. Sed videtur contrarius aliis, quia videntur alii dicere quod sedentes dixerunt; et Lucas XXII, 55 dicit quod unus de sedentibus. Quid ergo hic dicitur quod ancilla? Notandum, secundum Augustinum, quod quando negaverat, exivit: et dum esset in exeundo, dixit ei ancilla etc.; et tunc negavit; quod audiens Petrus reversus est intus. Tunc illi qui audierant ab ancilla, petierunt idem. Et potest esse quod unus, qui cognoscebat eum, magis urgebat eum. Et iterum *cum iuramento negavit, quia non novi hominem*;

And concerning this,
first, the denial is set down;
second, Peter's repentance, at *and immediately the cock crowed. And Peter remembered the word of Jesus*.

The first is divided into three parts, according to the three denials.

The second is at *and as he went out of the gate*; the third, at *and after a little while those came who stood by*.

2293. And first, the place is set down; second, the occasion; third, the denial.

It says therefore, *but Peter sat without in the court*, namely outside the place where Christ was suffering: for those who distance themselves from Christ are quickly confounded. *All who forsake you will be confounded* (Jer 17:13). On the contrary, *come to him and be enlightened: and your faces will not be confounded* (Ps 33:6). For the one who is outside of Christ's passion easily slips and falls.

Then the provocation to denial is set down: *and there came to him a servant maid, saying: you also were with Jesus the Galilean*. And Peter's fall lines up with the fall of the first man; *from the woman came the beginning of sin* (Sir 25:33). In the same way, Peter denied Christ at the words of a woman, by which the Lord wished to humiliate his presumption, because it was not at the words of a man, but of a woman. *You also were with Jesus the Galilean*. This used to be a glorious thing to him, but now it is terrible to him, and so he denies it: *but he denied before them all, saying: I do not know what you are saying*.

If we wish to make Peter's guilt worse, we can make it worse in three ways. It is made worse because right away, at a small fright, he denied Christ; *the sound of a flying leaf will terrify them* (Lev 26:36). Likewise, because he was not ashamed to do it before all. Likewise, by lying, because he said, *I do not know what you are saying*, and *I do not know the man*; contrary to: *for your soul be not ashamed to say the truth* (Sir 4:24).

2294. *And as he went out of the gate, another maid saw him, and she said to those who were there: this man also was with Jesus of Nazareth. And again he denied*. Here the second denial is set down. And first, he touches on the place; second, the provocation; third, the denial.

As regards history, according to Mark, the cock crowed after the first denial, and then he went out the door and another maid saw him, and he denied him again (Mark 14:66). But this seems contrary to the others, because the others seem to say that those who were sitting spoke; and Luke says that it was one of those sitting (Luke 22:55). What then is said here about a maid? One should note, according to Augustine, that when he had denied him, he went out, and while he was in the process of going out, a maid spoke to him, and then he denied him again; hearing, Peter turned back inside. Then those who had heard what the maid said asked the same thing. And it can be that one who knew him

contra illud Eccli. XXIII, 9: *iurationi ne assuescat os tuum*.

2295. Tunc sequitur tertia negatio. Et primo describitur tempus; secundo incitativum; tertio negatio. Dicit ergo **et post pusillum**. Lucas dicit quod *facto intervallo quasi unius horae*. Et hoc procurabat diabolus, ut respirationem non haberet. Unde dicunt ei **et tu ex illis es**; et hoc probant **nam et loquela tua manifestum te facit**.

2296. Sed constat quod omnes Iudaei erant; quomodo ergo dicit **nam et loquela tua manifestum te facit**? Solvit Hieronymus quod in eadem lingua saepe diversa locutio fit, sicut patet in Francia, et Picardia, et Burgundia, et tamen una loquela est. Sic Galilaei aliquam differentiam habebant a Ierosolymitanis. Sic et cuilibet potest dici: **nam et loquela tua manifestum te facit**; quia, ut dicitur Lc. VI, 45, *ex abundantia cordis os loquitur*; quia cum homo est carnalis, cito prorumpit in verba carnalia; cum spiritualis, in verba spiritualia.

2297. **Tunc coepit detestari et iurare** et cetera. Aliqui sunt qui volunt excusare Petrum, quod non peccavit; unde cum dixit **non novi hominem**, verum est hominem, sed hominem et Deum. Et hoc non est bonum, quia imponit mendacium Christo: quia dixerat Christus **tu me negabis**. Ideo melius est dicere quod Petrus potius mentitus est, quam Christus.

Item notandum quod non solum negavit Christum sed negavit se esse Christianum. Unde in una negatione dixit **non novi eum**, scilicet non sum Christianus.

2298. Item notandum quod qui cito non se retrahit in peius vadit; Eccli. XIX, 1: *qui spernit modica, paulatim defluit*. Unde negationi periurium addidit, periurio blasphemiam. Unde Gregorius: *peccatum quod per poenitentiam non diluitur, mox suo pondere ad aliud trahit*.

2299. Item notandum quod signatur triplex tentatio qua tentatur homo. Tentatur a concupiscentia carnis; Iac. I, 14: *unusquisque tentatur a concupiscentia sua*. Item tentatur a cupiditate terrenorum; Sap. XIV, 2: *illud enim cupiditas acquirendi excogitavit*. Item a daemonibus, et hoc signatur per illam negationem, in qua dicitur **post pusillum accesserunt qui stabant**. Ad Eph. VI, 12: *non est nobis colluctatio adversus carnem et sanguinem, sed adversus principes et potestates, adversus mundi rectores tenebrarum harum, contra spiritualia nequitiae in caelestibus*. De istis tribus habetur I Io. II, 6: *omne quod est in mundo, aut est concupiscentia carnis, aut concupiscentia oculorum, aut superbia vitae*.

Vel aliter, secundum Augustinum, dicendum est, quod per istas tres negationes omnium haereticorum

was pressing him more. **And again he denied with an oath, I do not know the man**; contrary to: *do not let your mouth be accustomed to swearing* (Sir 23:9).

2295. Then there follows the third denial. And first, the time is described; second, the provocation; third, the denial. It says then, **and after a little while**. Luke says, *and after the space, as it were of one hour* (Luke 22:59). And the devil obtained this, that he might have no time to breathe. Hence they say to him, **surely you also are one of them**, and they prove it, **for even your speech discovers you**.

2296. But since they were all Jews, why does it say, **for even your speech discovers you**? Jerome resolves it, saying that different phrases often occur in the same language, as is clear in France, and Picardy, and Burgundy, and yet there is one speech. In the same way, the Galileans had some things different from the Jerusalemites. So also it can be said to any man: **for even your speech discovers you**; for, as is said, *for out of the abundance of the heart the mouth speaks* (Luke 6:45), for when a man is carnal, he quickly breaks into carnal words; when he is spiritual, into spiritual words.

2297. **Then he began to curse and to swear**. There are some who wish to excuse Peter, saying that he did not sin. Hence when he said, **I do not know the man**, it is true that he did not know a man, but one who was man and God. And this is not good, because it places the lie on Christ: for Christ had said, **you will deny me** (Matt 26:34). So it is better to say that Peter lied, rather than Christ.

Also, one should notice that he not only denied Christ but denied that he was a Christian. For in one denial he said, **I do not know the man**, that is, I am not a Christian.

2298. Likewise, one should note that he who does not quickly draw himself back falls into something worse; *he who contemns small things, will fall by little and little* (Sir 19:1). Hence to the denial he added a perjury, and to the perjury a blasphemy. Hence Gregory says: *a sin which is not washed away by repentance soon, by its own weight, draws one to another*.

2299. Likewise, one should note that this signifies the three temptations by which a man is tempted. He is tempted by the concupiscence of the flesh; *every man is tempted by his own concupiscence* (Jas 1:14). Likewise, he is tempted by a desire for earthly things; *for this the desire of gain devised* (Wis 14:2). Likewise, by the demons, and this is signified by this denial, in which it says, **and after a little while those came who stood by**. For our wrestling is not against flesh and blood; but against principalities and power, against the rulers of the world of this darkness, against the spirits of wickedness in the high places (Eph 6:12). It says about these three, *for all that is in the world, is the concupiscence of the flesh, and the concupiscence of the eyes, and the pride of life* (1 John 2:16).

Or in another way, following Augustine, one should say that these three denials signify the error of all heretics. For

error signatur. Quidam enim Christi divinitatem negabant, ut Photinus; quidam autem humanitatem, ut Eunomius; quidam utrumque, ut Arius qui inaequalem Patri dicebat Filium.

Item, secundum Origenem, signatur persecutio, quam habitura erat Ecclesia. Prima fuit a Iudaeis, in qua multi mortui sunt; secunda a gentibus, in qua multi martyres facti sunt; tertia ab haereticis, quae multos seduxit, et aliqui etiam mortui sunt.

2300. Item notandum quod inveniuntur quaedam scripta, quae videntur excusare Petrum, quod non peccavit mortaliter, quia dicit Bernardus: *sopita fuit in eo caritas, non extincta*. Dicendum quod mortaliter peccavit, non tamen fuit ex malitia, sed timore mortis. Et hoc voluit dicere Bernardus, quod *sopita fuit* et cetera.

2301. *Et continuo gallus cantavit*. Hic agitur de poenitentia Petri. Et

primo ponitur motivum, sive excitativum;

secundo poenitentia eius, ibi *et egressus foras flevit amare*.

2302. Tanguntur duo, quibus fit excitatio. Primo cantus galli; unde *et continuo gallus cantavit*. Per gallum praedicator signatur, qui homines peccatores excitat ad poenitentiam; unde Apostolus, I Cor. XV, 34: *evigilate, iusti et nolite peccare*; et ad Eph. V, 14: *surge, qui dormis, et exurge a mortuis, et illuminabit te Christus*.

Secundum est memoria Petri *et recordatus est Petrus verbi Iesu, quod dixerat* et cetera. Ps. XXI, 28: *reminiscentur, et convertentur ad Dominum omnes fines terrae*. Et haec duo frequenter accidunt ad vocem praedicatoris, quia qui oblitus est Deum per peccata, ad vocem praedicatoris revertitur. De illo gallo dicitur in Iob XXXVIII, 36: *quis dedit gallo intelligentiam?*

Item Lucas ponit tertium, quia *Dominus respexit Petrum*. Apostolus ad Rom. c. III, 24: *iustificati gratis per gratiam ipsius*. Thren. V, 21: *converte nos, Domine, ad te, et convertemur*.

2303. Post agitur de poenitentia Petri: *et egressus foras flevit amare*. Et est poenitentia commendabilis ex tribus. Et primo, quia cito, quia statim egressus; Eccli. V, 8: *ne tardes converti ad Dominum*. Item prudens, quia declinavit a consortio eorum, qui induxerant eum ad negandum; sic et poenitentes debent occasionem vitare peccandi; II ad Cor. VI, 17: *exite de medio eorum, et separamini, dicit Dominus, et immundum ne tetigeritis, et ego recipiam vos*. Item quia efficax et vera; Ier. VI, 26: *luctum unigeniti fac tibi, planctum amarum*; Is. XXXVIII, 15: *recogitabo tibi omnes annos meos in amaritudine animae meae*.

some denied Christ's divinity, like Photinus; and some the humanity, like Eunomius; some both, like Arius, who said the Son is unequal to the Father.

Likewise, according to Origen, it signifies the persecution the Church was going to endure. First, it was from the Jews, in which many died; the second, from the gentiles, in which many were made martyrs; the third, from heretics, which seduced many, and some even died.

2300. Also, one should note that there are found certain things written which seem to excuse Peter, saying that he did not sin mortally, for Bernard says: *charity was stunned in him, but not extinquished*. One should say that he sinned mortally, yet it was not out of malice, but fear of death. And this is what Bernard wished to say, that it *was stunned*.

2301. *And immediately the cock crowed*. Here he treats of Peter's repentance. And

first, the motive is set down, or provocation;

second, his repentance, at *and going out, he wept bitterly*.

2302. Two things are touched upon by which he was provoked. First, the crowing of the cock; hence, *and immediately the cock crowed*. The cock signifies the preacher, who provokes sinners to repentance; hence the Apostle: *awake, you just, and sin not* (1 Cor 15:34); and, *rise you who sleep, and arise from the dead: and Christ will enlighten you* (Eph 5:14).

Second is Peter's memory: **and Peter remembered the word of Jesus which he had said**. *All the ends of the earth will remember, and will be converted to the Lord* (Ps 21:28). And these two things frequently occur at the voice of a preacher, because the one who has forgotten God through sin turns back at the voice of a preacher. It says about this cock, *who gave the cock understanding?* (Job 38:36).

Luke also sets down a third, namely that *the Lord looked at Peter* (Luke 22:61). The Apostle: *being justified freely by his grace* (Rom 3:24). *Convert us, O Lord, to yourself and we will be converted* (Lam 5:21).

2303. Then he treats of Peter's repentance: **and going out, he wept bitterly**. And his repentance is commendable for three reasons. And first, that it was quick, for he went out immediately; *do not delay to be converted to the Lord* (Sir 5:8). Likewise, it was prudent, for he left the company of those who had led him to denial; so also those who repent should avoid the occasion of sinning; *wherefore, go out from among them, and be separate, says the Lord, and do not touch the unclean thing: and I will receive you* (2 Cor 6:17–18). Likewise, because it was efficacious and true; *make you mourning as for an only son, a bitter lamentation* (Jer 6:26); *I will recount to you all my years in the bitterness of my soul* (Isa 38:15).

Chapter 27

Lecture 1

27:1 Mane autem facto consilium inierunt omnes principes sacerdotum et seniores populi adversus Iesum, ut eum morti traderent. [n. 2305]

27:2 Et vinctum adduxerunt eum, et tradiderunt Pontio Pilato praesidi. [n. 2306]

27:3 Tunc videns Iudas, qui eum tradidit, quod damnatus esset, poenitentia ductus, retulit triginta argenteos principibus sacerdotum et senioribus, [n. 2308]

27:4 dicens: peccavi, tradens sanguinem iustum. At illi dixerunt: quid ad nos? Tu videris. [n. 2312]

27:5 Et proiectis argenteis in templo recessit, et abiens laqueo se suspendit. [n. 2314]

27:6 Principes autem sacerdotum, acceptis argenteis, dixerunt: non licet eos mittere in corbanam, quia pretium sanguinis est. [n. 2316]

27:7 Consilio autem inito, emerunt ex illis agrum figuli in sepulturam peregrinorum. [n. 2319]

27:8 Propter hoc vocatus est ager ille Haceldama, hoc est ager sanguinis, usque in hodiernum diem. [n. 2320]

27:9 Tunc impletum est quod dictum est per Ieremiam prophetam dicentem: *et acceperunt triginta argenteos, pretium appretiati, quem appretiaverunt a filiis Israel*, [n. 2321]

27:10 *et dederunt eos in agrum figuli, sicut constituit mihi Dominus.* [n. 2321]

27:1 Πρωΐας δὲ γενομένης συμβούλιον ἔλαβον πάντες οἱ ἀρχιερεῖς καὶ οἱ πρεσβύτεροι τοῦ λαοῦ κατὰ τοῦ Ἰησοῦ ὥστε θανατῶσαι αὐτόν·

27:2 καὶ δήσαντες αὐτὸν ἀπήγαγον καὶ παρέδωκαν Πιλάτῳ τῷ ἡγεμόνι.

27:3 Τότε ἰδὼν Ἰούδας ὁ παραδιδοὺς αὐτὸν ὅτι κατεκρίθη, μεταμεληθεὶς ἔστρεψεν τὰ τριάκοντα ἀργύρια τοῖς ἀρχιερεῦσιν καὶ πρεσβυτέροις

27:4 λέγων· ἥμαρτον παραδοὺς αἷμα ἀθῶον. οἱ δὲ εἶπαν· τί πρὸς ἡμᾶς; σὺ ὄψῃ.

27:5 καὶ ῥίψας τὰ ἀργύρια εἰς τὸν ναὸν ἀνεχώρησεν, καὶ ἀπελθὼν ἀπήγξατο.

27:6 Οἱ δὲ ἀρχιερεῖς λαβόντες τὰ ἀργύρια εἶπαν· οὐκ ἔξεστιν βαλεῖν αὐτὰ εἰς τὸν κορβανᾶν, ἐπεὶ τιμὴ αἵματός ἐστιν.

27:7 συμβούλιον δὲ λαβόντες ἠγόρασαν ἐξ αὐτῶν τὸν ἀγρὸν τοῦ κεραμέως εἰς ταφὴν τοῖς ξένοις.

27:8 διὸ ἐκλήθη ὁ ἀγρὸς ἐκεῖνος ἀγρὸς αἵματος ἕως τῆς σήμερον.

27:9 τότε ἐπληρώθη τὸ ῥηθὲν διὰ Ἰερεμίου τοῦ προφήτου λέγοντος· καὶ ἔλαβον τὰ τριάκοντα ἀργύρια, τὴν τιμὴν τοῦ τετιμημένου ὃν ἐτιμήσαντο ἀπὸ υἱῶν Ἰσραήλ,

27:10 καὶ ἔδωκαν αὐτὰ εἰς τὸν ἀγρὸν τοῦ κεραμέως, καθὰ συνέταξέν μοι κύριος.

27:1 And when morning came, all the chief priests and elders of the people took counsel against Jesus, that they might put him to death. [n. 2305]

27:2 And they brought him bound, and delivered him to Pontius Pilate the governor. [n. 2306]

27:3 Then Judas, who betrayed him, seeing that he was condemned, repenting himself, brought back the thirty pieces of silver to the chief priests and elders, [n. 2308]

27:4 saying: I have sinned in betraying innocent blood. But they said: what is that to us? You look to it. [n. 2312]

27:5 And casting down the pieces of silver in the temple, he departed, and went and hung himself with a halter. [n. 2314]

27:6 But the chief priests, having taken the pieces of silver, said: it is not lawful to put them into the corbona, because it is the price of blood. [n. 2316]

27:7 And after they had consulted together, they bought the potter's field with it, to be a burying place for strangers. [n. 2319]

27:8 For this cause, the field was called Haceldama, that is, the field of blood, even to this day. [n. 2320]

27:9 Then was fulfilled that which was spoken by Jeremiah the prophet, saying: *and they took the thirty pieces of silver, the price of him who was prized, whom they prized of the children of Israel.* [n. 2321]

27:10 *And they gave them to the potter's field, as the Lord appointed to me.* [n. 2321]

27:11 Iesus autem stetit ante praesidem, et interrogavit eum praeses dicens: tu es rex Iudaeorum? Dicit illi Iesus: tu dicis. [n. 2322]	27:11 Ὁ δὲ Ἰησοῦς ἐστάθη ἔμπροσθεν τοῦ ἡγεμόνος· καὶ ἐπηρώτησεν αὐτὸν ὁ ἡγεμὼν λέγων· σὺ εἶ ὁ βασιλεὺς τῶν Ἰουδαίων; ὁ δὲ Ἰησοῦς ἔφη· σὺ λέγεις.	27:11 And Jesus stood before the governor, and the governor asked him, saying: are you the king of the Jews? Jesus said to him: you say it. [n. 2322]
27:12 Et cum accusaretur a principibus sacerdotum et senioribus, nihil respondit. [n. 2326]	27:12 καὶ ἐν τῷ κατηγορεῖσθαι αὐτὸν ὑπὸ τῶν ἀρχιερέων καὶ πρεσβυτέρων οὐδὲν ἀπεκρίνατο.	27:12 And when he was accused by the chief priests and elders, he answered nothing. [n. 2326]
27:13 Tunc dicit illi Pilatus: non audis quanta adversum te dicant testimonia? [n. 2327]	27:13 τότε λέγει αὐτῷ ὁ Πιλᾶτος· οὐκ ἀκούεις πόσα σου καταμαρτυροῦσιν;	27:13 Then Pilate said to him: do you not hear what great testimonies they allege against you? [n. 2327]
27:14 Et non respondit ei ad ullum verbum, ita ut miraretur praeses vehementer. [n. 2328]	27:14 καὶ οὐκ ἀπεκρίθη αὐτῷ πρὸς οὐδὲ ἓν ῥῆμα, ὥστε θαυμάζειν τὸν ἡγεμόνα λίαν.	27:14 And he did not answer to any word; so that the governor wondered exceedingly. [n. 2328]
27:15 Per diem autem solemnem consueverat praeses populo dimittere unum vinctum quem voluissent. [n. 2331]	27:15 Κατὰ δὲ ἑορτὴν εἰώθει ὁ ἡγεμὼν ἀπολύειν ἕνα τῷ ὄχλῳ δέσμιον ὃν ἤθελον.	27:15 Now, upon the solemn day, the governor was accustomed to release to the people one prisoner, whom they wished. [n. 2331]
27:16 Habebat autem tunc vinctum insignem, qui dicebatur Barabbas. [n. 2331]	27:16 εἶχον δὲ τότε δέσμιον ἐπίσημον λεγόμενον [Ἰησοῦν] Βαραββᾶν.	27:16 And he had then a notorious prisoner, who was called Barabbas. [n. 2331]
27:17 Congregatis ergo illis, dixit Pilatus: quem vultis dimittam vobis, Barabbam, an Iesum, qui dicitur Christus? [n. 2332]	27:17 συνηγμένων οὖν αὐτῶν εἶπεν αὐτοῖς ὁ Πιλᾶτος· τίνα θέλετε ἀπολύσω ὑμῖν, [Ἰησοῦν τὸν] Βαραββᾶν ἢ Ἰησοῦν τὸν λεγόμενον χριστόν;	27:17 They therefore being gathered together, Pilate said: whom do you wish that I release to you, Barabbas, or Jesus who is called the Christ? [n. 2332]
27:18 Sciebat enim quod per invidiam tradidissent eum. [n. 2333]	27:18 ᾔδει γὰρ ὅτι διὰ φθόνον παρέδωκαν αὐτόν.	27:18 For he knew that for envy they had delivered him. [n. 2333]
27:19 Sedentem autem illo pro tribunali, misit ad eum uxor eius dicens: nihil tibi et iusto illi. Multa enim passa sum hodie per visum propter eum. [n. 2334]	27:19 Καθημένου δὲ αὐτοῦ ἐπὶ τοῦ βήματος ἀπέστειλεν πρὸς αὐτὸν ἡ γυνὴ αὐτοῦ λέγουσα· μηδὲν σοὶ καὶ τῷ δικαίῳ ἐκείνῳ· πολλὰ γὰρ ἔπαθον σήμερον κατ' ὄναρ δι' αὐτόν.	27:19 And as he was sitting for the tribunal, his wife sent to him, saying: have nothing to do with that just man; for I have suffered many things this day in a vision because of him. [n. 2334]
27:20 Princeps autem sacerdotum et seniores persuaserunt populis, ut peterent Barabbam, Iesum vero perderent. [n. 2337]	27:20 Οἱ δὲ ἀρχιερεῖς καὶ οἱ πρεσβύτεροι ἔπεισαν τοὺς ὄχλους ἵνα αἰτήσωνται τὸν Βαραββᾶν, τὸν δὲ Ἰησοῦν ἀπολέσωσιν.	27:20 But the chief priests and elders persuaded the people, that they should ask for Barabbas, and make Jesus away. [n. 2337]
27:21 Respondens autem praeses ait illis: quem vultis vobis de duobus dimitti? At illi dixerunt: Barabbam. [n. 2338]	27:21 ἀποκριθεὶς δὲ ὁ ἡγεμὼν εἶπεν αὐτοῖς· τίνα θέλετε ἀπὸ τῶν δύο ἀπολύσω ὑμῖν; οἱ δὲ εἶπαν· τὸν Βαραββᾶν.	27:21 And the governor answering, said to them: which of the two do you wish to be released to you? But they said: Barabbas. [n. 2338]
27:22 Dicit illis Pilatus: quid igitur faciam de Iesu, qui dicitur Christus? [n. 2340]	27:22 λέγει αὐτοῖς ὁ Πιλᾶτος· τί οὖν ποιήσω Ἰησοῦν τὸν λεγόμενον χριστόν; λέγουσιν πάντες· σταυρωθήτω.	27:22 Pilate said to them: what should I do then with Jesus who is called the Christ? [n. 2340]

²⁷:²³ Dicunt omnes: crucifigatur. Ait illis praeses: quid enim mali fecit? At illi magis clamabant, dicentes: crucifigatur. [n. 2340]	²⁷:²³ ὁ δὲ ἔφη· τί γὰρ κακὸν ἐποίησεν; οἱ δὲ περισσῶς ἔκραζον λέγοντες· σταυρωθήτω.	²⁷:²³ They all said: let him be crucified. The governor said to them: why, what evil has he done? But they cried out the more, saying: let him be crucified. [n. 2340]
²⁷:²⁴ Videns autem Pilatus, quia nihil proficeret, sed magis tumultus fieret, accepta aqua lavit manus coram populo dicens: innocens ego sum a sanguine iusti huius, vos videritis. [n. 2342]	²⁷:²⁴ Ἰδὼν δὲ ὁ Πιλᾶτος ὅτι οὐδὲν ὠφελεῖ ἀλλὰ μᾶλλον θόρυβος γίνεται, λαβὼν ὕδωρ ἀπενίψατο τὰς χεῖρας ἀπέναντι τοῦ ὄχλου λέγων· ἀθῷός εἰμι ἀπὸ τοῦ αἵματος τούτου· ὑμεῖς ὄψεσθε.	²⁷:²⁴ And Pilate seeing that nothing prevailed, but rather that a tumult was made, taking water washed his hands before the people, saying: I am innocent of the blood of this just man; you look to it. [n. 2342]
²⁷:²⁵ Et respondens universus populus, dixit: sanguis eius super nos, et super filios nostros. [n. 2343]	²⁷:²⁵ καὶ ἀποκριθεὶς πᾶς ὁ λαὸς εἶπεν· τὸ αἷμα αὐτοῦ ἐφ᾽ ἡμᾶς καὶ ἐπὶ τὰ τέκνα ἡμῶν.	²⁷:²⁵ And the whole people answering, said: his blood be upon us and our children. [n. 2343]
²⁷:²⁶ Tunc dimisit illis Barabbam, Iesum autem flagellatum tradidit eis, ut crucifigeretur. [n. 2344]	²⁷:²⁶ τότε ἀπέλυσεν αὐτοῖς τὸν Βαραββᾶν, τὸν δὲ Ἰησοῦν φραγελλώσας παρέδωκεν ἵνα σταυρωθῇ.	²⁷:²⁶ Then he released to them Barabbas, and having scourged Jesus, delivered him to them to be crucified. [n. 2344]

2304. Supra Evangelista narravit quod passus est Christus a Iudaeis, hic narrat quod passus est a gentilibus: et quatuor facit.

Primo tangit quomodo traditus est gentibus;

secundo quomodo examinatur;
tertio quomodo condemnatur;
quarto quomodo patitur.

Secunda ibi *Iesus autem stetit ante praesidem* etc.; tertia ibi *per diem solemnem consueverat praeses* etc.; quarta ibi *tunc milites praesidis suscipientes Iesum in praetorium* et cetera.

Circa primum duo.

Primo narrat de assignatione, qua traditus est in manibus gentilium;

secundo de morte et peccato traditoris, ibi *tunc videns Iudas, qui eum tradidit, quod damnatus esset*.

Circa primum tria.

Primo motivum assignat;
secundo modum;
tertio factum.

2305. Causa fuit consilium habitum de morte: et secundum hoc tria tangit, ex quibus aggravatur eorum peccatum. Primo ex sollicitudine, et hoc tangit cum dicit **mane autem facto consilium inierunt**, quia cum tota nocte solliciti essent in illusione, tamen mane convenerunt. Unde bene solliciti erant; Iob XXIV, v. 14: *mane primo consurgit homicida*.

Item aggravatur ex communitate, quia **omnes principes**. Si enim unus, vel duo, excusabile esset; sed omnes convenerunt; Is. I, 6: *a planta pedis usque ad verticem non est in eo sanitas*; ideo dicit **omnes principes**;

2304. Above, the Evangelist recounted what Christ suffered from the Jews; here he recounts what he suffered from the gentiles: and he does four things:

first, he touches on how he is handed over to the gentiles;

second, how he is tried;
third, how he is condemned;
fourth, how he suffers.

The second is at **and Jesus stood before the governor**; the third, at **now, upon the solemn day, the governor was accustomed**; the fourth, at **then the soldiers of the governor taking Jesus into the praetorium** (Matt 27:27).

Concerning the first, two things:

first, he tells about the allotment by which he is given over into the hands of the gentiles;

second, about the death and sin of the betrayer, at **then Judas, who betrayed him, seeing that he was condemned**.

Concerning the first, three things:

first, he gives the motive;
second, the manner;
third, the deed.

2305. The cause was the plan they formed for his death: and in accord with this he touches on three things by which their sin is made worse. First, by solicitude, and he touches on this when he says, **and when morning came . . . they took counsel**, for while they had been solicitous at mockery the whole night, yet in the morning they came together. Hence they were quite solicitous; *the murderer rises at the very break of day* (Job 24:14).

Likewise, it is made worse by partnership, for **all the chief priests**. For if it had been one or two, it would have been excusable, but all came together; *from the sole of the foot unto the top of the head, there is no soundness therein*

Ezech. c. XI, 2: *Fili hominis, hi sunt viri qui cogitant iniquitatem, et tractant consilium pessimum.*

Item ex crudelitate, quia multa alia cogitare poterant, sed cogitabant quomodo *eum morti traderent*; Prov. I, 16: *pedes eorum ad malum currunt et festinant ut effundant sanguinem.*

2306. Sed quomodo? **Vinctum adduxerunt.** Haec erat consuetudo, quod tales vincti adducerentur et signarentur morti condemnati. Et signavit quod sicut mortem nostram sua morte destruxit, sic vincula peccatorum vinculis suis destruxit.

2307. Et tradiderunt Pontio Pilato. Et quare? Triplex est ratio. Una litteralis erat, quia vicarius erat imperatoris, et Iudaei non habebant iudicium sanguinis. Propter quod dicunt in Io. XVIII, 31: *nobis non licet interficere quemquam.*

Item ex intentione ipsorum: ipsi enim nolebant occulte interficere, sed manifeste, ut fama divulgaretur, secundum quod habetur Sap. c. II, 20: *morte turpissima condemnemus eum.*

Tertia causa est, quia pro omnibus voluit mori, ideo voluit ut omnes congregarentur, tam Iudaei quam gentiles, ita quod impletum est illud Ps. II, 2: *astiterunt reges terrae, et principes convenerunt in unum.*

2308. Tunc videns Iudas, qui eum tradidit, quod damnatus esset et cetera. Hic agitur de poenitentia et morte Iudae.

Et circa hoc duo facit.

Primo narrat de proditione;

secundo quid factum sit de pretio, ibi **principes autem sacerdotum, acceptis argenteis, dixerunt.**

Circa primum

primo agitur de poenitentia;

secundo de desperatione, ibi **et proiectis argenteis in templo, recessit.**

Circa primum tria facit.

Primo ponitur motivum;

secundo poenitentia;

tertio effectus.

2309. Motivum **tunc videns quod damnatus esset, poenitentia ductus, retulit triginta argenteos.** Potuit esse quod credidit Iudas, quando vendidit eum, quod non occideretur, sed quod flagellaretur; ideo videns quod damnatus esset, poenituit.

Sed est quaestio, quando traditus fuit praesidi, quomodo videre potuit quod esset damnatus. Hieronymus dicit quod hoc vidit oculo mentis, quia ex quo vidit quod a Iudaeis damnatus erat, et traditus Pilato, cogitavit quod Pilatus iudicaret ad voluntatem eorum, scilicet Iudaeorum. Origenes dixit quod quidam dixerunt: **videns**

(Isa 1:6); this is why he says, **all the chief priests**. *Son of man, these are the men that study iniquity, and frame a wicked counsel* (Ezek 11:2).

Likewise, by cruelty, because they could have considered many other things, but they considered how **they might put him to death**; as it is written: *for their feet run to evil, and make haste to shed blood* (Prov 1:16).

2306. But how? **They brought him bound**. This was the custom, that such men were brought bound, and were marked as condemned to death. And it signified that just as he destroyed our death by his death, so he destroyed the bonds of sinners by his own bonds.

2307. And delivered him to Pontius Pilate. And why? There are three reasons. One is literal, that he was the vicar of the emperor, and the Jews did not have judgment over blood. On account of which they say, *it is not lawful for us to put any man to death* (John 18:31).

Also, there is a reason from their intention: for they did not want to kill him in a hidden manner, but openly, that the story might become commonly known, in accord with what is said, *let us condemn him to a most shameful death* (Wis 2:20).

A third reason is because he wanted to die for all, so he desired that all should be gathered together, both the Jews and the gentiles, so that the Psalm was fulfilled, *the kings of the earth stood up, and the princes met together* (Ps 2:2).

2308. Then Judas, who betrayed him, seeing that he was condemned. Here he treats of the repentance and death of Judas.

And concerning this he does two things:

first, he tells about the betrayal;

second, what was done about the reward, at **but the chief priests, having taken the pieces of silver, said**.

Concerning the first,

first, he treats of the repentance;

second, of the despair, at **and casting down the pieces of silver in the temple, he departed**.

Concerning the first, he does three things:

first, the motive is set down;

second, the repentance;

third, the effect.

2309. The motive: **seeing that he was condemned, repenting himself, brought back the thirty pieces of silver**. It could be that Judas thought, when he sold him, that he would not be killed, but that he would be scourged; so seeing that he was condemned, he repented.

But there is a question, when he had been handed over to the governor, how he could think that he was condemned. Jerome says that he saw this with the eye of the mind, because having seen that he had been condemned by the Jews, and handed over to Pilate, he thought that Pilate would judge him as they wished, namely the Jews. Origen said that some have said: **Judas . . . seeing that he was**

Iudas quod esset damnatus, scilicet ipse Iudas, ex isto motus fuit ad poenitentiam.

2310. Unde ***poenitentia ductus retulit triginta argenteos***. Et haec poenitentia non fuit vera poenitentia; habuit tamen aliquid poenitentiae, quia poenitentia debet esse media inter spem et timorem; Iudas autem timorem et dolorem quidem habuit, quia de peccato praeterito doluit, sed spem non habuit. Et talis est poenitentia impiorum; Sap. V, 3: *poenitentiam agentes, et prae angustia spiritus gementes*.

2311. Et quare ductus poenitentia? Notandum quod dicit Origenes, quod aliquando accidit quod diabolus impellit hominem ad peccandum, aliquando homo; sed aliter et aliter, quia homo ut libidinem compleat, diabolus ut perdat. Et si diabolus immisit, non habuit ex creatione, et ideo poenitere potuit.

Et hoc est contra Manichaeos, qui dicunt quod duplex est creatio, bona et mala, et qui sunt de creatione mala, non possunt bene agere, et e converso. Et secundum eos Iudas fuit de creatione mala. Quomodo ergo potuit poenitere? Dicit ergo quod hoc quod desperavit, non fuit nisi quia negligens fuit.

2312. Sequitur effectus. Effectus poenitentiae est ut peccator studeat emendare. Peccaverat, quia vendiderat Christum, fecerat enim quod in se erat: ideo ***triginta denarios retulit***. Et primo ponitur retractatio; secundo poenitentia, ibi ***peccavi tradens sanguinem iustum***.

Retulit ergo ***triginta argenteos***; et in hoc retractavit, dicens ***peccavi***, idest vere deliqui. In hoc autem quod dicit ***tradens sanguinem iustum***, etsi bene dicit, non complete tamen, quia potest retorqueri ad hominem iustum. Unde Ier. XXVI, 15: *si occideritis me, sanguinem innocentem tradetis contra vosmetipsos*. Unde dicit Hieronymus quod si rectam fidem habuisset, non desperasset. Debuit enim dicere, tradens Deum. In hoc ergo quod dixit ***tradens sanguinem iustum***, minoravit eius potestatem, et ostendit se non habere rectam fidem.

2313. Tunc ponitur Iudaeorum obstinatio ***at illi dixerunt: quid ad nos?*** Iste iustum confitebatur, et tamen dicunt ***quid ad nos?*** Ier. VIII, 7: *populus meus non cognovit iudicium Domini*. ***Tu videris***, idest non sequimur conscientiam tuam. Remigius: ***quid ad nos?*** Tu primo vendidisti, et post iustum confiteris. Quis videris apud nos, qui ita mutas sententiam? Mutare enim de malo in bonum, bonum est: de malo autem in malum, malum; Eccli. XXVII, 12: *iustum in aeternum stat, stultus autem ut luna mutatur*.

2314. Tunc ponitur desperatio. Desperatus enim de bonis temporalibus nihil curat; et sic facit iste, quia ***proiectis argenteis in templo recessit***, non habuit curam de

condemned, namely Judas himself, and this moved him to repentance.

2310. Hence, ***repenting himself, brought back the thirty pieces of silver***. And this repentance was not true repentance, yet had something of repentance, because repentance should be a middle between hope and fear; but Judas had fear and sorrow, indeed, for he sorrowed over his past sin, but he did not have hope. And such is the repentance of the impious; *repenting, and groaning for anguish of spirit* (Wis 5:3).

2311. And why did he repent? One should note that Origen says that it sometimes happens that the devil urges a man on to sin, and sometimes that a man does; but in different ways, for a man does so to satisfy lust, the devil to destroy. And if the devil threw him down, he did not have this from his creation, and therefore he could have repented.

And this is against the Manichees, who say that there are two creations, a good and a bad, and that those who are of the bad creation cannot act well, and vice versa. And according to them, Judas was of the bad creation. How then could he have repented? He says therefore that the fact that he despaired only happened because he was negligent.

2312. There follows the effect. The effect of repentance is that the sinner is eager to repair his sin. He had sinned, because he had sold Christ, for he had done what was in himself: for this reason, he ***brought back the thirty pieces of silver***. And first, the bringing back is set down; second, the repentance, at ***I have sinned in betraying innocent blood***.

He brought back therefore ***the thirty pieces of silver***; and while doing so he retracted, saying, ***I have sinned***, i.e., I have truly offended. But when he says, ***betraying innocent blood***, although he speaks well, still he does not speak completely, because it can be referred to a righteous man. Hence, *if you put me to death, you will shed innocent blood against your own selves* (Jer 26:15). Hence Jerome says that if he had had the right faith, he would not have despaired. For he should have said: betraying God. Therefore, when he said, ***betraying innocent blood***, he lessened his power, and showed that he lacked the right faith.

2313. Then the Jews' obstinacy is set down: ***but they said: what is that to us?*** He professed that he was a just man, and yet they say, ***what is that to us?*** *My people have not known the judgment of the Lord* (Jer 8:7). ***You look to it***, i.e., we do not follow your conscience. Remigius: ***what is that to us?*** *You first sold him, and later you profess that he is a just man. Whom do you see among us, you who so change your opinion?* For to change from bad to good is good, but to change from bad to bad is bad. *A holy man continues in wisdom as the sun: but a fool is changed as the moon* (Sir 27:12).

2314. Then the desperation is set down. For a desperate man cares nothing for temporal goods; and this man acted the same way, for ***casting down the pieces of silver in***

the temple, he departed, for he had no care for money, *and went and hung himself with a halter*. Hence it says that *he hanged himself and burst open in the middle* (Acts 1:18).

And why? Origen says that it happens that the devil casts someone down into sin, and although he gives him room, yet he wishes to cast him down into another. And the Apostle wished to avoid this, saying, *you should rather forgive him and comfort him, lest perhaps such a one be swallowed up with overmuch sorrow* (2 Cor 2:7). Thus Judas came to such a great submersion that *he went and hung himself with a halter*. *Nor the deep swallow me up* (Ps 68:16). Origen recounts the opinion of certain men who said that since Judas had heard talk about the resurrection, he thought to run to meet Christ, and this is why he hung himself with a halter.

2315. Augustine asks when this happened. For if we wish to think about it, we find hardly any time before the passion in which this might happen, because the chief priests had been occupied the whole day with the death of Christ. Likewise on the following day it was the Sabbath, and they would not have accepted the money on that day. For this reason, Augustine seems to want that this happened after the resurrection. Yet it can be said that some had gone to Pilate, and pursued Christ's death, while others had remained in the temple, and Judas handed the thirty pieces of silver over to these.

2316. *But the chief priests having taken the pieces of silver, said*. He describes what was done with Judas's money. And

first, he says how it is excluded from the treasury;

second, he tells on what it was spent.

2317. It says therefore, *but the chief priests, having taken the pieces of silver, said: it is not lawful to put them into the corbona*. One should note that the offering of gratification, or the gift of grace, was put in the treasury. For there were some things which were offered voluntarily, and other things which were offered out of debt: the voluntary ones were put in the treasury, but the others elsewhere; *the Most High does not approve the gifts of the wicked* (Sir 34:23). Therefore, *it is not lawful to put them into the corbona, because it is the price of blood*. And in this the Lord's word is verified, above, *who strain out a gnat, and swallow a camel* (Matt 23:24). They did not want to put this money in the treasury, but they managed the death of the Son of God quite well.

2318. Then he tells what happened from there. And he tells

first, the deed;

second, what was done from there.

2319. It says, *and after they had consulted together*. Why did they do this? One should say that God arranged it this way, so that this deed would be held in memory. Hence, *they bought the potter's field with it, to be a burying place*

for strangers, not for those who belong to the homeland, but for others. It was fitting, according to a mystery, for by Christ's death not only was justification hastened, but rest for the dead; *from henceforth now, says the Spirit, that they may rest from their labors* (Rev 14:13). Or it can be that the strangers are those who do not have their own lodging; *woe is me, that my sojourning is prolonged!* (Ps 119:5). And these are buried with Christ. The Apostle: *we are buried together with him* (Rom 6:4). This field is holy Church. Hence above, *the kingdom of heaven is like a treasure hidden in a field* (Matt 13:44). This potter is Christ. Hence it says, *behold as clay is in the hand of the potter, so are you in my hand, O house of Israel* (Jer 18:6).

2320. Then a confirmation of the deed is set down. And first, by the name: *for this cause the field was called Haceldama, that is, the field of blood, even to this day*, namely even to the time at which this Gospel was written. Then he confirms it by authority: *then was fulfilled that which was spoken by Jeremiah the prophet*.

2321. But there is a question, why he says, *by Jeremiah the prophet*, when the words, according as they lie here, are not written anywhere in the Sacred Scriptures. Yet a similar thing is found: *and they weighed for my wages thirty pieces of silver* (Zech 11:12). Therefore, there is a question, why it is put down as *by Jeremiah*, when it was spoken through Zacharias. Augustine says that in another place what is written is found through a prophet, and not through Jeremiah, yet it seems that the man is Jeremiah, as is said in the text. Jerome touches on a solution, namely that the prophets wrote other books which were canonized among the Jews. For there are some books of the prophets which are not in the canon of the Bible, as for instance Jude names certain things in his canon, and all the apostles also accepted them. So he says that a certain man brought him a book of Jeremiah where these words were written verbatim, and the Evangelist wrote according as he found in the apocryphal book.

Augustine resolves it: it sometimes happens that, wishing to express the name of one author, another name occurs to him; so it can be that when he wished to write Zacharias, he wrote *Jeremiah*. But there were at the time many Jews who knew the law; why did they not correct it? Because they thought that it had been divinely spoken, because all the prophets spoke by the Holy Spirit, and the words of a prophet had efficacy only from the Holy Spirit; so, that they might imply this mystery, they did not correct it. Another solution which he states is that, although they are not the words of Jeremiah, yet something similar is done (Jer 32:6), that he received a command that he should buy a field. Or, the Holy Spirit moved Matthew to the same deed as that to which he moved Jeremiah.

But if we wish, we can take up the words of Jerome, in the book *On the Best Kind of Interpretation*, who says that the footman of Christ does not fall into a word of falsity: for

falsitatis: officium est enim boni interpretis non considerare verba, sed sensum. Ideo iste posuit sensum quorumdam scriptorum in Ieremia, quorundam in Zacharia, sicut habetur in Marco quod ponit auctoritatem Isaiae, cuius una pars est Malachiae, alia Isaiae. Sic et Matthaeus coniungit duas sententias, quarum una a Zacharia, altera a Ieremia ponitur, XXXII, 6. Quod enim est in Zacharia, scilicet quod *appenderunt*, idest acceperunt, *triginta argenteos*, in Ieremia non invenitur; sed quod agrum emit, quod signabat factum toti populo. '*Sicut constituit mihi Dominus,*' hoc expresse habetur ex eo quod praecipit Ieremiae, ubi supra, quod agrum emeret. Ideo secundum primam partem in Zacharia habetur, secundum secundam in Ieremia.

2322. *Iesus autem stetit ante praesidem, et interrogavit eum praeses*. Supra enarravit Evangelista quomodo Dominus assignatus est in manu gentium, hic autem agit de examinatione:

et circa hoc tria facit.

Primo narrat quomodo ante terrenum iudicem sistitur;

secundo quomodo examinatur;

tertio quomodo accusatur.

2323. Dicit ergo: ita dictum est de Iuda cum tradidisset praesidi Iesum. *Iesus* ergo **stetit ante praesidem**, idest tamquam reus et accusandus; Iob XXXVI, 17: *causa tua quasi impii iudicata est: causam iudiciumque recipies*. Per hoc enim meruit ut fieret iudex vivorum et mortuorum.

2324. Tunc sequitur examinatio; et primo ponitur interrogatio; secundo responsio, ibi **dicit illi Iesus**.

Pontifices in multis accusabant eum, scilicet de subversione legis, et quia regem se dicebat. Unde Pilatus non curavit quaerere de transgressione legis, sed potius de eo quod videbatur tangere laesionem maiestatis, scilicet **tu es rex Iudaeorum?** Quia Io. XIX, 12 habetur: *omnis qui se regem facit, contradicit Caesari*.

Tunc sequitur responsio **dicit ei Iesus: tu dicis**. Dicit Hieronymus quod Christus sic moderatur sermonem suum, quod non affirmat, nec negat, sed dicit: **tu dicis**. Prov. c. XVII, 27: *qui moderatur sermones suos prudens est*.

Item nota, secundum Hilarium, quod supra c. XXVI, 63, interrogatus a principe Iudaeorum, **si tu es Christus Filius Dei**, dixit **tu dixisti**: et respondit per praeteritum; cum autem respondit gentili, respondit per praesens. Et in hoc significatur quod confessio Christi a Iudaea est de praeterito, quia facta est per prophetas; Ier. XXIII, 5:

the duty of a good interpreter is not to consider the words, but the meaning. For this reason, this Evangelist set down the meaning of certain things written in Jeremiah, and of certain things in Zechariah, just as it is found in Mark that he sets down an authority of Isaiah, of which one part is from Malachias, and another from Isaiah (Mark 1:2). So also, Matthew joins two thoughts, of which one is set down by Zechariah, and the other by Jeremiah (Jer 32:6). For what is in Zechariah, namely that *they weighed out*, i.e., took, *thirty pieces of silver* (Zech 11:12), is not found in Jeremiah, but rather that he bought a field, which signified the deed of the whole people. '*As the Lord appointed to me*'; this is found explicitly in what he commanded Jeremiah, in the place above, that he buy a field. So as regards the first part it is found in Zechariah; as regards the second, in Jeremiah.

2322. *And Jesus stood before the governor, and the governor asked him*. Above, the Evangelist told how the Lord was delivered into the hand of a gentile; and here, he treats of the examination.

And concerning this he does three things:

first, he tells how he is made to stand before an earthly judge;

second, how he is examined;

third, how he is accused.

2323. It says therefore: thus it is said of Judas when he had handed Jesus over to the governor. *Jesus* therefore **stood before the governor**, i.e., as one guilty and to be charged with a crime; *your cause has been judged as that of the wicked, cause and judgment you will recover* (Job 36:17). For by this he merited to become the judge of the living and the dead.

2324. Then there follows the examination, and first, the interrogation is set down; second, the response, at **Jesus said to him**.

The high priests were accusing him of several things, namely of subversion of the law, and that he called himself a king. So Pilate did not care to question him about transgressions of the law, but rather about that which seemed to pertain to sedition, namely, **are you the king of the Jews?** For John says, *for whoever makes himself a king, speaks against Caesar* (John 19:12).

Then there follows the response: **Jesus said to him: you say it**. Jerome says that Christ moderates his words in such a way that he neither affirms nor denies, but says: **you say it**. He who sets bounds to his words is knowing and wise (Prov 17:27).

Notice also, following Hilary, that above, when asked by the high priest **if you are the Christ the Son of God**, he said, **you have said it** (Matt 26:63). And he responded with the past tense; but when he responded to a gentile, he responded with the present tense. And this signifies that the Jews' profession of Christ is from long before, because it was

regnabit rex, et sapiens erit. Sed loquens ad gentilem dicit *tu dicis*, quia gentilitas confitebatur.

2325. Consequenter agitur de accusatione. Et
primo ponitur accusatio;
secundo inductio ad respondendum, ibi *dixit autem Pilatus*.

2326. Dicit ergo *et cum accusaretur a principibus sacerdotum, nihil respondit*. Super quibus accusaretur, tacet Matthaeus, sed Lucas hoc dicit XXIII, 1 ss. Haec est consuetudo Evangelistarum, quia quod unus omittit, alter narrat. Unde ibi dicitur quod seduceret turbas etc., et quod prohibebat dari censum Caesari, item regem se diceret. Et hoc est falsum secundum intentionem suam, quia intendebant de regno temporali; sed ipse dicit, Io. c. XVIII, 36, *regnum meum non est de hoc mundo*. Sed Christus *nihil respondit*. Tunc impletum est quod dictum est per Is. LIII, 7: *quasi agnus coram tondente se obmutescet, et non aperiet os suum*. Et c. XLII, 2: *non audietur foris vox eius*.

2327. *Tunc dicit ei Pilatus*. Ex tunc conabatur Pilatus eum liberare, ideo conabatur ut responderet; unde dicebat *non audis quanta adversum te dicunt testimonia?* Et primo ponitur incitatio *non audis* et cetera. Hoc autem dicebat, quia volebat dimittere eum: ipsi enim qui erant accusatores, erant testes, et ideo noluit respondere.

2328. Quare autem non respondit, potest esse ratio ex parte Christi, quia noluit excusare passionem suam: poterat enim eam excusare loquendo; ideo noluit loqui. *Oblatus enim est quia voluit*, Is. LIII, 7. Item, ut daret nobis exemplum, quia cum malediceretur, non maledicebat. Item quia tot signa Iudaei viderant, quod converti poterant, et ideo reputavit eos indignos; Eccli. XXXII, 6: *ubi non est auditus, non effundas sermonem*.

Et notandum quod in multis loquitur, et in multis silet, quia si semper loqueretur, excusaret se; item si semper taceret, pertinax videretur. Pilato autem quandoque respondet, quandoque non; sed Iudaeis numquam respondet, quia Pilatus ignorabat, ideo veritatem aliquando dicebat, sed Iudaei obstinati erant.

2329. Tunc ponitur admiratio Pilati *ita ut praeses miraretur vehementer*. Et quare miratur? Quia audiebat eum facundissimum: et hoc est quod dicit David, Ps. XXXVII, v. 14: *ego autem tamquam surdus non audiebam, et sicut mutus non aperiens os suum*, idest ac si essem ignorans.

Et notate quod dicit *vehementer*: quod enim aliquis sapiens nihil respondeat, mirum est; sed quod in tali causa, ubi adiudicatur morti, non respondeat, hoc

done by the prophets; *and a king will reign, and will be wise* (Jer 23:5). But when speaking to a gentile, he says, *you say it*, for the gentiles were confessing then for the first time.

2325. Next, he treats of the accusation. And
first, the accusation is set down;
second, an exhortation to responding, at *then Pilate said to him*.

2326. It says then, *and when he was accused by the chief priests and elders, he answered nothing*. Matthew does not mention what he was accused of, but Luke tells this (Luke 23:1). This is the evangelists' usual practice, that what one leaves out, the other recounts. Hence it is said there that he was seducing the crowds, and that he forbade the census be given to Caesar, and that he called himself a king. And this is false, according to their meaning, because they mean it of a temporal kingdom; but he himself says, *my kingdom is not of this world* (John 18:36). But Christ gave no response. Then was fulfilled what was said, *he will be led as a sheep to the slaughter, and will be dumb as a lamb before his shearer, and he will not open his mouth* (Isa 53:7). And, *neither will his voice be heard abroad* (Isa 42:2).

2327. *Then Pilate said to him*. From that point on, Pilate was trying to free him, and this is why he tried to make him respond; hence he said, *do you not hear what great testimonies they allege against you?* And first, a provocation is set down: *do you not hear?* And he said this because he wanted to release him; for the very ones who were the accusers were the witnesses, and so he did not want to respond.

2328. As to why he did not respond, there can be a reason on Christ's part, because he did not want to avoid his passion: for he could have avoided it by speaking, and this is why he did not want to speak. For *he was offered because it was his own will* (Isa 53:7). Also, to give us an example, that one should not slander when one is slandered. Also, because the Jews had seen so many signs that they could have converted, and so he considered them unworthy; *where there is no hearing, pour not out words* (Sir 32:6).

And one should notice that he speaks on several occasions, and is silent on several occasions, for if he always spoke he would exonerate himself; likewise if he was always silent, he would seem stubborn. However, he responds to Pilate sometimes, but never responds to the Jews, because Pilate was ignorant, and so he sometimes spoke the truth, but the Jews were obstinate.

2329. Then Pilate's wonderment is set down: *so that the governor wondered exceedingly*. And why does he marvel? Because he heard that he was most eloquent; and this is what David says, *but I, as a deaf man, heard not: and as a dumb man not opening his mouth* (Ps 37:14), i.e., as though I were ignorant.

And notice that it says, *exceedingly*, for that a wise man should not respond is a marvel; but that he should not respond in such a case, where he is condemned to death, this

vehementer est admirandum. Item quia non videbat eum perterritum: in tali enim casu solent homines etiam perterreri.

2330. Tunc agitur de damnatione. Et

primo ponitur diversum studium volentium excusare ipsum;

secundo studium volentium condemnare, ibi ***principes autem sacerdotum et seniores persuaserunt populis ut peterent Barabbam***;

tertio condemnatio, ibi ***tunc dimisit illis Barabbam***.

Circa primum

primo ponitur studium Pilati ad liberandum;

secundo studium principum ad condemnandum.

Circa primum

primo ponit quasdam opportunitates;

secundo tractat de eius liberatione;

tertio dat causam.

Secunda ibi ***congregatis ergo illis, dixit Pilatus***; tertia ibi ***sciebat enim quod per invidiam tradidissent eum***.

2331. In prima ponit duas opportunitates. Dicit ergo ***per diem autem solemnem consueverat praeses populo dimittere unum vinctum***. Ista consuetudo non erat ex lege imperatoris, sed ex voluntate eius, ut redderet populum sibi magis devotum: quia in solemnitate debebant magis esse iucundi, nolebat quod illa die esset causa tristitiae. Sic et Romae in illo die quo imperator intrabat, nullus adiudicabatur morti. Item de novo acquisiverat praefecturam, ideo volebat sibi eos esse devotos. Aliquid tamen simile legitur in Veteri Testamento, scilicet quod Saul liberavit Ionatham, qui adiudicatus erat morti, I Reg. XIV, 44 ss.

Deinde ponit opportunitatem ex quodam latrone, qui dicebatur **Barabbas**, qui interpretatur filius patris, scilicet diaboli; Io. VIII, 44: *vos ex patre diabolo estis*.

2332. *Congregatis autem illis, dicit Pilatus: quem vultis dimittam vobis?* Hic facit Pilatus contra consuetudinem Iudaeorum, quia non solebat eos rogare, sed ipsi rogabant eum. Sed hoc faciebat, quia quaerebat eum dimittere, et videtur inducere, quia videbatur ei quod deberent praeeligere Christum quam Barabbam; quia iste erat reus laesae maiestatis, et multis nocuerat.

Item ex eo quod Christum nominat, dicens ***an Iesum, qui dicitur Christus?*** Christus enim dicitur 'unctus'. Unde regem appellabat eum, ideo credebat quod Christum deberent accipere; Eccli. XV, 18: *ante hominem vita et mors*. Sic Pilatus ante eos posuit bonum et

is greatly to be marveled at. Likewise, because he saw that he was not terrified; for in such a case men are usually also terrified.

2330. Then he treats of the condemnation. And

first, he sets down the various efforts of those wishing to excuse him;

second, the effort of those wishing to condemn him, at ***but the chief priests and elders persuaded the people, that they should ask Barabbas***;

third, the condemnation, at ***then he released to them Barabbas***.

Concerning the first,

first, Pilate's effort to free him is set down;

second, the effort of the chief priests to condemn him.

Concerning the first,

first, he sets out certain opportunities;

second, he discusses his liberation;

third, he gives the reason.

The second is at ***they therefore being gathered together, Pilate said***; the third, at ***for he knew that for envy they had delivered him***.

2331. In the first part, he sets out two opportunities. He says then, ***now, upon the solemn day, the governor was accustomed to release to the people one prisoner***. This custom was not from the emperor's law, but from his own will, that he might make the people more devoted to him: since they should rather be pleasant on the solemnity, he did not want that day to be a cause of sorrow. So also in Rome, on the day on which the emperor entered, no one was condemned to death. Also, he had acquired the office of prefect only recently, so he wanted them to be devoted to him. Yet something similar is written in the Old Testament, namely that Saul freed Jonathan, who had been condemned to death (1 Sam 14:44).

Then he sets out the opportunity from a certain thief, who was called **Barabbas**, which means son of the father, namely of the devil; *you are of your father the devil* (John 8:44).

2332. *They therefore being gathered together, Pilate said: whom do you wish that I release to you?* Pilate did this contrary to the custom of the Jews, for he did not usually ask them, but they themselves asked him. But he did this because he sought to release him, and he seems to lead them to release Jesus, because it seemed to him that they should choose Christ over Barabbas, for this man was guilty of sedition, and had harmed many.

Also from the fact that he called him Christ, saying, ***or Jesus who is called the Christ?*** For Christ means 'anointed.' Hence he called him a king, and so he thought that they would take the Christ; *before man is life and death, good and evil, that which he will choose will be given him* (Sir 15:18).

malum; et ipsi acceperunt malum, ideo eos semper sequitur malum.

2333. Deinde ponit causam *sciebat enim quod per invidiam tradidissent eum*. Ex quo sciebat? Audierat enim multa bona de eo, et videbat eum constantem; unde *sciebat quod per invidiam tradidissent eum*. Sicut enim invidia diaboli fuit inimica primo homini, sic debuit esse invidia istorum inimica Christo. Sic enim Ioseph ex invidia traditus est a fratribus, Gen. XXXVII, 28.

2334. *Sedente autem eo pro tribunali, misit ad eum uxor eius*. Supra posuit Evangelista unam causam, quare Pilatus nitebatur dimittere eum, hic autem ponit aliam causam, scilicet admonitionem uxoris. Et

primo ponitur admonitio;

secundo causa admonitionis, ibi *multa enim passa sum hodie per visum propter eum*.

2335. *Sedente autem eo pro tribunali*. Sicut dicit quaedam Glossa, tribunal est sedes iudicum. Prov. XX, 8: *rex qui sedet in solio iudicii dissipat omne malum intuitu suo*. Cathedra proprie doctorum; supra XXIII, 2: *super cathedram Moysi sederunt scribae et Pharisaei*. Et dicitur a 'tribunis,' quia primo tribuni electi sunt a Romanis ad facienda iudicia.

Et dicit *pro tribunali*: et est iste modus loquendi Graecus. Aliquando enim *pro* accipitur pro 'ante'; sicut, exercitus est pro castris, idest ante castra. Aliquando pro 'in'; unde *pro tribunali*, idest in tribunali.

Misit ad eum uxor eius dicens. Erat ista mulier gentilis, et signat ecclesiam gentilium, quae suscepit Christum, ut I ad Cor. I. *Nihil tibi et iusto illi*, idest non pertinet ad te iudicare, immo ipse debet esse iudex tuus; Act. c. X, 42: *qui constitutus est iudex vivorum et mortuorum*.

2336. *Multa enim passa sum hodie per visum propter eum*. Hic ponitur causa. Et est modus loquendi talis: quando enim abstrahitur quis a sensibus, aliqua secundum imaginationem apparent, et consuetum est quod visio refertur ad id quod apparet, cum sit alienatio a sensibus: hoc autem fit aliquando in vigilia, aliquando in somno. Quando in vigilia, visio dicitur; unde Num. XII, 6 dicitur: *si quis fuerit inter vos propheta Domini, in visione apparebo ei, vel per somnium loquar ad illum*. Hic autem ponitur propheta pro utroque.

Notandum quod huius causa quandoque corporalis intrinseca est, ut quando superabundat sanguis, fit apparitio corporum rubeorum, et sic de aliis. Aliquando ex causa extrinseca, ut ex frigore somniat aliquis quod sit in nive. Aliquando autem fit a causa spirituali, et hoc vel a Deo per bonum angelum; et de hoc Iob XXXIII, 15:

In the same way, Pilate set before them good and evil, and they themselves took the evil, and so evil always follows them.

2333. Then he sets down the reason: *for he knew that for envy they had delivered him*. How did he know? For he had heard many good things about him, and saw that he was resolute; from this *he knew that for envy they had delivered him*. For just as the devil's envy was hostile to the first man, so the envy of these men had to be hostile to Christ. For Joseph was handed over by his brothers in the same way, out of envy (Gen 37:28).

2334. *And as he was sitting for the tribunal, his wife sent to him*. Above, the Evangelist set down one reason why Pilate strove to release him, and here he sets down another reason, namely his wife's warning. And

first, the warning is set down;

second, the reason for the warning, at *for I have suffered many things this day in a vision because of him*.

2335. *And as he was sitting for the tribunal*. As a certain Gloss says, a tribunal is a judgment seat. *The king, who sits on the throne of judgment, scatters away all evil with his look* (Prov 20:8). A chair is properly for teachers; above, *the scribes and the Pharisees have sat on the chair of Moses* (Matt 23:2). And the name derives from 'tribune,' because the tribunes were first chosen by the Romans for passing judgment.

And he says, *for the tribunal*: and this is the Greek way of speaking. Sometimes *for* is taken as 'before,' as in, the army is for the field, i.e., before the field. Sometimes as 'on'; hence, *for the tribunal*, i.e., on the tribunal.

His wife sent to him, saying. This woman was a gentile, and signifies the church of the gentiles, which accepted Christ (1 Cor 1). *Have nothing to do with that just man*, i.e., it does not pertain to you to judge; on the contrary, he should be your judge. *Who was appointed by God, to be judge of the living and of the dead* (Acts 10:42).

2336. *For I have suffered many things this day in a vision because of him*. Here the reason is set down. And there is such a way of speaking: for when someone is withdrawn from the senses, things appear according to the imagination, and it is common that when there is a separation from the senses the power of vision is attributed to what appears. Sometimes this happens when one is awake, and sometimes while asleep. When it happens while one is awake, it is called a vision; hence, *if there is among you a prophet of the Lord, I will appear to him in a vision, or I will speak to him in a dream* (Num 12:6). But here a prophet is set down for both.

One should note that the cause of this is sometimes intrinsic to the body, as when there is an overabundance of blood, there comes an apparition of reddish bodies, and so on with the others. Sometimes it comes from an extrinsic cause, as someone may dream due to coldness that he is in the snow. But sometimes it comes from a spiritual cause,

per somnium in visione nocturna aperit aures vivorum. Et haec vera sunt, et veritatem habentia; non tamen multum debet confidere; Eccli. XXXIV, 7: *ne dederis in illis cor tuum, multos enim errare fecerunt somnia*. Aliquando fiunt a daemonibus, qui possunt imprimere in phantasiam, quia est virtus corporalis: unde divinationes et huiusmodi prohibentur in lege; Deut. XVIII, v. 10: *non inveniatur in te qui somnia observet, vel auguria* et cetera.

De hac visione possumus dicere quod facta est a Deo per bonos angelos; vel a diabolo, quia erat ad impediendum passionem: quia in passione erat peccatum occisionis. Et sic fiebat per angelos bonos; sed ex passione sequitur fructus, ideo diabolus iam percipiens eum esse Deum, et timens per passionem potestatem amittere, sicut in mente Iudae posuerat ut eum traderet, sic et modo voluit impedire, non quia vellet impedire peccatum, sed potius passionis fructum.

2337. Tunc ponit studium Iudaeorum volentium occidere Christum **principes autem sacerdotum et seniores persuaserunt populis ut peterent Barabbam**. In utroque enim se ostendunt abominabiles, quia principes qui alios corrigere deberent; Prov. XVII, 15: *qui iustificat impium abominabilis est*. Similiter eo quod seniores; Dan. XIII, 5: *egressa est iniquitas a senioribus populi*.

2338. *Respondens autem praeses ait illis.* Hic ponit conatum, quo conabatur Pilatus dimittere eum. Et primo ostendit quibus verbis egerit ad liberationem; secundo quibus factis, ibi **videns autem Pilatus quia nihil proficeret**.

Tribus modis est conatus liberare eum. Primo ex comparatione; secundo ex dignitate; tertio ex innocentia.

2339. Ex comparatione, quia comparavit eum malo actori, **respondens** scilicet petitioni populi, vel istis principibus qui instigabant eum **quem vultis vobis de duobus dimitti? At illi dixerunt: Barabbam**. Quod et populo improperat Petrus, Act. III, 13, dicens de Christo: *quem vos quidem tradidistis, et negastis ante faciem Pilati, iudicante illo dimitti. Vos autem Sanctum et Iustum negastis, et petistis virum homicidam donari vobis* et cetera.

2340. *Dicit ergo Pilatus: quid ergo faciam de Iesu, qui dicitur Christus?* Hic allegat dignitatem **quid faciam de Iesu**, quasi dicat: iniuriosum erit vobis, si illum occidatis, **qui dicitur Christus**. Sed isti vereri non potuerunt: immo dicunt omnes **crucifigatur**: haec enim erat mors turpissima. Ideo completur quod dicitur Sap. II, 20:

and this is either from God through a good angel; and Job says about this: *by a dream in a vision by night . . . he opens the ears of men* (Job 33:15). And these are true, and have truth; yet one should not put much confidence in them; *for dreams have deceived many, and they have failed who put their trust in them* (Sir 34:7). Sometimes they come from demons, who can impress them on a phantasm, since it is a bodily power. Hence divinations and suchlike are forbidden in the law; *neither let there be found among you any one who . . . observes dreams and omens* (Deut 18:10).

As regards this vision, we can say that it was caused by God through good angels; or by the devil, who was bent on preventing the passion: for in the passion there was the sin of murder. And in this way it came through good angels; but a good fruit comes out of the passion, so the devil, already perceiving that he was God, and afraid of losing power through the passion, just as he had put it in the mind of Judas to betray him, so also now he wished to prevent it, not because he wanted to prevent the sin, but rather to prevent the fruit of the passion.

2337. Then he sets down the effort of the Jews, who wished to kill Christ: **but the chief priests and elders persuaded the people, that they should ask for Barabbas**. For in either they show themselves to be detestable, for the chief priests are those who should correct others; *he who justifies the wicked, and he who condemns the just, both are abominable before God* (Prov 17:15). Similarly, by the fact that the elders did so; *iniquity came . . . from the ancient judges, that seemed to govern the people* (Dan 13:5).

2338. *And the governor answering, said to them.* Here he sets down the attempt with which Pilate attempted to release him. And first, he describes the words by which he acted for the release; second, the deeds, at **and Pilate seeing that nothing prevailed**.

He tried to free him in three ways: first, by a comparison; second, by Christ's dignity; third, by his innocence.

2339. By a comparison, because he compared him to an evildoer, **answering** namely to the people's request, or to the leaders who prompted him, **which of the two do you wish to be released to you? But they said, Barabbas**. For which Peter rebuked the people also, saying about Christ: *whom you indeed delivered up and denied before the face of Pilate, when he judged he should be released. But you denied the Holy One and the Just, and desired a murderer to be granted unto you* (Acts 3:13–14).

2340. Therefore, Pilate said: **what should I do then with Jesus who is called the Christ?** Here he appeals to his dignity: **what should I do then with Jesus**, as though to say: it will be harmful to you if you kill the one **who is called the Christ**. But these men were incapable of reverence; rather they all say, **let him be crucified**, for this was a most

morte turpissima condemnemus eum; Is. III, 8: *lingua eorum et adinventiones eorum contra Dominum*.

2341. *Ait illis praeses: quid enim mali fecit?* Hic allegat innocentiam eius, intendens eum liberare, quasi utens illo quod dicitur Ier. c. II, 5: *quid invenerunt patres vestri in me iniquitatis?* Et Io. VIII, 46: *quis ex vobis arguet me de peccato?* **At illi magis clamabant: crucifigatur**. Unde flecti non poterant, secundum illud Ier. VIII, 5: *apprehenderunt mendacium, et noluerunt reverti*. Unde pertinaces erant in malitia.

2342. *Videns autem Pilatus quod nihil proficeret*. Hic intendit liberationem eius per factum; et primo ponitur factum; secundo populi obligatio ad poenam.

Dicit **videns autem Pilatus quia nihil proficeret**. Per hoc dat intelligere quod multa alia dixerat, et quod nihil proficiebat. **Accepta autem aqua lavit manus suas**. Haec erat consuetudo quod quando quis volebat se ostendere innocentem, lavabat manus, sic et iste; unde dixit **ego innocens sum a sanguine iusti huius** et cetera. Secundum hunc modum habetur in Ps. XXV, 6: *lavabo inter innocentes manus meas*. Et vere ipse fuisset innocens, si in sua sententia permansisset, unde vocat eum **iustum**. **Vos videritis**, idest quid vobis accidere debeat. Unde Io. XVIII, 31 dicitur: *accipite eum vos, et secundum legem vestram iudicate eum*.

2343. Tunc sequitur oblatio ad poenam **sanguis eius super nos, et super filios nostros**. Et ita fiet quod sanguis Christi expetitur ab eis usque hodie; et bene convenit illis quod dictum est Gen. IV, 10: *sanguis fratris tui Abel clamat ad me de terra*. Sed sanguis Christi efficacior est quam sanguis Abel. Apostolus ad Hebraeos XII, 24: *habemus sanguinem melius clamantem quam sanguis Abel*; Ier. XXVI, 15: *verumtamen si occideritis me, sanguinem innocentem tradetis contra vosmetipsos*.

2344. *Tunc dimisit Barabbam*. **Dimisit**, idest absolvit a sententia mortis. *Iesum vero flagellatum tradidit eis ut crucifigerent*. Et quare flagellatum? Hieronymus dicit quia consuetudo erat Romanorum quod adiudicatus morti primo flagellabatur. Et sicut dicitur Io. c. XIX, 1 ipse flagellavit; unde completur in eo quod habetur in Ps. XXXVII, 18: *ego autem in flagella paratus sum*. Quidam dicunt quod flagellavit ut moverentur ad pietatem, et sic flagellatum dimitterent.

shameful death. So what is said is fulfilled, *let us condemn him to a most shameful death* (Wis 2:20); *their tongue, and their devices are against the Lord* (Isa 3:8).

2341. *The governor said to them: why, what evil has he done?* Here he appeals to his innocence, meaning to free him, as though using what is said, *what iniquity have your fathers found in me?* (Jer 2:5). And, *which of you will convince me of sin?* (John 8:46). **But they cried out the more, saying: let him be crucified**. Hence they could not be persuaded, in accord with, *they have laid hold on lying, and have refused to return* (Jer 8:5). Hence they were obstinate in malice.

2342. *And Pilate seeing that nothing prevailed*. Here he aims at his liberation by deed: and first, the deed is set down; second, the people's agreement to the punishment.

He says, **and Pilate seeing that nothing prevailed**. By this he gives one to understand that he had said many other things, and that it did no good. **Taking water washed his hands**. This was the custom, that when someone wanted to show himself innocent, he would wash his hands, as this man did; hence he said, **I am innocent of the blood of this just man**. In accord with this manner of acting, it says, *I will wash my hands among the innocent* (Ps 25:6). And truly, he would have been innocent if he had persevered in his judgment, hence he calls him a **just man**. **You look to it**, i.e., what should happen to you. Hence John says, *take him, and judge him according to your law* (John 18:31).

2343. Then there follows the agreement to the punishment: **his blood be upon us and our children**. And in this way it came about that Christ's blood is demanded of them even to this day; and what is said fits them well: *the voice of your brother's blood cries to me from the earth* (Gen 4:10). But Christ's blood is more efficacious than Abel's blood. The Apostle: *and to the sprinkling of blood which speaks better than that of Abel* (Heb 12:24); *if you put me to death, you will shed innocent blood against your own selves* (Jer 26:15).

2344. *Then he released to them Barabbas*. **He released**, i.e., he absolved him from the sentence of death. **And having scourged Jesus, delivered him to them to be crucified**. And why did he scourge him? Jerome says that it was the Romans' custom that those condemned to death were first scourged. And as it says, he himself scourged him (John 19:1); hence what is said is fulfilled in him: *I am ready for scourges* (Ps 37:18). Some say that he scourged him so that they would be moved to pity, and so release him scourged.

Lecture 2

27:27 Tunc milites praesidis suscipientes Iesum in praetorium, congregaverunt ad eum universam cohortem, [n. 2346]

27:28 et exuentes eum, chlamydem coccineam circumdederunt ei, [n. 2347]

27:29 et plectentes coronam de spinis posuerunt super caput eius, et arundinem in dextera eius, et genu flexo ante eum illudebant dicentes: ave, rex Iudaeorum. [n. 2350]

27:30 Et expuentes in eum acceperunt arundinem, et percutiebant caput eius. [n. 2353]

27:31 Et postquam illuserunt ei, exuerunt eum chlamyde, et induerunt eum vestimentis eius, et duxerunt eum, ut crucifigerent. [n. 2355]

27:32 Exeuntes autem invenerunt hominem Cyrenaeum, nomine Simonem: hunc angariaverunt, ut tolleret crucem eius. [n. 2356]

27:33 Et venerunt in locum, qui dicitur Golgotha, quod est Calvariae locus. [n. 2358]

27:34 Et dederunt ei vinum bibere cum felle mixtum, et cum gustasset noluit bibere. [n. 2360]

27:35 Postquam autem crucifixerunt eum, diviserunt vestimenta eius, sortem mittentes, ut impleretur quod dictum est per Prophetam dicentem: *diviserunt sibi vestimenta mea, et super vestem meam miserunt sortem*. [n. 2362]

27:36 Et sedentes servabant eum. [n. 2365]

27:37 Et imposuerunt super caput eius causam ipsius scriptam: Hic Est Iesus Rex Iudaeorum. [n. 2366]

27:38 Tunc crucifixi sunt cum eo duo latrones, unus a dextris, et unus a sinistris. [n. 2367]

27:27 Τότε οἱ στρατιῶται τοῦ ἡγεμόνος παραλαβόντες τὸν Ἰησοῦν εἰς τὸ πραιτώριον συνήγαγον ἐπ' αὐτὸν ὅλην τὴν σπεῖραν.

27:28 καὶ ἐκδύσαντες αὐτὸν χλαμύδα κοκκίνην περιέθηκαν αὐτῷ,

27:29 καὶ πλέξαντες στέφανον ἐξ ἀκανθῶν ἐπέθηκαν ἐπὶ τῆς κεφαλῆς αὐτοῦ καὶ κάλαμον ἐν τῇ δεξιᾷ αὐτοῦ, καὶ γονυπετήσαντες ἔμπροσθεν αὐτοῦ ἐνέπαιξαν αὐτῷ λέγοντες· χαῖρε, βασιλεῦ τῶν Ἰουδαίων,

27:30 καὶ ἐμπτύσαντες εἰς αὐτὸν ἔλαβον τὸν κάλαμον καὶ ἔτυπτον εἰς τὴν κεφαλὴν αὐτοῦ.

27:31 καὶ ὅτε ἐνέπαιξαν αὐτῷ, ἐξέδυσαν αὐτὸν τὴν χλαμύδα καὶ ἐνέδυσαν αὐτὸν τὰ ἱμάτια αὐτοῦ καὶ ἀπήγαγον αὐτὸν εἰς τὸ σταυρῶσαι.

27:32 Ἐξερχόμενοι δὲ εὗρον ἄνθρωπον Κυρηναῖον ὀνόματι Σίμωνα, τοῦτον ἠγγάρευσαν ἵνα ἄρῃ τὸν σταυρὸν αὐτοῦ.

27:33 Καὶ ἐλθόντες εἰς τόπον λεγόμενον Γολγοθᾶ, ὅ ἐστιν Κρανίου Τόπος λεγόμενος,

27:34 ἔδωκαν αὐτῷ πιεῖν οἶνον μετὰ χολῆς μεμιγμένον· καὶ γευσάμενος οὐκ ἠθέλησεν πιεῖν.

27:35 Σταυρώσαντες δὲ αὐτὸν διεμερίσαντο τὰ ἱμάτια αὐτοῦ βάλλοντες κλῆρον [ἵνα πληρωθῇ τὸ ῥηθὲν ὑπὸ τοῦ προφήτου, διεμερίσαντο τὰ ἱμάτιά μου ἑαυτοῖς, καὶ ἐπὶ τὸν ἱματισμόν μου ἔβαλον κλῆρον],

27:36 καὶ καθήμενοι ἐτήρουν αὐτὸν ἐκεῖ.

27:37 Καὶ ἐπέθηκαν ἐπάνω τῆς κεφαλῆς αὐτοῦ τὴν αἰτίαν αὐτοῦ γεγραμμένην· οὗτός ἐστιν Ἰησοῦς ὁ βασιλεὺς τῶν Ἰουδαίων.

27:38 Τότε σταυροῦνται σὺν αὐτῷ δύο λῃσταί, εἷς ἐκ δεξιῶν καὶ εἷς ἐξ εὐωνύμων.

27:27 Then the soldiers of the governor, taking Jesus into the praetorium, gathered together to him the whole cohort; [n. 2346]

27:28 and stripping him, they put a scarlet cloak about him. [n. 2347]

27:29 And plaiting a crown of thorns, they put it on his head, and a reed in his right hand. And bowing the knee before him, they mocked him, saying: hail, king of the Jews. [n. 2350]

27:30 And spitting upon him, they took the reed, and struck his head. [n. 2353]

27:31 And after they had mocked him, they took the cloak off of him, and put on him his own garments, and led him away to crucify him. [n. 2355]

27:32 And going out, they found a man of Cyrene, named Simon: him they forced to take up his cross. [n. 2356]

27:33 And they came to the place which is called Golgotha, which is the place of Calvary. [n. 2358]

27:34 And they gave him wine to drink mixed with gall. And when he had tasted, he would not drink. [n. 2360]

27:35 And after they had crucified him, they divided his garments, casting lots; that it might be fulfilled what was spoken by the Prophet, saying: *they divided my garments among them; and upon my vesture they cast lots*. [n. 2362]

27:36 And they sat and watched him. [n. 2365]

27:37 And they put over his head, his cause written: THIS IS JESUS THE KING OF THE JEWS. [n. 2366]

27:38 Then there were crucified with him two thieves, one on the right hand, and one on the left. [n. 2367]

27:39 Praetereuntes autem blasphemabant eum, moventes capita sua, [n. 2368]

27:40 et dicentes: vah qui destruis templum Dei, et in triduo illud reaedificas, salva temetipsum: si Filius Dei es, descende de cruce. [n. 2370]

27:41 Similiter et principes sacerdotum illudentes cum scribis et senioribus, dicentes: [n. 2371]

27:42 alios salvos fecit, seipsum non potest salvum facere. Si rex Israel est, descendat nunc de cruce, et credimus ei. [n. 2372]

27:43 Confidet in Deo, liberet nunc eum, si vult. Dixit enim: quia Dei Filius sum. [n. 2374]

27:44 Idipsum autem et latrones, qui fixi erant cum eo, improperabant ei. [n. 2375]

27:45 A sexta autem hora tenebrae factae sunt per universam terram usque ad horam nonam, [n. 2376]

27:46 et circa horam nonam clamavit Iesus voce magna dicens: Eli, Eli, lamma sabacthani? Hoc est: Deus meus, Deus meus, ut quid dereliquisti me? [n. 2381]

27:47 Quidam autem illic stantes et audientes dicebant: Eliam vocat iste. [n. 2384]

27:48 Et continuo currens unus ex eis, acceptam spongiam implevit aceto, et imposuit arundini; et dabat ei bibere. [n. 2386]

27:49 Caeteri vero dicebant: sine, videamus an veniat Elias liberans eum. [n. 2387]

27:50 Iesus autem iterum clamans voce magna, emisit spiritum. [n. 2388]

27:51 Et ecce velum templi scissum est in duas partes a summo usque deorsum, et terra mota est, et petrae scissae sunt, [n. 2391]

27:52 et monumenta aperta sunt, et multa corpora sanctorum, qui dormierant, surrexerunt, [n. 2393]

27:39 Οἱ δὲ παραπορευόμενοι ἐβλασφήμουν αὐτὸν κινοῦντες τὰς κεφαλὰς αὐτῶν

27:40 καὶ λέγοντες· ὁ καταλύων τὸν ναὸν καὶ ἐν τρισὶν ἡμέραις οἰκοδομῶν, σῶσον σεαυτόν, εἰ υἱὸς εἶ τοῦ θεοῦ, [καὶ] κατάβηθι ἀπὸ τοῦ σταυροῦ.

27:41 ὁμοίως καὶ οἱ ἀρχιερεῖς ἐμπαίζοντες μετὰ τῶν γραμματέων καὶ πρεσβυτέρων ἔλεγον·

27:42 ἄλλους ἔσωσεν, ἑαυτὸν οὐ δύναται σῶσαι· βασιλεὺς Ἰσραήλ ἐστιν, καταβάτω νῦν ἀπὸ τοῦ σταυροῦ καὶ πιστεύσομεν ἐπ᾽ αὐτόν.

27:43 πέποιθεν ἐπὶ τὸν θεόν, ῥυσάσθω νῦν εἰ θέλει αὐτόν· εἶπεν γὰρ ὅτι θεοῦ εἰμι υἱός.

27:44 Τὸ δ᾽ αὐτὸ καὶ οἱ λῃσταὶ οἱ συσταυρωθέντες σὺν αὐτῷ ὠνείδιζον αὐτόν.

27:45 Ἀπὸ δὲ ἕκτης ὥρας σκότος ἐγένετο ἐπὶ πᾶσαν τὴν γῆν ἕως ὥρας ἐνάτης.

27:46 περὶ δὲ τὴν ἐνάτην ὥραν ἀνεβόησεν ὁ Ἰησοῦς φωνῇ μεγάλῃ λέγων· ηλι ηλι λεμα σαβαχθανι; τοῦτ᾽ ἔστιν· θεέ μου θεέ μου, ἱνατί με ἐγκατέλιπες;

27:47 τινὲς δὲ τῶν ἐκεῖ ἑστηκότων ἀκούσαντες ἔλεγον ὅτι Ἠλίαν φωνεῖ οὗτος.

27:48 καὶ εὐθέως δραμὼν εἷς ἐξ αὐτῶν καὶ λαβὼν σπόγγον πλήσας τε ὄξους καὶ περιθεὶς καλάμῳ ἐπότιζεν αὐτόν.

27:49 οἱ δὲ λοιποὶ ἔλεγον· ἄφες ἴδωμεν εἰ ἔρχεται Ἠλίας σώσων αὐτόν.

27:50 ὁ δὲ Ἰησοῦς πάλιν κράξας φωνῇ μεγάλῃ ἀφῆκεν τὸ πνεῦμα.

27:51 Καὶ ἰδοὺ τὸ καταπέτασμα τοῦ ναοῦ ἐσχίσθη ἀπ᾽ ἄνωθεν ἕως κάτω εἰς δύο καὶ ἡ γῆ ἐσείσθη καὶ αἱ πέτραι ἐσχίσθησαν,

27:52 καὶ τὰ μνημεῖα ἀνεῴχθησαν καὶ πολλὰ σώματα τῶν κεκοιμημένων ἁγίων ἠγέρθησαν,

27:39 And those who passed by, blasphemed him, wagging their heads, [n. 2368]

27:40 and saying: vah, you who destroy the temple of God, and in three days rebuilds it, save your own self: if you are the Son of God, come down from the cross. [n. 2370]

27:41 In like manner also the chief priests, with the scribes and elders mocking, said: [n. 2371]

27:42 he saved others; himself he cannot save. If he is the king of Israel, let him now come down from the cross, and we will believe him. [n. 2372]

27:43 He trusted in God; let him now deliver him if he will have him; for he said: I am the Son of God. [n. 2374]

27:44 And with the same thing the thieves, who were crucified with him, also reproached him. [n. 2375]

27:45 Now from the sixth hour there was darkness over the whole earth, until the ninth hour. [n. 2376]

27:46 And about the ninth hour Jesus cried with a loud voice, saying: Eli, Eli, lamma sabacthani? That is: my God, my God, why have you forsaken me? [n. 2381]

27:47 And some who stood there and heard, said: this man calls Elijah. [n. 2384]

27:48 And immediately one of them, running, took a sponge, and filled it with vinegar; and put it on a reed, and gave him to drink. [n. 2386]

27:49 And the others said: wait, let us see whether Elijah will come to deliver him. [n. 2387]

27:50 And Jesus again crying with a loud voice, yielded up the spirit. [n. 2388]

27:51 And behold the veil of the temple was rent in two from the top even to the bottom, and the earth quaked, and the rocks were rent. [n. 2391]

27:52 And the graves were opened, and many bodies of the saints who had slept arose, [n. 2393]

27:53 et exeuntes de monumentis post resurrectionem eius, venerunt in sanctam civitatem et apparuerunt multis. [n. 2396]

27:54 Centurio autem, et qui cum eo erant, custodientes Iesum, viso terraemotu, et his quae fiebant, timuerunt valde, dicentes: vere Filius Dei erat iste. [n. 2397]

27:55 Erant autem ibi mulieres multae a longe, quae secutae erant Iesum a Galilaea ministrantes ei, [n. 2399]

27:56 inter quas erat Maria Magdalene, et Maria Iacobi, et Ioseph mater, et mater filiorum Zebedaei. [n. 2402]

27:57 Cum autem sero factum esset, venit quidam homo dives ab Arimathaea nomine Ioseph, qui et ipse discipulus erat Iesu. [n. 2404]

27:58 Hic accessit ad Pilatum, et petiit corpus Iesu. Tunc Pilatus iussit reddi corpus; [n. 2406]

27:59 et, accepto corpore, Ioseph involvit illud sindone munda, [n. 2407]

27:60 et posuit illud in monumento suo novo, quod exciderat in petra, et advolvit saxum magnum ad ostium monumenti, et abiit. [n. 2408]

27:61 Erat autem ibi Maria Magdalene, et altera Maria, sedentes contra sepulchrum. [n. 2409]

27:62 Altera autem die, quae est post Parasceven, convenerunt principes sacerdotum et Pharisaei ad Pilatum [n. 2410]

27:63 dicentes: Domine, recordati sumus quia seductor ille dixit adhuc vivens: post tres dies resurgam. [n. 2412]

27:53 καὶ ἐξελθόντες ἐκ τῶν μνημείων μετὰ τὴν ἔγερσιν αὐτοῦ εἰσῆλθον εἰς τὴν ἁγίαν πόλιν καὶ ἐνεφανίσθησαν πολλοῖς.

27:54 Ὁ δὲ ἑκατόνταρχος καὶ οἱ μετ' αὐτοῦ τηροῦντες τὸν Ἰησοῦν ἰδόντες τὸν σεισμὸν καὶ τὰ γενόμενα ἐφοβήθησαν σφόδρα, λέγοντες· ἀληθῶς θεοῦ υἱὸς ἦν οὗτος.

27:55 Ἦσαν δὲ ἐκεῖ γυναῖκες πολλαὶ ἀπὸ μακρόθεν θεωροῦσαι, αἵτινες ἠκολούθησαν τῷ Ἰησοῦ ἀπὸ τῆς Γαλιλαίας διακονοῦσαι αὐτῷ·

27:56 ἐν αἷς ἦν Μαρία ἡ Μαγδαληνὴ καὶ Μαρία ἡ τοῦ Ἰακώβου καὶ Ἰωσὴφ μήτηρ καὶ ἡ μήτηρ τῶν υἱῶν Ζεβεδαίου.

27:57 Ὀψίας δὲ γενομένης ἦλθεν ἄνθρωπος πλούσιος ἀπὸ Ἁριμαθαίας, τοὔνομα Ἰωσήφ, ὃς καὶ αὐτὸς ἐμαθητεύθη τῷ Ἰησοῦ·

27:58 οὗτος προσελθὼν τῷ Πιλάτῳ ᾐτήσατο τὸ σῶμα τοῦ Ἰησοῦ. τότε ὁ Πιλᾶτος ἐκέλευσεν ἀποδοθῆναι.

27:59 καὶ λαβὼν τὸ σῶμα ὁ Ἰωσὴφ ἐνετύλιξεν αὐτὸ [ἐν] σινδόνι καθαρᾷ

27:60 καὶ ἔθηκεν αὐτὸ ἐν τῷ καινῷ αὐτοῦ μνημείῳ ὃ ἐλατόμησεν ἐν τῇ πέτρᾳ καὶ προσκυλίσας λίθον μέγαν τῇ θύρᾳ τοῦ μνημείου ἀπῆλθεν.

27:61 Ἦν δὲ ἐκεῖ Μαριὰμ ἡ Μαγδαληνὴ καὶ ἡ ἄλλη Μαρία καθήμεναι ἀπέναντι τοῦ τάφου.

27:62 Τῇ δὲ ἐπαύριον, ἥτις ἐστὶν μετὰ τὴν παρασκευήν, συνήχθησαν οἱ ἀρχιερεῖς καὶ οἱ Φαρισαῖοι πρὸς Πιλᾶτον

27:63 λέγοντες· κύριε, ἐμνήσθημεν ὅτι ἐκεῖνος ὁ πλάνος εἶπεν ἔτι ζῶν· μετὰ τρεῖς ἡμέρας ἐγείρομαι.

27:53 and coming out of the tombs after his resurrection, came into the holy city, and appeared to many. [n. 2396]

27:54 Now the centurion, and those who were with him watching Jesus, having seen the earthquake, and the things that were done, were much afraid, saying: indeed this was the Son of God. [n. 2397]

27:55 And there were there many women afar off, who had followed Jesus from Galilee, ministering to him; [n. 2399]

27:56 among whom was Mary Magdalen, and Mary the mother of James and Joseph, and the mother of the sons of Zebedee. [n. 2402]

27:57 And when it was evening, there came a certain rich man of Arimathea, named Joseph, who himself was also a disciple of Jesus. [n. 2404]

27:58 He went to Pilate, and asked for the body of Jesus. Then Pilate commanded that the body should be delivered. [n. 2406]

27:59 And Joseph, taking the body, wrapped it up in a clean linen cloth, [n. 2407]

27:60 and laid it in his own new monument, which he had hewed out in a rock. And he rolled a great stone to the door of the monument, and went his way. [n. 2408]

27:61 And there was there Mary Magdalen, and the other Mary sitting over against the sepulchre. [n. 2409]

27:62 And the next day, which followed the Day of Preparation, the chief priests and the Pharisees came together to Pilate, [n. 2410]

27:63 saying: Lord, we have remembered, that that seducer said, while he was yet alive: after three days I will rise again. [n. 2412]

²⁷:⁶⁴ Iube ergo custodiri sepulchrum usque in diem tertium, ne forte veniant discipuli eius, et furentur eum, et dicant plebi: surrexit a mortuis, et erit novissimus error peior priore. [n. 2413]	²⁷:⁶⁴ κέλευσον οὖν ἀσφαλισθῆναι τὸν τάφον ἕως τῆς τρίτης ἡμέρας, μήποτε ἐλθόντες οἱ μαθηταὶ αὐτοῦ κλέψωσιν αὐτὸν καὶ εἴπωσιν τῷ λαῷ· ἠγέρθη ἀπὸ τῶν νεκρῶν, καὶ ἔσται ἡ ἐσχάτη πλάνη χείρων τῆς πρώτης.	²⁷:⁶⁴ Command therefore that the sepulchre be guarded until the third day, lest perhaps his disciples come and steal him away, and say to the people: he is risen from the dead; and the last error will be worse than the first. [n. 2413]
²⁷:⁶⁵ Ait illis Pilatus: habetis custodiam; ite, custodite sicut scitis. [n. 2415]	²⁷:⁶⁵ ἔφη αὐτοῖς ὁ Πιλᾶτος· ἔχετε κουστωδίαν· ὑπάγετε ἀσφαλίσασθε ὡς οἴδατε.	²⁷:⁶⁵ Pilate said to them: you have a guard; go, guard it as you know. [n. 2415]
²⁷:⁶⁶ Illi autem abeuntes, munierunt sepulchrum, signantes lapidem cum custodibus. [n. 2416]	²⁷:⁶⁶ οἱ δὲ πορευθέντες ἠσφαλίσαντο τὸν τάφον σφραγίσαντες τὸν λίθον μετὰ τῆς κουστωδίας.	²⁷:⁶⁶ And departing, they made the sepulchre sure, sealing the stone, and setting guards. [n. 2416]

2345. Postquam habitum est de condemnatione, hic agitur de passione et morte; secundo de sepultura, ibi *cum sero autem factum esset* et cetera.

Circa primum duo facit. Quia

primo narrat quae indigne pertulit;

secundo quae magnifice fecit, ibi *a sexta autem hora tenebrae factae sunt*.

Prima pars in tres. In

prima agit de illusione militum;

secundo de crucifixione;

tertio de crucifixi derisione per Iudaeos facta.

Secunda ibi *et postquam illuserunt ei*; tertia ibi *praetereuntes autem blasphemabant eum*.

Circa primum

primo describuntur illusores;

secundo illusio.

2346. Dicit ergo *milites congregaverunt universam cohortem*. Cohors societas militum dicitur, et quilibet, qui habebat iudiciariam potestatem, habebat cohortem militum ad exercendum iudicium. Praetorium dicitur esse locus ubi exercebantur iudicia. Unde congregati sunt ad eum et gentiles, et Iudaei, ut nulli essent immunes, quia omnes debebat redimere. Ideo competit quod habetur Rom. c. XI, 32: *conclusit Deus omnia in incredulitate, ut omnium misereatur*. Et in Ps. CXVII, v. 10: *circuierunt me sicut apes*.

2347. *Et exuentes eum, chlamydem coccineam circumdederunt ei*. Hic describitur illusio. Et

primo quoad habitum;

secundo quantum ad honorem;

tertio quantum ad opprobrium.

Secunda ibi *et genu flexo ante eum, illudebant ei*; tertia ibi *exeuntes autem invenerunt hominem Cyrenaeum, nomine Simonem* et cetera.

2348. Notandum quod licet accusassent eum de multis, tamen non propter aliud patiebatur, nisi quia regem se dicebat, sicut habetur Io. XIX, 12: *si eum dimittis, non es amicus Caesaris*. Unde ex hac causa magis timuit.

2345. After having dealt with the condemnation, here he treats of the passion and death; second, of the burial, at *and when it was evening*.

Concerning the first, he does two things. For

first, he recounts what he undeservedly suffered;

second, what he magnificently did, at *now from the sixth hour there was darkness*.

The first part is in three parts. In

the first, he treats of the soldiers' mockery;

second, of the crucifixion;

third, of the Jews' mockery of the crucified one.

The second is at *and after they had mocked him*; the third, at *and those who passed by*.

Concerning the first,

first, the mockers are described;

second, the mockery.

2346. It says then, *then the soldiers . . . gathered together to him the whole cohort*. A cohort means a company of soldiers, and anyone who had judicial power had a cohort of soldiers to carry out his judgment. The praetorium is said to be the place where judgments were carried out. Hence both gentiles and Jews were gathered together to him, that no one might be exempt, because he had to redeem all. For this reason, what is said is fitting: *God has concluded all in unbelief, that he may have mercy on all* (Rom 11:32). And, *they surrounded me like bees* (Ps 117:12).

2347. *And stripping him, they put a scarlet cloak about him*. Here the mockery is described. And

first, as regards clothing;

second, as regards honor;

third, as regards reproach.

The second is at *and bowing the knee before him, they mocked him*; the third, at *and going out, they found a man of Cyrene, named Simon*.

2348. One should note that although they had accused him of many things, yet he suffered for nothing else than that he called himself a king, as is found, *if you release this man, you are not Caesar's friend* (John 19:12). Hence Pilate

435

Ideo volentes illudere, imponunt ei signa regis. Consuetudo enim est quod reges purpura induantur; et isti loco huius veste coccinea eum induerunt. Item solent habere coronam; et loco huius fecerunt coronam spineam. Item solent habere sceptrum; et loco huius dederunt ei baculum arundineum.

2349. Dicit ergo *et chlamydem coccineam circumdederunt ei*, idest rubeam.

Sed quid est quod Marcus dicit XV, 17, quod eum purpura induerunt? Augustinus solvit quod hoc dixit propter similitudinem coloris. Vel potest dici, quod quamvis esset coccinea, tamen habebat aliquid de purpura.

Per hoc quod propriis vestibus exuitur, et alienis induitur, reprehenduntur haeretici, qui dixerunt eum non esse verum hominem. Ista chlamys potest signare carnem Christi sanguine proprio cruentatam: *ipse enim vulneratus est propter iniquitates nostras; attritus est propter scelera nostra*. Is. LIII, 5. Vel signat sanguinem martyrum, qui laverunt stolas suas in sanguine Agni. Vel peccatum gentilium.

2350. *Et plectentes coronam de spinis posuerunt super caput eius*. Unde pro corona gloriae imposuerunt ei coronam contumeliae; Is. XXII, 18: *coronate eum corona tribulationis*. Per istas spinas signantur aculei peccatorum, quibus conscientia vulneratur: et istas Christus accepit pro nobis, quia pro peccatis nostris mortuus est. Vel potest referri ad maledictum Adae, ubi dictum est: *spinas et tribulos germinabit tibi*. Unde signatum est quod solvebatur ista maledictio.

2351. Et loco sceptri *arundinem in dextera eius*. Et signatur potestas daemonum secundum Origenem, quam Christus de manibus eorum eripuit; IV Reg. XVIII, 21: *non confidas in baculo arundineo*. Potest enim signari inanitas gentilium, quam sibi tamen Christus assumpsit; Ps. II, 8: *postula a me, et dabo tibi gentes haereditatem tuam*. Et bene comparantur arundini, quia sicut arundo fertur in omnem ventum, sic gentilitas in omnem errorem.

Item arundine utebatur ad scribendum. Item ad venenosa occidendum. Sic Christus fideles ad se trahit et ascribit, sed persecutores ad mortem.

2352. Tunc agitur de illusorio honore, et istum exhibebant facto; unde dicitur *et genu flexo ante eum, illudebant ei*. Et licet hoc fecerint illudendo, tamen signabat quod omne genu ante eum flecti debebat; Phil. II, v. 10: *in nomine Iesu omne genu flectatur*. Unde illudebant verbo, dicentes ei: *ave, rex Iudaeorum*. Et signantur per istos illi qui *voce confitentur se nosse Deum, factis autem negant*, ad Tit. I, 16.

2353. Item varias contumelias intulerunt, quia inspuerunt in faciem eius; Is. l, 6: *faciem meam non averti*

was afraid more for this reason. So when they wished to mock him, they put on him the signs of a king. For it is the custom that kings are clothed in purple; and in place of this, they clothed him with a scarlet garment. Likewise, they usually have a crown; and in place of this they made a crown of thorns. Likewise, they usually have a scepter; and in place of this, they gave him a reed.

2349. It says therefore, **they put a scarlet cloak about him**, i.e., a red one.

But why does Mark say that they clothed him in purple? (Mark 15:17). Augustine resolves it: he said this owing to the likeness of the colors. Or it can be said that although it was scarlet, yet it had something of purple.

By the fact that he was stripped of his own clothes and clothed with another man's, those heretics are caught up who said that he was not a true man. The cloak can signify Christ's body, stained with his blood: for *he was wounded for our iniquities, he was bruised for our sins* (Isa 53:5). Or, it signifies the blood of the martyrs, who washed their robes in the blood of the Lamb (Rev 7:14). Or, the sin of the gentiles.

2350. And plaiting a crown of thorns, they put it on his head. Hence instead of a crown of glory, they imposed on him a crown of indignity; *he will crown you with a crown of tribulation* (Isa 22:18). These thorns signify the prickles of sinners, which prick their consciences: and Christ received these for us, for he died for our sins (1 Cor 15:3). Or it can be referred to Adam's curse, where it was said: *thorns and thistles will it bring forth to you* (Gen 3:18). Hence it signified that this curse was undone.

2351. And in place of a scepter, **a reed in his right hand**. And it signifies the power of the demons, according to Origen, which Christ tore from their hands; *do you trust in Egypt a staff of a broken reed?* (2 Kgs 18:21). For it can signify the uselessness of the gentiles, whom Christ still took to himself; *ask of me, and I will give you the gentiles for your inheritance* (Ps 2:8). And they are well compared to a reed, because as a reed is bent by every wind, so the gentiles by every error.

Also, a reed is used for writing. Also, for killing with poison. Thus Christ also drew and reckoned the faithful to himself, but the persecutors unto death.

2352. Then he treats of the mockery by honor, and they showed this by deed; hence it says, **and bowing the knee before him, they mocked him**. And although they did this by way of mockery, yet it signified that every knee should bend before him; *in the name of Jesus every knee should bow* (Phil 2:10). Then they mocked him by word, saying to him: **hail, king of the Jews**. And they signify those who *profess that they know God: but in their works they deny him* (Titus 1:16).

2353. Likewise, they inflicted various indignities, for they spat on his face; *I have not turned away my face from*

a conspuentibus in me. Item percutiebant caput eius tamquam stultus esset.

Et qui sunt illi qui caput Christi percutiunt? *Caput Christi est Deus*, ut habetur I Cor. XI, v. 3. Illi ergo caput Christi percutiunt, qui divinitatem Christi blasphemant. Per arundinem sacra Scriptura signatur. Tales errorem suum per sacram Scripturam confirmant.

2354. *Exeuntes autem invenerunt hominem Cyrenaeum, nomine Simonem*. Post illusionem agitur de crucifixione, et circa hoc duo facit. Primo determinat de loco crucifixionis; secundo de habitu, et de his, quae in eo loco sunt acta. Et

primo narrat quomodo Christus ductus est ad locum;

secundo quomodo crux est delata;

tertio quomodo pervenerunt ad passionem.

2355. *Et postquam illuserunt, exuerunt*, scilicet chlamydem, quam ei induerant.

Notate quod illuditur in veste aliena sed ducitur in propria; per quod signatur, quod non erat ei proprium illudi, sed occidi: quia, ut habetur ad Phil. II, 8, *humiliavit semetipsum factus obediens usque ad mortem*. Ibi enim apparuit virtus, Ps. CXVII, 16: *dextera Domini fecit virtutem*; Is. LIII, 7: *quasi ovis ad occisionem ducetur*.

2356. *Exeuntes autem invenerunt hominem Cyrenaeum*. Hic agitur de delatione crucis. Et per hoc signatur quod noluit pati in civitate, sed extra. Et ratio assignatur ad Hebr. ult., 12, ubi dicitur: *propter quod ut Iesus sanctificaret per suum sanguinem populum, extra portam passus est*.

Competit etiam figurae, quia, sicut habetur Lev. XVI, 19 ss. quod hircus, qui pro peccato debuit immolari, extra castra mittebatur; sic et Christus, quia erat hostia populi.

Item ad nostram aedificationem, ut det nobis intelligere, quod exire debemus ad eum extra conversationem nostram; ad Hebr. ult., *improperium eius portantes*. Item passus est extra portam, ut virtus passionis non includeretur ad unam gentem; Io. XI, 52, *mortuus est, ut omnes gentes congregaret in unum*.

2357. *Hunc angariaverunt ut tolleret crucem*. Hic videtur discordia, quia Io. XIX, v. 17 habetur quod *exivit baiulans sibi crucem*. Hic est quaedam solutio secundum Hieronymum, quod primo portavit, sed post incedentes obviaverunt Simoni, et angariaverunt et cetera. Origenes dicit quod e converso fuit, quod Simon primo portavit, et post Christus.

Et ratio est mystica quare primo tulit crucem. Unde supra XVI, 24: **qui vult venire post me, abneget semetipsum, et tollat crucem suam et sequatur me** et cetera.

them that rebuked me, and spit upon me (Isa 50:6). Likewise, they struck his head as though he were a fool.

And who are those who strike Christ's head? *The head of Christ is God*, as is said (1 Cor 11:3). Therefore, those strike Christ's head who blaspheme Christ's divinity. The reed signified the Sacred Scriptures. Such men support their error with Sacred Scripture.

2354. *And going out, they found a man of Cyrene, named Simon*. After the mockery, he treats of the crucifixion, and concerning this he does two things. First, he describes the place of the crucifixion; second, the condition, and the things which were done in that place.

first, he recounts how Christ was led to the place;

second, how the cross was carried;

third, how they arrived at the passion.

2355. *And after they had mocked him, they took off*, namely the cloak with which they had clothed him.

Note that he is mocked in another's clothing but led away in his own; which signifies that to be mocked was not his own, but to be killed: for, as is said, *he humbled himself, becoming obedient unto death* (Phil 2:8). For his strength was made apparent there, *the right hand of the Lord has wrought strength* (Ps 117:16); *he will be led as a sheep to the slaughter* (Isa 53:7).

2356. *And going out, they found a man of Cyrene*. Here he treats of the carrying of the cross. And this signified that he did not wish to suffer in the city, but outside. And the reason is given where it says, *wherefore Jesus also, that he might sanctify the people by his own blood, suffered outside the gate* (Heb 13:12).

It also agrees with a figure, for, as it is said that the goat which had to be offered for sin was cast outside the camp (Lev 16:19), so also Christ, for he was the people's sacrifice.

Likewise for our edification, that we might understand that we must go out to him outside our way of life; *let us go forth therefore to him outside the camp, bearing his reproach* (Heb 13:13). Also, he suffered outside the gate so that the strength of his passion would not be shut up in one nation; *he died that all nations might be gathered into one* (John 11:52).

2357. *Him they forced to take up his cross*. Here there seems to be a disharmony, because John says that *bearing his own cross, he went forth* (John 19:17). There is one solution here according to Jerome, that he carried it at first, but after they left they met Simon, and forced him. Origen says that it happened the other way around, that Simon carried it at first, and Christ later.

And there is a mystical reason why he carried the cross. For above, **if any man wants to come after me, let him deny himself, and take up his cross, and follow me** (Matt 16:24).

Et notandum quod iste Simon extraneus erat: et signat gentilem populum, qui crucem Domini tulit; I Cor. I, 18: *verbum crucis pereuntibus quidem stultitia: his autem qui salvi fiunt, idest nobis, virtus Dei est*. Et **Simon** dicitur 'obediens': et gentilis populus obedivit; Ps. XVII, 45: *populus quem non cognovi, servivit mihi, in auditu auris obedivit mihi*. Et veniebat de villa. Villa Latine, 'pagos' dicitur Graece. Unde ille de villa venit, qui de Paganismo venit.

Convenit et quod dicit **Cyrenaeum**, quod interpretatur 'haereditas pretii'; Ps. II, 8: *postula a me, et dabo tibi gentes haereditatem tuam*. Et quod dicit, quod coegerunt eum, signat illos, qui exterius crucem ferunt; interius autem coacte ferunt, quia non propter Deum, sed propter mundum. Ad Gal. V, 24: *qui Christi sunt, carnem suam crucifixerunt cum vitiis et concupiscentiis*.

2358. Consequenter ponitur locus *et venerunt in locum qui dicitur Golgotha, quod est Calvariae locus*. Calvaria dicitur apud homines denudatum, sicut patet in coemeteriis. Unde dicitur in Graeco 'cranios'. Et dicunt aliqui, quod in illo loco sepultus fuit Adam. Hieronymus istud improbat, quia sepultus fuit in Hebron, ut habetur in Iosue XIV.

Et quare ibi passus est? Notandum quod in qualibet civitate est aliquis locus, ubi solent damnati cruciari: unde ibi erat locus damnatorum.

2359. Tunc narratur quid actum est in sua crucifixione. Et

primo ponitur potatio eius;

secundo crucifixio;

tertio alia, quae facta sunt.

Et circa primum

primo ponitur quid sit oblatum;

secundo quomodo se habuit ad oblatum.

2360. Dicit ergo *et dederunt ei vinum bibere cum felle mixtum*. Voluerunt quod omnes sensus eius paterentur: visus passus est per sputa et vigilias, auditus per blasphemias et verba irrisoria, tactus, quia flagellatus; ideo voluerunt quod et gustus pateretur. Et completum est quod in Ps. LXVIII, 22 dicitur: *et dederunt in escam meam fel, et in siti mea potaverunt me aceto*: et Ier. II, 21: *quomodo conversa es in pravum, vinea aliena?*

Sed est quaestio: quia in Mc. XV, 23 habetur quod dederunt ei vinum myrrhatum. Dicendum quod myrrha amarissima est, et vinum felle mixtum est amarum. Sed consuetudo est omne amarum nominari sub specie fellis. Unde secundum veritatem vinum erat myrrhatum,

And one should notice that this Simon was a foreigner, and he signified the gentile people, who bore the Lord's cross; *for the word of the cross, to those indeed who perish, is foolishness; but to those who are saved, that is, to us, it is the power of God* (1 Cor 1:18). And **Simon** means 'obedient': and the gentile people obeyed; *a people, which I knew not, has served me: at the hearing of the ear they have obeyed me* (Ps 17:45). And he came from a village. What is called a village in Latin is called a 'pagos' in Greek. Hence he who comes from a village is one who came from paganism.

And it is also fitting that it says, **of Cyrene**, which means 'inheritance of a reward'; *ask of me, and I will give you the gentiles for your inheritance* (Ps 2:8). And when it says that they forced him, it signifies those who bear the cross exteriorly; but interiorly they bear it as one who is forced, for they do it not for God's sake, but for the world's. *And those who are Christ's, have crucified their flesh, with the vices and concupiscences* (Gal 5:24).

2358. Next, the place is set down: *and they came to the place that is called Golgotha, which is the place of the skull*. Among men, a skull is something said to be stripped bare, as is clear in cemeteries. Hence in Greek it is called 'kranios'. And some say that Adam was buried in that place. Jerome disproves this, since he was buried in Hebron (Josh 14).

And why did he suffer there? One should note that in any city there is a certain place where the condemned are usually tormented: hence it was the place of the condemned.

2359. Then what was done at his crucifixion is recounted. And

first, his drink;

second, his crucifixion;

third, other things which were done.

And concerning the first,

first, what was offered is set down;

second, how he dealt with the thing offered.

2360. It says therefore, *and they gave him wine to drink mixed with gall*. They wanted all his senses to suffer: his vision suffered by spittle and wakefulness, his hearing by blasphemies and mocking words, his touch because he was scourged; so they desired that his taste should also suffer. And what is said in the Psalm was fulfilled: *and they gave me gall for my food, and in my thirst they gave me vinegar to drink* (Ps 68:22); and, *how then are you turned unto me into that which is good for nothing, O strange vineyard?* (Jer 2:21).

But there is a question, for it says that they gave him wine mixed with myrrh (Mark 15:23). One should say that myrrh is most bitter, and wine mixed with gall is bitter. But usually everything bitter is named under the species of gall. So in fact it was wine mixed with myrrh, but it is named by

sed tamen ad similitudinem fellis dicitur. Et per hoc significabatur quod amaritudinem peccatorum nostrorum tulit.

2361. Postea ponitur quomodo se habuit, *quia cum gustasset, noluit bibere*.

Sed quid est quod dicit Marcus quod *accepit*, hic autem dicit quod gustavit? Potest dici quod non accepit, nisi ad gustandum. Et hoc signat, quia gustavit mortem: quia enim cito surrexit, vix visus est mortuus, quia fuit *inter mortuos liber*, Ps. LXXXVII, 6.

2362. *Postquam autem crucifixerunt eum* et cetera. Sed potest quaeri quare magis ista morte voluit mori.

Una ratio est ex parte crucifigentium, quia volebant quod per hoc infamaretur, secundum illud Sap. II, 20: *morte turpissima condemnemus eum* etc., et haec est crucis. Item ex parte ordinationis Dei, quia Christus voluit esse noster magister, ut daret nobis exemplum patiendi mortem. Unde passus est mortem ut per mortem liberaret nos, ut habetur ad Hebr. cap. II, 14 s. Sed multi sunt qui bene volunt pati mortem, sed mortem abiectam refugiunt; ideo Dominus dedit exemplum ne quodlibet genus mortis refugerent.

Item competebat redemptioni, quia ad satisfactionem pro peccato primi hominis: sed primus homo peccavit in ligno; ideo Dominus in ligno pati voluit; Sap. XIV, 7: *benedictum lignum, per quod fit iustitia*. Item Christus exaltandus erat per passionem, ideo exaltari voluit per passionem in cruce. Item volebat corda nostra trahere ad se; Io. XII, 32: *si exaltatus fuero a terra, omnia traham ad meipsum*. Item ut corda nostra elevarentur.

2363. *Diviserunt sibi vestimenta sua*. Hic ponuntur quae facta sunt in contumeliam crucifixi. Et

primo ponitur divisio vestimenti;
secundo superpositio tituli;
tertio associatio.
Circa primum
primo ponit factum;
secundo prophetiam.

2364. Dicit ergo ***diviserunt***. Chrysostomus dicit quod hoc factum fuit in magnum vituperium. Consuetudo enim erat quod condemnatus non denudabatur nisi vilissimus homo: ideo ut magnam contumeliam inferrent ei, denudaverunt ipsum, ut instruamur quod nos ab omni effectu actuum carnalium debemus nos denudare.

Quomodo hoc factum sit, Matthaeus transit, sed Ioannes narrat c. XIX, 23 s. quod quilibet miles accepit partem suam de alia veste; sed super tunica inconsutili miserunt sortem.

2365. Tunc ponitur prophetia *ut adimpleretur quod dictum est per prophetam*. Ly *ut* non ponitur causative, sed consecutive, quia Christo patiente accidit impleri

a likeness to gall. And this signified that he bore the bitterness of our sins.

2361. After this, how he dealt with it is set down: ***and when he had tasted, he would not drink***.

But why does Mark say that he did not take it, while here it says that he tasted it? One can say that he only took it to taste it. And this signifies that he tasted death: for he quickly arose, and hardly seemed dead, because he was *free among the dead* (Ps 87:6).

2362. *And after they had crucified him*. But one can ask why he wished to die by this death rather than another.

One reason is on the side of those who crucified him, that they wanted him to be defamed by this, in accord with, *let us condemn him to a most shameful death* (Wis 2:20), and this is the death of the cross. Also, on the part of God's decree, for Christ willed to be our teacher, that he might give us an example of suffering death. For he suffered death that he might free us through death, as is said (Heb 2:14). But there are many who are quite willing to suffer death, but flee from a base death; so the Lord gave an example, lest they should flee from any kind of death.

Likewise, it fits with the redemption, because he died to satisfy for the sin of the first man: but the first man sinned on a tree; for this reason, the Lord willed to suffer on a tree. *For blessed is the wood, by which justice comes* (Wis 14:7). Also, Christ was to be exalted through his suffering, so he willed to be lifted up by suffering on the cross. Again, he willed to draw our hearts to himself; *and I, if I be lifted up from the earth, will draw all things to myself* (John 12:32). Again, that our hearts might be raised up.

2363. *They divided his garments*. Here are set down the things which were done as an insult to the crucified one. And

first, the division of his garments is set down;
second, the placing of a title over him;
third, the association.
Concerning the first,
first, he sets down the deed;
second, a prophecy.

2364. He says therefore, ***they divided***. Chrysostom says that this was done as a great disparagement. For usually a condemned man was only stripped if he was a most vile man: so, to inflict a great insult on him, they stripped him, that we might learn that we should strip ourselves of every effect of carnal acts.

Matthew passes over when this was done, but John recounts that each soldier took his own part of the other garment; but they cast lots over the seamless tunic (John 19:23).

2365. Then a prophecy is set down: ***that it might be fulfilled what was spoken by the prophet***. The ***that*** is not set down causatively, but consecutively, for when Christ

istud quod dictum erat *et sedentes servabant eum* etc., ut scilicet non sepeliretur; Ps. XXI, 18: *ipsi vero consideraverunt et inspexerunt me*.

2366. Tunc sequitur titulus *et imposuerunt super caput eius causam ipsius scriptam* et cetera. Et attendendum quod illud quod ad ignominiam fecerunt ex ordinatione, cessit ad honorem eius. Unde *imposuerunt causam ipsius*, idest causam pro qua patiebatur; Apoc. c. XIX, 16 habetur scriptum: *Rex regum et Dominus dominantium*. Quod ergo dicit *Rex Iudaeorum*, hoc pertinet ad honorem, quia futurus erat rex super omnes gentes; Ps. II, 6: *ego autem constitutus sum rex ab eo super Sion montem sanctum eius*.

2367. Tunc ponitur societas *tunc crucifixi sunt cum eo duo latrones*. Haec fuit societas, quia in medio duorum latronum ut malefactor; unde Is. LIII, 12: *et cum iniquis deputatus est*. Sed *unus a dextris, alter a sinistris*. Crucem accepit ut iudex: sicut enim in iudicio quidam a dextris, quidam a sinistris, sic hic. Unde per hoc signatur iudex vivorum et mortuorum; ad Phil. II, 9: *propter quod exaltavit illum Deus, et dedit illi nomen quod est super omne nomen, ut in nomine Iesu omne genu flectatur, caelestium, terrestrium et infernorum*; Iob XXXVI, 17: *causa tua quasi impii iudicata est, causam iudiciumque recipies*. Item per hoc quod unus a dextris, alius a sinistris, signatur quod pro omnibus Christus passus est; sed tamen aliqui credunt, aliqui non; I ad Cor. I, 23: *nos autem praedicamus Christum crucifixum, Iudaeis quidem scandalum, gentibus autem stultitiam*. Vel potest dici quod quidam crucem patiuntur propter Deum, et hi a dextris; quidam autem non propter Deum, sed propter mundum, et hi a sinistris.

2368. Tunc agitur de illusione crucifixi *praetereuntes autem blasphemabant eum*; et

primo agitur de ea quae a populo;
secundo de ea, quae a principibus;
tertio de illa, quae a latronibus.
Circa primum
primo describit blasphemos;
secundo blasphemias.

2369. Primo ergo describit quia *praetereuntes*, idest praeter viam euntes: de talibus dicitur Is. XXX, 11: *declinate a me semitam, cesset a facie nostra Sanctus Israel*. Item describuntur, quia *movebant capita*: et hoc faciebant ad delusionem. Per caput significatur ratio, per pedes affectus; unde primo moverunt affectus ad malum, post movent capita, quia infatuantur in peccatis.

suffered it happened that what had been said was fulfilled. *And they sat and watched him*, namely so that he would not be buried; *and they have looked and stared upon me* (Ps 21:18).

2366. Then there follows the title: *and they put over his head, his cause written*. And one should note carefully that what they did in order to shame him fell to his honor. Hence *they put . . . his cause*, i.e., the cause for which he suffered; it is found written, *King of kings and Lord of lords* (Rev 19:16). Therefore, when it says, **KING OF THE JEWS**, this pertains to his honor, because he was going to be king over all nations; *but I am appointed king by him over Zion his holy mountain* (Ps 2:6).

2367. Then his company is set down: *then there were crucified with him two thieves*. These were his company, because he was in the middle of two thieves as though an evildoer; hence, *and was reputed with the wicked* (Isa 53:12). But one was at his right, the other at his left. He took up the cross as a judge: for just as in a judgment one is at the right and the other at the left, so it is here. Hence this signifies the judge of the living and the dead; *for which cause God also has exalted him, and has given him a name which is above all names: that in the name of Jesus every knee should bow, of those that are in heaven, on earth, and under the earth* (Phil 2:9); *your cause has been judged as that of the wicked, cause and judgment you will recover* (Job 36:17). Likewise, the fact that one was at the right and the other at the left signifies that Christ suffered for all; yet some believe, and some do not. *But we preach Christ crucified, unto the Jews indeed a stumblingblock, and unto the gentiles foolishness* (1 Cor 1:23). Or, it can be said that some suffer the cross for God's sake, and these are at the right; while others suffer the cross not for God's sake, but for the world's sake, and these are at the left.

2368. Then he treats of the mockery of the crucified one: *and those that passed by, blasphemed him, wagging their heads*; and

first, he treats of what the people did;
second, of what the rulers did;
third, of what the thieves did.
Concerning the first,
first, he describes the blasphemers;
second, the blasphemies.

2369. First therefore he describes them, at *those who passed by*, i.e., those going along the road. About such men it says, *turn away the path from me, let the Holy One of Israel cease from before us* (Isa 30:11). Likewise, they are described at *wagging their heads*: and they did this for mockery. The head signifies reason, and the feet signify the affections; hence first they moved their affections, then they moved their heads, because they are made foolish in sins.

2370. In tribus irrident eum. Primo in verbis; secundo de operibus quae fecit; tertio de dignitate quam sibi appropriavit.

De primo dicit **vah qui destruis templum Dei** et cetera. **Vah** est interiectio derisionis. Iam enim erat divulgatum, et non volebant credere; unde de his dicit Ier. VIII, 5: *apprehenderunt mendacium, et noluerunt reverti*. Quasi dicerent: *si vis reaedificare templum, reaedifica te*; sed non poterat reaedificare nisi primo solveretur; ideo primo voluit quod solveretur, quia de templo corporis sui hoc dixerat.

Deinde ex opere **salva teipsum**; quasi dicerent: *salvasti alios, salva te*. Sed non vere alios, nec poteris te salvare.

Item ex dignitate, quia **si Filius Dei es, descende nunc de cruce**. Haec conditionalis non est bona, immo potius, si Filius Dei est, debet esse obediens Patri. *Ipse enim factus est obediens usque ad mortem*, Phil. II, 8. Item potius deberent dicere: si Filius Dei es, ascende, et non **descende**; Io. III, 13: *nemo ascendit in caelum, nisi qui descendit de caelo, Filius hominis qui est in caelo*. Utuntur eodem verbo, quo diabolus usus est tentans eum supra IV, 6: **si filius Dei es, mitte te deorsum**. Non est enim Filii Dei descendere: unde persuasione diaboli loquebantur, volentes impedire passionem eius.

2371. Tunc sequitur de illusione principum **similiter et principes sacerdotum illudentes** et cetera. Unde non solum populus, sed principes illudebant ei. Aliquis non facit vim si a minimis condemnatur, sed derisionem maiorum tolerare non potest. Naturaliter enim homo appetit honorari, honor autem fit in testimonium virtutis; unde delusio fit propter opprobrium. Et describuntur isti ex auctoritate, quia **principes**. Item ex doctrina, quia **scribae**. Item ex vita, quia Pharisaei, qui praeeminebant in vita; Ier. V, 5: *ibo ad optimates, et loquar eis: ipsi enim cognoverunt viam Domini, et iudicium Dei sui. Et ecce magis hi simul confregerunt iugum, ruperunt vincula*.

Et tria dicunt.
Primo improperant miracula quae fecit;
secundo regiam dignitatem;
tertio quod Filium Dei se fecit.

2372. Quantum ad primum dicunt: **alios salvos fecit, seipsum non potest salvum facere**. Volebant dicere: si alios salvos fecit, se poterit salvare; sed se non potest: ergo nec alios salvos fecit. Sed nos e contrario debemus arguere: alios salvos fecit, ergo se salvare potest; sed se potuit salvare resurgendo: ergo et nos poterit salvare. Ad Hebr. c. V, 9: *factus est omnibus obtemperantibus sibi*

2370. They laugh at him for three things. First, for words; second, for the works he did; third, for the dignity which he claimed for himself.

About the first, it says, **vah, you who destroy the temple of God**. **Vah** is an interjection of derision. For he was already well known, and they did not want to believe; hence Jeremiah says about them, *they have laid hold on lying, and have refused to return* (Jer 8:5). As though to say: *if you wish to rebuild the temple, rebuild yourself*; but he could not have rebuilt unless he had first been destroyed; so he first willed that he be destroyed, because he had said this about the temple of his own body.

Then over the work: **save your own self**, as though to say: *you save others, save yourself*. But you did not truly save others, nor can you save yourself.

Likewise, over the dignity: **if you are the Son of God, come down from the cross**. This conditional statement is not a good one, but rather on the contrary, if he is the Son of God, he should be obedient to the Father. For he was *obedient unto death* (Phil 2:8). Likewise, they should rather say that: if you are the Son of God, ascend, and not **come down**; *no man has ascended into heaven, but he who descended from heaven, the Son of man who is in heaven* (John 3:13). They use the same words which the devil used when tempting him, above: **if you are the Son of God, cast yourself down** (Matt 4:6). For it does not belong to the Son of God to come down: hence the devil was speaking by way of persuasion, desiring to obstruct his passion.

2371. Then there follows the chief priests' mockery: **in like manner also the chief priests . . . mocking**. Hence not only the people, but even the chief priests were mocking him. Some are not disturbed if they are condemned by the least of men, but they cannot endure the scorn of the great. For man naturally desires to be honored, and honor comes in testimony to virtue; hence ridicule comes due to disgrace. And these men are described by authority, **the chief priests**. Likewise by teaching, **the scribes**. Likewise, by life, since they were Pharisees, who were preeminent in life; *I will go therefore to the great men, and I will speak to them: for they have known the way of the Lord, the judgment of their God: and behold these have together broken the yoke more, and have burst the bonds* (Jer 5:5).

And they say three things:
first, they scoff at the miracles he did;
second, his kingly dignity;
third, that he made himself the Son of God.

2372. As regards the first, they say: **he saved others; himself he cannot save**. They wished to say: if he saved others, he would have been able to save himself; but he cannot save himself, therefore neither did he save others. But we should argue the other way around: he saved others, therefore he can save himself; but he was able to save himself by rising again, therefore he was also able to save us. He

causa salutis aeternae. Unde isti non intendebant nisi salutem temporalem; Christus autem voluit ostendere quod salus aeterna praeponenda est; unde dicunt: *si rex Israel est, descendat nunc de cruce*.

2373. Hic improperant regiam dignitatem, et faciunt falsam promissionem, et faciunt malam consequentiam, quia si rex Israel est, non debet descendere, quia per crucem debet ascendere; Ps. XCV, 10: *Dominus regnavit a ligno*, et in Is. IX, 6: *factus est principatus* idest crux *super humerum eius*. Item fecit quod maius est, quia surrexit de sepulcro, et tamen non crediderunt, unde mendaces erant; Ier. XXIII, 16: *nolite audire verba prophetarum, qui prophetant vobis, et decipiunt vos*: et sequitur: *visionem enim cordis sui loquuntur vobis*.

2374. Item improperant quod dixit se Filium Dei *confidit in Deo, liberet eum si vult*. Ps. XXI, 9: *speravit in Domino, eripiat eum, salvum faciat eum, quoniam vult eum*. Poterat liberare, si vellet; sed nolebat, quia volebat eum ad tempus morti exponere, ut nobis salutem procuraret, et sibi honorem. Unde impletum fuit quod dicitur in Ier. XV, 10: *omnes male dicunt mihi*.

2375. *Idipsum autem et latrones improperabant ei*. Sed quid est quod dicitur hic quod ambo improperant ei, in Luca autem c. XXIII, 39, quod unus solus? Solvit Augustinus, quod aliquando consuetudo est in Scriptura quod plurale ponitur pro singulari, ut Hebr. II, 33: *obturaverunt ora leonum*, idest obturavit, scilicet Daniel. Et est loquendi modus, sicut dicitur: isti rustici mihi sunt infesti, etiam si unus solus sic infestet eum. Sic Matthaeus loquitur. Vel aliter, secundum Hieronymum, quod a principio ambo improperaverunt ei; sed unus videns miracula quae faciebat, poenituit. Et hoc, ut dicit Chrysostomus, divina dispensatione factum est. Unde significantur illi, qui post multa scelera ad Christum revertuntur.

2376. *A sexta autem hora tenebrae factae sunt per universam terram*. Supra narravit Evangelista quomodo Dominus passus est in cruce; hic quomodo operatus est magnifica. Et

primo ponit quae operatus est ante mortem;

secundo quae post mortem, ibi *Iesus autem iterum clamans voce magna, emisit spiritum*.

Circa primum duo facit.

Primo narrat obtenebrationem accidentem;

secundo clamorem, ibi *et circa horam nonam clamavit Iesus*.

2377. Dicit ergo *a sexta autem hora tenebrae factae sunt per universam terram*. Sicut narrat Origenes, gentiles audientes Evangelistam hoc narrantem pro miraculo, deridebant eum, et dicebant hoc factum fuisse

became, to all who obey him, the cause of eternal salvation (Heb 5:9). For these men meant nothing but temporal salvation, while Christ wished to show that eternal salvation should be put first; hence they say, *if he is the king of Israel, let him now come down from the cross*.

2373. Here they scoff at his kingly dignity, and they make a false promise, and draw a false consequence. For if he is the king of Israel, he should not come down, because he should ascend through the cross; *the Lord has reigned from the wood* (Ps 95:10), and *the government*, i.e., the cross, *is upon his shoulder* (Isa 9:6). Likewise, he did something greater, for he rose from the grave, and yet they did not believe; hence they were lying. *Hearken not to the words of the prophets that prophesy to you, and deceive you*, and there follows, *they speak a vision of their own heart* (Jer 23:19).

2374. Likewise, they scoff at the fact that he called himself the Son of God: *he trusted in God; let him now deliver him if he will have him*. He hoped in the Lord, let him deliver him: let him save him, seeing he delights in him (Ps 21:9). He could have freed him, if he wished; but he did not want to, for he wanted to abandon him to death for a time, that he might gain salvation for us, and honor for himself. Hence what is said, was fulfilled: *all curse me* (Jer 15:10).

2375. *And with the same thing the thieves who were crucified with him also reproached him*. But why does it say here that both scoffed at him, while in Luke it says that only one did? (Luke 23:39). Augustine resolves it, saying that sometimes it is the custom in the Scriptures that the plural is set down instead of the singular, as, *who . . . closed the mouths of lions* (Heb 11:33), i.e., he closed, namely Daniel. And this is a common way of speaking, as it is said that, these peasants have harassed me, even if only one is thus harassing him. This is how Matthew speaks. Or in another way, according to Jerome, that both scoffed at him at first, but one, seeing the miracles he was working, repented. And this, as Chrysostom says, was done by divine arrangement. Hence it signifies those who turn back to Christ after many sins.

2376. *Now from the sixth hour there was darkness over the whole earth*. Above, the Evangelist recounted how the Lord suffered on the cross; here, how he worked great things. And

first, he sets down the things he worked before death;

second, the things he worked after death, at *and Jesus again crying with a loud voice, yielded up the spirit*.

Concerning the first, he does two things:

first, he recounts darkness falling;

second, the cry, at *and about the ninth hour Jesus cried*.

2377. It says therefore, *now from the sixth hour there was darkness over the whole earth*. As Origen recounts, gentiles hearing the Evangelist recount this as a miracle laughed at him, and said that this had happened naturally;

naturaliter; ideo credebant, quod ut ignorans diceret, cum sol naturaliter pateretur. Sed non fuit haec eclipsis naturalis, sed miraculosa. Sed si vultis videre, audite quod Dionysius dicit, qui erat vigintiquinque annorum, et studebat in astris in civitate Heliopolis. Et dum viderent, admirati sunt ipse et Apollonius; et videbatur eis quod non erat naturalis, et consideraverunt quatuor miracula.

Primum ex tempore, quia cum esset dies qua Pascha debebat fieri, luna erat quintadecima, ubi luna est in oppositione ad solem; sed naturalis eclipsis fit ex coniunctione lunae ad solem. Secundum miraculum fuit, quod quando sol in occidente est, luna debet esse in oriente; sed hic mutatus est cursus lunae. Item tertium signum est quod semper obscuratio incipit a parte occidentis, quia omnes planetae habent duplicem motum, proprium et communem. Luna quoad proprium motum velocior est, et cum venit ad corpus solis, venit ab occidente; sed sic non fuit hic, quia ab oriente venit. Quartum miraculum fuit, quod ab eadem parte incipit obscuratio, et redit illuminatio; sed hoc tunc non fuit, quia illam partem quam primo occupavit, ultimo dimisit, quia luna ab oriente venit usque ad corpus solis, et tunc retrocessit, unde illa pars primo fuit illuminata. Et ideo ista considerans, in adventu Pauli se convertit et post convertit socium suum. Quintum miraculum, quod est maius, ut dicit, est quod quando naturalis eclipsis est, parum durat: non enim sol patitur, sed fit obscuratio per interpositionem lunae; sed corpus lunae non est maius quam solis, ideo moram non habet; sed istud duravit tribus horis, ideo magnum fuit miraculum.

2378. Sed quaerit Origenes: *si istud fuit ita magnum miraculum, quare aliquis astrologorum non descripsit?*

Respondit, et dixit quod ista obscuratio non fuit universalis, sed circa terram Iudaeae. Vel dicitur **super universam terram**, scilicet Iudaeam. Similis modus loquendi est, cum dicitur: *non est gens, aut regnum etc.*, intelligendum enim de illa gente, sic et hic. Chrysostomus vero dicit quod intelligitur **super universam terram**, idest super totum mundum, quia moriebatur pro universo mundo; ideo voluit per signum passionis omnibus innotescere. Sed Dionysius dicit, quod erat in Aegypto, et ipse vidit, et sic poterat intelligere quod durabat usque in Asiam: unde magis est ei credendum.

Narrat quidam astronomus de quadam eclipsi, quae facta fuit tempore Tiberii, sed non dicit quando, vel quantum duravit, vel quomodo; tamen potest dici quod quia tunc non erat tempus eclipsis, non perpenderunt modum. Unde aliqui dixerunt quod nubes multae interpositae fuerunt inter nos et solem; aliqui autem dixerunt,

for this reason they thought that he spoke as one ignorant, since the sun suffered naturally. But this was not a natural eclipse, but a miraculous one. But if you wish to see, hear what Dionysius says, who was twenty-five years old, and studying the heavenly bodies in the city of Heliopolis. And when they saw it, they marveled, he and Apollonius; and it seemed to them that it was not natural, and they carefully examined four miracles.

First, on the part of the time, for when it was the day on which the Pasch was supposed to take place, it was the fifteenth moon, where the moon stands opposite to the sun; but a natural eclipse comes from a conjoining of the moon to the sun. The second miracle was that when the sun is in the west, the moon should be in the east; but here the course of the moon was changed. Likewise a third sign is that darkening always begins from the western side, because all the planets have a double motion, their own proper motion and a common one. The moon is faster as regards its own proper motion, and when it approaches the body of the sun, it comes from the west; but it was not so here, for it came from the east. The fourth miracle was that a darkening of the sun begins and the illumination returns from the same part; but this did not happen then, for the part it occupied first was the part it left last, for the moon came from the east up to the sun's body, and then went backwards, hence that part was the first to be illuminated again. And this is why, considering these things, when Paul came he converted himself and later converted his companion. The fifth miracle, which as he says is greater, is that when there is a natural eclipse, it lasts only a little while: for the sun does not suffer, but rather a darkening is caused by the interposition of the moon; but the moon's body is not bigger than the sun's, so it has no delay. But this one went on for three hours, and so it was a great miracle.

2378. But Origen asks: *if this was such a great miracle, why does not any astronomer describe it?*

He responded, and said that this darkening was not universal, but around the land of Judea. Or, it says, **over the whole earth**, namely Judea. A similar way of speaking is when it says, *there is no nation or kingdom, where my lord has not sent to seek you* (1 Kgs 18:10), for it should be understood as about this nation; so it is here. But Chrysostom says that it is understood as **over the whole earth**, i.e., over the whole world, because he died for the whole world; so he willed to make it known to all through a sign of the passion. But Dionysius says that he was in Egypt, and he himself saw it, and so he could know that it reached all the way to Asia; hence one should believe him more.

A certain astronomer does tell of a certain eclipse which happened at the time of Tiberius, but he does not say when, or how long it lasted, or the manner of it; yet one can say that, since it was not then the time for an eclipse, he did not consider carefully the manner. Hence some have said that many clouds were positioned between us and the sun; but

quod sol retraxit radios suos; unde Amos VIII, 9: *occidit eis sol in meridie*.

2379. Sed est quaestio, quia hic dicitur quod crucifixus est hora sexta, Marcus vero dicit hora tertia, c. XV, 25.

Dicendum quod Matthaeus historiam narrat, quod crucifixus est hora sexta, et mortuus est hora nona. Et hoc mysterio competit, quia sol in meridie est in medio caeli; ideo competit Filio Dei, qui est verus Sol; Mal. c. IV, 2: *vobis timentibus nomen Dei orietur sol iustitiae*. Item competit transgressioni primi hominis; quia Adam post meridiem peccavit, Gen. III, 8, ideo Christus satisfacere voluit illa hora.

2380. Quare ergo dicit Marcus quod hora tertia?

Dicendum quod crucifixus fuit hora tertia lingua Iudaeorum, sed hora sexta manibus militum. Item tribus horis fuerunt tenebrae, et fuit figuratum per id quod scribitur Exod. X, v. 22, quod *Moyses tribus horis extendit manus suas in caelum, et factae sunt tenebrae tribus diebus in universa terra Aegypti*. Sic Christus in cruce expandit manus suas, et factae sunt tenebrae tribus horis, ad signandum quod privati erant lumine Trinitatis.

2381. *Et circa horam nonam clamavit Iesus voce magna*. Hic ponit clamorem Christi. Et

primo ponitur clamor;

secundo effectus, ibi *quidam autem de illic stantibus* et cetera.

2382. Dicit ergo *et circa horam nonam clamavit Iesus voce magna*. Secundum Origenem Christus voce magna clamat, et signat multitudinem mysteriorum. Is. VI, 3: *Seraphim clamabant alter ad alterum: sanctus, sanctus, sanctus Dominus Deus exercituum*. Unde qui vult hoc intelligere, quod taedio mortis clamavit, non intellexit mysterium; ideo non sic intelligendum est, sed quia voluit dare intelligere se aequalem Patri, lingua Hebraea dixit **Eli, Eli lamma sabacthani?** Item, quia voluit signare quod praenuntiata est a prophetis, ideo dixit illud Ps. XXI, 2: *Deus meus, respice in me, quare me dereliquisti?* Unde dicit Hieronymus quod impii sunt qui aliter Psalmum illum exponere volunt quam de passione Christi.

2383. Notate, quod quidam male intellexerunt. Unde debetis scire quod fuerunt duae haereses. Una quae in Christo non posuit Verbum unitum, sed quod Verbum fuit loco animae, et hoc posuit Arius. Alii vero, quod Verbum non fuit unitum naturaliter, sed per gratiam, sicut in aliquo iusto; ut in prophetis, et sic Nestorius. Unde exponebant **Deus, Deus meus, ut quid dereliquisti me?** Dicunt quod hoc dicebat Verbum Dei, et vocat eum Deum, quia creatura sua est, et conqueritur, quod

others have said the sun withdrew its rays, hence, *the sun will go down at midday* (Amos 8:9).

2379. But there is a question, because it says here that he was crucified in the sixth hour, while Mark says it was the third hour (Mark 15:25).

One should say that Matthew recounts the history, because he was crucified in the sixth hour, and died in the ninth hour. And this pertains to a mystery, for at noon the sun is in the middle of the sky; and so it befits the Son of God, who is the true sun. *But unto you who fear my name, the Sun of justice will arise* (Mal 4:2). Likewise it fits with the first man's transgression, for Adam sinned after noon (Gen 3:8); so Christ willed to make satisfaction in that hour.

2380. Why then does Mark say that it was in the third hour?

One should say that he was crucified in the third hour by the tongue of the Jews, but in the sixth hour by the hands of the soldiers. Likewise, there was darkness for three hours, and it was prefigured by what is written, that *Moses stretched out his hands to the sky for three hours, and a darkness was cast over the whole land of Egypt for three days* (Exod 10:22). Thus Christ spread out his hands on the cross, and a darkness was cast for three hours, to signify that they were deprived of the light of the Trinity.

2381. *And about the ninth hour Jesus cried with a loud voice*. Here he sets down Christ's cry. And

first, the cry is set down;

second, the effect, at *and some who stood there*.

2382. It says therefore, *and about the ninth hour Jesus cried with a loud voice*. According to Origen, Christ cries out in a loud voice, and signifies a multitude of mysteries. *They cried one to another, and said: holy, holy, holy, the Lord God of hosts* (Isa 6:3). Hence the one who wants to take it that he cried out from a weariness of death has not understood the mystery. So one should not understand it this way, but since he willed it to be understood that he is equal to the Father, he said in the Hebrew language, **Eli, Eli, lamma sabacthani?** Also, because he willed to signify that he was foretold by the prophets, and so he spoke the words of the Psalm: *O God, my God, look upon me: why have you forsaken me?* (Ps 21:2) Hence Jerome says that they are impious who wish to explain this Psalm otherwise than about Christ's passion.

2383. Note that some have understood this badly. Hence you should know that there have been two heresies. There was one which did not hold that the Word was united in Christ, but that the Word stood in place of a soul; and Arius held this. But there was another, that the Word was not united naturally, but through grace, as in any just man, as in the prophets; and this is what Nestorius said. Whence they explained **my God, my God, why have you forsaken me?** They say that the Word of God said this, and he calls him

hoc Verbum fecit sibi uniri, et post dereliquit eum. Sed haec est expositio impia, quia semper cum eo est; unde divinitas non dimisit carnem, nec animam: unde in Io. VII, v. 29: *qui me misit, mecum est*.

Quid ergo? Dicendum quod ex ipso modo loquendi manifestum est, quod de Christo debebat intelligi: dicitur enim de eo Io. ult., 17: *ascendo ad Patrem meum, et Patrem vestrum, Deum meum, et Deum vestrum*. Patrem nominat, eo quod Deus est; Deum nominat, eo quod homo est: ideo cum dicit **Deus meus, Deus meus** etc. manifestum est quod secundum quod est homo, loquitur; ideo ingeminat, ut magnitudinem affectus humani designet. Et quod dicitur **derelequisti me**, dicitur per similitudinem, quia quod habemus, a Deo habemus; unde sicut cum aliquis alicui malo exponitur, dicitur derelictus, sic quando Dominus dereliquit hominem cadere in malum poenae, vel culpae, dicitur derelictus; ideo Christus dicitur **derelictus** non quantum ad unionem, nec quantum ad gratiam, sed quantum ad passionem; Is. LIV, 7: *ad punctum dereliqui te*. Et dicit **ut quid?** Non quasi ex taedio, sed potest designare compassionem ad Iudaeos unde non dixit nisi postquam tenebrae essent; unde vult dicere: quare voluisti ut passioni traderer, et isti obtenebrarentur? Item signat admirationem, unde admirabilis est Dei caritas. Ad Rom. V, 8: *commendat Deus caritatem suam in nobis, quoniam cum adhuc peccatores essemus, secundum tempus Christus pro nobis mortuus est*.

2384. Tunc sequitur effectus **quidam autem illic stantes** et cetera. Et

primo ponitur effectus communis in omnibus;

secundo in uno eorum, ibi **et continuo currens unus ex eis** et cetera.

2385. Dicit ergo **quidam autem illic stantes et audientes, dicebant: Eliam vocat iste**.

Qui fuerunt isti? Credit Hieronymus quod isti fuerunt milites, qui nescierunt linguam Hebraeam, et propter hoc credebant quod Eliam vocaret, quia Elias multum erat famosus, quia raptus fuit in caelum, ut habetur IV Reg. II, v. 11. Vel potest dici quod illi fuerunt Iudaei, et volunt per hoc ostendere quod Christus est homo, et non Deus, qui auxilium alterius petit.

2386. Tunc ostenditur effectus in uno: et primo dicitur quid ipse fecerit; secundo quid alii.

Dicit ergo **unus autem ex eis acceptam spongiam implevit aceto**. Quare hoc fecerit, non dicitur hic, sed in Io. XIX, 28, quia Christus videns omnia consummata dixit, *sitio*: ideo iste volens ei satisfacere, dedit ei potum damnatorum. Unde impletum est quod in Ps. c. LXVIII, 22 dicitur: *et dederunt in escam meam fel, et in siti mea potaverunt me aceto*.

God, because he is his creature, and he laments because the Word united this creature to himself, and then abandoned him. But this is an impious explanation, because he is always with him; hence the divinity left neither the body nor the soul. Hence, *and he who sent me, is with me* (John 8:29).

What then? One should say that it is clear from the very manner of speaking that it should be understood as about Christ, for John says of him: *I ascend to my Father and to your Father, to my God and your God* (John 20:17). He calls him Father, because he is God; he calls him God, because he is man. And so when he says, **my God, my God**, it is clear that he speaks according as he is a man; this is why he repeats it, to indicate the magnitude of human feeling. And when he says, **why have you forsaken me**, he speaks by way of similitude, because what we have, we have from God; hence just as when someone is exposed to an evil he is called abandoned, in the same way when the Lord has left a man to fall into the evil of punishment, or of guilt, he is called abandoned. So Christ is called **forsaken** not as regards the union, nor as regards grace, but as regards the passion; *for a small moment have I forsaken you* (Isa 54:7). And he says, **why?** not as though out of weariness, but it can indicate his compassion for the Jews. Hence he only said it after there was darkness; so he wishes to say: why have you willed that I should be handed over to suffering, and that these men should be darkened? Likewise, it indicates astonishment, for the charity of God is astonishing. *But God commends his charity towards us; because when as yet we were sinners, according to the time, Christ died for us* (Rom 5:8–9).

2384. Then there follows the effect: **and some who stood there**. And

first, he sets down the effect common on all;

second, the effect on one of them, at **and immediately one of them, running**.

2385. It says then, **and some who stood there and heard, said: this man calls Elijah**.

Who were these men? Jerome believes that these were the soldiers, who did not know the Hebrew language, and owing to this thought that he called Elijah, because Elijah was very famous, since he was caught up into heaven (2 Kgs 2:11). Or, one can say that these men were Jews, and wished to show by this that Christ is a man, and not God, because he begs for the help of another.

2386. Then the effect on one man is described: and first, it says what he himself did; second, what the others did.

It says therefore, **and immediately one of them, running, took a sponge, and filled it with vinegar**. It does not say here why he did this, but in John it says that Christ, seeing that everything was finished, said: *I thirst* (John 19:28). So this man, wishing to satisfy him, gave him the drink of the condemned. Hence what is said in the Psalm was fulfilled, *and they gave me gall for my food, and in my thirst they gave me vinegar to drink* (Ps 68:22).

2387. Notandum quod erat vinum myrrhatum, sed dictum est fel et acetum, quia habebat amaritudinem. Mystice per vinum myrrhatum significantur illi, qui nihil habent de fide. Vel per acetum, quod fit per corruptionem vini, signatur corruptio humanae naturae. Istam autem amaritudinem Christus potavit. Vel per acetum malitia Iudaeorum signatur. Et ponitur in spongia, quae cavernosa est, et signat cautelas et versutias Iudaeorum. Sed imponunt calamo. Per calamum Sacra Scriptura signatur; unde suam malitiam per Scripturam confirmare volunt.

Et potest esse quod iste ex compassione movebatur; unde volebat iste facere ei auxilium, alii autem nolebant, ideo dicebant: *sine, videamus an veniat Elias liberans eum*.

2388. *Iesus autem iterum clamans voce magna, emisit spiritum*. Hic agitur de his, quae post mortem acta sunt. Et

primo ponitur mors Christi;

secundo quae acta sunt;

tertio effectus.

Secunda ibi *et ecce velum templi scissum est*; tertia ibi *centurio autem* et cetera.

Circa primum tangitur mors, et modus mortis.

2389. Causa mortis triplex assignatur: una causa fuit, ut ostenderet quantum nos amavit. Augustinus: *nulla maior est ratio amoris quam praeveniri amando*. Rom. V, v. 8: *commendat Deus caritatem suam in nobis, quoniam cum peccatores essemus, Christus pro nobis mortuus est*. Item, ut doceret nos contemnere mortem. Per mortem destruxit omnia peccata. Item ut poenam peccati Adae tolleret, ut scilicet liberaret a peccato Adae. Dictum enim fuit ei, Gen. II, 17: *quacumque hora comederitis, moriemini*: ab hac morte nos liberavit. Item, quia diabolus, qui est actor mortis, invaserat eum, qui non meruerat, ideo potestatem in aliis amisit; ideo animam suam morti tradidit, ut nostras liberaret.

2390. Item designatur conditio mortis *et clamans voce magna emisit spiritum*.

Quidam dixerunt quod divinitas mortua fuerat; sed hoc est falsum, quia vita non potest mori, sed Deus non solum est vivens, sed etiam vita. Aliqui dixerunt animam mori cum corpore: quod esse non potest, quia non posset apprehendere immortalitatem.

Item notandum quod omnes moriuntur ex necessitate; Christus autem propria voluntate. Unde non dicit *est mortuus* sed *emisit* quia ex voluntate, et hoc signat potestatem, sicut alibi dicitur Io. X, 18: *potestatem habeo ponendi animam meam, et potestatem habeo iterum sumendi eam*.

2387. One should note that it was wine mixed with myrrh, but it is called gall, or vinegar, because it is bitter. Mystically, the wine mixed with myrrh signifies those who have nothing of the faith. Or vinegar, which comes from the corruption of wine, signifies the corruption of human nature. And Christ drank this bitterness. Or, the vinegar signifies the Jews' malice. And it is put in a sponge, which is porous, and signifies the carefulness and cunning of the Jews. But he put it on a reed. The reed signifies the Sacred Scriptures; hence they wish to support their malice with Scripture.

And it can be that this man was moved by compassion; hence this man wished to give him help, while the others did not wish to, and so they said: *wait, let us see whether Elijah will come to deliver him*.

2388. *And Jesus again crying with a loud voice, yielded up the spirit*. Here he treats of those things which were done after his death. And

first, Christ's death is set down;

second, the things which were done;

third, the effect.

The second is at *and behold the veil of the temple was rent in two*; the third, at *now the centurion*.

Concerning the first, he touches on the death, and the manner of the death.

2389. Three reasons are given for the death. One reason was to show how much he loved us. Augustine: *there is no greater reason for love than to be preceded in loving*. God commends his charity towards us; because when as yet we were sinners, according to the time, Christ died for us (Rom 5:8–9). Likewise, to teach us to despise death. Through death he destroyed all sins. Likewise, to bear the penalty of Adam's sin, namely that he might free us from Adam's sin. For it was said to him, *for in whatever day you eat of it, you will die the death* (Gen 2:17); he freed us from this death. Likewise since the devil, who is the wielder of death, attacked him who had not deserved it, he lost his power over others; this is why he handed his soul over to death, that he might free us.

2390. Likewise, the condition of the death is indicated: *and Jesus again crying with a loud voice, yielded up the spirit*.

Some have said that the divinity had died; but this is false, because life cannot die, and God is not only living, but also life. Some have said that the soul died with the body: but this cannot be, because then it could not lay hold of immortality.

Also, one should note that all men die by necessity; but Christ by his own will. Hence it does not say *he died*, but rather he *yielded up*, because it was by will, and this indicates power, as is said in another place, *I have power to lay it down: and I have power to take it up again* (John 10:18).

Et voluit mori cum magna voce, ad signandum quod ex potestate, et non necessitate moriebatur: unde animam suam posuit cum voluit, et accepit cum voluit. Unde facilius fuit Christo ponere animam, et recipere, quam alicui dormire, et excitari. Sed quare imputatum est eis? Quia fecerunt quod in eis fuit.

2391. *Et ecce velum templi scissum est* et cetera. In parte ista agitur de effectu.

Primo agitur de his quae circa templum facta sunt;
secundo de his quae in elementis;
tertio de his quae in hominibus.

2392. Et videndum quod Matthaeus alio ordine narrat quam Lucas. Dicit Augustinus quod Matthaeus narrat ordinem historiae: et hoc patet, quia dicit *et ecce velum templi scissum est*. In Luca autem nihil tale habetur.

Et notandum quod in templo duplex velum erat, sicut in tabernaculo, quia erat velum intra sancta sanctorum, et erat velum aliud, quod non erat in sanctis. Et ista duo duplicem velationem signabant, quia velum interius significabat velationem mysteriorum caelestium, quae nobis revelabuntur: tunc enim similes ei erimus, cum apparuerit gloria sua. Aliud, quod exterius erat, significabat velationem mysteriorum, quae ad Ecclesiam pertinent. Unde istud exterius fuit scissum, alterum non, ad signandum quod mysteria manifestabantur per mortem Christi, quae ad Ecclesiam pertinent; sed aliud non fuit divisum, quia secreta caelestia adhuc remanent velata. Unde Apostolus II Cor. III, 16: *cum autem Israel conversus fuerit ad Deum, amovebitur velamen*. Unde per passionem omnia mysteria, quae in lege et prophetis scripta sunt, aperta fuerunt, ut habetur Luc. ult., 27: *incipiens a Moyse et omnibus prophetis, interpretabatur illis in omnibus Scripturis, quae de ipso erant*.

Vel significabat dispersionem populi Iudaeorum. Et quia gloria eorum erat in velo, quod in passione Domini scissum est, significabatur quod tota gloria dividebatur ab eis.

2393. *Et terra mota est, et petrae scissae sunt* et cetera. Supra positum est miraculum, quod factum est circa sacra templi; hic ponit miraculum quod factum est circa elementa. Et ista convenientia inveniuntur primo quantum ad virtutem passionis; secundo quantum ad effectum salutis; tertio quantum ad iudiciariam potestatem, quam Christus patiendo meruit.

Convenit quod *terra mota est* etc., quia non potest praesentiam tantae maiestatis sine tremore sustinere; unde in Ps. CIII, 32: *qui respicit terram et facit eam tremere*. *Et petrae scissae sunt*, per quod signatum est quod nulla virtus potest ei resistere; III Reg. XIX, 11: *transit Dominus subvertens montes, et conterens petras*.

And he willed to die with a loud voice to indicate that he died by his power, and not out of necessity: for he laid down his soul when he willed, and he took it up when he willed. So it was easier for Christ to lay down his soul and to take it up than for someone else to sleep and wake up. But why was it blamed on them? Because they did what was in them.

2391. *And behold the veil of the temple was rent in two*. In this part, he treats of the effect:

first, he treats of the things done concerning the temple;
second, of the things done in the elements;
third, of the things done in men.

2392. And it seems that Matthew tells things in an order different from what Luke says (Luke 23:44). Augustine says that Matthew recounts the order of history; and this is clear, because he says, *and behold the veil of the temple was rent in two*. But in Luke no such thing is found.

And one should note that there were two veils in the temple, as in the tabernacle, for there was a veil inside the holy of holies, and there was another veil which was not in the holies. And these two signified a double veiling, for the interior veiling signified the veiling of the heavenly mysteries, which will be revealed to us: for then we will be like him, when he appears in his glory. The other, which was exterior, signified the veiling of the mysteries which pertain to the Church. Hence this exterior one was split in two, not the other, to signify that those mysteries which pertain to the Church were manifested through Christ's death; but the other was not divided, because the heavenly secrets still remain veiled. Hence the Apostle: *but when they will be converted to the Lord, the veil will be taken away* (2 Cor 3:16). Hence through the passion all the mysteries which were written in the law and the prophets were opened, as is said, *and beginning at Moses and all the prophets, he expounded to them in all the Scriptures, the things that were concerning him* (Luke 24:27).

Or, it signified the dispersion of the Jewish people. And since their glory was in the veil which was torn in two during the Lord's passion, it signified that the whole glory was cut off from them.

2393. *And the earth quaked, and the rocks were rent*. Above was set down the miracle which was worked concerning the sacred temple; here he sets down the miracle which was worked concerning the elements. And these things are found to be fitting: first, as regards the power of the passion; second, as regards the effect of salvation; third, as regards the judicial power which Christ merited by suffering.

It is fitting that *the earth quaked*, because it cannot endure the presence of such great majesty without trembling; hence, *he looks upon the earth, and makes it tremble* (Ps 103:32). *And the rocks were rent*, which signified that no power can resist him; *and behold the Lord passes . . . overthrowing the mountains, and breaking the rocks in pieces*

Et monumenta aperta sunt. Monumenta sunt claustra corporum mortuorum. Unde signatur quod vincula mortis disrumpit; Os. XIII, 14: *ero mors tua, O mors, morsus tuus ero, inferne.* Item I Cor. XV, 54: *absorpta est mors in victoria.*

Item convenit quantum ad effectum. Commovetur terra dum quidquid terrenum est abiicitur. Ps. LIX, 4: *commovisti terram, et conturbasti eam, sana contritiones eius, quia commota est.* Item petrae scinduntur, quando duritia cordium ad compassionem movetur; Ier. c. XXIII, 29: *verba mea,* scilicet passionis, *quasi ignis, et quasi malleus conterens petras.* Item quod *monumenta aperta sunt,* signat quod mortui in peccatis debent resurgere; Eph. c. V, 14: *surge qui dormis, et exurge ex mortuis.*

Item convenit venienti ad iudicium, quia ipso veniente, terra movebitur; Agg. II, 7: *adhuc unum modicum est, et ego movebo caelum et terram.* Item petrae scinduntur, quia omnis altitudo virorum deprimetur. Item monumenta aperientur, quia mortui venient ad iudicium; Io. V, 28: *venit hora in qua omnes, qui in monumentis sunt, audient vocem Filii Dei.*

2394. Consequenter tangitur miraculum in hominibus. Et

primo tangit resurrectionem;
secundo manifestationem.

2395. Dicit ergo *et multa corpora sanctorum qui dormierant surrexerunt.*

De illis solet esse quaestio, utrum resurrexerint iterum morituri, vel non morituri. Constat aliquos resurrexisse, ut post morerentur, ut Lazarus. Sed de istis potest dici quod surrexerunt non iterum morituri, quia surrexerunt ad manifestationem resurrectionis Christi. Certum autem est quod *Christus resurgens ex mortuis, iam non moritur.* Item si surrexissent, non esset eis beneficium exhibitum, sed potius detrimentum; ideo surrexerunt tamquam intraturi cum Christo in caelum.

2396. *Et exeuntes de monumentis post resurrectionem eius, venerunt in sanctam civitatem.* Et notandum quod licet istud dictum sit in morte Christi, tamen intelligendum est per anticipationem esse dictum, quia post resurrectionem actum est; quia Christus *primogenitus mortuorum,* Apoc. I, 5.

Et venerunt in sanctam civitatem, non quod modo esset sancta, sed quia ante fuerat; Is. c. I, 21: *quomodo facta est meretrix civitas fidelis, plena iudicii?* Vel dicitur sancta, quia sancta ibi tractabantur. Vel, secundum Hieronymum *in sanctam civitatem,* scilicet caelestem, quia cum Christo venerunt in gloriam. *Et apparuerunt multis.* Sicut enim Christus potestatem habet se manifestandi quibus vult, sic intelligendum de corporibus glorificatis.

(1 Kgs 19:11). **And the graves were opened.** Graves are enclosures for dead bodies. Hence it signifies that he burst the bonds of death; *O death, I will be your death; O hell, I will be your bite* (Hos 13:14). Likewise, *death is swallowed up in victory* (1 Cor 15:54).

Likewise, it is fitting as regards the effect. The earth quakes when any part of the earth is thrown down. *You have moved the earth, and have troubled it: heal you the breaches thereof, for it has been moved* (Ps 59:4). Similarly, rocks are broken when hardness of heart is moved to compassion; *are not my words,* namely about the passion, *as a fire . . . and as a hammer that breaks the rock in pieces?* (Jer 23:29). Similarly, that graves were opened signifies that those who are dead in sin should rise again; *rise you who sleep, and arise from the dead* (Eph 5:14).

Likewise it fits with his coming for judgment, for when he comes the earth will be shaken; *yet one little while, and I will move the heaven and the earth* (Hag 2:7). Again, the rocks are broken, because the loftiness of men is humbled. Also, the graves are opened, because the dead will rise for the judgment; *the hour comes, in which all who are in the graves will hear the voice of the Son of God* (John 5:28).

2394. Next he treats of the miracle in men. And

first, he touches on the resurrection;
second, the manifestation.

2395. It says therefore, **and many bodies of the saints who had slept arose.**

There is usually a question about these people, whether they rose again and died again, or did not die. It is agreed that some have arisen and later died, like Lazarus. But one can say about these people that they rose and did not die again, because they rose for the manifestation of Christ's resurrection, and it is certain that *Christ rising again from the dead, dies now no more* (Rom 6:9). Also, if they had risen only to die again, it would not have been a kindness shown them but rather an injury; therefore they rose to enter into heaven with Christ.

2396. **And coming out of the tombs after his resurrection, came into the holy city.** And one should note that although this was said in the description of Christ's death, yet one should understand that it was said by way of anticipation, because it was done after the resurrection; for Christ is *the first begotten of the dead* (Rev 1:5).

And they came **into the holy city,** not because it was holy now, but because it had been before; *how is the faithful city, that was full of judgment, become a harlot?* (Isa 1:21). Or, it is called holy because holy things were done there. Or, following Jerome, **into the holy city,** namely the heavenly city, because they went with Christ into glory. **And appered to many.** For just as Christ has the power of manifesting himself to whom he wishes, so it should be understood with glorified bodies.

2397. *Centurio autem* et cetera. Hic agitur de effectu miraculorum. Et

primo in gentibus;

secundo in mulieribus, ibi *erant autem ibi mulieres multae*.

2398. Circa primum tria facit. Primo ponitur diligens consideratio; secundo timor; tertio vera confessio fidei proveniens ex timore.

Dicit ergo *centurio autem et qui cum eo erant custodientes Iesum, viso terraemotu et his quae fiebant, timuerunt valde*.

In Luca dicitur quod iste territus fuit ex hoc quod Christus clamans expiravit; hic autem dicitur, quod *viso terraemotu*. Et dicitur Augustinus quod non esset facile solvere nisi diceret *et his quae fiebant*. Iste autem signabat gentilem populum, qui salubri timore confessi sunt Dominum; unde Os. II, 24: *dicam non populo meo: populus meus es tu. Et ipse dicet: Deus meus es tu. Vocabo gentem meam, non gentem meam*. Is. XXVI, 18: *a facie tua, Domine, concepimus, et peperimus spiritum salutis*.

Deinde ponitur vera confessio, ibi *vere Filius Dei erat iste*. In hoc confunditur Arius, qui eum existentem in caelo non confitetur esse vere Filium Dei, quem centurio in morte confitetur; I Io. V, 20: *hic est vere Filius Dei, et vita aeterna*.

2399. Sequitur devotio mulierum *erant autem ibi mulieres multae* et cetera.

Et primo describuntur quoad praeterita, et quoad praesentia. In quo considerandum quod populis recedentibus, mulieres adhaeserunt, ita quod impletum est quod dicitur Is. l, 2: *non remansit vir mecum*.

2400. Sed considerandum, quod hic dicitur quod steterunt *a longe*. Io. autem XIX, v. 25 dicit quod *stabant iuxta crucem* et cetera. Augustinus dicit quod potest dici quod aliae mulieres essent quae prope, et quae longe; nisi diceretur utrobique, quod Maria Magdalena erat una.

Ideo aliter dicendum quod sicut multum et paucum dicuntur relative, sic prope et longe: et sicut idem potest dici multum et paucum respectu diversorum, sic prope et longe. Sic considerandum quod centurio et gentiles iuxta crucem erant; sed mulieres post eos, turbae vero magis a longe. Unde secundum diversam comparationem erant longe et prope: longe comparando ad centurionem et gentiles; prope comparando ad turbas.

Vel potest dici quod primo steterunt prope, sed cum emisit spiritum, steterunt longe.

2397. *Now the centurion*. Here he treats of the effect of the miracles. And

first, on the gentiles;

second, on the women, at *and there were there many women afar off*.

2398. Concerning the first, he does three things. First, their diligent consideration is set down; second, their fear; third, their true confession of the faith, which came from fear.

It says therefore, *now the centurion and they who were with him watching Jesus, having seen the earthquake, and the things that were done, were much afraid*.

In Luke, it says that this man was terrified by the fact that Christ expired while crying out (Luke 23:42); but here it says that it was after *having seen the earthquake*. And Augustine says that this would not be easy to resolve if it did not say, *and the things that were done*. Now, this man signified the gentile people, who confessed the Lord with a healthy fear; hence, *I will say to that which was not my people: you are my people: and they will say: you are my God* (Hos 2:24). *We have conceived by your face, O Lord, and we have born a spirit of salvation* (Isa 26:18).

Then the true confession is set down, at *indeed this was the Son of God*. By this Arius is confounded, who does not confess that he is truly the Son of God while he is in heaven, whom the centurion confessed while he was dead; *this is the true God and life eternal* (1 John 5:20).

2399. There follows the women's devotion: *and there were there many women*.

And first, they are described with respect to the past, and with respect to the present. In which one should consider that when the people drew back, the women clung to him, so that what is said in Isaiah was fulfilled: *I came, and there was not a man* (Isa 50:2).

2400. But one should consider that it says here that they stood *afar off*. Now, John says that they *stood by the cross* (John 19:25). Augustine says that one can say that there were some women there who were near, and some who were at a distance; except it says it of both, because Mary Magdalen was one of them.

So one should say otherwise, that just as many and few are said relatively, so are near and far: and just as the same thing can be called many and few with respect to different things, so it can be called near and far with respect to different things. Thus one should consider that the centurion and the gentiles were next to the cross; but the women were after them, and the crowds indeed further off. Hence they were near and far, according to different comparisons: far off in comparison to the centurion and the gentiles, but near in comparison to the crowds.

Or one can say that at first they stood near, but when he sent forth the spirit, they stood at a distance.

2401. Also, notice that it says that they **had followed Jesus from Galilee, ministering to him**. For he to whom angels were ministering permitted that the women minister to him. By this he gave an example to the apostles who were following that they should accept temporal things from those to whom they were ministering spiritual things. And this was an ancient custom, that teachers received the necessary things from the good people whom they taught. But Paul, since he preached to the gentiles, among whom there was not this custom, did not wish to accept anything, lest it seem that he preached for money.

2402. *Among whom was Mary Magdalen, and Mary the mother of James and Joseph*. Helvidius took an occasion for error from these words, who said that Jesus was born from the seed of Joseph. Jerome says to this that there were two Jameses: the Greater, who is called the brother of John, and the Lesser, who was the son of Alpheus, whose mother was also the mother of Joseph. Hence the woman who was the mother of James the Greater was not the mother of James the Lesser, for it immediately adds *and the mother of the sons of Zebedee*.

2403. But why does it say, *Mary of Cleophas, and Mary of Alpheus*? Jerome resolves it, that it could have been that this Mary had a husband who had two names: hence he was called Cleophas and Alpheus. Or, one can say that first she married Cleophas, and when he died she married Alpheus. Or, one can say that Cleophas was the father, and the mother was called Salome, because Mark says, *and Salome* (Mark 15:40); hence Salome is the name of a woman.

Hence the error of the teacher in the Gloss on the second chapter of Galatians is clear, that it was the name of a man. And also the error of the teacher in the histories, because in Greek it has *Salomei*, which is a feminine ending, which is never found in the masculine.

2404. *And when it was evening*. In this part,

first, he treats of the burial;

second, of the veneration;

third, of the watch.

The second is at *and Joseph taking the body, wrapped it up in a clean linen cloth*; the third, at *and the next day*.

Concerning the first,

first, he sets down the condition of the one who buried him;

second, his request.

2405. Four conditions are set down; hence *when it was evening*, for it was necessary that the body be removed, so it would not remain on the Sabbath, *there came a certain rich man of Arimathea*. And he is described by resources, *rich*; blessed is the rich man who is found without blemish: and who has not gone after gold, nor put his trust in money nor in treasures (Sir 31:8).

But why does he call him rich? One should say that he does not say this for the sake of his praise or boasting, but

quod potuit impetrare a Pilato quod non potuisset unus pauper.

Item describitur a patria, quia *ab Arimathaea*, quod idem est quod Ramatha, quae fuit Samuelis. Et signat 'excelsum,' et iste excelsus fuit. Item ex nomine, quia *Ioseph*, qui 'accrescens' signatur.

Item ex religione, *quia et ipse discipulus erat Iesu*, quia ex fide non excidetat; Io. XIII, v. 31: *si vos manseritis in sermone meo, vere discipuli mei eritis*.

2406. Tunc agitur de impetratione; et primo ponitur petitio; secundo impetratio. *Hic accessit ad Pilatum, et petiit corpus Iesu*. Et commendatur quia *accessit*. Sequitur impetratio *tunc Pilatus iussit reddi corpus*.

2407. Sequitur de sepultura: *et accepto corpore, Ioseph involvit illud in sindone munda*. Et agitur de cultu et sepultura.

De cultu: fuit simplex cultus, quia simplici sindone. Et ideo, secundum. Hieronymum, vituperatur cultus nimius sepulturae.

Per istam sindonem secundum mysterium tria signantur. Primo signatur caro Christi munda: fit enim de lino, quod per multam pressuram dealbatur; sic caro Christi per multam pressuram ad candorem resurrectionis pervenit; Lucae ult., 46: *sic oportuit Christum pati, et resurgere a mortuis tertia die*.

Vel signat Ecclesiam non habentem maculam neque rugam: et hoc signatur per istud linteum, quod ex diversis filis est contextum.

Item signatur munda conscientia ubi Christus quiescit.

2408. *Et posuit eum in monumento suo novo*. Et quatuor dicit de isto monumento. Primo quod erat suum. Et satis conveniebat quod qui pro peccatis aliorum mortuus erat, quod in monumento aliorum sepeliretur. Item dicit *novo*, quia si alia corpora posita fuissent, nesciretur quis surrexisset; Item dicit quod *in petra*, non in monumento ex diversis lapidibus constructo, ut omnis calumnia amoveretur.

Sed quare non sub terra? Ratio fuit ne crederetur, quod discipuli per cavenas terrae extraxissent eum.

Item dicit quod *advolvit saxum magnum*. Et ideo quia magnum, non poterat a paucis revolvi, et maxime cum essent ibi custodes.

2409. Tunc sequitur devotio mulierum. Unde mulieres, quae ardentius amabant, secutae sunt eum usque ad sepulcrum: unde dicitur *erat ibi Maria Magdalena et altera Maria*: et non nominatur Maria Zebedaei, quae non erat ibi, quia non ita ardenter amabat.

in this connection, that he was able to obtain the body from Pilate, which one poor man could not have done.

Likewise, he is described by homeland, *of Arimathea*, which is the same as Rama, which was Samuel's city of residence. And it means 'exalted,' and this man was exalted. Likewise by name, *Joseph*, which means 'increasing.'

Likewise, by religion, *who himself was also a disciple of Jesus*, for he had not fallen away from the faith; *if you continue in my word, you will be my disciples indeed* (John 8:31).

2406. Then he treats of the obtaining; and first the request is set down, second the obtaining. *He went to Pilate, and asked for the body of Jesus*. And he is commended, for *he went*. There follows the obtaining: *then Pilate commanded that the body should be delivered*.

2407. There follows the description of the burial: *and Joseph, taking the body, wrapped it up in a clean linen cloth*. And he treats of the veneration, and the burial.

Of the veneration: it was simple veneration, for it was a simple linen cloth. And for this reason, according to Jerome, veneration with excessively big sepulchres is censured.

According to a mystery, this linen cloth signifies three things. First, it signifies the clean flesh of Christ: for it comes from flax, which is whitened by great pressure; thus the flesh of Christ through great pressure arrived at the radiance of the resurrection; *thus it is written, and thus it behooved Christ to suffer, and to rise again from the dead* (Luke 24:46).

Or, it signifies the Church, which has neither spot nor wrinkle (Eph 5:27): and this is signified by the linen, which is woven together out of various fibers.

Likewise, it signifies a clean conscience, where Christ rests.

2408. *And laid it in his own new monument*. And he says four things about this tomb. First, that it was his own. And it was fitting enough that the one who had died for the sins of others should be buried in the tomb of others. Also, he says, *new*, for if another body had been placed there, it would not be known who had risen. Also, he says that it was *in a rock*, not in a tomb built out of different stones, that every false accusation might be removed.

But why not under the ground? The reason was lest it should be thought that the disciples had dragged him out through caves in the ground.

Also, he says that *he rolled a great stone*. And since it was big, it could not be rolled by a few men, and most of all since there were guards.

2409. Then there follows the women's devotion. For the women, who were more ardent, followed him all the way to the tomb: hence it says, *and there was there Mary Magdalen, and the other Mary*. And he does not mention Mary of Zebedee, who was not there, because she did not love as ardently.

2410. *Altera autem die* etc. Hic agitur de custodia sepulcri: et tria facit.

Primo ponitur petitio;

secundo concessio;

tertio executio.

Circa primum ponitur tempus; et causa; et petitio; et periculum imminens.

2411. Tempus *altera autem die, quae est post Parasceven*. Parasceves 'praeparatio' dicitur. Unde Iudaei, quia in Sabbato nihil agebant, praeparabant in praecedenti die, et ideo dicebatur Parasceves; unde quamvis aliquid solemnitatis haberent, tamen maioris observationis erat Sabbatum, unde nihil in Sabbato praeparabant ex praecepto, Exod. XVI, v. 22, ubi praecepit Dominus quod die Veneris colligerent de manna ad duos dies.

Tunc *convenerunt principes sacerdotum*, unde multum intenti erant ipsum persequi, quia non sufficit persequi usque ad mortem, sed etiam post mortem; unde voluerunt impedire resurrectionem.

2412. Sed quare convenerunt? Sequitur causa *Domine, recordati sumus quod seductor ille*. Seductorem vocant ilium; unde Io. c. VII, 12 dicitur, quod quidam ex eis dicebant, quia bonus est: alii autem non, sed seducit turbas. *Post tres dies resurgam*. Istud habebant ex hoc, quod dixerat supra c. XII, v. 40, *quod sicut Ionas fuit in ventre ceti tribus diebus et tribus noctibus, sic erit Filius hominis in corde terrae tribus diebus et tribus noctibus*. Et ponitur pars pro toto, sicut supra expositum est.

2413. Item ponitur petitio *iube ergo custodiri sepulcrum*. Ipsum studium Iudaeorum prodest nobis ad certitudinem; unde quanto magis nocere intendebant, tanto magis proficiebant ad salutem credentium; Iob v, 13: *apprehendit sapientes in astutia eorum*, quia quod intendunt, Dominus in aliud convertit.

2414. Deinde ponitur intentio petitionis *ne forte discipuli eius veniant, et furentur eum, et dicant plebi: resurrexit a mortuis*: et in hoc prophetaverunt, ideo magis peccaverunt, quia mirabilia viderunt, et tamen non crediderunt posse resurgere.

2415. Sequitur concessio: *ait illis Pilatus: habetis custodiam*; idest habeatis custodiam, quasi dicens: in vobis est, ut custodiatis eum.

2416. Sequitur executio *illi autem abeuntes munierunt sepulcrum signantes lapidem cum custodibus*. Unde non suffecit quod custodes ponerent, sed etiam sigillaverunt. Nec suffecit eis quod milites hoc facerent,

2410. *And the next day*; here he treats of the watch over the tomb: and he does three things:

first, the request is set down;

second, the consent;

third, the execution of the request.

Concerning the first, the time is set down; and the reason; and the request; and the threatening danger.

2411. The time: *and the next day, which followed the Day of Preparation*. 'Parasceves' means 'preparation.' For the Jews, who did nothing on the Sabbath, prepared on the day before, and for this reason it was called the Day of Preparation. For even though they might have some solemnity, still a greater observance belonged to the Sabbath, hence they prepared nothing on the Sabbath, due to the commandment, where the Lord commanded that Friday they should collect enough of the manna for two days (Exod 16:22).

Then *the chief priests and the Pharisees came together to Pilate*, for they intended to persecute him greatly, for it was not enough to persecute him until death, but they intended to persecute him even after death; hence they desired to prevent the resurrection.

2412. But why did they come together? The reason follows: *Lord, we have remembered, that that seducer said*. They call him a *seducer*; hence John says that some of them were saying that he is good, but others that he is not, but rather he seduces the crowds (John 7:12). *After three days I will rise again*. They knew this from what he had said above, that *as Jonas was in the whale's belly three days and three nights: so will the Son of man be in the heart of the earth for three days and three nights* (Matt 12:40). And the part is put down for the whole, as was explained above.

2413. Likewise, the request is set down: *command therefore that the sepulchre be guarded*. The very zeal of the Jews is profitable for us, for certitude: hence the more they meant to do harm, the more they were profitable for the salvation of those who believe. *Who catches the wise in their craftiness* (Job 5:13), because the Lord turns what they intend into something else.

2414. Then the intention behind the request is set down: *lest perhaps his disciples come and steal him away, and say to the people: he is risen from the dead*. And in this they prophesied, and so they sinned the more, for they had seen marvelous things, and yet did not believe that he could rise again.

2415. The consent follows: *Pilate said to them: you have a guard*, i.e., you should have guard, as though to say, it is on you to guard him.

2416. There follows the execution: *and departing, they made the sepulchre sure, sealing the stone, and setting guards*. Hence it was not enough that they should place guards around, but they also sealed it. Nor was it enough for them that the soldiers should do this, but they even

sed etiam ipsimet sigillaverunt; Ps. XXI, v. 17: *consilium malignantium obsedit me.*

sealed it themselves; *the council of the malignant has besieged me* (Ps 21:17).

Chapter 28

Lecture 1

²⁸:¹ Vespere autem Sabbati, quae lucescit in primam Sabbati, venit Maria Magdalene, et altera Maria, videre sepulchrum. [n. 2418]

²⁸:² Et ecce terraemotus factus est magnus. Angelus enim Domini descendit de caelo, et accedens revolvit lapidem, et sedebat super eum. [n. 2423]

²⁸:³ Erat autem aspectus eius sicut fulgur, et vestimentum eius sicut nix. [n. 2427]

²⁸:⁴ Prae timore autem eius exterriti sunt custodes, et facti sunt velut mortui. [n. 2428]

²⁸:⁵ Respondens autem angelus dixit mulieribus: nolite timere vos. Scio enim quod Iesum, qui crucifixus est, quaeritis. [n. 2429]

²⁸:⁶ Non est hic: surrexit enim, sicut dixit. Venite, videte locum ubi positus erat Dominus. [n. 2432]

²⁸:⁷ Et cito euntes dicite discipulis eius, quia surrexit, et ecce praecedit vos in Galilaeam. Ibi eum videbitis, ecce praedixi vobis. [n. 2433]

²⁸:⁸ Et exierunt cito de monumento cum timore et gaudio magno, currentes nuntiare discipulis eius. [n. 2434]

²⁸:⁹ Et ecce Iesus occurrit illis dicens: avete. Illae autem accesserunt, et tenuerunt pedes eius, et adoraverunt eum. [n. 2437]

²⁸:¹⁰ Tunc ait illis Iesus: nolite timere. Ite, nuntiate fratribus meis, ut eant in Galilaeam, ibi me videbunt. [n. 2440]

²⁸:¹ Ὀψὲ δὲ σαββάτων, τῇ ἐπιφωσκούσῃ εἰς μίαν σαββάτων ἦλθεν Μαριὰμ ἡ Μαγδαληνὴ καὶ ἡ ἄλλη Μαρία θεωρῆσαι τὸν τάφον.

²⁸:² καὶ ἰδοὺ σεισμὸς ἐγένετο μέγας· ἄγγελος γὰρ κυρίου καταβὰς ἐξ οὐρανοῦ καὶ προσελθὼν ἀπεκύλισεν τὸν λίθον καὶ ἐκάθητο ἐπάνω αὐτοῦ.

²⁸:³ ἦν δὲ ἡ εἰδέα αὐτοῦ ὡς ἀστραπὴ καὶ τὸ ἔνδυμα αὐτοῦ λευκὸν ὡς χιών.

²⁸:⁴ ἀπὸ δὲ τοῦ φόβου αὐτοῦ ἐσείσθησαν οἱ τηροῦντες καὶ ἐγενήθησαν ὡς νεκροί.

²⁸:⁵ ἀποκριθεὶς δὲ ὁ ἄγγελος εἶπεν ταῖς γυναιξίν· μὴ φοβεῖσθε ὑμεῖς, οἶδα γὰρ ὅτι Ἰησοῦν τὸν ἐσταυρωμένον ζητεῖτε·

²⁸:⁶ οὐκ ἔστιν ὧδε, ἠγέρθη γὰρ καθὼς εἶπεν· δεῦτε ἴδετε τὸν τόπον ὅπου ἔκειτο.

²⁸:⁷ καὶ ταχὺ πορευθεῖσαι εἴπατε τοῖς μαθηταῖς αὐτοῦ ὅτι ἠγέρθη ἀπὸ τῶν νεκρῶν, καὶ ἰδοὺ προάγει ὑμᾶς εἰς τὴν Γαλιλαίαν, ἐκεῖ αὐτὸν ὄψεσθε· ἰδοὺ εἶπον ὑμῖν.

²⁸:⁸ Καὶ ἀπελθοῦσαι ταχὺ ἀπὸ τοῦ μνημείου μετὰ φόβου καὶ χαρᾶς μεγάλης ἔδραμον ἀπαγγεῖλαι τοῖς μαθηταῖς αὐτοῦ.

²⁸:⁹ καὶ ἰδοὺ Ἰησοῦς ὑπήντησεν αὐταῖς λέγων· χαίρετε. αἱ δὲ προσελθοῦσαι ἐκράτησαν αὐτοῦ τοὺς πόδας καὶ προσεκύνησαν αὐτῷ.

²⁸:¹⁰ τότε λέγει αὐταῖς ὁ Ἰησοῦς· μὴ φοβεῖσθε· ὑπάγετε ἀπαγγείλατε τοῖς ἀδελφοῖς μου ἵνα ἀπέλθωσιν εἰς τὴν Γαλιλαίαν, κἀκεῖ με ὄψονται.

²⁸:¹ And in the evening of the Sabbath, when it began to dawn towards the first day of the week, Mary Magdalen and the other Mary came to see the sepulchre. [n. 2418]

²⁸:² And behold there was a great earthquake. For an angel of the Lord descended from heaven, and coming, rolled back the stone, and sat upon it. [n. 2423]

²⁸:³ And his countenance was as lightning, and his raiment as snow. [n. 2427]

²⁸:⁴ And for fear of him, the guards were struck with terror, and became as dead men. [n. 2428]

²⁸:⁵ And the angel answering, said to the women: fear not; for I know that you seek Jesus who was crucified. [n. 2429]

²⁸:⁶ He is not here, for he is risen, as he said. Come, and see the place where the Lord was laid. [n. 2432]

²⁸:⁷ And going quickly, tell his disciples that he is risen, and behold he will go before you into Galilee; there you will see him as he has foretold it to you. [n. 2433]

²⁸:⁸ And they went out quickly from the sepulchre with fear and great joy, running to tell his disciples. [n. 2434]

²⁸:⁹ And behold Jesus met them, saying: all hail. But they came up and took hold of his feet, and adored him. [n. 2437]

²⁸:¹⁰ Then Jesus said to them: fear not. Go, tell my brethren that they go into Galilee, there they will see me. [n. 2440]

28:11 Quae cum abiissent, ecce quidam de custodibus venerunt in civitatem, et nuntiaverunt principibus sacerdotum omnia quae facta fuerant. [n. 2444]

28:12 Et congregati cum senioribus, consilio accepto, pecuniam copiosam dederunt militibus [n. 2447]

28:13 dicentes: dicite quia discipuli eius nocte venerunt, et furati sunt eum, nobis dormientibus: [n. 2448]

28:14 et si hoc auditum fuerit a praeside, nos suadebimus ei, et securos vos faciemus. [n. 2449]

28:15 At illi, accepta pecunia fecerunt sicut erant edocti. Et divulgatum est verbum istud apud Iudaeos usque in hodiernum diem. [n. 2450]

28:16 Undecim autem discipuli abierunt in Galilaeam in montem, ubi constituerat illis Iesus. [n. 2451]

28:17 Et videntes eum adoraverunt: quidam autem dubitaverunt. [n. 2455]

28:18 Et accedens Iesus, locutus est eis dicens: data est mihi omnis potestas in caelo et in terra. [n. 2456]

28:19 Euntes ergo docete omnes gentes, baptizantes eos in nomine Patris, et Filii, et Spiritus Sancti, [n. 2462]

28:20 docentes eos servare omnia quaecumque mandavi vobis. Et ecce ego vobiscum sum omnibus diebus usque ad consummationem saeculi. [n. 2468]

28:11 Πορευομένων δὲ αὐτῶν ἰδού τινες τῆς κουστωδίας ἐλθόντες εἰς τὴν πόλιν ἀπήγγειλαν τοῖς ἀρχιερεῦσιν ἅπαντα τὰ γενόμενα.

28:12 καὶ συναχθέντες μετὰ τῶν πρεσβυτέρων συμβούλιόν τε λαβόντες ἀργύρια ἱκανὰ ἔδωκαν τοῖς στρατιώταις

28:13 λέγοντες· εἴπατε ὅτι οἱ μαθηταὶ αὐτοῦ νυκτὸς ἐλθόντες ἔκλεψαν αὐτὸν ἡμῶν κοιμωμένων.

28:14 καὶ ἐὰν ἀκουσθῇ τοῦτο ἐπὶ τοῦ ἡγεμόνος, ἡμεῖς πείσομεν [αὐτὸν] καὶ ὑμᾶς ἀμερίμνους ποιήσομεν.

28:15 οἱ δὲ λαβόντες τὰ ἀργύρια ἐποίησαν ὡς ἐδιδάχθησαν. καὶ διεφημίσθη ὁ λόγος οὗτος παρὰ Ἰουδαίοις μέχρι τῆς σήμερον [ἡμέρας].

28:16 Οἱ δὲ ἕνδεκα μαθηταὶ ἐπορεύθησαν εἰς τὴν Γαλιλαίαν εἰς τὸ ὄρος οὗ ἐτάξατο αὐτοῖς ὁ Ἰησοῦς,

28:17 καὶ ἰδόντες αὐτὸν προσεκύνησαν, οἱ δὲ ἐδίστασαν.

28:18 καὶ προσελθὼν ὁ Ἰησοῦς ἐλάλησεν αὐτοῖς λέγων· ἐδόθη μοι πᾶσα ἐξουσία ἐν οὐρανῷ καὶ ἐπὶ [τῆς] γῆς.

28:19 πορευθέντες οὖν μαθητεύσατε πάντα τὰ ἔθνη, βαπτίζοντες αὐτοὺς εἰς τὸ ὄνομα τοῦ πατρὸς καὶ τοῦ υἱοῦ καὶ τοῦ ἁγίου πνεύματος,

28:20 διδάσκοντες αὐτοὺς τηρεῖν πάντα ὅσα ἐνετειλάμην ὑμῖν· καὶ ἰδοὺ ἐγὼ μεθ' ὑμῶν εἰμι πάσας τὰς ἡμέρας ἕως τῆς συντελείας τοῦ αἰῶνος.

28:11 Who when they had departed, behold some of the guards came into the city, and told the chief priests all things that had been done. [n. 2444]

28:12 And they, being assembled together with the elders, taking counsel, gave a great sum of money to the soldiers, [n. 2447]

28:13 saying: say that his disciples came by night, and stole him away when we were asleep. [n. 2448]

28:14 And if the governor hears this, we will persuade him, and secure you. [n. 2449]

28:15 So they, taking the money, did as they were taught; and this word was spread abroad among the Jews even to this day. [n. 2450]

28:16 And the eleven disciples went into Galilee, to the mountain where Jesus had appointed them. [n. 2451]

28:17 And seeing him they adored: but some doubted. [n. 2455]

28:18 And Jesus coming, spoke to them, saying: all power is given to me in heaven and in earth. [n. 2456]

28:19 Going therefore, teach all nations, baptizing them in the name of the Father, and of the Son, and of the Holy Spirit, [n. 2462]

28:20 teaching them to observe all things whatsoever that I have commanded you; and behold I am with you all days, even to the consummation of the world. [n. 2468]

2417. Postquam complevit sacramenta Dominicae passionis, agit Evangelista de triumpho Dominicae resurrectionis: et dividitur. Quia

primo ostenditur, quomodo discipuli cognoverunt Christi resurrectionem per auditum;

secundo, quomodo per visum, ut per auditum et visum fiat testificatio certa.

Circa primum

primo ponitur quomodo per auditum a mulieribus;

2417. After having completed the mysteries of the Lord's passion, the Evangelist treats of the triumph of the Lord's resurrection: and it is divided. For

first, he describes how the disciples knew of Christ's resurrection through hearing;

second, how they knew through sight, that through hearing and sight sure testimony might be given.

Concerning the first,

first, he sets down how they knew through hearing from the women;

secundo quomodo a custodibus. Secunda ibi *quae cum abiissent, ecce quidam de custodibus venerunt in civitatem*.

Circa primum duo facit.

Primo dicit, quomodo mulieres cognoverunt per angelum;

secundo per Christi visionem, ibi *et exierunt cito de monumento*.

Circa primum tria.

Primo ponuntur personae, quibus facta fuit revelatio;

secundo angelus revelans;

tertio revelatio.

Secunda ibi *et ecce terraemotus factus est magnus*; tertia ibi *respondens autem angelus dixit*.

Circa primum tria facit.

Primo designat tempus; secundo personas; tertio studium.

2418. Tempus *vespere autem Sabbati*.

Et circa hoc duplex est dubitatio. Prima de hoc quod dicit *vespere*; secunda de hoc quod dicit *lucescit*.

Circa primum est dubitatio, quia videntur contrariari Matthaeus et Ioannes, quia Ioannes dicit quod *adhuc tenebrae erant*. Quid ergo dicit hic *vespere autem Sabbati*?

Hic est triplex solutio. Prima Hieronymi, quod venerunt vespere et mane. Et quod hic dicit *vespere*, ille autem *mane*, non est dissonantia, sed sedulitas sanctarum mulierum. Beda solvit sic, quod inceperunt venire in vespere, sed pervenerunt in mane. Sed numquid erat tantum spatium? Dicit quod non; sed tunc dicitur aliquis facere, quando praeparat se ad faciendum. Et hoc habetur in Lc. XXIII, 55 quod *videntes monumentum et quemadmodum positum erat corpus eius, revertentes paraverunt aromata*. In Parasceve emerunt aromata, et in Sabbato quieverunt, et in vespere paraverunt se ad eundum. Tertia solutio est Augustini, qui dicit quod modus consuetus in Sacra Scriptura est quod sumitur pars pro toto, unde intelligitur *vespere* pro tota nocte Sabbati; unde *vespere autem Sabbati*, idest quae est post Sabbatum, unde vespere quae est initium primae Sabbati. Simile habetur Gen. c. I, 5 in commemoratione operum Dei: *et factum est vespere et mane dies unus*. Unde venerunt vespere, quia in ultima parte noctis. Et haec est *quae lucescit in prima Sabbati*. Vespere non lucescit, quia vespere tenebrescit. Unde venerunt quando lucescit, idest in prima hora diei. Notate quod Iudaei omnes

second, how they knew from hearing from the guards. The second is at *who, when they had departed, behold some of the guards came into the city*.

Concerning the first, he does two things:

first, he tells how the women knew through an angel;

second, how they knew through seeing Christ, at *and they went out quickly from the sepulchre*.

Concerning the first, three things:

first, he sets down the persons to whom the revelation was made;

second, the angel who revealed it;

third, the revelation.

The second is at *and behold there was a great earthquake*; the third, at *and the angel answering, said*.

Concerning the first, he does three things:

first, he designates the time; second, the persons; third, their zeal.

2418. The time: *and in the evening of the Sabbath*.

And there are two difficulties about this. First, about when he says, *in the evening*; second, about when he says, *when it began to dawn*.

There is a difficulty about the first because Matthew and John seem contrary to one another, because John says that *it was yet dark* (John 20:1). So why does it say here, *and in the evening of the Sabbath*?

There are three solutions here. First, Jerome's, that they came both in the evening and in the morning. And that this one says, *in the evening*, and that one, *when it was yet dark*, is not a disharmony, but the unwearied diligence of the holy women. Bede resolves it this way, that they began to come in the evening, but arrived in the morning. But was there really that great a space of time? He says that there was not; but someone is said to do something when he prepares himself for doing it. And this is found, that they *saw the sepulchre, and how his body was laid. And returning, they prepared spices and ointments* (Luke 23:55–56). They bought spices on the Day of Preparation, and they rested on the Sabbath, and in the evening they prepared themselves for going. The third solution is Augustine's, who says that it is a common way of speaking in the Sacred Scriptures that the part is taken for the whole; hence *in the evening* is taken for the whole night of the Sabbath. Hence, *and in the evening of the Sabbath*, i.e., what is after the Sabbath, hence in the evening is the beginning of the first day of the week. A similar thing is found in the account of God's works: *and there was evening and morning one day* (Gen 1:5). So they came in the evening, because they came in the last part of

the night. And this is what ***it began to dawn towards the first day of the week*** means. It does not grow light in the evening, for in the evening it grows dark. Hence they came when it was growing light, i.e., in the first hour of the day. Note that the Jews begin the days of the week from the Sabbath, hence the first day of the week means the Lord's day.

And if you ask Augustine why Mark uses such a manner of speaking, he will say that they prepared the spices in the evening, and went in the morning; hence he goes back to the same thing Bede says.

2419. But how, according to Jerome, should one understand ***it began to dawn?*** For in the evening it grows dark. One should know that for the Jews, the day begins from evening. The reason is that they kept days by the moon, and the moon begins to shine late; this is why the day begins from evening, but grows light on the first day of the week. A similar way of speaking is, *and it was the Day of the Preparation, and the Sabbath drew on* (Luke 23:54).

2420. And this manner of speaking fits with a mystery. First, with the solemnity of the Lord's resurrection, for that night was made bright; *night will be light as day* (Ps 138:12). Likewise, it fits with the restoration of man which came about through Christ: in the first man there was a progress from day into night, namely the night of sin; and his condition was changed, namely from night into day. *For before you were darkness, but now light in the Lord* (Eph 5:8). Also, it signifies that whatever was dark in the law and the prophets all grew light through Christ's resurrection. *Dark waters in the clouds of the air* (Ps 17:12). But this was illuminated in the resurrection, as is found, *and beginning at Moses and all the prophets, he expounded to them in all the Scriptures, the things that were concerning him* (Luke 24:27).

2421. Next he treats of the persons: ***Mary Magdalen and the other Mary***, and she is understood to be the mother of James. Mark adds a third, *and Salome* (Mark 16:1); hence Salome is the name of a woman. But it was not without mystery that two women of the same name came; for he willed to appear to a woman first, because by this the female sex is in a certain way repaired: for just as a woman first heard death instead of life, so by divine arrangement she first saw life instead of death. *From the woman came the beginning of sin* (Sir 25:33). Also, of the same name, because this signifies the unity of the Church: for one was a gentile and the other a Jew, but now all are one Church; *one is my dove* (Song 6:8). Likewise, they are called **Mary**: for just as Mary received the child from a closed womb, so these women going out from the closed tomb merited to see him.

2422. Hence these women ***came to see the sepulchre***; and this indicates their devotion, because they could not be satisfied, so when they could not see him, they wished at least to see the tomb. ***Where your treasure is, there also is your heart*** (Matt 6:21).

2423. *And behold there was a great earthquake.* Here he treats of the angel who revealed it. And first, he touches

---

ferias incipiunt a Sabbato; unde prima Sabbati dicitur dies Dominica.

Et si quaeras ab Augustino, quare Marcus utitur tali modo loquendi, dicet quod vespere paraverunt aromata, et mane venerunt; unde redit in idem quod Beda dicit.

2419. Sed secundum Hieronymum quomodo intelligendum quod dicit ***quae lucescit?*** Quia vespere tenebrescit. Sciendum quod Iudaeis dies incipit esse a vespere. Et ratio est, quia a luna observabant dies; luna autem incipit lucere a sero; ideo illa dies incipit a vespere, sed lucescit in prima Sabbati. Similis modus loquendi Lc. XXIII, 54: *erat autem Parasceves, et Sabbatum illucescebat.*

2420. Et iste modus loquendi mysterio competit, primo, ad solemnitatem Dominicae resurrectionis, quia nox illa fuit lucida; Ps. CXXXVIII, 12: *et nox sicut dies illuminabitur.* Item competit humanae restaurationi, quae facta est per Christum: in primo enim homine fuit processus a die in noctem, scilicet peccati; et mutatus est status, scilicet a nocte in diem; ad Eph. V, 8: *eratis aliquando tenebrae, nunc autem lux in Domino.* Item signatur, quod quicquid erat tenebrosum in lege et prophetis, totum per resurrectionem Christi lucescit. *Tenebrosa aqua in nubibus aeris,* Ps. XVII, 12. Hoc autem in resurrectione illuminatur, ut habetur Lc. ult., 27: *incipiens a Moyse et omnibus prophetis interpretabatur illis in omnibus Scripturis, quae de ipso erant.*

2421. Consequenter agit de personis ***venit Maria Magdalena et altera Maria***; et intelligitur mater Iacobi; Marcus addit tertiam, *et Salome:* unde Salome est nomen mulieris. Sed non fuit sine mysterio, quod duae eiusdem nominis venerunt; unde mulieri primo voluit apparere, quia in hoc quodammodo reparatur sexus muliebris: quia sicut mulier primo in loco vitae prius audivit mortem, sic in loco mortis per ordinationem divinam primo vidit vitam; Eccli. XXV, 33: *a muliere initium peccati factum est.* Item eiusdem nominis, quia per has unitas signatur Ecclesiae: primo enim una fuit ex gentibus, una ex Iudaeis, sed modo omnes sunt una Ecclesia; Cant. VI, 8: *una est columba mea.* Item vocantur **Mariae**: sicut enim de utero clauso Maria suscepit puerum, sic istae exeuntem de tumulo clauso meruerunt videre eum.

2422. Unde istae venerunt ***videre sepulcrum***; et in hoc signatur devotio earum, quia non poterant satiari, ideo cum non possent eum videre, volebant saltem videre sepulcrum. ***Ubi est thesaurus tuus, ibi et cor tuum est,*** supra VI, 21.

2423. *Et ecce terrae motus factus est magnus.* Hic agitur de angelo revelante. Et primo tangitur adventus

angeli; secundo opus eius; tertio dispositio; quarto effectus.

Secunda ibi *et accedens revolvit lapidem*; tertia ibi *et sedebat super eum*; quarta ibi *prae timore autem eius exterriti sunt custodes*.

Et circa primum

primo praesignatur adventus;

secundo tangitur adventus causa, ibi *angelus autem Domini descendit de caelo*.

2424. Dicit ergo *et ecce terrae motus factus est magnus*. Hoc congruebat, et habet causam litteralem. Una ratio, secundum Chrysostomum, quia istae de nocte venerant, et ideo esse potuit quod dormierunt; ideo ut excitarentur, factus est terraemotus ad excitandum illas. Hieronymus dicit quod aliquid tactum erat de humanitate, ideo debebat aliquid tangi de divinitate; ideo cum agitur de sepulcro quod erat humanitatis, fit terraemotus, ut signaretur quod talis mortuus non poterat teneri sub terra. *Fuit enim inter mortuos liber*, Ps. LXXXVII, 6.

Mystice bis factus est terraemotus, ut per unum significetur motus cordium, quia per mortem eius liberati sumus a peccato; per alium translatio ad gloriam; Rom. IV, 25: *traditus est propter peccata nostra, et resurrexit propter iustificationem nostram*. Et in Ps. LIX, 4: *commovisti terram, et conturbasti eam*. Item huius resurrectio est quaedam praefiguratio resurrectionis futurae: in futura autem erit tremor terrae; Ps. LXXV, 9: *terra tremuit et quievit, cum exurgeret in iudicio Deus*.

2425. Et quare? Subiungitur *angelus Domini descendit de caelo*. Si terra non potuit angelum sustinere, multo minus poterit adventum Christi ad iudicium: et dicit *descendit*; licet enim angelus non circumscribatur loco, tamen definitur loco secundum suam operationem; ideo aliquis motus ei convenit. Item convenit quod per angelum denuntietur resurrectio, tum propter gloriam illius, per quem fit, ut dicit Paulus Act. XIII, 30: *Deus suscitavit eum a mortuis*. Eius autem ministri sunt angeli. Item ad denotandum dignitatem resurgentis. De isto dicitur supra c. IV, 11 quod *accesserunt angeli, et ministrabant ei*. Item competit, quia per resurrectionem caelestia terrestribus coniungebantur.

2426. Consequenter ponitur opus angeli *et accedens revolvit lapidem* et cetera. Et hoc secundum litteram, ut panderet iter mulieribus, quia secundum veritatem iam surrexerat Christus: sicut enim de utero clauso exivit, ita de signato sepulcro. Unde hoc factum est ad manifestandum mulieribus: unde *revolvit*, idest iterato volvit, ad signandum gloriam resurgentis; et haec revolutio

on the angel's coming; second, his work; third, his manner; fourth, the effect.

The second is at *and coming, rolled back the stone*; the third, at *and sat upon it*; the fourth, at *and for fear of him, the guards were struck with terror*.

And concerning the first,

first, there is a portent of his coming;

second, the reason for his coming is touched on, at *for an angel of the Lord descended from heaven*.

2424. It says therefore, *and behold there was a great earthquake*. This was fitting, and has a literal reason. One reason, according to Chrysostom, is because the women came at night, and so it could have been that they slept; and so that they would wake up, there was an earthquake to wake them. Jerome says that something had been said about the humanity, and so something had to be said about the divinity; so when the sepulchre is discussed, an earthquake happens, to signify that a dead man of this sort could not be held under the earth. For he was *free among the dead* (Ps 87:6).

Mystically, there were two earthquakes, so that one might signify the movement of hearts, since we were freed from sin through his death; the other, the change toward glory. *Who was delivered up for our sins, and rose again for our justification* (Rom 4:25). And, *you have moved the earth, and have troubled it* (Ps 59:4). Also, his resurrection is a certain prefiguration of the future resurrection: and in the future one, there will be a trembling of the earth; *the earth trembled and was still, when God arose in judgment* (Ps 75:9–10).

2425. And why? It adds next: *an angel of the Lord descended from heaven*. If the earth could not endure an angel, much less will it be able to endure the coming of Christ for judgment. And it says, *descended*, for although an angel is not confined by place, yet it is assigned to a place according to its operation; and this is why some motion befits him. Likewise, it is fitting that the resurrection should be proclaimed through an angel, both on account of the glory of the one through whom it was done, as Paul says, *God raised him up from the dead* (Acts 13:30). And his ministers are angels. Likewise, to indicate the dignity of the one rising. It says about this above, that *angels approached and ministered to him* (Matt 4:11). It was also fitting because by the resurrection the heavenly were conjoined with the earthly.

2426. Next the angel's work is set down: *and coming, rolled back the stone*. And this literally, that he might clear the way for the women, because in truth Christ had already risen by then: for just as he came out from a closed womb, so he came out from a sealed sepulchre. Hence this was done to manifest the resurrection to the women: hence he *rolled back the stone*, i.e., rolled it a second time, to signify the glory of the one who rose; and this turning back

significabat manifestationem legis, quae scripta erat in tabulis lapideis.

2427. Consequenter ponitur dispositio. Et primo quoad situm; secundo quantum ad aspectum; tertio quoad habitum.

Quantum ad situm, quia **sedebat**, non ut fessus, ad signandum quod doctor esset divinae resurrectionis. Item sedere est quiescentium: et per hoc signatur quies quam ex resurrectione habuit in gloria; Rom. VI, 9: *Christus exurgens ex mortuis, iam non moritur, mors illi ultra non dominabitur*. Item sedere est dominantis; Ps. CIX, 1: *dixit Dominus Domino meo: sede a dextris meis*. Et iste sedet *super lapidem*, scilicet diabolum, ad signandum, quod iam dominabatur et mortis et diaboli.

Erat autem aspectus eius sicut fulgur. Hic describitur ex aspectu; et in hoc patet quod apparuit in corpore assumpto. Sed quare ***sicut fulgur***? Quia sicut fulgur claritatem habet, sic et angeli cognitionem; Dan. X, 6: *et oculi eius quasi lampas*. Sed Christus est qui *omnem venientem in hunc mundum illuminat*, Io. I, 9. Item fulgur habet terrorem, sic aspectus angeli; unde Lc. I, 9 dicitur quod territus fuit Zacharias ad vocem angeli.

Item describitur ex habitu ***vestimenta eius sicut nix***, per quod candor iustorum. Mystice autem signatur gloria resurrectionis; Apoc. III, v. 5: *qui vicerit vestietur vestimentis albis*. Item claritas vitae; Eccle. IX, 8: *omni tempore vestimenta tua sint candida*.

Item nota quod dicit quod ***aspectus eius erat sicut fulgur et vestimenta eius sicut nix***, quia in iudicio erit terribilis malis, et demulcebit bonos; Io. XVI, 22: *videbo vos, et gaudebit cor vestrum*.

2428. ***Prae timore autem eius exterriti sunt custodes***. Hic ponitur effectus apparitionis, quia in eorum cordibus extitit timor; et merito, quia ex mala conscientia servabant eum, et semper timida est nequitia, Sap. XVII, 10. ***Et facti sunt quasi mortui***, qui Christum in morte quantum in ipsis fuit voluerunt detinere; Is. XXXIII, 3: *a voce angeli fugerunt populi*.

2429. ***Respondens autem angelus dixit mulieribus*** et cetera. Hic sequitur denuntiatio resurrectionis. Et
primo mulieres confortat;
secundo studium commendat;
tertio gaudium indicat;
quarto officium iniungit denuntiandi.

2430. Dicit ergo ***respondens autem angelus*** et cetera. Sed ad quid respondet? Intentioni mulierum. Non legitur eas aliquid fuisse locutas prae timore: semper enim ita est, quod homo semper turbatur in apparitione angeli, sive bonus, sive malus appareat angelus; quia natura

signified the manifestation of the law, which had been written on tablets of stone.

2427. Next, his manner is set down. And first, as regards his position; second, as regards his countenance; third, as regards his clothing.

As regards position: **and sat**, not as though fatigued, but to signify that he was the teacher of the divine resurrection. Likewise, to sit belongs to those who rest: and this signifies the rest which Christ had in glory from the resurrection; *knowing that Christ rising again from the dead, dies now no more, death will no more have dominion over him* (Rom 6:9). Also, to sit belongs to one who has dominion; *the Lord said to my Lord: sit at my right hand* (Ps 19:1). And he sits over the stone, namely the devil, to signify that now he has dominion over both death and the devil.

And his countenance was as lightning. Here he is described by countenance; and by this it is clear that he appeared in an assumed body. But why ***like lightning***? Because as lightning has brilliance, so also does an angel's knowledge; *his eyes as a burning lamp* (Dan 10:6). But Christ is the one who *enlightens every man who comes into this world* (John 1:9). Likewise, lightning causes terror, like an angel's countenance; hence Luke says that Zechariah was terrified at the voice of the angel (Luke 1:9).

Likewise, he is described by clothing: ***his raiment as snow***, through which the purity of the just is signified. And mystically, it signifies the glory of the resurrection; *he who will overcome, shall thus be clothed in white garments* (Rev 3:5). Likewise, clarity of life; *at all times let your garments be white* (Sir 9:8).

Likewise, note that it says that ***his countenance was as lightning, and his raiment as snow***, because at the judgment he will be terrifying to the wicked, and will soothe the good; *I will see you again, and your heart will rejoice* (John 16:22).

2428. ***And for fear of him, the guards were struck with terror***. Here the effect of the appearance is set down, for fear was in their hearts; and deservedly, because they were guarding him out of a bad conscience, and always, *wickedness is fearful* (Wis 17:10). ***And became as dead men***, who had wished as far as was in them to detain Christ in death; *at the voice of the angel the people fled* (Isa 33:3).

2429. ***And the angel answering, said to the women***. Here follows the proclamation of the resurrection. And
first, he comforts the women;
second, he commends their zeal;
third, he announces joy;
fourth, he lays on them the duty of proclaiming.

2430. It says therefore, ***and the angel answering***. But to what is he responding? To the intention of the women. Due to fear, they are not written to have said anything: for so it always is, for a man is always disturbed at the appearance of an angel, whether the angel appearing is good or bad;

humana fragilis est. Sed sicut dicit B. Antonius, si bonus est angelus, semper dimittit consolatum, ut patet in apparitione Zachariae et Virginis Mariae, utrique dictum est: *ne timeas* et cetera. Lc. I, 30. Sic et istas confortat. Et si dimittat desolatum hominem, constat quod non fuit bonus angelus. Ideo dixit **nolite timere vos**; quasi dicens: vestrum non est timere, quia amatis Christum. *Non enim accepistis spiritum servitutis in timore*, Rom. c. VIII, 15. Non enim confortavit custodes, quia non digni erant.

2431. Tunc commendat studium **scio enim quod Iesum, qui crucifixus est, quaeritis**.

Sed numquid angeli cognoscunt cogitationes? Videtur quod non; Ier. XVII, 9: *pravum est cor hominis et inscrutabile, quis cognoscet illud? Ego dominus scrutans corda et probans renes*. Dicendum est quod non, nisi per revelationem divinam; vel per signum, quia frequenter per gestus corporis habentur indicia voluntatis.

Iesum quaeritis. Nominat eum, ut significet eundem esse. Item **crucifixum**: et in hoc innuit parvam fidem earum, quia quaerebant eum in loco mortis, et credebant eum morte posse teneri.

2432. Tunc annuntiat resurrectionem: **surrexit**, scilicet propria virtute; Ps. III, 6: *ego dormivi, et somnum cepi, et exurrexi, quia Dominus suscepit me*. Et probat hoc per recordationem verbi Dei **sicut dixit**; qui supra c. XX, 19 dixerat: *et tertia die resurget*. Verbum enim Domini non potest deficere. Item indicat ex visu: **venite et videte locum ubi positus erat Dominus**, unde viderunt lapidem revolutum, et non viderunt Christum, quia surrexit clauso tumulo.

2433. Tunc indicit eis officium denuntiationis **et cito euntes dicite discipulis eius quia surrexit**. Et tria indicit. Primo, quia denuntient resurrectionem; secundo, quia locum; tertio quia visionem eis promittant. Et sicut prima mulier primo locuta est diabolo, sic cum bono angelo prima locuta est, ut omnia restaurarentur.

Secundo innuitur locus: **et praecedet vos in Galilaeam**.

Et quare primo in Galilaeam? Non enim prius visus est in Galilaea, sed in Ierusalem. Sed quare magis nominat Galilaeam? Ad signandum quod ipse idem est, qui solebat conversari in Galilaea. Item ut a timore liberarentur, quia securius habitabant in Galilaea, quam in Iudaea. Vel mystice dicitur Galilaea 'transmigratio,' et potest signare transitum ad gentes. Unde **videbitis in Galilaea**, idest nuntiabitis nomen meum gentibus. Hoc autem non facerent, nisi praecederet eos.

2434. *Ibi eum videbitis, sicut praedixit vobis*. Unde verbum Domini tantae potestatis est, quod non poterit aliter esse.

for human nature is frail. But as Blessed Antonius says, if the angel is good, he always sends one away consoled, as is clear in the appearance to Zecharias and to the Virgin Mary, to both of whom it was said: *fear not* (Luke 1:30). So also this one gives comfort. And if the angel sends one away desolate, it is certain that it was not a good angel. For this reason, he said, **fear not**; as though to say: yours is not to fear, because you love Christ. *For you have not received the spirit of bondage again in fear* (Rom 8:15). Indeed, he did not comfort the guards, because they were not worthy.

2431. Then he commends their zeal: **for I know that you seek Jesus who was crucified**.

But do angels know thoughts? It seems they do not; *the heart is perverse above all things, and unsearchable, who can know it? I am the Lord who search the heart and prove the reins* (Jer 17:9–10). One should say that they do not, except by divine revelation; or by a sign, for often an indication of the will is found in the movement of the body.

You seek Jesus. He names him, which signifies that he is the same. Also, the **crucified**; and in this he points out their little faith, for they sought him in the place of the dead, and believed that he was able to be held by death.

2432. Then he announces the resurrection: **he is risen**, namely by his own power; *I have slept and taken my rest: and I have risen up, because the Lord has protected me* (Ps 3:6). And he proves this by recalling God's word: **as he said**; for he had said above, **on the third day he will rise again** (Matt 20:19). For the word of the Lord cannot fail. Likewise, he shows it by what was seen: **come, and see the place where the Lord was laid**, for they had seen the stone rolled back, and had not seen Christ, because he rose from the closed tomb.

2433. Then he lays on them the duty of proclaiming: **and going quickly, tell his disciples that he is risen**. And he commands three things: first, that they should announce the resurrection; second, the place; third, that they should promise them that they will see him. And as the first woman first spoke to the devil, in the same way she first spoke with the good angel, that all things might be restored.

Second, the place is stated: **and behold he will go before you into Galilee**.

And why first into Galilee? For he was not seen first in Galilee, but in Jerusalem. But why does he name Galilee instead? To signify that he is the same one who used to pass his life in Galilee. Also, that they might be free of fear, because they dwelt more securely in Galilee than in Judea. Or mystically, Galilee means 'transmigration,' and can signify the passing over to the gentiles. Hence, **you will see him in Galilee**, i.e., you shall announce my name to the gentiles. Moreover, they would not have done this if he did not go before them.

2434. *There you will see him as he has foretold it to you*. For the Lord's word has such great power that it could not be otherwise.

Sed hic est quaestio litteralis, quia hic dicitur quod viderunt eum sedentem super lapidem; in alio Evangelista quod *introeuntes in monumentum viderunt iuvenem sedentem in dextris*. Solvit Augustinus, quod bis viderunt visionem angelorum: unde possibile fuit, quod unum viderunt extra, alium intra. Vel potest dici quod sepulcrum non solum dicitur lapis excisus, sed erat ibi aliqua materies, ubi includebatur monumentum; unde quod Marcus dicit, *introeuntes in monumentum*, non est intelligendum de lapide illo, sed de spatio in quo includebatur: et hoc patet, quia dicitur hic quod *exierunt cito de monumento cum timore et gaudio* et cetera.

2435. Supra nuntiata est resurrectio mulieribus, hic certificantur de ipsa per Christum: et tria facit Evangelista.

Primo describuntur mulieres;

secundo Christi occursus;

tertio iniungitur denuntiationis officium.

Secunda ibi *et ecce Iesus occurrit illis*; tertia ibi *nolite timere* et cetera.

2436. In prima tria notabilia est considerare. Primo mulierum statum; secundo affectum; tertio propositum.

Status tangitur cum dicitur *exierunt cito de monumento*. Quantum ad litteram monumentum non dicitur lapis excisus, sed illud spatium, quod aliquo munimine erat firmum. Secundum mysterium monumentum est locus mortuorum: et per hoc signatur status peccati; Ps. LXXXVII, 6: *sicut vulnerati dormientes in sepulcris*. Unde exire de monumento est exire de peccato; II ad Cor. VI, 17: *propter hoc exite de medio eorum* et cetera. Et notate quod dicit *cito*, quia de peccato est cito exeundum; Eccli. V, 8: *non tardes converti ad Dominum, et ne differas de die in diem*.

Item tangitur affectus duplex, scilicet timoris et gaudii. Timor de angeli visione, gaudium de resurrectione: timor ex fragilitate humana, gaudium a visione divina; Ps. XXIX, v. 6: *ad vesperum demorabitur fletus, et ad matutinum laetitia*. Sic peccator debet timere; Eccli. V, 5: *de propitiato peccato noli esse sine metu*. Sed gaudere debet de spe resurrectionis; Ps. II, 11: *servite Domino in timore, et exultate ei cum tremore*.

Tunc tangit propositum *currentes nuntiare discipulis* et cetera. Et istud poenitentibus competit, quia currere debent et festinare ut proficiant in bonis: I ad Cor. IX, 24: *sic currite ut comprehendatis*. Et ad Hebr. IV, 11: *festinemus ingredi in illam requiem*. Item tangit bonum propositum, quia voluit ut quod acceperant, aliis communicarent; I Petr. IV, 10: *unusquisque sicut accepit gratiam in alterutrum administrantes*.

2437. *Et ecce Iesus occurrit illis*. Hic ponitur occursus Christi.

But there is a literal question here, because it says here that they saw him sitting on the stone; in another Evangelist it says that *entering into the sepulchre, they saw a young man sitting on the right side* (Mark 16:5). Augustine resolves it, saying that they saw a vision of angels twice: hence it was possible that they saw one outside, and another inside. Or one can say that sepulchre means not only the rock hollowed out, but there was also some further thing in which the tomb was included; so when Mark says, *entering into the sepulchre*, one should not understand it to mean the rock, but rather the area in which it was included. And this is clear, because it says here that **they went out quickly from the sepulchre with fear and great joy**.

2435. Above, the resurrection was announced to the women; here they are assured of it by Christ; and the Evangelist does three things:

first, the women are described;

second, their meeting Christ;

third, the duty of proclaiming is laid on them.

The second is at **and behold Jesus met them**; the third, at **fear not**.

2436. In the first, there are three noteworthy things to consider: first, the women's position; second, their emotion; third, their intention.

The position is touched on when it says, **they went out quickly from the sepulchre**. Literally the tomb does not mean the rock hollowed out, but that area which was made firm by some support. According to a mystery, a tomb is the place of the dead, and this signifies the state of sin; *like the slain sleeping in the sepulchres* (Ps 87:6). Hence to go out from the tomb is to go out from sin; *wherefore, go out from among them* (2 Cor 6:17). And notice that it says, **quickly**, because one should get quickly out of sin; *do not delay to be converted to the Lord, and do not defer it from day to day* (Sir 5:8).

Likewise, two emotions are touched on, namely fear and joy. Fear at seeing an angel, joy at the resurrection: fear due to human fragility, joy from the divine vision; *in the evening weeping will have place, and in the morning gladness* (Ps 29:6). In this way, the sinner should fear; *do not be without fear about sin forgiven* (Sir 5:5). But he should rejoice over the hope of the resurrection; *serve the Lord with fear: and rejoice unto him with trembling* (Ps 2:11).

Then he touches on the intention: **running to tell his disciples**. And this is fitting for penitents, for they should run and make haste to progress in good things; *so run that you may obtain* (1 Cor 9:24). And, *let us hasten therefore to enter into that rest* (Heb 4:11). Likewise, he touches on a good intention, for he willed that they should communicate to others what they had received; *as every man has received grace, ministering the same one to another* (1 Pet 4:10).

2437. **And behold Jesus met them**. Here their meeting Christ is set down.

Et primo ponitur occursus; secundo salutatio; tertio mulierum reverentia.

Dicit ergo *et ecce Iesus occurrit illis*. Et recte dicit quod *occurrit*, quia ex insperato occurrit, dando gratiam; Sap. VI, 14: *praeoccupat qui se concupiscunt, ut illis se prior ostendat*; Is. LXIV, 5: *occurristi laetanti, et facienti iustitiam*.

Item salutavit eas, dicens *avete*. 'Avete' in Graeco gaudium signat; unde dictum est supra, quod cum gaudio ibant. Unde spirituale gaudium semper augetur in iustis, et hoc per spiritualem loquelam; Ps. LXXXIV, 5: *audiam quid loquatur in me Deus*. Et haec erant verba consolatoria, qui sicut prima mulier audivit maledictionem, sic istae mulieres audierunt benedictionem, et maledictioni benedictio respondet.

Et tunc *illae accesserunt et tenuerunt pedes eius, et adoraverunt eum*. Unde accedunt, tenent pedes, adorant. Sic anima peccatoris non debet gratiam Dei recipere in vanum: et hoc signatur, quia *accesserunt*; Ps. XXXIII, 6: *accedite ad eum, et illuminamini*. Item debent firmiter adhaerere: et hoc signatur in hoc quod *tenuerunt pedes eius*. Deut. XXXIII, 3: *qui appropinquant pedibus eius, accipient de doctrina illius*. Item tangit reverentiam in hoc quod dicit *et adoraverunt eum*, quia ipsum Deum recognoverunt; Ps. CXXXI, 7: *adorabimus in loco ubi steterunt pedes eius*.

2438. Sed potest esse quaestio, quia Io. ult., 12 dicitur ei: *noli me tangere*; hic autem dicitur, quod *tenuerunt pedes eius*. Ideo intelligendum, quod bis viderunt, et semel viderunt unum angelum, ut dicit Augustinus, et alia vice duos, sed etiam bis Christum. Primo vidit Maria Magdalena plorans, ut habetur Io. XX, 14. Sed post aliis supervenientibus occurrit eis, et tunc tenuerunt pedes eius; sed Maria Magdalena primo non potuit tenere eum; et hoc secundum Augustinum, quia primo dubitavit, et ideo digna non fuit; sed iam certificata, digna est effecta tangere Christum, ut tactus exterior concordaret interiori.

2439. Consequenter iniungit officium denuntiandi. Et ubi hoc facit,

primo excutit timorem;

secundo officium iniungit, ibi *ite, nuntiate fratribus meis*.

2440. Dicit ergo *tunc ait Iesus eis: nolite timere*. Et hoc factum est convenienter, quia qui ad officium praedicationis ponuntur non debent timere; unde Dominus mittens discipulos suos dixit: *nolite timere*. Timor autem est duplex, scilicet servilis, et initialis, et hic est bonus; Ps. CXVIII, v. 120: *confige timore tuo carnes meas*. Unde dixit *avete*, ut augeret caritatem in eis. Sed quia *perfecta caritas foras mittit timorem*, I Io. IV, 18, ideo dicit *nolite timere*.

And first, the meeting is set down; second, the greeting; third, the women's reverence.

It says therefore, *and behold Jesus met them*. And rightly does it say that he *met* them, for he meets one unexpectedly, by giving grace; *she prevents those who covet her, so that she first shows herself unto them* (Wis 6:14); *you have met him who rejoices, and does justice* (Isa 64:5).

Likewise he greeted them, saying, *all hail*. 'Hail' in Greek indicates joy; hence it is said above that they were going with joy. Hence spiritual joy is always increased in the just, and this is through spiritual conversation; *I will hear what the Lord God will speak in me* (Ps 84:9). And these were consoling words, for just as a woman first heard a curse, so these women heard a blessing, and the blessing answers to the curse.

And then *they came up and took hold of his feet, and adored him*. Hence they approached, took hold of his feet, and adored. Thus a sinner's soul should not receive God's grace in vain, and this is signified by *they came up*; *come to him and be enlightened* (Ps 33:6). Likewise, they should cling firmly, and this is signified by the fact that they *took hold of his feet*. *Those who approach to his feet, will receive of his doctrine* (Deut 33:3). Likewise, he touches on reverence when he says, *and adored him*, for they recognized him as God; *we will adore in the place where his feet stood* (Ps 131:7).

2438. But there can be a question, because in John she is told, *do not touch me* (John 20:17), while here it says that they *took hold of his feet*. So one should understand that they saw twice, and once they saw one angel, as Augustine says, and the other time two, but they also saw Christ twice. First, Mary Magdalene saw him as she wept (John 20:14). But later, when the others arrived, they met them, and then they took hold of his feet; but Mary Magdalene could not hold him at first, and according to Augustine this is because she doubted at first, and so was not worthy; but then being assured, she was made worthy to touch Christ, that the exterior sense of touch might be in harmony with the interior.

2439. Next he lays on them the duty of proclaiming. And where he does this,

first, he casts out fear;

second, he lays on the duty, at *go, tell my brethren*.

2440. It says therefore, *then Jesus said to them: fear not*. And this was fittingly done, for the one who is given the office of preaching should not fear; hence, when the Lord sent out his disciples, he said, *fear not* (Luke 12:32). Now, there are two fears, namely servile fear, and initial fear, and this is good; *pierce my flesh with your fear* (Ps 118:120). Hence, he said, *all hail*, to increase charity in them. But since *perfect charity casts out fear* (1 John 4:18), he says, *fear not*.

2441. And first, he gives the office of proclaiming; second, he shows perfect charity toward his own. And he lays the office of proclaiming on the women, for as a woman brought the words of death to the man, so the other way around it was fitting for a woman to be the messenger of salvation. And first, the proclamation is touched on; second, the place of the appearance.

He says therefore, *go, tell my brethren*.

And why does he say, *my*? To confirm the truth of his nature. For since he had come out from the sepulchre, and appeared glorious, someone might believe that he had not taken up true flesh, and so he says, *my brethren*. Also, owing to a likeness of grace, for he willed to become our brother for the sake of our justification; *that he might be the firstborn amongst many brethren* (Rom 8:29). Likewise *brethren*, i.e., coheirs: *heirs indeed of God, and joint heirs with Christ* (Rom 8:17). Hence with the inheritance now acquired, he calls them brothers.

2442. *That they go into Galilee*. These words seem to imply that he first appeared in Galilee. This Evangelist does not mention the other appearances; but Bede says that he appeared ten times. Five times on the very day of the resurrection. First, to Mary Magdalene, as is recounted in John (John 20:14). Second, to these two whom Matthew touches on here. Third, he appeared to Peter; yet how and when is not said, but that it happened is mentioned in Luke (Luke 24:12). Fourth, to the two disciples going into Emmaus. Fifth, when he appeared to all the disciples except Thomas. Indeed, after these five others are written down. The first after the others was when on the eighth day he appeared to all the disciples, and to Thomas. Second, when he appeared during the fishing, when Peter said, *I am going fishing* (John 21:3). Another, which is mentioned here. Another, when he reproached their unbelief. Last, when he appeared on the Mount of Olives, when he ascended into heaven (Mark 16:14). Yet there were others, as Paul says (1 Cor 15:5–8).

2443. But why is it that both the angel and Christ say that *he will go before you into Galilee*?

Chrysostom says that he says this because he used to pass his life there. Also, that they might be secure there, and might securely await him. Yet Augustine says, in accord with a mystery, that Galilee means 'transmigration': hence it signifies the transmigration to the gentiles, or of this world into glory. The Apostle: *while we are in the body, we are absent from the Lord* (2 Cor 5:6).

2444. *Who when they had departed, behold some of the guards came into the city, and told the chief priests*. Here he treats of the proclamation which was made through the guards. And

first, he sets down the proclamation;

second, an impediment, at *and they, being assembled together with the elders*.

2445. Dicit ergo *et cum abiissent* et cetera. Et quare tantum expectaverunt? Dicendum quod dictum est, quod *prae timore exterriti sunt custodes*. Et forte hoc fecit Dominus, ne molestiam mulieribus inferrent. *Ecce quidam de custodibus venerunt in civitatem, et nuntiaverunt principibus sacerdotum*. Et quare principibus? Quia habebant familiaritatem: item quia ab eis acceperant pretium. Nihilominus nuntiaverunt Pilato; unde in quadam epistola, quam misit Pilatus ad Tiberium, scriptum est, quomodo custodes nuntiaverunt Pilato et cetera. Et *nuntiaverunt*. Iam signabatur, quod per ora gentilium erat manifestanda Christi resurrectio.

2446. Tunc ponitur malitia impedientium. Et

primo tangitur malitia principum;
secundo corruptio custodum;
tertio plebis.

2447. Circa primum concurrunt quatuor ad exaggerandum malitiam istorum. Primo ponitur congregatio; unde dicit *et congregati cum senioribus* etc. quia non unus tantum; Dan. XII, 5: *egressa est iniquitas a senioribus populi*.

Item exaggeratur malitia, quia hoc non fecerunt ex infirmitate, sed ex malitia, sive ex maligno consilio; et hoc est consilium impiorum, de quo Ps. I, 1: *beatus vir, qui non abiit in consilio impiorum*.

Item fraudem fecerunt, quia oblatam pecuniam expenderunt in usum mendacii; unde sciebant illud Eccle. X, 19 quod *pecuniae obediunt omnia*; sicut dicit Hieronymus, similes sunt istis qui bona ecclesiastica expendunt ad faciendam voluptatem.

Item in hoc quod suaserunt mendacium. Et primo suadent, secundo impunitatem promittunt.

2448. Suadent mendacium *dicite, quia discipuli eius nocte venerunt, et furati sunt eum*. Ier. IX, 5: *docuerunt linguam suam loqui mendacium*. In Ps. XXVI, 12: *mentita est iniquitas sibi*. Et vere, ut ait Hieronymus, mendacium, quia discipuli ita stupefacti erant quod non ausi fuissent accedere. Item si debuissent accedere, accessissent primo die, quando non aderant custodes. Item hoc patet, quia remanserunt linteamina, unde si tulissent eum, non dimisissent. Item constat quod cum aromatibus sepultus est, unde linteamina adhaerebant ut colla, unde vix potuissent amovisse. Item lapis erat magnus; unde non potuissent sine magno adiutorio et sine strepitu multo solvisse.

Item arguit sic Augustinus: *aut venerunt vobis vigilantibus, aut dormientibus. Si vigilantibus, quare non eiecistis eos? Si dormientibus, quomodo vidistis?* Et sic apparet, quod mendacium fuit.

2449. Deinde impunitatem promittunt: unde possent dicere: erimus puniti, si praeses audiret. Unde dicit

2445. It says therefore, *when they had departed*. And why did they wait so long? One should say that it said that *for fear of him, the guards were struck with terror*. And perhaps the Lord did this, lest they should give the women trouble. *Behold some of the guards came into the city, and told the chief priests*. And why the chief priests? Because they were friendly with them; also, because they had received their pay from them. Nevertheless, they did tell Pilate; hence in a certain letter which Pilate sent to Tiberius, it is written how the guards had told Pilate; *and told*. Already it signified that Christ's resurrection was to be made known by the mouths of gentiles.

2446. Then he sets down the malice of those impeding the proclamation. And

first, the chief priests' malice is touched on;
second, the guards' corruption;
third, the people's.

2447. Concerning the first, four things combine to make their malice greater. First, the gathering is set down; hence it says, *and they, being assembled together with the elders*. So it was not just one; *iniquity came out . . . from the ancient judges* (Dan 13:5).

Likewise, their malice is made greater because they did not do this out of weakness, but out of malice, or out of malignant counsel; and this is the counsel of the ungodly, of which the Psalm says, *blessed is the man who has not walked in the counsel of the ungodly* (Ps 1:1).

Likewise, they were guilty of fraud, because they spent money from offerings to buy a lie; for they knew that, *all things obey money* (Eccl 10:19). As Jerome says, they are like those who expend ecclesiastical goods to obtain pleasure.

Likewise, by the fact that they urge a lie. And first they urge it; second, they promise impunity.

2448. They urge the lie: *say that, his disciples came by night, and stole him away*. *They have taught their tongue to speak lies* (Jer 9:5). *Iniquity has lied to itself* (Ps 26:12). And indeed, as Jerome says, it was a lie, because the disciples were so stunned that they would not have dared to draw near. Also, if they had dared to draw near, they would have done so on the first day, when there were no guards. This is also clear because the linen stuff remained; for if they had taken him, they would not have left them. Likewise, it is well known that he was buried with spices, so the linen stuff adhered like hard skins, so they could hardly have removed them. Likewise, the stone was huge, so they could not have opened it without a great deal of help and a lot of noise.

Likewise, Augustine argues this way: *either they came while you were awake, or while you slept. If while you were awake, why did you not drive them out? If while you slept, how did you see them?* And so it is apparent that it was a lie.

2449. Then they promise impunity: for they could say, we will be punished if the governor should hear. So it says,

si hoc auditum fuerit a praeside, nos suadebimus ei, et securos vos faciemus. Et quomodo potuerunt illud facere? Dicendum, quod praeses non multum curabat. Item sciebant quod non puniret eos, nisi ad petitionem eorum; ideo sciebant quod et cetera. In hoc signatur cautela diaboli.

2450. *At illi, accepta pecunia fecerunt sicut erant edocti.* Non est mirum si milites corrupti fuerunt pro pecunia, quia et unus de discipulis eius corruptus erat. Eccli. c. X, 9: *avaro nihil est scelestius.*

Et divulgatum est. Et non solum usquequo fuit scriptum hoc, sed etiam usque nunc.

2451. *Undecim autem discipuli abierunt in Galilaeam* et cetera. Supra auditum est quomodo notitia resurrectionis pervenit ad discipulos ex revelatione mulierum, hic quomodo ex eius visione.

Et dividitur: quia
primo ponitur Christi apparitio;
secundo apparentis instructio.
Secunda, ibi *et accedens Iesus locutus est eis.*
Circa primum tria facit.
Primo describitur locus visionis;
secundo visio;
tertio officium.

2452. Dicit ergo **undecim autem discipuli**, quia obedientes Christo, **abierunt in Galilaeam**. Quod dicit **undecim**, intelligendum, quod Iudas abierat: Io. VI, 71: *duodecim elegi vos, et unus ex vobis diabolus est.*

Sed duo sunt notanda, quod Christus videtur in Galilaea, et quod in monte. Galilaea interpretatur 'transmigratio.' Per hoc signatur quod nullus potest videre Deum, nisi ex duplici transmigratione transferatur, scilicet a vitio ad virtutem; supra V, 8: **beati mundo corde, quoniam ipsi Deum videbunt**. Item, a mortalitate ad immortalitatem; unde dicit Apostolus, Phil. I, 23: *coarctor autem e duobus, desiderium habens dissolvi, et esse cum Christo.* Item visus est in monte, ad signandum quod qui vult videre Deum, oportet quod tendat ad celsitudinem iustitiae; Ps. LXXXIII, 3: *ibunt de virtute in virtutem.*

Item quod in monte, significat excellentiam illam, ad quam exaltatus est per resurrectionem: quia dum fuit in mundo, fuit in valle mortalitatis, et ascendit in montem immortalitatis per resurrectionem. Is. II, 2: *elevabitur super colles, et fluent ad eum omnes gentes.*

2453. Et notate, quod apparet eis in loco **ubi constituerat**, in quo signatur obedientia, quia soli obedientes veniunt ad visionem divinam; in Io. XIV, 15: *si diligitis me, mandata mea servate*: et sequitur: *et ego diligam eum, et manifestabo ei meipsum.* Ps. CXVIII, 104: *a mandatis*

and if the governor hears this, we will persuade him, and secure you. And how were they able to do this? One should say that the governor did not care a great deal. Also, they knew that he would not punish them except at their request. This signifies the devil's carefulness.

2450. *So they, taking the money, did as they were taught.* It is no marvel if the soldiers were corrupted for money, for even one of his disciples had been corrupted. *But nothing is more wicked than the covetous man* (Sir 10:9).

And this word was spread abroad among the Jews even to this day. And not only until the time this was written, but even until now.

2451. *And the eleven disciples went into Galilee.* Above, it was heard how notice of the resurrection came to the disciples by the women's revelation; here, how it came by seeing him.

And it is divided, for
first, Christ's appearance is set down;
second, the instruction of the one appearing.
The second is at **and Jesus coming, spoke to them.**
Concerning the first, he does three things:
first, the place where they saw is described;
second, their seeing him;
third, their office.

2452. It says therefore, **and the eleven disciples**, since they were obedient to Christ, **went into Galilee**. When it says, **the eleven**, one must understand that Judas had left; *have I not chosen you twelve; and one of you is a devil?* (John 6:71).

But two things should be noticed, that Christ is seen in Galilee, and that it was on a mountain. Galilee means 'transmigration.' This signifies that no one can see God unless he is carried over by a twofold transmigration, namely from vice to virtue; above, **blessed are the clean of heart: for they will see God** (Matt 5:8). Also, from mortality to immortality; hence the Apostle says, *but I am straitened between two: having a desire to be dissolved and to be with Christ* (Phil 1:23). Likewise, he was seen on a mountain, to signify that the one who wishes to see God must tend toward the height of justice; *they will go from virtue to virtue* (Ps 83:8).

Likewise, that it was on a mountain signifies the excellence to which he was exalted through the resurrection: for while he was in the world, he was in the valley of mortality, and went up onto the mountain of immortality through the resurrection. *And it will be exalted above the hills, and all nations will flow unto it* (Isa 2:2).

2453. And notice that he appears to them in the place he **had appointed**, which indicates obedience, for only the obedient come to the divine vision; *if you love me, keep my commandments* (John 14:15), and there follows, *I will love him, and will manifest myself to him* (John 14:21). And

tuis intellexi; idest, ab observatione mandatorum; unde in veteri lege nemo poterat ascendere in montem: nova lex supplet. Et necessarium fuit, quod eis apparuerit, quia testes debebant ad tantum opus dari. Sed ipse dedit testes non solum de auditu, sed etiam de visu; I Io. I, 2: *quod videmus, et audivimus . . . hoc testamur.*

2454. Sed quaestio est, quando fuit facta haec apparitio: et secundum quod Augustinus dicit, in prima die resurrectionis non, quia in sero fuit visio ubi Thomas non erat. Item nec infra octavam, aut in octava die, quia in Ierusalem fuerunt octo diebus. Nec possumus dicere, quod statim post octo dies: quia contradiceremus Ioanni, qui dicit, quod quando manifestavit se ad mare Tiberiadis, *iam tertio manifestatus est Iesus*; et haec hic non est tertia, sed post hanc tertiam facta est.

2455. *Et videntes.* Notandum quod considerantium Dei magnalia duo sunt genera, quia quidam habent illa in reverentia: unde Abraham dixit, Gen. XVIII, 27: *loquar ad Dominum meum, cum sim pulvis et cinis*; et Iob IX, 14: *quantus sum ego ut respondeam ei, et loquar verbis meis cum eo?* Et sequitur: *ideo me reprehendo, et ago poenitentiam in favilla et cinere.* Item haec reverentia reperitur in angelis. Apoc. VII, 11: *omnes angeli ceciderunt in conspectu throni in facies suas, et adoraverunt Deum.* Et hoc est, quia quanto magis aliquis eum cognoscit, eo magis revereretur eum.

Sed aliqui in infidelitatem vertuntur: volunt enim omnia adaequare suo intellectui, unde quaecumque non intelligunt, blasphemant. Sic fuit de discipulis, quia *et videntes eum adoraverunt* Ps. XXXI, 7: *adorabimus in loco ubi steterunt pedes eius.* **Quidam autem dubitaverunt**, ideo Dominus tradidit se palpandum, ut dicitur Lc. XXIV, 39.

2456. *Et accedens Iesus locutus est eis.* Hic ponitur instructio facta a Christo.

Et tria sunt consideranda.
Primo potestatem denuntiat;
secundo officium iniungit;
tertio auxilium futurum promittit.

Secunda ibi **euntes ergo docete omnes gentes**; tertia ibi **ecce ego vobiscum sum omnibus diebus**.

2457. Dicit ergo *et accedens Iesus locutus est eis.* Discipuli dispartiti erant, quia quidam eum in reverentiam habebant, quidam autem dubitabant; ideo indigebant utroque, scilicet quod manifestaret se, et quod confortaret eos. Sic accessit ad totum populum; Is. c. IX, 2: *populus*, gentium, *qui ambulabat in tenebris, vidit lucem magnam.*

elsewhere: *by your commandments I have had understanding* (Ps 118:104), i.e., from the keeping of the commandments; hence in the old law, no one could go up onto the mountain: the new law completes it. And it was necessary that he appear to them, because witnesses had to be given for such a great work. But he gave witnesses who not only heard, but who also saw; *that which we have seen and have heard, we declare unto you* (1 John 1:3).

2454. But there is a question, when this appearance happened. And according to what Augustine says, it did not happen on the first day of the resurrection, because on the evening of that day there was the appearance where Thomas was not present. Likewise neither was it within the octave of the resurrection, or on the eighth day, because they were in Jerusalem for eight days. Nor can we say that it happened immediately after the eight days, because we would contradict John, who says that when he manifested himself at the sea of Tiberius, *this is now the third time that Jesus was manifested* (John 21:14); and this here is not the third, but the third happened after this.

2455. *And seeing.* One should note that there are two kinds of people who consider the great things of God, for some hold them in reverence: hence Abraham said, *I will speak to my Lord, whereas I am dust and ashes* (Gen 18:27); and *what am I then, that I should answer him, and have words with him?* (Job 9:14), and there follows *therefore I reprehend myself, and do penance in dust and ashes* (Job 42:6). This reverence is also found in the angels. *And all the angels . . . fell down before the throne upon their faces, and adored God* (Rev 7:11). And this is because the more someone knows him, the more he reveres him.

But others are turned toward infidelity: for they wish to make all things fit with their own understanding, so whatever they do not understand, they blaspheme. So it was with the disciples: *and seeing him they adored*; *we will adore in the place where his feet stood* (Ps 131:7). **But some doubted**; this is why the Lord offered himself to be touched (Luke 24:39).

2456. *And Jesus coming, spoke to them.* Here the instruction given by Christ is set down.

And there are three things to be considered:
first, he proclaims his power;
second, he confers an office;
third, he promises future help.

The second is at **going therefore, teach all nations**; the third, at **behold I am with you all days**.

2457. It says therefore, *and Jesus coming, spoke to them.* The disciples were divided, for some held him in reverence, while some doubted; so they needed both, namely that he should manifest himself and that he should comfort them. In this way he drew near to the whole people; *the people*, of the gentiles, *that walked in darkness, have seen a great light* (Isa 9:2).

2458. Item nuntiavit potestatem *data est mihi omnis potestas in caelo et in terra*. Et, sicut dicit Hieronymus, data est potestas ei qui a populo ante crucifixus est. Potentia Dei nihil aliud est quam omnipotentia; et haec data non est Christo, quia non convenit Christo secundum humanitatem. Convenit autem ei aliquid, et secundum quod homo, et secundum quod Deus: unde in Christo secundum quod homo, est scientia, voluntas et liberum arbitrium, et similiter secundum quod Deus. Duplex ergo in Christo est voluntas, scilicet creata et increata. Potest ergo argui quod duplex est potentia, et duplex scientia et cetera.

2459. Est ergo quaestio, quare sicut communicatur ei omnis scientia, quare non omnipotentia. Ratio est ista. Scientia et cognitio est secundum assimilationem cognoscentis ad cognitum, quia sufficit quod species cognitorum sint in cognoscente aliquo modo, vel ita quod per essentiam cognoscat vel quod sint inditae vel ita quod accipiantur a rebus: qualitercumque sint, sufficit ad cognitionem; ideo non oportet quod essentia sit omnium, sed quod sit capax omnium. Hoc autem est esse receptionis infinitae, sicut materia prima. Sed potentia activa sequitur actum, quia quantum est actu, tantum habet agere; ideo qui habet omnipotentiam activam, habet potentiam ad actum omnium. Hoc autem non est, nisi quia habeat potentiam infinitam, quod non convenit Christo inquantum homo, sed solum inquantum Deus.

2460. Quid ergo dicit quod *mihi est data omnis potestas in caelo et in terra?* Notandum, secundum Hilarium, quod datio potest intelligi sive quantum ad divinitatem, quia Pater ab aeterno suam essentiam communicavit Filio; et quia sua essentia est sua potentia, ideo ab aeterno dedit suam potentiam; vel potest etiam referri ad Christum, secundum humanitatem. Sed intelligendum quod humanitas Christi aliquid accepit gratia unionis, et haec sunt omnia quae sunt Deo propria; aliquid autem accepit consequens unionem, ut plenitudinem gratiae et huiusmodi, et est quasi effectus unionis; Io. I, 14: *vidimus eum quasi unigenitum a Patre plenum gratiae et veritatis*. In omnibus ergo his quae insunt Christo gratia unionis, non oportet quod omnia dicantur secundum duplicitatem, sed in aliis quae consequuntur. Unde dico quod potentia est data, non quia alia potentia sit data, sed data est secundum quod est unita Verbo, ut Filio Dei per naturam, sed Christo per gratiam unionis.

2461. Sed quare magis dicit post resurrectionem *data est mihi omnis potestas*, quam ante resurrectionem? Dicendum quod in Scriptura dicitur aliquid fieri,

2458. Likewise, he announced his power: *all power is given to me in heaven and in earth*. And, as Jerome says, the power is given to him who before was crucified by the people. The power of God is nothing other than omnipotence; and this was not given to Christ, because it does not belong to Christ according to his humanity. But something belongs to him both according as he is man and according as he is God: hence in Christ according as he is man there is knowledge, will, and free judgment, and similarly according as he is God. Therefore in Christ there are two wills, namely a created will and an uncreated will. Therefore one can argue that there are two powers, and two knowledges.

2459. Therefore there is a question as to why omnipotence is not communicated to him, the way all science is communicated to him. The reason is this. Science and knowledge exist according to an assimilation of the one knowing to the thing known, for it is enough that the species of the things known be in the one knowing in some way, or such that one may know through the essence either the things which are impressed or such as are received from things: however they may be, it is enough for knowledge. For this reason, it is not necessary that the essence of the knower be all things, but that it be capable of all things. Now, this is the being of infinite reception, such as prime matter. But an active power follows act, because it has the power to act to the degree that it is in act; for this reason, the one who has an active omnipotence has the power for every act. But this is only the case because he has an infinite power, which does not belong to Christ insofar as he is man, but only insofar as he is God.

2460. So why does he say that *all power is given to me in heaven and in earth*? One should note, following Hilary, that the giving can be understood either with regard to the divinity, for the Father from eternity has communicated his own essence to the Son, and since his essence is his power, then from eternity he has given his power; or it can also be referred to Christ according to his humanity. But one should understand that Christ's humanity received some things by the grace of union, and these are all things which are proper to God; and it received other things which follow on the union, such as the fullness of grace and suchlike, and this is as it were an effect of the union; *we saw his glory, the glory as it were of the only begotten of the Father, full of grace and truth* (John 1:14). Therefore, in all those things which are present in Christ by the grace of union, it is not necessary that everything be said according to a doubling, but rather it is necessary in the other things which follow. Hence I say that power is given not because another power is given, but it is given according as the humanity is united to the Word, as to the Son of God by nature, but to the Christ by the grace of union.

2461. By why does he say after the resurrection that *all power is given to me*, rather than before the resurrection? One should say that in Scripture a thing is said to happen

when it first becomes known: so before the resurrection his omnipotence was not so manifest, although he had it; but when he could convert the entire world, then it was made manifest.

We can also say otherwise, that **power** signifies a certain honor of leadership, as we say men are in power; and this is how this power is taken here. Now, it is agreed that Christ, who held rule over the world from eternity as the Son of God, received the execution of that rule from the resurrection; as though to say: now I am in possession. It says about this power: *and judgment will sit, that his power may be taken away, and be broken in pieces, and perish even to the end. And that the kingdom, and power, and the greatness of the kingdom, under the whole heaven, may be given to the people of the saints of the Most High: whose kingdom is an everlasting kingdom, and all kings shall serve him, and will obey him* (Dan 7:26–28). Hence a certain actual leadership is understood: as if the Son were exalted to the exercise of that power which he naturally possessed; *the Lamb that was slain is worthy to receive power and divinity* (Rev 5:12).

2462. *Going therefore, teach all nations*. Here he bestows an office; and he bestows a threefold office:

first, of teaching;

second, of baptizing;

third, the office of forming with regard to morals.

2463. He says therefore, *going therefore, teach all nations*. And this follows in this way, as though he said: **all power is given to me by God**, that not only the Jews but also the gentiles may be converted to me; therefore, since it is the time, *going . . . teach all nations*. *As the Father has sent me, I also send you* (John 20:21). And, *I dispose to you, as my Father has disposed to me, a kingdom* (Luke 22:29). And he says, **going therefore, teach**, because this is the first thing in which we should be instructed, namely in faith, because *without faith it is impossible to please God* (Heb 11:6). And from this it arose in the Church that she first catechizes those who are to be baptized, i.e., she instructs them in faith. And, the power being received, he sends them to all nations; and this is what **teach all nations** means. *I have given you to be the light of the gentiles, that you may be my salvation even to the farthest part of the earth* (Isa 49:6).

2464. And after they have been taught about faith, he gives the office of baptizing. **Baptizing them**, as though to say: the one who is advanced to such a dignity must first be made aware of the dignity, that afterward he may have reverence for it. *For as many of you as have been baptized in Christ, have put on Christ* (Gal 3:27).

2465. But what is the form of baptism? ***In the name of the Father, and of the Son, and of the Holy Spirit***.

There are two things in Christ, the humanity and the divinity. The humanity is the way, not the end; *I am the way, and the truth, and the life* (John 14:6): the truth, as though the end for the contemplative; the life, as though the end for

humanitate, maneatis, sed ulterius transeatis ad divinitatem. Ideo oportebat quod duo signarentur, humanitas et divinitas. Per baptismum humanitas; ad Rom. VI, 4: *consepulti enim sumus cum illo per baptismum in mortem*. Et per formam verborum, divinitas ita quod sanctificatio est per divinitatem. Et ideo dicit **in nomine Patris, et Filii, et Spiritus Sancti**.

Et ratio est, quia per baptismum fit regeneratio, et in regeneratione tria requiruntur. Primo, cui fiat; secundo, per quem; tertio, quo.

Cui, scilicet Deo Patri, ut dicit Apostolus Rom. VIII, 29: *quos praescivit, hos et praedestinavit conformes fieri imaginis Filii sui*. Et Io. I, 12: *dedit eis potestatem filios Dei fieri his qui credunt in nomine eius*. Per quem, quia per Filium; Gal. IV, 4: *misit Deus Filium suum . . . ut adoptionem filiorum reciperemus*, quia per adoptionem ad naturalem Filium sumus filii. Item quo, quia accepimus donum Spiritus Sancti; ad Rom. VIII, 15: *non accepistis Spiritum servitutis iterum in timore, sed accepistis spiritum adoptionis filiorum Dei*. Ideo oportuit fieri mentionem de Patre, Filio et Spiritu Sancto. Et ista in baptismo Christi fuerunt, quia fuit Filius per quem, Pater a quo, et Spiritus Sanctus in columba.

2466. Et dicitur **in nomine**, idest in invocatione nominis, vel in virtute nominis, quia virtutem habet; Ier. XIV, 9: *tu autem in nobis es, Domine, et nomen tuum invocatum est super nos, ne derelinquas nos*. Item dicit **in nomine**, non *in nominibus*, et confunduntur haereses, quae non ponunt distinctionem in hoc quod dicit **in nomine Patris, et Filii**. Sed confunditur Arius per hoc quod in singulari dicit **in nomine**.

2467. Notandum quod in primitiva Ecclesia baptizabatur in nomine Christi, et hoc ut redderetur nomen venerabile. Sed numquid modo sufficeret? Credo quod non, quia expressa requiritur invocatio Trinitatis. In Christo continetur implicite Trinitas.

Sic ergo inducit ut eos instrueret ad baptismum. Sed contra Apostolus dicit, quod non misit eum Deus baptizare, sed evangelizare, sed baptizare per alios, sicut Christus non baptizabat, sed discipuli eius.

2468. Docentes eos servare omnia quaecumque mandavi vobis. Sed numquid sufficit ad salutem credere et baptizari? Non; immo etiam requiritur instructio morum; ideo dicit **docentes servare omnia quaecumque mandavi vobis**. Ps. CXVIII, 4: *tu mandasti mandata tua*

the active. I do not will that you should remain in the way, namely in the humanity, but that you should at last pass over to the divinity. For this reason it was necessary that two things should be signified, the humanity and the divinity. Baptism signifies the humanity; *we are buried together with him by baptism into death* (Rom 6:4). And the divinity is signified through the form of words, such that sanctification is through the divinity. And this is why he says, **in the name of the Father, and of the Son, and of the Holy Spirit**.

And the reason is that through baptism comes a regeneration, and in a regeneration three things are required: first, to what it is made; second, through what; third, by what.

To what, namely to God the Father, as the Apostle says: *whom he foreknew, he also predestined to be made conformable to the image of his Son* (Rom 8:29). And, *he gave them power to be made the sons of God, to those who believe in his name* (John 1:12). Through what, namely through the Son; *God sent his Son . . . that we might receive the adoption of sons* (Gal 4:4), for through adoption to the natural Son we are made sons. Likewise by what, for we receive the gift of the Holy Spirit; *you have not received the spirit of bondage again in fear; but you have received the Spirit of adoption of sons* (Rom 8:15). Therefore mention had to be made of the Father, of the Son, and of the Holy Spirit. And these were in Christ's baptism: the Son was through whom, the Father from whom, and the Holy Spirit in the dove.

2466. And it says, **in the name**, i.e., in the invocation of the name, or in the power of the name, for it has power; *but you, O Lord, are among us, and your name is called upon by us, forsake us not* (Jer 14:9). Also, it says, **in the name**, not *in the names*, and those heresies are confounded which put no distinction in the fact that he says, **in the name of the Father, and of the Son**. But Arius is confounded by the fact that he says, **in the name**, in the singular.

2467. One should note that in the primitive Church they baptized in the name of Christ, and this was so that the name might be rendered venerable. But would this manner of baptizing be enough? I believe that it would not, because an express invocation of the Trinity is required. In Christ the Trinity is contained implicitly.

In this way then he brings in this formula to instruct them toward baptism. But the Apostle says to the contrary, that God did not send him to baptize, but to evangelize, and others to baptize, just as Christ himself did not baptize, but rather his disciples did.

2468. Teaching them to observe all things whatsoever that I have commanded you. But is it enough for salvation to believe and be baptized? No; on the contrary, an instruction in morals is required, and this is why he says, **teaching them to observe all things whatsoever that I have**

custodiri nimis. Et dicit *quae mandavi,* non *quae consului.* Unde supra X, 27: *quae vobis dico, omnibus dico.*

2469. Tunc ponit tertium *et ecce ego vobiscum sum omnibus diebus usque ad consummationem saeculi.* Hic promittit auxilium; quare respondet dicentibus: tu mandas quod doceamus omnes, non sumus sufficientes. Non timeatis, quia *ego vobiscum sum.*

Et notate quod sicut mandatum ponitur transire in omnes, sic et auxilium; quia promittit apostolis et aliis simile exequentibus: unde ipse ad Patrem orans dicit: *non pro eis autem rogo tantum,* scilicet discipulis, *sed et pro his qui credituri sunt per verbum eorum in me.* Unde omnibus communiter promittit; Io. XIV, 12: *qui credit in me, opera quae ego facio, et ipse faciet et maiora horum faciet.*

Item per omne tempus; unde dicit *omnibus diebus usque ad consummationem saeculi.* Non sic dicit, ut quasi post non sit nobiscum, nisi usque ad consummationem saeculi, sed quia tunc erimus per consummationem in gloria; Apoc. XXI, 3: *ecce tabernaculum Dei cum hominibus, et habitabit cum eis. Et ipsi populus eius erunt, et ipse Deus cum eis erit eorum Deus.* Unde etiam Is. VII, 14 dicitur quod *vocabitur nomen eius Emmanuel,* quod interpretatur 'nobiscum Deus,' *usque ad consummationem saeculi*; quasi dicat: generatio fidelium fortior est quam mundus. Non enim peribit mundus, donec omnia fiant, idest Ecclesia fidelium consummetur, et compleatur numerus electorum a Deo in vitam aeternam, cui est honor et potestas per infinita saecula saeculorum. Amen.

commanded you. You have commanded your commandments to be kept most diligently (Ps 118:4). And he says, *that I have commanded*, not *what I have counseled.* Hence above, *what I say to you, I say to all* (Mark 13:37).

2469. Then he sets down the third thing: *and behold I am with you all days, even to the consummation of the world.* Here he promises help; by which he responds to those who say, you command that we should teach all, but we are not sufficient. Do not fear, for *I am with you.*

And notice that, just as a command is laid down to go out unto all, so also help; for he makes a promise to the apostles and to others who similarly carry out his command: for, praying to the Father, he says, *not for them only do I pray*, namely the disciples, *but for those also who through their word will believe in me* (John 17:20). Hence he makes the promise commonly to all; *he who believes in me, the works that I do, he also will do; and greater than these will he do* (John 14:12).

Likewise, he is with us through all time; hence he says, *all days, even to the consummation of the world*. He does not speak this way as though he is only with us to the consummation of the world, but because then we will be in glory through the consummation; *behold the tabernacle of God with men, and he will dwell with them. And they will be his people; and God himself with them will be their God* (Rev 21:3). Hence also Isaiah says that *his name will be called Emmanuel* (Isa 7:14), which means 'God with us,' *even to the consummation of the world*; as though to say: the generation of the faithful is stronger than the world. For the world will not perish until all things come to pass, that is, until the Church of the faithful is consummated, and the number of the elect is completed by God unto eternal life, to whom is honor and power through infinite ages of ages. Amen.